# Texas
# Estates
# Code

2014 Edition

WITH TABLES
AND INDEX

*As Amended through the
2013 Regular and Called Sessions of
the 83rd Legislature*

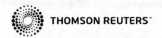

Mat #41273954

# PREFACE

This Pamphlet contains the text of the Texas Estates Code, as enacted and added by Acts 2009, 81st Leg., ch. 680, and Acts 2011, 82nd Leg., ch. 823 (H.B. 2759), effective January 1, 2014, and subsequent legislation. Also included in this pamphlet is Chapter 166 of the Health and Safety Code, Advance Directives, and an appendix containing the former Texas Probate Code, the predecessor to the Estates Code.

As part of the Texas Legislative Council's statutory revision program the Probate Code was redesignated and repealed and the Estates Code was enacted effective January 1, 2014, by Acts 2009, 81st Leg., ch. 680, and Acts 2011, 82nd Leg., ch. 823 (H.B. 2759).

A Disposition Table is included preceding the Estates Code providing a means of tracing former Probate Articles of the Civil Statutes into the Estates Code.

A detailed descriptive word Index is furnished to facilitate the search for specific textual provisions. A Table of Sections Affected indicates sections of the Estates Code affected through the 2013 Third Called Session of the 83rd Legislature.

For additional information or research assistance call the West reference attorneys at 1-800-REF-ATTY (1-800-733-2889). Contact West's editorial department directly with your questions and suggestions by e-mail at west.editor@thomson.com.

WEST

December, 2013

# THOMSON REUTERS PROVIEW™

**This title is one of many now available on your tablet as an eBook.**

Take your research mobile. Powered by the Thomson Reuters ProView™ app, our eBooks deliver the same trusted content as your print resources, but in a compact, on-the-go format.

ProView eBooks are designed for the way you work. You can add your own notes and highlights to the text, and all of your annotations will transfer electronically to every new edition of your eBook.

You can also instantly verify primary authority with built-in links to WestlawNext® and KeyCite®, so you can be confident that you're accessing the most current and accurate information.

**To find out more about ProView eBooks and available discounts, call 1-800-344-5009.**

# TABLE OF CONTENTS

## TEXAS ESTATES CODE

*Section Analysis, see beginning of each Chapter.*

### TITLE 1.   GENERAL PROVISIONS

### TITLE 2.   ESTATES OF DECEDENTS; DURABLE POWERS OF ATTORNEY
#### SUBTITLE A.   SCOPE, JURISDICTION, VENUE, AND COURTS

#### SUBTITLE B.   PROCEDURAL MATTERS

# TABLE OF CONTENTS

# TABLE OF CONTENTS

# TABLE OF CONTENTS

# TABLE OF CONTENTS

# TABLE OF CONTENTS

# TABLE OF CONTENTS

# TABLE OF CONTENTS

# TABLE OF CONTENTS

# TABLE OF CONTENTS

# TABLE OF CONTENTS

# TABLE OF CONTENTS

# TABLE OF CONTENTS

## SUBTITLE F.  EVALUATION, MODIFICATION, OR TERMINATION OF GUARDIANSHIP

# TABLE OF CONTENTS

XVIII

# TABLE OF CONTENTS

## HEALTH AND SAFETY CODE
### TITLE 2.   HEALTH
### Subtitle H.   Public Health Provisions

## APPENDIX: PROBATE CODE

(Page A–1)

## INDEX

(Page I–1)

*

# EFFECTIVE DATES

The following table shows the date of adjournment and the effective date of ninety day bills enacted at sessions of the legislature beginning with the year 1945:

| Year | Leg. | Session | Adjournment Date | Effective Date |
|------|------|---------|------------------|----------------|
| 1945 | 49 | Regular | June 5, 1945 | September 4, 1945 |
| 1947 | 50 | Regular | June 6, 1947 | September 5, 1947 |
| 1949 | 51 | Regular | June 6, 1949 | September 5, 1949 |
| 1951 | 52 | Regular | June 8, 1951 | September 7, 1951 |
| 1953 | 53 | Regular | May 27, 1953 | August 26, 1953 |
| 1954 | 53 | 1st C.S. | May 13, 1954 | August 12, 1954 |
| 1955 | 54 | Regular | June 7, 1955 | September 6, 1955 |
| 1957 | 55 | Regular | May 23, 1957 | August 22, 1957 |
| 1957 | 55 | 1st C.S. | November 12, 1957 | February 11, 1958 |
| 1957 | 55 | 2nd C.S. | December 3, 1957 | March 4, 1958 |
| 1959 | 56 | Regular | May 12, 1959 | August 11, 1959 |
| 1959 | 56 | 1st C.S. | June 16, 1959 | September 15, 1959 |
| 1959 | 56 | 2nd C.S. | July 16, 1959 | October 15, 1959 |
| 1959 | 56 | 3rd C.S. | August 6, 1959 | November 5, 1959 |
| 1961 | 57 | Regular | May 29, 1961 | August 28, 1961 |
| 1961 | 57 | 1st C.S. | August 8, 1961 | November 7, 1961 |
| 1961 | 57 | 2nd C.S. | August 14, 1961 | November 13, 1961 |
| 1962 | 57 | 3rd C.S. | February 1, 1962 | May 3, 1962 |
| 1963 | 58 | Regular | May 24, 1963 | August 23, 1963 |
| 1965 | 59 | Regular | May 31, 1965 | August 30, 1965 |
| 1966 | 59 | 1st C.S. | February 23, 1966 | * |
| 1967 | 60 | Regular | May 29, 1967 | August 28, 1967 |
| 1968 | 60 | 1st C.S. | July 3, 1968 | * |
| 1969 | 61 | Regular | June 2, 1969 | September 1, 1969 |
| 1969 | 61 | 1st C.S. | August 26, 1969 | * |
| 1969 | 61 | 2nd C.S. | September 9, 1969 | December 9, 1969 |
| 1971 | 62 | Regular | May 31, 1971 | August 30, 1971 |
| 1971 | 62 | 1st C.S. | June 4, 1971 | September 3, 1971 |
| 1972 | 62 | 2nd C.S. | March 30, 1972 | June 29, 1972 |
| 1972 | 62 | 3rd C.S. | July 7, 1972 | * |
| 1972 | 62 | 4th C.S. | October 17, 1972 | January 16, 1973 |
| 1973 | 63 | Regular | May 28, 1973 | August 27, 1973 |
| 1973 | 63 | 1st C.S. | December 20, 1973 | * |
| 1975 | 64 | Regular | June 2, 1975 | September 1, 1975 |
| 1977 | 65 | Regular | May 30, 1977 | August 29, 1977 |
| 1977 | 65 | 1st C.S. | July 21, 1977 | * |
| 1978 | 65 | 2nd C.S. | August 8, 1978 | November 7, 1978 |
| 1979 | 66 | Regular | May 28, 1979 | August 27, 1979 |
| 1981 | 67 | Regular | June 1, 1981 | August 31, 1981 |

# EFFECTIVE DATES

| Year | Leg. | Session | Adjournment Date | Effective Date |
|------|------|---------|------------------|----------------|
| 1981 | 67 | 1st C.S. | August 11, 1981 | November 10, 1981 |
| 1982 | 67 | 2nd C.S. | May 28, 1982 | * |
| 1982 | 67 | 3rd C.S. | September 9, 1982 | * |
| 1983 | 68 | Regular | May 30, 1983 | August 29, 1983 |
| 1983 | 68 | 1st C.S. | June 25, 1983 | September 23, 1983 |
| 1984 | 68 | 2nd C.S. | July 3, 1984 | October 2, 1984 |
| 1985 | 69 | Regular | May 27, 1985 | August 26, 1985 |
| 1985 | 69 | 1st C.S. | May 30, 1985 | August 29, 1985 |
| 1986 | 69 | 2nd C.S. | September 4, 1986 | December 4, 1986 |
| 1986 | 69 | 3rd C.S. | September 30, 1986 | December 30, 1986 |
| 1987 | 70 | Regular | June 1, 1987 | August 31, 1987 |
| 1987 | 70 | 1st C.S. | June 3, 1987 | September 2, 1987 |
| 1987 | 70 | 2nd C.S. | July 21, 1987 | October 20, 1987 |
| 1989 | 71 | Regular | May 29, 1989 | August 28, 1989 |
| 1989 | 71 | 1st C.S. | July 19, 1989 | October 18, 1989 |
| 1989 | 71 | 2nd C.S. | December 12, 1989 | * |
| 1990 | 71 | 3rd C.S. | March 28, 1990 | * |
| 1990 | 71 | 4th C.S. | May 1, 1990 | * |
| 1990 | 71 | 5th C.S. | May 30, 1990 | * |
| 1990 | 71 | 6th C.S. | June 7, 1990 | September 6, 1990 |
| 1991 | 72 | Regular | May 27, 1991 | August 26, 1991 |
| 1991 | 72 | 1st C.S. | August 13, 1991 | November 12, 1991 |
| 1991 | 72 | 2nd C.S. | August 25, 1991 | November 24, 1991 |
| 1992 | 72 | 3rd C.S. | January 8, 1992 | April 8, 1992 |
| 1992 | 72 | 4th C.S. | December 3, 1992 | * |
| 1993 | 73 | Regular | May 31, 1993 | August 30, 1993 |
| 1995 | 74 | Regular | May 29, 1995 | August 28, 1995 |
| 1997 | 75 | Regular | June 2, 1997 | September 1, 1997 |
| 1999 | 76 | Regular | May 31, 1999 | August 30, 1999 |
| 2001 | 77 | Regular | May 28, 2001 | September 1, 2001 |
| 2003 | 78 | Regular | June 2, 2003 | September 1, 2003 |
| 2003 | 78 | 1st C.S. | July 28, 2003 | * |
| 2003 | 78 | 2nd C.S. | August 26, 2003 | * |
| 2005 | 79 | 2nd C.S. | August 19, 2005 | November 18, 2005 |
| 2006 | 79 | 3rd C.S. | May 16, 2006 | August 15, 2006 |
| 2007 | 80 | Regular | May 28, 2007 | August 27, 2007 |
| 2009 | 81 | Regular | June 1, 2009 | August 31, 2009 |
| 2009 | 81 | 1st C.S. | July 2, 2009 | * |
| 2011 | 82 | Regular | May 30, 2011 | August 29, 2011 |
| 2011 | 82 | 1st C.S. | June 29, 2011 | September 28, 2011** |
| 2013 | 83 | Regular | May 27, 2013 | August 26, 2013 |
| 2013 | 83 | 1st C.S. | June 25, 2013 | September 24, 2013** |

# EFFECTIVE DATES

| Year | Leg. | Session | Adjournment Date | Effective Date |
|------|------|---------|------------------|----------------|
| 2013 | 83 | 2nd C.S. | July 30, 2013 | October 29, 2013** |
| 2013 | 83 | 3rd C.S. | August 5, 2013 | * |

\* No legislation for which the ninety day effective date is applicable.

\*\* Legislation effective on the 91st day after session.

\*

# DISPOSITION TABLE

Showing where the subject matter of sections of the Probate Code is covered in the Estates Code as originally enacted.

| Probate Code Section | Estates Code Section |
|---|---|
| 29 | 351.002 |
| 31 | 55.251 |
|  | 55.252 |
| 32 | 351.001 |
| 33(a), (b) | 51.001 |
| 33(c) | 51.002 |
|  | 51.003 |
| 33(d) | 51.151 |
| 33(e) | 51.056 |
| 33(f)(1) | 51.051 |
|  | 51.101 |
| 33(f)(2) | 51.053 |
| 33(f)(3) | 51.054 |
| 33(f)(4) | 51.052 |
| 33(g) | 51.104 |
| 33(h) | 51.102 |
| 33(i) | 51.103 |
| 33(j) | 51.202 |
| 34 | 51.055 |
| 34A | 53.104 |
|  | 1054.007 |
| 35 | 51.201 |
| 36(a) | 351.352 |
|  | 351.353 |
|  | 351.354 |
| 36(b) | 351.355 |
| 36B | 151.001 |
| 36C | 151.002 |
| 36D | 151.003 |
| 36E | 151.004 |
| 36F | 151.005 |
| 37 | 101.001 |
|  | 101.003 |
|  | 101.005 |
|  | 101.051 |
| 37A(a) | 122.002 |
| 37A(b) | 122.003 |
| 37A(c) | 122.101 |
| 37A(d) | 122.102 |
| 37A(e) | 122.001 |
| 37A(f) | 122.103 |
| 37A(g) | 122.051 |
| 37A(h) | 122.052 |
|  | 122.053 |
|  | 122.054 |
|  | 122.055 |
| 37A(i) | 122.056 |
| 37A(j) | 122.005 |
| 37A(k) | 122.004 |
| 37A(l) | 122.151 |
|  | 122.152 |
| 37A(m) | 122.153 |
| 37A(n) | 122.104 |
| 37A(o) | 122.105 |
|  | 122.106 |
| 37B(a) | 122.201 |
| 37B(b) | 122.202 |
|  | 122.203 |
| 37B(c) | 122.204 |
| 37B(d) | 122.205 |
| 37B(e) | 122.206 |
| 37C(a) | 255.101 |
| 37C(b) | 255.102 |
| 38(a) | 201.001 |
| 38(b) | 201.002 |
| 39 | 201.102 |
|  | 201.103 |
| 40 | 201.054 |
| 41(a) | 201.056 |
| 41(b) | 201.057 |
| 41(c) | 201.060 |
| 41(d) | 201.058 |
|  | 201.059 |
|  | 201.061 |
| 41(e), (f) | 201.062 |
| 42(a) | 201.051 |
| 42(b)(1) | 201.052 |
| 42(b)(2) | 201.053 |
| 42(c) | 102.001 |
|  | 353.001 |
| 42(d) | 201.055 |
| 43 | 201.101 |
| 44(a), (b) | 201.151 |
| 44(c) | 201.152 |
| 45 | 201.003 |
| 46(a) | 101.002 |
|  | 111.001 |
| 46(b) | 111.002 |
| 47(a) | 121.051 |
|  | 121.052 |
|  | 121.053 |
| 47(b) | 121.151 |
| 47(c) | 121.101 |
|  | 121.102 |
| 47(d) | 121.152 |
| 47(e) | 121.153 |
| 47(f) | 121.001 |
| 47A(a) | 123.101 |
| 47A(b), (c) | 123.102 |
| 47A(d), (e) | 123.103 |
| 47A(f) | 123.104 |
| 48(a) | 202.001 |
|  | 202.002 |
| 48(b) | 202.006 |
| 49(a) | 202.004 |
|  | 202.005 |
| 49(b) | 202.007 |
|  | 202.008 |
| 50(a) | 202.051 |
|  | 202.054 |
| 50(b) | 202.052 |
| 50(c) | 202.053 |
| 50(d) | 202.055 |
| 50(e) | 202.056 |
| 51 | 202.101 |
|  | 202.102 |
|  | 202.103 |
| 52 | 203.001 |
| 52A | 203.002 |
| 53(a) | 202.151 |
| 53(b), (c) | 202.009 |
| 53A(a) | 204.051 |
| 53A(b) | 204.052 |
| 53A(c), (d) | 204.053 |
| 53A(e) | 204.054 |
| 53A(f) | 204.055 |
| 53A(g) | 204.056 |
| 53B(a) | 204.101 |

# DISPOSITION TABLE

# DISPOSITION TABLE

# DISPOSITION TABLE

# DISPOSITION TABLE

# DISPOSITION TABLE

# DISPOSITION TABLE

| Probate Code Section | Estates Code Section | Probate Code Section | Estates Code Section |
|---|---|---|---|
| | 310.006 | 436(7) | 113.002 |
| 378B(i) | 310.002 | 436(8), (9) | 113.001 |
| 379 | 360.251 | 436(10) | 113.004 |
| 380(a) | 360.151 | 436(11) to (13) | 113.001 |
| 380(b) | 360.152 | 436(14) | 113.004 |
| 380(c) | 360.153 | 436(15) | 113.001 |
| 380(d) | 360.154 | 437 | 113.101 |
| 380(e) | 360.155 | 438(a) | 113.102 |
| 380(f) | 360.156 | 438(b) | 113.103 |
| 380(g) | 360.157 | 438(c) | 113.104 |
| 381(a) | 360.201 | 438A(a) | 113.104 |
| 381(b), (c) | 360.202 | 438A(b), (c) | 113.105 |
| 381(d) | 360.203 | 438A(d) | 113.154 |
| 382 | 360.252 | 438A(e) | 113.105 |
| 384 | 360.301 | 438A(f) | 113.206 |
| 385 | 360.253 | | 113.208 |
| 386 | 360.254 | 438A(g) | 113.208 |
| 387 | 360.103 | 438B | 113.106 |
| 398A | 351.105 | 438B(c) | 113.1541 |
| 399(a) | 359.001 | 439(a) | 113.151 |
| 399(b) | 359.002 | 439(b) | 113.152 |
| 399(c) | 359.003 | 439(c) | 113.153 |
| | 359.004 | 439(d) | 113.155 |
| 399(d) | 359.005 | 439A(a) | 113.051 |
| 400 | 359.101 | 439A(b) | 113.052 |
| 401(a) to (d) | 359.051 | 439A(c), (d) | 113.053 |
| 401(e) | 359.052 | 440 | 113.156 |
| | 359.053 | | 113.157 |
| | 359.054 | 441 | 113.158 |
| 402 | 359.006 | 442 | 113.251 |
| 403 | 359.102 | | 113.252 |
| 404 | 362.001 | | 113.253 |
| 405 | 362.003 | 443 | 113.201 |
| | 362.004 | 444 | 113.003 |
| 405A | 362.007 | | 113.005 |
| 406 | 362.051 | | 113.202 |
| 407 | 362.005 | 445 | 113.203 |
| 408(a) | 362.006 | | 113.207 |
| 408(b) | 362.011 | 446 | 113.204 |
| 408(c) | 362.012 | 447 | 113.205 |
| 408(d) | 362.013 | 448 | 113.209 |
| 409 | 362.009 | 449 | 113.210 |
| 410 | 362.010 | 450(a) | 111.051 |
| 412 | 362.008 | | 111.052 |
| 414 | 362.052 | 450(b) | 111.053 |
| 427 | 551.001 | 450(c) | 111.051 |
| | 551.002 | 451 | 112.051 |
| | 551.003 | 452 | 112.052 |
| | 551.004 | 453 | 112.151 |
| 428 | 551.005 | 454 | 112.152 |
| 429 | 551.101 | 455 | 112.054 |
| 430 | 551.006 | 456(a) | 112.053 |
| 431 | 551.102 | | 112.101 |
| 432 | 551.103 | 456(b) | 112.102 |
| 433(a) | 551.051 | 456(c) | 112.103 |
| | 551.052 | 456(d) | 112.101 |
| 433(b) | 551.052 | 457 | 112.104 |
| | 551.055 | 458 | 112.053 |
| 433(c) | 551.052 | | 112.105 |
| | 551.053 | 459 | 112.106 |
| 433(d) | 551.054 | 460(a) | 112.203 |
| 436(1) to (3) | 113.001 | 460(b) | 112.204 |
| 436(4), (5) | 113.004 | 460(c) | 112.206 |
| 436(6) | 113.003 | 460(d) | 112.205 |

# DISPOSITION TABLE

# DISPOSITION TABLE

# DISPOSITION TABLE

# DISPOSITION TABLE

# DISPOSITION TABLE

# DISPOSITION TABLE

\*

# ESTATES CODE
## TABLE OF SECTIONS AFFECTED
## BY THE 83rd LEGISLATURE,
## REGULAR AND CALLED SESSIONS

Acts 2013

| Sec. | Effect | Ch. | Sec. |
|---|---|---|---|
| 21.001(b) | Amended | 161 | 6.001 |
| 21.001(c) | Amended | 161 | 6.001 |
| 21.002(b) | Amended | 161 | 6.002 |
| 21.003(b) | Amended | 161 | 6.003 |
| 21.005 | Amended | 161 | 6.004 |
| | | 1136 | 1 |
| 21.005 note | — | 1136 | 62(a) |
| | | 63 | |
| 22.001(b) | Amended | 161 | 6.005 |
| 22.017 | Amended | 161 | 6.006 |
| 32.001(d) | Redes. from Probate 2(e) and amended | 1136 | 2 |
| 32.001 note | — | 1136 | 63 |
| 32.005(b) | Amended | 161 | 6.007 |
| 32.006 | Amended | 1136 | 3 |
| 32.006 note | — | 1136 | 62(d) |
| | | 63 | |
| Ch. 34 heading | Added | 161 | 6.008 |
| 34.001 | Redes. from Probate 5B and amended | 161 | 6.009 |
| 34.002 | Redes. from Probate 5C and amended | 161 | 6.009 |
| 51.203(c) | Amended | 1136 | 4 |
| 51.203 note | — | 1136 | 62(e) |
| | | 63 | |
| 53.104 | Amended | 1136 | 5 |
| 53.104 note | — | 1136 | 62(e) |
| | | 63 | |
| 53.107 | Added | 1136 | 6 |
| 53.107 note | — | 1136 | 62(d) |
| | | 63 | |
| 54.051 | Amended | 1136 | 7 |
| 54.051 note | — | 1136 | 63 |
| 102.004 | Amended | 1136 | 8 |
| 102.004 note | — | 1136 | 62(f) |
| | | 63 | |
| Title 2, Subtitle Y heading | Repealed | 161 | 6.078(b) |
| 111.051(1) | Amended | 1136 | 9 |
| 111.051(1–a) | Added | 1136 | 9 |
| 111.051 note | — | 1136 | 61 |
| | | 63 | |
| 111.054 | Added | 1136 | 10 |
| 111.054 note | — | 1136 | 61 |
| | | 63 | |
| 122.051 | Amended | 689 | 1 |
| 122.051 note | — | 689 | 3 |
| 122.057 | Repealed | 1136 | 60 |
| 122.057 note | — | 1136 | 63 |
| 122.107 | Added | 689 | 2 |
| 152.001(b) | Amended | 161 | 6.010 |
| 152.102(b) | Amended | 161 | 6.011 |
| 201.051 | Amended | 1136 | 11 |
| 201.051 note | — | 1136 | 62(f) |
| | | 63 | |

# TABLE OF SECTIONS AFFECTED

# ESTATES CODE

# TABLE OF SECTIONS AFFECTED

# ESTATES CODE

# TABLE OF SECTIONS AFFECTED

# TABLE OF SECTIONS AFFECTED

# ESTATES CODE

*The Estates Code was enacted, effective January 1, 2014, by Acts 2009, 81st Leg., ch. 680 and Acts 2011, 82nd Leg., ch. 823 (H.B. 2759).*

## TITLE 1.  GENERAL PROVISIONS

### CHAPTER 21.  PURPOSE AND CONSTRUCTION

### § 21.001.  Purpose of Code

(a) This code is enacted as a part of the state's continuing statutory revision program, begun by the Texas Legislative Council in 1963 as directed by the legislature in the law codified as Section 323.007, Government Code. The program contemplates a topic-by-topic revision of the state's general and permanent statute law without substantive change.

(b) Consistent with the objectives of the statutory revision program, the purpose of this code, except Subtitle X, Title 2, and Subtitles Y and Z, Title 3, is to make the law encompassed by this code, except Subtitle X, Title 2, and Subtitles Y and Z, Title 3, more accessible and understandable by:

(1) rearranging the statutes into a more logical order;

(2) employing a format and numbering system designed to facilitate citation of the law and to accommodate future expansion of the law;

(3) eliminating repealed, duplicative, unconstitutional, expired, executed, and other ineffective provisions; and

(4) restating the law in modern American English to the greatest extent possible.

(c) The provisions of Subtitle X, Title 2, and Subtitles Y and Z, Title 3, are transferred from the Texas Probate Code and redesignated as part of this code, but are not revised as part of the state's continuing statutory revision program.

Added by Acts 2009, 81st Leg., ch. 680, § 1, eff. Jan. 1, 2014. Amended by Acts 2011, 82nd Leg., ch. 823 (H.B. 2759), § 2.01, eff. Jan. 1, 2014; Acts 2013, 83rd Leg., ch. 161 (S.B. 1093), § 6.001, eff. Jan. 1, 2014.

Section 11 of Acts 2009, 81st Leg., ch. 680 provides:

"Legislative Intent.  This Act is enacted under Section 43, Article III, Texas Constitution.  This Act is intended as a recodification only, and no substantive change in law is intended by this Act."

### § 21.002.  Construction

(a) Except as provided by this section, Section 22.027, or Section 1002.023, Chapter 311, Government Code (Code Construction Act), applies to the construction of a provision of this code.

(b) Chapter 311, Government Code (Code Construction Act), does not apply to the construction of a provision of Subtitle X, Title 2, or Subtitle Y or Z, Title 3.

Added by Acts 2009, 81st Leg., ch. 680, § 1, eff. Jan. 1, 2014. Amended by Acts 2011, 82nd Leg., ch. 823 (H.B. 2759), § 2.02, eff. Jan. 1, 2014; Acts 2013, 83rd Leg., ch. 161 (S.B. 1093), § 6.002, eff. Jan. 1, 2014.

### § 21.003.  Statutory References

(a) A reference in a law other than in this code to a statute or a part of a statute revised by, or redesignated as part of, this code is considered to be a reference to the part of this code that revises that statute or part of that statute or contains the redesignated statute or part of the statute, as applicable.

(b) A reference in Subtitle X, Title 2, or Subtitle Y or Z, Title 3, to a chapter, a part, a subpart, a section, or any portion of a section "of this code" is a reference to the chapter, part, subpart, section, or portion of a section as redesignated in the Estates Code, except that:

(1) a reference in Subtitle X, Title 2, or Subtitle Y or Z, Title 3, to Chapter I is a reference to Chapter I, Estates Code, and to the revision of sections derived from Chapter I, Texas Probate Code, and any reenactments and amendments to those sections; and

(2) a reference in Subtitle X, Title 2, or Subtitle Y or Z, Title 3, to a chapter, part, subpart, section, or portion of a section that does not exist in the Estates Code is a reference to the revision or redesignation of the corresponding chapter, part, subpart, section, or portion of a section of the Texas Probate Code and any reenactments or amendments.

Added by Acts 2009, 81st Leg., ch. 680, § 1, eff. Jan. 1, 2014. Amended by Acts 2011, 82nd Leg., ch. 823 (H.B. 2759), § 2.03, eff. Jan. 1, 2014; Acts 2013, 83rd Leg., ch. 161 (S.B. 1093), § 6.003, eff. Jan. 1, 2014.

## § 21.004. Effect of Division of Law

The division of this code into titles, subtitles, chapters, subchapters, parts, subparts, sections, subsections, subdivisions, paragraphs, and subparagraphs is for convenience and does not have any legal effect.

Added by Acts 2009, 81st Leg., ch. 680, § 1, eff. Jan. 1, 2014.

## § 21.005. Applicability of Certain Laws

(a) Notwithstanding Section 21.002(b) of this code and Section 311.002, Government Code:

(1) Section 311.032(c), Government Code, applies to Subtitle X, Title 2, and Subtitles Y and Z, Title 3; and

(2) Sections 311.005(4) and 311.012(b) and (c), Government Code, apply to Subtitle X, Title 2, and Subtitles Y and Z, Title 3.

(b) Chapter 132, Civil Practice and Remedies Code, does not apply to Subchapter C, Chapter 251.

Added by Acts 2009, 81st Leg., ch. 680, § 1, eff. Jan. 1, 2014. Amended by Acts 2011, 82nd Leg., ch. 823 (H.B. 2759), § 2.04, eff. Jan. 1, 2014; Acts 2013, 83rd Leg., ch. 161 (S.B. 1093), § 6.004, eff. Jan. 1, 2014; Acts 2013, 83rd Leg., ch. 1136 (H.B. 2912), § 1, eff. Jan. 1, 2014.

Section 62(a) of Acts 2013, 83rd Leg., ch. 1136 (H.B. 2912) provides:

"Section 21.005(b), Estates Code, as added by this Act, applies only to a will executed on or after the effective date [Jan. 1, 2014] of this Act. A will executed before the effective date of this Act is governed by the law in effect on the date the will was executed, and the former law is continued in effect for that purpose."

## § 21.006. Applicability to Probate Proceedings

The procedure prescribed by Title 2 governs all probate proceedings.

Added by Acts 2009, 81st Leg., ch. 680, § 1, eff. Jan. 1, 2014.

## CHAPTER 22. DEFINITIONS

## § 22.001. Applicability of Definitions

(a) Except as provided by Subsection (b), the definition for a term provided by this chapter applies in this code unless a different meaning of the term is otherwise apparent from the context in which the term is used.

(b) If Title 3 provides a definition for a term that is different from the definition provided by this chapter, the definition for the term provided by Title 3 applies in that title.

Added by Acts 2009, 81st Leg., ch. 680, § 1, eff. Jan. 1, 2014. Amended by Acts 2013, 83rd Leg., ch. 161 (S.B. 1093), § 6.005, eff. Jan. 1, 2014.

## § 22.002. Authorized Corporate Surety

"Authorized corporate surety" means a domestic or foreign corporation authorized to engage in business in this state for the purpose of issuing surety, guaranty, or indemnity bonds that guarantee the fidelity of an executor or administrator.

Added by Acts 2009, 81st Leg., ch. 680, § 1, eff. Jan. 1, 2014.

## § 22.003. Charitable Organization

"Charitable organization" means:

(1) a nonprofit corporation, trust, community chest, fund, foundation, or other entity that is:

(A) exempt from federal income tax under Section 501(a), Internal Revenue Code of 1986, by being described by Section 501(c)(3) of that code; and

(B) organized and operated exclusively for:

(i) religious, charitable, scientific, educational, or literary purposes;

(ii) testing for public safety;

(iii) preventing cruelty to children or animals; or

(iv) promoting amateur sports competition; or

(2) any other entity that is organized and operated exclusively for the purposes listed in Section 501(c)(3), Internal Revenue Code of 1986.

Added by Acts 2009, 81st Leg., ch. 680, § 1, eff. Jan. 1, 2014.

### § 22.004. Child

(a) "Child" includes an adopted child, regardless of whether the adoption occurred through:

(1) an existing or former statutory procedure; or

(2) acts of estoppel.

(b) The term "child" does not include a child who does not have a presumed father unless a provision of this code expressly states that a child who does not have a presumed father is included.

Added by Acts 2009, 81st Leg., ch. 680, § 1, eff. Jan. 1, 2014.

### § 22.005. Claims

"Claims" includes:

(1) liabilities of a decedent that survive the decedent's death, including taxes, regardless of whether the liabilities arise in contract or tort or otherwise;

(2) funeral expenses;

(3) the expense of a tombstone;

(4) expenses of administration;

(5) estate and inheritance taxes; and

(6) debts due such estates.

Added by Acts 2009, 81st Leg., ch. 680, § 1, eff. Jan. 1, 2014.

### § 22.006. Corporate Fiduciary

"Corporate fiduciary" means a financial institution, as defined by Section 201.101, Finance Code, that:

(1) is existing or engaged in business under the laws of this state, another state, or the United States;

(2) has trust powers; and

(3) is authorized by law to act under the order or appointment of a court of record, without giving bond, as receiver, trustee, executor, administrator, or, although the financial institution does not have general depository powers, depository for any money paid into the court, or to become sole guarantor or surety in or on any bond required to be given under the laws of this state.

Added by Acts 2009, 81st Leg., ch. 680, § 1, eff. Jan. 1, 2014.

### § 22.007. Court; County Court, Probate Court, and Statutory Probate Court

(a) "Court" means and includes:

(1) a county court in the exercise of its probate jurisdiction;

(2) a court created by statute and authorized to exercise original probate jurisdiction; and

(3) a district court exercising original probate jurisdiction in a contested matter.

(b) The terms "county court" and "probate court" are synonymous and mean:

(1) a county court in the exercise of its probate jurisdiction;

(2) a court created by statute and authorized to exercise original probate jurisdiction; and

(3) a district court exercising probate jurisdiction in a contested matter.

(c) "Statutory probate court" means a court created by statute and designated as a statutory probate court under Chapter 25, Government Code. For purposes of this code, the term does not include a county court at law exercising probate jurisdiction unless the court is designated a statutory probate court under Chapter 25, Government Code.

Added by Acts 2009, 81st Leg., ch. 680, § 1, eff. Jan. 1, 2014.

### § 22.008. Devise

"Devise":

(1) used as a noun, includes a testamentary disposition of real property, personal property, or both; and

(2) used as a verb, means to dispose of real property, personal property, or both, by will.

Added by Acts 2009, 81st Leg., ch. 680, § 1, eff. Jan. 1, 2014.

### § 22.009. Devisee

"Devisee" includes a legatee.

Added by Acts 2009, 81st Leg., ch. 680, § 1, eff. Jan. 1, 2014.

### § 22.010. Distributee

"Distributee" means a person who is entitled to a part of the estate of a decedent under a lawful will or the statutes of descent and distribution.

Added by Acts 2009, 81st Leg., ch. 680, § 1, eff. Jan. 1, 2014.

### § 22.011. Docket

"Docket" means the probate docket.

Added by Acts 2009, 81st Leg., ch. 680, § 1, eff. Jan. 1, 2014.

## § 22.012. Estate

"Estate" means a decedent's property, as that property:

(1) exists originally and as the property changes in form by sale, reinvestment, or otherwise;

(2) is augmented by any accretions and other additions to the property, including any property to be distributed to the decedent's representative by the trustee of a trust that terminates on the decedent's death, and substitutions for the property; and

(3) is diminished by any decreases in or distributions from the property.

Added by Acts 2009, 81st Leg., ch. 680, § 1, eff. Jan. 1, 2014.

## § 22.013. Exempt Property

"Exempt property" means the property in a decedent's estate that is exempt from execution or forced sale by the constitution or laws of this state, and any allowance paid instead of that property.

Added by Acts 2009, 81st Leg., ch. 680, § 1, eff. Jan. 1, 2014.

## § 22.014. Governmental Agency of the State

"Governmental agency of the state" means:

(1) a municipality;

(2) a county;

(3) a public school district;

(4) a special-purpose district or authority;

(5) a board, commission, department, office, or other agency in the executive branch of state government, including an institution of higher education, as defined by Section 61.003, Education Code;

(6) the legislature or a legislative agency;

(7) the supreme court, the court of criminal appeals, a court of appeals, or a district, county, or justice of the peace court;

(8) a judicial agency having statewide jurisdiction; and

(9) the State Bar of Texas.

Added by Acts 2009, 81st Leg., ch. 680, § 1, eff. Jan. 1, 2014.

## § 22.015. Heir

"Heir" means a person who is entitled under the statutes of descent and distribution to a part of the estate of a decedent who dies intestate. The term includes the decedent's surviving spouse.

Added by Acts 2009, 81st Leg., ch. 680, § 1, eff. Jan. 1, 2014.

## § 22.016. Incapacitated Person

A person is "incapacitated" if the person:

(1) is a minor;

(2) is an adult who, because of a physical or mental condition, is substantially unable to:

(A) provide food, clothing, or shelter for himself or herself;

(B) care for the person's own physical health; or

(C) manage the person's own financial affairs; or

(3) must have a guardian appointed for the person to receive funds due the person from a governmental source.

Added by Acts 2009, 81st Leg., ch. 680, § 1, eff. Jan. 1, 2014.

## § 22.017. Independent Executor

"Independent executor" means the personal representative of an estate under independent administration as provided by Chapter 401 and Section 402.001. The term includes an independent administrator.

Added by Acts 2009, 81st Leg., ch. 680, § 1, eff. Jan. 1, 2014. Amended by Acts 2013, 83rd Leg., ch. 161 (S.B. 1093), § 6.006, eff. Jan. 1, 2014.

## § 22.018. Interested Person; Person Interested

"Interested person" or "person interested" means:

(1) an heir, devisee, spouse, creditor, or any other having a property right in or claim against an estate being administered; and

(2) anyone interested in the welfare of an incapacitated person, including a minor.

Added by Acts 2009, 81st Leg., ch. 680, § 1, eff. Jan. 1, 2014.

## § 22.019. Judge

"Judge" means the presiding judge of any court having original jurisdiction over probate proceedings, regardless of whether the court is:

(1) a county court in the exercise of its probate jurisdiction;

(2) a court created by statute and authorized to exercise probate jurisdiction; or

(3) a district court exercising probate jurisdiction in a contested matter.

Added by Acts 2009, 81st Leg., ch. 680, § 1, eff. Jan. 1, 2014.

## § 22.020. Legacy

"Legacy" includes a gift or devise of real or personal property made by a will.

Added by Acts 2009, 81st Leg., ch. 680, § 1, eff. Jan. 1, 2014.

## § 22.021. Legatee

"Legatee" includes a person who is entitled to a legacy under a will.

Added by Acts 2009, 81st Leg., ch. 680, § 1, eff. Jan. 1, 2014.

## § 22.022. Minor

"Minor" means a person younger than 18 years of age who:

(1) has never been married; and

(2) has not had the disabilities of minority removed for general purposes.

Added by Acts 2009, 81st Leg., ch. 680, § 1, eff. Jan. 1, 2014.

## § 22.023. [Blank]

## § 22.024. Mortgage; Lien

"Mortgage" and "lien" include:

(1) a deed of trust;

(2) a vendor's lien, a mechanic's, materialman's, or laborer's lien, an attachment or garnishment lien, and a federal or state tax lien;

(3) a chattel mortgage;

(4) a judgment; and

(5) a pledge by hypothecation.

Added by Acts 2009, 81st Leg., ch. 680, § 1, eff. Jan. 1, 2014.

## § 22.025. Net Estate

"Net estate" means a decedent's property excluding:

(1) homestead rights;

(2) exempt property;

(3) the family allowance; and

(4) an enforceable claim against the decedent's estate.

Added by Acts 2009, 81st Leg., ch. 680, § 1, eff. Jan. 1, 2014.

## § 22.026. Next of Kin

"Next of kin" includes:

(1) an adopted child or the adopted child's descendants; and

(2) the adoptive parent of the adopted child.

Added by Acts 2009, 81st Leg., ch. 680, § 1, eff. Jan. 1, 2014.

## § 22.027. Person

(a) "Person" includes a natural person and a corporation.

(b) The definition of "person" assigned by Section 311.005, Government Code, does not apply to any provision in this code.

Added by Acts 2009, 81st Leg., ch. 680, § 1, eff. Jan. 1, 2014.

## § 22.028. Personal Property

"Personal property" includes an interest in:

(1) goods;

(2) money;

(3) a chose in action;

(4) an evidence of debt; and

(5) a real chattel.

Added by Acts 2009, 81st Leg., ch. 680, § 1, eff. Jan. 1, 2014.

## § 22.029. Probate Matter; Probate Proceedings; Proceeding in Probate; Proceedings for Probate

The terms "probate matter," "probate proceedings," "proceeding in probate," and "proceedings for probate" are synonymous and include a matter or proceeding relating to a decedent's estate.

Added by Acts 2009, 81st Leg., ch. 680, § 1, eff. Jan. 1, 2014.

## § 22.030. Real Property

"Real property" includes estates and interests in land, whether corporeal or incorporeal or legal or equitable. The term does not include a real chattel.

Added by Acts 2009, 81st Leg., ch. 680, § 1, eff. Jan. 1, 2014.

## § 22.031. Representative; Personal Representative

(a) "Representative" and "personal representative" include:

(1) an executor and independent executor;

(2) an administrator, independent administrator, and temporary administrator; and

(3) a successor to an executor or administrator listed in Subdivision (1) or (2).

(b) The inclusion of an independent executor in Subsection (a) may not be construed to subject an independent executor to the control of the courts in probate matters with respect to settlement of estates, except as expressly provided by law.

Added by Acts 2009, 81st Leg., ch. 680, § 1, eff. Jan. 1, 2014.

## § 22.032. Surety

"Surety" includes a personal surety and a corporate surety.

Added by Acts 2009, 81st Leg., ch. 680, § 1, eff. Jan. 1, 2014.

## § 22.033. Ward

"Ward" means a person for whom a guardian has been appointed.

Added by Acts 2009, 81st Leg., ch. 680, § 1, eff. Jan. 1, 2014.

## § 22.034. Will

"Will" includes:

(1) a codicil; and

(2) a testamentary instrument that merely:

(A) appoints an executor or guardian;

(B) directs how property may not be disposed of; or

(C) revokes another will.

Added by Acts 2009, 81st Leg., ch. 680, § 1, eff. Jan. 1, 2014.

# TITLE 2. ESTATES OF DECEDENTS; DURABLE POWERS OF ATTORNEY

## SUBTITLE A. SCOPE, JURISDICTION, VENUE, AND COURTS

### CHAPTER 31. GENERAL PROVISIONS

## § 31.001. Scope of "Probate Proceeding" for Purposes of Code

The term "probate proceeding," as used in this code, includes:

(1) the probate of a will, with or without administration of the estate;

(2) the issuance of letters testamentary and of administration;

(3) an heirship determination or small estate affidavit, community property administration, and homestead and family allowances;

(4) an application, petition, motion, or action regarding the probate of a will or an estate administration, including a claim for money owed by the decedent;

(5) a claim arising from an estate administration and any action brought on the claim;

(6) the settling of a personal representative's account of an estate and any other matter related to the settlement, partition, or distribution of an estate; and

(7) a will construction suit.

Added by Acts 2009, 81st Leg., ch. 1351, § 13(a), eff. Jan. 1, 2014.

Sections 13(c) and 14 of Acts 2009, 81st Leg., ch. 1351 provide:

"[Sec. 13.] (c) Except as otherwise provided by this subsection, this section [Sec. 13] takes effect January 1, 2014. The changes in law made by this section take effect only if H.B. No. 2502, Acts of the 81st Legislature, Regular Session, 2009, is enacted and becomes law. If that bill does not become law, this section has no effect." H.B. No. 2502, Acts of the 81st Legislature, Regular Session, 2009, was signed by the Governor on June 19, 2009, effective January 1, 2014.

"Sec. 14. Except as otherwise provided by this Act, the changes in law made by this Act apply only to an action filed on or after the effective date of this Act. An action filed before the effective date of this Act is governed by the law applicable to the action immediately before the effective date of this Act, and the former law is continued in effect for that purpose."

## § 31.002. Matters Related to Probate Proceeding

(a) For purposes of this code, in a county in which there is no statutory probate court or county court at law exercising original probate jurisdiction, a matter related to a probate proceeding includes:

(1) an action against a personal representative or former personal representative arising out of the representative's performance of the duties of a personal representative;

(2) an action against a surety of a personal representative or former personal representative;

(3) a claim brought by a personal representative on behalf of an estate;

(4) an action brought against a personal representative in the representative's capacity as personal representative;

(5) an action for trial of title to real property that is estate property, including the enforcement of a lien against the property; and

(6) an action for trial of the right of property that is estate property.

(b) For purposes of this code, in a county in which there is no statutory probate court, but in which there is a county court at law exercising original probate jurisdiction, a matter related to a probate proceeding includes:

(1) all matters and actions described in Subsection (a);

(2) the interpretation and administration of a testamentary trust if the will creating the trust has been admitted to probate in the court; and

(3) the interpretation and administration of an inter vivos trust created by a decedent whose will has been admitted to probate in the court.

(c) For purposes of this code, in a county in which there is a statutory probate court, a matter related to a probate proceeding includes:

(1) all matters and actions described in Subsections (a) and (b); and

(2) any cause of action in which a personal representative of an estate pending in the statutory probate court is a party in the representative's capacity as personal representative.

Added by Acts 2009, 81st Leg., ch. 1351, § 13(a), eff. Jan. 1, 2014.

Sections 13(c) and 14 of Acts 2009, 81st Leg., ch. 1351 provide:

"[Sec. 13.] (c) Except as otherwise provided by this subsection, this section [Sec. 13] takes effect January 1, 2014. The changes in law made by this section take effect only if H.B. No. 2502, Acts of the 81st Legislature, Regular Session, 2009, is enacted and becomes law. If that bill does not become law, this section has no effect." H.B. No. 2502 [ch. 680], Acts of the 81st Legislature, Regular Session, 2009, was signed by the Governor on June 19, 2009, effective January 1, 2014.

"Sec. 14. Except as otherwise provided by this Act, the changes in law made by this Act apply only to an action filed on or after the effective date of this Act. An action filed before the effective date of this Act is governed by the law applicable to the action immediately before the effective date of this Act, and the former law is continued in effect for that purpose."

## CHAPTER 32. JURISDICTION

Section

## § 32.001. General Probate Court Jurisdiction; Appeals

(a) All probate proceedings must be filed and heard in a court exercising original probate jurisdiction. The court exercising original probate jurisdiction also has jurisdiction of all matters related to the probate proceeding as specified in Section 31.002 for that type of court.

(b) A probate court may exercise pendent and ancillary jurisdiction as necessary to promote judicial efficiency and economy.

(c) A final order issued by a probate court is appealable to the court of appeals.

(d) The administration of the estate of a decedent, from the filing of the application for probate and administration, or for administration, until the decree of final distribution and the discharge of the last personal representative, shall be considered as one proceeding for purposes of jurisdiction. The entire proceeding is a proceeding in rem.

Added by Acts 2009, 81st Leg., ch. 1351, § 13(a), eff. Jan. 1, 2014. Amended by Acts 2013, 83rd Leg., ch. 1136 (H.B. 2912), § 2, eff. Jan. 1, 2014.

Sections 13(c) and 14 of Acts 2009, 81st Leg., ch. 1351 provide:

"[Sec. 13.] (c) Except as otherwise provided by this subsection, this section [Sec. 13] takes effect January 1, 2014. The changes in law made by this section take effect only if H.B. No. 2502, Acts of the 81st Legislature, Regular Session, 2009, is enacted and becomes law. If that bill does not become law, this section has no effect." H.B. No. 2502, Acts of the 81st Legislature, Regular Session, 2009, was signed by the Governor on June 19, 2009, effective January 1, 2014.

"Sec. 14. Except as otherwise provided by this Act, the changes in law made by this Act apply only to an action filed on or after the effective date of this Act. An action filed before the effective date of this Act is governed by the law applicable to the action immediately before the effective date of this Act, and the former law is continued in effect for that purpose."

## § 32.002. Original Jurisdiction for Probate Proceedings

(a) In a county in which there is no statutory probate court or county court at law exercising original probate jurisdiction, the county court has original jurisdiction of probate proceedings.

(b) In a county in which there is no statutory probate court, but in which there is a county court at law exercising original probate jurisdiction, the county court at law exercising original probate jurisdiction and the county court have concurrent original jurisdiction of probate proceedings, unless otherwise provided by law. The judge of a county court may hear probate proceedings while sitting for the judge of any other county court.

(c) In a county in which there is a statutory probate court, the statutory probate court has original jurisdiction of probate proceedings.

Added by Acts 2009, 81st Leg., ch. 1351, § 13(a), eff. Jan. 1, 2014.

Sections 13(c) and 14 of Acts 2009, 81st Leg., ch. 1351 provide:

"[Sec. 13.] (c) Except as otherwise provided by this subsection, this section [Sec. 13] takes effect January 1, 2014. The changes in law made by this section take effect only if H.B. No. 2502, Acts of the 81st Legislature, Regular Session, 2009, is enacted and becomes law. If that bill does not become law, this section has no effect." H.B. No. 2502 [ch. 680], Acts of the 81st Legislature, Regular Session, 2009, was signed by the Governor on June 19, 2009, effective January 1, 2014.

"Sec. 14. Except as otherwise provided by this Act, the changes in law made by this Act apply only to an action filed on or after the effective date of this Act. An action filed before the effective date of this Act is governed by the law applicable to the action immediately before the effective date of this Act, and the former law is continued in effect for that purpose."

### § 32.003. Jurisdiction of Contested Probate Proceeding in County with No Statutory Probate Court or Statutory County Court

(a) In a county in which there is no statutory probate court or county court at law exercising original probate jurisdiction, when a matter in a probate proceeding is contested, the judge of the county court may, on the judge's own motion, or shall, on the motion of any party to the proceeding, according to the motion:

(1) request the assignment of a statutory probate court judge to hear the contested matter, as provided by Section 25.0022, Government Code; or

(2) transfer the contested matter to the district court, which may then hear the contested matter as if originally filed in the district court.

(b) If a party to a probate proceeding files a motion for the assignment of a statutory probate court judge to hear a contested matter in the proceeding before the judge of the county court transfers the contested matter to a district court under this section, the county judge shall grant the motion for the assignment of a statutory probate court judge and may not transfer the matter to the district court unless the party withdraws the motion.

(b–1) If a judge of a county court requests the assignment of a statutory probate court judge to hear a contested matter in a probate proceeding on the judge's own motion or on the motion of a party to the proceeding as provided by this section, the judge may request that the statutory probate court judge be assigned to the entire proceeding on the judge's own motion or on the motion of a party.

(c) A party to a probate proceeding may file a motion for the assignment of a statutory probate court judge under this section before a matter in the proceeding becomes contested, and the motion is given effect as a motion for assignment of a statutory probate court judge under Subsection (a) if the matter later becomes contested.

(d) Notwithstanding any other law, a transfer of a contested matter in a probate proceeding to a district court under any authority other than the authority provided by this section:

(1) is disregarded for purposes of this section; and

(2) does not defeat the right of a party to the proceeding to have the matter assigned to a statutory probate court judge in accordance with this section.

(e) A statutory probate court judge assigned to a contested matter in a probate proceeding or to the entire proceeding under this section has the jurisdiction and authority granted to a statutory probate court by this subtitle. A statutory probate court judge assigned to hear only the contested matter in a probate proceeding shall, on resolution of the matter, including any appeal of the matter, return the matter to the county court for further proceedings not inconsistent with the orders of the statutory probate court or court of appeals, as applicable. A statutory probate court judge assigned to the entire probate proceeding as provided by Subsection (b–1) shall, on resolution of the contested matter in the proceeding, including any appeal of the matter, return the entire proceeding to the county court for further proceedings not inconsistent with the orders of the statutory probate court or court of appeals, as applicable.

(f) A district court to which a contested matter is transferred under this section has the jurisdiction and authority granted to a statutory probate court by this subtitle. On resolution of a contested matter transferred to the district court under this section, including any appeal of the matter, the district court shall return the matter to the county court for further proceedings not inconsistent with the orders of the district court or court of appeals, as applicable.

(g) If only the contested matter in a probate proceeding is assigned to a statutory probate court judge under this section, or if the contested matter in a probate proceeding is transferred to a district court under this section, the county court shall continue to exercise jurisdiction over the management of the estate, other than a contested matter, until final disposition of the contested matter is made in accordance with this section. Any matter related to a probate proceeding in which a contested matter is transferred to a district court may be brought in the district court. The district court in which a matter related to the proceeding is filed may, on its own motion or on the motion of any party, find that the matter is not a contested matter and transfer the matter to the county court with jurisdiction of the management of the estate.

(h) If a contested matter in a probate proceeding is transferred to a district court under this section, the district court has jurisdiction of any contested matter in the proceeding that is subsequently filed, and the county court shall transfer those contested matters to the district court. If a statutory probate court judge is assigned under this section to hear a contested matter in a probate proceeding, the statutory probate court judge shall be assigned to hear any contested matter in the proceeding that is subsequently filed.

(i) The clerk of a district court to which a contested matter in a probate proceeding is transferred under this section may perform in relation to the contested matter any function a county clerk may perform with respect to that type of matter.

Added by Acts 2009, 81st Leg., ch. 1351, § 13(a), eff. Jan. 1, 2014. Amended by Acts 2011, 82nd Leg., ch. 1338 (S.B. 1198), § 2.02, eff. Jan. 1, 2014.

Sections 13(c) and 14 of Acts 2009, 81st Leg., ch. 1351 provide:

"[Sec. 13.] (c) Except as otherwise provided by this subsection, this section [Sec. 13] takes effect January 1, 2014. The changes in law made by this section take effect only if H.B. No. 2502, Acts of the 81st Legislature, Regular Session, 2009, is enacted and becomes law. If that bill does not become law, this section has no effect." H.B. No. 2502, Acts of the 81st Legislature, Regular Session, 2009, was signed by the Governor on June 19, 2009, effective January 1, 2014.

"Sec. 14. Except as otherwise provided by this Act, the changes in law made by this Act apply only to an action filed on or after the effective date of this Act. An action filed before the effective date of this Act is governed by the law applicable to the action immediately before the effective date of this Act, and the former law is continued in effect for that purpose."

### § 32.004. Jurisdiction of Contested Probate Proceeding in County with No Statutory Probate Court

(a) In a county in which there is no statutory probate court, but in which there is a county court at law exercising original probate jurisdiction, when a matter in a probate proceeding is contested, the judge of the county court may, on the judge's own motion, or shall, on the motion of any party to the proceeding, transfer the contested matter to the county court at law. In addition, the judge of the county court, on the judge's own motion or on the motion of a party to the proceeding, may transfer the entire proceeding to the county court at law.

(b) A county court at law to which a proceeding is transferred under this section may hear the proceeding as if originally filed in that court. If only a contested matter in the proceeding is transferred, on the resolution of the matter, the matter shall be returned to the county court for further proceedings not inconsistent with the orders of the county court at law.

Added by Acts 2009, 81st Leg., ch. 1351, § 13(a), eff. Jan. 1, 2014.

Sections 13(c) and 14 of Acts 2009, 81st Leg., ch. 1351 provide:

"[Sec. 13.] (c) Except as otherwise provided by this subsection, this section [Sec. 13] takes effect January 1, 2014. The changes in law made by this section take effect only if H.B. No. 2502, Acts of the 81st Legislature, Regular Session, 2009, is enacted and becomes law. If that bill does not become law, this section has no effect." H.B. No. 2502 [ch. 680], Acts of the 81st Legislature, Regular Session, 2009, was signed by the Governor on June 19, 2009, effective January 1, 2014.

"Sec. 14. Except as otherwise provided by this Act, the changes in law made by this Act apply only to an action filed on or after the effective date of this Act. An action filed before the effective date of this Act is governed by the law applicable to the action immediately before the effective date of this Act, and the former law is continued in effect for that purpose."

### § 32.005. Exclusive Jurisdiction of Probate Proceeding in County with Statutory Probate Court

(a) In a county in which there is a statutory probate court, the statutory probate court has exclusive jurisdiction of all probate proceedings, regardless of whether contested or uncontested. A cause of action related to the probate proceeding must be brought in a statutory probate court unless the jurisdiction of the statutory probate court is concurrent with the jurisdiction of a district court as provided by Section 32.007 or with the jurisdiction of any other court.

(b) This section shall be construed in conjunction and in harmony with Chapter 401 and Section 402.001 and all other sections of this title relating to independent executors, but may not be construed to expand the court's control over an independent executor.

Added by Acts 2009, 81st Leg., ch. 1351, § 13(a), eff. Jan. 1, 2014. Amended by Acts 2013, 83rd Leg., ch. 161 (S.B. 1093), § 6.007, eff. Jan. 1, 2014.

Sections 13(c) and 14 of Acts 2009, 81st Leg., ch. 1351 provide:

"[Sec. 13.] (c) Except as otherwise provided by this subsection, this section [Sec. 13] takes effect January 1, 2014. The changes in law made by this section take effect only if H.B. No. 2502, Acts of the 81st Legislature, Regular Session, 2009, is enacted and becomes law. If that bill does not become law, this section has no effect." H.B. No. 2502 [ch. 680], Acts of the 81st Legislature, Regular Session, 2009, was signed by the Governor on June 19, 2009, effective January 1, 2014.

"Sec. 14. Except as otherwise provided by this Act, the changes in law made by this Act apply only to an action filed on or after the effective date of this Act. An action filed before the effective date of this Act is governed by the law applicable to the action immediately before the effective date of this Act, and the former law is continued in effect for that purpose."

### § 32.006. Jurisdiction of Statutory Probate Court with Respect to Trusts and Powers of Attorney

In a county in which there is a statutory probate court, the statutory probate court has jurisdiction of:

(1) an action by or against a trustee;

(2) an action involving an inter vivos trust, testamentary trust, or charitable trust;

(3) an action by or against an agent or former agent under a power of attorney arising out of the agent's performance of the duties of an agent; and

(4) an action to determine the validity of a power of attorney or to determine an agent's rights, powers, or duties under a power of attorney.

Added by Acts 2009, 81st Leg., ch. 1351, § 13(a), eff. Jan. 1, 2014.  Amended by Acts 2013, 83rd Leg., ch. 1136 (H.B. 2912), § 3, eff. Jan. 1, 2014.

Sections 13(c) and 14 of Acts 2009, 81st Leg., ch. 1351 provide:

"[Sec. 13.]  (c) Except as otherwise provided by this subsection, this section [Sec. 13] takes effect January 1, 2014.  The changes in law made by this section take effect only if H.B. No. 2502, Acts of the 81st Legislature, Regular Session, 2009, is enacted and becomes law. If that bill does not become law, this section has no effect."  H.B. No. 2502 [ch. 680], Acts of the 81st Legislature, Regular Session, 2009, was signed by the Governor on June 19, 2009, effective January 1, 2014.

"Sec. 14.  Except as otherwise provided by this Act, the changes in law made by this Act apply only to an action filed on or after the effective date of this Act.  An action filed before the effective date of this Act is governed by the law applicable to the action immediately before the effective date of this Act, and the former law is continued in effect for that purpose."

Section 62(d) of Acts 2013, 83rd Leg., ch. 1136 (H.B. 2912) provides:

"The changes in law made by Sections 32.006, 256.052, 256.053, 256.054, 256.152(c), 256.153, 256.154, 256.155(a), 256.156, 256.203, 257.052, 257.053, 401.001(a), 401.004(d), and 401.006, Estates Code, as amended by this Act, and Section 53.107, Estates Code, as added by this Act, apply only to an action filed or other proceeding commenced on or after the effective date [Jan. 1, 2014] of this Act.  An action filed or other proceeding commenced before the effective date of this Act is governed by the law in effect on the date the action was filed or the proceeding was commenced, and the former law is continued in effect for that purpose."

## § 32.007.  Concurrent Jurisdiction with District Court

A statutory probate court has concurrent jurisdiction with the district court in:

(1) a personal injury, survival, or wrongful death action by or against a person in the person's capacity as a personal representative;

(2) an action by or against a trustee;

(3) an action involving an inter vivos trust, testamentary trust, or charitable trust, including a charitable trust as defined by Section 123.001, Property Code;

(4) an action involving a personal representative of an estate in which each other party aligned with the personal representative is not an interested person in that estate;

(5) an action against an agent or former agent under a power of attorney arising out of the agent's performance of the duties of an agent; and

(6) an action to determine the validity of a power of attorney or to determine an agent's rights, powers, or duties under a power of attorney.

Added by Acts 2009, 81st Leg., ch. 1351, § 13(a), eff. Jan. 1, 2014.  Amended by Acts 2011, 82nd Leg., ch. 1338 (S.B. 1198), § 2.03, eff. Jan. 1, 2014.

Sections 13(c) and 14 of Acts 2009, 81st Leg., ch. 1351 provide:

"[Sec. 13.]  (c) Except as otherwise provided by this subsection, this section [Sec. 13] takes effect January 1, 2014.  The changes in law made by this section take effect only if H.B. No. 2502, Acts of the 81st Legislature, Regular Session, 2009, is enacted and becomes law. If that bill does not become law, this section has no effect."  H.B. No. 2502 [ch. 680], Acts of the 81st Legislature, Regular Session, 2009, was signed by the Governor on June 19, 2009, effective January 1, 2014.

"Sec. 14.  Except as otherwise provided by this Act, the changes in law made by this Act apply only to an action filed on or after the effective date of this Act.  An action filed before the effective date of this Act is governed by the law applicable to the action immediately before the effective date of this Act, and the former law is continued in effect for that purpose."

## CHAPTER 33.  VENUE

### SUBCHAPTER A.  VENUE FOR CERTAIN PROCEEDINGS

### SUBCHAPTER A.  VENUE FOR CERTAIN PROCEEDINGS

## § 33.001.  Probate of Wills and Granting of Letters Testamentary and of Administration

Venue for a probate proceeding to admit a will to probate or for the granting of letters testamentary or of administration is:

(1) in the county in which the decedent resided, if the decedent had a domicile or fixed place of residence in this state; or

(2) with respect to a decedent who did not have a domicile or fixed place of residence in this state:

(A) if the decedent died in this state, in the county in which:

(i) the decedent's principal estate was located at the time of the decedent's death; or

(ii) the decedent died; or

(B) if the decedent died outside of this state:

(i) in any county in this state in which the decedent's nearest of kin reside; or

(ii) if there is no next of kin of the decedent in this state, in the county in which the decedent's principal estate was located at the time of the decedent's death.

Added by Acts 2011, 82nd Leg., ch. 1338 (S.B. 1198), § 2.04, eff. Jan. 1, 2014.

### § 33.002. Action Related to Probate Proceeding in Statutory Probate Court

Except as provided by Section 33.003, venue for any cause of action related to a probate proceeding pending in a statutory probate court is proper in the statutory probate court in which the decedent's estate is pending.

Added by Acts 2011, 82nd Leg., ch. 1338 (S.B. 1198), § 2.04, eff. Jan. 1, 2014.

### § 33.003. Certain Actions Involving Personal Representative

Notwithstanding any other provision of this chapter, the proper venue for an action by or against a personal representative for personal injury, death, or property damages is determined under Section 15.007, Civil Practice and Remedies Code.

Added by Acts 2011, 82nd Leg., ch. 1338 (S.B. 1198), § 2.04, eff. Jan. 1, 2014.

### § 33.004. Heirship Proceedings

(a) Venue for a proceeding to determine a decedent's heirs is in:

(1) the court of the county in which a proceeding admitting the decedent's will to probate or administering the decedent's estate was most recently pending; or

(2) the court of the county in which venue would be proper for commencement of an administration of the decedent's estate under Section 33.001 if:

(A) no will of the decedent has been admitted to probate in this state and no administration of the decedent's estate has been granted in this state; or

(B) the proceeding is commenced by the trustee of a trust holding assets for the benefit of the decedent.

(b) Notwithstanding Subsection (a) and Section 33.001, if there is no administration pending of the estate of a deceased ward who died intestate, venue for a proceeding to determine the deceased ward's heirs is in the probate court in which the guardianship proceedings with respect to the ward's estate were pending on the date of the ward's death. A proceeding described by this subsection may not be brought as part of the guardianship proceedings with respect to the ward's estate, but rather must be filed as a separate cause in which the court may determine the heirs' respective shares and interests in the estate as provided by the laws of this state.

Added by Acts 2011, 82nd Leg., ch. 1338 (S.B. 1198), § 2.04, eff. Jan. 1, 2014.

### § 33.005. Certain Actions Involving Breach of Fiduciary Duty

Notwithstanding any other provision of this chapter, venue for a proceeding brought by the attorney general alleging breach of a fiduciary duty by a charitable entity or a fiduciary or managerial agent of a charitable trust is determined under Section 123.005, Property Code.

Added by Acts 2011, 82nd Leg., ch. 1338 (S.B. 1198), § 2.04, eff. Jan. 1, 2014.

### SUBCHAPTER B. DETERMINATION OF VENUE

### § 33.051. Commencement of Proceeding

For purposes of this subchapter, a probate proceeding is considered commenced on the filing of an application for the proceeding that avers facts sufficient to confer venue on the court in which the application is filed.

Added by Acts 2011, 82nd Leg., ch. 1338 (S.B. 1198), § 2.04, eff. Jan. 1, 2014.

### § 33.052. Concurrent Venue

(a) If applications for probate proceedings involving the same estate are filed in two or more courts having concurrent venue, the court in which a proceeding involving the estate was first commenced has and retains jurisdiction of the proceeding to the exclusion of the other court or courts in which a proceeding involving the same estate was commenced.

(b) The first commenced probate proceeding extends to all of the decedent's property, including the decedent's estate property.

Added by Acts 2011, 82nd Leg., ch. 1338 (S.B. 1198), § 2.04, eff. Jan. 1, 2014.

### § 33.053. Probate Proceedings in More Than One County

If probate proceedings involving the same estate are commenced in more than one county, each proceeding commenced in a county other than the county in which a proceeding was first commenced is stayed until the court in which the proceeding was first commenced makes a final determination of venue.

Added by Acts 2011, 82nd Leg., ch. 1338 (S.B. 1198), § 2.04, eff. Jan. 1, 2014.

### § 33.054. Jurisdiction to Determine Venue

(a) Subject to Sections 33.052 and 33.053, a court in which an application for a probate proceeding is filed has jurisdiction to determine venue for the proceeding and for any matter related to the proceeding.

(b) A court's determination under this section is not subject to collateral attack.

Added by Acts 2011, 82nd Leg., ch. 1338 (S.B. 1198), § 2.04, eff. Jan. 1, 2014.

### § 33.055. Protection for Certain Purchasers

Notwithstanding Section 33.052, a bona fide purchaser of real property who relied on a probate proceeding that was not the first commenced proceeding, without knowledge that the proceeding was not the first commenced proceeding, shall be protected with respect to the purchase unless before the purchase an order rendered in the first commenced proceeding admitting the decedent's will to probate, determining the decedent's heirs, or granting administration of the decedent's estate was recorded in the office of the county clerk of the county in which the purchased property is located.

Added by Acts 2011, 82nd Leg., ch. 1338 (S.B. 1198), § 2.04, eff. Jan. 1, 2014.

### SUBCHAPTER C. TRANSFER OF PROBATE PROCEEDING

### § 33.101. Transfer to Other County in Which Venue Is Proper

If probate proceedings involving the same estate are commenced in more than one county and the court

making a determination of venue as provided by Section 33.053 determines that venue is proper in another county, the court clerk shall make and retain a copy of the entire file in the case and transmit the original file to the court in the county in which venue is proper. The court to which the file is transmitted shall conduct the proceeding in the same manner as if the proceeding had originally been commenced in that county.

Added by Acts 2011, 82nd Leg., ch. 1338 (S.B. 1198), § 2.04, eff. Jan. 1, 2014.

### § 33.102. Transfer for Want of Venue

(a) If it appears to the court at any time before the final order in a probate proceeding is rendered that the court does not have priority of venue over the proceeding, the court shall, on the application of an interested person, transfer the proceeding to the proper county by transmitting to the proper court in that county:

(1) the original file in the case; and

(2) certified copies of all entries that have been made in the judge's probate docket in the proceeding.

(b) The court of the county to which a probate proceeding is transferred under Subsection (a) shall complete the proceeding in the same manner as if the proceeding had originally been commenced in that county.

(c) If the question as to priority of venue is not raised before a final order in a probate proceeding is announced, the finality of the order is not affected by any error in venue.

Added by Acts 2011, 82nd Leg., ch. 1338 (S.B. 1198), § 2.04, eff. Jan. 1, 2014.

### § 33.103. Transfer for Convenience

(a) The court may order that a probate proceeding be transferred to the proper court in another county in this state if it appears to the court at any time before the proceeding is concluded that the transfer would be in the best interest of:

(1) the estate; or

(2) if there is no administration of the estate, the decedent's heirs or beneficiaries under the decedent's will.

(b) The clerk of the court from which the probate proceeding described by Subsection (a) is transferred shall transmit to the court to which the proceeding is transferred:

(1) the original file in the proceeding; and

(2) a certified copy of the index.

Added by Acts 2011, 82nd Leg., ch. 1338 (S.B. 1198), § 2.04, eff. Jan. 1, 2014.

### § 33.104. Validation of Previous Proceedings

All orders entered in connection with a probate proceeding that is transferred to another county under a provision of this subchapter are valid and shall be recognized in the court to which the proceeding is transferred if the orders were made and entered in conformance with the procedure prescribed by this code.

Added by Acts 2011, 82nd Leg., ch. 1338 (S.B. 1198), § 2.04, eff. Jan. 1, 2014.

### CHAPTER 34. MATTERS RELATING TO CERTAIN OTHER TYPES OF PROCEEDINGS

### § 34.001. Transfer of Proceeding

(a) A judge of a statutory probate court, on the motion of a party to the action or on the motion of a person interested in an estate, may transfer to the judge's court from a district, county, or statutory court a cause of action related to a probate proceeding pending in the statutory probate court or a cause of action in which a personal representative of an estate pending in the statutory probate court is a party and may consolidate the transferred cause of action with the other proceedings in the statutory probate court relating to that estate.

(b) Notwithstanding any other provision of this subtitle, Title 1, Subtitle X, Title 2, Chapter 51, 52, 53, 54, 55, or 151, or Section 351.001, 351.002, 351.053, 351.352, 351.353, 351.354, or 351.355, the proper venue for an action by or against a personal representative for personal injury, death, or property damages is determined under Section 15.007, Civil Practice and Remedies Code.

Added by Acts 1983, 68th Leg., p. 5228, ch. 958, § 1, eff. Sept. 1, 1983. Amended by Acts 1999, 76th Leg., ch. 1431, § 1, eff. Sept. 1, 1999; Acts 2003, 78th Leg., ch. 204, § 3.06, eff. Sept. 1, 2003; Subsec. (a) amended by Acts 2009, 81st Leg., ch. 1351, § 12(c), eff. Sept. 1, 2009. Redesignated from V.A.T.S. Probate Code, § 5B by Acts 2009, 81st Leg., ch. 680, § 2, eff. Jan. 1, 2014. Redesignated from V.T.C.A., Estates Code § 5B and amended by Acts 2013, 83rd Leg., ch. 161 (S.B. 1093), § 6.009, eff. Jan. 1, 2014.

Section 3 of Acts 1999, 76th Leg., ch. 1431 provides:

"This Act takes effect September 1, 1999, and applies only to a motion to transfer a cause of action filed on or after that date. A motion to transfer a cause of action filed before the effective date of this Act is governed by the law in effect on the date the motion was filed, and the former law is continued in effect for that purpose."

Section 12(i) of Acts 2009, 81st Leg., ch. 1351 provides:

"The changes in law made by this section apply only to an action filed or a proceeding commenced on or after the effective date [Jan. 1, 2014] of this Act. An action filed or proceeding commenced before the effective date of this Act is governed by the law in effect on the date the action was filed or the proceeding was commenced, and the former law is continued in effect for that purpose."

### § 34.002. Actions to Collect Delinquent Property Taxes

(a) This section applies only to a decedent's estate that:

(1) is being administered in a pending probate proceeding;

(2) owns or claims an interest in property against which a taxing unit has imposed ad valorem taxes that are delinquent; and

(3) is not being administered as an independent administration under Chapter 401 and Section 402.001.

(b) Notwithstanding any provision of this code to the contrary, if the probate proceedings are pending in a foreign jurisdiction or in a county other than the county in which the taxes were imposed, a suit to foreclose the lien securing payment of the taxes or to enforce personal liability for the taxes must be brought under Section 33.41, Tax Code, in a court of competent jurisdiction in the county in which the taxes were imposed.

(c) If the probate proceedings have been pending for four years or less in the county in which the taxes were imposed, the taxing unit may present a claim for the delinquent taxes against the estate to the personal representative of the estate in the probate proceedings.

(d) If the taxing unit presents a claim against the estate under Subsection (c):

(1) the claim of the taxing unit is subject to each applicable provision in Subchapter A, Chapter 124, Subchapter B, Chapter 308, Subchapter F, Chapter 351, and Chapters 355 and 356 that relates to a claim or the enforcement of a claim in a probate proceeding; and

(2) the taxing unit may not bring a suit in any other court to foreclose the lien securing payment of the taxes or to enforce personal liability for the delinquent taxes before the first day after the

fourth anniversary of the date the application for the probate proceeding was filed.

(e) To foreclose the lien securing payment of the delinquent taxes, the taxing unit must bring a suit under Section 33.41, Tax Code, in a court of competent jurisdiction for the county in which the taxes were imposed if:

(1) the probate proceedings have been pending in that county for more than four years; and

(2) the taxing unit did not present a delinquent tax claim under Subsection (c) against the estate in the probate proceeding.

(f) In a suit brought under Subsection (e), the taxing unit:

(1) shall make the personal representative of the decedent's estate a party to the suit; and

(2) may not seek to enforce personal liability for the taxes against the estate of the decedent.

Added by Acts 1999, 76th Leg., ch. 1481, § 36, eff. Sept. 1, 1999. Redesignated from V.A.T.S. Probate Code, § 5C by Acts 2009, 81st Leg., ch. 680, § 2, eff. Jan. 1, 2014. Redesignated from V.T.C.A., Estates Code § 5C and amended by Acts 2013, 83rd Leg., ch. 161 (S.B. 1093), § 6.009, eff. Jan. 1, 2014.

Section 52 of Acts 1999, 76th Leg., ch. 1481 provides:

"The changes in law made by Sections 36, 37, and 38 of this Act apply to the estates of all decedents, regardless of the date of death, and to the estates of all wards, regardless of the date the application for appointment of a guardian was filed, and to all causes of action pending on September 1, 1999, or brought after that date."

## SUBTITLE B. PROCEDURAL MATTERS

### CHAPTER 51. NOTICES AND PROCESS IN PROBATE PROCEEDINGS IN GENERAL

### SUBCHAPTER A. ISSUANCE AND FORM OF NOTICE OR PROCESS

#### § 51.001. Issuance of Notice or Process in General

(a) Except as provided by Subsection (b), a person is not required to be cited or otherwise given notice except in a situation in which this title expressly provides for citation or the giving of notice.

(b) If this title does not expressly provide for citation or the issuance or return of notice in a probate matter, the court may require that notice be given. A court that requires that notice be given may prescribe the form and manner of service of the notice and the return of service.

(c) Unless a court order is required by this title, the county clerk without a court order shall issue:

(1) necessary citations, writs, and other process in a probate matter; and

(2) all notices not required to be issued by a personal representative.

Added by Acts 2009, 81st Leg., ch. 680, § 1, eff. Jan. 1, 2014.

#### § 51.002. Direction of Writ or Other Process

(a) A writ or other process other than a citation or notice must be directed "To any sheriff or constable within the State of Texas."

(b) Notwithstanding Subsection (a), a writ or other process other than a citation or notice may not be held defective because the process is directed to the sheriff or a constable of a named county if the process is properly served within that county by the sheriff or constable.

Added by Acts 2009, 81st Leg., ch. 680, § 1, eff. Jan. 1, 2014.

### § 51.003.  Contents of Citation or Notice

(a) A citation or notice must:

(1) be directed to the person to be cited or notified;

(2) be dated;

(3) state the style and number of the proceeding;

(4) state the court in which the proceeding is pending;

(5) describe generally the nature of the proceeding or matter to which the citation or notice relates;

(6) direct the person being cited or notified to appear by filing a written contest or answer or to perform another required action; and

(7) state when and where the appearance or performance described by Subdivision (6) is required.

(b) A citation or notice issued by the county clerk must be styled "The State of Texas" and be signed by the clerk under the clerk's seal.

(c) A notice required to be given by a personal representative must be in writing and be signed by the representative in the representative's official capacity.

(d) A citation or notice is not required to contain a precept directed to an officer, but may not be held defective because the citation or notice contains a precept directed to an officer authorized to serve the citation or notice.

Added by Acts 2009, 81st Leg., ch. 680, § 1, eff. Jan. 1, 2014.

## SUBCHAPTER B.  METHODS OF SERVING CITATION OR NOTICE; PERSONS TO BE SERVED

### § 51.051.  Personal Service

(a) Except as otherwise provided by Subsection (b), if personal service of citation or notice is required, the citation or notice must be served on the attorney of record for the person to be cited or notified. Notwithstanding the requirement of personal service, service may be made on that attorney by any method specified by Section 51.055 for service on an attorney of record.

(b) If the person to be cited or notified does not have an attorney of record in the proceeding, or if an attempt to serve the person's attorney is unsuccessful:

(1) the sheriff or constable shall serve the citation or notice by delivering a copy of the citation or notice to the person to be cited or notified, in person, if the person to whom the citation or notice is directed is in this state; or

(2) any disinterested person competent to make an oath that the citation or notice was served may serve the citation or notice, if the person to be cited or notified is absent from or is not a resident of this state.

(c) The return day of the citation or notice served under Subsection (b) must be at least 10 days after the date of service, excluding the date of service.

(d) If citation or notice attempted to be served as provided by Subsection (b) is returned with the notation that the person sought to be served, whether inside or outside this state, cannot be found, the county clerk shall issue a new citation or notice. Service of the new citation or notice must be made by publication.

Added by Acts 2009, 81st Leg., ch. 680, § 1, eff. Jan. 1, 2014.

### § 51.052.  Service by Mail

(a) The county clerk, or the personal representative if required by statute or court order, shall serve a citation or notice required or permitted to be served by regular mail by mailing the original citation or notice to the person to be cited or notified.

(b) Except as provided by Subsection (c), the county clerk shall issue a citation or notice required or permitted to be served by registered or certified mail and shall serve the citation or notice by mailing the original citation or notice by registered or certified mail.

(c) A personal representative shall issue a notice required to be given by the representative by registered or certified mail and shall serve the notice by mailing the original notice by registered or certified mail.

(d) The county clerk or personal representative, as applicable, shall mail a citation or notice under Subsection (b) or (c) with an instruction to deliver the citation or notice to the addressee only and with return receipt requested. The clerk or representative, as applicable, shall address the envelope containing the citation or notice to:

(1) the attorney of record in the proceeding for the person to be cited or notified; or

(2) the person to be cited or notified, if the citation or notice to the attorney is returned unde-

livered or the person to be cited or notified has no attorney of record in the proceeding.

(e) Service by mail shall be made at least 20 days before the return day of the service, excluding the date of service. The date of service by mail is the date of mailing.

(f) A copy of a citation or notice served under Subsection (a), (b), or (c), together with a certificate of the person serving the citation or notice showing that the citation or notice was mailed and the date of the mailing, shall be filed and recorded. A returned receipt for a citation or notice served under Subsection (b) or (c) shall be attached to the certificate.

(g) If a citation or notice served by mail is returned undelivered, a new citation or notice shall be issued. Service of the new citation or notice must be made by posting.

Added by Acts 2009, 81st Leg., ch. 680, § 1, eff. Jan. 1, 2014.

### § 51.053. Service by Posting

(a) The county clerk shall deliver the original and a copy of a citation or notice required to be posted to the sheriff or a constable of the county in which the proceeding is pending. The sheriff or constable shall post the copy at the door of the county courthouse or the location in or near the courthouse where public notices are customarily posted.

(b) Citation or notice under this section must be posted for at least 10 days before the return day of the service, excluding the date of posting, except as provided by Section 51.102(b). The date of service of citation or notice by posting is the date of posting.

(c) A sheriff or constable who posts a citation or notice under this section shall return the original citation or notice to the county clerk and state the date and location of the posting in a written return on the citation or notice.

(d) The method of service prescribed by this section applies when a personal representative is required or permitted to post a notice. The notice must be:

(1) issued in the name of the representative;

(2) addressed and delivered to, and posted and returned by, the appropriate officer; and

(3) filed with the county clerk.

Added by Acts 2009, 81st Leg., ch. 680, § 1, eff. Jan. 1, 2014.

### § 51.054. Service by Publication

(a) Citation or notice to a person to be served by publication shall be published one time in a newspaper of general circulation in the county in which the proceeding is pending. The publication must be made at least 10 days before the return day of the service, excluding the date of publication.

(b) The date of service of citation or notice by publication is the date of publication printed on the newspaper in which the citation or notice is published.

(c) If no newspaper is published, printed, or of general circulation in the county in which the citation or notice is to be published, the citation or notice under Subsection (a) shall be served by posting.

Added by Acts 2009, 81st Leg., ch. 680, § 1, eff. Jan. 1, 2014.

### § 51.055. Service on Party's Attorney of Record

(a) If a party is represented by an attorney of record in a probate proceeding, each citation or notice required to be served on the party in that proceeding shall be served instead on that attorney. A notice under this subsection may be served by delivery to the attorney in person or by registered or certified mail.

(b) A notice may be served on an attorney of record under this section by:

(1) another party to the proceeding;

(2) the attorney of record for another party to the proceeding;

(3) the appropriate sheriff or constable; or

(4) any other person competent to testify.

(c) Each of the following is prima facie evidence of the fact that service has been made under this section:

(1) the written statement of an attorney of record showing service;

(2) the return of the officer showing service; and

(3) the affidavit of any other person showing service.

Added by Acts 2009, 81st Leg., ch. 680, § 1, eff. Jan. 1, 2014.

### § 51.056. Service on Personal Representative or Receiver

Unless this title expressly provides for another method of service, the county clerk who issues a citation or notice required to be served on a personal representative or receiver shall serve the citation or notice by mailing the original citation or notice by registered or certified mail to:

(1) the representative's or receiver's attorney of record; or

(2) the representative or receiver, if the representative or receiver does not have an attorney of record.

Added by Acts 2009, 81st Leg., ch. 680, § 1, eff. Jan. 1, 2014.

## SUBCHAPTER C. RETURN AND PROOF OF SERVICE OF CITATION OR NOTICE

### § 51.101. Requirements for Return on Citation or Notice Served by Personal Service

The return of the person serving a citation or notice under Section 51.051 must:

(1) be endorsed on or attached to the citation or notice;

(2) state the date and place of service;

(3) certify that a copy of the citation or notice was delivered to the person directed to be served;

(4) be subscribed and sworn to before, and under the hand and official seal of, an officer authorized by the laws of this state to take an affidavit; and

(5) be returned to the county clerk who issued the citation or notice.

Added by Acts 2009, 81st Leg., ch. 680, § 1, eff. Jan. 1, 2014.

### § 51.102. Validity of Service and Return on Citation or Notice Served by Posting

(a) A citation or notice in a probate matter that is required to be served by posting and is issued in conformity with this title, and the service and return of service of the citation or notice, is valid if:

(1) a sheriff or constable posts a copy of the citation or notice at the location or locations prescribed by this title; and

(2) the posting occurs on a day preceding the return day of service specified in the citation or notice that provides sufficient time for the period the citation or notice must be posted to expire before the specified return day.

(b) The fact that a sheriff or constable, as applicable, makes the return of service on the citation or notice described by Subsection (a) and returns the citation or notice on which the return has been made to the court before the expiration of the period the citation or notice must be posted does not affect the validity of the citation or notice or the service or return of service. This subsection applies even if the sheriff or constable makes the return of service and returns the citation or notice on which the return is

made to the court on the same day the citation or notice is issued.

Added by Acts 2009, 81st Leg., ch. 680, § 1, eff. Jan. 1, 2014.

### § 51.103. Proof of Service

(a) Proof of service in each case requiring citation or notice must be filed before the hearing.

(b) Proof of service consists of:

(1) if the service is made by a sheriff or constable, the return of service;

(2) if the service is made by a private person, the person's affidavit;

(3) if the service is made by mail:

(A) the certificate of the county clerk making the service, or the affidavit of the personal representative or other person making the service, stating that the citation or notice was mailed and the date of the mailing; and

(B) the return receipt attached to the certificate or affidavit, as applicable, if the mailing was by registered or certified mail and a receipt has been returned; and

(4) if the service is made by publication, an affidavit:

(A) made by the publisher of the newspaper in which the citation or notice was published or an employee of the publisher;

(B) that contains or to which is attached a copy of the published citation or notice; and

(C) that states the date of publication printed on the newspaper in which the citation or notice was published.

Added by Acts 2009, 81st Leg., ch. 680, § 1, eff. Jan. 1, 2014.

### § 51.104. Return to Court

A citation or notice issued by a county clerk must be returned to the court from which the citation or notice was issued on the first Monday after the service is perfected.

Added by Acts 2009, 81st Leg., ch. 680, § 1, eff. Jan. 1, 2014.

## SUBCHAPTER D. ALTERNATIVE MANNER OF ISSUANCE, SERVICE, AND RETURN

### § 51.151. Court–Ordered Issuance, Service, and Return Under Certain Circumstances

(a) A citation or notice required by this title shall be issued, served, and returned in the manner specified by written order of the court in accordance with this title and the Texas Rules of Civil Procedure if:

(1) an interested person requests that action;

(2) a specific method is not provided by this title for giving the citation or notice;

(3) a specific method is not provided by this title for the service and return of citation or notice; or

(4) a provision relating to a matter described by Subdivision (2) or (3) is inadequate.

(b) Citation or notice issued, served, and returned in the manner specified by a court order as provided by Subsection (a) has the same effect as if the manner of service and return had been specified by this title.

Added by Acts 2009, 81st Leg., ch. 680, § 1, eff. Jan. 1, 2014.

## SUBCHAPTER E.　ADDITIONAL NOTICE PROVISIONS

### § 51.201.　Waiver of Notice of Hearing

(a) A legally competent person who is interested in a hearing in a probate proceeding may waive notice of the hearing in writing either in person or through an attorney.

(b) A trustee of a trust may waive notice under Subsection (a) on behalf of a beneficiary of the trust as provided by that subsection.

(c) A consul or other representative of a foreign government whose appearance has been entered as provided by law on behalf of a person residing in a foreign country may waive notice under Subsection (a) on the person's behalf as provided by that subsection.

(d) A person who submits to the jurisdiction of the court in a hearing is considered to have waived notice of the hearing.

Added by Acts 2009, 81st Leg., ch. 680, § 1, eff. Jan. 1, 2014.

### § 51.202.　Request for Notice of Filing of Pleading

(a) At any time after an application is filed to commence a probate proceeding, including a proceeding for the probate of a will, the grant of letters testamentary or of administration, or a determination of heirship, a person interested in the estate may file with the county clerk a written request to be notified of all, or any specified, motions, applications, or pleadings filed with respect to the proceeding by any person or by one or more persons specifically named in the request. A person filing a request under this section is responsible for payment of the fees and other costs of providing a requested notice, and the clerk may require a deposit to cover the estimated

costs of providing the notice. Thereafter, the clerk shall send to the requestor by regular mail a copy of any requested document.

(b) A county clerk's failure to comply with a request under this section does not invalidate any proceeding.

Added by Acts 2009, 81st Leg., ch. 680, § 1, eff. Jan. 1, 2014.

### § 51.203.　Service of Notice of Intention to Take Depositions in Certain Matters

(a) If a will is to be probated, or in another probate matter in which there is no opposing party or attorney of record on whom to serve notice and copies of interrogatories, service may be made by posting notice of the intention to take depositions for a period of 10 days as provided by Section 51.053 governing a posting of notice.

(b) When notice by posting under Subsection (a) is filed with the county clerk, a copy of the interrogatories must also be filed.

(c) At the expiration of the 10–day period prescribed by Subsection (a):

(1) the depositions for which the notice was posted may be taken; and

(2) the judge may file cross-interrogatories if no person appears.

Added by Acts 2009, 81st Leg., ch. 680, § 1, eff. Jan. 1, 2014. Amended by Acts 2013, 83rd Leg., ch. 1136 (H.B. 2912), § 4, eff. Jan. 1, 2014.

Section 62(e) of Acts 2013, 83rd Leg., ch. 1136 (H.B. 2912) provides:

"The changes in law made by Sections 51.203(c), 53.104, 305.002(a), 305.003, 308.054(b), 309.051(a), 309.056, 309.103(a) and (b), 355.060, 361.155(b), 362.005, 362.011, 362.013, 404.001(a), 404.003, 404.005(b) and (c), and 551.001(a), Estates Code, as amended by this Act, and Sections 253.001(c), 301.155, 305.004, 309.057, 361.155(c), 404.0035, 404.0036, and 404.0037, Estates Code, as added by this Act, apply to the administration of the estate of a decedent that is pending or commenced on or after the effective date [Jan. 1, 2014] of this Act."

## CHAPTER 52.　FILING AND RECORDKEEPING

### SUBCHAPTER A.　RECORDKEEPING REQUIREMENTS

## SUBCHAPTER A. RECORDKEEPING REQUIREMENTS

### § 52.001. Probate Docket

(a) The county clerk shall maintain a record book titled "Judge's Probate Docket" and shall record in the book:

(1) the name of each person with respect to whom, or with respect to whose estate, proceedings are commenced or sought to be commenced;

(2) the name of each executor, administrator, or applicant for letters testamentary or of administration;

(3) the date each original application for probate proceedings is filed;

(4) a notation of each order, judgment, decree, and proceeding that occurs in each estate, including the date it occurs; and

(5) the docket number of each estate as assigned under Subsection (b).

(b) The county clerk shall assign a docket number to each estate in the order proceedings are commenced.

Added by Acts 2009, 81st Leg., ch. 680, § 1, eff. Jan. 1, 2014. Amended by Acts 2011, 82nd Leg., ch. 91 (S.B. 1303), § 8.001, eff. Jan. 1, 2014.

### § 52.002. Claim Docket

(a) The county clerk shall maintain a record book titled "Claim Docket" and shall record in the book each claim that is presented against an estate for the court's approval.

(b) The county clerk shall assign one or more pages of the record book to each estate.

(c) The claim docket must be ruled in 16 columns at proper intervals from top to bottom, with a short note of the contents at the top of each column. The county clerk shall record for each claim, in the order claims are filed, the following information in the respective columns, beginning with the first or marginal column:

(1) the name of the claimant;

(2) the amount of the claim;

(3) the date of the claim;

(4) the date the claim is filed;

(5) the date the claim is due;

(6) the date the claim begins bearing interest;

(7) the interest rate;

(8) the date the claim is allowed by the executor or administrator, if applicable;

(9) the amount allowed by the executor or administrator, if applicable;

(10) the date the claim is rejected, if applicable;

(11) the date the claim is approved, if applicable;

(12) the amount approved for the claim, if applicable;

(13) the date the claim is disapproved, if applicable;

(14) the class to which the claim belongs;

(15) the date the claim is established by a judgment of a court, if applicable; and

(16) the amount of the judgment established under Subdivision (15), if applicable.

Added by Acts 2009, 81st Leg., ch. 680, § 1, eff. Jan. 1, 2014.

### § 52.003. Probate Fee Book

(a) The county clerk shall maintain a record book titled "Probate Fee Book" and shall record in the book each item of cost that accrues to the officers of the court and any witness fees.

(b) Each record entry must include:

(1) the party to whom the cost or fee is due;

(2) the date the cost or fee accrued;

(3) the estate or party liable for the cost or fee; and

(4) the date the cost or fee is paid.

Added by Acts 2009, 81st Leg., ch. 680, § 1, eff. Jan. 1, 2014.

### § 52.004. Alternate Recordkeeping

Instead of maintaining the record books described by Sections 52.001, 52.002, and 52.003, the county clerk may maintain the information described by those sections relating to a person's or estate's probate proceedings:

(1) on a computer file;

(2) on microfilm;

(3) in the form of a digitized optical image; or

(4) in another similar form of data compilation.

Added by Acts 2009, 81st Leg., ch. 680, § 1, eff. Jan. 1, 2014.

## SUBCHAPTER B. FILES; INDEX

### § 52.051. Filing Procedures

(a) An application for a probate proceeding, complaint, petition, or other paper permitted or required by law to be filed with a court in a probate matter must be filed with the county clerk of the appropriate county.

(b) Each paper filed in an estate must be given the docket number assigned to the estate.

(c) On receipt of a paper described by Subsection (a), the county clerk shall:

(1) file the paper; and

(2) endorse on the paper:

(A) the date the paper is filed;

(B) the docket number; and

(C) the clerk's official signature.

Added by Acts 2009, 81st Leg., ch. 680, § 1, eff. Jan. 1, 2014.

## § 52.052. Case Files

(a) The county clerk shall maintain a case file for the estate of each decedent for which a probate proceeding has been filed.

(b) Each case file must contain each order, judgment, and proceeding of the court and any other probate filing with the court, including each:

(1) application for the probate of a will;

(2) application for the granting of administration;

(3) citation and notice, whether published or posted, including the return on the citation or notice;

(4) will and the testimony on which the will is admitted to probate;

(5) bond and official oath;

(6) inventory, appraisement, and list of claims;

(6-a) affidavit in lieu of the inventory, appraisement, and list of claims;

(7) exhibit and account;

(8) report of renting;

(9) application for sale or partition of real estate;

(10) report of sale;

(11) report of the commissioners of partition;

(12) application for authority to execute a lease for mineral development, or for pooling or unitization of lands, royalty, or other interest in minerals, or to lend or invest money; and

(13) report of lending or investing money.

(c) Only the substance of a deposition must be recorded under Subsection (b)(4).

Added by Acts 2009, 81st Leg., ch. 680, § 1, eff. Jan. 1, 2014. Amended by Acts 2011, 82nd Leg., ch. 1338 (S.B. 1198), § 2.05, eff. Jan. 1, 2014.

## § 52.053. Index

(a) The county clerk shall properly index the records required under this chapter.

(b) The county clerk shall keep the index open for public inspection, but may not release the index from the clerk's custody.

Added by Acts 2009, 81st Leg., ch. 680, § 1, eff. Jan. 1, 2014.

## CHAPTER 53. OTHER COURT DUTIES AND PROCEDURES

## SUBCHAPTER A.  ENFORCEMENT OF ORDERS

## § 53.001. Enforcement of Judge's Orders

A judge may enforce the judge's lawful orders against an executor or administrator by attachment and confinement. Unless this title expressly provides otherwise, the term of confinement for any one offense under this section may not exceed three days.

Added by Acts 2009, 81st Leg., ch. 680, § 1, eff. Jan. 1, 2014.

## SUBCHAPTER B.  COSTS AND SECURITY

## § 53.051. Applicability of Certain Laws

A law regulating costs in ordinary civil cases applies to a probate matter when not expressly provided for in this title.

Added by Acts 2009, 81st Leg., ch. 680, § 1, eff. Jan. 1, 2014.

## § 53.052. Security for Certain Costs

(a) The clerk may require a person who files an application, complaint, or opposition relating to an estate, other than the personal representative of the estate, to provide security for the probable costs of the proceeding before filing the application, complaint, or opposition.

(b) At any time before the trial of an application, complaint, or opposition described by Subsection (a), anyone interested in the estate or an officer of the court may, by written motion, obtain from the court an order requiring the person who filed the application, complaint, or opposition to provide security for the probable costs of the proceeding. The rules governing civil suits in the county court with respect to giving security for the probable costs of a proceeding control in cases described by Subsection (a) and this subsection.

(c) An executor or administrator appointed by a court of this state may not be required to provide security for costs in an action brought by the executor or administrator in the executor's or administrator's fiduciary capacity.

Added by Acts 2009, 81st Leg., ch. 680, § 1, eff. Jan. 1, 2014.

### § 53.053. Exemption from Probate Fees for Estates of Certain Military Servicemembers

(a) In this section, "combat zone" means an area that the president of the United States by executive order designates for purposes of 26 U.S.C. Section 112 as an area in which armed forces of the United States are or have engaged in combat.

(b) Notwithstanding any other law, the clerk of a county court may not charge, or collect from, the estate of a decedent any of the following fees if the decedent died while in active service as a member of the armed forces of the United States in a combat zone:

(1) a fee for or associated with the filing of the decedent's will for probate; and

(2) a fee for any service rendered by the probate court regarding the administration of the decedent's estate.

Added by Acts 2009, 81st Leg., ch. 680, § 1, eff. Jan. 1, 2014.

### § 53.054. Exemption from Probate Fees for Estates of Certain Law Enforcement Officers, Firefighters, and Others

(a) In this section:

(1) "Eligible decedent" means an individual listed in Section 615.003, Government Code.

(2) "Line of duty" and "personal injury" have the meanings assigned by Section 615.021(e), Government Code.

(b) Notwithstanding any other law, the clerk of a court may not charge, or collect from, the estate of an eligible decedent any of the following fees if the decedent died as a result of a personal injury sustained in the line of duty in the individual's position as described by Section 615.003, Government Code:

(1) a fee for or associated with the filing of the decedent's will for probate; and

(2) a fee for any service rendered by the court regarding the administration of the decedent's estate.

Added by Acts 2011, 82nd Leg., ch. 614 (S.B. 543), § 2.01, eff. Jan. 1, 2014.

## SUBCHAPTER C. PROCEDURES FOR PROBATE MATTERS

### § 53.101. Calling of Dockets

The judge in whose court probate proceedings are pending, at times determined by the judge, shall:

(1) call the estates of decedents in the estates' regular order on both the probate and claim dockets; and

(2) issue orders as necessary.

Added by Acts 2009, 81st Leg., ch. 680, § 1, eff. Jan. 1, 2014.

### § 53.102. Setting of Certain Hearings by Clerk

(a) If a judge is unable to designate the time and place for hearing a probate matter pending in the judge's court because the judge is absent from the county seat or is on vacation, disqualified, ill, or deceased, the county clerk of the county in which the matter is pending may:

(1) designate the time and place for hearing;

(2) enter the setting on the judge's docket; and

(3) certify on the docket the reason that the judge is not acting to set the hearing.

(b) If, after the perfection of the service of notices and citations required by law concerning the time and place of hearing, a qualified judge is not present for a hearing set under Subsection (a), the hearing is automatically continued from day to day until a qualified judge is present to hear and determine the matter.

Added by Acts 2009, 81st Leg., ch. 680, § 1, eff. Jan. 1, 2014.

## § 53.103. Rendering of Decisions, Orders, Decrees, and Judgments

The county court shall render all decisions, orders, decrees, and judgments in probate matters in open court, except as otherwise specially provided.

Added by Acts 2009, 81st Leg., ch. 680, § 1, eff. Jan. 1, 2014.

## § 53.104. Appointment of Attorneys ad Litem

(a) Except as provided by Section 202.009(b), the judge of a probate court may appoint an attorney ad litem in any probate proceeding to represent the interests of any person, including:

(1) a person who has a legal disability under state or federal law;

(2) a nonresident;

(3) an unborn or unascertained person;

(4) an unknown heir;

(5) a missing heir; or

(6) an unknown or missing person for whom cash is deposited into the court's registry under Section 362.011.

(b) An attorney ad litem appointed under this section is entitled to reasonable compensation for services provided in the amount set by the court. The court shall:

(1) tax the compensation as costs in the probate proceeding and order the compensation to be paid out of the estate or by any party at any time during the proceeding; or

(2) for an attorney ad litem appointed under Subsection (a)(6), order that the compensation be paid from the cash on deposit in the court's registry as provided by Section 362.011.

Added by Acts 2009, 81st Leg., ch. 680, § 1, eff. Jan. 1, 2014. Amended by Acts 2013, 83rd Leg., ch. 1136 (H.B. 2912), § 5, eff. Jan. 1, 2014.

Section 62(e) of Acts 2013, 83rd Leg., ch. 1136 (H.B. 2912) provides:
"The changes in law made by Sections 51.203(c), 53.104, 305.002(a), 305.003, 308.054(b), 309.051(a), 309.056, 309.103(a) and (b), 355.060, 361.155(b), 362.005, 362.011, 362.013, 404.001(a), 404.003, 404.005(b) and (c), and 551.001(a), Estates Code, as amended by this Act, and Sections 253.001(c), 301.155, 305.004, 309.057, 361.155(c), 404.0035, 404.0036, and 404.0037, Estates Code, as added by this Act, apply to the administration of the estate of a decedent that is pending or commenced on or after the effective date [Jan. 1, 2014] of this Act."

## § 53.105. [Blank]

## § 53.106. Executions in Probate Matters

(a) An execution in a probate matter must be:

(1) directed "to any sheriff or any constable within the State of Texas";

(2) attested and signed by the clerk officially under court seal; and

(3) made returnable in 60 days.

(b) A proceeding under an execution described by Subsection (a) is governed, to the extent applicable, by the laws regulating a proceeding under an execution issued by a district court.

(c) Notwithstanding Subsection (a), an execution directed to the sheriff or a constable of a specific county in this state may not be held defective if properly executed within that county by the sheriff or constable to whom the execution is directed.

Added by Acts 2009, 81st Leg., ch. 680, § 1, eff. Jan. 1, 2014.

## § 53.107. Inapplicability of Certain Rules of Civil Procedure

The following do not apply to probate proceedings:

(1) Rules 47(c) and 169, Texas Rules of Civil Procedure; and

(2) the portions of Rule 190.2, Texas Rules of Civil Procedure, concerning expedited actions under Rule 169, Texas Rules of Civil Procedure.

Added by Acts 2013, 83rd Leg., ch. 1136 (H.B. 2912), § 6, eff. Jan. 1, 2014.

Section 62(d) of Acts 2013, 83rd Leg., ch. 1136 (H.B. 2912) provides:
"The changes in law made by Sections 32.006, 256.052, 256.053, 256.054, 256.152(c), 256.153, 256.154, 256.155(a), 256.156, 256.203, 257.052, 257.053, 401.001(a), 401.004(d), and 401.006, Estates Code, as amended by this Act, and Section 53.107, Estates Code, as added by this Act, apply only to an action filed or other proceeding commenced on or after the effective date [Jan. 1, 2014] of this Act. An action filed or other proceeding commenced before the effective date of this Act is governed by the law in effect on the date the action was filed or the proceeding was commenced, and the former law is continued in effect for that purpose."

## CHAPTER 54. PLEADINGS AND EVIDENCE IN GENERAL

### SUBCHAPTER A. PLEADINGS

### SUBCHAPTER A. PLEADINGS

## § 54.001. Effect of Filing or Contesting Pleading

(a) The filing or contesting in probate court of a pleading relating to a decedent's estate does not constitute tortious interference with inheritance of the estate.

(b) This section does not abrogate any right of a person under Rule 13, Texas Rules of Civil Procedure, or Chapter 10, Civil Practice and Remedies Code.

Added by Acts 2009, 81st Leg., ch. 680, § 1, eff. Jan. 1, 2014.

### § 54.002. Defect in Pleading

A court may not invalidate a pleading in probate, or an order based on the pleading, on the basis of a defect of form or substance in the pleading unless a timely objection has been made against the defect and the defect has been called to the attention of the court in which the proceeding was or is pending.

Added by Acts 2009, 81st Leg., ch. 680, § 1, eff. Jan. 1, 2014.

## SUBCHAPTER B. EVIDENCE

### § 54.051. Applicability of Certain Rules Relating to Witnesses and Evidence

Except as provided by Section 51.203, the Texas Rules of Evidence apply in a proceeding arising under this title to the extent practicable.

Added by Acts 2009, 81st Leg., ch. 680, § 1, eff. Jan. 1, 2014. Amended by Acts 2013, 83rd Leg., ch. 1136 (H.B. 2912), § 7, eff. Jan. 1, 2014.

### § 54.052. Use of Certain Records as Evidence

The following are admissible as evidence in any court of this state:

(1) record books described by Sections 52.001, 52.002, and 52.003 and individual case files described by Section 52.052, including records maintained in a manner allowed under Section 52.004; and

(2) certified copies or reproductions of the records.

Added by Acts 2009, 81st Leg., ch. 680, § 1, eff. Jan. 1, 2014.

## CHAPTER 55. COMPLAINTS AND CONTESTS

## SUBCHAPTER A. CONTEST OF PROCEEDINGS IN PROBATE COURT

### § 55.001. Opposition in Probate Proceeding

A person interested in an estate may, at any time before the court decides an issue in a proceeding, file written opposition regarding the issue. The person is entitled to process for witnesses and evidence, and to be heard on the opposition, as in other suits.

Added by Acts 2009, 81st Leg., ch. 680, § 1, eff. Jan. 1, 2014.

### § 55.002. Trial by Jury

In a contested probate or mental illness proceeding in a probate court, a party is entitled to a jury trial as in other civil actions.

Added by Acts 2009, 81st Leg., ch. 680, § 1, eff. Jan. 1, 2014.

## SUBCHAPTER B. INSTITUTION OF HIGHER EDUCATION OR CHARITABLE ORGANIZATION AS PARTY TO CERTAIN ACTIONS

### § 55.051. Definition

In this subchapter, "institution of higher education" has the meaning assigned by Section 61.003, Education Code.

Added by Acts 2009, 81st Leg., ch. 680, § 1, eff. Jan. 1, 2014.

## § 55.052. Necessary Party

An institution of higher education, a private institution of higher education, or a charitable organization that is a distributee under a will is a necessary party to a will contest or will construction suit involving the will.

Added by Acts 2009, 81st Leg., ch. 680, § 1, eff. Jan. 1, 2014.

## § 55.053. Service of Process

The court shall serve an institution or organization that is a necessary party under Section 55.052 in the manner provided by this title for service on other parties.

Added by Acts 2009, 81st Leg., ch. 680, § 1, eff. Jan. 1, 2014.

### SUBCHAPTER C.    MENTAL CAPACITY OF DECEDENT

## § 55.101. Entitlement to Production of Communications and Records

Notwithstanding Subtitle B, Title 3, Occupations Code, a person who is a party to a will contest or proceeding in which a party relies on the mental or testamentary capacity of a decedent before the decedent's death as part of the party's claim or defense is entitled to production of all communications or records relevant to the decedent's condition before the decedent's death.

Added by Acts 2009, 81st Leg., ch. 680, § 1, eff. Jan. 1, 2014.

## § 55.102. Release of Records

On receipt of a subpoena for communications or records described by Section 55.101 and a file-stamped copy of the will contest or proceeding described by that section, the appropriate physician, hospital, medical facility, custodian of records, or other person in possession of the communications or records shall release the communications or records to the requesting party without further authorization.

Added by Acts 2009, 81st Leg., ch. 680, § 1, eff. Jan. 1, 2014.

### SUBCHAPTER D.    ATTACHMENT OF ESTATE PROPERTY

## § 55.151. Order for Issuance of Writ of Attachment

(a) If a person interested in an estate files with the judge a written complaint made under oath alleging that the executor or administrator of the estate is about to remove the estate or part of the estate outside of the state, the judge may order a writ of attachment to issue, directed "to any sheriff or any constable within the State of Texas." The writ must order the sheriff or constable to:

(1) seize the estate or a part of the estate; and

(2) hold that property subject to the judge's additional orders regarding the complaint.

(b) Notwithstanding Subsection (a), a writ of attachment directed to the sheriff or constable of a specific county within the state is not defective if the writ was properly executed in that county by that officer.

Added by Acts 2009, 81st Leg., ch. 680, § 1, eff. Jan. 1, 2014.

## § 55.152. Bond

Before a writ of attachment ordered under Section 55.151 may be issued, the complainant must execute a bond that is:

(1) payable to the executor or administrator of the estate;

(2) in an amount set by the judge; and

(3) conditioned for the payment of all damages and costs that are recovered for the wrongful suing out of the writ.

Added by Acts 2009, 81st Leg., ch. 680, § 1, eff. Jan. 1, 2014.

### SUBCHAPTER E.    SPECIFIC PERFORMANCE OF AGREEMENT TO TRANSFER TITLE

## § 55.201. Complaint and Citation

(a) If a person sold property and entered into a bond or other written agreement to transfer title to the property and then died without transferring the title, the owner of the bond or agreement or the owner's legal representative may:

(1) file a written complaint in the court of the county in which letters testamentary or of administration on the decedent's estate were granted; and

(2) have the personal representative of the estate cited to appear on a date stated in the citation and show cause why specific performance of the bond or agreement should not be ordered.

(b) Except as provided by Subsection (c), the bond or agreement must be filed with the complaint described by Subsection (a).

(c) If good cause under oath is shown why the bond or written agreement cannot be filed with the complaint, the bond or agreement or the substance of the bond or agreement must be stated in the complaint.

Added by Acts 2009, 81st Leg., ch. 680, § 1, eff. Jan. 1, 2014.

## § 55.202. Hearing and Order

(a) After service of the citation under Section 55.201, the court shall hear the complaint and the evidence on the complaint.

(b) The court shall order the personal representative to transfer title to the property, according to the tenor of the bond or agreement, to the complainant if the judge is satisfied from the proof that:

(1) the bond or agreement was legally executed by the decedent; and

(2) the complainant has a right to demand specific performance.

(c) The order must fully describe the property to be transferred.

Added by Acts 2009, 81st Leg., ch. 680, § 1, eff. Jan. 1, 2014.

## § 55.203. Conveyance

(a) A conveyance made under this subchapter must refer to and identify the court order authorizing the conveyance. On delivery of the conveyance, all the right and title to the property conveyed that the decedent had vests in the person to whom the conveyance is made.

(b) A conveyance under this subchapter is prima facie evidence that all requirements of the law for obtaining the conveyance have been complied with.

Added by Acts 2009, 81st Leg., ch. 680, § 1, eff. Jan. 1, 2014.

## SUBCHAPTER F. BILL OF REVIEW

## § 55.251. Revision and Correction of Order or Judgment in Probate Proceeding

(a) An interested person may, by a bill of review filed in the court in which the probate proceedings were held, have an order or judgment rendered by the court revised and corrected on a showing of error in the order or judgment, as applicable.

(b) A bill of review to revise and correct an order or judgment may not be filed more than two years after the date of the order or judgment, as applicable.

Added by Acts 2009, 81st Leg., ch. 680, § 1, eff. Jan. 1, 2014. Amended by Acts 2011, 82nd Leg., ch. 91 (S.B. 1303), § 8.002, eff. Jan. 1, 2014.

## § 55.252. Injunction

A process or action under a court order or judgment subject to a bill of review filed under Section 55.251 may be stayed only by writ of injunction.

Added by Acts 2009, 81st Leg., ch. 680, § 1, eff. Jan. 1, 2014. Amended by Acts 2011, 82nd Leg., ch. 91 (S.B. 1303), § 8.003, eff. Jan. 1, 2014.

## CHAPTER 56. CHANGE AND RESIGNATION OF RESIDENT AGENT OF PERSONAL REPRESENTATIVE FOR SERVICE OF PROCESS

## § 56.001. Change of Resident Agent

(a) A personal representative of an estate may change the representative's resident agent to accept service of process in a probate proceeding or other action relating to the estate by filing with the court in which the probate proceeding is pending a statement titled "Designation of Successor Resident Agent" that states the names and addresses of:

(1) the representative;

(2) the resident agent; and

(3) the successor resident agent.

(b) The designation of a successor resident agent takes effect on the date a statement under Subsection (a) is filed with the court.

Added by Acts 2009, 81st Leg., ch. 680, § 1, eff. Jan. 1, 2014.

## § 56.002. Resignation of Resident Agent

(a) A resident agent of a personal representative may resign as resident agent by giving notice to the representative and filing with the court in which the probate proceeding is pending a statement titled "Resignation of Resident Agent" that states:

(1) the name of the representative;

(2) the representative's address most recently known by the resident agent;

(3) that notice of the resignation has been given to the representative and the date that notice was given; and

(4) that the representative has not designated a successor resident agent.

(b) The resident agent shall send, by certified mail, return receipt requested, a copy of a resignation statement filed under Subsection (a) to:

(1) the personal representative at the address most recently known by the resident agent; and

(2) each party in the case or the party's attorney or other designated representative of record.

(c) The resignation of a resident agent takes effect on the date the court enters an order accepting the resignation. A court may not enter an order accepting the resignation unless the resident agent complies with this section.

Added by Acts 2009, 81st Leg., ch. 680, § 1, eff. Jan. 1, 2014.

## SUBTITLE C. PASSAGE OF TITLE AND DISTRIBUTION OF DECEDENTS' PROPERTY IN GENERAL

### CHAPTER 101. ESTATE ASSETS IN GENERAL

SUBCHAPTER A. PASSAGE AND POSSESSION OF DECEDENT'S ESTATE ON DEATH

## SUBCHAPTER A. PASSAGE AND POSSESSION OF DECEDENT'S ESTATE ON DEATH

### § 101.001. Passage of Estate on Decedent's Death

(a) Subject to Section 101.051, if a person dies leaving a lawful will:

(1) all of the person's estate that is devised by the will vests immediately in the devisees;

(2) all powers of appointment granted in the will vest immediately in the donees of those powers; and

(3) all of the person's estate that is not devised by the will vests immediately in the person's heirs at law.

(b) Subject to Section 101.051, the estate of a person who dies intestate vests immediately in the person's heirs at law.

Added by Acts 2009, 81st Leg., ch. 680, § 1, eff. Jan. 1, 2014.

### § 101.002. Effect of Joint Ownership of Property

If two or more persons hold an interest in property jointly and one joint owner dies before severance, the interest of the decedent in the joint estate:

(1) does not survive to the remaining joint owner or owners; and

(2) passes by will or intestacy from the decedent as if the decedent's interest had been severed.

Added by Acts 2009, 81st Leg., ch. 680, § 1, eff. Jan. 1, 2014.

### § 101.003. Possession of Estate by Personal Representative

On the issuance of letters testamentary or of administration on an estate described by Section 101.001, the executor or administrator has the right to possession of the estate as the estate existed at the death of the testator or intestate, subject to the exceptions provided by Section 101.051. The executor or administrator shall recover possession of the estate and hold the estate in trust to be disposed of in accordance with the law.

Added by Acts 2009, 81st Leg., ch. 680, § 1, eff. Jan. 1, 2014.

## SUBCHAPTER B. LIABILITY OF ESTATE FOR DEBTS

### § 101.051. Liability of Estate for Debts in General

(a) A decedent's estate vests in accordance with Section 101.001(a) subject to the payment of:

(1) the debts of the decedent, except as exempted by law; and

(2) any court-ordered child support payments that are delinquent on the date of the decedent's death.

(b) A decedent's estate vests in accordance with Section 101.001(b) subject to the payment of, and is still liable for:

(1) the debts of the decedent, except as exempted by law; and

(2) any court-ordered child support payments that are delinquent on the date of the decedent's death.

Added by Acts 2009, 81st Leg., ch. 680, § 1, eff. Jan. 1, 2014.

### § 101.052. Liability of Community Property for Debts of Deceased Spouse

(a) The community property subject to the sole or joint management, control, and disposition of a spouse during marriage continues to be subject to the liabilities of that spouse on death.

(b) The interest that the deceased spouse owned in any other nonexempt community property passes to the deceased spouse's heirs or devisees charged with the debts that were enforceable against the deceased spouse before death.

(c) This section does not prohibit the administration of community property under other provisions of this title relating to the administration of an estate.

Added by Acts 2009, 81st Leg., ch. 680, § 1, eff. Jan. 1, 2014.

# CHAPTER 102. PROBATE ASSETS: DECEDENT'S HOMESTEAD

## § 102.001. Treatment of Certain Children

For purposes of determining homestead rights, a child is a child of his or her mother and a child of his or her father, as provided by Sections 201.051, 201.052, and 201.053.

Added by Acts 2009, 81st Leg., ch. 680, § 1, eff. Jan. 1, 2014.

## § 102.002. Homestead Rights Not Affected by Character of the Homestead.

The homestead rights and the respective interests of the surviving spouse and children of a decedent are the same whether the homestead was the decedent's separate property or was community property between the surviving spouse and the decedent.

Added by Acts 2009, 81st Leg., ch. 680, § 1, eff. Jan. 1, 2014.

## § 102.003. Passage of Homestead

The homestead of a decedent who dies leaving a surviving spouse descends and vests on the decedent's death in the same manner as other real property of the decedent and is governed by the same laws of descent and distribution.

Added by Acts 2009, 81st Leg., ch. 680, § 1, eff. Jan. 1, 2014.

## § 102.004. Liability of Homestead for Debts

If the decedent was survived by a spouse or minor child, the homestead is not liable for the payment of any of the debts of the estate, other than:

(1) purchase money for the homestead;

(2) taxes due on the homestead;

(3) work and material used in constructing improvements on the homestead if the requirements of Section 50(a)(5), Article XVI, Texas Constitution, are met;

(4) an owelty of partition imposed against the entirety of the property by a court order or written agreement of the parties to the partition, including a debt of one spouse in favor of the other spouse resulting from a division or an award of a family homestead in a divorce proceeding;

(5) the refinance of a lien against the homestead, including a federal tax lien resulting from the tax debt of both spouses, if the homestead is a family homestead, or from the tax debt of the decedent;

(6) an extension of credit on the homestead if the requirements of Section 50(a)(6), Article XVI, Texas Constitution, are met; or

(7) a reverse mortgage.

Added by Acts 2009, 81st Leg., ch. 680, § 1, eff. Jan. 1, 2014. Amended by Acts 2013, 83rd Leg., ch. 1136 (H.B. 2912), § 8, eff. Jan. 1, 2014.

Section 62(f) of Acts 2013, 83rd Leg., ch. 1136 (H.B. 2912) provides:

"The changes in law made by Sections 102.004, 201.051, 201.052(b), 202. 004, 202.009, 202.056, 202.151, 353.101(d), 403.055, 403.056(a), and 405.001(b), Estates Code, as amended by this Act, and Sections 201.052(a–1), 202.0025, and 202.057, Estates Code, as added by this Act, apply only to the estate of a decedent who dies on or after the effective date [Jan. 1, 2014] of this Act. The estate of a decedent who dies before the effective date of this Act is governed by the law in effect on the date of the decedent's death, and the former law is continued in effect for that purpose."

## § 102.005. Prohibitions on Partition of Homestead

The homestead may not be partitioned among the decedent's heirs:

(1) during the lifetime of the surviving spouse for as long as the surviving spouse elects to use or occupy the property as a homestead; or

(2) during the period the guardian of the decedent's minor children is permitted to use and occupy the homestead under a court order.

Added by Acts 2009, 81st Leg., ch. 680, § 1, eff. Jan. 1, 2014.

## § 102.006. Circumstances Under Which Partition of Homestead Is Authorized

The homestead may be partitioned among the respective owners of the property in the same manner as other property held in common if:

(1) the surviving spouse dies, sells his or her interest in the homestead, or elects to no longer use or occupy the property as a homestead; or

(2) the court no longer permits the guardian of the minor children to use and occupy the property as a homestead.

Added by Acts 2009, 81st Leg., ch. 680, § 1, eff. Jan. 1, 2014.

## CHAPTER 111. NONPROBATE ASSETS IN GENERAL

### SUBCHAPTER A. RIGHT OF SURVIVORSHIP AGREEMENTS BETWEEN JOINT TENANTS

### SUBCHAPTER A. RIGHT OF SURVIVORSHIP AGREEMENTS BETWEEN JOINT TENANTS

### § 111.001. Right of Survivorship Agreements Authorized

(a) Notwithstanding Section 101.002, two or more persons who hold an interest in property jointly may agree in writing that the interest of a joint owner who dies survives to the surviving joint owner or owners.

(b) An agreement described by Subsection (a) may not be inferred from the mere fact that property is held in joint ownership.

Added by Acts 2009, 81st Leg., ch. 680, § 1, eff. Jan. 1, 2014.

### § 111.002. Agreements Concerning Community Property

(a) Section 111.001 does not apply to an agreement between spouses regarding the spouses' community property.

(b) An agreement between spouses regarding a right of survivorship in community property is governed by Chapter 112.

Added by Acts 2009, 81st Leg., ch. 680, § 1, eff. Jan. 1, 2014.

### SUBCHAPTER B. OTHER PROVISIONS FOR PAYMENT OR TRANSFER OF CERTAIN ASSETS ON DEATH

### § 111.051. Definitions

In this subchapter:

(1) "Contracting third party" means a financial institution, insurance company, plan custodian, plan administrator, or other person who is a party to an account agreement, insurance contract, annuity contract, retirement account, beneficiary designation, or other similar contract the terms of which control whether a nontestamentary transfer has occurred or to whom property passes as a result of a possible nontestamentary transfer. The term does not include a person who is:

(A) an owner of the property subject to a possible nontestamentary transfer; or

(B) a possible recipient of the property subject to a possible nontestamentary transfer.

(1–a) "Employees' trust" means:

(A) a trust that forms a part of a stock-bonus, pension, or profit-sharing plan under Section 401, Internal Revenue Code of 1954 (26 U.S. C. Section 401 (1986));

(B) a pension trust under Chapter 111, Property Code; and

(C) an employer-sponsored benefit plan or program, or any other retirement savings arrangement, including a pension plan created under Section 3, Employee Retirement Income Security Act of 1974 (29 U.S.C. Section 1002 (1986)), regardless of whether the plan, program, or arrangement is funded through a trust.

(2) "Financial institution" has the meaning assigned by Section 113.001.

(3) "Individual retirement account" means a trust, custodial arrangement, or annuity under Section 408(a) or (b), Internal Revenue Code of 1954 (26 U.S.C. Section 408 (1986)).

(4) "Retirement account" means a retirement-annuity contract, an individual retirement account, a simplified employee pension, or any other retirement savings arrangement.

(5) "Retirement-annuity contract" means an annuity contract under Section 403, Internal Revenue Code of 1954 (26 U.S.C. Section 403 (1986)).

(6) "Simplified employee pension" means a trust, custodial arrangement, or annuity under Section 408, Internal Revenue Code of 1954 (26 U.S.C. Section 408 (1986)).

Added by Acts 2009, 81st Leg., ch. 680, § 1, eff. Jan. 1, 2014. Amended by Acts 2013, 83rd Leg., ch. 1136 (H.B. 2912), § 9, eff. Jan. 1, 2014.

Section 61 of Acts 2013, 83rd Leg., ch. 1136 (H.B. 2912) provides:

"(a) The changes in law made by Section 111.051, Estates Code, as amended by this Act, and Section 111.054, Estates Code, as added by this Act, represent the fundamental policy of this state for the protection of its residents and are intended to prevail over the laws of another state or jurisdiction, to the extent those laws are in conflict with Texas law.

"(b) The changes in law made by Section 111.051, Estates Code, as amended by this Act, and Section 111.054, Estates Code, as added by this Act, apply to an account at a financial institution, an insurance contract, an annuity contract, a retirement account, a beneficiary designation, or another similar arrangement of a person who dies on or after the effective date [Jan. 1, 2014] of this Act."

## § 111.052. Validity of Certain Nontestamentary Instruments and Provisions

(a) This code does not invalidate:

(1) any provision in an insurance policy, employment contract, bond, mortgage, promissory note, deposit agreement, employees' trust, retirement account, deferred compensation arrangement, custodial agreement, pension plan, trust agreement, conveyance of property, security, account with a financial institution, mutual fund account, or any other written instrument effective as a contract, gift, conveyance, or trust, stating that:

(A) money or other benefits under the instrument due to or controlled or owned by a decedent shall be paid after the decedent's death, or property that is the subject of the instrument shall pass, to a person designated by the decedent in the instrument or in a separate writing, including a will, executed at the same time as the instrument or subsequently; or

(B) money due or to become due under the instrument shall cease to be payable if the promisee or promissor dies before payment or demand; or

(2) an instrument described by Subdivision (1).

(b) A provision described by Subsection (a)(1) is considered nontestamentary.

Added by Acts 2009, 81st Leg., ch. 680, § 1, eff. Jan. 1, 2014.

## § 111.053. Creditor's Rights Not Limited

Nothing in this subchapter limits the rights of a creditor under another law of this state.

Added by Acts 2009, 81st Leg., ch. 680, § 1, eff. Jan. 1, 2014.

## § 111.054. Application of State Law to Certain Nontestamentary Transfers

(a) This section applies if more than 50 percent of the:

(1) assets in an account at a financial institution, in a retirement account, or in another similar arrangement are owned, immediately before a possible nontestamentary transfer of the assets, by one or more persons domiciled in this state; or

(2) interests under an insurance contract, annuity contract, beneficiary designation, or other similar arrangement are owned, immediately before a possible nontestamentary transfer of the interests, by one or more persons domiciled in this state.

(b) Notwithstanding a choice of law or other contractual provision in an agreement prepared or provided by a contracting third party, Texas law applies to determine:

(1) whether a nontestamentary transfer of assets or interests described by Subsection (a) has occurred; and

(2) the ownership of the assets or interests following a possible nontestamentary transfer.

(c) Notwithstanding a choice of law or other contractual provision in an agreement prepared or provided by a contracting third party, any person, including a personal representative, who is asserting an ownership interest in assets or interests described by Subsection (a) subject to a possible nontestamentary transfer shall have access to the courts of this state for a judicial determination of:

(1) whether a nontestamentary transfer of the assets or interests has occurred; or

(2) the ownership of the assets or interests following a possible nontestamentary transfer.

(d) Subsections (a), (b), and (c) do not apply to an obligation:

(1) owed by a party to the contracting third party; or

(2) owed by the contracting third party to a party.

(e) This section applies to a community property survivorship agreement governed by Chapter 112 and a multiple-party account governed by Chapter 113.

Added by Acts 2013, 83rd Leg., ch. 1136 (H.B. 2912), § 10, eff. Jan. 1, 2014.

Section 61 of Acts 2013, 83rd Leg., ch. 1136 (H.B. 2912) provides:

"(a) The changes in law made by Section 111.051, Estates Code, as amended by this Act, and Section 111.054, Estates Code, as added by this Act, represent the fundamental policy of this state for the protection of its residents and are intended to prevail over the laws of another state or jurisdiction, to the extent those laws are in conflict with Texas law.

"(b) The changes in law made by Section 111.051, Estates Code, as amended by this Act, and Section 111.054, Estates Code, as added by this Act, apply to an account at a financial institution, an insurance contract, an annuity contract, a retirement account, a beneficiary designation, or another similar arrangement of a person who dies on or after the effective date [Jan. 1, 2014] of this Act."

## CHAPTER 112. COMMUNITY PROPERTY WITH RIGHT OF SURVIVORSHIP

### SUBCHAPTER A. GENERAL PROVISIONS

### § 112.001. Definition of Community Property Survivorship Agreement

In this chapter, "community property survivorship agreement" means an agreement between spouses creating a right of survivorship in community property.

Added by Acts 2009, 81st Leg., ch. 680, § 1, eff. Jan. 1, 2014.

### § 112.002. Applicability of Other Law to Community Property Held in Multiple–Party Accounts

Chapter 113 applies to multiple-party accounts held by spouses with a right of survivorship to the extent that chapter is not inconsistent with this chapter.

Added by Acts 2009, 81st Leg., ch. 680, § 1, eff. Jan. 1, 2014.

### SUBCHAPTER B. COMMUNITY PROPERTY SURVIVORSHIP AGREEMENTS

### § 112.051. Agreement for Right of Survivorship in Community Property

At any time, spouses may agree between themselves that all or part of their community property, then existing or to be acquired, becomes the property of the surviving spouse on the death of a spouse.

Added by Acts 2009, 81st Leg., ch. 680, § 1, eff. Jan. 1, 2014.

### § 112.052. Form of Agreement

(a) A community property survivorship agreement must be in writing and signed by both spouses.

(b) A written agreement signed by both spouses is sufficient to create a right of survivorship in the community property described in the agreement if the agreement includes any of the following phrases:

(1) "with right of survivorship";

(2) "will become the property of the survivor";

(3) "will vest in and belong to the surviving spouse"; or

(4) "shall pass to the surviving spouse."

(c) Notwithstanding Subsection (b), a community property survivorship agreement that otherwise meets the requirements of this chapter is effective without including any of the phrases listed in that subsection.

(d) A survivorship agreement may not be inferred from the mere fact that an account is a joint account or that an account is designated as JT TEN, Joint Tenancy, or joint, or with other similar language.

Added by Acts 2009, 81st Leg., ch. 680, § 1, eff. Jan. 1, 2014. Amended by Acts 2011, 82nd Leg., ch. 1338 (S.B. 1198), § 2.06, eff. Jan. 1, 2014.

### § 112.053. Adjudication Not Required

A community property survivorship agreement that satisfies the requirements of this chapter is effective and enforceable without an adjudication.

Added by Acts 2009, 81st Leg., ch. 680, § 1, eff. Jan. 1, 2014.

### § 112.054. Revocation of Agreement

(a) A community property survivorship agreement made in accordance with this chapter may be revoked as provided by the terms of the agreement.

(b) If a community property survivorship agreement does not provide a method of revocation, the agreement may be revoked by a written instrument:

(1) signed by both spouses; or

(2) signed by one spouse and delivered to the other spouse.

(c) A community property survivorship agreement may be revoked with respect to specific property subject to the agreement by the disposition of the property by one or both spouses if the disposition is not inconsistent with specific terms of the agreement and applicable law.

Added by Acts 2009, 81st Leg., ch. 680, § 1, eff. Jan. 1, 2014.

## SUBCHAPTER C. ADJUDICATION TO PROVE COMMUNITY PROPERTY SURVIVORSHIP AGREEMENT

### § 112.101. Application Authorized

(a) Notwithstanding Section 112.053, after the death of a spouse, the surviving spouse or the surviving spouse's personal representative may apply to the court for an order stating that a community property survivorship agreement satisfies the requirements of this chapter and is effective to create a right of survivorship in community property.

(b) An application under this section must include:

(1) the surviving spouse's name and domicile;

(2) the deceased spouse's name and former domicile;

(3) the fact, time, and place of the deceased spouse's death;

(4) facts establishing venue in the court; and

(5) the deceased spouse's social security number, if known.

(c) An application under this section must be filed in the county of proper venue for administration of the deceased spouse's estate.

(d) The original community property survivorship agreement shall be filed with an application under this section.

Added by Acts 2009, 81st Leg., ch. 680, § 1, eff. Jan. 1, 2014.

### § 112.102. Proof Required by Court

An applicant for an order under Section 112.101 must prove to the court's satisfaction that:

(1) the spouse whose community property interest is at issue is deceased;

(2) the court has jurisdiction and venue;

(3) the agreement was executed with the formalities required by law;

(4) the agreement was not revoked; and

(5) citation has been served and returned in the manner and for the length of time required by this title.

Added by Acts 2009, 81st Leg., ch. 680, § 1, eff. Jan. 1, 2014.

### § 112.103. Method of Proof of Signatures

(a) The deceased spouse's signature to an agreement that is the subject of an application under Section 112.101 may be proved by:

(1) the sworn testimony of one witness taken in open court;

(2) the affidavit of one witness; or

(3) the written or oral deposition of one witness taken in the same manner and under the same rules as depositions in other civil actions.

(b) If the surviving spouse is competent to make an oath, the surviving spouse's signature to the agreement may be proved by:

(1) the sworn testimony of the surviving spouse taken in open court;

(2) the surviving spouse's affidavit; or

(3) the written or oral deposition of the surviving spouse taken in the same manner and under the same rules as depositions in other civil actions.

(c) If the surviving spouse is not competent to make an oath, the surviving spouse's signature to the agreement may be proved in the manner provided by

Subsection (a) for proof of the deceased spouse's signature.

Added by Acts 2009, 81st Leg., ch. 680, § 1, eff. Jan. 1, 2014.

### § 112.104. Court Action; Issuance of Order

(a) On completion of a hearing on an application under Section 112.101, if the court is satisfied that the requisite proof has been made, the court shall enter an order adjudging the agreement valid.

(b) Certified copies of the agreement and order may be:

(1) recorded in other counties; and

(2) used in evidence, as the original agreement might be, on the trial of the same matter in any other court, on appeal or otherwise.

Added by Acts 2009, 81st Leg., ch. 680, § 1, eff. Jan. 1, 2014.

### § 112.105. Effect of Order

(a) An order under this subchapter adjudging a community property survivorship agreement valid constitutes sufficient authority to a person who:

(1) owes money, has custody of any property, or acts as registrar or transfer agent of any evidence of interest, indebtedness, property, or right that is subject to the terms of the agreement; or

(2) purchases from or otherwise deals with the surviving spouse for payment or transfer to the surviving spouse.

(b) The surviving spouse may enforce that spouse's right to a payment or transfer from a person described by Subsection (a)(2).

Added by Acts 2009, 81st Leg., ch. 680, § 1, eff. Jan. 1, 2014.

### § 112.106. Custody of Adjudicated Agreement

(a) An original community property survivorship agreement adjudicated under this subchapter, together with the order adjudging the agreement valid, shall be deposited in the office of the county clerk of the county in which the agreement was adjudicated and must remain at that office, except during a period when the agreement is moved to another location for inspection on order of the court in which the agreement was adjudicated.

(b) If the court orders an original community property survivorship agreement adjudicated under this subchapter to be moved to another location for inspection, the person moving the original agreement shall give a receipt for the agreement and the court clerk shall make and retain a copy of the original agreement.

Added by Acts 2009, 81st Leg., ch. 680, § 1, eff. Jan. 1, 2014.

## SUBCHAPTER D. OWNERSHIP AND TRANSFER OF COMMUNITY PROPERTY SUBJECT TO AGREEMENT

### § 112.151. Ownership of Property During Marriage; Management Rights

(a) Property subject to a community property survivorship agreement remains community property during the marriage of the spouses.

(b) Unless the agreement provides otherwise, a community property survivorship agreement does not affect the rights of the spouses concerning the management, control, and disposition of property subject to the agreement.

Added by Acts 2009, 81st Leg., ch. 680, § 1, eff. Jan. 1, 2014.

### § 112.152. Nontestamentary Nature of Transfers Under Agreement

(a) Transfers at death resulting from community property survivorship agreements made in accordance with this chapter are effective by reason of the agreements involved and are not testamentary transfers.

(b) Except as expressly provided otherwise by this title, transfers described by Subsection (a) are not subject to the provisions of this title applicable to testamentary transfers.

Added by Acts 2009, 81st Leg., ch. 680, § 1, eff. Jan. 1, 2014.

## SUBCHAPTER E. THIRD PARTIES DEALING WITH COMMUNITY PROPERTY SUBJECT TO RIGHT OF SURVIVORSHIP

### § 112.201. Definition of Certified Copy

In this subchapter, a "certified copy" means a copy of an official record or document that is:

(1) authorized by law to be recorded or filed and actually recorded or filed in a public office; and

(2) certified as correct in accordance with Rule 902, Texas Rules of Evidence.

Added by Acts 2009, 81st Leg., ch. 680, § 1, eff. Jan. 1, 2014.

### § 112.202. Actual Knowledge or Notice of Agreement

(a) In this subchapter, a person or entity has "actual knowledge" of a community property survivorship agreement or the revocation of a community property survivorship agreement only if the person or entity has received:

(1) written notice of the agreement or revocation; or

(2) the original or a certified copy of the agreement or revoking instrument.

(b) In this subchapter, a person or entity has "notice" of a community property survivorship agreement or the revocation of a community property survivorship agreement if:

(1) the person or entity has actual knowledge of the agreement or revocation; or

(2) with respect to real property, the agreement or revoking instrument is properly recorded in the county in which the real property is located.

Added by Acts 2009, 81st Leg., ch. 680, § 1, eff. Jan. 1, 2014.

### § 112.203. Personal Representative Without Actual Knowledge of Agreement

If the personal representative of a deceased spouse's estate has no actual knowledge of the existence of an agreement creating a right of survivorship in community property in the surviving spouse, the personal representative is not liable to the surviving spouse or any person claiming from the surviving spouse for selling, exchanging, distributing, or otherwise disposing of the property.

Added by Acts 2009, 81st Leg., ch. 680, § 1, eff. Jan. 1, 2014.

### § 112.204. Third–Party Purchaser Without Notice of Agreement

(a) This section applies only to a person or entity who for value purchases property:

(1) from a person claiming from a deceased spouse more than six months after the date of the deceased spouse's death or from the personal representative of the deceased spouse's estate; and

(2) without notice of the existence of an agreement creating a right of survivorship in the property in the surviving spouse.

(b) A purchaser of property from a person claiming from the deceased spouse has good title to the interest in the property that the person would have had in the absence of the agreement described by Subsection (a)(2), as against the claims of the surviving spouse or any person claiming from the surviving spouse.

(c) A purchaser of property from the personal representative of the deceased spouse's estate has good title to the interest in the property that the personal

representative would have had authority to convey in the absence of the agreement described by Subsection (a)(2), as against the claims of the surviving spouse or any person claiming from the surviving spouse.

Added by Acts 2009, 81st Leg., ch. 680, § 1, eff. Jan. 1, 2014.

### § 112.205. Debtors and Other Persons Without Notice of Agreement

(a) This section applies only to a person or entity who:

(1) owes money to a deceased spouse; or

(2) has custody of property or acts as registrar or transfer agent of any evidence of interest, indebtedness, property, or right owned by a deceased spouse before that spouse's death.

(b) A person or entity with no actual knowledge of the existence of an agreement creating a right of survivorship in property described by Subsection (a) in the surviving spouse may pay or transfer that property to the personal representative of the deceased spouse's estate or, if no administration of the deceased spouse's estate is pending, to the heirs or devisees of the estate and shall be discharged from all claims for those amounts or property paid or transferred.

Added by Acts 2009, 81st Leg., ch. 680, § 1, eff. Jan. 1, 2014.

### § 112.206. Third–party Purchaser Without Notice of Revocation of Agreement

(a) This section applies only to a person or entity who for value purchases property from a surviving spouse more than six months after the date of the deceased spouse's death and:

(1) with respect to personal property:

(A) the purchaser has received an original or certified copy of an agreement purporting to create a right of survivorship in the personal property in the surviving spouse, purportedly signed by both spouses; and

(B) the purchaser has no notice of the revocation of the agreement; or

(2) with respect to real property:

(A) the purchaser has received an original or certified copy of an agreement purporting to create a right of survivorship in the real property in the surviving spouse, purportedly signed by both spouses or such an agreement is properly recorded in a county in which any part of the real property is located; and

(B) the purchaser has no notice of the revocation of the agreement.

(b) A purchaser has good title to the interest in the property that the surviving spouse would have had in the absence of the revocation of the agreement, as against the claims of the personal representative of the deceased spouse's estate or any person claiming from the representative or the deceased spouse.

Added by Acts 2009, 81st Leg., ch. 680, § 1, eff. Jan. 1, 2014.

### § 112.207. Debtors and Other Persons Without Notice of Revocation of Agreement

(a) This section applies only to a person or entity who:

(1) owes money to a deceased spouse; or

(2) has custody of property or acts as registrar or transfer agent of any evidence of interest, indebtedness, property, or right owned by a deceased spouse before that spouse's death.

(b) If a person or entity is presented with the original or a certified copy of an agreement creating a right of survivorship in property described by Subsection (a) in the surviving spouse, purportedly signed by both spouses, and if the person or entity has no actual knowledge that the agreement was revoked, the person or entity may pay or transfer that property to the surviving spouse and shall be discharged from all claims for those amounts or property paid or transferred.

Added by Acts 2009, 81st Leg., ch. 680, § 1, eff. Jan. 1, 2014.

### § 112.208. Rights of Surviving Spouse Against Creditors

Except as expressly provided by this subchapter, this subchapter does not affect the rights of a surviving spouse or person claiming from the surviving spouse in disputes with persons claiming from a deceased spouse or the successors of any of them concerning a beneficial interest in property or the proceeds from a beneficial interest in property, subject to a right of survivorship under an agreement that satisfies the requirements of this chapter.

Added by Acts 2009, 81st Leg., ch. 680, § 1, eff. Jan. 1, 2014.

### SUBCHAPTER F.  RIGHTS OF CREDITORS

### § 112.251.  Multiple–Party Accounts

Chapter 113 governs the rights of creditors with respect to multiple-party accounts, as defined by Section 113. 004.

Added by Acts 2009, 81st Leg., ch. 680, § 1, eff. Jan. 1, 2014.

### § 112.252.  Liabilities of Deceased Spouse Not Affected by Right of Survivorship

(a) Except as expressly provided by Section 112.251, the community property subject to the sole or joint management, control, and disposition of a spouse during marriage continues to be subject to the liabilities of that spouse on that spouse's death without regard to a right of survivorship in the surviving spouse under an agreement made in accordance with this chapter.

(b) The surviving spouse is liable to account to the deceased spouse's personal representative for property received by the surviving spouse under a right of survivorship to the extent necessary to discharge the deceased spouse's liabilities.

(c) A proceeding to assert a liability under Subsection (b):

(1) may be commenced only if the deceased spouse's personal representative has received a written demand by a creditor; and

(2) must be commenced on or before the second anniversary of the deceased spouse's death.

(d) Property recovered by the deceased spouse's personal representative under this section shall be administered as part of the deceased spouse's estate.

Added by Acts 2009, 81st Leg., ch. 680, § 1, eff. Jan. 1, 2014.

### § 112.253.  Rights of Deceased Spouse's Creditors in Relation to Third Parties

This subchapter does not affect the protection afforded to a person or entity under Subchapter E unless, before payment or transfer to the surviving spouse, the person or entity received a written notice from the deceased spouse's personal representative stating the amount needed to discharge the deceased spouse's liabilities.

Added by Acts 2009, 81st Leg., ch. 680, § 1, eff. Jan. 1, 2014.

### CHAPTER 113.  MULTIPLE– PARTY ACCOUNTS

### SUBCHAPTER A.  GENERAL PROVISIONS

SUBCHAPTER A. GENERAL PROVISIONS

## § 113.001. General Definitions

In this chapter:

(1) "Account" means a contract of deposit of funds between a depositor and a financial institution. The term includes a checking account, savings account, certificate of deposit, share account, or other similar arrangement.

(2) "Beneficiary" means a person named in a trust account for whom a party to the account is named as trustee.

(2–a) "Charitable organization" means any corporation, community chest, fund, or foundation that is exempt from federal income tax under Section 501(a) of the Internal Revenue Code of 1986 by being listed as an exempt organization in Section 501(c)(3) of that code.

(3) "Financial institution" means an organization authorized to do business under state or federal laws relating to financial institutions. The term includes a bank or trust company, savings bank, building and loan association, savings and loan company or association, credit union, and brokerage firm that deals in the sale and purchase of stocks, bonds, and other types of securities.

(4) "Payment" of sums on deposit includes a withdrawal, a payment on a check or other directive of a party, and a pledge of sums on deposit by a party and any set-off, or reduction or other disposition of all or part of an account under a pledge.

(5) "P.O.D. payee" means a person or charitable organization designated on a P.O.D. account as a person to whom the account is payable on request after the death of one or more persons.

(6) "Proof of death" includes:

(A) a certified copy of a death certificate; or

(B) a judgment or order of a court in a proceeding in which the death of a person is proved to the satisfaction of the court by circumstantial evidence in accordance with Chapter 454.

(7) "Request" means a proper request for withdrawal, or a check or order for payment, that complies with all conditions of the account, including special requirements concerning necessary signatures and regulations of the financial institution. If a financial institution conditions withdrawal or payment on advance notice, for purposes of this chapter a request for withdrawal or payment is treated as

immediately effective and a notice of intent to withdraw is treated as a request for withdrawal.

(8) "Sums on deposit" means the balance payable on a multiple-party account including interest, dividends, and any deposit life insurance proceeds added to the account by reason of the death of a party.

(9) "Withdrawal" includes payment to a third person in accordance with a check or other directive of a party.

Added by Acts 2009, 81st Leg., ch. 680, § 1, eff. Jan. 1, 2014. Amended by Acts 2011, 82nd Leg., ch. 1338 (S.B. 1198), § 2.07, eff. Jan. 1, 2014.

## § 113.002. Definition of Party

(a) In this chapter, "party" means a person who, by the terms of a multiple-party account, has a present right, subject to request, to payment from the account. Except as otherwise required by the context, the term includes a guardian, personal representative, or assignee, including an attaching creditor, of a party. The term also includes a person identified as a trustee of an account for another regardless of whether a beneficiary is named. The term does not include a named beneficiary unless the beneficiary has a present right of withdrawal.

(b) A P.O.D. payee, including a charitable organization, or beneficiary of a trust account is a party only after the account becomes payable to the P.O.D. payee or beneficiary by reason of the P.O.D. payee or beneficiary surviving the original payee or trustee.

Added by Acts 2009, 81st Leg., ch. 680, § 1, eff. Jan. 1, 2014. Amended by Acts 2011, 82nd Leg., ch. 1338 (S.B. 1198), § 2.08, eff. Jan. 1, 2014.

## § 113.003. Definition of Net Contribution

(a) In this chapter, "net contribution" of a party to a joint account at any given time is the sum of all deposits made to that account by or for the party, less all withdrawals made by or for the party that have not been paid to or applied to the use of any other party, plus a pro rata share of any interest or dividends included in the current balance of the account. The term also includes any deposit life insurance proceeds added to the account by reason of the death of the party whose net contribution is in question.

(b) A financial institution may not be required to inquire, for purposes of establishing net contributions, about:

(1) the source of funds received for deposit to a multiple-party account; or

(2) the proposed application of an amount withdrawn from a multiple-party account.

Added by Acts 2009, 81st Leg., ch. 680, § 1, eff. Jan. 1, 2014.

## § 113.004. Types of Accounts

In this chapter:

(1) "Convenience account" means an account that:

(A) is established at a financial institution by one or more parties in the names of the parties and one or more convenience signers; and

(B) has terms that provide that the sums on deposit are paid or delivered to the parties or to the convenience signers "for the convenience" of the parties.

(2) "Joint account" means an account payable on request to one or more of two or more parties, regardless of whether there is a right of survivorship.

(3) "Multiple-party account" means a joint account, a convenience account, a P.O.D. account, or a trust account. The term does not include an account established for the deposit of funds of a partnership, joint venture, or other association for business purposes, or an account controlled by one or more persons as the authorized agent or trustee for a corporation, unincorporated association, charitable or civic organization, or a regular fiduciary or trust account in which the relationship is established other than by deposit agreement.

(4) "P.O.D. account" means an account payable on request to:

(A) one person during the person's lifetime and, on the person's death, to one or more P.O.D. payees; or

(B) one or more persons during their lifetimes and, on the death of all of those persons, to one or more P.O.D. payees.

(5) "Trust account" means an account in the name of one or more parties as trustee for one or more beneficiaries in which the relationship is established by the form of the account and the deposit agreement with the financial institution and in which there is no subject of the trust other than the sums on deposit in the account. The deposit agreement is not required to address payment to the beneficiary. The term does not include:

(A) a regular trust account under a testamentary trust or a trust agreement that has significance apart from the account; or

(B) a fiduciary account arising from a fiduciary relationship, such as the attorney-client relationship.

Added by Acts 2009, 81st Leg., ch. 680, § 1, eff. Jan. 1, 2014.

### § 113.005. Authority of Financial Institutions to Enter Into Certain Accounts

A financial institution may enter into a multiple-party account to the same extent that the institution may enter into a single-party account.

Added by Acts 2009, 81st Leg., ch. 680, § 1, eff. Jan. 1, 2014.

## SUBCHAPTER B. UNIFORM ACCOUNT FORM

### § 113.051. Establishment of Type of Account; Applicability of Certain Law

(a) A contract of deposit that contains provisions substantially the same as in the form provided by Section 113.052 establishes the type of account selected by a party. This chapter governs an account selected under the form.

(b) A contract of deposit that does not contain provisions substantially the same as in the form provided by Section 113.052 is governed by the provisions of this chapter applicable to the type of account that most nearly conforms to the depositor's intent.

Added by Acts 2009, 81st Leg., ch. 680, § 1, eff. Jan. 1, 2014. Amended by Acts 2011, 82nd Leg., ch. 91 (S.B. 1303), § 8.004, eff. Jan. 1, 2014.

### § 113.052. Form

A financial institution may use the following form to establish the type of account selected by a party:

UNIFORM SINGLE–PARTY OR MULTIPLE–PARTY ACCOUNT SELECTION FORM NOTICE: The type of account you select may determine how property passes on your death. Your will may not control the disposition of funds held in some of the following accounts. You may choose to designate one or more convenience signers on an account, even if the account is not a convenience account. A designated convenience signer may make transactions on your behalf during your lifetime, but does not own the account during your lifetime. The designated convenience signer owns the account on your death only if the convenience signer is also designated as a P.O.D. payee or trust account beneficiary.

Select one of the following accounts by placing your initials next to the account selected:

___ (1) SINGLE–PARTY ACCOUNT WITHOUT "P.O.D." (PAYABLE ON DEATH) DESIGNATION.

The party to the account owns the account. On the death of the party, ownership of the account passes as a part of the party's estate under the party's will or by intestacy.

Enter the name of the party:

_____

Enter the name(s) of the convenience signer(s), if you want one or more convenience signers on this account:

_____

_____

___ (2) SINGLE–PARTY ACCOUNT WITH "P.O.D." (PAYABLE ON DEATH) DESIGNATION. The party to the account owns the account. On the death of the party, ownership of the account passes to the P.O.D. beneficiaries of the account. The account is not a part of the party's estate.

Enter the name of the party:

_____

Enter the name or names of the P.O.D. beneficiaries:

_____

_____

Enter the name(s) of the convenience signer(s), if you want one or more convenience signers on this account:

_____

_____

___ (3) MULTIPLE–PARTY ACCOUNT WITHOUT RIGHT OF SURVIVORSHIP. The parties to the account own the account in proportion to the parties' net contributions to the account. The financial institution may pay any sum in the account to a party at any time. On the death of a party, the party's ownership of the account passes as a part of the party's estate under the party's will or by intestacy.

Enter the names of the parties:

_____

_____

_____

Enter the name(s) of the convenience signer(s), if you want one or more convenience signers on this account:

_____

_____

___ (4) MULTIPLE–PARTY ACCOUNT WITH RIGHT OF SURVIVORSHIP. The parties to the account own the account in proportion to the parties' net contributions to the account. The financial institution may pay any sum in the account to a party at any time. On the death of a party, the party's ownership of the account passes to the surviving parties.

Enter the names of the parties:

_____

_____

Enter the name(s) of the convenience signer(s), if you want one or more convenience signers on this account:

_____

_____

___ (5) MULTIPLE–PARTY ACCOUNT WITH RIGHT OF SURVIVORSHIP AND P.O.D. (PAYABLE ON DEATH) DESIGNATION. The parties to the account own the account in proportion to the parties' net contributions to the account. The financial institution may pay any sum in the account to a party at any time. On the death of the last surviving party, the ownership of the account passes to the P.O.D. beneficiaries.

Enter the names of the parties:

_____

_____

Enter the name or names of the P.O.D. beneficiaries:

_____

_____

Enter the name(s) of the convenience signer(s), if you want one or more convenience signers on this account:

_____

_____

___ (6) CONVENIENCE ACCOUNT. The parties to the account own the account. One or more convenience signers to the account may make account transactions for a party. A convenience signer does not own the account. On the death of the last surviving party, ownership of the account passes as a part of the last surviving party's estate under the last surviving party's will or by intestacy. The financial institution may pay funds in the account to a convenience signer before the financial institution receives notice of the death of the last surviving party. The payment to a convenience signer does not affect the parties' ownership of the account.

Enter the names of the parties:

_____

_____

Enter the name(s) of the convenience signer(s):

_____

_____

___ (7) TRUST ACCOUNT. The parties named as trustees to the account own the account in proportion to the parties' net contributions to the account. A trustee may withdraw funds from the account. A beneficiary may not withdraw funds from the account before all trustees are deceased. On the death of the last surviving trustee, the ownership of the account passes to the beneficiary. The trust account is not a part of a trustee's estate and does not pass under the trustee's will or by intestacy, unless the trustee survives all of the beneficiaries and all other trustees.

Enter the name or names of the trustees:

_____

_____

Enter the name or names of the beneficiaries:

_____

_____

Enter the name(s) of the convenience signer(s), if you want one or more convenience signers on this account:

_____

_____

Added by Acts 2009, 81st Leg., ch. 680, § 1, eff. Jan. 1, 2014. Amended by Acts 2011, 82nd Leg., ch. 91 (S.B. 1303), § 8.005, eff. Jan. 1, 2014.

§ 113.053.  Use of Form; Disclosure

(a) A financial institution is considered to have adequately disclosed the information provided in this subchapter if the financial institution uses the form provided by Section 113.052.

(b) If a financial institution varies the format of the form provided by Section 113.052, the financial institution may make disclosures in the account agreement or in any other form that adequately discloses the information provided by this subchapter.

(c) If the customer receives adequate disclosure of the ownership rights to an account and the names of the parties are appropriately indicated, a financial institution may combine any of the provisions in, and vary the format of, the form and notices described in Section 113.052 in:

(1) a universal account form with options listed for selection and additional disclosures provided in the account agreement; or

(2) any other manner that adequately discloses the information provided by this subchapter.

Added by Acts 2009, 81st Leg., ch. 680, § 1, eff. Jan. 1, 2014.

## SUBCHAPTER C.  OWNERSHIP AND OPERATION OF ACCOUNTS

### § 113.101.  Effect of Certain Provisions Regarding Ownership Between Parties and Others

The provisions of this subchapter and Subchapters B and D that relate to beneficial ownership between parties, or between parties and P.O.D. payees or beneficiaries of multiple-party accounts:

(1) are relevant only to controversies between those persons and those persons' creditors and other successors; and

(2) do not affect the withdrawal power of those persons under the terms of an account contract.

Added by Acts 2009, 81st Leg., ch. 680, § 1, eff. Jan. 1, 2014.

### § 113.102.  Ownership of Joint Account During Parties' Lifetimes

During the lifetime of all parties to a joint account, the account belongs to the parties in proportion to the net contributions by each party to the sums on deposit unless there is clear and convincing evidence of a different intent.

Added by Acts 2009, 81st Leg., ch. 680, § 1, eff. Jan. 1, 2014.

### § 113.103.  Ownership of P.O.D. Account During Original Payee's Lifetime

(a) During the lifetime of an original payee of a P.O.D. account, the account belongs to the original payee and does not belong to the P.O.D. payee or payees.

(b) If two or more parties are named as original payees of a P.O.D. account, during the parties' lifetimes rights between the parties are governed by Section 113.102.

Added by Acts 2009, 81st Leg., ch. 680, § 1, eff. Jan. 1, 2014.

### § 113.104.  Ownership of Trust Account During Trustee's Lifetime

(a) A trust account belongs beneficially to the trustee during the trustee's lifetime unless:

(1) the terms of the account or the deposit agreement manifest a contrary intent; or

(2) other clear and convincing evidence of an irrevocable trust exists.

(b) If two or more parties are named as trustees on a trust account, during the parties' lifetimes beneficial rights between the parties are governed by Section 113.102.

(c) An account that is an irrevocable trust belongs beneficially to the beneficiary.

Added by Acts 2009, 81st Leg., ch. 680, § 1, eff. Jan. 1, 2014.

### § 113.105.  Ownership of Convenience Account; Additions and Accruals

(a) The making of a deposit in a convenience account does not affect the title to the deposit.

(b) A party to a convenience account is not considered to have made a gift of the deposit, or of any additions or accruals to the deposit, to a convenience signer.

(c) An addition made to a convenience account by anyone other than a party, and accruals to the addition, are considered to have been made by a party.

Added by Acts 2009, 81st Leg., ch. 680, § 1, eff. Jan. 1, 2014.

### § 113.106.  Ownership and Operation of Other Account with Convenience Signer

(a) An account established by one or more parties at a financial institution that is not designated as a convenience account, but is instead designated as a single-party account or another type of multiple-party account, may provide that the sums on deposit may be paid or delivered to the parties or to one or more convenience signers "for the convenience of the parties."

(b) Except as provided by Section 113.1541:

(1) the provisions of Sections 113.105, 113.206, and 113.208 apply to an account described by Subsection (a), including provisions relating to the ownership of the account during the lifetimes and on the deaths of the parties and provisions relating to the powers and duties of the financial institution at which the account is established; and

(2) any other law relating to a convenience signer applies to a convenience signer designated as pro-

vided by this section to the extent the law applies to a convenience signer on a convenience account.

Added by Acts 2011, 82nd Leg., ch. 91 (S.B. 1303), § 8.006(a), eff. Jan. 1, 2014.

## SUBCHAPTER D. RIGHTS OF SURVIVORSHIP IN ACCOUNTS

### § 113.151. Establishment of Right of Survivorship in Joint Account; Ownership on Death of Party

(a) Sums remaining on deposit on the death of a party to a joint account belong to the surviving party or parties against the estate of the deceased party if the interest of the deceased party is made to survive to the surviving party or parties by a written agreement signed by the party who dies.

(b) Notwithstanding any other law, an agreement is sufficient under this section to confer an absolute right of survivorship on parties to a joint account if the agreement contains a statement substantially similar to the following: "On the death of one party to a joint account, all sums in the account on the date of the death vest in and belong to the surviving party as his or her separate property and estate."

(c) A survivorship agreement may not be inferred from the mere fact that the account is a joint account or that the account is designated as JT TEN, Joint Tenancy, or joint, or with other similar language.

(d) If there are two or more surviving parties to a joint account that is subject to a right of survivorship agreement:

(1) during the parties' lifetimes respective ownerships are in proportion to the parties' previous ownership interests under Sections 113.102, 113.103, and 113.104, as applicable, augmented by an equal share for each survivor of any interest a deceased party owned in the account immediately before that party's death; and

(2) the right of survivorship continues between the surviving parties if a written agreement signed by a party who dies provides for that continuation.

Added by Acts 2009, 81st Leg., ch. 680, § 1, eff. Jan. 1, 2014. Amended by Acts 2011, 82nd Leg., ch. 1338 (S.B. 1198), § 2.09, eff. Jan. 1, 2014.

### § 113.152. Ownership of P.O.D. Account on Death of Party

(a) If the account is a P.O.D. account and there is a written agreement signed by the original payee or payees, on the death of the original payee or on the death of the survivor of two or more original payees, any sums remaining on deposit belong to:

(1) the P.O.D. payee or payees if surviving; or

(2) the survivor of the P.O.D. payees if one or more P.O.D. payees die before the original payee.

(b) If two or more P.O.D. payees survive, no right of survivorship exists between the surviving P.O.D. payees unless the terms of the account or deposit agreement expressly provide for survivorship between those payees.

Added by Acts 2009, 81st Leg., ch. 680, § 1, eff. Jan. 1, 2014.

### § 113.153. Ownership of Trust Account on Death of Trustee

(a) If the account is a trust account and there is a written agreement signed by the trustee or trustees, on death of the trustee or the survivor of two or more trustees, any sums remaining on deposit belong to:

(1) the person or persons named as beneficiaries, if surviving; or

(2) the survivor of the persons named as beneficiaries if one or more beneficiaries die before the trustee.

(b) If two or more beneficiaries survive, no right of survivorship exists between the surviving beneficiaries unless the terms of the account or deposit agreement expressly provide for survivorship between those beneficiaries.

Added by Acts 2009, 81st Leg., ch. 680, § 1, eff. Jan. 1, 2014.

### § 113.154. Ownership of Convenience Account on Death of Party

On the death of the last surviving party to a convenience account:

(1) a convenience signer has no right of survivorship in the account; and

(2) ownership of the account remains in the estate of the last surviving party.

Added by Acts 2009, 81st Leg., ch. 680, § 1, eff. Jan. 1, 2014.

### § 113.1541. Ownership of Other Account with Convenience Signer on Death of Last Surviving Party

On the death of the last surviving party to an account that has a convenience signer designated as provided by Section 113.106, the convenience signer does not have a right of survivorship in the account and the estate of the last surviving party owns the account unless the convenience signer is also designated as a P.O.D. payee or as a beneficiary.

Added by Acts 2011, 82nd Leg., ch. 91 (S.B. 1303), § 8.006(b), eff. Jan. 1, 2014.

## § 113.155. Effect of Death of Party on Certain Accounts Without Rights of Survivorship

The death of a party to a multiple-party account to which Sections 113.151, 113.152, and 113.153 do not apply has no effect on the beneficial ownership of the account, other than to transfer the rights of the deceased party as part of the deceased party's estate.

Added by Acts 2009, 81st Leg., ch. 680, § 1, eff. Jan. 1, 2014.

## § 113.156. Applicability of Certain Provisions on Death of Party

Sections 113.151, 113.152, 113.153, and 113.155 as to rights of survivorship are determined by the form of the account at the death of a party.

Added by Acts 2009, 81st Leg., ch. 680, § 1, eff. Jan. 1, 2014.

## § 113.157. Written Notice to Financial Institutions Regarding Form of Account

Notwithstanding any other law, the form of an account may be altered by written order given by a party to the financial institution to change the form of the account or to stop or vary payment under the terms of the account. The order or request must be signed by a party, received by the financial institution during the party's lifetime, and not countermanded by another written order of the same party during the party's lifetime.

Added by Acts 2009, 81st Leg., ch. 680, § 1, eff. Jan. 1, 2014.

## § 113.158. Nontestamentary Nature of Certain Transfers

Transfers resulting from the application of Sections 113.151, 113.152, 113.153, and 113.155 are effective by reason of the account contracts involved and this chapter and are not to be considered testamentary transfers or subject to the testamentary provisions of this title.

Added by Acts 2009, 81st Leg., ch. 680, § 1, eff. Jan. 1, 2014.

## SUBCHAPTER E. PROTECTION OF FINANCIAL INSTITUTIONS

## § 113.201. Applicability of Subchapter

This subchapter and Section 113.003(b) govern:

(1) the liability of financial institutions that make payments as provided by this subchapter; and

(2) the set-off rights of those institutions.

Added by Acts 2009, 81st Leg., ch. 680, § 1, eff. Jan. 1, 2014.

## § 113.202. Payment of Multiple–Party Account

A multiple-party account may be paid, on request, to any one or more of the parties.

Added by Acts 2009, 81st Leg., ch. 680, § 1, eff. Jan. 1, 2014.

## § 113.203. Payment of Joint Account

(a) Subject to Subsection (b), amounts in a joint account may be paid, on request, to any party without regard to whether any other party is incapacitated or deceased at the time the payment is demanded.

(b) Payment may not be made to the personal representative or heir of a deceased party unless:

(1) proofs of death are presented to the financial institution showing that the deceased party was the last surviving party; or

(2) there is no right of survivorship under Sections 113.151, 113.152, 113.153, and 113.155.

Added by Acts 2009, 81st Leg., ch. 680, § 1, eff. Jan. 1, 2014.

## § 113.204. Payment of P.O.D. Account

(a) A P.O.D. account may be paid, on request, to any original payee of the account.

(b) Payment may be made, on request, to the P.O.D. payee or to the personal representative or heirs of a deceased P.O.D. payee on the presentation to the financial institution of proof of death showing that the P.O.D. payee survived each person named as an original payee.

(c) Payment may be made to the personal representative or heirs of a deceased original payee if proof of death is presented to the financial institution showing that the deceased original payee was the survivor of each other person named on the account as an original payee or a P.O.D. payee.

Added by Acts 2009, 81st Leg., ch. 680, § 1, eff. Jan. 1, 2014.

## § 113.205. Payment of Trust Account

(a) A trust account may be paid, on request, to any trustee.

(b) Unless a financial institution has received written notice that a beneficiary has a vested interest not dependent on the beneficiary's surviving the trustee, payment may be made to the personal representative or heirs of a deceased trustee if proof of death is presented to the financial institution showing that the deceased trustee was the survivor of each other person named on the account as a trustee or beneficiary.

(c) Payment may be made, on request, to a beneficiary if proof of death is presented to the financial institution showing that the beneficiary or beneficiaries survived all persons named as trustees.

Added by Acts 2009, 81st Leg., ch. 680, § 1, eff. Jan. 1, 2014.

### § 113.206.  Payment of Convenience Account

Deposits to a convenience account and additions and accruals to the deposits may be paid to a party or a convenience signer.

Added by Acts 2009, 81st Leg., ch. 680, § 1, eff. Jan. 1, 2014.

### § 113.207.  Liability for Payment from Joint Account After Death

A financial institution that pays an amount from a joint account to a surviving party to that account in accordance with a written agreement under Section 113.151 is not liable to an heir, devisee, or beneficiary of the deceased party's estate.

Added by Acts 2009, 81st Leg., ch. 680, § 1, eff. Jan. 1, 2014.

### § 113.208.  Liability for Payment from Convenience Account

(a) A financial institution is completely released from liability for a payment made from a convenience account before the financial institution receives notice in writing signed by a party not to make the payment in accordance with the terms of the account.  After receipt of the notice from a party, the financial institution may require a party to approve any further payments from the account.

(b) A financial institution that makes a payment of the sums on deposit in a convenience account to a convenience signer after the death of the last surviving party, but before the financial institution receives written notice of the last surviving party's death, is completely released from liability for the payment.

(c) A financial institution that makes a payment of the sums on deposit in a convenience account to the personal representative of the deceased last surviving party's estate after the death of the last surviving party, but before a court order prohibiting payment is served on the financial institution, is, to the extent of the payment, released from liability to any person claiming a right to the funds.  The personal represen-

tative's receipt of the funds is a complete release and discharge of the financial institution.

Added by Acts 2009, 81st Leg., ch. 680, § 1, eff. Jan. 1, 2014.

### § 113.209.  Discharge from Claims

(a) Payment made in accordance with Section 113.202, 113.203, 113.204, 113.205, or 113.207 discharges the financial institution from all claims for those amounts paid regardless of whether the payment is consistent with the beneficial ownership of the account between parties, P.O.D. payees, or beneficiaries, or their successors.

(b) The protection provided by Subsection (a) does not extend to payments made after a financial institution receives, from any party able to request present payment, written notice to the effect that withdrawals in accordance with the terms of the account should not be permitted.  Unless the notice is withdrawn by the person giving the notice, the successor of a deceased party must concur in a demand for withdrawal for the financial institution to be protected under Subsection (a).

(c) No notice, other than the notice described by Subsection (b), or any other information shown to have been available to a financial institution affects the institution's right to the protection provided by Subsection (a).

(d) The protection provided by Subsection (a) does not affect the rights of parties in disputes between the parties or the parties' successors concerning the beneficial ownership of funds in, or withdrawn from, multiple-party accounts.

Added by Acts 2009, 81st Leg., ch. 680, § 1, eff. Jan. 1, 2014.

### § 113.210.  Set–Off to Financial Institution

(a) Without qualifying any other statutory right to set-off or lien and subject to any contractual provision, if a party to a multiple-party account is indebted to a financial institution, the financial institution has a right to set-off against the account in which the party has, or had immediately before the party's death, a present right of withdrawal.

(b) The amount of the account subject to set-off under this section is that proportion to which the debtor is, or was immediately before the debtor's death, beneficially entitled, and in the absence of proof of net contributions, to an equal share with all parties having present rights of withdrawal.

Added by Acts 2009, 81st Leg., ch. 680, § 1, eff. Jan. 1, 2014.

## SUBCHAPTER F. RIGHTS OF CREDITORS; PLEDGE OF ACCOUNT

### § 113.251. Pledge of Account

(a) A party to a multiple-party account may pledge the account or otherwise create a security interest in the account without the joinder of, as applicable, a P.O.D. payee, a beneficiary, a convenience signer, or any other party to a joint account, regardless of whether a right of survivorship exists.

(b) A convenience signer may not pledge or otherwise create a security interest in an account.

(c) Not later than the 30th day after the date a security interest on a multiple-party account is perfected, a secured creditor that is a financial institution with accounts insured by the Federal Deposit Insurance Corporation shall provide written notice of the pledge of the account to any other party to the account who did not create the security interest. The notice must be sent by certified mail to each other party at the last address the party provided to the depository bank.

(d) The financial institution is not required to provide the notice described by Subsection (c) to a P.O.D. payee, beneficiary, or convenience signer.

Added by Acts 2009, 81st Leg., ch. 680, § 1, eff. Jan. 1, 2014.

### § 113.252. Rights of Creditors

(a) A multiple-party account is not effective against:

(1) an estate of a deceased party to transfer to a survivor amounts needed to pay debts, taxes, and expenses of administration, including statutory allowances to the surviving spouse and minor children, if other assets of the estate are insufficient; or

(2) the claim of a secured creditor who has a lien on the account.

(b) A party, P.O.D. payee, or beneficiary who receives payment from a multiple-party account after the death of a deceased party is liable to account to the deceased party's personal representative for amounts the deceased party owned beneficially immediately before the party's death to the extent necessary to discharge the claims and charges described by Subsection (a) that remain unpaid after application of the deceased party's estate. The party, P.O.D. payee, or beneficiary is not liable in an amount greater than the amount the party, P.O.D. payee, or beneficiary received from the multiple-party account.

(c) A proceeding to assert liability under Subsection (b):

(1) may only be commenced if the personal representative receives a written demand by a surviving spouse, a creditor, or one acting for a minor child of the deceased party; and

(2) must be commenced on or before the second anniversary of the death of the deceased party.

(d) Amounts recovered by the personal representative under this section must be administered as part of the decedent's estate.

Added by Acts 2009, 81st Leg., ch. 680, § 1, eff. Jan. 1, 2014.

### § 113.253. No Effect on Certain Rights and Liabilities of Financial Institutions

This subchapter does not:

(1) affect the right of a financial institution to make payment on multiple-party accounts according to the terms of the account; or

(2) make the financial institution liable to the estate of a deceased party unless, before payment, the institution received written notice from the personal representative stating the amounts needed to pay debts, taxes, claims, and expenses of administration.

Added by Acts 2009, 81st Leg., ch. 680, § 1, eff. Jan. 1, 2014.

## CHAPTER 121. SURVIVAL REQUIREMENTS

### SUBCHAPTER A. GENERAL PROVISIONS

## SUBCHAPTER A.   GENERAL PROVISIONS

### § 121.001.   Applicability of Chapter

This chapter does not apply if provision has been made by will, living trust, deed, or insurance contract, or in any other manner, for a disposition of property that is different from the disposition of the property that would be made if the provisions of this chapter applied.

Added by Acts 2009, 81st Leg., ch. 680, § 1, eff. Jan. 1, 2014.

## SUBCHAPTER B.   SURVIVAL REQUIREMENT FOR INTESTATE SUCCESSION AND CERTAIN OTHER PURPOSES

### § 121.051.   Applicability of Subchapter

This subchapter does not apply if the application of this subchapter would result in the escheat of an intestate estate.

Added by Acts 2009, 81st Leg., ch. 680, § 1, eff. Jan. 1, 2014.

### § 121.052.   Required Period of Survival for Intestate Succession and Certain Other Purposes

A person who does not survive a decedent by 120 hours is considered to have predeceased the decedent for purposes of the homestead allowance, exempt property, and intestate succession, and the decedent's heirs are determined accordingly, except as otherwise provided by this chapter.

Added by Acts 2009, 81st Leg., ch. 680, § 1, eff. Jan. 1, 2014.

### § 121.053.   Intestate Succession: Failure to Survive Presumed Under Certain Circumstances

A person who, if the person survived a decedent by 120 hours, would be the decedent's heir is considered not to have survived the decedent for the required period if:

(1) the time of death of the decedent or of the person, or the times of death of both, cannot be determined; and

(2) the person's survival for the required period after the decedent's death cannot be established.

Added by Acts 2009, 81st Leg., ch. 680, § 1, eff. Jan. 1, 2014.

## SUBCHAPTER C.   SURVIVAL REQUIREMENTS FOR CERTAIN BENEFICIARIES

### § 121.101.   Required Period of Survival for Devisee

A devisee who does not survive the testator by 120 hours is treated as if the devisee predeceased the testator unless the testator's will contains some language that:

(1) deals explicitly with simultaneous death or deaths in a common disaster; or

(2) requires the devisee to survive the testator, or to survive the testator for a stated period, to take under the will.

Added by Acts 2009, 81st Leg., ch. 680, § 1, eff. Jan. 1, 2014.

### § 121.102.   Required Period of Survival for Contingent Beneficiary

(a) If property is disposed of in a manner that conditions the right of a beneficiary to succeed to an interest in the property on the beneficiary surviving another person, the beneficiary is considered not to have survived the other person unless the beneficiary survives the person by 120 hours, except as provided by Subsection (b).

(b) If an interest in property is given alternatively to one of two or more beneficiaries, with the right of each beneficiary to take being dependent on that beneficiary surviving the other beneficiary or beneficiaries, and all of the beneficiaries die within a period of less than 120 hours, the property shall be divided into as many equal portions as there are beneficiaries. The portions shall be distributed respectively to those who would have taken if each beneficiary had survived.

Added by Acts 2009, 81st Leg., ch. 680, § 1, eff. Jan. 1, 2014.

## SUBCHAPTER D.   DISTRIBUTION OF CERTAIN PROPERTY ON PERSON'S FAILURE TO SURVIVE FOR REQUIRED PERIOD

### § 121.151.   Distribution of Community Property

(a) This section applies to community property, including the proceeds of life or accident insurance that are community property and become payable to the estate of either the husband or wife.

(b) If a husband and wife die leaving community property but neither survives the other by 120 hours, one-half of all community property shall be distributed as if the husband had survived, and the other one-half shall be distributed as if the wife had survived.

Added by Acts 2009, 81st Leg., ch. 680, § 1, eff. Jan. 1, 2014.

## § 121.152. Distribution of Property Owned by Joint Owners

If property, including community property with a right of survivorship, is owned so that one of two joint owners is entitled to the whole of the property on the death of the other, but neither survives the other by 120 hours, one-half of the property shall be distributed as if one joint owner had survived, and the other one-half shall be distributed as if the other joint owner had survived. If there are more than two joint owners and all of the joint owners die within a period of less than 120 hours, the property shall be divided into as many equal portions as there are joint owners and the portions shall be distributed respectively to those who would have taken if each joint owner survived.

Added by Acts 2009, 81st Leg., ch. 680, § 1, eff. Jan. 1, 2014.

## § 121.153. Distribution of Certain Insurance Proceeds

(a) If the insured under a life or accident insurance policy and a beneficiary of the proceeds of that policy die within a period of less than 120 hours, the insured is considered to have survived the beneficiary for the purpose of determining the rights under the policy of the beneficiary or beneficiaries as such.

(b) This section does not prevent the applicability of Section 121.151 to proceeds of life or accident insurance that are community property.

Added by Acts 2009, 81st Leg., ch. 680, § 1, eff. Jan. 1, 2014.

## CHAPTER 122. DISCLAIMERS AND ASSIGNMENTS

### SUBCHAPTER A. GENERAL PROVISIONS RELATING TO DISCLAIMER

## SUBCHAPTER A. GENERAL PROVISIONS RELATING TO DISCLAIMER

### § 122.001. Definitions

In this chapter, other than Subchapter E:

(1) "Beneficiary" includes a person who would have been entitled, if the person had not made a disclaimer, to receive property as a result of the death of another person:

(A) by inheritance;

(B) under a will;

(C) by an agreement between spouses for community property with a right of survivorship;

(D) by a joint tenancy with a right of survivorship;

(E) by a survivorship agreement, account, or interest in which the interest of the decedent passes to a surviving beneficiary;

(F) by an insurance, annuity, endowment, employment, deferred compensation, or other contract or arrangement; or

(G) under a pension, profit sharing, thrift, stock bonus, life insurance, survivor income, incentive, or other plan or program providing retirement, welfare, or fringe benefits with respect to an employee or a self-employed individual.

(2) "Disclaimer" includes renunciation.

(3) "Property" includes all legal and equitable interests, powers, and property, present or future,

vested or contingent, and beneficial or burdensome, in whole or in part.

Added by Acts 2009, 81st Leg., ch. 680, § 1, eff. Jan. 1, 2014.

### § 122.002. Who May Disclaim

(a) A person who may be entitled to receive property as a beneficiary who on or after September 1, 1977, intends to irrevocably disclaim all or any part of the property shall evidence the disclaimer as provided by this chapter.

(b) Subject to Subsection (c), the legally authorized representative of a person who may be entitled to receive property as a beneficiary who on or after September 1, 1977, intends to irrevocably disclaim all or any part of the property on the beneficiary's behalf shall evidence the disclaimer as provided by this chapter.

(c) A disclaimer made by a legally authorized representative described by Subsection (d)(1), (2), or (3), other than an independent executor, must be made with prior court approval of the court that has or would have jurisdiction over the legally authorized representative. A disclaimer made by an independent executor on behalf of a decedent may be made without prior court approval.

(d) In this section, "legally authorized representative" means:

(1) a guardian if the person entitled to receive the property as a beneficiary is an incapacitated person;

(2) a guardian ad litem if the person entitled to receive the property as a beneficiary is an unborn or unascertained person;

(3) a personal representative, including an independent executor, if the person entitled to receive the property as a beneficiary is a decedent; or

(4) an attorney in fact or agent appointed under a durable power of attorney authorizing disclaimers if the person entitled to receive the property as a beneficiary executed the power of attorney as a principal.

Added by Acts 2009, 81st Leg., ch. 680, § 1, eff. Jan. 1, 2014.

### § 122.003. Effective Date; Creditors' Claims

(a) A disclaimer evidenced as provided by this chapter is effective for all purposes as of the date of the decedent's death.

(b) Property disclaimed in accordance with this chapter is not subject to the claims of a creditor of the disclaimant.

Added by Acts 2009, 81st Leg., ch. 680, § 1, eff. Jan. 1, 2014.

### § 122.004. Disclaimer Irrevocable

A disclaimer that is filed and served as provided by this chapter is irrevocable.

Added by Acts 2009, 81st Leg., ch. 680, § 1, eff. Jan. 1, 2014.

### § 122.005. Power to Provide Method of Disclaimer

A will, insurance policy, employee benefit agreement, or other instrument may provide for the making of a disclaimer by a beneficiary of an interest receivable under that instrument and for the disposition of disclaimed property in a manner different than provided by this chapter.

Added by Acts 2009, 81st Leg., ch. 680, § 1, eff. Jan. 1, 2014.

## SUBCHAPTER B. FORM, FILING, AND NOTICE OF DISCLAIMER

### § 122.051. Form and Contents

(a) A disclaimer of property receivable by a beneficiary must be evidenced by written memorandum acknowledged before:

(1) a notary public; or

(2) another person authorized to take acknowledgments of conveyances of real estate.

(b) A disclaimer of property receivable by a beneficiary must include a statement regarding whether the beneficiary is a child support obligor described by Section 122.107.

Added by Acts 2009, 81st Leg., ch. 680, § 1, eff. Jan. 1, 2014. Amended by Acts 2013, 83rd Leg., ch. 689 (H.B. 2621), § 1, eff. Jan. 1, 2014.

Section 3 of Acts 2013, 83rd Leg., ch. 689 (H.B. 2621) provides:

"The change in law made by this Act applies only to a disclaimer filed on or after the effective date [Jan. 1, 2014] of this Act. A disclaimer filed before the effective date of this Act is governed by the law in effect on the date the disclaimer was filed, and the former law is continued in effect for that purpose."

### § 122.052. Filing in Probate Court

Except as provided by Sections 122.053 and 122.054, the written memorandum of disclaimer must be filed in the probate court in which:

(1) the decedent's will has been probated;

(2) proceedings have commenced for the administration of the decedent's estate; or

(3) an application has been filed for probate of the decedent's will or administration of the decedent's estate.

Added by Acts 2009, 81st Leg., ch. 680, § 1, eff. Jan. 1, 2014.

## § 122.053. Filing in County of Decedent's Residence

The written memorandum of disclaimer must be filed with the county clerk of the county of the decedent's residence on the date of the decedent's death if:

(1) the administration of the decedent's estate is closed;

(2) one year has expired since the date letters testamentary were issued in an independent administration;

(3) a will of the decedent has not been probated or filed for probate;

(4) administration of the decedent's estate has not commenced; or

(5) an application for administration of the decedent's estate has not been filed.

Added by Acts 2009, 81st Leg., ch. 680, § 1, eff. Jan. 1, 2014.

## § 122.054. Nonresident Decedent

If the decedent is not a resident of this state on the date of the decedent's death and the disclaimer is of real property that is located in this state, the written memorandum of disclaimer must be:

(1) filed with the county clerk of the county in which the real property is located; and

(2) recorded by the county clerk in the deed records of that county.

Added by Acts 2009, 81st Leg., ch. 680, § 1, eff. Jan. 1, 2014.

## § 122.055. Filing Deadline

(a) Except as provided by Subsection (c), a written memorandum of disclaimer of a present interest must be filed not later than nine months after the date of the decedent's death.

(b) Except as provided by Subsection (c), a written memorandum of disclaimer of a future interest may be filed not later than nine months after the date of the event determining that the taker of the property or interest is finally ascertained and the taker's interest is indefeasibly vested.

(c) If the beneficiary is a charitable organization or a governmental agency of the state, a written memorandum of disclaimer of a present or future interest must be filed not later than the later of:

(1) the first anniversary of the date the beneficiary receives the notice required by Subchapter A, Chapter 308; or

(2) the expiration of the six-month period following the date the personal representative files:

(A) the inventory, appraisement, and list of claims due or owing to the estate; or

(B) the affidavit in lieu of the inventory, appraisement, and list of claims.

Added by Acts 2009, 81st Leg., ch. 680, § 1, eff. Jan. 1, 2014. Amended by Acts 2011, 82nd Leg., ch. 1338 (S.B. 1198), § 2.10, eff. Jan. 1, 2014.

## § 122.056. Notice

(a) Except as provided by Subsection (b), a copy of the written memorandum of disclaimer shall be delivered in person to, or mailed by registered or certified mail to and received by, the legal representative of the transferor of the interest or the holder of legal title to the property to which the disclaimer relates not later than nine months after:

(1) the date of the decedent's death; or

(2) if the interest is a future interest, the date the person who will receive the property or interest is finally ascertained and the person's interest is indefeasibly vested.

(b) If the beneficiary is a charitable organization or a governmental agency of this state, notice of a disclaimer required by Subsection (a) must be filed not later than the later of:

(1) the first anniversary of the date the beneficiary receives the notice required by Subchapter A, Chapter 308; or

(2) the expiration of the six-month period following the date the personal representative files:

(A) the inventory, appraisement, and list of claims due or owing to the estate; or

(B) the affidavit in lieu of the inventory, appraisement, and list of claims.

Added by Acts 2009, 81st Leg., ch. 680, § 1, eff. Jan. 1, 2014. Amended by Acts 2011, 82nd Leg., ch. 1338 (S.B. 1198), § 2.11, eff. Jan. 1, 2014.

## SUBCHAPTER C. EFFECT OF DISCLAIMER

## § 122.101. Effect

Unless the decedent's will provides otherwise:

(1) property subject to a disclaimer passes as if the person disclaiming or on whose behalf a disclaimer is made had predeceased the decedent; and

(2) a future interest that would otherwise take effect in possession or enjoyment after the termination of the estate or interest that is disclaimed takes effect as if the disclaiming beneficiary had predeceased the decedent.

Added by Acts 2009, 81st Leg., ch. 680, § 1, eff. Jan. 1, 2014.

### § 122.102. Ineffective Disclaimer

(a) Except as provided by Subsection (b), a disclaimer that does not comply with this chapter is ineffective.

(b) A disclaimer otherwise ineffective under Subsection (a) is effective as an assignment of the disclaimed property to those who would have received the property had the person attempting the disclaimer died before the decedent.

Added by Acts 2009, 81st Leg., ch. 680, § 1, eff. Jan. 1, 2014.

### § 122.103. Subsequent Disclaimer

This chapter does not prevent a person who is entitled to property as the result of a disclaimer from subsequently disclaiming the property.

Added by Acts 2009, 81st Leg., ch. 680, § 1, eff. Jan. 1, 2014.

### § 122.104. Disclaimer After Acceptance

A disclaimer is not effective if the person making the disclaimer has previously accepted the property by taking possession or exercising dominion and control of the property as a beneficiary.

Added by Acts 2009, 81st Leg., ch. 680, § 1, eff. Jan. 1, 2014.

### § 122.105. Interest in Trust Property

A beneficiary who accepts an interest in a trust is not considered to have a direct or indirect interest in trust property that relates to a licensed or permitted business and over which the beneficiary exercises no control.

Added by Acts 2009, 81st Leg., ch. 680, § 1, eff. Jan. 1, 2014.

### § 122.106. Interest in Securities

Direct or indirect beneficial ownership of not more than five percent of any class of equity securities that is registered under the Securities Exchange Act of 1934 (15 U.S.C. Section 78a et seq.) is not considered an ownership interest in the business of the issuer of the securities within the meaning of any statute, pursuant thereto.

Added by Acts 2009, 81st Leg., ch. 680, § 1, eff. Jan. 1, 2014.

### § 122.107. Attempted Disclaimers by Certain Child Support Obligors Ineffective

(a) A disclaimer made by a beneficiary who is a child support obligor of estate property that could be applied to satisfy the beneficiary's child support obligation is not effective if the beneficiary owes child support arrearages that have been:

(1) administratively determined by the Title IV–D agency as defined by Section 101.033, Family Code, in a Title IV–D case as defined by Section 101. 034, Family Code; or

(2) confirmed and reduced to judgment as provided by Section 157.263, Family Code.

(b) After distribution of estate property to a beneficiary described by Subsection (a), the child support obligee to whom the child support arrearages are owed may enforce the child support obligation by a lien or by any other remedy provided by law.

Added by Acts 2013, 83rd Leg., ch. 689 (H.B. 2621), § 2, eff. Jan. 1, 2014.

Section 3 of Acts 2013, 83rd Leg., ch. 689 (H.B. 2621) provides:

"The change in law made by this Act applies only to a disclaimer filed on or after the effective date [Jan. 1, 2014] of this Act. A disclaimer filed before the effective date of this Act is governed by the law in effect on the date the disclaimer was filed, and the former law is continued in effect for that purpose."

## SUBCHAPTER D.  PARTIAL DISCLAIMER

### § 122.151. Partial Disclaimer

A person who may be entitled to receive property as a beneficiary may wholly or partly disclaim the property, including:

(1) specific powers of invasion;

(2) powers of appointment; and

(3) fee estate in favor of life estates.

Added by Acts 2009, 81st Leg., ch. 680, § 1, eff. Jan. 1, 2014.

### § 122.152. Effect of Partial Disclaimer

A partial disclaimer in accordance with this chapter is effective whether the property disclaimed constitutes a portion of a single, aggregate gift or constitutes part or all of a separate, independent gift, except that:

(1) a partial disclaimer is effective only with respect to property expressly described or referred to by category in the disclaimer; and

(2) a partial disclaimer of property subject to a burdensome interest created by the decedent's will

is not effective unless the property constitutes a gift separate and distinct from undisclaimed gifts.

Added by Acts 2009, 81st Leg., ch. 680, § 1, eff. Jan. 1, 2014.

### § 122.153. Partial Disclaimer by Spouse

A disclaimer by the decedent's surviving spouse of a transfer by the decedent is not a disclaimer by the surviving spouse of all or any part of any other transfer from the decedent to or for the benefit of the surviving spouse, regardless of whether the property or interest that would have passed under the disclaimed transfer passes because of the disclaimer to or for the benefit of the surviving spouse by the other transfer.

Added by Acts 2009, 81st Leg., ch. 680, § 1, eff. Jan. 1, 2014.

### SUBCHAPTER E. ASSIGNMENT OF INTEREST

### § 122.201. Assignment

A person who is entitled to receive property or an interest in property from a decedent under a will, by inheritance, or as a beneficiary under a life insurance contract, and does not disclaim the property under this chapter may assign the property or interest in property to any person.

Added by Acts 2009, 81st Leg., ch. 680, § 1, eff. Jan. 1, 2014.

### § 122.202. Filing of Assignment

An assignment may, at the request of the assignor, be filed as provided for the filing of a disclaimer under Subchapter B.

Added by Acts 2009, 81st Leg., ch. 680, § 1, eff. Jan. 1, 2014.

### § 122.203. Notice

Notice of the filing of an assignment as provided by Section 122.202 must be served as required by Section 122.056 for notice of a disclaimer.

Added by Acts 2009, 81st Leg., ch. 680, § 1, eff. Jan. 1, 2014.

### § 122.204. Failure to Comply

Failure to comply with Subchapters A, B, C, and D does not affect an assignment.

Added by Acts 2009, 81st Leg., ch. 680, § 1, eff. Jan. 1, 2014.

### § 122.205. Gift

An assignment under this subchapter is a gift to the assignee and is not a disclaimer under Subchapters A, B, C, and D.

Added by Acts 2009, 81st Leg., ch. 680, § 1, eff. Jan. 1, 2014.

### § 122.206. Spendthrift Provision

An assignment of property or interest that would defeat a spendthrift provision imposed in a trust may not be made under this subchapter.

Added by Acts 2009, 81st Leg., ch. 680, § 1, eff. Jan. 1, 2014.

## CHAPTER 123. DISSOLUTION OF MARRIAGE

### SUBCHAPTER A. EFFECT OF DISSOLUTION OF MARRIAGE ON WILL

### § 123.001. Will Provisions Made Before Dissolution of Marriage

(a) In this section, "relative" means an individual related to another individual by:

(1) consanguinity, as determined under Section 573.022, Government Code; or

(2) affinity, as determined under Section 573.024, Government Code.

(b) If, after the testator makes a will, the testator's marriage is dissolved by divorce, annulment, or a declaration that the marriage is void, all provisions in the will, including all fiduciary appointments, shall be read as if the former spouse and each relative of the former spouse who is not a relative of the testator failed to survive the testator, unless the will expressly provides otherwise.

Added by Acts 2009, 81st Leg., ch. 680, § 1, eff. Jan. 1, 2014.

### § 123.002. Treatment of Decedent's Former Spouse

A person is not a surviving spouse of a decedent if the person's marriage to the decedent has been dissolved by divorce, annulment, or a declaration that the marriage is void, unless:

(1) as the result of a subsequent marriage, the person is married to the decedent at the time of death; and

(2) the subsequent marriage is not declared void under Subchapter C.

Added by Acts 2009, 81st Leg., ch. 680, § 1, eff. Jan. 1, 2014.

### SUBCHAPTER B. EFFECT OF DISSOLUTION OF MARRIAGE ON CERTAIN NONTESTAMENTARY TRANSFERS

### § 123.051. Definitions

In this subchapter:

(1) "Disposition or appointment of property" includes a transfer of property to or a provision of another benefit to a beneficiary under a trust instrument.

(2) "Divorced individual" means an individual whose marriage has been dissolved by divorce, annulment, or a declaration that the marriage is void.

(2–a) "Relative" means an individual who is related to another individual by consanguinity or affinity, as determined under Sections 573.022 and 573.024, Government Code, respectively.

(3) "Revocable," with respect to a disposition, appointment, provision, or nomination, means a disposition to, appointment of, provision in favor of, or nomination of an individual's spouse that is contained in a trust instrument executed by the individual before the dissolution of the individual's marriage to the spouse and that the individual was solely empowered by law or by the trust instrument to revoke regardless of whether the individual had the capacity to exercise the power at that time.

Added by Acts 2009, 81st Leg., ch. 680, § 1, eff. Jan. 1, 2014. Amended by Acts 2011, 82nd Leg., ch. 1338 (S.B. 1198), § 2.13, eff. Jan. 1, 2014.

### § 123.052. Revocation of Certain Nontestamentary Transfers; Treatment of Former Spouse as Beneficiary Under Certain Policies or Plans

(a) The dissolution of the marriage revokes a provision in a trust instrument that was executed by a divorced individual before the divorced individual's marriage was dissolved and that:

(1) is a revocable disposition or appointment of property made to the divorced individual's former spouse or any relative of the former spouse who is not a relative of the divorced individual;

(2) confers a general or special power of appointment on the divorced individual's former spouse or any relative of the former spouse who is not a relative of the divorced individual; or

(3) nominates the divorced individual's former spouse or any relative of the former spouse who is not a relative of the divorced individual to serve:

(A) as a personal representative, trustee, conservator, agent, or guardian; or

(B) in another fiduciary or representative capacity.

(b) Subsection (a) does not apply if one of the following provides otherwise:

(1) a court order;

(2) the express terms of a trust instrument executed by the divorced individual before the individual's marriage was dissolved; or

(3) an express provision of a contract relating to the division of the marital estate entered into between the divorced individual and the individual's former spouse before, during, or after the marriage.

(c) Sections 9.301 and 9.302, Family Code, govern the designation of a former spouse as a beneficiary of certain life insurance policies or as a beneficiary under certain retirement benefit plans or other financial plans.

Added by Acts 2009, 81st Leg., ch. 680, § 1, eff. Jan. 1, 2014. Amended by Acts 2011, 82nd Leg., ch. 1338 (S.B. 1198), § 2.14, eff. Jan. 1, 2014.

### § 123.053. Effect of Revocation

(a) An interest granted in a provision of a trust instrument that is revoked under Section 123.052(a)(1) or (2) passes as if the former spouse of the divorced individual who executed the trust instrument and each relative of the former spouse who is not a relative of the divorced individual disclaimed the interest granted in the provision.

(b) An interest granted in a provision of a trust instrument that is revoked under Section 123.052(a)(3) passes as if the former spouse and each relative of the former spouse who is not a relative of the divorced individual died immediately before the dissolution of the marriage.

Added by Acts 2009, 81st Leg., ch. 680, § 1, eff. Jan. 1, 2014. Amended by Acts 2011, 82nd Leg., ch. 1338 (S.B. 1198), § 2.15, eff. Jan. 1, 2014.

### § 123.054. Liability of Certain Purchasers or Recipients of Certain Payments, Benefits, or Property

A bona fide purchaser of property from a divorced individual's former spouse or any relative of the former spouse who is not a relative of the divorced individual or a person who receives from the former spouse or any relative of the former spouse who is not a relative of the divorced individual a payment, benefit, or property in partial or full satisfaction of an enforceable obligation:

(1) is not required by this subchapter to return the payment, benefit, or property; and

(2) is not liable under this subchapter for the amount of the payment or the value of the property or benefit.

Added by Acts 2009, 81st Leg., ch. 680, § 1, eff. Jan. 1, 2014. Amended by Acts 2011, 82nd Leg., ch. 1338 (S.B. 1198), § 2.16, eff. Jan. 1, 2014.

### § 123.055. Liability of Former Spouse for Certain Payments, Benefits, or Property

A divorced individual's former spouse or any relative of the former spouse who is not a relative of the divorced individual who, not for value, receives a payment, benefit, or property to which the former spouse or the relative of the former spouse who is not a relative of the divorced individual is not entitled as a result of Sections 123.052(a) and (b):

(1) shall return the payment, benefit, or property to the person who is entitled to the payment, benefit, or property under this subchapter; or

(2) is personally liable to the person described by Subdivision (1) for the amount of the payment or the value of the benefit or property received, as applicable.

Added by Acts 2009, 81st Leg., ch. 680, § 1, eff. Jan. 1, 2014. Amended by Acts 2011, 82nd Leg., ch. 1338 (S.B. 1198), § 2.17, eff. Jan. 1, 2014.

## SUBCHAPTER C. CERTAIN MARRIAGES VOIDABLE AFTER DEATH

### § 123.101. Proceeding to Void Marriage Based on Mental Capacity Pending at Time of Death

(a) If a proceeding under Chapter 6, Family Code, to declare a marriage void based on the lack of mental capacity of one of the parties to the marriage is pending on the date of death of one of those parties, or if a guardianship proceeding in which a court is requested under Chapter 6, Family Code, to declare a ward's or proposed ward's marriage void based on the lack of mental capacity of the ward or proposed ward is pending on the date of the ward's or proposed ward's death, the court may make the determination and declare the marriage void after the decedent's death.

(b) In making a determination described by Subsection (a), the court shall apply the standards for an annulment prescribed by Section 6.108(a), Family Code.

Added by Acts 2009, 81st Leg., ch. 680, § 1, eff. Jan. 1, 2014.

### § 123.102. Application to Void Marriage After Death

(a) Subject to Subsection (c), if a proceeding described by Section 123.101(a) is not pending on the date of a decedent's death, an interested person may file an application with the court requesting that the court void the marriage of the decedent if:

(1) on the date of the decedent's death, the decedent was married; and

(2) that marriage commenced not earlier than three years before the date of the decedent's death.

(b) The notice applicable to a proceeding for a declaratory judgment under Chapter 37, Civil Practice and Remedies Code, applies to a proceeding under Subsection (a).

(c) An application authorized by Subsection (a) may not be filed after the first anniversary of the date of the decedent's death.

Added by Acts 2009, 81st Leg., ch. 680, § 1, eff. Jan. 1, 2014.

### § 123.103. Action on Application to Void Marriage after Death

(a) Except as provided by Subsection (b), in a proceeding brought under Section 123.102, the court shall declare the decedent's marriage void if the court finds that, on the date the marriage occurred, the decedent did not have the mental capacity to:

(1) consent to the marriage; and

(2) understand the nature of the marriage ceremony, if a ceremony occurred.

(b) A court that makes a finding described by Subsection (a) may not declare the decedent's marriage void if the court finds that, after the date the marriage occurred, the decedent:

(1) gained the mental capacity to recognize the marriage relationship; and

(2) did recognize the marriage relationship.

Added by Acts 2009, 81st Leg., ch. 680, § 1, eff. Jan. 1, 2014.

### § 123.104. Effect of Voided Marriage

If the court declares a decedent's marriage void in a proceeding described by Section 123.101(a) or brought under Section 123.102, the other party to the marriage is not considered the decedent's surviving spouse for purposes of any law of this state.

Added by Acts 2009, 81st Leg., ch. 680, § 1, eff. Jan. 1, 2014.

## CHAPTER 124. VALUATION AND TAXATION OF ESTATE PROPERTY

### SUBCHAPTER A. APPORTIONMENT OF TAXES

### SUBCHAPTER B. SATISFACTION OF CERTAIN PECUNIARY GIFTS

### SUBCHAPTER A. APPORTIONMENT OF TAXES

### § 124.001. Definitions

In this subchapter:

(1) "Court" means:

(A) a court in which proceedings for administration of an estate are pending or have been completed; or

(B) if no proceedings are pending or have been completed, a court in which venue lies for the administration of an estate.

(2) "Estate" means the gross estate of a decedent as determined for the purpose of estate taxes.

(3) "Estate tax" means any estate, inheritance, or death tax levied or assessed on the property of a decedent's estate because of the death of a person and imposed by federal, state, local, or foreign law, including the federal estate tax and the inheritance tax imposed by Chapter 211, Tax Code, and including interest and penalties imposed in addition to those taxes. The term does not include a tax imposed under Section 2701(d)(1)(A), Internal Revenue Code of 1986 (26 U.S.C. Section 2701(d)).

(4) "Person" includes a trust, natural person, partnership, association, joint stock company, corporation, government, political subdivision, or governmental agency.

(5) "Person interested in the estate" means a person, or a fiduciary on behalf of that person, who is entitled to receive or who has received, from a decedent or because of the death of the decedent, property included in the decedent's estate for purposes of the estate tax. The term does not include a creditor of the decedent or of the decedent's estate.

(6) "Representative" means the representative, executor, or administrator of an estate, or any other person who is required to pay estate taxes assessed against the estate.

Added by Acts 2009, 81st Leg., ch. 680, § 1, eff. Jan. 1, 2014.

### § 124.002. References to Internal Revenue Code

A reference in this subchapter to a section of the Internal Revenue Code of 1986 refers to that section as it exists at the time in question. The reference also includes a corresponding section of a subsequent Internal Revenue Code and, if the referenced section is renumbered, the section as renumbered.

Added by Acts 2009, 81st Leg., ch. 680, § 1, eff. Jan. 1, 2014.

### § 124.003. Apportionment Directed by Federal Law

If federal law directs the apportionment of the federal estate tax, a similar state tax shall be apportioned in the same manner.

Added by Acts 2009, 81st Leg., ch. 680, § 1, eff. Jan. 1, 2014.

### § 124.004. Effect of Disclaimers

This subchapter shall be applied after giving effect to any disclaimers made in accordance with Subchapters A, B, C, and D, Chapter 122.

Added by Acts 2009, 81st Leg., ch. 680, § 1, eff. Jan. 1, 2014.

### § 124.005. General Apportionment of Estate Tax; Exceptions

(a) A representative shall charge each person interested in the estate a portion of the total estate tax assessed against the estate. The portion charged to each person must represent the same ratio as the taxable value of that person's interest in the estate included in determining the amount of the tax bears to the total taxable value of all the interests of all persons interested in the estate included in determining the amount of the tax. In apportioning an estate tax under this subsection, the representative shall disregard a portion of the tax that is:

(1) apportioned under the law imposing the tax;

(2) otherwise apportioned by federal law; or

(3) apportioned as otherwise provided by this subchapter.

(b) Subsection (a) does not apply to the extent the decedent, in a written inter vivos or testamentary instrument disposing of or creating an interest in property, specifically directs the manner of apportionment of estate tax or grants a discretionary power of apportionment to another person. A direction for the apportionment or nonapportionment of estate tax is limited to the estate tax on the property passing under the instrument unless the instrument is a will that provides otherwise.

(c) If directions under Subsection (b) for the apportionment of an estate tax are provided in two or more instruments executed by the same person and the directions in those instruments conflict, the instrument disposing of or creating an interest in the property to be taxed controls. If directions for the apportionment of estate tax are provided in two or more instruments executed by different persons and the directions in those instruments conflict, the direction of the person in whose estate the property is included controls.

(d) Subsections (b) and (c) do not:

(1) grant or enlarge the power of a person to apportion estate tax to property passing under an instrument created by another person in excess of the estate tax attributable to the property; or

(2) apply to the extent federal law directs a different manner of apportionment.

Added by Acts 2009, 81st Leg., ch. 680, § 1, eff. Jan. 1, 2014.

### § 124.006. Effect of Tax Deductions, Exemptions, or Credits

(a) A deduction, exemption, or credit allowed by law in connection with the estate tax inures to a person interested in the estate as provided by this section.

(b) If the deduction, exemption, or credit is allowed because of the relationship of the person interested in the estate to the decedent, or because of the purpose of the gift, the deduction, exemption, or credit inures to the person having the relationship or receiving the gift, unless that person's interest in the estate is subject to a prior present interest that is not allowable as a deduction. The estate tax apportionable to the person having the present interest shall be paid from the corpus of the gift or the interest of the person having the relationship.

(c) A deduction for property of the estate that was previously taxed and a credit for gift taxes or death taxes of a foreign country that were paid by the decedent or the decedent's estate inure proportionally to all persons interested in the estate who are liable for a share of the estate tax.

(d) A credit for inheritance, succession, or estate taxes, or for similar taxes applicable to property or interests includable in the estate, inures to the persons interested in the estate who are chargeable with payment of a portion of those taxes to the extent that the credit proportionately reduces those taxes.

Added by Acts 2009, 81st Leg., ch. 680, § 1, eff. Jan. 1, 2014.

## § 124.007. Exclusion of Certain Property from Apportionment

(a) To the extent that property passing to or in trust for a surviving spouse or a charitable, public, or similar gift or devise is not an allowable deduction for purposes of the estate tax solely because of an inheritance tax or other death tax imposed on and deductible from the property:

(1) the property is not included in the computation provided for by Section 124.005; and

(2) no apportionment is made against the property.

(b) The exclusion provided by this section does not apply if the result would be to deprive the estate of a deduction otherwise allowable under Section 2053(d), Internal Revenue Code of 1986, for a state death tax on a transfer for a public, charitable, or religious use.

Added by Acts 2009, 81st Leg., ch. 680, § 1, eff. Jan. 1, 2014.

## § 124.008. Exclusion of Certain Temporary Interests from Apportionment.

(a) Except as provided by Section 124.009(c), the following temporary interests are not subject to apportionment:

(1) an interest in income;

(2) an estate for years or for life; or

(3) another temporary interest in any property or fund.

(b) The estate tax apportionable to a temporary interest described by Subsection (a) and the remainder, if any, is chargeable against the corpus of the property or the funds that are subject to the temporary interest and remainder.

Added by Acts 2009, 81st Leg., ch. 680, § 1, eff. Jan. 1, 2014.

## § 124.009. Qualified Real Property

(a) In this section, "qualified real property" has the meaning assigned by Section 2032A, Internal Revenue Code of 1986 (26 U.S.C. Section 2032A).

(b) If an election is made under Section 2032A, Internal Revenue Code of 1986 (26 U.S.C. Section 2032A), the representative shall apportion estate taxes according to the amount of federal estate tax that would be payable if the election were not made. The representative shall apply the amount of the reduction of the estate tax resulting from the election to reduce the amount of the estate tax allocated based on the value of the qualified real property that is the subject of the election. If the amount of that reduction is greater than the amount of the taxes allocated based on the value of the qualified real property, the representative shall:

(1) apply the excess amount to the portion of the taxes allocated for all other property; and

(2) apportion the amount described by Subdivision (1) under Section 124.005(a).

(c) If additional federal estate tax is imposed under Section 2032A(c), Internal Revenue Code of 1986 (26 U.S.C. Section 2032A), because of an early disposition or cessation of a qualified use, the additional tax shall be equitably apportioned among the persons who have an interest in the portion of the qualified real property to which the additional tax is attributable in proportion to their interests. The additional tax is a charge against that qualified real property. If the qualified real property is split between one or more life or term interests and remainder interests, the additional tax shall be apportioned to each person whose action or cessation of use caused the imposition of additional tax, unless all persons with an interest in the qualified real property agree in writing to dispose of the property, in which case the additional tax shall be apportioned among the remainder interests.

Added by Acts 2009, 81st Leg., ch. 680, § 1, eff. Jan. 1, 2014.

## § 124.010. Effect of Extension or Deficiency in Payment of Estate Taxes; Liability of Representative

(a) If the date for the payment of any portion of an estate tax is extended:

(1) the amount of the extended tax shall be apportioned to the persons who receive the specific property that gives rise to the extension; and

(2) those persons are entitled to the benefits and shall bear the burdens of the extension.

(b) Except as provided by Subsection (c), interest on an extension of estate tax and interest and penalties on a deficiency shall be apportioned equitably to reflect the benefits and burdens of the extension or deficiency and of any tax deduction associated with the interest and penalties.

(c) A representative shall be charged with the amount of any penalty or interest that is assessed due to delay caused by the representative's negligence.

Added by Acts 2009, 81st Leg., ch. 680, § 1, eff. Jan. 1, 2014.

## § 124.011. Apportionment of Interest and Penalties

(a) Interest and penalties assessed against an estate by a taxing authority shall be apportioned among and charged to the persons interested in the estate in the manner provided by Section 124.005 unless, on application by any person interested in the estate, the court determines that:

(1) the proposed apportionment is not equitable; or

(2) the assessment of interest or penalties was caused by a breach of fiduciary duty of a representative.

(b) If the apportionment is not equitable, the court may apportion interest and penalties in an equitable manner.

(c) If the assessment of interest or penalties was caused by a breach of fiduciary duty of a representative, the court may charge the representative with the amount of the interest and penalties assessed attributable to the representative's conduct.

Added by Acts 2009, 81st Leg., ch. 680, § 1, eff. Jan. 1, 2014.

## § 124.012. Apportionment of Representative's Expenses

(a) Expenses reasonably incurred by a representative in determination of the amount, apportionment, or collection of the estate tax shall be apportioned among and charged to persons interested in the estate in the manner provided by Section 124.005 unless, on application by any person interested in the estate, the court determines that the proposed apportionment is not equitable.

(b) If the court determines that the proposed apportionment is not equitable, the court may apportion the expenses in an equitable manner.

Added by Acts 2009, 81st Leg., ch. 680, § 1, eff. Jan. 1, 2014.

## § 124.013. Withholding of Estate Tax Share by Representative

A representative who has possession of any estate property that is distributable to a person interested in the estate may withhold from that property an amount equal to the person's apportioned share of the estate tax.

Added by Acts 2009, 81st Leg., ch. 680, § 1, eff. Jan. 1, 2014.

## § 124.014. Recovery of Estate Tax Share Not Withheld

(a) If property includable in an estate does not come into possession of a representative obligated to pay the estate tax, the representative shall:

(1) recover from each person interested in the estate the amount of the estate tax apportioned to the person under this subchapter; or

(2) assign to persons affected by the tax obligation the representative's right of recovery.

(b) The obligation to recover a tax under Subsection (a) does not apply if:

(1) the duty is waived by the parties affected by the tax obligation or by the instrument under which the representative derives powers; or

(2) in the reasonable judgment of the representative, proceeding to recover the tax is not cost-effective.

Added by Acts 2009, 81st Leg., ch. 680, § 1, eff. Jan. 1, 2014.

## § 124.015. Recovery of Unpaid Estate Tax; Reimbursement

(a) A representative shall recover from any person interested in the estate the unpaid amount of the estate tax apportioned and charged to the person under this subchapter unless the representative determines in good faith that an attempt to recover the amount would be economically impractical.

(b) A representative who cannot collect from a person interested in the estate an unpaid amount of estate tax apportioned to that person shall apportion the amount not collected in the manner provided by Section 124.005(a) among the other persons interested in the estate who are subject to apportionment.

(c) A person who is charged with or who pays an apportioned amount under Subsection (b) has a right of reimbursement for that amount from the person who failed to pay the tax. The representative may enforce the right of reimbursement, or the person who is charged with or who pays an apportioned amount under Subsection (b) may enforce the right of reimbursement directly by an assignment from the representative. A person assigned the right under this subsection is subrogated to the rights of the representative.

(d) A representative who has a right of reimbursement may petition a court to determine the right of reimbursement.

Added by Acts 2009, 81st Leg., ch. 680, § 1, eff. Jan. 1, 2014.

## § 124.016. Time to Initiate Actions to Recover Unpaid Estate Tax

(a) A representative required to recover unpaid amounts of estate tax apportioned to persons interested in the estate under this subchapter may not be required to initiate the necessary actions until the expiration of the 90th day after the date of the final determination by the Internal Revenue Service of the amount of the estate tax.

(b) A representative who initiates an action under this subchapter within a reasonable time after the expiration of the 90–day period is not subject to any liability or surcharge because a portion of the estate tax apportioned to a person interested in the estate was collectible during a period after the death of the decedent but thereafter became uncollectible.

Added by Acts 2009, 81st Leg., ch. 680, § 1, eff. Jan. 1, 2014.

## § 124.017. Tax or Death Duty Payable to Another State

(a) A representative acting in another state may initiate an action in a court of this state to recover from a person interested in the estate who is domiciled in this state or owns property in this state subject to attachment or execution, a proportionate amount of:

(1) the federal estate tax;

(2) an estate tax payable to another state; or

(3) a death duty due by a decedent's estate to another state.

(b) In the action, a determination of apportionment by the court having jurisdiction of the administration of the decedent's estate in the other state is prima facie correct.

(c) This section applies only if the state in which the determination of apportionment was made provides a substantially similar remedy.

Added by Acts 2009, 81st Leg., ch. 680, § 1, eff. Jan. 1, 2014.

## § 124.018. Payment of Expenses and Attorney's Fees

The court shall award necessary expenses, including reasonable attorney's fees, to the prevailing party in an action initiated by a person for the collection of estate taxes from a person interested in the estate to whom estate taxes were apportioned and charged under Section 124.005.

Added by Acts 2009, 81st Leg., ch. 680, § 1, eff. Jan. 1, 2014.

## SUBCHAPTER B. SATISFACTION OF CERTAIN PECUNIARY GIFTS

## § 124.051. Valuation of Property Distributed in Kind in Satisfaction of Pecuniary Gift

Unless the governing instrument provides otherwise, if a will or trust contains a pecuniary devise or transfer that may be satisfied by distributing assets in kind and the executor, administrator, or trustee determines to fund the devise or transfer by distributing assets in kind, the property shall be valued, for the purpose of funding the devise or transfer, at the value of the property on the date or dates of distribution.

Added by Acts 2009, 81st Leg., ch. 680, § 1, eff. Jan. 1, 2014.

## § 124.052. Satisfaction of Marital Deduction Pecuniary Gifts with Assets in Kind

(a) This section applies to an executor, administrator, or trustee authorized under the will or trust of a decedent to satisfy a pecuniary devise or transfer in trust in kind with assets at their value for federal estate tax purposes, in satisfaction of a gift intended to qualify, or that otherwise would qualify, for a United States estate tax marital deduction.

(b) Unless the governing instrument provides otherwise, an executor, administrator, or trustee, in order to implement a devise or transfer described by Subsection (a), shall distribute assets, including cash, fairly representative of appreciation or depreciation in the value of all property available for distribution in satisfaction of the devise or transfer.

Added by Acts 2009, 81st Leg., ch. 680, § 1, eff. Jan. 1, 2014.

## SUBTITLE D. PROCEEDINGS BEFORE ADMINISTRATION OF ESTATE

## CHAPTER 151. EXAMINATION OF DOCUMENTS AND SAFE DEPOSIT BOXES

## § 151.001.  Examination of Documents or Safe Deposit Box with Court Order

(a) A judge of a court that has probate jurisdiction of a decedent's estate may order a person to permit a court representative named in the order to examine a decedent's documents or safe deposit box if it is shown to the judge that:

(1) the person may possess or control the documents or that the person leased the safe deposit box to the decedent; and

(2) the documents or safe deposit box may contain:

(A) a will of the decedent;

(B) a deed to a burial plot in which the decedent is to be buried; or

(C) an insurance policy issued in the decedent's name and payable to a beneficiary named in the policy.

(b) The court representative shall examine the decedent's documents or safe deposit box in the presence of:

(1) the judge ordering the examination or an agent of the judge; and

(2) the person who has possession or control of the documents or who leased the safe deposit box or, if that person is a corporation, an officer of the corporation or an agent of an officer.

Added by Acts 2009, 81st Leg., ch. 680, § 1, eff. Jan. 1, 2014.

## § 151.002.  Delivery of Document with Court Order

(a) A judge who orders an examination of a decedent's documents or safe deposit box under Section 151.001 may order the person who possesses or controls the documents or who leases the safe deposit box to permit the court representative to take possession of a document described by Section 151.001(a)(2).

(b) The court representative shall deliver:

(1) a will to the clerk of a court that:

(A) has probate jurisdiction; and

(B) is located in the same county as the court of the judge who ordered the examination under Section 151.001;

(2) a burial plot deed to the person designated by the judge in the order for the examination; or

(3) an insurance policy to a beneficiary named in the policy.

(c) A court clerk to whom a will is delivered under Subsection (b) shall issue a receipt for the will to the court representative.

Added by Acts 2009, 81st Leg., ch. 680, § 1, eff. Jan. 1, 2014.

## § 151.003.  Examination of Document or Safe Deposit Box Without Court Order

(a) A person who possesses or controls a document delivered by a decedent for safekeeping or who leases a safe deposit box to a decedent may permit examination of the document or the contents of the safe deposit box by:

(1) the decedent's spouse;

(2) a parent of the decedent;

(3) a descendant of the decedent who is at least 18 years of age; or

(4) a person named as executor of the decedent's estate in a copy of a document that the person has and that appears to be a will of the decedent.

(b) An examination under Subsection (a) shall be conducted in the presence of the person who possesses or controls the document or who leases the safe deposit box or, if the person is a corporation, an officer of the corporation.

Added by Acts 2009, 81st Leg., ch. 680, § 1, eff. Jan. 1, 2014.

## § 151.004.  Delivery of Document Without Court Order

(a) Subject to Subsection (c), a person who permits an examination of a decedent's document or safe deposit box under Section 151.003 may deliver:

(1) a document appearing to be the decedent's will to:

(A) the clerk of a court that:

(i) has probate jurisdiction; and

(ii) is located in the county in which the decedent resided; or

(B) a person named in the document as an executor of the decedent's estate;

(2) a document appearing to be a deed to a burial plot in which the decedent is to be buried, or appearing to give burial instructions, to the person conducting the examination; or

(3) a document appearing to be an insurance policy on the decedent's life to a beneficiary named in the policy.

(b) A person who has leased a safe deposit box to the decedent shall keep a copy of a document delivered by the person under Subsection (a)(1) until the fourth anniversary of the date of delivery.

(c) A person may not deliver a document under Subsection (a) unless the person examining the document:

(1) requests delivery of the document; and

(2) issues a receipt for the document to the person delivering the document.

Added by Acts 2009, 81st Leg., ch. 680, § 1, eff. Jan. 1, 2014.

## § 151.005. Restriction on Removal of Contents of Safe Deposit Box

A person may not remove the contents of a decedent's safe deposit box except as provided by Section 151.002, Section 151.004, or another law.

Added by Acts 2009, 81st Leg., ch. 680, § 1, eff. Jan. 1, 2014.

## CHAPTER 152. EMERGENCY INTERVENTION

SUBCHAPTER A.  EMERGENCY INTERVENTION

## SUBCHAPTER A.  EMERGENCY INTERVENTION

### § 152.001.  Application Authorized

(a) Subject to Subsection (b), a person qualified to serve as an administrator under Section 304.001 may file an application requesting emergency intervention by a court exercising probate jurisdiction to provide for:

(1) the payment of the decedent's funeral and burial expenses; or

(2) the protection and storage of personal property owned by the decedent that, on the date of the decedent's death, was located in accommodations rented by the decedent.

(b) An applicant may file an application under this section only if:

(1) an application or affidavit has not been filed and is not pending under Section 256.052, 256.054, or 301.052 or Chapter 205 or 401; and

(2) the applicant needs to:

(A) obtain funds for the payment of the decedent's funeral and burial expenses; or

(B) gain access to accommodations rented by the decedent that contain the decedent's personal property and the applicant has been denied access to those accommodations.

Added by Acts 2009, 81st Leg., ch. 680, § 1, eff. Jan. 1, 2014. Amended by Acts 2013, 83rd Leg., ch. 161 (S.B. 1093), § 6.010, eff. Jan. 1, 2014.

### § 152.002.  Contents of Application

(a) An emergency intervention application must be sworn and must contain:

(1) the applicant's name, address, and interest;

(2) facts showing an immediate necessity for the issuance of an emergency intervention order under Subchapter B;

(3) the decedent's date of death, place of death, and residential address on the date of death;

(4) the name and address of the funeral home holding the decedent's remains; and

(5) the names of any known or ascertainable heirs and devisees of the decedent.

(b) In addition to the information required under Subsection (a), if emergency intervention is requested to obtain funds needed for the payment of the decedent's funeral and burial expenses, the application must also contain:

(1) the reason any known or ascertainable heirs and devisees of the decedent:

(A) cannot be contacted; or

(B) have refused to assist in the decedent's burial;

(2) a description of necessary funeral and burial procedures and a statement from the funeral home that contains a detailed and itemized description of the cost of those procedures; and

(3) the name and address of an individual, entity, or financial institution, including an employer, in possession of any funds of or due to the decedent, and related account numbers and balances, if known by the applicant.

(c) In addition to the information required under Subsection (a), if emergency intervention is requested to gain access to accommodations rented by a decedent that at the time of the decedent's death contain the decedent's personal property, the application must also contain:

(1) the reason any known or ascertainable heirs and devisees of the decedent:

(A) cannot be contacted; or

(B) have refused to assist in the protection of the decedent's personal property;

(2) the type and location of the decedent's personal property and the name of the person in possession of the property; and

(3) the name and address of the owner or manager of the accommodations and a statement regarding whether access to the accommodations is necessary.

Added by Acts 2009, 81st Leg., ch. 680, § 1, eff. Jan. 1, 2014.

### § 152.003. Additional Contents of Application: Instructions Regarding Decedent's Funeral and Remains

(a) In addition to the information required under Section 152.002, if emergency intervention is requested to obtain funds needed for the payment of a decedent's funeral and burial expenses, the application must also state whether there are any written instructions from the decedent relating to the type and manner of funeral or burial preferred by the decedent. The applicant shall:

(1) attach the instructions, if available, to the application; and

(2) fully comply with the instructions.

(b) If written instructions do not exist, the applicant may not permit the decedent's remains to be cremated unless the applicant obtains the court's permission to cremate the remains.

Added by Acts 2009, 81st Leg., ch. 680, § 1, eff. Jan. 1, 2014.

### § 152.004. Time and Place of Filing

An emergency intervention application must be filed:

(1) with the court clerk in the county in which:

(A) the decedent was domiciled; or

(B) the accommodations rented by the decedent that contain the decedent's personal property are located; and

(2) not earlier than the third day after the date of the decedent's death and not later than the 90th day after the date of the decedent's death.

Added by Acts 2009, 81st Leg., ch. 680, § 1, eff. Jan. 1, 2014.

## SUBCHAPTER B. ORDER FOR EMERGENCY INTERVENTION

### § 152.051. Issuance of Order Regarding Funeral and Burial Expenses

If on review of an application filed under Section 152.001 the court determines that emergency intervention is necessary to obtain funds needed for the payment of a decedent's funeral and burial expenses, the court may order funds of the decedent that are being held by an individual, an employer, or a financial institution to be paid directly to a funeral home only for:

(1) reasonable and necessary attorney's fees for the attorney who obtained the order;

(2) court costs for obtaining the order; and

(3) funeral and burial expenses not to exceed $5,000 as ordered by the court to provide the decedent with a reasonable, dignified, and appropriate funeral and burial.

Added by Acts 2009, 81st Leg., ch. 680, § 1, eff. Jan. 1, 2014.

### § 152.052. Issuance of Order Regarding Access to Certain Personal Property

If on review of an application filed under Section 152.001 the court determines that emergency intervention is necessary to gain access to accommodations rented by the decedent that, at the time of the decedent's death, contain the decedent's personal property, the court may order one or more of the following:

(1) that the owner or agent of the accommodations shall grant the applicant access to the accommodations at a reasonable time and in the presence of the owner or agent;

(2) that the applicant and owner or agent of the accommodations shall jointly prepare and file with the court a list that generally describes the decedent's property found at the premises;

(3) that the applicant or the owner or agent of the accommodations may remove and store the

decedent's property at another location until claimed by the decedent's heirs;

(4) that the applicant has only the powers that are specifically stated in the order and that are necessary to protect the decedent's property that is the subject of the application; or

(5) that funds of the decedent held by an individual, an employer, or a financial institution be paid to the applicant for reasonable and necessary attorney's fees and court costs for obtaining the order.

Added by Acts 2009, 81st Leg., ch. 680, § 1, eff. Jan. 1, 2014.

### § 152.053.  Duration of Order

The authority of an applicant under an emergency intervention order expires on the earlier of:

(1) the 90th day after the date the order is issued; or

(2) the date a personal representative of the decedent's estate qualifies.

Added by Acts 2009, 81st Leg., ch. 680, § 1, eff. Jan. 1, 2014.

### § 152.054.  Certified Copies of Order

The court clerk may issue certified copies of an emergency intervention order on request of the applicant only until the earlier of:

(1) the 90th day after the date the order is signed; or

(2) the date a personal representative of the decedent's estate qualifies.

Added by Acts 2009, 81st Leg., ch. 680, § 1, eff. Jan. 1, 2014.

### § 152.055.  Liability of Certain Persons in Connection with Order

(a) A person who is provided a certified copy of an emergency intervention order within the period prescribed by Section 152.054 is not personally liable for an action taken by the person in accordance with and in reliance on the order.

(b) If a personal representative has not been appointed when an emergency intervention order issued under Section 152.052 expires, a person in possession of the decedent's personal property that is the subject of the order, without incurring civil liability, may:

(1) release the property to the decedent's heirs; or

(2) dispose of the property under Subchapter C, Chapter 54, Property Code, or Section 7.209 or 7.210, Business & Commerce Code.

Added by Acts 2009, 81st Leg., ch. 680, § 1, eff. Jan. 1, 2014.

### SUBCHAPTER C.  LIMITATION ON RIGHT OF DECEDENT'S SURVIVING SPOUSE TO CONTROL DECEDENT'S BURIAL OR CREMATION

### § 152.101.  Application Authorized

(a) The executor of a decedent's will or the decedent's next of kin may file an application for an order limiting the right of the decedent's surviving spouse to control the decedent's burial or cremation.

(b) For purposes of Subsection (a), the decedent's next of kin:

(1) is determined in accordance with order of descent, with the person nearest in order of descent first, and so on; and

(2) includes the decedent's descendants who legally adopted the decedent or who have been legally adopted by the decedent.

(c) An application under this section must be under oath and must establish:

(1) whether the decedent died intestate or testate;

(2) that the surviving spouse is alleged to be a principal or accomplice in a wilful act that resulted in the decedent's death; and

(3) that good cause exists to limit the surviving spouse's right to control the decedent's burial or cremation.

Added by Acts 2009, 81st Leg., ch. 680, § 1, eff. Jan. 1, 2014.

### § 152.102.  Hearing;  Issuance of Order

(a) If the court finds that there is good cause to believe that the decedent's surviving spouse is the principal or an accomplice in a wilful act that resulted in the decedent's death, the court may, after notice and a hearing, limit the surviving spouse's right to control the decedent's burial or cremation.

(b) Subsection (a) applies:

(1) without regard to whether the decedent died intestate or testate;

(2) regardless of whether the surviving spouse is designated by the decedent's will as the executor of the decedent's estate; and

(3) subject to the prohibition described by Section 711.002(*l*), Health and Safety Code.

(c) If the court limits the surviving spouse's right of control as provided by Subsection (a), the court shall designate and authorize a person to make burial or cremation arrangements.

Added by Acts 2009, 81st Leg., ch. 680, § 1, eff. Jan. 1, 2014. Amended by Acts 2013, 83rd Leg., ch. 161 (S.B. 1093), § 6.011, eff. Jan. 1, 2014.

## SUBTITLE E. INTESTATE SUCCESSION

### CHAPTER 201. DESCENT AND DISTRIBUTION

#### SUBCHAPTER A. INTESTATE SUCCESSION

### SUBCHAPTER A. INTESTATE SUCCESSION

### § 201.001. Estate of an Intestate Not Leaving Spouse

(a) If a person who dies intestate does not leave a spouse, the estate to which the person had title descends and passes in parcenary to the person's kindred in the order provided by this section.

(b) The person's estate descends and passes to the person's children and the children's descendants.

(c) If no child or child's descendant survives the person, the person's estate descends and passes in equal portions to the person's father and mother.

(d) If only the person's father or mother survives the person, the person's estate shall:

(1) be divided into two equal portions, with:

(A) one portion passing to the surviving parent; and

(B) one portion passing to the person's siblings and the siblings' descendants; or

(2) be inherited entirely by the surviving parent if there is no sibling of the person or siblings' descendants.

(e) If neither the person's father nor mother survives the person, the person's entire estate passes to the person's siblings and the siblings' descendants.

(f) If none of the kindred described by Subsections (b)–(e) survive the person, the person's estate shall be divided into two moieties, with:

(1) one moiety passing to the person's paternal kindred as provided by Subsection (g); and

(2) one moiety passing to the person's maternal kindred as provided by Subsection (h).

(g) The moiety passing to the person's paternal kindred passes in the following order:

(1) if both paternal grandparents survive the person, equal portions pass to the person's paternal grandfather and grandmother;

(2) if only the person's paternal grandfather or grandmother survives the person, the person's estate shall:

(A) be divided into two equal portions, with:

(i) one portion passing to the surviving grandparent; and

(ii) one portion passing to the descendants of the deceased grandparent; or

(B) pass entirely to the surviving grandparent if no descendant of the deceased grandparent survives the person; and

(3) if neither the person's paternal grandfather nor grandmother survives the person, the moiety passing to the decedent's paternal kindred passes to the descendants of the person's paternal grandfather and grandmother, and so on without end, passing in like manner to the nearest lineal ancestors and their descendants.

(h) The moiety passing to the person's maternal kindred passes in the same order and manner as the other moiety passes to the decedent's paternal kindred under Subsection (g).

Added by Acts 2009, 81st Leg., ch. 680, § 1, eff. Jan. 1, 2014.

## § 201.002. Separate Estate of an Intestate

(a) If a person who dies intestate leaves a surviving spouse, the estate, other than a community estate, to which the person had title descends and passes as provided by this section.

(b) If the person has one or more children or a descendant of a child:

(1) the surviving spouse takes one-third of the personal estate;

(2) two-thirds of the personal estate descends to the person's child or children, and the descendants of a child or children; and

(3) the surviving spouse is entitled to a life estate in one-third of the person's land, with the remainder descending to the person's child or children and the descendants of a child or children.

(c) Except as provided by Subsection (d), if the person has no child and no descendant of a child:

(1) the surviving spouse is entitled to all of the personal estate;

(2) the surviving spouse is entitled to one-half of the person's land without a remainder to any person; and

(3) one-half of the person's land passes and is inherited according to the rules of descent and distribution.

(d) If the person described by Subsection (c) does not leave a surviving parent or one or more surviving siblings, or their descendants, the surviving spouse is entitled to the entire estate.

Added by Acts 2009, 81st Leg., ch. 680, § 1, eff. Jan. 1, 2014.

## § 201.003. Community Estate of an Intestate

(a) If a person who dies intestate leaves a surviving spouse, the community estate of the deceased spouse passes as provided by this section.

(b) The community estate of the deceased spouse passes to the surviving spouse if:

(1) no child or other descendant of the deceased spouse survives the deceased spouse; or

(2) all of the surviving children and descendants of the deceased spouse are also children or descendants of the surviving spouse.

(c) If the deceased spouse is survived by a child or other descendant who is not also a child or descendant of the surviving spouse, one-half of the community estate is retained by the surviving spouse and the other one-half passes to the deceased spouse's children or descendants. The descendants inherit only the portion of that estate to which they would be entitled under Section 201.101. In every case, the community estate passes charged with the debts against the community estate.

Added by Acts 2009, 81st Leg., ch. 680, § 1, eff. Jan. 1, 2014.

## SUBCHAPTER B. MATTERS AFFECTING INHERITANCE

### § 201.051. Maternal Inheritance

For purposes of inheritance, a child is the child of the child's biological or adopted mother, and the child and the child's issue shall inherit from the child's mother and the child's maternal kindred, both descendants, ascendants, and collateral kindred in all degrees, and they may inherit from the child and the child's issue. However, if a child has intended parents, as defined by Section 160.102, Family Code, under a gestational agreement validated under Subchapter I, Chapter 160, Family Code, the child is the child of the intended mother and not the biological mother or gestational mother unless the biological mother is also the intended mother.

Added by Acts 2009, 81st Leg., ch. 680, § 1, eff. Jan. 1, 2014. Amended by Acts 2013, 83rd Leg., ch. 1136 (H.B. 2912), § 11, eff. Jan. 1, 2014.

Section 62(f) of Acts 2013, 83rd Leg., ch. 1136 (H.B. 2912) provides:

"The changes in law made by Sections 102.004, 201.051, 201.052(b), 202. 004, 202.009, 202.056, 202.151, 353.101(d), 403.055, 403.056(a), and 405.001(b), Estates Code, as amended by this Act, and Sections 201.052(a–1), 202.0025, and 202.057, Estates Code, as added by this Act, apply only to the estate of a decedent who dies on or after the effective date [Jan. 1, 2014] of this Act. The estate of a decedent who dies before the effective date of this Act is governed by the law in effect on the date of the decedent's death, and the former law is continued in effect for that purpose."

### § 201.052. Paternal Inheritance

(a) For purposes of inheritance, a child is the child of the child's biological father if:

(1) the child is born under circumstances described by Section 160.201, Family Code;

(2) the child is adjudicated to be the child of the father by court decree under Chapter 160, Family Code;

(3) the child was adopted by the child's father; or

(4) the father executed an acknowledgment of paternity under Subchapter D, Chapter 160, Family Code, or a similar statement properly executed in another jurisdiction.

(a–1) Notwithstanding Subsection (a), if a child has intended parents, as defined by Section 160.102, Family Code, under a gestational agreement validated under Subchapter I, Chapter 160, Family Code, the child is the child of the intended father and not the biological father unless the biological father is also the intended father.

(b) A child described by Subsection (a) or (a–1) and the child's issue shall inherit from the child's father and the child's paternal kindred, both descendants, ascendants, and collateral kindred in all degrees, and they may inherit from the child and the child's issue.

(c) A person may petition the probate court for a determination of right of inheritance from a decedent if the person:

(1) claims to be a biological child of the decedent and is not otherwise presumed to be a child of the decedent; or

(2) claims inheritance through a biological child of the decedent who is not otherwise presumed to be a child of the decedent.

(d) If under Subsection (c) the court finds by clear and convincing evidence that the purported father was the biological father of the child:

(1) the child is treated as any other child of the decedent for purposes of inheritance; and

(2) the child and the child's issue may inherit from the child's paternal kindred, both descendants, ascendants, and collateral kindred in all degrees, and they may inherit from the child and the child's issue.

(e) This section does not permit inheritance by a purported father of a child, recognized or not, if the purported father's parental rights have been terminated.

Added by Acts 2009, 81st Leg., ch. 680, § 1, eff. Jan. 1, 2014. Amended by Acts 2013, 83rd Leg., ch. 1136 (H.B. 2912), § 12, eff. Jan. 1, 2014.

Section 62(f) of Acts 2013, 83rd Leg., ch. 1136 (H.B. 2912) provides:

"The changes in law made by Sections 102.004, 201.051, 201.052(b), 202. 004, 202.009, 202.056, 202.151, 353.101(d), 403.055, 403.056(a), and 405.001(b), Estates Code, as amended by this Act, and Sections 201.052(a–1), 202.0025, and 202.057, Estates Code, as added by this Act, apply only to the estate of a decedent who dies on or after the effective date [Jan. 1, 2014] of this Act. The estate of a decedent who dies before the effective date of this Act is governed by the law in effect on the date of the decedent's death, and the former law is continued in effect for that purpose."

### § 201.053. Effect of Reliance on Affidavit of Heirship

(a) A person who purchases for valuable consideration any interest in property of the heirs of a decedent acquires good title to the interest that the person would have received, as purchaser, in the absence of a claim of the child described by Subdivision (1), if the person:

(1) in good faith relies on the declarations in an affidavit of heirship that does not include a child who at the time of the sale or contract of sale of the property:

(A) is not a presumed child of the decedent; and

(B) has not under a final court decree or judgment been found to be entitled to treatment under Section 201.052 as a child of the decedent; and

(2) is without knowledge of the claim of the child described by Subdivision (1).

(b) Subsection (a) does not affect any liability of the heirs for the proceeds of a sale described by Subsection (a) to the child who was not included in the affidavit of heirship.

Added by Acts 2009, 81st Leg., ch. 680, § 1, eff. Jan. 1, 2014.

### § 201.054. Adopted Child

(a) For purposes of inheritance under the laws of descent and distribution, an adopted child is regarded as the child of the adoptive parent or parents, and the adopted child and the adopted child's descendants inherit from and through the adoptive parent or parents and their kindred as if the adopted child were the natural child of the adoptive parent or parents. The adoptive parent or parents and their kindred inherit from and through the adopted child as if the adopted child were the natural child of the adoptive parent or parents.

(b) The natural parent or parents of an adopted child and the kindred of the natural parent or parents may not inherit from or through the adopted child, but the adopted child inherits from and through the child's natural parent or parents, except as provided by Section 162.507(c), Family Code.

(c) This section does not prevent an adoptive parent from disposing of the parent's property by will according to law.

(d) This section does not diminish the rights of an adopted child under the laws of descent and distribution or otherwise that the adopted child acquired by virtue of inclusion in the definition of "child" under Section 22.004.

Added by Acts 2009, 81st Leg., ch. 680, § 1, eff. Jan. 1, 2014.

### § 201.055. Issue of Void or Voidable Marriage

The issue of a marriage declared void or voided by annulment shall be treated in the same manner as the issue of a valid marriage.

Added by Acts 2009, 81st Leg., ch. 680, § 1, eff. Jan. 1, 2014.

## § 201.056. Persons Not in Being

No right of inheritance accrues to any person other than to a child or lineal descendant of an intestate, unless the person is in being and capable in law to take as an heir at the time of the intestate's death.

Added by Acts 2009, 81st Leg., ch. 680, § 1, eff. Jan. 1, 2014.

## § 201.057. Collateral Kindred of Whole and Half Blood

If the inheritance from an intestate passes to the collateral kindred of the intestate and part of the collateral kindred are of whole blood and the other part are of half blood of the intestate, each of the collateral kindred who is of half blood inherits only half as much as that inherited by each of the collateral kindred who is of whole blood. If all of the collateral kindred are of half blood of the intestate, each of the collateral kindred inherits a whole portion.

Added by Acts 2009, 81st Leg., ch. 680, § 1, eff. Jan. 1, 2014.

## § 201.058. Convicted Persons

(a) No conviction shall work corruption of blood or forfeiture of estate except as provided by Subsection (b).

(b) If a beneficiary of a life insurance policy or contract is convicted and sentenced as a principal or accomplice in wilfully bringing about the death of the insured, the proceeds of the insurance policy or contract shall be paid in the manner provided by the Insurance Code.

Added by Acts 2009, 81st Leg., ch. 680, § 1, eff. Jan. 1, 2014.

## § 201.059. Person Who Dies by Casualty

Death by casualty does not result in forfeiture of estate.

Added by Acts 2009, 81st Leg., ch. 680, § 1, eff. Jan. 1, 2014.

## § 201.060. Alienage

A person is not disqualified to take as an heir because the person, or another person through whom the person claims, is or has been an alien.

Added by Acts 2009, 81st Leg., ch. 680, § 1, eff. Jan. 1, 2014.

## § 201.061. Estate of Person Who Dies by Suicide

The estate of a person who commits suicide descends or vests as if the person died a natural death.

Added by Acts 2009, 81st Leg., ch. 680, § 1, eff. Jan. 1, 2014.

## § 201.062. Treatment of Certain Parent–Child Relationships

(a) A probate court may enter an order declaring that the parent of a child under 18 years of age may not inherit from or through the child under the laws of descent and distribution if the court finds by clear and convincing evidence that the parent has:

(1) voluntarily abandoned and failed to support the child in accordance with the parent's obligation or ability for at least three years before the date of the child's death, and did not resume support for the child before that date;

(2) voluntarily and with knowledge of the pregnancy:

(A) abandoned the child's mother beginning at a time during her pregnancy with the child and continuing through the birth;

(B) failed to provide adequate support or medical care for the mother during the period of abandonment before the child's birth; and

(C) remained apart from and failed to support the child since birth; or

(3) been convicted or has been placed on community supervision, including deferred adjudication community supervision, for being criminally responsible for the death or serious injury of a child under the following sections of the Penal Code or adjudicated under Title 3, Family Code, for conduct that caused the death or serious injury of a child and that would constitute a violation of one of the following sections of the Penal Code:

(A) Section 19.02 (murder);

(B) Section 19.03 (capital murder);

(C) Section 19.04 (manslaughter);

(D) Section 21.11 (indecency with a child);

(E) Section 22.01 (assault);

(F) Section 22.011 (sexual assault);

(G) Section 22.02 (aggravated assault);

(H) Section 22.021 (aggravated sexual assault);

(I) Section 22.04 (injury to a child, elderly individual, or disabled individual);

(J) Section 22.041 (abandoning or endangering child);

(K) Section 25.02 (prohibited sexual conduct);

(L) Section 43.25 (sexual performance by a child); or

(M) Section 43.26 (possession or promotion of child pornography).

(b) On a determination under Subsection (a) that the parent of a child may not inherit from or through the child, the parent shall be treated as if the parent predeceased the child for purposes of:

(1) inheritance under the laws of descent and distribution; and

(2) any other cause of action based on parentage.

Added by Acts 2009, 81st Leg., ch. 680, § 1, eff. Jan. 1, 2014.

## SUBCHAPTER C. DISTRIBUTION TO HEIRS

### § 201.101. Determination of Per Capita with Representation Distribution

(a) The children, descendants, brothers, sisters, uncles, aunts, or other relatives of an intestate who stand in the first or same degree of relationship alone and come into the distribution of the intestate's estate take per capita, which means by persons.

(b) If some of the persons described by Subsection (a) are dead and some are living, each descendant of those persons who have died is entitled to a distribution of the intestate's estate. Each descendant inherits only that portion of the property to which the parent through whom the descendant inherits would be entitled if that parent were alive.

Added by Acts 2009, 81st Leg., ch. 680, § 1, eff. Jan. 1, 2014.

### § 201.102. No Distinction Based on Property's Source

A distinction may not be made, in regulating the descent and distribution of an estate of a person dying intestate, between property derived by gift, devise, or descent from the intestate's father, and property derived by gift, devise, or descent from the intestate's mother.

Added by Acts 2009, 81st Leg., ch. 680, § 1, eff. Jan. 1, 2014.

### § 201.103. Treatment of Intestate's Estate

All of the estate to which an intestate had title at the time of death descends and vests in the intestate's heirs in the same manner as if the intestate had been the original purchaser.

Added by Acts 2009, 81st Leg., ch. 680, § 1, eff. Jan. 1, 2014.

## SUBCHAPTER D. ADVANCEMENTS

### § 201.151. Determination of Advancement; Date of Valuation

(a) If a decedent dies intestate as to all or part of the decedent's estate, property that the decedent gave during the decedent's lifetime to a person who, on the date of the decedent's death, is the decedent's heir, or property received by the decedent's heir under a nontestamentary transfer under Subchapter B, Chapter 111, or Chapter 112 or 113, is an advancement against the heir's intestate share of the estate only if:

(1) the decedent declared in a contemporaneous writing, or the heir acknowledged in writing, that the gift or nontestamentary transfer is an advancement; or

(2) the decedent's contemporaneous writing or the heir's written acknowledgment otherwise indicates that the gift or nontestamentary transfer is to be considered in computing the division and distribution of the decedent's intestate estate.

(b) For purposes of Subsection (a), property that is advanced is valued as of the earlier of:

(1) the time that the heir came into possession or enjoyment of the property; or

(2) the time of the decedent's death.

Added by Acts 2009, 81st Leg., ch. 680, § 1, eff. Jan. 1, 2014.

### § 201.152. Survival of Recipient Required

If the recipient of property described by Section 201.151 does not survive the decedent, the property is not considered in computing the division and distribution of the decedent's intestate estate unless the decedent's contemporaneous writing provides otherwise.

Added by Acts 2009, 81st Leg., ch. 680, § 1, eff. Jan. 1, 2014.

## CHAPTER 202. DETERMINATION OF HEIRSHIP

### SUBCHAPTER A. AUTHORIZATION AND PROCEDURES FOR COMMENCEMENT OF PROCEEDING TO DECLARE HEIRSHIP

## SUBCHAPTER A. AUTHORIZATION AND PROCEDURES FOR COMMENCEMENT OF PROCEEDING TO DECLARE HEIRSHIP

### § 202.001. General Authorization for and Nature of Proceeding to Declare Heirship

In the manner provided by this chapter, a court may determine through a proceeding to declare heirship:

(1) the persons who are a decedent's heirs and only heirs; and

(2) the heirs' respective shares and interests under the laws of this state in the decedent's estate or, if applicable, in the trust.

Added by Acts 2009, 81st Leg., ch. 680, § 1, eff. Jan. 1, 2014. Amended by Acts 2011, 82nd Leg., ch. 1338 (S.B. 1198), § 2.18, eff. Jan. 1, 2014.

### § 202.002. Circumstances Under Which Proceeding to Declare Heirship Is Authorized

A court may conduct a proceeding to declare heirship when:

(1) a person dies intestate owning or entitled to property in this state and there has been no administration in this state of the person's estate;

(2) there has been a will probated in this state or elsewhere or an administration in this state of a decedent's estate, but:

(A) property in this state was omitted from the will or administration; or

(B) no final disposition of property in this state has been made in the administration; or

(3) it is necessary for the trustee of a trust holding assets for the benefit of a decedent to determine the heirs of the decedent.

Added by Acts 2009, 81st Leg., ch. 680, § 1, eff. Jan. 1, 2014. Amended by Acts 2011, 82nd Leg., ch. 1338 (S.B. 1198), § 2.19, eff. Jan. 1, 2014.

### § 202.0025. Action Brought After Decedent's Death

Notwithstanding Section 16.051, Civil Practice and Remedies Code, a proceeding to declare heirship of a decedent may be brought at any time after the decedent's death.

Added by Acts 2013, 83rd Leg., ch. 1136 (H.B. 2912), § 13, eff. Jan. 1, 2014.

Section 62(f) of Acts 2013, 83rd Leg., ch. 1136 (H.B. 2912) provides:

"The changes in law made by Sections 102.004, 201.051, 201.052(b), 202. 004, 202.009, 202.056, 202.151, 353.101(d), 403.055, 403.056(a), and 405.001(b), Estates Code, as amended by this Act, and Sections 201.052(a–1), 202.0025, and 202.057, Estates Code, as added by this Act, apply only to the estate of a decedent who dies on or after the effective date [Jan. 1, 2014] of this Act. The estate of a decedent who dies before the effective date of this Act is governed by the law in effect on the date of the decedent's death, and the former law is continued in effect for that purpose."

Section 62(g) of Acts 2013, 83rd Leg., ch. 1136 (H.B. 2912) provides:

"Section 202.0025, Estates Code, as added by this Act, is intended to clarify current law in regard to the commencement of proceedings to declare heirship, and an inference may not be made regarding the statute of limitations for a proceeding to declare heirship filed before the effective date [Jan. 1, 2014] of this Act."

### § 202.003. [Blank]

### § 202.004. Persons Who May Commence Proceeding to Declare Heirship

A proceeding to declare heirship of a decedent may be commenced and maintained under a circumstance specified by Section 202.002 by:

(1) the personal representative of the decedent's estate;

(2) a person claiming to be a creditor or the owner of all or part of the decedent's estate;

(3) if the decedent was a ward with respect to whom a guardian of the estate had been appointed, the guardian of the estate, provided that the proceeding is commenced and maintained in the probate court in which the proceedings for the guardianship of the estate were pending at the time of the decedent's death;

(4) a party seeking the appointment of an independent administrator under Section 401.003; or

(5) the trustee of a trust holding assets for the benefit of a decedent.

Added by Acts 2009, 81st Leg., ch. 680, § 1, eff. Jan. 1, 2014. Amended by Acts 2011, 82nd Leg., ch. 1338 (S.B. 1198), § 2.20, eff. Jan. 1, 2014; Acts 2013, 83rd Leg., ch. 1136 (H.B. 2912), § 14, eff. Jan. 1, 2014.

Section 62(f) of Acts 2013, 83rd Leg., ch. 1136 (H.B. 2912) provides:

"The changes in law made by Sections 102.004, 201.051, 201.052(b), 202. 004, 202.009, 202.056, 202.151, 353.101(d), 403.055, 403.056(a), and 405.001(b), Estates Code, as amended by this Act, and Sections 201.052(a–1), 202.0025, and 202.057, Estates Code, as added by this Act, apply only to the estate of a decedent who dies on or after the effective date [Jan. 1, 2014] of this Act. The estate of a decedent who dies before the effective date of this Act is governed by the law in effect on the date of the decedent's death, and the former law is continued in effect for that purpose."

## § 202.005. Application for Proceeding to Declare Heirship

A person authorized by Section 202.004 to commence a proceeding to declare heirship must file an application in a court specified by Section 33.004 to commence the proceeding. The application must state:

(1) the decedent's name and time and place of death;

(2) the names and residences of the decedent's heirs, the relationship of each heir to the decedent, and the true interest of the applicant and each of the heirs in the decedent's estate or in the trust, as applicable;

(3) if the time or place of the decedent's death or the name or residence of an heir is not definitely known to the applicant, all the material facts and circumstances with respect to which the applicant has knowledge and information that might reasonably tend to show the time or place of the decedent's death or the name or residence of the heir;

(4) that all children born to or adopted by the decedent have been listed;

(5) that each of the decedent's marriages has been listed with:

(A) the date of the marriage;

(B) the name of the spouse;

(C) the date and place of termination if the marriage was terminated; and

(D) other facts to show whether a spouse has had an interest in the decedent's property;

(6) whether the decedent died testate and, if so, what disposition has been made of the will;

(7) a general description of all property belonging to the decedent's estate or held in trust for the benefit of the decedent, as applicable; and

(8) an explanation for the omission from the application of any of the information required by this section.

Added by Acts 2009, 81st Leg., ch. 680, § 1, eff. Jan. 1, 2014. Amended by Acts 2011, 82nd Leg., ch. 1338 (S.B. 1198), § 2.21, eff. Jan. 1, 2014.

## § 202.006. Request for Determination of Necessity for Administration

A person who files an application under Section 202.005 not later than the fourth anniversary of the date of the death of the decedent who is the subject of the application may request that the court determine whether there is a need for administration of the decedent's estate. The court shall hear evidence on the issue and, in the court's judgment, make a determination of the issue.

Added by Acts 2009, 81st Leg., ch. 680, § 1, eff. Jan. 1, 2014.

## § 202.007. Affidavit Supporting Application Required

(a) An application filed under Section 202.005 must be supported by the affidavit of each applicant.

(b) An affidavit of an applicant under Subsection (a) must state that, to the applicant's knowledge:

(1) all the allegations in the application are true; and

(2) no material fact or circumstance has been omitted from the application.

Added by Acts 2009, 81st Leg., ch. 680, § 1, eff. Jan. 1, 2014.

## § 202.008. Required Parties to Proceeding to Declare Heirship

Each of the following persons must be made a party to a proceeding to declare heirship:

(1) each unknown heir of the decedent who is the subject of the proceeding;

· (2) each person who is named as an heir of the decedent in the application filed under Section 202.005; and

(3) each person who is, on the filing date of the application, shown as owning a share or interest in any real property described in the application by the deed records of the county in which the property is located.

Added by Acts 2009, 81st Leg., ch. 680, § 1, eff. Jan. 1, 2014.

### § 202.009. Attorney ad Litem

(a) The court shall appoint an attorney ad litem in a proceeding to declare heirship to represent the interests of heirs whose names or locations are unknown.

(b) The court may expand the appointment of the attorney ad litem appointed under Subsection (a) to include representation of an heir who is an incapacitated person on a finding that the appointment is necessary to protect the interests of the heir.

Added by Acts 2009, 81st Leg., ch. 680, § 1, eff. Jan. 1, 2014. Amended by Acts 2013, 83rd Leg., ch. 1136 (H.B. 2912), § 15, eff. Jan. 1, 2014.

Section 62(f) of Acts 2013, 83rd Leg., ch. 1136 (H.B. 2912) provides:

"The changes in law made by Sections 102.004, 201.051, 201.052(b), 202. 004, 202.009, 202.056, 202.151, 353.101(d), 403.055, 403.056(a), and 405.001(b), Estates Code, as amended by this Act, and Sections 201.052(a-1), 202.0025, and 202.057, Estates Code, as added by this Act, apply only to the estate of a decedent who dies on or after the effective date [Jan. 1, 2014] of this Act. The estate of a decedent who dies before the effective date of this Act is governed by the law in effect on the date of the decedent's death, and the former law is continued in effect for that purpose."

## SUBCHAPTER B.  NOTICE OF PROCEEDING TO DECLARE HEIRSHIP

### § 202.051. Service of Citation by Mail When Recipient's Name and Address Are Known or Ascertainable

Except as provided by Section 202.054, citation in a proceeding to declare heirship must be served by registered or certified mail on:

(1) each distributee who is 12 years of age or older and whose name and address are known or can be ascertained through the exercise of reasonable diligence; and

(2) the parent, managing conservator, or guardian of each distributee who is younger than 12 years of age if the name and address of the parent,

managing conservator, or guardian are known or can be reasonably ascertained.

Added by Acts 2009, 81st Leg., ch. 680, § 1, eff. Jan. 1, 2014.

### § 202.052. Service of Citation by Publication When Recipient's Name or Address Is Not Ascertainable

If the address of a person or entity on whom citation is required to be served cannot be ascertained, citation must be served on the person or entity by publication in the county in which the proceeding to declare heirship is commenced and in the county of the last residence of the decedent who is the subject of the proceeding, if that residence was in a county other than the county in which the proceeding is commenced. To determine whether a decedent has any other heirs, citation must be served on unknown heirs by publication in the manner provided by this section.

Added by Acts 2009, 81st Leg., ch. 680, § 1, eff. Jan. 1, 2014.

### § 202.053. Required Posting of Citation

Except in a proceeding in which citation is served by publication as provided by Section 202.052, citation in a proceeding to declare heirship must be posted in:

(1) the county in which the proceeding is commenced; and

(2) the county of the last residence of the decedent who is the subject of the proceeding.

Added by Acts 2009, 81st Leg., ch. 680, § 1, eff. Jan. 1, 2014.

### § 202.054. Personal Service of Citation May Be Required

The court may require that service of citation in a proceeding to declare heirship be made by personal service on some or all of those named as distributees in the application filed under Section 202.005.

Added by Acts 2009, 81st Leg., ch. 680, § 1, eff. Jan. 1, 2014.

### § 202.055. Service of Citation on Certain Persons Not Required

A party to a proceeding to declare heirship who executed the application filed under Section 202.005 is not required to be served by any method.

Added by Acts 2009, 81st Leg., ch. 680, § 1, eff. Jan. 1, 2014.

### § 202.056. Waiver of Service of Citation

A parent, managing conservator, guardian, attorney ad litem, or guardian ad litem of a minor distributee who:

(1) is younger than 12 years of age may waive citation required by this subchapter to be served on the distributee; and

(2) is 12 years of age or older may not waive citation required by this subchapter to be served on the distributee.

Added by Acts 2009, 81st Leg., ch. 680, § 1, eff. Jan. 1, 2014. Amended by Acts 2013, 83rd Leg., ch. 1136 (H.B. 2912), § 16, eff. Jan. 1, 2014.

Section 62(f) of Acts 2013, 83rd Leg., ch. 1136 (H.B. 2912) provides:

"The changes in law made by Sections 102.004, 201.051, 201.052(b), 202. 004, 202.009, 202.056, 202.151, 353.101(d), 403.055, 403.056(a), and 405.001(b), Estates Code, as amended by this Act, and Sections 201.052(a–1), 202.0025, and 202.057, Estates Code, as added by this Act, apply only to the estate of a decedent who dies on or after the effective date [Jan. 1, 2014] of this Act. The estate of a decedent who dies before the effective date of this Act is governed by the law in effect on the date of the decedent's death, and the former law is continued in effect for that purpose."

## § 202.057. Affidavit of Service of Citation

(a) A person who files an application under Section 202.005 shall file with the court:

(1) a copy of any citation required by this subchapter and the proof of delivery of service of the citation; and

(2) an affidavit sworn to by the applicant or a certificate signed by the applicant's attorney stating:

(A) that the citation was served as required by this subchapter;

(B) the name of each person to whom the citation was served, if the person's name is not shown on the proof of delivery; and

(C) the name of each person who waived citation under Section 202.056.

(b) The court may not enter an order in the proceeding to declare heirship under Subchapter E until the affidavit or certificate required by Subsection (a) is filed.

Added by Acts 2013, 83rd Leg., ch. 1136 (H.B. 2912), § 17, eff. Jan. 1, 2014.

Section 62(f) of Acts 2013, 83rd Leg., ch. 1136 (H.B. 2912) provides:

"The changes in law made by Sections 102.004, 201.051, 201.052(b), 202. 004, 202.009, 202.056, 202.151, 353.101(d), 403.055, 403.056(a), and 405.001(b), Estates Code, as amended by this Act, and Sections 201.052(a–1), 202.0025, and 202.057, Estates Code, as added by this Act, apply only to the estate of a decedent who dies on or after the effective date [Jan. 1, 2014] of this Act. The estate of a decedent who dies before the effective date of this Act is governed by the law in effect on the date of the decedent's death, and the former law is continued in effect for that purpose."

## SUBCHAPTER C. TRANSFER OF PENDING PROCEEDING TO DECLARE HEIRSHIP

### § 202.101. Required Transfer of Pending Proceeding to Declare Heirship Under Certain Circumstances

If, after a proceeding to declare heirship is commenced, an administration of the estate of the decedent who is the subject of the proceeding is granted in this state or the decedent's will is admitted to probate in this state, the court in which the proceeding to declare heirship is pending shall, by an order entered of record in the proceeding, transfer the proceeding to the court in which the administration was granted or the will was probated.

Added by Acts 2009, 81st Leg., ch. 680, § 1, eff. Jan. 1, 2014.

### § 202.102. Transfer of Records

The clerk of the court from which a proceeding to declare heirship is transferred under Section 202.101 shall, on entry of the order under that section, send to the clerk of the court named in the order a certified transcript of all pleadings, entries in the judge's probate docket, and orders of the court in the proceeding. The clerk of the court to which the proceeding is transferred shall:

(1) file the transcript;

(2) record the transcript in the judge's probate docket of that court; and

(3) docket the proceeding.

Added by Acts 2009, 81st Leg., ch. 680, § 1, eff. Jan. 1, 2014. Amended by Acts 2011, 82nd Leg., ch. 91 (S.B. 1303), § 8.007, eff. Jan. 1, 2014.

### § 202.103. Procedures Applicable to Transferred Proceeding to Declare Heirship; Consolidation with Other Proceeding

A proceeding to declare heirship that is transferred under Section 202.101 shall proceed as though the proceeding was originally filed in the court to which the proceeding is transferred. The court may consolidate the proceeding with the other proceeding pending in that court.

Added by Acts 2009, 81st Leg., ch. 680, § 1, eff. Jan. 1, 2014.

## SUBCHAPTER D. EVIDENCE RELATING TO DETERMINATION OF HEIRSHIP

### § 202.151. Evidence in Proceeding to Declare Heirship

(a) The court may require that any testimony admitted as evidence in a proceeding to declare heirship be reduced to writing and subscribed and sworn to by the witnesses, respectively.

(b) Testimony in a proceeding to declare heirship must be taken in open court, by deposition in accordance with Section 51.203, or in accordance with the Texas Rules of Civil Procedure.

Added by Acts 2009, 81st Leg., ch. 680, § 1, eff. Jan. 1, 2014. Amended by Acts 2011, 82nd Leg., ch. 91 (S.B. 1303), § 8.008, eff. Jan. 1, 2014; Acts 2013, 83rd Leg., ch. 1136 (H.B. 2912), § 18, eff. Jan. 1, 2014.

Section 62(f) of Acts 2013, 83rd Leg., ch. 1136 (H.B. 2912) provides:

"The changes in law made by Sections 102.004, 201.051, 201.052(b), 202. 004, 202.009, 202.056, 202.151, 353.101(d), 403.055, 403.056(a), and 405.001(b), Estates Code, as amended by this Act, and Sections 201.052(a–1), 202.0025, and 202.057, Estates Code, as added by this Act, apply only to the estate of a decedent who dies on or after the effective date [Jan. 1, 2014] of this Act. The estate of a decedent who dies before the effective date of this Act is governed by the law in effect on the date of the decedent's death, and the former law is continued in effect for that purpose."

## SUBCHAPTER E. JUDGMENT IN PROCEEDING TO DECLARE HEIRSHIP

### § 202.201. Required Statements in Judgment

(a) The judgment in a proceeding to declare heirship must state:

(1) the names and places of residence of the heirs of the decedent who is the subject of the proceeding; and

(2) the heirs' respective shares and interests in the decedent's property.

(b) If the proof in a proceeding to declare heirship is in any respect deficient, the judgment in the proceeding must state that.

Added by Acts 2009, 81st Leg., ch. 680, § 1, eff. Jan. 1, 2014.

### § 202.202. Finality and Appeal of Judgment

(a) The judgment in a proceeding to declare heirship is a final judgment.

(b) At the request of an interested person, the judgment in a proceeding to declare heirship may be appealed or reviewed within the same time limits and in the same manner as other judgments in probate matters.

Added by Acts 2009, 81st Leg., ch. 680, § 1, eff. Jan. 1, 2014.

### § 202.203. Correction of Judgment at Request of Heir Not Properly Served

If an heir of a decedent who is the subject of a proceeding to declare heirship is not served with citation by registered or certified mail or personal service in the proceeding, the heir may:

(1) have the judgment in the proceeding corrected by bill of review:

(A) at any time, but not later than the fourth anniversary of the date of the judgment; or

(B) after the passage of any length of time, on proof of actual fraud; and

(2) recover the heir's just share of the property or the value of that share from:

(A) the heirs named in the judgment; and

(B) those who claim under the heirs named in the judgment and who are not bona fide purchasers for value.

Added by Acts 2009, 81st Leg., ch. 680, § 1, eff. Jan. 1, 2014.

### § 202.204. Limitation of Liability of Certain Persons Acting in Accordance with Judgment

(a) The judgment in a proceeding to declare heirship is conclusive in a suit between an heir omitted from the judgment and a bona fide purchaser for value who purchased property after entry of the judgment without actual notice of the claim of the omitted heir, regardless of whether the judgment is subsequently modified, set aside, or nullified.

(b) A person is not liable to another person for the following actions performed in good faith after a judgment is entered in a proceeding to declare heirship:

(1) delivering the property of the decedent who was the subject of the proceeding to the persons named as heirs in the judgment; or

(2) engaging in any other transaction with the persons named as heirs in the judgment.

Added by Acts 2009, 81st Leg., ch. 680, § 1, eff. Jan. 1, 2014.

### § 202.205. Effect of Certain Judgments on Liability to Creditors

(a) A judgment in a proceeding to declare heirship stating that there is no necessity for administration of the estate of the decedent who is the subject of the proceeding constitutes authorization for a person who owes money to the estate, has custody of estate property, acts as registrar or transfer agent of an evidence of interest, indebtedness, property, or right belonging to the estate, or purchases from or otherwise deals with an heir named in the judgment to take the following actions without liability to a creditor of the estate or other person:

(1) to pay, deliver, or transfer the property or the evidence of property rights to an heir named in the judgment; or

(2) to purchase property from an heir named in the judgment.

(b) An heir named in a judgment in a proceeding to declare heirship is entitled to enforce the heir's right to payment, delivery, or transfer described by Subsection (a) by suit.

(c) Except as provided by this section, this chapter does not affect the rights or remedies of the creditors of a decedent who is the subject of a proceeding to declare heirship.

Added by Acts 2009, 81st Leg., ch. 680, § 1, eff. Jan. 1, 2014.

### § 202.206. Filing and Recording of Judgment

(a) A certified copy of the judgment in a proceeding to declare heirship may be:

(1) filed for record in the office of the county clerk of the county in which any real property described in the judgment is located;

(2) recorded in the deed records of that county; and

(3) indexed in the name of the decedent who was the subject of the proceeding as grantor and in the names of the heirs named in the judgment as grantees.

(b) On the filing of a judgment in accordance with Subsection (a), the judgment constitutes constructive notice of the facts stated in the judgment.

Added by Acts 2009, 81st Leg., ch. 680, § 1, eff. Jan. 1, 2014.

## CHAPTER 203. NONJUDICIAL EVIDENCE OF HEIRSHIP

Section

### § 203.001. Recorded Statement of Facts as Prima Facie Evidence of Heirship

(a) A court shall receive in a proceeding to declare heirship or a suit involving title to property a statement of facts concerning the family history, genealogy, marital status, or the identity of the heirs of a decedent as prima facie evidence of the facts contained in the statement if:

(1) the statement is contained in:

(A) an affidavit or other instrument legally executed and acknowledged or sworn to before, and certified by, an officer authorized to take acknowledgments or oaths, as applicable; or

(B) a judgment of a court of record; and

(2) the affidavit or instrument containing the statement has been of record for five years or more in the deed records of a county in this state in which the property is located at the time the suit involving title to property is commenced, or in the deed records of a county in this state in which the decedent was domiciled or had a fixed place of residence at the time of the decedent's death.

(b) If there is an error in a statement of facts in a recorded affidavit or instrument described by Subsection (a), anyone interested in a proceeding in which the affidavit or instrument is offered in evidence may prove the true facts.

(c) An affidavit of facts concerning the identity of a decedent's heirs as to an interest in real property that is filed in a proceeding or suit described by Subsection (a) may be in the form prescribed by Section 203.002.

(d) An affidavit of facts concerning the identity of a decedent's heirs does not affect the rights of an omitted heir or creditor of the decedent as otherwise provided by law. This section is cumulative of all other statutes on the same subject and may not be construed as abrogating any right to present evidence or rely on an affidavit of facts conferred by any other statute or rule.

Added by Acts 2009, 81st Leg., ch. 680, § 1, eff. Jan. 1, 2014.

### § 203.002. Form of Affidavit Concerning Identity of Heirs

An affidavit of facts concerning the identity of a decedent's heirs may be in substantially the following form:

### AFFIDAVIT OF FACTS CONCERNING THE IDENTITY OF HEIRS

Before me, the undersigned authority, on this day personally appeared _____ ("Affiant") (insert name of affiant) who, being first duly sworn, upon his/her oath states:

1. My name is _____ (insert name of affiant), and I live at _____ (insert address of affiant's residence). I am personally familiar with the family and marital history of _____ ("Decedent") (insert name of decedent), and I have personal knowledge of the facts stated in this affidavit.

2. I knew decedent from _____ (insert date) until _____ (insert date). Decedent died on

_____ (insert date of death). Decedent's place of death was _____ (insert place of death). At the time of decedent's death, decedent's residence was _____ (insert address of decedent's residence).

3. Decedent's marital history was as follows: _____ (insert marital history and, if decedent's spouse is deceased, insert date and place of spouse's death).

4. Decedent had the following children: _____ (insert name, birth date, name of other parent, and current address of child or date of death of child and descendants of deceased child, as applicable, for each child).

5. Decedent did not have or adopt any other children and did not take any other children into decedent's home or raise any other children, except: _____ (insert name of child or names of children, or state "none").

6. (Include if decedent was not survived by descendants.) Decedent's mother was: _____ (insert name, birth date, and current address or date of death of mother, as applicable).

7. (Include if decedent was not survived by descendants.) Decedent's father was: _____ (insert name, birth date, and current address or date of death of father, as applicable).

8. (Include if decedent was not survived by descendants or by both mother and father.) Decedent had the following siblings: _____ (insert name, birth date, and current address or date of death of each sibling and parents of each sibling and descendants of each deceased sibling, as applicable, or state "none").

9. (Optional.) The following persons have knowledge regarding the decedent, the identity of decedent's children, if any, parents, or siblings, if any: _____ (insert names of persons with knowledge, or state "none").

10. Decedent died without leaving a written will. (Modify statement if decedent left a written will.)

11. There has been no administration of decedent's estate. (Modify statement if there has been administration of decedent's estate.)

12. Decedent left no debts that are unpaid, except: _____ (insert list of debts, or state "none").

13. There are no unpaid estate or inheritance taxes, except: _____ (insert list of unpaid taxes, or state "none").

14. To the best of my knowledge, decedent owned an interest in the following real property: _____ (insert list of real property in which decedent owned an interest, or state "none").

15. (Optional.) The following were the heirs of decedent: _____ (insert names of heirs).

16. (Insert additional information as appropriate, such as size of the decedent's estate.)

Signed this ___ day of _____, ___.

_____
(signature of affiant)

State of _____

County of _____

Sworn to and subscribed to before me on _____ by
(date)

_____
(insert name of affiant).

_____
(signature of notarial officer)

(Seal, if any, of notary) _____
(printed name)

My commission expires: _____

Added by Acts 2009, 81st Leg., ch. 680, § 1, eff. Jan. 1, 2014.

## CHAPTER 204. GENETIC TESTING IN PROCEEDINGS TO DECLARE HEIRSHIP

### SUBCHAPTER A. GENERAL PROVISIONS

### SUBCHAPTER B. COURT ORDERS FOR GENETIC TESTING IN PROCEEDINGS TO DECLARE HEIRSHIP

### SUBCHAPTER C. RESULTS OF GENETIC TESTING

## SUBCHAPTER A. GENERAL PROVISIONS

### § 204.001. Proceedings and Records Public

A proceeding under this chapter or Chapter 202 involving genetic testing is open to the public as in other civil cases. Papers and records in the proceeding are available for public inspection.

Added by Acts 2009, 81st Leg., ch. 680, § 1, eff. Jan. 1, 2014.

## SUBCHAPTER B. COURT ORDERS FOR GENETIC TESTING IN PROCEEDINGS TO DECLARE HEIRSHIP

### § 204.051. Order for Genetic Testing

(a) In a proceeding to declare heirship under Chapter 202, the court may, on the court's own motion, and shall, on the request of a party to the proceeding, order one or more specified individuals to submit to genetic testing as provided by Subchapter F, Chapter 160, Family Code. If two or more individuals are ordered to be tested, the court may order that the testing of those individuals be done concurrently or sequentially.

(b) The court may enforce an order under this section by contempt.

Added by Acts 2009, 81st Leg., ch. 680, § 1, eff. Jan. 1, 2014.

### § 204.052. Advancement of Costs

Subject to any assessment of costs following a proceeding to declare heirship in accordance with Rule 131, Texas Rules of Civil Procedure, the cost of genetic testing ordered under Section 204.051 must be advanced:

(1) by a party to the proceeding who requests the testing;

(2) as agreed by the parties and approved by the court; or

(3) as ordered by the court.

Added by Acts 2009, 81st Leg., ch. 680, § 1, eff. Jan. 1, 2014.

### § 204.053. Order and Advancement of Costs for Subsequent Genetic Testing

(a) Subject to Subsection (b), the court shall order genetic testing subsequent to the testing conducted under Section 204.051 if:

(1) a party to the proceeding to declare heirship contests the results of the genetic testing ordered under Section 204.051; and

(2) the party contesting the results requests that additional testing be conducted.

(b) If the results of the genetic testing ordered under Section 204.051 identify a tested individual as an heir of the decedent, the court may order additional genetic testing in accordance with Subsection (a) only if the party contesting those results pays for the additional testing in advance.

Added by Acts 2009, 81st Leg., ch. 680, § 1, eff. Jan. 1, 2014.

### § 204.054. Submission of Genetic Material by Other Relative Under Certain Circumstances

If a sample of an individual's genetic material that could identify another individual as the decedent's heir is not available for purposes of conducting genetic testing under this subchapter, the court, on a finding of good cause and that the need for genetic testing outweighs the legitimate interests of the individual to be tested, may order any of the following individuals to submit a sample of genetic material for the testing under circumstances the court considers just:

(1) a parent, sibling, or child of the individual whose genetic material is not available; or

(2) any other relative of that individual, as necessary to conduct the testing.

Added by Acts 2009, 81st Leg., ch. 680, § 1, eff. Jan. 1, 2014.

### § 204.055. Genetic Testing of Deceased Individual

On good cause shown, the court may order:

(1) genetic testing of a deceased individual under this subchapter; and

(2) if necessary, removal of the remains of the deceased individual as provided by Section 711.004, Health and Safety Code, for that testing.

Added by Acts 2009, 81st Leg., ch. 680, § 1, eff. Jan. 1, 2014.

### § 204.056. Criminal Penalty

(a) An individual commits an offense if:

(1) the individual intentionally releases an identifiable sample of the genetic material of another

individual that was provided for purposes of genetic testing ordered under this subchapter; and

(2) the release:

(A) is for a purpose not related to the proceeding to declare heirship; and

(B) was not ordered by the court or done in accordance with written permission obtained from the individual who provided the sample.

(b) An offense under this section is a Class A misdemeanor.

Added by Acts 2009, 81st Leg., ch. 680, § 1, eff. Jan. 1, 2014.

## SUBCHAPTER C. RESULTS OF GENETIC TESTING

### § 204.101. Results of Genetic Testing; Admissibility

A report of the results of genetic testing ordered under Subchapter B:

(1) must comply with the requirements for a report prescribed by Section 160.504, Family Code; and

(2) is admissible in a proceeding to declare heirship under Chapter 202 as evidence of the truth of the facts asserted in the report.

Added by Acts 2009, 81st Leg., ch. 680, § 1, eff. Jan. 1, 2014.

### § 204.102. Presumption Regarding Results of Genetic Testing; Rebuttal

The presumption under Section 160.505, Family Code:

(1) applies to the results of genetic testing ordered under Subchapter B; and

(2) may be rebutted as provided by Section 160.505, Family Code.

Added by Acts 2009, 81st Leg., ch. 680, § 1, eff. Jan. 1, 2014.

### § 204.103. Contesting Results of Genetic Testing

(a) A party to a proceeding to declare heirship who contests the results of genetic testing may call one or more genetic testing experts to testify in person or by telephone, videoconference, deposition, or another method approved by the court.

(b) Unless otherwise ordered by the court, the party offering the testimony under Subsection (a) bears the expense for the expert testifying.

Added by Acts 2009, 81st Leg., ch. 680, § 1, eff. Jan. 1, 2014.

## SUBCHAPTER D. USE OF RESULTS OF GENETIC TESTING IN CERTAIN PROCEEDINGS TO DECLARE HEIRSHIP

### § 204.151. Applicability of Subchapter

This subchapter applies in a proceeding to declare heirship of a decedent only with respect to an individual who claims to be a biological child of the decedent or claims to inherit through a biological child of the decedent.

Added by Acts 2009, 81st Leg., ch. 680, § 1, eff. Jan. 1, 2014. Amended by Acts 2013, 83rd Leg., ch. 1136 (H.B. 2912), § 19, eff. Jan. 1, 2014.

Section 62(b) of Acts 2013, 83rd Leg., ch. 1136 (H.B. 2912) provides:

"The changes in law made by this Act to Sections 204.151 and 204.152, Estates Code, apply only to a proceeding to declare heirship commenced on or after January 1, 2014. A proceeding to declare heirship commenced before that date is governed by the law in effect on the date the proceeding was commenced, and the former law is continued in effect for that purpose."

### § 204.152. Presumption; Rebuttal

The presumption under Section 160.505, Family Code, that applies in establishing a parent-child relationship also applies in determining heirship in the probate court using the results of genetic testing ordered with respect to an individual described by Section 204.151, and the presumption may be rebutted in the same manner provided by Section 160.505, Family Code.

Added by Acts 2009, 81st Leg., ch. 680, § 1, eff. Jan. 1, 2014. Amended by Acts 2013, 83rd Leg., ch. 1136 (H.B. 2912), § 19, eff. Jan. 1, 2014.

Section 62(b) of Acts 2013, 83rd Leg., ch. 1136 (H.B. 2912) provides:

"The changes in law made by this Act to Sections 204.151 and 204.152, Estates Code, apply only to a proceeding to declare heirship commenced on or after January 1, 2014. A proceeding to declare heirship commenced before that date is governed by the law in effect on the date the proceeding was commenced, and the former law is continued in effect for that purpose."

### § 204.153. Effect of Inconclusive Results of Genetic Testing

If the results of genetic testing ordered under Subchapter B do not identify or exclude a tested individual as the ancestor of the individual described by Section 204.151:

(1) the court may not dismiss the proceeding to declare heirship; and

(2) the results of the genetic testing and other relevant evidence are admissible in the proceeding.

Added by Acts 2009, 81st Leg., ch. 680, § 1, eff. Jan. 1, 2014.

## SUBCHAPTER E. ADDITIONAL ORDERS FOLLOWING RESULTS OF GENETIC TESTING

### § 204.201. Order for Change of Name

On the request of an individual determined by the results of genetic testing to be the heir of a decedent and for good cause shown, the court may:

(1) order the name of the individual to be changed; and

(2) if the court orders a name change under Subdivision (1), order the bureau of vital statistics to issue an amended birth record for the individual.

Added by Acts 2009, 81st Leg., ch. 680, § 1, eff. Jan. 1, 2014.

## CHAPTER 205. SMALL ESTATE AFFIDAVIT

Section
205.001. Entitlement to Estate Without Appointment of Personal Representative.
205.002. Affidavit Requirements.
205.003. Examination and Approval of Affidavit.
205.004. Copy of Affidavit to Certain Persons.
205.005. Affidavit as Local Government Record.
205.006. Title to Homestead Transferred Under Affidavit.
205.007. Liability of Certain Persons.
205.008. Effect of Chapter.

### § 205.001. Entitlement to Estate Without Appointment of Personal Representative

The distributees of the estate of a decedent who dies intestate are entitled to the decedent's estate without waiting for the appointment of a personal representative of the estate to the extent the estate assets, excluding homestead and exempt property, exceed the known liabilities of the estate, excluding any liabilities secured by homestead and exempt property, if:

(1) 30 days have elapsed since the date of the decedent's death;

(2) no petition for the appointment of a personal representative is pending or has been granted;

(3) the value of the estate assets, excluding homestead and exempt property, does not exceed $50,000;

(4) an affidavit that meets the requirements of Section 205.002 is filed with the clerk of the court that has jurisdiction and venue of the estate;

(5) the judge approves the affidavit as provided by Section 205.003; and

(6) the distributees comply with Section 205.004.

Added by Acts 2009, 81st Leg., ch. 680, § 1, eff. Jan. 1, 2014.

### § 205.002. Affidavit Requirements

An affidavit filed under Section 205.001 must:

(1) be sworn to by:

(A) two disinterested witnesses;

(B) each distributee of the estate who has legal capacity; and

(C) if warranted by the facts, the natural guardian or next of kin of any minor distributee or the guardian of any other incapacitated distributee;

(2) show the existence of the conditions prescribed by Sections 205.001(1), (2), and (3); and

(3) include:

(A) a list of all known estate assets and liabilities;

(B) the name and address of each distributee; and

(C) the relevant family history facts concerning heirship that show each distributee's right to receive estate money or other property or to have any evidence of money, property, or other right of the estate as is determined to exist transferred to the distributee as an heir or assignee.

Added by Acts 2009, 81st Leg., ch. 680, § 1, eff. Jan. 1, 2014.

### § 205.003. Examination and Approval of Affidavit

The judge shall examine an affidavit filed under Section 205.001. The judge may approve the affidavit if the judge determines that the affidavit conforms to the requirements of this chapter.

Added by Acts 2009, 81st Leg., ch. 680, § 1, eff. Jan. 1, 2014.

### § 205.004. Copy of Affidavit to Certain Persons

The distributees of the estate shall provide a copy of the affidavit under this chapter, certified by the court clerk, to each person who:

(1) owes money to the estate;

(2) has custody or possession of estate property; or

(3) acts as a registrar, fiduciary, or transfer agent of or for an evidence of interest, indebtedness, property, or other right belonging to the estate.

Added by Acts 2009, 81st Leg., ch. 680, § 1, eff. Jan. 1, 2014.

### § 205.005. Affidavit as Local Government Record

(a) If the judge approves an affidavit under Section 205.003, the affidavit shall be maintained as a local

75

government record under Subtitle C, Title 6, Local Government Code.

(b) If the county does not maintain local government records in a manner authorized under Subtitle C, Title 6, Local Government Code, the county clerk shall provide and keep in the clerk's office an appropriate book labeled "Small Estates" in which the clerk shall, on payment of the legal recording fee, record each affidavit filed under this chapter. The small estates book must contain an accurate index that shows the decedent's name and references to any land involved.

Added by Acts 2009, 81st Leg., ch. 680, § 1, eff. Jan. 1, 2014.

### § 205.006.　Title to Homestead Transferred Under Affidavit

(a) If a decedent's homestead is the only real property in the decedent's estate, title to the homestead may be transferred under an affidavit that meets the requirements of this chapter. The affidavit used to transfer title to the homestead must be recorded in the deed records of a county in which the homestead is located.

(b) A bona fide purchaser for value may rely on an affidavit recorded under this section. A bona fide purchaser for value without actual or constructive notice of an heir who is not disclosed in the recorded affidavit acquires title to a homestead free of the interests of the undisclosed heir, but remains subject to any claim a creditor of the decedent has by law. A purchaser has constructive notice of an heir who is not disclosed in the recorded affidavit if an affidavit, judgment of heirship, or title transaction in the chain of title in the deed records identifies that heir as the decedent's heir.

(c) An heir who is not disclosed in an affidavit recorded under this section may recover from an heir who receives consideration from a purchaser in a transfer for value of title to a homestead passing under the affidavit.

Added by Acts 2009, 81st Leg., ch. 680, § 1, eff. Jan. 1, 2014.

### § 205.007.　Liability of Certain Persons

(a) A person making a payment, delivery, transfer, or issuance under an affidavit described by this chapter is released to the same extent as if made to a personal representative of the decedent. The person may not be required to:

(1) see to the application of the affidavit; or

(2) inquire into the truth of any statement in the affidavit.

(b) The distributees to whom payment, delivery, transfer, or issuance is made are:

(1) answerable for the payment, delivery, transfer, or issuance to any person having a prior right; and

(2) accountable to any personal representative appointed after the payment, delivery, transfer, or issuance.

(c) Each person who executed the affidavit is liable for any damage or loss to any person that arises from a payment, delivery, transfer, or issuance made in reliance on the affidavit.

(d) If a person to whom the affidavit is delivered refuses to pay, deliver, transfer, or issue property as provided by this section, the property may be recovered in an action brought for that purpose by or on behalf of the distributees entitled to the property on proof of the facts required to be stated in the affidavit.

Added by Acts 2009, 81st Leg., ch. 680, § 1, eff. Jan. 1, 2014.

### § 205.008.　Effect of Chapter

(a) This chapter does not affect the disposition of property under a will or other testamentary document.

(b) Except as provided by Section 205.006, this chapter does not transfer title to real property.

Added by Acts 2009, 81st Leg., ch. 680, § 1, eff. Jan. 1, 2014.

## SUBTITLE F.　WILLS

### CHAPTER 251.　FUNDAMENTAL REQUIREMENTS AND PROVISIONS RELATING TO WILLS

## SUBCHAPTER A.  WILL FORMATION

### § 251.001.  Who May Execute Will

Under the rules and limitations prescribed by law, a person of sound mind has the right and power to make a last will and testament if, at the time the will is made, the person:

(1) is 18 years of age or older;

(2) is or has been married;  or

(3) is a member of the armed forces of the United States, an auxiliary of the armed forces of the United States, or the United States Maritime Service.

Added by Acts 2009, 81st Leg., ch. 680, § 1, eff. Jan. 1, 2014.

### § 251.002.  Interests That May Pass by Will;  Disinheritance

(a) Subject to limitations prescribed by law, a person competent to make a last will and testament may devise under the will and testament all the estate, right, title, and interest in property the person has at the time of the person's death.

(b) A person who makes a last will and testament may:

(1) disinherit an heir;  and

(2) direct the disposition of property or an interest passing under the will or by intestacy.

Added by Acts 2009, 81st Leg., ch. 680, § 1, eff. Jan. 1, 2014.

## SUBCHAPTER B.  WILL REQUIREMENTS

### § 251.051.  Written, Signed, and Attested

Except as otherwise provided by law, a last will and testament must be:

(1) in writing;

(2) signed by:

(A) the testator in person;  or

(B) another person on behalf of the testator:

(i) in the testator's presence;  and

(ii) under the testator's direction;  and

(3) attested by two or more credible witnesses who are at least 14 years of age and who subscribe their names to the will in their own handwriting in the testator's presence.

Added by Acts 2009, 81st Leg., ch. 680, § 1, eff. Jan. 1, 2014.

### § 251.052.  Exception for Holographic Wills

Notwithstanding Section 251.051, a will written wholly in the testator's handwriting is not required to be attested by subscribing witnesses.

Added by Acts 2009, 81st Leg., ch. 680, § 1, eff. Jan. 1, 2014.

## SUBCHAPTER C.  SELF–PROVED WILLS

### § 251.101.  Self–Proved Will

A self-proved will is a will:

(1) to which a self-proving affidavit subscribed and sworn to by the testator and witnesses is attached or annexed;  or

(2) that is simultaneously executed, attested, and made self-proved as provided by Section 251.1045.

Added by Acts 2009, 81st Leg., ch. 680, § 1, eff. Jan. 1, 2014. Amended by Acts 2011, 82nd Leg., ch. 1338 (S.B. 1198), § 2.22, eff. Jan. 1, 2014.

### § 251.102.  Probate and Treatment of Self–Proved Will

(a) A self-proved will may be admitted to probate without the testimony of any subscribing witnesses if:

(1) the testator and witnesses execute a self-proving affidavit;  or

(2) the will is simultaneously executed, attested, and made self-proved as provided by Section 251.1045.

(b) A self-proved will may not otherwise be treated differently than a will that is not self-proved.

Added by Acts 2009, 81st Leg., ch. 680, § 1, eff. Jan. 1, 2014. Amended by Acts 2011, 82nd Leg., ch. 1338 (S.B. 1198), § 2.23, eff. Jan. 1, 2014.

### § 251.103.  Period for Making Attested Wills Self–Proved

A will or testament that meets the requirements of Section 251.051 may be made self-proved at:

(1) the time of the execution of the will or testament;  or

(2) a later date during the lifetime of the testator and the witnesses.

Added by Acts 2009, 81st Leg., ch. 680, § 1, eff. Jan. 1, 2014.

## § 251.104. Requirements for Self–Proving Affidavit

(a) An affidavit that is in form and content substantially as provided by Subsection (e) is a self-proving affidavit.

(b) A self-proving affidavit must be made by the testator and by the attesting witnesses before an officer authorized to administer oaths. The officer shall affix the officer's official seal to the self-proving affidavit.

(c) The self-proving affidavit shall be attached or annexed to the will or testament.

(d) An affidavit that is in substantial compliance with the form of the affidavit provided by Subsection (e), that is subscribed and acknowledged by the testator, and that is subscribed and sworn to by the attesting witnesses is sufficient to self-prove the will. No other affidavit or certificate of a testator is required to self-prove a will or testament other than the affidavit provided by Subsection (e).

(e) The form and content of the self-proving affidavit must be substantially as follows:

THE STATE OF TEXAS

COUNTY OF _____

Before me, the undersigned authority, on this day personally appeared _____, _____, and _____, known to me to be the testator and the witnesses, respectively, whose names are subscribed to the annexed or foregoing instrument in their respective capacities, and, all of said persons being by me duly sworn, the said _____, testator, declared to me and to the said witnesses in my presence that said instrument is [his/her] last will and testament, and that [he/she] had willingly made and executed it as [his/her] free act and deed; and the said witnesses, each on [his/her] oath stated to me, in the presence and hearing of the said testator, that the said testator had declared to them that said instrument is [his/her] last will and testament, and that [he/she] executed same as such and wanted each of them to sign it as a witness; and upon their oaths each witness stated further that they did sign the same as witnesses in the presence of the said testator and at [his/her] request; that [he/she] was at that time eighteen years of age or over (or being under such age, was or had been lawfully married, or was then a member of the armed forces of the United States, or an auxiliary of the armed forces of the United States, or the United States Maritime Service) and was of sound mind; and that each of said witnesses was then at least fourteen years of age.

_____

Testator

_____

Witness

_____

Witness

Subscribed and sworn to before me by the said _____, testator, and by the said _____ and _____, witnesses, this ___ day of _____ A.D. _____.

(SEAL)

(Signed) _____

(Official Capacity of Officer)

Added by Acts 2009, 81st Leg., ch. 680, § 1, eff. Jan. 1, 2014. Amended by Acts 2011, 82nd Leg., ch. 1338 (S.B. 1198), § 2.24, eff. Jan. 1, 2014.

## § 251.1045. Simultaneous Execution, Attestation, and Self–Proving

(a) As an alternative to the self-proving of a will by the affidavits of the testator and the attesting witnesses as provided by Section 251.104, a will may be simultaneously executed, attested, and made self-proved before an officer authorized to administer oaths, and the testimony of the witnesses in the probate of the will may be made unnecessary, with the inclusion in the will of the following in form and contents substantially as follows:

I, _____, as testator, after being duly sworn, declare to the undersigned witnesses and to the undersigned authority that this instrument is my will, that I have willingly made and executed it in the presence of the undersigned witnesses, all of whom were present at the same time, as my free act and deed, and that I have requested each of the undersigned witnesses to sign this will in my presence and in the presence of each other. I now sign this will in the presence of the attesting witnesses and the undersigned authority on this _____ day of _____, 20_____.

_____

Testator

The undersigned, _____ and _____, each being at least fourteen years of age, after being duly sworn, declare to the testator and to the undersigned authority that the testator declared to us that this instrument is the testator's will and that the testator requested us to act as witnesses to the testator's will and signature. The testator then signed this will in our presence, all of us being present at the same time. The testator is eighteen years of age or over (or being under such age, is or has been lawfully married, or is a member of the armed forces of the United States or of an auxiliary of the armed forces of the United States or of the United States Maritime Service), and we believe the testator to be of sound mind. We now sign our names as attesting witnesses in the presence of the testator, each other, and the undersigned authority on this _____ day of _____, 20_____.

_____
Witness

_____
Witness

Subscribed and sworn to before me by the said _____, testator, and by the said _____ and _____, witnesses, this ___ day of _____ A.D. _____.

(SEAL)

(Signed) _____
(Official Capacity of Officer)

(b) A will that is in substantial compliance with the form provided by Subsection (a) is sufficient to self-prove a will.

Added by Acts 2011, 82nd Leg., ch. 1338 (S.B. 1198), § 2.25, eff. Jan. 1, 2014.

## § 251.105. Effect of Signature on Self–Proving Affidavit

A signature on a self-proving affidavit is considered a signature to the will if necessary to prove that the will was signed by the testator or witnesses or both, except that, in that case, the will may not be considered a self-proved will.

Added by Acts 2009, 81st Leg., ch. 680, § 1, eff. Jan. 1, 2014.

## § 251.106. Contest, Revocation, or Amendment of Self–Proved Will

A self-proved will may be contested, revoked, or amended by a codicil in the same manner as a will that is not self-proved.

Added by Acts 2009, 81st Leg., ch. 680, § 1, eff. Jan. 1, 2014.

## § 251.107. Self–Proved Holographic Will

Notwithstanding any other provision of this subchapter, a will written wholly in the testator's handwriting may be made self-proved at any time during the testator's lifetime by the attachment or annexation to the will of an affidavit by the testator to the effect that:

(1) the instrument is the testator's last will;

(2) the testator was 18 years of age or older at the time the will was executed or, if the testator was younger than 18 years of age, that the testator:

(A) was or had been married; or

(B) was a member of the armed forces of the United States, an auxiliary of the armed forces of the United States, or the United States Maritime Service at the time the will was executed;

(3) the testator was of sound mind; and

(4) the testator has not revoked the will.

Added by Acts 2009, 81st Leg., ch. 680, § 1, eff. Jan. 1, 2014.

## CHAPTER 252. SAFEKEEPING AND CUSTODY OF WILLS

### SUBCHAPTER A. DEPOSIT OF WILL WITH COUNTY CLERK

### SUBCHAPTER B. WILL DELIVERY DURING LIFE OF TESTATOR

### SUBCHAPTER C. ACTIONS BY COUNTY CLERK ON DEATH OF TESTATOR

### SUBCHAPTER D. LEGAL EFFECT OF WILL DEPOSIT

### SUBCHAPTER E. DUTY AND LIABILITY OF CUSTODIAN OF ESTATE PAPERS

## SUBCHAPTER A. DEPOSIT OF WILL WITH COUNTY CLERK

### § 252.001. Will Deposit; Certificate

(a) A testator, or another person for the testator, may deposit the testator's will with the county clerk of the county of the testator's residence. Before accepting the will for deposit, the clerk may require proof satisfactory to the clerk concerning the testator's identity and residence.

(b) The county clerk shall receive and keep the will on the payment of a $5 fee.

(c) On the deposit of the will, the county clerk shall issue a certificate of deposit for the will.

Added by Acts 2009, 81st Leg., ch. 680, § 1, eff. Jan. 1, 2014.

### § 252.002. Sealed Wrapper Required

(a) A will intended to be deposited with a county clerk shall be enclosed in a sealed wrapper.

(b) The wrapper must be endorsed with:

(1) "Will of," followed by the name, address, and signature of the testator; and

(2) the name and current address of each person who is to be notified of the deposit of the will after the testator's death.

Added by Acts 2009, 81st Leg., ch. 680, § 1, eff. Jan. 1, 2014.

### § 252.003. Numbering of Filed Wills and Corresponding Certificates

(a) A county clerk shall number wills deposited with the clerk in consecutive order.

(b) A certificate of deposit issued under Section 252.001(c) on receipt of a will must bear the same number as the will for which the certificate is issued.

Added by Acts 2009, 81st Leg., ch. 680, § 1, eff. Jan. 1, 2014.

### § 252.004. Index

A county clerk shall keep an index of all wills deposited with the clerk under Section 252.001.

Added by Acts 2009, 81st Leg., ch. 680, § 1, eff. Jan. 1, 2014.

## SUBCHAPTER B. WILL DELIVERY DURING LIFE OF TESTATOR

### § 252.051. Will Delivery

During the lifetime of the testator, a will deposited with a county clerk under Subchapter A may be delivered only to:

(1) the testator; or

(2) another person authorized by the testator by a sworn written order.

Added by Acts 2009, 81st Leg., ch. 680, § 1, eff. Jan. 1, 2014.

### § 252.052. Surrender of Certificate of Deposit; Exception

(a) Except as provided by Subsection (b), on delivery of a will to the testator or a person authorized by the testator under Section 252.051, the certificate of deposit issued for the will must be surrendered by the person to whom delivery of the will is made.

(b) A county clerk may instead accept and file an affidavit by the testator stating that the certificate of deposit issued for the will has been lost, stolen, or destroyed.

Added by Acts 2009, 81st Leg., ch. 680, § 1, eff. Jan. 1, 2014.

## SUBCHAPTER C. ACTIONS BY COUNTY CLERK ON DEATH OF TESTATOR

### § 252.101. Notification by County Clerk

A county clerk shall notify, by registered mail, return receipt requested, each person named on the endorsement of the will wrapper that the will is on deposit in the clerk's office if:

(1) an affidavit is submitted to the clerk stating that the testator has died; or

(2) the clerk receives other notice or proof of the testator's death sufficient to convince the clerk that the testator has died.

Added by Acts 2009, 81st Leg., ch. 680, § 1, eff. Jan. 1, 2014.

### § 252.102. Will Delivery on Testator's Death

On the request of one or more persons notified under Section 252.101, the county clerk shall deliver the will that is the subject of the notice to the person or persons. The clerk shall obtain a receipt for delivery of the will.

Added by Acts 2009, 81st Leg., ch. 680, § 1, eff. Jan. 1, 2014.

### § 252.103. Inspection of Will by County Clerk

A county clerk shall open a will wrapper and inspect the will if:

(1) the notice required by Section 252.101 is returned as undelivered; or

(2) the clerk has accepted for deposit a will that does not specify on the will wrapper the person to

whom the will is to be delivered on the testator's death.

Added by Acts 2009, 81st Leg., ch. 680, § 1, eff. Jan. 1, 2014.

### § 252.104. Notice and Delivery of Will to Executor

If a county clerk inspects a will under Section 252.103 and the will names an executor, the clerk shall:

(1) notify the person named as executor, by registered mail, return receipt requested, that the will is on deposit with the clerk; and

(2) deliver, on request, the will to the person named as executor.

Added by Acts 2009, 81st Leg., ch. 680, § 1, eff. Jan. 1, 2014.

### § 252.105. Notice and Delivery of Will to Devisees

(a) If a county clerk inspects a will under Section 252.103, the clerk shall notify by registered mail, return receipt requested, the devisees named in the will that the will is on deposit with the clerk if:

(1) the will does not name an executor;

(2) the person named as executor in the will:

(A) has died; or

(B) fails to take the will before the 31st day after the date the notice required by Section 252.104 is mailed to the person; or

(3) the notice mailed to the person named as executor is returned as undelivered.

(b) On request, the county clerk shall deliver the will to any or all of the devisees notified under Subsection (a).

Added by Acts 2009, 81st Leg., ch. 680, § 1, eff. Jan. 1, 2014.

### SUBCHAPTER D. LEGAL EFFECT OF WILL DEPOSIT

### § 252.151. Deposit Has No Legal Significance

The provisions of Subchapter A providing for the deposit of a will with a county clerk during the lifetime of a testator are solely for the purpose of providing a safe and convenient repository for a will. For purposes of probate, a will deposited as provided by Subchapter A may not be treated differently than a will that has not been deposited.

Added by Acts 2009, 81st Leg., ch. 680, § 1, eff. Jan. 1, 2014.

### § 252.152. Prior Deposited Will in Relation to Later Will

A will that is not deposited as provided by Subchapter A shall be admitted to probate on proof that the will is the last will and testament of the testator, notwithstanding the fact that the testator has a prior will that has been deposited in accordance with Subchapter A.

Added by Acts 2009, 81st Leg., ch. 680, § 1, eff. Jan. 1, 2014.

### § 252.153. Will Deposit Does Not Constitute Notice

The deposit of a will as provided by Subchapter A does not constitute notice, constructive or otherwise, to any person as to the existence or the contents of the will.

Added by Acts 2009, 81st Leg., ch. 680, § 1, eff. Jan. 1, 2014.

### SUBCHAPTER E. DUTY AND LIABILITY OF CUSTODIAN OF ESTATE PAPERS

### § 252.201. Will Delivery

On receiving notice of a testator's death, the person who has custody of the testator's will shall deliver the will to the clerk of the court that has jurisdiction of the testator's estate.

Added by Acts 2009, 81st Leg., ch. 680, § 1, eff. Jan. 1, 2014.

### § 252.202. Personal Service on Custodian of Estate Papers

On a sworn written complaint that a person has custody of the last will of a testator or any papers belonging to the estate of a testator or intestate, the judge of the court that has jurisdiction of the estate shall have the person cited by personal service to appear and show cause why the person should not deliver:

(1) the will to the court for probate; or

(2) the papers to the executor or administrator.

Added by Acts 2009, 81st Leg., ch. 680, § 1, eff. Jan. 1, 2014.

### § 252.203. Arrest; Confinement

On the return of a citation served under Section 252.202, if the judge is satisfied that the person served with the citation had custody of the will or papers at the time the complaint under that section was filed and the person does not deliver the will or papers or show good cause why the will or papers have not been delivered, the judge may have the person arrested and confined until the person delivers the will or papers.

Added by Acts 2009, 81st Leg., ch. 680, § 1, eff. Jan. 1, 2014.

### § 252.204. Damages

(a) A person who refuses to deliver a will or papers described by Section 252.202 is liable to any person aggrieved by the refusal for all damages sustained as a result of the refusal.

(b) Damages may be recovered under this section in any court of competent jurisdiction.

Added by Acts 2009, 81st Leg., ch. 680, § 1, eff. Jan. 1, 2014.

## CHAPTER 253. CHANGE AND REVOCATION OF WILLS

**Section**
253.001.   Court May Not Prohibit Changing a Will.
253.002.   Revocation of Will.

### § 253.001. Court May Not Prohibit Changing a Will

(a) Notwithstanding Section 22.007(a), in this section, "court" means a constitutional county court, district court, or statutory county court, including a statutory probate court.

(b) A court may not prohibit a person from executing a new will or a codicil to an existing will.

(c) Any portion of a court order that purports to prohibit a person from executing a new will or a codicil to an existing will is void and may be disregarded without penalty or sanction of any kind.

Added by Acts 2009, 81st Leg., ch. 680, § 1, eff. Jan. 1, 2014. Amended by Acts 2013, 83rd Leg., ch. 1136 (H.B. 2912), § 20, eff. Jan. 1, 2014.

Section 62(e) of Acts 2013, 83rd Leg., ch. 1136 (H.B. 2912) provides:

"The changes in law made by Sections 51.203(c), 53.104, 305.002(a), 305.003, 308.054(b), 309.051(a), 309.056, 309.103(a) and (b), 355.060, 361.155(b), 362.005, 362.011, 362.013, 404.001(a), 404.003, 404.005(b) and (c), and 551.001(a), Estates Code, as amended by this Act, and Sections 253.001(c), 301.155, 305.004, 309.057, 361.155(c), 404.0035, 404.0036, and 404.0037, Estates Code, as added by this Act, apply to the administration of the estate of a decedent that is pending or commenced on or after the effective date [Jan. 1, 2014] of this Act."

### § 253.002. Revocation of Will

A written will, or a clause or devise in a written will, may not be revoked, except by a subsequent will, codicil, or declaration in writing that is executed with like formalities, or by the testator destroying or canceling the same, or causing it to be destroyed or canceled in the testator's presence.

Added by Acts 2009, 81st Leg., ch. 680, § 1, eff. Jan. 1, 2014.

## CHAPTER 254. VALIDITY OF CERTAIN PROVISIONS IN, AND CONTRACTS RELATING TO, WILLS

**Section**
254.001.   Devises to Trustees.
254.002.   Bequests to Certain Subscribing Witnesses.
254.003.   Devises to Certain Attorneys and Other Persons.
254.004.   Contracts Concerning Wills or Devises; Joint or Reciprocal Wills.
254.005.   Forfeiture Clause.

### § 254.001. Devises to Trustees

(a) A testator may validly devise property in a will to the trustee of a trust established or to be established:

(1) during the testator's lifetime by the testator, the testator and another person, or another person, including a funded or unfunded life insurance trust in which the settlor has reserved any or all rights of ownership of the insurance contracts; or

(2) at the testator's death by the testator's devise to the trustee, regardless of the existence, size, or character of the corpus of the trust, if:

(A) the trust is identified in the testator's will; and

(B) the terms of the trust are in:

(i) a written instrument, other than a will, executed before, with, or after the execution of the testator's will; or

(ii) another person's will if that person predeceased the testator.

(b) A devise under Subsection (a) is not invalid because the trust:

(1) is amendable or revocable; or

(2) was amended after the execution of the will or the testator's death.

(c) Unless the testator's will provides otherwise, property devised to a trust described by Subsection (a) is not held under a testamentary trust of the testator. The property:

(1) becomes part of the trust to which the property is devised; and

(2) must be administered and disposed of according to the provisions of the instrument establishing the trust, including any amendment to the instrument made before or after the testator's death.

(d) Unless the testator's will provides otherwise, a revocation or termination of the trust before the testator's death causes the devise to lapse.

Added by Acts 2009, 81st Leg., ch. 680, § 1, eff. Jan. 1, 2014.

## § 254.002. Bequests to Certain Subscribing Witnesses

(a) Except as provided by Subsection (c), if a devisee under a will is also a subscribing witness to the will and the will cannot be otherwise established:

(1) the bequest is void; and

(2) the subscribing witness shall be allowed and compelled to appear and give the witness's testimony in the same manner as if the bequest to the witness had not been made.

(b) Notwithstanding Subsection (a), if the subscribing witness described by that subsection would have been entitled to a share of the testator's estate had the testator died intestate, the witness is entitled to as much of that share as does not exceed the value of the bequest to the witness under the will.

(c) If the testimony of a subscribing witness described by Subsection (a) proving the will is corroborated by at least one disinterested and credible person who testifies that the subscribing witness's testimony is true and correct:

(1) the bequest to the subscribing witness is not void under Subsection (a); and

(2) the subscribing witness is not regarded as an incompetent or noncredible witness under Subchapters B and C, Chapter 251.

Added by Acts 2009, 81st Leg., ch. 680, § 1, eff. Jan. 1, 2014.

## § 254.003. Devises to Certain Attorneys and Other Persons

(a) A devise of property in a will is void if the devise is made to:

(1) an attorney who prepares or supervises the preparation of the will;

(2) a parent, descendant of a parent, or employee of the attorney described by Subdivision (1); or

(3) the spouse of a person described by Subdivision (1) or (2).

(b) This section does not apply to:

(1) a devise made to a person who:

(A) is the testator's spouse;

(B) is an ascendant or descendant of the testator; or

(C) is related within the third degree by consanguinity or affinity to the testator; or

(2) a bona fide purchaser for value from a devisee in a will.

Added by Acts 2009, 81st Leg., ch. 680, § 1, eff. Jan. 1, 2014.

## § 254.004. Contracts Concerning Wills or Devises; Joint or Reciprocal Wills

(a) A contract executed or entered into on or after September 1, 1979, to make a will or devise, or not to revoke a will or devise, may be established only by:

(1) a written agreement that is binding and enforceable; or

(2) a will stating:

(A) that a contract exists; and

(B) the material provisions of the contract.

(b) The execution of a joint will or reciprocal wills does not constitute by itself sufficient evidence of the existence of a contract.

Added by Acts 2009, 81st Leg., ch. 680, § 1, eff. Jan. 1, 2014.

## § 254.005. Forfeiture Clause

A provision in a will that would cause a forfeiture of or void a devise or provision in favor of a person for bringing any court action, including contesting a will, is enforceable unless in a court action determining whether the forfeiture clause should be enforced, the person who brought the action contrary to the forfeiture clause establishes by a preponderance of the evidence that:

(1) just cause existed for bringing the action; and

(2) the action was brought and maintained in good faith.

Added by Acts 2011, 82nd Leg., ch. 91 (S.B. 1303), § 8.009(a), eff. Jan. 1, 2014; Acts 2011, 82nd Leg., ch. 1338 (S.B 1198), § 2.26, eff. Jan. 1, 2014. Amended by Acts 2013, 83rd Leg., ch. 351 (H.B. 2380), § 2.01, eff. Jan. 1, 2014.

## CHAPTER 255. CONSTRUCTION AND INTERPRETATION OF WILLS

### SUBCHAPTER A. CERTAIN PERSONAL PROPERTY EXCLUDED FROM DEVISE OR LEGACY

## SUBCHAPTER A. CERTAIN PERSONAL PROPERTY EXCLUDED FROM DEVISE OR LEGACY

### § 255.001. Definitions

In this subchapter:

(1) "Contents" means tangible personal property, other than titled personal property, found inside of or on a specifically devised item. The term includes clothing, pictures, furniture, coin collections, and other items of tangible personal property that:

(A) do not require a formal transfer of title; and

(B) are located in another item of tangible personal property such as a cedar chest or other furniture.

(2) "Titled personal property" includes all tangible personal property represented by a certificate of title, certificate of ownership, written label, marking, or designation that signifies ownership by a person. The term includes a motor vehicle, motor home, motorboat, or other similar property that requires a formal transfer of title.

Added by Acts 2009, 81st Leg., ch. 680, § 1, eff. Jan. 1, 2014.

### § 255.002. Certain Personal Property Excluded from Devise of Real Property

A devise of real property does not include any personal property located on, or associated with, the real property or any contents of personal property located on the real property unless the will directs that the personal property or contents are included in the devise.

Added by Acts 2009, 81st Leg., ch. 680, § 1, eff. Jan. 1, 2014.

### § 255.003. Contents Excluded from Legacy of Personal Property

A legacy of personal property does not include any contents of the property unless the will directs that the contents are included in the legacy.

Added by Acts 2009, 81st Leg., ch. 680, § 1, eff. Jan. 1, 2014.

## SUBCHAPTER B. SUCCESSION BY PRETERMITTED CHILD

### § 255.051. Definition

In this subchapter, "pretermitted child" means a testator's child who is born or adopted:

(1) during the testator's lifetime or after the testator's death; and

(2) after the execution of the testator's will.

Added by Acts 2009, 81st Leg., ch. 680, § 1, eff. Jan. 1, 2014.

### § 255.052. Applicability and Construction

(a) Sections 255.053 and 255.054 apply only to a pretermitted child who is not:

(1) mentioned in the testator's will;

(2) provided for in the testator's will; or

(3) otherwise provided for by the testator.

(b) For purposes of this subchapter, a child is provided for or a provision is made for a child if a disposition of property to or for the benefit of the pretermitted child, whether vested or contingent, is made:

(1) in the testator's will, including a devise to a trustee under Section 254.001; or

(2) outside the testator's will and is intended to take effect at the testator's death.

Added by Acts 2009, 81st Leg., ch. 680, § 1, eff. Jan. 1, 2014.

### § 255.053. Succession by Pretermitted Child If Testator Has Living Child at Will's Execution

(a) If no provision is made in the testator's last will for any child of the testator who is living when the testator executes the will, a pretermitted child succeeds to the portion of the testator's separate and community estate, other than any portion of the estate devised to the pretermitted child's other parent, to which the pretermitted child would have been entitled under Section 201.001 if the testator had died intestate without a surviving spouse, except as limited by Section 255.056.

(b) If a provision, whether vested or contingent, is made in the testator's last will for one or more children of the testator who are living when the testator executes the will, a pretermitted child is entitled only to a portion of the disposition made to children under the will that is equal to the portion the child would have received if the testator had:

(1) included all of the testator's pretermitted children with the children on whom benefits were conferred under the will; and

(2) given an equal share of those benefits to each child.

(c) To the extent feasible, the interest in the testator's estate to which the pretermitted child is entitled under Subsection (b) must be of the same character, whether an equitable or legal life estate or in fee, as the interest that the testator conferred on the testator's children under the will.

Added by Acts 2009, 81st Leg., ch. 680, § 1, eff. Jan. 1, 2014. Amended by Acts 2011, 82nd Leg., ch. 1338 (S.B. 1198), § 2.27, eff. Jan. 1, 2014.

### § 255.054. Succession by Pretermitted Child If Testator Has No Living Child at Will's Execution

If a testator has no child living when the testator executes the testator's last will, a pretermitted child succeeds to the portion of the testator's separate and community estate, other than any portion of the estate devised to the pretermitted child's other parent, to which the pretermitted child would have been entitled under Section 201.001 if the testator had died intestate without a surviving spouse, except as limited by Section 255.056.

Added by Acts 2009, 81st Leg., ch. 680, § 1, eff. Jan. 1, 2014. Amended by Acts 2011, 82nd Leg., ch. 1338 (S.B. 1198), § 2.28, eff. Jan. 1, 2014.

### § 255.055. Ratable Recovery by Pretermitted Child from Portions Passing to Other Beneficiaries

(a) A pretermitted child may recover the share of the testator's estate to which the child is entitled from the testator's other children under Section 255.053(b) or from the testamentary beneficiaries under Sections 255.053(a) and 255.054, other than the pretermitted child's other parent, ratably, out of the portions of the estate passing to those persons under the will.

(b) In abating the interests of the beneficiaries described by Subsection (a), the character of the testamentary plan adopted by the testator must be preserved to the maximum extent possible.

Added by Acts 2009, 81st Leg., ch. 680, § 1, eff. Jan. 1, 2014.

### § 255.056. Limitation on Reduction of Estate Passing to Surviving Spouse

If a pretermitted child's other parent is not the surviving spouse of the testator, the portion of the testator's estate to which the pretermitted child is entitled under Section 255.053(a) or 255.054 may not reduce the portion of the testator's estate passing to the testator's surviving spouse by more than one-half.

Added by Acts 2011, 82nd Leg., ch. 1338 (S.B. 1198), § 2.29, eff. Jan. 1, 2014.

## SUBCHAPTER C. LIFETIME GIFTS AS SATISFACTION OF DEVISE

### § 255.101. Certain Lifetime Gifts Considered Satisfaction of Devise

Property that a testator gives to a person during the testator's lifetime is considered a satisfaction, either wholly or partly, of a devise to the person if:

(1) the testator's will provides for deduction of the lifetime gift from the devise;

(2) the testator declares in a contemporaneous writing that the lifetime gift is to be deducted from, or is in satisfaction of, the devise; or

(3) the devisee acknowledges in writing that the lifetime gift is in satisfaction of the devise.

Added by Acts 2009, 81st Leg., ch. 680, § 1, eff. Jan. 1, 2014.

### § 255.102. Valuation of Property

Property given in partial satisfaction of a devise shall be valued as of the earlier of:

(1) the date the devisee acquires possession of or enjoys the property; or

(2) the date of the testator's death.

Added by Acts 2009, 81st Leg., ch. 680, § 1, eff. Jan. 1, 2014.

## SUBCHAPTER D.   FAILURE OF DEVISE; DISPOSITION OF PROPERTY TO DEVISEE WHO PREDECEASES TESTATOR

### § 255.151.   Applicability of Subchapter

This subchapter applies unless the testator's last will and testament provides otherwise. For example, a devise in the testator's will stating "to my surviving children" or "to such of my children as shall survive me" prevents the application of Sections 255.153 and 255.154.

Added by Acts 2009, 81st Leg., ch. 680, § 1, eff. Jan. 1, 2014.

### § 255.152.   Failure of Devise; Effect on Residuary Estate

(a) Except as provided by Sections 255.153 and 255.154, if a devise, other than a residuary devise, fails for any reason, the devise becomes a part of the residuary estate.

(b) Except as provided by Sections 255.153 and 255.154, if the residuary estate is devised to two or more persons and the share of one of the residuary devisees fails for any reason, that residuary devisee's share passes to the other residuary devisees, in proportion to the residuary devisee's interest in the residuary estate.

(c) Except as provided by Sections 255.153 and 255.154, the residuary estate passes as if the testator had died intestate if all residuary devisees:

(1) are deceased at the time the testator's will is executed;

(2) fail to survive the testator; or

(3) are treated as if the residuary devisees predeceased the testator.

Added by Acts 2009, 81st Leg., ch. 680, § 1, eff. Jan. 1, 2014.

### § 255.153.   Disposition of Property to Certain Devisees Who Predecease Testator

(a) If a devisee who is a descendant of the testator or a descendant of a testator's parent is deceased at the time the will is executed, fails to survive the testator, or is treated as if the devisee predeceased the testator by Chapter 121 or otherwise, the descendants of the devisee who survived the testator by 120 hours take the devised property in place of the devisee.

(b) Devised property to which Subsection (a) applies shall be divided into the number of shares equal to the total number of surviving descendants in the nearest degree of kinship to the devisee and deceased persons in the same degree of kinship to the devisee whose descendants survived the testator. Each surviving descendant in the nearest degree of kinship to the devisee receives one share, and the share of each deceased person in the same degree of kinship to the devisee whose descendants survived the testator is divided among the descendants by representation.

Added by Acts 2009, 81st Leg., ch. 680, § 1, eff. Jan. 1, 2014.

### § 255.154.   Devisee Under Class Gift

For purposes of this subchapter, a person who would have been a devisee under a class gift if the person had survived the testator is treated as a devisee unless the person died before the date the will was executed.

Added by Acts 2009, 81st Leg., ch. 680, § 1, eff. Jan. 1, 2014.

## SUBCHAPTER E.   [BLANK]

## SUBCHAPTER F.   DEVISE OF SECURITIES

### § 255.251.   Definitions

In this subchapter:

(1) "Securities" has the meaning assigned by Section 4, The Securities Act (Article 581–4, Vernon's Texas Civil Statutes).

(2) "Stock" means securities.

Added by Acts 2009, 81st Leg., ch. 680, § 1, eff. Jan. 1, 2014.

### § 255.252.   Increase in Securities; Accessions

Unless the will of a testator clearly provides otherwise, a devise of securities that are owned by the testator on the date the will is executed includes the following additional securities subsequently acquired by the testator as a result of the testator's ownership of the devised securities:

(1) securities of the same organization acquired because of an action initiated by the organization or any successor, related, or acquiring organization, including stock splits, stock dividends, and new issues of stock acquired in a reorganization, redemption, or exchange, other than securities acquired through the exercise of purchase options or through a plan of reinvestment; and

(2) securities of another organization acquired as a result of a merger, consolidation, reorganization, or other distribution by the organization or any

successor, related, or acquiring organization, including stock splits, stock dividends, and new issues of stock acquired in a reorganization, redemption, or exchange, other than securities acquired through the exercise of purchase options or through a plan of reinvestment.

Added by Acts 2009, 81st Leg., ch. 680, § 1, eff. Jan. 1, 2014.

### § 255.253.  Cash Distribution Not Included in Devise

Unless the will of a testator clearly provides otherwise, a devise of securities does not include a cash distribution relating to the securities that accrues before the testator's death, regardless of whether the distribution is paid before the testator's death.

Added by Acts 2009, 81st Leg., ch. 680, § 1, eff. Jan. 1, 2014.

## SUBCHAPTER G.  EXONERATION OF DEBTS SECURED BY SPECIFIC DEVISES

### § 255.301.  No Right to Exoneration of Debts

Except as provided by Section 255.302, a specific devise passes to the devisee subject to each debt secured by the property that exists on the date of the testator's death, and the devisee is not entitled to exoneration from the testator's estate for payment of the debt.

Added by Acts 2009, 81st Leg., ch. 680, § 1, eff. Jan. 1, 2014.

### § 255.302.  Exception

A specific devise does not pass to the devisee subject to a debt described by Section 255.301 if the will in which the devise is made specifically states that the devise passes without being subject to the debt.  A general provision in the will stating that debts are to be paid is not a specific statement for purposes of this section.

Added by Acts 2009, 81st Leg., ch. 680, § 1, eff. Jan. 1, 2014.

### § 255.303.  Rights of Certain Creditors and Other Persons

(a) Section 255.301 does not affect the rights of creditors provided under this title or the rights of other persons or entities provided under Chapters 102 and 353.

(b) A debt described by Section 255.301 that a creditor elects to have allowed and approved as a matured secured claim shall be paid in accordance with Sections 355.153(b), (c), (d), and (e).

Added by Acts 2009, 81st Leg., ch. 680, § 1, eff. Jan. 1, 2014.

## SUBCHAPTER H.  EXERCISE OF POWER OF APPOINTMENT THROUGH WILL

### § 255.351.  Exercise of Power of Appointment Through Will

A testator may not exercise a power of appointment through a residuary clause in the testator's will or through a will providing for general disposition of all of the testator's property unless:

(1) the testator makes a specific reference to the power in the will;  or

(2) there is some other indication in writing that the testator intended to include the property subject to the power in the will.

Added by Acts 2009, 81st Leg., ch. 680, § 1, eff. Jan. 1, 2014.

## CHAPTER 256.  PROBATE OF WILLS GENERALLY

### SUBCHAPTER A.  EFFECTIVENESS OF WILL; PERIOD FOR PROBATE

SUBCHAPTER E.  ADMISSION OF WILL TO, AND
PROCEDURES FOLLOWING, PROBATE

SUBCHAPTER A.  EFFECTIVENESS OF
WILL; PERIOD FOR PROBATE

### § 256.001.  Will Not Effective Until Probated

Except as provided by Subtitle K with respect to foreign wills, a will is not effective to prove title to, or the right to possession of, any property disposed of by the will until the will is admitted to probate.

Added by Acts 2009, 81st Leg., ch. 680, § 1, eff. Jan. 1, 2014.

### § 256.002.  Probate Before Death Void

The probate of a will of a living person is void.

Added by Acts 2009, 81st Leg., ch. 680, § 1, eff. Jan. 1, 2014.

### § 256.003.  Period for Admitting Will to Probate; Protection for Certain Purchasers

(a) A will may not be admitted to probate after the fourth anniversary of the testator's death unless it is shown by proof that the applicant for the probate of the will was not in default in failing to present the will for probate on or before the fourth anniversary of the testator's death.

(b) Letters testamentary may not be issued if a will is admitted to probate after the fourth anniversary of the testator's death.

(c) A person who for value, in good faith, and without knowledge of the existence of a will purchases property from a decedent's heirs after the fourth anniversary of the decedent's death shall be held to have good title to the interest that the heir or heirs would have had in the absence of a will, as against the claim of any devisee under any will that is subsequently offered for probate.

Added by Acts 2009, 81st Leg., ch. 680, § 1, eff. Jan. 1, 2014.

SUBCHAPTER B.  APPLICATION
REQUIREMENTS

### § 256.051.  Eligible Applicants for Probate of Will

(a) An executor named in a will or an interested person may file an application with the court for an order admitting a will to probate, whether the will is:

(1) written or unwritten;

(2) in the applicant's possession or not;

(3) lost;

(4) destroyed; or

(5) outside of this state.

(b) An application for the probate of a will may be combined with an application for the appointment of an executor or administrator.  A person interested in either the probate or the appointment may apply for both.

Added by Acts 2009, 81st Leg., ch. 680, § 1, eff. Jan. 1, 2014.

### § 256.052.  Contents of Application for Probate of Will

(a) An application for the probate of a will must state and aver the following to the extent each is known to the applicant or can, with reasonable diligence, be ascertained by the applicant:

(1) each applicant's name and domicile;

(2) the testator's name, domicile, and, if known, age, on the date of the testator's death;

(3) the fact, time, and place of the testator's death;

(4) facts showing that the court with which the application is filed has venue;

(5) that the testator owned property, including a statement generally describing the property and the property's probable value;

(6) the date of the will;

(7) the name, state of residence, and physical address where service can be had of the executor named in the will or other person to whom the applicant desires that letters be issued;

(8) the name of each subscribing witness to the will, if any;

(9) whether one or more children born to or adopted by the testator after the testator executed the will survived the testator and, if so, the name of each of those children;

(10) whether a marriage of the testator was ever dissolved after the will was made and, if so, when and from whom;

(11) whether the state, a governmental agency of the state, or a charitable organization is named in the will as a devisee; and

(12) that the executor named in the will, the applicant, or another person to whom the applicant desires that letters be issued is not disqualified by law from accepting the letters.

(b) If an applicant does not state or aver any matter required by Subsection (a) in the application, the application must state the reason the matter is not stated and averred.

Added by Acts 2009, 81st Leg., ch. 680, § 1, eff. Jan. 1, 2014. Amended by Acts 2011, 82nd Leg., ch. 1338 (S.B. 1198), § 2.30(a), eff. Jan. 1, 2014; Acts 2013, 83rd Leg., ch. 1136 (H.B. 2912), §§ 21, 22, eff. Jan. 1, 2014.

Section 62(d) of Acts 2013, 83rd Leg., ch. 1136 (H.B. 2912) provides:

"The changes in law made by Sections 32.006, 256.052, 256.053, 256.054, 256.152(c), 256.153, 256.154, 256.155(a), 256.156, 256.203, 257.052, 257.053, 401.001(a), 401.004(d), and 401.006, Estates Code, as amended by this Act, and Section 53.107, Estates Code, as added by this Act, apply only to an action filed or other proceeding commenced on or after the effective date [Jan. 1, 2014] of this Act. An action filed or other proceeding commenced before the effective date of this Act is governed by the law in effect on the date the action was filed or the proceeding was commenced, and the former law is continued in effect for that purpose."

### § 256.053. Filing of Will with Application for Probate Generally Required

(a) An applicant for the probate of a will shall file the will with the application if the will is in the applicant's control.

(b) A will filed under Subsection (a) must remain in the custody of the county clerk unless removed from the clerk's custody by a court order.

Added by Acts 2009, 81st Leg., ch. 680, § 1, eff. Jan. 1, 2014. Amended by Acts 2013, 83rd Leg., ch. 1136 (H.B. 2912), §§ 23, 24, eff. Jan. 1, 2014.

Section 62(d) of Acts 2013, 83rd Leg., ch. 1136 (H.B. 2912) provides:

"The changes in law made by Sections 32.006, 256.052, 256.053, 256.054, 256.152(c), 256.153, 256.154, 256.155(a), 256.156, 256.203, 257.052, 257.053, 401.001(a), 401.004(d), and 401.006, Estates Code, as amended by this Act, and Section 53.107, Estates Code, as added by this Act, apply only to an action filed or other proceeding commenced on or after the effective date [Jan. 1, 2014] of this Act. An action filed or other proceeding commenced before the effective date of this Act is governed by the law in effect on the date the action was filed or the proceeding was commenced, and the former law is continued in effect for that purpose."

### § 256.054. Additional Application Requirements When No Will Is Produced

In addition to the requirements for an application under Section 256.052, if an applicant for the probate of a will cannot produce the will in court, the application must state:

(1) the reason the will cannot be produced;

(2) the contents of the will, as far as known; and

(3) the name, age, marital status, and address, if known, and the relationship to the testator, if any, of:

(A) each devisee;

(B) each person who would inherit as an heir of the testator in the absence of a valid will; and

(C) in the case of partial intestacy, each heir of the testator.

Added by Acts 2009, 81st Leg., ch. 680, § 1, eff. Jan. 1, 2014. Amended by Acts 2013, 83rd Leg., ch. 1136 (H.B. 2912), § 25, eff. Jan. 1, 2014.

Section 62(d) of Acts 2013, 83rd Leg., ch. 1136 (H.B. 2912) provides:

"The changes in law made by Sections 32.006, 256.052, 256.053, 256.054, 256.152(c), 256.153, 256.154, 256.155(a), 256.156, 256.203, 257.052, 257.053, 401.001(a), 401.004(d), and 401.006, Estates Code, as amended by this Act, and Section 53.107, Estates Code, as added by this Act, apply only to an action filed or other proceeding commenced on or after the effective date [Jan. 1, 2014] of this Act. An action filed or other proceeding commenced before the effective date of this Act is governed by the law in effect on the date the action was filed or the proceeding was commenced, and the former law is continued in effect for that purpose."

## SUBCHAPTER C. PROCEDURES FOR SECOND APPLICATION

### § 256.101. Procedure on Filing of Second Application When Original Application Has Not Been Heard

(a) If, after an application for the probate of a decedent's will or the appointment of a personal representative for the decedent's estate has been filed but before the application is heard, an application is filed for the probate of a will of the same decedent that has not previously been presented for probate, the court shall:

(1) hear both applications together; and

(2) determine:

(A) if both applications are for the probate of a will, which will should be admitted to probate, if either, or whether the decedent died intestate; or

(B) if only one application is for the probate of a will, whether the will should be admitted to probate or whether the decedent died intestate.

(b) The court may not sever or bifurcate the proceeding on the applications described in Subsection (a).

Added by Acts 2009, 81st Leg., ch. 680, § 1, eff. Jan. 1, 2014. Amended by Acts 2011, 82nd Leg., ch. 1338 (S.B. 1198), § 2.31, eff. Jan. 1, 2014.

### § 256.102. Procedure on Filing of Second Application for Probate After First Will Has Been Admitted

If, after a decedent's will has been admitted to probate, an application is filed for the probate of a will of the same decedent that has not previously been presented for probate, the court shall determine:

(1) whether the former probate should be set aside; and

(2) if the former probate is to be set aside, whether:

(A) the other will should be admitted to probate; or

(B) the decedent died intestate.

Added by Acts 2009, 81st Leg., ch. 680, § 1, eff. Jan. 1, 2014.

### § 256.103.  Procedure When Application for Probate Is Filed After Letters of Administration Have Been Granted

(a) A lawful will of a decedent that is discovered after letters of administration have been granted on the decedent's estate may be proved in the manner provided for the proof of wills.

(b) The court shall allow an executor named in a will described by Subsection (a) who is not disqualified to qualify and accept as executor.  The court shall revoke the previously granted letters of administration.

(c) If an executor is not named in a will described by Subsection (a), or if the executor named is disqualified or dead, renounces the executorship, fails or is unable to accept and qualify before the 21st day after the date of the probate of the will, or fails to present the will for probate before the 31st day after the discovery of the will, the court, as in other cases, shall grant an administration with the will annexed of the testator's estate.

(d) An act performed by the first administrator before the executor described by Subsection (b) or the administrator with the will annexed described by Subsection (c) qualifies is as valid as if no will had been discovered.

Added by Acts 2009, 81st Leg., ch. 680, § 1, eff. Jan. 1, 2014.

### SUBCHAPTER D.  REQUIRED PROOF FOR PROBATE OF WILL

### § 256.151.  General Proof Requirements

An applicant for the probate of a will must prove to the court's satisfaction that:

(1) the testator is dead;

(2) four years have not elapsed since the date of the testator's death and before the application;

(3) the court has jurisdiction and venue over the estate;

(4) citation has been served and returned in the manner and for the period required by this title; and

(5) the person for whom letters testamentary or of administration are sought is entitled by law to the letters and is not disqualified.

Added by Acts 2009, 81st Leg., ch. 680, § 1, eff. Jan. 1, 2014.

### § 256.152.  Additional Proof Required for Probate of Will

(a) An applicant for the probate of a will must prove the following to the court's satisfaction, in addition to the proof required by Section 256.151, to obtain the probate:

(1) the testator did not revoke the will; and

(2) if the will is not self-proved, the testator:

(A) executed the will with the formalities and solemnities and under the circumstances required by law to make the will valid; and

(B) at the time of executing the will, was of sound mind and:

(i) was 18 years of age or older;

(ii) was or had been married; or

(iii) was a member of the armed forces of the United States, an auxiliary of the armed forces of the United States, or the United States Maritime Service.

(b) A will that is self-proved as provided by Subchapter C, Chapter 251, or, if executed in another state or a foreign country, is self-proved in accordance with the laws of the state or foreign country of the testator's domicile at the time of the execution is not required to have any additional proof that the will was executed with the formalities and solemnities and under the circumstances required to make the will valid.

(c) As an alternative to Subsection (b), a will executed in another state or a foreign country is considered self-proved without further evidence of the law of the other state or foreign country if the will, or an affidavit of the testator and attesting witnesses attached or annexed to the will, provides that:

(1) the testator declared that the testator signed the instrument as the testator's will, the testator signed it willingly or willingly directed another to sign for the testator, the testator executed the will as the testator's free and voluntary act for the purposes expressed in the instrument, the testator is of sound mind and under no constraint or undue influence, and the testator is eighteen years of age or over or, if under that age, was or had been lawfully married, or was then a member of the armed forces of the United States, an auxiliary of

the armed forces of the United States, or the United States Maritime Service; and

(2) the witnesses declared that the testator signed the instrument as the testator's will, the testator signed it willingly or willingly directed another to sign for the testator, each of the witnesses, in the presence and hearing of the testator, signed the will as witness to the testator's signing, and to the best of their knowledge the testator was of sound mind and under no constraint or undue influence, and the testator was eighteen years of age or over or, if under that age, was or had been lawfully married, or was then a member of the armed forces of the United States, an auxiliary of the armed forces of the United States, or the United States Maritime Service.

Added by Acts 2009, 81st Leg., ch. 680, § 1, eff. Jan. 1, 2014. Amended by Acts 2011, 82nd Leg., ch. 1338 (S.B. 1198), § 2.32, eff. Jan. 1, 2014; Acts 2013, 83rd Leg., ch. 1136 (H.B. 2912), § 26, eff. Jan. 1, 2014.

Section 62(d) of Acts 2013, 83rd Leg., ch. 1136 (H.B. 2912) provides:

"The changes in law made by Sections 32.006, 256.052, 256.053, 256.054, 256.152(c), 256.153, 256.154, 256.155(a), 256.156, 256.203, 257.052, 257.053, 401.001(a), 401.004(d), and 401.006, Estates Code, as amended by this Act, and Section 53.107, Estates Code, as added by this Act, apply only to an action filed or other proceeding commenced on or after the effective date [Jan. 1, 2014] of this Act. An action filed or other proceeding commenced before the effective date of this Act is governed by the law in effect on the date the action was filed or the proceeding was commenced, and the former law is continued in effect for that purpose."

## § 256.153. Proof of Execution of Attested Will

(a) An attested will produced in court that is not self-proved as provided by this title may be proved in the manner provided by this section.

(b) A will described by Subsection (a) may be proved by the sworn testimony or affidavit of one or more of the subscribing witnesses to the will taken in open court.

(c) If all the witnesses to a will described by Subsection (a) are nonresidents of the county or the witnesses who are residents of the county are unable to attend court, the will may be proved:

(1) by the sworn testimony of one or more of the witnesses by written or oral deposition taken in accordance with Section 51.203 or the Texas Rules of Civil Procedure;

(2) if no opposition in writing to the will is filed on or before the date set for the hearing on the will, by the sworn testimony or affidavit of two witnesses taken in open court, or by deposition as provided by Subdivision (1), to the signature or the handwriting evidenced by the signature of:

(A) one or more of the attesting witnesses; or

(B) the testator, if the testator signed the will; or

(3) if it is shown under oath to the court's satisfaction that, after a diligent search was made, only one witness can be found who can make the required proof, by the sworn testimony or affidavit of that witness taken in open court, or by deposition as provided by Subdivision (1), to a signature, or the handwriting evidenced by a signature, described by Subdivision (2).

(d) If none of the witnesses to a will described by Subsection (a) are living, or if each of the witnesses is a member of the armed forces or the armed forces reserves of the United States, an auxiliary of the armed forces or armed forces reserves, or the United States Maritime Service and is beyond the court's jurisdiction, the will may be proved:

(1) by two witnesses to the handwriting of one or both of the subscribing witnesses to the will or the testator, if the testator signed the will, by:

(A) sworn testimony or affidavit taken in open court; or

(B) written or oral deposition taken in accordance with Section 51.203 or the Texas Rules of Civil Procedure; or

(2) if it is shown under oath to the court's satisfaction that, after a diligent search was made, only one witness can be found who can make the required proof, by the sworn testimony or affidavit of that witness taken in open court, or by deposition as provided by Subdivision (1), to a signature or the handwriting described by Subdivision (1).

(e) A witness being deposed for purposes of proving the will as provided by Subsection (c) or (d) may testify by referring to a certified copy of the will, without the judge requiring the original will to be removed from the court's file and shown to the witness.

Added by Acts 2009, 81st Leg., ch. 680, § 1, eff. Jan. 1, 2014. Amended by Acts 2013, 83rd Leg., ch. 1136 (H.B. 2912), § 27, eff. Jan. 1, 2014.

Section 62(d) of Acts 2013, 83rd Leg., ch. 1136 (H.B. 2912) provides:

"The changes in law made by Sections 32.006, 256.052, 256.053, 256.054, 256.152(c), 256.153, 256.154, 256.155(a), 256.156, 256.203, 257.052, 257.053, 401.001(a), 401.004(d), and 401.006, Estates Code, as amended by this Act, and Section 53.107, Estates Code, as added by this Act, apply only to an action filed or other proceeding commenced on or after the effective date [Jan. 1, 2014] of this Act. An action filed or other proceeding commenced before the effective date of this Act is governed by the law in effect on the date the action was filed or the proceeding was commenced, and the former law is continued in effect for that purpose."

## § 256.154. Proof of Execution of Holographic Will

(a) A will wholly in the handwriting of the testator that is not self-proved as provided by this title may be proved by two witnesses to the testator's handwriting. The evidence may be by:

(1) sworn testimony or affidavit taken in open court; or

(2) if the witnesses are nonresidents of the county or are residents who are unable to attend court, written or oral deposition taken in accordance with Section 51.203 or the Texas Rules of Civil Procedure.

(b) A witness being deposed for purposes of proving the will as provided by Subsection (a)(2) may testify by referring to a certified copy of the will, without the judge requiring the original will to be removed from the court's file and shown to the witness.

Added by Acts 2009, 81st Leg., ch. 680, § 1, eff. Jan. 1, 2014. Amended by Acts 2013, 83rd Leg., ch. 1136 (H.B. 2912), § 28, eff. Jan. 1, 2014.

Section 62(d) of Acts 2013, 83rd Leg., ch. 1136 (H.B. 2912) provides:

"The changes in law made by Sections 32.006, 256.052, 256.053, 256.054, 256.152(c), 256.153, 256.154, 256.155(a), 256.156, 256.203, 257.052, 257.053, 401.001(a), 401.004(d), and 401.006, Estates Code, as amended by this Act, and Section 53.107, Estates Code, as added by this Act, apply only to an action filed or other proceeding commenced on or after the effective date [Jan. 1, 2014] of this Act. An action filed or other proceeding commenced before the effective date of this Act is governed by the law in effect on the date the action was filed or the proceeding was commenced, and the former law is continued in effect for that purpose."

## § 256.155. Procedures for Depositions When No Contest Is Filed

(a) This section, rather than Sections 256.153(c) and (d) and 256.154 regarding the taking of depositions, applies if no contest has been filed with respect to an application for the probate of a will.

(b) Depositions for the purpose of establishing a will may be taken in the manner provided by Section 51.203 for the taking of depositions when there is no opposing party or attorney of record on whom notice and copies of interrogatories may be served.

Added by Acts 2009, 81st Leg., ch. 680, § 1, eff. Jan. 1, 2014. Amended by Acts 2013, 83rd Leg., ch. 1136 (H.B. 2912), § 29, eff. Jan. 1, 2014.

Section 62(d) of Acts 2013, 83rd Leg., ch. 1136 (H.B. 2912) provides:

"The changes in law made by Sections 32.006, 256.052, 256.053, 256.054, 256.152(c), 256.153, 256.154, 256.155(a), 256.156, 256.203, 257.052, 257.053, 401.001(a), 401.004(d), and 401.006, Estates Code, as amended by this Act, and Section 53.107, Estates Code, as added by this Act, apply only to an action filed or other proceeding commenced on or after the effective date [Jan. 1, 2014] of this Act. An action filed or other proceeding commenced before the effective date of this Act is governed by the law in effect on the date the action was filed or the proceeding was commenced, and the former law is continued in effect for that purpose."

## § 256.156. Proof of Will Not Produced in Court

(a) A will that cannot be produced in court must be proved in the same manner as provided in Section 256.153 for an attested will or Section 256.154 for a holographic will, as applicable. The same amount and character of testimony is required to prove the will not produced in court as is required to prove a will produced in court.

(b) In addition to the proof required by Subsection (a):

(1) the cause of the nonproduction of a will not produced in court must be proved, which must be sufficient to satisfy the court that the will cannot by any reasonable diligence be produced; and

(2) the contents of the will must be substantially proved by the testimony of a credible witness who has read either the original or a copy of the will, has heard the will read, or can identify a copy of the will.

Added by Acts 2009, 81st Leg., ch. 680, § 1, eff. Jan. 1, 2014. Amended by Acts 2013, 83rd Leg., ch. 1136 (H.B. 2912), § 30, eff. Jan. 1, 2014.

Section 62(d) of Acts 2013, 83rd Leg., ch. 1136 (H.B. 2912) provides:

"The changes in law made by Sections 32.006, 256.052, 256.053, 256.054, 256.152(c), 256.153, 256.154, 256.155(a), 256.156, 256.203, 257.052, 257.053, 401.001(a), 401.004(d), and 401.006, Estates Code, as amended by this Act, and Section 53.107, Estates Code, as added by this Act, apply only to an action filed or other proceeding commenced on or after the effective date [Jan. 1, 2014] of this Act. An action filed or other proceeding commenced before the effective date of this Act is governed by the law in effect on the date the action was filed or the proceeding was commenced, and the former law is continued in effect for that purpose."

## § 256.157. Testimony Regarding Probate to Be Committed to Writing

(a) Except as provided by Subsection (b), all testimony taken in open court on the hearing of an application to probate a will must be:

(1) committed to writing at the time the testimony is taken;

(2) subscribed and sworn to in open court by the witness; and

(3) filed by the clerk.

(b) In a contested case, the court, on the agreement of the parties or, if there is no agreement, on the court's own motion, may waive the requirements of Subsection (a).

Added by Acts 2009, 81st Leg., ch. 680, § 1, eff. Jan. 1, 2014.

## SUBCHAPTER E. ADMISSION OF WILL TO, AND PROCEDURES FOLLOWING, PROBATE

### § 256.201. Admission of Will to Probate

If the court is satisfied on the completion of hearing an application for the probate of a will that the will should be admitted to probate, the court shall enter an order admitting the will to probate. Certified copies of the will and the order admitting the will to probate, or of the record of the will and order, and the record of testimony, may be:

(1) recorded in other counties; and

(2) used in evidence, as the originals may be used, on the trial of the same matter in any other court when taken to that court by appeal or otherwise.

Added by Acts 2009, 81st Leg., ch. 680, § 1, eff. Jan. 1, 2014.

### § 256.202. Custody of Probated Will

An original will and the probate of the will shall be deposited in the office of the county clerk of the county in which the will was probated. The will and probate of the will shall remain in that office except during a time the will and the probate of the will are removed for inspection to another place on an order of the court where the will was probated. If that court orders the original will to be removed to another place for inspection:

(1) the person removing the will shall give a receipt for the will; and

(2) the court clerk shall make and retain a copy of the will.

Added by Acts 2009, 81st Leg., ch. 680, § 1, eff. Jan. 1, 2014.

### § 256.203. Establishing Contents of Will Not in Court's Custody

If for any reason a will is not in the court's custody, the court shall find the contents of the will by written order. Certified copies of the contents as established by the order may be:

(1) recorded in other counties; and

(2) used in evidence, as certified copies of wills in the custody of the court may be used.

Added by Acts 2009, 81st Leg., ch. 680, § 1, eff. Jan. 1, 2014. Amended by Acts 2013, 83rd Leg., ch. 1136 (H.B. 2912), § 31, eff. Jan. 1, 2014.

Section 62(d) of Acts 2013, 83rd Leg., ch. 1136 (H.B. 2912) provides:
"The changes in law made by Sections 32.006, 256.052, 256.053, 256.054, 256.152(c), 256.153, 256.154, 256.155(a), 256.156, 256.203, 257.052, 257.053, 401.001(a), 401.004(d), and 401.006, Estates Code, as amended by this Act, and Section 53.107, Estates Code, as added by this Act, apply only to an action filed or other proceeding commenced on or after the effective date [Jan. 1, 2014] of this Act. An action filed or other proceeding commenced before the effective date of this Act is governed by the law in effect on the date the action was filed or the proceeding was commenced, and the former law is continued in effect for that purpose."

### § 256.204. Period for Contest

(a) After a will is admitted to probate, an interested person may commence a suit to contest the validity thereof not later than the second anniversary of the date the will was admitted to probate, except that an interested person may commence a suit to cancel a will for forgery or other fraud not later than the second anniversary of the date the forgery or fraud was discovered.

(b) Notwithstanding Subsection (a), an incapacitated person may commence the contest under that subsection on or before the second anniversary of the date the person's disabilities are removed.

Added by Acts 2009, 81st Leg., ch. 680, § 1, eff. Jan. 1, 2014.

## CHAPTER 257. PROBATE OF WILL AS MUNIMENT OF TITLE

### SUBCHAPTER A. AUTHORIZATION

### SUBCHAPTER A. AUTHORIZATION

### § 257.001. Probate of Will as Muniment of Title Authorized

A court may admit a will to probate as a muniment of title if the court is satisfied that the will should be admitted to probate and the court:

(1) is satisfied that the testator's estate does not owe an unpaid debt, other than any debt secured by a lien on real estate; or

(2) finds for another reason that there is no necessity for administration of the estate.

Added by Acts 2009, 81st Leg., ch. 680, § 1, eff. Jan. 1, 2014.

## SUBCHAPTER B.  APPLICATION AND PROOF REQUIREMENTS

### § 257.051.  Contents of Application Generally

(a) An application for the probate of a will as a muniment of title must state and aver the following to the extent each is known to the applicant or can, with reasonable diligence, be ascertained by the applicant:

(1) each applicant's name and domicile;

(2) the testator's name, domicile, and, if known, age, on the date of the testator's death;

(3) the fact, time, and place of the testator's death;

(4) facts showing that the court with which the application is filed has venue;

(5) that the testator owned property, including a statement generally describing the property and the property's probable value;

(6) the date of the will;

(7) the name and residence of:

(A) any executor named in the will;  and

(B) each subscribing witness to the will, if any;

(8) whether one or more children born to or adopted by the testator after the testator executed the will survived the testator and, if so, the name of each of those children;

(9) that the testator's estate does not owe an unpaid debt, other than any debt secured by a lien on real estate;

(10) whether a marriage of the testator was ever dissolved after the will was made and, if so, when and from whom;  and

(11) whether the state, a governmental agency of the state, or a charitable organization is named in the will as a devisee.

(b) If an applicant does not state or aver any matter required by Subsection (a) in the application, the application must state the reason the matter is not stated and averred.

Added by Acts 2009, 81st Leg., ch. 680, § 1, eff. Jan. 1, 2014. Amended by Acts 2011, 82nd Leg., ch. 1338 (S.B. 1198), § 2.33(a), eff. Jan. 1, 2014.

### § 257.052.  Filing of Will with Application Generally Required

(a) An applicant for the probate of a will as a muniment of title shall file the will with the application if the will is in the applicant's control.

(b) A will filed under Subsection (a) must remain in the custody of the county clerk unless removed from the clerk's custody by court order.

Added by Acts 2009, 81st Leg., ch. 680, § 1, eff. Jan. 1, 2014. Amended by Acts 2013, 83rd Leg., ch. 1136 (H.B. 2912), § 32, eff. Jan. 1, 2014.

Section 62(d) of Acts 2013, 83rd Leg., ch. 1136 (H.B. 2912) provides:

"The changes in law made by Sections 32.006, 256.052, 256.053, 256.054, 256.152(c), 256.153, 256.154, 256.155(a), 256.156, 256.203, 257.052, 257.053, 401.001(a), 401.004(d), and 401.006, Estates Code, as amended by this Act, and Section 53.107, Estates Code, as added by this Act, apply only to an action filed or other proceeding commenced on or after the effective date [Jan. 1, 2014] of this Act.  An action filed or other proceeding commenced before the effective date of this Act is governed by the law in effect on the date the action was filed or the proceeding was commenced, and the former law is continued in effect for that purpose."

### § 257.053.  Additional Application Requirements When No Will Is Produced

In addition to the requirements for an application under Section 257.051, if an applicant for the probate of a will as a muniment of title cannot produce the will in court, the application must state:

(1) the reason the will cannot be produced;

(2) the contents of the will, to the extent known;  and

(3) the name, age, marital status, and address, if known, and the relationship to the testator, if any, of:

(A) each devisee;

(B) each person who would inherit as an heir of the testator in the absence of a valid will;  and

(C) in the case of partial intestacy, each heir of the testator.

Added by Acts 2009, 81st Leg., ch. 680, § 1, eff. Jan. 1, 2014. Amended by Acts 2013, 83rd Leg., ch. 1136 (H.B. 2912), § 33, eff. Jan. 1, 2014.

Section 62(d) of Acts 2013, 83rd Leg., ch. 1136 (H.B. 2912) provides:

"The changes in law made by Sections 32.006, 256.052, 256.053, 256.054, 256.152(c), 256.153, 256.154, 256.155(a), 256.156, 256.203, 257.052, 257.053, 401.001(a), 401.004(d), and 401.006, Estates Code, as amended by this Act, and Section 53.107, Estates Code, as added by this Act, apply only to an action filed or other proceeding commenced on or after the effective date [Jan. 1, 2014] of this Act.  An action filed or other proceeding commenced before the effective date of this Act is governed by the law in effect on the date the action was filed or the proceeding was commenced, and the former law is continued in effect for that purpose."

## § 257.054. Proof Required

An applicant for the probate of a will as a muniment of title must prove to the court's satisfaction that:

(1) the testator is dead;

(2) four years have not elapsed since the date of the testator's death and before the application;

(3) the court has jurisdiction and venue over the estate;

(4) citation has been served and returned in the manner and for the period required by this title;

(5) the testator's estate does not owe an unpaid debt, other than any debt secured by a lien on real estate;

(6) the testator did not revoke the will; and

(7) if the will is not self-proved in the manner provided by this title, the testator:

(A) executed the will with the formalities and solemnities and under the circumstances required by law to make the will valid; and

(B) at the time of executing the will was of sound mind and:

(i) was 18 years of age or older;

(ii) was or had been married; or

(iii) was a member of the armed forces of the United States, an auxiliary of the armed forces of the United States, or the United States Maritime Service.

Added by Acts 2009, 81st Leg., ch. 680, § 1, eff. Jan. 1, 2014.

### SUBCHAPTER C. ORDER ADMITTING WILL; REPORT

## § 257.101. Declaratory Judgment Construing Will

(a) On application and notice as provided by Chapter 37, Civil Practice and Remedies Code, the court may hear evidence and include in an order probating a will as a muniment of title a declaratory judgment:

(1) construing the will, if a question of construction of the will exists; or

(2) determining those persons who are entitled to receive property under the will and the persons' shares or interests in the estate, if a person who is entitled to property under the provisions of the will cannot be ascertained solely by reference to the will.

(b) A declaratory judgment under this section is conclusive in any suit between a person omitted from the judgment and a bona fide purchaser for value who purchased property after entry of the judgment without actual notice of the claim of the omitted person to an interest in the estate.

(c) A person who delivered the testator's property to a person declared to be entitled to the property under the declaratory judgment under this section or engaged in any other transaction with the person in good faith after entry of the judgment is not liable to any person for actions taken in reliance on the judgment.

Added by Acts 2009, 81st Leg., ch. 680, § 1, eff. Jan. 1, 2014.

## § 257.102. Authority of Certain Persons Acting in Accordance with Order

(a) An order admitting a will to probate as a muniment of title constitutes sufficient legal authority for each person who owes money to the testator's estate, has custody of property, acts as registrar or transfer agent of any evidence of interest, indebtedness, property, or right belonging to the estate, or purchases from or otherwise deals with the estate, to pay or transfer without administration the applicable asset without liability to a person described in the will as entitled to receive the asset.

(b) A person who is entitled to property under the provisions of a will admitted to probate as a muniment of title is entitled to deal with and treat the property in the same manner as if the record of title to the property was vested in the person's name.

Added by Acts 2009, 81st Leg., ch. 680, § 1, eff. Jan. 1, 2014.

## § 257.103. Report by Applicant After Probate

(a) Except as provided by Subsection (b), not later than the 180th day after the date a will is admitted to probate as a muniment of title, the applicant for the probate of the will shall file with the court clerk a sworn affidavit stating specifically the terms of the will that have been fulfilled and the terms that have not been fulfilled.

(b) The court may:

(1) waive the requirement under Subsection (a); or

(2) extend the time for filing the affidavit under Subsection (a).

(c) The failure of an applicant for probate of a will to file the affidavit required by Subsection (a) does not affect title to property passing under the terms of the will.

Added by Acts 2009, 81st Leg., ch. 680, § 1, eff. Jan. 1, 2014.

# CHAPTER 258. CITATIONS AND NOTICES RELATING TO PROBATE OF WILL

## SUBCHAPTER A. CITATIONS WITH RESPECT TO APPLICATIONS FOR PROBATE OF WILL

## SUBCHAPTER A. CITATIONS WITH RESPECT TO APPLICATIONS FOR PROBATE OF WILL

### § 258.001. Citation on Application for Probate of Will Produced in Court

(a) On the filing with the clerk of an application for the probate of a written will produced in court, the clerk shall issue a citation to all parties interested in the estate.

(b) The citation required by Subsection (a) shall be served by posting and must state:

(1) that the application has been filed;

(2) the nature of the application;

(3) the testator's name;

(4) the applicant's name;

(5) the time when the court will act on the application; and

(6) that any person interested in the estate may appear at the time stated in the citation to contest the application.

Added by Acts 2009, 81st Leg., ch. 680, § 1, eff. Jan. 1, 2014.

### § 258.002. Citation on Application for Probate of Will Not Produced in Court

(a) On the filing of an application for the probate of a written will that cannot be produced in court, the clerk shall issue a citation to all parties interested in the estate. The citation must:

(1) contain substantially the statements made in the application for probate;

(2) identify the court that will act on the application; and

(3) state the time and place of the court's action on the application.

(b) The citation required by Subsection (a) shall be served on the testator's heirs by personal service if the heirs are residents of this state and their addresses are known.

(c) Service of the citation required by Subsection (a) may be made by publication if:

(1) the heirs are not residents of this state;

(2) the names or addresses of the heirs are unknown; or

(3) the heirs are transient persons.

Added by Acts 2009, 81st Leg., ch. 680, § 1, eff. Jan. 1, 2014.

### § 258.003. Court Action Prohibited Before Service of Citation

A court may not act on an application for the probate of a will until service of citation has been made in the manner provided by this subchapter.

Added by Acts 2009, 81st Leg., ch. 680, § 1, eff. Jan. 1, 2014.

## SUBCHAPTER B. NOTICES WITH RESPECT TO APPLICATION TO PROBATE WILL AFTER THE PERIOD FOR PROBATE

### § 258.051. Notice to Heirs

(a) Except as provided by Subsection (c), an applicant for the probate of a will under Section 256.003(a) must give notice by service of process to each of the testator's heirs whose address can be ascertained by the applicant with reasonable diligence.

(b) The notice required by Subsection (a) must:

(1) contain a statement that:

(A) the testator's property will pass to the testator's heirs if the will is not admitted to probate; and

(B) the person offering the testator's will for probate may not be in default for failing to present the will for probate during the four-year period immediately following the testator's death; and

(2) be given before the probate of the testator's will.

(c) Notice otherwise required by Subsection (a) is not required to be given to an heir who has delivered to the court an affidavit signed by the heir that:

(1) contains the statement described by Subsection (b)(1); and

(2) states that the heir does not object to the offer of the testator's will for probate.

Added by Acts 2009, 81st Leg., ch. 680, § 1, eff. Jan. 1, 2014.

### § 258.052. Appointment of Attorney ad Litem

If an applicant described by Section 258.051(a) cannot, with reasonable diligence, ascertain the address of any of the testator's heirs, the court shall appoint an attorney ad litem to protect the interests of the testator's unknown heirs after an application for the probate of a will is made under Section 256.003(a).

Added by Acts 2009, 81st Leg., ch. 680, § 1, eff. Jan. 1, 2014.

### § 258.053. Previously Probated Will

With respect to an application under Section 256.003(a) for the probate of a will of a testator who has had another will admitted to probate, this subchapter applies so as to require notice to the beneficiaries of the testator's probated will instead of to the testator's heirs.

Added by Acts 2009, 81st Leg., ch. 680, § 1, eff. Jan. 1, 2014.

## SUBCHAPTER C. SERVICE BY PUBLICATION OR OTHER SUBSTITUTED SERVICE

### § 258.101. Service by Publication or Other Substituted Service

Notwithstanding any other provision of this chapter, if an attempt to make service under this chapter is unsuccessful, service may be made in the manner provided by Rule 109 or 109a, Texas Rules of Civil Procedure, for the service of a citation on a party by publication or other substituted service.

Added by Acts 2009, 81st Leg., ch. 680, § 1, eff. Jan. 1, 2014.

## SUBTITLE G. INITIAL APPOINTMENT OF PERSONAL REPRESENTATIVE AND OPENING OF ADMINISTRATION

## CHAPTER 301. APPLICATION FOR LETTERS TESTAMENTARY OR OF ADMINISTRATION

### SUBCHAPTER A. PERIOD FOR APPLICATION FOR LETTERS

### SUBCHAPTER B. APPLICATION REQUIREMENTS

### SUBCHAPTER C. OPPOSITION TO CERTAIN APPLICATIONS

### SUBCHAPTER D. REQUIRED PROOF FOR ISSUANCE OF LETTERS

### SUBCHAPTER E. PREVENTION OF ADMINISTRATION

## SUBCHAPTER A. PERIOD FOR APPLICATION FOR LETTERS

### § 301.001. Administration Before Death Void

The administration of an estate of a living person is void.

Added by Acts 2009, 81st Leg., ch. 680, § 1, eff. Jan. 1, 2014.

### § 301.002. Period for Filing Application for Letters Testamentary or of Administration

(a) Except as provided by Subsection (b), an application for the grant of letters testamentary or of administration of an estate must be filed not later than the fourth anniversary of the decedent's death.

(b) This section does not apply if administration is necessary to receive or recover property due a decedent's estate.

Added by Acts 2009, 81st Leg., ch. 680, § 1, eff. Jan. 1, 2014.

## SUBCHAPTER B. APPLICATION REQUIREMENTS

### § 301.051. Eligible Applicants for Letters

An executor named in a will or an interested person may file an application with the court for:

(1) the appointment of the executor named in the will; or

(2) the appointment of an administrator, if:

(A) there is a will, but:

(i) no executor is named in the will; or

(ii) the executor named in the will is disqualified, refuses to serve, is dead, or resigns; or

(B) there is no will.

Added by Acts 2009, 81st Leg., ch. 680, § 1, eff. Jan. 1, 2014.

### § 301.052. Contents of Application for Letters of Administration

An application for letters of administration when no will is alleged to exist must state:

(1) the applicant's name, domicile, and, if any, relationship to the decedent;

(2) the decedent's name and that the decedent died intestate;

(3) the fact, time, and place of the decedent's death;

(4) facts necessary to show that the court with which the application is filed has venue;

(5) whether the decedent owned property and, if so, include a statement of the property's probable value;

(6) the name, age, marital status, and address, if known, and the relationship to the decedent of each of the decedent's heirs;

(7) if known by the applicant at the time the applicant files the application, whether one or more children were born to or adopted by the decedent and, if so, the name, birth date, and place of birth of each child;

(8) if known by the applicant at the time the applicant files the application, whether the decedent was ever divorced and, if so, when and from whom;

(9) that a necessity exists for administration of the decedent's estate and an allegation of the facts that show that necessity; and

(10) that the applicant is not disqualified by law from acting as administrator.

Added by Acts 2009, 81st Leg., ch. 680, § 1, eff. Jan. 1, 2014.

### SUBCHAPTER C. OPPOSITION TO CERTAIN APPLICATIONS

### § 301.101. Opposition to Application for Letters of Administration

An interested person may, at any time before an application for letters of administration is granted, file an opposition to the application in writing and may apply for the grant of letters to the interested person or any other person. On the trial, the court, considering the applicable provisions of this code, shall grant letters to the person that seems best entitled to the letters without notice other than the notice given on the original application.

Added by Acts 2009, 81st Leg., ch. 680, § 1, eff. Jan. 1, 2014.

### SUBCHAPTER D. REQUIRED PROOF FOR ISSUANCE OF LETTERS

### § 301.151. General Proof Requirements

An applicant for the issuance of letters testamentary or of administration of an estate must prove to the court's satisfaction that:

(1) the person whose estate is the subject of the application is dead;

(2) four years have not elapsed since the date of the decedent's death and before the application;

(3) the court has jurisdiction and venue over the estate;

(4) citation has been served and returned in the manner and for the period required by this title; and

(5) the person for whom letters testamentary or of administration are sought is entitled by law to the letters and is not disqualified.

Added by Acts 2009, 81st Leg., ch. 680, § 1, eff. Jan. 1, 2014.

### § 301.152. Additional Proof Required for Letters Testamentary

If letters testamentary are to be granted, it must appear to the court that:

(1) the proof required for the probate of the will has been made; and

(2) the person to whom the letters are to be granted is named as executor in the will.

Added by Acts 2009, 81st Leg., ch. 680, § 1, eff. Jan. 1, 2014.

### § 301.153. Additional Proof Required for Letters of Administration; Effect of Finding No Necessity for Administration Exists

(a) If letters of administration are to be granted, the applicant for the letters must prove to the court's satisfaction that a necessity for an administration of the estate exists.

(b) If an application is filed for letters of administration but the court finds that no necessity for an administration of the estate exists, the court shall recite in the court's order refusing the application that no necessity for an administration exists.

(c) A court order containing a recital that no necessity for an administration of the estate exists constitutes sufficient legal authority for each person who owes money, has custody of property, or acts as registrar or transfer agent of any evidence of interest, indebtedness, property, or right belonging to the estate, and to each person purchasing or otherwise dealing with the estate, for payment or transfer to the distributees.

(d) A distributee is entitled to enforce by suit the distributee's right to payment or transfer described by Subsection (c).

Added by Acts 2009, 81st Leg., ch. 680, § 1, eff. Jan. 1, 2014.

### § 301.154. Proof Required When Letters Have Previously Been Granted

If letters testamentary or of administration have previously been granted with respect to an estate, an applicant for the granting of subsequent letters must show only that the person for whom the letters are sought is entitled by law to the letters and is not disqualified.

Added by Acts 2009, 81st Leg., ch. 680, § 1, eff. Jan. 1, 2014.

### § 301.155. Authorized Methods of Proof

A fact contained in an application for issuance of letters testamentary or of administration or any other fact required to be proved by this subchapter may be proved by the sworn testimony of a witness with personal knowledge of the fact that is:

(1) taken in open court; or

(2) if proved under oath to the satisfaction of the court that the witness is unavailable, taken by deposition on written questions in accordance with Section 51.203 or the Texas Rules of Civil Procedure.

Added by Acts 2013, 83rd Leg., ch. 1136 (H.B. 2912), § 34, eff. Jan. 1, 2014.

Section 62(e) of Acts 2013, 83rd Leg., ch. 1136 (H.B. 2912) provides:

"The changes in law made by Sections 51.203(c), 53.104, 305.002(a), 305.003, 308.054(b), 309.051(a), 309.056, 309.103(a) and (b), 355.060, 361.155(b), 362.005, 362.011, 362.013, 404.001(a), 404.003, 404.005(b) and (c), and 551.001(a), Estates Code, as amended by this Act, and Sections 253.001(c), 301.155, 305.004, 309.057, 361.155(c), 404.0035, 404.0036, and 404.0037, Estates Code, as added by this Act, apply to the administration of the estate of a decedent that is pending or commenced on or after the effective date [Jan. 1, 2014] of this Act."

## SUBCHAPTER E. PREVENTION OF ADMINISTRATION

### § 301.201. Method of Preventing Administration Requested by Creditor

(a) If a creditor files an application for letters of administration of an estate, another interested person who does not desire the administration can defeat the application by:

(1) paying the creditor's claim;

(2) proving to the court's satisfaction that the creditor's claim is fictitious, fraudulent, illegal, or barred by limitation; or

(3) executing a bond that is:

(A) payable to, and to be approved by, the judge in an amount that is twice the amount of the creditor's claim; and

(B) conditioned on the obligors paying the claim on the establishment of the claim by suit in any court in the county having jurisdiction of the amount.

(b) A bond executed and approved under Subsection (a)(3) must be filed with the county clerk.

Added by Acts 2009, 81st Leg., ch. 680, § 1, eff. Jan. 1, 2014.

### § 301.202. Suit on Bond

Any creditor for whose protection a bond is executed under Section 301.201(a)(3) may sue on the bond in the creditor's own name to recover the creditor's claim.

Added by Acts 2009, 81st Leg., ch. 680, § 1, eff. Jan. 1, 2014.

### § 301.203. Bond Secured by Lien

If a bond is executed and approved under Section 301.201(a)(3), a lien exists on all of the estate in the possession of the distributees, and those claiming under the distributees with notice of the lien, to secure the ultimate payment of the bond.

Added by Acts 2009, 81st Leg., ch. 680, § 1, eff. Jan. 1, 2014.

## CHAPTER 303. CITATIONS AND NOTICES IN GENERAL ON OPENING OF ADMINISTRATION

### § 303.001. Citation on Application for Issuance of Letters of Administration

(a) On the filing with the clerk of an application for letters of administration, the clerk shall issue a citation to all parties interested in the estate.

(b) The citation required by Subsection (a) shall be served by posting and must state:

(1) that the application has been filed;

(2) the nature of the application;

(3) the decedent's name;

(4) the applicant's name;

(5) the time when the court will act on the application; and

(6) that any person interested in the estate may appear at the time stated in the citation to contest the application.

Added by Acts 2009, 81st Leg., ch. 680, § 1, eff. Jan. 1, 2014.

### § 303.002. Court Action Prohibited Before Service of Citation

A court may not act on an application for the issuance of letters of administration until service of citation has been made in the manner provided by this chapter.

Added by Acts 2009, 81st Leg., ch. 680, § 1, eff. Jan. 1, 2014.

### § 303.003. Service by Publication or Other Substituted Service

Notwithstanding any other provision of this chapter, if an attempt to make service under this chapter is unsuccessful, service may be made in the manner provided by Rule 109 or 109a, Texas Rules of Civil Procedure, for the service of a citation on a party by publication or other substituted service.

Added by Acts 2009, 81st Leg., ch. 680, § 1, eff. Jan. 1, 2014.

## CHAPTER 304. PERSONS WHO MAY SERVE AS PERSONAL REPRESENTATIVES

### § 304.001. Order of Persons Qualified to Serve as Personal Representative

(a) The court shall grant letters testamentary or of administration to persons qualified to act, in the following order:

(1) the person named as executor in the decedent's will;

(2) the decedent's surviving spouse;

(3) the principal devisee of the decedent;

(4) any devisee of the decedent;

(5) the next of kin of the decedent;

(6) a creditor of the decedent;

(7) any person of good character residing in the county who applies for the letters;

(8) any other person who is not disqualified under Section 304.003; and

(9) any appointed public probate administrator.

(b) For purposes of Subsection (a)(5), the decedent's next of kin:

(1) is determined in accordance with order of descent, with the person nearest in order of descent first, and so on; and

(2) includes a person and the person's descendants who legally adopted the decedent or who have been legally adopted by the decedent.

(c) If persons are equally entitled to letters testamentary or of administration, the court:

(1) shall grant the letters to the person who, in the judgment of the court, is most likely to administer the estate advantageously; or

(2) may grant the letters to two or more of those persons.

Added by Acts 2009, 81st Leg., ch. 680, § 1, eff. Jan. 1, 2014. Amended by Acts 2013, 83rd Leg., ch. 671 (H.B. 1755), § 3, eff. Jan. 1, 2014; Acts 2013, 83rd Leg., ch. 1136 (H.B. 2912), § 35, eff. Jan. 1, 2014.

Section 62(c) of Acts 2013, 83rd Leg., ch. 1136 (H.B. 2912) provides:

"The changes in law made by this Act to Section 304.001(c), Estates Code, apply only to an application for the grant of letters testamentary or of administration of a decedent's estate filed on or after January 1, 2014. An application for the grant of letters testamentary or of administration of a decedent's estate filed before that date is governed by the law in effect on the date the application was filed, and the former law is continued in effect for that purpose."

### § 304.002. Renouncing Right to Serve as Personal Representative

A decedent's surviving spouse, or, if there is no surviving spouse, the heirs or any one of the heirs of the decedent to the exclusion of any person not equally entitled to letters testamentary or of administration, may renounce the right to the letters in favor of another qualified person in open court or by a power of attorney authenticated and filed with the county clerk of the county where the application for the letters is filed. After the right to the letters has been renounced, the court may grant the letters to the other qualified person.

Added by Acts 2009, 81st Leg., ch. 680, § 1, eff. Jan. 1, 2014.

### § 304.003. Persons Disqualified to Serve as Executor or Administrator

A person is not qualified to serve as an executor or administrator if the person is:

(1) incapacitated;

(2) a felon convicted under the laws of the United States or of any state of the United States unless, in accordance with law, the person has been pardoned or has had the person's civil rights restored;

(3) a nonresident of this state who:

(A) is a natural person or corporation; and

(B) has not:

(i) appointed a resident agent to accept service of process in all actions or proceedings with respect to the estate; or

(ii) had that appointment filed with the court;

(4) a corporation not authorized to act as a fiduciary in this state; or

(5) a person whom the court finds unsuitable.

Added by Acts 2009, 81st Leg., ch. 680, § 1, eff. Jan. 1, 2014.

## CHAPTER 305. QUALIFICATION OF PERSONAL REPRESENTATIVE

### SUBCHAPTER A. GENERAL PROVISIONS

### SUBCHAPTER A. GENERAL PROVISIONS

### § 305.001. Definitions

In this chapter:

(1) "Bond" means a bond required by this chapter to be given by a person appointed to serve as a personal representative.

(2) "Oath" means an oath required by this chapter to be taken by a person appointed to serve as a personal representative.

Added by Acts 2009, 81st Leg., ch. 680, § 1, eff. Jan. 1, 2014.

### § 305.002. Manner of Qualification of Personal Representative

(a) A personal representative, other than an executor described by Subsection (b), is considered to have qualified when the representative has:

(1) taken and filed the oath prescribed by Subchapter B;

(2) filed the required bond with the clerk; and

(3) obtained the judge's approval of the bond.

(b) An executor who is not required to give a bond is considered to have qualified when the executor has taken and filed the oath prescribed by Subchapter B.

Added by Acts 2009, 81st Leg., ch. 680, § 1, eff. Jan. 1, 2014. Amended by Acts 2013, 83rd Leg., ch. 1136 (H.B. 2912), § 36, eff. Jan. 1, 2014.

Section 62(e) of Acts 2013, 83rd Leg., ch. 1136 (H.B. 2912) provides:

"The changes in law made by Sections 51.203(c), 53.104, 305.002(a), 305.003, 308.054(b), 309.051(a), 309.056, 309.103(a) and (b), 355.060, 361.155(b), 362.005, 362.011, 362.013, 404.001(a), 404.003, 404.005(b) and (c), and 551.001(a), Estates Code, as amended by this Act, and Sections 253.001(c), 301.155, 305.004, 309.057, 361.155(c), 404.0035, 404.0036, and 404.0037, Estates Code, as added by this Act, apply to the administration of the estate of a decedent that is pending or commenced on or after the effective date [Jan. 1, 2014] of this Act."

### § 305.003. Period for Taking Oath

An oath may be taken and subscribed at any time before:

(1) the 21st day after the date of the order granting letters testamentary or of administration, as applicable; or

(2) the letters testamentary or of administration, as applicable, are revoked for a failure to qualify within the period allowed.

Added by Acts 2009, 81st Leg., ch. 680, § 1, eff. Jan. 1, 2014. Amended by Acts 2013, 83rd Leg., ch. 1136 (H.B. 2912), § 37, eff. Jan. 1, 2014.

Section 62(e) of Acts 2013, 83rd Leg., ch. 1136 (H.B. 2912) provides:

"The changes in law made by Sections 51.203(c), 53.104, 305.002(a), 305.003, 308.054(b), 309.051(a), 309.056, 309.103(a) and (b), 355.060, 361.155(b), 362.005, 362.011, 362.013, 404.001(a), 404.003, 404.005(b) and (c), and 551.001(a), Estates Code, as amended by this Act, and Sections 253.001(c), 301.155, 305.004, 309.057, 361.155(c), 404.0035, 404.0036, and 404.0037, Estates Code, as added by this Act, apply to the administration of the estate of a decedent that is pending or commenced on or after the effective date [Jan. 1, 2014] of this Act."

### § 305.004. Period for Giving Bond

(a) A bond may be filed with the clerk at any time before:

(1) the 21st day after:

(A) the date of the order granting letters testamentary or of administration, as applicable; or

(B) the date of any order modifying the bond requirement; or

(2) the date letters testamentary or of administration, as applicable, are revoked for a failure to qualify within the period allowed.

(b) The court shall act promptly to review a bond filed as provided by Subsection (a) and, if acceptable, shall approve the bond.

(c) If no action has been taken by the court on the bond before the 21st day after the date the bond is filed, the person appointed personal representative may file a motion requiring the judge of the court in which the bond was filed to specify on the record the reason or reasons for the judge's failure to act on the bond. The hearing on the motion must be held before the 11th day after the date the motion is filed.

Added by Acts 2013, 83rd Leg., ch. 1136 (H.B. 2912), § 38, eff. Jan. 1, 2014.

Section 62(e) of Acts 2013, 83rd Leg., ch. 1136 (H.B. 2912) provides:

"The changes in law made by Sections 51.203(c), 53.104, 305.002(a), 305.003, 308.054(b), 309.051(a), 309.056, 309.103(a) and (b), 355.060, 361.155(b), 362.005, 362.011, 362.013, 404.001(a), 404.003, 404.005(b) and (c), and 551.001(a), Estates Code, as amended by this Act, and Sections 253.001(c), 301.155, 305.004, 309.057, 361.155(c), 404.0035, 404.0036, and 404.0037, Estates Code, as added by this Act, apply to the administration of the estate of a decedent that is pending or commenced on or after the effective date [Jan. 1, 2014] of this Act."

## SUBCHAPTER B.  OATHS

### § 305.051. Oath of Executor or Administrator with Will Annexed

Before the issuance of letters testamentary or letters of administration with the will annexed, the person named as executor or appointed as administrator with the will annexed shall take and subscribe an oath in substantially the following form:

I do solemnly swear that the writing offered for probate is the last will of _____ (insert name of testator), so far as I know or believe, and that I will well and truly perform all the duties of _____ (insert "executor of the will" or "administrator with the will annexed," as applicable) for the estate of _____ (insert name of testator).

Added by Acts 2009, 81st Leg., ch. 680, § 1, eff. Jan. 1, 2014.

### § 305.052. Oath of Administrator

Before the issuance of letters of administration, the person appointed as administrator shall take and subscribe an oath in substantially the following form:

I do solemnly swear that _____ (insert name of decedent), deceased, died _____ (insert "without leaving any lawful will" or "leaving a lawful will, but the executor named in the will is dead or has failed to offer the will for probate or to accept and qualify as executor, within the period required," as applicable), so far as I know or believe, and that I will well and truly perform all the duties of administrator of the estate of the deceased.

Added by Acts 2009, 81st Leg., ch. 680, § 1, eff. Jan. 1, 2014.

### § 305.053.  Oath of Temporary Administrator

Before the issuance of temporary letters of administration, the person appointed as temporary administrator shall take and subscribe an oath in substantially the following form:

I do solemnly swear that I will well and truly perform the duties of temporary administrator of the estate of _____ (insert name of decedent), deceased, in accordance with the law, and with the order of the court appointing me as temporary administrator.

Added by Acts 2009, 81st Leg., ch. 680, § 1, eff. Jan. 1, 2014.

### § 305.054.  Administration of Oath

An oath may be taken before any person authorized to administer oaths under the laws of this state.

Added by Acts 2009, 81st Leg., ch. 680, § 1, eff. Jan. 1, 2014.

### § 305.055.  Filing and Recording of Oath

An oath shall be:

(1) filed with the clerk of the court granting the letters testamentary or of administration, as applicable; and

(2) recorded in the judge's probate docket.

Added by Acts 2009, 81st Leg., ch. 680, § 1, eff. Jan. 1, 2014. Amended by Acts 2011, 82nd Leg., ch. 91 (S.B. 1303), § 8.012, eff. Jan. 1, 2014.

### SUBCHAPTER C.  GENERAL PROVISIONS RELATING TO BONDS

### § 305.101.  Bond Generally Required; Exceptions

(a) Except as otherwise provided by this title, a person to whom letters testamentary or of administration will be issued must enter into a bond before issuance of the letters.

(b) Letters testamentary shall be issued without the requirement of a bond to a person named as executor in a will probated in a court of this state if:

(1) the will directs that no bond or security be required of the person; and

(2) the court finds that the person is qualified.

(c) A bond is not required if a personal representative is a corporate fiduciary.

Added by Acts 2009, 81st Leg., ch. 680, § 1, eff. Jan. 1, 2014.

### § 305.102.  Bond Required from Executor Otherwise Exempt

(a) This section applies only to an estate for which an executor was appointed under a will, but from whom no bond was required.

(b) A person who has a debt, claim, or demand against the estate, with respect to the justice of which the person or the person's agent or attorney has made an oath, or another person interested in the estate, whether in person or as the representative of another, may file a written complaint in the court where the will is probated.

(c) On the filing of the complaint, the court shall cite the executor to appear and show cause why the executor should not be required to give a bond.

(d) On hearing the complaint, the court shall enter an order requiring the executor to give a bond not later than the 10th day after the date of the order if it appears to the court that:

(1) the executor is wasting, mismanaging, or misapplying the estate; and

(2) as a result of conduct described by Subdivision (1):

(A) a creditor may probably lose the creditor's debt; or

(B) a person's interest in the estate may be diminished or lost.

(e) A bond required under this section must be:

(1) in an amount sufficient to protect the estate and the estate's creditors;

(2) payable to and approved by the judge; and

(3) conditioned that the executor:

(A) will well and truly administer the estate; and

(B) will not waste, mismanage, or misapply the estate.

(f) If the executor fails to give a bond required under this section on or before the 10th day after the date of the order and the judge has not extended the period for giving the bond, the judge, without citation, shall remove the executor and appoint a competent person in the executor's place who shall administer the estate according to the will and law. Before entering into the administration of the estate, the appointed person must:

(1) take the oath required of an administrator with the will annexed under Section 305.051; and

(2) give a bond in the manner and amount provided by this chapter for the issuance of original letters of administration.

Added by Acts 2009, 81st Leg., ch. 680, § 1, eff. Jan. 1, 2014.

### § 305.103. Bonds of Joint Personal Representatives

If two or more persons are appointed as personal representatives of an estate and are required by this chapter or by the court to give a bond, the court may require:

(1) a separate bond from each person; or

(2) a joint bond from all of the persons.

Added by Acts 2009, 81st Leg., ch. 680, § 1, eff. Jan. 1, 2014.

### § 305.104. Bond of Married Person

(a) A married person appointed as a personal representative may execute a bond required by law:

(1) jointly with the person's spouse; or

(2) separately without the person's spouse.

(b) A bond executed by a married person binds the person's separate estate, but does not bind the person's spouse unless the spouse signed the bond.

Added by Acts 2009, 81st Leg., ch. 680, § 1, eff. Jan. 1, 2014.

### § 305.105. Bond of Married Person Under 18 Years of Age

Any bond required to be executed by a person who is under 18 years of age, is or has been married, and accepts and qualifies as an executor or administrator is as valid and binding for all purposes as if the person were of legal age.

Added by Acts 2009, 81st Leg., ch. 680, § 1, eff. Jan. 1, 2014.

### § 305.106. General Formalities

A bond required under Section 305.101(a) must:

(1) be conditioned as required by law;

(2) be payable to the judge and the judge's successors in office;

(3) bear the written approval of the judge in the judge's official capacity; and

(4) be executed and approved in accordance with this chapter.

Added by Acts 2009, 81st Leg., ch. 680, § 1, eff. Jan. 1, 2014.

### § 305.107. Subscription of Bond by Principals and Sureties

A bond required under Section 305.101 shall be subscribed by both principals and sureties.

Added by Acts 2009, 81st Leg., ch. 680, § 1, eff. Jan. 1, 2014.

### § 305.108. Form of Bond

The following form, or a form with the same substance, may be used for the bond of a personal representative:

The State of Texas

County of _____

Know all persons by these presents that we, _____ (insert name of each principal), as principal, and _____ (insert name of each surety), as sureties, are held and firmly bound unto the judge of _____ (insert reference to appropriate judge), and that judge's successors in office, in the sum of _____ dollars, conditioned that the above bound principal or principals, appointed as _____ (insert "executor of the last will and testament," "administrator with the will annexed of the estate," "administrator of the estate," or "temporary administrator of the estate," as applicable) of _____ (insert name of decedent), deceased, shall well and truly perform all of the duties required of the principal or principals by law under that appointment.

Added by Acts 2009, 81st Leg., ch. 680, § 1, eff. Jan. 1, 2014.

### § 305.109. Filing of Bond

A bond required under Section 305.101 shall be filed with the clerk after the court approves the bond.

Added by Acts 2009, 81st Leg., ch. 680, § 1, eff. Jan. 1, 2014.

### § 305.110. Failure to Give Bond

Another person may be appointed as personal representative to replace a personal representative who at any time fails to give a bond as required by the court in the period prescribed by this chapter.

Added by Acts 2009, 81st Leg., ch. 680, § 1, eff. Jan. 1, 2014.

### § 305.111. Bond Not Void on First Recovery

A personal representative's bond does not become void on the first recovery but may be put in suit and prosecuted from time to time until the entire amount of the bond has been recovered.

Added by Acts 2009, 81st Leg., ch. 680, § 1, eff. Jan. 1, 2014.

## SUBCHAPTER D.  AMOUNT OF BOND AND ASSOCIATED DEPOSITS

### § 305.151.  General Standard Regarding Amount of Bond

(a) The judge shall set the amount of a bond, in an amount considered sufficient to protect the estate and the estate's creditors, as provided by this chapter.

(b) Notwithstanding Subsection (a) or other provisions generally applicable to bonds of personal representatives, if the person to whom letters testamentary or of administration are granted is entitled to all of the decedent's estate after payment of debts, a bond shall be in an amount sufficient to protect creditors only.

Added by Acts 2009, 81st Leg., ch. 680, § 1, eff. Jan. 1, 2014.

### § 305.152.  Evidentiary Hearing on Amount of Bond

Before setting the amount of a bond, the court shall hear evidence and determine:

(1) the amount of cash on hand and where that cash is deposited;

(2) the amount of cash estimated to be needed for administrative purposes, including operation of a business, factory, farm, or ranch owned by the estate, and expenses of administration for one year;

(3) the revenue anticipated to be received in the succeeding 12 months from dividends, interest, rentals, or use of property belonging to the estate and the aggregate amount of any installments or periodic payments to be collected;

(4) the estimated value of certificates of stock, bonds, notes, or other securities of the estate and the name of the depository, if any, in which those assets are deposited;

(5) the face value of life insurance or other policies payable to the person on whose estate administration is sought or to the estate;

(6) the estimated value of other personal property owned by the estate;  and

(7) the estimated amount of debts due and owing by the estate.

Added by Acts 2009, 81st Leg., ch. 680, § 1, eff. Jan. 1, 2014.

### § 305.153.  Specific Bond Amount

(a) Except as otherwise provided by this section, the judge shall set the bond in an amount equal to the sum of:

(1) the estimated value of all personal property belonging to the estate;  and

(2) an additional amount to cover revenue anticipated to be derived during the succeeding 12 months from:

(A) interest and dividends;

(B) collectible claims;

(C) the aggregate amount of any installments or periodic payments, excluding income derived or to be derived from federal social security payments;  and

(D) rentals for the use of property.

(b) The judge shall reduce the amount of the original bond under Subsection (a) in proportion to the amount of cash or the value of securities or other assets:

(1) authorized or required to be deposited by court order;  or

(2) voluntarily deposited by the personal representative or the sureties on the representative's bond, as provided by Sections 305.155 and 305.156.

(c) A bond required to be given by a temporary administrator shall be in the amount that the judge directs.

Added by Acts 2009, 81st Leg., ch. 680, § 1, eff. Jan. 1, 2014.

### § 305.154.  Agreement Regarding Deposit of Estate Assets

(a) A personal representative may agree with the surety or sureties on a bond, either corporate or personal, for the deposit of any cash and other estate assets in a depository described by Subsection (c), if the deposit is otherwise proper, in a manner that prevents the withdrawal of the cash or other assets without:

(1) the written consent of the surety or sureties;  or

(2) a court order entered after notice to the surety or sureties as directed by the court.

(b) The court may require the action described by Subsection (a) if the court considers that action to be in the best interest of the estate.

(c) Cash and assets must be deposited under this section in a financial institution, as defined by Section 201.101, Finance Code, that:

(1) has its main office or a branch office in this state; and

(2) is qualified to act as a depository in this state under the laws of this state or the United States.

(d) An agreement under this section may not release the principal or sureties from liability, or change the liability of the principal or sureties, as established by the terms of the bond.

Added by Acts 2009, 81st Leg., ch. 680, § 1, eff. Jan. 1, 2014.

### § 305.155. Deposit of Estate Assets on Terms Prescribed by Court

(a) Cash, securities, or other personal assets of an estate or to which the estate is entitled may or, if considered by the court to be in the best interest of the estate, shall, be deposited in one or more depositories described by Section 305.154(c) on terms prescribed by the court.

(b) The court in which the proceedings are pending may authorize or require additional estate assets currently on hand or that accrue during the pendency of the proceedings to be deposited as provided by Subsection (a) on:

(1) the court's own motion; or

(2) the written application of the personal representative or any other person interested in the estate.

(c) The amount of the bond required to be given by the personal representative shall be reduced in proportion to the amount of the cash and the value of the securities or other assets deposited under this section.

(d) Cash, securities, or other assets deposited under this section may be withdrawn in whole or in part from the depository only in accordance with a court order, and the amount of the personal representative's bond shall be increased in proportion to the amount of the cash and the value of the securities or other assets authorized to be withdrawn.

Added by Acts 2009, 81st Leg., ch. 680, § 1, eff. Jan. 1, 2014.

### § 305.156. Deposits of Personal Representative

(a) Instead of giving a surety or sureties on a bond, or to reduce the amount of a bond, a personal representative may deposit the representative's own cash or securities acceptable to the court with a depository described by Subsection (b), if the deposit is otherwise proper.

(b) Cash or securities must be deposited under this section in:

(1) a depository described by Section 305.154(c); or

(2) any other corporate depository approved by the court.

(c) A deposit may be in an amount or value equal to the amount of the bond required or in a lesser amount or value, in which case the amount of the bond is reduced by the amount or value of the deposit.

(d) The amount of cash or securities on deposit may be increased or decreased, by court order from time to time, as the interest of the estate requires.

(e) A deposit of cash or securities made instead of a surety or sureties on a bond may be withdrawn or released only on order of a court having jurisdiction.

(f) A creditor has the same rights against a personal representative and deposits made under this section as are provided for recovery against sureties on a bond.

Added by Acts 2009, 81st Leg., ch. 680, § 1, eff. Jan. 1, 2014.

### § 305.157. Receipt for Deposits of Personal Representative

(a) A depository that receives a deposit made under Section 305.156 instead of a surety or sureties on a bond shall issue a receipt for the deposit that:

(1) shows the amount of cash deposited or the amount and description of the securities deposited, as applicable; and

(2) states that the depository agrees to disburse or deliver the cash or securities only on receipt of a certified copy of an order of the court in which the proceedings are pending.

(b) A receipt issued by a depository under Subsection (a) shall be attached to the personal representative's bond and be delivered to and filed by the county clerk after approval by the judge.

Added by Acts 2009, 81st Leg., ch. 680, § 1, eff. Jan. 1, 2014.

### § 305.158. Bond Required Instead of Deposits by Personal Representative

(a) The court may on its own motion or on the written application by the personal representative or any other person interested in the estate:

(1) require that an adequate bond be given instead of a deposit under Section 305.156; or

(2) authorize withdrawal of a deposit made under Section 305.156 and substitution of a bond with sureties.

(b) Not later than the 20th day after the date of entry of the court's motion or the date the personal representative is personally served with notice of the filing of an application by another person interested in the estate, the representative shall file a sworn statement showing the condition of the estate.

(c) A personal representative who fails to comply with Subsection (b) is subject to removal as in other cases.

(d) The personal representative's deposit under Section 305.156 may not be released or withdrawn until the court has:

(1) been satisfied as to the condition of the estate;

(2) determined the amount of the bond;  and

(3) received and approved the bond.

Added by Acts 2009, 81st Leg., ch. 680, § 1, eff. Jan. 1, 2014.

### § 305.159. Withdrawal of Deposits on Closing of Administration

(a) Any deposit of assets of the personal representative, the estate, or a surety that remains at the time an estate is closed shall be released by court order and paid to the person or persons entitled to the deposit.

(b) Except as provided by Subsection (c), a writ of attachment or garnishment does not lie against a deposit described by Subsection (a).

(c) A writ of attachment or garnishment may lie against a deposit described by Subsection (a) as to a claim of a creditor of the estate being administered or a person interested in the estate, including a distributee or ward, to the extent the court has ordered distribution.

Added by Acts 2009, 81st Leg., ch. 680, § 1, eff. Jan. 1, 2014.

### § 305.160. Increased or Additional Bonds in Certain Circumstances

The provisions of this subchapter regarding the deposit of cash and securities govern, to the extent the provisions may be applicable, the court orders to be entered when:

(1) one of the following circumstances occurs:

(A) estate property has been authorized to be sold or rented;

(B) money has been borrowed on estate property;  or

(C) real property, or an interest in real property, has been authorized to be leased for mineral development or subjected to unitization;  and

(2) the general bond has been found to be insufficient.

Added by Acts 2009, 81st Leg., ch. 680, § 1, eff. Jan. 1, 2014.

## SUBCHAPTER E. BOND SURETIES

### § 305.201. Personal or Authorized Corporate Sureties

(a) The surety or sureties on a bond may be personal or authorized corporate sureties.

(b) A bond with sureties who are individuals must have at least two sureties, each of whom must:

(1) execute an affidavit in the manner provided by this subchapter;  and

(2) own property in this state, excluding property exempt by law, that the judge is satisfied is sufficient to qualify the person as a surety as required by law.

(c) A bond with an authorized corporate surety is only required to have one surety, except as provided by law.

Added by Acts 2009, 81st Leg., ch. 680, § 1, eff. Jan. 1, 2014.

### § 305.202. Sureties for Certain Bonds

(a) If the amount of a bond exceeds $50,000, the court may require that the bond be signed by:

(1) at least two authorized corporate sureties;  or

(2) one authorized corporate surety and at least two good and sufficient personal sureties.

(b) The estate shall pay the cost of a bond with corporate sureties.

Added by Acts 2009, 81st Leg., ch. 680, § 1, eff. Jan. 1, 2014.

### § 305.203. Affidavit of Personal Surety

(a) Before a judge may consider a bond with personal sureties, each person offered as surety must execute an affidavit stating the amount by which the person's assets that are reachable by creditors exceeds the person's liabilities, and each affidavit must be presented to the judge for consideration.

(b) The total worth of the personal sureties on a bond must equal at least twice the amount of the bond.

(c) An affidavit presented to and approved by the judge under this section shall be attached to and form part of the bond.

Added by Acts 2009, 81st Leg., ch. 680, § 1, eff. Jan. 1, 2014.

## § 305.204. Lien on Real Property Owned by Personal Sureties

(a) If a judge finds that the estimated value of personal property of the estate that cannot be deposited, as provided by Subchapter D, is such that personal sureties cannot be accepted without the creation of a specific lien on real property owned by each of the sureties, the judge shall enter an order requiring each surety to:

(1) designate real property that:

(A) is owned by the surety and located in this state;

(B) is subject to execution; and

(C) has a value that exceeds all liens and unpaid taxes by an amount at least equal to the amount of the bond; and

(2) give an adequate legal description of the real property designated under Subdivision (1).

(b) The surety shall incorporate the information required in the order under Subsection (a) in an affidavit. Following approval by the judge, the affidavit shall be attached to and form part of the bond.

(c) A lien arises as security for the performance of the obligation of the bond only on the real property designated in the affidavit.

(d) Before letters testamentary or of administration are issued to the personal representative whose bond includes an affidavit under this section, the court clerk shall mail a statement to the office of the county clerk of each county in which any real property designated in the affidavit is located. The statement must be signed by the court clerk and include:

(1) a sufficient description of the real property located in that county;

(2) the names of the principal and sureties on the bond;

(3) the amount of the bond; and

(4) the name of the estate and court in which the bond is given.

(e) Each county clerk who receives a statement required by Subsection (d) shall record the statement in the county deed records. Each recorded statement shall be indexed in a manner that permits the convenient determination of the existence and character of the liens described in the statements.

(f) The recording and indexing required by Subsection (e) constitutes constructive notice to all persons regarding the existence of the lien on real property located in the county, effective as of the date of the indexing.

(g) If each personal surety subject to a court order under this section does not comply with the order, the judge may require that the bond be signed by:

(1) an authorized corporate surety; or

(2) an authorized corporate surety and at least two personal sureties.

Added by Acts 2009, 81st Leg., ch. 680, § 1, eff. Jan. 1, 2014.

## § 305.205. Subordination of Lien on Real Property Owned by Personal Sureties

(a) A personal surety required to create a lien on specific real property under Section 305.204 who wishes to lease the real property for mineral development may file a written application in the court in which the proceedings are pending requesting subordination of the lien to the proposed lease.

(b) The judge may enter an order granting the application.

(c) A certified copy of the order, filed and recorded in the deed records of the proper county, is sufficient to subordinate the lien to the rights of a lessee under the proposed lease.

Added by Acts 2009, 81st Leg., ch. 680, § 1, eff. Jan. 1, 2014.

## § 305.206. Release of Lien on Real Property Owned by Personal Sureties

(a) A personal surety who has given a lien under Section 305.204 may apply to the court to have the lien released.

(b) The court shall order the lien released if:

(1) the court is satisfied that the bond is sufficient without the lien; or

(2) sufficient other real or personal property of the surety is substituted on the same terms required for the lien that is to be released.

(c) If the personal surety does not offer a lien on other substituted property under Subsection (b)(2) and the court is not satisfied that the bond is sufficient without the substitution of other property, the court shall order the personal representative to appear and give a new bond.

(d) A certified copy of the court's order releasing the lien and describing the property that was subject to the lien has the effect of cancelling the lien if the order is filed with the county clerk of the county in which the property is located and recorded in the deed records of that county.

Added by Acts 2009, 81st Leg., ch. 680, § 1, eff. Jan. 1, 2014.

### § 305.207.  Deposits by Personal Surety

Instead of executing an affidavit under Section 305.203 or creating a lien under Section 305.204 when required, a personal surety may deposit the surety's own cash or securities instead of pledging real property as security.  The deposit:

(1) must be made in the same manner a personal representative deposits the representative's own cash or securities;  and

(2) is subject, to the extent applicable, to the provisions governing the same type of deposits made by personal representatives.

Added by Acts 2009, 81st Leg., ch. 680, § 1, eff. Jan. 1, 2014.

### SUBCHAPTER F.  NEW BONDS

### § 305.251.  Grounds for Requiring New Bond

(a) A personal representative may be required to give a new bond if:

(1) a surety on a bond dies, removes beyond the limits of this state, or becomes insolvent;

(2) in the court's opinion:

(A) the sureties on a bond are insufficient;  or

(B) a bond is defective;

(3) the amount of a bond is insufficient;

(4) a surety on a bond petitions the court to be discharged from future liability on the bond;  or

(5) a bond and the record of the bond have been lost or destroyed.

(b) Any person interested in the estate may have the personal representative cited to appear and show cause why the representative should not be required to give a new bond by filing a written application with the county clerk of the county in which the probate proceedings are pending.  The application must allege that:

(1) the bond is insufficient or defective;  or

(2) the bond and the record of the bond have been lost or destroyed.

Added by Acts 2009, 81st Leg., ch. 680, § 1, eff. Jan. 1, 2014. Amended by Acts 2011, 82nd Leg., ch. 91 (S.B. 1303), § 8.013, eff. Jan. 1, 2014.

### § 305.252.  Court Order or Citation on New Bond

(a) When a judge becomes aware that a bond is in any respect insufficient or that a bond and the record of the bond have been lost or destroyed, the judge shall:

(1) without delay and without notice enter an order requiring the personal representative to give a new bond;  or

(2) without delay have the representative cited to show cause why the representative should not be required to give a new bond.

(b) An order entered under Subsection (a)(1) must state:

(1) the reasons for requiring a new bond;

(2) the amount of the new bond;  and

(3) the period within which the new bond must be given, which may not be earlier than the 10th day after the date of the order.

(c) A personal representative who opposes an order entered under Subsection (a)(1) may demand a hearing on the order.  The hearing must be held before the expiration of the period within which the new bond must be given.

Added by Acts 2009, 81st Leg., ch. 680, § 1, eff. Jan. 1, 2014.

### § 305.253.  Show Cause Hearing on New Bond Requirement

(a) On the return of a citation ordering a personal representative to show cause why the representative should not be required to give a new bond, the judge shall, on the date specified for the hearing of the matter, inquire into the sufficiency of the reasons for requiring a new bond.

(b) If the judge is satisfied that a new bond should be required, the judge shall enter an order requiring a new bond.  The order must state:

(1) the amount of the new bond;  and

(2) the period within which the new bond must be given, which may not be later than the 20th day after the date of the order.

Added by Acts 2009, 81st Leg., ch. 680, § 1, eff. Jan. 1, 2014.

### § 305.254.  Effect of Order Requiring New Bond

(a) An order requiring a personal representative to give a new bond has the effect of suspending the representative's powers.

(b) After the order is entered, the personal representative may not pay out any of the estate's money or take any other official action, except to preserve estate property, until the new bond is given and approved.

Added by Acts 2009, 81st Leg., ch. 680, § 1, eff. Jan. 1, 2014.

### § 305.255.  New Bond in Decreased Amount

(a) A personal representative required to give a bond may at any time file with the clerk a written application requesting that the court reduce the amount of the bond.

(b) On the filing of an application under Subsection (a), the clerk shall promptly issue and have notice posted to all interested persons and the sureties on the bond.  The notice must inform the interested persons and sureties of:

(1) the fact that the application has been filed;

(2) the nature of the application; and

(3) the time the judge will hear the application.

(c) The judge may permit the filing of a new bond in a reduced amount if:

(1) proof is submitted that a bond in an amount less than the bond in effect will be adequate to meet the requirements of law and protect the estate;  and

(2) the judge approves an accounting filed at the time of the application.

Added by Acts 2009, 81st Leg., ch. 680, § 1, eff. Jan. 1, 2014.

### § 305.256.  Request by Surety for New Bond

(a) A surety on a bond may at any time file with the clerk a petition requesting that the court in which the proceedings are pending:

(1) require the personal representative to give a new bond;  and

(2) discharge the petitioner from all liability for the future acts of the representative.

(b) On the filing of a petition under Subsection (a), the personal representative shall be cited to appear and give a new bond.

Added by Acts 2009, 81st Leg., ch. 680, § 1, eff. Jan. 1, 2014.

### § 305.257.  Discharge of Former Sureties on Execution of New Bond

When a new bond has been given and approved, the court shall enter an order discharging the sureties on the former bond from all liability for the future acts of the principal on the bond.

Added by Acts 2009, 81st Leg., ch. 680, § 1, eff. Jan. 1, 2014.

## CHAPTER 306.  GRANTING AND ISSUANCE OF LETTERS

Section

### § 306.001.  Granting of Letters Testamentary

(a) Before the 21st day after the date a will has been probated, the court shall grant letters testamentary, if permitted by law, to each executor appointed by the will who:

(1) is not disqualified;  and

(2) is willing to accept the trust and qualify according to law.

(b) Failure of the court to issue letters testamentary within the period prescribed by this section does not affect the validity of any letters testamentary issued in accordance with law after that period.

Added by Acts 2009, 81st Leg., ch. 680, § 1, eff. Jan. 1, 2014.

### § 306.002.  Granting of Letters of Administration

(a) Subject to Subsection (b), the court hearing an application under Chapter 301 shall grant:

(1) the administration of a decedent's estate if the decedent died intestate;  or

(2) the administration of the decedent's estate with the will annexed if the decedent died leaving a will but:

(A) the will does not name an executor;  or

(B) the executor named in the will:

(i) is deceased;

(ii) fails to accept and qualify before the 21st day after the date the will is probated;  or

(iii) fails to present the will for probate before the 31st day after the date of the decedent's death and the court finds there was no good cause for that failure.

(b) The court may not grant any administration of an estate unless a necessity for the administration exists, as determined by the court.

(c) The court may find other instances of necessity for an administration based on proof before the court, but a necessity is considered to exist if:

(1) there are two or more debts against the estate;

(2) there is a desire for the county court to partition the estate among the distributees; or

(3) the administration is necessary to receive or recover funds or other property due the estate.

Added by Acts 2009, 81st Leg., ch. 680, § 1, eff. Jan. 1, 2014.

### § 306.003.   Order Granting Letters

When letters testamentary or of administration are granted, the court shall enter an order to that effect stating:

(1) the name of the decedent;

(2) the name of the person to whom the letters are granted;

(3) the amount of any required bond;

(4) the name of at least one but not more than three disinterested persons appointed to appraise the estate and return the appraisement to the court, if:

(A) any interested person applies to the court for the appointment of an appraiser; or

(B) the court considers an appraisement to be necessary; and

(5) that the clerk shall issue letters in accordance with the order when the person to whom the letters are granted has qualified according to law.

Added by Acts 2009, 81st Leg., ch. 680, § 1, eff. Jan. 1, 2014.

### § 306.004.   Issuance of Original Letters

When an executor or administrator has qualified in the manner required by law, the clerk of the court granting the letters testamentary or of administration shall promptly issue and deliver the letters to the executor or administrator. If more than one person qualifies as executor or administrator, the clerk shall issue the letters to each person who qualifies.

Added by Acts 2009, 81st Leg., ch. 680, § 1, eff. Jan. 1, 2014.

### § 306.005.   Form and Content of Letters

Letters testamentary or of administration shall be in the form of a certificate of the clerk of the court granting the letters, attested by the court's seal, that states:

(1) the executor or administrator, as applicable, has qualified as executor or administrator in the manner required by law;

(2) the date of the qualification; and

(3) the name of the decedent.

Added by Acts 2009, 81st Leg., ch. 680, § 1, eff. Jan. 1, 2014.

### § 306.006.   Replacement and Other Additional Letters

When letters testamentary or of administration have been destroyed or lost, the clerk shall issue other letters to replace the original letters, which have the same effect as the original letters. The clerk shall also issue any number of letters as and when requested by the person or persons who hold the letters.

Added by Acts 2009, 81st Leg., ch. 680, § 1, eff. Jan. 1, 2014.

### § 306.007.   Effect of Letters or Certificate

Letters testamentary or of administration or a certificate of the clerk of the court that granted the letters, under the court's seal, indicating that the letters have been issued, is sufficient evidence of:

(1) the appointment and qualification of the personal representative of an estate; and

(2) the date of qualification.

Added by Acts 2009, 81st Leg., ch. 680, § 1, eff. Jan. 1, 2014.

## CHAPTER 307.   VALIDITY OF CERTAIN ACTS OF EXECUTORS AND ADMINISTRATORS

### § 307.001.   Rights of Good Faith Purchasers

(a) This section applies only to an act performed by a qualified executor or administrator in that capacity and in conformity with the law and the executor's or administrator's authority.

(b) An act continues to be valid for all intents and purposes in regard to the rights of an innocent purchaser who purchases any of the estate property from the executor or administrator for valuable consideration, in good faith, and without notice of any illegality in the title to the property, even if the act or the authority under which the act was performed is subsequently set aside, annulled, and declared invalid.

Added by Acts 2009, 81st Leg., ch. 680, § 1, eff. Jan. 1, 2014.

### § 307.002.   Joint Executors or Administrators

(a) Except as provided by Subsection (b), if there is more than one executor or administrator of an estate at the same time, the acts of one of the executors or administrators in that capacity are valid as if all the executors or administrators had acted jointly. If one of the executors or administrators dies, resigns, or is removed, a co-executor or co-administrator of the estate shall proceed with the administration as if the death, resignation, or removal had not occurred.

(b) If there is more than one executor or administrator of an estate at the same time, all of the qualified executors or administrators who are acting in that capacity must join in the conveyance of real estate unless the court, after due hearing, authorizes fewer than all to act.

Added by Acts 2009, 81st Leg., ch. 680, § 1, eff. Jan. 1, 2014.

## CHAPTER 308. NOTICE TO BENEFICIARIES AND CLAIMANTS

### SUBCHAPTER A. NOTICE TO CERTAIN BENEFICIARIES AFTER PROBATE OF WILL

### SUBCHAPTER A. NOTICE TO CERTAIN BENEFICIARIES AFTER PROBATE OF WILL

### § 308.001. Definition

In this subchapter, "beneficiary" means a person, entity, state, governmental agency of the state, charitable organization, or trustee of a trust entitled to receive property under the terms of a decedent's will, to be determined for purposes of this subchapter with the assumption that each person who is alive on the date of the decedent's death survives any period required to receive the bequest as specified by the terms of the will. The term does not include a person, entity, state, governmental agency of the state, charitable organization, or trustee of a trust that would be entitled to receive property under the terms of a decedent's will on the occurrence of a contingency that has not occurred as of the date of the decedent's death.

Added by Acts 2009, 81st Leg., ch. 680, § 1, eff. Jan. 1, 2014. Amended by Acts 2011, 82nd Leg., ch. 1338 (S.B. 1198), § 2.34, eff. Jan. 1, 2014.

### § 308.0015. Application

This subchapter does not apply to the probate of a will as a muniment of title.

Added by Acts 2011, 82nd Leg., ch. 1338 (S.B. 1198), § 2.35, eff. Jan. 1, 2014.

### § 308.002. Required Notice to Certain Beneficiaries After Probate of Will

(a) Except as provided by Subsection (c), not later than the 60th day after the date of an order admitting a decedent's will to probate, the personal representative of the decedent's estate, including an independent executor or independent administrator, shall give notice that complies with Section 308.003 to each beneficiary named in the will whose identity and address are known to the representative or, through reasonable diligence, can be ascertained. If, after the 60th day after the date of the order, the representative becomes aware of the identity and address of a beneficiary who was not given notice on or before the 60th day, the representative shall give the notice as soon as possible after becoming aware of that information.

(b) Notwithstanding the requirement under Subsection (a) that the personal representative give the notice to the beneficiary, the representative shall give the notice with respect to a beneficiary described by this subsection as follows:

(1) if the beneficiary is a trustee of a trust, to the trustee, unless the representative is the trustee, in which case the representative shall, except as provided by Subsection (b–1), give the notice to the person or class of persons first eligible to receive the trust income, to be determined for purposes of this subdivision as if the trust were in existence on the date of the decedent's death;

(2) if the beneficiary has a court-appointed guardian or conservator, to that guardian or conservator;

(3) if the beneficiary is a minor for whom no guardian or conservator has been appointed, to a parent of the minor; and

(4) if the beneficiary is a charity that for any reason cannot be notified, to the attorney general.

(b–1) The personal representative is not required to give the notice otherwise required by Subsection (b)(1) to a person eligible to receive trust income at the sole discretion of the trustee of a trust if:

(1) the representative has given the notice to an ancestor of the person who has a similar interest in the trust; and

(2) no apparent conflict exists between the ancestor and the person eligible to receive trust income.

(c) A personal representative is not required to give the notice otherwise required by this section to a beneficiary who:

(1) has made an appearance in the proceeding with respect to the decedent's estate before the will was admitted to probate;

(2) is entitled to receive aggregate gifts under the will with an estimated value of $2,000 or less;

(3) has received all gifts to which the beneficiary is entitled under the will not later than the 60th day after the date of the order admitting the decedent's will to probate; or

(4) has received a copy of the will that was admitted to probate or a written summary of the gifts to the beneficiary under the will and has waived the right to receive the notice in an instrument that:

(A) either acknowledges the receipt of the copy of the will or includes the written summary of the gifts to the beneficiary under the will;

(B) is signed by the beneficiary; and

(C) is filed with the court.

(d) The notice required by this section must be sent by registered or certified mail, return receipt requested.

Added by Acts 2009, 81st Leg., ch. 680, § 1, eff. Jan. 1, 2014. Amended by Acts 2011, 82nd Leg., ch. 1338 (S.B. 1198), § 2.36, eff. Jan. 1, 2014.

### § 308.003. Contents of Notice

The notice required by Section 308.002 must include:

(1) the name and address of the beneficiary to whom the notice is given or, for a beneficiary described by Section 308.002(b), the name and address of the beneficiary for whom the notice is given and of the person to whom the notice is given;

(2) the decedent's name;

(3) a statement that the decedent's will has been admitted to probate;

(4) a statement that the beneficiary to whom or for whom the notice is given is named as a beneficiary in the will;

(5) the personal representative's name and contact information; and

(6) either:

(A) a copy of the will that was admitted to probate and of the order admitting the will to probate; or

(B) a summary of the gifts to the beneficiary under the will, the court in which the will was admitted to probate, the docket number assigned to the estate, the date the will was admitted to probate, and, if different, the date the court appointed the personal representative.

Added by Acts 2009, 81st Leg., ch. 680, § 1, eff. Jan. 1, 2014. Amended by Acts 2011, 82nd Leg., ch. 1338 (S.B. 1198), § 2.37, eff. Jan. 1, 2014.

### § 308.004. Affidavit or Certificate

(a) Not later than the 90th day after the date of an order admitting a will to probate, the personal representative shall file with the clerk of the court in which the decedent's estate is pending a sworn affidavit of the representative or a certificate signed by the representative's attorney stating:

(1) for each beneficiary to whom notice was required to be given under this subchapter, the name and address of the beneficiary to whom the representative gave the notice or, for a beneficiary described by Section 308.002(b), the name and address of the beneficiary and of the person to whom the notice was given;

(2) the name and address of each beneficiary to whom notice was not required to be given under Section 308.002(c)(2), (3), or (4);

(3) the name of each beneficiary whose identity or address could not be ascertained despite the representative's exercise of reasonable diligence; and

(4) any other information necessary to explain the representative's inability to give the notice to or for any beneficiary as required by this subchapter.

(b) The affidavit or certificate required by Subsection (a) may be included with any pleading or other document filed with the court clerk, including the inventory, appraisement, and list of claims, an affidavit in lieu of the inventory, appraisement, and list of claims, or an application for an extension of the deadline to file the inventory, appraisement, and list of claims or an affidavit in lieu of the inventory, appraisement, and list of claims, provided that the pleading or other document is filed not later than the date the affidavit or certificate is required to be filed under Subsection (a).

Added by Acts 2009, 81st Leg., ch. 680, § 1, eff. Jan. 1, 2014. Amended by Acts 2011, 82nd Leg., ch. 1338 (S.B. 1198), § 2.38, eff. Jan. 1, 2014.

## SUBCHAPTER B. NOTICE TO CLAIMANTS

### § 308.051. Required Notice Regarding Presentment of Claims in General

(a) Within one month after receiving letters testamentary or of administration, a personal representative of an estate shall provide notice requiring each person who has a claim against the estate to present the claim within the period prescribed by law by:

(1) having the notice published in a newspaper printed in the county in which the letters were issued; and

(2) if the decedent remitted or should have remitted taxes administered by the comptroller, sending the notice to the comptroller by certified or registered mail.

(b) Notice provided under Subsection (a) must include:

(1) the date the letters testamentary or of administration were issued to the personal representative;

(2) the address to which a claim may be presented; and

(3) an instruction of the representative's choice that the claim be addressed in care of:

(A) the representative;

(B) the representative's attorney; or

(C) "Representative, Estate of _____" (naming the estate).

(c) If a newspaper is not printed in the county in which the letters testamentary or of administration were issued, the notice must be posted and the return made and filed as otherwise required by this title.

Added by Acts 2009, 81st Leg., ch. 680, § 1, eff. Jan. 1, 2014.

### § 308.052. Proof of Publication

A copy of the published notice required by Section 308.051(a)(1), together with the publisher's affidavit, sworn to and subscribed before a proper officer, to the effect that the notice was published as provided in this title for the service of citation or notice by publication, shall be filed in the court in which the cause is pending.

Added by Acts 2009, 81st Leg., ch. 680, § 1, eff. Jan. 1, 2014.

### § 308.053. Required Notice to Secured Creditor

(a) Within two months after receiving letters testamentary or of administration, a personal representative of an estate shall give notice of the issuance of the letters to each person the representative knows to have a claim for money against the estate that is secured by estate property.

(b) Within a reasonable period after a personal representative obtains actual knowledge of the existence of a person who has a secured claim for money against the estate and to whom notice was not previously given, the representative shall give notice to the person of the issuance of the letters testamentary or of administration.

(c) Notice provided under this section must be:

(1) sent by certified or registered mail, return receipt requested; and

(2) addressed to the record holder of the claim at the record holder's last known post office address.

(d) The following shall be filed with the clerk of the court in which the letters testamentary or of administration were issued:

(1) a copy of each notice and of each return receipt; and

(2) the personal representative's affidavit stating:

(A) that the notice was mailed as required by law; and

(B) the name of the person to whom the notice was mailed, if that name is not shown on the notice or receipt.

Added by Acts 2009, 81st Leg., ch. 680, § 1, eff. Jan. 1, 2014.

### § 308.054. Permissive Notice to Unsecured Creditor

(a) At any time before an estate administration is closed, a personal representative may give notice by certified or registered mail, return receipt requested, to an unsecured creditor who has a claim for money against the estate.

(b) Notice given under Subsection (a) must:

(1) expressly state that the creditor must present the claim before the 121st day after the date of the receipt of the notice or the claim is barred, if the claim is not barred by the general statutes of limitation; and

(2) include:

(A) the date the letters testamentary or of administration held by the personal representative were issued to the representative;

(B) the address to which the claim may be presented; and

(C) an instruction of the representative's choice that the claim be addressed in care of:

(i) the representative;

(ii) the representative's attorney; or

(iii) "Representative, Estate of _____" (naming the estate).

Added by Acts 2009, 81st Leg., ch. 680, § 1, eff. Jan. 1, 2014. Amended by Acts 2013, 83rd Leg., ch. 1136 (H.B. 2912), § 39, eff. Jan. 1, 2014.

Section 62(e) of Acts 2013, 83rd Leg., ch. 1136 (H.B. 2912) provides:

"The changes in law made by Sections 51.203(c), 53.104, 305.002(a), 305.003, 308.054(b), 309.051(a), 309.056, 309.103(a) and (b), 355.060, 361.155(b), 362.005, 362.011, 362.013, 404.001(a), 404.003, 404.005(b) and (c), and 551.001(a), Estates Code, as amended by this Act, and Sections 253.001(c), 301.155, 305.004, 309.057, 361.155(c), 404.0035, 404.0036, and 404.0037, Estates Code, as added by this Act, apply to the administration of the estate of a decedent that is pending or commenced on or after the effective date [Jan. 1, 2014] of this Act."

### § 308.055. One Notice Sufficient

A personal representative is not required to give a notice required by Section 308.051 or 308.053 if another person also appointed as personal representative of the estate or a former personal representative of the estate has given that notice.

Added by Acts 2009, 81st Leg., ch. 680, § 1, eff. Jan. 1, 2014.

### § 308.056. Liability for Failure to Give Required Notice

A personal representative who fails to give a notice required by Section 308.051 or 308.053, or to cause the notice to be given, and the sureties on the representative's bond are liable for any damage a person suffers due to that neglect, unless it appears that the person otherwise had notice.

Added by Acts 2009, 81st Leg., ch. 680, § 1, eff. Jan. 1, 2014.

## CHAPTER 309. INVENTORY, APPRAISEMENT, AND LIST OF CLAIMS

### SUBCHAPTER A. APPRAISERS

### SUBCHAPTER A. APPRAISERS

### § 309.001. Appointment of Appraisers

(a) At any time after letters testamentary or of administration are granted, the court, for good cause, on the court's own motion or on the motion of an interested party shall appoint at least one but not more than three disinterested persons who are residents of the county in which the letters were granted to appraise the estate property.

(b) At any time after letters testamentary or of administration are granted, the court, for good cause shown, on the court's own motion or on the motion of an interested person shall appoint at least one but not more than three disinterested persons who are residents of the county in which the letters were granted to appraise the estate property.

(c) If the court makes an appointment under Subsection (a) or (b) and part of the estate is located in a county other than the county in which the letters were granted, the court, if the court considers necessary, may appoint at least one but not more than three disinterested persons who are residents of the county in which the relevant part of the estate is located to appraise the estate property located in that county.

Added by Acts 2009, 81st Leg., ch. 680, § 1, eff. Jan. 1, 2014.

## § 309.002.  Appraisers' Fees

An appraiser appointed by the court as herein authorized is entitled to receive compensation, payable out of the estate, of at least $5 for each day the appraiser actually serves in performing the appraiser's duties.

Added by Acts 2009, 81st Leg., ch. 680, § 1, eff. Jan. 1, 2014.

## § 309.003.  Failure or Refusal to Act by Appraisers

If an appraiser appointed under Section 309.001 fails or refuses to act, the court by one or more similar orders shall remove the appraiser and appoint one or more other appraisers, as the case requires.

Added by Acts 2009, 81st Leg., ch. 680, § 1, eff. Jan. 1, 2014.

## SUBCHAPTER B.  REQUIREMENTS FOR INVENTORY, APPRAISEMENT, AND LIST OF CLAIMS; AFFIDAVIT IN LIEU OF INVENTORY, APPRAISEMENT, AND LIST OF CLAIMS

## § 309.051.  Inventory and Appraisement

(a) Except as provided by Subsection (c) or Section 309.056 or unless a longer period is granted by the court, before the 91st day after the date the personal representative qualifies, the representative shall prepare and file with the court clerk a single written instrument that contains a verified, full, and detailed inventory of all estate property that has come into the representative's possession or of which the representative has knowledge.  The inventory must:

(1) include:

(A) all estate real property located in this state; and

(B) all estate personal property regardless of where the property is located;  and

(2) specify which portion of the property, if any, is separate property and which, if any, is community property.

(b) The personal representative shall:

(1) set out in the inventory the representative's appraisement of the fair market value on the date of the decedent's death of each item in the inventory;  or

(2) if the court has appointed one or more appraisers for the estate:

(A) determine the fair market value of each item in the inventory with the assistance of the appraiser or appraisers;  and

(B) set out that appraisement in the inventory.

(c) The court for good cause shown may require the personal representative to file the inventory and appraisement within a shorter period than the period prescribed by Subsection (a).

(d) The inventory, when approved by the court and filed with the court clerk, is for all purposes the inventory and appraisement of the estate referred to in this title.

Added by Acts 2009, 81st Leg., ch. 680, § 1, eff. Jan. 1, 2014. Amended by Acts 2011, 82nd Leg., ch. 91 (S.B. 1303), § 8.014, eff. Jan. 1, 2014;  Acts 2011, 82nd Leg., ch. 1338 (S.B. 1198), § 2.40, eff. Jan. 1, 2014;  Acts 2013, 83rd Leg., ch. 1136 (H.B. 2912), § 40, eff. Jan. 1, 2014.

Section 62(e) of Acts 2013, 83rd Leg., ch. 1136 (H.B. 2912) provides:

"The changes in law made by Sections 51.203(c), 53.104, 305.002(a), 305.003, 308.054(b), 309.051(a), 309.056, 309.103(a) and (b), 355.060, 361.155(b), 362.005, 362.011, 362.013, 404.001(a), 404.003, 404.005(b) and (c), and 551.001(a), Estates Code, as amended by this Act, and Sections 253.001(c), 301.155, 305.004, 309.057, 361.155(c), 404.0035, 404.0036, and 404.0037, Estates Code, as added by this Act, apply to the administration of the estate of a decedent that is pending or commenced on or after the effective date [Jan. 1, 2014] of this Act."

## § 309.052.  List of Claims

A complete list of claims due or owing to the estate must be attached to the inventory and appraisement required by Section 309.051.  The list of claims must state:

(1) the name and, if known, address of each person indebted to the estate;  and

(2) regarding each claim:

(A) the nature of the debt, whether by note, bill, bond, or other written obligation, or by account or verbal contract;

(B) the date the debt was incurred;

(C) the date the debt was or is due;

(D) the amount of the claim, the rate of interest on the claim, and the period for which the claim bears interest;  and

(E) whether the claim is separate property or community property.

Added by Acts 2009, 81st Leg., ch. 680, § 1, eff. Jan. 1, 2014. Amended by Acts 2011, 82nd Leg., ch. 1338 (S.B. 1198), § 2.41, eff. Jan. 1, 2014.

## § 309.053.  Affidavit of Personal Representative

The personal representative shall attach to the inventory, appraisement, and list of claims the representative's affidavit, subscribed and sworn to before an officer in the county authorized by law to administer oaths, that the inventory, appraisement, and list of claims are a true and complete statement of the property and claims of the estate of which the representative has knowledge.

Added by Acts 2009, 81st Leg., ch. 680, § 1, eff. Jan. 1, 2014.

### § 309.054. Approval or Disapproval by the Court

(a) On the filing of the inventory, appraisement, and list of claims with the court clerk, the judge shall examine and approve or disapprove the inventory, appraisement, and list of claims.

(b) If the judge approves the inventory, appraisement, and list of claims, the judge shall enter an order to that effect.

(c) If the judge does not approve the inventory, appraisement, or list of claims, the judge:

(1) shall enter an order to that effect requiring the filing of another inventory, appraisement, or list of claims, whichever is not approved, within a period specified in the order not to exceed 20 days after the date the order is entered; and

(2) may, if considered necessary, appoint new appraisers.

Added by Acts 2009, 81st Leg., ch. 680, § 1, eff. Jan. 1, 2014.

### § 309.055. Failure of Joint Personal Representatives to File Inventory, Appraisement, and List of Claims or Affidavit in Lieu of Inventory, Appraisement, and List of Claims

(a) If more than one personal representative qualifies to serve, any one or more of the representatives, on the neglect of the other representatives, may make and file an inventory, appraisement, and list of claims or an affidavit in lieu of an inventory, appraisement, and list of claims.

(b) A personal representative who neglects to make or file an inventory, appraisement, and list of claims or an affidavit in lieu of an inventory, appraisement, and list of claims may not interfere with and does not have any power over the estate after another representative makes and files an inventory, appraisement, and list of claims or an affidavit in lieu of an inventory, appraisement, and list of claims.

(c) The personal representative who files the inventory, appraisement, and list of claims or the affidavit in lieu of an inventory, appraisement, and list of claims is entitled to the whole administration unless, before the 61st day after the date the representative files the

inventory, appraisement, and list of claims or the affidavit in lieu of an inventory, appraisement, and list of claims, one or more delinquent representatives file with the court a written, sworn, and reasonable excuse that the court considers satisfactory. The court shall enter an order removing one or more delinquent representatives and revoking those representatives' letters if:

(1) an excuse is not filed; or

(2) the court does not consider the filed excuse sufficient.

Added by Acts 2009, 81st Leg., ch. 680, § 1, eff. Jan. 1, 2014. Amended by Acts 2011, 82nd Leg., ch. 1338 (S.B. 1198), § 2.42, eff. Jan. 1, 2014.

### § 309.056. Affidavit in Lieu of Inventory, Appraisement, and List of Claims

(a) In this section, "beneficiary" means a person, entity, state, governmental agency of the state, charitable organization, or trust entitled to receive property:

(1) under the terms of a decedent's will, to be determined for purposes of this section with the assumption that each person who is alive on the date of the decedent's death survives any period required to receive the bequest as specified by the terms of the will; or

(2) as an heir of the decedent.

(b) Notwithstanding Sections 309.051 and 309.052, or any contrary provision in a decedent's will that does not specifically prohibit the filing of an affidavit described by this subsection, if there are no unpaid debts, except for secured debts, taxes, and administration expenses, at the time the inventory is due, including any extensions, an independent executor may file with the court clerk, in lieu of the inventory, appraisement, and list of claims, an affidavit stating that all debts, except for secured debts, taxes, and administration expenses, are paid and that all beneficiaries have received a verified, full, and detailed inventory and appraisement. The affidavit in lieu of the inventory, appraisement, and list of claims must be filed within the 90–day period prescribed by Section 309.051(a), unless the court grants an extension.

(c) If the independent executor files an affidavit in lieu of the inventory, appraisement, and list of claims as authorized under Subsection (b):

(1) any person interested in the estate, including a possible heir of the decedent or a beneficiary under a prior will of the decedent, is entitled to receive a copy of the inventory, appraisement, and

list of claims from the independent executor on written request;

(2) the independent executor may provide a copy of the inventory, appraisement, and list of claims to any person the independent executor believes in good faith may be a person interested in the estate without liability to the estate or its beneficiaries; and

(3) a person interested in the estate may apply to the court for an order compelling compliance with Subdivision (1), and the court, in its discretion, may compel the independent executor to provide a copy of the inventory, appraisement, and list of claims to the interested person or may deny the application.

(d) An independent executor is not liable for choosing to file:

(1) an affidavit under this section in lieu of filing an inventory, appraisement, and list of claims, if permitted by law; or

(2) an inventory, appraisement, and list of claims in lieu of filing an affidavit under this section.

Added by Acts 2011, 82nd Leg., ch. 1338 (S.B. 1198), § 2.43, eff. Jan. 1, 2014. Amended by Acts 2013, 83rd Leg., ch. 1136 (H.B. 2912), § 41, eff. Jan. 1, 2014.

Section 62(e) of Acts 2013, 83rd Leg., ch. 1136 (H.B. 2912) provides:
"The changes in law made by Sections 51.203(c), 53.104, 305.002(a), 305.003, 308.054(b), 309.051(a), 309.056, 309.103(a) and (b), 355.060, 361.155(b), 362.005, 362.011, 362.013, 404.001(a), 404.003, 404.005(b) and (c), and 551.001(a), Estates Code, as amended by this Act, and Sections 253.001(c), 301.155, 305.004, 309.057, 361.155(c), 404.0035, 404.0036, and 404.0037, Estates Code, as added by this Act, apply to the administration of the estate of a decedent that is pending or commenced on or after the effective date [Jan. 1, 2014] of this Act."

### § 309.057. Penalty for Failure to Timely File Inventory, Appraisement, and List of Claims or Affidavit in Lieu of

(a) This section applies only to a personal representative, including an independent executor or administrator, who does not file an inventory, appraisement, and list of claims or affidavit in lieu of the inventory, appraisement, and list of claims, as applicable, within the period prescribed by Section 309.051 or any extension granted by the court.

(b) Any person interested in the estate on written complaint, or the court on the court's own motion, may have a personal representative to whom this section applies cited to file the inventory, appraisement, and list of claims or affidavit in lieu of the inventory, appraisement, and list of claims, as applicable, and show cause for the failure to timely file.

(c) If the personal representative does not file the inventory, appraisement, and list of claims or affidavit

in lieu of the inventory, appraisement, and list of claims, as applicable, after being cited or does not show good cause for the failure to timely file, the court on hearing may fine the representative in an amount not to exceed $1,000.

(d) The personal representative and the representative's sureties, if any, are liable for any fine imposed under this section and for all damages and costs sustained by the representative's failure. The fine, damages, and costs may be recovered in any court of competent jurisdiction.

Added by Acts 2013, 83rd Leg., ch. 1136 (H.B. 2912), § 42, eff. Jan. 1, 2014.

Section 62(e) of Acts 2013, 83rd Leg., ch. 1136 (H.B. 2912) provides:
"The changes in law made by Sections 51.203(c), 53.104, 305.002(a), 305.003, 308.054(b), 309.051(a), 309.056, 309.103(a) and (b), 355.060, 361.155(b), 362.005, 362.011, 362.013, 404.001(a), 404.003, 404.005(b) and (c), and 551.001(a), Estates Code, as amended by this Act, and Sections 253.001(c), 301.155, 305.004, 309.057, 361.155(c), 404.0035, 404.0036, and 404.0037, Estates Code, as added by this Act, apply to the administration of the estate of a decedent that is pending or commenced on or after the effective date [Jan. 1, 2014] of this Act."

## SUBCHAPTER C. CHANGES TO INVENTORY, APPRAISEMENT, AND LIST OF CLAIMS

### § 309.101. Discovery of Additional Property or Claims

(a) If after the filing of the inventory, appraisement, and list of claims the personal representative acquires possession or knowledge of property or claims of the estate not included in the inventory, appraisement, and list of claims the representative shall promptly file with the court clerk a verified, full, and detailed supplemental inventory, appraisement, and list of claims.

(b) If after the filing of the affidavit in lieu of the inventory, appraisement, and list of claims the personal representative acquires possession or knowledge of property or claims of the estate not included in the inventory and appraisement given to the beneficiaries, the representative shall promptly file with the court clerk a supplemental affidavit in lieu of the inventory, appraisement, and list of claims stating that all beneficiaries have received a verified, full, and detailed supplemental inventory and appraisement.

Added by Acts 2009, 81st Leg., ch. 680, § 1, eff. Jan. 1, 2014. Amended by Acts 2011, 82nd Leg., ch. 1338 (S.B. 1198), § 2.44, eff. Jan. 1, 2014.

### § 309.102. Additional Inventory and Appraisement or List of Claims

(a) On the written complaint of any interested person that property or claims of the estate have not been included in the filed inventory, appraisement, and list of claims, the personal representative shall be cited to appear before the court in which the cause is pending and show cause why the representative should not be required to make and file an additional inventory and appraisement or list of claims, or both, as applicable.

(b) After hearing the complaint, if the court is satisfied of the truth of the complaint, the court shall enter an order requiring the personal representative to make and file an additional inventory and appraisement or list of claims, or both, as applicable. The additional inventory and appraisement or list of claims:

    (1) must be made and filed in the same manner as the original inventory and appraisement or list of claims within the period prescribed by the court, not to exceed 20 days after the date the order is entered; and

    (2) may include only property or claims not previously included in the inventory and appraisement or list of claims.

Added by Acts 2009, 81st Leg., ch. 680, § 1, eff. Jan. 1, 2014.

## § 309.103. Correction of Inventory, Appraisement, or List of Claims for Erroneous or Unjust Item

(a) Any interested person who considers an inventory, appraisement, or list of claims or an affidavit in lieu of the inventory, appraisement, and list of claims to be erroneous or unjust in any particular may:

    (1) file a written complaint setting forth the alleged erroneous or unjust item; and

    (2) have the personal representative cited to appear before the court and show cause why the item should not be corrected.

(b) On the hearing of the complaint, if the court is satisfied from the evidence that the inventory, appraisement, or list of claims or an affidavit in lieu of the inventory, appraisement, and list of claims is erroneous or unjust as alleged in the complaint, the court shall enter an order:

    (1) specifying the erroneous or unjust item and the corrections to be made; and

    (2) if the complaint relates to an inventory, appraisement, or list of claims, appointing appraisers to make a new appraisement correcting the erroneous or unjust item and requiring the filing of the new appraisement before the 21st day after the date of the order.

(c) The court on the court's own motion or that of the personal representative may also have a new appraisement made for the purposes described by this section.

Added by Acts 2009, 81st Leg., ch. 680, § 1, eff. Jan. 1, 2014. Amended by Acts 2013, 83rd Leg., ch. 1136 (H.B. 2912), § 43, eff. Jan. 1, 2014.

Section 62(e) of Acts 2013, 83rd Leg., ch. 1136 (H.B. 2912) provides:

"The changes in law made by Sections 51.203(c), 53.104, 305.002(a), 305.003, 308.054(b), 309.051(a), 309.056, 309.103(a) and (b), 355.060, 361.155(b), 362.005, 362.011, 362.013, 404.001(a), 404.003, 404.005(b) and (c), and 551.001(a), Estates Code, as amended by this Act, and Sections 253.001(c), 301.155, 305.004, 309.057, 361.155(c), 404.0035, 404.0036, and 404.0037, Estates Code, as added by this Act, apply to the administration of the estate of a decedent that is pending or commenced on or after the effective date [Jan. 1, 2014] of this Act."

## § 309.104. Reappraisement

(a) A reappraisement made, filed, and approved by the court replaces the original appraisement. Not more than one reappraisement may be made.

(b) Notwithstanding Subsection (a), an interested person may object to a reappraisement regardless of whether the court has approved the reappraisement. If the court finds that the reappraisement is erroneous or unjust, the court shall appraise the property on the basis of the evidence before the court.

Added by Acts 2009, 81st Leg., ch. 680, § 1, eff. Jan. 1, 2014.

## SUBCHAPTER D. USE OF INVENTORY, APPRAISEMENT, AND LIST OF CLAIMS AS EVIDENCE

## § 309.151. Use of Inventory, Appraisement, and List of Claims as Evidence

Each inventory, appraisement, and list of claims that has been made, filed, and approved in accordance with law, the record of the inventory, appraisement, and list of claims, or a copy of an original or the record that has been certified under the seal of the county court affixed by the clerk:

    (1) may be given in evidence in any court of this state in any suit by or against the personal representative; and

    (2) is not conclusive for or against the representative if it is shown that:

        (A) any property or claim of the estate is not shown in the originals, the record, or the copies; or

        (B) the value of the property or claim of the estate exceeded the value shown in the appraisement or list of claims.

Added by Acts 2009, 81st Leg., ch. 680, § 1, eff. Jan. 1, 2014.

# CHAPTER 310. ALLOCATION OF ESTATE INCOME AND EXPENSES

## § 310.001. Definition

In this chapter, "undistributed assets" includes funds used to pay debts, administration expenses, and federal and state estate, inheritance, succession, and generation-skipping transfer taxes until the date the debts, expenses, and taxes are paid.

Added by Acts 2009, 81st Leg., ch. 680, § 1, eff. Jan. 1, 2014.

## § 310.002. Applicability of Other Law

Chapter 116, Property Code, controls to the extent of any conflict between this chapter and Chapter 116, Property Code.

Added by Acts 2009, 81st Leg., ch. 680, § 1, eff. Jan. 1, 2014.

## § 310.003. Allocation of Expenses

(a) Except as provided by Section 310.004(a) and unless the will provides otherwise, all expenses incurred in connection with the settlement of a decedent's estate shall be charged against the principal of the estate, including:

(1) debts;

(2) funeral expenses;

(3) estate taxes and penalties relating to estate taxes; and

(4) family allowances.

(b) Fees and expenses of an attorney, accountant, or other professional advisor, commissions and expenses of a personal representative, court costs, and all other similar fees or expenses relating to the administration of the estate and interest relating to estate taxes shall be allocated between the income and principal of the estate as the executor determines in the executor's discretion to be just and equitable.

Added by Acts 2009, 81st Leg., ch. 680, § 1, eff. Jan. 1, 2014.

## § 310.004. Income Determination and Distribution

(a) Unless a will provides otherwise, income from the assets of a decedent's estate that accrues after the death of the testator and before distribution, including income from property used to discharge liabilities, shall be:

(1) determined according to the rules applicable to a trustee under the Texas Trust Code (Subtitle B, Title 9, Property Code); and

(2) distributed as provided by Subsections (b) and (c) and by Chapter 116, Property Code.

(b) Income from property devised to a specific devisee shall be distributed to the devisee after reduction for:

(1) property taxes;

(2) other taxes, including taxes imposed on income that accrues during the period of administration and that is payable to the devisee;

(3) ordinary repairs;

(4) insurance premiums;

(5) interest accrued after the testator's death; and

(6) other expenses of management and operation of the property.

(c) The balance of the net income shall be distributed to all other devisees after reduction for the balance of property taxes, ordinary repairs, insurance premiums, interest accrued, other expenses of management and operation of all property from which the estate is entitled to income, and taxes imposed on income that accrues during the period of administration and that is payable or allocable to the devisees, in proportion to the devisees' respective interests in the undistributed assets of the estate.

Added by Acts 2009, 81st Leg., ch. 680, § 1, eff. Jan. 1, 2014.

## § 310.005. Treatment of Income Received by Trustee

Income received by a trustee under this chapter shall be treated as income of the trust as provided by Section 116.101, Property Code.

Added by Acts 2009, 81st Leg., ch. 680, § 1, eff. Jan. 1, 2014.

## § 310.006. Frequency and Method of Determining Interests in Certain Estate Assets

Except as required by Sections 2055 and 2056, Internal Revenue Code of 1986 (26 U.S.C. Sections 2055 and 2056), the frequency and method of determining the beneficiaries' respective interests in the undistributed assets of an estate are in the sole and absolute discretion of the executor of the estate. The executor may consider all relevant factors, including administrative convenience and expense and the interests of the various beneficiaries of the estate, to reach a fair and equitable result among beneficiaries.

Added by Acts 2009, 81st Leg., ch. 680, § 1, eff. Jan. 1, 2014.

# SUBTITLE H.  CONTINUATION OF ADMINISTRATION

## CHAPTER 351.  POWERS AND DUTIES OF PERSONAL REPRESENTATIVES IN GENERAL

### SUBCHAPTER A.  GENERAL PROVISIONS

### SUBCHAPTER B.  GENERAL AUTHORITY OF PERSONAL REPRESENTATIVES

### SUBCHAPTER C.  POSSESSION AND CARE OF ESTATE PROPERTY

### SUBCHAPTER D.  COLLECTION OF CLAIMS; RECOVERY OF PROPERTY

### SUBCHAPTER E.  OPERATION OF BUSINESS

### SUBCHAPTER F.  AUTHORITY TO ENGAGE IN CERTAIN BORROWING

### SUBCHAPTER G.  PAYMENT OF INCOME OF CERTAIN ESTATES DURING ADMINISTRATION

### SUBCHAPTER H.  CERTAIN ADMINISTERED ESTATES

### SUBCHAPTER A.  GENERAL PROVISIONS

#### § 351.001.  Applicability of Common Law

The rights, powers, and duties of executors and administrators are governed by common law principles to the extent that those principles do not conflict with the statutes of this state.

Added by Acts 2009, 81st Leg., ch. 680, § 1, eff. Jan. 1, 2014.

#### § 351.002.  Appeal Bond

(a) Except as provided by Subsection (b), an appeal bond is not required if an appeal is taken by an executor or administrator.

(b) An executor or administrator must give an appeal bond if the appeal personally concerns the executor or administrator.

Added by Acts 2009, 81st Leg., ch. 680, § 1, eff. Jan. 1, 2014.

#### § 351.003.  Certain Costs Adjudged Against Personal Representative

If a personal representative neglects to perform a required duty or is removed for cause, the representative and the sureties on the representative's bond are liable for:

(1) the costs of removal and other additional costs incurred that are not expenditures authorized by this title; and

(2) reasonable attorney's fees incurred in:

(A) removing the representative; or

(B) obtaining compliance regarding any statutory duty the representative has neglected.

Added by Acts 2009, 81st Leg., ch. 680, § 1, eff. Jan. 1, 2014.

## SUBCHAPTER B. GENERAL AUTHORITY OF PERSONAL REPRESENTATIVES

### § 351.051. Exercise of Authority Under Court Order

(a) A personal representative of an estate may renew or extend any obligation owed by or to the estate on application and order authorizing the renewal or extension. If a personal representative considers it in the interest of the estate, the representative may, on written application to the court and if authorized by court order:

(1) purchase or exchange property;

(2) take claims or property for the use and benefit of the estate in payment of a debt due or owed to the estate;

(3) compound bad or doubtful debts due or owed to the estate;

(4) make a compromise or settlement in relation to property or a claim in dispute or litigation;

(5) compromise or pay in full any secured claim that has been allowed and approved as required by law against the estate by conveying to the holder of the claim the real estate or personal property securing the claim:

(A) in full payment, liquidation, and satisfaction of the claim; and

(B) in consideration of cancellation of notes, deeds of trust, mortgages, chattel mortgages, or other evidences of liens securing the payment of the claim; or

(6) abandon the administration of burdensome or worthless estate property.

(b) Abandoned property may be foreclosed on by a mortgagee or other secured party or a trustee without further court order.

Added by Acts 2009, 81st Leg., ch. 680, § 1, eff. Jan. 1, 2014.

### § 351.052. Exercise of Authority Without Court Order

(a) A personal representative of an estate may, without application to or order of the court:

(1) release a lien on payment at maturity of the debt secured by the lien;

(2) vote stocks by limited or general proxy;

(3) pay calls and assessments;

(4) insure the estate against liability in appropriate cases;

(5) insure estate property against fire, theft, and other hazards; or

(6) pay taxes, court costs, and bond premiums.

(b) A personal representative who is under court control may apply and obtain a court order if the representative has doubts regarding the propriety of the exercise of any power listed in Subsection (a).

Added by Acts 2009, 81st Leg., ch. 680, § 1, eff. Jan. 1, 2014.

### § 351.053. Authority to Serve Pending Appeal of Appointment

Pending an appeal from an order or judgment appointing an administrator or temporary administrator, the appointee shall continue to:

(1) act as administrator or temporary administrator; and

(2) prosecute any suit then pending in favor of the estate.

Added by Acts 2009, 81st Leg., ch. 680, § 1, eff. Jan. 1, 2014.

### § 351.054. Authority to Commence Suits

(a) An executor or administrator appointed in this state may commence a suit for:

(1) recovery of personal property, debts, or damages; or

(2) title to or possession of land, any right attached to or arising from that land, or an injury or damage done to that land.

(b) A judgment in a suit described by Subsection (a) is conclusive, but may be set aside by any interested person for fraud or collusion on the executor's or administrator's part.

Added by Acts 2009, 81st Leg., ch. 680, § 1, eff. Jan. 1, 2014.

## SUBCHAPTER C. POSSESSION AND CARE OF ESTATE PROPERTY

### § 351.101. Duty of Care

An executor or administrator of an estate shall take care of estate property as a prudent person would take of that person's own property, and if any buildings belong to the estate, the executor or administrator shall keep those buildings in good repair, except for extraordinary casualties, unless directed by a court order not to do so.

Added by Acts 2009, 81st Leg., ch. 680, § 1, eff. Jan. 1, 2014.

## § 351.102. Possession of Personal Property and Records

(a) Immediately after receiving letters testamentary or of administration, the personal representative of an estate shall collect and take possession of the estate's personal property, record books, title papers, and other business papers.

(b) The personal representative shall deliver the property, books, and papers described by Subsection (a) that are in the representative's possession to the person or persons legally entitled to the property, books, and papers when:

(1) the administration of the estate is closed; or

(2) a successor personal representative receives letters testamentary or of administration.

Added by Acts 2009, 81st Leg., ch. 680, § 1, eff. Jan. 1, 2014.

## § 351.103. Possession of Property Held in Common Ownership

If an estate holds or owns any property in common or as part owner with another, the personal representative of the estate is entitled to possession of the property in common with the other part owner or owners in the same manner as other owners in common or joint owners are entitled to possession of the property.

Added by Acts 2009, 81st Leg., ch. 680, § 1, eff. Jan. 1, 2014.

## § 351.104. Administration of Partnership Interest

(a) If a decedent was a partner in a general partnership and the partnership agreement or articles of partnership provide that, on the death of a partner, the partner's personal representative is entitled to that partner's place in the partnership, a personal representative accordingly contracting to enter the partnership under the partnership agreement or articles of partnership is, to the extent allowed by law, liable to a third person only to the extent of:

(1) the deceased partner's capital in the partnership; and

(2) the estate's assets held by the representative.

(b) This section does not exonerate a personal representative from liability for the representative's negligence.

Added by Acts 2009, 81st Leg., ch. 680, § 1, eff. Jan. 1, 2014.

## § 351.105. Holding of Stocks, Bonds, and Other Personal Property in Nominee's Name

(a) Unless otherwise provided by the will, a personal representative of an estate may cause stocks, bonds, and other personal property of the estate to be registered and held in the name of a nominee without mentioning the fiduciary relationship in any instrument or record constituting or evidencing title to that property. The representative is liable for the acts of the nominee with respect to property registered in this manner. The representative's records must at all times show the ownership of the property.

(b) Any property registered in the manner described by Subsection (a) shall be kept:

(1) in the possession and control of the personal representative at all times; and

(2) separate from the representative's individual property.

Added by Acts 2009, 81st Leg., ch. 680, § 1, eff. Jan. 1, 2014.

## SUBCHAPTER D. COLLECTION OF CLAIMS; RECOVERY OF PROPERTY

## § 351.151. Ordinary Diligence Required

(a) If there is a reasonable prospect of collecting the claims or recovering the property of an estate, the personal representative of the estate shall use ordinary diligence to:

(1) collect all claims and debts due the estate; and

(2) recover possession of all property to which the estate has claim or title.

(b) If a personal representative wilfully neglects to use the ordinary diligence required under Subsection (a), the representative and the sureties on the representative's bond are liable, on the suit of any person interested in the estate, for the use of the estate, for the amount of those claims or the value of that property lost by the neglect.

Added by Acts 2009, 81st Leg., ch. 680, § 1, eff. Jan. 1, 2014.

## § 351.152. Contingent Interest for Certain Attorney's Fees; Court Approval

(a) Except as provided by Subsection (b) and subject only to the approval of the court in which the estate is being administered, a personal representative may convey or enter into a contract to convey for attorney services a contingent interest in any property sought to be recovered, not to exceed a one-third interest in the property.

(b) A personal representative, including an independent executor or independent administrator, may convey or enter into a contract to convey for attorney services a contingent interest in any property sought to be recovered under this subchapter in an amount that exceeds a one-third interest in the property only on the approval of the court in which the estate is being administered. The court must approve a contract entered into or conveyance made under this section before an attorney performs any legal services. A contract entered into or a conveyance made in violation of this section is void unless the court ratifies or reforms the contract or documents relating to the conveyance to the extent necessary to make the contract or conveyance meet the requirements of this section.

(c) In approving a contract or conveyance under this section, the court shall consider:

(1) the time and labor required, the novelty and difficulty of the questions involved, and the skill required to perform the legal services properly;

(2) the fee customarily charged in the locality for similar legal services;

(3) the value of the property recovered or sought to be recovered by the personal representative under this subchapter;

(4) the benefits to the estate that the attorney will be responsible for securing; and

(5) the experience and ability of the attorney who will perform the services.

Added by Acts 2009, 81st Leg., ch. 680, § 1, eff. Jan. 1, 2014.

### § 351.153.  Recovery of Certain Expenses

On proof satisfactory to the court, a personal representative of an estate is entitled to all necessary and reasonable expenses incurred by the representative in:

(1) collecting or attempting to collect a claim or debt owed to the estate; or

(2) recovering or attempting to recover property to which the estate has a title or claim.

Added by Acts 2009, 81st Leg., ch. 680, § 1, eff. Jan. 1, 2014.

SUBCHAPTER E.  OPERATION OF BUSINESS

### § 351.201.  Definition

In this subchapter, "business" includes a farm, ranch, or factory.

Added by Acts 2009, 81st Leg., ch. 680, § 1, eff. Jan. 1, 2014.

### § 351.202.  Order Requiring Personal Representative to Operate Business.

(a) A court, after notice to all interested persons and a hearing, may order the personal representative of an estate to operate a business that is part of the estate and may grant the representative the powers to operate the business that the court determines are appropriate, after considering the factors listed in Subsection (b), if:

(1) the disposition of the business has not been specifically directed by the decedent's will;

(2) it is not necessary to sell the business at once for the payment of debts or for any other lawful purpose; and

(3) the court determines that the operation of the business by the representative is in the best interest of the estate.

(b) In determining which powers to grant a personal representative in an order entered under Subsection (a), the court shall consider:

(1) the condition of the estate and the business;

(2) the necessity that may exist for the future sale of the business or of business property to provide for payment of debts or claims against the estate or other lawful expenditures with respect to the estate;

(3) the effect of the order on the speedy settlement of the estate; and

(4) the best interests of the estate.

Added by Acts 2009, 81st Leg., ch. 680, § 1, eff. Jan. 1, 2014.

### § 351.203.  Powers of Personal Representative Regarding Business

(a) A personal representative granted authority to operate a business in an order entered under Section 351.202(a) has the powers granted under Section 351.052, regardless of whether the order specifies that the representative has those powers, unless the order specifically provides that the representative does not have one or more of the powers listed in Section 351.052.

(b) In addition to the powers granted to the personal representative under Section 351.052, subject to any specific limitation on those powers in accordance with Subsection (a), an order entered under Section 351.202(a) may grant the representative one or more of the following powers:

(1) the power to hire, pay, and terminate the employment of employees of the business;

(2) the power to incur debt on behalf of the business, including debt secured by liens against assets of the business or estate, if permitted or directed by the order;

(3) the power to purchase and sell property in the ordinary course of the operation of the business, including the power to purchase and sell real property if the court finds that the principal purpose of the business is the purchasing and selling of real property and the order states that finding;

(4) the power to enter into a lease or contract, the term of which may extend beyond the settlement of the estate, but only to the extent that granting the power appears to be consistent with the speedy settlement of the estate; and

(5) any other power the court finds necessary with respect to the operation of the business.

(c) If the order entered under Section 351.202(a) gives the personal representative the power to purchase, sell, lease, or otherwise encumber property:

(1) the purchase, sale, lease, or encumbrance is governed by the terms of the order; and

(2) the representative is not required to comply with any other provision of this title regarding the purchase, sale, lease, or encumbrance, including any provision requiring citation or notice.

Added by Acts 2009, 81st Leg., ch. 680, § 1, eff. Jan. 1, 2014.

### § 351.204.  Fiduciary Duties of Personal Representative Regarding Business

(a) A personal representative who operates a business under an order entered under Section 351.202(a) has the same fiduciary duties as a representative who does not operate a business that is part of an estate.

(b) In operating a business under an order entered under Section 351.202(a), a personal representative shall consider:

(1) the condition of the estate and the business;

(2) the necessity that may exist for the future sale of the business or of business property to provide for payment of debts or claims against the estate or other lawful expenditures with respect to the estate;

(3) the effect of the order on the speedy settlement of the estate; and

(4) the best interests of the estate.

(c) A personal representative who operates a business under an order entered under Section 351.202(a) shall report to the court with respect to the operation

and condition of the business as part of the accounts required by Chapters 359 and 362, unless the court orders the reports regarding the business to be made more frequently or in a different manner or form.

Added by Acts 2009, 81st Leg., ch. 680, § 1, eff. Jan. 1, 2014.

### § 351.205.  Real Property of Business; Notice

(a) A personal representative shall file a notice in the real property records of the county in which the real property is located before purchasing, selling, leasing, or otherwise encumbering any real property of the business in accordance with an order entered under Section 351.202(a).

(b) The notice filed under Subsection (a) must:

(1) state:

(A) the decedent's name;

(B) the county of the court in which the decedent's estate is pending;

(C) the cause number assigned to the pending estate; and

(D) that one or more orders have been entered under Section 351.202(a); and

(2) include a description of the property that is the subject of the purchase, sale, lease, or other encumbrance.

(c) For purposes of determining a personal representative's authority with respect to a purchase, sale, lease, or other encumbrance of real property of a business that is part of an estate, a third party who deals in good faith with the representative with respect to the transaction may rely on the notice filed under Subsection (a) and an order entered under Section 351.202(a) and filed as part of the estate records maintained by the clerk of the court in which the estate is pending.

Added by Acts 2009, 81st Leg., ch. 680, § 1, eff. Jan. 1, 2014.

### SUBCHAPTER F.  AUTHORITY TO ENGAGE IN CERTAIN BORROWING

### § 351.251.  Mortgage or Pledge of Estate Property Authorized in Certain Circumstances

Under order of the court, a personal representative of an estate may mortgage or pledge by deed of trust or otherwise as security for an indebtedness any property of the estate as necessary for:

(1) the payment of any ad valorem, income, gift, estate, inheritance, or transfer taxes on the transfer of an estate or due from a decedent or the estate, regardless of whether those taxes are assessed by a

state, a political subdivision of a state, the federal government, or a foreign country;

(2) the payment of expenses of administration, including amounts necessary for operation of a business, farm, or ranch owned by the estate;

(3) the payment of claims allowed and approved, or established by suit, against the estate; or

(4) the renewal and extension of an existing lien.

Added by Acts 2009, 81st Leg., ch. 680, § 1, eff. Jan. 1, 2014.

### § 351.252. Application; Order

(a) If necessary to borrow money for a purpose described by Section 351.251 or to create or extend a lien on estate property as security, the personal representative of the estate shall file a sworn application for that authority with the court. The application must state fully and in detail the circumstances that the representative believes make the granting of the authority necessary.

(b) On the filing of an application under Subsection (a), the clerk shall issue and have posted a citation to all interested persons, stating the nature of the application and requiring any interested person who chooses to do so to appear and show cause, if any, why the application should not be granted.

(c) If satisfied by the evidence adduced at the hearing on an application filed under Subsection (a) that it is in the interest of the estate to borrow money or to extend and renew an existing lien, the court shall issue an order to that effect that sets out the terms of the authority granted under the order.

(d) If a new lien is created on estate property, the court may require, for the protection of the estate and the creditors, that the personal representative's general bond be increased or an additional bond given, as for the sale of real property belonging to the estate.

Added by Acts 2009, 81st Leg., ch. 680, § 1, eff. Jan. 1, 2014.

### § 351.253. Term of Loan or Lien Extension

Except as otherwise provided by this section, the term of a loan or lien renewal authorized under Section 351.252 may not exceed a period of three years from the date original letters testamentary or of administration are granted to the personal representative of the affected estate. The court may authorize an extension of a lien renewed under Section 351.252 for not more than one additional year without further citation or notice.

Added by Acts 2009, 81st Leg., ch. 680, § 1, eff. Jan. 1, 2014.

## SUBCHAPTER G. PAYMENT OF INCOME OF CERTAIN ESTATES DURING ADMINISTRATION

### § 351.301. Applicability of Subchapter

This subchapter applies only to the estate of a decedent that is being administered under the direction, control, and orders of a court in the exercise of the court's probate jurisdiction.

Added by Acts 2009, 81st Leg., ch. 680, § 1, eff. Jan. 1, 2014.

### § 351.302. Application and Order for Payment of Certain Estate Income

(a) On the application of the executor or administrator of an estate or of any interested party, and after notice of the application has been given by posting, the court may order and direct the executor or administrator to pay, or credit to the account of, those persons who the court finds will own the estate assets when administration on the estate is completed, and in the same proportions, that part of the annual net income received by or accruing to the estate that the court finds can conveniently be paid to those owners without prejudice to the rights of creditors, legatees, or other interested parties, if:

(1) it appears from evidence introduced at a hearing on the application, and the court finds, that the reasonable market value of the estate assets on hand at that time, excluding the annual income from the estate assets, is at least twice the aggregate amount of all unpaid debts, administration expenses, and legacies; and

(2) no estate creditor or legatee has appeared and objected.

(b) Except as otherwise provided by this title, nothing in this subchapter authorizes the court to order paid over to the owners of the estate any part of the principal of the estate.

Added by Acts 2009, 81st Leg., ch. 680, § 1, eff. Jan. 1, 2014.

### § 351.303. Treatment of Certain Amounts Received from Mineral Lease

For the purposes of this subchapter, bonuses, rentals, and royalties received for or from an oil, gas, or other mineral lease shall be treated as income rather than as principal.

Added by Acts 2009, 81st Leg., ch. 680, § 1, eff. Jan. 1, 2014.

## SUBCHAPTER H.  CERTAIN ADMINISTERED ESTATES

### § 351.351.  Applicability

This subchapter does not apply to:

(1) the appointment of an independent executor or administrator under Section 401.002 or 401.003(a); or

(2) the appointment of a successor independent executor under Section 404.005 .

Added by Acts 2009, 81st Leg., ch. 680, § 1, eff. Jan. 1, 2014. Amended by Acts 2013, 83rd Leg., ch. 161 (S.B. 1093), § 6.012, eff. Jan. 1, 2014.

### § 351.352.  Ensuring Compliance with Law

A county or probate court shall use reasonable diligence to see that personal representatives of estates administered under court orders and other officers of the court perform the duty enjoined on them by law applicable to those estates.

Added by Acts 2009, 81st Leg., ch. 680, § 1, eff. Jan. 1, 2014.

### § 351.353.  Annual Examination of Certain Estates; Bond of Personal Representative

For each estate administered under orders of a county or probate court, the judge shall, if the judge considers it necessary, annually examine the condition of the estate and the solvency of the bond of the estate's personal representative.  If the judge finds the representative's bond is not sufficient to protect the estate, the judge shall require the representative to execute a new bond in accordance with law.  In each case, the judge, as provided by law, shall notify the representative and the sureties on the representative's bond.

Added by Acts 2009, 81st Leg., ch. 680, § 1, eff. Jan. 1, 2014.

### § 351.354.  Judge's Liability

A judge is liable on the judge's bond to those damaged if damage or loss results to an estate administered under orders of a county or probate court from the gross neglect of the judge to use reasonable diligence in the performance of the judge's duty under this subchapter.

Added by Acts 2009, 81st Leg., ch. 680, § 1, eff. Jan. 1, 2014.

### § 351.355.  Identifying Information

(a) The court may request an applicant or court-appointed fiduciary to produce other information identifying an applicant, decedent, or personal representa-tive, including a social security number, in addition to identifying information the applicant or fiduciary is required to produce under this title.

(b) The court shall maintain any information required under this section, and the information may not be filed with the clerk.

Added by Acts 2009, 81st Leg., ch. 680, § 1, eff. Jan. 1, 2014.

## CHAPTER 352.  COMPENSATION AND EXPENSES OF PERSONAL REPRESENTATIVES AND OTHERS

### SUBCHAPTER A.  COMPENSATION OF PERSONAL REPRESENTATIVES

### SUBCHAPTER A.  COMPENSATION OF PERSONAL REPRESENTATIVES

### § 352.001.  Definition

In this subchapter, "financial institution" means an organization authorized to engage in business under state or federal laws relating to financial institutions, including:

(1) a bank;

(2) a trust company;

(3) a savings bank;

(4) a building and loan association;

(5) a savings and loan company or association; and

(6) a credit union.

Added by Acts 2009, 81st Leg., ch. 680, § 1, eff. Jan. 1, 2014.

### § 352.002.  Standard Compensation

(a) An executor, administrator, or temporary administrator a court finds to have taken care of and managed an estate in compliance with the standards of this title is entitled to receive a five percent commission on all amounts that the executor or administrator actually receives or pays out in cash in the administration of the estate.

(b) The commission described by Subsection (a):

(1) may not exceed, in the aggregate, more than five percent of the gross fair market value of the estate subject to administration; and

(2) is not allowed for:

(A) receiving funds belonging to the testator or intestate that were, at the time of the testator's or intestate's death, either on hand or held for the testator or intestate in a financial institution or a brokerage firm, including cash or a cash equivalent held in a checking account, savings account, certificate of deposit, or money market account;

(B) collecting the proceeds of a life insurance policy; or

(C) paying out cash to an heir or legatee in that person's capacity as an heir or legatee.

Added by Acts 2009, 81st Leg., ch. 680, § 1, eff. Jan. 1, 2014.

### § 352.003. Alternate Compensation

(a) The court may allow an executor, administrator, or temporary administrator reasonable compensation for the executor's or administrator's services, including unusual efforts to collect funds or life insurance, if:

(1) the executor or administrator manages a farm, ranch, factory, or other business of the estate; or

(2) the compensation calculated under Section 352.002 is unreasonably low.

(b) The county court has jurisdiction to receive, consider, and act on applications from independent executors for purposes of this section.

Added by Acts 2009, 81st Leg., ch. 680, § 1, eff. Jan. 1, 2014.

### § 352.004. Denial of Compensation

The court may, on application of an interested person or on the court's own motion, wholly or partly deny a commission allowed by this subchapter if:

(1) the court finds that the executor or administrator has not taken care of and managed estate property prudently; or

(2) the executor or administrator has been removed under Section 404.003 or Subchapter B, Chapter 361.

Added by Acts 2009, 81st Leg., ch. 680, § 1, eff. Jan. 1, 2014. Amended by Acts 2011, 82nd Leg., ch. 1338 (S.B. 1198), § 2.45, eff. Jan. 1, 2014; Acts 2013, 83rd Leg., ch. 161 (S.B. 1093), § 6.013, eff. Jan. 1, 2014.

## SUBCHAPTER B. EXPENSES OF PERSONAL REPRESENTATIVES AND OTHERS

### § 352.051. Expenses; Attorney's Fees

On proof satisfactory to the court, a personal representative of an estate is entitled to:

(1) necessary and reasonable expenses incurred by the representative in:

(A) preserving, safekeeping, and managing the estate;

(B) collecting or attempting to collect claims or debts; and

(C) recovering or attempting to recover property to which the estate has a title or claim; and

(2) reasonable attorney's fees necessarily incurred in connection with the proceedings and management of the estate.

Added by Acts 2009, 81st Leg., ch. 680, § 1, eff. Jan. 1, 2014.

### § 352.052. Allowance for Defense of Will

(a) A person designated as executor in a will or an alleged will, or as administrator with the will or alleged will annexed, who, for the purpose of having the will or alleged will admitted to probate, defends the will or alleged will or prosecutes any proceeding in good faith and with just cause, whether or not successful, shall be allowed out of the estate the executor's or administrator's necessary expenses and disbursements in those proceedings, including reasonable attorney's fees.

(b) A person designated as a devisee in or beneficiary of a will or an alleged will, or as administrator with the will or alleged will annexed, who, for the purpose of having the will or alleged will admitted to probate, defends the will or alleged will or prosecutes any proceeding in good faith and with just cause, whether or not successful, may be allowed out of the estate the person's necessary expenses and disbursements in those proceedings, including reasonable attorney's fees.

Added by Acts 2009, 81st Leg., ch. 680, § 1, eff. Jan. 1, 2014.

### § 352.053. Expense Charges

(a) The court shall act on expense charges in the same manner as other claims against the estate.

(b) All expense charges shall be:

(1) made in writing, showing specifically each item of expense and the date of the expense;

(2) verified by the personal representative's affidavit;

(3) filed with the clerk; and

(4) entered on the claim docket.

Added by Acts 2009, 81st Leg., ch. 680, § 1, eff. Jan. 1, 2014.

## CHAPTER 353. EXEMPT PROPERTY AND FAMILY ALLOWANCE

### SUBCHAPTER A. GENERAL PROVISIONS

## SUBCHAPTER A.  GENERAL PROVISIONS

### § 353.001.  Treatment of Certain Children

For purposes of distributing exempt property and making a family allowance, a child is a child of his or her mother and a child of his or her father, as provided by Sections 201.051, 201.052, and 201.053.

Added by Acts 2009, 81st Leg., ch. 680, § 1, eff. Jan. 1, 2014.

## SUBCHAPTER B.  EXEMPT PROPERTY; ALLOWANCE IN LIEU OF EXEMPT PROPERTY

### § 353.051.  Exempt Property to Be Set Aside

(a) Unless an application and verified affidavit are filed as provided by Subsection (b), immediately after the inventory, appraisement, and list of claims of an estate are approved or after the affidavit in lieu of the inventory, appraisement, and list of claims is filed, the court by order shall set aside:

(1) the homestead for the use and benefit of the decedent's surviving spouse and minor children; and

(2) all other estate property that is exempt from execution or forced sale by the constitution and laws of this state for the use and benefit of the decedent's:

(A) surviving spouse and minor children;

(B) unmarried adult children remaining with the decedent's family; and

(C) each other adult child who is incapacitated.

(b) Before the inventory, appraisement, and list of claims of an estate are approved or, if applicable, before the affidavit in lieu of the inventory, appraisement, and list of claims is filed:

(1) the decedent's surviving spouse or any other person authorized to act on behalf of the decedent's minor children may apply to the court to have exempt property, including the homestead, set aside by filing an application and a verified affidavit listing all property that the applicant claims is exempt; and

(2) any of the decedent's unmarried adult children remaining with the decedent's family, any other adult child of the decedent who is incapacitated, or a person who is authorized to act on behalf of the adult incapacitated child may apply to the court to have all exempt property, other than the homestead, set aside by filing an application and a verified affidavit listing all property, other than the homestead, that the applicant claims is exempt.

(c) At a hearing on an application filed under Subsection (b), the applicant has the burden of proof by a preponderance of the evidence.  The court shall set aside property of the decedent's estate that the court finds is exempt.

Added by Acts 2009, 81st Leg., ch. 680, § 1, eff. Jan. 1, 2014. Amended by Acts 2011, 82nd Leg., ch. 810 (H.B. 2492), § 2.01, eff. Jan. 1, 2014; Acts 2011, 82nd Leg., ch. 1338 (S.B. 1198), § 2.46, eff. Jan. 1, 2014.

### § 353.052.  Delivery of Exempt Property

(a) The executor or administrator of an estate shall deliver, without delay, exempt property that has been set aside for the decedent's surviving spouse and children in accordance with this section.

(b) If there is a surviving spouse and there are no children of the decedent, or if all the children, including any adult incapacitated children, of the decedent are also the children of the surviving spouse, the executor or administrator shall deliver all exempt property to the surviving spouse.

(c) If there is a surviving spouse and there are children of the decedent who are not also children of the surviving spouse, the executor or administrator shall deliver the share of those children in exempt property, other than the homestead, to:

(1) the children, if the children are of legal age;

(2) the children's guardian, if the children are minors; or

(3) the guardian of each of the children who is an incapacitated adult, or to another appropriate person, as determined by the court, on behalf of the adult incapacitated child if there is no guardian.

(d) If there is no surviving spouse and there are children of the decedent, the executor or administrator shall deliver exempt property, other than the homestead, to:

(1) the children, if the children are of legal age;

(2) the children's guardian, if the children are minors; or

(3) the guardian of each of the children who is an incapacitated adult, or to another appropriate person, as determined by the court, on behalf of the adult incapacitated child if there is no guardian.

(e) In all cases, the executor or administrator shall deliver the homestead to:

(1) the decedent's surviving spouse, if there is a surviving spouse; or

(2) the guardian of the decedent's minor children, if there is not a surviving spouse.

Added by Acts 2009, 81st Leg., ch. 680, § 1, eff. Jan. 1, 2014. Amended by Acts 2011, 82nd Leg., ch. 810 (H.B. 2492), § 2.02, eff. Jan. 1, 2014.

### § 353.053.  Allowance in Lieu of Exempt Property

(a) If all or any of the specific articles exempt from execution or forced sale by the constitution and laws of this state are not among the decedent's effects, the court shall make, in lieu of the articles not among the effects, a reasonable allowance to be paid to the decedent's surviving spouse and children as provided by Section 353.054.

(b) The allowance in lieu of a homestead may not exceed $45,000, and the allowance in lieu of other exempt property may not exceed $30,000, excluding the family allowance for the support of the surviving

spouse, minor children, and adult incapacitated children provided by Subchapter C.

Added by Acts 2009, 81st Leg., ch. 680, § 1, eff. Jan. 1, 2014. Amended by Acts 2011, 82nd Leg., ch. 810 (H.B. 2492), § 2.03, eff. Jan. 1, 2014;  Acts 2013, 83rd Leg., ch. 647 (H.B. 789), § 2.01, eff. Jan. 1, 2014.

### § 353.054.  Payment of Allowance in Lieu of Exempt Property

(a) The executor or administrator of an estate shall pay an allowance in lieu of exempt property in accordance with this section.

(b) If there is a surviving spouse and there are no children of the decedent, or if all the children, including any adult incapacitated children, of the decedent are also the children of the surviving spouse, the executor or administrator shall pay the entire allowance to the surviving spouse.

(c) If there is a surviving spouse and there are children of the decedent who are not also children of the surviving spouse, the executor or administrator shall pay the surviving spouse one-half of the entire allowance plus the shares of the decedent's children of whom the surviving spouse is the parent.  The remaining shares must be paid to:

(1) the decedent's adult children of whom the surviving spouse is not a parent and who are not incapacitated;

(2) the guardian of the children of whom the surviving spouse is not a parent and who are minors; or

(3) the guardian or another appropriate person, as determined by the court, if there is no guardian, of each child who is an incapacitated adult.

(d) If there is no surviving spouse and there are children of the decedent, the executor or administrator shall divide the entire allowance equally among the children and pay the children's shares to:

(1) each of those children who are adults and who are not incapacitated;

(2) the guardian of each of those children who are minors; or

(3) the guardian or another appropriate person, as determined by the court, if there is no guardian, of each of those children who is an incapacitated adult.

Added by Acts 2009, 81st Leg., ch. 680, § 1, eff. Jan. 1, 2014. Amended by Acts 2011, 82nd Leg., ch. 810 (H.B. 2492), § 2.04, eff. Jan. 1, 2014.

## § 353.055. Method of Paying Allowance in Lieu of Exempt Property

(a) An allowance in lieu of any exempt property shall be paid in the manner selected by the decedent's surviving spouse or children of legal age, or by the guardian of the decedent's minor children, or by the guardian of each adult incapacitated child or other appropriate person, as determined by the court, if there is no guardian, as follows:

(1) in money out of estate funds that come into the executor's or administrator's possession;

(2) in any of the decedent's property or a part of the property chosen by those individuals at the appraisement; or

(3) part in money described by Subdivision (1) and part in property described by Subdivision (2).

(b) Property specifically devised to another may be taken as provided by Subsection (a) only if other available property is insufficient to pay the allowance.

Added by Acts 2009, 81st Leg., ch. 680, § 1, eff. Jan. 1, 2014. Amended by Acts 2011, 82nd Leg., ch. 810 (H.B. 2492), § 2.05, eff. Jan. 1, 2014.

## § 353.056. Sale of Property to Raise Funds for Allowance in Lieu of Exempt Property

(a) On the written application of the decedent's surviving spouse and children, or of a person authorized to represent any of those children, the court shall order the sale of estate property for cash in an amount that will be sufficient to raise the amount of the allowance provided under Section 353.053 or a portion of that amount, as necessary, if:

(1) the decedent had no property that the surviving spouse or children are willing to take for the allowance or the decedent had insufficient property; and

(2) there are not sufficient estate funds in the executor's or administrator's possession to pay the amount of the allowance or a portion of that amount, as applicable.

(b) Property specifically devised to another may be sold to raise cash as provided by Subsection (a) only if other available property is insufficient to pay the allowance.

Added by Acts 2009, 81st Leg., ch. 680, § 1, eff. Jan. 1, 2014. Amended by Acts 2011, 82nd Leg., ch. 810 (H.B. 2492), § 2.06, eff. Jan. 1, 2014.

## SUBCHAPTER C.  FAMILY ALLOWANCE

### § 353.101.  Family Allowance

(a) Unless an application and verified affidavit are filed as provided by Subsection (b), immediately after the inventory, appraisement, and list of claims of an estate are approved or after the affidavit in lieu of the inventory, appraisement, and list of claims is filed, the court shall fix a family allowance for the support of the decedent's surviving spouse, minor children, and adult incapacitated children.

(b) Before the inventory, appraisement, and list of claims of an estate are approved or, if applicable, before the affidavit in lieu of the inventory, appraisement, and list of claims is filed, the decedent's surviving spouse or any other person authorized to act on behalf of the decedent's minor children or adult incapacitated children may apply to the court to have the court fix the family allowance by filing an application and a verified affidavit describing:

(1) the amount necessary for the maintenance of the surviving spouse, the decedent's minor children, and the decedent's adult incapacitated children for one year after the date of the decedent's death; and

(2) the surviving spouse's separate property and any property that the decedent's minor children or adult incapacitated children have in their own right.

(c) At a hearing on an application filed under Subsection (b), the applicant has the burden of proof by a preponderance of the evidence. The court shall fix a family allowance for the support of the decedent's surviving spouse, minor children, and adult incapacitated children.

(d) A family allowance may not be made for:

(1) the decedent's surviving spouse, if the surviving spouse has separate property adequate for the surviving spouse's maintenance;

(2) the decedent's minor children, if the minor children have property in their own right adequate for the children's maintenance; or

(3) any of the decedent's adult incapacitated children, if:

(A) the adult incapacitated child has property in the person's own right adequate for the person's maintenance; or

(B) at the time of the decedent's death, the decedent was not supporting the adult incapacitated child.

Added by Acts 2009, 81st Leg., ch. 680, § 1, eff. Jan. 1, 2014. Amended by Acts 2011, 82nd Leg., ch. 810 (H.B. 2492), § 2.07, eff. Jan. 1, 2014; Acts 2011, 82nd Leg., ch. 1338 (S.B. 1198), § 2.47, eff. Jan. 1, 2014; Acts 2013, 83rd Leg., ch. 1136 (H.B. 2912), § 44, eff. Jan. 1, 2014.

Section 62(f) of Acts 2013, 83rd Leg., ch. 1136 (H.B. 2912) provides:

"The changes in law made by Sections 102.004, 201.051, 201.052(b), 202.004, 202.009, 202.056, 202.151, 353.101(d), 403.055, 403.056(a), and 405.001(b), Estates Code, as amended by this Act, and Sections 201.052(a–1), 202.0025, and 202.057, Estates Code, as added by this Act, apply only to the estate of a decedent who dies on or after the effective date [Jan. 1, 2014] of this Act. The estate of a decedent who dies before the effective date of this Act is governed by the law in effect on the date of the decedent's death, and the former law is continued in effect for that purpose."

### § 353.102. Amount and Method of Payment of Family Allowance

(a) The amount of the family allowance must be sufficient for the maintenance of the decedent's surviving spouse, minor children, and adult incapacitated children for one year from the date of the decedent's death.

(b) The allowance must be fixed with regard to the facts or circumstances then existing and the facts and circumstances anticipated to exist during the first year after the decedent's death.

(c) The allowance may be paid in a lump sum or in installments, as ordered by the court.

Added by Acts 2009, 81st Leg., ch. 680, § 1, eff. Jan. 1, 2014. Amended by Acts 2011, 82nd Leg., ch. 810 (H.B. 2492), § 2.08, eff. Jan. 1, 2014.

### § 353.103. Order Fixing Family Allowance

When a family allowance has been fixed, the court shall enter an order that:

(1) states the amount of the allowance;

(2) provides how the allowance shall be payable; and

(3) directs the executor or administrator to pay the allowance in accordance with law.

Added by Acts 2009, 81st Leg., ch. 680, § 1, eff. Jan. 1, 2014.

### § 353.104. Preference of Family Allowance

The family allowance made for the support of the decedent's surviving spouse, minor children, and adult incapacitated children shall be paid in preference to all other debts of or charges against the estate, other than Class 1 claims.

Added by Acts 2009, 81st Leg., ch. 680, § 1, eff. Jan. 1, 2014. Amended by Acts 2011, 82nd Leg., ch. 810 (H.B. 2492), § 2.09, eff. Jan. 1, 2014.

### § 353.105. Payment of Family Allowance

(a) The executor or administrator of an estate shall apportion and pay the family allowance in accordance with this section.

(b) If there is a surviving spouse and there are no minor children or adult incapacitated children of the decedent, the executor or administrator shall pay the entire family allowance to the surviving spouse.

(c) If there is a surviving spouse and all of the minor children and adult incapacitated children of the decedent are also the children of the surviving spouse, the executor or administrator shall pay the entire family allowance to the surviving spouse for use by the surviving spouse, the decedent's minor children, and adult incapacitated children.

(d) If there is a surviving spouse and some or all of the minor children or adult incapacitated children of the decedent are not also children of the surviving spouse, the executor or administrator shall pay:

(1) the portion of the entire family allowance necessary for the support of those minor children to the guardian of those children; and

(2) the portion of the entire family allowance necessary for the support of each of those adult incapacitated children to the guardian of the adult incapacitated child or another appropriate person, as determined by the court, on behalf of the adult incapacitated child if there is no guardian.

(e) If there is no surviving spouse and there are minor children or adult incapacitated children of the decedent, the executor or administrator shall pay the family allowance:

(1) for the minor children, to the guardian of those children; and

(2) for each adult incapacitated child, to the guardian of the adult incapacitated child or another appropriate person, as determined by the court, on behalf of the adult incapacitated child if there is no guardian.

Added by Acts 2009, 81st Leg., ch. 680, § 1, eff. Jan. 1, 2014. Amended by Acts 2011, 82nd Leg., ch. 810 (H.B. 2492), § 2.10, eff. Jan. 1, 2014.

### § 353.106. Surviving Spouse, Minor Children, or Adult Incapacitated Children May Take Personal Property for Family Allowance

(a) A decedent's surviving spouse, the guardian of the decedent's minor children, or the guardian of an adult incapacitated child of the decedent or another appropriate person, as determined by the court, on behalf of the adult incapacitated child if there is no guardian, as applicable, is entitled to take, at the property's appraised value as shown by the appraisement, any of the estate's personal property in full or partial payment of the family allowance.

(b) Property specifically devised to another may be taken as provided by Subsection (a) only if other available property is insufficient to pay the allowance.

Added by Acts 2009, 81st Leg., ch. 680, § 1, eff. Jan. 1, 2014. Amended by Acts 2011, 82nd Leg., ch. 810 (H.B. 2492), §§ 2.11, 2.12, eff. Jan. 1, 2014.

### § 353.107.  Sale of Estate Property to Raise Funds for Family Allowance

(a) The court shall, as soon as the inventory, appraisement, and list of claims are returned and approved or the affidavit in lieu of the inventory, appraisement, and list of claims is filed, order the sale of estate property for cash in an amount that will be sufficient to raise the amount of the family allowance, or a portion of that amount, as necessary, if:

(1) the decedent had no personal property that the surviving spouse, the guardian of the decedent's minor children, or the guardian of the decedent's adult incapacitated child or other appropriate person acting on behalf of the adult incapacitated child is willing to take for the family allowance, or the decedent had insufficient personal property; and

(2) there are not sufficient estate funds in the executor's or administrator's possession to pay the amount of the family allowance or a portion of that amount, as applicable.

(b) Property specifically devised to another may be sold to raise cash as provided by Subsection (a) only if other available property is insufficient to pay the family allowance.

Added by Acts 2009, 81st Leg., ch. 680, § 1, eff. Jan. 1, 2014. Amended by Acts 2011, 82nd Leg., ch. 810 (H.B. 2492), § 2.13, eff. Jan. 1, 2014; Acts 2011, 82nd Leg., ch. 1338 (S.B. 1198), § 2.48, eff. Jan. 1, 2014.

Section 3.01 of Acts 2011, 82nd Leg., ch. 1338 (S.B. 1198) provides:
"To the extent of any conflict, this Act prevails over another Act of the 82nd Legislature, Regular Session, 2011, relating to nonsubstantive additions to and corrections in enacted codes."

### SUBCHAPTER D.  LIENS ON AND DISPOSITION OF EXEMPT PROPERTY AND PROPERTY TAKEN AS ALLOWANCE

### § 353.151.  Liens

(a) This section applies to all estates, whether solvent or insolvent.

(b) If property on which there is a valid subsisting lien or encumbrance is set aside as exempt for the surviving spouse or children or is appropriated to

make an allowance in lieu of exempt property or for the support of the surviving spouse or children, the debts secured by the lien shall, if necessary, be either paid or continued against the property.

Added by Acts 2009, 81st Leg., ch. 680, § 1, eff. Jan. 1, 2014.

### § 353.152.  Distribution of Exempt Property of Solvent Estate

If on final settlement of an estate it appears that the estate is solvent, the exempt property, other than the homestead or any allowance made in lieu of the homestead, is subject to partition and distribution among the heirs of the decedent and the distributees in the same manner as other estate property.

Added by Acts 2009, 81st Leg., ch. 680, § 1, eff. Jan. 1, 2014.

### § 353.153.  Title to Property of Insolvent Estate

If on final settlement an estate proves to be insolvent, the decedent's surviving spouse and children have absolute title to all property and allowances set aside or paid to them under this title.  The property and allowances may not be taken for any of the estate debts except as provided by Section 353.155.

Added by Acts 2009, 81st Leg., ch. 680, § 1, eff. Jan. 1, 2014.

### § 353.154.  Certain Property Not Considered in Determining Solvency

In determining whether an estate is solvent or insolvent, the exempt property set aside for the decedent's surviving spouse or children, any allowance made in lieu of that exempt property, and the family allowance under Subchapter C may not be estimated or considered as estate assets.

Added by Acts 2009, 81st Leg., ch. 680, § 1, eff. Jan. 1, 2014.

### § 353.155.  Exempt Property Liable for Certain Debts

The exempt property, other than the homestead or any allowance made in lieu of the homestead:

(1) is liable for the payment of Class 1 claims; and

(2) is not liable for any estate debts other than the claims described by Subdivision (1).

Added by Acts 2009, 81st Leg., ch. 680, § 1, eff. Jan. 1, 2014.

### CHAPTER 354.  SUMMARY PROCEEDINGS FOR, OR WITHDRAWAL FROM ADMINISTRATION OF, CERTAIN ESTATES

SUBCHAPTER A.  SUMMARY PROCEEDINGS FOR CERTAIN SMALL ESTATES

## SUBCHAPTER A. SUMMARY PROCEEDINGS FOR CERTAIN SMALL ESTATES

### § 354.001. Summary Proceedings for Certain Small Estates

(a) If, after a personal representative of an estate has filed the inventory, appraisement, and list of claims or the affidavit in lieu of the inventory, appraisement, and list of claims as provided by Chapter 309, it is established that the decedent's estate, excluding any homestead, exempt property, and family allowance to the decedent's surviving spouse, minor children, and adult incapacitated children, does not exceed the amount sufficient to pay the claims against the estate classified as Classes 1 through 4 under Section 355.102, the representative shall:

(1) on order of the court, pay those claims in the order provided and to the extent permitted by the assets of the estate subject to the payment of those claims; and

(2) after paying the claims in accordance with Subdivision (1), present to the court the representative's account with an application for the settlement and allowance of the account.

(b) On presentation of the personal representative's account and application under Subsection (a), the court, with or without notice, may adjust, correct, settle, allow, or disallow the account.

(c) If the court settles and allows the personal representative's account under Subsection (b), the court may:

(1) decree final distribution;

(2) discharge the representative; and

(3) close the administration.

Added by Acts 2009, 81st Leg., ch. 680, § 1, eff. Jan. 1, 2014. Amended by Acts 2011, 82nd Leg., ch. 810 (H.B. 2492), § 2.14, eff. Jan. 1, 2014; Acts 2011, 82nd Leg., ch. 1338 (S.B. 1198), § 2.49, eff. Jan. 1, 2014.

## SUBCHAPTER B. WITHDRAWAL FROM ADMINISTRATION OF CERTAIN ESTATES

### § 354.051. Required Report on Condition of Estate

At any time after the return of the inventory, appraisement, and list of claims of an estate required by Chapter 309, anyone entitled to a portion of the estate, by a written complaint filed in the court in which the case is pending, may have the estate's executor or administrator cited to appear and render under oath an exhibit of the condition of the estate.

Added by Acts 2009, 81st Leg., ch. 680, § 1, eff. Jan. 1, 2014.

### § 354.052. Bond Required to Withdraw Estate From Administration

After the executor or administrator has rendered the exhibit of the condition of the estate if required under Section 354.051, one or more persons entitled to the estate, or other persons for them, may execute and deliver a bond to the court. The bond must be:

(1) conditioned that the persons executing the bond shall:

(A) pay all unpaid debts against the estate that have been or are:

(i) allowed by the executor or administrator and approved by the court; or

(ii) established by suit against the estate; and

(B) pay to the executor or administrator any balance that the court in its judgment on the exhibit finds to be due the executor or administrator;

(2) payable to the judge and the judge's successors in office in an amount equal to at least twice the gross appraised value of the estate as shown by the inventory, appraisement, and list of claims returned under Chapter 309; and

(3) approved by the court.

Added by Acts 2009, 81st Leg., ch. 680, § 1, eff. Jan. 1, 2014.

### § 354.053. Order for Delivery of Estate

On the giving and approval of the bond under Section 354.052, the court shall enter an order requiring the executor or administrator to promptly deliver to each person entitled to any portion of the estate that portion to which the person is entitled.

Added by Acts 2009, 81st Leg., ch. 680, § 1, eff. Jan. 1, 2014.

### § 354.054. Order of Discharge

After an estate has been withdrawn from administration under Section 354.053, the court shall enter an order:

(1) discharging the executor or administrator; and

(2) declaring the administration closed.

Added by Acts 2009, 81st Leg., ch. 680, § 1, eff. Jan. 1, 2014.

### § 354.055. Lien on Property of Estate Withdrawn From Administration

A lien exists on all of the estate withdrawn from administration under Section 354.053 and in the possession of the distributees and those claiming under the distributees with notice of that lien, to secure the ultimate payment of:

(1) the bond under Section 354.052; and

(2) debts and claims secured by the bond.

Added by Acts 2009, 81st Leg., ch. 680, § 1, eff. Jan. 1, 2014.

### § 354.056. Partition of Estate Withdrawn From Administration

On written application to the court, any person entitled to any portion of an estate withdrawn from administration under Section 354.053 may cause a partition and distribution of the estate to be made among those persons entitled to the estate in accordance with the provisions of this title that relate to the partition and distribution of an estate.

Added by Acts 2009, 81st Leg., ch. 680, § 1, eff. Jan. 1, 2014.

### § 354.057. Creditors Entitled to Sue on Bond

A creditor of an estate withdrawn from administration under Section 354.053 whose debt or claim against the estate is unpaid and not barred by limitation is entitled to:

(1) commence a suit in the person's own name on the bond under Section 354.052; and

(2) obtain a judgment on the bond for the debt or claim the creditor establishes against the estate.

Added by Acts 2009, 81st Leg., ch. 680, § 1, eff. Jan. 1, 2014.

### § 354.058. Creditors May Sue Distributees

(a) A creditor of an estate withdrawn from administration under Section 354.053 whose debt or claim against the estate is unpaid and not barred by limitation may sue:

(1) any distributee who has received any of the estate; or

(2) all the distributees jointly.

(b) A distributee is not liable for more than the distributee's just proportion according to the amount of the estate the distributee received in the distribution.

Added by Acts 2009, 81st Leg., ch. 680, § 1, eff. Jan. 1, 2014.

## CHAPTER 355. PRESENTMENT AND PAYMENT OF CLAIMS

### SUBCHAPTER A. PRESENTMENT OF CLAIMS AGAINST ESTATES IN GENERAL

### SUBCHAPTER B. ACTION ON CLAIMS

### SUBCHAPTER C. PAYMENT OF CLAIMS, ALLOWANCES, AND EXPENSES

## SUBCHAPTER A.  PRESENTMENT OF CLAIMS AGAINST ESTATES IN GENERAL

### § 355.001.  Presentment of Claim to Personal Representative

A claim may be presented to a personal representative of an estate at any time before the estate is closed if suit on the claim has not been barred by the general statutes of limitation.

Added by Acts 2009, 81st Leg., ch. 680, § 1, eff. Jan. 1, 2014.

### § 355.002.  Presentment of Claim to Clerk

(a) A claim may also be presented by depositing the claim with the clerk with vouchers and the necessary exhibits and affidavit attached to the claim. On receiving a claim deposited under this subsection, the clerk shall advise the personal representative or the representative's attorney of the deposit of the claim by a letter mailed to the representative's last known address.

(b) A claim deposited under Subsection (a) is presumed to be rejected if the personal representative fails to act on the claim on or before the 30th day after the date the claim is deposited.

(c) Failure of the clerk to give the notice required under Subsection (a) does not affect the validity of the presentment or the presumption of rejection because the personal representative does not act on the claim within the 30–day period prescribed by Subsection (b).

(d) The clerk shall enter a claim deposited under Subsection (a) on the claim docket.

Added by Acts 2009, 81st Leg., ch. 680, § 1, eff. Jan. 1, 2014.

### § 355.003.  Inclusion of Attorney's Fees in Claim

If the instrument evidencing or supporting a claim provides for attorney's fees, the claimant may include as a part of the claim the portion of attorney's fees the claimant has paid or contracted to pay to an attorney to prepare, present, and collect the claim.

Added by Acts 2009, 81st Leg., ch. 680, § 1, eff. Jan. 1, 2014.

### § 355.004.  Affidavit Authenticating Claim for Money in General

(a) Except as provided by Section 355.005, a claim for money against an estate must be supported by an affidavit that states:

(1) that the claim is just;

(2) that all legal offsets, payments, and credits known to the affiant have been allowed; and

(3) if the claim is not founded on a written instrument or account, the facts on which the claim is founded.

(b) A photostatic copy of an exhibit or voucher necessary to prove a claim may be offered with and attached to the claim instead of attaching the original.

Added by Acts 2009, 81st Leg., ch. 680, § 1, eff. Jan. 1, 2014.

### § 355.005.  Affidavit Authenticating Claim of Corporation or Other Entity

(a) An authorized officer or representative of a corporation or other entity shall make the affidavit required to authenticate a claim of the corporation or entity.

(b) In an affidavit made by an officer of a corporation, or by an executor, administrator, trustee, assignee, agent, representative, or attorney, it is sufficient to state that the affiant has made diligent inquiry and examination and believes the claim is just and that all legal offsets, payments, and credits made known to the affiant have been allowed.

Added by Acts 2009, 81st Leg., ch. 680, § 1, eff. Jan. 1, 2014.

### § 355.006. Lost or Destroyed Evidence Concerning Claim

If evidence of a claim is lost or destroyed, the claimant or an authorized representative or agent of the claimant may make an affidavit to the fact of the loss or destruction. The affidavit must state:

(1) the amount, date, and nature of the claim;

(2) the due date of the claim;

(3) that the claim is just;

(4) that all legal offsets, payments, and credits known to the affiant have been allowed; and

(5) that the claimant is still the owner of the claim.

Added by Acts 2009, 81st Leg., ch. 680, § 1, eff. Jan. 1, 2014.

### § 355.007. Waiver of Certain Defects of Form or Claims of Insufficiency

A defect of form or a claim of insufficiency of a presented exhibit or voucher is considered waived by the personal representative unless a written objection to the defect or insufficiency is made not later than the 30th day after the date the claim is presented and is filed with the county clerk.

Added by Acts 2009, 81st Leg., ch. 680, § 1, eff. Jan. 1, 2014.

### § 355.008. Effect on Statutes of Limitation of Presentment of or Suit on Claim

The general statutes of limitation are tolled on the date:

(1) a claim for money is filed or deposited with the clerk; or

(2) suit is brought against the personal representative of an estate with respect to a claim of the estate that is not required to be presented to the representative.

Added by Acts 2009, 81st Leg., ch. 680, § 1, eff. Jan. 1, 2014.

### SUBCHAPTER B. ACTION ON CLAIMS

### § 355.051. Allowance or Rejection of Claim

A personal representative of an estate shall, not later than the 30th day after the date an authenticated claim against the estate is presented to the representative, or deposited with the clerk as provided under Section 355.002, endorse on the claim, attach to the claim, or file with the clerk a memorandum signed by the representative stating:

(1) the date the claim was presented or deposited; and

(2) whether the representative allows or rejects the claim, or if the representative allows or rejects a part of the claim, the portion the representative allows or rejects.

Added by Acts 2009, 81st Leg., ch. 680, § 1, eff. Jan. 1, 2014.

### § 355.052. Failure to Timely Allow or Reject Claim

The failure of a personal representative to timely allow or reject a claim under Section 355.051 constitutes a rejection of the claim. If the claim is established by suit after that rejection:

(1) the costs shall be taxed against the representative, individually; or

(2) the representative may be removed on the written complaint of any person interested in the claim after personal service of citation, hearing, and proof, as in other cases of removal.

Added by Acts 2009, 81st Leg., ch. 680, § 1, eff. Jan. 1, 2014.

### § 355.053. Claim Entered on Claim Docket

After a claim against an estate has been presented to the personal representative and allowed or rejected, wholly or partly, by the representative, the claim must be filed with the county clerk of the proper county. The clerk shall enter the claim on the claim docket.

Added by Acts 2009, 81st Leg., ch. 680, § 1, eff. Jan. 1, 2014.

### § 355.054. Contest of Claim

(a) A person interested in an estate may, at any time before the court has acted on a claim, appear and object in writing to the approval of the claim or any part of the claim.

(b) If a person objects under Subsection (a):

(1) the parties are entitled to process for witnesses; and

(2) the court shall hear evidence and render judgment as in ordinary suits.

Added by Acts 2009, 81st Leg., ch. 680, § 1, eff. Jan. 1, 2014.

### § 355.055. Court's Action on Claim

The court shall:

(1) act on each claim that has been allowed and entered on the claim docket for a period of 10 days

either approving the claim wholly or partly or disapproving the claim; and

(2) concurrently classify the claim.

Added by Acts 2009, 81st Leg., ch. 680, § 1, eff. Jan. 1, 2014.

### § 355.056. Hearing on Certain Claims

(a) If a claim is properly authenticated and allowed but the court is not satisfied that the claim is just, the court shall:

(1) examine the claimant and the personal representative under oath; and

(2) hear other evidence necessary to determine the issue.

(b) If after conducting the examination and hearing the evidence under Subsection (a) the court is not convinced that the claim is just, the court shall disapprove the claim.

Added by Acts 2009, 81st Leg., ch. 680, § 1, eff. Jan. 1, 2014.

### § 355.057. Court Order Regarding Action on Claim

(a) The court acting on a claim shall state the exact action taken on the claim, whether the claim is approved or disapproved, or approved in part and disapproved in part, and the classification of the claim by endorsing on or attaching to the claim a written memorandum that is dated and officially signed.

(b) An order under Subsection (a) has the effect of a final judgment.

Added by Acts 2009, 81st Leg., ch. 680, § 1, eff. Jan. 1, 2014.

### § 355.058. Appeal of Court's Action on Claim

A claimant or any person interested in an estate who is dissatisfied with the court's action on a claim may appeal the action to the court of appeals in the manner other judgments of the county court in probate matters are appealed.

Added by Acts 2009, 81st Leg., ch. 680, § 1, eff. Jan. 1, 2014.

### § 355.059. Allowance and Approval Prohibited Without Affidavit

A personal representative of an estate may not allow, and the court may not approve, a claim for money against the estate unless the claim is supported by an affidavit that meets the applicable requirements of Sections 355.004(a) and 355.005.

Added by Acts 2009, 81st Leg., ch. 680, § 1, eff. Jan. 1, 2014.

### § 355.060. Unsecured Claims Barred Under Certain Circumstances

If a personal representative gives a notice permitted by Section 308.054 to an unsecured creditor for money and the creditor's claim is not presented before the 121st day after the date of receipt of the notice, the claim is barred.

Added by Acts 2009, 81st Leg., ch. 680, § 1, eff. Jan. 1, 2014. Amended by Acts 2013, 83rd Leg., ch. 1136 (H.B. 2912), § 45, eff. Jan. 1, 2014.

Section 62(e) of Acts 2013, 83rd Leg., ch. 1136 (H.B. 2912) provides:

"The changes in law made by Sections 51.203(c), 53.104, 305.002(a), 305.003, 308.054(b), 309.051(a), 309.056, 309.103(a) and (b), 355.060, 361.155(b), 362.005, 362.011, 362.013, 404.001(a), 404.003, 404.005(b) and (c), and 551.001(a), Estates Code, as amended by this Act, and Sections 253.001(c), 301.155, 305.004, 309.057, 361.155(c), 404.0035, 404.0036, and 404.0037, Estates Code, as added by this Act, apply to the administration of the estate of a decedent that is pending or commenced on or after the effective date [Jan. 1, 2014] of this Act."

### § 355.061. Allowing Barred Claim Prohibited: Court Disapproval

(a) A personal representative may not allow a claim for money against a decedent or the decedent's estate if a suit on the claim is barred:

(1) under Section 355.060, 355.064, or 355.201(b); or

(2) by an applicable general statute of limitation.

(b) A claim for money that is allowed by the personal representative shall be disapproved if the court is satisfied that the claim is barred, including because the limitation has run.

Added by Acts 2009, 81st Leg., ch. 680, § 1, eff. Jan. 1, 2014.

### § 355.062. Certain Actions on Claims With Lost or Destroyed Evidence Void

(a) Before a claim the evidence for which is lost or destroyed is approved, the claim must be proved by disinterested testimony taken in open court or by oral or written deposition.

(b) The allowance or approval of a claim the evidence for which is lost or destroyed is void if the claim is:

(1) allowed or approved without the affidavit under Section 355.006; or

(2) approved without satisfactory proof.

Added by Acts 2009, 81st Leg., ch. 680, § 1, eff. Jan. 1, 2014.

### § 355.063. Claims Not Allowed After Order for Partition and Distribution

After an order for final partition and distribution of an estate has been made:

(1) a claim for money against the estate may not be allowed by a personal representative;

(2) a suit may not be commenced against the representative on a claim for money against the estate; and

(3) the owner of any claim that is not barred by the laws of limitation has a right of action on the claim against the heirs, devisees, or creditors of the estate, limited to the value of the property received by those heirs, devisees, or creditors in distributions from the estate.

Added by Acts 2009, 81st Leg., ch. 680, § 1, eff. Jan. 1, 2014.

### § 355.064. Suit on Rejected Claim

(a) A claim or part of a claim that has been rejected by the personal representative is barred unless not later than the 90th day after the date of rejection the claimant commences suit on the claim in the court of original probate jurisdiction in which the estate is pending.

(b) In a suit commenced on the rejected claim, the memorandum endorsed on or attached to the claim, or any other memorandum of rejection filed with respect to the claim, is taken to be true without further proof unless denied under oath.

Added by Acts 2009, 81st Leg., ch. 680, § 1, eff. Jan. 1, 2014.

### § 355.065. Presentment of Claim Prerequisite for Judgment

A judgment may not be rendered in favor of a claimant on a claim for money that has not been:

(1) legally presented to the personal representative of an estate; and

(2) wholly or partly rejected by the representative or disapproved by the court.

Added by Acts 2009, 81st Leg., ch. 680, § 1, eff. Jan. 1, 2014.

### § 355.066. Judgment in Suit on Rejected Claim

No execution may issue on a rejected claim or part of a claim that is established by suit. The judgment in the suit shall be:

(1) filed in the court in which the estate is pending;

(2) entered on the claim docket;

(3) classified by the court; and

(4) handled as if originally allowed and approved in due course of administration.

Added by Acts 2009, 81st Leg., ch. 680, § 1, eff. Jan. 1, 2014.

## SUBCHAPTER C. PAYMENT OF CLAIMS, ALLOWANCES, AND EXPENSES

### § 355.101. Approval or Establishment of Claim Required for Payment

A claim or any part of a claim for money against an estate may not be paid until the claim or part of the claim has been approved by the court or established by the judgment of a court of competent jurisdiction.

Added by Acts 2009, 81st Leg., ch. 680, § 1, eff. Jan. 1, 2014.

### § 355.102. Claims Classification; Priority of Payment

(a) Claims against an estate shall be classified and have priority of payment as provided by this section.

(b) Class 1 claims are composed of funeral expenses and expenses of the decedent's last illness for a reasonable amount approved by the court, not to exceed a total of $15,000. Any excess shall be classified and paid as other unsecured claims.

(c) Class 2 claims are composed of expenses of administration, expenses incurred in preserving, safekeeping, and managing the estate, including fees and expenses awarded under Section 352.052, and unpaid expenses of administration awarded in a guardianship of the decedent.

(d) Class 3 claims are composed of each secured claim for money under Section 355.151(a)(1), including a tax lien, to the extent the claim can be paid out of the proceeds of the property subject to the mortgage or other lien. If more than one mortgage, lien, or security interest exists on the same property, the claims shall be paid in order of priority of the mortgage, lien, or security interest securing the debt.

(e) Class 4 claims are composed of claims for the principal amount of and accrued interest on delinquent child support and child support arrearages that have been confirmed and reduced to money judgment, as determined under Subchapter F, Chapter 157, Family Code, and claims for unpaid child support obligations under Section 154.015, Family Code.

(f) Class 5 claims are composed of claims for taxes, penalties, and interest due under Title 2, Tax Code, Chapter 2153, Occupations Code, Section 81.111, Natural Resources Code, the Municipal Sales and Use Tax Act (Chapter 321, Tax Code), Section 451.404, Transportation Code, or Subchapter I, Chapter 452, Transportation Code.

(g) Class 6 claims are composed of claims for the cost of confinement established by the Texas Department of Criminal Justice under Section 501.017, Government Code.

(h) Class 7 claims are composed of claims for repayment of medical assistance payments made by the state under Chapter 32, Human Resources Code, to or for the benefit of the decedent.

(i) Class 8 claims are composed of any other claims not described by Subsections (b)–(h).

Added by Acts 2009, 81st Leg., ch. 680, § 1, eff. Jan. 1, 2014. Amended by Acts 2011, 82nd Leg., ch. 91 (S.B. 1303), § 8.015, eff. Jan. 1, 2014.

## § 355.103. Priority of Certain Payments

When a personal representative has estate funds in the representative's possession, the representative shall pay in the following order:

(1) funeral expenses and expenses of the decedent's last illness, in an amount not to exceed $15,000;

(2) allowances made to the decedent's surviving spouse and children, or to either the surviving spouse or children;

(3) expenses of administration and expenses incurred in preserving, safekeeping, and managing the estate; and

(4) other claims against the estate in the order of the claims' classifications.

Added by Acts 2009, 81st Leg., ch. 680, § 1, eff. Jan. 1, 2014.

## § 355.104. Payment of Proceeds From Sale of Property Securing Debt

(a) If a personal representative has the proceeds of a sale made to satisfy a mortgage, lien, or security interest, and the proceeds or any part of the proceeds are not required for the payment of any debts against the estate that have a preference over the mortgage, lien, or security interest, the representative shall pay the proceeds to any holder of a mortgage, lien, or security interest. If there is more than one mortgage, lien, or security interest against the property, the representative shall pay the proceeds to the holders of the mortgages, liens, or security interests in the order of priority of the holders' mortgages, liens, or security interests.

(b) A holder of a mortgage, lien, or security interest, on proof of a personal representative's failure to pay proceeds under this section, may obtain an order from the court directing the payment to be made.

Added by Acts 2009, 81st Leg., ch. 680, § 1, eff. Jan. 1, 2014.

## § 355.105. Claimant's Petition for Allowance and Payment of Claim

A claimant whose claim has not been paid may:

(1) petition the court for determination of the claim at any time before the claim is barred by an applicable statute of limitations; and

(2) procure on due proof an order for the claim's allowance and payment from the estate.

Added by Acts 2009, 81st Leg., ch. 680, § 1, eff. Jan. 1, 2014.

## § 355.106. Order for Payment of Claim Obtained by Personal Representative

After the sixth month after the date letters testamentary or of administration are granted, the court may order a personal representative to pay any claim that is allowed and approved on application by the representative stating that the representative has no actual knowledge of any outstanding enforceable claim against the estate other than the claims already approved and classified by the court.

Added by Acts 2009, 81st Leg., ch. 680, § 1, eff. Jan. 1, 2014.

## § 355.107. Order for Payment of Claim Obtained by Creditor

(a) At any time after the first anniversary of the date letters testamentary are granted for an estate, a creditor of the estate whose claim or part of a claim has been approved by the court or established by suit may obtain an order directing that payment of the claim or part of the claim be made on written application and proof, except as provided by Subsection (b), showing that the estate has sufficient available funds.

(b) If the estate does not have available funds to pay a claim or part of a claim described by Subsection (a) and waiting for the estate to receive funds from other sources would unreasonably delay the payment, the court shall order the sale of estate property sufficient to make the payment.

(c) The personal representative of the estate must first be cited on a written application under Subsection (a) to appear and show cause why the order should not be made.

Added by Acts 2009, 81st Leg., ch. 680, § 1, eff. Jan. 1, 2014.

## § 355.108. Payment When Assets Insufficient to Pay Claims of Same Class

(a) If there are insufficient assets to pay all claims of the same class, other than secured claims for money, the claims in that class shall be paid pro rata, as directed by the court, and in the order directed.

(b) A personal representative may not be allowed to pay a claim under Subsection (a) other than with the pro rata amount of the estate funds that have come into the representative's possession, regardless of whether the estate is solvent or insolvent.

Added by Acts 2009, 81st Leg., ch. 680, § 1, eff. Jan. 1, 2014.

### § 355.109.  Abatement of Bequests

(a) Except as provided by Subsections (b), (c), and (d), a decedent's property is liable for debts and expenses of administration other than estate taxes, and bequests abate in the following order:

(1) property not disposed of by will, but passing by intestacy;

(2) personal property of the residuary estate;

(3) real property of the residuary estate;

(4) general bequests of personal property;

(5) general devises of real property;

(6) specific bequests of personal property;  and

(7) specific devises of real property.

(b) This section does not affect the requirements for payment of a claim of a secured creditor who elects to have the claim continued as a preferred debt and lien against specific property under Subchapter D.

(c) A decedent's intent expressed in a will controls over the abatement of bequests provided by this section.

(d) This section does not apply to the payment of estate taxes under Subchapter A, Chapter 124.

Added by Acts 2009, 81st Leg., ch. 680, § 1, eff. Jan. 1, 2014.

### § 355.110.  Allocation of Funeral Expenses

A personal representative paying a claim for funeral expenses and for items incident to the funeral, such as a tombstone, grave marker, crypt, or burial plot:

(1) shall charge all of the claim to the decedent's estate;  and

(2) may not charge any part of the claim to the community share of a surviving spouse.

Added by Acts 2009, 81st Leg., ch. 680, § 1, eff. Jan. 1, 2014.

### § 355.111.  Payment of Court Costs Relating to Claim

All costs incurred in the probate court with respect to a claim shall be taxed as follows:

(1) if the claim is allowed and approved, the estate shall pay the costs;

(2) if the claim is allowed but disapproved, the claimant shall pay the costs;

(3) if the claim is rejected but established by suit, the estate shall pay the costs;

(4) if the claim is rejected and not established by suit, the claimant shall pay the costs, except as provided by Section 355.052;  and

(5) if the claim is rejected in part and the claimant fails, in a suit to establish the claim, to recover a judgment for a greater amount than was allowed or approved for the claim, the claimant shall pay all costs in the suit.

Added by Acts 2009, 81st Leg., ch. 680, § 1, eff. Jan. 1, 2014.

### § 355.112.  Joint Obligation for Payment of Certain Debts

On the death of a person jointly bound with one or more other persons for the payment of a debt or for any other purpose, the decedent's estate shall be charged by virtue of the obligation in the same manner as if the obligors had been bound severally as well as jointly.

Added by Acts 2009, 81st Leg., ch. 680, § 1, eff. Jan. 1, 2014.

### § 355.113.  Liability for Nonpayment of Claim

(a) A person or claimant, except the state treasury, entitled to payment from an estate of money the court orders to be paid is authorized to have execution issued against the estate property for the amount due, with interest and costs, if:

(1) the personal representative fails to pay the money on demand;

(2) estate funds are available to make the payment;  and

(3) the person or claimant makes an affidavit of the demand for payment and the representative's failure to pay.

(b) The court may cite the personal representative and the sureties on the representative's bond to show cause why the representative and sureties should not be held liable under Subsection (a) for the debt, interest, costs, and damages:

(1) on return of the execution not satisfied;  or

(2) on the affidavit of demand and failure to pay under Subsection (a).

(c) On the return of citation served under Subsection (b), the court shall render judgment against the cited personal representative and sureties, in favor of the claim holder, if good cause why the representative and sureties should not be held liable is not shown. The judgment must be for:

(1) the amount previously ordered to be paid or established by suit that remains unpaid, together with interest and costs; and

(2) damages on the amount neglected to be paid at the rate of five percent per month for each month, or fraction of a month, that the payment was neglected to be paid after demand was made.

(d) Damages ordered under Subsection (c)(2) may be collected in any court of competent jurisdiction.

Added by Acts 2009, 81st Leg., ch. 680, § 1, eff. Jan. 1, 2014.

## SUBCHAPTER D. PRESENTMENT AND PAYMENT OF SECURED CLAIMS FOR MONEY

### § 355.151. Option to Treat Claim as Matured Secured Claim or Preferred Debt and Lien

(a) If a secured claim for money against an estate is presented, the claimant shall specify in the claim, in addition to all other matters required to be specified in the claim, whether the claimant desires to have the claim:

(1) allowed and approved as a matured secured claim to be paid in due course of administration, in which case the claim shall be paid in that manner if allowed and approved; or

(2) allowed, approved, and fixed as a preferred debt and lien against the specific property securing the indebtedness and paid according to the terms of the contract that secured the lien, in which case the claim shall be so allowed and approved if it is a valid lien.

(b) Notwithstanding Subsection (a)(2), the personal representative may pay a claim that the claimant desired to have allowed, approved, and fixed as a preferred debt and lien as described by Subsection (a)(2) before maturity if that payment is in the best interest of the estate.

Added by Acts 2009, 81st Leg., ch. 680, § 1, eff. Jan. 1, 2014.

### § 355.152. Period for Specifying Treatment of Secured Claim

(a) A secured creditor may present the creditor's claim for money and shall specify within the later of six months after the date letters testamentary or of administration are granted, or four months after the date notice required to be given under Section 308.053

is received, whether the claim is to be allowed and approved under Section 355.151(a)(1) or (2).

(b) A secured claim for money that is not presented within the period prescribed by Subsection (a) or that is presented without specifying how the claim is to be paid under Section 355.151 shall be treated as a claim to be paid in accordance with Section 355.151(a)(2).

Added by Acts 2009, 81st Leg., ch. 680, § 1, eff. Jan. 1, 2014.

### § 355.153. Payment of Matured Secured Claim

(a) A claim allowed and approved as a matured secured claim under Section 355.151(a)(1) shall be paid in due course of administration, and the secured creditor is not entitled to exercise any other remedy in a manner that prevents the preferential payment of claims and allowances described by Sections 355.103(1), (2), and (3).

(b) If a claim is allowed and approved as a matured secured claim under Section 355.151(a)(1) for a debt that would otherwise pass with the property securing the debt to one or more devisees in accordance with Section 255.301, the personal representative shall:

(1) collect from the devisees the amount of the debt; and

(2) pay that amount to the claimant in satisfaction of the claim.

(c) Each devisee's share of the debt under Subsection (b) is an amount equal to a fraction representing the devisee's ownership interest in the property securing the debt, multiplied by the amount of the debt.

(d) If the personal representative is unable to collect from the devisees an amount sufficient to pay the debt under Subsection (b), the representative shall, subject to Chapter 356, sell the property securing the debt. The representative shall:

(1) use the sale proceeds to pay the debt and any expenses associated with the sale; and

(2) distribute the remaining sale proceeds to each devisee in an amount equal to a fraction representing the devisee's ownership interest in the property, multiplied by the amount of the remaining sale proceeds.

(e) If the sale proceeds under Subsection (d) are insufficient to pay the debt and any expenses associated with the sale, the difference between the sale proceeds and the sum of the amount of the debt and the expenses associated with the sale shall be paid in the manner prescribed by Subsection (a).

Added by Acts 2009, 81st Leg., ch. 680, § 1, eff. Jan. 1, 2014.

## § 355.154. Preferred Debt and Lien

When a claim for a debt is allowed and approved under Section 355.151(a)(2):

(1) a further claim for the debt may not be made against other estate assets;

(2) the debt thereafter remains a preferred lien against the property securing the debt; and

(3) the property remains security for the debt in any distribution or sale of the property before final maturity and payment of the debt.

Added by Acts 2009, 81st Leg., ch. 680, § 1, eff. Jan. 1, 2014.

## § 355.155. Payment of Maturities on Preferred Debt and Lien

(a) If property securing a debt for which a claim is allowed, approved, and fixed under Section 355.151(a)(2) is not sold or distributed within six months from the date letters testamentary or of administration are granted, the personal representative of the estate shall:

(1) promptly pay all maturities that have accrued on the debt according to the terms of the debt; and

(2) perform all the terms of any contract securing the debt.

(b) If the personal representative defaults in payment or performance under Subsection (a), on application of the claim holder, the court shall:

(1) require the sale of the property subject to the unmatured part of the debt and apply the proceeds of the sale to the liquidation of the maturities;

(2) require the sale of the property free of the lien and apply the proceeds to the payment of the whole debt; or

(3) authorize foreclosure by the claim holder as provided by this subchapter.

Added by Acts 2009, 81st Leg., ch. 680, § 1, eff. Jan. 1, 2014.

## § 355.156. Affidavit Required for Foreclosure

An application by a claim holder under Section 355.155(b)(3) to foreclose the claim holder's mortgage, lien, or security interest on property securing a claim allowed, approved, and fixed under Section 355.151(a)(2) must be supported by the claim holder's affidavit that:

(1) describes the property or part of the property to be sold by foreclosure;

(2) describes the amounts of the claim holder's outstanding debt;

(3) describes the maturities that have accrued on the debt according to the terms of the debt;

(4) describes any other debts secured by a mortgage, lien, or security interest against the property that are known by the claim holder;

(5) contains a statement that the claim holder has no knowledge of the existence of any debt secured by the property other than those described by the application; and

(6) requests permission for the claim holder to foreclose the claim holder's mortgage, lien, or security interest.

Added by Acts 2009, 81st Leg., ch. 680, § 1, eff. Jan. 1, 2014.

## § 355.157. Citation on Application

(a) The clerk shall issue citation on the filing of an application by:

(1) personal service to:

(A) the personal representative; and

(B) any person described by the application as having other debts secured by a mortgage, lien, or security interest against the property; and

(2) posting to any other person interested in the estate.

(b) A citation issued under Subsection (a) must require the person cited to appear and show cause why foreclosure should or should not be permitted.

Added by Acts 2009, 81st Leg., ch. 680, § 1, eff. Jan. 1, 2014.

## § 355.158. Hearing on Application

(a) The clerk shall immediately notify the judge when an application is filed. The judge shall schedule in writing a date for a hearing on the application.

(b) The judge may, by entry on the docket or otherwise, continue a hearing on an application for a reasonable time to allow an interested person to obtain an appraisal or other evidence concerning the fair market value of the property that is the subject of the application. If the interested person requests an unreasonable time for a continuance, the interested person must show good cause for the continuance.

(c) If the court finds at the hearing that there is a default in payment of maturities that have accrued on a debt described by Section 355.155(a) or performance under the contract securing the debt, the court shall:

(1) require the sale of the property subject to the unmatured part of the debt and apply the proceeds of the sale to the liquidation of the maturities;

(2) require the sale of the property free of the lien and apply the proceeds to the payment of the whole debt; or

(3) authorize foreclosure by the claim holder as provided by Section 355. 156.

(d) A person interested in the estate may appeal an order issued under Subsection (c)(3).

Added by Acts 2009, 81st Leg., ch. 680, § 1, eff. Jan. 1, 2014.

### § 355.159. Manner of Foreclosure; Minimum Price

(a) When the court grants a claim holder the right of foreclosure at a hearing under Section 355.158, the court shall authorize the claim holder to foreclose the claim holder's mortgage, lien, or security interest:

(1) in accordance with the provisions of the document creating the mortgage, lien, or security interest; or

(2) in any other manner allowed by law.

(b) Based on the evidence presented at the hearing, the court may set a minimum price for the property to be sold by foreclosure that does not exceed the fair market value of the property. If the court sets a minimum price, the property may not be sold at the foreclosure sale for a lower price.

Added by Acts 2009, 81st Leg., ch. 680, § 1, eff. Jan. 1, 2014.

### § 355.160. Unsuccessful Foreclosure; Subsequent Application

If property that is the subject of a foreclosure sale authorized and conducted under this subchapter is not sold because no bid at the sale met the minimum price set by the court, the claim holder may file a subsequent application for foreclosure under Section 355.155(b)(3). The court may eliminate or modify the minimum price requirement and grant permission for another foreclosure sale.

Added by Acts 2009, 81st Leg., ch. 680, § 1, eff. Jan. 1, 2014.

### SUBCHAPTER E. CLAIMS INVOLVING PERSONAL REPRESENTATIVES

### § 355.201. Claim by Personal Representative

(a) The provisions of this chapter regarding the presentment of claims against a decedent's estate may not be construed to apply to any claim of a personal representative against the decedent.

(b) A personal representative holding a claim against the decedent shall file the claim in the court granting the letters testamentary or of administration,

verified by affidavit as required in other cases, within six months after the date the representative qualifies, or the claim is barred.

(c) A claim by a personal representative that has been filed with the court within the required period shall be entered on the claim docket and acted on by the court in the same manner as in other cases.

(d) A personal representative may appeal a judgment of the court acting on a claim under this section as in other cases.

(e) The previous provisions regarding the presentment of claims may not be construed to apply to a claim:

(1) of any heir or devisee who claims in that capacity;

(2) that accrues against the estate after the granting of letters testamentary or of administration and for which the personal representative has contracted; or

(3) for delinquent ad valorem taxes against a decedent's estate that is being administered in probate in:

(A) a county other than the county in which the taxes were imposed; or

(B) the same county in which the taxes were imposed, if the probate proceedings have been pending for more than four years.

Added by Acts 2009, 81st Leg., ch. 680, § 1, eff. Jan. 1, 2014.

### § 355.202. Claims Against Personal Representatives

(a) The naming of an executor in a will does not extinguish a just claim that the decedent had against the person named as executor.

(b) If a personal representative is indebted to the decedent, the representative shall account for the debt in the same manner as if the debt were cash in the representative's possession.

(c) Notwithstanding Subsection (b), a personal representative is required to account for the debt only from the date the debt becomes due if the debt was not due at the time the representative received letters testamentary or of administration.

Added by Acts 2009, 81st Leg., ch. 680, § 1, eff. Jan. 1, 2014.

### § 355.203. Purchase of Claim by Personal Representative Prohibited

(a) It is unlawful, and cause for removal, for a personal representative, whether acting under appointment by will or court orders, to purchase a claim against the estate the representative represents for the representative's own use or any other purpose.

(b) On written complaint by a person interested in the estate and on satisfactory proof of a violation of Subsection (a), the court after citation and hearing:

(1) shall enter an order canceling the claim described by Subsection (a); and

(2) may remove the personal representative who is found to have violated Subsection (a).

(c) No part of a claim canceled under Subsection (b) may be paid out of the estate.

Added by Acts 2009, 81st Leg., ch. 680, § 1, eff. Jan. 1, 2014.

# CHAPTER 356. SALE OF ESTATE PROPERTY

## SUBCHAPTER A. GENERAL PROVISIONS

### § 356.001. Court Order Authorizing Sale

(a) Except as provided by this chapter, estate property may not be sold without a court order authorizing the sale.

(b) Except as otherwise specially provided by this chapter, the court may order estate property to be sold for cash or on credit, at public auction or privately, as the court considers most advantageous to the estate.

Added by Acts 2009, 81st Leg., ch. 680, § 1, eff. Jan. 1, 2014.

### § 356.002.　Sale Authorized by Will

(a) Subject to Subsection (b), if a will authorizes the executor to sell the testator's property:

(1) a court order is not required to authorize the executor to sell the property; and

(2) the executor may sell the property:

(A) at public auction or privately as the executor considers to be in the best interest of the estate; and

(B) for cash or on credit terms determined by the executor.

(b) Any particular directions in the testator's will regarding the sale of estate property shall be followed unless the directions have been annulled or suspended by court order.

Added by Acts 2009, 81st Leg., ch. 680, § 1, eff. Jan. 1, 2014.

### SUBCHAPTER B.　CERTAIN ESTATE PROPERTY REQUIRED TO BE SOLD

### § 356.051.　Sale of Certain Personal Property Required

(a) After approval of the inventory, appraisement, and list of claims, the personal representative of an estate promptly shall apply for a court order to sell, at public auction or privately, for cash or on credit for a term not to exceed six months, all estate property that is liable to perish, waste, or deteriorate in value, or that will be an expense or disadvantage to the estate if kept.

(b) The following may not be included in a sale under Subsection (a):

(1) property exempt from forced sale;

(2) property that is the subject of a specific legacy; and

(3) personal property necessary to carry on a farm, ranch, factory, or other business that is thought best to operate.

(c) In determining whether to order the sale of an asset under Subsection (a), the court shall consider:

(1) the personal representative's duty to take care of and manage the estate in the manner a person of ordinary prudence, discretion, and intelligence would manage the person's own affairs; and

(2) whether the asset constitutes an asset that a trustee is authorized to invest under Subchapter F, Chapter 113, Property Code, or Chapter 117, Property Code.　(Tex. Prob. Code, Sec. 333.)

Added by Acts 2009, 81st Leg., ch. 680, § 1, eff. Jan. 1, 2014.

### SUBCHAPTER C.　SALE OF PERSONAL PROPERTY

### § 356.101.　Order for Sale

(a) Except as provided by Subsection (b), on the application of the personal representative of an estate or any interested person, the court may order the sale of any estate personal property not required to be sold by Section 356.051, including livestock or growing or harvested crops, if the court finds that the sale of the property is in the estate's best interest to pay, from the proceeds of the sale:

(1) expenses of administration;

(2) the decedent's funeral expenses;

(3) expenses of the decedent's last illness;

(4) allowances; or

(5) claims against the estate.

(b) The court may not order under this section the sale of exempt property or property that is the subject of a specific legacy.

Added by Acts 2009, 81st Leg., ch. 680, § 1, eff. Jan. 1, 2014.

### § 356.102.　Requirements for Application and Order

To the extent possible, an application and order for the sale of personal property under Section 356.101 must conform to the requirements under Subchapter F for an application and order for the sale of real estate.

Added by Acts 2009, 81st Leg., ch. 680, § 1, eff. Jan. 1, 2014.

### § 356.103.　Sale at Public Auction

Unless the court directs otherwise, before estate personal property is sold at public auction, notice must be:

(1) issued by the personal representative of the estate; and

(2) posted in the manner notice is posted for original proceedings in probate.

Added by Acts 2009, 81st Leg., ch. 680, § 1, eff. Jan. 1, 2014.

### §  356.104.   Sale on Credit

(a) Estate personal property may not be sold on credit at public auction for a term of more than six months from the date of sale.

(b) Estate personal property purchased on credit at public auction may not be delivered to the purchaser until the purchaser gives a note for the amount due, with good and solvent personal security.  The requirement that security be provided may be waived if the property will not be delivered until the note, with interest, has been paid.

Added by Acts 2009, 81st Leg., ch. 680, § 1, eff. Jan. 1, 2014.

### §  356.105.   Report; Evidence of Title

(a) A sale of estate personal property shall be reported to the court.  The laws regulating the confirmation or disapproval of a sale of real estate apply to the sale, except that a conveyance is not required.

(b) The court's order confirming the sale of estate personal property:

(1) vests the right and title of the intestate's estate in the purchaser who has complied with the terms of the sale; and

(2) is prima facie evidence that all requirements of the law in making the sale have been met.

(c) The personal representative of an estate, on request, may issue a bill of sale without warranty to the purchaser of estate personal property as evidence of title.  The purchaser shall pay for the issuance of the bill of sale.

Added by Acts 2009, 81st Leg., ch. 680, § 1, eff. Jan. 1, 2014.

### SUBCHAPTER D.   SALE OF LIVESTOCK

### §  356.151.   Authority for Sale

(a) A personal representative of an estate who has possession of livestock and who considers selling the livestock to be necessary or to the estate's advantage may, in addition to any other method provided by law for the sale of personal property, obtain authority from the court in which the estate is pending to sell the livestock through:

(1) a bonded livestock commission merchant; or

(2) a bonded livestock auction commission merchant.

(b) The court may authorize the sale of livestock in the manner described by Subsection (a) on a written and sworn application by the personal representative or any person interested in the estate.

Added by Acts 2009, 81st Leg., ch. 680, § 1, eff. Jan. 1, 2014.

### §  356.152.   Contents of Application; Hearing

(a)  An application under Section 356.151 must:

(1)  describe the livestock sought to be sold;  and

(2)  state why granting the application is necessary or to the estate's advantage.

(b)  The court:

(1)  shall promptly consider the application;  and

(2)  may hear evidence for or against the application, with or without notice, as the facts warrant.

Added by Acts 2009, 81st Leg., ch. 680, § 1, eff. Jan. 1, 2014.

### §  356.153.   Grant of Application

If the court grants an application for the sale of livestock, the court shall:

(1)  enter an order to that effect;  and

(2)  authorize delivery of the livestock to a commission merchant described by Section 356.151 for sale in the regular course of business.

Added by Acts 2009, 81st Leg., ch. 680, § 1, eff. Jan. 1, 2014.

### §  356.154.   Report; Passage of Title

The personal representative of the estate shall promptly report to the court a sale of livestock authorized under this subchapter, supported by a verified copy of the commission merchant's account of the sale.  A court order of confirmation is not required to pass title to the purchaser of the livestock.

Added by Acts 2009, 81st Leg., ch. 680, § 1, eff. Jan. 1, 2014.

### §  356.155.   Commission Merchant Fees

A commission merchant shall be paid the merchant's usual and customary charges, not to exceed five percent of the sale price, for the sale of livestock authorized under this subchapter.

Added by Acts 2009, 81st Leg., ch. 680, § 1, eff. Jan. 1, 2014.

### SUBCHAPTER E.   SALE OF MORTGAGED PROPERTY

### §  356.201.   Application  for  Sale  of  Mortgaged Property

A creditor holding a claim that is secured by a valid mortgage or other lien and that has been allowed and approved or established by suit may, by filing a written application, obtain from the court in which the estate is pending an order requiring that the property securing the lien, or as much of the property as is necessary to satisfy the claim, be sold.

Added by Acts 2009, 81st Leg., ch. 680, § 1, eff. Jan. 1, 2014.

### § 356.202.  Citation

On the filing of an application under Section 356.201, the clerk shall issue a citation requiring the personal representative of the estate to appear and show cause why the application should not be granted.

Added by Acts 2009, 81st Leg., ch. 680, § 1, eff. Jan. 1, 2014.

### § 356.203.  Order

The court may order the lien securing the claim of a creditor who files an application under Section 356.201 to be discharged out of general estate assets or refinanced if the discharge or refinance of the lien appears to the court to be advisable.  Otherwise, the court shall grant the application and order that the property securing the lien be sold at public or private sale, as considered best, as in an ordinary sale of real estate.

Added by Acts 2009, 81st Leg., ch. 680, § 1, eff. Jan. 1, 2014.

## SUBCHAPTER F.  SALE OF REAL PROPERTY: APPLICATION AND ORDER FOR SALE

### § 356.251.  Application for Order of Sale

An application may be made to the court for an order to sell estate property if the sale appears necessary or advisable to:

(1) pay:

(A) expenses of administration;

(B) the decedent's funeral expenses;

(C) expenses of the decedent's last illness;

(D) allowances; and

(E) claims against the estate; or

(2) dispose of an interest in estate real property if selling the interest is considered in the estate's best interest.

Added by Acts 2009, 81st Leg., ch. 680, § 1, eff. Jan. 1, 2014.

### § 356.252.  Contents of Application

An application for the sale of real estate must:

(1) be in writing;

(2) describe:

(A) the real estate sought to be sold; or

(B) the interest in or part of the real estate sought to be sold; and

(3) be accompanied by an exhibit, verified by an affidavit, showing:

(A) the estate's condition fully and in detail;

(B) the charges and claims that have been approved or established by suit or that have been rejected and may yet be established;

(C) the amount of each claim described by Paragraph (B);

(D) the estate property remaining on hand that is liable for the payment of the claims described by Paragraph (B); and

(E) any other facts showing the necessity for or advisability of the sale.

Added by Acts 2009, 81st Leg., ch. 680, § 1, eff. Jan. 1, 2014.

### § 356.253.  Citation

On the filing of an application and exhibit described by Section 356.252, the clerk shall issue a citation to all persons interested in the estate.  The citation must:

(1) describe the real estate or the interest in or part of the real estate sought to be sold;

(2) inform the interested persons of the right under Section 356.254 to file an opposition to the sale during the period prescribed by the court in the citation; and

(3) be served by posting.

Added by Acts 2009, 81st Leg., ch. 680, § 1, eff. Jan. 1, 2014.

### § 356.254.  Opposition to Sale

During the period prescribed in a citation issued under Section 356.253, any person interested in the estate may file:

(1) a written opposition to the sale; or

(2) an application for the sale of other estate property.

Added by Acts 2009, 81st Leg., ch. 680, § 1, eff. Jan. 1, 2014.

### § 356.255.  Hearing on Application and Any Opposition

(a) The clerk of the court in which an application for an order of sale is filed shall immediately call to the judge's attention any opposition to the sale that is filed during the period prescribed in the citation issued under Section 356.253.  The court shall hold a hearing on the application if an opposition to the sale is filed during the period prescribed in the citation.

(b) A hearing on an application for an order of sale is not required under this section if no opposition to the application is filed during the period prescribed in the citation. The court may determine that a hearing on the application is necessary even if no opposition is filed during that period.

(c) If the court orders a hearing under Subsection (a) or (b), the court shall designate in writing a date and time for the hearing on the application and any opposition, together with the evidence pertaining to the application and any opposition. The clerk shall issue a notice of the date and time of the hearing to the applicant and to each person who files an opposition to the sale, if applicable.

(d) The judge, by entries on the docket, may continue a hearing held under this section from time to time until the judge is satisfied concerning the application.

Added by Acts 2009, 81st Leg., ch. 680, § 1, eff. Jan. 1, 2014.

### § 356.256. Order

(a) The court shall order the sale of the estate property described in an application for an order of sale if the court is satisfied that the sale is necessary or advisable. Otherwise, the court may deny the application and, if the court considers it best, may order the sale of other estate property the sale of which would be more advantageous to the estate.

(b) An order for the sale of real estate under this section must specify:

(1) the property to be sold, including a description that identifies that property;

(2) whether the property is to be sold at public auction or private sale and, if at public auction, the time and place of the sale;

(3) the necessity or advisability of, and the purpose of, the sale;

(4) except in a case in which a personal representative was not required to give a general bond, that the court, after examining the general bond given by the representative, finds that:

(A) the bond is sufficient as required by law; or

(B) the bond is insufficient;

(5) if the court finds that the general bond is insufficient under Subdivision (4)(B), the amount of the necessary or increased bond, as applicable;

(6) that the sale is to be made and the report returned in accordance with law; and

(7) the terms of the sale.

Added by Acts 2009, 81st Leg., ch. 680, § 1, eff. Jan. 1, 2014.

### § 356.257. Sale for Payment of Debts

Estate real property selected to be sold for the payment of expenses or claims must be that property the sale of which the court considers most advantageous to the estate.

Added by Acts 2009, 81st Leg., ch. 680, § 1, eff. Jan. 1, 2014.

## SUBCHAPTER G. SALE OF REAL ESTATE: TERMS OF SALE

### § 356.301. Permissible Terms

Real estate of an estate may be sold for cash, part cash and part credit, or the equity in land securing an indebtedness may be sold subject to the indebtedness, or with an assumption of the indebtedness, at public or private sale, as appears to the court to be in the estate's best interest.

Added by Acts 2009, 81st Leg., ch. 680, § 1, eff. Jan. 1, 2014.

### § 356.302. Sale on Credit

(a) The cash payment for real estate of an estate sold partly on credit may not be less than one-fifth of the purchase price. The purchaser shall execute a note for the deferred payments, payable in monthly, quarterly, semiannual, or annual installments, in amounts that appear to the court to be in the estate's best interest. The note must bear interest from the date at a rate of not less than four percent per year, payable as provided in the note.

(b) A note executed by a purchaser under Subsection (a) must be secured by a vendor's lien retained in the deed and in the note on the property sold, and be further secured by a deed of trust on the property sold, with the usual provisions for foreclosure and sale on failure to make the payments provided in the deed and the note.

(c) At the election of the holder of a note executed by a purchaser under Subsection (a), default in the payment of principal, interest, or any part of the principal or interest, when due matures the entire debt.

Added by Acts 2009, 81st Leg., ch. 680, § 1, eff. Jan. 1, 2014.

## SUBCHAPTER H. RECONVEYANCE OF REAL ESTATE FOLLOWING FORECLOSURE

### § 356.351. Applicability of Subchapter

This subchapter applies only to real estate owned by an estate as a result of the foreclosure of a vendor's lien or mortgage belonging to the estate:

(1) by a judicial sale;

(2) by a foreclosure suit;

(3) through a sale under a deed of trust; or

(4) by acceptance of a deed in cancellation of a lien or mortgage owned by the estate.

Added by Acts 2009, 81st Leg., ch. 680, § 1, eff. Jan. 1, 2014.

## § 356.352. Application and Order for Reconveyance

On proper application and proof, the court may dispense with the requirements for a credit sale prescribed by Section 356.302 and order the reconveyance of foreclosed real estate to the former mortgage debtor or former owner if it appears to the court that:

(1) an application to redeem the real estate has been made by the former owner to a corporation or agency created by an Act of the United States Congress or of this state in connection with legislation for the relief of owners of mortgaged or encumbered homes, farms, ranches, or other real estate; and

(2) owning bonds of one of those federal or state corporations or agencies instead of the real estate would be in the estate's best interest.

Added by Acts 2009, 81st Leg., ch. 680, § 1, eff. Jan. 1, 2014.

## § 356.353. Exchange for Bonds

(a) If a court orders the reconveyance of foreclosed real estate as provided by Section 356.352, vendor's lien notes shall be reserved for the total amount of the indebtedness due or for the total amount of bonds that the corporation or agency to which the application to redeem the real estate was submitted as described by Section 356.352(1) is allowed to advance under the corporation's or agency's rules or regulations.

(b) On obtaining the order for reconveyance, it shall be proper for the personal representative of the estate to indorse and assign the reserved vendor's lien notes over to any one of the corporations or agencies described by Section 356.352(1) in exchange for bonds of that corporation or agency.

Added by Acts 2009, 81st Leg., ch. 680, § 1, eff. Jan. 1, 2014.

## SUBCHAPTER I. SALE OF REAL ESTATE: PUBLIC SALE

## § 356.401. Required Notice

(a) Except as otherwise provided by Section 356.403(c), the personal representative of an estate shall advertise a public sale of real estate of the estate by a notice published in the county in which the estate is pending, as provided by this title for publication of notices or citations. The notice must:

(1) include a reference to the order of sale;

(2) include the time, place, and required terms of sale; and

(3) briefly describe the real estate to be sold.

(b) The notice required by Subsection (a) is not required to contain field notes, but if the real estate to be sold is rural property, the notice must include:

(1) the name of the original survey of the real estate;

(2) the number of acres comprising the real estate;

(3) the location of the real estate in the county; and

(4) any name by which the real estate is generally known.

Added by Acts 2009, 81st Leg., ch. 680, § 1, eff. Jan. 1, 2014.

## § 356.402. Method of Sale

A public sale of real estate of an estate shall be made at public auction to the highest bidder.

Added by Acts 2009, 81st Leg., ch. 680, § 1, eff. Jan. 1, 2014.

## § 356.403. Time and Place of Sale

(a) Except as provided by Subsection (c), a public sale of real estate of an estate shall be made at:

(1) the courthouse door in the county in which the proceedings are pending; or

(2) another place in that county at which sales of real estate are specifically authorized to be made.

(b) The sale must occur between 10 a.m. and 4 p.m. on the first Tuesday of the month after publication of notice has been completed.

(c) If the court considers it advisable, the court may order the sale to be made in the county in which the real estate is located, in which event notice shall be published both in that county and in the county in which the proceedings are pending.

Added by Acts 2009, 81st Leg., ch. 680, § 1, eff. Jan. 1, 2014.

## § 356.404. Continuance of Sale

(a) A public sale of real estate of an estate that is not completed on the day advertised may be continued from day to day by an oral public announcement of the continuance made at the conclusion of the sale each day.

(b) A continued sale must occur within the hours prescribed by Section 356.403(b).

(c) The continuance of a sale under this section shall be shown in the report of the sale made to the court.

Added by Acts 2009, 81st Leg., ch. 680, § 1, eff. Jan. 1, 2014.

### § 356.405. Failure of Bidder to Comply

(a) If a person bids off real estate of the estate offered for sale at public auction and fails to comply with the terms of the sale, the property shall be readvertised and sold without any further order.

(b) The person defaulting on a bid as described by Subsection (a) is liable for payment to the personal representative of the estate, for the estate's benefit, of:

(1) 10 percent of the amount of the bid; and

(2) the amount of any deficiency in price on the second sale.

(c) The personal representative may recover the amounts under Subsection (b) by suit in any court in the county in which the sale was made that has jurisdiction of the amount claimed.

Added by Acts 2009, 81st Leg., ch. 680, § 1, eff. Jan. 1, 2014.

### SUBCHAPTER J. SALE OF REAL ESTATE: PRIVATE SALE

### § 356.451. Manner of Sale

A private sale of real estate of the estate shall be made in the manner the court directs in the order of sale. Unless the court directs otherwise, additional advertising, notice, or citation concerning the sale is not required.

Added by Acts 2009, 81st Leg., ch. 680, § 1, eff. Jan. 1, 2014.

### SUBCHAPTER K. SALE OF EASEMENT OR RIGHT–OF–WAY

### § 356.501. Authorization

Easements and rights-of-way on, under, and over the land of an estate that is being administered under court order may be sold and conveyed regardless of whether the sale proceeds are required to pay charges or claims against the estate or for other lawful purposes.

Added by Acts 2009, 81st Leg., ch. 680, § 1, eff. Jan. 1, 2014.

### § 356.502. Procedure

The procedure for the sale of an easement or right-of-way authorized under Section 356.501 is the same as the procedure provided by law for a sale of estate real property at private sale.

Added by Acts 2009, 81st Leg., ch. 680, § 1, eff. Jan. 1, 2014.

### SUBCHAPTER L. CONFIRMATION OF SALE OF REAL PROPERTY AND TRANSFER OF TITLE

### § 356.551. Report

A sale of estate real property shall be reported to the court ordering the sale not later than the 30th day after the date the sale is made. The report must:

(1) be sworn to, in writing, and filed with the clerk;

(2) include:

(A) the date of the order of sale;

(B) a description of the property sold;

(C) the time and place of sale;

(D) the purchaser's name;

(E) the amount for which each parcel of property or interest in property was sold;

(F) the terms of the sale;

(G) whether the sale was made at public auction or privately; and

(H) whether the purchaser is ready to comply with the order of sale; and

(3) be noted on the probate docket.

Added by Acts 2009, 81st Leg., ch. 680, § 1, eff. Jan. 1, 2014.

### § 356.552. Action of Court on Report of Sale

After the expiration of five days from the date a report of sale is filed under Section 356.551, the court shall:

(1) inquire into the manner in which the sale was made;

(2) hear evidence in support of or against the report; and

(3) determine the sufficiency or insufficiency of the personal representative's general bond, if any has been required and given.

Added by Acts 2009, 81st Leg., ch. 680, § 1, eff. Jan. 1, 2014.

## § 356.553. Confirmation of Sale When Bond Not Required

If the personal representative of an estate is not required by this title to give a general bond, the court may confirm the sale of estate real property in the manner provided by Section 356.556(a) if the court finds that the sale is satisfactory and made in accordance with law.

Added by Acts 2009, 81st Leg., ch. 680, § 1, eff. Jan. 1, 2014.

## § 356.554. Sufficiency of Bond

(a) If the personal representative of an estate is required by this title to give a general bond, before the court confirms any sale of real estate, the court shall determine whether the bond is sufficient to protect the estate after the sale proceeds are received.

(b) If the court finds that the general bond is sufficient, the court may confirm the sale as provided by Section 356.556(a).

(c) If the court finds that the general bond is insufficient, the court may not confirm the sale until the general bond is increased to the amount required by the court, or an additional bond is given, and approved by the court.

(d) An increase in the amount of the general bond, or the additional bond, as applicable under Subsection (c), must be equal to the sum of:

(1) the amount for which the real estate is sold; and

(2) any additional amount the court finds necessary and sets for the estate's protection.

Added by Acts 2009, 81st Leg., ch. 680, § 1, eff. Jan. 1, 2014.

## § 356.555. Increased or Additional Bond Not Required

Notwithstanding Sections 356.554(c) and (d), if the real estate sold is encumbered by a lien to secure a claim against the estate and is sold to the owner or holder of the secured claim in full payment, liquidation, and satisfaction of the claim, an increased general bond or additional bond may not be required except for the amount of any cash paid to the personal representative of the estate in excess of the amount necessary to pay, liquidate, and satisfy the claim in full.

Added by Acts 2009, 81st Leg., ch. 680, § 1, eff. Jan. 1, 2014.

## § 356.556. Confirmation or Disapproval Order

(a) If the court is satisfied that a sale reported under Section 356.551 was for a fair price, properly made, and in conformity with law, and the court has approved any increased or additional bond that the court found necessary to protect the estate, the court shall enter an order:

(1) confirming the sale;

(2) showing conformity with this chapter;

(3) detailing the terms of the sale; and

(4) authorizing the personal representative to convey the property on the purchaser's compliance with the terms of the sale.

(b) If the court is not satisfied that the sale was for a fair price, properly made, and in conformity with law, the court shall enter an order setting aside the sale and ordering a new sale to be made, if necessary.

(c) The court's action in confirming or disapproving a report of a sale has the effect of a final judgment. Any person interested in the estate or in the sale is entitled to have an order entered under this section reviewed as in other final judgments in probate proceedings.

Added by Acts 2009, 81st Leg., ch. 680, § 1, eff. Jan. 1, 2014.

## § 356.557. Deed

Real estate of an estate that is sold shall be conveyed by a proper deed that refers to and identifies the court order confirming the sale. The deed:

(1) vests in the purchaser all right and title of the estate to, and all interest of the estate in, the property; and

(2) is prima facie evidence that the sale has met all applicable requirements of the law.

Added by Acts 2009, 81st Leg., ch. 680, § 1, eff. Jan. 1, 2014.

## § 356.558. Delivery of Deed

(a) After the court has confirmed a sale and the purchaser has complied with the terms of the sale, the personal representative of the estate shall promptly execute and deliver to the purchaser a proper deed conveying the property.

(b) If the sale is made partly on credit:

(1) the vendor's lien securing one or more purchase money notes must be expressly retained in the deed and may not be waived; and

(2) before actual delivery of the deed to the purchaser, the purchaser shall execute and deliver to the personal representative of the estate one or

more vendor's lien notes, with or without personal sureties as ordered by the court, and a deed of trust or mortgage on the property as additional security for the payment of the notes.

(c) On completion of the transaction, the personal representative of the estate shall promptly file or cause to be filed and recorded the deed of trust or mortgage in the appropriate records in the county in which the land is located.

Added by Acts 2009, 81st Leg., ch. 680, § 1, eff. Jan. 1, 2014.

### § 356.559.  Damages; Removal

(a) If the personal representative of an estate neglects to comply with Section 356.558, including to file the deed of trust securing a lien in the proper county, the representative and the sureties on the representative's bond shall, after complaint and citation, be held liable for the use of the estate and for all damages resulting from the representative's neglect, and the court may remove the representative.

(b) Damages under this section may be recovered in any court of competent jurisdiction.

Added by Acts 2009, 81st Leg., ch. 680, § 1, eff. Jan. 1, 2014.

### SUBCHAPTER M.  PROCEDURE ON FAILURE TO APPLY FOR SALE

### § 356.601.  Failure to Apply for Sale

If the personal representative of an estate neglects to apply for an order to sell sufficient estate property to pay charges and claims against the estate that have been allowed and approved or established by suit, any interested person, on written application, may have the representative cited to appear and make a full exhibit of the estate's condition and show cause why a sale of the property should not be ordered.

Added by Acts 2009, 81st Leg., ch. 680, § 1, eff. Jan. 1, 2014.

### § 356.602.  Court Order

On hearing an application under Section 356.601, if the court is satisfied that a sale of estate property is necessary or advisable to satisfy the charges and claims described by Section 356.601, the court shall enter an order of sale as provided by Section 356.256.

Added by Acts 2009, 81st Leg., ch. 680, § 1, eff. Jan. 1, 2014.

### SUBCHAPTER N.  PURCHASE OF PROPERTY BY PERSONAL REPRESENTATIVE

### § 356.651.  General Prohibition on Purchase

Except as otherwise provided by this subchapter, the personal representative of an estate may not purchase, directly or indirectly, any estate property sold by the representative or any co-representative of the estate.

Added by Acts 2009, 81st Leg., ch. 680, § 1, eff. Jan. 1, 2014.

### § 356.652.  Exception: Authorization in Will

A personal representative of an estate may purchase estate property if the representative was appointed in a will that:

(1) has been admitted to probate;  and

(2) expressly authorizes the sale.

Added by Acts 2009, 81st Leg., ch. 680, § 1, eff. Jan. 1, 2014.

### § 356.653.  Exception: Executory Contract

A personal representative of a decedent's estate may purchase estate property in compliance with the terms of a written executory contract signed by the decedent, including:

(1) a contract for deed;

(2) an earnest money contract;

(3) a buy/sell agreement;  and

(4) a stock purchase or redemption agreement.

Added by Acts 2009, 81st Leg., ch. 680, § 1, eff. Jan. 1, 2014.

### § 356.654.  Exception: Best Interest of Estate

(a) Subject to Subsection (b), the personal representative of an estate, including an independent administrator, may purchase estate property on the court's determination that the sale is in the estate's best interest.

(b) Before purchasing estate property as authorized by Subsection (a), the personal representative shall give notice of the purchase by certified mail, return receipt requested, unless the court requires another form of notice, to:

(1) each distributee of the estate;  and

(2) each creditor whose claim remains unsettled after being presented within six months of the date letters testamentary or of administration are originally granted.

(c) The court may require additional notice or allow for the waiver of the notice required for a sale made under this section.

Added by Acts 2009, 81st Leg., ch. 680, § 1, eff. Jan. 1, 2014.

### § 356.655.  Purchase in Violation of Subchapter

(a) If a personal representative of an estate purchases estate property in violation of this subchapter, any person interested in the estate may file a written complaint with the court in which the proceedings are pending.

(b) On service of citation on the personal representative on a complaint filed under Subsection (a) and after hearing and proof, the court shall:

    (1) declare the sale void;

    (2) set aside the sale; and

    (3) order the reconveyance of the property to the estate.

(c) The court shall adjudge against the personal representative all costs of the sale, protest, and suit found necessary.

Added by Acts 2009, 81st Leg., ch. 680, § 1, eff. Jan. 1, 2014.

## CHAPTER 357. RENTING ESTATE PROPERTY

### SUBCHAPTER A. RENTAL AND RETURN OF ESTATE PROPERTY

### SUBCHAPTER A. RENTAL AND RETURN OF ESTATE PROPERTY

#### § 357.001. Renting Estate Property Without Court Order

(a) The personal representative of an estate, without a court order, may rent any of the estate property for one year or less, at public auction or privately, as is considered to be in the best interest of the estate.

(b) On the sworn complaint of any person interested in the estate, the court shall require a personal representative who, without a court order, rents estate property to account to the estate for the reasonable value of the rent of the property, to be ascertained by the court on satisfactory evidence.

Added by Acts 2009, 81st Leg., ch. 680, § 1, eff. Jan. 1, 2014.

#### § 357.002. Renting Estate Property With Court Order

(a) The personal representative of an estate may, if the representative prefers, and shall, if the proposed rental period is more than one year, file a written application with the court setting forth the property the representative seeks to rent.

(b) If the court finds that granting an application filed under Subsection (a) is in the interest of the estate, the court shall grant the application and issue an order that:

    (1) describes the property to be rented; and

    (2) states whether the property will be rented at public auction or privately, whether for cash or on credit, and if on credit, the extent of the credit and the period for which the property may be rented.

(c) If, under Subsection (b), the court orders property to be rented at public auction, the court shall prescribe whether notice of the auction shall be published or posted.

Added by Acts 2009, 81st Leg., ch. 680, § 1, eff. Jan. 1, 2014. Amended by Acts 2011, 82nd Leg., ch. 91 (S.B. 1303), § 8.016, eff. Jan. 1, 2014.

#### § 357.003. Estate Property Rented on Credit

Possession of estate property rented on credit may not be delivered until the renter executes and delivers to the personal representative a note with good personal security for the amount of the rent. If the property is delivered without the representative receiving the required security, the representative and the sureties on the representative's bond are liable for the full amount of the rent. When a rental is payable in installments, in advance of the period to which the installments relate, this section does not apply.

Added by Acts 2009, 81st Leg., ch. 680, § 1, eff. Jan. 1, 2014.

#### § 357.004. Condition of Returned Estate Property

(a) Estate property that is rented, with or without a court order, must be returned to the estate's possession in as good a condition, except for reasonable wear and tear, as when the property was rented.

(b) The personal representative of an estate shall:

    (1) ensure that rented estate property is returned in the condition required by Subsection (a);

    (2) report to the court any damage to, or loss or destruction of, the property; and

    (3) ask the court for the authority to take any necessary action.

(c) A personal representative who fails to act as required by this section and the sureties on the representative's bond are liable to the estate for any loss or damage suffered as a result of the representative's failure.

Added by Acts 2009, 81st Leg., ch. 680, § 1, eff. Jan. 1, 2014.

## § 357.005. Complaint for Failure to Rent

(a) Any person interested in an estate may:

(1) file a written and sworn complaint in the court in which the estate is pending; and

(2) have the personal representative cited to appear and show cause why the representative did not rent any estate property.

(b) The court, on hearing the complaint, shall issue an order that appears to be in the best interest of the estate.

Added by Acts 2009, 81st Leg., ch. 680, § 1, eff. Jan. 1, 2014.

## SUBCHAPTER B. REPORT ON RENTED ESTATE PROPERTY

## § 357.051. Reports Concerning Rentals

(a) A personal representative of an estate who rents estate property with an appraised value of $3,000 or more shall, not later than the 30th day after the date the property is rented, file with the court a sworn and written report stating:

(1) the property rented and the property's appraised value;

(2) the date the property was rented and whether the rental occurred at public auction or privately;

(3) the name of each person renting the property;

(4) the rental amount; and

(5) whether the rental was for cash or on credit and, if on credit, the length of time, the terms, and the security received for the credit.

(b) A personal representative of an estate who rents estate property with an appraised value of less than $3,000 may report the rental in the next annual or final account that must be filed as required by law.

Added by Acts 2009, 81st Leg., ch. 680, § 1, eff. Jan. 1, 2014.

## § 357.052. Court Action on Report

(a) At any time after the fifth day after the date the report of renting is filed, the court shall:

(1) examine the report; and

(2) by order approve and confirm the report if found just and reasonable.

(b) If the court disapproves the report, the estate is not bound and the court may order another offering for rent of the property that is the subject of the

report, in the same manner and subject to the provisions of this chapter.

(c) If the court approves the report and it later appears that, by reason of any fault of the personal representative, the property was not rented for the property's reasonable value, the court shall have the representative and the sureties on the representative's bond appear and show cause why the reasonable value of the rent of the property should not be adjudged against the representative.

Added by Acts 2009, 81st Leg., ch. 680, § 1, eff. Jan. 1, 2014.

## CHAPTER 358. MATTERS RELATING TO MINERAL PROPERTIES

### SUBCHAPTER A. GENERAL PROVISIONS

SUBCHAPTER F. PROCEDURE IF PERSONAL
REPRESENTATIVE OF ESTATE NEGLECTS
TO APPLY FOR AUTHORITY

## SUBCHAPTER A.   GENERAL PROVISIONS

### § 358.001.   Definitions

In this chapter:

(1) "Gas" includes all liquid hydrocarbons in the gaseous phase in the reservoir.

(2) "Land" and "interest in land" include minerals or an interest in minerals in place.

(3) "Mineral development" includes exploration for, whether by geophysical or other means, drilling for, mining for, development of, operations in connection with, production of, and saving of oil, other liquid hydrocarbons, gas, gaseous elements, sulphur, metals, and all other minerals, whether solid or otherwise.

(4) "Property" includes land, minerals in place, whether solid, liquid, or gaseous, and an interest of any kind in that property, including a royalty interest, owned by an estate.

Added by Acts 2009, 81st Leg., ch. 680, § 1, eff. Jan. 1, 2014.

## SUBCHAPTER B.   MINERAL LEASES AFTER PUBLIC NOTICE

### § 358.051.   Authorization for Leasing of Minerals

(a) The court in which probate proceedings on a decedent's estate are pending may authorize the personal representative of the estate, appointed and qualified under the laws of this state and acting solely under court orders, to make, execute, and deliver a lease, with or without a unitization clause or pooling provision, providing for the exploration for and development and production of oil, other liquid hydrocarbons, gas, metals and other solid minerals, and other minerals, or any of those minerals in place, belonging to the estate.

(b) A lease described by Subsection (a) must be made and entered into under and in conformity with this subchapter.

Added by Acts 2009, 81st Leg., ch. 680, § 1, eff. Jan. 1, 2014.

### § 358.052.   Lease Application

(a) The personal representative of an estate shall file with the county clerk of the county in which the probate proceeding is pending a written application, addressed to the court or the judge of the court, for authority to lease estate property for mineral exploration and development, with or without a pooling provision or unitization clause.

(b) The lease application must:

(1) describe the property fully by reference to the amount of acreage, the survey name or number, or the abstract number, or by another method adequately identifying the property and the property's location in the county in which the property is situated;

(2) specify the interest thought to be owned by the estate, if less than the whole, but requesting authority to include all of the interest owned by the estate, if that is the intention;  and

(3) set out the reasons the estate property described in the application should be leased.

(c) The lease application is not required to set out or suggest:

(1) the name of any proposed lessee;  or

(2) the terms, provisions, or form of any desired lease.

Added by Acts 2009, 81st Leg., ch. 680, § 1, eff. Jan. 1, 2014.

### § 358.053.   Scheduling of Hearing on Application; Continuance

(a) Immediately after the filing of a lease application under Section 358.052, the county clerk shall call the filing of the application to the court's attention, and the judge shall promptly make and enter a brief order designating the time and place for hearing the application.

(b) If the hearing is not held at the time originally designated by the court or by a timely continuance order entered, the hearing shall be continued automatically without further notice to the same time on the following day, other than Sundays and holidays on which the county courthouse is officially closed, and from day to day until the lease application is finally acted on and disposed of by court order.  Notice of an automatic continuance is not required.

Added by Acts 2009, 81st Leg., ch. 680, § 1, eff. Jan. 1, 2014.

## § 358.054. Notice of Hearing on Application

(a) At least 10 days before the date set for the hearing on a lease application filed under Section 358.052, excluding the date of notice and the date set for the hearing, the personal representative shall give notice of the hearing by:

(1) publishing the notice in one issue of a newspaper of general circulation in the county in which the proceeding is pending; or

(2) if there is no newspaper described by Subdivision (1), posting the notice or having the notice posted.

(b) If notice is published, the date of notice is the date printed on the newspaper.

(c) The notice must:

(1) be dated;

(2) be directed to all persons interested in the estate;

(3) state the date on which the lease application was filed;

(4) describe briefly the property sought to be leased, specifying the fractional interest sought to be leased if less than the entire interest in the tract or tracts identified; and

(5) state the time and place designated by the judge for the hearing.

Added by Acts 2009, 81st Leg., ch. 680, § 1, eff. Jan. 1, 2014.

## § 358.055. Requirements Regarding Order and Notice Mandatory

An order of the judge or court authorizing any act to be performed under a lease application filed under Section 358.052 is void in the absence of:

(1) a written order originally designating a time and place for hearing;

(2) a notice issued by the personal representative of the estate in compliance with the order described by Subdivision (1); and

(3) proof of the publication or posting of the notice as required under Section 358.054.

Added by Acts 2009, 81st Leg., ch. 680, § 1, eff. Jan. 1, 2014.

## § 358.056. Hearing on Application; Order

(a) At the time and place designated for the hearing under Section 358.053(a), or at the time to which the hearing is continued as provided by Section 358.053(b), the judge shall:

(1) hear a lease application filed under Section 358.052; and

(2) require proof as to the necessity or advisability of leasing for mineral development the property described in the application and the notice.

(b) The judge shall enter an order authorizing one or more leases affecting and covering the property or portions of property described in the application, with or without pooling provisions or unitization clauses, and with or without cash consideration if considered by the court to be in the best interest of the estate, if the judge is satisfied that:

(1) the application is in proper form;

(2) notice has been given in the manner and for the time required by law;

(3) proof of necessity or advisability of leasing is sufficient; and

(4) the application should be granted.

(c) The order must contain:

(1) the name of the lessee;

(2) any actual cash consideration to be paid by the lessee;

(3) a finding that the requirements of Subsection (b) have been satisfied; and

(4) one of the following findings:

(A) a finding that the personal representative is exempted by law from giving bond; or

(B) if the representative is not exempted by law from giving bond, a finding as to whether the representative's general bond on file is sufficient to protect the personal property on hand, including any cash bonus to be paid.

(d) If the court finds the general bond insufficient to meet the requirements of Subsection (c)(4)(B), the order must show the amount of increased or additional bond required to cover the deficiency.

(e) A complete exhibit copy, either written or printed, of each authorized lease must be set out in the order or attached to the order and incorporated by reference and made part of the order. The exhibit copy must show:

(1) the name of the lessee;

(2) the date of the lease;

(3) an adequate description of the property being leased;

(4) any delay rental to be paid to defer commencement of operations; and

(5) all other authorized terms and provisions.

(f) If the date of a lease does not appear in the exhibit copy of the lease or in the order, the date of the order is considered for all purposes to be the date of the lease.

(g) If the name or address of the depository bank for receiving rental is not shown in the exhibit copy of a lease, the estate's personal representative may insert that information, or cause that information to be inserted, in the lease at the time of the lease's execution or at any other time agreeable to the lessee or the lessee's successors or assignees.

Added by Acts 2009, 81st Leg., ch. 680, § 1, eff. Jan. 1, 2014.

### § 358.057.　Making of Lease on Granting of Application

(a) If the court grants an application as provided by Section 358.056, the personal representative of the estate may make the lease or leases, as evidenced by the exhibit copies described by Section 358.056, in accordance with the order.

(b) The lease or leases must be made not later than the 30th day after the date of the order unless an extension is granted by the court on sworn application showing good cause.

(c) It is not necessary for the judge to make an order confirming the lease or leases.

Added by Acts 2009, 81st Leg., ch. 680, § 1, eff. Jan. 1, 2014.

### § 358.058.　Bond Requirements

(a) Unless the personal representative of the estate is not required to give a general bond, a lease for which a cash consideration is required, although ordered, executed, and delivered, is not valid:

(1) unless the order authorizing the lease makes findings with respect to the general bond; and

(2) if the general bond has been found insufficient, unless and until:

(A) the bond has been increased or an additional bond given, as required by the order, with the sureties required by law; and

(B) the increased bond or additional bond has been approved by the judge and filed with the clerk of the court in which the proceedings are pending.

(b) If two or more leases of different land are authorized by the same order, the general bond must be increased, or additional bonds given, to cover all of the leases.

Added by Acts 2009, 81st Leg., ch. 680, § 1, eff. Jan. 1, 2014.

### § 358.059.　Term of Lease Binding

(a) A lease executed and delivered in compliance with this subchapter is valid and binding on the property or interest in property owned by the estate and covered by the lease for the full term provided by the lease, subject only to the lease's terms and conditions, even if the primary term extends beyond the date the estate is closed in accordance with law.

(b) The authorized primary term of the lease may not exceed five years, subject to the lease terms and provisions extending the lease beyond the primary term by:

(1) paying production;

(2) bona fide drilling or reworking operations, whether in or on the same well or wells or an additional well or wells, without a cessation of operations of more than 60 consecutive days before production has been restored or obtained; or

(3) a shut-in gas well.

Added by Acts 2009, 81st Leg., ch. 680, § 1, eff. Jan. 1, 2014.

### § 358.060.　Amendment of Lease Regarding Effect of Shut–in Gas Well

(a) An oil, gas, and mineral lease executed by a personal representative under the former Texas Probate Code or this code may be amended by an instrument that provides that a shut-in gas well on the land covered by the lease or on land pooled with all or part of the land covered by the lease continues the lease in effect after the lease's five-year primary term.

(b) The personal representative, with the approval of the court, shall execute the instrument according to the terms and conditions prescribed by the instrument.

Added by Acts 2009, 81st Leg., ch. 680, § 1, eff. Jan. 1, 2014.

## SUBCHAPTER C.　MINERAL LEASES AT PRIVATE SALE

### § 358.101.　Authorization for Leasing of Minerals at Private Sale

(a) Notwithstanding the mandatory requirements of Subchapter B for setting a time and place for hearing of a lease application filed under Section 358.052 and the issuance, service, and return of notice, the court may authorize the making of oil, gas, and mineral leases at private sale without public notice or advertising if, in the court's opinion, facts are set out in the application required by Subchapter B sufficient to show that it would be more advantageous to the estate that a lease be made privately and without compliance with those mandatory requirements.

(b) Leases authorized by this section may include pooling provisions or unitization clauses as in other cases.

Added by Acts 2009, 81st Leg., ch. 680, § 1, eff. Jan. 1, 2014.

### § 358.102. Action of Court if Public Advertising Not Required

(a) At any time after the fifth day and before the 11th day after the filing date of an application to lease at private sale and without an order setting the hearing time and place, the court shall:

(1) hear the application;

(2) inquire into the manner in which the proposed lease has been or will be made; and

(3) hear evidence for or against the application.

(b) If satisfied that the lease has been or will be made for a fair and sufficient consideration and on fair terms and has been or will be properly made in conformity with law, the court shall enter an order authorizing the execution of the lease without the necessity of advertising, notice, or citation. The order must comply in all other respects with the requirements essential to the validity of mineral leases as set out in Subchapter B, as if advertising or notice were required.

(c) The issuance of an order confirming a lease or leases made at private sale is not required, but such a lease is not valid until any increased or additional bond required by the court has been approved by the court and filed with the court clerk.

Added by Acts 2009, 81st Leg., ch. 680, § 1, eff. Jan. 1, 2014.

## SUBCHAPTER D. POOLING OR UNITIZATION OF ROYALTIES OR MINERALS

### § 358.151. Authorization for Pooling or Unitization

(a) If an existing lease or leases on property owned by an estate being administered do not adequately provide for pooling or unitization, the court in which the proceedings are pending may, in the manner provided by this subchapter, authorize the commitment of royalty or mineral interests in oil, liquid hydrocarbons, gas, gaseous elements, and other minerals, or any one or more of them, owned by the estate, to agreements that provide for the operation of areas as a pool or unit for the exploration for, develop-

ment of, and production of all of those minerals, if the court finds that:

(1) the pool or unit to which the agreement relates will be operated in a manner that protects correlative rights or prevents the physical or economic waste of oil, liquid hydrocarbons, gas, gaseous elements, or other minerals subject to the agreement; and

(2) it is in the best interest of the estate to execute the agreement.

(b) An agreement authorized under Subsection (a) may, among other things, provide that:

(1) operations incident to the drilling of or production from a well on any portion of a pool or unit shall be considered for all purposes to be the conduct of operations on or production from each separately owned tract in the pool or unit;

(2) any lease covering any part of the area committed to a pool or unit continues in effect in its entirety as long as:

(A) oil, gas, or other minerals subject to the agreement are produced in paying quantities from any part of the pooled or unitized area;

(B) operations are conducted as provided in the lease on any part of the pooled or unitized area; or

(C) there is a shut-in gas well on any part of the pooled or unitized area, if the presence of the shut-in gas well is a ground for continuation of the lease under the terms of the lease;

(3) the production allocated by the agreement to each tract included in a pool or unit shall, when produced, be considered for all purposes to have been produced from the tract by a well drilled on the tract;

(4) the royalties provided for on production from any tract or portion of a tract within the pool or unit shall be paid only on that portion of the production allocated to the tract in accordance with the agreement;

(5) the dry gas, before or after extraction of hydrocarbons, may be returned to a formation underlying any land or leases committed to the agreement, and that royalties are not required to be paid on the gas returned; and

(6) gas obtained from other sources or other land may be injected into a formation underlying any land or leases committed to the agreement, and that royalties are not required to be paid on the gas injected when the gas is produced from the unit.

Added by Acts 2009, 81st Leg., ch. 680, § 1, eff. Jan. 1, 2014.

## § 358.152. Pooling or Unitization Application

(a) The personal representative of an estate shall file with the county clerk of the county in which the probate proceeding is pending a written application for authority to:

(1) enter into pooling or unitization agreements supplementing, amending, or otherwise relating to any existing lease or leases covering property owned by the estate; or

(2) commit royalties or other interests in minerals, whether or not subject to a lease, to a pooling or unitization agreement.

(b) The pooling or unitization application must also:

(1) sufficiently describe the property as required in an original lease application;

(2) describe briefly any lease or leases to which the interest of the estate is subject; and

(3) set out the reasons the proposed agreement concerning the property should be entered into.

(c) A copy of the proposed agreement must be attached to the application and made a part of the application by reference.

(d) The agreement may not be recorded in the judge's probate docket.

(e) Immediately after the pooling or unitization application is filed, the clerk shall call the application to the judge's attention.

Added by Acts 2009, 81st Leg., ch. 680, § 1, eff. Jan. 1, 2014. Amended by Acts 2011, 82nd Leg., ch. 91 (S.B. 1303), § 8.017, eff. Jan. 1, 2014.

## § 358.153. Notice Not Required

Notice by advertising, citation, or otherwise of the filing of a pooling or unitization application under Section 358.152 is not required.

Added by Acts 2009, 81st Leg., ch. 680, § 1, eff. Jan. 1, 2014.

## § 358.154. Hearing on Application

(a) The judge may hold a hearing on a pooling or unitization application filed under Section 358.152 at any time agreeable to the parties to the proposed agreement.

(b) The judge shall hear evidence and determine to the judge's satisfaction whether it is in the best interest of the estate that the proposed agreement be authorized.

(c) The hearing may be continued from day to day and from time to time as the court finds necessary.

Added by Acts 2009, 81st Leg., ch. 680, § 1, eff. Jan. 1, 2014.

## § 358.155. Action of Court and Contents of Order

(a) The court shall enter an order setting out the court's findings and authorizing execution of the proposed pooling or unitization agreement, with or without payment of cash consideration according to the agreement, if the court finds that:

(1) the pool or unit to which the agreement relates will be operated in a manner that protects correlative rights or prevents the physical or economic waste of oil, liquid hydrocarbons, gas, gaseous elements, or other minerals subject to the agreement;

(2) it is in the best interest of the estate that the agreement be executed; and

(3) the agreement conforms substantially with the permissible provisions of Section 358.151.

(b) If cash consideration is to be paid for the agreement, the court shall also make findings as to the necessity of increased or additional bond, as in the making of leases on payment of the cash bonus for the lease. Such an agreement is not valid until any required increased or additional bond has been approved by the judge and filed with the clerk.

(c) If the effective date of the agreement is not stipulated in the agreement, the effective date of the agreement is the date of the court's order.

Added by Acts 2009, 81st Leg., ch. 680, § 1, eff. Jan. 1, 2014.

## SUBCHAPTER E. SPECIAL ANCILLARY INSTRUMENTS THAT MAY BE EXECUTED WITHOUT COURT ORDER

### § 358.201. Authorization for Execution of Agreements

As to any mineral lease or pooling or unitization agreement, executed on behalf of an estate before January 1, 1956, or on or after that date under the provisions of the former Texas Probate Code or this code, or executed by a former owner of land, minerals, or royalty affected by the lease or agreement, the personal representative of the estate being administered may, without further court order and without consideration, execute:

(1) division orders;

(2) transfer orders;

(3) instruments of correction;

(4) instruments designating depository banks for the receipt of delay rentals or shut-in gas well royalty to accrue or become payable under the terms of the lease; and

(5) similar instruments relating to the lease or agreement and the property covered by the lease or agreement.

Added by Acts 2009, 81st Leg., ch. 680, § 1, eff. Jan. 1, 2014.

## SUBCHAPTER F. PROCEDURE IF PERSONAL REPRESENTATIVE OF ESTATE NEGLECTS TO APPLY FOR AUTHORITY

### § 358.251. Application to Show Cause

If the personal representative of an estate neglects to apply for authority to subject estate property to a lease for mineral development, pooling, or unitization, or to commit royalty or another interest in minerals to pooling or unitization, any person interested in the estate may, on written application filed with the county clerk, have the representative cited to show cause why it is not in the best interest of the estate to make such a lease or enter into such an agreement.

Added by Acts 2009, 81st Leg., ch. 680, § 1, eff. Jan. 1, 2014.

### § 358.252. Hearing on Application

(a) The county clerk shall immediately call the filing of an application under Section 358.251 to the attention of the judge of the court in which the probate proceedings are pending.

(b) The judge shall set a time and place for a hearing on the application, and the personal representative of the estate shall be cited to appear and show cause why the execution of a lease or agreement described by Section 358.251 should not be ordered.

Added by Acts 2009, 81st Leg., ch. 680, § 1, eff. Jan. 1, 2014.

### § 358.253. Order

On a hearing conducted under Section 358.252, if satisfied from the evidence that it would be in the best interest of the estate, the court shall enter an order requiring the personal representative promptly to file an application to subject the estate property to a lease for mineral development, with or without pooling or unitization provisions, or to commit royalty or other minerals to pooling or unitization, as appropriate.

Added by Acts 2009, 81st Leg., ch. 680, § 1, eff. Jan. 1, 2014.

### § 358.254. Procedure to be Followed After Entry of Order

After entry of an order under Section 358.253, the procedure prescribed with respect to an original lease application, or with respect to an original application for authority to commit royalty or minerals to pooling or unitization, whichever is appropriate, shall be followed.

Added by Acts 2009, 81st Leg., ch. 680, § 1, eff. Jan. 1, 2014.

## CHAPTER 359. ANNUAL ACCOUNT AND OTHER EXHIBITS AND REPORTS

### SUBCHAPTER A. ANNUAL ACCOUNT AND OTHER EXHIBITS

### SUBCHAPTER A. ANNUAL ACCOUNT AND OTHER EXHIBITS

### § 359.001. Account of Estate Required

(a) On the expiration of 12 months from the date a personal representative qualifies and receives letters testamentary or of administration to administer a decedent's estate under court order, the representative shall file with the court an account consisting of a written exhibit made under oath that lists all claims against the estate presented to the representative during the period covered by the account. The exhibit must specify:

(1) the claims allowed by the representative;

(2) the claims paid by the representative;

(3) the claims rejected by the representative and the date the claims were rejected; and

(4) the claims for which a lawsuit has been filed and the status of that lawsuit.

(b) The account must:

(1) show all property that has come to the personal representative's knowledge or into the representative's possession that was not previously listed or inventoried as estate property;

(2) show any changes in estate property that have not been previously reported;

(3) provide a complete account of receipts and disbursements for the period covered by the account, including the source and nature of the receipts and disbursements, with separate listings for principal and income receipts;

(4) provide a complete, accurate, and detailed description of:

(A) the property being administered;

(B) the condition of the property and the use being made of the property; and

(C) if rented, the terms on which and the price for which the property was rented;

(5) show the cash balance on hand and the name and location of the depository where the balance is kept;

(6) show any other cash held in a savings account or other manner that was deposited subject to court order and the name and location of the depository for that cash;

(7) provide a detailed description of the personal property of the estate that shows how and where the property is held for safekeeping;

(8) provide a statement that during the period covered by the account all tax returns due have been filed and all taxes due and owing have been paid, including:

(A) a complete account of the amount of the taxes;

(B) the date the taxes were paid; and

(C) the governmental entity to which the taxes were paid;

(9) if on the filing of the account a tax return due to be filed or any taxes due to be paid are delinquent, provide the reasons for, and include a description of, the delinquency; and

(10) provide a statement that the representative has paid all the required bond premiums for the accounting period.

(c) For bonds, notes, and other securities, the description required by Subsection (b)(7) must include:

(1) the names of the obligor and obligee or, if payable to bearer, a statement that the bond, note, or other security is payable to bearer;

(2) the date of issue and maturity;

(3) the interest rate;

(4) the serial number or other identifying numbers;

(5) the manner in which the property is secured; and

(6) other information necessary to fully identify the bond, note, or other security.

Added by Acts 2009, 81st Leg., ch. 680, § 1, eff. Jan. 1, 2014.

### § 359.002. Annual Account Required Until Estate Closed

(a) Each personal representative of the estate of a decedent shall continue to file an annual account conforming to the essential requirements of Section 359.001 regarding changes in the estate assets occurring since the date the most recent previous account was filed.

(b) The annual account must be filed in a manner that allows the court or an interested person to ascertain the true condition of the estate, with respect to money, securities, and other property, by adding to the balances forwarded from the most recent previous account the amounts received during the period covered by the account and subtracting the disbursements made during that period.

(c) The description of property sufficiently described in an inventory or previous account may be made in the annual account by reference to that description.

Added by Acts 2009, 81st Leg., ch. 680, § 1, eff. Jan. 1, 2014.

### § 359.003. Supporting Vouchers and Other Documents Attached to Account.

(a) The personal representative of an estate shall attach to each annual account:

(1) a voucher for each item of credit claimed in the account or, to support the item in the absence of the voucher, other evidence satisfactory to the court;

(2) an official letter from the bank or other depository where the estate money on hand is deposited that shows the amounts in general or special deposits; and

(3) proof of the existence and possession of:

(A) securities owned by the estate or shown by the account; and

(B) other assets held by a depository subject to court order.

(b) An original voucher submitted to the court may on application be returned to the personal representative after approval of the account.

(c) The court may require:

(1) additional evidence of the existence and custody of the securities and other personal property as the court considers proper; and

(2) the personal representative at any time to exhibit the securities and other personal property to the court or another person designated by the court at the place where the securities and other personal property are held for safekeeping.

Added by Acts 2009, 81st Leg., ch. 680, § 1, eff. Jan. 1, 2014.

### § 359.004. Method of Proof for Securities and Other Assets

(a) The proof required by Section 359.003(a)(3) must be by:

(1) an official letter from the bank or other depository where the securities or other assets are held for safekeeping, and if the depository is the personal representative, the official letter must be signed by a representative of the depository other than the one verifying the account;

(2) a certificate of an authorized representative of a corporation that is surety on the personal representative's bonds;

(3) a certificate of the clerk or a deputy clerk of a court of record in this state; or

(4) an affidavit of any other reputable person designated by the court on request of the personal representative or other interested party.

(b) The certificate or affidavit described by Subsection (a) must:

(1) state that the affiant has examined the assets that the personal representative exhibited to the affiant as assets of the estate;

(2) describe the assets by reference to the account or in another manner that sufficiently identifies the assets exhibited; and

(3) state the time and the place the assets were exhibited.

(c) Instead of attaching a certificate or an affidavit, the personal representative may exhibit the securities to the judge, who shall endorse on the account, or include in the judge's order with respect to the account, a statement that the securities shown in the account as on hand were exhibited to the judge and that the securities were the same as those shown in the account, or note any variance.

(d) If the securities are exhibited at a location other than where the securities are deposited for safekeeping, that exhibit is at the personal representative's own expense and risk.

Added by Acts 2009, 81st Leg., ch. 680, § 1, eff. Jan. 1, 2014.

### § 359.005. Verification of Account

The personal representative shall attach to the annual account the representative's affidavit that the account contains a correct and complete statement of the matters to which it relates.

Added by Acts 2009, 81st Leg., ch. 680, § 1, eff. Jan. 1, 2014.

### § 359.006. Additional Accounts

(a) At any time after the expiration of 15 months from the date original letters testamentary or of administration are granted to an executor or administrator, an interested person may file a written complaint in the court in which the estate is pending to have the representative cited to appear and make a written exhibit under oath that sets forth fully, in connection with previous exhibits, the condition of the estate.

(b) If it appears to the court, from the exhibit or other evidence, that the executor or administrator has estate funds in the representative's possession that are subject to distribution among the creditors of the estate, the court shall order the funds to be paid out to the creditors in accordance with this title.

(c) A personal representative may voluntarily present to the court the exhibit described by Subsection (a). If the representative has any estate funds in the representative's possession that are subject to distribution among the creditors of the estate, the court shall issue an order similar to the order entered under Subsection (b).

Added by Acts 2009, 81st Leg., ch. 680, § 1, eff. Jan. 1, 2014.

## SUBCHAPTER B. ACTION ON ANNUAL ACCOUNT

### § 359.051. Filing and Consideration of Annual Account

(a) The personal representative of an estate shall file an annual account with the county clerk. The county clerk shall promptly note the filing on the judge's docket.

(b) At any time after the account has remained on file for 10 days following the date the account is filed, the judge shall consider the account and may continue the hearing on the account until fully advised on all account items.

(c) The court may not approve the account unless possession of cash, listed securities, or other assets held in safekeeping or on deposit under court order has been proven as required by law.

Added by Acts 2009, 81st Leg., ch. 680, § 1, eff. Jan. 1, 2014.

### § 359.052.  Correction of Annual Account

(a) If the court finds an annual account is incorrect, the account must be corrected.

(b) The court by order shall approve an annual account that is corrected to the satisfaction of the court and shall act with respect to unpaid claims in accordance with Sections 359.053 and 359.054.

Added by Acts 2009, 81st Leg., ch. 680, § 1, eff. Jan. 1, 2014.

### § 359.053.  Order for Payment of Claims in Full

After approval of an annual account as provided by Section 359.052, if it appears to the court from the exhibit or other evidence that the estate is wholly solvent and that the personal representative has in the representative's possession sufficient funds to pay every character of claims against the estate, the court shall order immediate payment of all claims allowed and approved or established by judgment.

Added by Acts 2009, 81st Leg., ch. 680, § 1, eff. Jan. 1, 2014.

### § 359.054.  Order for Pro Rata Payment of Claims

After approval of an annual account as provided by Section 359.052, if it appears to the court from the account or other evidence that the funds on hand are not sufficient to pay every character of claims against the estate or if the estate is insolvent and the personal representative has any funds on hand, the court shall order the funds to be applied:

(1) first to the payment of any unpaid claims having a preference in the order of their priority; and

(2) then to the pro rata payment of the other claims allowed and approved or established by final judgment, considering:

(A) claims that were presented before the first anniversary of the date administration was granted; and

(B) claims that are in litigation or on which a lawsuit may be filed.

Added by Acts 2009, 81st Leg., ch. 680, § 1, eff. Jan. 1, 2014.

## SUBCHAPTER C.  PENALTIES

### § 359.101.  Penalty for Failure to File Annual Account

(a) If the personal representative of an estate does not file an annual account required by Section 359.001 or 359.002, any person interested in the estate on written complaint, or the court on the court's own motion, may have the representative cited to file the account and show cause for the failure.

(b) If the personal representative does not file the account after being cited or does not show good cause for the failure, the court on hearing may:

(1) revoke the representative's letters testamentary or of administration; and

(2) fine the representative in an amount not to exceed $500.

(c) The personal representative and the representative's sureties are liable for any fine imposed and for all damages and costs sustained by the representative's failure.  The fine, damages, and costs may be recovered in any court of competent jurisdiction.

Added by Acts 2009, 81st Leg., ch. 680, § 1, eff. Jan. 1, 2014.

### § 359.102.  Penalty for Failure to File Exhibit or Report

(a) If a personal representative does not file an exhibit or report required by this title, any person interested in the estate on written complaint filed with the court clerk may have the representative cited to appear and show cause why the representative should not file the exhibit or report.

(b) On hearing, the court may:

(1) order the personal representative to file the exhibit or report; and

(2) unless good cause is shown for the failure, revoke the representative's letters testamentary or of administration and fine the representative in an amount not to exceed $1,000.

Added by Acts 2009, 81st Leg., ch. 680, § 1, eff. Jan. 1, 2014.

## CHAPTER 360.  PARTITION AND DISTRIBUTION OF ESTATE

### SUBCHAPTER A.  APPLICATION FOR PARTITION AND DISTRIBUTION

Section
360.001.  General Application.

## SUBCHAPTER A. APPLICATION FOR PARTITION AND DISTRIBUTION

### § 360.001. General Application

(a) At any time after the first anniversary of the date original letters testamentary or of administration are granted, an executor, administrator, heir, or devisee of a decedent's estate, by written application filed in the court in which the estate is pending, may request the partition and distribution of the estate.

(b) An application under Subsection (a) must state:

(1) the decedent's name;

(2) the name and residence of each person entitled to a share of the estate and whether the person is an adult or a minor;

(3) if the applicant does not know a fact required by Subdivision (2); and

(4) the reasons why the estate should be partitioned and distributed.

Added by Acts 2009, 81st Leg., ch. 680, § 1, eff. Jan. 1, 2014.

### § 360.002. Application for Partial Distribution

(a) At any time after original letters testamentary or of administration are granted and the inventory, appraisement, and list of claims are filed and approved, an executor, administrator, heir, or devisee of a decedent's estate, by written application filed in the court in which the estate is pending, may request a distribution of any portion of the estate.

(b) All interested parties, including known creditors, must be personally cited as in other distributions.

(c) Except as provided by Subsection (d), the court, on proper citation and hearing, may distribute any portion of the estate the court considers advisable.

(d) If a distribution is to be made to one or more heirs or devisees, but not to all heirs or devisees, the court shall require a refunding bond in an amount determined by the court to be filed with the court, unless a written waiver of the bond requirement is filed with the court by all interested parties. On approving the bond, if required, the court shall order the distribution of the relevant portion of the estate.

(e) This section applies to corpus as well as income, notwithstanding any other provision of this title.

Added by Acts 2009, 81st Leg., ch. 680, § 1, eff. Jan. 1, 2014.

## SUBCHAPTER B. CITATION

### § 360.051. Citation of Interested Persons

(a) On the filing of the application, the clerk shall issue a citation that:

(1) states:

(A) the decedent's name; and

(B) the date the court will hear the application; and

(2) requires all persons interested in the estate to appear and show cause why the estate should not be partitioned and distributed.

(b) A citation under this section must be:

(1) personally served on each person residing in the state who is entitled to a share of the estate and whose address is known; and

(2) served by publication on any person entitled to a share of the estate:

(A) whose identity or address is not known;

(B) who is not a resident of this state; or

(C) who is a resident of this state but is absent from this state.

Added by Acts 2009, 81st Leg., ch. 680, § 1, eff. Jan. 1, 2014.

### § 360.052.  Citation of Executor or Administrator

When a person other than the executor or administrator applies for partition and distribution, the executor or administrator must also be cited to appear and answer the application and file in court a verified exhibit and account of the condition of the estate, as in the case of a final settlement.

Added by Acts 2009, 81st Leg., ch. 680, § 1, eff. Jan. 1, 2014.

## SUBCHAPTER C.  PROCEEDINGS; EXPENSES

### § 360.101.  Hearing on Application

(a) At the hearing on an application for partition and distribution, the court shall determine:

(1) the residue of the estate that is subject to partition and distribution;

(2) the persons entitled by law to partition and distribution and those persons' respective shares; and

(3) whether an advancement has been made to any of the persons described by Subdivision (2), and if so, the nature and value of the advancement.

(b) For purposes of Subsection (a)(1), the residue of the estate is determined by deducting from the entire assets of the estate remaining on hand:

(1) the amount of all debts and expenses that:

(A) have been approved or established by judgment but not paid; or

(B) may be established by judgment in the future; and

(2) the probable future expenses of administration.

(c) If an advancement described by Subsection (a)(3) has been made, the court shall require the advancement to be placed in hotchpotch as required by the law governing intestate succession.

Added by Acts 2009, 81st Leg., ch. 680, § 1, eff. Jan. 1, 2014.

### § 360.102.  Court Decree

If the court determines that the estate should be partitioned and distributed, the court shall enter a decree stating:

(1) the name and address, if known, of each person entitled to a share of the estate, specifying:

(A) which of those persons are known to be minors;

(B) the name of the minors' guardian or guardian ad litem; and

(C) the name of the attorney appointed to represent those persons who are unknown or who are not residents of this state;

(2) the proportional part of the estate to which each person is entitled;

(3) a full description of all the estate to be distributed; and

(4) that the executor or administrator must retain possession of a sufficient amount of money or property to pay all debts, taxes, and expenses of administration and specifying the amount of money or the property to be retained.

Added by Acts 2009, 81st Leg., ch. 680, § 1, eff. Jan. 1, 2014.

### § 360.103.  Expenses of Partition

(a) The distributees shall pay the expense of the estate's partition pro rata.

(b) The portion of the estate allotted to a distributee is liable for the distributee's portion of the partition expense, and, if not paid, the court may order execution for the expense in the names of the persons entitled to payment of the expense.

Added by Acts 2009, 81st Leg., ch. 680, § 1, eff. Jan. 1, 2014.

## SUBCHAPTER D.  PARTITION AND DISTRIBUTION IF ESTATE PROPERTY IS CAPABLE OF DIVISION

### § 360.151.  Appointment of Commissioners

If the estate does not consist entirely of money or debts due to the estate and the court has not previously determined that the estate is incapable of partition, the court shall appoint three or more discreet and disinterested persons as commissioners to make a partition and distribution of the estate.

Added by Acts 2009, 81st Leg., ch. 680, § 1, eff. Jan. 1, 2014.

## § 360.152.  Writ of Partition

(a) When commissioners are appointed under Section 360.151, the clerk shall issue a writ of partition directed to the commissioners, commanding the commissioners to:

(1) proceed promptly to make the partition and distribution in accordance with the court decree; and

(2) return the writ, with the commissioners' proceedings under the writ, on a date stated in the writ.

(b) A copy of the court decree must accompany the writ.

(c) The writ must be served by:

(1) delivering the writ and the accompanying copy of the court decree to one of the commissioners; and

(2) notifying the other commissioners, verbally or otherwise, of the commissioners' appointment.

(d) Service under Subsection (c) may be made by any person.

Added by Acts 2009, 81st Leg., ch. 680, § 1, eff. Jan. 1, 2014.

## § 360.153.  Partition by Commissioners

(a) The commissioners shall make a fair, just, and impartial partition and distribution of the estate in the following order and manner:

(1) if the real estate is capable of being divided without manifest injury to all or any of the distributees, the commissioners shall partition and distribute the land or other property by allotting to each distributee:

(A) a share in each parcel;

(B) shares in one or more parcels; or

(C) one or more parcels separately, with or without the addition of a share of other parcels;

(2) if the real estate is not capable of a fair, just, and equal division in kind, but may be made capable of a fair, just, and equal division in kind by allotting to one or more of the distributees a proportion of the money or other personal property to supply the deficiency, the commissioners may make, as nearly as possible, an equal division of the real estate and supply the deficiency of any share from the money or other personal property; and

(3) the commissioners shall:

(A) make a like division in kind, as nearly as possible, of the money and other personal property; and

(B) determine by lot, among equal shares, to whom each share shall belong.

(b) The commissioners shall allot the land or other property under Subsection (a)(1) in the manner described by that subsection that is most in the interest of the distributees.

Added by Acts 2009, 81st Leg., ch. 680, § 1, eff. Jan. 1, 2014.

## § 360.154.  Commissioners' Report

(a) After dividing all or any part of the estate, at least a majority of the commissioners shall make a written, sworn report to the court that:

(1) states the property divided by the commissioners; and

(2) describes in particular the property allotted to each distributee and the value of that property.

(b) If real estate was divided, the report must also contain a general plat of the land with:

(1) the division lines plainly set down; and

(2) the number of acres in each share.

Added by Acts 2009, 81st Leg., ch. 680, § 1, eff. Jan. 1, 2014.

## § 360.155.  Court Action on Commissioners' Report

(a) On the return of a commissioners' report under Section 360.154, the court shall:

(1) examine the report carefully; and

(2) hear:

(A) all exceptions and objections to the report; and

(B) all evidence in favor of or against the report.

(b) If the report is informal, the court shall have the informality corrected.

(c) If the division appears to have been fairly made according to law and no valid exceptions are taken to the division, the court shall approve the division and enter a decree vesting title in the distributees of the distributees' respective shares or portions of the property as set apart to the distributees by the commissioners.

(d) If the division does not appear to have been fairly made according to law or a valid exception is taken to the division, the court may:

(1) set aside the report and division; and

(2) order a new partition to be made.

Added by Acts 2009, 81st Leg., ch. 680, § 1, eff. Jan. 1, 2014.

## § 360.156.  Delivery of Property

When the commissioners' report has been approved and ordered to be recorded, the court shall order the executor or administrator to deliver to the distributees on demand the distributees' respective shares of the estate, including all the title deeds and documents belonging to the distributees.

Added by Acts 2009, 81st Leg., ch. 680, § 1, eff. Jan. 1, 2014.

## § 360.157.  Commissioners' Fees

A commissioner who partitions and distributes an estate under this subchapter is entitled to $5 for each day the commissioner necessarily engages in performing the commissioner's duties, to be taxed and paid as other costs in cases of partition.

Added by Acts 2009, 81st Leg., ch. 680, § 1, eff. Jan. 1, 2014.

## SUBCHAPTER E.  PARTITION AND DISTRIBUTION IF ESTATE PROPERTY IS INCAPABLE OF DIVISION

## § 360.201.  Court Finding

If, in the court's opinion, all or part of an estate is not capable of a fair and equal partition and distribution, the court shall make a special written finding specifying the property incapable of division.

Added by Acts 2009, 81st Leg., ch. 680, § 1, eff. Jan. 1, 2014.

## § 360.202.  Sale of Estate Property

(a) When the court has found that all or part of an estate is not capable of fair and equal division, the court shall order the sale of all estate property not capable of fair and equal division.

(b) The sale must be made by the executor or administrator in the manner provided for the sale of real estate to satisfy estate debts.

(c) The court shall distribute the proceeds collected from the sale to the persons entitled to the proceeds.

(d) A distributee who buys property at the sale is required to pay or secure only the amount by which the distributee's bid exceeds the amount of the distributee's share of the property.

Added by Acts 2009, 81st Leg., ch. 680, § 1, eff. Jan. 1, 2014.

## § 360.203.  Applicability of Provisions Relating to Sale of Real Estate.

The provisions of this title relating to reports of sales of real estate, the giving of an increased general or additional bond on the sale of real estate, and the vesting of title to property sold by decree or by deed apply to sales made under this subchapter.

Added by Acts 2009, 81st Leg., ch. 680, § 1, eff. Jan. 1, 2014.

## SUBCHAPTER F.  CERTAIN TYPES OF ESTATE PROPERTY

## § 360.251.  Estate Consisting Only of Money or Debts

If the estate to be distributed consists only of money or debts due to the estate, the court shall:

(1) set the amount to which each distributee is entitled; and

(2) order the executor or administrator to pay and deliver that amount.

Added by Acts 2009, 81st Leg., ch. 680, § 1, eff. Jan. 1, 2014.

## § 360.252.  Estate Property Located in Another County

(a) If any portion of the estate to be partitioned is located in another county and cannot be fairly partitioned without prejudice to the distributees' interests, the commissioners may report those facts to the court in writing.

(b) On the making of a report under Subsection (a), if the court is satisfied that the property cannot be fairly divided or that the sale of the property would be more advantageous to the distributees, the court may order a sale of the property.  The sale must be conducted in the manner provided by Subchapter E for the sale of property that is not capable of fair and equal division.

(c) If the court is not satisfied that the property cannot be fairly and advantageously divided, or that the sale of the property would be more advantageous to the distributees, the court may appoint three or more commissioners in each county in which the property is located.  If the court appoints commissioners under this subsection, the proceedings under Subchapter D for partition by commissioners must be followed.

Added by Acts 2009, 81st Leg., ch. 680, § 1, eff. Jan. 1, 2014.

## § 360.253.  Community Property

(a) If a spouse dies leaving community property, the surviving spouse, at any time after letters testamentary or of administration have been granted and an inventory, appraisement, and list of claims of the estate have been returned or an affidavit in lieu of the inventory, appraisement, and list of claims has been filed, may apply in writing to the court that granted the letters for a partition of the community property.

(b) The surviving spouse shall execute and deliver a bond to the judge of the court described by Subsection (a). The bond must be:

(1) with a corporate surety or at least two good and sufficient personal sureties;

(2) payable to and approved by the judge;

(3) in an amount equal to the value of the surviving spouse's interest in the community property; and

(4) conditioned for the payment of half of all debts existing against the community property.

(c) The court shall proceed to partition the community property into two equal moieties, one to be delivered to the surviving spouse and the other to be delivered to the executor or administrator of the deceased spouse's estate.

(d) If a partition is made under this section:

(1) a lien exists on the property delivered to the surviving spouse to secure the payment of the bond required under Subsection (b); and

(2) any creditor of the community estate:

(A) may sue in the creditor's own name on the bond; and

(B) is entitled:

(i) to have judgment on the bond for half of the debt the creditor establishes; and

(ii) to be paid by the executor or administrator of the deceased spouse's estate for the other half.

(e) The provisions of this title relating to the partition and distribution of an estate apply to a partition under this section to the extent applicable.

Added by Acts 2009, 81st Leg., ch. 680, § 1, eff. Jan. 1, 2014. Amended by Acts 2011, 82nd Leg., ch. 1338 (S.B. 1198), § 2.50, eff. Jan. 1, 2014.

## § 360.254. Jointly Owned Property

(a) A person who has a joint interest with a decedent's estate in any property may apply to the court that granted letters testamentary or of administration on the estate for a partition of the property.

(b) On application under Subsection (a), the court shall partition the property between the applicant and the decedent's estate.

(c) The provisions of this title relating to the partition and distribution of an estate govern a partition under this section to the extent applicable.

Added by Acts 2009, 81st Leg., ch. 680, § 1, eff. Jan. 1, 2014.

## SUBCHAPTER G. ENFORCEMENT

### § 360.301. Liability for Failure to Deliver Estate Property

(a) If an executor or administrator neglects, when demanded, to deliver a portion of an estate ordered to be delivered to a person entitled to that portion, the person may file with the court clerk a written complaint alleging:

(1) the fact of the neglect;

(2) the date of the person's demand; and

(3) other relevant facts.

(b) On the filing of a complaint under Subsection (a), the court clerk shall issue a citation to be served personally on the executor or administrator. The citation must:

(1) apprise the executor or administrator of the complaint; and

(2) cite the executor or administrator to appear before the court and answer, if the executor or administrator desires, at the time designated in the citation.

(c) If at the hearing the court finds that the citation was properly served and returned and that the executor or administrator is guilty of the neglect alleged, the court shall enter an order to that effect.

(d) An executor or administrator found guilty under Subsection (c) is liable to the complainant for damages at the rate of 10 percent of the amount or the appraised value of the portion of the estate neglectfully withheld, per month, for each month or fraction of a month that the portion is or has been neglectfully withheld after the date of demand. Damages under this subsection may be recovered in any court of competent jurisdiction.

Added by Acts 2009, 81st Leg., ch. 680, § 1, eff. Jan. 1, 2014.

## CHAPTER 361. DEATH, RESIGNATION, OR REMOVAL OF PERSONAL REPRESENTATIVES; APPOINTMENT OF SUCCESSORS

### SUBCHAPTER A. RESIGNATION OF PERSONAL REPRESENTATIVE

## SUBCHAPTER A. RESIGNATION OF PERSONAL REPRESENTATIVE

### § 361.001. Resignation Application

A personal representative who wishes to resign the representative's trust shall file a written application with the court clerk, accompanied by a complete and verified exhibit and final account showing the true condition of the estate entrusted to the representative's care.

Added by Acts 2009, 81st Leg., ch. 680, § 1, eff. Jan. 1, 2014.

### § 361.002. Immediate Appointment of Successor; Discharge and Release

(a) If the necessity exists, the court may immediately accept the resignation of a personal representative and appoint a successor representative.

(b) The court may not discharge a person whose resignation is accepted under Subsection (a), or release the person or the sureties on the person's bond, until a final order has been issued or judgment has been rendered on the final account required under Section 361.001.

Added by Acts 2009, 81st Leg., ch. 680, § 1, eff. Jan. 1, 2014.

### § 361.003. Hearing Date; Citation

(a) When an application to resign as personal representative is filed under Section 361.001, supported by the exhibit and final account required under that section, the court clerk shall bring the application to the judge's attention and the judge shall set a date for a hearing on the matter.

(b) After a hearing is set under Subsection (a), the clerk shall issue a citation to all interested persons, showing:

(1) that an application that complies with Section 361.001 has been filed; and

(2) the time and place set for the hearing at which the interested persons may appear and contest the exhibit and final account supporting the application.

(c) Unless the court directs that the citation under Subsection (b) be published, the citation must be posted.

Added by Acts 2009, 81st Leg., ch. 680, § 1, eff. Jan. 1, 2014.

### § 361.004. Hearing

(a) At the time set for the hearing under Section 361.003, unless the court continues the hearing, and if the court finds that the citation required under that section has been properly issued and served, the court shall:

(1) examine the exhibit and final account required by Section 361.001;

(2) hear all evidence for and against the exhibit and final account; and

(3) if necessary, restate and audit and settle the exhibit and final account.

(b) If the court is satisfied that the matters entrusted to the personal representative applying to resign have been handled and accounted for in accordance with the law, the court shall:

(1) enter an order approving the exhibit and final account; and

(2) require that any estate property remaining in the applicant's possession be delivered to the persons entitled by law to receive the property.

Added by Acts 2009, 81st Leg., ch. 680, § 1, eff. Jan. 1, 2014.

### § 361.005.  Requirements for Discharge

(a) A personal representative applying to resign may not be discharged until:

(1) the resignation application has been heard;

(2) the exhibit and final account required under Section 361.001 have been examined, settled, and approved; and

(3) the applicant has satisfied the court that the applicant has:

(A) delivered any estate property remaining in the applicant's possession; or

(B) complied with all lawful orders of the court with relation to the applicant's trust as representative.

(b) When a personal representative applying to resign has fully complied with the orders of the court, the court shall enter an order:

(1) accepting the resignation; and

(2) discharging the applicant, and, if the applicant is under bond, the applicant's sureties.

Added by Acts 2009, 81st Leg., ch. 680, § 1, eff. Jan. 1, 2014.

## SUBCHAPTER B.  REMOVAL AND REINSTATEMENT OF PERSONAL REPRESENTATIVE

### § 361.051.  Removal Without Notice

The court, on the court's own motion or on the motion of any interested person, and without notice, may remove a personal representative appointed under this title who:

(1) neglects to qualify in the manner and time required by law;

(2) fails to return, before the 91st day after the date the representative qualifies, an inventory of the estate property and a list of claims that have come to the representative's knowledge, unless that deadline is extended by court order;

(3) if required, fails to give a new bond within the time prescribed;

(4) is absent from the state for a consecutive period of three or more months without the court's permission, or moves out of state;

(5) cannot be served with notices or other processes because:

(A) the representative's whereabouts are unknown;

(B) the representative is eluding service; or

(C) the representative is a nonresident of this state who does not have a resident agent to accept service of process in any probate proceeding or other action relating to the estate; or

(6) subject to Section 361.054(a), has misapplied, embezzled, or removed from the state, or is about to misapply, embezzle, or remove from the state, all or part of the property entrusted to the representative's care.

Added by Acts 2009, 81st Leg., ch. 680, § 1, eff. Jan. 1, 2014.

### § 361.052.  Removal With Notice

The court may remove a personal representative on the court's own motion, or on the complaint of any interested person, after the representative has been cited by personal service to answer at a time and place fixed in the notice, if:

(1) sufficient grounds appear to support a belief that the representative has misapplied, embezzled, or removed from the state, or is about to misapply, embezzle, or remove from the state, all or part of the property entrusted to the representative's care;

(2) the representative fails to return any account required by law to be made;

(3) the representative fails to obey a proper order of the court that has jurisdiction with respect to the performance of the representative's duties;

(4) the representative is proved to have been guilty of gross misconduct, or mismanagement in the performance of the representative's duties;

(5) the representative:

(A) becomes incapacitated;

(B) is sentenced to the penitentiary; or

(C) from any other cause, becomes incapable of properly performing the duties of the representative's trust; or

(6) the representative, as executor or administrator, fails to:

(A) make a final settlement by the third anniversary of the date letters testamentary or of administration are granted, unless that period is extended by the court on a showing of sufficient cause supported by oath; or

(B) timely file the affidavit or certificate required by Section 308.004.

Added by Acts 2009, 81st Leg., ch. 680, § 1, eff. Jan. 1, 2014.

### § 361.053. Removal Order

An order removing a personal representative must:

(1) state the cause of the removal;

(2) require that, if the removed representative has been personally served with citation, any letters testamentary or of administration issued to the removed representative be surrendered, and that, regardless of whether the letters have been delivered, all the letters be canceled of record; and

(3) require the removed representative to deliver any estate property in the representative's possession to the persons entitled to the property or to the person who has been appointed and has qualified as successor representative.

Added by Acts 2009, 81st Leg., ch. 680, § 1, eff. Jan. 1, 2014.

### § 361.054. Removal and Reinstatement of Personal Representative Under Certain Circumstances

(a) The court may remove a personal representative under Section 361.051(6) only on the presentation of clear and convincing evidence given under oath.

(b) Not later than the 10th day after the date the court signs the order of removal, a personal representative who is removed under Section 361.051(6) may file an application with the court for a hearing to determine whether the representative should be reinstated.

(c) On the filing of an application under Subsection (b), the court clerk shall issue to the applicant and to the successor representative of the decedent's estate a notice stating:

(1) that an application for reinstatement has been filed;

(2) the name of the decedent from whose estate the applicant was removed as personal representative; and

(3) the name of the applicant for reinstatement.

(d) The notice required by Subsection (c) must cite all persons interested in the estate to appear at the time and place stated in the notice if the persons wish to contest the application.

(e) If, at the conclusion of a hearing under this section, the court is satisfied by a preponderance of the evidence that the personal representative applying for reinstatement did not engage in the conduct that directly led to the applicant's removal, the court shall:

(1) set aside any order appointing a successor representative; and

(2) enter an order reinstating the applicant as personal representative of the estate.

(f) If the court sets aside the appointment of a successor representative under this section, the court may require the successor representative to prepare and file, under oath, an accounting of the estate and to detail the disposition the successor has made of the estate property.

Added by Acts 2009, 81st Leg., ch. 680, § 1, eff. Jan. 1, 2014.

## SUBCHAPTER C. APPOINTMENT OF SUCCESSOR REPRESENTATIVE

### § 361.101. Requirements for Revocation of Letters

Except as otherwise expressly provided by this title, the court may revoke letters testamentary or of administration and grant other letters only:

(1) on application; and

(2) after personal service of citation on the person, if living, whose letters are sought to be revoked, requiring the person to appear and show cause why the application should not be granted.

Added by Acts 2009, 81st Leg., ch. 680, § 1, eff. Jan. 1, 2014.

### § 361.102. Appointment Because of Death, Resignation, or Removal

(a) If a person appointed as personal representative fails to qualify or, after qualifying, dies, resigns, or is removed, the court may, on application, appoint a successor representative if the appointment of a successor is necessary. The appointment may be made before a final accounting is filed or before any action on a final accounting is taken. In the event of death, the legal representatives of the deceased personal representative shall account for, pay, and deliver all estate property that was entrusted to the deceased personal representative's care to the persons legally entitled to receive the property, at the time and in the manner ordered by the court.

(b) The court may appoint a successor representative under this section without citation or notice if the court finds that the immediate appointment of a successor representative is necessary.

Added by Acts 2009, 81st Leg., ch. 680, § 1, eff. Jan. 1, 2014.

### § 361.103.  Appointment Because of Existence of Prior Right

If letters testamentary or of administration have been granted to a person and another person applies for letters, the court shall revoke the initial letters and grant letters to the second applicant if the second applicant:

(1) is qualified;

(2) has a prior right to the letters;  and

(3) has not waived the prior right to the letters.

Added by Acts 2009, 81st Leg., ch. 680, § 1, eff. Jan. 1, 2014.

### § 361.104.  Appointment When Named Executor Becomes an Adult

(a) A person named as executor in a will who was not an adult when the will was probated is entitled to have letters testamentary or of administration that were granted to another person revoked and appropriate letters granted to the named executor on proof that the named executor has become an adult and is not otherwise disqualified.

(b) This subsection applies only if a will names two or more persons as executor.  A person named as an executor in the will who was a minor when the will was probated may, on becoming an adult, qualify and receive letters if:

(1) letters have been issued only to the named executors in the will who were adults when the will was probated;  and

(2) the person is not otherwise disqualified from receiving letters.

Added by Acts 2009, 81st Leg., ch. 680, § 1, eff. Jan. 1, 2014.

### § 361.105.  Appointment of Formerly Sick or Absent Executor

(a) This section applies only to a person named as executor in a will who was sick or absent from the state when the testator died or the will was proved and, as a result, could not:

(1) present the will for probate before the 31st day after the date of the testator's death;  or

(2) accept and qualify as executor before the 21st day after the date the will is probated.

(b) A person to whom this section applies may accept and qualify as executor before the 61st day

after the date the person returns to the state or recovers from illness if proof is presented to the court that the person was ill or absent.

(c) If a person accepts and qualifies as executor under Subsection (b) and letters testamentary or of administration have been issued to another person, the court shall revoke the other person's letters.

Added by Acts 2009, 81st Leg., ch. 680, § 1, eff. Jan. 1, 2014.

### § 361.106.  Appointment When Will Discovered After Grant of Administration

If, after letters of administration have been issued, it is discovered that the decedent left a lawful will, the court shall revoke the letters of administration and issue proper letters to any persons entitled to the letters.

Added by Acts 2009, 81st Leg., ch. 680, § 1, eff. Jan. 1, 2014.

## SUBCHAPTER D.  PROCEDURES AFTER DEATH, RESIGNATION, OR REMOVAL OF PERSONAL REPRESENTATIVE

### § 361.151.  Payment to Estate While Office of Personal Representative is Vacant

(a) A debtor, obligor, or payor may pay or tender money or another thing of value falling due to an estate while the office of personal representative of the estate is vacant to the court clerk for the credit of the estate.

(b) Payment or tender under Subsection (a) discharges the debtor, obligor, or payor of the obligation for all purposes to the extent and purpose of the payment or tender.

(c) If the court clerk accepts payment or tender under this section, the court clerk shall issue a receipt for the payment or tender.

Added by Acts 2009, 81st Leg., ch. 680, § 1, eff. Jan. 1, 2014.

### § 361.152.  Further Administration With or Without Notice or Will Annexed

(a) If an estate is unrepresented as a result of the death, removal, or resignation of the estate's personal representative, and on application by a qualified person interested in the estate, the court shall grant further administration of the estate if necessary, and with the will annexed if there is a will.

(b) An appointment under Subsection (a) shall be made on notice and after a hearing, as in the case of an original appointment, except that, if the court finds that the immediate appointment of a successor representative is necessary, the court may appoint the successor on application but without citation or notice.

Added by Acts 2009, 81st Leg., ch. 680, § 1, eff. Jan. 1, 2014.

### § 361.153.  Rights, Powers, and Duties of Successor Representative

(a) If a personal representative of an estate not administered succeeds another personal representative, the successor representative has all rights, powers, and duties of the predecessor, other than those rights and powers conferred on the predecessor by will that are different from those conferred by this title on personal representatives generally.  Subject to that exception, the successor representative shall administer the estate as if the successor's administration were a continuation of the former administration.

(b) A successor representative shall account for all the estate property that came into the predecessor's possession, and is entitled to any order or remedy that the court has the power to give to enforce the delivery of the estate property and the liability of the predecessor's sureties for any portion of the estate property that is not delivered.  The successor is not required to account for any portion of the estate property that the successor failed to recover after due diligence.

(c) In addition to the powers granted under Subsections (a) and (b), a successor representative may:

(1) make himself or herself, and may be made, a party to a suit prosecuted by or against the successor's predecessors;

(2) settle with the predecessor, and receive and give a receipt for any portion of the estate property that remains in the predecessor's possession;  or

(3) commence a suit on the bond or bonds of the predecessor, in the successor's own name and capacity, for all the estate property that:

(A) came into the predecessor's possession; and

(B) has not been accounted for by the predecessor.

Added by Acts 2009, 81st Leg., ch. 680, § 1, eff. Jan. 1, 2014.

### § 361.154.  Successor Executor Also Succeeds to Prior Rights and Duties.

An executor who accepts appointment and qualifies after letters of administration have been granted on the estate shall, in the manner prescribed by Section 361.153, succeed to the previous administrator, and shall administer the estate as if the executor's administration were a continuation of the former administration, subject to any legal directions of the testator with respect to the estate that are contained in the will.

Added by Acts 2009, 81st Leg., ch. 680, § 1, eff. Jan. 1, 2014.

### § 361.155.  Successor Representative to Return Inventory, Appraisement, and List of Claims or Affidavit in Lieu of Inventory, Appraisement, and List of Claims

(a) An appointee who has qualified to succeed a former personal representative, before the 91st day after the date the personal representative qualifies, shall make and return to the court an inventory, appraisement, and list of claims of the estate or, if the appointee is an independent executor, shall make and return to the court that document or file an affidavit in lieu of the inventory, appraisement, and list of claims, in the manner provided for an original appointee, and shall also return additional inventories, appraisements, and lists of claims and additional affidavits in the manner provided for an original appointee.

(b) Except as otherwise provided by this subsection, an appointee who files an inventory, appraisement, and list of claims under Subsection (a) shall set out in the inventory the appointee's appraisement of the fair market value of each item in the inventory on the date of the appointee's qualification.  If an inventory, appraisement, and list of claims has not been filed by any former personal representative, the appointee shall set out the inventory as provided by Sections 309.051 and 309.052.

(c) On the application of any person interested in the estate, the court shall, in an order appointing a successor representative of an estate, appoint appraisers as in an original appointment.

Added by Acts 2009, 81st Leg., ch. 680, § 1, eff. Jan. 1, 2014. Amended by Acts 2011, 82nd Leg., ch. 1338 (S.B. 1198), §§ 2.51, 2.52, eff. Jan. 1, 2014; Acts 2013, 83rd Leg., ch. 1136 (H.B. 2912), § 46, eff. Jan. 1, 2014.

Section 62(e) of Acts 2013, 83rd Leg., ch. 1136 (H.B. 2912) provides:

"The changes in law made by Sections 51.203(c), 53.104, 305.002(a), 305.003, 308.054(b), 309.051(a), 309.056, 309.103(a) and (b), 355.060, 361.155(b), 362.005, 362.011, 362.013, 404.001(a), 404.003, 404.005(b) and (c), and 551.001(a), Estates Code, as amended by this Act, and Sections 253.001(c), 301.155, 305.004, 309.057, 361.155(c), 404.0035, 404.0036, and 404.0037, Estates Code, as added by this Act, apply to the administration of the estate of a decedent that is pending or commenced on or after the effective date [Jan. 1, 2014] of this Act."

## CHAPTER 362.  CLOSING ADMINISTRATION OF ESTATE

### SUBCHAPTER A.  SETTLING AND CLOSING ESTATE

## SUBCHAPTER A.  SETTLING AND CLOSING ESTATE

### § 362.001.  Settling and Closing Administration of Estate

The administration of an estate shall be settled and closed when:

(1) all the debts known to exist against the estate have been paid, or have been paid to the extent permitted by the assets in the personal representative's possession; and

(2) no further need for administration exists.

Added by Acts 2009, 81st Leg., ch. 680, § 1, eff. Jan. 1, 2014.

### § 362.002.  Compelling Settlement of Estate

A person interested in the administration of an estate for which letters testamentary or of administration have been granted may proceed, after any period of time, to compel settlement of the estate if it does not appear from the record that the administration of the estate has been closed.

Added by Acts 2009, 81st Leg., ch. 680, § 1, eff. Jan. 1, 2014.

### § 362.003.  Verified Account Required

The personal representative of an estate shall present to the court the representative's verified account for final settlement when the administration of the estate is to be settled and closed.

Added by Acts 2009, 81st Leg., ch. 680, § 1, eff. Jan. 1, 2014.

### § 362.004.  Contents of Account

(a) Except as provided by Subsection (b), it is sufficient for an account for final settlement to:

(1) refer to the inventory without describing each item of property in detail; and

(2) refer to and adopt any proceeding had in the administration concerning a sale, renting, leasing for mineral development, or any other transaction on behalf of the estate, including an exhibit, account, or voucher previously filed and approved, without restating the particular items thereof.

(b) An account for final settlement must be accompanied by proper vouchers supporting each item included in the account for which the personal representative has not already accounted and, either by reference to any proceeding described by Subsection (a) or by a statement of the facts, must show:

(1) the estate property that has come into the representative's possession and the disposition of that property;

(2) the debts that have been paid;

(3) any debts and expenses still owing by the estate;

(4) any estate property still in the representative's possession;

(5) the persons entitled to receive that estate and, for each of those persons:

(A) the person's relationship to the decedent;

(B) the person's residence, if known; and

(C) whether the person is an adult or a minor and, if the person is a minor, the name of each of the minor's guardians, if any;

(6) any advancement or payment made by the representative from that estate to any person entitled to receive part of that estate;

(7) the tax returns due that have been filed and the taxes due and owing that have been paid, including:

(A) a complete account of the amount of taxes;

(B) the date the taxes were paid; and

(C) the governmental entity to which the taxes were paid;

(8) if on the filing of the account a tax return due to be filed or any taxes due to be paid are delinquent, the reasons for, and include a description of, the delinquency; and

(9) that the representative has paid all required bond premiums.

Added by Acts 2009, 81st Leg., ch. 680, § 1, eff. Jan. 1, 2014.

## § 362.005.　Citation and Notice on Presentation of Account

(a) On the presentation of an account for final settlement by a temporary or permanent personal representative, the county clerk shall issue citation to the persons and in the manner provided by Subsection (b).

(b) Citation issued under Subsection (a) must:

(1) contain:

(A) a statement that an account for final settlement has been presented;

(B) the time and place the court will consider the account; and

(C) a statement requiring the person cited to appear and contest the account, if the person wishes to contest the account; and

(2) be given to each heir or beneficiary of the decedent by certified mail, return receipt requested, unless the court by written order directs another method of service to be given.

(c) The personal representative shall also provide to each person entitled to citation under Subsection (b) a copy of the account for final settlement either by:

(1) certified mail, return receipt requested; or

(2) electronic delivery, including facsimile or e-mail.

(d) The court by written order shall require additional notice if the court considers the additional notice necessary.

(e) The court may allow the waiver of citation of an account for final settlement in a proceeding concerning a decedent's estate.

(f) The personal representative shall file an affidavit sworn to by the personal representative or a certificate signed by the personal representative's attorney stating:

(1) that the citation was given as required by this section;

(2) the name of each person to whom the citation was given, if the person's name is not shown on the proof of delivery;

(3) the name of each person executing a waiver of citation; and

(4) that each person entitled to citation was provided a copy of the account for final settlement, indicating the method of delivery for each person.

Added by Acts 2009, 81st Leg., ch. 680, § 1, eff. Jan. 1, 2014. Amended by Acts 2013, 83rd Leg., ch. 1136 (H.B. 2912), § 47, eff. Jan. 1, 2014.

Section 62(e) of Acts 2013, 83rd Leg., ch. 1136 (H.B. 2912) provides:

"The changes in law made by Sections 51.203(c), 53.104, 305.002(a), 305.003, 308.054(b), 309.051(a), 309.056, 309.103(a) and (b), 355.060, 361.155(b), 362.005, 362.011, 362.013, 404.001(a), 404.003, 404.005(b) and (c), and 551.001(a), Estates Code, as amended by this Act, and Sections 253.001(c), 301.155, 305.004, 309.057, 361.155(c), 404.0035, 404.0036, and 404.0037, Estates Code, as added by this Act, apply to the administration of the estate of a decedent that is pending or commenced on or after the effective date [Jan. 1, 2014] of this Act."

## § 362.006.　Examination of and Hearing on Account

(a) On the court's satisfaction that citation has been properly served on all persons interested in the estate, the court shall examine the account for final settlement and the accompanying vouchers.

(b) After hearing all exceptions or objections to the account for final settlement and accompanying vouchers and the evidence in support of or against the account, the court shall audit and settle the account and, if necessary, restate the account.

Added by Acts 2009, 81st Leg., ch. 680, § 1, eff. Jan. 1, 2014.

## § 362.007.　Delivery of Certain Property to Guardian

The court may permit a resident personal representative who has possession of any of a ward's estate to deliver the estate to a qualified and acting guardian of the ward.

Added by Acts 2009, 81st Leg., ch. 680, § 1, eff. Jan. 1, 2014.

## § 362.008.　Certain Debts Excluded from Settlement Computation

In the settlement of any of the accounts of the personal representative, all debts due the estate that the court is satisfied could not have been collected by due diligence and that have not been collected shall be excluded from the computation.

Added by Acts 2009, 81st Leg., ch. 680, § 1, eff. Jan. 1, 2014.

## § 362.009.　Money Due to Estate Pending Final Discharge

Money or another thing of value that becomes due to the estate while an account for final settlement is pending may be paid, delivered, or tendered to the personal representative until the order of final discharge of the representative is entered in the judge's probate docket. The representative shall issue a receipt for the money or other thing of value to the obligor or payor. On issuance of the receipt, the obligor or payor is discharged of the obligation for all purposes.

Added by Acts 2009, 81st Leg., ch. 680, § 1, eff. Jan. 1, 2014. Amended by Acts 2011, 82nd Leg., ch. 91 (S.B. 1303), § 8.018, eff. Jan. 1, 2014.

### § 362.010. Payment of Inheritance Taxes Required

A personal representative's account for final settlement of an estate may not be approved, and the estate may not be closed, unless the account shows and the court finds that all inheritance taxes due and owing to this state with respect to all interests and properties passing through the representative's possession have been paid.

Added by Acts 2009, 81st Leg., ch. 680, § 1, eff. Jan. 1, 2014.

### § 362.011. Partition and Distribution of Estate; Deposit in Court's Registry

(a) If, on final settlement of an estate, any of the estate remains in the personal representative's possession, the court shall order that a partition and distribution be made among the persons entitled to receive that part of the estate.

(b) The court shall order the personal representative to convert into money any remaining nonmonetary assets to which a person who is unknown or missing is entitled. The procedures in Chapter 356 apply to the conversion of nonmonetary assets under this subsection.

(c) The court shall order the personal representative to deposit in an account in the court's registry all money, including the proceeds of any conversion under Subsection (b), to which a person who is unknown or missing is entitled. The court shall hold money deposited in an account under this subsection until the court renders:

(1) an order requiring money in the account to be paid to the previously unknown or missing person who is entitled to the money; or

(2) another order regarding the disposition of the money.

Added by Acts 2009, 81st Leg., ch. 680, § 1, eff. Jan. 1, 2014. Amended by Acts 2013, 83rd Leg., ch. 1136 (H.B. 2912), § 48, eff. Jan. 1, 2014.

Section 62(e) of Acts 2013, 83rd Leg., ch. 1136 (H.B. 2912) provides:

"The changes in law made by Sections 51.203(c), 53.104, 305.002(a), 305.003, 308.054(b), 309.051(a), 309.056, 309.103(a) and (b), 355.060, 361.155(b), 362.005, 362.011, 362.013, 404.001(a), 404.003, 404.005(b) and (c), and 551.001(a), Estates Code, as amended by this Act, and Sections 253.001(c), 301.155, 305.004, 309.057, 361.155(c), 404.0035, 404.0036, and 404.0037, Estates Code, as added by this Act, apply to the administration of the estate of a decedent that is pending or commenced on or after the effective date [Jan. 1, 2014] of this Act."

### § 362.012. Discharge of Personal Representative When No Estate Property Remains

The court shall enter an order discharging a personal representative from the representative's trust and closing the estate if, on final settlement of the estate, none of the estate remains in the representative's possession.

Added by Acts 2009, 81st Leg., ch. 680, § 1, eff. Jan. 1, 2014.

### § 362.013. Discharge of Personal Representative When Estate Fully Administered

The court shall enter an order discharging a personal representative from the representative's trust and declaring the estate closed when:

(1) the representative has fully administered the estate in accordance with this title and the court's orders;

(2) the representative's account for final settlement has been approved; and

(3) the representative has:

(A) delivered all of the estate remaining in the representative's possession to the person or persons entitled to receive that part of the estate; and

(B) with respect to the portion of the estate distributable to an unknown or missing person, complied with an order of the court under Section 362.011.

Added by Acts 2009, 81st Leg., ch. 680, § 1, eff. Jan. 1, 2014. Amended by Acts 2013, 83rd Leg., ch. 1136 (H.B. 2912), § 49, eff. Jan. 1, 2014.

Section 62(e) of Acts 2013, 83rd Leg., ch. 1136 (H.B. 2912) provides:

"The changes in law made by Sections 51.203(c), 53.104, 305.002(a), 305.003, 308.054(b), 309.051(a), 309.056, 309.103(a) and (b), 355.060, 361.155(b), 362.005, 362.011, 362.013, 404.001(a), 404.003, 404.005(b) and (c), and 551.001(a), Estates Code, as amended by this Act, and Sections 253.001(c), 301.155, 305.004, 309.057, 361.155(c), 404.0035, 404.0036, and 404.0037, Estates Code, as added by this Act, apply to the administration of the estate of a decedent that is pending or commenced on or after the effective date [Jan. 1, 2014] of this Act."

## SUBCHAPTER B. FAILURE OF PERSONAL REPRESENTATIVE TO ACT

### § 362.051. Failure to Present Account

(a) The court, on the court's own motion or on the written complaint of anyone interested in a decedent's estate that has been administered, shall have the personal representative who is charged with the duty of presenting an account for final settlement cited to appear and present the account within the time specified in the citation if the representative failed or neglected to present the account at the proper time.

(b) On or after the fourth anniversary of the date the court clerk last issues letters testamentary or of administration for a decedent's estate, the court may close the estate without an account for final settlement and without appointing a successor personal representative if:

(1) the whereabouts of the personal representative and heirs of the decedent are unknown; and

(2) a complaint has not been filed by anyone interested in the decedent's estate.

Added by Acts 2009, 81st Leg., ch. 680, § 1, eff. Jan. 1, 2014.

### § 362.052. Liability for Failure to Deliver Estate Property

(a) On the final settlement of an estate, if the personal representative neglects on demand to deliver a portion of the estate or any money in the representative's possession ordered to be delivered to a person entitled to that property, the person may file with the court clerk a written complaint alleging:

(1) the fact of the neglect;

(2) the date of the person's demand; and

(3) other relevant facts.

(b) On the filing of a complaint under Subsection (a), the court clerk shall issue a citation to be served personally on the personal representative. The citation must:

(1) apprise the representative of the complaint; and

(2) cite the representative to appear before the court and answer, if the representative desires, at a time designated in the citation.

(c) If at the hearing the court finds that the citation was properly served and returned, and that the personal representative is guilty of the neglect charged, the court shall enter an order to that effect.

(d) A personal representative found guilty under Subsection (c) is liable to the person who filed the complaint under Subsection (a) for damages at the rate of 10 percent of the amount of the money or the appraised value of the portion of the estate neglectfully withheld, per month, for each month or fraction of a month that the money or portion of the estate is or has been neglectfully withheld after the date of de-

mand. Damages under this subsection may be recovered in any court of competent jurisdiction.

Added by Acts 2009, 81st Leg., ch. 680, § 1, eff. Jan. 1, 2014.

## SUBTITLE I.  INDEPENDENT ADMINISTRATION
### CHAPTER 401.  CREATION

### § 401.001.  Expression of Testator's Intent in Will

(a) Any person capable of making a will may provide in the person's will that no other action shall be had in the probate court in relation to the settlement of the person's estate than the probating and recording of the will and the return of any required inventory, appraisement, and list of claims of the person's estate.

(b) Any person capable of making a will may provide in the person's will that no independent administration of his or her estate may be allowed. In such case the person's estate, if administered, shall be administered and settled under the direction of the probate court as other estates are required to be settled and not as an independent administration.

Added by Acts 2011, 82nd Leg., ch. 1338 (S.B. 1198), § 2.53, eff. Jan. 1, 2014. Amended by Acts 2013, 83rd Leg., ch. 1136 (H.B. 2912), § 50, eff. Jan. 1, 2014.

Section 62(d) of Acts 2013, 83rd Leg., ch. 1136 (H.B. 2912) provides:
"The changes in law made by Sections 32.006, 256.052, 256.053, 256.054, 256.152(c), 256.153, 256.154, 256.155(a), 256.156, 256.203, 257.052, 257.053, 401.001(a), 401.004(d), and 401.006, Estates Code, as amended by this Act, and Section 53.107, Estates Code, as added by this Act, apply only to an action filed or other proceeding commenced on or after the effective date [Jan. 1, 2014] of this Act. An action filed or other proceeding commenced before the effective date of this Act is governed by the law in effect on the date the action was filed or the proceeding was commenced, and the former law is continued in effect for that purpose."

### § 401.002.  Creation in Testate Estate by Agreement

(a) Except as provided in Section 401.001(b), if a decedent's will names an executor but the will does not provide for independent administration as provided in Section 401.001(a), all of the distributees of the decedent may agree on the advisability of having an independent administration and collectively designate in the application for probate of the decedent's will the executor named in the will to serve as independent executor and request in the application that no other action shall be had in the probate court in relation to the settlement of the decedent's estate other than the probating and recording of the decedent's will and the return of an inventory, appraisement, and list of claims of the decedent's estate. In such case the probate court shall enter an order granting independent administration and appointing the person, firm, or corporation designated in the application as independent executor, unless the court finds that it would not be in the best interest of the estate to do so.

(b) Except as provided in Section 401.001(b), in situations where no executor is named in the decedent's will, or in situations where each executor named in the will is deceased or is disqualified to serve as executor or indicates by affidavit filed with the application for administration of the decedent's estate the executor's inability or unwillingness to serve as executor, all of the distributees of the decedent may agree on the advisability of having an independent administration and collectively designate in the application for probate of the decedent's will a qualified person, firm, or corporation to serve as independent administrator and request in the application that no other action shall be had in the probate court in relation to the settlement of the decedent's estate other than the probating and recording of the decedent's will and the return of an inventory, appraisement, and list of claims of the decedent's estate. In such case the probate court shall enter an order granting independent administration and appointing the person, firm, or corporation designated in the application as independent administrator, unless the court finds that it would not be in the best interest of the estate to do so.

Added by Acts 2011, 82nd Leg., ch. 1338 (S.B. 1198), § 2.53, eff. Jan. 1, 2014.

## § 401.003. Creation in Intestate Estate by Agreement

(a) All of the distributees of a decedent dying intestate may agree on the advisability of having an independent administration and collectively designate in the application for administration of the decedent's estate a qualified person, firm, or corporation to serve as independent administrator and request in the application that no other action shall be had in the probate court in relation to the settlement of the decedent's estate other than the return of an inventory, appraisement, and list of claims of the decedent's estate. In such case the probate court shall enter an order

granting independent administration and appointing the person, firm, or corporation designated in the application as independent administrator, unless the court finds that it would not be in the best interest of the estate to do so.

(b) The court may not appoint an independent administrator to serve in an intestate administration unless and until the parties seeking appointment of the independent administrator have been determined, through a proceeding to declare heirship under Chapter 202, to constitute all of the decedent's heirs.

Added by Acts 2011, 82nd Leg., ch. 1338 (S.B. 1198), § 2.53, eff. Jan. 1, 2014.

## § 401.004. Means of Establishing Distributee Consent

(a) This section applies to the creation of an independent administration under Section 401.002 or 401.003.

(b) All distributees shall be served with citation and notice of the application for independent administration unless the distributee waives the issuance or service of citation or enters an appearance in court.

(c) If a distributee is an incapacitated person, the guardian of the person of the distributee may sign the application on behalf of the distributee. If the probate court finds that either the granting of independent administration or the appointment of the person, firm, or corporation designated in the application as independent executor would not be in the best interest of the incapacitated person, then, notwithstanding anything to the contrary in Section 401.002 or 401.003, the court may not enter an order granting independent administration of the estate. If a distributee who is an incapacitated person has no guardian of the person, the probate court may appoint a guardian ad litem to make application on behalf of the incapacitated person if the court considers such an appointment necessary to protect the interest of the distributees. Alternatively, if the distributee who is an incapacitated person is a minor and has no guardian of the person, the natural guardian or guardians of the minor may consent on the minor's behalf if there is no conflict of interest between the minor and the natural guardian or guardians.

(d) If a trust is created in the decedent's will or if the decedent's will devises property to a trustee as described by Section 254.001, the person or class of persons entitled to receive property outright from the trust on the decedent's death and those first eligible to receive the income from the trust, when determined as if the trust were to be in existence on the date of the decedent's death, shall, for the purposes of Section 401.002, be considered to be the distributee or distributees on behalf of the trust, and any other trust or trusts coming into existence on the termination of the trust, and are authorized to apply for independent administration on behalf of the trusts without the consent or agreement of the trustee or any other beneficiary of the trust, or the trustee or any beneficiary of any other trust which may come into existence on the termination of the trust. If a trust beneficiary who is considered to be a distributee under this subsection is an incapacitated person, the trustee or cotrustee may file the application or give the consent, provided that the trustee or cotrustee is not the person proposed to serve as the independent executor.

(e) If a life estate is created either in the decedent's will or by law, the life tenant or life tenants, when determined as if the life estate were to commence on the date of the decedent's death, shall, for the purposes of Section 401.002 or 401.003, be considered to be the distributee or distributees on behalf of the entire estate created, and are authorized to apply for independent administration on behalf of the estate without the consent or approval of any remainderman.

(f) If a decedent's will contains a provision that a distributee must survive the decedent by a prescribed period of time in order to take under the decedent's will, then, for the purposes of determining who shall be the distributee under Section 401.002 and under Subsection (c), it shall be presumed that the distributees living at the time of the filing of the application for probate of the decedent's will survived the decedent by the prescribed period.

(g) In the case of all decedents, whether dying testate or intestate, for the purposes of determining who shall be the distributees under Section 401.002 or 401.003 and under Subsection (c), it shall be presumed that no distributee living at the time the application for independent administration is filed shall subsequently disclaim any portion of the distributee's interest in the decedent's estate.

(h) If a distributee of a decedent's estate dies and if by virtue of the distributee's death the distributee's share of the decedent's estate becomes payable to the distributee's estate, the deceased distributee's personal representative may sign the application for independent administration of the decedent's estate under Section 401.002 or 401.003 and under Subsection (c).

Added by Acts 2011, 82nd Leg., ch. 1338 (S.B. 1198), § 2.53, eff. Jan. 1, 2014. Amended by Acts 2013, 83rd Leg., ch. 1136 (H.B. 2912), § 51, eff. Jan. 1, 2014.

Section 62(d) of Acts 2013, 83rd Leg., ch. 1136 (H.B. 2912) provides:

"The changes in law made by Sections 32.006, 256.052, 256.053, 256.054, 256.152(c), 256.153, 256.154, 256.155(a), 256.156, 256.203, 257.052, 257.053, 401.001(a), 401.004(d), and 401.006, Estates Code, as amended by this Act, and Section 53.107, Estates Code, as added by this Act, apply only to an action filed or other proceeding commenced on or after the effective date [Jan. 1, 2014] of this Act. An action filed or other proceeding commenced before the effective date of this Act is governed by the law in effect on the date the action was filed or the proceeding was commenced, and the former law is continued in effect for that purpose."

### § 401.005. Bond; Waiver of Bond

(a) If an independent administration of a decedent's estate is created under Section 401.002 or 401.003, then, unless the probate court waives bond on application for waiver, the independent executor shall be required to enter into bond payable to and to be approved by the judge and the judge's successors in a sum that is found by the judge to be adequate under all circumstances, or a bond with one surety in a sum that is found by the judge to be adequate under all circumstances, if the surety is an authorized corporate surety.

(b) This section does not repeal any other section of this title.

Added by Acts 2011, 82nd Leg., ch. 1338 (S.B. 1198), § 2.53, eff. Jan. 1, 2014.

### § 401.006. Granting Power of Sale by Agreement

In a situation in which a decedent does not have a will, or a decedent's will does not contain language authorizing the personal representative to sell property or contains language that is not sufficient to grant the representative that authority, the court may include in an order appointing an independent executor under Section 401.002 or 401.003 any general or specific authority regarding the power of the independent executor to sell property that may be consented to by the beneficiaries who are to receive any interest in the property in the application for independent administration or in their consents to the independent administration. The independent executor, in such event, may sell the property under the authority granted in the court order without the further consent of those beneficiaries.

Added by Acts 2011, 82nd Leg., ch. 1338 (S.B. 1198), § 2.53, eff. Jan. 1, 2014. Amended by Acts 2013, 83rd Leg., ch. 1136 (H.B. 2912), § 52, eff. Jan. 1, 2014.

Section 62(h) of Acts 2013, 83rd Leg., ch. 1136 (H.B. 2912) provides:

"An inference may not be made from the changes in law made by this Act to Section 401.006, Estates Code, as to whether an independent executor had the authority to sell personal property of the estate in a probate proceeding filed before the effective date [Jan. 1, 2014] of this Act."

Section 62(d) of Acts 2013, 83rd Leg., ch. 1136 (H.B. 2912) provides:

"The changes in law made by Sections 32.006, 256.052, 256.053, 256.054, 256.152(c), 256.153, 256.154, 256.155(a), 256.156, 256.203, 257.052, 257.053, 401.001(a), 401.004(d), and 401.006, Estates Code, as amended by this Act, and Section 53.107, Estates Code, as added by this Act, apply only to an action filed or other proceeding commenced on or after the effective date [Jan. 1, 2014] of this Act. An action filed or other proceeding commenced before the effective date of this Act is governed by the law in effect on the date the action was filed or the proceeding was commenced, and the former law is continued in effect for that purpose."

### § 401.007. No Liability of Judge

Absent proof of fraud or collusion on the part of a judge, no judge may be held civilly liable for the commission of misdeeds or the omission of any required act of any person, firm, or corporation designated as an independent executor under Section 401.002 or 401.003. Section 351.354 does not apply to the appointment of an independent executor under Section 401.002 or 401.003.

Added by Acts 2011, 82nd Leg., ch. 1338 (S.B. 1198), § 2.53, eff. Jan. 1, 2014.

### § 401.008. Person Declining to Serve

A person who declines to serve or resigns as independent executor of a decedent's estate may be appointed an executor or administrator of the estate if the estate will be administered and settled under the direction of the court.

Added by Acts 2011, 82nd Leg., ch. 1338 (S.B. 1198), § 2.53, eff. Jan. 1, 2014.

## CHAPTER 402. ADMINISTRATION

### SUBCHAPTER A. GENERAL PROVISIONS

### SUBCHAPTER A. GENERAL PROVISIONS

### § 402.001. General Scope and Exercise of Powers

When an independent administration has been created, and the order appointing an independent executor has been entered by the probate court, and the inventory, appraisement, and list of claims has been filed by the independent executor and approved by the court or an affidavit in lieu of the inventory, appraisement, and list of claims has been filed by the indepen-

dent executor, as long as the estate is represented by an independent executor, further action of any nature may not be had in the probate court except where this title specifically and explicitly provides for some action in the court.

Added by Acts 2011, 82nd Leg., ch. 1338 (S.B. 1198), § 2.53, eff. Jan. 1, 2014.

### § 402.002. Independent Executors May Act Without Court Approval

Unless this title specifically provides otherwise, any action that a personal representative subject to court supervision may take with or without a court order may be taken by an independent executor without a court order. The other provisions of this subtitle are designed to provide additional guidance regarding independent administrations in specified situations, and are not designed to limit by omission or otherwise the application of the general principles set forth in this chapter.

Added by Acts 2011, 82nd Leg., ch. 1338 (S.B. 1198), § 2.53, eff. Jan. 1, 2014.

### SUBCHAPTER B. POWER OF SALE

### § 402.051. Definition of Independent Executor

In this subchapter, "independent executor" does not include an independent administrator.

Added by Acts 2011, 82nd Leg., ch. 1338 (S.B. 1198), § 2.53, eff. Jan. 1, 2014.

### § 402.052. Power of Sale of Estate Property Generally

Unless limited by the terms of a will, an independent executor, in addition to any power of sale of estate property given in the will, and an independent administrator have the same power of sale for the same purposes as a personal representative has in a supervised administration, but without the requirement of court approval. The procedural requirements applicable to a supervised administration do not apply.

Added by Acts 2011, 82nd Leg., ch. 1338 (S.B. 1198), § 2.53, eff. Jan. 1, 2014.

### § 402.053. Protection of Person Purchasing Estate Property

(a) A person who is not a devisee or heir is not required to inquire into the power of sale of estate property of the independent executor or independent administrator or the propriety of the exercise of the power of sale if the person deals with the independent executor or independent administrator in good faith and:

(1) a power of sale is granted to the independent executor in the will;

(2) a power of sale is granted under Section 401.006 in the court order appointing the independent executor or independent administrator; or

(3) the independent executor or independent administrator provides an affidavit, executed and sworn to under oath and recorded in the deed records of the county where the property is located, that the sale is necessary or advisable for any of the purposes described in Section 356.251(1).

(b) As to acts undertaken in good faith reliance, the affidavit described by Subsection (a)(3) is conclusive proof, as between a purchaser of property from the estate, and the personal representative of an estate or the heirs and distributees of the estate, with respect to the authority of the independent executor or independent administrator to sell the property. The signature or joinder of a devisee or heir who has an interest in the property being sold as described in this section is not necessary for the purchaser to obtain all right, title, and interest of the estate in the property being sold.

(c) This subchapter does not relieve the independent executor or independent administrator from any duty owed to a devisee or heir in relation, directly or indirectly, to the sale.

Added by Acts 2011, 82nd Leg., ch. 1338 (S.B. 1198), § 2.53, eff. Jan. 1, 2014.

### § 402.054. No Limitation on Other Action

This subchapter does not limit the authority of an independent executor to take any other action without court supervision or approval with respect to estate assets that may take place in a supervised administration, for purposes and within the scope otherwise authorized by this title, including the authority to enter into a lease and to borrow money.

Added by Acts 2011, 82nd Leg., ch. 1338 (S.B. 1198), § 2.53, eff. Jan. 1, 2014.

## CHAPTER 403. EXEMPTIONS AND ALLOWANCES; CLAIMS

### SUBCHAPTER A. EXEMPTIONS AND ALLOWANCES

### SUBCHAPTER B. CLAIMS

## SUBCHAPTER A. EXEMPTIONS AND ALLOWANCES

### § 403.001. Setting Aside Exempt Property and Allowances

The independent executor shall set aside and deliver to those entitled exempt property and allowances for support, and allowances in lieu of exempt property, as prescribed in this title, to the same extent and result as if the independent executor's actions had been accomplished in, and under orders of, the court.

Added by Acts 2011, 82nd Leg., ch. 1338 (S.B. 1198), § 2.53, eff. Jan. 1, 2014.

## SUBCHAPTER B. CLAIMS

### § 403.051. Duty of Independent Executor

(a) An independent executor, in the administration of an estate, independently of and without application to, or any action in or by the court:

(1) shall give the notices required under Sections 308.051 and 308.053;

(2) may give the notice to an unsecured creditor with a claim for money permitted under Section 308.054 and bar a claim under Section 403.055; and

(3) may approve or reject any claim, or take no action on a claim, and shall classify and pay claims approved or established by suit against the estate in the same order of priority, classification, and proration prescribed in this title.

(b) To be effective, the notice prescribed under Subsection (a)(2) must include, in addition to the other information required by Section 308.054, a statement that a claim may be effectively presented by only one of the methods prescribed by this subchapter.

Added by Acts 2011, 82nd Leg., ch. 1338 (S.B. 1198), § 2.53, eff. Jan. 1, 2014.

## § 403.052. Secured Claims for Money

Within six months after the date letters are granted or within four months after the date notice is received under Section 308.053, whichever is later, a creditor with a claim for money secured by property of the estate must give notice to the independent executor of the creditor's election to have the creditor's claim approved as a matured secured claim to be paid in due course of administration. In addition to giving the notice within this period, a creditor whose claim is secured by real property shall record a notice of the creditor's election under this section in the deed records of the county in which the real property is located. If no election to be a matured secured creditor is made, or the election is made, but not within the prescribed period, or is made within the prescribed period but the creditor has a lien against real property and fails to record notice of the claim in the deed records as required within the prescribed period, the claim shall be a preferred debt and lien against the specific property securing the indebtedness and shall be paid according to the terms of the contract that secured the lien, and the claim may not be asserted against other assets of the estate. The independent executor may pay the claim before maturity if it is determined to be in the best interest of the estate to do so.

Added by Acts 2011, 82nd Leg., ch. 1338 (S.B. 1198), § 2.53, eff. Jan. 1, 2014.

## § 403.053. Matured Secured Claims

(a) A claim approved as a matured secured claim under Section 403.052 remains secured by any lien or security interest against the specific property securing payment of the claim but subordinated to the payment from the property of claims having a higher classification under Section 355.102. However, the secured creditor:

(1) is not entitled to exercise any remedies in a manner that prevents the payment of the higher priority claims and allowances; and

(2) during the administration of the estate, is not entitled to exercise any contractual collection rights, including the power to foreclose, without either the prior written approval of the independent executor or court approval.

(b) Subsection (a) may not be construed to suspend or otherwise prevent a creditor with a matured secured claim from seeking judicial relief of any kind or from executing any judgment against an independent executor. Except with respect to real property, any

third party acting in good faith may obtain good title with respect to an estate asset acquired through a secured creditor's extrajudicial collection rights, without regard to whether the creditor had the right to collect the asset or whether the creditor acted improperly in exercising those rights during an estate administration due to having elected matured secured status.

(c) If a claim approved or established by suit as a matured secured claim is secured by property passing to one or more devisees in accordance with Subchapter G, Chapter 255, the independent executor shall collect from the devisees the amount of the debt and pay that amount to the claimant or shall sell the property and pay out of the sale proceeds the claim and associated expenses of sale consistent with the provisions of Sections 355.153(b), (c), (d), and (e) applicable to court supervised administrations.

Added by Acts 2011, 82nd Leg., ch. 1338 (S.B. 1198), § 2.53, eff. Jan. 1, 2014.

## § 403.054. Preferred Debt and Lien Claims

During an independent administration, a secured creditor whose claim is a preferred debt and lien against property securing the indebtedness under Section 403.052 is free to exercise any judicial or extrajudicial collection rights, including the right to foreclosure and execution; provided, however, that the creditor does not have the right to conduct a nonjudicial foreclosure sale within six months after letters are granted.

Added by Acts 2011, 82nd Leg., ch. 1338 (S.B. 1198), § 2.53, eff. Jan. 1, 2014.

## § 403.055. Certain Unsecured Claims; Barring of Claims

An unsecured creditor who has a claim for money against an estate and who receives a notice under Section 308.054 shall give to the independent executor notice of the nature and amount of the claim before the 121st day after the date the notice is received or the claim is barred.

Added by Acts 2011, 82nd Leg., ch. 1338 (S.B. 1198), § 2.53, eff. Jan. 1, 2014. Amended by Acts 2013, 83rd Leg., ch. 1136 (H.B. 2912), § 53, eff. Jan. 1, 2014.

Section 62(f) of Acts 2013, 83rd Leg., ch. 1136 (H.B. 2912) provides:

"The changes in law made by Sections 102.004, 201.051, 201.052(b), 202. 004, 202.009, 202.056, 202.151, 353.101(d), 403.055, 403.056(a), and 405.001(b), Estates Code, as amended by this Act, and Sections 201.052(a–1), 202.0025, and 202.057, Estates Code, as added by this Act, apply only to the estate of a decedent who dies on or after the effective date [Jan. 1, 2014] of this Act. The estate of a decedent who dies before the effective date of this Act is governed by the law in effect on the date of the decedent's death, and the former law is continued in effect for that purpose."

## § 403.056.  Notices Required by Creditors

(a) Notice to the independent executor required by Sections 403.052 and 403.055 must be contained in:

(1) a written instrument that complies with Section 355.004 and is hand-delivered with proof of receipt, or mailed by certified mail, return receipt requested with proof of receipt, to the independent executor or the executor's attorney;

(2) a pleading filed in a lawsuit with respect to the claim; or

(3) a written instrument that complies with Section 355.004 or a pleading filed in the court in which the administration of the estate is pending.

(b) This section does not exempt a creditor who elects matured secured status from the filing requirements of Section 403.052, to the extent those requirements are applicable.

Added by Acts 2011, 82nd Leg., ch. 1338 (S.B. 1198), § 2.53, eff. Jan. 1, 2014.  Amended by Acts 2013, 83rd Leg., ch. 1136 (H.B. 2912), § 54, eff. Jan. 1, 2014.

Section 62(f) of Acts 2013, 83rd Leg., ch. 1136 (H.B. 2912) provides: "The changes in law made by Sections 102.004, 201.051, 201.052(b), 202. 004, 202.009, 202.056, 202.151, 353.101(d), 403.055, 403.056(a), and 405.001(b), Estates Code, as amended by this Act, and Sections 201.052(a–1), 202.0025, and 202.057, Estates Code, as added by this Act, apply only to the estate of a decedent who dies on or after the effective date [Jan. 1, 2014] of this Act.  The estate of a decedent who dies before the effective date of this Act is governed by the law in effect on the date of the decedent's death, and the former law is continued in effect for that purpose."

## § 403.057.  Statute of Limitations

Except as otherwise provided by Section 16.062, Civil Practice and Remedies Code, the running of the statute of limitations shall be tolled only by a written approval of a claim signed by an independent executor, a pleading filed in a suit pending at the time of the decedent's death, or a suit brought by the creditor against the independent executor.  In particular, the presentation of a statement or claim, or a notice with respect to a claim, to an independent executor does not toll the running of the statute of limitations with respect to that claim.

Added by Acts 2011, 82nd Leg., ch. 1338 (S.B. 1198), § 2.53, eff. Jan. 1, 2014.

## § 403.058.  Other Claim Procedures Generally Do Not Apply

Except as otherwise provided by this subchapter, the procedural provisions of this title governing creditor claims in supervised administrations do not apply to independent administrations.  By way of example, but not as a limitation:

(1) Sections 355.064 and 355.066 do not apply to independent administrations, and consequently a creditor's claim may not be barred solely because the creditor failed to file a suit not later than the 90th day after the date an independent executor rejected the claim or with respect to a claim for which the independent executor takes no action; and

(2) Sections 355.156, 355.157, 355.158, 355.159, and 355.160 do not apply to independent administrations.

Added by Acts 2011, 82nd Leg., ch. 1338 (S.B. 1198), § 2.53, eff. Jan. 1, 2014.

## § 403.0585.  Liability of Independent Executor for Payment of a Claim

An independent executor, in the administration of an estate, may pay at any time and without personal liability a claim for money against the estate to the extent approved and classified by the independent executor if:

(1) the claim is not barred by limitations; and

(2) at the time of payment, the independent executor reasonably believes the estate will have sufficient assets to pay all claims against the estate.

Added by Acts 2011, 82nd Leg., ch. 1338 (S.B. 1198), § 2.53, eff. Jan. 1, 2014.

## § 403.059.  Enforcement of Claims by Suit

Any person having a debt or claim against the estate may enforce the payment of the same by suit against the independent executor;  and, when judgment is recovered against the independent executor, the execution shall run against the estate of the decedent in the possession of the independent executor that is subject to the debt.  The independent executor shall not be required to plead to any suit brought against the executor for money until after six months after the date that an independent administration was created and the order appointing the executor was entered by the probate court.

Added by Acts 2011, 82nd Leg., ch. 1338 (S.B. 1198), § 2.53, eff. Jan. 1, 2014.

## § 403.060.  Requiring Heirs to Give Bond

When an independent administration is created and the order appointing an independent executor is entered by the probate court, any person having a debt against the estate may, by written complaint filed in the probate court in which the order was entered, cause all distributees of the estate, heirs at law, and other persons entitled to any portion of the estate under the will, if any, to be cited by personal service to appear before the court and execute a bond for an amount equal to the amount of the creditor's claim or the full value of the estate, as shown by the inventory and list of claims, whichever is smaller. The bond must be payable to the judge, and the judge's successors, and be approved by the judge, and conditioned that all obligors shall pay all debts that shall be established against the estate in the manner provided by law. On the return of the citation served, unless a person so entitled to any portion of the estate, or some of them, or some other person for them, shall execute the bond to the satisfaction of the probate court, the estate shall be administered and settled under the direction of the probate court as other estates are required to be settled. If the bond is executed and approved, the independent administration shall proceed. Creditors of the estate may sue on the bond, and shall be entitled to judgment on the bond for the amount of their debt, or they may have their action against those in possession of the estate.

Added by Acts 2011, 82nd Leg., ch. 1338 (S.B. 1198), § 2.53, eff. Jan. 1, 2014.

## CHAPTER 404. ACCOUNTINGS, SUCCESSORS, AND OTHER REMEDIES

## § 404.001. Accounting

(a) At any time after the expiration of 15 months after the date that the court clerk first issues letters testamentary or of administration to any personal representative of an estate, any person interested in the estate may demand an accounting from the independent executor. The independent executor shall furnish to the person or persons making the demand an exhibit in writing, sworn and subscribed by the independent executor, setting forth in detail:

(1) the property belonging to the estate that has come into the executor's possession as executor;

(2) the disposition that has been made of the property described by Subdivision (1);

(3) the debts that have been paid;

(4) the debts and expenses, if any, still owing by the estate;

(5) the property of the estate, if any, still remaining in the executor's possession;

(6) other facts as may be necessary to a full and definite understanding of the exact condition of the estate; and

(7) the facts, if any, that show why the administration should not be closed and the estate distributed.

(a–1) Any other interested person shall, on demand, be entitled to a copy of any exhibit or accounting that has been made by an independent executor in compliance with this section.

(b) Should the independent executor not comply with a demand for an accounting authorized by this section within 60 days after receipt of the demand, the person making the demand may compel compliance by an action in the probate court. After a hearing, the court shall enter an order requiring the accounting to be made at such time as it considers proper under the circumstances.

(c) After an initial accounting has been given by an independent executor, any person interested in an estate may demand subsequent periodic accountings at intervals of not less than 12 months, and such subsequent demands may be enforced in the same manner as an initial demand.

(d) The right to an accounting accorded by this section is cumulative of any other remedies which persons interested in an estate may have against the independent executor of the estate.

Added by Acts 2011, 82nd Leg., ch. 1338 (S.B. 1198), § 2.53, eff. Jan. 1, 2014. Amended by Acts 2013, 83rd Leg., ch. 1136 (H.B. 2912), § 55, eff. Jan. 1, 2014.

Section 62(e) of Acts 2013, 83rd Leg., ch. 1136 (H.B. 2912) provides:

"The changes in law made by Sections 51.203(c), 53.104, 305.002(a), 305.003, 308.054(b), 309.051(a), 309.056, 309.103(a) and (b), 355.060, 361.155(b), 362.005, 362.011, 362.013, 404.001(a), 404.003, 404.005(b) and (c), and 551.001(a), Estates Code, as amended by this Act, and Sections 253.001(c), 301.155, 305.004, 309.057, 361.155(c), 404.0035, 404.0036, and 404.0037, Estates Code, as added by this Act, apply to the administration of the estate of a decedent that is pending or commenced on or after the effective date [Jan. 1, 2014] of this Act."

## § 404.002. Requiring Independent Executor to Give Bond

When it has been provided by will, regularly probated, that an independent executor appointed by the will shall not be required to give bond for the management of the estate devised by the will, or the independent executor is not required to give bond because bond has been waived by court order as authorized under Section 401.005, then the independent executor may be required to give bond, on proper proceedings had for that purpose as in the case of personal representatives in a supervised administration, if it be made to appear at any time that the independent executor is mismanaging the property, or has betrayed or is about to betray the independent executor's trust, or has in some other way become disqualified.

Added by Acts 2011, 82nd Leg., ch. 1338 (S.B. 1198), § 2.53, eff. Jan. 1, 2014.

## § 404.003. Removal of Independent Executor Without Notice

The probate court, on the court's own motion or on the motion of any interested person, and without notice, may remove an independent executor appointed under this subtitle when:

(1) the independent executor cannot be served with notice or other processes because:

(A) the independent executor's whereabouts are unknown;

(B) the independent executor is eluding service; or

(C) the independent executor is a nonresident of this state without a designated resident agent; or

(2) sufficient grounds appear to support a belief that the independent executor has misapplied or embezzled, or is about to misapply or embezzle, all or part of the property committed to the independent executor's care.

Added by Acts 2011, 82nd Leg., ch. 1338 (S.B. 1198), § 2.53, eff. Jan. 1, 2014. Amended by Acts 2013, 83rd Leg., ch. 1136 (H.B. 2912), § 56, eff. Jan. 1, 2014.

Section 62(e) of Acts 2013, 83rd Leg., ch. 1136 (H.B. 2912) provides:

"The changes in law made by Sections 51.203(c), 53.104, 305.002(a), 305.003, 308.054(b), 309.051(a), 309.056, 309.103(a) and (b), 355.060, 361.155(b), 362.005, 362.011, 362.013, 404.001(a), 404.003, 404.005(b) and (c), and 551.001(a), Estates Code, as amended by this Act, and Sections 253.001(c), 301.155, 305.004, 309.057, 361.155(c), 404.0035, 404.0036, and 404.0037, Estates Code, as added by this Act, apply to the administration of the estate of a decedent that is pending or commenced on or after the effective date [Jan. 1, 2014] of this Act."

## § 404.0035. Removal of Independent Executor with Notice

(a) The probate court, on the court's own motion, may remove an independent executor appointed under this subtitle after providing 30 days' written notice of the court's intent to remove the independent executor, by certified mail, return receipt requested, to the independent executor's last known address and to the last known address of the independent executor's attorney of record, if the independent executor:

(1) neglects to qualify in the manner and time required by law; or

(2) fails to return, before the 91st day after the date the independent executor qualifies, either an inventory of the estate property and a list of claims that have come to the independent executor's knowledge or an affidavit in lieu of the inventory, appraisement, and list of claims, unless that deadline is extended by court order.

(b) The probate court, on its own motion or on motion of any interested person, after the independent executor has been cited by personal service to answer at a time and place fixed in the notice, may remove an independent executor when:

(1) the independent executor fails to make an accounting which is required by law to be made;

(2) the independent executor fails to timely file the affidavit or certificate required by Section 308.004;

(3) the independent executor is proved to have been guilty of gross misconduct or gross mismanagement in the performance of the independent executor's duties;

(4) the independent executor becomes an incapacitated person, or is sentenced to the penitentiary, or from any other cause becomes legally incapacitated from properly performing the independent executor's fiduciary duties; or

(5) the independent executor becomes incapable of properly performing the independent executor's fiduciary duties due to a material conflict of interest.

Added by Acts 2013, 83rd Leg., ch. 1136 (H.B. 2912), § 56, eff. Jan. 1, 2014.

Section 62(e) of Acts 2013, 83rd Leg., ch. 1136 (H.B. 2912) provides:

"The changes in law made by Sections 51.203(c), 53.104, 305.002(a), 305.003, 308.054(b), 309.051(a), 309.056, 309.103(a) and (b), 355.060, 361.155(b), 362.005, 362.011, 362.013, 404.001(a), 404.003, 404.005(b) and (c), and 551.001(a), Estates Code, as amended by this Act, and Sections 253.001(c), 301.155, 305.004, 309.057, 361.155(c), 404.0035, 404.0036, and 404.0037, Estates Code, as added by this Act, apply to the administration of the estate of a decedent that is pending or commenced on or after the effective date [Jan. 1, 2014] of this Act."

### § 404.0036.   Removal Order

(a)  The order of removal of an independent executor shall state the cause of removal and shall direct by order the disposition of the assets remaining in the name or under the control of the removed independent executor.  The order of removal shall require that letters issued to the removed independent executor shall be surrendered and that all letters shall be canceled of record.

(b) If an independent executor is removed by the court under Section 404.003 or 404.0035, the court may, on application, appoint a successor independent executor as provided by Section 404.005.

Added by Acts 2013, 83rd Leg., ch. 1136 (H.B. 2912), § 56, eff. Jan. 1, 2014.

Section 62(e) of Acts 2013, 83rd Leg., ch. 1136 (H.B. 2912) provides:

"The changes in law made by Sections 51.203(c), 53.104, 305.002(a), 305.003, 308.054(b), 309.051(a), 309.056, 309.103(a) and (b), 355.060, 361.155(b), 362.005, 362.011, 362.013, 404.001(a), 404.003, 404.005(b) and (c), and 551.001(a), Estates Code, as amended by this Act, and Sections 253.001(c), 301.155, 305.004, 309.057, 361.155(c), 404.0035, 404.0036, and 404.0037, Estates Code, as added by this Act, apply to the administration of the estate of a decedent that is pending or commenced on or after the effective date [Jan. 1, 2014] of this Act."

### § 404.0037.   Costs and Expenses Related to Removal of Independent Executor

(a) An independent executor who defends an action for the independent executor's removal in good faith, whether successful or not, shall be allowed out of the estate the independent executor's necessary expenses and disbursements, including reasonable attorney's fees, in the removal proceedings.

(b) Costs and expenses incurred by the party seeking removal that are incident to removal of an independent executor appointed without bond, including reasonable attorney's fees and expenses, may be paid out of the estate.

Added by Acts 2013, 83rd Leg., ch. 1136 (H.B. 2912), § 56, eff. Jan. 1, 2014.

Section 62(e) of Acts 2013, 83rd Leg., ch. 1136 (H.B. 2912) provides:

"The changes in law made by Sections 51.203(c), 53.104, 305.002(a), 305.003, 308.054(b), 309.051(a), 309.056, 309.103(a) and (b), 355.060, 361.155(b), 362.005, 362.011, 362.013, 404.001(a), 404.003, 404.005(b) and (c), and 551.001(a), Estates Code, as amended by this Act, and Sections 253.001(c), 301.155, 305.004, 309.057, 361.155(c), 404.0035, 404.0036, and 404.0037, Estates Code, as added by this Act, apply to the administration of the estate of a decedent that is pending or commenced on or after the effective date [Jan. 1, 2014] of this Act."

### § 404.004.   Powers of an Administrator Who Succeeds an Independent Executor

(a) Whenever a person has died, or shall die, testate, owning property in this state, and the person's will has been or shall be admitted to probate by the court, and the probated will names an independent executor or executors, or trustees acting in the capacity of independent executors, to execute the terms and provisions of that will, and the will grants to the independent executor, or executors, or trustees acting in the capacity of independent executors, the power to raise or borrow money and to mortgage, and the independent executor, or executors, or trustees, have died or shall die, resign, fail to qualify, or be removed from office, leaving unexecuted parts or portions of the will of the testator, and an administrator with the will annexed is appointed by the probate court, and an administrator's bond is filed and approved by the court, then in all such cases, the court may, in addition to the powers conferred on the administrator under other provisions of the laws of this state, authorize, direct, and empower the administrator to do and perform the acts and deeds, clothed with the rights, powers, authorities, and privileges, and subject to the limitations, set forth in the subsequent provisions of this section.

(b) The court, on application, citation, and hearing, may, by its order, authorize, direct, and empower the administrator to raise or borrow such sums of money and incur such obligations and debts as the court shall, in its said order, direct, and to renew and extend same from time to time, as the court, on application and order, shall provide;  and, if authorized by the court's order, to secure such loans, obligations, and debts, by pledge or mortgage on property or assets of the estate, real, personal, or mixed, on such terms and conditions, and for such duration of time, as the court shall consider to be in the best interests of the estate, and by its order shall prescribe;  and all such loans, obligations, debts, pledges, and mortgages shall be valid and enforceable against the estate and against the administrator in the administrator's official capacity.

(c) The court may order and authorize the administrator to have and exercise the powers and privileges set forth in Subsection (a) or (b) only to the extent that same are granted to or possessed by the independent executor, or executors, or trustees acting in the capacity of independent executors, under the terms of the probated will of the decedent, and then only in such cases as it appears, at the hearing of the application, that at the time of the appointment of the administrator, there are outstanding and unpaid obligations and debts of the estate, or of the independent executor, or executors, or trustees, chargeable against the estate, or unpaid expenses of administration, or when the court appointing the administrator orders the business of the estate to be carried on and it becomes necessary, from time to time, under orders of the court, for the administrator to borrow money and incur obligations and indebtedness in order to protect and preserve the estate.

(d) The court, in addition, may, on application, citation, and hearing, order, authorize, and empower the administrator to assume, exercise, and discharge, under the orders and directions of the court, made from time to time, all or such part of the rights, powers, and authorities vested in and delegated to, or possessed by, the independent executor, or executors, or trustees acting in the capacity of independent executors, under the terms of the will of the decedent, as the court finds to be in the best interests of the estate and shall, from time to time, order and direct.

(e) The granting to the administrator by the court of some, or all, of the powers and authorities set forth in this section shall be on application filed by the administrator with the county clerk, setting forth such facts as, in the judgment of the administrator, require the granting of the power or authority requested.

(f) On the filing of an application under Subsection (e), the clerk shall issue citation to all persons interested in the estate, stating the nature of the application, and requiring those persons to appear on the return day named in such citation and show cause why the application should not be granted, should they choose to do so. The citation shall be served by posting.

(g) The court shall hear the application and evidence on the application, on or after the return day named in the citation, and, if satisfied a necessity exists and that it would be in the best interests of the estate to grant the application in whole or in part, the court shall so order; otherwise, the court shall refuse the application.

Added by Acts 2011, 82nd Leg., ch. 1338 (S.B. 1198), § 2.53, eff. Jan. 1, 2014.

### § 404.005.  Court-Appointed Successor Independent Executor

(a) If the will of a person who dies testate names an independent executor who, having qualified, fails for any reason to continue to serve, or is removed for cause by the court, and the will does not name a successor independent executor or if each successor executor named in the will fails for any reason to qualify as executor or indicates by affidavit filed with the application for an order continuing independent administration the successor executor's inability or unwillingness to serve as successor independent executor, all of the distributees of the decedent as of the filing of the application for an order continuing independent administration may apply to the probate court for the appointment of a qualified person, firm, or corporation to serve as successor independent executor. If the probate court finds that continued administration of the estate is necessary, the court shall enter an order continuing independent administration and appointing the person, firm, or corporation designated in the application as successor independent executor, unless the probate court finds that it would not be in the best interest of the estate to do so. The successor independent executor shall serve with all of the powers and privileges granted to the successor's predecessor independent executor.

(b) Except as otherwise provided by this subsection, if a distributee described in this section is an incapacitated person, the guardian of the person of the distributee may sign the application on behalf of the distributee. If the probate court finds that either the continuing of independent administration or the appointment of the person, firm, or corporation designated in the application as successor independent executor would not be in the best interest of the incapacitated person, then, notwithstanding Subsection (a), the court may not enter an order continuing independent administration of the estate. If the distributee is an incapacitated person and has no guardian of the person, the court may appoint a guardian ad litem to make application on behalf of the incapacitated person if the probate court considers such an appointment necessary to protect the interest of that distributee. If a distributee described in this section is a minor and has no guardian of the person, a natural guardian of the minor may sign the application for the order continuing independent administration on the minor's behalf unless a conflict of interest exists between the minor and the natural guardian.

(c) Except as otherwise provided by this subsection, if a trust is created in the decedent's will or if the decedent's will devises property to a trustee as described by Section 254.001, the person or class of persons entitled to receive property outright from the trust on the decedent's death and those first eligible to receive the income from the trust, determined as if the trust were to be in existence on the date of the filing of the application for an order continuing independent administration, shall, for the purposes of this section, be considered to be the distributee or distributees on behalf of the trust, and any other trust or trusts coming into existence on the termination of the trust, and are authorized to apply for an order continuing independent administration on behalf of the trust without the consent or agreement of the trustee or any other beneficiary of the trust, or the trustee or any beneficiary of any other trust which may come into existence on the termination of the trust. If a person considered to be a distributee under this subsection is an incapacitated person, the trustee or cotrustee may apply for the order continuing independent administration or sign the application on the incapacitated person's behalf if the trustee or cotrustee is not the person proposed to serve as the independent executor.

(d) If a life estate is created either in the decedent's will or by law, and if a life tenant is living at the time of the filing of the application for an order continuing independent administration, then the life tenant or life tenants, determined as if the life estate were to commence on the date of the filing of the application for an order continuing independent administration, shall, for the purposes of this section, be considered to be the distributee or distributees on behalf of the entire estate created, and are authorized to apply for an order continuing independent administration on behalf of the estate without the consent or approval of any remainderman.

(e) If a decedent's will contains a provision that a distributee must survive the decedent by a prescribed period of time in order to take under the decedent's will, for the purposes of determining who shall be the distributee under this section, it shall be presumed that the distributees living at the time of the filing of the application for an order continuing independent administration of the decedent's estate survived the decedent for the prescribed period.

(f) In the case of all decedents, for the purposes of determining who shall be the distributees under this section, it shall be presumed that no distributee living at the time the application for an order continuing independent administration of the decedent's estate is filed shall subsequently disclaim any portion of the distributee's interest in the decedent's estate.

(g) If a distributee of a decedent's estate should die, and if by virtue of the distributee's death the distributee's share of the decedent's estate shall become payable to the distributee's estate, then the deceased distributee's personal representative may sign the application for an order continuing independent administration of the decedent's estate under this section.

(h) If a successor independent executor is appointed under this section, then, unless the probate court shall waive bond on application for waiver, the successor independent executor shall be required to enter into bond payable to and to be approved by the judge and the judge's successors in a sum that is found by the judge to be adequate under all circumstances, or a bond with one surety in an amount that is found by the judge to be adequate under all circumstances, if the surety is an authorized corporate surety.

(i) Absent proof of fraud or collusion on the part of a judge, the judge may not be held civilly liable for the commission of misdeeds or the omission of any required act of any person, firm, or corporation designated as a successor independent executor under this section. Section 351.354 does not apply to an appointment of a successor independent executor under this section.

Added by Acts 2011, 82nd Leg., ch. 1338 (S.B. 1198), § 2.53, eff. Jan. 1, 2014. Amended by Acts 2013, 83rd Leg., ch. 1136 (H.B. 2912), § 57, eff. Jan. 1, 2014.

Section 62(e) of Acts 2013, 83rd Leg., ch. 1136 (H.B. 2912) provides:

"The changes in law made by Sections 51.203(c), 53.104, 305.002(a), 305.003, 308.054(b), 309.051(a), 309.056, 309.103(a) and (b), 355.060, 361.155(b), 362.005, 362.011, 362.013, 404.001(a), 404.003, 404.005(b) and (c), and 551.001(a), Estates Code, as amended by this Act, and Sections 253.001(c), 301.155, 305.004, 309.057, 361.155(c), 404.0035, 404.0036, and 404.0037, Estates Code, as added by this Act, apply to the administration of the estate of a decedent that is pending or commenced on or after the effective date [Jan. 1, 2014] of this Act."

## CHAPTER 405. CLOSING AND DISTRIBUTIONS

## § 405.001.  Accounting and Distribution

(a) In addition to or in lieu of the right to an accounting provided by Section 404.001, at any time after the expiration of two years after the date the court clerk first issues letters testamentary or of administration to any personal representative of an estate, a person interested in the estate then subject to independent administration may petition the court for an accounting and distribution.  The court may order an accounting to be made with the court by the independent executor at such time as the court considers proper.  The accounting shall include the information that the court considers necessary to determine whether any part of the estate should be distributed.

(b) On receipt of the accounting and, after notice to the independent executor and a hearing, unless the court finds a continued necessity for administration of the estate, the court shall order its distribution by the independent executor to the distributees entitled to the property.  If the court finds there is a continued necessity for administration of the estate, the court shall order the distribution of any portion of the estate that the court finds should not be subject to further administration by the independent executor.  If any portion of the estate that is ordered to be distributed is incapable of distribution without prior partition or sale, the court may:

(1) order partition and distribution, or sale, in the manner provided for the partition and distribution of property incapable of division in supervised estates; or

(2) order distribution of that portion of the estate incapable of distribution without prior partition or sale in undivided interests.

(c) If all the property in the estate is ordered distributed by the court and the estate is fully administered, the court may also order the independent executor to file a final account with the court and may enter an order closing the administration and terminating the power of the independent executor to act as executor.

Added by Acts 2011, 82nd Leg., ch. 1338 (S.B. 1198), § 2.53, eff. Jan. 1, 2014.  Amended by Acts 2013, 83rd Leg., ch. 1136 (H.B. 2912), § 58, eff. Jan. 1, 2014.

Section 62(f) of Acts 2013, 83rd Leg., ch. 1136 (H.B. 2912) provides:

"The changes in law made by Sections 102.004, 201.051, 201.052(b), 202. 004, 202.009, 202.056, 202.151, 353.101(d), 403.055, 403.056(a), and 405.001(b), Estates Code, as amended by this Act, and Sections 201.052(a–1), 202.0025, and 202.057, Estates Code, as added by this Act, apply only to the estate of a decedent who dies on or after the effective date [Jan. 1, 2014] of this Act.  The estate of a decedent who dies before the effective date of this Act is governed by the law in effect on the date of the decedent's death, and the former law is continued in effect for that purpose."

## § 405.002.  Receipts and Releases for Distributions by Independent Executor

(a) An independent executor may not be required to deliver tangible or intangible personal property to a distributee unless the independent executor receives, at or before the time of delivery of the property, a signed receipt or other proof of delivery of the property to the distributee.

(b) An independent executor may not require a waiver or release from the distributee as a condition of delivery of property to a distributee.

Added by Acts 2011, 82nd Leg., ch. 1338 (S.B. 1198), § 2.53, eff. Jan. 1, 2014.

## § 405.003.  Judicial Discharge of Independent Executor

(a) After an estate has been administered and if there is no further need for an independent administration of the estate, the independent executor of the estate may file an action for declaratory judgment under Chapter 37, Civil Practice and Remedies Code, seeking to discharge the independent executor from any liability involving matters relating to the past administration of the estate that have been fully and fairly disclosed.

(b) On the filing of an action under this section, each beneficiary of the estate shall be personally served with citation, except for a beneficiary who has waived the issuance and service of citation.

(c) In a proceeding under this section, the court may require the independent executor to file a final account that includes any information the court considers necessary to adjudicate the independent executor's request for a discharge of liability.  The court may audit, settle, or approve a final account filed under this subsection.

(d) On or before filing an action under this section, the independent executor must distribute to the beneficiaries of the estate any of the remaining assets or property of the estate that remains in the independent executor's possession after all of the estate's debts have been paid, except for a reasonable reserve of assets that the independent executor may retain in a fiduciary capacity pending court approval of the final account.  The court may review the amount of assets on reserve and may order the independent executor to make further distributions under this section.

(e) Except as ordered by the court, the independent executor is entitled to pay from the estate legal fees, expenses, or other costs incurred in relation to a proceeding for judicial discharge filed under this section. The independent executor shall be personally liable to refund any amount of such fees, expenses, or other costs not approved by the court as a proper charge against the estate.

Added by Acts 2011, 82nd Leg., ch. 1338 (S.B. 1198), § 2.53, eff. Jan. 1, 2014.

## § 405.004. Closing Independent Administration by Closing Report or Notice of Closing Estate

When all of the debts known to exist against the estate have been paid, or when they have been paid so far as the assets in the independent executor's possession will permit, when there is no pending litigation, and when the independent executor has distributed to the distributees entitled to the estate all assets of the estate, if any, remaining after payment of debts, the independent executor may file with the court a closing report or a notice of closing of the estate.

Added by Acts 2011, 82nd Leg., ch. 1338 (S.B. 1198), § 2.53, eff. Jan. 1, 2014.

## § 405.005. Closing Report

An independent executor may file a closing report verified by affidavit that:

(1) shows:

(A) the property of the estate that came into the independent executor's possession;

(B) the debts that have been paid;

(C) the debts, if any, still owing by the estate;

(D) the property of the estate, if any, remaining on hand after payment of debts; and

(E) the names and addresses of the distributees to whom the property of the estate, if any, remaining on hand after payment of debts has been distributed; and

(2) includes signed receipts or other proof of delivery of property to the distributees named in the closing report if the closing report reflects that there was property remaining on hand after payment of debts.

Added by Acts 2011, 82nd Leg., ch. 1338 (S.B. 1198), § 2.53, eff. Jan. 1, 2014.

## § 405.006. Notice of Closing Estate

(a) Instead of filing a closing report under Section 405.005, an independent executor may file a notice of closing estate verified by affidavit that states:

(1) that all debts known to exist against the estate have been paid or have been paid to the extent permitted by the assets in the independent executor's possession;

(2) that all remaining assets of the estate, if any, have been distributed; and

(3) the names and addresses of the distributees to whom the property of the estate, if any, remaining on hand after payment of debts has been distributed.

(b) Before filing the notice, the independent executor shall provide to each distributee of the estate a copy of the notice of closing estate. The notice of closing estate filed by the independent executor must include signed receipts or other proof that all distributees have received a copy of the notice of closing estate.

Added by Acts 2011, 82nd Leg., ch. 1338 (S.B. 1198), § 2.53, eff. Jan. 1, 2014.

## § 405.007. Effect of Filing Closing Report or Notice of Closing Estate

(a) The independent administration of an estate is considered closed 30 days after the date of the filing of a closing report or notice of closing estate unless an interested person files an objection with the court within that time. If an interested person files an objection within the 30–day period, the independent administration of the estate is closed when the objection has been disposed of or the court signs an order closing the estate.

(b) The closing of an independent administration by filing of a closing report or notice of closing estate terminates the power and authority of the independent executor, but does not relieve the independent executor from liability for any mismanagement of the estate or from liability for any false statements contained in the report or notice.

(c) When a closing report or notice of closing estate has been filed, persons dealing with properties of the estate, or with claims against the estate, shall deal directly with the distributees of the estate; and the acts of the distributees with respect to the properties or claims shall in all ways be valid and binding as regards the persons with whom they deal, notwithstanding any false statements made by the independent executor in the report or notice.

(d) If the independent executor is required to give bond, the independent executor's filing of the closing report and proof of delivery, if required, automatically releases the sureties on the bond from all liability for the future acts of the principal. The filing of a notice of closing estate does not release the sureties on the bond of an independent executor.

(e) An independent executor's closing report or notice of closing estate shall constitute sufficient legal authority to all persons owing any money, having custody of any property, or acting as registrar or transfer agent or trustee of any evidence of interest, indebtedness, property, or right that belongs to the estate, for payment or transfer without additional administration to the distributees described in the will as entitled to receive the particular asset or who as heirs at law are entitled to receive the asset. The distributees described in the will as entitled to receive the particular asset or the heirs at law entitled to receive the asset may enforce their right to the payment or transfer by suit.

Added by Acts 2011, 82nd Leg., ch. 1338 (S.B. 1198), § 2.53, eff. Jan. 1, 2014.

## § 405.008. Partition and Distribution or Sale of Property Incapable of Division

If the will does not distribute the entire estate of the testator or provide a means for partition of the estate, or if no will was probated, the independent executor may, but may not be required to, petition the probate court for either a partition and distribution of the estate or an order of sale of any portion of the estate alleged by the independent executor and found by the court to be incapable of a fair and equal partition and distribution, or both. The estate or portion of the estate shall either be partitioned and distributed or sold, or both, in the manner provided for the partition and distribution of property and the sale of property incapable of division in supervised estates.

Added by Acts 2011, 82nd Leg., ch. 1338 (S.B. 1198), § 2.53, eff. Jan. 1, 2014.

## § 405.009. Closing Independent Administration on Application by Distributee

(a) At any time after an estate has been fully administered and there is no further need for an independent administration of the estate, any distributee may file an application to close the administration;

and, after citation on the independent executor, and on hearing, the court may enter an order:

(1) requiring the independent executor to file a closing report meeting the requirements of Section 405.005;

(2) closing the administration;

(3) terminating the power of the independent executor to act as independent executor; and

(4) releasing the sureties on any bond the independent executor was required to give from all liability for the future acts of the principal.

(b) The order of the court closing the independent administration shall constitute sufficient legal authority to all persons owing any money, having custody of any property, or acting as registrar or transfer agent or trustee of any evidence of interest, indebtedness, property, or right that belongs to the estate, for payment or transfer without additional administration to the distributees described in the will as entitled to receive the particular asset or who as heirs at law are entitled to receive the asset. The distributees described in the will as entitled to receive the particular asset or the heirs at law entitled to receive the asset may enforce their right to the payment or transfer by suit.

Added by Acts 2011, 82nd Leg., ch. 1338 (S.B. 1198), § 2.53, eff. Jan. 1, 2014.

## § 405.010. Issuance of Letters

At any time before the authority of an independent executor has been terminated in the manner set forth in this subtitle, the clerk shall issue such number of letters testamentary as the independent executor shall request.

Added by Acts 2011, 82nd Leg., ch. 1338 (S.B. 1198), § 2.53, eff. Jan. 1, 2014.

## § 405.011. Rights and Remedies Cumulative

The rights and remedies conferred by this chapter are cumulative of other rights and remedies to which a person interested in the estate may be entitled under law.

Added by Acts 2011, 82nd Leg., ch. 1338 (S.B. 1198), § 2.53, eff. Jan. 1, 2014.

## § 405.012. Closing Procedures Not Required

An independent executor is not required to close the independent administration of an estate under Section 405.003 or Sections 405.004 through 405.007.

Added by Acts 2011, 82nd Leg., ch. 1338 (S.B. 1198), § 2.53, eff. Jan. 1, 2014.

SUBTITLE J. ADDITIONAL MATTERS RELATING TO THE ADMINISTRATION OF CERTAIN ESTATES

## CHAPTER 451. ORDER OF NO ADMINISTRATION

### § 451.001. Application for Family Allowance and Order of no Administration

(a) If the value of the entire assets of an estate, excluding homestead and exempt property, does not exceed the amount to which the surviving spouse, minor children, and adult incapacitated children of the decedent are entitled as a family allowance, an application may be filed by or on behalf of the surviving spouse, minor children, or adult incapacitated children requesting a court to make a family allowance and to enter an order that no administration of the decedent's estate is necessary.

(b) The application may be filed:

(1) in any court in which venue is proper for administration; or

(2) if an application for the appointment of a personal representative has been filed but not yet granted, in the court in which the application is filed.

(c) The application must:

(1) state the names of the heirs or devisees;

(2) list, to the extent known, estate creditors together with the amounts of the claims; and

(3) describe all property belonging to the estate, together with:

(A) the estimated value of the property according to the best knowledge and information of the applicant; and

(B) the liens and encumbrances on the property.

(d) The application must also include a prayer that the court make a family allowance and that, if the family allowance exhausts the entire assets of the estate, excluding homestead and exempt property, the entire assets of the estate be set aside to the surviving spouse, minor children, and adult incapacitated chil-dren, as with other family allowances provided for by Subchapter C, Chapter 353.

Added by Acts 2009, 81st Leg., ch. 680, § 1, eff. Jan. 1, 2014. Amended by Acts 2011, 82nd Leg., ch. 810 (H.B. 2492), § 2.15, eff. Jan. 1, 2014.

### § 451.002. Hearing and Order

(a) On the filing of an application under Section 451.001, the court may hear the application:

(1) promptly without notice; or

(2) at a time and with notice as required by the court.

(b) On the hearing of the application, if the court finds that the facts contained in the application are true and that the expenses of last illness, funeral charges, and expenses of the proceeding have been paid or secured, the court shall:

(1) make a family allowance; and

(2) if the entire assets of the estate, excluding homestead and exempt property, are exhausted by the family allowance made under Subdivision (1):

(A) assign to the surviving spouse, minor children, and adult incapacitated children the entire estate in the same manner and with the same effect as provided in Subchapter C, Chapter 353, for the making of a family allowance to the surviving spouse, minor children, and adult incapacitated children; and

(B) order that there shall be no administration of the estate.

Added by Acts 2009, 81st Leg., ch. 680, § 1, eff. Jan. 1, 2014. Amended by Acts 2011, 82nd Leg., ch. 810 (H.B. 2492), § 2.16, eff. Jan. 1, 2014.

### § 451.003. Effect of Order

(a) An order of no administration issued under Section 451.002(b) constitutes sufficient legal authority to each person who owes money, has custody of property, or acts as registrar or transfer agent of any evidence of interest, indebtedness, property, or right, belonging to the estate, and to each person purchasing from or otherwise dealing with the estate, for payment or transfer without administration to the persons described in the order as entitled to receive the estate.

(b) The persons described in the order are entitled to enforce by suit their right to payment or transfer described by this section.

Added by Acts 2009, 81st Leg., ch. 680, § 1, eff. Jan. 1, 2014.

## § 451.004. Proceeding to Revoke Order

(a) At any time, but not later than the first anniversary of the date of entry of an order of no administration under Section 451.002(b), any interested person may file an application to revoke the order.

(b) An application to revoke the order must allege that:

(1) other estate property has been discovered, property belonging to the estate was not included in the application for no administration, or the property described in the application for no administration was incorrectly valued; and

(2) if that property were added, included, or correctly valued, as applicable, the total value of the property would exceed the amount necessary to justify the court in ordering no administration.

(c) The court shall revoke the order on proof of any of the grounds described by Subsection (b).

(d) If the value of any property is contested, the court may appoint two appraisers to appraise the property in accordance with the procedure prescribed for inventories and appraisements under Chapter 309. The appraisement of the appointed appraisers shall be received in evidence but is not conclusive.

Added by Acts 2009, 81st Leg., ch. 680, § 1, eff. Jan. 1, 2014.

# CHAPTER 452. TEMPORARY ADMINISTRATION OF ESTATES

## SUBCHAPTER A. APPOINTMENT OF TEMPORARY ADMINISTRATOR GENERALLY

### § 452.001. Duty to Appoint Temporary Administrator

A judge who determines that the interest of a decedent's estate requires the immediate appointment of a personal representative shall, by written order, appoint a temporary administrator with powers limited as the circumstances of the case require.

Added by Acts 2009, 81st Leg., ch. 680, § 1, eff. Jan. 1, 2014.

### § 452.002. Application for Appointment

(a) A person may file with the court clerk a written application for the appointment of a temporary administrator of a decedent's estate under this subchapter.

(b) The application must:

(1) be verified;

(2) include the information required by:

(A) Sections 256.052, 256.053, and 256.054, if the decedent died testate; or

(B) Section 301.052, if the decedent died intestate; and

(3) include an affidavit that:

(A) states the name, address, and interest of the applicant;

(B) states the facts showing an immediate necessity for the appointment of a temporary administrator;

(C) lists the requested powers and duties of the temporary administrator;

(D) states that the applicant is entitled to letters of temporary administration and is not disqualified by law from serving as a temporary administrator; and

(E) describes the property that the applicant believes to be in the decedent's estate.

Added by Acts 2009, 81st Leg., ch. 680, § 1, eff. Jan. 1, 2014.

### § 452.003. Order of Appointment; Requirements

The order appointing a temporary administrator must:

(1) designate the appointee as "temporary administrator" of the decedent's estate;

(2) specify the period of the appointment, which may not exceed 180 days unless the appointment is made permanent under Section 452.008;

(3) define the powers given to the appointee; and

(4) set the amount of bond to be given by the appointee.

Added by Acts 2009, 81st Leg., ch. 680, § 1, eff. Jan. 1, 2014.

### § 452.004.  Temporary Administrator's Bond

(a) In this section, "business day" means a day other than a Saturday, Sunday, or holiday recognized by this state.

(b) Not later than the third business day after the date of the order appointing a temporary administrator, the appointee shall file with the county clerk a bond in the amount ordered by the court.

Added by Acts 2009, 81st Leg., ch. 680, § 1, eff. Jan. 1, 2014.

### § 452.005.  Issuance of Letters of Temporary Administration

Not later than the third day after the date an appointee qualifies as temporary administrator, the county clerk shall issue to the appointee letters of temporary administration that list the powers to be exercised by the appointee as ordered by the court.

Added by Acts 2009, 81st Leg., ch. 680, § 1, eff. Jan. 1, 2014.

### § 452.006.  Notice of Appointment

(a) On the date the county clerk issues letters of temporary administration:

(1) the county clerk shall post on the courthouse door a notice of the appointment to all interested persons; and

(2) the appointee shall notify, by certified mail, return receipt requested, the decedent's known heirs of the appointment.

(b) A notice required under Subsection (a) must state that:

(1) an heir or other interested person may request a hearing to contest the appointment not later than the 15th day after the date the letters of temporary administration are issued;

(2) if no contest is made during the period specified by the notice, the appointment continues for the period specified in the order appointing a temporary administrator; and

(3) the court may make the appointment permanent.

Added by Acts 2009, 81st Leg., ch. 680, § 1, eff. Jan. 1, 2014.

### § 452.007.  Hearing to Contest Appointment

(a) A hearing shall be held and a determination made not later than the 10th day after the date an heir or other interested person requests a hearing to contest the appointment of a temporary administrator. If a request is not made on or before the 15th day after the date the letters of temporary administration are issued, the appointment of a temporary administrator continues for the period specified in the order, unless the appointment is made permanent under Section 452.008.

(b) While a contest of the appointment of a temporary administrator is pending, the temporary appointee shall continue to act as administrator of the estate to the extent of the powers given by the appointment.

(c) A court that sets aside a temporary administrator's appointment may require the temporary administrator to prepare and file, under oath, a complete exhibit of the condition of the estate and detail any disposition of the estate property made by the temporary administrator.

Added by Acts 2009, 81st Leg., ch. 680, § 1, eff. Jan. 1, 2014.

### § 452.008.  Permanent Appointment

At the end of a temporary administrator's period of appointment, the court by written order may make the appointment permanent if the permanent appointment is in the interest of the estate.

Added by Acts 2009, 81st Leg., ch. 680, § 1, eff. Jan. 1, 2014.

## SUBCHAPTER B.  TEMPORARY ADMINISTRATION PENDING CONTEST OF A WILL OR ADMINISTRATION

### § 452.051.  Appointment of Temporary Administrator

(a) If a contest related to probating a will or granting letters of administration is pending, the court may appoint a temporary administrator, with powers limited as the circumstances of the case require.

(b) The appointment may continue until the contest is terminated and an executor or administrator with full powers is appointed.

(c) The power of appointment under this section is in addition to the court's power of appointment under Subchapter A.

Added by Acts 2009, 81st Leg., ch. 680, § 1, eff. Jan. 1, 2014.

### § 452.052.  Additional Powers Regarding Claims

(a) A court that grants temporary administration pending a will contest or a contest on an application for letters of administration may, at any time while the contest is pending, give the temporary administrator all the powers of a permanent administrator regarding claims against the estate.

(b) If the court gives the temporary administrator powers described by Subsection (a), the court and the temporary administrator shall act in the same manner as in permanent administration in matters such as:

(1) approving or disapproving claims;

(2) paying claims;  and

(3) selling property to pay claims.

(c) The court shall require a temporary administrator given powers described by Subsection (a) to give bond in the full amount required of a permanent administrator.

(d) This section is cumulative and does not affect the court's right to order a temporary administrator to perform any action described by this section in other cases if the action is necessary or expedient to preserve the estate pending the contest's final determination.

Added by Acts 2009, 81st Leg., ch. 680, § 1, eff. Jan. 1, 2014.

### SUBCHAPTER C.  POWERS AND DUTIES OF TEMPORARY ADMINISTRATOR

### § 452.101.  Limited Powers of Temporary Administrator

(a) A temporary administrator may exercise only the rights and powers:

(1) specifically expressed in the court's order appointing the temporary administrator;  or

(2) expressed in the court's subsequent orders.

(b) An act performed by a temporary administrator is void unless expressly authorized by the court's orders.

Added by Acts 2009, 81st Leg., ch. 680, § 1, eff. Jan. 1, 2014.

### § 452.102.  Additional Bond for Extension of Rights and Powers

A court that extends the rights and powers of a temporary administrator in an order subsequent to the order appointing the temporary administrator may require additional bond commensurate with the extension.

Added by Acts 2009, 81st Leg., ch. 680, § 1, eff. Jan. 1, 2014.

### SUBCHAPTER D.  EXPIRATION AND CLOSING OF TEMPORARY ADMINISTRATION

### § 452.151.  Accounting

At the expiration of a temporary appointment, the temporary administrator shall file with the court clerk:

(1) a sworn list of all estate property that has come into the temporary administrator's possession;

(2) a return of all sales made by the temporary administrator;  and

(3) a full exhibit and account of all the temporary administrator's acts as temporary administrator.

Added by Acts 2009, 81st Leg., ch. 680, § 1, eff. Jan. 1, 2014.

### § 452.152.  Closing Temporary Administration

(a) The court shall act on the list, return, exhibit, and account filed under Section 452.151.

(b) When letters of temporary administration expire or become ineffective for any cause, the court immediately shall enter an order requiring the temporary administrator to promptly deliver the estate remaining in the temporary administrator's possession to the person legally entitled to possession of the estate.

(c) On proof of delivery under Subsection (b), the temporary administrator shall be discharged and the sureties on the temporary administrator's bond shall be released as to any future liability.

Added by Acts 2009, 81st Leg., ch. 680, § 1, eff. Jan. 1, 2014.

### CHAPTER 453.  ADMINISTRATION OF COMMUNITY PROPERTY

## § 453.001. Effect of Chapter

This chapter does not prohibit the administration of community property under other provisions of this title relating to the administration of an estate.

Added by Acts 2009, 81st Leg., ch. 680, § 1, eff. Jan. 1, 2014.

## § 453.002. Administration of Community Property Not Necessary

If a spouse dies intestate and the community property passes to the surviving spouse, no administration of the community property is necessary.

Added by Acts 2009, 81st Leg., ch. 680, § 1, eff. Jan. 1, 2014.

## § 453.003. General Powers of Surviving Spouse if no Administration is Pending

(a) If there is no qualified executor or administrator of a deceased spouse's estate, the surviving spouse, as the surviving partner of the marital partnership, may:

(1) sue and be sued to recover community property;

(2) sell, mortgage, lease, and otherwise dispose of community property to pay community debts;

(3) collect claims due to the community estate; and

(4) exercise other powers as necessary to:

(A) preserve the community property;

(B) discharge community obligations; and

(C) wind up community affairs.

(b) This section does not affect the disposition of the deceased spouse's property.

Added by Acts 2009, 81st Leg., ch. 680, § 1, eff. Jan. 1, 2014.

## § 453.004. Collection of Unpaid Wages if no Administration is Pending

(a) If a person who owes money to the community estate for current wages at the time of a deceased spouse's death is provided an affidavit stating that the affiant is the surviving spouse and that no one has qualified as executor or administrator of the deceased spouse's estate, the person who pays or delivers to the affiant the deceased spouse's final paycheck for the wages, including any unpaid sick pay or vacation pay, is released from liability to the same extent as if the payment or delivery is made to the deceased spouse's personal representative. The person is not required to inquire into the truth of the affidavit.

(b) An affiant to whom the payment or delivery is made under Subsection (a) is answerable to a person having a prior right and is accountable to a personal representative who is appointed. The affiant is liable for any damage or loss to a person that arises from a payment or delivery made in reliance on the affidavit.

(c) This section does not affect the disposition of the deceased spouse's property.

Added by Acts 2009, 81st Leg., ch. 680, § 1, eff. Jan. 1, 2014.

## § 453.005. Remarriage of Surviving Spouse

The remarriage of a surviving spouse does not terminate the surviving spouse's powers as a surviving partner.

Added by Acts 2009, 81st Leg., ch. 680, § 1, eff. Jan. 1, 2014.

## § 453.006. Account of Community Debts and Disposition of Community Property

(a) The surviving spouse shall keep a fair and full account and statement of:

(1) all community debts and expenses paid by the surviving spouse; and

(2) the disposition made of the community property.

(b) The surviving spouse or personal representative shall keep a separate, distinct account of all community debts allowed or paid in the administration and settlement of an estate described by Sections 101.052(a) and (b).

Added by Acts 2009, 81st Leg., ch. 680, § 1, eff. Jan. 1, 2014.

## § 453.007. Delivery of Community Estate on Final Partition

On final partition of the community estate, the surviving spouse shall deliver to the deceased spouse's heirs or devisees their interest in the estate, and the increase in and profits of the interest, after deducting from the interest:

(1) the proportion of the community debts chargeable to the interest;

(2) unavoidable losses;

(3) necessary and reasonable expenses; and

(4) a reasonable commission for the management of the interest.

Added by Acts 2009, 81st Leg., ch. 680, § 1, eff. Jan. 1, 2014.

### § 453.008. Liability of Surviving Spouse for Loss

A surviving spouse is not liable for a loss sustained by the community estate unless the surviving spouse is guilty of gross negligence or bad faith.

Added by Acts 2009, 81st Leg., ch. 680, § 1, eff. Jan. 1, 2014.

### § 453.009. Distribution of Powers Between Personal Representative and Surviving Spouse

(a) A qualified personal representative of a deceased spouse's estate may administer:

(1) the separate property of the deceased spouse;

(2) the community property that was by law under the management of the deceased spouse during the marriage; and

(3) the community property that was by law under the joint control of the spouses during the marriage.

(b) The surviving spouse, as surviving partner of the marital partnership, is entitled to:

(1) retain possession and control of the community property that was legally under the sole management of the surviving spouse during the marriage; and

(2) exercise over that property any power this chapter authorizes the surviving spouse to exercise if there is no administration pending on the deceased spouse's estate.

(c) The surviving spouse, by written instrument filed with the clerk, may waive any right to exercise powers as community survivor. If the surviving spouse files a waiver under this subsection, the deceased spouse's personal representative may administer the entire community estate.

Added by Acts 2009, 81st Leg., ch. 680, § 1, eff. Jan. 1, 2014.

### CHAPTER 454. ADMINISTRATION OF ESTATE OF PERSON PRESUMED DEAD

SUBCHAPTER A.  ESTATES OF PERSONS
PRESUMED DEAD

SUBCHAPTER B.  PERSONS PRESUMED DEAD
BUT SUBSEQUENTLY PROVED LIVING

SUBCHAPTER A.  ESTATES OF PERSONS
PRESUMED DEAD

### § 454.001. Applicability; Determination of Death

(a) This subchapter applies in a proceeding to probate a person's will or administer a person's estate if there is no direct evidence that the person is dead.

(b) The court has jurisdiction to determine the fact, time, and place of the person's death.

Added by Acts 2009, 81st Leg., ch. 680, § 1, eff. Jan. 1, 2014.

### § 454.002. Grant of Letters on Proof of Death

On application for the grant of letters testamentary or of administration for the estate of a person presumed to be dead, the court shall grant the letters if the death of the person is proved by circumstantial evidence to the court's satisfaction.

Added by Acts 2009, 81st Leg., ch. 680, § 1, eff. Jan. 1, 2014.

### § 454.003. Citation and Search

(a) If the fact of a person's death must be proved by circumstantial evidence under Section 454.002, at the request of any interested person, the court may order that a citation be issued to the person presumed dead and that the citation be served on the person by publication and posting and by additional methods as directed by the order.

(b) After letters testamentary or of administration are issued, the court may also direct:

(1) the personal representative to search for the person presumed dead by notifying law enforcement agencies and public welfare agencies in appropriate locations that the person has disappeared; and

(2) the applicant to engage the services of an investigative agency to search for the person presumed dead.

(c) The expense of a search or notice under this section shall be taxed to the estate as a cost and paid out of the estate property.

Added by Acts 2009, 81st Leg., ch. 680, § 1, eff. Jan. 1, 2014.

## § 454.004. Distribution of Estate

The personal representative of the estate of a person presumed dead may not distribute the estate to the persons entitled to the estate until the third anniversary of the date the court granted the letters under Section 454.002.

Added by Acts 2009, 81st Leg., ch. 680, § 1, eff. Jan. 1, 2014.

## SUBCHAPTER B. PERSONS PRESUMED DEAD BUT SUBSEQUENTLY PROVED LIVING

### § 454.051. Restoration of Estate

(a) Except as provided by Subsection (b), a person who was proved by circumstantial evidence to be dead under Section 454.002 and who, in a subsequent action, is proved by direct evidence to have been living at any time after the date the court granted the letters under that section, is entitled to restoration of the person's estate or the residue of the person's estate, including the rents and profits from the estate.

(b) For estate property sold by the personal representative of the estate, a distributee, or a distributee's successors or assignees to a bona fide purchaser for value, the right of a person to restoration is limited to the proceeds of the sale or the residue of the sold property with any increase of the proceeds or the residue.

Added by Acts 2009, 81st Leg., ch. 680, § 1, eff. Jan. 1, 2014.

### § 454.052. Liability of Personal Representative and Others Acting Under Court Order; Bonds Not Voided

(a) Anyone, including a personal representative, who delivered to another the estate or any part of the estate of a person who was proved by circumstantial evidence to be dead under Section 454.002 and who, in a subsequent action, is proved by direct evidence to have been living at any time after the date the court granted the letters testamentary or of administration under that section is not liable for any part of the estate delivered in accordance with the court's order.

(b) Subject to Subsection (c), the bond of a personal representative of the estate of a person described by Subsection (a) is not void in any event.

(c) A surety is not liable for any act of the personal representative that was done in compliance with or approved by the court's order.

Added by Acts 2009, 81st Leg., ch. 680, § 1, eff. Jan. 1, 2014.

## CHAPTER 455. PUBLIC PROBATE ADMINISTRATOR

### § 455.001. Definition

In this chapter, "public probate administrator" means the public probate administrator appointed under Section 25.00251, Government Code.

Added by Acts 2013, 83rd Leg., ch. 671 (H.B. 1755), § 2, eff. Jan. 1, 2014.

### § 455.002. Bond of Public Probate Administrator

(a) The public probate administrator must execute an official bond of at least $100,000 conditioned as required by law and payable to the statutory probate court judge who appointed the public probate administrator.

(b) In addition to the official bond of office, at any time, for good cause, the statutory probate court judge who appointed the public probate administrator may require the administrator to post an additional corporate surety bond for individual estates. The additional bonds shall bear the written approval of the judge requesting the additional bond.

(c) The county may choose to self-insure the public probate administrator for the minimum bond amount required by this section.

Added by Acts 2013, 83rd Leg., ch. 671 (H.B. 1755), § 2, eff. Jan. 1, 2014.

### § 455.003. Funding of Public Probate Administrator's Office

A public probate administrator is entitled to commissions under Subchapter A, Chapter 352, to be paid into the county treasury. The public probate administrator's office, including salaries, is funded, in part, by the commissions.

Added by Acts 2013, 83rd Leg., ch. 671 (H.B. 1755), § 2, eff. Jan. 1, 2014.

## § 455.004.  Powers and Duties

(a) On receipt of notice of a decedent for whose estate a personal representative has not been appointed and who has no known or suitable next of kin, the public probate administrator shall take prompt possession or control of the decedent's property located in the county that:

(1) is considered by the public probate administrator to be subject to loss, injury, waste, or misappropriation; or

(2) the court orders into the possession and control of the public probate administrator after notice to the public probate administrator.

(b) The public probate administrator is responsible for determining if the decedent has any heirs or a will and, if necessary, shall make burial arrangements with the appropriate county facility in charge of indigent burial if there are no known personal representatives.

(c) If the public probate administrator determines the decedent executed a will, the administrator shall file the will with the county clerk.

(d) The public probate administrator has all of the powers and duties of an administrator under this title.

(e) The public probate administrator may dispose of any unclaimed property by public auction or private sale, or donation to a charity, if appropriate.

(f) The statutory probate court judge or commissioners court may request accountings in addition to accountings otherwise required by this title.

Added by Acts 2013, 83rd Leg., ch. 671 (H.B. 1755), § 2, eff. Jan. 1, 2014.

## § 455.005.  Informing Public Probate Administrator

(a) If a public officer or employee knows of a decedent without known or suitable next of kin or knows of property of a decedent that is subject to loss, injury, waste, or misappropriation, the officer or employee may inform the public probate administrator of that fact.

(b) If a person dies in a hospital, mental health facility, or board and care facility without known or suitable next of kin, the person in charge of the hospital or facility may give immediate notice of that fact to the public probate administrator of the county in which the hospital or facility is located.

(c) A funeral director in control of a decedent's remains may notify the public probate administrator if:

(1) none of the persons listed in Section 711.002, Health and Safety Code, can be found after a reasonable inquiry or contacted by reasonable means; or

(2) any of the persons listed in Section 711.002, Health and Safety Code, refuses to act.

Added by Acts 2013, 83rd Leg., ch. 671 (H.B. 1755), § 2, eff. Jan. 1, 2014.

## § 455.006.  Public Probate Administrator's Initiation of Administration

(a) The public probate administrator shall investigate a decedent's estate and circumstances to determine if the opening of an administration is necessary if the public probate administrator has reasonable cause to believe that the decedent found in the county or believed to be domiciled in the county in which the administrator is appointed does not have a personal representative appointed for the decedent's estate.

(b) The public probate administrator shall secure a decedent's estate or resolve any other circumstances related to a decedent, if, after the investigation, the public probate administrator determines that:

(1) the decedent has an estate that may be subject to loss, injury, waste, or misappropriation; or

(2) there are other circumstances relating to the decedent that require action by the public probate administrator.

(c) To establish reasonable cause under Subsection (a), the public probate administrator may require an information letter about the decedent that contains the following:

(1) the name, address, date of birth, and county of residence of the decedent;

(2) a description of the relationship between the interested person and the decedent;

(3) a statement of the suspected cause of death of the decedent;

(4) the names and telephone numbers of any known friends or relatives of the decedent;

(5) a description of any known property of the decedent, including the estimated value of the property; and

(6) a statement of whether the property is subject to loss, injury, waste, or misappropriation.

Added by Acts 2013, 83rd Leg., ch. 671 (H.B. 1755), § 2, eff. Jan. 1, 2014.

## § 455.007. Access to Information

(a) A public probate administrator who has made an investigation under Section 455.006 may present to the statutory probate court judge a statement of the known facts relating to a decedent with a request for permission to take possession or control of property of the decedent and further investigate the matter.

(b) On presentation of a statement under Subsection (a), a statutory probate court judge may issue an order authorizing the public probate administrator to take possession or control of property under this chapter. A public probate administrator may record the order in any county in which property subject to the order is located.

(c) On presentation of an order issued under this section, a financial institution, governmental or private agency, retirement fund administrator, insurance company, licensed securities dealer, or any other person shall perform the following without requiring a death certificate or letters of administration and without inquiring into the truth of the order:

(1) provide the public probate administrator complete information concerning property held in the name of the decedent referenced in the order, without charge, including the names and addresses of any beneficiaries and any evidence of a beneficiary designation; and

(2) grant the public probate administrator access to a safe deposit box rented in the name of the decedent referenced in the order, without charge, for the purpose of inspection and removal of its contents.

(d) Costs and expenses incurred in drilling or forcing a safe deposit box open under Subsection (c) shall be paid by the decedent's estate.

Added by Acts 2013, 83rd Leg., ch. 671 (H.B. 1755), § 2, eff. Jan. 1, 2014.

## § 455.008. Small Estates

(a) If gross assets of an estate do not exceed 10 percent of the maximum amount authorized for a small estate affidavit under Section 205.001, the public probate administrator may act without issuance of letters testamentary or of administration if the court approves a statement of administration stating:

(1) the name and domicile of the decedent;

(2) the date and place of death of the decedent; and

(3) the name, address, and relationship of each known heir or devisee of the decedent.

(b) On approval of the statement of administration, the public probate administrator may:

(1) take possession of, collect, manage, and secure the personal property of the decedent;

(2) sell the decedent's personal property at private or public sale or auction, without a court order;

(3) distribute personal property to the estate's personal representative if one is appointed after the statement of administration is filed;

(4) distribute personal property to a distributee of the decedent who presents an affidavit complying with Chapter 205;

(5) sell or abandon perishable property of the decedent if necessary to preserve the estate;

(6) make necessary funeral arrangements for the decedent and pay reasonable funeral charges with estate assets;

(7) distribute to a minor heir or devisee for whom a guardian has not been appointed the share of an intestate estate or a devise to which the heir or devisee is entitled; and

(8) distribute allowances and exempt property as provided by this title.

(c) On the distribution of property and internment of the decedent under this section, the public probate administrator shall file with the clerk an affidavit, to be approved by the court, detailing:

(1) the property collected;

(2) the property's distribution;

(3) the cost of internment; and

(4) the place of internment.

Added by Acts 2013, 83rd Leg., ch. 671 (H.B. 1755), § 2, eff. Jan. 1, 2014.

## § 455.009. Small Estate Affidavit

(a) If gross assets of an estate do not exceed the maximum amount authorized for a small estate affidavit under Section 205.001, the public probate administrator may file an affidavit that complies with Chapter 205 for approval by the statutory probate court judge.

(b) If the statutory probate court judge approves the affidavit, the affidavit:

(1) must be maintained or recorded as provided by Section 205.005; and

(2) has the effect described by Section 205.007.

Added by Acts 2013, 83rd Leg., ch. 671 (H.B. 1755), § 2, eff. Jan. 1, 2014.

## § 455.010.   Grant of Administration

(a) A public probate administrator shall file an application for letters of administration or administration with will annexed as provided by this title:

(1) if gross assets of an estate exceed the maximum amount authorized for a small estate affidavit under Section 205.001;

(2) if the property of the decedent cannot be disposed of using other methods detailed in this chapter; or

(3) at the discretion of the public probate administrator or on order of the statutory probate court judge.

(b) After issuance of letters of administration, the public probate administrator is considered a personal representative under this title and has all of the powers and duties of a personal representative under this title.

Added by Acts 2013, 83rd Leg., ch. 671 (H.B. 1755), § 2, eff. Jan. 1, 2014.

## § 455.011.   Withdrawal of Public Probate Administrator and Appointment of Successor

(a) If a public probate administrator has taken any action under Section 455.008, 455.009, or 455.010 and a qualified person more entitled to serve as a personal representative under Section 304.001 comes forward or a will of a decedent is found naming an executor, the public probate administrator may surrender the administration of the estate and the assets of the estate to the person once the person has qualified under this title.

(b) Before surrendering the administration of the estate, the public probate administrator must file a verified affidavit that shows fully and in detail:

(1) the condition of the estate;

(2) the charges and claims that have been approved or established by suit or that have been rejected and may be established later;

(3) the amount of each claim that has been rejected and may be established later;

(4) the property of the estate in the administrator's possession; and

(5) any other facts that are necessary in determining the condition of the estate.

(c) The court may require any other filing from the public probate administrator that the court considers appropriate to fully show the condition of the estate before surrendering the estate under this section.

Added by Acts 2013, 83rd Leg., ch. 671 (H.B. 1755), § 2, eff. Jan. 1, 2014.

## § 455.012.   Deposit of Funds into the County Treasury

The public probate administrator shall deposit all funds coming into the custody of the administrator in the county treasury.  Funds deposited must be dispersed at the direction of the public probate administrator and according to the guidelines of the county treasurer or auditor.

Added by Acts 2013, 83rd Leg., ch. 671 (H.B. 1755), § 2, eff. Jan. 1, 2014.

# SUBTITLE K.   FOREIGN WILLS, OTHER TESTAMENTARY INSTRUMENTS, AND FIDUCIARIES

## CHAPTER 501.   ANCILLARY PROBATE OF FOREIGN WILL

Section
501.001.   Authority for Ancillary Probate of Foreign Will.
501.002.   Application for Ancillary Probate of Foreign Will.
501.003.   Citation and Notice.
501.004.   Recording by Clerk.
501.005.   Effect of Filing and Recording Foreign Will.
501.006.   Ancillary Letters Testamentary.
501.007.   Effect on Property.
501.008.   Setting Aside of Certain Foreign Wills.

## § 501.001.   Authority for Ancillary Probate of Foreign Will

The written will of a testator who was not domiciled in this state at the time of the testator's death may be admitted to probate in this state if:

(1) the will would affect any property in this state;  and

(2) proof is presented that the will stands probated or otherwise established in any state of the United States or a foreign nation.

Added by Acts 2009, 81st Leg., ch. 680, § 1, eff. Jan. 1, 2014.

## § 501.002.   Application for Ancillary Probate of Foreign Will

(a) An application for ancillary probate in this state of a foreign will admitted to probate or otherwise established in the jurisdiction in which the testator was domiciled at the time of the testator's death is required to indicate only that probate in this state is requested on the basis of the authenticated copy of the foreign proceedings in which the will was admitted to probate or otherwise established.

(b) An application for ancillary probate in this state of a foreign will that has been admitted to probate or otherwise established in a jurisdiction other than the jurisdiction in which the testator was domiciled at the time of the testator's death must:

(1) include all information required for an application for probate of a domestic will; and

(2) state the name and address of:

(A) each devisee; and

(B) each person who would be entitled to a portion of the estate as an heir in the absence of a will.

(c) An application described by Subsection (a) or (b) must include for filing a copy of the foreign will and the judgment, order, or decree by which the will was admitted to probate or otherwise established. The copy must:

(1) be attested by and with the original signature of the court clerk or other official who has custody of the will or who is in charge of probate records;

(2) include a certificate with the original signature of the judge or presiding magistrate of the court stating that the attestation is in proper form; and

(3) have the court seal affixed, if a court seal exists.

Added by Acts 2009, 81st Leg., ch. 680, § 1, eff. Jan. 1, 2014.

### § 501.003. Citation and Notice

(a) Citation or notice is not required for an application described by Section 501.002(a).

(b) For an application described by Section 501.002(b), a citation shall be issued and served by registered or certified mail on each devisee and heir identified in the application.

Added by Acts 2009, 81st Leg., ch. 680, § 1, eff. Jan. 1, 2014.

### § 501.004. Recording by Clerk

(a) If a foreign will submitted for ancillary probate in this state has been admitted to probate or otherwise established in the jurisdiction in which the testator was domiciled at the time of the testator's death, it is the ministerial duty of the court clerk to record the will and the evidence of the will's probate or other establishment in the judge's probate docket.

(b) If a foreign will submitted for ancillary probate in this state has been admitted to probate or otherwise established in a jurisdiction other than the juris-

diction in which the testator was domiciled at the time of the testator's death, and a contest against the ancillary probate is not filed as authorized by Chapter 504, the court clerk shall record the will and the evidence of the will's probate or other establishment in the judge's probate docket.

(c) A court order is not necessary for the recording of a foreign will in accordance with this section.

Added by Acts 2009, 81st Leg., ch. 680, § 1, eff. Jan. 1, 2014. Amended by Acts 2011, 82nd Leg., ch. 91 (S.B. 1303), § 8.019, eff. Jan. 1, 2014.

### § 501.005. Effect of Filing and Recording Foreign Will

On filing and recording a foreign will in accordance with this chapter, the foreign will:

(1) is considered to be admitted to probate; and

(2) has the same effect for all purposes as if the original will had been admitted to probate by order of a court of this state, subject to contest in the manner and to the extent provided by Chapter 504.

Added by Acts 2009, 81st Leg., ch. 680, § 1, eff. Jan. 1, 2014.

### § 501.006. Ancillary Letters Testamentary

(a) On application, an executor named in a foreign will admitted to ancillary probate in this state in accordance with this chapter is entitled to receive ancillary letters testamentary on proof made to the court that:

(1) the executor has qualified to serve as executor in the jurisdiction in which the will was previously admitted to probate or otherwise established; and

(2) the executor is not disqualified from serving in that capacity in this state.

(b) After the proof required by Subsection (a) is made, the court shall enter an order directing that ancillary letters testamentary be issued to the executor. The court shall revoke any letters of administration previously issued by the court to any other person on application of the executor after personal service of citation on the person to whom the letters were issued.

Added by Acts 2009, 81st Leg., ch. 680, § 1, eff. Jan. 1, 2014.

### § 501.007. Effect on Property

A foreign will admitted to ancillary probate in this state as provided by this chapter after having been admitted to probate or otherwise established in the jurisdiction in which the testator was domiciled at the time of the testator's death is effective to dispose of property in this state regardless of whether the will was executed with the formalities required by this title.

Added by Acts 2009, 81st Leg., ch. 680, § 1, eff. Jan. 1, 2014.

### § 501.008. Setting Aside of Certain Foreign Wills

(a) This section applies only to a foreign will admitted to ancillary probate in this state, in accordance with the procedures prescribed by this chapter, based on the previous probate or other establishment of the will in the jurisdiction in which the testator was domiciled at the time of the testator's death.

(b) The admission to probate in this state of a foreign will to which this section applies shall be set aside if it is subsequently proven in a proceeding brought for that purpose that the foreign jurisdiction in which the will was admitted to probate or otherwise established was not in fact the domicile of the testator at the time of the testator's death.

(c) The title or rights of a person who, before commencement of a proceeding to set aside the admission to probate of a foreign will under this section, purchases property in good faith and for value from the personal representative or a devisee or otherwise deals in good faith with the personal representative or a devisee are not affected by the subsequent setting aside of the admission to probate in this state.

Added by Acts 2009, 81st Leg., ch. 680, § 1, eff. Jan. 1, 2014.

## CHAPTER 502.  ORIGINAL PROBATE OF FOREIGN WILL

### § 502.001.  Original Probate of Foreign Will Authorized

(a) This section applies only to a will of a testator who dies domiciled outside of this state that:

(1) on probate, may operate on any property in this state; and

(2) is valid under the laws of this state.

(b) A court may grant original probate of a will described by Subsection (a) in the same manner as the court grants the probate of other wills under this title if the will:

(1) has not been rejected from probate or establishment in the jurisdiction in which the testator died domiciled; or

(2) has been rejected from probate or establishment in the jurisdiction in which the testator died domiciled solely for a cause that is not a ground for rejection of a will of a testator who died domiciled in this state.

(c) A court may delay passing on an application for probate of a foreign will pending the result of probate or establishment, or of a contest of probate or establishment, in the jurisdiction in which the testator died domiciled.

Added by Acts 2009, 81st Leg., ch. 680, § 1, eff. Jan. 1, 2014.

### § 502.002.  Proof of Foreign Will in Original Probate Proceeding

(a) A copy of the will of a testator who dies domiciled outside of this state, authenticated in the manner required by this title, is sufficient proof of the contents of the will to admit the will to probate in an original proceeding in this state if an objection to the will is not made.

(b) This section does not:

(1) authorize the probate of a will that would not otherwise be admissible to probate; or

(2) if an objection is made to a will, relieve the proponent from offering proof of the contents and legal sufficiency of the will as otherwise required.

(c) Subsection (b)(2) does not require the proponent to produce the original will unless ordered by the court.

Added by Acts 2009, 81st Leg., ch. 680, § 1, eff. Jan. 1, 2014.

## CHAPTER 503.  RECORDING OF FOREIGN TESTAMENTARY INSTRUMENT

### SUBCHAPTER A.  REQUIREMENTS FOR RECORDING FOREIGN TESTAMENTARY INSTRUMENT

### SUBCHAPTER B.  EFFECTS OF RECORDED FOREIGN TESTAMENTARY INSTRUMENT

# CONTEST OF FOREIGN TESTAMENTARY INSTRUMENT

### § 503.001. Authorization to Record Certain Foreign Testamentary Instruments in Deed Records

(a) A copy of a will or other testamentary instrument that conveys, or in any other manner disposes of, land in this state and that has been probated according to the laws of any state of the United States or a country other than the United States, along with a copy of the judgment, order, or decree by which the instrument was admitted to probate that has the attestation, seal, and certificate required by Section 501.002(c), may be filed and recorded in the deed records in any county in this state in which the land is located:

(1) without further proof or authentication, subject to Section 503.003; and

(2) in the same manner as a deed or conveyance is required to be recorded under the laws of this state.

(b) A copy of a will or other testamentary instrument described by Subsection (a), along with a copy of the judgment, order, or decree by which the instrument was admitted to probate that has the attestation and certificate required by Section 501.002(c), is:

(1) prima facie evidence that the instrument has been admitted to probate according to the laws of the state or country in which it was allegedly admitted to probate; and

(2) sufficient to authorize the instrument and the judgment, order, or decree to be recorded in the deed records in the proper county or counties in this state.

Added by Acts 2009, 81st Leg., ch. 680, § 1, eff. Jan. 1, 2014.

### § 503.002. Original Signatures Not Required

Notwithstanding Section 501.002(c), the original signatures required by that section may not be required for a recordation in the deed records in accordance with Section 503.001 or for a purpose described by Section 503.051 or 503.052.

Added by Acts 2009, 81st Leg., ch. 680, § 1, eff. Jan. 1, 2014.

### § 503.003. Contest of Recorded Foreign Testamentary Instrument Permitted

The validity of a will or other testamentary instrument, a copy of which is filed and recorded as provided by Section 503.001, may be contested in the manner and to the extent provided by Subchapter A, Chapter 504.

Added by Acts 2009, 81st Leg., ch. 680, § 1, eff. Jan. 1, 2014.

## SUBCHAPTER B. EFFECTS OF RECORDED FOREIGN TESTAMENTARY INSTRUMENT

### § 503.051. Recorded Foreign Testamentary Instrument as Conveyance

A copy of a foreign will or other testamentary instrument described by Section 503.001 and the copy of the judgment, order, or decree by which the instrument was admitted to probate that are attested and proved as provided by that section and delivered to the county clerk of the proper county in this state to be recorded in the deed records:

(1) take effect and are valid as a deed of conveyance of all property in this state covered by the instrument; and

(2) have the same effect as a recorded deed or other conveyance of land beginning at the time the instrument is delivered to the clerk to be recorded.

Added by Acts 2009, 81st Leg., ch. 680, § 1, eff. Jan. 1, 2014.

### § 503.052. Recorded Foreign Testamentary Instrument as Notice of Title.

A copy of a foreign will or other testamentary instrument described by Section 503.001 and the copy of the judgment, order, or decree by which the instrument was admitted to probate that is attested and proved as provided by that section and filed for recording in the deed records of the proper county in this state constitute notice to all persons of the:

(1) existence of the instrument; and

(2) title or titles conferred by the instrument.

Added by Acts 2009, 81st Leg., ch. 680, § 1, eff. Jan. 1, 2014.

## CHAPTER 504. CONTEST OF OR OTHER CHALLENGE TO FOREIGN TESTAMENTARY INSTRUMENT

### SUBCHAPTER A. CONTEST OR SETTING ASIDE PROBATE OF FOREIGN WILL IN THIS STATE

## SUBCHAPTER A.  CONTEST OR SETTING ASIDE PROBATE OF FOREIGN WILL IN THIS STATE

### § 504.001.  Grounds for Contesting Foreign Will Probated in Domiciliary Jurisdiction

(a) Subject to Subsection (b), an interested person may contest a foreign will that has been:

(1) admitted to probate or established in the jurisdiction in which the testator was domiciled at the time of the testator's death; and

(2) admitted to probate in this state or filed in the deed records of any county of this state.

(b) A will described by Subsection (a) may be contested only on the grounds that:

(1) the proceedings in the jurisdiction in which the testator was domiciled at the time of the testator's death were not authenticated in the manner required for ancillary probate or recording in the deed records in this state;

(2) the will has been finally rejected for probate in this state in another proceeding; or

(3) the probate of the will has been set aside in the jurisdiction in which the testator was domiciled at the time of the testator's death.

Added by Acts 2009, 81st Leg., ch. 680, § 1, eff. Jan. 1, 2014.

### § 504.002.  Grounds for Contesting Foreign Will Probated in Non–domiciliary Jurisdiction

A foreign will admitted to probate or established in any jurisdiction other than the jurisdiction in which the testator was domiciled at the time of the testator's death may be contested on any grounds that are the basis for the contest of a domestic will.

Added by Acts 2009, 81st Leg., ch. 680, § 1, eff. Jan. 1, 2014.

### § 504.003.  Procedures and Time Limits for Contesting Foreign Will

(a) The probate in this state of a foreign will probated or established in a jurisdiction other than the jurisdiction in which the testator was domiciled at the time of the testator's death may be contested in the manner that would apply if the testator had been domiciled in this state at the time of the testator's death.

(b) A foreign will admitted to ancillary probate in this state or filed in the deed records of any county of this state may be contested using the same procedures and within the same time limits applicable to the contest of a will admitted to original probate in this state.

Added by Acts 2009, 81st Leg., ch. 680, § 1, eff. Jan. 1, 2014.

### § 504.004.  Probate of Foreign Will Set Aside for Lack of Service

(a) The probate in this state of a foreign will shall be set aside if:

(1) the will was probated in this state:

(A) in accordance with the procedure applicable to the probate of a will admitted to probate in the jurisdiction in which the testator was domiciled at the time of the testator's death; and

(B) without the service of citation required for a will admitted to probate in another jurisdiction that was not the testator's domicile at the time of the testator's death; and

(2) it is proved that the foreign jurisdiction in which the will was probated was not the testator's domicile at the time of the testator's death.

(b) If otherwise entitled, a will the probate of which is set aside in accordance with Subsection (a) may be:

(1) reprobated in accordance with the procedure prescribed for the probate of a will admitted in a jurisdiction that was not the testator's domicile at the time of the testator's death; or

(2) admitted to original probate in this state in the proceeding in which the ancillary probate was set aside or in a subsequent proceeding.

Added by Acts 2009, 81st Leg., ch. 680, § 1, eff. Jan. 1, 2014.

## SUBCHAPTER B.  CONTEST OR FINAL REJECTION IN FOREIGN JURISDICTION

### § 504.051.  Notice of Will Contest in Foreign Jurisdiction

Verified notice that a proceeding to contest a will probated or established in a foreign jurisdiction has been commenced in that jurisdiction may be filed and recorded in the judge's probate docket of the court in this state in which the foreign will was probated, or in the deed records of any county of this state in which the foreign will was recorded, within the time limits for the contest of a foreign will in this state.

Added by Acts 2009, 81st Leg., ch. 680, § 1, eff. Jan. 1, 2014. Amended by Acts 2011, 82nd Leg., ch. 91 (S.B. 1303), § 8.020, eff. Jan. 1, 2014.

### § 504.052. Effect of Notice

After a notice is filed and recorded under Section 504.051, the probate or recording in this state of the foreign will that is the subject of the notice has no effect until verified proof is filed and recorded that the foreign proceedings:

(1) have been terminated in favor of the will; or

(2) were never commenced.

Added by Acts 2009, 81st Leg., ch. 680, § 1, eff. Jan. 1, 2014.

### § 504.053. Effect of Rejection of Testamentary Instrument by Foreign Jurisdiction

(a) Except as provided by Subsection (b), final rejection of a will or other testamentary instrument from probate or establishment in a foreign jurisdiction in which the testator was domiciled at the time of the testator's death is conclusive in this state.

(b) A will or other testamentary instrument that is finally rejected from probate or establishment in a foreign jurisdiction in which the testator was domiciled at the time of the testator's death may be admitted to probate or continue to be effective in this state if the will or other instrument was rejected solely for a cause that is not a ground for rejection of a will of a testator who died domiciled in this state.

Added by Acts 2009, 81st Leg., ch. 680, § 1, eff. Jan. 1, 2014.

## CHAPTER 505. FOREIGN PERSONAL REPRESENTATIVES, TRUSTEES, AND FIDUCIARIES

### SUBCHAPTER A. FOREIGN CORPORATE FIDUCIARY

### SUBCHAPTER B. FOREIGN EXECUTORS AND TRUSTEES

### SUBCHAPTER C. RECOVERY OF DEBTS BY FOREIGN EXECUTOR OR ADMINISTRATOR

### SUBCHAPTER A. FOREIGN CORPORATE FIDUCIARY

### § 505.001. Definition

In this subchapter, "foreign corporate fiduciary" means a corporate fiduciary that does not have its main office or a branch office in this state.

Added by Acts 2009, 81st Leg., ch. 680, § 1, eff. Jan. 1, 2014.

### § 505.002. Applicability of Other Law

(a) A foreign corporate fiduciary acting in a fiduciary capacity in this state in strict accordance with this subchapter:

(1) is not transacting business in this state within the meaning of Section 9.001, Business Organizations Code; and

(2) is qualified to serve in that capacity under Section 501.006.

(b) This subchapter is in addition to, and not a limitation on, Subtitles F and G, Title 3, Finance Code.

Added by Acts 2009, 81st Leg., ch. 680, § 1, eff. Jan. 1, 2014.

### § 505.003. Authority of Foreign Corporate Fiduciary to Serve in Fiduciary Capacity

(a) Subject to Subsections (b) and (c) and Section 505.004, a foreign corporate fiduciary may be appointed by will, deed, agreement, declaration, indenture, court order or decree, or otherwise and may serve in this state in any fiduciary capacity, including as:

(1) trustee of a personal or corporate trust;

(2) executor;

(3) administrator; or

(4) guardian of the estate.

(b) A foreign corporate fiduciary appointed to serve in a fiduciary capacity in this state must have the corporate power to act in that capacity.

(c) This section applies only to the extent that the home state of the foreign corporate fiduciary appointed to serve in a fiduciary capacity in this state grants to a corporate fiduciary whose home state is this state the authority to serve in like fiduciary capacity.

Added by Acts 2009, 81st Leg., ch. 680, § 1, eff. Jan. 1, 2014.

### § 505.004.  Filing Requirements; Designation

(a) A foreign corporate fiduciary must file the following documents with the secretary of state before qualifying or serving in this state in a fiduciary capacity as authorized by Section 505.003:

(1) a copy of the fiduciary's charter, articles of incorporation or of association, and all amendments to those documents, certified by the fiduciary's secretary under the fiduciary's corporate seal;

(2) a properly executed written instrument that by the instrument's terms is of indefinite duration and irrevocable, appointing the secretary of state and the secretary of state's successors as the fiduciary's agent for service of process on whom notices and processes issued by a court of this state may be served in an action or proceeding relating to a trust, estate, fund, or other matter within this state with respect to which the fiduciary is acting in a fiduciary capacity, including the acts or defaults of the fiduciary with respect to that trust, estate, or fund; and

(3) a written certificate of designation specifying the name and address of the officer, agent, or other person to whom the secretary of state shall forward notices and processes described by Subdivision (2).

(b) A foreign corporate fiduciary may change the certificate of designation under Subsection (a)(3) by filing a new certificate.

Added by Acts 2009, 81st Leg., ch. 680, § 1, eff. Jan. 1, 2014.

### § 505.005.  Service of Notice or Process on Secretary of State

(a) On receipt of a notice or process described by Section 505.004(a)(2), the secretary of state shall promptly forward the notice or process by registered or certified mail to the officer, agent, or other person designated by the foreign corporate fiduciary under Section 505.004 to receive the notice or process.

(b) Service of notice or process described by Section 505.004(a)(2) on the secretary of state as agent for a foreign corporate fiduciary has the same effect as if personal service had been had in this state on the foreign corporate fiduciary.

Added by Acts 2009, 81st Leg., ch. 680, § 1, eff. Jan. 1, 2014.

### § 505.006.  Criminal Penalty; Effect of Conviction

(a) A foreign corporate fiduciary commits an offense if the fiduciary violates this subchapter.

(b) An offense under this section is a misdemeanor punishable by a fine not to exceed $5,000.

(c) On conviction, the court may prohibit a foreign corporate fiduciary convicted of an offense under this section from thereafter serving in any fiduciary capacity in this state.

Added by Acts 2009, 81st Leg., ch. 680, § 1, eff. Jan. 1, 2014.

## SUBCHAPTER B.  FOREIGN EXECUTORS AND TRUSTEES

### § 505.051.  Applicability of Bond Requirement

(a) A foreign executor is not required to give bond if the will appointing the foreign executor provides that the executor may serve without bond.

(b) The bond provisions of this title applicable to domestic representatives apply to a foreign executor if the will appointing the foreign executor does not exempt the foreign executor from giving bond.

Added by Acts 2009, 81st Leg., ch. 680, § 1, eff. Jan. 1, 2014.

### § 505.052.  Power to Sell Property

(a) If a foreign will has been recorded in the deed records of a county in this state in the manner provided by this subtitle and the will gives an executor or trustee the power to sell property located in this state:

(1) an order of a court of this state is not necessary to authorize the executor or trustee to make the sale and execute proper conveyance; and

(2) any specific directions the testator gave in the foreign will respecting the sale of the estate property must be followed unless the directions have been annulled or suspended by an order of a court of competent jurisdiction.

(b) Notwithstanding Section 501.002(c), the original signatures required by that section may not be required for purposes of this section.

Added by Acts 2009, 81st Leg., ch. 680, § 1, eff. Jan. 1, 2014.

## SUBCHAPTER C. RECOVERY OF DEBTS BY FOREIGN EXECUTOR OR ADMINISTRATOR

### § 505.101. Suit to Recover Debt

(a) On giving notice by registered or certified mail to all creditors of a decedent in this state who have filed a claim against the decedent's estate for a debt due to the creditor, a foreign executor or administrator of a person who was a nonresident at the time of death may maintain a suit in this state for the recovery of debts due to the decedent.

(b) The plaintiff's letters testamentary or of administration granted by a competent tribunal, properly authenticated, must be filed with the suit.

Added by Acts 2009, 81st Leg., ch. 680, § 1, eff. Jan. 1, 2014.

### § 505.102. Jurisdiction

(a) A foreign executor or administrator who files a suit authorized by Section 505.101 submits personally to the jurisdiction of the courts of this state in a proceeding relating to the recovery of a debt owed to a resident of this state by the decedent whose estate the executor or administrator represents.

(b) Jurisdiction under this section is limited to the amount of money or value of personal property recovered in this state by the foreign executor or administrator.

Added by Acts 2009, 81st Leg., ch. 680, § 1, eff. Jan. 1, 2014.

### § 505.103. Restriction on Suit Brought by Foreign Executor or Administrator

A suit may not be maintained in this state by a foreign executor or administrator for a decedent's estate under this subchapter if there is:

(1) an executor or administrator of the decedent's estate qualified by a court of this state; or

(2) a pending application in this state for the appointment of an executor or administrator of the decedent's estate.

Added by Acts 2009, 81st Leg., ch. 680, § 1, eff. Jan. 1, 2014.

# SUBTITLE L. PAYMENT OF ESTATES INTO TREASURY

## CHAPTER 551. PAYMENT OF CERTAIN ESTATES TO STATE

### SUBCHAPTER A. PAYMENT OF CERTAIN FUNDS TO STATE

### SUBCHAPTER B. RECOVERY OF FUNDS PAID TO STATE

### SUBCHAPTER C. PENALTIES; ENFORCEMENT

### SUBCHAPTER A. PAYMENT OF CERTAIN FUNDS TO STATE

### § 551.001. Payment of Certain Shares of Estate to State

(a) The court, by written order, shall require the executor or administrator of an estate to pay to the comptroller as provided by this subchapter the share of that estate of a person entitled to that share who does not demand the share, including any portion deposited in an account in the court's registry under Section 362.011(c), from the executor or administrator within six months after the date of, as applicable:

(1) a court order approving the report of the commissioners of partition made under Section 360.154; or

(2) the settlement of the final account of the executor or administrator.

(b) This section does not apply to the share of an estate to which a resident minor without a guardian is entitled.

Added by Acts 2009, 81st Leg., ch. 680, § 1, eff. Jan. 1, 2014. Amended by Acts 2013, 83rd Leg., ch. 1136 (H.B. 2912), § 59, eff. Jan. 1, 2014.

Section 62(e) of Acts 2013, 83rd Leg., ch. 1136 (H.B. 2912) provides:

"The changes in law made by Sections 51.203(c), 53.104, 305.002(a), 305.003, 308.054(b), 309.051(a), 309.056, 309.103(a) and (b), 355.060, 361.155(b), 362.005, 362.011, 362.013, 404.001(a), 404.003, 404.005(b) and (c), and 551.001(a), Estates Code, as amended by this Act, and Sections 253.001(c), 301.155, 305.004, 309.057, 361.155(c), 404.0035, 404.0036, and 404.0037, Estates Code, as added by this Act, apply to the administration of the estate of a decedent that is pending or commenced on or after the effective date [Jan. 1, 2014] of this Act."

## § 551.002. Payment of Portion That is in Money

The executor or administrator shall pay the portion of the share subject to Section 551.001 that is in money to the comptroller.

Added by Acts 2009, 81st Leg., ch. 680, § 1, eff. Jan. 1, 2014.

## § 551.003. Payment of Portion That is Not in Money

(a) The court's order under Section 551.001 must require the executor or administrator to:

(1) sell, on terms determined best by the court, the portion of a share subject to that section that is in property other than money; and

(2) on collection of the proceeds of the sale, pay the proceeds to the comptroller.

(b) An action to recover the proceeds of a sale under this section is governed by Subchapter B.

Added by Acts 2009, 81st Leg., ch. 680, § 1, eff. Jan. 1, 2014.

## § 551.004. Compensation to Executor or Administrator

The executor or administrator is entitled to reasonable compensation for services performed under Section 551.003.

Added by Acts 2009, 81st Leg., ch. 680, § 1, eff. Jan. 1, 2014.

## § 551.005. Comptroller Indispensable Party

(a) The comptroller is an indispensable party to a judicial or administrative proceeding concerning the disposition and handling of any share of an estate that is or may be payable to the comptroller under Section 551.001.

(b) The clerk of a court that orders an executor or administrator to pay funds to the comptroller under Section 551.001 shall serve on the comptroller, by personal service of citation, a certified copy of the court order not later than the fifth day after the date the order is issued.

Added by Acts 2009, 81st Leg., ch. 680, § 1, eff. Jan. 1, 2014.

## § 551.006. Comptroller's Receipt

(a) An executor or administrator who pays to the comptroller under this subchapter any funds of the estate represented by the executor or administrator shall:

(1) obtain from the comptroller a receipt for the payment, with official seal attached; and

(2) file the receipt with the clerk of the court that orders the payment.

(b) The court clerk shall record the comptroller's receipt in the judge's probate docket.

Added by Acts 2009, 81st Leg., ch. 680, § 1, eff. Jan. 1, 2014. Amended by Acts 2011, 82nd Leg., ch. 91 (S.B. 1303), § 8.021, eff. Jan. 1, 2014.

## SUBCHAPTER B. RECOVERY OF FUNDS PAID TO STATE

## § 551.051. Recovery of Funds

If funds of an estate have been paid to the comptroller under this chapter, an heir or devisee or an assignee of an heir or devisee may recover the share of the funds to which the heir, devisee, or assignee is entitled.

Added by Acts 2009, 81st Leg., ch. 680, § 1, eff. Jan. 1, 2014.

## § 551.052. Action for Recovery

(a) A person claiming funds under Section 551.051 must bring an action, on or before the fourth anniversary of the date of the order requiring payment under this chapter to the comptroller, by filing a petition in the district court of Travis County against the comptroller. The petition must set forth:

(1) the plaintiff's right to the funds; and

(2) the amount claimed by the plaintiff.

(b) On the filing of a petition under Subsection (a), the court clerk shall issue a citation for the comptroller to appear and represent the interest of this state in the action. The citation must be served by personal service.

(c) Proceedings in an action brought under this section are governed by the rules applicable to other civil actions.

Added by Acts 2009, 81st Leg., ch. 680, § 1, eff. Jan. 1, 2014.

## § 551.053. Judgment

(a) If a plaintiff establishes the plaintiff's right to funds claimed under this subchapter, the court shall award a judgment that specifies the amount to which the plaintiff is entitled.

(b) A certified copy of the judgment constitutes sufficient authority for the comptroller to pay the judgment.

Added by Acts 2009, 81st Leg., ch. 680, § 1, eff. Jan. 1, 2014.

## § 551.054.  Payment of Costs

The costs of an action brought under this subchapter shall be adjudged against the plaintiff.  The plaintiff may be required to secure the costs.

Added by Acts 2009, 81st Leg., ch. 680, § 1, eff. Jan. 1, 2014.

## § 551.055.  Representation of Comptroller

As the comptroller elects and with the approval of the attorney general, the attorney general, the county attorney or criminal district attorney for the county, or the district attorney for the district shall represent the comptroller in an action brought under this subchapter.

Added by Acts 2009, 81st Leg., ch. 680, § 1, eff. Jan. 1, 2014.

## SUBCHAPTER C.  PENALTIES; ENFORCEMENT

## § 551.101.  Liability of Court Clerk; Penalty

(a) A court clerk who fails to timely comply with Section 551.005(b) is liable for a $100 penalty.

(b) The penalty under Subsection (a) shall be recovered through an action brought in the name of this state, after personal service of citation, on the information of any resident.  Half of the penalty shall be paid to the informer and the other half to this state.

Added by Acts 2009, 81st Leg., ch. 680, § 1, eff. Jan. 1, 2014.

## § 551.102.  Damages for Failure to Make Payments

(a) An executor or administrator who fails to pay funds of an estate to the comptroller as required by an order under Section 551.001 on or before the 30th day after the date of the order is liable, after personal service of citation charging that failure and after proof of the failure, for damages.  The damages:

(1) accrue at the rate of five percent of the amount of the funds per month for each month or fraction of a month after the 30th day after the date of the order that the executor or administrator fails to make the payment; and

(2) must be paid to the comptroller out of the executor's or administrator's own estate.

(b) Damages under this section may be recovered in any court of competent jurisdiction.

Added by Acts 2009, 81st Leg., ch. 680, § 1, eff. Jan. 1, 2014.

## § 551.103.  Enforcement of Payment and Damages; Recovery on Bond

(a) The comptroller may apply in the name of this state to the court that issued an order for the payment of funds of an estate under this chapter to enforce the payment of:

(1) funds the executor or administrator has failed to pay to the comptroller under the order; and

(2) any damages that have accrued under Section 551.102.

(b) The court shall enforce the payment under Subsection (a) in the manner prescribed for enforcement of other payment orders.

(c) In addition to the action under Subsection (a), the comptroller may bring an action in the name of this state against the executor or administrator and the sureties on the executor's or administrator's bond for the recovery of the funds ordered to be paid and any accrued damages.

(d) The county attorney or criminal district attorney for the county, the district attorney for the district, or the attorney general, at the election of the comptroller and with the approval of the attorney general, shall represent the comptroller in all proceedings under this section, and shall also represent the interests of this state in all other matters arising under this code.

Added by Acts 2009, 81st Leg., ch. 680, § 1, eff. Jan. 1, 2014.

## SUBTITLE P.  DURABLE POWERS OF ATTORNEY

## CHAPTER 751.  GENERAL PROVISIONS REGARDING DURABLE POWERS OF ATTORNEY

### SUBCHAPTER A.  GENERAL PROVISIONS

## SUBCHAPTER A.  GENERAL PROVISIONS

### § 751.001.  Short Title

This subtitle may be cited as the Durable Power of Attorney Act.

Added by Acts 2011, 82nd Leg., ch. 823 (H.B. 2759), § 1.01, eff. Jan. 1, 2014.

### § 751.002.  Definition of Durable Power of Attorney

A "durable power of attorney" means a written instrument that:

(1) designates another person as attorney in fact or agent;

(2) is signed by an adult principal;

(3) contains:

(A) the words:

(i) "This power of attorney is not affected by subsequent disability or incapacity of the principal"; or

(ii) "This power of attorney becomes effective on the disability or incapacity of the principal";  or

(B) words similar to those of Paragraph (A) that show the principal's intent that the authority con-

ferred on the attorney in fact or agent shall be exercised notwithstanding the principal's subsequent disability or incapacity;  and

(4) is acknowledged by the principal before an officer authorized under the laws of this state or another state to:

(A) take acknowledgments to deeds of conveyance; and

(B) administer oaths.

Added by Acts 2011, 82nd Leg., ch. 823 (H.B. 2759), § 1.01, eff. Jan. 1, 2014.

### § 751.003.  Uniformity of Application and Construction

This subtitle shall be applied and construed to effect the general purpose of this subtitle, which is to make uniform the law with respect to the subject of this subtitle among states enacting these provisions.

Added by Acts 2011, 82nd Leg., ch. 823 (H.B. 2759), § 1.01, eff. Jan. 1, 2014.

### § 751.004.  Duration of Durable Power of Attorney

A durable power of attorney does not lapse because of the passage of time unless the instrument creating the power of attorney specifically states a time limitation.

Added by Acts 2011, 82nd Leg., ch. 823 (H.B. 2759), § 1.01, eff. Jan. 1, 2014.

### § 751.005.  Extension of Principal's Authority to Other Persons

If, in this subtitle, a principal is given an authority to act, that authority includes:

(1) any person designated by the principal;

(2) a guardian of the estate of the principal;  or

(3) another personal representative of the principal.

Added by Acts 2011, 82nd Leg., ch. 823 (H.B. 2759), § 1.01, eff. Jan. 1, 2014.

### § 751.006.  Rights Cumulative

The rights set out under this subtitle are cumulative of any other rights or remedies the principal may have at common law or other applicable statutes and are not in derogation of those rights.

Added by Acts 2011, 82nd Leg., ch. 823 (H.B. 2759), § 1.01, eff. Jan. 1, 2014.

## SUBCHAPTER B. EFFECT OF CERTAIN ACTS ON EXERCISE OF DURABLE POWER OF ATTORNEY

### § 751.051. Effect of Acts Performed by Attorney in Fact or Agent During Principal's Disability or Incapacity

Each act performed by an attorney in fact or agent under a durable power of attorney during a period of the principal's disability or incapacity has the same effect, and inures to the benefit of and binds the principal and the principal's successors in interest, as if the principal were not disabled or incapacitated.

Added by Acts 2011, 82nd Leg., ch. 823 (H.B. 2759), § 1.01, eff. Jan. 1, 2014.

### § 751.052. Relation of Attorney in Fact or Agent to Court–appointed Guardian of Estate

(a) If, after execution of a durable power of attorney, a court of the principal's domicile appoints a permanent guardian of the estate of the principal, the powers of the attorney in fact or agent terminate on the qualification of the guardian of the estate. The attorney in fact or agent shall:

(1) deliver to the guardian of the estate all assets of the ward's estate that are in the possession of the attorney in fact or agent; and

(2) account to the guardian of the estate as the attorney in fact or agent would account to the principal if the principal had terminated the powers of the attorney in fact or agent.

(b) If, after execution of a durable power of attorney, a court of the principal's domicile appoints a temporary guardian of the estate of the principal, the court may suspend the powers of the attorney in fact or agent on the qualification of the temporary guardian of the estate until the date the term of the temporary guardian expires. This subsection may not be construed to prohibit the application for or issuance of a temporary restraining order under applicable law.

Added by Acts 2011, 82nd Leg., ch. 823 (H.B. 2759), § 1.01, eff. Jan. 1, 2014.

### § 751.053. Effect of Principal's Divorce or Marriage Annulment if Former Spouse is Attorney in Fact or Agent

Unless otherwise expressly provided by the durable power of attorney, if, after execution of a durable power of attorney, the principal is divorced from a person who has been appointed the principal's attorney in fact or agent or the principal's marriage to a person who has been appointed the principal's attorney in fact or agent is annulled, the powers of the attorney in fact or agent granted to the principal's former spouse terminate on the date the divorce or annulment of marriage is granted by a court.

Added by Acts 2011, 82nd Leg., ch. 823 (H.B. 2759), § 1.01, eff. Jan. 1, 2014.

### § 751.054. Knowledge of Termination of Power; Good–Faith Acts

(a) The revocation by, the death of, or the qualification of a guardian of the estate of a principal who has executed a durable power of attorney does not revoke or terminate the agency as to the attorney in fact, agent, or other person who acts in good faith under or in reliance on the power without actual knowledge of the termination of the power by:

(1) the revocation;

(2) the principal's death; or

(3) the qualification of a guardian of the estate of the principal.

(b) The divorce of a principal from a person who has been appointed the principal's attorney in fact or agent before the date the divorce is granted, or the annulment of the marriage of a principal and a person who has been appointed the principal's attorney in fact or agent before the date the annulment is granted, does not revoke or terminate the agency as to a person other than the principal's former spouse if the person acts in good faith under or in reliance on the power of attorney.

(c) An action taken under this section, unless otherwise invalid or unenforceable, binds the principal's successors in interest.

Added by Acts 2011, 82nd Leg., ch. 823 (H.B. 2759), § 1.01, eff. Jan. 1, 2014.

### § 751.055. Affidavit Regarding Lack of Knowledge of Termination of Power or of Disability or Incapacity; Good–faith Reliance

(a) As to an act undertaken in good-faith reliance on a durable power of attorney, an affidavit executed by the attorney in fact or agent under the durable power of attorney stating that the attorney in fact or agent did not have, at the time the power was exercised, actual knowledge of the termination of the power by revocation, the principal's death, the principal's divorce or the annulment of the principal's marriage if the attorney in fact or agent was the principal's spouse, or the qualification of a guardian of the estate of the principal, is conclusive proof as between the attorney in fact or agent and a person other than the principal or the principal's personal representative dealing with the attorney in fact or agent of the nonrevocation or nontermination of the power at that time.

(b) As to an act undertaken in good-faith reliance on a durable power of attorney, an affidavit executed by the attorney in fact or agent under the durable power of attorney stating that the principal is disabled or incapacitated, as defined by the power of attorney, is conclusive proof as between the attorney in fact or agent and a person other than the principal or the principal's personal representative dealing with the attorney in fact or agent of the principal's disability or incapacity at that time.

(c) If the exercise of the power of attorney requires execution and delivery of an instrument that is to be recorded, an affidavit executed under Subsection (a) or (b), authenticated for record, may also be recorded.

(d) This section and Section 751.056 do not affect a provision in a durable power of attorney for the termination of the power by:

(1) expiration of time; or

(2) the occurrence of an event other than express revocation.

Added by Acts 2011, 82nd Leg., ch. 823 (H.B. 2759), § 1.01, eff. Jan. 1, 2014.

### § 751.056.  Nonliability of Third Party on Good-Faith Reliance

If a durable power of attorney is used, a third party who relies in good faith on the acts of an attorney in fact or agent performed within the scope of the power of attorney is not liable to the principal.

Added by Acts 2011, 82nd Leg., ch. 823 (H.B. 2759), § 1.01, eff. Jan. 1, 2014.

### § 751.057.  Effect of Bankruptcy Proceeding

(a) The filing of a voluntary or involuntary petition in bankruptcy in connection with the debts of a principal who has executed a durable power of attorney does not revoke or terminate the agency as to the principal's attorney in fact or agent.

(b) Any act the attorney in fact or agent may undertake with respect to the principal's property is subject to the limitations and requirements of the United States Bankruptcy Code (11 U.S.C. Section 101 et seq.) until a final determination is made in the bankruptcy proceeding.

Added by Acts 2011, 82nd Leg., ch. 823 (H.B. 2759), § 1.01, eff. Jan. 1, 2014.

### § 751.058.  Effect of Revocation of Durable Power of Attorney on Third Party

Unless otherwise provided by the durable power of attorney, a revocation of a durable power of attorney is not effective as to a third party relying on the power of attorney until the third party receives actual notice of the revocation.

Added by Acts 2011, 82nd Leg., ch. 823 (H.B. 2759), § 1.01, eff. Jan. 1, 2014.

### SUBCHAPTER C.  DUTY TO INFORM AND ACCOUNT

### § 751.101.  Fiduciary Duties

An attorney in fact or agent is a fiduciary and has a duty to inform and to account for actions taken under the power of attorney.

Added by Acts 2011, 82nd Leg., ch. 823 (H.B. 2759), § 1.01, eff. Jan. 1, 2014.

### § 751.102.  Duty to Timely Inform Principal

(a) The attorney in fact or agent shall timely inform the principal of each action taken under the power of attorney.

(b) Failure of an attorney in fact or agent to timely inform, as to third parties, does not invalidate any action of the attorney in fact or agent.

Added by Acts 2011, 82nd Leg., ch. 823 (H.B. 2759), § 1.01, eff. Jan. 1, 2014.

### § 751.103.  Maintenance of Records

(a) The attorney in fact or agent shall maintain records of each action taken or decision made by the attorney in fact or agent.

(b) The attorney in fact or agent shall maintain all records until delivered to the principal, released by the principal, or discharged by a court.

Added by Acts 2011, 82nd Leg., ch. 823 (H.B. 2759), § 1.01, eff. Jan. 1, 2014.

### § 751.104.  Accounting

(a) The principal may demand an accounting by the attorney in fact or agent.

(b) Unless otherwise directed by the principal, an accounting under Subsection (a) must include:

(1) the property belonging to the principal that has come to the attorney in fact's or agent's knowledge or into the attorney in fact's or agent's possession;

(2) each action taken or decision made by the attorney in fact or agent;

(3) a complete account of receipts, disbursements, and other actions of the attorney in fact or agent that includes the source and nature of each receipt, disbursement, or action, with receipts of principal and income shown separately;

(4) a listing of all property over which the attorney in fact or agent has exercised control that includes:

(A) an adequate description of each asset; and

(B) the asset's current value, if the value is known to the attorney in fact or agent;

(5) the cash balance on hand and the name and location of the depository at which the cash balance is kept;

(6) each known liability; and

(7) any other information and facts known to the attorney in fact or agent as necessary for a full and definite understanding of the exact condition of the property belonging to the principal.

(c) Unless directed otherwise by the principal, the attorney in fact or agent shall also provide to the principal all documentation regarding the principal's property.

Added by Acts 2011, 82nd Leg., ch. 823 (H.B. 2759), § 1.01, eff. Jan. 1, 2014.

### § 751.105. Effect of Failure to Comply; Suit

If the attorney in fact or agent fails or refuses to inform the principal, provide documentation, or deliver an accounting under Section 751.104 within 60 days of a demand under that section, or a longer or shorter period as demanded by the principal or ordered by a court, the principal may file suit to:

(1) compel the attorney in fact or agent to deliver the accounting or the assets; or

(2) terminate the power of attorney.

Added by Acts 2011, 82nd Leg., ch. 823 (H.B. 2759), § 1.01, eff. Jan. 1, 2014.

### § 751.106. Effect of Subchapter on Principal's Rights

This subchapter does not limit the right of the principal to terminate the power of attorney or to make additional requirements of or to give additional instructions to the attorney in fact or agent.

Added by Acts 2011, 82nd Leg., ch. 823 (H.B. 2759), § 1.01, eff. Jan. 1, 2014.

## SUBCHAPTER D. RECORDING DURABLE POWER OF ATTORNEY FOR CERTAIN REAL PROPERTY TRANSACTIONS

### § 751.151. Recording for Real Property Transactions Requiring Execution and Delivery of Instruments

A durable power of attorney for a real property transaction requiring the execution and delivery of an instrument that is to be recorded, including a release, assignment, satisfaction, mortgage, security agreement, deed of trust, encumbrance, deed of conveyance, oil, gas, or other mineral lease, memorandum of a lease, lien, or other claim or right to real property, must be recorded in the office of the county clerk of the county in which the property is located.

Added by Acts 2011, 82nd Leg., ch. 823 (H.B. 2759), § 1.01, eff. Jan. 1, 2014.

## CHAPTER 752. STATUTORY DURABLE POWER OF ATTORNEY

### SUBCHAPTER A. GENERAL PROVISIONS REGARDING STATUTORY DURABLE POWER OF ATTORNEY

## SUBCHAPTER A. GENERAL PROVISIONS REGARDING STATUTORY DURABLE POWER OF ATTORNEY

### § 752.001. Use, Meaning, and Effect of Statutory Durable Power of Attorney

(a) A person may use a statutory durable power of attorney to grant an attorney in fact or agent powers with respect to a person's property and financial matters.

(b) A power of attorney in substantially the form prescribed by Section 752.051 has the meaning and effect prescribed by this subtitle.

Added by Acts 2011, 82nd Leg., ch. 823 (H.B. 2759), § 1.01, eff. Jan. 1, 2014.

### § 752.002. Validity Not Affected

A power of attorney is valid with respect to meeting the requirements for a statutory durable power of attorney regardless of the fact that:

(1) one or more of the categories of optional powers listed in the form prescribed by Section 752.051 are not initialed; or

(2) the form includes specific limitations on, or additions to, the powers of the attorney in fact or agent.

Added by Acts 2011, 82nd Leg., ch. 823 (H.B. 2759), § 1.01, eff. Jan. 1, 2014. Amended by Acts 2013, 83rd Leg., ch. 700 (H.B. 2918), § 2, eff. Jan. 1, 2014.

Section 3 of Acts 2013, 83rd Leg., ch. 700 (H.B. 2918) provides:

"The changes in law made by this Act apply only to a power of attorney executed on or after the effective date [Jan. 1, 2014] of this Act. A power of attorney executed before the effective date of this Act is governed by the law in effect on the date the power of attorney was executed, and that law is continued in effect for that purpose."

### § 752.003. Prescribed Form Not Exclusive

The form prescribed by Section 752.051 is not exclusive, and other forms of power of attorney may be used.

Added by Acts 2011, 82nd Leg., ch. 823 (H.B. 2759), § 1.01, eff. Jan. 1, 2014.

### § 752.004. Legal Sufficiency of Statutory Durable Power of Attorney

A statutory durable power of attorney is legally sufficient under this subtitle if:

(1) the wording of the form complies substantially with the wording of the form prescribed by Section 752.051;

(2) the form is properly completed; and

(3) the signature of the principal is acknowledged.

Added by Acts 2011, 82nd Leg., ch. 823 (H.B. 2759), § 1.01, eff. Jan. 1, 2014.

## SUBCHAPTER B. FORM OF STATUTORY DURABLE POWER OF ATTORNEY

### § 752.051. Form

The following form is known as a "statutory durable power of attorney":

### STATUTORY DURABLE POWER OF ATTORNEY

NOTICE: THE POWERS GRANTED BY THIS DOCUMENT ARE BROAD AND SWEEPING. THEY ARE EXPLAINED IN THE DURABLE POWER OF ATTORNEY ACT, SUBTITLE P, TITLE 2, ESTATES CODE. IF YOU HAVE ANY QUESTIONS ABOUT THESE POWERS, OBTAIN COMPETENT LEGAL ADVICE. THIS DOCUMENT DOES NOT AUTHORIZE ANYONE TO MAKE MEDICAL AND OTHER HEALTH–CARE DECISIONS FOR YOU. YOU MAY REVOKE THIS POWER OF ATTORNEY IF YOU LATER WISH TO DO SO.

You should select someone you trust to serve as your agent (attorney in fact). Unless you specify otherwise, generally the agent's (attorney in fact's) authority will continue until:

(1) you die or revoke the power of attorney;

(2) your agent (attorney in fact) resigns or is unable to act for you; or

(3) a guardian is appointed for your estate.

I, _____ (insert your name and address), appoint _____ (insert the name and address of the person appointed) as my agent (attorney in fact) to act for me in any lawful way with respect to all of the following powers that I have initialed below.

TO GRANT ALL OF THE FOLLOWING POWERS, INITIAL THE LINE IN FRONT OF (N)

AND IGNORE THE LINES IN FRONT OF THE OTHER POWERS LISTED IN (A) THROUGH (M).

TO GRANT A POWER, YOU MUST INITIAL THE LINE IN FRONT OF THE POWER YOU ARE GRANTING.

TO WITHHOLD A POWER, DO NOT INITIAL THE LINE IN FRONT OF THE POWER. YOU MAY, BUT DO NOT NEED TO, CROSS OUT EACH POWER WITHHELD.

___ (A) Real property transactions;

___ (B) Tangible personal property transactions;

___ (C) Stock and bond transactions;

___ (D) Commodity and option transactions;

___ (E) Banking and other financial institution transactions;

___ (F) Business operating transactions;

___ (G) Insurance and annuity transactions;

___ (H) Estate, trust, and other beneficiary transactions;

___ (I) Claims and litigation;

___ (J) Personal and family maintenance;

___ (K) Benefits from social security, Medicare, Medicaid, or other governmental programs or civil or military service;

___ (L) Retirement plan transactions;

___ (M) Tax matters;

___ (N) ALL OF THE POWERS LISTED IN (A) THROUGH (M). YOU DO NOT HAVE TO INITIAL THE LINE IN FRONT OF ANY OTHER POWER IF YOU INITIAL LINE (N).

SPECIAL INSTRUCTIONS:

Special instructions applicable to gifts (initial in front of the following sentence to have it apply):

___ I grant my agent (attorney in fact) the power to apply my property to make gifts outright to or for the benefit of a person, including by the exercise of a presently exercisable general power of appointment held by me, except that the amount of a gift to an individual may not exceed the amount of annual exclusions allowed from the federal gift tax for the calendar year of the gift.

ON THE FOLLOWING LINES YOU MAY GIVE SPECIAL INSTRUCTIONS LIMITING OR EXTENDING THE POWERS GRANTED TO YOUR AGENT.

_____
_____
_____
_____
_____
_____
_____
_____

UNLESS YOU DIRECT OTHERWISE ABOVE, THIS POWER OF ATTORNEY IS EFFECTIVE IMMEDIATELY AND WILL CONTINUE UNTIL IT IS REVOKED.

CHOOSE ONE OF THE FOLLOWING ALTERNATIVES BY CROSSING OUT THE ALTERNATIVE NOT CHOSEN:

(A) This power of attorney is not affected by my subsequent disability or incapacity.

(B) This power of attorney becomes effective upon my disability or incapacity.

YOU SHOULD CHOOSE ALTERNATIVE (A) IF THIS POWER OF ATTORNEY IS TO BECOME EFFECTIVE ON THE DATE IT IS EXECUTED.

IF NEITHER (A) NOR (B) IS CROSSED OUT, IT WILL BE ASSUMED THAT YOU CHOSE ALTERNATIVE (A).

If Alternative (B) is chosen and a definition of my disability or incapacity is not contained in this power of attorney, I shall be considered disabled or incapacitated for purposes of this power of attorney if a physician certifies in writing at a date later than the date this power of attorney is executed that, based on the physician's medical examination of me, I am mentally incapable of managing my financial affairs. I authorize the physician who examines me for this purpose to disclose my physical or mental condition to another person for purposes of this power of attorney. A third party who accepts this power of attorney is fully protected from any action taken under this power of attorney that is based on the determination made by a physician of my disability or incapacity.

I agree that any third party who receives a copy of this document may act under it. Revocation of the durable power of attorney is not effective as to a third party until the third party receives actual notice of the revocation. I agree to indemnify the third party for any claims that arise against the third party because of reliance on this power of attorney.

If any agent named by me dies, becomes legally disabled, resigns, or refuses to act, I name the following (each to act alone and successively, in the order named) as successor(s) to that agent: _____.

Signed this _____ day of _____, _____

_____
(your signature)

State of _____
County of _____

This document was acknowledged before me on _____(date) by

_____
(name of principal)

_____
(signature of notarial officer)

(Seal, if any, of notary) _____
(printed name)

My commission expires: _____

## IMPORTANT INFORMATION FOR AGENT (ATTORNEY IN FACT)

Agent's Duties

When you accept the authority granted under this power of attorney, you establish a "fiduciary" relationship with the principal. This is a special legal relationship that imposes on you legal duties that continue until you resign or the power of attorney is terminated or revoked by the principal or by operation of law. A fiduciary duty generally includes the duty to:

(1) act in good faith;

(2) do nothing beyond the authority granted in this power of attorney;

(3) act loyally for the principal's benefit;

(4) avoid conflicts that would impair your ability to act in the principal's best interest; and

(5) disclose your identity as an agent or attorney in fact when you act for the principal by writing or printing the name of the principal and signing your own name as "agent" or "attorney in fact" in the following manner:

(Principal's Name) by (Your Signature) as Agent (or as Attorney in Fact)

In addition, the Durable Power of Attorney Act (Subtitle P, Title 2, Estates Code) requires you to:

(1) maintain records of each action taken or decision made on behalf of the principal;

(2) maintain all records until delivered to the principal, released by the principal, or discharged by a court; and

(3) if requested by the principal, provide an accounting to the principal that, unless otherwise directed by the principal or otherwise provided in the Special Instructions, must include:

(A) the property belonging to the principal that has come to your knowledge or into your possession;

(B) each action taken or decision made by you as agent or attorney in fact;

(C) a complete account of receipts, disbursements, and other actions of you as agent or attorney in fact that includes the source and nature of each receipt, disbursement, or action, with receipts of principal and income shown separately;

(D) a listing of all property over which you have exercised control that includes an adequate description of each asset and the asset's current value, if known to you;

(E) the cash balance on hand and the name and location of the depository at which the cash balance is kept;

(F) each known liability;

(G) any other information and facts known to you as necessary for a full and definite understanding of the exact condition of the property belonging to the principal; and

(H) all documentation regarding the principal's property.

Termination of Agent's Authority

You must stop acting on behalf of the principal if you learn of any event that terminates this power of attorney or your authority under this power of attorney. An event that terminates this power of attorney or your authority to act under this power of attorney includes:

(1) the principal's death;

(2) the principal's revocation of this power of attorney or your authority;

(3) the occurrence of a termination event stated in this power of attorney;

(4) if you are married to the principal, the dissolution of your marriage by court decree of divorce or annulment;

(5) the appointment and qualification of a permanent guardian of the principal's estate; or

(6) if ordered by a court, the suspension of this power of attorney on the appointment and qualification of a temporary guardian until the date the term

of the temporary guardian expires.Liability of Agent

The authority granted to you under this power of attorney is specified in the Durable Power of Attorney Act (Subtitle P, Title 2, Estates Code). If you violate the Durable Power of Attorney Act or act beyond the authority granted, you may be liable for any damages caused by the violation or subject to prosecution for misapplication of property by a fiduciary under Chapter 32 of the Texas Penal Code.

THE ATTORNEY IN FACT OR AGENT, BY ACCEPTING OR ACTING UNDER THE APPOINTMENT, ASSUMES THE FIDUCIARY AND OTHER LEGAL RESPONSIBILITIES OF AN AGENT.

Added by Acts 2011, 82nd Leg., ch. 823 (H.B. 2759), § 1.01, eff. Jan. 1, 2014. Amended by Acts 2013, 83rd Leg., ch. 700 (H.B. 2918), § 1, eff. Jan. 1, 2014.

Section 3 of Acts 2013, 83rd Leg., ch. 700 (H.B. 2918) provides:

"The changes in law made by this Act apply only to a power of attorney executed on or after the effective date [Jan. 1, 2014] of this Act. A power of attorney executed before the effective date of this Act is governed by the law in effect on the date the power of attorney was executed, and that law is continued in effect for that purpose."

## SUBCHAPTER C. CONSTRUCTION OF POWERS RELATED TO STATUTORY DURABLE POWER OF ATTORNEY

### § 752.101. Construction in General

By executing a statutory durable power of attorney that confers authority with respect to any class of transactions, the principal empowers the attorney in fact or agent for that class of transactions to:

(1) demand, receive, and obtain by litigation, action, or otherwise any money or other thing of value to which the principal is, may become, or may claim to be entitled;

(2) conserve, invest, disburse, or use any money or other thing of value received on behalf of the principal for the purposes intended;

(3) contract in any manner with any person, on terms agreeable to the attorney in fact or agent, to accomplish a purpose of a transaction and perform, rescind, reform, release, or modify that contract or another contract made by or on behalf of the principal;

(4) execute, acknowledge, seal, and deliver a deed, revocation, mortgage, lease, notice, check, release, or other instrument the attorney in fact or agent considers desirable to accomplish a purpose of a transaction;

(5) with respect to a claim existing in favor of or against the principal:

(A) prosecute, defend, submit to arbitration, settle, and propose or accept a compromise; or

(B) intervene in an action or litigation relating to the claim;

(6) seek on the principal's behalf the assistance of a court to carry out an act authorized by the power of attorney;

(7) engage, compensate, and discharge an attorney, accountant, expert witness, or other assistant;

(8) keep appropriate records of each transaction, including an accounting of receipts and disbursements;

(9) prepare, execute, and file a record, report, or other document the attorney in fact or agent considers necessary or desirable to safeguard or promote the principal's interest under a statute or governmental regulation;

(10) reimburse the attorney in fact or agent for an expenditure made in exercising the powers granted by the durable power of attorney; and

(11) in general, perform any other lawful act that the principal may perform with respect to the transaction.

Added by Acts 2011, 82nd Leg., ch. 823 (H.B. 2759), § 1.01, eff. Jan. 1, 2014.

### § 752.102. Real Property Transactions

The language conferring authority with respect to real property transactions in a statutory durable power of attorney empowers the attorney in fact or agent, without further reference to a specific description of the real property, to:

(1) accept as a gift or as security for a loan or reject, demand, buy, lease, receive, or otherwise acquire an interest in real property or a right incident to real property;

(2) sell, exchange, convey with or without covenants, quitclaim, release, surrender, mortgage, encumber, partition or consent to partitioning, subdivide, apply for zoning, rezoning, or other governmental permits, plat or consent to platting, develop, grant options concerning, lease or sublet, or otherwise dispose of an estate or interest in real property or a right incident to real property;

(3) release, assign, satisfy, and enforce by litigation, action, or otherwise a mortgage, deed of trust,

encumbrance, lien, or other claim to real property that exists or is claimed to exist;

(4) perform any act of management or of conservation with respect to an interest in real property, or a right incident to real property, owned or claimed to be owned by the principal, including the authority to:

(A) insure against a casualty, liability, or loss;

(B) obtain or regain possession or protect the interest or right by litigation, action, or otherwise;

(C) pay, compromise, or contest taxes or assessments or apply for and receive refunds in connection with the taxes or assessments;

(D) purchase supplies, hire assistance or labor, or make repairs or alterations to the real property; and

(E) manage and supervise an interest in real property, including the mineral estate, by, for example:

(i) entering into a lease for oil, gas, and mineral purposes;

(ii) making contracts for development of the mineral estate; or

(iii) making pooling and unitization agreements;

(5) use, develop, alter, replace, remove, erect, or install structures or other improvements on real property in which the principal has or claims to have an estate, interest, or right;

(6) participate in a reorganization with respect to real property or a legal entity that owns an interest in or right incident to real property, receive and hold shares of stock or obligations received in a plan or reorganization, and act with respect to the shares or obligations, including:

(A) selling or otherwise disposing of the shares or obligations;

(B) exercising or selling an option, conversion, or similar right with respect to the shares or obligations; and

(C) voting the shares or obligations in person or by proxy;

(7) change the form of title of an interest in or right incident to real property; and

(8) dedicate easements or other real property in which the principal has or claims to have an interest to public use, with or without consideration.

Added by Acts 2011, 82nd Leg., ch. 823 (H.B. 2759), § 1.01, eff. Jan. 1, 2014.

## § 752.103. Tangible Personal Property Transactions

The language conferring general authority with respect to tangible personal property transactions in a statutory durable power of attorney empowers the attorney in fact or agent to:

(1) accept tangible personal property or an interest in tangible personal property as a gift or as security for a loan or reject, demand, buy, receive, or otherwise acquire ownership or possession of tangible personal property or an interest in tangible personal property;

(2) sell, exchange, convey with or without covenants, release, surrender, mortgage, encumber, pledge, create a security interest in, pawn, grant options concerning, lease or sublet to others, or otherwise dispose of tangible personal property or an interest in tangible personal property;

(3) release, assign, satisfy, or enforce by litigation, action, or otherwise a mortgage, security interest, encumbrance, lien, or other claim on behalf of the principal, with respect to tangible personal property or an interest in tangible personal property; and

(4) perform an act of management or conservation with respect to tangible personal property or an interest in tangible personal property on behalf of the principal, including:

(A) insuring the property or interest against casualty, liability, or loss;

(B) obtaining or regaining possession or protecting the property or interest by litigation, action, or otherwise;

(C) paying, compromising, or contesting taxes or assessments or applying for and receiving refunds in connection with taxes or assessments;

(D) moving the property;

(E) storing the property for hire or on a gratuitous bailment; and

(F) using, altering, and making repairs or alterations to the property.

Added by Acts 2011, 82nd Leg., ch. 823 (H.B. 2759), § 1.01, eff. Jan. 1, 2014.

## § 752.104. Stock and Bond Transactions

The language conferring authority with respect to stock and bond transactions in a statutory durable power of attorney empowers the attorney in fact or agent to:

(1) buy, sell, and exchange:

(A) stocks;

(B) bonds;

(C) mutual funds; and

(D) all other types of securities and financial instruments other than commodity futures contracts and call and put options on stocks and stock indexes;

(2) receive certificates and other evidences of ownership with respect to securities;

(3) exercise voting rights with respect to securities in person or by proxy;

(4) enter into voting trusts; and

(5) consent to limitations on the right to vote.

Added by Acts 2011, 82nd Leg., ch. 823 (H.B. 2759), § 1.01, eff. Jan. 1, 2014.

## § 752.105.  Commodity and Option Transactions

The language conferring authority with respect to commodity and option transactions in a statutory durable power of attorney empowers the attorney in fact or agent to:

(1) buy, sell, exchange, assign, settle, and exercise commodity futures contracts and call and put options on stocks and stock indexes traded on a regulated options exchange; and

(2) establish, continue, modify, or terminate option accounts with a broker.

Added by Acts 2011, 82nd Leg., ch. 823 (H.B. 2759), § 1.01, eff. Jan. 1, 2014.

## § 752.106.  Banking and Other Financial Institution Transactions

The language conferring authority with respect to banking and other financial institution transactions in a statutory durable power of attorney empowers the attorney in fact or agent to:

(1) continue, modify, or terminate an account or other banking arrangement made by or on behalf of the principal;

(2) establish, modify, or terminate an account or other banking arrangement with a bank, trust company, savings and loan association, credit union, thrift company, brokerage firm, or other financial institution selected by the attorney in fact or agent;

(3) rent a safe deposit box or space in a vault;

(4) contract to procure other services available from a financial institution as the attorney in fact or agent considers desirable;

(5) withdraw by check, order, or otherwise money or property of the principal deposited with or left in the custody of a financial institution;

(6) receive bank statements, vouchers, notices, or similar documents from a financial institution and act with respect to those documents;

(7) enter a safe deposit box or vault and withdraw from or add to its contents;

(8) borrow money at an interest rate agreeable to the attorney in fact or agent and pledge as security the principal's property as necessary to borrow, pay, renew, or extend the time of payment of a debt of the principal;

(9) make, assign, draw, endorse, discount, guarantee, and negotiate promissory notes, bills of exchange, checks, drafts, or other negotiable or nonnegotiable paper of the principal, or payable to the principal or the principal's order to receive the cash or other proceeds of those transactions, to accept a draft drawn by a person on the principal, and to pay the principal when due;

(10) receive for the principal and act on a sight draft, warehouse receipt, or other negotiable or nonnegotiable instrument;

(11) apply for and receive letters of credit, credit cards, and traveler's checks from a financial institution and give an indemnity or other agreement in connection with letters of credit; and

(12) consent to an extension of the time of payment with respect to commercial paper or a financial transaction with a financial institution.

Added by Acts 2011, 82nd Leg., ch. 823 (H.B. 2759), § 1.01, eff. Jan. 1, 2014.

## § 752.107.  Business Operation Transactions

The language conferring authority with respect to business operating transactions in a statutory durable power of attorney empowers the attorney in fact or agent to:

(1) operate, buy, sell, enlarge, reduce, or terminate a business interest;

(2) do the following, to the extent that an attorney in fact or agent is permitted by law to act for a principal and subject to the terms of a partnership agreement:

(A) perform a duty, discharge a liability, or exercise a right, power, privilege, or option that the principal has, may have, or claims to have under the partnership agreement, whether or not the principal is a general or limited partner;

(B) enforce the terms of the partnership agreement by litigation, action, or otherwise; and

(C) defend, submit to arbitration, settle, or compromise litigation or an action to which the principal is a party because of membership in the partnership;

(3) exercise in person or by proxy, or enforce by litigation, action, or otherwise, a right, power, privilege, or option the principal has or claims to have as the holder of a bond, share, or other similar instrument and defend, submit to arbitration, settle, or compromise a legal proceeding to which the principal is a party because of a bond, share, or similar instrument;

(4) with respect to a business owned solely by the principal:

(A) continue, modify, renegotiate, extend, and terminate a contract made before execution of the power of attorney with an individual, legal entity, firm, association, or corporation by or on behalf of the principal with respect to the business;

(B) determine:

(i) the location of the business's operation;

(ii) the nature and extent of the business;

(iii) the methods of manufacturing, selling, merchandising, financing, accounting, and advertising employed in the business's operation;

(iv) the amount and types of insurance carried; and

(v) the method of engaging, compensating, and dealing with the business's accountants, attorneys, and other agents and employees;

(C) change the name or form of organization under which the business is operated and enter into a partnership agreement with other persons or organize a corporation to take over all or part of the operation of the business; and

(D) demand and receive money due or claimed by the principal or on the principal's behalf in the operation of the business and control and disburse the money in the operation of the business;

(5) put additional capital into a business in which the principal has an interest;

(6) join in a plan of reorganization, consolidation, or merger of the business;

(7) sell or liquidate a business or part of the business at the time and on the terms that the attorney in fact or agent considers desirable;

(8) establish the value of a business under a buyout agreement to which the principal is a party;

(9) do the following:

(A) prepare, sign, file, and deliver reports, compilations of information, returns, or other papers with respect to a business:

(i) that are required by a governmental agency, department, or instrumentality; or

(ii) that the attorney in fact or agent considers desirable; and

(B) make related payments; and

(10) pay, compromise, or contest taxes or assessments and perform any other act that the attorney in fact or agent considers desirable to protect the principal from illegal or unnecessary taxation, fines, penalties, or assessments with respect to a business, including attempts to recover, in any manner permitted by law, money paid before or after the execution of the power of attorney.

Added by Acts 2011, 82nd Leg., ch. 823 (H.B. 2759), § 1.01, eff. Jan. 1, 2014.

## § 752.108.   Insurance and Annuity Transactions

(a) The language conferring authority with respect to insurance and annuity transactions in a statutory durable power of attorney empowers the attorney in fact or agent to:

(1) continue, pay the premium or assessment on, modify, rescind, release, or terminate a contract procured by or on behalf of the principal that insures or provides an annuity to either the principal or another person, whether or not the principal is a beneficiary under the contract;

(2) procure new, different, or additional insurance contracts and annuities for the principal or the principal's spouse, children, and other dependents and select the amount, type of insurance or annuity, and method of payment;

(3) pay the premium or assessment on, or modify, rescind, release, or terminate, an insurance contract or annuity procured by the attorney in fact or agent;

(4) designate the beneficiary of the insurance contract, except as provided by Subsection (b);

(5) apply for and receive a loan on the security of the insurance contract or annuity;

(6) surrender and receive the cash surrender value;

(7) exercise an election;

(8) change the manner of paying premiums;

(9) change or convert the type of insurance contract or annuity with respect to which the principal

has or claims to have a power described by this section;

(10) change the beneficiary of an insurance contract or annuity, except that the attorney in fact or agent may be designated a beneficiary only to the extent authorized by Subsection (b);

(11) apply for and procure government aid to guarantee or pay premiums of an insurance contract on the life of the principal;

(12) collect, sell, assign, borrow on, or pledge the principal's interest in an insurance contract or annuity; and

(13) pay from proceeds or otherwise, compromise or contest, or apply for refunds in connection with a tax or assessment imposed by a taxing authority with respect to an insurance contract or annuity or the proceeds of the contract or annuity or liability accruing because of the tax or assessment.

(b) An attorney in fact or agent may be named a beneficiary of an insurance contract or an extension, renewal, or substitute for the contract only to the extent the attorney in fact or agent was named as a beneficiary under a contract procured by the principal before executing the power of attorney.

Added by Acts 2011, 82nd Leg., ch. 823 (H.B. 2759), § 1.01, eff. Jan. 1, 2014.

## § 752.109. Estate, Trust, and Other Beneficiary Transactions

The language conferring authority with respect to estate, trust, and other beneficiary transactions in a statutory durable power of attorney empowers the attorney in fact or agent to act for the principal in all matters that affect a trust, probate estate, guardianship, conservatorship, escrow, custodianship, or other fund from which the principal is, may become, or claims to be entitled, as a beneficiary, to a share or payment, including to:

(1) accept, reject, disclaim, receive, receipt for, sell, assign, release, pledge, exchange, or consent to a reduction in or modification of a share in or payment from the fund;

(2) demand or obtain by litigation, action, or otherwise money or any other thing of value to which the principal is, may become, or claims to be entitled because of the fund;

(3) initiate, participate in, or oppose a legal or judicial proceeding to:

(A) ascertain the meaning, validity, or effect of a deed, will, declaration of trust, or other instrument or transaction affecting the interest of the principal; or

(B) remove, substitute, or surcharge a fiduciary;

(4) conserve, invest, disburse, or use anything received for an authorized purpose; and

(5) transfer all or part of the principal's interest in real property, stocks, bonds, accounts with financial institutions, insurance, and other property to the trustee of a revocable trust created by the principal as settlor.

Added by Acts 2011, 82nd Leg., ch. 823 (H.B. 2759), § 1.01, eff. Jan. 1, 2014.

## § 752.110. Claims and Litigation

The language conferring general authority with respect to claims and litigation in a statutory durable power of attorney empowers the attorney in fact or agent to:

(1) assert and prosecute before a court or administrative agency a claim, a claim for relief, a counterclaim, or an offset, or defend against an individual, a legal entity, or a government, including an action to:

(A) recover property or other thing of value;

(B) recover damages sustained by the principal;

(C) eliminate or modify tax liability; or

(D) seek an injunction, specific performance, or other relief;

(2) bring an action to determine an adverse claim, intervene in an action or litigation, and act as an amicus curiae;

(3) in connection with an action or litigation:

(A) procure an attachment, garnishment, libel, order of arrest, or other preliminary, provisional, or intermediate relief and use an available procedure to effect or satisfy a judgment, order, or decree; and

(B) perform any lawful act the principal could perform, including:

(i) acceptance of tender;

(ii) offer of judgment;

(iii) admission of facts;

(iv) submission of a controversy on an agreed statement of facts;

(v) consent to examination before trial; and

(vi) binding of the principal in litigation;

(4) submit to arbitration, settle, and propose or accept a compromise with respect to a claim or litigation;

(5) waive the issuance and service of process on the principal, accept service of process, appear for the principal, designate persons on whom process directed to the principal may be served, execute and file or deliver stipulations on the principal's behalf, verify pleadings, seek appellate review, procure and give surety and indemnity bonds, contract and pay for the preparation and printing of records and briefs, or receive and execute and file or deliver a consent, waiver, release, confession of judgment, satisfaction of judgment, notice, agreement, or other instrument in connection with the prosecution, settlement, or defense of a claim or litigation;

(6) act for the principal regarding voluntary or involuntary bankruptcy or insolvency proceedings concerning:

(A) the principal; or

(B) another person, with respect to a reorganization proceeding or a receivership or application for the appointment of a receiver or trustee that affects the principal's interest in property or other thing of value; and

(7) pay a judgment against the principal or a settlement made in connection with a claim or litigation and receive and conserve money or other thing of value paid in settlement of or as proceeds of a claim or litigation.

Added by Acts 2011, 82nd Leg., ch. 823 (H.B. 2759), § 1.01, eff. Jan. 1, 2014.

### § 752.111. Personal and Family Maintenance

The language conferring authority with respect to personal and family maintenance in a statutory durable power of attorney empowers the attorney in fact or agent to:

(1) perform the acts necessary to maintain the customary standard of living of the principal, the principal's spouse and children, and other individuals customarily or legally entitled to be supported by the principal, including:

(A) providing living quarters by purchase, lease, or other contract; or

(B) paying the operating costs, including interest, amortization payments, repairs, and taxes on premises owned by the principal and occupied by those individuals;

(2) provide for the individuals described by Subdivision (1):

(A) normal domestic help;

(B) usual vacations and travel expenses; and

(C) money for shelter, clothing, food, appropriate education, and other living costs;

(3) pay necessary medical, dental, and surgical care, hospitalization, and custodial care for the individuals described by Subdivision (1);

(4) continue any provision made by the principal for the individuals described by Subdivision (1) for automobiles or other means of transportation, including registering, licensing, insuring, and replacing the automobiles or other means of transportation;

(5) maintain or open charge accounts for the convenience of the individuals described by Subdivision (1) and open new accounts the attorney in fact or agent considers desirable to accomplish a lawful purpose; and

(6) continue:

(A) payments incidental to the membership or affiliation of the principal in a church, club, society, order, or other organization; or

(B) contributions to those organizations.

Added by Acts 2011, 82nd Leg., ch. 823 (H.B. 2759), § 1.01, eff. Jan. 1, 2014.

### § 752.112. Benefits From Certain Governmental Programs or Civil or Military Service

The language conferring authority with respect to benefits from social security, Medicare, Medicaid, or other governmental programs or civil or military service in a statutory durable power of attorney empowers the attorney in fact or agent to:

(1) execute a voucher in the principal's name for an allowance or reimbursement payable by the United States, a foreign government, or a state or subdivision of a state to the principal, including an allowance or reimbursement for:

(A) transportation of the individuals described by Section 752.111(1); and

(B) shipment of the household effects of those individuals;

(2) take possession and order the removal and shipment of the principal's property from a post, warehouse, depot, dock, or other governmental or private place of storage or safekeeping and execute and deliver a release, voucher, receipt, bill of lading, shipping ticket, certificate, or other instrument for that purpose;

(3) prepare, file, and prosecute a claim of the principal for a benefit or assistance, financial or

otherwise, to which the principal claims to be entitled under a statute or governmental regulation;

(4) prosecute, defend, submit to arbitration, settle, and propose or accept a compromise with respect to any benefits the principal may be entitled to receive; and

(5) receive the financial proceeds of a claim of the type described by this section and conserve, invest, disburse, or use anything received for a lawful purpose.

Added by Acts 2011, 82nd Leg., ch. 823 (H.B. 2759), § 1.01, eff. Jan. 1, 2014.

### § 752.113.  Retirement Plan Transactions

(a) In this section, "retirement plan" means:

(1) an employee pension benefit plan as defined by Section 3, Employee Retirement Income Security Act of 1974 (29 U.S.C. Section 1002), without regard to the provisions of Section (2)(B) of that section;

(2) a plan that does not meet the definition of an employee benefit plan under the Employee Retirement Income Security Act of 1974 (29 U.S.C. Section 1001 et seq.) because the plan does not cover common law employees;

(3) a plan that is similar to an employee benefit plan under the Employee Retirement Income Security Act of 1974 (29 U.S.C. Section 1001 et seq.), regardless of whether the plan is covered by Title 1 of that Act, including a plan that provides death benefits to the beneficiary of employees; and

(4) an individual retirement account or annuity, a self-employed pension plan, or a similar plan or account.

(b) The language conferring authority with respect to retirement plan transactions in a statutory durable power of attorney empowers the attorney in fact or agent to perform any lawful act the principal may perform with respect to a transaction relating to a retirement plan, including to:

(1) apply for service or disability retirement benefits;

(2) select payment options under any retirement plan in which the principal participates, including plans for self-employed individuals;

(3) designate or change the designation of a beneficiary or benefits payable by a retirement plan, except as provided by Subsection (c);

(4) make voluntary contributions to retirement plans if authorized by the plan;

(5) exercise the investment powers available under any self-directed retirement plan;

(6) make rollovers of plan benefits into other retirement plans;

(7) borrow from, sell assets to, and purchase assets from retirement plans if authorized by the plan;

(8) waive the principal's right to be a beneficiary of a joint or survivor annuity if the principal is a spouse who is not employed;

(9) receive, endorse, and cash payments from a retirement plan;

(10) waive the principal's right to receive all or a portion of benefits payable by a retirement plan; and

(11) request and receive information relating to the principal from retirement plan records.

(c) An attorney in fact or agent may be named a beneficiary under a retirement plan only to the extent the attorney in fact or agent was a named beneficiary under the retirement plan before the durable power of attorney was executed.

Added by Acts 2011, 82nd Leg., ch. 823 (H.B. 2759), § 1.01, eff. Jan. 1, 2014.

### § 752.114.  Tax Matters

The language conferring authority with respect to tax matters in a statutory durable power of attorney empowers the attorney in fact or agent to:

(1) prepare, sign, and file:

(A) federal, state, local, and foreign income, gift, payroll, Federal Insurance Contributions Act (26 U.S.C. Chapter 21), and other tax returns;

(B) claims for refunds;

(C) requests for extensions of time;

(D) petitions regarding tax matters; and

(E) any other tax-related documents, including:

(i) receipts;

(ii) offers;

(iii) waivers;

(iv) consents, including consents and agreements under Section 2032A, Internal Revenue Code of 1986 (26 U.S.C. Section 2032A);

(v) closing agreements; and

(vi) any power of attorney form required by the Internal Revenue Service or other taxing authority with respect to a tax year on which the statute of limitations has not run and 25 tax years following that tax year;

(2) pay taxes due, collect refunds, post bonds, receive confidential information, and contest deficiencies determined by the Internal Revenue Service or other taxing authority;

(3) exercise any election available to the principal under federal, state, local, or foreign tax law; and

(4) act for the principal in all tax matters, for all periods, before the Internal Revenue Service and any other taxing authority.

Added by Acts 2011, 82nd Leg., ch. 823 (H.B. 2759), § 1.01, eff. Jan. 1, 2014.

### § 752.115.  Existing Interests; Foreign Interests

The powers described by Sections 752.102–752.114 may be exercised equally with respect to an interest the principal has at the time the durable power of attorney is executed or acquires later, whether or not:

(1) the property is located in this state; or

(2) the powers are exercised or the durable power of attorney is executed in this state.

Added by Acts 2011, 82nd Leg., ch. 823 (H.B. 2759), § 1.01, eff. Jan. 1, 2014.

## TITLE 3.  GUARDIANSHIP AND RELATED PROCEDURES

## SUBTITLE A.  GENERAL PROVISIONS

### CHAPTER 1001.  PURPOSE AND CONSTRUCTION

**Section**
1001.001.    Policy; Purpose of Guardianship.
1001.002.    Laws Applicable to Guardianships.
1001.003.    References in Law Meaning Incapacitated Person.

### § 1001.001.  Policy; Purpose of Guardianship

(a) A court may appoint a guardian with either full or limited authority over an incapacitated person as indicated by the incapacitated person's actual mental or physical limitations and only as necessary to promote and protect the well-being of the incapacitated person.

(b) In creating a guardianship that gives a guardian limited authority over an incapacitated person, the court shall design the guardianship to encourage the development or maintenance of maximum self-reliance and independence in the incapacitated person.

Added by Acts 2011, 82nd Leg., ch. 823 (H.B. 2759), § 1.02, eff. Jan. 1, 2014.

### § 1001.002.  Laws Applicable to Guardianships

To the extent applicable and not inconsistent with other provisions of this code, the laws and rules governing estates of decedents apply to guardianships.

Added by Acts 2011, 82nd Leg., ch. 823 (H.B. 2759), § 1.02, eff. Jan. 1, 2014.

### § 1001.003.  References in Law Meaning Incapacitated Person

In this code or any other law, a reference to any of the following means an incapacitated person:

(1) a person who is mentally, physically, or legally incompetent;

(2) a person who is judicially declared incompetent;

(3) an incompetent or an incompetent person;

(4) a person of unsound mind; or

(5) a habitual drunkard.

Added by Acts 2011, 82nd Leg., ch. 823 (H.B. 2759), § 1.02, eff. Jan. 1, 2014.

## CHAPTER 1002.  DEFINITIONS

**Section**
1002.001.    Applicability of Definitions.
1002.002.    Attorney ad Litem.
1002.003.    Authorized Corporate Surety.
1002.004.    Child.
1002.005.    Claim.
1002.006.    Community Administrator.
1002.007.    Corporate Fiduciary.
1002.008.    Court; Probate Court; Statutory Probate Court.
1002.009.    Court Investigator.
1002.010.    Estate; Guardianship Estate.
1002.011.    Exempt Property.
1002.012.    Guardian.
1002.013.    Guardian ad Litem.
1002.014.    Guardianship Certification Board.
1002.014.    Guardianship Certification Program of the Judicial Branch Certification Commission.
1002.015.    Guardianship Proceeding.
1002.016.    Guardianship Program.
1002.016.    Guardianship Program.
1002.017.    Incapacitated Person.
1002.018.    Interested Person; Person Interested.
1002.019.    Minor.
1002.020.    Mortgage; Lien.
1002.021.    Next of Kin.
1002.022.    Parent.
1002.023.    Person.
1002.024.    Personal Property.
1002.025.    Private Professional Guardian.
1002.025.    Private Professional Guardian.
1002.026.    Proposed Ward.
1002.027.    Real Property.
1002.028.    Representative; Personal Representative.
1002.029.    Surety.

Section
1002.030. Ward.

## § 1002.001. Applicability of Definitions

The definition for a term provided by this chapter applies in this title.

Added by Acts 2011, 82nd Leg., ch. 823 (H.B. 2759), § 1.02, eff. Jan. 1, 2014.

## § 1002.002. Attorney ad Litem

"Attorney ad litem" means an attorney appointed by a court to represent and advocate on behalf of a proposed ward, an incapacitated person, an unborn person, or another person described by Section 1054.007 in a guardianship proceeding.

Added by Acts 2011, 82nd Leg., ch. 823 (H.B. 2759), § 1.02, eff. Jan. 1, 2014. Amended by Acts 2013, 83rd Leg., ch. 982 (H.B. 2080), § 1, eff. Jan. 1, 2014.

Section 36 of Acts 2013, 83rd Leg., ch. 982 (H.B. 2080) provides:

"(a) Except as otherwise provided by this section, the changes in law made by this Act apply to:

"(1) a guardianship created before, on, or after the effective date [Jan. 1, 2014] of this Act; and

"(2) an application for a guardianship pending on, or filed on or after the effective date of this Act.

"(b) The changes in law made by this Act to Sections 1301.054, 1301.055, 1301.057(b), (c), and (d), 1301.058, 1301.101, and 1301.102(a), Estates Code, apply only to an application for the creation, modification, or termination of a management trust that is filed on or after the effective date of this Act. An application described by this subsection that is filed before the effective date of this Act is governed by the law in effect on the date the application was filed, and the former law is continued in effect for that purpose.

"(c) The changes in law made by this Act to Sections 1301.103 and 1301.154(a), Estates Code, and by Section 1301.202(a–1), Estates Code, as added by this Act, apply to a management trust created before, on, or after the effective date of this Act.

"(d) The changes in law made by this Act to Section 1102.003, Estates Code, apply to a guardianship proceeding that is commenced on or after the effective date of this Act. A guardianship proceeding commenced before that date is governed by the law in effect on the date the proceeding was commenced, and the former law is continued in effect for that purpose."

Section 38 of Acts 2013, 83rd Leg., ch. 982 (H.B. 2080) provides:

"To the extent of any conflict, this Act prevails over another Act of the 83rd Legislature, Regular Session, 2013, relating to nonsubstantive additions to and corrections in enacted codes."

## § 1002.003. Authorized Corporate Surety

"Authorized corporate surety" means a domestic or foreign corporation authorized to engage in business in this state to issue surety, guaranty, or indemnity bonds that guarantee the fidelity of a guardian.

Added by Acts 2011, 82nd Leg., ch. 823 (H.B. 2759), § 1.02, eff. Jan. 1, 2014.

## § 1002.004. Child

"Child" includes a biological child and an adopted child, regardless of whether the child was adopted by a parent under a statutory procedure or by acts of estoppel.

Added by Acts 2011, 82nd Leg., ch. 823 (H.B. 2759), § 1.02, eff. Jan. 1, 2014.

## § 1002.005. Claim

"Claim" includes:

(1) a liability against the estate of an incapacitated person; and

(2) a debt due to the estate of an incapacitated person.

Added by Acts 2011, 82nd Leg., ch. 823 (H.B. 2759), § 1.02, eff. Jan. 1, 2014.

## § 1002.006. Community Administrator

"Community administrator" means a spouse who, on the judicial declaration of incapacity of the other spouse, is authorized to manage, control, and dispose of the entire community estate, including the part of the community estate the incapacitated spouse legally has the power to manage in the absence of the incapacity.

Added by Acts 2011, 82nd Leg., ch. 823 (H.B. 2759), § 1.02, eff. Jan. 1, 2014.

## § 1002.007. Corporate Fiduciary

"Corporate fiduciary" means a financial institution, as defined by Section 201. 101, Finance Code, that:

(1) is existing or engaged in business under the laws of this state, another state, or the United States;

(2) has trust powers; and

(3) is authorized by law to act under the order or appointment of a court of record, without giving bond, as guardian, receiver, trustee, executor, administrator, or, although the financial institution does not have general depository powers, depository for any money paid into the court, or to become sole guarantor or surety in or on any bond required to be given under the laws of this state.

Added by Acts 2011, 82nd Leg., ch. 823 (H.B. 2759), § 1.02, eff. Jan. 1, 2014.

## § 1002.008. Court; Probate Court; Statutory Probate Court

(a) "Court" or "probate court" means:

(1) a county court exercising its probate jurisdiction;

(2) a court created by statute and authorized to exercise original probate jurisdiction; or

(3) a district court exercising original probate jurisdiction in a contested matter.

(b) "Statutory probate court" means a court created by statute and designated as a statutory probate court under Chapter 25, Government Code. The term does not include a county court at law exercising probate jurisdiction unless the court is designated a statutory probate court under Chapter 25, Government Code.

Added by Acts 2011, 82nd Leg., ch. 823 (H.B. 2759), § 1.02, eff. Jan. 1, 2014.

### § 1002.009. Court Investigator

"Court investigator" means a person appointed by the judge of a statutory probate court under Section 25.0025, Government Code.

Added by Acts 2011, 82nd Leg., ch. 823 (H.B. 2759), § 1.02, eff. Jan. 1, 2014.

### § 1002.010. Estate; Guardianship Estate

"Estate" or "guardianship estate" means a ward's or deceased ward's property, as that property:

(1) exists originally and changes in form by sale, reinvestment, or otherwise;

(2) is augmented by any accretions and other additions to the property, including any property to be distributed to the deceased ward's representative by the trustee of a trust that terminates on the ward's death, or substitutions for the property; and

(3) is diminished by any decreases in or distributions from the property.

Added by Acts 2011, 82nd Leg., ch. 823 (H.B. 2759), § 1.02, eff. Jan. 1, 2014.

### § 1002.011. Exempt Property

"Exempt property" means the property in a deceased ward's estate that is exempt from execution or forced sale by the constitution or laws of this state, and any allowance paid instead of that property.

Added by Acts 2011, 82nd Leg., ch. 823 (H.B. 2759), § 1.02, eff. Jan. 1, 2014.

### § 1002.012. Guardian

(a) "Guardian" means a person appointed as a:

(1) guardian under Subchapter D, Chapter 1101;

(2) successor guardian; or

(3) temporary guardian.

(b) Except as expressly provided otherwise, "guardian" includes:

(1) the guardian of the estate of an incapacitated person; and

(2) the guardian of the person of an incapacitated person.

Added by Acts 2011, 82nd Leg., ch. 823 (H.B. 2759), § 1.02, eff. Jan. 1, 2014.

### § 1002.013. Guardian ad Litem

"Guardian ad litem" means a person appointed by a court to represent the best interests of an incapacitated person in a guardianship proceeding.

Added by Acts 2011, 82nd Leg., ch. 823 (H.B. 2759), § 1.02, eff. Jan. 1, 2014.

### § 1002.014. Guardianship Certification Board

*Text of section effective until Sept. 1, 2014. See, also, text of § 1002.014 effective Sept. 1, 2014.*

"Guardianship Certification Board" means the Guardianship Certification Board established under Chapter 111, Government Code.

Added by Acts 2011, 82nd Leg., ch. 823 (H.B. 2759), § 1.02, eff. Jan. 1, 2014.

### § 1002.014. Guardianship Certification Program of the Judicial Branch Certification Commission

*Text of section effective Sept. 1, 2014. See, also, text of § 1002.014 effective until Sept. 1, 2014.*

"Guardianship certification program of the Judicial Branch Certification Commission" means the program established under Chapter 155, Government Code.

Added by Acts 2011, 82nd Leg., ch. 823 (H.B. 2759), § 1.02, eff. Jan. 1, 2014. Amended by Acts 2013, 83rd Leg., ch. 42 (S.B. 966), § 2.04, eff. Sept. 1, 2014.

### § 1002.015. Guardianship Proceeding

The term "guardianship proceeding" means a matter or proceeding related to a guardianship or any other matter covered by this title, including:

(1) the appointment of a guardian of a minor or other incapacitated person, including an incapacitated adult for whom another court obtained continuing, exclusive jurisdiction in a suit affecting the parent-child relationship when the person was a child;

(2) an application, petition, or motion regarding guardianship or an alternative to guardianship under this title;

(3) a mental health action; and

(4) an application, petition, or motion regarding a trust created under Chapter 1301.

Added by Acts 2011, 82nd Leg., ch. 823 (H.B. 2759), § 1.02, eff. Jan. 1, 2014. Amended by Acts 2013, 83rd Leg., ch. 161 (S.B. 1093), § 6.014, eff. Jan. 1, 2014.

### § 1002.016. Guardianship Program

*Text of section effective until Sept. 1, 2014. See, also, text of § 1002.016 effective Sept. 1, 2014.*

"Guardianship program" has the meaning assigned by Section 111.001, Government Code.

Added by Acts 2011, 82nd Leg., ch. 823 (H.B. 2759), § 1.02, eff. Jan. 1, 2014.

### § 1002.016. Guardianship Program

*Text of section effective Sept. 1, 2014. See, also, text of § 1002.016 effective until Sept. 1, 2014.*

"Guardianship program" has the meaning assigned by Section 155.001, Government Code.

Added by Acts 2011, 82nd Leg., ch. 823 (H.B. 2759), § 1.02, eff. Jan. 1, 2014. Amended by Acts 2013, 83rd Leg., ch. 42 (S.B. 966), § 2.05, eff. Sept. 1, 2014.

### § 1002.017. Incapacitated Person

"Incapacitated person" means:

(1) a minor;

(2) an adult who, because of a physical or mental condition, is substantially unable to:

(A) provide food, clothing, or shelter for himself or herself;

(B) care for the person's own physical health; or

(C) manage the person's own financial affairs; or

(3) a person who must have a guardian appointed for the person to receive funds due the person from a governmental source.

Added by Acts 2011, 82nd Leg., ch. 823 (H.B. 2759), § 1.02, eff. Jan. 1, 2014.

### § 1002.018. Interested Person; Person Interested

"Interested person" or "person interested" means:

(1) an heir, devisee, spouse, creditor, or any other person having a property right in or claim against an estate being administered; or

(2) a person interested in the welfare of an incapacitated person.

Added by Acts 2011, 82nd Leg., ch. 823 (H.B. 2759), § 1.02, eff. Jan. 1, 2014.

### § 1002.019. Minor

"Minor" means a person younger than 18 years of age who:

(1) has never been married; and

(2) has not had the disabilities of minority removed for general purposes.

Added by Acts 2011, 82nd Leg., ch. 823 (H.B. 2759), § 1.02, eff. Jan. 1, 2014.

### § 1002.020. Mortgage; Lien

"Mortgage" and "lien" include:

(1) a deed of trust;

(2) a vendor's lien;

(3) a mechanic's, materialman's, or laborer's lien;

(4) a judgment, attachment, or garnishment lien;

(5) a federal or state tax lien;

(6) a chattel mortgage; and

(7) a pledge by hypothecation.

Added by Acts 2011, 82nd Leg., ch. 823 (H.B. 2759), § 1.02, eff. Jan. 1, 2014.

### § 1002.021. Next of Kin

"Next of kin" includes:

(1) an adopted child;

(2) an adopted child's descendants; and

(3) the adoptive parent of an adopted child.

Added by Acts 2011, 82nd Leg., ch. 823 (H.B. 2759), § 1.02, eff. Jan. 1, 2014.

### § 1002.022. Parent

"Parent" means the mother of a child, a man presumed to be the biological father of a child, a man who has been adjudicated to be the biological father of a child by a court of competent jurisdiction, or an adoptive mother or father of a child, but does not include a parent as to whom the parent-child relationship has been terminated.

Added by Acts 2011, 82nd Leg., ch. 823 (H.B. 2759), § 1.02, eff. Jan. 1, 2014.

### § 1002.023. Person

(a) "Person" includes a natural person, a corporation, and a guardianship program.

(b) The definition of "person" assigned by Section 311.005, Government Code, does not apply to any provision in this title.

Added by Acts 2011, 82nd Leg., ch. 823 (H.B. 2759), § 1.02, eff. Jan. 1, 2014.

## § 1002.024.  Personal Property

"Personal property" includes an interest in:

(1) goods;

(2) money;

(3) a chose in action;

(4) an evidence of debt;  and

(5) a real chattel.

Added by Acts 2011, 82nd Leg., ch. 823 (H.B. 2759), § 1.02, eff. Jan. 1, 2014.

## § 1002.025.  Private Professional Guardian

*Text of section effective until Sept. 1, 2014. See, also, text of § 1002.025 effective Sept. 1, 2014.*

"Private professional guardian" has the meaning assigned by Section 111.001, Government Code.

Added by Acts 2011, 82nd Leg., ch. 823 (H.B. 2759), § 1.02, eff. Jan. 1, 2014.

## § 1002.025.  Private Professional Guardian

*Text of section effective Sept. 1, 2014.  See, also, text of § 1002.025 effective until Sept. 1, 2014.*

"Private professional guardian" has the meaning assigned by Section 155.001 , Government Code.

Added by Acts 2011, 82nd Leg., ch. 823 (H.B. 2759), § 1.02, eff. Jan. 1, 2014.  Amended by Acts 2013, 83rd Leg., ch. 42 (S.B. 966), § 2.06, eff. Sept. 1, 2014.

## § 1002.026.  Proposed Ward

"Proposed ward" means a person alleged in a guardianship proceeding to be incapacitated.

Added by Acts 2011, 82nd Leg., ch. 823 (H.B. 2759), § 1.02, eff. Jan. 1, 2014.

## § 1002.027.  Real Property

"Real property" includes estates and interests in land, whether corporeal or incorporeal or legal or equitable.  The term does not include a real chattel.

Added by Acts 2011, 82nd Leg., ch. 823 (H.B. 2759), § 1.02, eff. Jan. 1, 2014.

## § 1002.028.  Representative; Personal Representative

"Representative" and "personal representative" include:

(1) a guardian;  and

(2) a successor guardian.

Added by Acts 2011, 82nd Leg., ch. 823 (H.B. 2759), § 1.02, eff. Jan. 1, 2014.

## § 1002.029.  Surety

"Surety" includes a personal surety and a corporate surety.

Added by Acts 2011, 82nd Leg., ch. 823 (H.B. 2759), § 1.02, eff. Jan. 1, 2014.

## § 1002.030.  Ward

"Ward" means a person for whom a guardian has been appointed.

Added by Acts 2011, 82nd Leg., ch. 823 (H.B. 2759), § 1.02, eff. Jan. 1, 2014.

# SUBTITLE B.  SCOPE, JURISDICTION, AND VENUE

## CHAPTER 1021.  GENERAL PROVISIONS

Section
1021.001.  Matters Related to Guardianship Proceeding.

## § 1021.001.  Matters Related to Guardianship Proceeding

(a) For purposes of this code, in a county in which there is no statutory probate court, a matter related to a guardianship proceeding includes:

(1) the granting of letters of guardianship;

(2) the settling of an account of a guardian and all other matters relating to the settlement, partition, or distribution of a ward's estate;

(3) a claim brought by or against a guardianship estate;

(4) an action for trial of title to real property that is guardianship estate property, including the enforcement of a lien against the property;

(5) an action for trial of the right of property that is guardianship estate property;

(6) after a guardianship of the estate of a ward is required to be settled as provided by Section 1204.001:

(A) an action brought by or on behalf of the former ward against a former guardian of the ward for alleged misconduct arising from the performance of the person's duties as guardian;

(B) an action calling on the surety of a guardian or former guardian to perform in place of the guardian or former guardian, which may include the award of a judgment against the guardian or former guardian in favor of the surety;

(C) an action against a former guardian of the former ward that is brought by a surety that is called on to perform in place of the former guardian;

(D) a claim for the payment of compensation, expenses, and court costs, and any other matter authorized under Chapter 1155 and Subpart H, Part 2, Subtitle Z; and

(E) a matter related to an authorization made or duty performed by a guardian under Chapter 1204; and

(7) the appointment of a trustee for a trust created under Section 1301.053 or 1301.054, the settling of an account of the trustee, and all other matters relating to the trust.

(b) For purposes of this code, in a county in which there is a statutory probate court, a matter related to a guardianship proceeding includes:

(1) all matters and actions described in Subsection (a);

(2) a suit, action, or application filed against or on behalf of a guardianship or a trustee of a trust created under Section 1301.053 or 1301.054; and

(3) a cause of action in which a guardian in a guardianship pending in the statutory probate court is a party.

Added by Acts 2013, 83rd Leg., ch. 161 (S.B. 1093), § 6.015(a), eff. Jan. 1, 2014.

## CHAPTER 1022. JURISDICTION

## § 1022.001. General Probate Court Jurisdiction in Guardianship Proceedings; Appeals

(a) All guardianship proceedings must be filed and heard in a court exercising original probate jurisdiction. The court exercising original probate jurisdiction also has jurisdiction of all matters related to the guardianship proceeding as specified in Section 1021.001 for that type of court.

(b) A probate court may exercise pendent and ancillary jurisdiction as necessary to promote judicial efficiency and economy.

(c) A final order issued by a probate court is appealable to the court of appeals.

Added by Acts 2013, 83rd Leg., ch. 161 (S.B. 1093), § 6.015(a), eff. Jan. 1, 2014.

## § 1022.002. Original Jurisdiction for Guardianship Proceedings

(a) In a county in which there is no statutory probate court or county court at law exercising original probate jurisdiction, the county court has original jurisdiction of guardianship proceedings.

(b) In a county in which there is no statutory probate court, but in which there is a county court at law exercising original probate jurisdiction, the county court at law exercising original probate jurisdiction and the county court have concurrent original jurisdiction of guardianship proceedings, unless otherwise provided by law. The judge of a county court may hear guardianship proceedings while sitting for the judge of any other county court.

(c) In a county in which there is a statutory probate court, the statutory probate court has original jurisdiction of guardianship proceedings.

(d) From the filing of the application for the appointment of a guardian of the estate or person, or both, until the guardianship is settled and closed under this chapter, the administration of the estate of a minor or other incapacitated person is one proceeding for purposes of jurisdiction and is a proceeding in rem.

Added by Acts 2013, 83rd Leg., ch. 161 (S.B. 1093), § 6.015(a), eff. Jan. 1, 2014. Amended by Acts 2013, 83rd Leg., ch. 982 (H.B. 2080), § 2(a), eff. Jan. 1, 2014.

Section 2(b) of Acts 2013, 83rd Leg., ch. 982 (H.B. 2080) provides in part that the transfer and redesignation of Section 604, Texas Probate Code, to subsection (d) of this section is effective "notwithstanding the transfer of Section 604, Texas Probate Code, to the Estates Code and redesignation as Section 604 of that code effective January 1, 2014, by Section 3.01(a), Chapter 823 (H.B. 2759), Acts of the 82nd Legislature, Regular Session, 2011". Section 2(b) of Acts 2013, 83rd Leg., ch. 982 (H.B. 2080) provides:

"(b) This section takes effect only if H.B. 3862 or S.B. 1093, 83rd Legislature, Regular Session, 2013, is enacted and becomes law and adds Section 1022.002, Estates Code. If that legislation does not become law, or becomes law but does not add that section, this section has no effect."

S.B. 1093, 83rd Legislature, Regular Session, 2013, was enacted and became law as Chapter 161. Section 6.015(a) of Chapter 161 added Section 1022.002, Estates Code.

Section 36 of Acts 2013, 83rd Leg., ch. 982 (H.B. 2080) provides:

"(a) Except as otherwise provided by this section, the changes in law made by this Act apply to:

"(1) a guardianship created before, on, or after the effective date [Jan. 1, 2014] of this Act; and

"(2) an application for a guardianship pending on, or filed on or after, the effective date of this Act.

"(b) The changes in law made by this Act to Sections 1301.054, 1301.055, 1301.057(b), (c), and (d), 1301.058, 1301.101, and 1301.102(a), Estates Code, apply only to an application for the creation, modification, or termination of a management trust that is filed on or after the effective date of this Act. An application described by this subsection that is filed before the effective date of this Act is governed by the law in effect on the date the application was filed, and the former law is continued in effect for that purpose.

"(c) The changes in law made by this Act to Sections 1301.103 and 1301.154(a), Estates Code, and by Section 1301.202(a-1), Estates Code, as added by this Act, apply to a management trust created before, on, or after the effective date of this Act.

"(d) The changes in law made by this Act to Section 1102.003, Estates Code, apply to a guardianship proceeding that is commenced on or after the effective date of this Act. A guardianship proceeding commenced before that date is governed by the law in effect on the date the proceeding was commenced, and the former law is continued in effect for that purpose."

## § 1022.003. Jurisdiction of Contested Guardianship Proceeding in County With No Statutory Probate Court or County Court at Law

(a) In a county in which there is no statutory probate court or county court at law exercising original probate jurisdiction, when a matter in a guardianship proceeding is contested, the judge of the county court may, on the judge's own motion, or shall, on the motion of any party to the proceeding, according to the motion:

(1) request the assignment of a statutory probate court judge to hear the contested matter, as provided by Section 25.0022, Government Code; or

(2) transfer the contested matter to the district court, which may then hear the contested matter as if originally filed in the district court.

(b) If a party to a guardianship proceeding files a motion for the assignment of a statutory probate court judge to hear a contested matter in the proceeding before the judge of the county court transfers the contested matter to a district court under this section, the county judge shall grant the motion for the assignment of a statutory probate court judge and may not transfer the matter to the district court unless the party withdraws the motion.

(c) If a judge of a county court requests the assignment of a statutory probate court judge to hear a contested matter in a guardianship proceeding on the judge's own motion or on the motion of a party to the proceeding as provided by this section, the judge may request that the statutory probate court judge be assigned to the entire proceeding on the judge's own motion or on the motion of a party.

(d) A party to a guardianship proceeding may file a motion for the assignment of a statutory probate court judge under this section before a matter in the proceeding becomes contested, and the motion is given effect as a motion for assignment of a statutory probate court judge under Subsection (a) if the matter later becomes contested.

(e) Notwithstanding any other law, a transfer of a contested matter in a guardianship proceeding to a district court under any authority other than the authority provided by this section:

(1) is disregarded for purposes of this section; and

(2) does not defeat the right of a party to the proceeding to have the matter assigned to a statutory probate court judge in accordance with this section.

(f) A statutory probate court judge assigned to a contested matter in a guardianship proceeding or to the entire proceeding under this section has the jurisdiction and authority granted to a statutory probate court by this code. A statutory probate court judge assigned to hear only the contested matter in a guardianship proceeding shall, on resolution of the matter, including any appeal of the matter, return the matter to the county court for further proceedings not inconsistent with the orders of the statutory probate court or court of appeals, as applicable. A statutory probate court judge assigned to the entire guardianship proceeding as provided by Subsection (c) shall, on resolution of the contested matter in the proceeding, including any appeal of the matter, return the entire proceeding to the county court for further proceedings not inconsistent with the orders of the statutory probate court or court of appeals, as applicable.

(g) A district court to which a contested matter in a guardianship proceeding is transferred under this section has the jurisdiction and authority granted to a statutory probate court by this code. On resolution of a contested matter transferred to the district court under this section, including any appeal of the matter, the district court shall return the matter to the county court for further proceedings not inconsistent with the orders of the district court or court of appeals, as applicable.

(h) If only the contested matter in a guardianship proceeding is assigned to a statutory probate court judge under this section, or if the contested matter in a guardianship proceeding is transferred to a district court under this section, the county court shall continue to exercise jurisdiction over the management of the guardianship, other than a contested matter, until final disposition of the contested matter is made in accordance with this section. Any matter related to a guardianship proceeding in which a contested matter is transferred to a district court may be brought in the district court. The district court in which a matter related to the proceeding is filed may, on the court's own motion or on the motion of any party, find that the matter is not a contested matter and transfer the matter to the county court with jurisdiction of the management of the guardianship.

(i) If a contested matter in a guardianship proceeding is transferred to a district court under this section, the district court has jurisdiction of any contested matter in the proceeding that is subsequently filed, and the county court shall transfer those contested matters to the district court. If a statutory probate court judge is assigned under this section to hear a contested matter in a guardianship proceeding, the statutory probate court judge shall be assigned to hear any contested matter in the proceeding that is subsequently filed.

(j) The clerk of a district court to which a contested matter in a guardianship proceeding is transferred under this section may perform in relation to the transferred matter any function a county clerk may perform with respect to that type of matter.

Added by Acts 2013, 83rd Leg., ch. 161 (S.B. 1093), § 6.015(a), eff. Jan. 1, 2014.

## § 1022.004. Jurisdiction of Contested Guardianship Proceeding in County With no Statutory Probate Court

(a) In a county in which there is no statutory probate court, but in which there is a county court at law exercising original probate jurisdiction, when a matter in a guardianship proceeding is contested, the judge of the county court may, on the judge's own motion, or shall, on the motion of any party to the proceeding, transfer the contested matter to the coun-

ty court at law. In addition, the judge of the county court, on the judge's own motion or on the motion of a party to the proceeding, may transfer the entire proceeding to the county court at law.

(b) A county court at law to which a proceeding is transferred under this section may hear the proceeding as if originally filed in that court. If only a contested matter in the proceeding is transferred, on the resolution of the matter, the matter shall be returned to the county court for further proceedings not inconsistent with the orders of the county court at law.

Added by Acts 2013, 83rd Leg., ch. 161 (S.B. 1093), § 6.015(a), eff. Jan. 1, 2014.

## § 1022.005. Exclusive Jurisdiction of Guardianship Proceeding in County With Statutory Probate Court

(a) In a county in which there is a statutory probate court, the statutory probate court has exclusive jurisdiction of all guardianship proceedings, regardless of whether contested or uncontested.

(b) A cause of action related to a guardianship proceeding of which the statutory probate court has exclusive jurisdiction as provided by Subsection (a) must be brought in the statutory probate court unless the jurisdiction of the statutory probate court is concurrent with the jurisdiction of a district court as provided by Section 1022.006 or with the jurisdiction of any other court.

Added by Acts 2013, 83rd Leg., ch. 161 (S.B. 1093), § 6.015(a), eff. Jan. 1, 2014.

## § 1022.006. Concurrent Jurisdiction with District Court

A statutory probate court has concurrent jurisdiction with the district court in:

(1) a personal injury, survival, or wrongful death action by or against a person in the person's capacity as a guardian; and

(2) an action involving a guardian in which each other party aligned with the guardian is not an interested person in the guardianship.

Added by Acts 2013, 83rd Leg., ch. 161 (S.B. 1093), § 6.015(a), eff. Jan. 1, 2014.

## § 1022.007. Transfer of Proceeding by Statutory Probate Court

(a) A judge of a statutory probate court, on the motion of a party to the action or of a person interested in the guardianship, may:

(1) transfer to the judge's court from a district, county, or statutory court a cause of action that is a matter related to a guardianship proceeding pending in the statutory probate court, including a cause of action that is a matter related to a guardianship proceeding pending in the statutory probate court and in which the guardian, ward, or proposed ward in the pending guardianship proceeding is a party; and

(2) consolidate the transferred cause of action with the guardianship proceeding to which it relates and any other proceedings in the statutory probate court that are related to the guardianship proceeding.

(b) Notwithstanding any other provision of this title, the proper venue for an action by or against a guardian, ward, or proposed ward for personal injury, death, or property damages is determined under Section 15.007, Civil Practice and Remedies Code.

Added by Acts 2013, 83rd Leg., ch. 161 (S.B. 1093), § 6.015(a), eff. Jan. 1, 2014.

### § 1022.008.   Transfer of Contested Guardianship of the Person of a Minor

(a) If an interested person contests an application for the appointment of a guardian of the person of a minor or an interested person seeks the removal of a guardian of the person of a minor, the judge, on the judge's own motion, may transfer all matters related to the guardianship proceeding to a court of competent jurisdiction in which a suit affecting the parent-child relationship under the Family Code is pending.

(b) The probate court that transfers a proceeding under this section to a court with proper jurisdiction over suits affecting the parent-child relationship shall send to the court to which the transfer is made the complete files in all matters affecting the guardianship of the person of the minor and certified copies of all entries in the judge's guardianship docket. The transferring court shall keep a copy of the transferred files. If the transferring court retains jurisdiction of the guardianship of the estate of the minor or of another minor who was the subject of the suit, the court shall send a copy of the complete files to the court to which the transfer is made and shall keep the original files.

(c) The court to which a transfer is made under this section shall apply the procedural and substantive provisions of the Family Code, including Sections 155.005 and 155.205, in regard to enforcing an order rendered by the court from which the proceeding was transferred.

Added by Acts 1993, 73rd Leg., ch. 957, § 1, eff. Sept. 1, 1993. Amended by Acts 1997, 75th Leg., ch. 77, § 1, eff. Sept. 1, 1997; Acts 1997, 75th Leg., ch. 165, § 7.55, eff. Sept. 1, 1997; Acts 2009, 81st Leg., ch. 602, § 12, eff. June 19, 2009; Acts 2011, 82nd Leg., ch. 1085 (S.B. 1196), §§ 5, 6, eff. Sept. 1, 2011. Added by and redesignated from V.A.T.S. Probate Code, § 609(b), (c) by Acts 2013, 83rd Leg., ch. 161 (S.B.1093), § 6.015(a), (b), eff. Jan. 1, 2014.

## CHAPTER 1023.   VENUE

### § 1023.001.   Venue for Appointment of Guardian

(a) Except as otherwise authorized by this section, a proceeding for the appointment of a guardian for the person or estate, or both, of an incapacitated person shall be brought in the county in which the proposed ward resides or is located on the date the application is filed or in the county in which the principal estate of the proposed ward is located.

(b) A proceeding for the appointment of a guardian for the person or estate, or both, of a minor may be brought:

(1) in the county in which both the minor's parents reside;

(2) if the parents do not reside in the same county, in the county in which the parent who is the sole managing conservator of the minor resides, or in the county in which the parent who is the joint managing conservator with the greater period of physical possession of and access to the minor resides;

(3) if only one parent is living and the parent has custody of the minor, in the county in which that parent resides;

(4) if both parents are dead but the minor was in the custody of a deceased parent, in the county in which the last surviving parent having custody resided; or

(5) if both parents of a minor child have died in a common disaster and there is no evidence that the parents died other than simultaneously, in the county in which both deceased parents resided at the time of their simultaneous deaths if they resided in the same county.

(c) A proceeding for the appointment of a guardian who was appointed by will may be brought in the county in which the will was admitted to probate or in the county of the appointee's residence if the appointee resides in this state.

Added by Acts 1993, 73rd Leg., ch. 957, § 1, eff. Sept. 1, 1993. Amended by Acts 1999, 76th Leg., ch. 379, § 10, eff. Sept. 1, 1999. Redesignated from V.A.T.S. Probate Code, § 610 by Acts 2013, 83rd Leg., ch. 161 (S.B. 1093), § 6.015(c), eff. Jan. 1, 2014.

### § 1023.002. Concurrent Venue and Transfer for Want of Venue

(a) If two or more courts have concurrent venue of a guardianship proceeding, the court in which an application for a guardianship proceeding is initially filed has and retains jurisdiction of the proceeding. A proceeding is considered commenced by the filing of an application alleging facts sufficient to confer venue, and the proceeding initially legally commenced extends to all of the property of the guardianship estate.

(b) If a guardianship proceeding is commenced in more than one county, it shall be stayed except in the county in which it was initially commenced until final determination of proper venue is made by the court in the county in which it was initially commenced.

(c) If it appears to the court at any time before the guardianship is closed that the proceeding was commenced in a court that did not have venue over the proceeding, the court shall, on the application of any interested person, transfer the proceeding to the proper county.

(d) When a proceeding is transferred to another county under a provision of this chapter, all orders entered in connection with the proceeding shall be valid and shall be recognized in the court to which the guardianship was ordered transferred, if the orders were made and entered in conformance with the procedures prescribed by this code.

Added by Acts 1993, 73rd Leg., ch. 957, § 1, eff. Sept. 1, 1993. Amended by Acts 2011, 82nd Leg., ch. 1085 (S.B. 1196), § 7, eff. Sept. 1, 2011. Added by and redesignated from V.A.T.S. Probate Code, § 611(b) to (d) by Acts 2013, 83rd Leg., ch. 161 (S.B.1093), § 6.015(a), (d), eff. Jan. 1, 2014.

### § 1023.003. Application for Transfer of Guardianship to Another County

When a guardian or any other person desires to transfer the transaction of the business of the guardianship from one county to another, the person shall file a written application in the court in which the guardianship is pending stating the reason for the transfer.

Added by Acts 2013, 83rd Leg., ch. 161 (S.B. 1093), § 6.015(a), eff. Jan. 1, 2014.

### § 1023.004. Notice

(a) On filing an application to transfer a guardianship to another county, the sureties on the bond of the guardian shall be cited by personal service to appear and show cause why the application should not be granted.

(b) If an application is filed by a person other than the guardian, the guardian shall be cited by personal service to appear and show cause why the application should not be granted.

Added by Acts 1993, 73rd Leg., ch. 957, § 1, eff. Sept. 1, 1993. Amended by Acts 2011, 82nd Leg., 1st C.S., ch. 4 (S.B. 1), § 66.02, eff. Sept. 28, 2011. Added by and redesignated from V.A.T.S. Probate Code, §613(b) by Acts 2013, 83rd Leg., ch. 161 (S.B. 1093), § 6.015(a), (e), eff. Jan. 1, 2014.

### § 1023.005. Court Action

(a) On hearing an application under Section 1023.003, if good cause is not shown to deny the application and it appears that transfer of the guardianship is in the best interests of the ward, the court shall enter an order authorizing the transfer on payment on behalf of the estate of all accrued costs.

(b) In an order entered under Subsection (a), the court shall require the guardian, not later than the 20th day after the date the order is entered, to:

(1) give a new bond payable to the judge of the court to which the guardianship is transferred; or

(2) file a rider to an existing bond noting the court to which the guardianship is transferred.

Added by Acts 2013, 83rd Leg., ch. 161 (S.B. 1093), § 6.015(a), eff. Jan. 1, 2014.

### § 1023.006. Transfer of Record

When an order of transfer is made under Section 1023.005, the clerk shall record any unrecorded papers of the guardianship required to be recorded. On payment of the clerk's fee, the clerk shall transmit to the county clerk of the county to which the guardianship was ordered transferred:

(1) the case file of the guardianship proceedings; and

(2) a certified copy of the index of the guardianship records.

Added by Acts 2013, 83rd Leg., ch. 161 (S.B. 1093), § 6.015(a), eff. Jan. 1, 2014.

### § 1023.007.  Transfer Effective

The order transferring a guardianship does not take effect until:

(1) the case file and a certified copy of the index required by Section 1023.006 are filed in the office of the county clerk of the county to which the guardianship was ordered transferred; and

(2) a certificate under the clerk's official seal and reporting the filing of the case file and a certified copy of the index is filed in the court ordering the transfer by the county clerk of the county to which the guardianship was ordered transferred.

Added by Acts 2013, 83rd Leg., ch. 161 (S.B. 1093), § 6.015(a), eff. Jan. 1, 2014.

### § 1023.008.  Continuation of Guardianship

When a guardianship is transferred from one county to another in accordance with this chapter, the guardianship proceeds in the court to which it was transferred as if it had been originally commenced in that court.  It is not necessary to record in the receiving court any of the papers in the case that were recorded in the court from which the case was transferred.

Added by Acts 2013, 83rd Leg., ch. 161 (S.B. 1093), § 6.015(a), eff. Jan. 1, 2014.

### § 1023.009.  New Guardian Appointed on Transfer

If it appears to the court that transfer of the guardianship is in the best interests of the ward, but that because of the transfer it is not in the best interests of the ward for the guardian of the estate to continue to serve in that capacity, the court may in its order of transfer revoke the letters of guardianship and appoint a new guardian, and the former guardian shall account for and deliver the estate as provided by this title in a case in which a guardian resigns.

Added by Acts 2013, 83rd Leg., ch. 161 (S.B. 1093), § 6.015(a), eff. Jan. 1, 2014.

### § 1023.010.  Review of Transferred Guardianship

Not later than the 90th day after the date the transfer of the guardianship takes effect under Section 1023.007, the court to which the guardianship was transferred shall hold a hearing to consider modifying the rights, duties, and powers of the guardian or any other provisions of the transferred guardianship.

Added by Acts 2013, 83rd Leg., ch. 161 (S.B. 1093), § 6.015(a), eff. Jan. 1, 2014.

## SUBTITLE C.  PROCEDURAL MATTERS

## CHAPTER 1051.  NOTICES AND PROCESS IN GUARDIANSHIP PROCEEDINGS IN GENERAL

### SUBCHAPTER A.  ISSUANCE AND FORM OF NOTICE OR PROCESS

### SUBCHAPTER B.  METHODS OF SERVING CITATION OR NOTICE; PERSONS TO BE SERVED

### SUBCHAPTER C.  NOTICE AND CITATION REQUIRED FOR APPLICATION FOR GUARDIANSHIP

### SUBCHAPTER D.  RETURN AND PROOF OF SERVICE OF CITATION OR NOTICE

### SUBCHAPTER E.  ALTERNATIVE MANNER OF ISSUANCE, SERVICE, AND RETURN

### SUBCHAPTER F.  ADDITIONAL NOTICE PROVISIONS

## SUBCHAPTER A.  ISSUANCE AND FORM OF NOTICE OR PROCESS

### § 1051.001.  Issuance of Notice or Process in General

(a) Except as provided by Subsection (b), a person is not required to be cited or otherwise given notice in a guardianship proceeding except in a situation in which this title expressly provides for citation or the giving of notice.

(b) If this title does not expressly provide for citation or the issuance or return of notice in a guardianship proceeding, the court may require that notice be given.  A court that requires that notice be given shall prescribe the form and manner of service of the notice and the return of service.

(c) Unless a court order is required by this title, the county clerk without a court order shall issue:

(1) necessary citations, writs, and other process in a guardianship proceeding ;  and

(2) all notices not required to be issued by a guardian.

Added by Acts 2011, 82nd Leg., ch. 823 (H.B. 2759), § 1.02, eff. Jan. 1, 2014.  Amended by Acts 2013, 83rd Leg., ch. 161 (S.B. 1093), § 6.016, eff. Jan. 1, 2014.

### § 1051.002.  Direction of Writ or Other Process

(a) A writ or other process other than a citation or notice must be directed "To any sheriff or constable within the State of Texas."

(b) Notwithstanding Subsection (a), a writ or other process other than a citation or notice may not be held defective because the process is directed to the sheriff or a constable of a named county if the process is properly served within that county by an officer authorized to serve the process.

Added by Acts 2011, 82nd Leg., ch. 823 (H.B. 2759), § 1.02, eff. Jan. 1, 2014.

### § 1051.003.  Contents of Citation or Notice

(a) A citation or notice must:

(1) be directed to the person to be cited or notified;

(2) be dated;

(3) state the style and number of the proceeding;

(4) state the court in which the proceeding is pending;

(5) describe generally the nature of the proceeding or matter to which the citation or notice relates;

(6) direct the person being cited or notified to appear by filing a written contest or answer or to perform another required action;  and

(7) state when and where the appearance or performance described by Subdivision (6) is required.

(b) A citation or notice issued by the county clerk must be styled "The State of Texas" and be signed by the clerk under the clerk's seal.

(c) A notice required to be given by a guardian must be in writing and be signed by the guardian in the guardian's official capacity.

(d) A citation or notice is not required to contain a precept directed to an officer, but may not be held defective because the citation or notice contains a precept directed to an officer authorized to serve the citation or notice.

Added by Acts 2011, 82nd Leg., ch. 823 (H.B. 2759), § 1.02, eff. Jan. 1, 2014.

## SUBCHAPTER B.  METHODS OF SERVING CITATION OR NOTICE; PERSONS TO BE SERVED

### § 1051.051.  Personal Service

(a) Except as otherwise provided by Subsection (b), if personal service of citation or notice is required, the citation or notice must be served on the attorney of record for the person to be cited or notified.  Notwithstanding the requirement of personal service, service may be made on that attorney by any method specified by Section 1051.055 for service on an attorney of record.

(b) If the person to be cited or notified does not have an attorney of record in the proceeding, or if an attempt to serve the person's attorney is unsuccessful:

(1) the sheriff or constable shall serve the citation or notice by delivering a copy of the citation or notice to the person to be cited or notified, in person, if the person to whom the citation or notice is directed is in this state; or

(2) a disinterested person competent to make an oath that the citation or notice was served may serve the citation or notice, if the person to be cited or notified is absent from or is not a resident of this state.

(c) The return day of the citation or notice served under Subsection (b) must be at least 10 days after the date of service, excluding the date of service.

(d) If the citation or notice attempted to be served as provided by Subsection (b) is returned with the notation that the person sought to be served, whether inside or outside this state, cannot be found, the county clerk shall issue a new citation or notice. Service of the new citation or notice must be made by publication.

Added by Acts 2011, 82nd Leg., ch. 823 (H.B. 2759), § 1.02, eff. Jan. 1, 2014.

### § 1051.052.　Service by Mail

(a) The county clerk, or the guardian if required by statute or court order, shall serve a citation or notice required or permitted to be served by regular mail by mailing the original citation or notice to the person to be cited or notified.

(b) Except as provided by Subsection (c), the county clerk shall issue a citation or notice required or permitted to be served by registered or certified mail and shall serve the citation or notice by mailing the original citation or notice by registered or certified mail.

(c) A guardian shall issue a notice required to be given by the guardian by registered or certified mail and shall serve the notice by mailing the original notice by registered or certified mail.

(d) The county clerk or guardian, as applicable, shall mail a citation or notice under Subsection (b) or (c) with an instruction to deliver the citation or notice to the addressee only and with return receipt requested. The clerk or guardian, as applicable, shall address the envelope containing the citation or notice to:

(1) the attorney of record in the proceeding for the person to be cited or notified; or

(2) the person to be cited or notified, if the citation or notice to the attorney is returned undelivered or the person to be cited or notified has no attorney of record in the proceeding.

(e) Service by mail must be made at least 20 days before the return day of the citation or notice, excluding the date of service. The date of service by mail is the date of mailing.

(f) A copy of a citation or notice served under Subsection (a), (b), or (c) and a certificate of the person serving the citation or notice showing that the citation or notice was mailed and the date of the mailing shall be filed and recorded. A returned receipt for a citation or notice served under Subsection (b) or (c) shall be attached to the certificate.

(g) If a citation or notice served by mail is returned undelivered, a new citation or notice shall be issued. Service of the new citation or notice must be made by posting.

Added by Acts 2011, 82nd Leg., ch. 823 (H.B. 2759), § 1.02, eff. Jan. 1, 2014.

### § 1051.053.　Service by Posting

(a) The county clerk shall deliver the original and a copy of a citation or notice required to be posted to the sheriff or a constable of the county in which the proceeding is pending. The sheriff or constable shall post the copy at the door of the county courthouse or the location in or near the courthouse where public notices are customarily posted.

(b) Citation or notice under this section must be posted for at least 10 days before the return day of the citation or notice, excluding the date of posting, except as provided by Section 1051.152(b). The date of service of citation or notice by posting is the date of posting.

(c) A sheriff or constable who posts a copy of a citation or notice under this section shall return the original citation or notice to the county clerk and state the date and location of the posting in a written return of the copy of the citation or notice.

(d) The method of service prescribed by this section applies when a guardian is required or permitted to post a notice. The notice must be:

(1) issued in the name of the guardian;

(2) addressed and delivered to, and posted and returned by, the appropriate officer; and

(3) filed with the county clerk.

Added by Acts 2011, 82nd Leg., ch. 823 (H.B. 2759), § 1.02, eff. Jan. 1, 2014.

### § 1051.054.　Service by Publication

(a) Citation or notice to a person to be served by publication shall be published one time in a newspaper of general circulation in the county in which the proceeding is pending. The publication must be made at least 10 days before the return day of the citation or notice, excluding the date of publication.

(b) The date of service of citation or notice by publication is the date of publication printed on the newspaper in which the citation or notice is published.

(c) If there is not a newspaper of general circulation published or printed in the county in which the citation or notice is to be published, the citation or notice under Subsection (a) shall be served by posting.

Added by Acts 2011, 82nd Leg., ch. 823 (H.B. 2759), § 1.02, eff. Jan. 1, 2014.

### § 1051.055. Service on Party's Attorney of Record

(a) If a party is represented by an attorney of record in a guardianship proceeding, a citation or notice required to be served on the party shall be served instead on that attorney.

(b) A notice served on an attorney under this section may be served by:

(1) delivery to the attorney in person;

(2) registered or certified mail, return receipt requested; or

(3) any other form of mail that requires proof of delivery.

(c) A notice or citation may be served on an attorney under this section by:

(1) another party to the proceeding;

(2) the attorney of record for another party to the proceeding;

(3) an appropriate sheriff or constable; or

(4) another person competent to testify.

(d) Each of the following is prima facie evidence of the fact that service has been made under this section:

(1) the written statement of an attorney of record showing service;

(2) the return of the officer showing service; and

(3) the affidavit of a person showing service.

(e) Except as provided by Section 1051.105, an attorney ad litem may not waive personal service of citation.

Added by Acts 2011, 82nd Leg., ch. 823 (H.B. 2759), § 1.02, eff. Jan. 1, 2014.

### § 1051.056. Service on Guardian or Receiver

Unless this title expressly provides for another method of service, the county clerk who issues a citation or notice required to be served on a guardian or receiver shall serve the citation or notice by mailing the original citation or notice by registered or certified mail to:

(1) the guardian's or receiver's attorney of record; or

(2) the guardian or receiver, if the guardian or receiver does not have an attorney of record.

Added by Acts 2011, 82nd Leg., ch. 823 (H.B. 2759), § 1.02, eff. Jan. 1, 2014.

## SUBCHAPTER C. NOTICE AND CITATION REQUIRED FOR APPLICATION FOR GUARDIANSHIP

### § 1051.101. Notice Required for Application for Guardianship; Citation of Applicant Not Required

(a) On the filing of an application for guardianship, notice shall be issued and served as provided by this subchapter.

(b) It is not necessary to serve a citation on a person who files an application for the creation of a guardianship under this title or for that person to waive the issuance and personal service of citation under this subchapter.

Added by Acts 2011, 82nd Leg., ch. 823 (H.B. 2759), § 1.02, eff. Jan. 1, 2014.

### § 1051.102. Issuance of Citation for Application for Guardianship

(a) On the filing of an application for guardianship, the court clerk shall issue a citation stating:

(1) that the application was filed;

(2) the name of the proposed ward;

(3) the name of the applicant; and

(4) the name of the person to be appointed guardian as provided in the application, if that person is not the applicant.

(b) The citation must cite all persons interested in the welfare of the proposed ward to appear at the time and place stated in the notice if the persons wish to contest the application.

(c) The citation shall be posted.

(d) The citation must contain a clear and conspicuous statement informing those interested persons of the right provided under Section 1051.252 to be notified of any or all motions, applications, or pleadings relating to the application for the guardianship or any subsequent guardianship proceeding involving the ward after the guardianship is created, if any.

Added by Acts 2011, 82nd Leg., ch. 823 (H.B. 2759), § 1.02, eff. Jan. 1, 2014. Amended by Acts 2013, 83rd Leg., ch. 161 (S.B. 1093), § 6.017, eff. Jan. 1, 2014.

## § 1051.103. Service of Citation for Application for Guardianship

(a) The sheriff or other officer shall personally serve citation to appear and answer an application for guardianship on:

(1) a proposed ward who is 12 years of age or older;

(2) the proposed ward's parents, if the whereabouts of the parents are known or can be reasonably ascertained;

(3) any court-appointed conservator or person having control of the care and welfare of the proposed ward;

(4) the proposed ward's spouse, if the whereabouts of the spouse are known or can be reasonably ascertained; and

(5) the person named in the application to be appointed guardian, if that person is not the applicant.

(b) A citation served as provided by Subsection (a) must contain the statement regarding the right under Section 1051.252 that is required in the citation issued under Section 1051.102.

Added by Acts 2011, 82nd Leg., ch. 823 (H.B. 2759), § 1.02, eff. Jan. 1, 2014. Amended by Acts 2013, 83rd Leg., ch. 161 (S.B. 1093), § 6.018, eff. Jan. 1, 2014.

## § 1051.104. Notice by Applicant for Guardianship

(a) The person filing an application for guardianship shall mail a copy of the application and a notice containing the information required in the citation issued under Section 1051.102 by registered or certified mail, return receipt requested, or by any other form of mail that provides proof of delivery, to the following persons, if their whereabouts are known or can be reasonably ascertained:

(1) each adult child of the proposed ward;

(2) each adult sibling of the proposed ward;

(3) the administrator of a nursing home facility or similar facility in which the proposed ward resides;

(4) the operator of a residential facility in which the proposed ward resides;

(5) a person whom the applicant knows to hold a power of attorney signed by the proposed ward;

(6) a person designated to serve as guardian of the proposed ward by a written declaration under Subchapter E, Chapter 1104, if the applicant knows of the existence of the declaration;

(7) a person designated to serve as guardian of the proposed ward in the probated will of the last surviving parent of the proposed ward;

(8) a person designated to serve as guardian of the proposed ward by a written declaration of the proposed ward's last surviving parent, if the declarant is deceased and the applicant knows of the existence of the declaration; and

(9) each person named as another relative within the third degree by consanguinity in the application as required by Section 1101.001(b)(11) or (13) if the proposed ward's spouse and each of the proposed ward's parents, adult siblings, and adult children are deceased or there is no spouse, parent, adult sibling, or adult child.

(b) The applicant shall file with the court:

(1) a copy of any notice required by Subsection (a) and the proofs of delivery of the notice; and

(2) an affidavit sworn to by the applicant or the applicant's attorney stating:

(A) that the notice was mailed as required by Subsection (a); and

(B) the name of each person to whom the notice was mailed, if the person's name is not shown on the proof of delivery.

(c) Failure of the applicant to comply with Subsections (a)(2)–(9) does not affect the validity of a guardianship created under this title.

Added by Acts 2011, 82nd Leg., ch. 823 (H.B. 2759), § 1.02, eff. Jan. 1, 2014. Amended by Acts 2013, 83rd Leg., ch. 161 (S.B. 1093), § 6.019, eff. Jan. 1, 2014.

## § 1051.105. Waiver of Notice of Application for Guardianship

A person other than the proposed ward who is entitled to receive notice or personal service of citation under Sections 1051.103 and 1051.104(a) may, by writing filed with the clerk, waive the receipt of notice or the issuance and personal service of citation either in person or through an attorney ad litem.

Added by Acts 2011, 82nd Leg., ch. 823 (H.B. 2759), § 1.02, eff. Jan. 1, 2014.

## § 1051.106. Action by Court on Application for Guardianship

The court may not act on an application for the creation of a guardianship until the applicant has complied with Section 1051.104(b) and not earlier than the Monday following the expiration of the 10–day period beginning on the date service of notice and citation has been made as provided by Sections 1051.102, 1051.103, and 1051.104(a)(1).

Added by Acts 2011, 82nd Leg., ch. 823 (H.B. 2759), § 1.02, eff. Jan. 1, 2014.

## SUBCHAPTER D.  RETURN AND PROOF OF SERVICE OF CITATION OR NOTICE

### § 1051.151.  Requirements for Return on Citation or Notice Served by Personal Service

The return of the person serving a citation or notice under Section 1051.051 must:

(1) be endorsed on or attached to the citation or notice;

(2) state the date and place of service;

(3) certify that a copy of the citation or notice was delivered to the person directed to be served;

(4) be subscribed and sworn to before, and under the hand and official seal of, an officer authorized by the laws of this state to take an affidavit; and

(5) be returned to the county clerk who issued the citation or notice.

Added by Acts 2011, 82nd Leg., ch. 823 (H.B. 2759), § 1.02, eff. Jan. 1, 2014.

### § 1051.152.  Validity of Service and Return on Citation or Notice Served by Posting

(a) A citation or notice in a guardianship proceeding that is required to be served by posting and is issued in conformity with this title, and the service of and return of the citation or notice, is valid if:

(1) a sheriff or constable posts a copy of the citation or notice at the location or locations prescribed by this title; and

(2) the posting occurs on a day preceding the return day of service specified in the citation or notice that provides sufficient time for the period the citation or notice must be posted to expire before the specified return day.

(b) The fact that the sheriff or constable, as applicable, makes the return of service on the citation or notice described by Subsection (a) and returns the citation or notice on which the return has been made to the court before the expiration of the period the citation or notice must be posted does not affect the validity of the citation or notice or the service or return of service.  This subsection applies even if the sheriff or constable makes the return of service and returns the citation or notice to the court on the same day the citation or notice is issued.

Added by Acts 2011, 82nd Leg., ch. 823 (H.B. 2759), § 1.02, eff. Jan. 1, 2014.  Amended by Acts 2013, 83rd Leg., ch. 161 (S.B. 1093), § 6.020, eff. Jan. 1, 2014.

### § 1051.153.  Proof of Service

(a) Proof of service in each case requiring citation or notice must be filed before a hearing.

(b) Proof of service consists of:

(1) if the service is made by a sheriff or constable, the return of service;

(2) if the service is made by a private person, the person's affidavit;

(3) if the service is made by mail:

(A) the certificate of the county clerk making the service, or the affidavit of the guardian or other person making the service that states that the citation or notice was mailed and the date of the mailing; and

(B) the return receipt attached to the certificate, if the mailing was by registered or certified mail and a receipt has been returned; and

(4) if the service is made by publication, an affidavit that:

(A) is made by the publisher of the newspaper in which the citation or notice was published or an employee of the publisher;

(B) contains or to which is attached a copy of the published citation or notice; and

(C) states the date of publication printed on the newspaper in which the citation or notice was published.

Added by Acts 2011, 82nd Leg., ch. 823 (H.B. 2759), § 1.02, eff. Jan. 1, 2014.

### § 1051.154.  Return to Court

A citation or notice issued by a county clerk must be returned to the court from which the citation or notice was issued on the first Monday after the service is perfected.

Added by Acts 2011, 82nd Leg., ch. 823 (H.B. 2759), § 1.02, eff. Jan. 1, 2014.

## SUBCHAPTER E.  ALTERNATIVE MANNER OF ISSUANCE, SERVICE, AND RETURN

### § 1051.201.  Court–ordered Issuance, Service, and Return Under Certain Circumstances

(a) A citation or notice required by this title shall be issued, served, and returned in the manner speci-

241

fied by written order of the court in accordance with this title and the Texas Rules of Civil Procedure if:

(1) an interested person requests that action;

(2) a specific method is not provided by this title for giving the citation or notice;

(3) a specific method is not provided by this title for the service and return of citation or notice; or

(4) a provision with respect to a matter relating to citation or notice is inadequate.

(b) Citation or notice issued, served, and returned in the manner specified by a court order as provided by Subsection (a) has the same effect as if the manner of service and return had been specified by this title.

Added by Acts 2011, 82nd Leg., ch. 823 (H.B. 2759), § 1.02, eff. Jan. 1, 2014.

## SUBCHAPTER F. ADDITIONAL NOTICE PROVISIONS

### § 1051.251. Waiver of Notice of Hearing

(a) A competent person who is interested in a hearing in a guardianship proceeding may waive notice of the hearing in writing either in person or through an attorney.

(b) A consul or other representative of a foreign government whose appearance has been entered as provided by law on behalf of a person residing in a foreign country may waive notice on the person's behalf.

(c) A person who submits to the jurisdiction of the court in a hearing is considered to have waived notice of the hearing.

Added by Acts 2011, 82nd Leg., ch. 823 (H.B. 2759), § 1.02, eff. Jan. 1, 2014.

### § 1051.252. Request for Notice of Filing of Pleading

(a) At any time after an application is filed to commence a guardianship proceeding, a person interested in the estate or welfare of a ward or incapacitated person may file with the county clerk a written request to be notified of all, or any specified, motions, applications, or pleadings filed with respect to the proceeding by any person or by a person specifically designated in the request. A person filing a request under this section is responsible for payment of the fees and other costs of providing the requested documents, and the clerk may require a deposit to cover the estimated costs of providing the notice. The clerk

shall send to the requestor by regular mail a copy of any requested document.

(b) A county clerk's failure to comply with a request under this section does not invalidate a proceeding.

Added by Acts 2011, 82nd Leg., ch. 823 (H.B. 2759), § 1.02, eff. Jan. 1, 2014.

### § 1051.253. Service of Notice of Intention to Take Depositions in Certain Proceedings

(a) In a guardianship proceeding in which there is no opposing party or attorney of record on whom to serve notice and copies of interrogatories, service may be made by posting notice of the intention to take depositions for a period of 10 days as provided by Section 1051.053 governing a posting of notice.

(b) When notice by posting under Subsection (a) is filed with the clerk, a copy of the interrogatories must also be filed.

(c) At the expiration of the 10–day period prescribed by Subsection (a):

(1) the depositions for which the notice was posted may be taken; and

(2) the judge may file cross-interrogatories if no person appears.

Added by Acts 2011, 82nd Leg., ch. 823 (H.B. 2759), § 1.02, eff. Jan. 1, 2014. Amended by Acts 2013, 83rd Leg., ch. 161 (S.B. 1093), § 6.021, eff. Jan. 1, 2014; Acts 2013, 83rd Leg., ch. 982 (H.B. 2080), § 3, eff. Jan. 1, 2014.

Section 36 of Acts 2013, 83rd Leg., ch. 982 (H.B. 2080) provides:

"(a) Except as otherwise provided by this section, the changes in law made by this Act apply to:

"(1) a guardianship created before, on, or after the effective date [Jan. 1, 2014] of this Act; and

"(2) an application for a guardianship pending on, or filed on or after, the effective date of this Act.

"(b) The changes in law made by this Act to Sections 1301.054, 1301.055, 1301.057(b), (c), and (d), 1301.058, 1301.101, and 1301.102(a), Estates Code, apply only to an application for the creation, modification, or termination of a management trust that is filed on or after the effective date of this Act. An application described by this subsection that is filed before the effective date of this Act is governed by the law in effect on the date the application was filed, and the former law is continued in effect for that purpose.

"(c) The changes in law made by this Act to Sections 1301.103 and 1301.154(a), Estates Code, and by Section 1301.202(a–1), Estates Code, as added by this Act, apply to a management trust created before, on, or after the effective date of this Act.

"(d) The changes in law made by this Act to Section 1102.003, Estates Code, apply to a guardianship proceeding that is commenced on or after the effective date of this Act. A guardianship proceeding commenced before that date is governed by the law in effect on the date the proceeding was commenced, and the former law is continued in effect for that purpose."

Section 38 of Acts 2013, 83rd Leg., ch. 982 (H.B. 2080) provides:

"To the extent of any conflict, this Act prevails over another Act of the 83rd Legislature, Regular Session, 2013, relating to nonsubstantive additions to and corrections in enacted codes."

## CHAPTER 1052. FILING AND RECORDKEEPING

## SUBCHAPTER A. RECORDKEEPING REQUIREMENTS

### § 1052.001. Guardianship Docket

(a) The county clerk shall maintain a record book titled "Judge's Guardianship Docket" and shall record in the book:

(1) the name of each person with respect to whom, or with respect to whose estate, a proceeding is commenced or sought to be commenced;

(2) the name of the guardian of the estate or person or of the applicant for letters of guardianship;

(3) the date each original application for a guardianship proceeding is filed;

(4) a notation of each order, judgment, decree, and proceeding that occurs in each estate, including the date it occurs; and

(5) the docket number of each guardianship as assigned under Subsection (b).

(b) The county clerk shall assign a docket number to each guardianship in the order a proceeding is commenced.

Added by Acts 2011, 82nd Leg., ch. 823 (H.B. 2759), § 1.02, eff. Jan. 1, 2014.

### § 1052.002. Claim Docket

(a) The county clerk shall maintain a record book titled "Claim Docket" and shall record in the book each claim that is presented against a guardianship for the court's approval.

(b) The county clerk shall assign one or more pages of the record book to each guardianship.

(c) The claim docket must be ruled in 16 columns at proper intervals from top to bottom, with a short note of the contents at the top of each column. The county clerk shall record for each claim, in the order the claims are filed, the following information in the respective columns, beginning with the first or marginal column:

(1) the name of the claimant;

(2) the amount of the claim;

(3) the date of the claim;

(4) the date the claim is filed;

(5) the date the claim is due;

(6) the date the claim begins bearing interest;

(7) the interest rate;

(8) the date the claim is allowed by the guardian, if applicable;

(9) the amount allowed by the guardian, if applicable;

(10) the date the claim is rejected, if applicable;

(11) the date the claim is approved, if applicable;

(12) the amount approved for the claim, if applicable;

(13) the date the claim is disapproved, if applicable;

(14) the class to which the claim belongs;

(15) the date the claim is established by a judgment of a court, if applicable; and

(16) the amount of the judgment established under Subdivision (15), if applicable.

Added by Acts 2011, 82nd Leg., ch. 823 (H.B. 2759), § 1.02, eff. Jan. 1, 2014.

### § 1052.003. Guardianship Fee Book

(a) The county clerk shall maintain a record book titled "Guardianship Fee Book" and shall record in the book each item of cost that accrues to the officers of the court and any witness fees.

(b) Each record entry must include:

(1) the party to whom the cost or fee is due;

(2) the date the cost or fee accrued;

(3) the guardianship or party liable for the cost or fee; and

(4) the date the cost or fee is paid.

Added by Acts 2011, 82nd Leg., ch. 823 (H.B. 2759), § 1.02, eff. Jan. 1, 2014.

## § 1052.004.  Alternate Recordkeeping

Instead of maintaining the record books described by Sections 1052.001, 1052.002, and 1052.003, the county clerk may maintain the information described by those sections relating to a person's guardianship proceeding:

(1) on a computer file;

(2) on microfilm;

(3) in the form of a digitized optical image;  or

(4) in another similar form of data compilation.

Added by Acts 2011, 82nd Leg., ch. 823 (H.B. 2759), § 1.02, eff. Jan. 1, 2014.

### SUBCHAPTER B.  FILES; INDEX

## § 1052.051.  Filing Procedures

(a) An application for a guardianship proceeding or a complaint, petition, or other paper permitted or required by law to be filed with a court in a guardianship proceeding must be filed with the county clerk of the appropriate county.

(b) Each paper filed in a guardianship proceeding must be given the docket number assigned to the estate.

(c) On receipt of a paper described by Subsection (a), the county clerk shall:

(1) file the paper;  and

(2) endorse on the paper:

(A) the date the paper is filed;

(B) the docket number;  and

(C) the clerk's official signature.

(d) Except as provided by Subsection (e), the court clerk shall collect a filing fee, including a deposit for payment to an attorney ad litem, required by law to be paid on the filing of any document described by Subsection (a) from the person or entity filing the document.

(e) Notwithstanding any other law requiring the payment of a filing fee for the document, the following are not required to pay a fee on the filing of a document described by Subsection (a):

(1) a guardian;

(2) an attorney ad litem;

(3) a guardian ad litem;

(4) a person or entity who files an affidavit of inability to pay under Rule 145, Texas Rules of Civil Procedure;

(5) a guardianship program;

(6) a governmental entity;  and

(7) a government agency or nonprofit agency providing guardianship services.

(f) After the creation of a guardianship, a person or entity is entitled to be reimbursed for a filing fee described by Subsection (d), other than a deposit for payment to an attorney ad litem, from:

(1) the guardianship estate;  or

(2) the county treasury, if the guardianship estate is insufficient to pay the amount of the filing fee.

Added by Acts 2011, 82nd Leg., ch. 823 (H.B. 2759), § 1.02, eff. Jan. 1, 2014.  Amended by Acts 2013, 83rd Leg., ch. 161 (S.B. 1093), § 6.022, eff. Jan. 1, 2014;  Acts 2013, 83rd Leg., ch. 982 (H.B. 2080), § 4, eff. Jan. 1, 2014.

Section 36 of Acts 2013, 83rd Leg., ch. 982 (H.B. 2080) provides:

"(a) Except as otherwise provided by this section, the changes in law made by this Act apply to:

"(1) a guardianship created before, on, or after the effective date [Jan. 1, 2014] of this Act;  and

"(2) an application for a guardianship pending on, or filed on or after, the effective date of this Act.

"(b) The changes in law made by this Act to Sections 1301.054, 1301.055, 1301.057(b), (c), and (d), 1301.058, 1301.101, and 1301.102(a), Estates Code, apply only to an application for the creation, modification, or termination of a management trust that is filed on or after the effective date of this Act.  An application described by this subsection that is filed before the effective date of this Act is governed by the law in effect on the date the application was filed, and the former law is continued in effect for that purpose.

"(c) The changes in law made by this Act to Sections 1301.103 and 1301.154(a), Estates Code, and by Section 1301.202(a–1), Estates Code, as added by this Act, apply to a management trust created before, on, or after the effective date of this Act.

"(d) The changes in law made by this Act to Section 1102.003, Estates Code, apply to a guardianship proceeding that is commenced on or after the effective date of this Act.  A guardianship proceeding commenced before that date is governed by the law in effect on the date the proceeding was commenced, and the former law is continued in effect for that purpose."

Section 38 of Acts 2013, 83rd Leg., ch. 982 (H.B. 2080) provides:

"To the extent of any conflict, this Act prevails over another Act of the 83rd Legislature, Regular Session, 2013, relating to nonsubstantive additions to and corrections in enacted codes."

## § 1052.052.  Case Files

(a) The county clerk shall maintain a case file for each person's filed guardianship proceedings.

(b) Each case file must contain each order, judgment, and proceeding of the court and any other guardianship filing with the court, including each:

(1) application for the granting of guardianship;

(2) citation and notice, whether published or posted, including the return on the citation or notice;

(3) bond and official oath;

(4) inventory, appraisement, and list of claims;

(5) exhibit and account;

(6) report of renting;

(7) application for sale or partition of real estate;

(8) report of sale;

(9) application for authority to execute a lease for mineral development, or for pooling or unitization of lands, royalty, or other interest in minerals, or to lend or invest money;

(10) report of lending or investing money;  and

(11) report of guardians of the persons.

Added by Acts 2011, 82nd Leg., ch. 823 (H.B. 2759), § 1.02, eff. Jan. 1, 2014.

### § 1052.053.   Index

(a) The county clerk shall properly index the records required under this chapter.

(b) The county clerk shall keep the index open for public inspection but may not release the index from the clerk's custody.

Added by Acts 2011, 82nd Leg., ch. 823 (H.B. 2759), § 1.02, eff. Jan. 1, 2014.

## CHAPTER 1053.   OTHER COURT DUTIES AND PROCEDURES

## SUBCHAPTER A.   ENFORCEMENT OF ORDERS

### § 1053.001.   Enforcement of Orders

A judge may enforce an order entered against a guardian by attachment and confinement.  Unless this title expressly provides otherwise, the term of confinement for any one offense under this section may not exceed three days.

Added by Acts 2011, 82nd Leg., ch. 823 (H.B. 2759), § 1.02, eff. Jan. 1, 2014.

## SUBCHAPTER B.   COSTS AND SECURITY

### § 1053.051.   Applicability of Certain Laws

A law regulating costs in ordinary civil cases applies to a guardianship proceeding unless otherwise expressly provided by this title.

Added by Acts 2011, 82nd Leg., ch. 823 (H.B. 2759), § 1.02, eff. Jan. 1, 2014.  Amended by Acts 2013, 83rd Leg., ch. 161 (S.B. 1093), § 6.023, eff. Jan. 1, 2014.

### § 1053.052.   Security for Certain Costs

(a) The clerk may require a person who files an application, complaint, or opposition relating to a guardianship proceeding, other than a guardian, attorney ad litem, or guardian ad litem, to provide security for the probable costs of the proceeding before filing the application, complaint, or opposition.

(b) At any time before the trial of an application, complaint, or opposition described by Subsection (a), an officer of the court or a person interested in the guardianship or in the welfare of the ward may, by written motion, obtain from the court an order requiring the person who filed the application, complaint, or opposition to provide security for the probable costs of the proceeding.  The rules governing civil suits in the county court with respect to providing security for the probable costs of a proceeding control in cases described by Subsection (a) and this subsection.

(c) A guardian, attorney ad litem, or guardian ad litem appointed under this title by a court of this state may not be required to provide security for costs in an action brought by the guardian, attorney ad litem, or guardian ad litem in the guardian's, attorney ad litem's, or guardian ad litem's fiduciary capacity.

Added by Acts 2011, 82nd Leg., ch. 823 (H.B. 2759), § 1.02, eff. Jan. 1, 2014.  Amended by Acts 2013, 83rd Leg., ch. 161 (S.B. 1093), § 6.024, eff. Jan. 1, 2014.

## SUBCHAPTER C.   PROCEDURES FOR GUARDIANSHIP PROCEEDINGS

### § 1053.101.   Calling of Dockets

The judge in whose court a guardianship proceeding is pending, as determined by the judge, shall:

(1) call guardianship proceedings in the proceedings' regular order on both the guardianship and claim dockets;  and

(2) issue necessary orders.

Added by Acts 2011, 82nd Leg., ch. 823 (H.B. 2759), § 1.02, eff. Jan. 1, 2014.  Amended by Acts 2013, 83rd Leg., ch. 161 (S.B. 1093), § 6.026, eff. Jan. 1, 2014.

## § 1053.102. Setting of Certain Hearings by Clerk

(a) If a judge is unable to designate the time and place for hearing a guardianship proceeding pending in the judge's court because the judge is absent from the county seat or is on vacation, disqualified, ill, or deceased, the county clerk of the county in which the proceeding is pending may:

(1) designate the time and place for hearing;

(2) enter the setting on the judge's docket; and

(3) certify on the docket the reason that the judge is not acting to set the hearing.

(b) If, after the perfection of the service of notices and citations required by law concerning the time and place of hearing, a qualified judge is not present for a hearing set under Subsection (a), the hearing is automatically continued from day to day until a qualified judge is present to hear and make a determination in the proceeding.

Added by Acts 2011, 82nd Leg., ch. 823 (H.B. 2759), § 1.02, eff. Jan. 1, 2014. Amended by Acts 2013, 83rd Leg., ch. 161 (S.B. 1093), § 6.027, eff. Jan. 1, 2014.

## § 1053.103. Rendering of Decisions, Orders, Decrees, and Judgments

The court shall render a decision, order, decree, or judgment in a guardianship proceeding in open court, except as otherwise expressly provided.

Added by Acts 2011, 82nd Leg., ch. 823 (H.B. 2759), § 1.02, eff. Jan. 1, 2014. Amended by Acts 2013, 83rd Leg., ch. 161 (S.B. 1093), § 6.028, eff. Jan. 1, 2014.

## § 1053.104. Confidentiality of Certain Information

(a) On request by a person protected by a protective order issued under Chapter 85, Family Code, or a guardian, attorney ad litem, or member of the family or household of a person protected by an order, the court may exclude from any document filed in a guardianship proceeding:

(1) the address and phone number of the person protected by the protective order;

(2) the place of employment or business of the person protected by the protective order;

(3) the school attended by the person protected by the protective order or the day-care center or other child-care facility the person attends or in which the person resides; and

(4) the place at which service of process on the person protected by the protective order was effectuated.

(b) On granting a request for confidentiality under this section, the court shall order the clerk to:

(1) strike the information described by Subsection (a) from the public records of the court; and

(2) maintain a confidential record of the information for use only by the court.

Added by Acts 2013, 83rd Leg., ch. 982 (H.B. 2080), § 5, eff. Jan. 1, 2014.

Section 36 of Acts 2013, 83rd Leg., ch. 982 (H.B. 2080) provides:

"(a) Except as otherwise provided by this section, the changes in law made by this Act apply to:

"(1) a guardianship created before, on, or after the effective date [Jan. 1, 2014] of this Act; and

"(2) an application for a guardianship pending on, or filed on or after, the effective date of this Act.

"(b) The changes in law made by this Act to Sections 1301.054, 1301.055, 1301.057(b), (c), and (d), 1301.058, 1301.101, and 1301.102(a), Estates Code, apply only to an application for the creation, modification, or termination of a management trust that is filed on or after the effective date of this Act. An application described by this subsection that is filed before the effective date of this Act is governed by the law in effect on the date the application was filed, and the former law is continued in effect for that purpose.

"(c) The changes in law made by this Act to Sections 1301.103 and 1301.154(a), Estates Code, and by Section 1301.202(a–1), Estates Code, as added by this Act, apply to a management trust created before, on, or after the effective date of this Act.

"(d) The changes in law made by this Act to Section 1102.003, Estates Code, apply to a guardianship proceeding that is commenced on or after the effective date of this Act. A guardianship proceeding commenced before that date is governed by the law in effect on the date the proceeding was commenced, and the former law is continued in effect for that purpose."

## § 1053.105. Inapplicability of Certain Rules of Civil Procedure

The following do not apply to guardianship proceedings:

(1) Rules 47(c) and 169, Texas Rules of Civil Procedure; and

(2) the portions of Rule 190.2, Texas Rules of Civil Procedure, concerning expedited actions under Rule 169, Texas Rules of Civil Procedure.

Added by Acts 2013, 83rd Leg., ch. 982 (H.B. 2080), § 5, eff. Jan. 1, 2014.

Section 36 of Acts 2013, 83rd Leg., ch. 982 (H.B. 2080) provides:

"(a) Except as otherwise provided by this section, the changes in law made by this Act apply to:

"(1) a guardianship created before, on, or after the effective date [Jan. 1, 2014] of this Act; and

"(2) an application for a guardianship pending on, or filed on or after, the effective date of this Act.

"(b) The changes in law made by this Act to Sections 1301.054, 1301.055, 1301.057(b), (c), and (d), 1301.058, 1301.101, and 1301.102(a), Estates Code, apply only to an application for the creation, modification, or termination of a management trust that is filed on or after the effective date of this Act. An application described by this subsection that is filed before the effective date of this Act is governed by the law in effect on the date the application was filed, and the former law is continued in effect for that purpose.

"(c) The changes in law made by this Act to Sections 1301.103 and 1301.154(a), Estates Code, and by Section 1301.202(a–1), Estates Code, as added by this Act, apply to a management trust created before, on, or after the effective date of this Act.

"(d) The changes in law made by this Act to Section 1102.003, Estates Code, apply to a guardianship proceeding that is commenced on or after the effective date of this Act. A guardianship proceeding commenced before that date is governed by the law in effect on the date the proceeding was commenced, and the former law is continued in effect for that purpose."

## CHAPTER 1054. COURT OFFICERS AND COURT–APPOINTED PERSONS

## SUBCHAPTER A. ATTORNEYS AD LITEM AND INTERPRETERS

### § 1054.001. Appointment of Attorney ad Litem in Proceeding for Appointment of Guardian

In a proceeding under this title for the appointment of a guardian, the court shall appoint an attorney ad litem to represent the proposed ward's interests.

Added by Acts 2011, 82nd Leg., ch. 823 (H.B. 2759), § 1.02, eff. Jan. 1, 2014.

### § 1054.002. Term of Appointment

(a) Unless the court determines that the continued appointment of an attorney ad litem appointed under Section 1054.001 is in the ward's best interests, the attorney's term of appointment expires, without a court order, on the date the court:

(1) appoints a guardian in accordance with Subchapter D, Chapter 1101;

(2) appoints a successor guardian; or

(3) denies the application for appointment of a guardian.

(b) The term of appointment of an attorney ad litem appointed under Section 1054.001 continues after the court appoints a temporary guardian under Chapter 1251 unless a court order provides for the termination or expiration of the attorney ad litem's appointment.

Added by Acts 2011, 82nd Leg., ch. 823 (H.B. 2759), § 1.02, eff. Jan. 1, 2014. Amended by Acts 2013, 83rd Leg., ch. 161 (S.B. 1093), § 6.029, eff. Jan. 1, 2014.

### § 1054.003. Access to Records

An attorney ad litem appointed under Section 1054.001 shall be provided copies of all of the current records in the guardianship case. The attorney may have access to all of the proposed ward's relevant medical, psychological, and intellectual testing records.

Added by Acts 2011, 82nd Leg., ch. 823 (H.B. 2759), § 1.02, eff. Jan. 1, 2014.

### § 1054.004. Duties

(a) An attorney ad litem appointed under Section 1054.001 shall interview the proposed ward within a reasonable time before the hearing in the proceeding for the appointment of a guardian. To the greatest extent possible, the attorney shall discuss with the proposed ward:

(1) the law and facts of the case;

(2) the proposed ward's legal options regarding disposition of the case; and

(3) the grounds on which guardianship is sought.

(b) Before the hearing, the attorney ad litem shall review:

(1) the application for guardianship;

(2) certificates of current physical, medical, and intellectual examinations; and

(3) all of the proposed ward's relevant medical, psychological, and intellectual testing records.

Added by Acts 2011, 82nd Leg., ch. 823 (H.B. 2759), § 1.02, eff. Jan. 1, 2014.

### § 1054.005.　Appointment of Interpreter

At the time the court appoints the attorney ad litem under Section 1054.001, the court shall appoint a language interpreter or sign interpreter if necessary to ensure effective communication between the proposed ward and the attorney.

Added by Acts 2011, 82nd Leg., ch. 823 (H.B. 2759), § 1.02, eff. Jan. 1, 2014.

### § 1054.006.　Representation of Ward or Proposed Ward by Attorney

(a) The following persons may at any time retain an attorney who holds a certificate required by Subchapter E to represent the person's interests in a guardianship proceeding instead of having those interests represented by an attorney ad litem appointed under Section 1054.001 or another provision of this title:

(1) a ward who retains the power to enter into a contract under the terms of the guardianship, subject to Section 1202.103; and

(2) a proposed ward for purposes of a proceeding for the appointment of a guardian as long as the proposed ward has capacity to contract.

(b) If the court finds that the ward or the proposed ward has capacity to contract, the court may remove an attorney ad litem appointed under Section 1054.001 or any other provision of this title that requires the court to appoint an attorney ad litem to represent the interests of a ward or proposed ward and appoint a ward or a proposed ward's retained counsel.

Added by Acts 2013, 83rd Leg., ch. 161 (S.B. 1093), § 6.030, eff. Jan. 1, 2014.

### § 1054.007.　Attorneys ad Litem

(a) Except in a situation in which this title requires the appointment to represent the interests of the person, a court may appoint an attorney ad litem in any guardianship proceeding to represent the interests of:

(1) an incapacitated person or another person who has a legal disability;

(2) a proposed ward;

(3) a nonresident;

(4) an unborn or unascertained person; or

(5) an unknown or missing potential heir.

(b) An attorney ad litem appointed under this section is entitled to reasonable compensation for services provided in the amount set by the court, to be taxed as costs in the proceeding.

Added by Acts 2013, 83rd Leg., ch. 982 (H.B. 2080), § 6, eff. Jan. 1, 2014.

Section 36 of Acts 2013, 83rd Leg., ch. 982 (H.B. 2080) provides:

"(a) Except as otherwise provided by this section, the changes in law made by this Act apply to:

"(1) a guardianship created before, on, or after the effective date [Jan. 1, 2014] of this Act; and

"(2) an application for a guardianship pending on, or filed on or after, the effective date of this Act.

"(b) The changes in law made by this Act to Sections 1301.054, 1301.055, 1301.057(b), (c), and (d), 1301.058, 1301.101, and 1301.102(a), Estates Code, apply only to an application for the creation, modification, or termination of a management trust that is filed on or after the effective date of this Act. An application described by this subsection that is filed before the effective date of this Act is governed by the law in effect on the date the application was filed, and the former law is continued in effect for that purpose.

"(c) The changes in law made by this Act to Sections 1301.103 and 1301.154(a), Estates Code, and by Section 1301.202(a–1), Estates Code, as added by this Act, apply to a management trust created before, on, or after the effective date of this Act.

"(d) The changes in law made by this Act to Section 1102.003, Estates Code, apply to a guardianship proceeding that is commenced on or after the effective date of this Act. A guardianship proceeding commenced before that date is governed by the law in effect on the date the proceeding was commenced, and the former law is continued in effect for that purpose."

## SUBCHAPTER B.　GUARDIANS AD LITEM

### § 1054.051.　Appointment of Guardian ad Litem in Guardianship Proceeding

The judge may appoint a guardian ad litem to represent the interests of an incapacitated person in a guardianship proceeding.

Added by Acts 2011, 82nd Leg., ch. 823 (H.B. 2759), § 1.02, eff. Jan. 1, 2014.

### § 1054.052.　Appointment of Guardian ad Litem Relating to Certain Other Suits

In the interest of judicial economy, the court may appoint as guardian ad litem under Section 1104.354(1) the person who has been appointed attorney ad litem under Section 1054.001 or the person who is serving as an ad litem for the ward's benefit in any other proceeding.

Added by Acts 2011, 82nd Leg., ch. 823 (H.B. 2759), § 1.02, eff. Jan. 1, 2014.

### § 1054.053. Term of Certain Appointments

Unless the court determines that the continued appointment of a guardian ad litem appointed in a proceeding for the appointment of a guardian is in the ward's best interests, the guardian ad litem's term of appointment expires, without a court order, on the date the court:

(1) appoints a guardian; or

(2) denies the application for appointment of a guardian.

Added by Acts 2011, 82nd Leg., ch. 823 (H.B. 2759), § 1.02, eff. Jan. 1, 2014.

### § 1054.054. Duties

(a) A guardian ad litem is an officer of the court.

(b) A guardian ad litem shall protect the incapacitated person whose interests the guardian has been appointed to represent in a manner that will enable the court to determine the action that will be in that person's best interests.

Added by Acts 2011, 82nd Leg., ch. 823 (H.B. 2759), § 1.02, eff. Jan. 1, 2014.

### § 1054.055. Compensation and Expenses

(a) A guardian ad litem is entitled to reasonable compensation for services provided in the amount set by the court, to be taxed as costs in the proceeding.

(b) The fees and expenses of a guardian ad litem appointed under Section 1104.354(1) are costs of the litigation proceeding that made the appointment necessary.

Added by Acts 2011, 82nd Leg., ch. 823 (H.B. 2759), § 1.02, eff. Jan. 1, 2014.

### § 1054.056. Immunity

(a) Subject to Subsection (b), a guardian ad litem appointed under this subchapter or Section 1102.001 or 1202.054 to represent the interests of an incapacitated person in a guardianship proceeding involving the creation, modification, or termination of a guardianship is not liable for civil damages arising from a recommendation made or an opinion given in the capacity of guardian ad litem.

(b) This section does not apply to a recommendation or opinion that is:

(1) wilfully wrongful;

(2) given:

(A) with conscious indifference to or reckless disregard for the safety of another;

(B) with malice; or

(C) in bad faith; or

(3) grossly negligent.

Added by Acts 2011, 82nd Leg., ch. 823 (H.B. 2759), § 1.02, eff. Jan. 1, 2014.

## SUBCHAPTER C. COURT VISITORS

### § 1054.101. Inapplicability of Subchapter to Certain Guardianships

This subchapter does not apply to a guardianship created only because the appointment of a guardian for a person is necessary for the person to receive funds from a governmental source.

Added by Acts 2011, 82nd Leg., ch. 823 (H.B. 2759), § 1.02, eff. Jan. 1, 2014.

### § 1054.102. Operation of Court Visitor Program

(a) Each statutory probate court shall operate a court visitor program to assess the conditions of wards and proposed wards.

(b) A court, other than a statutory probate court, that has jurisdiction of a guardianship proceeding may operate a court visitor program in accordance with the population needs and financial abilities of the area the court serves.

Added by Acts 2011, 82nd Leg., ch. 823 (H.B. 2759), § 1.02, eff. Jan. 1, 2014.

### § 1054.103. Evaluation of Ward or Proposed Ward

A court, at any time before a guardian is appointed for a proposed ward or during the pendency of a guardianship of the person or estate, may appoint a court visitor to evaluate the ward or proposed ward and provide a written report that substantially complies with Section 1054.104(b) on:

(1) the request of any interested person, including the ward or proposed ward; or

(2) the court's own motion.

Added by Acts 2011, 82nd Leg., ch. 823 (H.B. 2759), § 1.02, eff. Jan. 1, 2014.

### § 1054.104. Evaluation Report

(a) A court visitor appointed under Section 1054.103 shall file the report on the evaluation of a ward or proposed ward not later than the 14th day after the date the court visitor conducts the evaluation. The court visitor shall swear under penalty of perjury that the report is accurate to the best of the court visitor's knowledge and belief.

(b) A court visitor's report must include:

(1) a description of the nature and degree of the ward's or proposed ward's capacity and incapacity, including a description of the ward's or proposed ward's medical history, if reasonably available and not waived by the court;

(2) a medical prognosis and list of the ward's or proposed ward's treating physicians, when appropriate;

(3) a description of the ward's or proposed ward's living conditions and circumstances;

(4) a description of the ward's or proposed ward's social, intellectual, physical, and educational conditions;

(5) a statement that the court visitor has personally visited or observed the ward or proposed ward;

(6) a statement of the date of the guardian's most recent visit, if a guardian has been appointed;

(7) a recommendation as to any modification needed in the guardianship or proposed guardianship, including removal or denial of the guardianship; and

(8) any other information required by the court.

Added by Acts 2011, 82nd Leg., ch. 823 (H.B. 2759), § 1.02, eff. Jan. 1, 2014.

### § 1054.105. Compensation

(a) A court that operates a court visitor program shall use persons willing to serve as court visitors without compensation to the greatest extent possible.

(b) A court visitor who has not expressed a willingness to serve without compensation is entitled to reasonable compensation for services provided in an amount set by the court, to be taxed as costs in the proceeding.

Added by Acts 2011, 82nd Leg., ch. 823 (H.B. 2759), § 1.02, eff. Jan. 1, 2014.

## SUBCHAPTER D. COURT INVESTIGATORS

### § 1054.151. Investigation of Guardianship Application

On the filing of an application for guardianship under Section 1101.001, a court investigator shall investigate the circumstances alleged in the application to determine whether a less restrictive alternative to guardianship is appropriate.

Added by Acts 2011, 82nd Leg., ch. 823 (H.B. 2759), § 1.02, eff. Jan. 1, 2014.

### § 1054.152. General Duties

A court investigator shall:

(1) supervise a court visitor program established under Subchapter C and, in that capacity, serve as the chief court visitor;

(2) investigate a complaint received from any person about a guardianship and report to the judge, if necessary; and

(3) perform other duties as assigned by the judge or required by this title.

Added by Acts 2011, 82nd Leg., ch. 823 (H.B. 2759), § 1.02, eff. Jan. 1, 2014.

### § 1054.153. Investigation Report

(a) A court investigator shall file with the court a report containing the court investigator's findings and conclusions after conducting an investigation under Section 1054.151 or 1054.152.

(b) In a contested case, the court investigator shall provide copies of the report of the court investigator's findings and conclusions to the attorneys for the parties before the earlier of:

(1) the seventh day after the date the court investigator completes the report; or

(2) the 10th day before the date the trial is scheduled to begin.

(c) Disclosure to a jury of the contents of a court investigator's report is subject to the Texas Rules of Evidence.

Added by Acts 2011, 82nd Leg., ch. 823 (H.B. 2759), § 1.02, eff. Jan. 1, 2014.

### § 1054.154. Effect of Subchapter on Other Law

Nothing in this subchapter supersedes any duty or obligation of another to report or investigate abuse or neglect under any statute of this state.

Added by Acts 2011, 82nd Leg., ch. 823 (H.B. 2759), § 1.02, eff. Jan. 1, 2014.

## SUBCHAPTER E. QUALIFICATIONS TO SERVE AS COURT–APPOINTED ATTORNEY

### § 1054.201. Certification Required

(a) A court-appointed attorney in a guardianship proceeding, including an attorney ad litem, must be certified by the State Bar of Texas, or a person or other entity designated by the state bar, as having successfully completed a course of study in guardianship law and procedure sponsored by the state bar or the state bar's designee.

(b) The State Bar of Texas shall require three hours of credit for certification under this subchapter.

Added by Acts 2011, 82nd Leg., ch. 823 (H.B. 2759), § 1.02, eff. Jan. 1, 2014.

### § 1054.202. Certificate Expiration

(a) Except as provided by Subsection (b), a certificate issued under this subchapter expires on the second anniversary of the date the certificate is issued.

(b) A new certificate obtained by a person to whom a certificate under this subchapter was previously issued expires on the fourth anniversary of the date the new certificate is issued if the person has been certified each of the four years immediately preceding the date the new certificate is issued.

Added by Acts 2011, 82nd Leg., ch. 823 (H.B. 2759), § 1.02, eff. Jan. 1, 2014.

### § 1054.203. Eligibility for Appointment on Expiration of Certificate

An attorney whose certificate issued under this subchapter has expired must obtain a new certificate to be eligible for appointment by a court to represent a person at a guardianship proceeding, including as an attorney ad litem.

Added by Acts 2011, 82nd Leg., ch. 823 (H.B. 2759), § 1.02, eff. Jan. 1, 2014.

## CHAPTER 1055. TRIAL AND HEARING MATTERS

## SUBCHAPTER A. STANDING AND PLEADINGS

### § 1055.001. Standing to Commence or Contest Proceeding

(a) Except as provided by Subsection (b), any person has the right to:

(1) commence a guardianship proceeding, including a proceeding for complete restoration of a ward's capacity or modification of a ward's guardianship; or

(2) appear and contest a guardianship proceeding or the appointment of a particular person as guardian.

(b) A person who has an interest that is adverse to a proposed ward or incapacitated person may not:

(1) file an application to create a guardianship for the proposed ward or incapacitated person;

(2) contest the creation of a guardianship for the proposed ward or incapacitated person;

(3) contest the appointment of a person as a guardian of the proposed ward or incapacitated person; or

(4) contest an application for complete restoration of a ward's capacity or modification of a ward's guardianship.

(c) The court shall determine by motion in limine the standing of a person who has an interest that is adverse to a proposed ward or incapacitated person.

Added by Acts 2011, 82nd Leg., ch. 823 (H.B. 2759), § 1.02, eff. Jan. 1, 2014.

### § 1055.002. Defect in Pleading

A court may not invalidate a pleading in a guardianship proceeding, or an order based on the pleading, on the basis of a defect of form or substance in the pleading unless a timely objection has been made against the defect and the defect has been called to the attention of the court in which the proceeding was or is pending.

Added by Acts 2011, 82nd Leg., ch. 823 (H.B. 2759), § 1.02, eff. Jan. 1, 2014. Amended by Acts 2013, 83rd Leg., ch. 161 (S.B. 1093), § 6.031, eff. Jan. 1, 2014.

## SUBCHAPTER B. TRIAL AND HEARING

### § 1055.051. Hearing by Submission

(a) A court may consider by submission a motion or application filed under this title unless the proceeding is:

(1) contested; or

(2) an application for the appointment of a guardian.

(b) The party seeking relief under a motion or application being considered by the court on submission has the burden of proof at the hearing.

(c) The court may consider a person's failure to file a response to a motion or application that may be considered on submission as a representation that the person does not oppose the motion or application.

(d) A person's request for oral argument is not a response to a motion or application under this section.

(e) The court, on the court's own motion, may order oral argument on a motion or application that may be considered by submission.

Added by Acts 2011, 82nd Leg., ch. 823 (H.B. 2759), § 1.02, eff. Jan. 1, 2014.

### § 1055.052.   Trial by Jury

A party in a contested guardianship proceeding is entitled to a jury trial on request.

Added by Acts 2011, 82nd Leg., ch. 823 (H.B. 2759), § 1.02, eff. Jan. 1, 2014.

### § 1055.053.   Location of Hearing

(a) Except as provided by Subsection (b), the judge may hold a hearing on a guardianship proceeding involving an adult ward or adult proposed ward at any suitable location in the county in which the guardianship proceeding is pending.  The hearing should be held in a physical setting that is not likely to have a harmful effect on the ward or proposed ward.

(b) On the request of the adult proposed ward, the adult ward, or the attorney of the proposed ward or ward, the hearing may not be held under the authority of this section at a place other than the courthouse.

Added by Acts 2013, 83rd Leg., ch. 161 (S.B. 1093), § 6.032, eff. Jan. 1, 2014.

### SUBCHAPTER C.  EVIDENCE

### § 1055.101.   Applicability of Certain Rules Relating to Witnesses and Evidence

The rules relating to witnesses and evidence that apply in the district court apply in a guardianship proceeding to the extent practicable.

Added by Acts 2011, 82nd Leg., ch. 823 (H.B. 2759), § 1.02, eff. Jan. 1, 2014.

### § 1055.102.   Use of Certain Records as Evidence

The following are admissible as evidence in any court of this state:

(1) record books described by Sections 1052.001, 1052.002, and 1052.003 and individual case files described by Section 1052.052, including records maintained in a manner allowed under Section 1052.004; and

(2) certified copies or reproductions of the records.

Added by Acts 2011, 82nd Leg., ch. 823 (H.B. 2759), § 1.02, eff. Jan. 1, 2014.

### SUBCHAPTER D.  MEDIATION

### § 1055.151.   Mediation of Contested Guardianship Proceeding

(a) On the written agreement of the parties or on the court's own motion, the court may refer a contested guardianship proceeding to mediation.

(b) A mediated settlement agreement is binding on the parties if the agreement:

(1) provides, in a prominently displayed statement that is in boldfaced type, in capital letters, or underlined, that the agreement is not subject to revocation by the parties;

(2) is signed by each party to the agreement; and

(3) is signed by the party's attorney, if any, who is present at the time the agreement is signed.

(c) If a mediated settlement agreement meets the requirements of this section, a party is entitled to judgment on the mediated settlement agreement notwithstanding Rule 11, Texas Rules of Civil Procedure, or another rule or law.

(d) Notwithstanding Subsections (b) and (c), a court may decline to enter a judgment on a mediated settlement agreement if the court finds that the agreement is not in the ward's or proposed ward's best interests.

Added by Acts 2013, 83rd Leg., ch. 982 (H.B. 2080), § 7, eff. Jan. 1, 2014.

Section 36 of Acts 2013, 83rd Leg., ch. 982 (H.B. 2080) provides:

"(a) Except as otherwise provided by this section, the changes in law made by this Act apply to:

"(1) a guardianship created before, on, or after the effective date [Jan. 1, 2014] of this Act; and

"(2) an application for a guardianship pending on, or filed on or after, the effective date of this Act.

"(b) The changes in law made by this Act to Sections 1301.054, 1301.055, 1301.057(b), (c), and (d), 1301.058, 1301.101, and 1301.102(a), Estates Code, apply only to an application for the creation, modification, or termination of a management trust that is filed on or after the effective date of this Act. An application described by this subsection that is filed before the effective date of this Act is governed by the law in effect on the date the application was filed, and the former law is continued in effect for that purpose.

"(c) The changes in law made by this Act to Sections 1301.103 and 1301.154(a), Estates Code, and by Section 1301.202(a–1), Estates Code, as added by this Act, apply to a management trust created before, on, or after the effective date of this Act.

"(d) The changes in law made by this Act to Section 1102.003, Estates Code, apply to a guardianship proceeding that is commenced on or after the effective date of this Act. A guardianship proceeding commenced before that date is governed by the law in effect on the date the proceeding was commenced, and the former law is continued in effect for that purpose."

## CHAPTER 1056. EXECUTION, ATTACHMENT, AND BILL OF REVIEW

### SUBCHAPTER A. EXECUTION

### SUBCHAPTER A. EXECUTION

#### § 1056.001. Executions in Guardianship Proceedings

(a) An execution in a guardianship proceeding must be:

(1) directed "to any sheriff or any constable within the State of Texas";

(2) attested and signed by the clerk officially under court seal; and

(3) made returnable in 60 days.

(b) A proceeding under an execution in a guardianship proceeding is governed, to the extent applicable, by the laws regulating a proceeding under an execution issued by a district court.

(c) Notwithstanding Subsection (a), an execution directed to the sheriff or a constable of a specific county in this state may not be held defective if properly executed within that county by the sheriff or constable to whom the execution is directed.

Added by Acts 2011, 82nd Leg., ch. 823 (H.B. 2759), § 1.02, eff. Jan. 1, 2014. Amended by Acts 2013, 83rd Leg., ch. 161 (S.B. 1093), §§ 6.033, 6.034, eff. Jan. 1, 2014.

### SUBCHAPTER B. ATTACHMENT OF ESTATE PROPERTY

#### § 1056.051. Order for Issuance of Writ of Attachment

(a) If a person interested in the estate of an incapacitated person files with the judge a written complaint made under oath alleging that the guardian is about to remove the estate or a part of the estate outside of the state, the judge may order a writ of attachment to issue, directed "to any sheriff or any constable within the State of Texas." The writ must order the sheriff or constable to:

(1) seize the estate or a part of the estate; and

(2) hold that property subject to further court order.

(b) Notwithstanding Subsection (a), a writ of attachment directed to the sheriff or constable of a specific county in this state is not defective if the writ was properly executed within that county by the sheriff or constable to whom the writ is directed.

Added by Acts 2011, 82nd Leg., ch. 823 (H.B. 2759), § 1.02, eff. Jan. 1, 2014.

#### § 1056.052. Bond

Before a judge may issue a writ of attachment ordered under Section 1056.051, the complainant must execute a bond that is:

(1) payable to the guardian of the estate;

(2) in an amount set by the judge; and

(3) conditioned on the payment of all damages and costs that are recovered for a wrongful suit out of the writ.

Added by Acts 2011, 82nd Leg., ch. 823 (H.B. 2759), § 1.02, eff. Jan. 1, 2014.

### SUBCHAPTER C. BILL OF REVIEW

#### § 1056.101. Revision and Correction of Order or Judgment in Guardianship Proceeding

(a) An interested person, including a ward, may, by a bill of review filed in the court in which the guardianship proceeding was held, have an order or judgment rendered by the court revised and corrected on a showing of error in the order or judgment.

(b) Except as provided by Subsection (c), a bill of review to revise and correct an order or judgment may not be filed more than two years after the date of the order or judgment.

(c) A bill of review to revise and correct an order or judgment filed by a person whose disability has been removed must be filed not later than the second anniversary of the date the person's disability was removed.

Added by Acts 2011, 82nd Leg., ch. 823 (H.B. 2759), § 1.02, eff. Jan. 1, 2014.

### § 1056.102.  Injunction

A process or action under a court order or judgment subject to a bill of review filed under Section 1056.101 may be stayed only by writ of injunction.

Added by Acts 2011, 82nd Leg., ch. 823 (H.B. 2759), § 1.02, eff. Jan. 1, 2014.

### CHAPTER 1057.  CHANGE AND RESIGNATION OF RESIDENT AGENT OF GUARDIAN FOR SERVICE OF PROCESS

### § 1057.001.  Change of Resident Agent

(a) A guardian may change the guardian's resident agent to accept service of process in a guardianship proceeding or other matter relating to the guardianship by filing with the court in which the guardianship proceeding is pending a statement titled "Designation of Successor Resident Agent" that states the names and addresses of:

(1) the guardian;

(2) the resident agent; and

(3) the successor resident agent.

(b) The designation of a successor resident agent takes effect on the date the statement is filed with the court.

Added by Acts 2011, 82nd Leg., ch. 823 (H.B. 2759), § 1.02, eff. Jan. 1, 2014.

### § 1057.002.  Resignation of Resident Agent

(a) A resident agent of a guardian may resign as resident agent by giving notice to the guardian and filing with the court in which the guardianship proceeding is pending a statement titled "Resignation of Resident Agent" that states:

(1) the name of the guardian;

(2) the guardian's address most recently known by the resident agent;

(3) that notice of the resignation has been given to the guardian and the date that notice was given; and

(4) that the guardian does not have a resident agent.

(b) The resident agent shall send, by certified mail, return receipt requested, a copy of a resignation statement filed under Subsection (a) to:

(1) the guardian at the address most recently known by the resident agent; and

(2) each party in the case or the party's attorney or other designated representative of record.

(c) The resignation of the resident agent takes effect on the date the court enters an order accepting the resignation.  A court may not enter an order accepting the resignation unless the resident agent complies with this section.

Added by Acts 2011, 82nd Leg., ch. 823 (H.B. 2759), § 1.02, eff. Jan. 1, 2014.

## SUBTITLE D.  CREATION OF GUARDIANSHIP

### CHAPTER 1101.  GENERAL PROCEDURE TO APPOINT GUARDIAN

## SUBCHAPTER A. INITIATION OF PROCEEDING FOR APPOINTMENT OF GUARDIAN

### § 1101.001. Application for Appointment of Guardian; Contents

(a) Any person may commence a proceeding for the appointment of a guardian by filing a written application in a court having jurisdiction and venue.

(b) The application must be sworn to by the applicant and state:

(1) the proposed ward's name, sex, date of birth, and address;

(2) the name, relationship, and address of the person the applicant seeks to have appointed as guardian;

(3) whether guardianship of the person or estate, or both, is sought;

(4) the nature and degree of the alleged incapacity, the specific areas of protection and assistance requested, and the limitation or termination of rights requested to be included in the court's order of appointment, including a termination of:

(A) the right of a proposed ward who is 18 years of age or older to vote in a public election; and

(B) the proposed ward's eligibility to hold or obtain a license to operate a motor vehicle under Chapter 521, Transportation Code;

(5) the facts requiring the appointment of a guardian;

(6) the interest of the applicant in the appointment of a guardian;

(7) the nature and description of any kind of guardianship existing for the proposed ward in any other state;

(8) the name and address of any person or institution having the care and custody of the proposed ward;

(9) the approximate value and description of the proposed ward's property, including any compensation, pension, insurance, or allowance to which the proposed ward may be entitled;

(10) the name and address of any person whom the applicant knows to hold a power of attorney signed by the proposed ward and a description of the type of power of attorney;

(11) for a proposed ward who is a minor, the following information if known by the applicant:

(A) the name of each of the proposed ward's parents and either the parent's address or that the parent is deceased;

(B) the name and age of each of the proposed ward's siblings, if any, and either the sibling's address or that the sibling is deceased; and

(C) if each of the proposed ward's parents and adult siblings are deceased, the names and addresses of the proposed ward's other living relatives who are related to the proposed ward within the third degree by consanguinity and who are adults;

(12) for a proposed ward who is a minor, whether the minor was the subject of a legal or conservatorship proceeding in the preceding two years and, if so:

(A) the court involved;

(B) the nature of the proceeding; and

(C) any final disposition of the proceeding;

(13) for a proposed ward who is an adult, the following information if known by the applicant:

(A) the name of the proposed ward's spouse, if any, and either the spouse's address or that the spouse is deceased;

(B) the name of each of the proposed ward's parents and either the parent's address or that the parent is deceased;

(C) the name and age of each of the proposed ward's siblings, if any, and either the sibling's address or that the sibling is deceased;

(D) the name and age of each of the proposed ward's children, if any, and either the child's address or that the child is deceased; and

(E) if there is no living spouse, parent, adult sibling, or adult child of the proposed ward, the names and addresses of the proposed ward's other living relatives who are related to the proposed ward within the third degree by consanguinity and who are adults;

(14) facts showing that the court has venue of the proceeding; and

*Text of subsec. (b)(15) effective until Sept. 1, 2014*

(15) if applicable, that the person whom the applicant seeks to have appointed as a guardian is a private professional guardian who is certified under Subchapter C, Chapter 111, Government Code, and

has complied with the requirements of Subchapter G, Chapter 1104.

*Text of subsec. (b)(15) effective Sept. 1, 2015*

(15) if applicable, that the person whom the applicant seeks to have appointed as a guardian is a private professional guardian who is certified under Subchapter C, Chapter 155, Government Code, and has complied with the requirements of Subchapter G, Chapter 1104.

Added by Acts 2011, 82nd Leg., ch. 823 (H.B. 2759), § 1.02, eff. Jan. 1, 2014.  Amended by Acts 2013, 83rd Leg., ch. 42 (S.B. 966), § 2.07, eff. Sept. 1, 2014;  Acts 2013, 83rd Leg., ch. 161 (S.B. 1093), § 6.035, eff. Jan. 1, 2014.

### § 1101.002. Contents of Application; Confidentiality of Certain Addresses

An application filed under Section 1101.001 may omit the address of a person named in the application if:

(1) the application states that the person is protected by a protective order issued under Chapter 85, Family Code;

(2) a copy of the protective order is attached to the application as an exhibit;

(3) the application states the county in which the person resides;

(4) the application indicates the place where notice to or the issuance and service of citation on the person may be made or sent;  and

(5) the application is accompanied by a request for an order under Section 1051.201 specifying the manner of issuance, service, and return of citation or notice on the person.

Added by Acts 2013, 83rd Leg., ch. 982 (H.B. 2080), § 8, eff. Jan. 1, 2014.

Section 36 of Acts 2013, 83rd Leg., ch. 982 (H.B. 2080) provides:

"(a) Except as otherwise provided by this section, the changes in law made by this Act apply to:

"(1) a guardianship created before, on, or after the effective date [Jan. 1, 2014] of this Act;  and

"(2) an application for a guardianship pending on, or filed on or after, the effective date of this Act.

"(b) The changes in law made by this Act to Sections 1301.054, 1301.055, 1301.057(b), (c), and (d), 1301.058, 1301.101, and 1301.102(a), Estates Code, apply only to an application for the creation, modification, or termination of a management trust that is filed on or after the effective date of this Act.  An application described by this subsection that is filed before the effective date of this Act is governed by the law in effect on the date the application was filed, and the former law is continued in effect for that purpose.

"(c) The changes in law made by this Act to Sections 1301.103 and 1301.154(a), Estates Code, and by Section 1301.202(a-1), Estates Code, as added by this Act, apply to a management trust created before, on, or after the effective date of this Act.

"(d) The changes in law made by this Act to Section 1102.003, Estates Code, apply to a guardianship proceeding that is commenced on or after the effective date of this Act.  A guardianship proceeding commenced before that date is governed by the law in effect on the date the proceeding was commenced, and the former law is continued in effect for that purpose."

## SUBCHAPTER B. HEARING; JURY TRIAL

### § 1101.051. Hearing

(a) At a hearing for the appointment of a guardian, the court shall:

(1) inquire into the ability of any allegedly incapacitated adult to:

(A) feed, clothe, and shelter himself or herself;

(B) care for his or her own physical health;  and

(C) manage his or her property or financial affairs;

(2) ascertain the age of any proposed ward who is a minor;

(3) inquire into the governmental reports for any person who must have a guardian appointed to receive funds due the person from any governmental source;  and

(4) inquire into the qualifications, abilities, and capabilities of the person seeking to be appointed guardian.

(b) A proposed ward must be present at the hearing unless the court, on the record or in the order, determines that a personal appearance is not necessary.

(c) The court may close the hearing at the request of the proposed ward or the proposed ward's counsel.

Added by Acts 2011, 82nd Leg., ch. 823 (H.B. 2759), § 1.02, eff. Jan. 1, 2014.

### § 1101.052. Jury Trial

A proposed ward is entitled to a jury trial on request.

Added by Acts 2011, 82nd Leg., ch. 823 (H.B. 2759), § 1.02, eff. Jan. 1, 2014.

### § 1101.053. Provision of Records Required; Use of Records

(a) Before a hearing may be held for the appointment of a guardian, current and relevant medical, psychological, and intellectual testing records of the proposed ward must be provided to the attorney ad litem appointed to represent the proposed ward unless:

(1) the proposed ward is a minor or a person who must have a guardian appointed to receive funds due the person from any governmental source; or

(2) the court makes a finding on the record that:

(A) current or relevant records do not exist; and

(B) examining the proposed ward for the purpose of creating the records is impractical.

(b) Current medical, psychological, and intellectual testing records are a sufficient basis for a determination of guardianship.

(c) The findings and recommendations contained in the medical, psychological, and intellectual testing records are not binding on the court.

Added by Acts 2011, 82nd Leg., ch. 823 (H.B. 2759), § 1.02, eff. Jan. 1, 2014.

## SUBCHAPTER C. DETERMINATION OF NECESSITY OF GUARDIANSHIP; FINDINGS AND PROOF

### § 1101.101. Findings and Proof Required

(a) Before appointing a guardian for a proposed ward, the court must:

(1) find by clear and convincing evidence that:

(A) the proposed ward is an incapacitated person;

(B) it is in the proposed ward's best interest to have the court appoint a person as the proposed ward's guardian; and

(C) the proposed ward's rights or property will be protected by the appointment of a guardian; and

(2) find by a preponderance of the evidence that:

(A) the court has venue of the case;

(B) the person to be appointed guardian is eligible to act as guardian and is entitled to appointment, or, if no eligible person entitled to appointment applies, the person appointed is a proper person to act as guardian;

(C) if a guardian is appointed for a minor, the guardianship is not created for the primary purpose of enabling the minor to establish residency for enrollment in a school or school district for which the minor is not otherwise eligible for enrollment; and

(D) the proposed ward:

(i) is totally without capacity as provided by this title to care for himself or herself and to manage his or her property; or

(ii) lacks the capacity to do some, but not all, of the tasks necessary to care for himself or herself or to manage his or her property.

(b) The court may not grant an application to create a guardianship unless the applicant proves each element required by this title.

Added by Acts 2011, 82nd Leg., ch. 823 (H.B. 2759), § 1.02, eff. Jan. 1, 2014.

### § 1101.102. Determination of Incapacity of Certain Adults: Recurring Acts or Occurrences

A determination of incapacity of an adult proposed ward, other than a person who must have a guardian appointed to receive funds due the person from any governmental source, must be evidenced by recurring acts or occurrences in the preceding six months and not by isolated instances of negligence or bad judgment.

Added by Acts 2011, 82nd Leg., ch. 823 (H.B. 2759), § 1.02, eff. Jan. 1, 2014.

### § 1101.103. Determination of Incapacity of Certain Adults: Physician Examination

(a) Except as provided by Section 1101.104, the court may not grant an application to create a guardianship for an incapacitated person, other than a minor or person for whom it is necessary to have a guardian appointed only to receive funds from a governmental source, unless the applicant presents to the court a written letter or certificate from a physician licensed in this state that is:

(1) dated not earlier than the 120th day before the date the application is filed; and

(2) based on an examination the physician performed not earlier than the 120th day before the date the application is filed.

(b) The letter or certificate must:

(1) describe the nature, degree, and severity of the proposed ward's incapacity, including any functional deficits regarding the proposed ward's ability to:

(A) handle business and managerial matters;

(B) manage financial matters;

(C) operate a motor vehicle;

(D) make personal decisions regarding residence, voting, and marriage; and

(E) consent to medical, dental, psychological, or psychiatric treatment;

(2) in providing a description under Subdivision (1) regarding the proposed ward's ability to operate a motor vehicle and make personal decisions regarding voting, state whether in the physician's opinion the proposed ward:

(A) has the mental capacity to vote in a public election; and

(B) has the ability to safely operate a motor vehicle;

(3) provide an evaluation of the proposed ward's physical condition and mental function and summarize the proposed ward's medical history if reasonably available;

(4) state how or in what manner the proposed ward's ability to make or communicate responsible decisions concerning himself or herself is affected by the proposed ward's physical or mental health, including the proposed ward's ability to:

(A) understand or communicate;

(B) recognize familiar objects and individuals;

(C) perform simple calculations;

(D) reason logically; and

(E) administer to daily life activities;

(5) state whether any current medication affects the proposed ward's demeanor or the proposed ward's ability to participate fully in a court proceeding;

(6) describe the precise physical and mental conditions underlying a diagnosis of a mental disability, and state whether the proposed ward would benefit from supports and services that would allow the individual to live in the least restrictive setting; and

(7) include any other information required by the court.

(c) If the court determines it is necessary, the court may appoint the necessary physicians to examine the proposed ward. The court must make its determination with respect to the necessity for a physician's examination of the proposed ward at a hearing held for that purpose. Not later than the fourth day before the date of the hearing, the applicant shall give to the proposed ward and the proposed ward's attorney ad litem written notice specifying the purpose and the date and time of the hearing.

(d) A physician who examines the proposed ward, other than a physician or psychologist who examines the proposed ward under Section 1101.104(2), shall make available for inspection by the attorney ad litem appointed to represent the proposed ward a written

letter or certificate from the physician that complies with the requirements of Subsections (a) and (b).

Added by Acts 2011, 82nd Leg., ch. 823 (H.B. 2759), § 1.02, eff. Jan. 1, 2014.

### § 1101.104. Examinations and Documentation Regarding Intellectual Disability

If an intellectual disability is the basis of the proposed ward's alleged incapacity, the court may not grant an application to create a guardianship for the proposed ward unless the applicant presents to the court a written letter or certificate that:

(1) complies with Sections 1101.103(a) and (b); or

(2) shows that not earlier than 24 months before the hearing date:

(A) the proposed ward has been examined by a physician or psychologist licensed in this state or certified by the Department of Aging and Disability Services to perform the examination, in accordance with rules of the executive commissioner of the Health and Human Services Commission governing examinations of that kind, and the physician's or psychologist's written findings and recommendations include a determination of an intellectual disability; or

(B) a physician or psychologist licensed in this state or certified by the Department of Aging and Disability Services to perform examinations described by Paragraph (A) updated or endorsed in writing a prior determination of an intellectual disability for the proposed ward made by a physician or psychologist licensed in this state or certified by the department.

Added by Acts 2011, 82nd Leg., ch. 823 (H.B. 2759), § 1.02, eff. Jan. 1, 2014. Amended by Acts 2013, 83rd Leg., ch. 780 (S.B. 1235), § 2, eff. Jan. 1, 2014.

Sections 3 and 4 of Acts 2013, 83rd Leg., ch. 780 (S.B. 1235) provide:

"Sec. 3. The changes in law made by this Act to Section 1101.104, Estates Code, as effective January 1, 2014, apply only to an application to create a guardianship filed on or after the effective date of this Act. An application to create a guardianship filed before the effective date of this Act is governed by the law in effect on the date the application was filed, and the former law is continued in effect for that purpose.

"Sec. 4. To the extent of any conflict, this Act prevails over another Act [Acts 2013, 83rd Leg., ch. 161 (S.B. 1093)] of the 83rd Legislature, Regular Session, 2013, relating to nonsubstantive additions to and corrections in enacted codes. [An amendment by Acts 2013, 83rd Leg., ch. 161 (S.B. 1093), § 6.036 failed because of conflict with Acts 2013, 83rd Leg., ch. 780 (S.B. 1235).]"

## § 1101.105. Prohibition Against Consideration of Age as Sole Factor in Appointment of Guardian for Adults

In determining whether to appoint a guardian for an incapacitated person who is not a minor, the court may not use age as the sole factor.

Added by Acts 2011, 82nd Leg., ch. 823 (H.B. 2759), § 1.02, eff. Jan. 1, 2014.

## § 1101.106. Evidence of Necessity of Guardianship to Receive Governmental Funds

A certificate of the executive head or a representative of a bureau, department, or agency of the government, to the effect that the appointment of a guardian is a condition precedent to the payment of any funds due the proposed ward from that governmental entity, is prima facie evidence of the necessity for the appointment of a guardian.

Added by Acts 2011, 82nd Leg., ch. 823 (H.B. 2759), § 1.02, eff. Jan. 1, 2014.

## SUBCHAPTER D. COURT ACTION

## § 1101.151. Order Appointing Guardian With Full Authority

(a) If it is found that the proposed ward is totally without capacity to care for himself or herself, manage his or her property, operate a motor vehicle, and vote in a public election, the court may appoint a guardian of the proposed ward's person or estate, or both, with full authority over the incapacitated person except as provided by law.

(b) An order appointing a guardian under this section must contain findings of fact and specify:

(1) the information required by Section 1101.153(a);

(2) that the guardian has full authority over the incapacitated person;

(3) if necessary, the amount of funds from the corpus of the person's estate the court will allow the guardian to spend for the education and maintenance of the person under Subchapter A, Chapter 1156;

(4) whether the person is totally incapacitated because of a mental condition;

(5) that the person does not have the capacity to operate a motor vehicle and to vote in a public election; and

(6) if it is a guardianship of the person of the ward or of both the person and the estate of the ward, the rights of the guardian with respect to the person as specified in Section 1151.051(c)(1).

(c) An order appointing a guardian under this section that includes the rights of the guardian with respect to the person as specified in Section 1151.051(c)(1) must also contain the following prominently displayed statement in boldfaced type, in capital letters, or underlined:

"NOTICE TO ANY PEACE OFFICER OF THE STATE OF TEXAS: YOU MAY USE REASONABLE EFFORTS TO ENFORCE THE RIGHT OF A GUARDIAN OF THE PERSON OF A WARD TO HAVE PHYSICAL POSSESSION OF THE WARD OR TO ESTABLISH THE WARD'S LEGAL DOMICILE AS SPECIFIED IN THIS ORDER. A PEACE OFFICER WHO RELIES ON THE TERMS OF A COURT ORDER AND THE OFFICER'S AGENCY ARE ENTITLED TO THE APPLICABLE IMMUNITY AGAINST ANY CIVIL OR OTHER CLAIM REGARDING THE OFFICER'S GOOD FAITH ACTS PERFORMED IN THE SCOPE OF THE OFFICER'S DUTIES IN ENFORCING THE TERMS OF THIS ORDER THAT RELATE TO THE ABOVE–MENTIONED RIGHTS OF THE COURT–APPOINTED GUARDIAN OF THE PERSON OF THE WARD. ANY PERSON WHO KNOWINGLY PRESENTS FOR ENFORCEMENT AN ORDER THAT IS INVALID OR NO LONGER IN EFFECT COMMITS AN OFFENSE THAT MAY BE PUNISHABLE BY CONFINEMENT IN JAIL FOR AS LONG AS TWO YEARS AND A FINE OF AS MUCH AS $10,000."

Added by Acts 2011, 82nd Leg., ch. 823 (H.B. 2759), § 1.02, eff. Jan. 1, 2014. Amended by Acts 2013, 83rd Leg., ch. 982 (H.B. 2080), § 9, eff. Jan. 1, 2014.

Section 36 of Acts 2013, 83rd Leg., ch. 982 (H.B. 2080) provides:

"(a) Except as otherwise provided by this section, the changes in law made by this Act apply to:

"(1) a guardianship created before, on, or after the effective date [Jan. 1, 2014] of this Act; and

"(2) an application for a guardianship pending on, or filed on or after, the effective date of this Act.

"(b) The changes in law made by this Act to Sections 1301.054, 1301.055, 1301.057(b), (c), and (d), 1301.058, 1301.101, and 1301.102(a), Estates Code, apply only to an application for the creation, modification, or termination of a management trust that is filed on or after the effective date of this Act. An application described by this subsection that is filed before the effective date of this Act is governed by the law in effect on the date the application was filed, and the former law is continued in effect for that purpose.

"(c) The changes in law made by this Act to Sections 1301.103 and 1301.154(a), Estates Code, and by Section 1301.202(a–1), Estates Code, as added by this Act, apply to a management trust created before, on, or after the effective date of this Act.

"(d) The changes in law made by this Act to Section 1102.003, Estates Code, apply to a guardianship proceeding that is commenced on or after the effective date of this Act. A guardianship proceeding commenced before that date is governed by the law in effect on the date the proceeding was commenced, and the former law is continued in effect for that purpose."

## § 1101.152. Order Appointing Guardian With Limited Authority

(a) If it is found that the proposed ward lacks the capacity to do some, but not all, of the tasks necessary to care for himself or herself or to manage his or her property, the court may appoint a guardian with limited powers and permit the proposed ward to care for himself or herself or to manage his or her property commensurate with the proposed ward's ability.

(b) An order appointing a guardian under this section must contain findings of fact and specify:

(1) the information required by Section 1101.153(a);

(2) the specific powers, limitations, or duties of the guardian with respect to the person's care or the management of the person's property by the guardian;

(3) if necessary, the amount of funds from the corpus of the person's estate the court will allow the guardian to spend for the education and maintenance of the person under Subchapter A, Chapter 1156; and

(4) whether the person is incapacitated because of a mental condition and, if so, whether the person retains the right to vote in a public election or maintains eligibility to hold or obtain a license to operate a motor vehicle under Chapter 521, Transportation Code.

(c) An order appointing a guardian under this section that includes the right of the guardian to have physical possession of the ward or to establish the ward's legal domicile as specified in Section 1151.051(c)(1) must also contain the following prominently displayed statement in boldfaced type, in capital letters, or underlined:

"NOTICE TO ANY PEACE OFFICER OF THE STATE OF TEXAS: YOU MAY USE REASONABLE EFFORTS TO ENFORCE THE RIGHT OF A GUARDIAN OF THE PERSON OF A WARD TO HAVE PHYSICAL POSSESSION OF THE WARD OR TO ESTABLISH THE WARD'S LEGAL DOMICILE AS SPECIFIED IN THIS ORDER. A PEACE OFFICER WHO RELIES ON THE TERMS OF A COURT ORDER AND THE OFFICER'S AGENCY ARE ENTITLED TO THE APPLICABLE IMMUNITY AGAINST ANY CIVIL OR OTHER CLAIM REGARDING THE OFFICER'S GOOD FAITH ACTS PERFORMED IN THE SCOPE OF THE OFFICER'S DUTIES IN ENFORCING THE TERMS OF THIS ORDER THAT RELATE TO THE ABOVE–MENTIONED RIGHTS OF THE COURT–APPOINTED GUARDIAN OF THE PERSON OF THE WARD. ANY PERSON WHO KNOWINGLY PRESENTS FOR ENFORCEMENT AN ORDER THAT IS INVALID OR NO LONGER IN EFFECT COMMITS AN OFFENSE THAT MAY BE PUNISHABLE BY CONFINEMENT IN JAIL FOR AS LONG AS TWO YEARS AND A FINE OF AS MUCH AS $10,000."

Added by Acts 2011, 82nd Leg., ch. 823 (H.B. 2759), § 1.02, eff. Jan. 1, 2014. Amended by Acts 2013, 83rd Leg., ch. 982 (H.B. 2080), § 10, eff. Jan. 1, 2014.

Section 36 of Acts 2013, 83rd Leg., ch. 982 (H.B. 2080) provides:

"(a) Except as otherwise provided by this section, the changes in law made by this Act apply to:

"(1) a guardianship created before, on, or after the effective date [Jan. 1, 2014] of this Act; and

"(2) an application for a guardianship pending on, or filed on or after, the effective date of this Act.

"(b) The changes in law made by this Act to Sections 1301.054, 1301.055, 1301.057(b), (c), and (d), 1301.058, 1301.101, and 1301.102(a), Estates Code, apply only to an application for the creation, modification, or termination of a management trust that is filed on or after the effective date of this Act. An application described by this subsection that is filed before the effective date of this Act is governed by the law in effect on the date the application was filed, and the former law is continued in effect for that purpose.

"(c) The changes in law made by this Act to Sections 1301.103 and 1301.154(a), Estates Code, and by Section 1301.202(a–1), Estates Code, as added by this Act, apply to a management trust created before, on, or after the effective date of this Act.

"(d) The changes in law made by this Act to Section 1102.003, Estates Code, apply to a guardianship proceeding that is commenced on or after the effective date of this Act. A guardianship proceeding commenced before that date is governed by the law in effect on the date the proceeding was commenced, and the former law is continued in effect for that purpose."

## § 1101.153. General Contents of Order Appointing Guardian

(a) A court order appointing a guardian must specify:

(1) the name of the person appointed;

(2) the name of the ward;

(3) whether the guardian is of the person or estate of the ward, or both;

(4) the amount of any bond required;

(5) if it is a guardianship of the estate of the ward and the court considers an appraisal to be necessary, one, two, or three disinterested persons to appraise the estate and to return the appraisement to the court; and

(6) that the clerk will issue letters of guardianship to the person appointed when the person has qualified according to law.

(b) An order appointing a guardian may not duplicate or conflict with the powers and duties of any other guardian.

(c) An order appointing a guardian or a successor guardian may specify as authorized by Section 1202.001(c) a period during which a petition for adjudication that the ward no longer requires the guardianship may not be filed without special leave.

Added by Acts 2011, 82nd Leg., ch. 823 (H.B. 2759), § 1.02, eff. Jan. 1, 2014.

### § 1101.154. Appointment of Guardian of Estate for Certain Minors Prohibited

A court may not appoint a guardian of the estate of a minor when a payment of claims is made under Chapter 1355.

Added by Acts 2011, 82nd Leg., ch. 823 (H.B. 2759), § 1.02, eff. Jan. 1, 2014.

### § 1101.155. Dismissal of Application

If it is found that a proposed ward who is an adult possesses the capacity to care for himself or herself and manage his or her property as would a reasonably prudent person, the court shall dismiss an application for guardianship.

Added by Acts 2011, 82nd Leg., ch. 823 (H.B. 2759), § 1.02, eff. Jan. 1, 2014.

## CHAPTER 1102. COURT–INITIATED PROCEDURE TO APPOINT GUARDIAN

Section

### § 1102.001. Court–initiated Investigation

If a court has probable cause to believe that a person domiciled or found in the county in which the court is located is an incapacitated person, and the person does not have a guardian in this state, the court shall appoint a guardian ad litem or court investigator to investigate the person's conditions and circumstances to determine whether:

(1) the person is an incapacitated person; and

(2) a guardianship is necessary.

Added by Acts 2011, 82nd Leg., ch. 823 (H.B. 2759), § 1.02, eff. Jan. 1, 2014.

### § 1102.002. Establishment of Probable Cause for Investigation

To establish probable cause under Section 1102.001, the court may require:

(1) an information letter about the person believed to be incapacitated that is submitted by an interested person and satisfies the requirements of Section 1102.003; or

(2) a written letter or certificate from a physician who has examined the person believed to be incapacitated that satisfies the requirements of Section 1101.103, except that the letter must be:

(A) dated not earlier than the 120th day before the date of the appointment of a guardian ad litem or court investigator under Section 1102.001; and

(B) based on an examination the physician performed not earlier than the 120th day before that date.

Added by Acts 2011, 82nd Leg., ch. 823 (H.B. 2759), § 1.02, eff. Jan. 1, 2014.

### § 1102.003. Information Letter

(a) An interested person who submits an information letter under Section 1102.002(1) about a person believed to be incapacitated must, to the best of the interested person's knowledge:

(1) state the person's name, address, telephone number, county of residence, and date of birth;

(2) state whether the person's residence is a private residence, health care facility, or other type of residence;

(3) describe the relationship between the person and the interested person submitting the letter;

(4) state the names and telephone numbers of any known friends and relatives of the person;

(5) state whether a guardian of the person or estate has been appointed in this state for the person;

(6) state whether the person has executed a power of attorney and, if so, the designee's name, address, and telephone number;

(7) describe any property of the person, including the estimated value of that property;

(8) list the amount and source of any monthly income of the person;

(9) describe the nature and degree of the person's alleged incapacity; and

(10) state whether the person is in imminent danger of serious impairment to the person's physical health, safety, or estate.

(b) In addition to the requirements of Subsection (a), if an information letter under that subsection is submitted by an interested person who is a family member of the person believed to be incapacitated, the information letter must:

(1) be signed and sworn to before a notary public by the interested person; or

(2) include a written declaration signed by the interested person under penalty of perjury that the information contained in the information letter is true to the best of the person's knowledge.

Added by Acts 2011, 82nd Leg., ch. 823 (H.B. 2759), § 1.02, eff. Jan. 1, 2014. Amended by Acts 2013, 83rd Leg., ch. 982 (H.B. 2080), § 11, eff. Jan. 1, 2014.

Section 36 of Acts 2013, 83rd Leg., ch. 982 (H.B. 2080) provides:

"(a) Except as otherwise provided by this section, the changes in law made by this Act apply to:

"(1) a guardianship created before, on, or after the effective date [Jan. 1, 2014] of this Act; and

"(2) an application for a guardianship pending on, or filed on or after, the effective date of this Act.

"(b) The changes in law made by this Act to Sections 1301.054, 1301.055, 1301.057(b), (c), and (d), 1301.058, 1301.101, and 1301.102(a), Estates Code, apply only to an application for the creation, modification, or termination of a management trust that is filed on or after the effective date of this Act. An application described by this subsection that is filed before the effective date of this Act is governed by the law in effect on the date the application was filed, and the former law is continued in effect for that purpose.

"(c) The changes in law made by this Act to Sections 1301.103 and 1301.154(a), Estates Code, and by Section 1301.202(a–1), Estates Code, as added by this Act, apply to a management trust created before, on, or after the effective date of this Act.

"(d) The changes in law made by this Act to Section 1102.003, Estates Code, apply to a guardianship proceeding that is commenced on or after the effective date of this Act. A guardianship proceeding commenced before that date is governed by the law in effect on the date the proceeding was commenced, and the former law is continued in effect for that purpose."

## § 1102.004.  Application for Guardianship Following Investigation

A guardian ad litem or court investigator who, after an investigation as prescribed by Section 1102.001, believes that the person is an incapacitated person and that a guardianship is necessary shall file an application for the appointment of a guardian of the person or estate, or both, for the person.

Added by Acts 2011, 82nd Leg., ch. 823 (H.B. 2759), § 1.02, eff. Jan. 1, 2014.

## § 1102.005.  Compensation of Guardian ad Litem

(a) A court that appoints a guardian ad litem under Section 1102.001 may authorize compensation of the guardian ad litem from available funds of the proposed ward's estate, regardless of whether a guardianship is created for the proposed ward.

(b) After examining the proposed ward's assets and determining that the proposed ward is unable to pay for services provided by the guardian ad litem, the court may authorize compensation from the county treasury.

Added by Acts 2011, 82nd Leg., ch. 823 (H.B. 2759), § 1.02, eff. Jan. 1, 2014. Amended by Acts 2013, 83rd Leg., ch. 982 (H.B. 2080), § 12, eff. Jan. 1, 2014.

Section 36 of Acts 2013, 83rd Leg., ch. 982 (H.B. 2080) provides:

"(a) Except as otherwise provided by this section, the changes in law made by this Act apply to:

"(1) a guardianship created before, on, or after the effective date [Jan. 1, 2014] of this Act; and

"(2) an application for a guardianship pending on, or filed on or after, the effective date of this Act.

"(b) The changes in law made by this Act to Sections 1301.054, 1301.055, 1301.057(b), (c), and (d), 1301.058, 1301.101, and 1301.102(a), Estates Code, apply only to an application for the creation, modification, or termination of a management trust that is filed on or after the effective date of this Act. An application described by this subsection that is filed before the effective date of this Act is governed by the law in effect on the date the application was filed, and the former law is continued in effect for that purpose.

"(c) The changes in law made by this Act to Sections 1301.103 and 1301.154(a), Estates Code, and by Section 1301.202(a–1), Estates Code, as added by this Act, apply to a management trust created before, on, or after the effective date of this Act.

"(d) The changes in law made by this Act to Section 1102.003, Estates Code, apply to a guardianship proceeding that is commenced on or after the effective date of this Act. A guardianship proceeding commenced before that date is governed by the law in effect on the date the proceeding was commenced, and the former law is continued in effect for that purpose."

## CHAPTER 1103.  PROCEDURE TO APPOINT GUARDIAN FOR CERTAIN MINORS REQUIRING GUARDIANSHIPS AS ADULTS

## § 1103.001.  Application for Appointment of Guardian

Not earlier than the 180th day before the proposed ward's 18th birthday, a person may file an application under Section 1101.001 for the appointment of a guardian of the person or estate, or both, of a proposed ward who:

(1) is a minor; and

(2) because of incapacity will require a guardianship after the proposed ward is no longer a minor.

Added by Acts 2011, 82nd Leg., ch. 823 (H.B. 2759), § 1.02, eff. Jan. 1, 2014.

### § 1103.002. Appointment of Conservator as Guardian Without Hearing

(a) Notwithstanding any other law, if the applicant who files an application under Section 1101.001 or 1103.001 is a person who was appointed conservator of a disabled child and the proceeding is a guardianship proceeding described by Section 1002.015(1) in which the proposed ward is the incapacitated adult with respect to whom another court obtained continuing, exclusive jurisdiction in a suit affecting the parent-child relationship when the person was a child , the applicant may present to the court a written letter or certificate that meets the requirements of Sections 1101. 103(a) and (b).

(b) If, on receipt of the letter or certificate described by Subsection (a), the court is able to make the findings required by Section 1101.101, the court, notwithstanding Subchapter C, Chapter 1104, shall:

(1) appoint the conservator as guardian without conducting a hearing; and

(2) to the extent possible preserve the terms of possession and access to the ward that applied before the court obtained jurisdiction of the guardianship proceeding.

Added by Acts 2011, 82nd Leg., ch. 823 (H.B. 2759), § 1.02, eff. Jan. 1, 2014. Amended by Acts 2013, 83rd Leg., ch. 161 (S.B. 1093), § 6.037, eff. Jan. 1, 2014.

### § 1103.003. Effective Date of Guardianship

If the application filed under Section 1103.001 is heard before the proposed ward's 18th birthday, a guardianship created under this chapter may not take effect and the person appointed guardian may not take the oath as required under Section 1105.051 or give a bond as required under Section 1105.101 until the proposed ward's 18th birthday.

Added by Acts 2011, 82nd Leg., ch. 823 (H.B. 2759), § 1.02, eff. Jan. 1, 2014.

### § 1103.004. Settlement and Closing of Prior Guardianship

Notwithstanding Section 1202.001(b), the guardianship of the person of a minor who is the subject of an application for the appointment of a guardian of the person filed under Section 1103.001 is settled and closed when:

(1) the court, after a hearing on the application, determines that the appointment of a guardian of the person for the proposed ward is not necessary; or

(2) the guardian appointed by the court, after a hearing on the application, has qualified under Section 1105.002.

Added by Acts 2011, 82nd Leg., ch. 823 (H.B. 2759), § 1.02, eff. Jan. 1, 2014.

## CHAPTER 1104. SELECTION OF AND ELIGIBILITY TO SERVE AS GUARDIAN

SUBCHAPTER A. GENERAL PROVISIONS RELATING TO APPOINTMENT OF GUARDIAN

## SUBCHAPTER A.  GENERAL PROVISIONS RELATING TO APPOINTMENT OF GUARDIAN

### § 1104.001.  Guardian of the Person or Estate

(a) Only one person may be appointed as guardian of the person or estate, but one person may be appointed guardian of the person and another person may be appointed guardian of the estate, if it is in the best interest of the incapacitated person or ward.

(b) Subsection (a) does not prohibit the joint appointment, if the court finds it to be in the best interest of the incapacitated person or ward, of:

(1) a husband and wife;

(2) joint managing conservators;

(3) co-guardians appointed under the laws of a jurisdiction other than this state; or

(4) both parents of an adult who is incapacitated if the incapacitated person:

(A) has not been the subject of a suit affecting the parent-child relationship; or

(B) has been the subject of a suit affecting the parent-child relationship and both of the incapacitated person's parents were named as joint managing conservators in the suit but are no longer serving in that capacity.

Added by Acts 2011, 82nd Leg., ch. 823 (H.B. 2759), § 1.02, eff. Jan. 1, 2014.

### § 1104.002.  Preference of Incapacitated Person

Before appointing a guardian, the court shall make a reasonable effort to consider the incapacitated person's preference of the person to be appointed guardian and, to the extent consistent with other provisions of this title, shall give due consideration to the preference indicated by the incapacitated person.

Added by Acts 2011, 82nd Leg., ch. 823 (H.B. 2759), § 1.02, eff. Jan. 1, 2014.

### SUBCHAPTER B.  SELECTION OF GUARDIAN FOR MINOR

### § 1104.051.  Guardian of Minor Children

(a) If the parents live together, both parents are the natural guardians of the person of the minor children by the marriage, and one of the parents is entitled to be appointed guardian of the children's estates.  If the parents disagree as to which parent should be appointed, the court shall make the appointment on the basis of which parent is better qualified to serve in that capacity.

(b) The rights of parents who do not live together are equal.  The court shall assign the guardianship of their minor children to one parent considering only the best interests of the children.

(c) If one parent is deceased, the surviving parent is the natural guardian of the person of the minor children and is entitled to be appointed guardian of the minor children's estates.

Added by Acts 2011, 82nd Leg., ch. 823 (H.B. 2759), § 1.02, eff. Jan. 1, 2014.

### § 1104.052.  Guardian for Minor Orphan

In appointing a guardian for a minor orphan:

(1) if the last surviving parent did not appoint a guardian, the nearest ascendant in the direct line of the minor is entitled to guardianship of both the person and the estate of the minor;

(2) if more than one ascendant exists in the same degree in the direct line of the minor, the court shall appoint one ascendant according to circumstances and considering the minor's best interests;

(3) if the minor does not have an ascendant in the direct line of the minor:

(A) the court shall appoint the nearest of kin;  or

(B) if two or more persons are in the same degree of kinship to the minor, the court shall appoint one of those persons according to circumstances and considering the minor's best interests;  and

(4) if the minor does not have a relative who is eligible to be guardian, or if none of the eligible persons apply to be guardian, the court shall appoint a qualified person as guardian.

Added by Acts 2011, 82nd Leg., ch. 823 (H.B. 2759), § 1.02, eff. Jan. 1, 2014.

### § 1104.053.  Guardian Designated by Will or Written Declaration

(a) Notwithstanding Section 1104.001 or 1104.051, the surviving parent of a minor may by will or written declaration appoint any eligible person to be guardian of the person of the parent's minor children after the parent dies or in the event of the parent's incapacity.

(b) After the surviving parent of a minor dies or if the court finds the surviving parent is an incapacitated person, the court shall appoint the person designated in the will or declaration to serve as guardian of the person of the parent's minor children in preference to another otherwise entitled to serve as guardian under this title, unless the court finds that the person designated to serve as guardian:

(1) is disqualified;

(2) is deceased;

(3) refuses to serve;  or

(4) would not serve the minor children's best interests.

(c) On compliance with this title, an eligible person is also entitled to be appointed guardian of the minor children's estates after the surviving parent dies or in the event of the surviving parent's incapacity.

Added by Acts 2011, 82nd Leg., ch. 823 (H.B. 2759), § 1.02, eff. Jan. 1, 2014.

### § 1104.054.  Selection of Guardian by Minor

(a) Notwithstanding any other provision of this subchapter, if an application is filed for the guardianship of the person or estate, or both, of a minor at least 12 years of age, the minor may select the guardian by a writing filed with the clerk, if the court finds that the selection is in the minor's best interest and approves the selection.

(b) Notwithstanding any other provision of this subchapter, a minor at least 12 years of age may select another guardian of the minor's person or estate, or both, if the minor has a guardian appointed by the court, by will of the minor's parent, or by written declaration of the minor's parent, and that guardian dies, resigns, or is removed from guardianship. The minor must make the selection by filing an application in open court in person or by an attorney. The court shall make the appointment and revoke the letters of guardianship of the former guardian if the court is satisfied that:

(1) the person selected is suitable and competent; and

(2) the appointment of the person is in the minor's best interest.

Added by Acts 2011, 82nd Leg., ch. 823 (H.B. 2759), § 1.02, eff. Jan. 1, 2014.

## SUBCHAPTER C. SELECTION OF GUARDIAN FOR INCAPACITATED PERSON OTHER THAN MINOR

### § 1104.101. Appointment According to Circumstances and Best Interests

The court shall appoint a guardian for an incapacitated person other than a minor according to the circumstances and considering the incapacitated person's best interests.

Added by Acts 2011, 82nd Leg., ch. 823 (H.B. 2759), § 1.02, eff. Jan. 1, 2014.

### § 1104.102. Appointment Preferences

If the court finds that two or more eligible persons are equally entitled to be appointed guardian of an incapacitated person:

(1) the incapacitated person's spouse is entitled to the guardianship in preference to any other person, if the spouse is one of the eligible persons;

(2) the eligible person nearest of kin to the incapacitated person is entitled to the guardianship, if the incapacitated person's spouse is not one of the eligible persons; or

(3) the court shall appoint the eligible person who is best qualified to serve as guardian if:

(A) the persons entitled to serve under Subdivisions (1) and (2) refuse to serve;

(B) two or more persons entitled to serve under Subdivision (2) are related in the same degree of kinship to the incapacitated person; or

(C) neither the incapacitated person's spouse nor any person related to the incapacitated person is an eligible person.

Added by Acts 2011, 82nd Leg., ch. 823 (H.B. 2759), § 1.02, eff. Jan. 1, 2014.

### § 1104.103. Designation of Guardian by Will or Written Declaration

(a) The surviving parent of an adult individual who is an incapacitated person may, if the parent is the guardian of the person of the adult individual, by will or written declaration appoint an eligible person to serve as guardian of the person of the adult individual after the parent dies or in the event of the parent's incapacity.

(b) After the surviving parent dies or if the court finds the surviving parent has become an incapacitated person after being appointed the adult individual's guardian, the court shall appoint the person designated in the will or declaration to serve as guardian in preference to any other person otherwise entitled to serve as guardian under this title, unless the court finds that the person designated to serve as guardian:

(1) is disqualified;

(2) is deceased;

(3) refuses to serve; or

(4) would not serve the adult individual's best interests.

(c) On compliance with this title, the eligible person appointed under Subsection (b) is also entitled to be appointed guardian of the estate of the adult individual after the surviving parent dies or in the event of the surviving parent's incapacity, if the surviving parent is the guardian of the estate of the adult individual.

Added by Acts 2011, 82nd Leg., ch. 823 (H.B. 2759), § 1.02, eff. Jan. 1, 2014.

## SUBCHAPTER D. WRITTEN DECLARATION BY CERTAIN PARENTS TO APPOINT GUARDIAN FOR THEIR CHILDREN

### § 1104.151. Definitions

In this subchapter:

(1) "Declaration" means a written declaration of a person that:

(A) appoints a guardian for the person's child under Section 1104.053(a) or 1104.103(a); and

(B) satisfies the requirements of this subdivision and Sections 1104.152, 1104.153, 1104.154, 1104.156, 1104.159, and 1104.160.

(2) "Self-proving affidavit" means an affidavit the form and content of which substantially comply with the requirements of Section 1104.153.

(3) "Self-proving declaration" includes a self-proving affidavit that is attached or annexed to a declaration.

Added by Acts 2011, 82nd Leg., ch. 823 (H.B. 2759), § 1.02, eff. Jan. 1, 2014.

### § 1104.152. Requirements for Declaration

(a) A declaration appointing an eligible person to be guardian of the person of a parent's child under Section 1104.053(a) or 1104.103(a) must be signed by the declarant and be:

(1) written wholly in the declarant's handwriting; or

(2) attested to in the declarant's presence by at least two credible witnesses who are:

(A) 14 years of age or older; and

(B) not named as guardian or alternate guardian in the declaration.

(b) Notwithstanding Subsection (a), a declaration that is not written wholly in the declarant's handwriting may be signed by another person for the declarant under the direction of and in the presence of the declarant.

(c) A declaration described by Subsection (a)(2) may have attached a self-proving affidavit signed by the declarant and the witnesses attesting to:

(1) the competence of the declarant; and

(2) the execution of the declaration.

Added by Acts 2011, 82nd Leg., ch. 823 (H.B. 2759), § 1.02, eff. Jan. 1, 2014.

### § 1104.153. Form and Content of Declaration and Self–proving Affidavit.

(a) A declaration and affidavit may be in any form adequate to clearly indicate the declarant's intention to designate a guardian for the declarant's child.

(b) The following form may be used but is not required to be used:

DECLARATION OF APPOINTMENT OF
GUARDIAN FOR MY CHILDREN
IN THE EVENT OF MY DEATH
OR INCAPACITY

I, _____, make this Declaration to appoint as guardian for my child or children, listed as follows, in the event of my death or incapacity:

_____

_____

_____

_____

_____

_____

(add blanks as appropriate)

I designate _____ to serve as guardian of the person of my (child or children), _____ as first alternate guardian of the person of my (child or children), _____ as second alternate guardian of the person of my (child or children), and _____ as third alternate guardian of the person of my (child or children).

I direct that the guardian of the person of my (child or children) serve (with or without) bond.

(If applicable) I designate _____ to serve as guardian of the estate of my (child or children), _____ as first alternate guardian of the estate of my (child or children), _____ as second alternate guardian of the estate of my (child or children), and _____ as third alternate guardian of the estate of my (child or children).

If any guardian or alternate guardian dies, does not qualify, or resigns, the next named alternate guardian becomes guardian of my (child or children).

Signed this _____ day of _____, 20___.

_____
Declarant

_____
Witness

_____
Witness

SELF–PROVING AFFIDAVIT

Before me, the undersigned authority, on this date personally appeared _____, the declarant, and _____ and _____ as witnesses, and all being duly sworn, the declarant said that the above instrument was his or her Declaration of Appointment of Guardian for the Declarant's Children in the Event of Declarant's Death or Incapacity and that the declarant had made and executed it for the purposes expressed in the declaration. The witnesses declared to me that they are each 14 years of age or older, that they saw the declarant sign the declaration, that they signed the declaration as witnesses, and that the declarant appeared to them to be of sound mind.

_____

Declarant

_____

Affiant

_____

Affiant

Subscribed and sworn to before me by _____, the above named declarant, and _____ (names of affiants) affiants, on this ___ day of _____, 20___.

_____
Notary Public in and for the
State of Texas
My Commission expires:
_____

(Tex. Prob. Code, Sec. 677A(g).)

Added by Acts 2011, 82nd Leg., ch. 823 (H.B. 2759), § 1.02, eff. Jan. 1, 2014.

## § 1104.154.  Alternative to Self–proving Affidavit

(a) As an alternative to the self-proving affidavit authorized by Section 1104.153, a declaration of appointment of a guardian for the declarant's children in the event of the declarant's death or incapacity may be simultaneously executed, attested, and made self-proved by including the following in substantially the same form and with substantially the same contents:

I, _____, as declarant, after being duly sworn, declare to the undersigned witnesses and to the undersigned authority that this instrument is my Declaration of Appointment of Guardian for My Children in the Event of My Death or Incapacity, and that I have made and executed it for the purposes expressed in the declaration. I now sign this declaration in the presence of the attesting witnesses and the undersigned authority on this _____ day of _____, 20___.

_____
Declarant

The undersigned, _____ and _____, each being 14 years of age or older, after being duly sworn, declare to the declarant and to the undersigned authority that the declarant declared to us that this instrument is the declarant's Declaration of Appointment of Guardian for the Declarant's Children in the Event of Declarant's Death or Incapacity and that the declarant executed it for the purposes expressed in the declaration. The declarant then signed this declaration and we believe the declarant to be of sound mind. We now sign our names as attesting witnesses on this _____ day of _____, 20___.

_____
Witness

_____
Witness

Subscribed and sworn to before me by the above named declarant, and affiants, this _____ day of _____, 20___.

_____
Notary Public in and for the
State of Texas
My Commission expires:
_____

(b) A declaration that is executed as provided by Subsection (a) is considered self-proved to the same extent a declaration executed with a self-proving affidavit under Section 1104.153 is considered self-proved.

Added by Acts 2011, 82nd Leg., ch. 823 (H.B. 2759), § 1.02, eff. Jan. 1, 2014.

## § 1104.155.  Alternate Self–proving of Declaration

At any time during the declarant's lifetime, a declaration described by Section 1104.152(a)(1) may be made self-proved in the same form and manner that a will written wholly in the testator's handwriting is made self-proved under Section 251.107.

Added by Acts 2011, 82nd Leg., ch. 823 (H.B. 2759), § 1.02, eff. Jan. 1, 2014.

## § 1104.156.  Filing of Declaration and Self–proving Affidavit

The declaration and any self-proving affidavit may be filed with the court at any time after the application for appointment of a guardian is filed and before a guardian is appointed.

Added by Acts 2011, 82nd Leg., ch. 823 (H.B. 2759), § 1.02, eff. Jan. 1, 2014.

## § 1104.157.  Proof of Declaration

(a) The court may admit a declaration that is self-proved into evidence without the testimony of witnesses attesting to the competency of the declarant and the execution of the declaration. Additional proof of the execution of the declaration with the formalities and solemnities and under the circumstances required to make it a valid declaration is not necessary.

(b) A declaration described by Section 1104.152(a)(1) that is not self-proved may be proved in the same manner that a will written wholly in the testator's handwriting is proved under Section 256.154.

(c) A declaration described by Section 1104.152(a)(2) that is not self-proved may be proved in the same manner that an attested written will produced in court is proved under Section 256.153.

Added by Acts 2011, 82nd Leg., ch. 823 (H.B. 2759), § 1.02, eff. Jan. 1, 2014.

### § 1104.158.  Prima Facie Evidence

A properly executed and witnessed self-proving declaration, including a declaration and self-proving affidavit described by Section 1104.152(c), is prima facie evidence that:

(1) the declarant was competent at the time the declarant executed the declaration; and

(2) the guardian named in the declaration would serve the best interests of the ward or incapacitated person.

Added by Acts 2011, 82nd Leg., ch. 823 (H.B. 2759), § 1.02, eff. Jan. 1, 2014.

### § 1104.159.  Revocation of Declaration

The declarant may revoke a declaration in any manner provided for the revocation of a will under Section 253.002, including the subsequent re-execution of the declaration in the manner required for the original declaration.

Added by Acts 2011, 82nd Leg., ch. 823 (H.B. 2759), § 1.02, eff. Jan. 1, 2014.

### § 1104.160.  Alternate or Other Court–appointed Guardian

(a) The court shall appoint the next eligible designated alternate guardian named in a declaration if the designated guardian does not qualify, is deceased, refuses to serve, resigns, or dies after being appointed guardian, or is otherwise unavailable to serve as guardian.

(b) The court shall appoint another person to serve as guardian as otherwise provided by this title if the designated guardian and all designated alternate guardians named in the declaration:

(1) do not qualify;

(2) are deceased;

(3) refuse to serve; or

(4) later die or resign.

Added by Acts 2011, 82nd Leg., ch. 823 (H.B. 2759), § 1.02, eff. Jan. 1, 2014.

## SUBCHAPTER E.  WRITTEN DECLARATION TO DESIGNATE GUARDIAN BEFORE NEED ARISES

### § 1104.201.  Definitions

In this subchapter:

(1) "Declaration" means a written declaration of a person that:

(A) designates another person to serve as a guardian of the person or estate of the declarant; and

(B) satisfies the requirements of this subdivision and Sections 1104.202, 1104.203, 1104.204, 1104.205, 1104.207, 1104.210, 1104.211, and 1104.212.

(2) "Self-proving affidavit" means an affidavit the form and content of which substantially comply with the requirements of Section 1104.204.

(3) "Self-proving declaration" includes a self-proving affidavit that is attached or annexed to a declaration.

Added by Acts 2011, 82nd Leg., ch. 823 (H.B. 2759), § 1.02, eff. Jan. 1, 2014.

### § 1104.202.  Designation of Guardian for Declarant

(a) A person other than an incapacitated person may designate by declaration a person to serve as guardian of the person or estate of the declarant if the declarant becomes incapacitated.  The court shall appoint the person designated in the declaration to serve as guardian in preference to any other person otherwise entitled to serve as guardian under this title, unless the court finds that the person designated to serve as guardian:

(1) is disqualified; or

(2) would not serve the ward's best interests.

(b) A declarant may, in the declaration, disqualify a named person from serving as guardian of the declarant's person or estate.  The court may not under any circumstances appoint as guardian a person named under this subsection.

Added by Acts 2011, 82nd Leg., ch. 823 (H.B. 2759), § 1.02, eff. Jan. 1, 2014.

### § 1104.203.  Requirements for Declaration

(a) A declaration under this subchapter must be signed by the declarant and be:

(1) written wholly in the declarant's handwriting; or

(2) attested to in the declarant's presence by at least two credible witnesses who are:

(A) 14 years of age or older;  and

(B) not named as guardian or alternate guardian in the declaration.

(b) Notwithstanding Subsection (a), a declaration that is not written wholly in the declarant's handwriting may be signed by another person for the declarant under the direction of and in the presence of the declarant.

(c) A declaration described by Subsection (a)(2) may have attached a self-proving affidavit signed by the declarant and the witnesses attesting to:

(1) the competence of the declarant;  and

(2) the execution of the declaration.

Added by Acts 2011, 82nd Leg., ch. 823 (H.B. 2759), § 1.02, eff. Jan. 1, 2014.

### § 1104.204.  Form and Content of Declaration and Self–proving Affidavit.

(a) A declaration and affidavit may be in any form adequate to clearly indicate the declarant's intention to designate a guardian.

(b) The following form may be used but is not required to be used:

DECLARATION OF GUARDIAN

IN THE EVENT OF LATER INCAPACITY
OR NEED OF GUARDIAN

I, _____, make this Declaration of Guardian, to operate if the need for a guardian for me later arises.

1.  I designate _____ to serve as guardian of my person, _____ as first alternate guardian of my person, _____ as second alternate guardian of my person, and _____ as third alternate guardian of my person.

2.  I designate _____ to serve as guardian of my estate, _____ as first alternate guardian of my estate, _____ as second alternate guardian of my estate, and _____ as third alternate guardian of my estate.

3.  If any guardian or alternate guardian dies, does not qualify, or resigns, the next named alternate guardian becomes my guardian.

4.  I expressly disqualify the following persons from serving as guardian of my person: _____, _____, and _____.

5.  I expressly disqualify the following persons from serving as guardian of my estate: _____, _____, and _____.

Signed this ___ day of _____, 20___.

_____
Declarant

_____
Witness

_____
Witness

SELF–PROVING AFFIDAVIT

Before me, the undersigned authority, on this date personally appeared _____, the declarant, and _____ and _____ as witnesses, and all being duly sworn, the declarant said that the above instrument was his or her Declaration of Guardian and that the declarant had made and executed it for the purposes expressed in the declaration.  The witnesses declared to me that they are each 14 years of age or older, that they saw the declarant sign the declaration, that they signed the declaration as witnesses, and that the declarant appeared to them to be of sound mind.

_____
Declarant

_____
Affiant

_____
Affiant

Subscribed and sworn to before me by the above named declarant and affiants on this ___ day of _____, 20___.

_____
Notary Public in and for the
State of Texas
My Commission expires:

_____

Added by Acts 2011, 82nd Leg., ch. 823 (H.B. 2759), § 1.02, eff. Jan. 1, 2014.

### § 1104.205.  Alternative to Self–proving Affidavit

(a) As an alternative to the self-proving affidavit authorized by Section 1104.204, a declaration of guardian in the event of later incapacity or need of guardian may be simultaneously executed, attested, and made self-proved by including the following in substantially the same form and with substantially the same contents:

I, _____, as declarant, after being duly sworn, declare to the undersigned witnesses and to the undersigned authority that this instrument is my Declaration of Guardian in the Event of Later Incapacity or Need of Guardian, and that I have made and executed it for the purposes expressed in the declaration. I now sign this declaration in the presence of the attesting witnesses and the undersigned authority on this ___ day of _____, 20___.

_____
Declarant

The undersigned, _____ and _____, each being 14 years of age or older, after being duly sworn, declare to the declarant and to the undersigned authority that the declarant declared to us that this instrument is the declarant's Declaration of Guardian in the Event of Later Incapacity or Need of Guardian and that the declarant executed it for the purposes expressed in the declaration. The declarant then signed this declaration and we believe the declarant to be of sound mind. We now sign our names as attesting witnesses on this _____ day of _____, 20___.

_____
Witness

_____
Witness

Subscribed and sworn to before me by the above named declarant, and affiants, this ___ day of _____, 20___.

_____
Notary Public in and for the
State of Texas
My Commission expires:

_____

(b) A declaration that is executed as provided by Subsection (a) is considered self-proved to the same extent a declaration executed with a self-proving affidavit under Section 1104.204 is considered self-proved.

Added by Acts 2011, 82nd Leg., ch. 823 (H.B. 2759), § 1.02, eff. Jan. 1, 2014.

## § 1104.206. Alternate Self–proving of Declaration

At any time during the declarant's lifetime, a declaration described by Section 1104.203(a)(1) may be made self-proved in the same form and manner that a will written wholly in the testator's handwriting is made self-proved under Section 251.107.

Added by Acts 2011, 82nd Leg., ch. 823 (H.B. 2759), § 1.02, eff. Jan. 1, 2014.

## § 1104.207. Filing of Declaration and Self–proving Affidavit

The declaration and any self-proving affidavit may be filed with the court at any time after the application for appointment of a guardian is filed and before a guardian is appointed.

Added by Acts 2011, 82nd Leg., ch. 823 (H.B. 2759), § 1.02, eff. Jan. 1, 2014.

## § 1104.208. Proof of Declaration

(a) The court may admit a declaration that is self-proved into evidence without the testimony of witnesses attesting to the competency of the declarant and the execution of the declaration. Additional proof of the execution of the declaration with the formalities and solemnities and under the circumstances required to make it a valid declaration is not necessary.

(b) A declaration described by Section 1104.203(a)(1) that is not self-proved may be proved in the same manner that a will written wholly in the testator's handwriting is proved under Section 256.154.

(c) A declaration described by Section 1104.203(a)(2) that is not self-proved may be proved in the same manner that an attested written will produced in court is proved under Section 256.153.

Added by Acts 2011, 82nd Leg., ch. 823 (H.B. 2759), § 1.02, eff. Jan. 1, 2014.

## § 1104.209. Prima Facie Evidence

A properly executed and witnessed self-proving declaration, including a declaration and self-proving affidavit described by Section 1104.203(c), is prima facie evidence that:

(1) the declarant was competent at the time the declarant executed the declaration; and

(2) the guardian named in the declaration would serve the best interests of the ward or incapacitated person.

Added by Acts 2011, 82nd Leg., ch. 823 (H.B. 2759), § 1.02, eff. Jan. 1, 2014.

## § 1104.210. Revocation of Declaration

The declarant may revoke a declaration in any manner provided for the revocation of a will under Section 253.002, including the subsequent re-execution of the declaration in the manner required for the original declaration.

Added by Acts 2011, 82nd Leg., ch. 823 (H.B. 2759), § 1.02, eff. Jan. 1, 2014.

### § 1104.211. Effect of Divorce on Designation of Spouse

If a declarant designates the declarant's spouse to serve as guardian under this subchapter, and the declarant is subsequently divorced from that spouse before a guardian is appointed, the provision of the declaration designating the spouse has no effect.

Added by Acts 2011, 82nd Leg., ch. 823 (H.B. 2759), § 1.02, eff. Jan. 1, 2014.

### § 1104.212. Alternate or Other Court–appointed Guardian

(a) The court shall appoint the next eligible designated alternate guardian named in a declaration if the designated guardian does not qualify, is deceased, refuses to serve, resigns, or dies after being appointed guardian, or is otherwise unavailable to serve as guardian.

(b) The court shall appoint another person to serve as guardian as otherwise provided by this title if the designated guardian and all designated alternate guardians named in the declaration:

(1) do not qualify;

(2) are deceased;

(3) refuse to serve; or

(4) later die or resign.

Added by Acts 2011, 82nd Leg., ch. 823 (H.B. 2759), § 1.02, eff. Jan. 1, 2014.

## SUBCHAPTER F. CERTIFICATION REQUIREMENTS FOR CERTAIN GUARDIANS

### § 1104.251. Certification Required for Certain Guardians

*Text of subsec. (a) effective until Sept. 1, 2014*

(a) An individual must be certified under Subchapter C, Chapter 111, Government Code, if the individual:

(1) is a private professional guardian;

(2) will represent the interests of a ward as a guardian on behalf of a private professional guardian;

(3) is providing guardianship services to a ward of a guardianship program on the program's behalf, except as provided by Section 1104.254; or

(4) is an employee of the Department of Aging and Disability Services providing guardianship services to a ward of the department.

*Text of subsec. (a) effective Sept. 1, 2014*

(a) An individual must be certified under Subchapter C, Chapter 155, Government Code, if the individual:

(1) is a private professional guardian;

(2) will represent the interests of a ward as a guardian on behalf of a private professional guardian;

(3) is providing guardianship services to a ward of a guardianship program on the program's behalf, except as provided by Section 1104.254; or

(4) is an employee of the Department of Aging and Disability Services providing guardianship services to a ward of the department.

(b) An individual employed by or contracting with a guardianship program must be certified as provided by Subsection (a) to provide guardianship services to a ward of the program.

Added by Acts 2011, 82nd Leg., ch. 823 (H.B. 2759), § 1.02, eff. Jan. 1, 2014. Amended by Acts 2013, 83rd Leg., ch. 42 (S.B. 966), § 2.08, eff. Sept. 1, 2014.

### § 1104.252. Effect of Provisional Certificate

*Text of section effective until Sept. 1, 2014. See, also, text of § 1104.252 effective Sept. 1, 2014.*

For purposes of this subchapter, a person who holds a provisional certificate issued under Section 111.0421, Government Code, is considered to be certified.

Added by Acts 2011, 82nd Leg., ch. 823 (H.B. 2759), § 1.02, eff. Jan. 1, 2014.

### § 1104.252. Effect of Provisional Certificate

*Text of section effective Sept. 1, 2014. See, also, text of § 1104.252 effective until Sept. 1, 2014.*

For purposes of this subchapter, a person who holds a provisional certificate issued under Section 155.103, Government Code, is considered to be certified.

Added by Acts 2011, 82nd Leg., ch. 823 (H.B. 2759), § 1.02, eff. Jan. 1, 2014. Amended by Acts 2013, 83rd Leg., ch. 42 (S.B. 966), § 2.09, eff. Sept. 1, 2014.

## § 1104.253. Exception for Family Members and Friends

*Text of section effective until Sept. 1, 2014. See, also, text of § 1104.253 effective Sept. 1, 2014.*

A family member or friend of an incapacitated person is not required to be certified under Subchapter C, Chapter 111, Government Code, or any other law to serve as the person's guardian.

Added by Acts 2011, 82nd Leg., ch. 823 (H.B. 2759), § 1.02, eff. Jan. 1, 2014.

## § 1104.253. Exception for Family Members and Friends

*Text of section effective Sept. 1, 2014. See, also, text of § 1104.253 effective until Sept. 1, 2014.*

A family member or friend of an incapacitated person is not required to be certified under Subchapter C, Chapter 155, Government Code, or any other law to serve as the person's guardian.

Added by Acts 2011, 82nd Leg., ch. 823 (H.B. 2759), § 1.02, eff. Jan. 1, 2014. Amended by Acts 2013, 83rd Leg., ch. 42 (S.B. 966), § 2.10, eff. Sept. 1, 2014.

## § 1104.254. Exception for Certain Volunteers

An individual volunteering with a guardianship program or with the Department of Aging and Disability Services is not required to be certified as provided by Section 1104.251 to provide guardianship services or other services under Section 161.114, Human Resources Code, on the program's or the department's behalf.

Added by Acts 2011, 82nd Leg., ch. 823 (H.B. 2759), § 1.02, eff. Jan. 1, 2014. Amended by Acts 2013, 83rd Leg., ch. 161 (S.B. 1093), § 6.038, eff. Jan. 1, 2014.

## § 1104.255. Expiration of Certification

*Text of section effective until Sept. 1, 2014. See, also, text of § 1104.255 effective Sept. 1, 2014.*

A person whose certification under Subchapter C, Chapter 111, Government Code, has expired must obtain a new certification under that subchapter to provide or continue providing guardianship services to a ward or incapacitated person under this title.

Added by Acts 2011, 82nd Leg., ch. 823 (H.B. 2759), § 1.02, eff. Jan. 1, 2014.

## § 1104.255. Expiration of Certification

*Text of section effective Sept. 1, 2014. See, also, text of § 1104.255 effective until Sept. 1, 2014.*

A person whose certification under Subchapter C, Chapter 155, Government Code, has expired must obtain a new certification under that subchapter to provide or continue providing guardianship services to a ward or incapacitated person under this title.

Added by Acts 2011, 82nd Leg., ch. 823 (H.B. 2759), § 1.02, eff. Jan. 1, 2014. Amended by Acts 2013, 83rd Leg., ch. 42 (S.B. 966), § 2.11, eff. Sept. 1, 2014.

## § 1104.256. Failure to Comply; Court's Duty to Notify

*Text of section effective until Sept. 1, 2014. See, also, text of § 1104.256 effective Sept. 1, 2014.*

The court shall notify the Guardianship Certification Board if the court becomes aware of a person who is not complying with:

(1) the terms of a certification issued under Subchapter C, Chapter 111, Government Code; or

(2) the standards and rules adopted under that subchapter.

Added by Acts 2011, 82nd Leg., ch. 823 (H.B. 2759), § 1.02, eff. Jan. 1, 2014.

## § 1104.256. Failure to Comply; Court's Duty to Notify

*Text of section effective Sept. 1, 2014. See, also, text of § 1104.256 effective until Sept. 1, 2014.*

The court shall notify the guardianship certification program of the Judicial Branch Certification Commission if the court becomes aware of a person who is not complying with:

(1) the terms of a certification issued under Subchapter C, Chapter 155, Government Code; or

(2) the standards and rules adopted under that subchapter.

Added by Acts 2011, 82nd Leg., ch. 823 (H.B. 2759), § 1.02, eff. Jan. 1, 2014. Amended by Acts 2013, 83rd Leg., ch. 42 (S.B. 966), § 2.12, eff. Sept. 1, 2014.

## § 1104.257. Information Regarding Services Provided by Guardianship Program

*Text of section effective until Sept. 1, 2014. See, also, text of § 1104.257 effective Sept. 1, 2014.*

Not later than January 31 of each year, each guardianship program operating in a county shall submit to the county clerk a copy of the report submitted to the Guardianship Certification Board under Section 111.044, Government Code.

Added by Acts 2011, 82nd Leg., ch. 823 (H.B. 2759), § 1.02, eff. Jan. 1, 2014.

### § 1104.257. Information Regarding Services Provided by Guardianship Program

*Text of section effective Sept. 1, 2014. See, also, text of § 1104.257 effective until Sept. 1, 2014.*

Not later than January 31 of each year, each guardianship program operating in a county shall submit to the county clerk a copy of the report submitted to the guardianship certification program of the Judicial Branch Certification Commission under Section 155.105, Government Code.

Added by Acts 2011, 82nd Leg., ch. 823 (H.B. 2759), § 1.02, eff. Jan. 1, 2014. Amended by Acts 2013, 83rd Leg., ch. 42 (S.B. 966), § 2.13, eff. Sept. 1, 2014.

### § 1104.258. Information Regarding Certain State Employees Providing Guardianship Services

*Text of section effective until Sept. 1, 2014. See, also, text of § 1104.258 effective Sept. 1, 2014.*

Not later than January 31 of each year, the Department of Aging and Disability Services shall submit to the Guardianship Certification Board a statement containing:

(1) the name, address, and telephone number of each department employee who is or will be providing guardianship services to a ward or proposed ward on the department's behalf; and

(2) the name of each county in which each employee named in Subdivision (1) is providing or is authorized to provide those services.

Added by Acts 2011, 82nd Leg., ch. 823 (H.B. 2759), § 1.02, eff. Jan. 1, 2014.

### § 1104.258. Information Regarding Certain State Employees Providing Guardianship Services

*Text of section effective Sept. 1, 2014. See, also, text of § 1104.258 effective until Sept. 1, 2014.*

Not later than January 31 of each year, the Department of Aging and Disability Services shall submit to the guardianship certification program of the Judicial Branch Certification Commission a statement containing:

(1) the name, address, and telephone number of each department employee who is or will be providing guardianship services to a ward or proposed ward on the department's behalf; and

(2) the name of each county in which each employee named in Subdivision (1) is providing or is authorized to provide those services.

Added by Acts 2011, 82nd Leg., ch. 823 (H.B. 2759), § 1.02, eff. Jan. 1, 2014. Amended by Acts 2013, 83rd Leg., ch. 42 (S.B. 966), § 2.14, eff. Sept. 1, 2014.

## SUBCHAPTER G.   PRIVATE PROFESSIONAL GUARDIANS

### § 1104.301. Certification and Registration Required

A court may not appoint a private professional guardian to serve as a guardian or permit a private professional guardian to continue to serve as a guardian under this title if the private professional guardian is not:

(1) certified as provided by Section 1104.251(a), 1104.252, 1104.255, or 1104.256; or

(2) in compliance with the registration requirements of this subchapter.

Added by Acts 2011, 82nd Leg., ch. 823 (H.B. 2759), § 1.02, eff. Jan. 1, 2014.

### § 1104.302. Annual Certificate of Registration

A private professional guardian must annually apply for a certificate of registration.

Added by Acts 2011, 82nd Leg., ch. 823 (H.B. 2759), § 1.02, eff. Jan. 1, 2014.

### § 1104.303. Requirements of Application

(a) An application for a certificate of registration must include a sworn statement containing the following information concerning a private professional guardian or each person who represents or plans to represent the interests of a ward as a guardian on behalf of the private professional guardian:

(1) place of residence;

(2) business address and business telephone number;

(3) educational background and professional experience;

(4) three or more professional references;

*Text of subsec. (a)(5) effective until Sept. 1, 2014*

(5) the name of each ward the private professional guardian or person is or will be serving as a guardian;

*Text of subsec. (a)(5) effective Sept. 1, 2014*

(5) the name of each ward for whom the private professional guardian or person is or will be serving as a guardian;

(6) the aggregate fair market value of the property of all wards that is or will be managed by the private professional guardian or person;

(7) whether the private professional guardian or person has ever been removed as a guardian by the court or resigned as a guardian in a particular case, and, if so:

(A) a description of the circumstances causing the removal or resignation; and

(B) the style of the suit, the docket number, and the court having jurisdiction over the proceeding; and

*Text of subsec. (a)(8) effective until Sept. 1, 2014*

(8) the certification number or provisional certification number issued to the private professional guardian or person by the Guardianship Certification Board.

*Text of subsec. (a)(8) effective Sept. 1, 2014*

(8) the certification number or provisional certification number issued to the private professional guardian or person by the guardianship certification program of the Judicial Branch Certification Commission.

(b) The application must be:

(1) made to the clerk of the county having venue of the proceeding for the appointment of a guardian; and

(2) accompanied by a nonrefundable fee of $40 to cover the cost of administering this subchapter.

Added by Acts 2011, 82nd Leg., ch. 823 (H.B. 2759), § 1.02, eff. Jan. 1, 2014. Amended by Acts 2013, 83rd Leg., ch. 42 (S.B. 966), § 2.15, eff. Sept. 1, 2014; Acts 2013, 83rd Leg., ch. 982 (H.B. 2080), § 13, eff. Jan. 1, 2014.

Section 36 of Acts 2013, 83rd Leg., ch. 982 (H.B. 2080) provides:

"(a) Except as otherwise provided by this section, the changes in law made by this Act apply to:

"(1) a guardianship created before, on, or after the effective date [Jan. 1, 2014] of this Act; and

"(2) an application for a guardianship pending on, or filed on or after, the effective date of this Act.

"(b) The changes in law made by this Act to Sections 1301.054, 1301.055, 1301.057(b), (c), and (d), 1301.058, 1301.101, and 1301.102(a), Estates Code, apply only to an application for the creation, modification, or termination of a management trust that is filed on or after the effective date of this Act. An application described by this subsection that is filed before the effective date of this Act is governed by the law in effect on the date the application was filed, and the former law is continued in effect for that purpose.

"(c) The changes in law made by this Act to Sections 1301.103 and 1301.154(a), Estates Code, and by Section 1301.202(a–1), Estates Code, as added by this Act, apply to a management trust created before, on, or after the effective date of this Act.

"(d) The changes in law made by this Act to Section 1102.003, Estates Code, apply to a guardianship proceeding that is commenced on or after the effective date of this Act. A guardianship proceeding commenced before that date is governed by the law in effect on the date the proceeding was commenced, and the former law is continued in effect for that purpose."

Section 37 of Acts 2013, 83rd Leg., ch. 982 (H.B. 2080) provides:

"Section 51.607, Government Code, does not apply to the change in the amount of a fee made by Section 1104.303(b), Estates Code, as amended by this Act."

## § 1104.304. Term of Registration; Renewal

(a) The term of an initial registration begins on the date the requirements under Section 1104.303 are met and extends through December 31 of the year in which the application is made. After the term of the initial registration, the term of registration begins on January 1 and extends through December 31 of each year.

(b) An application to renew a registration must be completed during December of the year preceding the year for which the renewal is requested.

Added by Acts 2011, 82nd Leg., ch. 823 (H.B. 2759), § 1.02, eff. Jan. 1, 2014.

## § 1104.305. Use of Registration Information

(a) The clerk shall bring the information received under Section 1104.303 to the judge's attention for review.

(b) The judge shall use the information only to determine whether to appoint, remove, or continue the appointment of a private professional guardian.

Added by Acts 2011, 82nd Leg., ch. 823 (H.B. 2759), § 1.02, eff. Jan. 1, 2014.

## § 1104.306. Use of Names and Business Addresses

*Text of section effective until Sept. 1, 2014.*
*See, also, text of § 1104.306 effective Sept. 1, 2014.*

Not later than January 31 of each year, the clerk shall submit to the Guardianship Certification Board the name and business address of each private professional guardian who has satisfied the registration requirements of this subchapter during the preceding year.

Added by Acts 2011, 82nd Leg., ch. 823 (H.B. 2759), § 1.02, eff. Jan. 1, 2014.

### § 1104.306. Use of Names and Business Addresses

*Text of section effective Sept. 1, 2014. See, also, text of § 1104.306 effective until Sept. 1, 2014.*

Not later than January 31 of each year, the clerk shall submit to the guardianship certification program of the Judicial Branch Certification Commission the name and business address of each private professional guardian who has satisfied the registration requirements of this subchapter during the preceding year.

Added by Acts 2011, 82nd Leg., ch. 823 (H.B. 2759), § 1.02, eff. Jan. 1, 2014. Amended by Acts 2013, 83rd Leg., ch. 42 (S.B. 966), § 2.16, eff. Sept. 1, 2014.

## SUBCHAPTER H. GROUNDS FOR DISQUALIFICATION

### § 1104.351. Incapacity or Inexperience

A person may not be appointed guardian if the person is:

(1) a minor or other incapacitated person; or

(2) a person who, because of inexperience, lack of education, or other good reason, is incapable of properly and prudently managing and controlling the person or estate of the ward.

Added by Acts 2011, 82nd Leg., ch. 823 (H.B. 2759), § 1.02, eff. Jan. 1, 2014.

### § 1104.352. Unsuitability

A person may not be appointed guardian if the person is a person, institution, or corporation found by the court to be unsuitable.

Added by Acts 2011, 82nd Leg., ch. 823 (H.B. 2759), § 1.02, eff. Jan. 1, 2014. Amended by Acts 2013, 83rd Leg., ch. 161 (S.B. 1093), § 6.039, eff. Jan. 1, 2014.

### § 1104.353. Notoriously Bad Conduct; Presumption Concerning Best Interest

(a) A person may not be appointed guardian if the person's conduct is notoriously bad.

(b) It is presumed to be not in the best interests of a ward or incapacitated person to appoint as guardian of the ward or incapacitated person a person who has been finally convicted of:

(1) any sexual offense, including sexual assault, aggravated sexual assault, and prohibited sexual conduct;

(2) aggravated assault;

(3) injury to a child, elderly individual, or disabled individual;

(4) abandoning or endangering a child;

(5) terroristic threat; or

(6) continuous violence against the family of the ward or incapacitated person.

Added by Acts 2011, 82nd Leg., ch. 823 (H.B. 2759), § 1.02, eff. Jan. 1, 2014. Amended by Acts 2013, 83rd Leg., ch. 982 (H.B. 2080), § 14, eff. Jan. 1, 2014.

Section 36 of Acts 2013, 83rd Leg., ch. 982 (H.B. 2080) provides:

"(a) Except as otherwise provided by this section, the changes in law made by this Act apply to:

"(1) a guardianship created before, on, or after the effective date [Jan. 1, 2014] of this Act; and

"(2) an application for a guardianship pending on, or filed on or after, the effective date of this Act.

"(b) The changes in law made by this Act to Sections 1301.054, 1301.055, 1301.057(b), (c), and (d), 1301.058, 1301.101, and 1301.102(a), Estates Code, apply only to an application for the creation, modification, or termination of a management trust that is filed on or after the effective date of this Act. An application described by this subsection that is filed before the effective date of this Act is governed by the law in effect on the date the application was filed, and the former law is continued in effect for that purpose.

"(c) The changes in law made by this Act to Sections 1301.103 and 1301.154(a), Estates Code, and by Section 1301.202(a–1), Estates Code, as added by this Act, apply to a management trust created before, on, or after the effective date of this Act.

"(d) The changes in law made by this Act to Section 1102.003, Estates Code, apply to a guardianship proceeding that is commenced on or after the effective date of this Act. A guardianship proceeding commenced before that date is governed by the law in effect on the date the proceeding was commenced, and the former law is continued in effect for that purpose."

### § 1104.354. Conflict of Interest

A person may not be appointed guardian if the person:

(1) is a party or is a person whose parent is a party to a lawsuit concerning or affecting the welfare of the proposed ward, unless the court:

(A) determines that the lawsuit claim of the person who has applied to be appointed guardian is not in conflict with the lawsuit claim of the proposed ward; or

(B) appoints a guardian ad litem to represent the interests of the proposed ward throughout the litigation of the ward's lawsuit claim;

(2) is indebted to the proposed ward, unless the person pays the debt before appointment; or

(3) asserts a claim adverse to the proposed ward or the proposed ward's property.

Added by Acts 2011, 82nd Leg., ch. 823 (H.B. 2759), § 1.02, eff. Jan. 1, 2014.

### § 1104.355. Disqualified in Declaration

A person may not be appointed guardian if the person is disqualified in a declaration under Section 1104.202(b).

Added by Acts 2011, 82nd Leg., ch. 823 (H.B. 2759), § 1.02, eff. Jan. 1, 2014.

### § 1104.356. Lack of Certain Required Certification

A person may not be appointed guardian if the person does not have the certification to serve as guardian that is required by Subchapter F.

Added by Acts 2011, 82nd Leg., ch. 823 (H.B. 2759), § 1.02, eff. Jan. 1, 2014.

### § 1104.357. Nonresident Without Resident Agent

A person may not be appointed guardian if the person is a nonresident who has failed to file with the court the name of a resident agent to accept service of process in all actions or proceedings relating to the guardianship.

Added by Acts 2011, 82nd Leg., ch. 823 (H.B. 2759), § 1.02, eff. Jan. 1, 2014.

### § 1104.358. Subject to Protective Order for Family Violence

A person found to have committed family violence who is subject to a protective order issued under Chapter 85, Family Code, may not be appointed guardian of a proposed ward or ward who is protected by the protective order.

Added by Acts 2013, 83rd Leg., ch. 982 (H.B. 2080), § 15, eff. Jan. 1, 2014.

Section 36 of Acts 2013, 83rd Leg., ch. 982 (H.B. 2080) provides:

"(a) Except as otherwise provided by this section, the changes in law made by this Act apply to:

"(1) a guardianship created before, on, or after the effective date [Jan. 1, 2014] of this Act; and

"(2) an application for a guardianship pending on, or filed on or after, the effective date of this Act.

"(b) The changes in law made by this Act to Sections 1301.054, 1301.055, 1301.057(b), (c), and (d), 1301.058, 1301.101, and 1301.102(a), Estates Code, apply only to an application for the creation, modification, or termination of a management trust that is filed on or after the effective date of this Act. An application described by this subsection that is filed before the effective date of this Act is governed by the law in effect on the date the application was filed, and the former law is continued in effect for that purpose.

"(c) The changes in law made by this Act to Sections 1301.103 and 1301.154(a), Estates Code, and by Section 1301.202(a–1), Estates

Code, as added by this Act, apply to a management trust created before, on, or after the effective date of this Act.

"(d) The changes in law made by this Act to Section 1102.003, Estates Code, apply to a guardianship proceeding that is commenced on or after the effective date of this Act. A guardianship proceeding commenced before that date is governed by the law in effect on the date the proceeding was commenced, and the former law is continued in effect for that purpose."

## SUBCHAPTER I. ACCESS TO CRIMINAL HISTORY RECORDS

### § 1104.401. Definition

In this subchapter, "department" means the Department of Aging and Disability Services.

Added by Acts 2011, 82nd Leg., ch. 823 (H.B. 2759), § 1.02, eff. Jan. 1, 2014.

### § 1104.402. Court Clerk's Duty to Obtain Criminal History Record Information; Authority to Charge Fee

(a) Except as provided by Section 1104.403, 1104.404, or 1104.406(a), the clerk of the county having venue of the proceeding for the appointment of a guardian shall obtain criminal history record information that is maintained by the Department of Public Safety or the Federal Bureau of Investigation identification division relating to:

(1) a private professional guardian;

(2) each person who represents or plans to represent the interests of a ward as a guardian on behalf of the private professional guardian;

(3) each person employed by a private professional guardian who will:

(A) have personal contact with a ward or proposed ward;

(B) exercise control over and manage a ward's estate; or

(C) perform any duties with respect to the management of a ward's estate;

(4) each person employed by or volunteering or contracting with a guardianship program to provide guardianship services to a ward of the program on the program's behalf; or

(5) any other person proposed to serve as a guardian under this title, including a proposed temporary guardian and a proposed successor guardian, other than the ward's or proposed ward's family member or an attorney.

(b) The clerk may charge a $10 fee to recover the costs of obtaining criminal history record information under Subsection (a).

Added by Acts 2011, 82nd Leg., ch. 823 (H.B. 2759), § 1.02, eff. Jan. 1, 2014.

### § 1104.403. Submission of Criminal History Record Information by Proposed Guardian

Not later than the 10th day before the date of the hearing to appoint a guardian, a person may submit to the clerk a copy of the person's criminal history record information required under Section 1104. 402(a)(5) that the person obtains not earlier than the 30th day before the date of the hearing from:

(1) the Department of Public Safety; or

(2) the Federal Bureau of Investigation.

Added by Acts 2011, 82nd Leg., ch. 823 (H.B. 2759), § 1.02, eff. Jan. 1, 2014.

### § 1104.404. Exception for Information Concerning Certain Persons Holding a Certificate

*Text of subsec. (a) effective until Sept. 1, 2014*

(a) The clerk described by Section 1104.402 is not required to obtain criminal history record information for a person who holds a certificate issued under Section 111.042, Government Code, or a provisional certificate issued under Section 111.0421, Government Code, if the Guardianship Certification Board conducted a criminal history check on the person before issuing or renewing the certificate.

*Text of subsec. (a) effective Sept. 1, 2014*

(a) The clerk described by Section 1104.402 is not required to obtain criminal history record information for a person who holds a certificate issued under Section 155.102, Government Code, or a provisional certificate issued under Section 155.103, Government Code, if the guardianship certification program of the Judicial Branch Certification Commission conducted a criminal history check on the person before issuing or renewing the certificate.

(b) The board shall provide to the clerk at the court's request the criminal history record information that was obtained from the Department of Public Safety or the Federal Bureau of Investigation.

Added by Acts 2011, 82nd Leg., ch. 823 (H.B. 2759), § 1.02, eff. Jan. 1, 2014. Amended by Acts 2013, 83rd Leg., ch. 42 (S.B. 966), § 2.17, eff. Sept. 1, 2014.

### § 1104.405. Information for Exclusive Use of Court

(a) Criminal history record information obtained or provided under Section 1104.402, 1104. 403, or 1104.404 is privileged and confidential and is for the exclusive use of the court. The criminal history record information may not be released or otherwise disclosed to any person or agency except on court order or consent of the person being investigated.

(b) The county clerk may destroy the criminal history record information after the information is used for the purposes authorized by this subchapter.

Added by Acts 2011, 82nd Leg., ch. 823 (H.B. 2759), § 1.02, eff. Jan. 1, 2014.

### § 1104.406. Department's Duty to Obtain Criminal History Record Information

(a) The department shall obtain criminal history record information that is maintained by the Department of Public Safety or the Federal Bureau of Investigation identification division relating to each individual who is or will be providing guardianship services to a ward of or referred by the department, including:

(1) an employee of or an applicant selected for an employment position with the department;

(2) a volunteer or an applicant selected to volunteer with the department;

(3) an employee of or an applicant selected for an employment position with a business entity or other person who contracts with the department to provide guardianship services to a ward referred by the department; and

(4) a volunteer or an applicant selected to volunteer with a business entity or other person described by Subdivision (3).

(b) The department must obtain the information in Subsection (a) before:

(1) making an offer of employment to an applicant for an employment position; or

(2) a volunteer contacts a ward of or referred by the department.

(c) The department must annually obtain the information in Subsection (a) regarding employees or volunteers providing guardianship services.

Added by Acts 2011, 82nd Leg., ch. 823 (H.B. 2759), § 1.02, eff. Jan. 1, 2014.

## § 1104.407. Duty to Provide Information on Request

*Text of section effective until Sept. 1, 2014. See, also, text of § 1104.407 effective Sept. 1, 2014.*

The department shall provide the information obtained under Section 1102.406(a) to:

(1) the clerk of the county having venue of the guardianship proceeding at the court's request; and

(2) the Guardianship Certification Board at the board's request.

Added by Acts 2011, 82nd Leg., ch. 823 (H.B. 2759), § 1.02, eff. Jan. 1, 2014.

## § 1104.407. Duty to Provide Information on Request

*Text of section effective Sept. 1, 2014. See, also, text of § 1104.407 effective until Sept. 1, 2014.*

The department shall provide the information obtained under Section 1104.406(a) to:

(1) the clerk of the county having venue of the guardianship proceeding at the court's request; and

(2) the guardianship certification program of the Judicial Branch Certification Commission at the commission's request.

Added by Acts 2011, 82nd Leg., ch. 823 (H.B. 2759), § 1.02, eff. Jan. 1, 2014. Amended by Acts 2013, 83rd Leg., ch. 42 (S.B. 966), § 2.18, eff. Sept. 1, 2014.

## § 1104.408. Information for Exclusive Use of Court or Guardianship Certification Board

*Text of section effective until Sept. 1, 2014. See, also, text of § 1104.408 effective Sept. 1, 2014.*

(a) Criminal history record information obtained under Section 1104.407 is privileged and confidential and is for the exclusive use of the court or Guardianship Certification Board, as appropriate. The information may not be released or otherwise disclosed to any person or agency except:

(1) on court order;

(2) with the consent of the person being investigated; or

(3) as authorized by Section 1104.404 of this code or Section 411.1386(a–6), Government Code.

(b) The county clerk or Guardianship Certification Board may destroy the criminal history record information after the information is used for the purposes authorized by this subchapter.

Added by Acts 2011, 82nd Leg., ch. 823 (H.B. 2759), § 1.02, eff. Jan. 1, 2014.

## § 1104.408. Information for Exclusive Use of Court or Guardianship Certification Program of Judicial Branch Certification Commission

*Text of section effective Sept. 1, 2014. See, also, text of § 1104.408 effective until Sept. 1, 2014.*

(a) Criminal history record information obtained under Section 1104.407 is privileged and confidential and is for the exclusive use of the court or guardianship certification program of the Judicial Branch Certification Commission, as appropriate. The information may not be released or otherwise disclosed to any person or agency except:

(1) on court order;

(2) with the consent of the person being investigated; or

(3) as authorized by Section 1104.404 of this code or Section 411.1386(a–6), Government Code.

(b) The county clerk or guardianship certification program of the Judicial Branch Certification Commission may destroy the criminal history record information after the information is used for the purposes authorized by this subchapter.

Added by Acts 2011, 82nd Leg., ch. 823 (H.B. 2759), § 1.02, eff. Jan. 1, 2014. Amended by Acts 2013, 83rd Leg., ch. 42 (S.B. 966), § 2.19, eff. Sept. 1, 2014.

## § 1104.409. Use of Information by Court

The court shall use the information obtained under this subchapter only in determining whether to:

(1) appoint, remove, or continue the appointment of a private professional guardian, a guardianship program, or the department; or

(2) appoint any other person proposed to serve as a guardian under this title, including a proposed temporary guardian and a proposed successor guardian, other than the ward's or proposed ward's family member or an attorney.

Added by Acts 2011, 82nd Leg., ch. 823 (H.B. 2759), § 1.02, eff. Jan. 1, 2014.

## § 1104.410. Use of Information by Guardianship Certification Board

*Text of section effective until Sept. 1, 2014. See, also, text of § 1104.410 effective Sept. 1, 2014.*

Criminal history record information obtained by the Guardianship Certification Board under Section 1104.407(2) may be used for any purpose related to the issuance, denial, renewal, suspension, or revocation of a certificate issued by the board.

Added by Acts 2011, 82nd Leg., ch. 823 (H.B. 2759), § 1.02, eff. Jan. 1, 2014.

## § 1104.410. Use of Information by Guardianship Certification Program of Judicial Branch Certification Commission

*Text of section effective Sept. 1, 2014. See, also, text of § 1104.410 effective until Sept. 1, 2014.*

Criminal history record information obtained by the guardianship certification program of the Judicial Branch Certification Commission under Section 1104.407(2) may be used for any purpose related to the issuance, denial, renewal, suspension, or revocation of a certificate issued by the commission.

Added by Acts 2011, 82nd Leg., ch. 823 (H.B. 2759), § 1.02, eff. Jan. 1, 2014. Amended by Acts 2013, 83rd Leg., ch. 42 (S.B. 966), § 2.20, eff. Sept. 1, 2014.

## § 1104.411. Criminal Offense for Unauthorized Release or Disclosure

(a) A person commits an offense if the person releases or discloses any information received under this subchapter without the authorization prescribed by Section 1104.405 or 1104.408.

(b) An offense under this section is a Class A misdemeanor.

Added by Acts 2011, 82nd Leg., ch. 823 (H.B. 2759), § 1.02, eff. Jan. 1, 2014.

## § 1104.412. Effect of Subchapter on Department's Authority to Obtain or Use Information

This subchapter does not prohibit the department from obtaining and using criminal history record information as provided by other law.

Added by Acts 2011, 82nd Leg., ch. 823 (H.B. 2759), § 1.02, eff. Jan. 1, 2014.

## CHAPTER 1105. QUALIFICATION OF GUARDIANS

### SUBCHAPTER A. GENERAL PROVISIONS

## SUBCHAPTER A. GENERAL PROVISIONS

### § 1105.001. Definitions

In this chapter:

(1) "Bond" means a bond required by this chapter to be given by a person appointed to serve as a guardian.

(2) "Oath" means an oath required by this chapter to be taken by a person appointed to serve as a guardian.

Added by Acts 2011, 82nd Leg., ch. 823 (H.B. 2759), § 1.02, eff. Jan. 1, 2014.

### § 1105.002. Manner of Qualification of Guardian

(a) Except as provided by Subsection (b), a guardian is considered to have qualified when the guardian has:

(1) taken and filed the oath required under Section 1105.051;

(2) given the required bond;

(3) filed the bond with the clerk; and

(4) obtained the judge's approval of the bond.

(b) A guardian who is not required to give a bond is considered to have qualified when the guardian has taken and filed the required oath.

Added by Acts 2011, 82nd Leg., ch. 823 (H.B. 2759), § 1.02, eff. Jan. 1, 2014.

### § 1105.003. Period for Taking Oath and Giving Bond

(a) Except as provided by Section 1103.003, an oath may be taken and subscribed and a bond may be given and approved at any time before:

(1) the 21st day after the date of the order granting letters of guardianship; or

(2) the letters of guardianship are revoked for a failure to qualify within the period allowed.

(b) A guardian of an estate must give a bond before being issued letters of guardianship unless a bond is not required under this title.

Added by Acts 2011, 82nd Leg., ch. 823 (H.B. 2759), § 1.02, eff. Jan. 1, 2014.

## SUBCHAPTER B. OATHS

### § 1105.051. Oath of Guardian

(a) A guardian shall take an oath to discharge faithfully the duties of guardian for the person or estate, or both, of a ward.

(b) If the Department of Aging and Disability Services is appointed guardian, a department representative shall take the oath required by Subsection (a).

Added by Acts 2011, 82nd Leg., ch. 823 (H.B. 2759), § 1.02, eff. Jan. 1, 2014.

### § 1105.052. Administration of Oath

An oath may be taken before any person authorized to administer oaths under the laws of this state.

Added by Acts 2011, 82nd Leg., ch. 823 (H.B. 2759), § 1.02, eff. Jan. 1, 2014.

## SUBCHAPTER C. GENERAL PROVISIONS RELATING TO BONDS

### § 1105.101. Bond Generally Required; Exceptions

(a) Except as provided by this section, a guardian of the person or the estate of a ward shall give a bond.

(b) A bond is not required if the guardian is:

(1) a corporate fiduciary; or

(2) a guardianship program operated by a county.

(c) The court shall issue letters of guardianship of the person to a person without the requirement of a bond if:

(1) the person is named to be appointed guardian in a will made by a surviving parent that is probated by a court in this state, or in a written declaration made by a surviving parent, and the will or declaration directs that the guardian serve without a bond; and

(2) the court finds that the guardian is qualified.

(d) The court may not waive the requirement of bond for the guardian of the estate of a ward, regardless of whether a surviving parent's will or written declaration directs the court to waive the bond.

Added by Acts 2011, 82nd Leg., ch. 823 (H.B. 2759), § 1.02, eff. Jan. 1, 2014.

### § 1105.102. Bond for Certain Guardians of the Person

(a) This section applies only to a bond required to be posted by a guardian of the person of a ward when there is no guardian of the ward's estate.

(b) To ensure the performance of the guardian's duties, a court may accept only:

(1) a corporate surety bond;

(2) a personal surety bond;

(3) a deposit of money instead of a surety bond; or

(4) a personal bond.

(c) In determining the appropriate type and amount of bond to set for the guardian, the court shall consider:

(1) the familial relationship of the guardian to the ward;

(2) the guardian's ties to the community;

(3) the guardian's financial condition;

(4) the guardian's past history of compliance with the court; and

(5) the reason the guardian may have previously been denied a corporate surety bond.

Added by Acts 2011, 82nd Leg., ch. 823 (H.B. 2759), § 1.02, eff. Jan. 1, 2014.

### § 1105.103.  Bond Required From Guardian Otherwise Exempt

(a) This section applies only to an individual guardian of the estate from whom a bond was not required.

(b) A person who has a debt, claim, or demand against the guardianship, with respect to the justice of which an oath has been made by the person, the person's agent or attorney, or another person interested in the guardianship, in person or as the representative of another person, may file a written complaint under oath in the court in which the guardian was appointed.

(c) After a complaint is filed under Subsection (b), the court shall cite the guardian to appear and show cause why the guardian should not be required to give a bond.

(d) On hearing a complaint filed under Subsection (b), if it appears to the court that the guardian is wasting, mismanaging, or misapplying the guardianship estate and that a creditor may probably lose the creditor's debt, or that a person's interest in the guardianship may be diminished or lost, the court shall enter an order requiring the guardian to give a bond not later than the 10th day after the date of the order.

(e) A bond required under Subsection (d) must be:

(1) in an amount sufficient to protect the guardianship and the guardianship's creditors;

(2) approved by and payable to the judge; and

(3) conditioned that the guardian:

(A) will well and truly administer the guardianship; and

(B) will not waste, mismanage, or misapply the guardianship estate.

(f) If the guardian fails to give the bond required under Subsection (d) and the judge has not extended the period for giving the bond, the judge, without citation, shall remove the guardian and appoint a competent person as guardian, who shall:

(1) administer the guardianship according to the provisions of a will or law;

(2) take the oath required of a guardian under Section 1105.051 before the person enters on the administration of the guardianship; and

(3) give bond in the same manner and in the same amount provided by this title for the issuance of original letters of guardianship.

Added by Acts 2011, 82nd Leg., ch. 823 (H.B. 2759), § 1.02, eff. Jan. 1, 2014.

### § 1105.104.  Bonds of Joint Guardians

If two or more persons are appointed as guardians and are required to give a bond by the court or under this title, the court may require:

(1) a separate bond from each person; or

(2) a joint bond from all of the persons.

Added by Acts 2011, 82nd Leg., ch. 823 (H.B. 2759), § 1.02, eff. Jan. 1, 2014.

### § 1105.105.  Bond of Married Person

(a) A married person appointed as guardian may jointly execute, with or without, the person's spouse, a bond required by law.

(b) A bond executed by a married person:

(1) binds the person's separate estate; and

(2) may bind the person's spouse only if the spouse signs the bond.

Added by Acts 2011, 82nd Leg., ch. 823 (H.B. 2759), § 1.02, eff. Jan. 1, 2014.

### § 1105.106.  Bond of Married Person Younger Than 18 Years of Age

A bond required to be executed by a person who is younger than 18 years of age, is or has been married, and accepts and qualifies as guardian is as valid and binding for all purposes as if the person were of legal age.

Added by Acts 2011, 82nd Leg., ch. 823 (H.B. 2759), § 1.02, eff. Jan. 1, 2014.

### § 1105.107. Bond of Guardianship Program

The judge may require a guardianship program appointed guardian under this title to file one bond that:

(1) meets all the conditions required under this title; and

(2) is in an amount sufficient to protect all of the guardianships and the creditors of the guardianships of the wards receiving services from the guardianship program.

Added by Acts 2011, 82nd Leg., ch. 823 (H.B. 2759), § 1.02, eff. Jan. 1, 2014.

### § 1105.108. Subscription of Bond by Principals and Sureties

A bond required under this title shall be subscribed by the principals and sureties.

Added by Acts 2011, 82nd Leg., ch. 823 (H.B. 2759), § 1.02, eff. Jan. 1, 2014.

### § 1105.109. Form of Bond

The following form, or a form with the same substance, may be used for the bond of a guardian:

"The State of Texas

"County of _____

"Know all persons by these presents that we, _____ (insert name of each principal), as principal, and ___ (insert name of each surety), as sureties, are held and firmly bound to the judge of ___ (insert reference to appropriate judge), and that judge's successors in office, in the sum of $_____; conditioned that the above bound principal or principals, appointed by the judge as guardian or temporary guardian of the person or of the estate, or both, of _____ (insert name of ward, stating in each case whether the person is a minor or an incapacitated person other than a minor), shall well and truly perform all of the duties required of the guardian or temporary guardian by law under appointment."

Added by Acts 2011, 82nd Leg., ch. 823 (H.B. 2759), § 1.02, eff. Jan. 1, 2014.

### § 1105.110. Filing of Bond

A bond required under this title shall be filed with the clerk after the court approves the bond.

Added by Acts 2011, 82nd Leg., ch. 823 (H.B. 2759), § 1.02, eff. Jan. 1, 2014.

### § 1105.111. Failure to Give Bond

Another person may be appointed as guardian to replace a guardian who fails to give the bond required by the court within the period required under this title.

Added by Acts 2011, 82nd Leg., ch. 823 (H.B. 2759), § 1.02, eff. Jan. 1, 2014.

### § 1105.112. Bond Not Void on First Recovery

A guardian's bond is not void on the first recovery, but the bond may be sued on and prosecuted from time to time until the entire amount of the bond is recovered.

Added by Acts 2011, 82nd Leg., ch. 823 (H.B. 2759), § 1.02, eff. Jan. 1, 2014.

## SUBCHAPTER D. OTHER PROVISIONS RELATING TO BONDS OF GUARDIANS OF THE ESTATE

### § 1105.151. General Formalities

A bond given by a guardian of the estate must:

(1) be conditioned as required by law;

(2) be payable to the judge or that judge's successors in office;

(3) have the written approval of the judge in the judge's official capacity; and

(4) be executed and approved in accordance with this subchapter.

Added by Acts 2011, 82nd Leg., ch. 823 (H.B. 2759), § 1.02, eff. Jan. 1, 2014.

### § 1105.152. General Standard Regarding Amount of Bond

(a) The judge shall set the amount of a bond for a guardian of an estate in an amount sufficient to protect the guardianship and the guardianship's creditors, as provided by this title.

(b) In determining the amount of the bond, the court may not consider estate assets placed in a management trust under Chapter 1301.

Added by Acts 2011, 82nd Leg., ch. 823 (H.B. 2759), § 1.02, eff. Jan. 1, 2014.

### § 1105.153. Evidentiary Hearing on Amount of Bond

Before setting the amount of a bond required of a guardian of an estate, the court shall hear evidence and determine:

(1) the amount of cash on hand and where that cash is deposited;

(2) the amount of cash estimated to be needed for administrative purposes, including the operation of a business, factory, farm, or ranch owned by the guardianship estate, and administrative expenses for one year;

(3) the revenue anticipated to be received in the succeeding 12 months from dividends, interest, rentals, or use of property belonging to the guardianship estate and the aggregate amount of any installments or periodic payments to be collected;

(4) the estimated value of certificates of stock, bonds, notes, or other securities of the ward, and the name of the depository in which the stocks, bonds, notes, or other securities are deposited;

(5) the face value of life insurance or other policies payable to the ward or the ward's estate;

(6) the estimated value of other personal property that is owned by the guardianship, or by a person with a disability; and

(7) the estimated amount of debts due and owing by the ward.

Added by Acts 2011, 82nd Leg., ch. 823 (H.B. 2759), § 1.02, eff. Jan. 1, 2014.

### § 1105.154. Specific Bond Amount

(a) Except as otherwise provided by this section, the judge shall set the amount of a bond of a guardian of an estate in an amount equal to the sum of:

(1) the estimated value of all personal property belonging to the ward; and

(2) an additional amount to cover revenue anticipated to be derived during the succeeding 12 months from:

(A) interest and dividends;

(B) collectible claims;

(C) the aggregate amount of any installments or periodic payments, excluding income derived or to be derived from federal social security payments; and

(D) rentals for the use of property.

(b) The judge shall reduce the amount of the original bond under Subsection (a) in proportion to the amount of cash or the value of securities or other assets:

(1) authorized or required to be deposited by court order; or

(2) voluntarily deposited by the guardian or the sureties on the guardian's bond as provided in Sections 1105.156 and 1105.157(a).

(c) The judge shall set the amount of the bond for a temporary guardian.

Added by Acts 2011, 82nd Leg., ch. 823 (H.B. 2759), § 1.02, eff. Jan. 1, 2014.

### § 1105.155. Agreement Regarding Deposit of Estate Assets

(a) If the court considers it to be in the best interests of the ward, the court may require the guardian of the estate and the corporate or personal sureties on the guardian's bond to agree to deposit cash and other assets of the guardianship estate in a depository described by Subsection (b). If the depository is otherwise proper, the court may require the deposit to be made in a manner so as to prevent the withdrawal of the money or other assets in the guardianship estate without the written consent of the surety or on court order made after notice to the surety.

(b) Cash and assets must be deposited under this section in a financial institution as defined by Section 201.101, Finance Code, that:

(1) has its main office or a branch office in this state; and

(2) is qualified to act as a depository in this state under the laws of this state or the United States.

(c) An agreement made by a guardian and the sureties on the guardian's bond under this section does not release the principal or sureties from liability, or change the liability of the principal or sureties, as established by the terms of the bond.

Added by Acts 2011, 82nd Leg., ch. 823 (H.B. 2759), § 1.02, eff. Jan. 1, 2014.

### § 1105.156. Deposit of Estate Assets on Terms Prescribed by Court

(a) Cash, securities, or other personal assets of a ward to which the ward is entitled may, or if considered by the court to be in the best interests of the ward, shall, be deposited in one or more depositories described by this subchapter on terms prescribed by the court.

(b) The court in which the guardianship proceeding is pending may authorize or require additional estate assets currently on hand or that accrue during the pendency of the proceeding to be deposited as provided by Subsection (a) on:

(1) the court's own motion; or

(2) the written application of the guardian or any other person interested in the ward.

(c) The amount of the bond required to be given by the guardian of the estate shall be reduced in proportion to the amount of the cash or the value of the securities or other assets deposited under this section.

(d) Cash, securities, or other assets deposited under this section may be withdrawn wholly or partly from the depository only in accordance with a court order, and the amount of the guardian's bond shall be increased in proportion to the amount of the cash or the value of the securities or other assets authorized to be withdrawn.

Added by Acts 2011, 82nd Leg., ch. 823 (H.B. 2759), § 1.02, eff. Jan. 1, 2014.

### § 1105.157.  Deposits of Guardian

(a) Instead of giving a surety or sureties on a bond, or to reduce the amount of a bond, the guardian of an estate may deposit the guardian's own cash or securities acceptable to the court with a financial institution as defined by Section 201.101, Finance Code, that has its main office or a branch office in this state.

(b) If the deposit is otherwise proper, the deposit must be in an amount or value equal to the amount of the bond required or the bond shall be reduced by the value of assets that are deposited.

(c) A depository that receives a deposit made under Subsection (a) shall issue a receipt for the deposit that:

(1) shows the amount of cash deposited or the amount and description of the securities deposited, as applicable; and

(2) states that the depository agrees to disburse or deliver the cash or securities only on receipt of a certified copy of an order of the court in which the proceeding is pending.

(d) A receipt issued by a depository under Subsection (c) must be attached to the guardian's bond and be delivered to and filed by the county clerk after the receipt is approved by the judge.

(e) The amount of cash or securities on deposit may be increased or decreased, by court order from time to time, as the interests of the guardianship require.

(f) A deposit of cash or securities made instead of a surety on the bond may be withdrawn or released only on order of a court that has jurisdiction.

(g) A creditor has the same rights against a guardian of the estate and the deposits as are provided for recovery against sureties on a bond.

Added by Acts 2011, 82nd Leg., ch. 823 (H.B. 2759), § 1.02, eff. Jan. 1, 2014.

### § 1105.158.  Bond Required Instead of Deposits

(a) The court may on its own motion or on the written application by the guardian of an estate or any other person interested in the guardianship:

(1) require the guardian to give adequate bond instead of the deposit; or

(2) authorize withdrawal of the deposit and substitution of a bond with sureties.

(b) Before the 21st day after the date the guardian is personally served with notice of the filing of the application or the date the court enters the court's motion, the guardian shall file a sworn statement showing the condition of the guardianship.

(c) A guardian who fails to comply with Subsection (b) is subject to removal as in other cases.

(d) The deposit may not be released or withdrawn until the court:

(1) is satisfied as to the condition of the guardianship estate;

(2) determines the amount of the bond; and

(3) receives and approves the bond.

Added by Acts 2011, 82nd Leg., ch. 823 (H.B. 2759), § 1.02, eff. Jan. 1, 2014.

### § 1105.159.  Withdrawal of Deposits on Closing of Guardianship

(a) Any deposit of assets of the guardian of an estate, the guardianship, or a surety that remains at the time a guardianship is closed shall be released by court order and paid to the person entitled to the assets.

(b) Except as provided by Subsection (c), a writ of attachment or garnishment does not lie against a deposit described by Subsection (a).

(c) A writ of attachment or garnishment may lie against a deposit described by Subsection (a) as to a claim of a creditor of the guardianship or a person interested in the guardianship, including a distributee or ward, only to the extent the court has ordered distribution.

Added by Acts 2011, 82nd Leg., ch. 823 (H.B. 2759), § 1.02, eff. Jan. 1, 2014.

## § 1105.160. Authorized Corporate or Personal Sureties

(a) The surety on a bond of a guardian of an estate may be an authorized corporate or personal surety.

(b) A bond of a guardian of an estate with sureties who are individuals must have at least two sureties, each of whom must:

(1) execute an affidavit in the manner provided by Subchapter E; and

(2) own property in this state, excluding property exempt by law, that the judge is satisfied is sufficient to qualify the person as a surety as required by law.

(c) A bond with an authorized corporate surety is only required to have one surety, except as otherwise provided by law.

Added by Acts 2011, 82nd Leg., ch. 823 (H.B. 2759), § 1.02, eff. Jan. 1, 2014.

## § 1105.161. Sureties for Certain Bonds

(a) If the amount of the bond of a guardian of an estate exceeds $50,000, the court may require that the bond be signed by:

(1) at least two authorized corporate sureties; or

(2) one corporate surety and at least two good and sufficient personal sureties.

(b) The guardianship shall pay the cost of a bond with corporate sureties.

Added by Acts 2011, 82nd Leg., ch. 823 (H.B. 2759), § 1.02, eff. Jan. 1, 2014.

## § 1105.162. Deposits by Personal Surety

Instead of executing an affidavit under Section 1105.201 or creating a lien under Section 1105.202 when required, a personal surety may deposit the surety's own cash or securities in the same manner as a guardian instead of pledging real property as security, subject to the provisions governing the deposits if made by a guardian.

Added by Acts 2011, 82nd Leg., ch. 823 (H.B. 2759), § 1.02, eff. Jan. 1, 2014.

## § 1105.163. Applicability of Subchapter to Certain Court Orders

To the extent applicable, the provisions of this subchapter relating to the deposit of cash and securities cover the orders entered by the court when:

(1) property of a guardianship has been authorized to be sold or rented;

(2) money is borrowed from the guardianship;

(3) real property, or an interest in real property, has been authorized to be leased for mineral development or made subject to unitization;

(4) the general bond has been found insufficient; or

(5) money is borrowed or invested on behalf of a ward.

Added by Acts 2011, 82nd Leg., ch. 823 (H.B. 2759), § 1.02, eff. Jan. 1, 2014.

## SUBCHAPTER E. PROVISIONS RELATING TO PERSONAL SURETIES

## § 1105.201. Affidavit of Personal Surety

(a) Before a judge considers a bond with a personal surety, each personal surety must execute an affidavit stating the amount by which the surety's assets that are reachable by creditors exceeds the surety's liabilities. The total of the surety's worth must equal at least twice the amount of the bond.

(b) Each affidavit must be presented to the judge for consideration and, if approved, shall be attached to and form part of the bond.

Added by Acts 2011, 82nd Leg., ch. 823 (H.B. 2759), § 1.02, eff. Jan. 1, 2014.

## § 1105.202. Lien on Real Property Owned by Personal Surety

(a) If a judge finds that the estimated value of personal property of the guardianship that cannot be deposited, as provided by Subchapter D, is such that personal sureties cannot be accepted without the creation of a specific lien on the real property owned by the sureties, the judge shall enter an order requiring each surety to designate real property that is owned by the surety, located in this state, and subject to execution. The designated property must have a value that exceeds all liens and unpaid taxes by an amount at least equal to the amount of the bond and must have an adequate legal description, all of which the surety shall incorporate in an affidavit. Following approval by the judge, the affidavit shall be attached to and form part of the bond.

(b) A lien arises as security for the performance of the obligation of the bond only on the real property designated in the affidavit.

(c) Before letters of guardianship are issued to the guardian whose bond includes an affidavit under this section, the court clerk shall mail a statement to the office of the county clerk of each county in which any real property designated in the affidavit is located. The statement must be signed by the court clerk and include:

(1) a sufficient description of the real property;

(2) the names of the principal and sureties on the bond;

(3) the amount of the bond;

(4) the name of the guardianship; and

(5) the name of the court in which the bond is given.

(d) Each county clerk who receives a statement required by Subsection (c) shall record the statement in the county deed records. Each recorded statement shall be indexed in a manner that permits the convenient determination of the existence and character of the lien described in the statement.

(e) The recording and indexing required by Subsection (d) is constructive notice to a person regarding the existence of the lien on the real property located in the county, effective as of the date of the indexing.

(f) If each personal surety subject to a court order under this section does not comply with the order, the judge may require that the bond be signed by:

(1) an authorized corporate surety; or

(2) an authorized corporate surety and at least two personal sureties.

Added by Acts 2011, 82nd Leg., ch. 823 (H.B. 2759), § 1.02, eff. Jan. 1, 2014.

### § 1105.203. Subordination of Lien on Real Property Owned by Personal Surety

(a) A personal surety required to create a lien on specific real property under Section 1105.202 who wishes to lease the real property for mineral development may file a written application in the court in which the proceeding is pending requesting subordination of the lien to the proposed lease.

(b) The judge may enter an order granting the application.

(c) A certified copy of an order entered under this section that is filed and recorded in the deed records of the proper county is sufficient to subordinate the lien to the rights of a lessee under the proposed lease.

Added by Acts 2011, 82nd Leg., ch. 823 (H.B. 2759), § 1.02, eff. Jan. 1, 2014.

### § 1105.204. Release of Lien on Real Property Owned by Personal Sureties

(a) A personal surety who has given a lien under Section 1105.202 may apply to the court to have the lien released.

(b) The court shall order the lien released if:

(1) the court is satisfied that the bond is sufficient without the lien; or

(2) sufficient other real or personal property of the surety is substituted on the same terms required for the lien that is to be released.

(c) If the personal surety does not offer a lien on other substituted property under Subsection (b)(2) and the court is not satisfied that the bond is sufficient without the substitution of other property, the court shall order the guardian to appear and give a new bond.

(d) A certified copy of the court's order releasing the lien and describing the property that was subject to the lien has the effect of canceling the lien if the order is filed with the county clerk and recorded in the deed records of the county in which the property is located.

Added by Acts 2011, 82nd Leg., ch. 823 (H.B. 2759), § 1.02, eff. Jan. 1, 2014.

### SUBCHAPTER F. NEW BONDS

### § 1105.251. Grounds for Requiring New Bond

(a) A guardian may be required to give a new bond if:

(1) a surety on a bond dies, removes beyond the limits of this state, or becomes insolvent;

(2) in the court's opinion:

(A) the sureties on a bond are insufficient; or

(B) a bond is defective;

(3) the amount of a bond is insufficient;

(4) a surety on a bond petitions the court to be discharged from future liability on the bond; or

(5) a bond and the record of the bond have been lost or destroyed.

(b) A person interested in the guardianship may have the guardian cited to appear and show cause why the guardian should not be required to give a new bond by filing a written application with the county clerk of the county in which the guardianship proceeding is pending. The application must allege that:

(1) the bond is insufficient or defective; or

(2) the bond and the record of the bond have been lost or destroyed.

Added by Acts 2011, 82nd Leg., ch. 823 (H.B. 2759), § 1.02, eff. Jan. 1, 2014.

### § 1105.252. Court Order or Citation on New Bond

(a) When a judge is made aware that a bond is insufficient or that a bond and the record of the bond have been lost or destroyed, the judge shall:

(1) without delay and without notice enter an order requiring the guardian to give a new bond; or

(2) without delay have the guardian cited to show cause why the guardian should not be required to give a new bond.

(b) An order entered under Subsection (a)(1) must state:

(1) the reasons for requiring a new bond;

(2) the amount of the new bond; and

(3) the period within which the new bond must be given, which may not expire earlier than the 10th day after the date of the order.

(c) A guardian who opposes an order entered under Subsection (a)(1) may demand a hearing on the order. The hearing must be held before the expiration of the period within which the new bond must be given.

Added by Acts 2011, 82nd Leg., ch. 823 (H.B. 2759), § 1.02, eff. Jan. 1, 2014.

### § 1105.253. Show Cause Hearing on New Bond Requirement

(a) On the return of a citation ordering a guardian to show cause why the guardian should not be required to give a new bond, the judge shall, on the date specified in the return of citation for the hearing of the matter, inquire into the sufficiency of the reasons for requiring a new bond.

(b) If the judge is satisfied that a new bond should be required, the judge shall enter an order requiring a new bond. The order must state:

(1) the amount of the new bond; and

(2) the period within which the new bond must be given, which may not expire later than the 20th day after the date of the order.

Added by Acts 2011, 82nd Leg., ch. 823 (H.B. 2759), § 1.02, eff. Jan. 1, 2014.

### § 1105.254. Effect of Order Requiring New Bond

(a) An order requiring a guardian to give a new bond has the effect of suspending the guardian's powers.

(b) After the order is entered, the guardian may not pay out any of the guardianship's money or take any other official action, except to preserve the guardianship's property, until the new bond is given and approved.

Added by Acts 2011, 82nd Leg., ch. 823 (H.B. 2759), § 1.02, eff. Jan. 1, 2014.

### § 1105.255. New Bond in Decreased Amount

(a) A guardian required to give a bond may at any time file with the clerk a written application requesting that the court reduce the amount of the bond.

(b) After the guardian files an application under Subsection (a), the clerk shall issue and have posted notice to all persons interested in the estate and to a surety on the bond. The notice must inform the interested persons and surety of:

(1) the fact that the application has been filed;

(2) the nature of the application; and

(3) the time the judge will hear the application.

(c) The judge may permit the filing of a new bond in a reduced amount if:

(1) proof is submitted that a bond in an amount less than the bond in effect will be adequate to meet the requirements of law and protect the guardianship; and

(2) the judge approves an accounting filed at the time of the application.

Added by Acts 2011, 82nd Leg., ch. 823 (H.B. 2759), § 1.02, eff. Jan. 1, 2014.

### § 1105.256. Request by Surety for New Bond

(a) A surety on a guardian's bond may at any time file with the clerk a petition requesting that the court in which the proceeding is pending:

(1) require the guardian to give a new bond; and

(2) discharge the petitioner from all liability for the future acts of the guardian.

(b) If a petition is filed under Subsection (a), the guardian shall be cited to appear and give a new bond.

Added by Acts 2011, 82nd Leg., ch. 823 (H.B. 2759), § 1.02, eff. Jan. 1, 2014.

### § 1105.257. Discharge of Former Sureties on Approval of New Bond

When a new bond has been given and approved, the judge shall enter an order discharging the sureties on the former bond from all liability for the future acts of the principal on the bond.

Added by Acts 2011, 82nd Leg., ch. 823 (H.B. 2759), § 1.02, eff. Jan. 1, 2014.

## CHAPTER 1106. LETTERS OF GUARDIANSHIP

### § 1106.001. Issuance of Certificate as Letters of Guardianship

(a) When a person who is appointed guardian has qualified under Section 1105.002, the clerk shall issue to the guardian a certificate under seal stating:

(1) the fact of the appointment and of the qualification;

(2) the date of the appointment and of the qualification; and

(3) the date the letters of guardianship expire.

(b) The certificate issued by the clerk under Subsection (a) constitutes letters of guardianship.

Added by Acts 2011, 82nd Leg., ch. 823 (H.B. 2759), § 1.02, eff. Jan. 1, 2014.

### § 1106.002. Expiration of Letters of Guardianship

Letters of guardianship expire one year and four months after the date the letters are issued, unless renewed.

Added by Acts 2011, 82nd Leg., ch. 823 (H.B. 2759), § 1.02, eff. Jan. 1, 2014.

### § 1106.003. Renewal of Letters of Guardianship

(a) The clerk may not renew letters of guardianship relating to the appointment of a guardian of the estate until the court receives and approves the guardian's annual account.

(b) The clerk may not renew letters of guardianship relating to the appointment of a guardian of the person until the court receives and approves the guardian's annual report.

(c) If a guardian's annual account or annual report is disapproved or is not timely filed, the clerk may not issue further letters of guardianship to the delinquent guardian unless ordered by the court.

(d) Except as otherwise provided by this subsection, regardless of the date the court approves an annual account or annual report for purposes of this section, a renewal of letters of guardianship relates back to the date the original letters were issued. If the accounting period has been changed as provided by this title, a renewal relates back to the first day of the accounting period.

Added by Acts 2011, 82nd Leg., ch. 823 (H.B. 2759), § 1.02, eff. Jan. 1, 2014.

### § 1106.004. Replacement and Other Additional Letters of Guardianship

When letters of guardianship have been destroyed or lost, the clerk shall issue new letters that have the same effect as the original letters. The clerk shall also issue any number of letters on request of the person who holds the letters.

Added by Acts 2011, 82nd Leg., ch. 823 (H.B. 2759), § 1.02, eff. Jan. 1, 2014.

### § 1106.005. Effect of Letters or Certificate

(a) Letters of guardianship or a certificate issued under Section 1106.001 under seal of the clerk of the court that granted the letters is sufficient evidence of:

(1) the appointment and qualification of the guardian; and

(2) the date of qualification.

(b) The court order that appoints the guardian is evidence of the authority granted to the guardian and of the scope of the powers and duties that the guardian may exercise only after the date letters of guardianship or a certificate has been issued under Section 1106.001.

Added by Acts 2011, 82nd Leg., ch. 823 (H.B. 2759), § 1.02, eff. Jan. 1, 2014.

## § 1106.006. Validation of Certain Letters of Guardianship

(a) Letters of guardianship existing on September 1, 1993, that were issued to a nonresident guardian without the procedure or any part of the procedure provided in this chapter, or without a notice or citation required of a resident guardian, are validated as of the letters' dates, to the extent that the absence of the procedure, notice, or citation is concerned. An otherwise valid conveyance, mineral lease, or other act of a nonresident guardian qualified and acting in connection with the letters of guardianship and under supporting orders of a county or probate court of this state is validated.

(b) This section does not apply to letters of guardianship, a conveyance, a lease, or another act of a nonresident guardian under this section if the absence of the procedure, notice, or citation involving the letters, conveyance, lease, or other act of the nonresident guardian is an issue in a lawsuit pending in this state on September 1, 1993.

Added by Acts 2011, 82nd Leg., ch. 823 (H.B. 2759), § 1.02, eff. Jan. 1, 2014.

# SUBTITLE E. ADMINISTRATION OF GUARDIANSHIP

## CHAPTER 1151. RIGHTS, POWERS, AND DUTIES UNDER GUARDIANSHIP

### SUBCHAPTER A. RIGHTS, POWERS, AND DUTIES IN GENERAL

### SUBCHAPTER A. RIGHTS, POWERS, AND DUTIES IN GENERAL

## § 1151.001. Rights and Powers Retained by Ward

An incapacitated person for whom a guardian is appointed retains all legal and civil rights and powers except those designated by court order as legal disabilities by virtue of having been specifically granted to the guardian.

Added by Acts 2011, 82nd Leg., ch. 823 (H.B. 2759), § 1.02, eff. Jan. 1, 2014.

## § 1151.002. Rights of Good Faith Purchasers

(a) This section applies only to a guardian who has qualified acting as guardian and in conformity with the law and the guardian's authority.

(b) A guardian's act is valid for all purposes regarding the rights of an innocent purchaser of property of the guardianship estate who purchased the property from the guardian for valuable consideration, in good faith, and without notice of any illegality in the title to the property, regardless of whether the guardian's act or the authority under which the act was performed is subsequently set aside, annulled, or declared invalid.

Added by Acts 2011, 82nd Leg., ch. 823 (H.B. 2759), § 1.02, eff. Jan. 1, 2014.

### § 1151.003. Guardian May Not Dispute Ward's Right to Property; Exception

A guardian, or an heir, executor, administrator, or assignee of a guardian, may not dispute the right of the ward to any property that came into the guardian's possession as guardian of the ward, except property:

   (1) that is recovered from the guardian; or

   (2) on which there is a personal action pending.

Added by Acts 2011, 82nd Leg., ch. 823 (H.B. 2759), § 1.02, eff. Jan. 1, 2014.

### § 1151.004. Powers and Duties of Person Serving as Guardian of Both Person and Estate

The guardian of both the person and the estate of a ward has all the rights and powers and shall perform all the duties of the guardian of the person and the guardian of the estate.

Added by Acts 2011, 82nd Leg., ch. 823 (H.B. 2759), § 1.02, eff. Jan. 1, 2014.

## SUBCHAPTER B. POWERS AND DUTIES OF GUARDIANS RELATING TO CARE OF WARD

### § 1151.051. General Powers and Duties of Guardians of the Person

(a) The guardian of the person of a ward is entitled to take charge of the person of the ward.

(b) The duties of the guardian of the person correspond with the rights of the guardian.

(c) A guardian of the person has:

   (1) the right to have physical possession of the ward and to establish the ward's legal domicile;

   (2) the duty to provide care, supervision, and protection for the ward;

   (3) the duty to provide the ward with clothing, food, medical care, and shelter;

   (4) the power to consent to medical, psychiatric, and surgical treatment other than the inpatient psychiatric commitment of the ward;

   (5) on application to and order of the court, the power to establish a trust in accordance with 42 U.S.C. Section 1396p(d)(4)(B) and direct that the income of the ward as defined by that section be paid directly to the trust, solely for the purpose of the ward's eligibility for medical assistance under Chapter 32, Human Resources Code; and

   (6) the power to sign documents necessary or appropriate to facilitate employment of the ward if:

     (A) the guardian was appointed with full authority over the person of the ward under Section 1101.151; or

     (B) the power is specified in the court order appointing the guardian with limited powers over the person of the ward under Section 1101.152.

(d) Notwithstanding Subsection (c)(4), a guardian of the person of a ward has the power to personally transport the ward or to direct the ward's transport by emergency medical services or other means to an inpatient mental health facility for a preliminary examination in accordance with Subchapters A and C, Chapter 573, Health and Safety Code.

Added by Acts 2011, 82nd Leg., ch. 823 (H.B. 2759), § 1.02, eff. Jan. 1, 2014. Amended by Acts 2013, 83rd Leg., ch. 982 (H.B. 2080), § 16, eff. Jan. 1, 2014.

Section 36 of Acts 2013, 83rd Leg., ch. 982 (H.B. 2080) provides:

"(a) Except as otherwise provided by this section, the changes in law made by this Act apply to:

"(1) a guardianship created before, on, or after the effective date [Jan. 1, 2014] of this Act; and

"(2) an application for a guardianship pending on, or filed on or after, the effective date of this Act.

"(b) The changes in law made by this Act to Sections 1301.054, 1301.055, 1301.057(b), (c), and (d), 1301.058, 1301.101, and 1301.102(a), Estates Code, apply only to an application for the creation, modification, or termination of a management trust that is filed on or after the effective date of this Act. An application described by this subsection that is filed before the effective date of this Act is governed by the law in effect on the date the application was filed, and the former law is continued in effect for that purpose.

"(c) The changes in law made by this Act to Sections 1301.103 and 1301.154(a), Estates Code, and by Section 1301.202(a–1), Estates Code, as added by this Act, apply to a management trust created before, on, or after the effective date of this Act.

"(d) The changes in law made by this Act to Section 1102.003, Estates Code, apply to a guardianship proceeding that is commenced on or after the effective date of this Act. A guardianship proceeding commenced before that date is governed by the law in effect on the date the proceeding was commenced, and the former law is continued in effect for that purpose."

Section 38 of Acts 2013, 83rd Leg., ch. 982 (H.B. 2080) provides:

"To the extent of any conflict, this Act prevails over another Act of the 83rd Legislature, Regular Session, 2013, relating to nonsubstantive additions to and corrections in enacted codes."

### § 1151.052. Care of Adult Ward

(a) The guardian of an adult ward may spend funds of the guardianship as provided by court order to care for and maintain the ward.

(b) The guardian of an adult ward who has decision-making ability may apply on the ward's behalf for residential care and services provided by a public or private facility if the ward agrees to be placed in the facility. The guardian shall report the condition of the ward to the court at regular intervals at least annually, unless the court orders more frequent reports. The guardian shall include in a report of an adult ward who is receiving residential care in a public or private residential care facility a statement as to the necessity for continued care in the facility.

Added by Acts 2011, 82nd Leg., ch. 823 (H.B. 2759), § 1.02, eff. Jan. 1, 2014.

### § 1151.053. Commitment of Ward

(a) Except as provided by Subsection (b) or (c), a guardian may not voluntarily admit a ward to a public or private inpatient psychiatric facility operated by the Department of State Health Services for care and treatment or to a residential facility operated by the Department of Aging and Disability Services for care and treatment. If care and treatment in a psychiatric or residential facility is necessary, the ward or the ward's guardian may:

(1) apply for services under Section 593.027 or 593.028, Health and Safety Code;

(2) apply to a court to commit the person under Subtitle C or D, Title 7, Health and Safety Code, or Chapter 462, Health and Safety Code; or

(3) transport the ward to an inpatient mental health facility for a preliminary examination in accordance with Subchapters A and C, Chapter 573, Health and Safety Code.

(b) A guardian of a person younger than 18 years of age may voluntarily admit the ward to a public or private inpatient psychiatric facility for care and treatment.

(c) A guardian of a person may voluntarily admit an incapacitated person to a residential care facility for emergency care or respite care under Section 593.027 or 593.028, Health and Safety Code.

Added by Acts 2011, 82nd Leg., ch. 823 (H.B. 2759), § 1.02, eff. Jan. 1, 2014. Amended by Acts 2013, 83rd Leg., ch. 161 (S.B. 1093), § 6.040, eff. Jan. 1, 2014.

### § 1151.054. Administration of Medication

(a) In this section, "psychoactive medication" has the meaning assigned by Section 574.101, Health and Safety Code.

(b) The guardian of the person of a ward who is not a minor and who is under a protective custody order as provided by Subchapter B, Chapter 574, Health and Safety Code, may consent to the administration of psychoactive medication as prescribed by the ward's treating physician regardless of the ward's expressed preferences regarding treatment with psychoactive medication.

Added by Acts 2011, 82nd Leg., ch. 823 (H.B. 2759), § 1.02, eff. Jan. 1, 2014.

## SUBCHAPTER C. GENERAL POWERS AND DUTIES OF GUARDIANS OF THE ESTATE

### § 1151.101. General Powers and Duties

(a) Subject to Subsection (b), the guardian of the estate of a ward is entitled to:

(1) possess and manage all property belonging to the ward;

(2) collect all debts, rentals, or claims that are due to the ward;

(3) enforce all obligations in favor of the ward; and

(4) bring and defend suits by or against the ward.

(b) In the management of a ward's estate, the guardian of the estate is governed by the provisions of this title.

Added by Acts 2011, 82nd Leg., ch. 823 (H.B. 2759), § 1.02, eff. Jan. 1, 2014.

### § 1151.102. Exercise of Authority Under Court Order

(a) The guardian of the estate may renew or extend any obligation owed by or to the ward on application and if authorized by order.

(b) On written application to the court, a guardian of the estate may take an action described by Subsection (c) if:

(1) the guardian considers the action in the best interests of the estate; and

(2) the action is authorized by court order.

(c) A guardian of the estate who complies with Subsection (b) may:

(1) purchase or exchange property;

(2) take a claim or property for the use and benefit of the estate in payment of a debt due or owing to the estate;

(3) compound a bad or doubtful debt due or owing to the estate;

(4) make a compromise or a settlement in relation to property or a claim in dispute or litigation;

(5) compromise or pay in full any secured claim that has been allowed and approved as required by law against the estate by conveying to the holder of the secured claim the real estate or personal property securing the claim:

(A) in full payment, liquidation, and satisfaction of the claim; and

(B) in consideration of cancellation of a note, deed of trust, mortgage, chattel mortgage, or other evidence of a lien that secures the payment of the claim;

(6) abandon worthless or burdensome property and the administration of that property;

(7) purchase a prepaid funeral benefits contract; and

(8) establish a trust in accordance with 42 U.S.C. Section 1396p(d)(4)(B), and direct that the income of the ward as defined by that section be paid directly to the trust, solely for the purpose of the ward's eligibility for medical assistance under Chapter 32, Human Resources Code.

(d) A mortgagee, another secured party, or a trustee may foreclose on property abandoned under Subsection (c)(6) without further court order.

Added by Acts 2011, 82nd Leg., ch. 823 (H.B. 2759), § 1.02, eff. Jan. 1, 2014.

## § 1151.103.  Exercise of Authority Without Court Order

(a) The guardian of the estate of a ward may, without application to or order of the court:

(1) release a lien on payment at maturity of the debt secured by the lien;

(2) vote stocks by limited or general proxy;

(3) pay calls and assessments;

(4) insure the estate against liability in appropriate cases;

(5) insure estate property against fire, theft, and other hazards; and

(6) pay taxes, court costs, and bond premiums.

(b) A guardian of the estate may apply and obtain a court order if the guardian doubts the propriety of the exercise of any power listed in Subsection (a).

Added by Acts 2011, 82nd Leg., ch. 823 (H.B. 2759), § 1.02, eff. Jan. 1, 2014.

## § 1151.104.  Authority to Commence Suits

(a) The guardian of the estate of a ward appointed in this state may commence a suit for:

(1) the recovery of personal property, debts, or damages; or

(2) title to or possession of land, any right attached to or arising from that land, or injury or damage done.

(b) A judgment in a suit described by Subsection (a) is conclusive, but may be set aside by any person interested for fraud or collusion on the guardian's part.

Added by Acts 2011, 82nd Leg., ch. 823 (H.B. 2759), § 1.02, eff. Jan. 1, 2014.

## § 1151.105.  Ordinary Diligence Required

(a) If there is a reasonable prospect of collecting the claims or recovering the property, the guardian of the estate shall use ordinary diligence to:

(1) collect all claims and debts due the ward; and

(2) recover possession of all property to which the ward has claim or title.

(b) If the guardian wilfully neglects to use ordinary diligence, the guardian and the sureties on the guardian's bond are liable, on the suit of any person interested in the estate, for the use of the estate, the amount of the claims, or the value of the property that has been lost due to the guardian's neglect.

Added by Acts 2011, 82nd Leg., ch. 823 (H.B. 2759), § 1.02, eff. Jan. 1, 2014.

## SUBCHAPTER D.  POSSESSION AND CARE OF WARD'S PROPERTY BY GUARDIAN OF THE ESTATE

## § 1151.151.  Duty of Care

(a) The guardian of the estate shall take care of and manage the estate as a prudent person would manage the person's own property, except as otherwise provided by this title.

(b) The guardian of the estate shall account for all rents, profits, and revenues that the estate would have produced by prudent management as required by Subsection (a).

Added by Acts 2011, 82nd Leg., ch. 823 (H.B. 2759), § 1.02, eff. Jan. 1, 2014.

## § 1151.152.  Possession of Personal Property and Records

(a) Immediately after receiving letters of guardianship, the guardian of the estate shall collect and take possession of the ward's personal property, record books, title papers, and other business papers.

(b) The guardian of the estate shall deliver the ward's personal property, record books, title papers, and other business papers to a person legally entitled to that property when:

(1) the guardianship has been closed; or

(2) a successor guardian has received letters of guardianship.

Added by Acts 2011, 82nd Leg., ch. 823 (H.B. 2759), § 1.02, eff. Jan. 1, 2014.

### § 1151.153. Possession of Property Held in Common Ownership

The guardian of the estate is entitled to possession of a ward's property held or owned in common with a part owner in the same manner as another owner in common or joint owner is entitled.

Added by Acts 2011, 82nd Leg., ch. 823 (H.B. 2759), § 1.02, eff. Jan. 1, 2014.

### § 1151.154. Administration of Partnership Interest

(a) This section applies only to a general partnership governed by a partnership agreement or articles of partnership that provide that, on the incapacity of a partner, the guardian of the estate of the partner is entitled to the place of the incapacitated partner in the partnership.

(b) If a ward was a partner in a general partnership, the guardian who contracts to come into the partnership is, to the extent allowed by law, liable to a third person only to the extent of:

(1) the incapacitated partner's capital in the partnership; and

(2) the assets of the incapacitated partner's estate that are held by the guardian.

(c) This section does not exonerate a guardian from liability for the guardian's negligence.

Added by Acts 2011, 82nd Leg., ch. 823 (H.B. 2759), § 1.02, eff. Jan. 1, 2014.

### § 1151.155. Operation or Rental of Farm, Ranch, Factory, or Other Business

(a) If the ward owns a farm, ranch, factory, or other business that is not required to be immediately sold for the payment of a debt or other lawful purpose, the guardian of the estate on order of the court shall, as it appears to be in the estate's best interests:

(1) continue to operate, or cause the continued operation of, the farm, ranch, factory, or other business; or

(2) rent the farm, ranch, factory, or other business.

(b) In deciding whether to issue an order under Subsection (a), the court:

(1) shall consider:

(A) the condition of the estate; and

(B) the necessity that may exist for the future sale of the property or business for the payment of a debt, claim, or other lawful expenditure; and

(2) may not extend the time of renting any of the property beyond what appears consistent with the maintenance and education of a ward or the settlement of the ward's estate.

Added by Acts 2011, 82nd Leg., ch. 823 (H.B. 2759), § 1.02, eff. Jan. 1, 2014.

## SUBCHAPTER E.   AUTHORITY OF GUARDIAN TO ENGAGE IN CERTAIN BORROWING

### § 1151.201. Mortgage or Pledge of Estate Property Authorized in Certain Circumstances

(a) Under court order, the guardian may mortgage or pledge any property of a guardianship estate by deed of trust or otherwise as security for an indebtedness when necessary for:

(1) the payment of any ad valorem, income, gift, or transfer tax due from a ward, regardless of whether the tax is assessed by a state, a political subdivision of the state, the federal government, or a foreign country;

(2) the payment of any expense of administration, including amounts necessary for the operation of a business, farm, or ranch owned by the estate;

(3) the payment of any claim allowed and approved, or established by suit, against the ward or the ward's estate;

(4) the renewal and extension of an existing lien;

(5) an improvement or repair to the ward's real estate if:

(A) the real estate is not revenue producing but could be made revenue producing by certain improvements and repairs; or

(B) the revenue from the real estate could be increased by making improvements or repairs to the real estate;

(6) the purchase of a residence for the ward or a dependent of the ward, if the court finds that borrowing money for that purpose is in the ward's best interests; and

(7) funeral expenses of the ward and expenses of the ward's last illness, if the guardianship is kept open after the ward's death.

(b) Under court order, the guardian of the estate may also receive an extension of credit on the ward's behalf that is wholly or partly secured by a lien on real property that is the ward's homestead when necessary to:

(1) make an improvement or repair to the homestead; or

(2) pay for the ward's education or medical expenses.

(c) Proceeds of a home equity loan described by Subsection (b) may be used only for the purposes authorized under Subsection (b) and to pay the outstanding balance of the loan.

Added by Acts 2011, 82nd Leg., ch. 823 (H.B. 2759), § 1.02, eff. Jan. 1, 2014.

### § 1151.202.   Application; Order

(a) The guardian of the estate must file a sworn application with the court for authority to:

(1) borrow money for a purpose authorized by Section 1151.201(a) or (b); or

(2) create or extend a lien on estate property as security.

(b) The application must state fully and in detail the circumstances that the guardian of the estate believes make the granting of the authority necessary.

(c) On the filing of an application under Subsection (a), the clerk shall issue and have posted a citation to all interested persons stating the nature of the application and requiring the interested persons to appear and show cause why the application should not be granted.

(d) If the court is satisfied by the evidence presented at the hearing on an application filed under Subsection (a) that it is in the interest of the ward or the ward's estate to borrow money or to extend and renew an existing lien, the court shall issue an order to that effect, setting out the terms of the authority granted.

(e) If a new lien is created on guardianship estate property, the court may require, for the protection of the guardianship estate and the estate's creditors, that the guardian's general bond be increased or an additional bond be given, as for the sale of real property belonging to the estate.

Added by Acts 2011, 82nd Leg., ch. 823 (H.B. 2759), § 1.02, eff. Jan. 1, 2014.

### § 1151.203.   Term of Loan or Renewal

The term of a loan or renewal authorized under Section 1151.202 must be for the length of time that the court determines to be in the best interests of the ward or the ward's estate.

Added by Acts 2011, 82nd Leg., ch. 823 (H.B. 2759), § 1.02, eff. Jan. 1, 2014.

## SUBCHAPTER F.   GUARDIANS APPOINTED FOR WARD TO RECEIVE GOVERNMENT FUNDS

### § 1151.251.   Powers and Duties of Guardian Appointed as Necessary for Ward to Receive Government Funds

(a) A guardian of the person for whom it is necessary to have a guardian appointed to receive funds from a governmental source may:

(1) administer only:

(A) the funds received from the governmental source;

(B) all earnings, interest, or profits derived from the funds; and

(C) all property acquired with the funds; and

(2) receive the funds and pay the expenses of administering the guardianship and the expenses for the support, maintenance, or education of the ward or the ward's dependents.

(b) Expenditures under Subsection (a)(2) for the support, maintenance, or education of the ward or the ward's dependents may not exceed $12,000 during any 12–month period without the court's approval.

Added by Acts 2011, 82nd Leg., ch. 823 (H.B. 2759), § 1.02, eff. Jan. 1, 2014.

### § 1151.252.   Validation of Certain Prior Acts of Guardian

An act performed before September 1, 1993, by a guardian of the estate of a person for whom it is necessary to have a guardian appointed to receive and disburse funds that are due the person from a governmental source is validated if the act was performed in conformance with an order of a court that has venue with respect to the support, maintenance, and education of the ward or the ward's dependents and the investment of surplus funds of the ward under this title and if the validity of the act was not an issue in a probate proceeding or civil lawsuit that was pending on September 1, 1993.

Added by Acts 2011, 82nd Leg., ch. 823 (H.B. 2759), § 1.02, eff. Jan. 1, 2014.

## SUBCHAPTER G.   NOTICE BY GUARDIAN TO DEPARTMENT OF VETERANS AFFAIRS

### § 1151.301.   Notice of Filing Required; Hearing Date

(a) This section applies only to:

(1) a filing by a guardian whose ward is a beneficiary of the Department of Veterans Affairs of:

(A) an annual or other account of funds;  or

(B) an application for the expenditure or investment of funds;  or

(2) a filing of a claim against the estate of a ward who is a beneficiary of the Department of Veterans Affairs.

(b) The court shall set a date for a hearing of a matter initiated by a filing to which this section applies not earlier than 20 days from the date of the filing.

(c) Not later than the fifth day after the date of a filing to which this section applies, the person who makes the filing shall give notice of the date of the filing by mailing a certified copy of the filing to the office of the Department of Veterans Affairs in whose territory the court is located.

(d) An office of the Department of Veterans Affairs through its attorney may waive the service of notice or the time required for setting a hearing under this section.

Added by Acts 2011, 82nd Leg., ch. 823 (H.B. 2759), § 1.02, eff. Jan. 1, 2014.

## CHAPTER 1152.   GUARDIANSHIP PENDING APPEAL OF APPOINTMENT

Section
1152.001.  Guardian to Serve Pending Appeal of Appointment.
1152.002.  Appeal Bond.

### § 1152.001.   Guardian to Serve Pending Appeal of Appointment

Pending an appeal from an order or judgment appointing a guardian, the appointee shall continue to:

(1) act as guardian;  and

(2) prosecute a pending suit in favor of the guardianship.

Added by Acts 2011, 82nd Leg., ch. 823 (H.B. 2759), § 1.02, eff. Jan. 1, 2014.

### § 1152.002.   Appeal Bond

(a) Except as provided by Subsection (b), if a guardian appeals, an appeal bond is not required.

(b) A guardian must give an appeal bond if the appeal personally concerns the guardian.

Added by Acts 2011, 82nd Leg., ch. 823 (H.B. 2759), § 1.02, eff. Jan. 1, 2014.

## CHAPTER 1153.   NOTICE TO CLAIMANTS

Section
1153.001.  Required Notice Regarding Presentment of Claims in General.
1153.002.  Proof of Publication.
1153.003.  Required Notice to Certain Claimants.
1153.004.  Permissive Notice to Unsecured Creditor Regarding Period for Presentment of Claim.
1153.005.  One Notice Sufficient;  Liability for Failure to Give Required Notice.

### § 1153.001.   Required Notice Regarding Presentment of Claims in General.

(a) Within one month after receiving letters of guardianship, a guardian of an estate shall provide notice requiring each person who has a claim against the estate to present the claim within the period prescribed by law.  The notice must be:

(1) published in a newspaper printed in the county in which the letters were issued;  and

(2) sent to the comptroller by certified or registered mail, if the ward remitted or should have remitted taxes administered by the comptroller.

(b) Notice provided under Subsection (a) must include:

(1) the date the letters of guardianship were issued to the guardian of the estate;

(2) the address to which a claim may be presented;  and

(3) an instruction of the guardian's choice that the claim be addressed in care of:

(A) the guardian;

(B) the guardian's attorney;  or

(C) "Guardian, Estate of _____" (naming the estate).

(c) If a newspaper is not printed in the county in which the letters of guardianship were issued, the notice must be posted and the return made and filed as otherwise required by this title.

Added by Acts 2011, 82nd Leg., ch. 823 (H.B. 2759), § 1.02, eff. Jan. 1, 2014.

### § 1153.002.  Proof of Publication

A copy of the published notice required by Section 1153.001(a)(1), with the publisher's affidavit, sworn to and subscribed before a proper officer, to the effect that the notice was published as provided in this title for the service of citation or notice by publication, shall be filed in the court in which the cause is pending.

Added by Acts 2011, 82nd Leg., ch. 823 (H.B. 2759), § 1.02, eff. Jan. 1, 2014.

### § 1153.003.  Required Notice to Certain Claimants

(a) Within four months after receiving letters of guardianship, the guardian of an estate shall give notice of the issuance of the letters to each person who has a claim for money against the ward's estate:

(1) that is secured by a deed of trust, mortgage, or vendor's, mechanic's, or other contractor's lien on real estate belonging to the estate; or

(2) about which the guardian has actual knowledge.

(b) Notice provided under this section must be:

(1) sent by certified or registered mail, return receipt requested; and

(2) addressed to the record holder of the claim at the record holder's last known post office address.

(c) The following shall be filed in the court from which the letters of guardianship were issued:

(1) a copy of each notice required by Subsection (a)(1) with the return receipt; and

(2) the guardian's affidavit stating:

(A) that the notice was mailed as required by law; and

(B) the name of the person to whom the notice was mailed, if that name is not shown on the notice or receipt.

Added by Acts 2011, 82nd Leg., ch. 823 (H.B. 2759), § 1.02, eff. Jan. 1, 2014.

### § 1153.004.  Permissive Notice to Unsecured Creditor Regarding Period for Presentment of Claim

The guardian of the estate may expressly state in a notice given to an unsecured creditor under Section 1153.003(a)(2) that the creditor must present a claim not later than the 120th day after the date the creditor receives the notice or the claim is barred, if the claim is not barred by the general statutes of limitation.  A statement under this section must include:

(1) the address to which the claim may be presented; and

(2) an instruction that the claim be filed with the clerk of the court that issued the letters of guardianship.

Added by Acts 2011, 82nd Leg., ch. 823 (H.B. 2759), § 1.02, eff. Jan. 1, 2014.

### § 1153.005.  One Notice Sufficient; Liability for Failure to Give Required Notice

(a) A guardian of an estate is not required to give a notice required by Section 1153.003 if another person also appointed as guardian or a former guardian has given that notice.

(b) If the guardian fails to give a notice required by other sections of this title or to cause the notice to be given, the guardian and the sureties on the guardian's bond are liable for any damage a person suffers because of the neglect, unless it appears that the person otherwise had notice.

Added by Acts 2011, 82nd Leg., ch. 823 (H.B. 2759), § 1.02, eff. Jan. 1, 2014.

## CHAPTER 1154.  INVENTORY, APPRAISEMENT, AND LIST OF CLAIMS

### SUBCHAPTER A.  APPRAISERS

### SUBCHAPTER B.  REQUIREMENTS FOR INVENTORY, APPRAISEMENT, AND LIST OF CLAIMS

### SUBCHAPTER C.  CHANGES TO INVENTORY, APPRAISEMENT, AND LIST OF CLAIMS

### SUBCHAPTER A.   APPRAISERS

**§ 1154.001.   Appointment of Appraisers**

(a) After letters of guardianship of the estate are granted, the court, for good cause shown, on the court's own motion or the motion of any interested person, shall appoint at least one but not more than three disinterested persons who are residents of the county in which the letters were granted to appraise the ward's property.

(b) If the court makes an appointment under Subsection (a) and part of the estate is located in a county other than the county in which the letters were granted, the court, if the court considers it necessary, may appoint at least one but not more than three disinterested persons who are residents of the county in which the relevant part of the estate is located to appraise the estate property located in that county.

Added by Acts 2011, 82nd Leg., ch. 823 (H.B. 2759), § 1.02, eff. Jan. 1, 2014.

**§ 1154.002.   Appraisers' Fees**

An appraiser appointed by the court is entitled to receive a reasonable fee, payable out of the estate, for the performance of the appraiser's duties as an appraiser.

Added by Acts 2011, 82nd Leg., ch. 823 (H.B. 2759), § 1.02, eff. Jan. 1, 2014.

**§ 1154.003.   Failure or Refusal to Act by Appraisers**

If an appraiser appointed under Section 1154.001 fails or refuses to act, the court shall remove the appraiser and appoint one or more appraisers.

Added by Acts 2011, 82nd Leg., ch. 823 (H.B. 2759), § 1.02, eff. Jan. 1, 2014.

### SUBCHAPTER B.   REQUIREMENTS FOR INVENTORY, APPRAISEMENT, AND LIST OF CLAIMS

**§ 1154.051.   Inventory and Appraisement**

(a) Not later than the 30th day after the date the guardian of the estate qualifies, unless a longer period is granted by the court, the guardian shall file with the court clerk a single written instrument that contains a verified, full, and detailed inventory of all the ward's property that has come into the guardian's possession or of which the guardian has knowledge. The inventory must:

(1) include:

(A) all the ward's real property located in this state; and

(B) all the ward's personal property regardless of where the property is located; and

(2) specify:

(A) which portion of the property is separate property and which is community property; and

(B) if the property is owned in common with other persons, the ward's interest in that property.

(b) The guardian shall:

(1) set out in the inventory the guardian's appraisement of the fair market value of each item in the inventory on the date of the grant of letters of guardianship; or

(2) if the court has appointed an appraiser for the estate:

(A) determine the fair market value of each item in the inventory with the assistance of the appraiser; and

(B) set out in the inventory the appraisement made by the appraiser.

(c) The court for good cause shown may require the guardian to file the inventory and appraisement not later than the 30th day after the date of qualification of the guardian.

(d) The inventory, when approved by the court and filed with the court clerk, is for all purposes the inventory and appraisement of the estate referred to in this title.

Added by Acts 2011, 82nd Leg., ch. 823 (H.B. 2759), § 1.02, eff. Jan. 1, 2014.  Amended by Acts 2013, 83rd Leg., ch. 161 (S.B. 1093), § 6.041, eff. Jan. 1, 2014.

**§ 1154.052.   List of Claims**

The guardian of the estate shall make and attach to the inventory and appraisement required by Section 1154.051 a complete list of claims due or owing to the ward.  The list of claims must state:

(1) the name and, if known, address of each person indebted to the ward; and

(2) regarding each claim:

(A) the nature of the debt, whether it is a note, bill, bond, or other written obligation, or whether it is an account or verbal contract;

(B) the date the debt was incurred;

(C) the date the debt was or is due;

(D) the amount of the claim, the rate of interest on the claim, and the period for which the claim bears interest; and

(E) if any portion of the claim is held in common with others, the interest of the estate in the claim.

Added by Acts 2011, 82nd Leg., ch. 823 (H.B. 2759), § 1.02, eff. Jan. 1, 2014. Amended by Acts 2013, 83rd Leg., ch. 161 (S.B. 1093), § 6.042, eff. Jan. 1, 2014.

### § 1154.053. Affidavit of Guardian

The guardian of the estate shall attach to the inventory, appraisement, and list of claims the guardian's affidavit, subscribed and sworn to before an officer in the county authorized by law to administer oaths, that the inventory, appraisement, and list of claims are a true and complete statement of the property and claims of the estate of which the guardian has knowledge.

Added by Acts 2011, 82nd Leg., ch. 823 (H.B. 2759), § 1.02, eff. Jan. 1, 2014.

### § 1154.054. Approval or Disapproval by the Court

(a) On the filing of the inventory, appraisement, and list of claims with the court clerk, the judge shall examine and approve or disapprove the inventory, appraisement, and list of claims.

(b) If the judge approves the inventory, appraisement, and list of claims, the judge shall enter an order to that effect.

(c) If the judge does not approve the inventory, appraisement, or list of claims, the judge:

(1) shall enter an order to that effect requiring the filing of another inventory, appraisement, or list of claims, whichever is not approved, within a period specified in the order not to exceed 20 days after the date the order is entered; and

(2) may, if considered necessary, appoint new appraisers.

Added by Acts 2011, 82nd Leg., ch. 823 (H.B. 2759), § 1.02, eff. Jan. 1, 2014.

### § 1154.055. Failure of Joint Guardians to File Inventory, Appraisement, and List of Claims

(a) If more than one guardian of the estate qualifies to serve, any one or more of the guardians, on the

neglect of the other guardians, may make and file an inventory, appraisement, and list of claims.

(b) A guardian who neglects to make or file an inventory, appraisement, and list of claims may not interfere with and does not have any power over the estate after another guardian makes and files an inventory, appraisement, and list of claims.

(c) The guardian who files the inventory, appraisement, and list of claims is entitled to the whole administration unless, not later than the 60th day after the date the guardian files the inventory, appraisement, and list of claims, each of the delinquent guardians files with the court a written, sworn, and reasonable excuse that the court considers satisfactory. The court shall enter an order removing one or more delinquent guardians and revoking those guardians' letters if:

(1) an excuse is not filed; or

(2) the court does not consider the filed excuse sufficient.

Added by Acts 2011, 82nd Leg., ch. 823 (H.B. 2759), § 1.02, eff. Jan. 1, 2014.

## SUBCHAPTER C. CHANGES TO INVENTORY, APPRAISEMENT, AND LIST OF CLAIMS

### § 1154.101. Discovery of Additional Property or Claims

If after the filing of the inventory, appraisement, and list of claims the guardian of the estate acquires possession or knowledge of property or claims of the estate not included in the inventory, appraisement, and list of claims, the guardian shall promptly file with the court clerk a verified, full, and detailed supplemental inventory, appraisement, and list of claims.

Added by Acts 2011, 82nd Leg., ch. 823 (H.B. 2759), § 1.02, eff. Jan. 1, 2014.

### § 1154.102. Additional Inventory and Appraisement or List of Claims

(a) On the written complaint of any interested person that property or claims of the estate have not been included in the filed inventory, appraisement, and list of claims, the guardian of the estate shall be cited to appear before the court in which the cause is pending and show cause why the guardian should not be required to make and file an additional inventory and appraisement or list of claims, or both.

(b) After hearing the complaint, if the court is satisfied of the truth of the complaint, the court shall enter an order requiring the guardian to make and file an additional inventory and appraisement or list of claims, or both.　The additional inventory and appraisement or list of claims:

(1) must be made and filed in the same manner as the original inventory and appraisement or list of claims within the period prescribed by the court, not to exceed 20 days after the date of the order; and

(2) may include only property or claims not previously included in the inventory and appraisement or list of claims.

Added by Acts 2011, 82nd Leg., ch. 823 (H.B. 2759), § 1.02, eff. Jan. 1, 2014.

### § 1154.103.　Correction of Inventory, Appraisement, or List of Claims for Erroneous or Unjust Item

(a) A person interested in an estate who considers an inventory, appraisement, or list of claims filed by the guardian of the estate to be erroneous or unjust in any particular form may:

(1) file a written complaint setting forth the alleged erroneous or unjust item; and

(2) have the guardian cited to appear before the court and show cause why the item should not be corrected.

(b) On the hearing of the complaint, if the court is satisfied from the evidence that the inventory, appraisement, or list of claims is erroneous or unjust as alleged in the complaint, the court shall enter an order:

(1) specifying the erroneous or unjust item and the corrections to be made; and

(2) appointing an appraiser to make a new appraisement correcting the erroneous or unjust item and requiring the filing of the new appraisement not later than the 20th day after the date of the order.

(c) The court, on the court's own motion or a motion of the guardian of the estate, may also have a new appraisement made for the purposes described by this section.

Added by Acts 2011, 82nd Leg., ch. 823 (H.B. 2759), § 1.02, eff. Jan. 1, 2014.

### § 1154.104.　Reappraisement

(a) A reappraisement made, filed, and approved by the court replaces the original appraisement.　Not more than one reappraisement may be made.

(b) Notwithstanding Subsection (a), a person interested in an estate may object to a reappraisement regardless of whether the court has approved the reappraisement.　If the court finds that the reappraisement is erroneous or unjust, the court shall appraise the property on the basis of the evidence before the court.

Added by Acts 2011, 82nd Leg., ch. 823 (H.B. 2759), § 1.02, eff. Jan. 1, 2014.

## SUBCHAPTER D.　USE OF INVENTORY, APPRAISEMENT, AND LIST OF CLAIMS AS EVIDENCE

### § 1154.151.　Use of Inventory, Appraisement, and List of Claims as Evidence

Each inventory, appraisement, and list of claims that has been made, filed, and approved in accordance with law; the record of the inventory, appraisement, and list of claims; or a copy of an original or the record that has been certified under the seal of the county court affixed by the clerk:

(1) may be given in evidence in any court of this state in any suit by or against the guardian of the estate; and

(2) is not conclusive for or against the guardian of the estate if it is shown that:

(A) any property or claim of the estate is not shown in the inventory, appraisement, or list of claims; or

(B) the value of the property or claim of the estate exceeded the value shown in the appraisement or list of claims.

Added by Acts 2011, 82nd Leg., ch. 823 (H.B. 2759), § 1.02, eff. Jan. 1, 2014.

## CHAPTER 1155.　COMPENSATION, EXPENSES, AND COURT COSTS

### SUBCHAPTER A.　COMPENSATION OF GUARDIANS IN GENERAL

## SUBCHAPTER A.  COMPENSATION OF GUARDIANS IN GENERAL

### § 1155.001.  Definitions

In this subchapter:

(1) "Gross income" does not include United States Department of Veterans Affairs or social security benefits received by a ward.

(2) "Money paid out" does not include any money loaned, invested, or paid over on the settlement of a guardianship or a tax-motivated gift made by a ward.

Added by Acts 2011, 82nd Leg., ch. 823 (H.B. 2759), § 1.02, eff. Jan. 1, 2014.

### § 1155.002.  Compensation for Certain Guardians of the Person

(a) The court may authorize compensation for a guardian serving as a guardian of the person alone from available funds of the ward's estate or other funds available for that purpose. The court may set the compensation in an amount not to exceed five percent of the ward's gross income.

(b) If the ward's estate is insufficient to pay for the services of a private professional guardian or a licensed attorney serving as a guardian of the person, the court may authorize compensation for that guardian if funds in the county treasury are budgeted for that purpose.

Added by Acts 2011, 82nd Leg., ch. 823 (H.B. 2759), § 1.02, eff. Jan. 1, 2014.

### § 1155.003.  Compensation for Guardian of the Estate

(a) The guardian of an estate is entitled to reasonable compensation on application to the court at the time the court approves an annual or final accounting filed by the guardian under this title.

(b) A fee of five percent of the gross income of the ward's estate and five percent of all money paid out of the estate, subject to the award of an additional amount under Section 1155.006(a) following a review under Section 1155.006(a)(1), is considered reasonable under this section if the court finds that the guardian has taken care of and managed the estate in compliance with the standards of this title.

Added by Acts 2011, 82nd Leg., ch. 823 (H.B. 2759), § 1.02, eff. Jan. 1, 2014.

### § 1155.004.  Considerations in Authorizing Compensation

In determining whether to authorize compensation for a guardian under this subchapter, the court shall consider:

(1) the ward's monthly income from all sources; and

(2) whether the ward receives medical assistance under the state Medicaid program.

Added by Acts 2011, 82nd Leg., ch. 823 (H.B. 2759), § 1.02, eff. Jan. 1, 2014.

### § 1155.005.  Maximum Aggregate Compensation

Except as provided by Section 1155.006(a) for a fee the court determines is unreasonably low, the aggregate fee of the guardian of the person and guardian of the estate may not exceed an amount equal to five percent of the gross income of the ward's estate plus five percent of all money paid out of the estate.

Added by Acts 2011, 82nd Leg., ch. 823 (H.B. 2759), § 1.02, eff. Jan. 1, 2014.

### § 1155.006.  Modification of Unreasonably Low Compensation; Authorization for Payment of Estimated Quarterly Compensation

(a) On application of an interested person or on the court's own motion, the court may:

(1) review and modify the amount of compensation authorized under Section 1155.002(a) or 1155.003 if the court finds that the amount is unreasonably low when considering the services provided as guardian; and

(2) authorize compensation for the guardian in an estimated amount the court finds reasonable, to be paid on a quarterly basis before the guardian files an annual or final accounting, if the court finds that delaying the payment of compensation until the guardian files an accounting would create a hardship for the guardian.

(b) A finding of unreasonably low compensation may not be established under Subsection (a) solely because the amount of compensation is less than the usual and customary charges of the person or entity serving as guardian.

Added by Acts 2011, 82nd Leg., ch. 823 (H.B. 2759), § 1.02, eff. Jan. 1, 2014.

## § 1155.007. Reduction or Elimination of Estimated Quarterly Compensation

(a) A court that authorizes payment of estimated quarterly compensation under Section 1155.006(a) may later reduce or eliminate the guardian's compensation if, on review of an annual or final accounting or otherwise, the court finds that the guardian:

(1) received compensation in excess of the amount permitted under this subchapter;

(2) has not adequately performed the duties required of a guardian under this title; or

(3) has been removed for cause.

(b) If a court reduces or eliminates a guardian's compensation as provided by Subsection (a), the guardian and the surety on the guardian's bond are liable to the guardianship estate for any excess compensation received.

Added by Acts 2011, 82nd Leg., ch. 823 (H.B. 2759), § 1.02, eff. Jan. 1, 2014.

## § 1155.008. Denial of Compensation

On application of an interested person or on the court's own motion, the court may wholly or partly deny a fee authorized under this subchapter if:

(1) the court finds that the guardian has not adequately performed the duties required of a guardian under this title; or

(2) the guardian has been removed for cause.

Added by Acts 2011, 82nd Leg., ch. 823 (H.B. 2759), § 1.02, eff. Jan. 1, 2014.

## SUBCHAPTER B. COMPENSATION FOR PROFESSIONAL SERVICES

## § 1151.051. [Blank]

## § 1155.052. Attorney Serving as Guardian and Providing Related Legal Services

(a) Notwithstanding any other provision of this chapter, an attorney who serves as guardian and who also provides legal services in connection with the guardianship is not entitled to compensation for the guardianship services or payment of attorney's fees for the legal services from the ward's estate or other funds available for that purpose unless the attorney files with the court a detailed description of the services performed that identifies which of the services provided were guardianship services and which were legal services.

(b) An attorney described by Subsection (a) is not entitled to payment of attorney's fees for guardianship services that are not legal services.

(c) The court shall set the compensation of an attorney described by Subsection (a) for the performance of guardianship services in accordance with Subchapter A. The court shall set attorney's fees for an attorney described by Subsection (a) for legal services provided in accordance with Sections 1155.054, 1155.101, and 1155.151.

Added by Acts 2011, 82nd Leg., ch. 823 (H.B. 2759), § 1.02, eff. Jan. 1, 2014. Amended by Acts 2013, 83rd Leg., ch. 982 (H.B. 2080), § 17, eff. Jan. 1, 2014.

## § 1155.053. Compensation for Services to Recover Property

(a) Subject only to the approval of the court in which the estate is being administered and except as provided by Subsection (b), a guardian of an estate may convey or contract to convey a contingent interest in any property sought to be recovered, not to exceed one-third of the property for services of attorneys.

(b) A guardian of an estate may convey or contract to convey for services of attorneys a contingent interest that exceeds one-third of the property sought to be recovered under this section only on the approval of the court in which the estate is being administered. The court must approve a contract entered into or conveyance made under this section before an attorney performs any legal services. A contract entered into or conveyance made in violation of this section is void unless the court ratifies or reforms the contract or documents relating to the conveyance to the extent necessary to cause the contract or conveyance to meet the requirements of this section.

(c) In approving a contract or conveyance under Subsection (a) or (b) for services of an attorney, the court shall consider:

(1) the time and labor that will be required, the novelty and difficulty of the questions to be involved, and the skill that will be required to perform the legal services properly;

(2) the fee customarily charged in the locality for similar legal services;

(3) the value of property recovered or sought to be recovered by the guardian under this section;

(4) the benefits to the estate that the attorney will be responsible for securing; and

(5) the experience and ability of the attorney who will be performing the services.

Added by Acts 2011, 82nd Leg., ch. 823 (H.B. 2759), § 1.02, eff. Jan. 1, 2014.

### § 1155.054. Payment of Attorney's Fees to Certain Attorneys

(a) A court that creates a guardianship or creates a management trust under Chapter 1301 for a ward, on request of a person who filed an application to be appointed guardian of the proposed ward, an application for the appointment of another suitable person as guardian of the proposed ward, or an application for the creation of the management trust, may authorize the payment of reasonable and necessary attorney's fees, as determined by the court, in amounts the court considers equitable and just, to an attorney who represents the person who filed the application at the application hearing, regardless of whether the person is appointed the ward's guardian or whether a management trust is created, from available funds of the ward's estate or management trust, if created, subject to Subsections (b) and (d).

(b) The court may authorize amounts that otherwise would be paid from the ward's estate or the management trust as provided by Subsection (a) to instead be paid from the county treasury, subject to Subsection (e), if:

(1) the ward's estate or management trust is insufficient to pay the amounts; and

(2) funds in the county treasury are budgeted for that purpose.

(c) The court may not authorize attorney's fees under this section unless the court finds that the applicant acted in good faith and for just cause in the filing and prosecution of the application.

(d) If the court finds that a party in a guardianship proceeding acted in bad faith or without just cause in prosecuting or objecting to an application in the proceeding, the court may require the party to reimburse the ward's estate for all or part of the attorney's fees awarded under this section and shall issue judgment against the party and in favor of the estate for the amount of attorney's fees required to be reimbursed to the estate.

(e) The court may authorize the payment of attorney's fees from the county treasury under Subsection (b) only if the court is satisfied that the attorney to whom the fees will be paid has not received, and is not seeking, payment for the services described by that subsection from any other source.

Added by Acts 1995, 74th Leg., ch. 1039, § 28, eff. Sept. 1, 1995. Amended by Acts 1999, 76th Leg., ch. 905, § 2, eff. Sept. 1, 1999; Acts 2003, 78th Leg., ch. 549, § 10, eff. Sept. 1, 2003; Acts 2009, 81st Leg., ch. 314, § 1, eff. Sept. 1, 2009; Acts 2009, 81st Leg., ch. 930, §§ 2, 3, eff. Sept. 1, 2009. Redesignated as V.T.C.A., Estates Code § 665B by Acts 2011, 82nd Leg., ch. 823 (H.B. 2759), § 3.01(e), eff. Jan. 1, 2014. Redesignated from V.A.T.S. Probate Code, § 665B and amended by Acts 2013, 83rd Leg., ch. 982 (H.B. 2080), § 18, eff. Jan. 1, 2014.

Section 36 of Acts 2013, 83rd Leg., ch. 982 (H.B. 2080) provides:

"(a) Except as otherwise provided by this section, the changes in law made by this Act apply to:

"(1) a guardianship created before, on, or after the effective date [Jan. 1, 2014] of this Act; and

"(2) an application for a guardianship pending on, or filed on or after, the effective date of this Act.

"(b) The changes in law made by this Act to Sections 1301.054, 1301.055, 1301.057(b), (c), and (d), 1301.058, 1301.101, and 1301.102(a), Estates Code, apply only to an application for the creation, modification, or termination of a management trust that is filed on or after the effective date of this Act. An application described by this subsection that is filed before the effective date of this Act is governed by the law in effect on the date the application was filed, and the former law is continued in effect for that purpose.

"(c) The changes in law made by this Act to Sections 1301.103 and 1301.154(a), Estates Code, and by Section 1301.202(a–1), Estates Code, as added by this Act, apply to a management trust created before, on, or after the effective date of this Act.

"(d) The changes in law made by this Act to Section 1102.003, Estates Code, apply to a guardianship proceeding that is commenced on or after the effective date of this Act. A guardianship proceeding commenced before that date is governed by the law in effect on the date the proceeding was commenced, and the former law is continued in effect for that purpose."

## SUBCHAPTER C. EXPENSES

### § 1155.101. Reimbursement of Expenses in General

A guardian is entitled to reimbursement from the guardianship estate for all necessary and reasonable expenses incurred in performing any duty as a guardian, including reimbursement for the payment of reasonable attorney's fees necessarily incurred by the guardian in connection with the management of the estate or any other matter in the guardianship.

Added by Acts 2011, 82nd Leg., ch. 823 (H.B. 2759), § 1.02, eff. Jan. 1, 2014. Amended by Acts 2013, 83rd Leg., ch. 161 (S.B. 1093), § 6.043, eff. Jan. 1, 2014.

### § 1155.102. Reimbursement of Expenses for Collection of Claim or Debt

On satisfactory proof to the court, a guardian of an estate is entitled to all necessary and reasonable expenses incurred by the guardian in collecting or attempting to collect a claim or debt owed to the estate or in recovering or attempting to recover property to which the estate has title or a claim.

Added by Acts 2011, 82nd Leg., ch. 823 (H.B. 2759), § 1.02, eff. Jan. 1, 2014.

### § 1155.103. Expense Charges: Requirements

All expense charges shall be:

(1) in writing, showing specifically each item of expense and the date of the expense;

(2) verified by affidavit of the guardian;

(3) filed with the clerk; and

(4) paid only if the payment is authorized by court order.

Added by Acts 2011, 82nd Leg., ch. 823 (H.B. 2759), § 1.02, eff. Jan. 1, 2014.

### SUBCHAPTER D.  COSTS IN GENERAL

### § 1155.151. Costs in Guardianship Proceeding Generally

(a) In a guardianship proceeding, the court costs of the proceeding, including the cost of the guardians ad litem, attorneys ad litem, court visitor, mental health professionals, and interpreters appointed under this title, shall be set in an amount the court considers equitable and just and, except as provided by Subsection (c), shall be paid out of the guardianship estate, or the county treasury if the estate is insufficient to pay the cost, and the court shall issue the judgment accordingly.

(b) The costs attributable to the services of a person described by Subsection (a) shall be paid under this section at any time after the commencement of the proceeding as ordered by the court.

(c) If the court finds that a party in a guardianship proceeding acted in bad faith or without just cause in prosecuting or objecting to an application in the proceeding, the court may order the party to pay all or part of the costs of the proceeding. If the party found to be acting in bad faith or without just cause was required to provide security for the probable costs of the proceeding under Section 1053.052, the court shall first apply the amount provided as security as payment for costs ordered by the court under this subsection. If the amount provided as security is insufficient to pay the entire amount ordered by the court, the court shall render judgment in favor of the estate against the party for the remaining amount.

Added by Acts 2011, 82nd Leg., ch. 823 (H.B. 2759), § 1.02, eff. Jan. 1, 2014. Amended by Acts 2013, 83rd Leg., ch. 161 (S.B. 1093), §§ 6.044, 6.045, eff. Jan. 1, 2014; Acts 2013, 83rd Leg., ch. 982 (H.B. 2080), § 19, eff. Jan. 1, 2014.

Section 36 of Acts 2013, 83rd Leg., ch. 982 (H.B. 2080) provides:

"(a) Except as otherwise provided by this section, the changes in law made by this Act apply to:

"(1) a guardianship created before, on, or after the effective date [Jan. 1, 2014] of this Act; and

"(2) an application for a guardianship pending on, or filed on or after, the effective date of this Act.

"(b) The changes in law made by this Act to Sections 1301.054, 1301.055, 1301.057(b), (c), and (d), 1301.058, 1301.101, and 1301.102(a), Estates Code, apply only to an application for the creation, modification, or termination of a management trust that is filed on or after the effective date of this Act. An application described by this subsection that is filed before the effective date of this Act is governed by the law in effect on the date the application was filed, and the former law is continued in effect for that purpose.

"(c) The changes in law made by this Act to Sections 1301.103 and 1301.154(a), Estates Code, and by Section 1301.202(a–1), Estates Code, as added by this Act, apply to a management trust created before, on, or after the effective date of this Act.

"(d) The changes in law made by this Act to Section 1102.003, Estates Code, apply to a guardianship proceeding that is commenced on or after the effective date of this Act. A guardianship proceeding commenced before that date is governed by the law in effect on the date the proceeding was commenced, and the former law is continued in effect for that purpose."

### § 1155.152. Certain Costs Adjudged Against Guardian

If costs are incurred because a guardian neglects to perform a required duty or is removed for cause, the guardian and the sureties on the guardian's bond are liable for:

(1) any costs of removal and other additional costs incurred that are not expenditures authorized under this title; and

(2) reasonable attorney's fees incurred in:

(A) removing the guardian; or

(B) obtaining compliance regarding any statutory duty the guardian has neglected.

Added by Acts 2011, 82nd Leg., ch. 823 (H.B. 2759), § 1.02, eff. Jan. 1, 2014.

## SUBCHAPTER E. COMPENSATION AND COSTS IN GUARDIANSHIPS FOR CERTAIN MEDICAL ASSISTANCE RECIPIENTS

### § 1155.201. Definitions

In this subchapter:

(1) "Applied income" means the portion of the earned and unearned income of a recipient of medical assistance, or if applicable the recipient and the recipient's spouse, that is paid under the medical assistance program to an institution or long-term care facility in which the recipient resides.

(2) "Medical assistance" has the meaning assigned by Section 32.003, Human Resources Code.

Added by Acts 2011, 82nd Leg., ch. 823 (H.B. 2759), § 1.02, eff. Jan. 1, 2014. Amended by Acts 2013, 83rd Leg., ch. 161 (S.B. 1093), § 6.046, eff. Jan. 1, 2014.

### § 1155.202. Compensation and Costs Payable Under Medical Assistance Program

(a) Notwithstanding any other provision of this title and to the extent permitted by federal law, a court that appoints a guardian for a recipient of medical assistance who has applied income may order the following to be deducted as an additional personal needs allowance in the computation of the recipient's applied income in accordance with Section 32.02451, Human Resources Code:

(1) compensation to the guardian in an amount not to exceed $175 per month;

(2) costs directly related to establishing or terminating the guardianship, not to exceed $1,000 except as provided by Subsection (b); and

(3) other administrative costs related to the guardianship, not to exceed $1,000 during any three-year period.

(b) Costs ordered to be deducted under Subsection (a)(2) may include compensation and expenses for an attorney ad litem or guardian ad litem and reasonable attorney's fees for an attorney representing the guardian. The costs ordered to be paid may exceed $1,000 if the costs in excess of that amount are supported by documentation acceptable to the court and the costs are approved by the court.

(c) A court may not order:

(1) that the deduction for compensation and costs under Subsection (a) take effect before the later of:

(A) the month in which the court order issued under that subsection is signed; or

(B) the first month of medical assistance eligibility for which the recipient is subject to a copayment; or

(2) a deduction for services provided before the effective date of the deduction as provided by Subdivision (1).

Added by Acts 2011, 82nd Leg., ch. 823 (H.B. 2759), § 1.02, eff. Jan. 1, 2014. Amended by Acts 2013, 83rd Leg., ch. 161 (S.B. 1093), § 6.047, eff. Jan. 1, 2014.

## CHAPTER 1156. EDUCATION AND MAINTENANCE ALLOWANCES PAID FROM WARD'S ESTATE

### SUBCHAPTER A. ALLOWANCES FOR WARD

### SUBCHAPTER A. ALLOWANCES FOR WARD

### § 1156.001. Application for Allowance

(a) Subject to Section 1156.051, if a monthly allowance for a ward was not ordered in the court's order appointing a guardian, the guardian of the estate of the ward shall file with the court an application requesting a monthly allowance to be spent from the income and corpus of the ward's estate for:

(1) the education and maintenance of the ward; and

(2) the maintenance of the ward's property.

(b) The guardian must file the application not later than the 30th day after the date the guardian qualifies as guardian or the date specified by the court, whichever is later.

(c) The application must clearly separate amounts requested for the ward's education and maintenance from amounts requested for maintenance of the ward's property.

Added by Acts 2011, 82nd Leg., ch. 823 (H.B. 2759), § 1.02, eff. Jan. 1, 2014.

### § 1156.002. Court Determination of Allowance Amount

In determining the amount of the monthly allowance for the ward and the ward's property, the court shall consider the condition of the estate and the income and corpus of the estate necessary to pay the reasonably anticipated regular education and maintenance expenses of the ward and maintenance expenses of the ward's property.

Added by Acts 2011, 82nd Leg., ch. 823 (H.B. 2759), § 1.02, eff. Jan. 1, 2014.

### § 1156.003. Court Order Setting Allowance

(a) The court's order setting a monthly allowance must specify the types of expenditures the guardian may make on a monthly basis for the ward or the ward's property.

(b) If different persons have the guardianship of the person and of the estate of a ward, the court's order setting a monthly allowance must specify:

    (1) the amount, if any, set by the court for the ward's education and maintenance that the guardian of the estate shall pay; and

    (2) the amount, if any, that the guardian of the estate shall pay to the guardian of the person, at a time specified by the court, for the ward's education and maintenance.

(c) If the guardian of the estate fails to pay to the guardian of the person the monthly allowance set by the court, the guardian of the estate shall be compelled by court order to make the payment after the guardian is cited to appear.

(d) An order setting a monthly allowance does not affect the guardian's duty to account for expenditures of the allowance in the annual account required by Subchapter A, Chapter 1163.

Added by Acts 2011, 82nd Leg., ch. 823 (H.B. 2759), § 1.02, eff. Jan. 1, 2014.

### § 1156.004. Expenditures Exceeding Allowance

If a guardian in good faith has spent money from the income and corpus of the estate of the ward for the ward's support and maintenance and the expenditures exceed the monthly allowance authorized by the court, the guardian shall file a motion with the court requesting approval of the expenditures. The court may approve the excess expenditures if:

    (1) the expenditures were made when it was not convenient or possible for the guardian to first secure court approval;

    (2) the proof is clear and convincing that the expenditures were reasonable and proper;

    (3) the court would have granted authority in advance to make the expenditures; and

    (4) the ward received the benefits of the expenditures.

Added by Acts 2011, 82nd Leg., ch. 823 (H.B. 2759), § 1.02, eff. Jan. 1, 2014.

## SUBCHAPTER B. ALLOWANCES FOR WARD'S FAMILY

### § 1156.051. Certain Allowances Prohibited When Parent is Guardian of Minor Ward

(a) Except as provided by Subsection (b), a parent who is the guardian of the person of a ward who is 17 years of age or younger may not use the income or the corpus from the ward's estate for the ward's support, education, or maintenance.

(b) A court with proper jurisdiction may authorize the guardian of the person to spend the income or the corpus from the ward's estate to support, educate, or maintain the ward if the guardian presents to the court clear and convincing evidence that the ward's parents are unable without unreasonable hardship to pay for all of the expenses related to the ward's support.

Added by Acts 2011, 82nd Leg., ch. 823 (H.B. 2759), § 1.02, eff. Jan. 1, 2014.

### § 1156.052. Allowance for Ward's Spouse or Dependent

(a) Subject to Section 1156.051 and on application to the court, the court may order the guardian of the estate of a ward to spend money from the ward's estate for the education and maintenance of the ward's spouse or dependent.

(b) In determining whether to order the expenditure of money from a ward's estate for the ward's spouse or dependent, as appropriate, under this section, the court shall consider:

    (1) the circumstances of the ward, the ward's spouse, and the ward's dependents;

(2) the ability and duty of the ward's spouse to support himself or herself and the ward's dependent;

(3) the size of the ward's estate;

(4) a beneficial interest the ward or the ward's spouse or dependent has in a trust; and

(5) an existing estate plan, including a trust or will, that provides a benefit to the ward's spouse or dependent.

(c) A person who makes an application to the court under this section shall mail notice of the application by certified mail to all interested persons.

Added by Acts 2011, 82nd Leg., ch. 823 (H.B. 2759), § 1.02, eff. Jan. 1, 2014.

## CHAPTER 1157. PRESENTMENT AND PAYMENT OF CLAIMS

### SUBCHAPTER A. PRESENTMENT OF CLAIMS AGAINST GUARDIANSHIP ESTATE IN GENERAL

### SUBCHAPTER A. PRESENTMENT OF CLAIMS AGAINST GUARDIANSHIP ESTATE IN GENERAL

### § 1157.001. Presentment of Claim to Guardian of the Estate

A claim may be presented to the guardian of the estate at any time if:

(1) the estate has not been closed; and

(2) suit on the claim has not been barred by the general statutes of limitation.

Added by Acts 2011, 82nd Leg., ch. 823 (H.B. 2759), § 1.02, eff. Jan. 1, 2014.

### § 1157.002. Presentment of Claim to Clerk

(a) A claim may also be presented by depositing the claim with the clerk with vouchers and the necessary exhibits and affidavit attached to the claim. On receiving a claim deposited under this subsection, the clerk shall advise the guardian of the estate or the guardian's attorney of the deposit of the claim by a letter mailed to the guardian's last known address.

(b) A claim deposited under Subsection (a) is presumed to be rejected if the guardian fails to act on the claim on or before the 30th day after the date the claim is filed.

(c) Failure of the clerk to give the notice required under Subsection (a) does not affect the validity of the presentment or the presumption of rejection of the claim because the guardian does not act on the claim within the 30–day period prescribed by Subsection (b).

Added by Acts 2011, 82nd Leg., ch. 823 (H.B. 2759), § 1.02, eff. Jan. 1, 2014.

### § 1157.003. Inclusion of Attorney's Fees in Claim

If the instrument evidencing or supporting a claim provides for attorney's fees, the claimant may include as a part of the claim the portion of the attorney's fees the claimant has paid or contracted to pay to an attorney to prepare, present, and collect the claim.

Added by Acts 2011, 82nd Leg., ch. 823 (H.B. 2759), § 1.02, eff. Jan. 1, 2014.

### § 1157.004. Affidavit Authenticating Claim for Money in General

(a) Except as provided by Sections 1157.005 and 1157.102, a claim for money against an estate must be supported by an affidavit that states:

(1) that the claim is just;

(2) that all legal offsets, payments, and credits known to the affiant have been allowed; and

(3) if the claim is not founded on a written instrument or account, the facts on which the claim is founded.

(b) A photostatic copy of an exhibit or voucher necessary to prove a claim under this section may be offered with and attached to the claim instead of attaching the original.

Added by Acts 2011, 82nd Leg., ch. 823 (H.B. 2759), § 1.02, eff. Jan. 1, 2014.

### § 1157.005. Affidavit Authenticating Claim of Corporation or by Certain Other Representatives

(a) The cashier, treasurer, or managing official of a corporation shall make the affidavit required to authenticate a claim of the corporation.

(b) In an affidavit made by an officer of a corporation, or by an executor, administrator, guardian, trustee, assignee, agent, or attorney, it is sufficient to state that the affiant has made diligent inquiry and examination and believes the claim is just and that all legal offsets, payments, and credits made known to the affiant have been allowed.

Added by Acts 2011, 82nd Leg., ch. 823 (H.B. 2759), § 1.02, eff. Jan. 1, 2014.

### § 1157.006. Lost or Destroyed Evidence Concerning Claim

If evidence of a claim is lost or destroyed, the claimant or the claimant's representative may make an affidavit to the fact of the loss or destruction. The affidavit must state:

(1) the amount, date, and nature of the claim;

(2) the due date of the claim;

(3) that the claim is just;

(4) that all legal offsets, payments, and credits known to the affiant have been allowed; and

(5) that the claimant is still the owner of the claim.

Added by Acts 2011, 82nd Leg., ch. 823 (H.B. 2759), § 1.02, eff. Jan. 1, 2014.

### § 1157.007. Waiver of Certain Defects of Form or Claims of Insufficiency

A defect of form or a claim of insufficiency of a presented exhibit or voucher is considered waived by the guardian of the estate unless a written objection to the form, exhibit, or voucher is:

(1) made not later than the 30th day after the date the claim is presented; and

(2) filed with the county clerk.

Added by Acts 2011, 82nd Leg., ch. 823 (H.B. 2759), § 1.02, eff. Jan. 1, 2014.

### § 1157.008. Effect on Statutes of Limitation of Filing of or Suit on Claim

The general statutes of limitation are tolled by:

(1) filing a claim that is legally allowed and approved; or

(2) bringing a suit on a rejected and disapproved claim not later than the 90th day after the date the claim is rejected or disapproved.

Added by Acts 2011, 82nd Leg., ch. 823 (H.B. 2759), § 1.02, eff. Jan. 1, 2014.

### SUBCHAPTER B. ACTION ON CLAIMS

### § 1157.051. Allowance or Rejection of Claim

A guardian of the estate shall, not later than the 30th day after the date an authenticated claim against the guardianship estate is presented to the guardian or filed with the clerk as provided by this chapter, endorse on or attach to the claim a memorandum signed by the guardian stating:

(1) the date of presentation or filing of the claim; and

(2) whether the guardian allows or rejects the claim, or, if the guardian allows or rejects a part of the claim, the portion of the claim the guardian allows or rejects.

Added by Acts 2011, 82nd Leg., ch. 823 (H.B. 2759), § 1.02, eff. Jan. 1, 2014.

### § 1157.052. Failure to Endorse or Attach Memorandum or Allow or Reject Claim

The failure of a guardian of the estate to endorse on or attach to a claim presented to the guardian the memorandum required by Section 1157.051 or, not later than the 30th day after the date a claim is presented, to allow or reject the claim or portion of the claim constitutes a rejection of the claim. If the claim is later established by suit:

(1) the costs shall be taxed against the guardian, individually; or

(2) the guardian may be removed as in other cases of removal on the written complaint of any person interested in the claim after personal service of citation, hearing, and proof.

Added by Acts 2011, 82nd Leg., ch. 823 (H.B. 2759), § 1.02, eff. Jan. 1, 2014.

### § 1157.053. Claim Entered on Claim Docket

After a claim against a ward's estate has been presented to and allowed by the guardian of the estate, wholly or partly, the claim must be filed with the county clerk of the proper county. The clerk shall enter the claim on the claim docket.

Added by Acts 2011, 82nd Leg., ch. 823 (H.B. 2759), § 1.02, eff. Jan. 1, 2014.

### § 1157.054. Contest of Claim

(a) A person interested in a ward may, at any time before the court has acted on a claim, appear and object in writing to the approval of the claim or any part of the claim.

(b) If a person objects under Subsection (a):

(1) the parties are entitled to process for witnesses; and

(2) the court shall hear evidence and render judgment as in ordinary suits.

Added by Acts 2011, 82nd Leg., ch. 823 (H.B. 2759), § 1.02, eff. Jan. 1, 2014.

### § 1157.055. Court's Action on Claim

The court shall:

(1) approve, wholly or partly, or reject a claim that has been allowed and entered on the claim docket for a period of 10 days; and

(2) concurrently classify the claim.

Added by Acts 2011, 82nd Leg., ch. 823 (H.B. 2759), § 1.02, eff. Jan. 1, 2014.

### § 1157.056. Hearing on Certain Claims

(a) If a claim is properly authenticated and allowed, but the court is not satisfied that the claim is just, the court shall:

(1) examine the claimant and the guardian of the estate under oath; and

(2) hear other evidence necessary to determine the issue.

(b) If after the examination and hearing the court is not convinced that the claim is just, the court shall disapprove the claim.

Added by Acts 2011, 82nd Leg., ch. 823 (H.B. 2759), § 1.02, eff. Jan. 1, 2014.

### § 1157.057. Court Order Regarding Action on Claim

(a) The court acting on a claim shall endorse on or attach to the claim a written memorandum that:

(1) is dated and officially signed; and

(2) states:

(A) the exact action taken by the court on the claim, whether the claim is approved or disapproved, or is approved in part and rejected in part; and

(B) the classification of the claim.

(b) An order under Subsection (a) has the effect of a final judgment.

Added by Acts 2011, 82nd Leg., ch. 823 (H.B. 2759), § 1.02, eff. Jan. 1, 2014.

### § 1157.058. Appeal of Court's Action on Claim

If a claimant or any person interested in a ward is dissatisfied with the court's action on a claim, the claimant or interested person may appeal the action to the court of appeals in the manner other judgments of the county court in probate matters are appealed.

Added by Acts 2011, 82nd Leg., ch. 823 (H.B. 2759), § 1.02, eff. Jan. 1, 2014.

## § 1157.059. Allowance and Approval Prohibited Without Affidavit

Except as provided by Section 1157.102, a guardian of the estate may not allow, and the court may not approve, a claim for money against the estate unless the claim is supported by an affidavit that meets the applicable requirements of Sections 1157.004 and 1157.005.

Added by Acts 2011, 82nd Leg., ch. 823 (H.B. 2759), § 1.02, eff. Jan. 1, 2014.

## § 1157.060. Unsecured Claims Barred Under Certain Circumstances

A claim of an unsecured creditor for money that is not presented within the time prescribed by the notice of presentment permitted by Section 1153.004 is barred.

Added by Acts 2011, 82nd Leg., ch. 823 (H.B. 2759), § 1.02, eff. Jan. 1, 2014.

## § 1157.061. Allowing Barred Claim Prohibited; Court Disapproval

A guardian of the estate may not allow a claim against a ward if a suit on the claim is barred by an applicable general statute of limitation. A claim against a ward that is allowed by the guardian shall be disapproved if the court is satisfied that the limitation has run.

Added by Acts 2011, 82nd Leg., ch. 823 (H.B. 2759), § 1.02, eff. Jan. 1, 2014.

## § 1157.062. Certain Actions on Claims With Lost or Destroyed Evidence Void

(a) Before a claim the evidence for which is lost or destroyed is approved, the claim must be proved by disinterested testimony taken in open court or by oral or written deposition.

(b) The allowance or approval of a claim the evidence for which is lost or destroyed is void if the claim is:

(1) allowed or approved without the affidavit under Section 1157.006; or

(2) approved without satisfactory proof.

Added by Acts 2011, 82nd Leg., ch. 823 (H.B. 2759), § 1.02, eff. Jan. 1, 2014.

## § 1157.063. Suit on Rejected Claim

(a) A claim or part of a claim that has been rejected by the guardian of the estate is barred unless not later than the 90th day after the date of rejection the claimant commences suit on the claim in the court of original probate jurisdiction in which the guardianship is pending or in any other court of proper jurisdiction.

(b) In a suit commenced on the rejected claim, the memorandum endorsed on or attached to the claim is taken to be true without further proof unless denied under oath.

Added by Acts 2011, 82nd Leg., ch. 823 (H.B. 2759), § 1.02, eff. Jan. 1, 2014.

## § 1157.064. Presentment of Claim Prerequisite for Judgment

(a) Except as provided by Subsection (b), a judgment may not be rendered in favor of a claimant on a claim for money that has not been:

(1) legally presented to the guardian of the estate of the ward; and

(2) wholly or partly rejected by the guardian or the court.

(b) Subsection (a) does not apply to a claim against the estate of a ward for delinquent ad valorem taxes that is being administered in probate in a county other than the county in which the taxes were imposed.

Added by Acts 2011, 82nd Leg., ch. 823 (H.B. 2759), § 1.02, eff. Jan. 1, 2014.

## § 1157.065. Judgment in Suit on Rejected Claim

No execution may issue on a rejected claim or part of a claim that is established by suit. The judgment in the suit shall be:

(1) certified not later than the 30th day after the date of rendition, if the judgment is from a court other than the court of original probate jurisdiction;

(2) filed in the court in which the guardianship is pending;

(3) entered on the claim docket;

(4) classified by the court; and

(5) handled as if originally allowed and approved in due course of administration.

Added by Acts 2011, 82nd Leg., ch. 823 (H.B. 2759), § 1.02, eff. Jan. 1, 2014.

## SUBCHAPTER C. PAYMENT OF CLAIMS, ALLOWANCES, AND EXPENSES

## § 1157.101. Payment of Approved or Established Claim

Except as provided for payment of an unauthenticated claim at the risk of a guardian, a claim or any part of a claim for money against the estate of a ward may not be paid until the claim or part of the claim has been approved by the court or established by the judgment of a court of competent jurisdiction.

Added by Acts 2011, 82nd Leg., ch. 823 (H.B. 2759), § 1.02, eff. Jan. 1, 2014.

### § 1157.102.  Payment of Unauthenticated Claim

(a) Subject to Subsection (b), a guardian of the estate may pay an unauthenticated claim against the ward's estate if the guardian believes the claim to be just.

(b) A guardian who pays a claim under Subsection (a) and the sureties on the guardian's bond are liable for the amount of any payment of the claim if the court finds that the claim is not just.

Added by Acts 2011, 82nd Leg., ch. 823 (H.B. 2759), § 1.02, eff. Jan. 1, 2014.

### § 1157.103.  Priority of Payment of Claims

(a) Except as provided by Subsection (b), the guardian of the estate shall pay a claim against the ward's estate that has been allowed and approved or established by suit, as soon as practicable and in the following order:

(1) expenses for the care, maintenance, and education of the ward or the ward's dependents;

(2) funeral expenses of the ward and expenses of the ward's last illness, if the guardianship is kept open after the ward's death as provided under this title, except that any claim against the ward's estate that has been allowed and approved or established by suit before the ward's death shall be paid before the funeral expenses and expenses of the last illness;

(3) expenses of administration; and

(4) other claims against the ward or the ward's estate.

(b) If the estate is insolvent, the guardian shall give first priority to the payment of a claim relating to the administration of the guardianship. The guardian shall pay other claims against the ward's estate in the order prescribed by Subsection (a).

Added by Acts 2011, 82nd Leg., ch. 823 (H.B. 2759), § 1.02, eff. Jan. 1, 2014.

### § 1157.104.  Payment of Proceeds From Sale of Property Securing Debt

(a) If a guardian of the estate has on hand the proceeds of a sale made to satisfy a mortgage or other lien and the proceeds or any part of the proceeds are not required for the payment of any debts against the estate that have a preference over the mortgage or other lien, the guardian shall pay the proceeds to a holder of the mortgage or other lien.

(b) If the guardian fails to pay the proceeds as required by this section, the holder of a mortgage or other lien, on proof of the mortgage or other lien, may obtain an order from the court directing the payment of proceeds to be made.)

Added by Acts 2011, 82nd Leg., ch. 823 (H.B. 2759), § 1.02, eff. Jan. 1, 2014.

### § 1157.105.  Claimant's Petition for Allowance and Payment of Claim

A claimant whose claim has not been paid may:

(1) petition the court for determination of the claim at any time before the claim is barred by an applicable statute of limitations; and

(2) procure on due proof an order for the claim's allowance and payment from the estate.

Added by Acts 2011, 82nd Leg., ch. 823 (H.B. 2759), § 1.02, eff. Jan. 1, 2014.

### § 1157.106.  Payment When Assets Insufficient to Pay Certain Claims

(a) If there are insufficient assets to pay all claims of the same class, the claims in that class shall be paid pro rata, as directed by the court, and in the order directed.

(b) A guardian of the estate may not be allowed to pay any claims other than with the pro rata amount of the estate funds that have come into the guardian's possession, regardless of whether the estate is solvent or insolvent.

Added by Acts 2011, 82nd Leg., ch. 823 (H.B. 2759), § 1.02, eff. Jan. 1, 2014.

### § 1157.107.  Payment of Court Costs Relating to Claim

All costs incurred in the probate court with respect to a claim are taxed as follows:

(1) if the claim is allowed and approved, the guardianship estate shall pay the costs;

(2) if the claim is allowed but disapproved, the claimant shall pay the costs;

(3) if the claim is rejected but established by suit, the guardianship estate shall pay the costs;

(4) if the claim is rejected but not established by suit, the claimant shall pay the costs; or

(5) in a suit to establish the claim after the claim is rejected in part, if the claimant fails to recover judgment for a greater amount than was allowed or

approved for the claim, the claimant shall pay all costs.

Added by Acts 2011, 82nd Leg., ch. 823 (H.B. 2759), § 1.02, eff. Jan. 1, 2014.

### § 1157.108. Liability for Nonpayment of Claim

(a) A person or claimant, except the state treasury, entitled to payment from a guardianship estate of money the court orders to be paid is authorized to have execution issued against the property of the guardianship for the amount due, with interest and costs, if:

(1) a guardian of the estate fails to pay the money on demand;

(2) guardianship estate funds are available to make the payment; and

(3) the person or claimant makes an affidavit of the demand for payment and the guardian's failure to pay.

(b) The court may cite the guardian and the sureties on the guardian's bond to show cause why the guardian or sureties should not be held liable for the debt, interest, costs, or damages:

(1) on return of the execution under Subsection (a) not satisfied; or

(2) on the affidavit of demand and failure to pay under Subsection (a).

(c) On the return of citation served under Subsection (b), the court shall render judgment against the cited guardian and sureties, in favor of the claim holder, if good cause why the guardian and sureties should not be held liable is not shown. The judgment must be for:

(1) the unpaid amount ordered to be paid or established by suit, with interest and costs; and

(2) damages on the amount neglected to be paid at the rate of five percent per month for each month, or fraction of a month, that the payment was neglected to be paid after demand for payment was made.

(d) Damages ordered under Subsection (c)(2) may be collected in any court of competent jurisdiction.

Added by Acts 2011, 82nd Leg., ch. 823 (H.B. 2759), § 1.02, eff. Jan. 1, 2014.

### SUBCHAPTER D. PRESENTMENT AND PAYMENT OF SECURED CLAIMS

### § 1157.151. Option to Treat Claim as Matured Secured Claim or Preferred Debt and Lien

(a) If a secured claim against a ward is presented, the claimant shall specify in the claim, in addition to all other matters required to be specified in the claim, whether the claim shall be:

(1) allowed and approved as a matured secured claim to be paid in due course of administration, in which case the claim shall be paid in that manner if allowed and approved; or

(2) allowed, approved, and fixed as a preferred debt and lien against the specific property securing the indebtedness and paid according to the terms of the contract that secured the lien, in which case the claim shall be so allowed and approved if it is a valid lien.

(b) Notwithstanding Subsection (a)(2), the guardian of the estate may pay a claim that the claimant specified as a claim to be allowed, approved, and fixed as a preferred debt and lien as described by Subsection (a)(2) before maturity if that payment is in the best interests of the estate.

(c) If a secured claim is not presented within the time provided by law, the claim shall be treated as a claim to be paid in accordance with Subsection (a)(2).

Added by Acts 2011, 82nd Leg., ch. 823 (H.B. 2759), § 1.02, eff. Jan. 1, 2014.

### § 1157.152. Preferred Debt and Lien

When a claim for a debt has been allowed and approved under Section 1157.151(a)(2):

(1) a further claim for the debt may not be made against other estate assets;

(2) the claim remains a preferred lien against the property securing the claim; and

(3) the property remains security for the debt in any distribution or sale of the property before final maturity and payment of the debt.

Added by Acts 2011, 82nd Leg., ch. 823 (H.B. 2759), § 1.02, eff. Jan. 1, 2014.

### § 1157.153. Payment of Maturities on Preferred Debt and Lien

(a) If, not later than the 12th month after the date letters of guardianship are granted, the property securing a debt for which a claim is allowed, approved, and fixed under Section 1157.151(a)(2) is not sold or distributed, the guardian of the estate shall:

(1) promptly pay all maturities that have accrued on the debt according to the terms of the maturities; and

(2) perform all the terms of any contract securing the maturities.

(b) If the guardian defaults in payment or performance under Subsection (a):

(1) on the motion of the claim holder, the court shall require the sale of the property subject to the unmatured part of the debt and apply the proceeds of the sale to the liquidation of the maturities; or

(2) at the claim holder's option, a motion may be made in the same manner as a motion under Subdivision (1) to require the sale of the property free of the lien and apply the proceeds to the payment of the whole debt.

Added by Acts 2011, 82nd Leg., ch. 823 (H.B. 2759), § 1.02, eff. Jan. 1, 2014.

## SUBCHAPTER E. CLAIMS INVOLVING GUARDIANS

### § 1157.201. Claim by Guardian

(a) A claim that a guardian of the person or estate held against the ward at the time of the guardian's appointment, or that accrues after the appointment, shall be verified by affidavit as required in other cases and presented to the clerk of the court in which the guardianship is pending. The clerk shall enter the claim on the claim docket and the claim shall take the same course as other claims.

(b) A claim by a guardian that has been filed with the court within the required period shall be entered on the claim docket and acted on by the court in the same manner as in other cases.

(c) An appeal from a judgment of the court acting on a claim under this section may be taken as in other cases.

Added by Acts 2011, 82nd Leg., ch. 823 (H.B. 2759), § 1.02, eff. Jan. 1, 2014.

### § 1157.202. Purchase of Claim by Guardian Prohibited

(a) A guardian may not purchase, for the guardian's own use or for any other purpose, a claim against the guardianship the guardian represents.

(b) On written complaint by a person interested in the guardianship estate and on satisfactory proof of a violation of Subsection (a), the court after citation and hearing shall enter an order canceling the claim described by Subsection (a). No part of the canceled claim may be paid out of the guardianship.

(c) The court may remove a guardian for a violation of this section.

Added by Acts 2011, 82nd Leg., ch. 823 (H.B. 2759), § 1.02, eff. Jan. 1, 2014.

## CHAPTER 1158. SALE OR PARTITION OF WARD'S PROPERTY

## SUBCHAPTER A.  GENERAL PROVISIONS

### § 1158.001.  Court Order Authorizing Sale

(a) Except as provided by this chapter, any property of a ward may not be sold without a court order authorizing the sale.

(b) Except as otherwise specifically provided by this title, the court may order property of a ward to be sold for cash or on credit, at public auction or privately, as the court considers most advantageous to the estate.

Added by Acts 2011, 82nd Leg., ch. 823 (H.B. 2759), § 1.02, eff. Jan. 1, 2014.

## SUBCHAPTER B.  CERTAIN ESTATE PROPERTY REQUIRED TO BE SOLD

### § 1158.051.  Sale of Certain Personal Property Required

(a) After approval of the inventory, appraisement, and list of claims, the guardian of the estate of a ward promptly shall apply for a court order to sell, at public auction or privately, for cash or on credit for a term not to exceed six months, all estate property that is liable to perish, waste, or deteriorate in value, or that will be an expense or disadvantage to the estate if kept.

(b) The following may not be included in a sale under Subsection (a):

(1) property exempt from forced sale;

(2) property that is the subject of a specific legacy; and

(3) personal property necessary to carry on a farm, ranch, factory, or other business that is thought best to operate.

(c) In determining whether to order the sale of an asset under Subsection (a), the court shall consider:

(1) the guardian's duty to take care of and manage the estate in the manner a person of ordinary prudence, discretion, and intelligence would manage the person's own affairs; and

(2) whether the asset constitutes an asset that a trustee is authorized to invest under Subchapter F, Chapter 113, Property Code, or Chapter 117, Property Code.

Added by Acts 2011, 82nd Leg., ch. 823 (H.B. 2759), § 1.02, eff. Jan. 1, 2014.

## SUBCHAPTER C.  SALE OF PERSONAL PROPERTY

### § 1158.101.  Order for Sale

(a) Except as provided by Subsection (b), on the application of the guardian of the estate of a ward or any interested person, the court may order the sale of any estate personal property not required to be sold by Section 1158.051, including livestock or growing or harvested crops, if the court finds that the sale of the property is in the best interests of the ward or the ward's estate to pay, from the proceeds of the sale:

(1) expenses of the care, maintenance, and education of the ward or the ward's dependents;

(2) expenses of administration;

(3) allowances;

(4) claims against the ward or the ward's estate; and

(5) if the guardianship is kept open after the death of the ward, the ward's funeral expenses and expenses of the ward's last illness.

(b) The court may not order under this section the sale of exempt property.

Added by Acts 2011, 82nd Leg., ch. 823 (H.B. 2759), § 1.02, eff. Jan. 1, 2014.

### § 1158.102. Requirements for Application and Order

To the extent possible, an application and order for the sale of estate personal property under Section 1158.101 must conform to the requirements under Subchapter F for an application and order for the sale of real estate.

Added by Acts 2011, 82nd Leg., ch. 823 (H.B. 2759), § 1.02, eff. Jan. 1, 2014.

### § 1158.103. Sale at Public Auction

Unless the court directs otherwise, before estate personal property is sold at public auction, notice must be:

(1) issued by the guardian of the estate; and

(2) posted in the manner notice is posted for original proceedings in probate.

Added by Acts 2011, 82nd Leg., ch. 823 (H.B. 2759), § 1.02, eff. Jan. 1, 2014.

### § 1158.104. Sale on Credit

(a) Estate personal property may not be sold on credit at public auction for a term of more than six months from the date of sale.

(b) Estate personal property purchased on credit at public auction may not be delivered to the purchaser until the purchaser gives a note for the amount due, with good and solvent personal security. The requirement that security be provided may be waived if the property will not be delivered until the note, with interest, has been paid.

Added by Acts 2011, 82nd Leg., ch. 823 (H.B. 2759), § 1.02, eff. Jan. 1, 2014.

### § 1158.105. Report; Evidence of Title

(a) A sale of estate personal property shall be reported to the court. The laws regulating the confirmation or disapproval of a sale of real estate apply to the sale of personal property, except that a conveyance is not required.

(b) The court's order confirming the sale of estate personal property:

(1) vests the right and title of the ward's estate in the purchaser who has complied with the terms of the sale; and

(2) is prima facie evidence that all requirements of the law in making the sale have been met.

(c) The guardian of the estate, on request, may issue a bill of sale without warranty to the purchaser of estate personal property as evidence of title. The expense of the bill of sale if requested must be paid by the purchaser.

Added by Acts 2011, 82nd Leg., ch. 823 (H.B. 2759), § 1.02, eff. Jan. 1, 2014.

## SUBCHAPTER D.   SALE OF LIVESTOCK

### § 1158.151. Authority for Sale

(a) A guardian of the estate who has possession of livestock and who considers selling the livestock to be necessary or to the estate's advantage may, in addition to any other method provided by law for the sale of personal property, obtain authority from the court in which the estate is pending to sell the livestock through:

(1) a bonded livestock commission merchant; or

(2) a bonded livestock auction commission merchant.

(b) The court may authorize the sale of livestock in the manner described by Subsection (a) on a written and sworn application by the guardian or any person interested in the estate.

Added by Acts 2011, 82nd Leg., ch. 823 (H.B. 2759), § 1.02, eff. Jan. 1, 2014.

### § 1158.152. Contents of Application; Hearing

(a) An application under Section 1158.151 must:

(1) describe the livestock sought to be sold; and

(2) state why granting the application is necessary or to the estate's advantage.

(b) The court:

(1) shall consider the application; and

(2) may hear evidence for or against the application, with or without notice, as the facts warrant.

Added by Acts 2011, 82nd Leg., ch. 823 (H.B. 2759), § 1.02, eff. Jan. 1, 2014.

### § 1158.153.  Grant of Application

If the court grants an application for the sale of livestock, the court shall:

(1) enter an order to that effect; and

(2) authorize delivery of the livestock to a commission merchant described by Section 1158.151(a) for sale in the regular course of business.

Added by Acts 2011, 82nd Leg., ch. 823 (H.B. 2759), § 1.02, eff. Jan. 1, 2014.

### § 1158.154.  Report; Passage of Title

The guardian of the estate shall promptly report to the court a sale of livestock, supported by a verified copy of the commission merchant's account of the sale. A court order of confirmation is not required to pass title to the purchaser of the livestock.

Added by Acts 2011, 82nd Leg., ch. 823 (H.B. 2759), § 1.02, eff. Jan. 1, 2014.

### § 1158.155.  Commission Merchant Charges

The commission merchant shall be paid the commission merchant's usual and customary charges, not to exceed five percent of the sale price, for the sale of the livestock.

Added by Acts 2011, 82nd Leg., ch. 823 (H.B. 2759), § 1.02, eff. Jan. 1, 2014.

### SUBCHAPTER E.  SALE OF MORTGAGED PROPERTY

### § 1158.201.  Application for Sale of Mortgaged Property

On the filing of a written application, a creditor holding a claim that is secured by a valid mortgage or other lien and that has been allowed and approved or established by suit may obtain from the court in which the guardianship is pending an order requiring that the property securing the lien, or as much of the property as is necessary to satisfy the creditor's claim, be sold.

Added by Acts 2011, 82nd Leg., ch. 823 (H.B. 2759), § 1.02, eff. Jan. 1, 2014.

### § 1158.202.  Citation

On the filing of an application under Section 1158.201, the clerk shall issue a citation requiring the guardian of the estate to appear and show cause why the application should not be granted.

Added by Acts 2011, 82nd Leg., ch. 823 (H.B. 2759), § 1.02, eff. Jan. 1, 2014.

### § 1158.203.  Order

The court may order the lien securing the claim of a creditor who files an application under Section 1158.201 to be discharged out of general estate assets or refinanced if the discharge or refinance of the lien appears to the court to be advisable.  Otherwise, the court shall grant the application and order that the property securing the lien be sold at public or private sale, as the court considers best, as in an ordinary sale of real estate.

Added by Acts 2011, 82nd Leg., ch. 823 (H.B. 2759), § 1.02, eff. Jan. 1, 2014.

### SUBCHAPTER F.  SALE OF REAL PROPERTY: APPLICATION AND ORDER FOR SALE

### § 1158.251.  Application for Order of Sale

An application may be made to the court for an order to sell real property of a ward's estate if the sale appears necessary or advisable to:

(1) pay:

(A) expenses of administration, allowances, and claims against the ward or the ward's estate; and

(B) if the guardianship is kept open after the death of the ward, the ward's funeral expenses and expenses of the ward's last illness;

(2) make up the deficiency if the income of a ward's estate, the personal property of the estate, and the proceeds of previous sales are insufficient to pay for the education and maintenance of the ward or to pay debts against the estate;

(3) dispose of property of the ward's estate that consists wholly or partly of an undivided interest in real estate if considered in the best interests of the estate to sell the interest;

(4) dispose of real estate of a ward, any part of which is nonproductive or does not produce suffi-

cient revenue to make a fair return on the value of the real estate, if:

(A) the improvement of the real estate with a view to making the property productive is not considered advantageous or advisable; and

(B) the sale of the real estate and the investment of the money derived from that sale appears to be in the estate's best interests; or

(5) conserve the ward's estate by selling mineral interest or royalties on minerals in place owned by the ward.

Added by Acts 2011, 82nd Leg., ch. 823 (H.B. 2759), § 1.02, eff. Jan. 1, 2014.

### § 1158.252.  Contents of Application

An application for the sale of real estate must:

(1) be in writing;

(2) describe:

(A) the real estate sought to be sold; or

(B) the interest in or part of the real estate sought to be sold; and

(3) be accompanied by an exhibit, verified by an affidavit, showing fully and in detail:

(A) the estate's condition;

(B) the charges and claims that have been approved or established by suit or that have been rejected and may be established later;

(C) the amount of each claim described by Paragraph (B);

(D) the estate property remaining on hand that is liable for the payment of the claims described by Paragraph (B); and

(E) any other facts showing the necessity for or advisability of the sale.

Added by Acts 2011, 82nd Leg., ch. 823 (H.B. 2759), § 1.02, eff. Jan. 1, 2014.

### § 1158.253.  Citation

On the filing of an application for the sale of real estate under Section 1158.251, accompanied by an exhibit described by Section 1158.252, the clerk shall issue a citation to all persons interested in the guardianship. The citation must:

(1) describe the real estate or the interest in or part of the real estate sought to be sold;

(2) inform the interested persons of the right under Section 1158.254 to file an opposition to the sale during the period prescribed by the court in the citation; and

(3) be served by posting.

Added by Acts 2011, 82nd Leg., ch. 823 (H.B. 2759), § 1.02, eff. Jan. 1, 2014.

### § 1158.254.  Opposition to Sale

During the period prescribed in a citation issued under Section 1158.253, a person interested in the guardianship may file:

(1) a written opposition to the sale; or

(2) an application for the sale of other estate property.

Added by Acts 2011, 82nd Leg., ch. 823 (H.B. 2759), § 1.02, eff. Jan. 1, 2014.

### § 1158.255.  Hearing on Application and Any Opposition

(a) The clerk of the court in which an application for an order of sale is filed shall immediately call to the judge's attention any opposition to the sale that is filed during the period prescribed in the citation issued under Section 1158. 253. The court shall hold a hearing on the application if an opposition to the sale is filed during the period prescribed in the citation.

(b) A hearing on an application for an order of sale is not required under this section if no opposition to the application is filed during the period prescribed in the citation. The court may determine that a hearing on the application is necessary even if no opposition is filed during that period.

(c) If the court orders a hearing under Subsection (a) or (b), the court shall designate in writing a date and time for the hearing on the application and any opposition, together with the evidence pertaining to the application and any opposition. The clerk shall issue a notice of the date and time of the hearing to the applicant and to each person who files an opposition to the sale, if applicable.

(d) The judge, by entries on the docket, may continue a hearing held under this section from time to time until the judge is satisfied concerning the application.

Added by Acts 2011, 82nd Leg., ch. 823 (H.B. 2759), § 1.02, eff. Jan. 1, 2014.

### § 1158.256.  Order

(a) The court shall order the sale of the property of the estate described in an application under Section 1158.251 if the court is satisfied that the sale is necessary or advisable. Otherwise, the court may deny the application and, if the court considers it best, may order the sale of other estate property the sale of which would be more advantageous to the estate.

(b) An order for the sale of real estate under this section must specify:

(1) the property to be sold, including a description that identifies that property;

(2) whether the property is to be sold at public auction or private sale and, if at public auction, the time and place of the sale;

(3) the necessity or advisability of, and the purpose of, the sale;

(4) except in a case in which a guardian of the estate was not required to give a general bond, that the court, after examining the general bond given by the guardian, finds that:

(A) the bond is sufficient as required by law; or

(B) the bond is insufficient;

(5) if the court finds that the general bond is insufficient under Subdivision (4)(B), the amount of the necessary or increased bond, as applicable;

(6) that the sale is to be made and the report returned in accordance with law; and

(7) the terms of the sale.

Added by Acts 2011, 82nd Leg., ch. 823 (H.B. 2759), § 1.02, eff. Jan. 1, 2014.

### § 1158.257. Sale for Payment of Debts

Real property of a ward selected to be sold for the payment of expenses or claims must be that property the sale of which the court considers most advantageous to the guardianship.

Added by Acts 2011, 82nd Leg., ch. 823 (H.B. 2759), § 1.02, eff. Jan. 1, 2014.

## SUBCHAPTER G. SALE OF REAL ESTATE: TERMS OF SALE

### § 1158.301. Permissible Terms

Real estate of an estate may be sold for cash, or for part cash and part credit, or the equity in land securing an indebtedness may be sold subject to the indebtedness, or with an assumption of the indebtedness, at public or private sale, as appears to the court to be in the estate's best interests.

Added by Acts 2011, 82nd Leg., ch. 823 (H.B. 2759), § 1.02, eff. Jan. 1, 2014.

### § 1158.302. Sale on Credit

(a) The cash payment for real estate of an estate sold partly on credit may not be less than one-fifth of the purchase price. The purchaser shall execute a note for the deferred payments, payable in monthly, quarterly, semiannual, or annual installments, in amounts that appear to the court to be in the guardianship's best interests. The note must bear interest from the date at a rate of not less than four percent per year, payable as provided in the note.

(b) A note executed by a purchaser under Subsection (a) must be secured by a vendor's lien retained in the deed and in the note on the property sold, and be additionally secured by a deed of trust on the property sold, with the usual provisions for foreclosure and sale on failure to make the payments provided in the deed and the note.

(c) At the election of the holder of a note executed by a purchaser under Subsection (a), default in the payment of principal or interest or any part of the payment when due matures the entire debt.

Added by Acts 2011, 82nd Leg., ch. 823 (H.B. 2759), § 1.02, eff. Jan. 1, 2014.

## SUBCHAPTER H. RECONVEYANCE OF REAL ESTATE FOLLOWING FORECLOSURE

### § 1158.351. Applicability of Subchapter

This subchapter applies only to real estate owned by an estate as a result of the foreclosure of a vendor's lien or mortgage belonging to the estate:

(1) by a judicial sale;

(2) by a foreclosure suit;

(3) through a sale under a deed of trust; or

(4) by acceptance of a deed in cancellation of a lien or mortgage owned by the estate.

Added by Acts 2011, 82nd Leg., ch. 823 (H.B. 2759), § 1.02, eff. Jan. 1, 2014.

### § 1158.352. Application and Order for Reconveyance

On proper application and proof, the court may dispense with the requirements for a credit sale prescribed by Section 1158.302 and order the reconveyance of foreclosed real estate to the former mortgage debtor or former owner if it appears to the court that:

(1) an application to redeem the real estate has been made by the former owner to a corporation or agency created by an act of the United States Congress or of this state in connection with legislation for the relief of owners of mortgaged or encumbered homes, farms, ranches, or other real estate; and

(2) owning bonds of one of those federal or state corporations or agencies instead of the real estate would be in the estate's best interests.

Added by Acts 2011, 82nd Leg., ch. 823 (H.B. 2759), § 1.02, eff. Jan. 1, 2014.

### § 1158.353. Exchange for Bonds

(a) If a court orders the reconveyance of foreclosed real estate under Section 1158.352, vendor's lien notes shall be reserved for the total amount of the indebtedness due or for the total amount of bonds that the corporation or agency to which the application to redeem the real estate was submitted as described by Section 1158.352(1) is allowed to advance under the corporation's or agency's rules or regulations.

(b) On obtaining the order for reconveyance, it shall be proper for the guardian to endorse and assign the reserved vendor's lien notes over to any one of the corporations or agencies described by Section 1158.352(1) in exchange for bonds of that corporation or agency.

Added by Acts 2011, 82nd Leg., ch. 823 (H.B. 2759), § 1.02, eff. Jan. 1, 2014.

### SUBCHAPTER I. SALE OF REAL ESTATE: PUBLIC SALE

### § 1158.401. Required Notice

(a) Except as otherwise provided by this title, the guardian of the estate shall advertise a public sale of real estate of the estate by a notice published in the county in which the estate is pending, as provided by this title for publication of notices or citations. The notice must include a reference to:

(1) the order of sale;

(2) the time, place, and required terms of sale; and

(3) a brief description of the real estate to be sold.

(b) The reference described by Subsection (a)(1) is not required to contain field notes, but if the real estate to be sold is rural property, the reference must include:

(1) the name of the original survey of the real estate;

(2) the number of acres the real estate consists of;

(3) the location of the real estate in the county; and

(4) the name by which the real estate is generally known.

Added by Acts 2011, 82nd Leg., ch. 823 (H.B. 2759), § 1.02, eff. Jan. 1, 2014.

### § 1158.402. Method of Sale

A public sale of real estate of an estate shall be made at public auction to the highest bidder.

Added by Acts 2011, 82nd Leg., ch. 823 (H.B. 2759), § 1.02, eff. Jan. 1, 2014.

### § 1158.403. Time and Place of Sale

(a) Except as provided by Subsection (c), a public sale of real estate of an estate shall be made at:

(1) the courthouse door in the county in which the guardianship proceedings are pending; or

(2) another place in that county at which sales of real estate are specifically authorized to be made.

(b) The sale must occur between 10 a.m. and 4 p.m. on the first Tuesday of the month after publication of notice has been completed.

(c) If the court considers it advisable, the court may order the sale to be made in the county in which the real estate is located, in which event notice shall be published both in that county and in the county in which the proceedings are pending.

Added by Acts 2011, 82nd Leg., ch. 823 (H.B. 2759), § 1.02, eff. Jan. 1, 2014.

### § 1158.404. Continuance of Sale

(a) A public sale of real estate of an estate that is not completed on the day advertised may be continued from day to day by an oral public announcement of the continuance made at the conclusion of the sale each day.

(b) A continued sale must occur within the hours prescribed by Section 1158.403(b).

(c) The continuance of a sale under this section shall be shown in the report of the sale made to the court.

Added by Acts 2011, 82nd Leg., ch. 823 (H.B. 2759), § 1.02, eff. Jan. 1, 2014.

### § 1158.405. Failure of Bidder to Comply

(a) If a person who bids on real estate of the guardianship estate offered for sale at public auction fails to comply with the terms of the sale, the real estate shall be readvertised and sold without any further order.

(b) The person defaulting on a bid as described by Subsection (a) is liable for payment to the guardian of the estate, for the estate's benefit, of:

(1) 10 percent of the amount of the bid; and

(2) the amount of any deficiency in price on the second sale.

(c) The guardian shall recover the amounts under Subsection (b) by suit in any court in the county in which the sale was made that has jurisdiction over the amount claimed.

Added by Acts 2011, 82nd Leg., ch. 823 (H.B. 2759), § 1.02, eff. Jan. 1, 2014.

## SUBCHAPTER J. SALE OF REAL ESTATE: PRIVATE SALE

### § 1158.451. Manner of Sale

A private sale of real estate of the estate shall be made in the manner the court directs in the order of sale. Unless the court directs otherwise, additional advertising, notice, or citation concerning the sale is not required.

Added by Acts 2011, 82nd Leg., ch. 823 (H.B. 2759), § 1.02, eff. Jan. 1, 2014.

## SUBCHAPTER K. SALE OF EASEMENT OR RIGHT–OF–WAY

### § 1158.501. Authorization

The guardian may sell and convey easements and rights-of-way on, under, and over the land of a guardianship estate that is being administered under court order, regardless of whether the sale proceeds are required to pay charges or claims against the estate, or for other lawful purposes.

Added by Acts 2011, 82nd Leg., ch. 823 (H.B. 2759), § 1.02, eff. Jan. 1, 2014.

### § 1158.502. Procedure

The procedure for the sale of an easement or right-of-way authorized under Section 1158.501 is the same as the procedure provided by law for a sale of real property of a ward at private sale.

Added by Acts 2011, 82nd Leg., ch. 823 (H.B. 2759), § 1.02, eff. Jan. 1, 2014.

## SUBCHAPTER L. CONFIRMATION OF SALE OF REAL PROPERTY AND TRANSFER OF TITLE

### § 1158.551. Report

A sale of estate real property shall be reported to the court ordering the sale not later than the 30th day after the date the sale is made. The report must:

(1) be in writing, sworn to, and filed with the clerk;

(2) include:

(A) the date of the order of sale;

(B) a description of the property sold;

(C) the time and place of sale;

(D) the purchaser's name;

(E) the amount for which each parcel of property or interest in the parcel of property was sold;

(F) the terms of the sale;

(G) whether the sale was made at public auction or privately; and

(H) whether the purchaser is ready to comply with the order of sale; and

(3) be noted on the guardianship docket.

Added by Acts 2011, 82nd Leg., ch. 823 (H.B. 2759), § 1.02, eff. Jan. 1, 2014.

### § 1158.552. Action of Court on Report of Sale

After the expiration of five days from the date a report of sale is filed under Section 1158.551, the court shall:

(1) inquire into the manner in which the sale was made;

(2) hear evidence in support of or against the report; and

(3) determine the sufficiency or insufficiency of the guardian's general bond, if any has been required and given.

Added by Acts 2011, 82nd Leg., ch. 823 (H.B. 2759), § 1.02, eff. Jan. 1, 2014.

### § 1158.553. Confirmation of Sale When Bond Not Required

If the guardian of the estate of a ward is not required by Subtitle D to give a general bond, the court may confirm the sale of estate real property in the manner provided by Section 1158.556(a) if the court finds that the sale is satisfactory and made in accordance with law.

Added by Acts 2011, 82nd Leg., ch. 823 (H.B. 2759), § 1.02, eff. Jan. 1, 2014.

### § 1158.554. Sufficiency of Bond

(a) If the guardian of an estate is required by Subtitle D to give a general bond, before the court confirms any sale of real estate, the court shall determine whether the bond is sufficient to protect the estate after the sale proceeds are received.

(b) If the court finds that the general bond is sufficient, the court may confirm the sale as provided by Section 1158.556(a).

(c) If the court finds that the general bond is insufficient, the court may not confirm the sale until the general bond is increased to the amount required by the court, or an additional bond is given, and approved by the court.

(d) An increase in the amount of the general bond, or the additional bond, as applicable under Subsection (c), must be equal to the sum of:

(1) the amount for which the real estate is sold; and

(2) any additional amount the court finds necessary and sets for the estate's protection.

Added by Acts 2011, 82nd Leg., ch. 823 (H.B. 2759), § 1.02, eff. Jan. 1, 2014.

### § 1158.555. Increased or Additional Bond Not Required

Notwithstanding Sections 1158.554(c) and (d), if the real estate sold is encumbered by a lien to secure a claim against the estate and is sold to the owner or holder of the secured claim in full payment, liquidation, and satisfaction of the claim, an increased general bond or additional bond may not be required except for the amount of any cash paid to the guardian of the estate in excess of the amount necessary to pay, liquidate, and satisfy the claim in full.

Added by Acts 2011, 82nd Leg., ch. 823 (H.B. 2759), § 1.02, eff. Jan. 1, 2014.

### § 1158.556. Confirmation or Disapproval Order

(a) If the court is satisfied that a sale reported under Section 1158.551 was for a fair price, was properly made, and was in conformity with law, and the court has approved any increased or additional bond that the court found necessary to protect the estate, the court shall enter an order:

(1) confirming the sale;

(2) showing conformity with the provisions of this chapter relating to the sale;

(3) detailing the terms of the sale; and

(4) authorizing the guardian of the estate to convey the property on the purchaser's compliance with the terms of the sale.

(b) If the court is not satisfied that the sale was for a fair price, was properly made, and was in conformity with law, the court shall issue an order setting aside the sale and ordering a new sale to be made, if necessary.

(c) The court's action in confirming or disapproving a report of a sale has the effect of a final judgment. Any person interested in the guardianship estate or in the sale is entitled to have an order entered under this section reviewed as in other final judgments in probate proceedings.

Added by Acts 2011, 82nd Leg., ch. 823 (H.B. 2759), § 1.02, eff. Jan. 1, 2014.

### § 1158.557. Deed

Real estate of an estate that is sold shall be conveyed by a proper deed that refers to and identifies the court order confirming the sale. The deed:

(1) vests in the purchaser all right and title of the estate to, and all interest of the estate in, the property; and

(2) is prima facie evidence that the sale has met all applicable requirements of law.

Added by Acts 2011, 82nd Leg., ch. 823 (H.B. 2759), § 1.02, eff. Jan. 1, 2014.

### § 1158.558. Delivery of Deed

(a) After the court has confirmed a sale and one purchaser has complied with the terms of the sale, the guardian of the estate shall execute and deliver to the purchaser a proper deed conveying the property.

(b) If the sale is made partly on credit:

(1) the vendor's lien securing a purchase money note must be expressly retained in the deed and may not be waived; and

(2) before actual delivery of the deed to the purchaser, the purchaser shall execute and deliver to the guardian of the estate a vendor's lien note, with or without personal sureties as ordered by the court, and a deed of trust or mortgage on the property as additional security for the payment of the note.

(c) On completion of the transaction, the guardian of the estate shall promptly file and record the deed of trust or mortgage in the appropriate records in the county in which the land is located.

Added by Acts 2011, 82nd Leg., ch. 823 (H.B. 2759), § 1.02, eff. Jan. 1, 2014.

### § 1158.559. Damages; Removal

(a) If the guardian of the estate neglects to comply with Section 1158.558, including to file the deed of trust securing a lien in the proper county, the guardian and the sureties on the guardian's bond shall, after complaint and citation, be held liable for the use of the estate and for all damages resulting from the guardian's neglect, and the court may remove the guardian.

(b) Damages under this section may be recovered in a court of competent jurisdiction.

Added by Acts 2011, 82nd Leg., ch. 823 (H.B. 2759), § 1.02, eff. Jan. 1, 2014.

### SUBCHAPTER M. PROCEDURE ON FAILURE TO APPLY FOR SALE

#### § 1158.601. Failure to Apply for Sale

If the guardian of the estate of a ward neglects to apply for an order to sell sufficient property to pay charges and claims against the estate that have been allowed and approved or established by suit, an interested person, on written application, may have the guardian cited to appear and make a full exhibit of the estate's condition and show cause why a sale of the property should not be ordered.

Added by Acts 2011, 82nd Leg., ch. 823 (H.B. 2759), § 1.02, eff. Jan. 1, 2014.

#### § 1158.602. Court Order

On hearing an application under Section 1158. 601, if the court is satisfied that a sale of estate property is necessary or advisable to satisfy the charges and claims described by Section 1158.601, the court shall enter an order of sale as provided by Section 1158. 256.

Added by Acts 2011, 82nd Leg., ch. 823 (H.B. 2759), § 1.02, eff. Jan. 1, 2014.

### SUBCHAPTER N. PURCHASE OF ESTATE PROPERTY BY GUARDIAN

#### § 1158.651. General Prohibition on Purchase

Except as otherwise provided by Section 1158.652 or 1158.653, the guardian of the estate of a ward may not purchase, directly or indirectly, any estate property sold by the guardian or any co-representative of the guardian.

Added by Acts 2011, 82nd Leg., ch. 823 (H.B. 2759), § 1.02, eff. Jan. 1, 2014.

#### § 1158.652. Exception: Executory Contract

The guardian of the estate of a ward may purchase estate property in compliance with the terms of a written executory contract signed by the ward before the ward became incapacitated, including:

(1) a contract for deed;

(2) an earnest money contract;

(3) a buy/sell agreement; and

(4) a stock purchase or redemption agreement.

Added by Acts 2011, 82nd Leg., ch. 823 (H.B. 2759), § 1.02, eff. Jan. 1, 2014.

#### § 1158.653. Exception: Best Interest of Estate

(a) The guardian of the estate may purchase estate property on the court's determination that the sale is in the estate's best interest.

(b) In the case of an application filed by the guardian of the estate of a ward, the court shall appoint an attorney ad litem to represent the ward with respect to the sale.

(c) The court may require notice for a sale made under this section.

Added by Acts 2011, 82nd Leg., ch. 823 (H.B. 2759), § 1.02, eff. Jan. 1, 2014.

#### § 1158.654. Purchase in Violation of Subchapter

(a) If the guardian of the estate of a ward purchases estate property in violation of this subchapter, a person interested in the estate may file a written complaint with the court in which the guardianship proceedings are pending.

(b) On service of citation on the guardian on a complaint filed under Subsection (a) and after hearing and proof, the court shall:

(1) declare the sale void;

(2) set aside the sale; and

(3) order the reconveyance of the property to the estate.

(c) The court shall adjudge against the guardian all costs of the sale, protest, and suit, if found necessary.

Added by Acts 2011, 82nd Leg., ch. 823 (H.B. 2759), § 1.02, eff. Jan. 1, 2014.

### SUBCHAPTER O. PARTITION OF WARD'S INTEREST IN REAL ESTATE

#### § 1158.701. Partition by Agreement

(a) The guardian of the estate of a ward may agree to a partition of real estate in which the ward owns an interest in common with one or more other part owners if, in the opinion of the guardian, it is in the best interests of the ward's estate to partition the real estate.

(b) An agreement under Subsection (a) is subject to the approval of the court in which the guardianship proceeding is pending.

Added by Acts 2011, 82nd Leg., ch. 823 (H.B. 2759), § 1.02, eff. Jan. 1, 2014.

### § 1158.702. Application for Approval of Partition Agreement

(a) When a guardian has reached an agreement with the other part owners on how to partition real estate as described by Section 1158.701, the guardian shall file with the court in which the guardianship proceedings are pending an application to have the agreement approved by the court.

(b) The application must:

(1) describe the real estate to be divided;

(2) state why it is in the best interests of the ward's estate to partition the real estate; and

(3) show that the proposed partition agreement is fair and just to the ward's estate.

Added by Acts 2011, 82nd Leg., ch. 823 (H.B. 2759), § 1.02, eff. Jan. 1, 2014.

### § 1158.703. Hearing

(a) The county clerk shall immediately call to the attention of the judge of the court in which the guardianship proceeding is pending the filing of an application required by Section 1158.702. The judge shall designate a day to hear the application.

(b) The application must remain on file at least 10 days before any orders are entered.

(c) The judge may continue a hearing held under this section from time to time until the judge is satisfied concerning the application.

Added by Acts 2011, 82nd Leg., ch. 823 (H.B. 2759), § 1.02, eff. Jan. 1, 2014.

### § 1158.704. Order

If the judge is satisfied that the proposed partition of the real estate is in the best interests of the ward's estate, the court shall enter an order approving the partition and directing the guardian to execute the necessary agreement for the purpose of implementing the order and partition.

Added by Acts 2011, 82nd Leg., ch. 823 (H.B. 2759), § 1.02, eff. Jan. 1, 2014.

### § 1158.705. Partition Without Court Approval; Ratification of Partition Agreement

(a) If a guardian, without court approval as provided by this subchapter, executes or intends to execute an agreement to partition any real estate in which the ward has an interest, the guardian shall file with the court in which the guardianship proceedings are pending an application for the approval and ratification of the partition agreement.

(b) The application must:

(1) refer to the agreement in a manner in which the court can fully understand the nature of the partition and the real estate being divided; and

(2) state that, in the opinion of the guardian, the agreement is fair and just to the ward's estate and is in the best interests of the estate.

(c) On the filing of an application under Subsection (a), the court shall hold a hearing on the application as provided by Section 1158.703. The court shall enter an order ratifying and approving the partition agreement if the court is of the opinion that the partition is:

(1) fairly made; and

(2) in the best interests of the ward's estate.

(d) On ratification and approval, the partition is effective and binding as if originally executed after a court order.

Added by Acts 2011, 82nd Leg., ch. 823 (H.B. 2759), § 1.02, eff. Jan. 1, 2014.

### § 1158.706. Partition by Suit

(a) The guardian of the estate of a ward may bring a suit in the court in which the guardianship proceeding is pending for the partition of any real estate that the ward owns in common with one or more other part owners if the guardian is of the opinion that it is in the best interests of the ward's estate that the real estate be partitioned.

(b) The court may enter an order partitioning the real estate to the owner of the real estate, if after hearing the suit, the court is satisfied that the partition of the real estate is necessary.

Added by Acts 2011, 82nd Leg., ch. 823 (H.B. 2759), § 1.02, eff. Jan. 1, 2014.

## CHAPTER 1159. RENTING ESTATE PROPERTY

### SUBCHAPTER A. RENTAL AND RETURN OF ESTATE PROPERTY

Section
1159.001. Renting Estate Property Without Court Order.

## SUBCHAPTER A.   RENTAL AND RETURN OF ESTATE PROPERTY

### § 1159.001.   Renting Estate Property Without Court Order

(a) The guardian of an estate, without a court order, may rent any of the estate property for one year or less, at public auction or privately, as is considered to be in the best interests of the estate.

(b) On the sworn complaint of any person interested in the estate, the court shall require a guardian of the estate who, without a court order, rents estate property to account to the estate for the reasonable value of the rent of the property, to be ascertained by the court on satisfactory evidence.

Added by Acts 2011, 82nd Leg., ch. 823 (H.B. 2759), § 1.02, eff. Jan. 1, 2014.

### § 1159.002.   Renting Estate Property With Court Order

(a) The guardian of an estate may file a written application with the court setting forth the property the guardian seeks to rent.  If the proposed rental period is one year or more, the guardian of the estate shall file a written application with the court setting forth the property the guardian seeks to rent.

(b) If the court finds that granting an application filed under Subsection (a) is in the interests of the estate, the court shall grant the application and issue an order that:

(1) describes the property to be rented; and

(2) states whether the property will be rented at public auction or privately, whether for cash or on credit, and if on credit, the extent of the credit and the period for which the property may be rented.

(c) If, under Subsection (b), the court orders property to be rented at public auction, the court shall prescribe whether notice of the auction shall be published or posted.

Added by Acts 2011, 82nd Leg., ch. 823 (H.B. 2759), § 1.02, eff. Jan. 1, 2014.

### § 1159.003.   Estate Property Rented on Credit

(a) Possession of estate property rented on credit may not be delivered until the renter executes and delivers to the guardian of the estate a note with good personal security for the amount of the rent.  If the property is delivered without the guardian receiving the required security, the guardian and the sureties on the guardian's bond are liable for the full amount of the rent.

(b) Subsection (a) does not apply to a rental that is paid in installments in advance of the period to which the installments relate.

Added by Acts 2011, 82nd Leg., ch. 823 (H.B. 2759), § 1.02, eff. Jan. 1, 2014.

### § 1159.004.   Condition of Returned Estate Property

(a) Estate property that is rented must be returned to the estate's possession in as good a condition, except for reasonable wear and tear, as when the property was rented.

(b) The guardian of the estate shall:

(1) ensure that rented estate property is returned in the condition required by Subsection (a);

(2) report to the court any damage to, or loss or destruction of, estate property rented under this chapter; and

(3) ask the court for the authority to take any necessary action.

(c) A guardian who fails to act as required by this section and the sureties on the guardian's bond are liable to the estate for any loss or damage suffered as a result of the guardian's failure.

Added by Acts 2011, 82nd Leg., ch. 823 (H.B. 2759), § 1.02, eff. Jan. 1, 2014.

### § 1159.005.   Complaint for Failure to Rent

(a) A person interested in a guardianship may:

(1) file a written and sworn complaint in the court in which the estate is pending; and

(2) have the guardian of the estate cited to appear and show cause why the guardian did not rent any estate property.

(b) The court, on hearing the complaint, shall issue an order that is in the best interests of the estate.

Added by Acts 2011, 82nd Leg., ch. 823 (H.B. 2759), § 1.02, eff. Jan. 1, 2014.

## SUBCHAPTER B. REPORT ON RENTED ESTATE PROPERTY

### § 1159.051. Reports Concerning Rentals

(a) A guardian of an estate who rents estate property with an appraised value of $3,000 or more, not later than the 30th day after the date of the rental, shall file with the court a sworn and written report stating:

(1) the property rented and the property's appraised value;

(2) the date the property was rented and whether the rental occurred at public auction or privately;

(3) the name of the person renting the property;

(4) the rental amount;

(5) whether the rental was for cash or on credit; and

(6) if the rental was on credit, the length of time, the terms, and the security received for the credit.

(b) A guardian of an estate who rents estate property with an appraised value of less than $3,000 may report the rental in the next annual or final account that must be filed as required by law.

Added by Acts 2011, 82nd Leg., ch. 823 (H.B. 2759), § 1.02, eff. Jan. 1, 2014.

### § 1159.052. Court Action on Report

(a) After the fifth day after the date the report of the rental is filed, the court shall:

(1) examine the report; and

(2) by order approve and confirm the rental if the court finds the rental just and reasonable.

(b) If the court disapproves the rental, the guardianship is not bound and the court may order another offering for rent of the property in the same manner and subject to the provisions of this chapter.

(c) If the court approves the rental and it later appears that, by reason of the fault of the guardian of the estate, the property was not rented for the property's reasonable value, the court shall have the guardian and the sureties on the guardian's bond appear and show cause why the reasonable value of the rental of the property should not be adjudged against the guardian or sureties.

Added by Acts 2011, 82nd Leg., ch. 823 (H.B. 2759), § 1.02, eff. Jan. 1, 2014.

## CHAPTER 1160. MATTERS RELATING TO MINERAL PROPERTIES

### SUBCHAPTER A. GENERAL PROVISIONS

### SUBCHAPTER A. GENERAL PROVISIONS

### § 1160.001. Definitions

In this chapter:

(1) "Gas" includes all liquid hydrocarbons in the gaseous phase in the reservoir.

(2) "Land" includes minerals or an interest in minerals in place.

(3) "Mineral development" includes exploration for, whether by geophysical or other means, drilling for, mining for, development of, operations in connection with, production of, and saving of oil, other liquid hydrocarbons, gas, gaseous elements, sulphur, metals, and all other minerals, whether solid or otherwise.

(4) "Property" includes land, minerals in place, whether solid, liquid, or gaseous, and an interest of any kind in the property, including a royalty interest, owned by an estate.

Added by Acts 2011, 82nd Leg., ch. 823 (H.B. 2759), § 1.02, eff. Jan. 1, 2014,

## SUBCHAPTER B. MINERAL LEASES AFTER PUBLIC NOTICE

### § 1160.051. Authorization for Leasing of Minerals

(a) The court in which a guardianship proceeding is pending may authorize the guardian, acting solely under a court order, to make, execute, and deliver a lease, with or without a unitization clause or pooling provision, providing for the exploration for and development and production of oil, other liquid hydrocarbons, gas, metals and other solid minerals, and other minerals, or any of those minerals in place, belonging to the estate.

(b) A lease authorized by Subsection (a) must be made and entered into under and in conformity with this subchapter.

Added by Acts 2011, 82nd Leg., ch. 823 (H.B. 2759), § 1.02, eff. Jan. 1, 2014.

### § 1160.052. Lease Application

(a) The guardian of the estate shall file with the court a written application for authority to lease estate property for mineral exploration and development, with or without a pooling provision or unitization clause.

(b) The lease application must:

(1) describe the property fully enough by reference to the amount of acreage, the survey name or number, or the abstract number, or by another method that adequately identifies the property and the property's location in the county in which the property is located;

(2) specify the interest thought to be owned by the estate, if less than the whole, but request au-

thority to include all of the interest owned by the estate if that is the intention; and

(3) set out the reasons the estate property described in the application should be leased.

(c) The lease application is not required to set out or suggest:

(1) the name of any proposed lessee; or

(2) the terms, provisions, or form of any desired lease.

Added by Acts 2011, 82nd Leg., ch. 823 (H.B. 2759), § 1.02, eff. Jan. 1, 2014.

### § 1160.053. Scheduling of Hearing on Application; Continuance

(a) Immediately after the filing of a lease application under Section 1160.052, the county clerk shall call the filing of the application to the court's attention. The judge shall promptly make and enter a brief order designating the time and place for hearing the application.

(b) If the hearing is not held at the time originally designated by the court or by a timely continuance order entered, the hearing shall be continued automatically without further notice to the same time on the following day, other than Sundays and holidays on which the county courthouse is officially closed, and from day to day until the lease application is finally acted on and disposed of by court order. Notice of an automatic continuance is not required.

Added by Acts 2011, 82nd Leg., ch. 823 (H.B. 2759), § 1.02, eff. Jan. 1, 2014.

### § 1160.054. Notice of Hearing on Application

(a) At least 10 days before the date set for the hearing on a lease application filed under Section 1160.052, excluding the date of notice and the date set for the hearing, the guardian of the estate shall give notice of the hearing by:

(1) publishing the notice in one issue of a newspaper of general circulation in the county in which the proceeding is pending; or

(2) if there is no newspaper in the county, posting the notice or having the notice posted.

(b) If the notice is published, the date of notice is the date printed on the newspaper.

(c) The notice must:

(1) be dated;

(2) be directed to all persons interested in the estate;

(3) state the date on which the lease application was filed;

(4) describe briefly the property sought to be leased;

(5) specify the fractional interest sought to be leased if less than the entire interest in the tract identified; and

(6) state the time and place designated by the judge for the hearing.

Added by Acts 2011, 82nd Leg., ch. 823 (H.B. 2759), § 1.02, eff. Jan. 1, 2014.

## § 1160.055. Requirements Regarding Order and Notice Mandatory

A court order authorizing any act to be performed in accordance with a lease application filed under Section 1160.052 is void in the absence of:

(1) a written order originally designating a time and place for the hearing;

(2) a notice issued by the guardian of the estate in compliance with the order; and

(3) proof of publication or posting of the notice as required under Section 1160.054.

Added by Acts 2011, 82nd Leg., ch. 823 (H.B. 2759), § 1.02, eff. Jan. 1, 2014.

## § 1160.056. Hearing on Application; Order

(a) At the time and place designated for the hearing under Section 1160.053(a), or at the time to which the hearing is continued as provided by Section 1160.053(b), the judge shall:

(1) hear a lease application filed under Section 1160.052; and

(2) require proof as to the necessity or advisability of leasing for mineral development the property described in the application and the notice.

(b) The judge shall enter an order authorizing one or more leases affecting and covering the property or portions of property described in the lease application, with or without pooling provisions or unitization clauses, and with or without cash consideration if considered by the court to be in the best interest of the estate, if the judge is satisfied that:

(1) the application is in proper form;

(2) notice has been given in the manner and for the time required by law;

(3) proof of necessity or advisability of leasing is sufficient; and

(4) the application should be granted.

(c) The order must contain:

(1) the name of the lessee;

(2) any actual cash consideration to be paid by the lessee;

(3) a finding that the requirements of Subsection (b) have been satisfied; and

(4) one of the following findings:

(A) a finding that the guardian of the estate is exempt by law from giving a bond; or

(B) if the guardian of the estate is required to give a bond, a finding as to whether the guardian's general bond on file is sufficient to protect the personal property on hand, including any cash bonus to be paid.

(d) If the court finds the general bond insufficient to meet the requirements of Subsection (c)(4)(B), the order must show the amount of increased or additional bond required to cover the deficiency.

(e) A complete exhibit copy, either written or printed, of each authorized lease must be set out in, attached to, incorporated by reference in, or made part of the order. The exhibit copy must show:

(1) the name of the lessee;

(2) the date of the lease;

(3) an adequate description of the property being leased;

(4) any delay rental to be paid to defer commencement of operations; and

(5) all other authorized terms and provisions.

(f) If the date of a lease does not appear in the exhibit copy of the lease or in the order, the date of the order is considered for all purposes to be the date of the lease.

(g) If the name or address of a depository bank for receiving rental is not shown in the exhibit copy of a lease, the guardian of the estate may insert the name or address, or cause the name or address to be inserted, in the lease at the time of the lease's execution or at any other time agreeable to the lessee or the lessee's successors or assigns.

Added by Acts 2011, 82nd Leg., ch. 823 (H.B. 2759), § 1.02, eff. Jan. 1, 2014.

## § 1160.057. Making of Lease on Granting of Application

(a) If on the hearing of a lease application filed under Section 1160.052 the court grants the application, the guardian of the estate may make the lease, as evidenced by the exhibit copies, in accordance with the order.

(b) The lease must be made not later than the 30th day after the date of the order unless an extension is granted by the court on a sworn application showing good cause.

(c) It is not necessary for the judge to make an order confirming the lease.

Added by Acts 2011, 82nd Leg., ch. 823 (H.B. 2759), § 1.02, eff. Jan. 1, 2014.

## § 1160.058.  Bond Requirements

(a) Unless the guardian of the estate is not required to give a general bond, a lease for which a cash consideration is required, although ordered, executed, and delivered, is not valid:

(1) unless the order authorizing the lease makes a finding with respect to the general bond;  and

(2) if the general bond has been found insufficient, until:

(A) the bond has been increased or an additional bond given with the sureties required by law, as required by the order;  and

(B) the increased or additional bond has been approved by the judge and filed with the clerk of the court in which the proceeding is pending.

(b) If two or more leases of different land are authorized by the same order, the general bond shall be increased or additional bonds given to cover all of the leases.

Added by Acts 2011, 82nd Leg., ch. 823 (H.B. 2759), § 1.02, eff. Jan. 1, 2014.

## § 1160.059.  Term of Lease Binding

A lease executed and delivered in compliance with this subchapter is valid and binding on the property or interest owned by the estate and covered by the lease for the full term provided by the lease, subject only to the lease's terms and conditions, even if the primary term extends beyond the date the estate is closed in accordance with law.  For the lease to be valid and binding under this subchapter, the authorized primary term of the lease may not exceed five years, subject to the lease terms and provisions extending the lease beyond the primary term by:

(1) paying production;

(2) bona fide drilling or reworking operations, whether in or on the same well or wells or an additional well or wells without a cessation of opera-

tions of more than 60 consecutive days before production has been restored or obtained;  or

(3) a shut-in gas well.

Added by Acts 2011, 82nd Leg., ch. 823 (H.B. 2759), § 1.02, eff. Jan. 1, 2014.

## § 1160.060.  Amendment of Lease Regarding Effect of Shut–in Gas Well

(a) An oil, gas, and mineral lease executed by a guardian of an estate under this chapter or former Chapter XIII, Texas Probate Code, may be amended by an instrument that provides that a shut-in gas well on the land covered by the lease or on land pooled with all or part of the land covered by the lease continues the lease in effect after the lease's five-year primary term.

(b) The guardian of the estate, with court approval, shall execute the instrument according to the terms and conditions prescribed in the instrument.

Added by Acts 2011, 82nd Leg., ch. 823 (H.B. 2759), § 1.02, eff. Jan. 1, 2014.

## SUBCHAPTER C.  MINERAL LEASES AT PRIVATE SALE

## § 1160.101.  Authorization for Leasing of Minerals at Private Sale

(a) Notwithstanding the mandatory requirements for setting a time and place for hearing a lease application under Subchapter B and the issuance, service, and return of notice, the court may authorize the making of oil, gas, and mineral leases at a private sale without public notice or advertising if, in the court's opinion, facts are set out in the application sufficient to show that it would be more advantageous to the estate that a lease be made privately and without compliance with those mandatory requirements.

(b) Leases authorized under this subchapter may include pooling provisions or unitization clauses as in other cases.

Added by Acts 2011, 82nd Leg., ch. 823 (H.B. 2759), § 1.02, eff. Jan. 1, 2014.

## § 1160.102.  Action of Court if Public Advertising Not Required

(a) At any time after the fifth day and before the 11th day after the filing date of an application to lease at a private sale and without an order setting the hearing time and place, the court shall:

(1) hear the application;

(2) inquire into the manner in which the proposed lease has been or will be made; and

(3) hear evidence for or against the application.

(b) If the court is satisfied that the lease has been or will be made for a fair and sufficient consideration and on fair terms and has been or will be properly made in conformity with law, the court shall enter an order authorizing the execution of the lease without the necessity of advertising, notice, or citation. The order must comply in all other respects with the requirements essential to the validity of mineral leases set out in Subchapter B as if advertising or notice were required.

(c) An order that confirms a lease made at a private sale does not need to be issued. A lease made at a private sale is not valid until any increased or additional bond required by the court has been approved by the court and filed with the court clerk.

Added by Acts 2011, 82nd Leg., ch. 823 (H.B. 2759), § 1.02, eff. Jan. 1, 2014.

## SUBCHAPTER D. POOLING OR UNITIZATION OF ROYALTIES OR MINERALS

### § 1160.151. Authorization for Pooling or Unitization

(a) If an existing lease on property owned by an estate being administered does not adequately provide for pooling or unitization, the court in which the proceeding is pending may, in the manner provided by this subchapter, authorize the commitment of royalty or mineral interests in oil, liquid hydrocarbons, gas, gaseous elements, and other minerals or any one or more of them owned by the estate to agreements that provide for the operation of areas as a pool or unit for the exploration for, development of, and production of all of those minerals, if the court finds that:

(1) the pool or unit to which the agreement relates will be operated in a manner that protects correlative rights or prevents the physical or economic waste of oil, liquid hydrocarbons, gas, gaseous elements, or other minerals subject to the agreement; and

(2) it is in the best interests of the estate to execute the agreement.

(b) An agreement authorized under Subsection (a) may provide that:

(1) operations incident to the drilling of or production from a well on any portion of a pool or unit are considered for all purposes to be the conduct of

operations on or production from each separately owned tract in the pool or unit;

(2) any lease covering any part of the area committed to a pool or unit continues in effect in its entirety as long as:

(A) oil, gas, or other minerals subject to the agreement are produced in paying quantities from any part of the pooled or unitized area;

(B) operations are conducted as provided in the lease on any part of the pooled or unitized area; or

(C) there is a shut-in gas well on any part of the pooled or unitized area, if the presence of the shut-in gas well is a ground for continuation of the lease under the terms of the lease;

(3) the production allocated by the agreement to each tract included in a pool or unit shall, when produced, be considered for all purposes to have been produced from the tract by a well drilled on the tract;

(4) the royalties provided for on production from any tract or portion of a tract within the pool or unit shall be paid only on that portion of the production allocated to the tract in accordance with the agreement;

(5) the dry gas, before or after extraction of hydrocarbons, may be returned to a formation underlying any land or leases committed to the agreement, and that royalties are not required to be paid on the gas returned; and

(6) gas obtained from other sources or another tract of land may be injected into a formation underlying any land or lease committed to the agreement, and that royalties are not required to be paid on the gas injected when the gas is produced from the unit.

Added by Acts 2011, 82nd Leg., ch. 823 (H.B. 2759), § 1.02, eff. Jan. 1, 2014.

### § 1160.152. Pooling or Unitization Application

(a) The guardian of the estate shall file with the county clerk of the county in which the guardianship proceeding is pending a written application for authority to:

(1) enter into a pooling or unitization agreement supplementing, amending, or otherwise relating to any existing lease covering property owned by the estate; or

(2) commit royalties or other interests in minerals, whether or not subject to a lease, to a pooling or unitization agreement.

(b) The pooling or unitization application must also:

(1) sufficiently describe the property as required in an original lease application;

(2) describe briefly the lease to which the interest of the estate is subject; and

(3) set out the reasons the proposed agreement concerning the property should be entered into.

(c) A copy of the proposed agreement must be attached to the pooling or unitization application and made a part of the application by reference.

(d) The agreement may not be recorded in the judge's guardianship docket.

(e) Immediately after the pooling or unitization application is filed, the clerk shall call the application to the judge's attention.

Added by Acts 2011, 82nd Leg., ch. 823 (H.B. 2759), § 1.02, eff. Jan. 1, 2014.

### § 1160.153.　Notice Not Required

Notice by advertising, citation, or otherwise of the filing of a pooling or unitization application under Section 1160.152 is not required.

Added by Acts 2011, 82nd Leg., ch. 823 (H.B. 2759), § 1.02, eff. Jan. 1, 2014.

### § 1160.154.　Hearing on Application

(a) The judge may hold a hearing on a pooling or unitization application filed under Section 1160.152 at any time agreeable to the parties to the proposed agreement.

(b) The judge shall hear evidence and determine to the judge's satisfaction whether it is in the best interests of the estate that the proposed agreement be authorized.

(c) The hearing may be continued from day to day and from time to time as the court finds necessary.

Added by Acts 2011, 82nd Leg., ch. 823 (H.B. 2759), § 1.02, eff. Jan. 1, 2014.

### § 1160.155.　Action of Court and Contents of Order

(a) The court shall enter an order setting out the court's findings and authorizing execution of the proposed pooling or unitization agreement, with or without payment of cash consideration according to the agreement, if the court finds that:

(1) the pool or unit to which the agreement relates will be operated in a manner that protects correlative rights or prevents the physical or economic waste of oil, liquid hydrocarbons, gas, gas-

eous elements, or other minerals subject to the pool or unit;

(2) it is in the best interests of the estate that the agreement be executed; and

(3) the agreement conforms substantially with the permissible provisions of Section 1160.151.

(b) If cash consideration is to be paid for the pooling or unitization agreement, the court shall make a finding as to the necessity of increased or additional bond as a finding is made in the making of leases on payment of the cash bonus for the lease. The agreement is not valid until any required increased or additional bond has been approved by the judge and filed with the clerk.

(c) If the effective date of the pooling or unitization agreement is not stipulated in the agreement, the effective date of the agreement is the date of the court's order.

Added by Acts 2011, 82nd Leg., ch. 823 (H.B. 2759), § 1.02, eff. Jan. 1, 2014.

## SUBCHAPTER E.　SPECIAL ANCILLARY INSTRUMENTS THAT MAY BE EXECUTED WITHOUT COURT ORDER

### § 1160.201.　Authorization for Execution of Certain Instruments

As to any mineral lease or pooling or unitization agreement, executed on behalf of an estate before September 1, 1993, pursuant to provisions, or executed by a former owner of land, minerals, or royalty affected by the lease or agreement, the guardian of the estate being administered, without further court order and without consideration, may execute:

(1) division orders;

(2) transfer orders;

(3) instruments of correction;

(4) instruments designating depository banks for the receipt of delay rentals or shut-in gas well royalty to accrue or become payable under the terms of the lease; or

(5) similar instruments relating to the lease or agreement and the property covered by the lease or agreement.

Added by Acts 2011, 82nd Leg., ch. 823 (H.B. 2759), § 1.02, eff. Jan. 1, 2014.

## SUBCHAPTER F. PROCEDURE IF GUARDIAN OF ESTATE NEGLECTS TO APPLY FOR AUTHORITY

### § 1160.251. Application to Show Cause

If a guardian of an estate neglects to apply for authority to subject estate property to a lease for mineral development, pooling, or unitization, or authority to commit royalty or another interest in minerals to pooling or unitization, any person interested in the estate may, on written application filed with the county clerk, have the guardian cited to show cause why it is not in the best interests of the estate to make the lease or enter into an agreement.

Added by Acts 2011, 82nd Leg., ch. 823 (H.B. 2759), § 1.02, eff. Jan. 1, 2014.

### § 1160.252. Hearing on Application

(a) The county clerk shall immediately call the filing of an application under Section 1160.251 to the attention of the judge of the court in which the guardianship proceeding is pending.

(b) The judge shall set a time and place for a hearing on the application, and the guardian of the estate shall be cited to appear and show cause why the execution of a lease or agreement described by Section 1160.251 should not be ordered.

Added by Acts 2011, 82nd Leg., ch. 823 (H.B. 2759), § 1.02, eff. Jan. 1, 2014.

### § 1160.253. Order

On a hearing conducted under Section 1160.252 and if satisfied from the evidence that it would be in the best interests of the estate, the court shall enter an order requiring the guardian of the estate to file an application to subject the estate property to a lease for mineral development, with or without pooling or unitization provisions, or to commit royalty or other minerals to pooling or unitization, as appropriate.

Added by Acts 2011, 82nd Leg., ch. 823 (H.B. 2759), § 1.02, eff. Jan. 1, 2014.

### § 1160.254. Procedure to be Followed After Entry of Order

After entry of an order under Section 1160.253, the procedures prescribed with respect to an original lease application, or with respect to an original application for authority to commit royalty or minerals to pooling or unitization, shall be followed.

Added by Acts 2011, 82nd Leg., ch. 823 (H.B. 2759), § 1.02, eff. Jan. 1, 2014.

## CHAPTER 1161. INVESTMENTS AND LOANS OF ESTATES OF WARDS

### SUBCHAPTER A. GENERAL PROVISIONS

### SUBCHAPTER A. GENERAL PROVISIONS

### § 1161.001. Guardian's Duty to Keep Estate Invested

(a) The guardian of the estate shall invest any funds and assets of a ward's estate available for investment except:

(1) if the court orders otherwise under this chapter; or

(2) as provided by Subsection (b).

(b) The guardian of the estate is not required to invest funds that are immediately necessary for the education, support, and maintenance of the ward or any others the ward supports as provided by this title.

Added by Acts 2011, 82nd Leg., ch. 823 (H.B. 2759), § 1.02, eff. Jan. 1, 2014.

## § 1161.002. Standard for Management and Investment of Estate

(a) In acquiring, investing, reinvesting, exchanging, retaining, selling, supervising, and managing a ward's estate, a guardian of the estate shall exercise the judgment and care under the circumstances then prevailing that a person of ordinary prudence, discretion, and intelligence exercises in the management of the person's own affairs, considering the probable income from, probable increase in value of, and safety of the person's capital. The guardian shall also consider all other relevant factors, including:

(1) the anticipated costs of supporting the ward;

(2) the ward's age, education, current income, ability to earn additional income, net worth, and liabilities;

(3) the nature of the ward's estate; and

(4) any other resources reasonably available to the ward.

(b) In determining whether a guardian of the estate has exercised the standard of investment required by this section with respect to an investment decision, the court shall, absent fraud or gross negligence, consider the investment of all the estate assets over which the guardian has management or control, rather than considering the prudence of only a single investment made by the guardian.

Added by Acts 2011, 82nd Leg., ch. 823 (H.B. 2759), § 1.02, eff. Jan. 1, 2014.

## § 1161.003. Investments That Meet Standard for Investment

A guardian of the estate is considered to have exercised the standard required by Section 1161.002(a) with respect to investing the ward's estate if the guardian invests in the following:

(1) bonds or other obligations of the United States;

(2) tax-supported bonds of this state;

(3) except as limited by Sections 1161.004(b) and (c), tax-supported bonds of a county, district, political subdivision, or municipality in this state;

(4) if the payment of the shares or share accounts is insured by the Federal Deposit Insurance Corporation, shares or share accounts of:

(A) a state savings and loan association or savings bank that has its main office or a branch office in this state; or

(B) a federal savings and loan association or savings bank that has its main office or a branch office in this state;

(5) collateral bonds that:

(A) are issued by a company incorporated under the laws of this state that has a paid-in capital of $1 million or more;

(B) are a direct obligation of the company; and

(C) are specifically secured by first mortgage real estate notes or other securities pledged with a trustee; or

(6) interest-bearing time deposits that may be withdrawn on or before one year after demand in a bank that does business in this state, if the payment of the time deposits is insured by the Federal Deposit Insurance Corporation.

Added by Acts 2011, 82nd Leg., ch. 823 (H.B. 2759), § 1.02, eff. Jan. 1, 2014.

## § 1161.004. Restrictions on Investment in Certain Bonds

(a) In this section, "net funded debt" means the total funded debt less sinking funds on hand.

(b) A guardian of the estate may purchase the bonds of a county, district, or political subdivision other than a municipality only if the net funded debt of the county, district, or political subdivision that issues the bonds does not exceed 10 percent of the assessed value of taxable property in the county, district, or political subdivision.

(c) A guardian of the estate may purchase the bonds of a municipality only if the net funded debt of the municipality does not exceed 10 percent of the assessed value of taxable property in the municipality less that part of the debt incurred for acquisition or improvement of revenue-producing utilities, the revenue of which is not pledged to support other obligations of the municipality.

(d) Subsections (b) and (c) do not apply to bonds issued for road purposes in this state under Section 52, Article III, Texas Constitution, that are supported by a tax unlimited as to rate or amount.

Added by Acts 2011, 82nd Leg., ch. 823 (H.B. 2759), § 1.02, eff. Jan. 1, 2014.

## § 1161.005. Modification or Elimination of Duty or Standard

On a showing by clear and convincing evidence that the action is in the best interests of the ward and the ward's estate, the court may modify or eliminate:

(1) the duty of the guardian of the estate to keep the estate invested; or

(2) the standard required by Section 1161.002(a) with regard to investments of estate assets.

Added by Acts 2011, 82nd Leg., ch. 823 (H.B. 2759), § 1.02, eff. Jan. 1, 2014.

## § 1161.006. Retention of Certain Assets

(a) Without court approval a guardian of the estate may retain until the first anniversary of the date of receipt any property received into the guardianship estate at the estate's inception or added to the estate by gift, devise, inheritance, mutation, or increase, without regard to diversification of investments and without liability for any depreciation or loss resulting from the retention.

(b) The guardian shall care for and manage the retained assets as a person of ordinary prudence, discretion, and intelligence would in caring for and managing the person's own affairs.

(c) On application and a hearing, the court may issue an order authorizing the guardian to continue retaining the property after the period prescribed by Subsection (a) if the retention is an element of the guardian's investment plan as provided by Subchapter B.

Added by Acts 2011, 82nd Leg., ch. 823 (H.B. 2759), § 1.02, eff. Jan. 1, 2014.

## § 1161.007. Hearing to Protect Estate

(a) The court may, on the court's own motion or on written request of a person interested in the guardianship, cite the guardian of the estate to appear and show cause why the estate is not invested or not properly invested.

(b) Except as provided by Subsection (d), at any time after giving notice to all parties, the court may conduct a hearing to protect the estate.

(c) On the hearing of the court's motion or a request made under this section, the court shall issue an order the court considers to be in the ward's best interests.

(d) The court may not hold a final hearing on whether the estate is properly invested until the 31st day after the date the guardian is originally cited to appear under Subsection (a).

(e) The court may appoint a guardian ad litem for the limited purpose of representing the ward's best interests with respect to the investment of the ward's property at a hearing under this section.

Added by Acts 2011, 82nd Leg., ch. 823 (H.B. 2759), § 1.02, eff. Jan. 1, 2014.

## § 1161.008. Liability of Guardian and Guardian's Surety

(a) In addition to any other remedy authorized by law, if the guardian of the estate fails to invest or lend estate assets in the manner provided by this chapter, the guardian and the guardian's surety are liable for the principal and the greater of:

(1) the highest legal rate of interest on the principal during the period the guardian failed to invest or lend the assets; or

(2) the overall return that would have been made on the principal if the principal were invested in the manner provided by this chapter.

(b) In addition to the liability under Subsection (a), the guardian and the guardian's surety are liable for attorney's fees, litigation expenses, and costs related to a proceeding brought to enforce this section.

Added by Acts 2011, 82nd Leg., ch. 823 (H.B. 2759), § 1.02, eff. Jan. 1, 2014.

## SUBCHAPTER B. PROCEDURE FOR MAKING INVESTMENTS OR LOANS OR RETAINING ESTATE ASSETS

## § 1161.051. Procedure in General

(a) Not later than the 180th day after the date the guardian of the estate qualifies as guardian or another date specified by the court, the guardian shall:

(1) invest estate assets according to Section 1161.003; or

(2) file a written application with the court for an order:

(A) authorizing the guardian to:

(i) develop and implement an investment plan for estate assets;

(ii) invest in or sell securities under an investment plan developed under Subparagraph (i);

(iii) declare that one or more estate assets must be retained, despite being underproductive with respect to income or overall return; or

(iv) loan estate funds, invest in real estate or make other investments, or purchase a life, term, or endowment insurance policy or an annuity contract; or

(B) modifying or eliminating the guardian's duty to invest the estate.

(b) The court may approve an investment plan under Subsection (a)(2) without a hearing.

Added by Acts 2011, 82nd Leg., ch. 823 (H.B. 2759), § 1.02, eff. Jan. 1, 2014.

### § 1161.052. Court Action

(a) If the court determines that the action requested in the application is in the best interests of the ward and the ward's estate, the court shall issue an order:

(1) granting the authority requested in the application; or

(2) modifying or eliminating the guardian's duty to keep the estate invested.

(b) An order under Subsection (a) must state in reasonably specific terms:

(1) the nature of the investment, investment plan, or other action requested in the application and authorized by the court, including any authority to invest in and sell securities in accordance with the investment plan's objectives;

(2) when an investment must be reviewed and reconsidered by the guardian; and

(3) whether the guardian must report the guardian's review and recommendations to the court.

(c) A citation or notice is not necessary to invest in or sell securities under an investment plan authorized by the court under this section.

Added by Acts 2011, 82nd Leg., ch. 823 (H.B. 2759), § 1.02, eff. Jan. 1, 2014.

### § 1161.053. Applicability of Procedure to Certain Assets

The fact that an account or other asset is the subject of a specific or general gift under a ward's will, if any, or that a ward has funds, securities, or other property held with a right of survivorship does not prevent:

(1) the guardian of the estate from taking possession and control of the asset or closing the account; or

(2) the court from authorizing an action or modifying or eliminating a duty with respect to the possession, control, or investment of the account or other asset.

Added by Acts 2011, 82nd Leg., ch. 823 (H.B. 2759), § 1.02, eff. Jan. 1, 2014.

### § 1161.054. Inapplicability of Procedure to Certain Assets

(a) The procedure prescribed by this subchapter does not apply if a different procedure is prescribed for an investment or sale by a guardian.

(b) A guardian of the estate is not required to follow the procedure prescribed by this subchapter with respect to an investment or sale that is specifically authorized by other law.

Added by Acts 2011, 82nd Leg., ch. 823 (H.B. 2759), § 1.02, eff. Jan. 1, 2014.

SUBCHAPTER C. INVESTMENTS
IN CERTAIN INSURANCE OR
ANNUITIES

### § 1161.101. Definition

In this subchapter, "authorized life insurance company" means a stock or mutual legal reserve life insurance company that:

(1) is licensed by the Texas Department of Insurance to transact the business of life insurance in this state; and

(2) maintains the legal reserve required by the laws of this state.

Added by Acts 2011, 82nd Leg., ch. 823 (H.B. 2759), § 1.02, eff. Jan. 1, 2014.

### § 1161.102. Authority to Invest in Certain Insurance or Annuities

Subject to this subchapter, the guardian of the estate may invest in life, term, or endowment insurance policies, in annuity contracts, or in both, issued by an authorized life insurance company or administered by the Department of Veterans Affairs.

Added by Acts 2011, 82nd Leg., ch. 823 (H.B. 2759), § 1.02, eff. Jan. 1, 2014.

### § 1161.103. Investment Requirements

(a) An insurance policy in which the guardian of the estate invests must be issued on the life of:

(1) the ward;

(2) the ward's parent, spouse, child, sibling, or grandparent; or

(3) another person in whose life the ward may have an insurable interest.

(b) The ward must be the annuitant in the annuity contract in which the guardian of the estate invests.

(c) Only the ward, the ward's estate, or the ward's parent, spouse, child, sibling, or grandparent may be a beneficiary of the insurance policy or of the death benefit of the annuity contract.

(d) The insurance policy or annuity contract may not be amended or changed during the ward's life and disability, except on application to and order of the court.

Added by Acts 2011, 82nd Leg., ch. 823 (H.B. 2759), § 1.02, eff. Jan. 1, 2014.

## § 1161.104. Procedure for Investing in Insurance or Annuities

(a) Before the guardian of the estate may invest in life, term, or endowment insurance policies, in annuity contracts, or in both, the guardian must first apply to the court for an order that authorizes the investment.

(b) The application must include a report that shows:

(1) in detail the estate's financial condition on the date the application is filed;

(2) the name and address of the authorized life insurance company from which the insurance policy or annuity contract is to be purchased and that:

(A) the company is licensed by the Texas Department of Insurance to transact that business in this state on the date the application is filed; or

(B) the policy or contract is administered by the Department of Veterans Affairs;

(3) a statement of:

(A) the face amount and plan of the insurance policy sought to be purchased; and

(B) the amount, frequency, and duration of the annuity payments to be provided by the annuity contract sought to be purchased;

(4) a statement of the amount, frequency, and duration of the premiums required by the insurance policy or annuity contract; and

(5) a statement of the cash value of the insurance policy or annuity contract at the policy's or contract's anniversary nearest the ward's 21st birthday, assuming that all premiums to the anniversary are paid and that there is no indebtedness against the policy or contract incurred in accordance with its terms.

(c) If satisfied by the application and the evidence presented at the hearing that it is in the ward's interests to grant the application, the court shall enter an order granting the application.

Added by Acts 2011, 82nd Leg., ch. 823 (H.B. 2759), § 1.02, eff. Jan. 1, 2014.

## § 1161.105. Continuation of Preexisting Policies or Annuities

(a) A life, term, or endowment insurance policy or an annuity contract owned by the ward when a proceeding for the appointment of a guardian of the estate is commenced may be continued in full effect if it is shown that:

(1) the company issuing the policy or contract is an authorized life insurance company; or

(2) the policy or contract is administered by the Department of Veterans Affairs.

(b) All future premiums for an insurance policy or annuity contract described by Subsection (a) may be paid out of surplus funds of the ward's estate.

(c) The guardian of the estate must apply to the court for an order to:

(1) continue the policy, the contract, or both according to the existing terms of the policy or contract; or

(2) modify the policy or contract to fit any new developments affecting the ward's welfare.

(d) Before the court grants an application filed under Subsection (c), the guardian must file a report in the court that shows in detail the financial condition of the ward's estate on the date the application is filed.

Added by Acts 2011, 82nd Leg., ch. 823 (H.B. 2759), § 1.02, eff. Jan. 1, 2014.

## § 1161.106. Control and Ownership of Policies or Annuities

(a) Control of an insurance policy or an annuity contract and of the incidents of ownership in the policy or contract is vested in the guardian of the estate during the ward's life and disability.

(b) A right, benefit, or interest that accrues under an insurance policy or annuity contract subject to this subchapter becomes the ward's exclusive property when the ward's disability is terminated.

Added by Acts 2011, 82nd Leg., ch. 823 (H.B. 2759), § 1.02, eff. Jan. 1, 2014.

## SUBCHAPTER D. INVESTMENTS IN REAL ESTATE

### § 1161.151. Authority to Invest in Real Estate; Procedure and Requirements

(a) The guardian of the estate may invest estate assets in real estate if:

(1) the guardian believes that the investment is in the ward's best interests;

(2) there are on hand sufficient additional assets to provide a return sufficient to provide for:

(A) the education, support, and maintenance of the ward and others the ward supports, if applicable; and

(B) the maintenance, insurance, and taxes on the real estate in which the guardian wishes to invest;

(3) the guardian files a written application with the court requesting a court order authorizing the guardian to make the desired investment and stating the reasons why, in the guardian's opinion, the investment would be for the ward's benefit; and

(4) the court issues an order authorizing the investment as provided by this subchapter.

(b) If the ward's money is invested in real estate, the title to the real estate shall be made to the ward. The guardian shall inventory, appraise, manage, and account for the real estate as the guardian does with other real estate of the ward.

Added by Acts 2011, 82nd Leg., ch. 823 (H.B. 2759), § 1.02, eff. Jan. 1, 2014.

### § 1161.152. Court Authorization to Make Investments

(a) If the guardian of the estate files an application under this subchapter, the judge shall investigate as necessary to obtain all the facts concerning the investment.

(b) Subject to Subsection (c), on the hearing of the application, the court shall issue an order that authorizes the guardian to make the investment if the court is satisfied that the investment benefits the ward. The order must specify the investment to be made and contain other directions the court considers advisable.

(c) The judge may not issue an opinion or order on the application until after the 10th day after the date the application is filed.

Added by Acts 2011, 82nd Leg., ch. 823 (H.B. 2759), § 1.02, eff. Jan. 1, 2014.

### § 1161.153. Court Approval of Contracts Required

(a) If a contract is made for the investment of money in real estate under a court order, the guardian of the estate shall report the contract in writing to the court.

(b) The court shall inquire fully into the contract. If satisfied that the investment will benefit the ward's estate and that the title of the real estate is valid and unencumbered, the court may approve the contract and authorize the guardian to pay money in performance of the contract.

(c) The guardian may not pay any money on the contract until the contract is approved by a court order to that effect.

Added by Acts 2011, 82nd Leg., ch. 823 (H.B. 2759), § 1.02, eff. Jan. 1, 2014.

## SUBCHAPTER E. LOANS AND SECURITY FOR LOANS

### § 1161.201. Inapplicability of Subchapter

This subchapter does not apply to an investment in a debenture, bond, or other publicly traded debt security.

Added by Acts 2011, 82nd Leg., ch. 823 (H.B. 2759), § 1.02, eff. Jan. 1, 2014.

### § 1161.202. Authority to Make Loans

(a) If, at any time, the guardian of the estate has on hand money belonging to the ward in an amount that provides a return that is more than is necessary for the education, support, and maintenance of the ward and others the ward supports, if applicable, the guardian may lend the money for a reasonable interest rate.

(b) The guardian of the estate is considered to have obtained a reasonable interest rate for a loan for purposes of Subsection (a) if the interest rate is at least equal to 120 percent of the applicable short-term, midterm, or long-term interest rate under Section 7520, Internal Revenue Code of 1986, for the month during which the loan was made.

Added by Acts 2011, 82nd Leg., ch. 823 (H.B. 2759), § 1.02, eff. Jan. 1, 2014.

### § 1161.203. Loan Requirements

(a) Except as provided by Subsection (b), the guardian of the estate shall take as collateral the borrower's note for the money that is loaned, secured by:

(1) a mortgage with a power of sale on unencumbered real estate located in this state worth at least twice the amount of the note; or

(2) collateral notes secured by vendor's lien notes.

(b) The guardian may purchase vendor's lien notes if at least one-half has been paid in cash or its equivalent on the land for which the notes were given.

(c) Except as provided by Subsection (d), a guardian of the estate who lends estate money may not pay or transfer any money to consummate the loan until the guardian:

(1) submits to a reputable attorney for examination all bonds, notes, mortgages, abstracts, and other documents relating to the loan; and

(2) receives a written opinion from the attorney stating that the documents under Subdivision (1) are regular and that the title to relevant bonds, notes, or real estate is clear.

(d) A guardian of the estate may obtain a mortgagee's title insurance policy on any real estate loan instead of an abstract and attorney's opinion under Subsection (c).

(e) The borrower shall pay attorney's fees for any legal services required by Subsection (c).

Added by Acts 2011, 82nd Leg., ch. 823 (H.B. 2759), § 1.02, eff. Jan. 1, 2014.

## § 1161.204. Guardian's Duty to Report Loan to Court

(a) Not later than the 30th day after the date the guardian of the estate loans money from the estate, the guardian shall file with the court a written report, accompanied and verified by an affidavit, stating fully the facts related to the loan.

(b) This section does not apply to a loan made in accordance with a court order.

Added by Acts 2011, 82nd Leg., ch. 823 (H.B. 2759), § 1.02, eff. Jan. 1, 2014.

## § 1161.205. Guardian's Liability

(a) Except as provided by Subsection (b), a guardian of the estate who loans estate money with the court's approval on security approved by the court is not personally liable if the borrower is unable to repay the money and the security fails.

(b) If the guardian committed fraud or was negligent in making or managing the loan, including in collecting the loan, the guardian and the guardian's surety are liable for the loss sustained by the guardianship estate as a result of the fraud or negligence.

Added by Acts 2011, 82nd Leg., ch. 823 (H.B. 2759), § 1.02, eff. Jan. 1, 2014.

## CHAPTER 1162. TAX–MOTIVATED, CHARITABLE, NONPROFIT, AND OTHER GIFTS

### SUBCHAPTER A. CERTAIN GIFTS AND TRANSFERS

### SUBCHAPTER A. CERTAIN GIFTS AND TRANSFERS

## § 1162.001. Authority to Establish Estate or Other Transfer Plan

On application of the guardian of the estate or any interested person, after the posting of notice and hearing, and on a showing that the ward will probably remain incapacitated during the ward's lifetime, the court may enter an order that authorizes the guardian to apply the principal or income of the ward's estate that is not required for the support of the ward or the ward's family during the ward's lifetime toward the establishment of an estate plan for the purpose of minimizing income, estate, inheritance, or other taxes payable out of the ward's estate, or to transfer a portion of the ward's estate as necessary to qualify the ward for government benefits and only to the extent allowed by applicable state or federal laws, including rules, regarding those benefits. On the ward's behalf, the court may authorize the guardian to make gifts or transfers described by this section, outright or in trust, of the ward's property to or for the benefit of:

(1) an organization to which charitable contributions may be made under the Internal Revenue Code of 1986 and in which it is shown the ward would reasonably have an interest;

(2) the ward's spouse, descendant, or other person related to the ward by blood or marriage who is identifiable at the time of the order;

(3) a devisee under the ward's last validly executed will, trust, or other beneficial instrument, if the instrument exists; and

(4) a person serving as guardian of the ward, if the person is eligible under Subdivision (2) or (3).

Added by Acts 2011, 82nd Leg., ch. 823 (H.B. 2759), § 1.02, eff. Jan. 1, 2014. Amended by Acts 2013, 83rd Leg., ch. 161 (S.B. 1093), § 6.050, eff. Jan. 1, 2014.

### § 1162.002. Estate or Other Transfer Plan: Contents and Modification

(a) The person making an application to the court under Section 1162.001 shall:

(1) outline the proposed estate or other transfer plan; and

(2) state all the benefits that are to be derived from the plan.

(b) The application must indicate that the planned disposition is consistent with the ward's intentions, if the ward's intentions can be ascertained. If the ward's intentions cannot be ascertained, the ward will be presumed to favor reduction in the incidence of the various forms of taxation, the qualification for government benefits, and the partial distribution of the ward's estate as provided by Sections 1162.001 and 1162.004.

(c) A subsequent modification of an approved plan may be made by similar application to the court.

Added by Acts 2011, 82nd Leg., ch. 823 (H.B. 2759), § 1.02, eff. Jan. 1, 2014. Amended by Acts 2013, 83rd Leg., ch. 161 (S.B. 1093), § 6.051, eff. Jan. 1, 2014.

### § 1162.003. Notice of Application for Establishment of Estate or Other Transfer Plan

A person who makes an application to the court under Section 1162.001 shall mail notice of the application by certified mail to:

(1) all devisees under a will, trust, or other beneficial instrument relating to the ward's estate;

(2) the ward's spouse;

(3) the ward's dependents; and

(4) any other person as directed by the court.

Added by Acts 2011, 82nd Leg., ch. 823 (H.B. 2759), § 1.02, eff. Jan. 1, 2014. Amended by Acts 2013, 83rd Leg., ch. 161 (S.B. 1093), § 6.052, eff. Jan. 1, 2014.

### § 1162.004. Authority to Make Periodic Gifts

(a) In an order entered under Section 1162.001, the court may authorize the guardian to make, without subsequent application to or order of the court, gifts as provided by that section on an annual or other periodic basis if the court finds it to be in the best interest of the ward and the ward's estate.

(b) The court, on the court's own motion or on the motion of a person interested in the welfare of the ward, may modify or set aside an order entered under Subsection (a) if the court finds that the ward's financial condition has changed in such a manner that authorizing the guardian to make gifts of the estate on a continuing basis is no longer in the best interest of the ward and the ward's estate.

Added by Acts 2011, 82nd Leg., ch. 823 (H.B. 2759), § 1.02, eff. Jan. 1, 2014.

### § 1162.005. Application for Inspection of Certain Documents

(a) On the filing of an application under Section 1162.001 and for the purpose of establishing an estate plan under that section, the guardian of the ward's estate may apply to the court for an order to seek an in camera inspection of a copy of a will, codicil, trust, or other estate planning instrument of the ward as a means of obtaining access to the instrument.

(b) An application filed under this section must:

(1) be sworn to by the guardian;

(2) list each instrument requested for inspection; and

(3) state one or more reasons supporting the necessity to inspect each requested instrument for the purpose described by Subsection (a).

Added by Acts 2011, 82nd Leg., ch. 823 (H.B. 2759), § 1.02, eff. Jan. 1, 2014.

### § 1162.006. Notice of Application for Inspection

(a) A person who files an application under Section 1162.005 shall send a copy of the application to:

(1) each person who has custody of an instrument listed in the application;

(2) the ward's spouse;

(3) the ward's dependents;

(4) all devisees under a will, trust, or other beneficial instrument relating to the ward's estate; and

(5) any other person as directed by the court.

(b) Notice required by Subsection (a) must be delivered by:

(1) registered or certified mail to a person described by Subsection (a)(1); and

(2) certified mail to a person described by Subsection (a)(2), (3), (4), or (5).

Added by Acts 2011, 82nd Leg., ch. 823 (H.B. 2759), § 1.02, eff. Jan. 1, 2014.

### § 1162.007. Hearing on Application for Inspection; Inspection

(a) After the 10th day after the date on which the applicant complies with the notice requirement under Section 1162.006, the applicant may request that a hearing be held on the application. Notice of the date, time, and place of the hearing must be given by the applicant to each person described by Section 1162.006(a)(1) when the court sets a date for a hearing on the application.

(b) After the conclusion of a hearing on the application for inspection and on a finding that good cause exists for an in camera inspection of a requested instrument, the court shall direct the person that has custody of the requested will, codicil, trust, or other estate planning instrument to deliver a copy of the instrument to the court for in camera inspection only. After conducting an in camera inspection of the instrument, the court, if good cause exists, shall release all or part of the instrument to the applicant only for the purpose described by Section 1162.005(a).

(c) An attorney does not violate the attorney-client privilege solely by complying with a court order to release an instrument subject to this section and Sections 1162.005 and 1162.006. Notwithstanding Section 22.004, Government Code, the supreme court may not amend or adopt rules in conflict with this subsection.

Added by Acts 2011, 82nd Leg., ch. 823 (H.B. 2759), § 1.02, eff. Jan. 1, 2014.

### § 1162.008. Guardian ad Litem

The court may appoint a guardian ad litem for the ward or an interested party at any stage of proceedings under this subchapter if it is considered advisable for the protection of the ward or the interested party.

Added by Acts 2011, 82nd Leg., ch. 823 (H.B. 2759), § 1.02, eff. Jan. 1, 2014.

### SUBCHAPTER B. CHARITABLE AND NONPROFIT GIFTS

### § 1162.051. Application to Make Gift

The guardian of the estate may at any time file with the county clerk the guardian's sworn, written application requesting from the court in which the guardianship is pending an order authorizing the guardian to contribute from the income of the ward's estate the specific amount of money stated in the application to one or more designated:

(1) corporations, trusts, or community chests, funds, or foundations, organized and operated exclusively for religious, charitable, scientific, literary, or educational purposes; or

(2) nonprofit federal, state, county, or municipal projects operated exclusively for public health or welfare.

Added by Acts 2011, 82nd Leg., ch. 823 (H.B. 2759), § 1.02, eff. Jan. 1, 2014.

### § 1162.052. Hearing on Application to Make Gift

(a) The county clerk shall immediately call the filing of an application under Section 1162.051 to the attention of the judge of the court.

(b) The judge shall designate, by written order filed with the clerk, a day to hear the application. The application must remain on file for at least 10 days before the hearing is held.

(c) The judge may postpone or continue the hearing from time to time until the judge is satisfied concerning the application.

Added by Acts 2011, 82nd Leg., ch. 823 (H.B. 2759), § 1.02, eff. Jan. 1, 2014.

### § 1162.053. Order Authorizing Gift

On the conclusion of a hearing under Section 1162.052, the court may enter an order authorizing the guardian to make a contribution from the income of the ward's estate to a particular donee designated in the application and order if the court is satisfied and finds from the evidence that:

(1) the amount of the proposed contribution stated in the application will probably not exceed 20 percent of the net income of the ward's estate for the current calendar year;

(2) the net income of the ward's estate for the current calendar year exceeds, or probably will exceed, $25,000;

(3) the full amount of the contribution, if made, will probably be deductible from the ward's gross income in determining the net income of the ward under applicable federal income tax laws and rules;

(4) the condition of the ward's estate justifies a contribution in the proposed amount; and

(5) the proposed contribution is reasonable in amount and is for a worthy cause.

Added by Acts 2011, 82nd Leg., ch. 823 (H.B. 2759), § 1.02, eff. Jan. 1, 2014.

## CHAPTER 1163.　ANNUAL ACCOUNT AND OTHER EXHIBITS AND REPORTS

## SUBCHAPTER A.　ANNUAL ACCOUNT AND OTHER EXHIBITS BY GUARDIAN OF THE ESTATE

### § 1163.001.　Initial Annual Account of Estate

(a) Not later than the 60th day after the first anniversary of the date the guardian of the estate of a ward qualifies, unless the court extends that period, the guardian shall file with the court an account consisting of a written exhibit made under oath that:

(1) lists all claims against the estate presented to the guardian during the period covered by the account; and

(2) specifies:

(A) which claims have been:

(i) allowed by the guardian;

(ii) paid by the guardian; or

(iii) rejected by the guardian and the date the claims were rejected; and

(B) which claims have been the subject of a lawsuit and the status of that lawsuit.

(b) The account must:

(1) show all property that has come to the guardian's knowledge or into the guardian's possession that was not previously listed or inventoried as the ward's property;

(2) show any change in the ward's property that was not previously reported;

(3) provide a complete account of receipts and disbursements for the period covered by the account, including the source and nature of the receipts and disbursements, with separate listings for principal and income receipts;

(4) provide a complete, accurate, and detailed description of:

(A) the property being administered;

(B) the condition of the property and the use being made of the property; and

(C) if rented, the terms on which and the price for which the property was rented;

(5) show the cash balance on hand and the name and location of the depository where the balance is kept;

(6) show any other cash held in a savings account or other manner that was deposited subject to court order and the name and location of the depository for that cash; and

(7) provide a detailed description of the personal property of the estate that shows how and where the property is held for safekeeping.

(c) For bonds, notes, and other securities, the description required by Subsection (b)(7) must include:

(1) the names of the obligor and obligee or, if payable to bearer, a statement that the bond, note, or other security is payable to bearer;

(2) the date of issue and maturity;

(3) the interest rate;

(4) the serial number or other identifying numbers;

(5) the manner in which the property is secured; and

(6) other information necessary to fully identify the bond, note, or other security.

Added by Acts 2011, 82nd Leg., ch. 823 (H.B. 2759), § 1.02, eff. Jan. 1, 2014.

## § 1163.002. Annual Account Required Until Estate Closed

(a) A guardian of the estate shall file an annual account conforming to the essential requirements of Section 1163.001 regarding changes in the estate assets occurring since the date the most recent previous account was filed.

(b) The annual account must be filed in a manner that allows the court or an interested person to ascertain the true condition of the estate, with respect to money, securities, and other property, by adding to the balances forwarded from the most recent previous account the amounts received during the period covered by the account and subtracting the disbursements made during that period.

(c) The description of property sufficiently described in an inventory or previous account may be made in the annual account by reference to the property.

Added by Acts 2011, 82nd Leg., ch. 823 (H.B. 2759), § 1.02, eff. Jan. 1, 2014.

## § 1163.003. Supporting Vouchers and Other Documents Attached to Account

(a) The guardian of the estate shall attach to each annual account:

(1) a voucher for each item of credit claimed in the account or, to support the item in the absence of the voucher, other evidence satisfactory to the court;

(2) an official letter from the bank or other depository where the money on hand of the estate or ward is deposited that shows the amounts in general or special deposits; and

(3) proof of the existence and possession of:

(A) securities owned by the estate or shown by the account; and

(B) other assets held by a depository subject to court order.

(b) An original voucher submitted to the court may on application be returned to the guardian after approval of the annual account.

Added by Acts 2011, 82nd Leg., ch. 823 (H.B. 2759), § 1.02, eff. Jan. 1, 2014.

## § 1163.004. Method of Proof for Securities and Other Assets

(a) The proof required by Section 1163.003(a)(3) must be by:

(1) an official letter from the bank or other depository where the securities or other assets are held for safekeeping, and if the depository is the guardian, the official letter must be signed by a representative of the depository other than the depository verifying the annual account;

(2) a certificate of an authorized representative of a corporation that is surety on the guardian's bonds;

(3) a certificate of the clerk or a deputy clerk of a court of record in this state; or

(4) an affidavit of any other reputable person designated by the court on request of the guardian or other interested party.

(b) A certificate or affidavit described by Subsection (a) must:

(1) state that the affiant has examined the assets that the guardian exhibited to the affiant as assets of the estate for which the annual account is made;

(2) describe the assets by reference to the account or in another manner that sufficiently identifies the assets exhibited; and

(3) state the time and the place the assets were exhibited.

(c) Instead of attaching a certificate or an affidavit, the guardian may exhibit the securities to the judge of the court, who shall endorse on the annual account, or include in the judge's order with respect to the account, a statement that the securities shown to the judge as on hand were exhibited to the judge and that the securities were the same as those shown in the account, or note any variance. If the securities are exhibited at a location other than where the securities are deposited for safekeeping, that exhibit is at the guardian's own expense and risk.

(d) The judge of the court may require:

(1) additional evidence of the existence and custody of the securities and other personal property as the judge considers proper; and

(2) the guardian at any time to exhibit the securities to the judge or another person designated by the judge at the place where the securities are held for safekeeping.

Added by Acts 2011, 82nd Leg., ch. 823 (H.B. 2759), § 1.02, eff. Jan. 1, 2014.

### § 1163.005. Verification of Account and Statement Regarding Taxes and Status as Guardian

(a) The guardian of the estate shall attach to an account the guardian's affidavit stating:

(1) that the account contains a correct and complete statement of the matters to which the account relates;

(2) that the guardian has paid the bond premium for the next accounting period;

(3) that the guardian has filed all tax returns of the ward due during the accounting period;

(4) that the guardian has paid all taxes the ward owed during the accounting period, the amount of the taxes, the date the guardian paid the taxes, and the name of the governmental entity to which the guardian paid the taxes; and

(5) if the guardian is a private professional guardian, a guardianship program, or the Department of Aging and Disability Services, whether the guardian or an individual certified under Subchapter C, Chapter 111, Government Code, who is providing guardianship services to the ward and who is swearing to the account on the guardian's behalf, is or has been the subject of an investigation conducted by the Guardianship Certification Board during the accounting period.

(b) If on the filing of the account the guardian of the estate has failed on the ward's behalf to file a tax return or pay taxes due, the guardian shall attach to the account a description of the taxes and the reasons for the guardian's failure to file the return or pay the taxes.

Added by Acts 2011, 82nd Leg., ch. 823 (H.B. 2759), § 1.02, eff. Jan. 1, 2014. Amended by Acts 2013, 83rd Leg., ch. 982 (H.B. 2080), §§ 20, 21, eff. Jan. 1, 2014.

Section 36 of Acts 2013, 83rd Leg., ch. 982 (H.B. 2080) provides:

"(a) Except as otherwise provided by this section, the changes in law made by this Act apply to:

"(1) a guardianship created before, on, or after the effective date [Jan. 1, 2014] of this Act; and

"(2) an application for a guardianship pending on, or filed on or after, the effective date of this Act.

"(b) The changes in law made by this Act to Sections 1301.054, 1301.055, 1301.057(b), (c), and (d), 1301.058, 1301.101, and 1301.102(a), Estates Code, apply only to an application for the creation, modifica-

tion, or termination of a management trust that is filed on or after the effective date of this Act. An application described by this subsection that is filed before the effective date of this Act is governed by the law in effect on the date the application was filed, and the former law is continued in effect for that purpose.

"(c) The changes in law made by this Act to Sections 1301.103 and 1301.154(a), Estates Code, and by Section 1301.202(a–1), Estates Code, as added by this Act, apply to a management trust created before, on, or after the effective date of this Act.

"(d) The changes in law made by this Act to Section 1102.003, Estates Code, apply to a guardianship proceeding that is commenced on or after the effective date of this Act. A guardianship proceeding commenced before that date is governed by the law in effect on the date the proceeding was commenced, and the former law is continued in effect for that purpose."

### § 1163.006. Waiver of Account Filing

If the ward's estate produces negligible or fixed income, the court may waive the filing of annual accounts and may permit the guardian to:

(1) receive all estate income and apply the income to the support, maintenance, and education of the ward; and

(2) account to the court for the estate income and corpus when the estate must be closed.

Added by Acts 2011, 82nd Leg., ch. 823 (H.B. 2759), § 1.02, eff. Jan. 1, 2014.

## SUBCHAPTER B. ACTION ON ANNUAL ACCOUNT

### § 1163.051. Filing and Consideration of Annual Account

(a) The guardian of the estate shall file an annual account with the county clerk. The county clerk shall note the filing on the judge's docket.

(b) An annual account must remain on file for 10 days after the date the account is filed before being considered by the judge. After the expiration of that period, the judge shall consider the account and may continue the hearing on the account until fully advised on all account items.

(c) The court may not approve the annual account unless possession of cash, listed securities, or other assets held in safekeeping or on deposit under court order has been proven as required by law.

Added by Acts 2011, 82nd Leg., ch. 823 (H.B. 2759), § 1.02, eff. Jan. 1, 2014.

### § 1163.052. Correction and Approval of Annual Account

(a) If an annual account is found to be incorrect, the account shall be corrected.

(b) The court by order shall approve an annual account that is corrected to the satisfaction of the court and shall act with respect to unpaid claims in accordance with Sections 1163.053 and 1163.054.

Added by Acts 2011, 82nd Leg., ch. 823 (H.B. 2759), § 1.02, eff. Jan. 1, 2014.

## § 1163.053.  Order for Payment of Claims in Full

After approval of an annual account as provided by Section 1163.052, if it appears to the court from the exhibit or other evidence that the estate is wholly solvent and that the guardian has sufficient funds to pay every claim against the estate, the court shall order immediate payment of all claims allowed and approved or established by judgment.

Added by Acts 2011, 82nd Leg., ch. 823 (H.B. 2759), § 1.02, eff. Jan. 1, 2014.

## § 1163.054.  Order for Pro Rata Payment of Claims

After approval of an annual account as provided by Section 1163.052, if it appears to the court from the account or other evidence that the funds on hand are not sufficient to pay all claims against the estate or if the estate is insolvent and the guardian has any funds on hand, the court shall order the funds to be applied:

(1) first to the payment of any unpaid claims having a preference in the order of their priority; and

(2) then to the pro rata payment of the other claims allowed and approved or established by final judgment, considering also:

(A) claims that were presented not later than the first anniversary of the date letters of guardianship were granted; and

(B) claims that are in litigation or on which a lawsuit may be filed.

Added by Acts 2011, 82nd Leg., ch. 823 (H.B. 2759), § 1.02, eff. Jan. 1, 2014.

## SUBCHAPTER C.  ANNUAL REPORT BY GUARDIAN OF THE PERSON

## § 1163.101.  Annual Report Required

(a) Once each year for the duration of the guardianship, a guardian of the person shall file with the court a report that contains the information required by this section.

(b) The guardian of the person shall file a sworn, written report that shows each receipt and disbursement for:

(1) the support and maintenance of the ward;

(2) when necessary, the education of the ward; and

(3) when authorized by court order, the support and maintenance of the ward's dependents.

(c) The guardian of the person shall file a sworn affidavit that contains:

(1) the guardian's current name, address, and telephone number;

(2) the ward's date of birth and current name, address, telephone number, and age;

(3) a description of the type of home in which the ward resides, which shall be described as:

(A) the ward's own home;

(B) a nursing home;

(C) a guardian's home;

(D) a foster home;

(E) a boarding home;

(F) a relative's home, in which case the description must specify the relative's relationship to the ward;

(G) a hospital or medical facility;  or

(H) another type of residence;

(4) statements indicating:

(A) the length of time the ward has resided in the present home;

(B) the reason for a change in the ward's residence, if a change in the ward's residence has occurred in the past year;

(C) the date the guardian most recently saw the ward;

(D) how frequently the guardian has seen the ward in the past year;

(E) whether the guardian has possession or control of the ward's estate;

(F) whether the ward's mental health has improved, deteriorated, or remained unchanged during the past year, including a description of the change if a change has occurred;

(G) whether the ward's physical health has improved, deteriorated, or remained unchanged during the past year, including a description of the change if a change has occurred;

(H) whether the ward has regular medical care; and

(I) the ward's treatment or evaluation by any of the following persons during the past year, including the person's name and a description of the treatment:

(i) a physician;

(ii) a psychiatrist, psychologist, or other mental health care provider;

(iii) a dentist;

(iv) a social or other caseworker; or

(v) any other individual who provided treatment;

(5) a description of the ward's activities during the past year, including recreational, educational, social, and occupational activities, or a statement that no activities were available or that the ward was unable or refused to participate in activities;

(6) the guardian's evaluation of:

(A) the ward's living arrangements as excellent, average, or below average, including an explanation if the conditions are below average;

(B) whether the ward is content or unhappy with the ward's living arrangements; and

(C) unmet needs of the ward;

(7) a statement indicating whether the guardian's power should be increased, decreased, or unaltered, including an explanation if a change is recommended;

(8) a statement indicating that the guardian has paid the bond premium for the next reporting period;

(9) if the guardian is a private professional guardian, a guardianship program, or the Department of Aging and Disability Services, whether the guardian or an individual certified under Subchapter C, Chapter 111, Government Code, who is providing guardianship services to the ward and who is swearing to the affidavit on the guardian's behalf, is or has been the subject of an investigation conducted by the Guardianship Certification Board during the preceding year; and

(10) any additional information the guardian desires to share with the court regarding the ward, including:

(A) whether the guardian has filed for emergency detention of the ward under Subchapter A, Chapter 573, Health and Safety Code; and

(B) if applicable, the number of times the guardian has filed for emergency detention and the dates of the applications for emergency detention.

Added by Acts 2011, 82nd Leg., ch. 823 (H.B. 2759), § 1.02, eff. Jan. 1, 2014. Amended by Acts 2013, 83rd Leg., ch. 982 (H.B. 2080), § 22, eff. Jan. 1, 2014.

Section 36 of Acts 2013, 83rd Leg., ch. 982 (H.B. 2080) provides:

"(a) Except as otherwise provided by this section, the changes in law made by this Act apply to:

"(1) a guardianship created before, on, or after the effective date [Jan. 1, 2014] of this Act; and

"(2) an application for a guardianship pending on, or filed on or after, the effective date of this Act.

"(b) The changes in law made by this Act to Sections 1301.054, 1301.055, 1301.057(b), (c), and (d), 1301.058, 1301.101, and 1301.102(a), Estates Code, apply only to an application for the creation, modification, or termination of a management trust that is filed on or after the effective date of this Act. An application described by this subsection that is filed before the effective date of this Act is governed by the law in effect on the date the application was filed, and the former law is continued in effect for that purpose.

"(c) The changes in law made by this Act to Sections 1301.103 and 1301.154(a), Estates Code, and by Section 1301.202(a–1), Estates Code, as added by this Act, apply to a management trust created before, on, or after the effective date of this Act.

"(d) The changes in law made by this Act to Section 1102.003, Estates Code, apply to a guardianship proceeding that is commenced on or after the effective date of this Act. A guardianship proceeding commenced before that date is governed by the law in effect on the date the proceeding was commenced, and the former law is continued in effect for that purpose."

### § 1163.1011. Use of Unsworn Declaration for Electronic Filing of Annual Report

(a) A guardian of the person who files the annual report required by Section 1163.101 electronically with the court may use an unsworn declaration made as provided by this section instead of a written sworn declaration or affidavit required by Section 1163.101.

(b) An unsworn declaration authorized by this section must be:

(1) in writing; and

(2) subscribed by the person making the declaration as true under penalty of perjury.

(c) The form of an unsworn declaration authorized by this section must be substantially as follows:

I, (insert name of guardian of the person), the guardian of the person for (insert name of ward) in _____ County, Texas, declare under penalty of perjury that the foregoing is true and correct.

Executed on (insert date)

_____

(signature)

(d) An unsworn declaration authorized by Section 132.001, Civil Practice and Remedies Code, may not be used instead of a written sworn declaration or affidavit required by Section 1163.101.

Added by Acts 2013, 83rd Leg., ch. 982 (H.B. 2080), § 23, eff. Jan. 1, 2014.

Section 36 of Acts 2013, 83rd Leg., ch. 982 (H.B. 2080) provides:

"(a) Except as otherwise provided by this section, the changes in law made by this Act apply to:

"(1) a guardianship created before, on, or after the effective date [Jan. 1, 2014] of this Act; and

"(2) an application for a guardianship pending on, or filed on or after, the effective date of this Act.

"(b) The changes in law made by this Act to Sections 1301.054, 1301.055, 1301.057(b), (c), and (d), 1301.058, 1301.101, and 1301.102(a), Estates Code, apply only to an application for the creation, modification, or termination of a management trust that is filed on or after the effective date of this Act. An application described by this subsection that is filed before the effective date of this Act is governed by the law in effect on the date the application was filed, and the former law is continued in effect for that purpose.

"(c) The changes in law made by this Act to Sections 1301.103 and 1301.154(a), Estates Code, and by Section 1301.202(a–1), Estates Code, as added by this Act, apply to a management trust created before, on, or after the effective date of this Act.

"(d) The changes in law made by this Act to Section 1102.003, Estates Code, apply to a guardianship proceeding that is commenced on or after the effective date of this Act. A guardianship proceeding commenced before that date is governed by the law in effect on the date the proceeding was commenced, and the former law is continued in effect for that purpose."

## § 1163.102. Reporting Period

(a) Except as provided under Subsection (b), an annual report required by Section 1163.101 must cover a 12–month reporting period that begins on the date or the anniversary of the date the guardian of the person qualifies to serve.

(b) The court may change a reporting period for purposes of this subchapter but may not extend a reporting period so that it covers more than 12 months.

(c) Each report is due not later than the 60th day after the date the reporting period ends.

Added by Acts 2011, 82nd Leg., ch. 823 (H.B. 2759), § 1.02, eff. Jan. 1, 2014.

## § 1163.103. Report in Case of Deceased Ward

If the ward is deceased, the guardian of the person shall provide the court with the date and place of death, if known, instead of the information about the ward otherwise required to be provided in the annual report.

Added by Acts 2011, 82nd Leg., ch. 823 (H.B. 2759), § 1.02, eff. Jan. 1, 2014.

## § 1163.104. Approval of Report

(a) If the judge is satisfied that the facts stated in the report are true, the court shall approve the report.

(b) Unless the judge is satisfied that the facts stated in the report are true, the judge shall issue orders necessary for the ward's best interests.

(c) The court on the court's own motion may waive the costs and fees related to the filing of a report approved under Subsection (a).

Added by Acts 2011, 82nd Leg., ch. 823 (H.B. 2759), § 1.02, eff. Jan. 1, 2014.

## § 1163.105. Attorney Not Required

A guardian of the person may complete and file the report required under this subchapter without the assistance of an attorney.

Added by Acts 2011, 82nd Leg., ch. 823 (H.B. 2759), § 1.02, eff. Jan. 1, 2014.

## SUBCHAPTER D. PENALTIES

### § 1163.151. Penalty for Failure to File Required Account, Exhibit, or Report

(a) If a guardian does not file an account, an exhibit, a report of the guardian of the person, or another report required by this title, any person interested in the estate, on written complaint filed with the court clerk, or the court on the court's own motion, may have the guardian cited to appear and show cause why the guardian should not file the account, exhibit, or report.

(b) On hearing, the court may:

(1) order the guardian to file the account, exhibit, or report; and

(2) unless good cause is shown for the failure to file:

(A) revoke the guardian's letters of guardianship;

(B) fine the guardian in an amount not to exceed $1,000; or

(C) revoke the guardian's letters of guardianship and fine the guardian in an amount not to exceed $1,000.

Added by Acts 2011, 82nd Leg., ch. 823 (H.B. 2759), § 1.02, eff. Jan. 1, 2014.

## CHAPTER 1164. LIABILITY OF GUARDIAN OR GUARDIANSHIP PROGRAM

Section
1164.001. Liability of Guardian.

## § 1164.001.  Liability of Guardian

A person is not liable to a third person solely because the person has been appointed guardian of a ward under this title.

Added by Acts 2011, 82nd Leg., ch. 823 (H.B. 2759), § 1.02, eff. Jan. 1, 2014.

## § 1164.002.  Immunity of Guardianship Program

A guardianship program is not liable for civil damages arising from an action taken or omission made by a person while providing guardianship services to a ward on behalf of the guardianship program, unless the action or omission was:

(1) wilfully wrongful;

(2) taken or made:

(A) with conscious indifference to or reckless disregard for the safety of the ward or another;

(B) in bad faith; or

(C) with malice; or

(3) grossly negligent.

Added by Acts 2011, 82nd Leg., ch. 823 (H.B. 2759), § 1.02, eff. Jan. 1, 2014.

# SUBTITLE F.  EVALUATION, MODIFICATION, OR TERMINATION OF GUARDIANSHIP

## CHAPTER 1201.  EVALUATION OF GUARDIANSHIP

## SUBCHAPTER A.  REVIEW OF GUARDIANSHIP

## § 1201.001.  Determining Guardian's Performance of Duties

The court shall use reasonable diligence to determine whether a guardian is performing all of the duties required of the guardian that relate to the guardian's ward.

Added by Acts 2011, 82nd Leg., ch. 823 (H.B. 2759), § 1.02, eff. Jan. 1, 2014.

## § 1201.002.  Annual Examination of Guardianship; Bond of Guardian

(a) At least annually, the judge shall examine the well-being of each ward of the court and the solvency of the bond of the guardian of the ward's estate.

(b) If after examining the solvency of a guardian's bond as provided by Subsection (a) the judge determines that the guardian's bond is not sufficient to protect the ward or the ward's estate, the judge shall require the guardian to execute a new bond.

(c) The judge shall notify the guardian and the sureties on the guardian's bond as provided by law.

Added by Acts 2011, 82nd Leg., ch. 823 (H.B. 2759), § 1.02, eff. Jan. 1, 2014.

## § 1201.003.  Judge's Liability

A judge is liable on the judge's bond to those damaged if damage or loss results to a guardianship or ward because of the gross neglect of the judge to use reasonable diligence in the performance of the judge's duty under this subchapter.

Added by Acts 2011, 82nd Leg., ch. 823 (H.B. 2759), § 1.02, eff. Jan. 1, 2014.

## § 1201.004.  Identifying Information

(a) The court may request an applicant or court-appointed fiduciary to produce other information identifying an applicant, ward, or guardian, including a social security number, in addition to identifying information the applicant or fiduciary is required to produce under this title.

(b) The court shall maintain any information required under this section, and the information may not be filed with the clerk.

Added by Acts 2011, 82nd Leg., ch. 823 (H.B. 2759), § 1.02, eff. Jan. 1, 2014.

## SUBCHAPTER B.  ANNUAL DETERMINATION TO CONTINUE, MODIFY, OR TERMINATE GUARDIANSHIP

### § 1201.051.  Applicability

This subchapter does not apply to a guardianship that is created only because it is necessary for a person to have a guardian appointed to receive funds from a governmental source.

Added by Acts 2011, 82nd Leg., ch. 823 (H.B. 2759), § 1.02, eff. Jan. 1, 2014.

### § 1201.052.  Annual Determination

To determine whether a guardianship should be continued, modified, or terminated, the court in which the guardianship proceeding is pending:

(1) shall review annually each guardianship in which the application to create the guardianship was filed after September 1, 1993; and

(2) may review annually any other guardianship.

Added by Acts 2011, 82nd Leg., ch. 823 (H.B. 2759), § 1.02, eff. Jan. 1, 2014.

### § 1201.053.  Method of Determination

(a) In reviewing a guardianship under Section 1201.052, a statutory probate court may:

(1) review any report prepared by:

(A) a court investigator under Section 1054.153 or 1202.054;

(B) a guardian ad litem under Section 1202.054; or

(C) a court visitor under Section 1054.104;

(2) conduct a hearing;  or

(3) review an annual account prepared under Subchapter A, Chapter 1163, or a report prepared under Subchapter C, Chapter 1163.

(b) A court that is not a statutory probate court may use any method to review a guardianship under Section 1201.052 that is determined appropriate by the court according to the court's caseload and available resources.

Added by Acts 2011, 82nd Leg., ch. 823 (H.B. 2759), § 1.02, eff. Jan. 1, 2014.

### § 1201.054.  Form of Determination

A determination under this subchapter must be in writing and filed with the clerk.

Added by Acts 2011, 82nd Leg., ch. 823 (H.B. 2759), § 1.02, eff. Jan. 1, 2014.

## CHAPTER 1202.  MODIFICATION OR TERMINATION OF GUARDIANSHIP

### SUBCHAPTER A.  TERMINATION AND SETTLEMENT OF GUARDIANSHIP

### § 1202.001.  Term of Guardian or Guardianship

(a) Unless otherwise discharged as provided by law, a guardian remains in office until the estate is closed.

(b) A guardianship shall be settled and closed when the ward:

(1) dies and, if the ward was married, the ward's spouse qualifies as survivor in community;

(2) is found by the court to have full capacity to care for himself or herself and to manage the ward's property;

(3) is no longer a minor; or

(4) no longer must have a guardian appointed to receive funds due the ward from any governmental source.

(c) An order appointing a guardian or a successor guardian may specify a period of not more than one year during which a petition for adjudication that the ward no longer requires the guardianship may not be filed without special leave.

(d) A request for an order under this section may be made by informal letter to the court. A person who knowingly interferes with the transmission of the request to the court may be adjudged guilty of contempt of court.

(e) If a nonresident guardian of a nonresident ward qualifies as guardian under this title, any resident guardian's guardianship may be terminated.

Added by Acts 2011, 82nd Leg., ch. 823 (H.B. 2759), § 1.02, eff. Jan. 1, 2014.

### § 1202.002. Termination of Guardianship if Parent Is No Longer Incapacitated

(a) The powers of a person appointed to serve as the designated guardian of the person or estate, or both, of a minor child solely because of the incapacity of the minor's surviving parent and in accordance with Section 1104.053 and Subchapter D, Chapter 1104, terminate when a probate court enters an order finding that the surviving parent is no longer an incapacitated person.

(b) The powers of a person appointed to serve as the designated guardian of the person or estate, or both, of an adult individual solely because of the incapacity of the individual's surviving parent and in accordance with Section 1104.103 and Subchapter D, Chapter 1104, terminate when a probate court enters an order finding that the surviving parent is no longer an incapacitated person and reappointing the surviving parent as the individual's guardian.

Added by Acts 2011, 82nd Leg., ch. 823 (H.B. 2759), § 1.02, eff. Jan. 1, 2014.

## SUBCHAPTER B. APPLICATION FOR COMPLETE RESTORATION OF WARD'S CAPACITY OR MODIFICATION OF GUARDIANSHIP

### § 1202.051. Application Authorized

A ward or any person interested in the ward's welfare may file a written application with the court for an order:

(1) finding that the ward is no longer an incapacitated person and ordering the settlement and closing of the guardianship;

(2) finding that the ward lacks the capacity to do some or all of the tasks necessary to provide food, clothing, or shelter for himself or herself, to care for the ward's own physical health, or to manage the ward's own financial affairs and granting additional powers or duties to the guardian; or

(3) finding that the ward has the capacity to do some, but not all, of the tasks necessary to provide food, clothing, or shelter for himself or herself, to care for the ward's own physical health, or to manage the ward's own financial affairs and:

(A) limiting the guardian's powers or duties; and

(B) permitting the ward to care for himself or herself or to manage the ward's own financial affairs commensurate with the ward's ability.

Added by Acts 2011, 82nd Leg., ch. 823 (H.B. 2759), § 1.02, eff. Jan. 1, 2014.

### § 1202.052. Contents of Application

An application filed under Section 1202.051 must be sworn to by the applicant and must state:

(1) the ward's name, sex, date of birth, and address;

(2) the name and address of any person serving as guardian of the person of the ward on the date the application is filed;

(3) the name and address of any person serving as guardian of the estate of the ward on the date the application is filed;

(4) the nature and description of the ward's guardianship;

(5) the specific areas of protection and assistance and any limitation of rights that exist;

(6) whether the relief being sought is:

(A) a restoration of the ward's capacity because the ward is no longer an incapacitated person;

(B) the granting of additional powers or duties to the guardian; or

(C) the limitation of powers granted to or duties performed by the guardian;

(7) if the relief being sought under the application is described by Subdivision (6)(B) or (C):

(A) the nature and degree of the ward's incapacity;

(B) the specific areas of protection and assistance to be provided to the ward and requested to be included in the court's order; and

(C) any limitation of the ward's rights requested to be included in the court's order;

(8) the approximate value and description of the ward's property, including any compensation, pension, insurance, or allowance to which the ward is or may be entitled; and

(9) if the ward is 60 years of age or older, the names and addresses, to the best of the applicant's knowledge, of the ward's spouse, siblings, and children or, if there is no known spouse, sibling, or child, the names and addresses of the ward's next of kin.

Added by Acts 2011, 82nd Leg., ch. 823 (H.B. 2759), § 1.02, eff. Jan. 1, 2014.

### § 1202.053.  Citation Required

When an application is filed under Section 1202.051, citation shall be served on:

(1) the ward's guardian; and

(2) the ward if the ward is not the applicant.

Added by Acts 2011, 82nd Leg., ch. 823 (H.B. 2759), § 1.02, eff. Jan. 1, 2014.

### § 1202.054.  Informal Request for Order by Ward; Investigation and Report

(a) A ward may request an order under Section 1202.051 by informal letter to the court.  A person who knowingly interferes with the transmission of the request to the court may be adjudged guilty of contempt of court.

(b) On receipt of an informal letter under Subsection (a), the court shall appoint the court investigator or a guardian ad litem to investigate the ward's circumstances, including any circumstances alleged in the letter, to determine whether:

(1) the ward is no longer an incapacitated person; or

(2) a modification of the guardianship is necessary.

(c) The court investigator or guardian ad litem shall file with the court a report of the investigation's findings and conclusions.  If the court investigator or guardian ad litem determines that it is in the best interest of the ward to terminate or modify the guardianship, the court investigator or guardian ad litem shall file an application under Section 1202.051 on the ward's behalf.

(d) A guardian ad litem appointed under this section may also be appointed by the court to serve as attorney ad litem under Section 1202.101.

Added by Acts 2011, 82nd Leg., ch. 823 (H.B. 2759), § 1.02, eff. Jan. 1, 2014.

### § 1202.055.  Restriction on Subsequent Application Regarding Capacity or Modification

A person may not reapply for complete restoration of a ward's capacity or modification of a ward's guardianship before the first anniversary of the date of the hearing on the last preceding application, except as otherwise provided by the court on good cause shown by the applicant.

Added by Acts 2011, 82nd Leg., ch. 823 (H.B. 2759), § 1.02, eff. Jan. 1, 2014.

### SUBCHAPTER C. REPRESENTATION OF WARD IN PROCEEDING FOR COMPLETE RESTORATION OF WARD'S CAPACITY OR MODIFICATION OF GUARDIANSHIP

### § 1202.101.  Appointment of Attorney ad Litem

The court shall appoint an attorney ad litem to represent a ward in a proceeding for the complete restoration of the ward's capacity or for the modification of the ward's guardianship.  Unless otherwise provided by the court, the attorney ad litem shall represent the ward only for purposes of the restoration or modification proceeding.

Added by Acts 2011, 82nd Leg., ch. 823 (H.B. 2759), § 1.02, eff. Jan. 1, 2014.

### § 1202.102.  Compensation for Attorney ad Litem and Guardian ad Litem

(a) An attorney ad litem appointed under Section 1202.101 is entitled to reasonable compensation for services in the amount set by the court to be taxed as costs in the proceeding, regardless of whether the proceeding results in the restoration of the ward's capacity or a modification of the ward's guardianship.

(b) A guardian ad litem appointed in a proceeding involving the complete restoration of a ward's capacity or modification of a ward's guardianship is entitled to reasonable compensation, as provided by Section 1054.055(a), regardless of whether the proceeding results in the restoration of the ward's capacity or a modification of the ward's guardianship.

Added by Acts 2011, 82nd Leg., ch. 823 (H.B. 2759), § 1.02, eff. Jan. 1, 2014.

### § 1202.103.  Retention and Compensation of Attorney for Ward

(a) A ward may retain an attorney for a proceeding involving the complete restoration of the ward's capacity or modification of the ward's guardianship.

(b) The court may order that compensation for services provided by an attorney retained under this section be paid from funds in the ward's estate only if the court finds that the attorney had a good faith belief that the ward had the capacity necessary to retain the attorney's services.

Added by Acts 2011, 82nd Leg., ch. 823 (H.B. 2759), § 1.02, eff. Jan. 1, 2014.

## SUBCHAPTER D.  HEARING, EVIDENCE, AND ORDERS IN PROCEEDING FOR COMPLETE RESTORATION OF WARD'S CAPACITY OR MODIFICATION OF GUARDIANSHIP

### § 1202.151.  Evidence and Burden of Proof at Hearing

(a) Except as provided by Section 1202.201, at a hearing on an application filed under Section 1202.051, the court shall consider only evidence regarding the ward's mental or physical capacity at the time of the hearing that is relevant to the complete restoration of the ward's capacity or modification of the ward's guardianship.

(b) The party who filed the application has the burden of proof at the hearing.

Added by Acts 2011, 82nd Leg., ch. 823 (H.B. 2759), § 1.02, eff. Jan. 1, 2014.  Amended by Acts 2013, 83rd Leg., ch. 684 (H.B. 2407), § 2, eff. Jan. 1, 2014.

### § 1202.152.  Physician's Letter or Certificate Required

(a) The court may not grant an order completely restoring a ward's capacity or modifying a ward's guardianship under an application filed under Section 1202.051 unless the applicant presents to the court a written letter or certificate from a physician licensed in this state that is dated:

(1) not earlier than the 120th day before the date the application was filed; or

(2) after the date the application was filed but before the date of the hearing.

(b) A letter or certificate presented under Subsection (a) must:

(1) describe the nature and degree of incapacity, including the medical history if reasonably available, or state that, in the physician's opinion, the ward has the capacity to:

(A) provide food, clothing, and shelter for himself or herself;

(B) care for the ward's own physical health; and

(C) manage the ward's financial affairs;

(2) provide a medical prognosis specifying the estimated severity of any incapacity;

(3) state how or in what manner the ward's ability to make or communicate responsible decisions concerning himself or herself is affected by the ward's physical or mental health;

(4) state whether any current medication affects the ward's demeanor or the ward's ability to participate fully in a court proceeding;

(5) describe the precise physical and mental conditions underlying a diagnosis of senility, if applicable; and

(6) include any other information required by the court.

(c) If the court determines it is necessary, the court may appoint the necessary physicians to examine the ward in the same manner and to the same extent as a ward is examined by a physician under Section 1101.103 or 1101.104.

Added by Acts 2011, 82nd Leg., ch. 823 (H.B. 2759), § 1.02, eff. Jan. 1, 2014.

### § 1202.153.  Findings Required

(a) Before ordering the settlement and closing of a guardianship under an application filed under Section 1202.051, the court must find by a preponderance of the evidence that the ward is no longer partially or fully incapacitated.

(b) Before granting additional powers to the guardian or requiring the guardian to perform additional duties under an application filed under Section 1202.051, the court must find by a preponderance of the evidence that the current nature and degree of the ward's incapacity warrants a modification of the guardianship and that some or all of the ward's rights need to be further restricted.

(c) Before limiting the powers granted to or duties required to be performed by the guardian under an application filed under Section 1202.051, the court must find by a preponderance of the evidence that the current nature and degree of the ward's incapacity warrants a modification of the guardianship and that some of the ward's rights need to be restored.

Added by Acts 2011, 82nd Leg., ch. 823 (H.B. 2759), § 1.02, eff. Jan. 1, 2014.

### § 1202.154.   General Requirements for Order

(a) A court order entered with respect to an application filed under Section 1202.051 to completely restore a ward's capacity or modify a ward's guardianship must state:

(1) the guardian's name;

(2) the ward's name; and

(3) whether the type of guardianship being addressed at the proceeding is a:

(A) guardianship of the person;

(B) guardianship of the estate; or

(C) guardianship of both the person and the estate.

(b) In an order described by this section, the court may not grant a power to a guardian or require the guardian to perform a duty that is a power granted to or a duty required to be performed by another guardian.

Added by Acts 2011, 82nd Leg., ch. 823 (H.B. 2759), § 1.02, eff. Jan. 1, 2014.

### § 1202.155.   Additional Requirements for Order Restoring Ward's Capacity

If the court finds that a ward is no longer an incapacitated person, the order completely restoring the ward's capacity must contain findings of fact and specify, in addition to the information required by Section 1202.154:

(1) that the ward is no longer an incapacitated person;

(2) that there is no further need for a guardianship of the person or estate of the ward;

(3) if the ward's incapacity resulted from a mental condition, that the ward's mental capacity is completely restored;

(4) that the guardian is required to:

(A) immediately settle the guardianship in accordance with this title; and

(B) deliver all of the remaining guardianship estate to the ward; and

(5) that the clerk shall revoke letters of guardianship when the guardianship is finally settled and closed.

Added by Acts 2011, 82nd Leg., ch. 823 (H.B. 2759), § 1.02, eff. Jan. 1, 2014.

### § 1202.156.   Additional Requirements for Order Modifying Guardianship

If the court finds that a guardian's powers or duties should be expanded or limited, the order modifying the guardianship must contain findings of fact and specify, in addition to the information required by Section 1202.154:

(1) the specific powers, limitations, or duties of the guardian with respect to the care of the ward or the management of the ward's property, as appropriate;

(2) the specific areas of protection and assistance to be provided to the ward;

(3) any limitation of the ward's rights;

(4) if the ward's incapacity resulted from a mental condition, whether the ward retains the right to vote; and

(5) that the clerk shall modify the letters of guardianship to the extent applicable to conform to the order.

Added by Acts 2011, 82nd Leg., ch. 823 (H.B. 2759), § 1.02, eff. Jan. 1, 2014.

### § 1202.157.   Additional Requirements for Order Dismissing Application

If the court finds that a modification of the ward's guardianship is not necessary or that the ward's capacity has not been restored, the court shall dismiss the application and enter an order that contains findings of fact and specifies, in addition to the information required by Section 1202.154, that the guardian's powers, limitations, or duties with respect to the ward's care or the management of the ward's property remain unchanged.

Added by Acts 2011, 82nd Leg., ch. 823 (H.B. 2759), § 1.02, eff. Jan. 1, 2014.

## SUBCHAPTER E.   RESTORATION OF RIGHTS ON TERMINATION OF GUARDIANSHIP

### § 1202.201.   Removal of Firearm Disability on Complete Restoration of Ward's Capacity

(a) A person whose guardianship was terminated because the person's capacity was completely restored may file an application with the court that created the guardianship for an order requesting the removal of the person's disability to purchase a firearm imposed under 18 U.S.C. Section 922(g)(4).

(b) At a proceeding involving the complete restoration of the ward's capacity under Subchapter B, the ward or a person interested in the ward's welfare may request an order seeking relief from a firearms disability described by Subsection (a).

(c) In determining whether to grant the relief sought under Subsection (a) or (b), the court must hear and consider evidence about:

(1) the circumstances that led to imposition of the firearms disability;

(2) the person's mental history;

(3) the person's criminal history; and

(4) the person's reputation.

(d) A court may not grant relief under this section unless the court makes and enters in the record the following affirmative findings:

(1) the person or ward is no longer likely to act in a manner dangerous to public safety; and

(2) removing the person's or ward's disability to purchase a firearm is in the public interest.

Added by Acts 2013, 83rd Leg., ch. 684 (H.B. 2407), § 1, eff. Jan. 1, 2014.

## CHAPTER 1203. RESIGNATION, REMOVAL, OR DEATH OF GUARDIAN; APPOINTMENT OF SUCCESSOR

### SUBCHAPTER A. RESIGNATION OF GUARDIAN

### SUBCHAPTER A. RESIGNATION OF GUARDIAN

### § 1203.001.  Resignation Application

A guardian of the estate or guardian of the person who wishes to resign the guardian's trust shall file a written application with the court clerk, accompanied by:

(1) in the case of a guardian of the estate, a complete and verified exhibit and final account showing the true condition of the guardianship estate entrusted to the guardian's care; or

(2) in the case of a guardian of the person, a verified report containing the information required in the annual report required under Subchapter C,

Chapter 1163, showing the condition of the ward entrusted to the guardian's care.

Added by Acts 2011, 82nd Leg., ch. 823 (H.B. 2759), § 1.02, eff. Jan. 1, 2014.

## § 1203.002.  Immediate Acceptance of Resignation; Discharge and Release

(a) If the necessity exists, the court may immediately accept the resignation of a guardian and appoint a successor guardian as provided by Section 1203.102(b).

(b) The court may not discharge a person resigning as guardian of the estate whose resignation is accepted under Subsection (a), or release the person or the sureties on the person's bond, until a final order has been issued, or a final judgment has been rendered, on the final account required under Section 1203.001.

Added by Acts 2011, 82nd Leg., ch. 823 (H.B. 2759), § 1.02, eff. Jan. 1, 2014.

## § 1203.003.  Delivery of Estate Property to Successor Guardian Following Resignation

The court at any time may order a resigning guardian who has any part of a ward's estate to deliver any part of the estate to a person who has been appointed and has qualified as successor guardian.

Added by Acts 2011, 82nd Leg., ch. 823 (H.B. 2759), § 1.02, eff. Jan. 1, 2014.

## § 1203.004.  Hearing Date; Citation

(a) When an application to resign as guardian is filed under Section 1203.001, supported by the exhibit and final account or report required under that section, the court clerk shall bring the application to the judge's attention and the judge shall set a date for a hearing on the matter.

(b) After a hearing is set under Subsection (a), the clerk shall issue a citation to all interested persons, showing:

(1) that an application that complies with Section 1203.001 has been filed; and

(2) the time and place set for the hearing at which the interested persons may appear and contest the exhibit and final account or report supporting the application.

(c) Unless the court directs that the citation under Subsection (b) be published, the citation must be posted.

Added by Acts 2011, 82nd Leg., ch. 823 (H.B. 2759), § 1.02, eff. Jan. 1, 2014.

## § 1203.005.  Hearing

(a) At the time set for the hearing under Section 1203.004, unless the court continues the hearing, and if the court finds that the citation required under that section has been properly issued and served, the court shall:

(1) examine the exhibit and final account or report required by Section 1203.001;

(2) hear all evidence for and against the exhibit, final account, or report; and

(3) if necessary, restate and audit and settle the exhibit, final account, or report.

(b) If the court is satisfied that the matters entrusted to the guardian applying to resign have been handled and accounted for in accordance with the law, the court shall:

(1) enter an order approving the exhibit and final account or report; and

(2) require that any estate property remaining in the applicant's possession be delivered to the person entitled by law to receive the property.

(c) A guardian of the person shall comply with all court orders concerning the guardian's ward.

Added by Acts 2011, 82nd Leg., ch. 823 (H.B. 2759), § 1.02, eff. Jan. 1, 2014.

## § 1203.006.  Requirements for Discharge

(a) A guardian applying to resign may not be discharged until:

(1) the resignation application has been heard;

(2) the exhibit and final account or report required under Section 1203.001 has been examined, settled, and approved; and

(3) the applicant has satisfied the court that the applicant has:

(A) delivered any estate property remaining in the applicant's possession; or

(B) complied with all court orders relating to the applicant's trust as guardian.

(b) When a guardian applying to resign has fully complied with the court orders, the court shall enter an order:

(1) accepting the resignation; and

(2) discharging the applicant and, if the applicant is under bond, the applicant's sureties.

Added by Acts 2011, 82nd Leg., ch. 823 (H.B. 2759), § 1.02, eff. Jan. 1, 2014.

## SUBCHAPTER B. REMOVAL AND REINSTATEMENT OF GUARDIAN

### § 1203.051. Removal Without Notice; Appointment of Guardian Ad Litem and Attorney Ad Litem

(a) The court, on the court's own motion or on the motion of an interested person, including the ward, and without notice, may remove a guardian appointed under this title who:

(1) neglects to qualify in the manner and time required by law;

(2) fails to return, not later than the 30th day after the date the guardian qualifies, an inventory of the guardianship estate property and a list of claims that have come to the guardian's knowledge, unless that deadline is extended by court order;

(3) if required, fails to give a new bond within the period prescribed;

(4) is absent from the state for a consecutive period of three or more months without the court's permission, or removes from the state;

(5) cannot be served with notices or other processes because:

(A) the guardian's whereabouts are unknown;

(B) the guardian is eluding service; or

(C) the guardian is a nonresident of this state who does not have a resident agent to accept service of process in any guardianship proceeding or other matter relating to the guardianship;

(6) subject to Section 1203.056(a):

(A) has misapplied, embezzled, or removed from the state, or is about to misapply, embezzle, or remove from the state, any of the property entrusted to the guardian's care; or

(B) has engaged in conduct with respect to the ward that would be considered to be abuse, neglect, or exploitation, as those terms are defined by Section 48.002, Human Resources Code, if engaged in with respect to an elderly or disabled person, as defined by that section; or

(7) has neglected to educate or maintain the ward as liberally as the means of the ward and the condition of the ward's estate permit.

(b) In a proceeding to remove a guardian under Subsection (a)(6) or (7), the court shall appoint a guardian ad litem as provided by Subchapter B, Chapter 1054, and an attorney ad litem. The attorney ad litem has the duties prescribed by Section 1054.004. In the interest of judicial economy, the court may appoint the same person as guardian ad litem and attorney ad litem unless a conflict exists between the interests to be represented by the guardian ad litem and attorney ad litem.

Added by Acts 2011, 82nd Leg., ch. 823 (H.B. 2759), § 1.02, eff. Jan. 1, 2014. Amended by Acts 2013, 83rd Leg., ch. 161 (S.B. 1093), § 6.053, eff. Jan. 1, 2014.

### § 1203.052. Removal With Notice

(a) The court may remove a guardian on the court's own motion, or on the complaint of an interested person, after the guardian has been cited by personal service to answer at a time and place set in the notice, if:

(1) sufficient grounds appear to support a belief that the guardian has misapplied, embezzled, or removed from the state, or is about to misapply, embezzle, or remove from the state, any of the property entrusted to the guardian's care;

(2) the guardian fails to return any account or report that is required by law to be made;

(3) the guardian fails to obey a proper order of the court that has jurisdiction with respect to the performance of the guardian's duties;

(4) the guardian is proved to have been guilty of gross misconduct or mismanagement in the performance of the guardian's duties;

(5) the guardian:

(A) becomes incapacitated;

(B) is sentenced to the penitentiary; or

(C) from any other cause, becomes incapable of properly performing the duties of the guardian's trust;

(6) the guardian has engaged in conduct with respect to the ward that would be considered to be abuse, neglect, or exploitation, as those terms are defined by Section 48.002, Human Resources Code, if engaged in with respect to an elderly or disabled person, as defined by that section;

(7) the guardian neglects to educate or maintain the ward as liberally as the means of the ward's estate and the ward's ability or condition permit;

(8) the guardian interferes with the ward's progress or participation in programs in the community;

(9) the guardian fails to comply with the requirements of Subchapter G, Chapter 1104;

(10) the court determines that, because of the dissolution of the joint guardians' marriage, the termination of the guardians' joint appointment and the continuation of only one of the joint guardians as the sole guardian is in the best interest of the ward; or

(11) the guardian would be ineligible for appointment as a guardian under Subchapter H, Chapter 1104.

*Text of subsec. (b) effective until Sept. 1, 2014*

(b) In addition to the authority granted to the court under Subsection (a), the court may, on the complaint of the Guardianship Certification Board, remove a guardian who would be ineligible for appointment under Subchapter H, Chapter 1104, because of the guardian's failure to maintain the certification required under Subchapter F, Chapter 1104. The guardian shall be cited to appear and contest the request for removal under this subsection in the manner provided by Subsection (a).

*Text of subsec. (b) effective Sept. 1, 2014*

(b) In addition to the authority granted to the court under Subsection (a), the court may, on the complaint of the guardianship certification program of the Judicial Branch Certification Commission, remove a guardian who would be ineligible for appointment under Subchapter H, Chapter 1104, because of the guardian's failure to maintain the certification required under Subchapter F, Chapter 1104. The guardian shall be cited to appear and contest the request for removal under this subsection in the manner provided by Subsection (a).

Added by Acts 2011, 82nd Leg., ch. 823 (H.B. 2759), § 1.02, eff. Jan. 1, 2014. Amended by Acts 2013, 83rd Leg., ch. 42 (S.B. 966), § 2.21, eff. Sept. 1, 2014; Acts 2013, 83rd Leg., ch. 161 (S.B. 1093), § 6.054, eff. Jan. 1, 2014.

### § 1203.053. Removal Order

An order removing a guardian shall:

(1) state the cause of the removal;

(2) require that, if the removed guardian has been personally served with citation, any letters of guardianship issued to the removed guardian be surrendered and that, regardless of whether the letters have been delivered, all the letters be canceled of record; and

(3) require the removed guardian to:

(A) deliver any estate property in the guardian's possession to the persons entitled to the property or to one who has been appointed and has qualified as successor guardian; and

(B) relinquish control of the ward's person as required in the order.

Added by Acts 2011, 82nd Leg., ch. 823 (H.B. 2759), § 1.02, eff. Jan. 1, 2014.

### § 1203.0531. Notice of Removal Order

The court clerk shall issue notice of an order rendered by the court removing a guardian under Section 1203.051(a)(1), (2), (3), (4), (6), or (7). The notice must:

(1) state the names of the ward and the removed guardian;

(2) state the date the court signed the order of removal;

(3) contain the following statement printed in 12–point bold font:

"If you have been removed from serving as guardian under Section 1203.051(a)(6)(A) or (B), Estates Code, you have the right to contest the order of removal by filing an application with the court for a hearing under Section 1203.056, Estates Code, to determine whether you should be reinstated as guardian. The application must be filed not later than the 30th day after the date the court signed the order of removal.";

(4) contain as an attachment a copy of the order of removal; and

(5) be personally served on the removed guardian not later than the seventh day after the date the court signed the order of removal.

Added by Acts 2013, 83rd Leg., ch. 161 (S.B. 1093), § 6.055, eff. Jan. 1, 2014.

### § 1203.054. Discharge and Release Following Removal

With respect to a person who is removed as guardian of the estate and whose successor is appointed without citation or notice as provided by Section 1203.102(b), the court may not discharge the person or release the person or the sureties on the person's bond until a final order has been issued or final judgment has been rendered on the guardian's final account.

Added by Acts 2011, 82nd Leg., ch. 823 (H.B. 2759), § 1.02, eff. Jan. 1, 2014.

### § 1203.055. Delivery of Estate Property to Successor Guardian Following Removal

The court at any time may order a person removed as guardian under this subchapter who has any part of a ward's estate to deliver any part of the estate to a person who has been appointed and has qualified as successor guardian.

Added by Acts 2011, 82nd Leg., ch. 823 (H.B. 2759), § 1.02, eff. Jan. 1, 2014.

### § 1203.056. Removal and Reinstatement of Guardian Under Certain Circumstances

(a) The court may remove a guardian under Section 1203.051(a)(6)(A) or (B) only on the presentation of clear and convincing evidence given under oath.

(b) Not later than the 30th day after the date the court signs the order of removal, a guardian who is removed under Section 1203.051(a)(6)(A) or (B) may file an application with the court for a hearing to determine whether the guardian should be reinstated.

(c) On the filing of an application under Subsection (b), the court clerk shall issue to the applicant, the ward, a person interested in the ward's welfare or estate, and, if applicable, a person who has control of the care and custody of the ward a notice stating:

(1) that an application for reinstatement has been filed;

(2) the name of the ward; and

(3) the name of the applicant for reinstatement.

(d) The notice required by Subsection (c) must cite all persons interested in the ward's welfare or estate to appear at the time and place stated in the notice if the persons wish to contest the application.

(e) The court shall hold a hearing on an application for reinstatement under this section as soon as practicable after the application is filed, but not later than the 60th day after the date the court signed the order of removal. If, at the conclusion of the hearing, the court is satisfied by a preponderance of the evidence that the applicant did not engage in the conduct that directly led to the applicant's removal, the court shall:

(1) set aside any order appointing a successor guardian; and

(2) enter an order reinstating the applicant as guardian of the ward or estate.

(f) If the court sets aside the appointment of a successor guardian under this section, the court may require the successor guardian to prepare and file, under oath, an accounting of the estate and to detail the disposition the successor has made of the estate property.

Added by Acts 2011, 82nd Leg., ch. 823 (H.B. 2759), § 1.02, eff. Jan. 1, 2014. Amended by Acts 2013, 83rd Leg., ch. 161 (S.B. 1093), § 6.056, eff. Jan. 1, 2014.

### § 1203.057. Removal of Joint Guardian

If a joint guardian is removed under Section 1203.052(a)(10), the other joint guardian is entitled to continue to serve as the sole guardian unless removed for a reason other than the dissolution of the joint guardians' marriage.

Added by Acts 2011, 82nd Leg., ch. 823 (H.B. 2759), § 1.02, eff. Jan. 1, 2014.

## SUBCHAPTER C. APPOINTMENT OF SUCCESSOR GUARDIAN; REVOCATION OF LETTERS

### § 1203.101. Requirements for Revocation of Letters

Except as otherwise expressly provided by this title, letters of guardianship may be revoked only:

(1) on application; and

(2) after personal service of citation on the person whose letters are sought to be revoked requiring the person to appear and show cause why the application should not be granted.

Added by Acts 2011, 82nd Leg., ch. 823 (H.B. 2759), § 1.02, eff. Jan. 1, 2014.

### § 1203.102. Appointment Because of Resignation, Removal, or Death; Hearing to Set Aside Immediate Appointment

(a) If a guardian resigns, is removed, or dies, the court may appoint a successor guardian on application and on service of notice as directed by the court, except as provided by Subsection (b). In the event the guardian of the person or of the estate of a ward dies, a personal representative of the deceased guardian, at the time and in the manner ordered by the court, shall account for, pay, and deliver all guardianship property entrusted to the representative's care to a person legally entitled to receive the property.

(b) The court may appoint a successor guardian under this section without citation or notice if the court finds that a necessity exists for the immediate appointment. Subject to an order of the court, a successor guardian has the rights and powers of the removed guardian.

(c) The appointment of a successor guardian under Subsection (b) does not preclude an interested person from filing an application to be appointed guardian of the ward for whom the successor guardian was appointed. The court shall hold a hearing on an application filed under the circumstances described by this subsection. At the conclusion of the hearing, the court may set aside the appointment of the successor guardian and appoint the applicant as the ward's guardian if the applicant is not disqualified and after considering the requirements of Subchapter B or C, Chapter 1104, as applicable.

(d) If the court sets aside the appointment of the successor guardian under this section, the court may require the successor guardian to prepare and file, under oath, an accounting of the estate and to detail the disposition the successor has made of the estate property.

Added by Acts 2011, 82nd Leg., ch. 823 (H.B. 2759), § 1.02, eff. Jan. 1, 2014. Amended by Acts 2013, 83rd Leg., ch. 161 (S.B. 1093), §§ 6.057, 6.058, eff. Jan. 1, 2014.

## § 1203.103. Appointment Because of Existence of Prior Right

If letters of guardianship have been granted to a person and another person applies for letters, the previously issued letters shall be revoked, and letters shall be granted to the subsequent applicant if that applicant:

(1) is qualified;

(2) has a prior right to be appointed successor guardian; and

(3) has not waived that prior right.

Added by Acts 2011, 82nd Leg., ch. 823 (H.B. 2759), § 1.02, eff. Jan. 1, 2014.

## § 1203.104. Appointment When Guardian Named in Will Becomes an Adult

(a) A person named as guardian in a will who was not an adult when the will was probated is entitled to have letters of guardianship that were granted to another person revoked and appropriate letters granted to the named guardian on proof that the named guardian has become an adult and is not otherwise disqualified from serving as a guardian.

(b) This subsection applies only if a will names two or more persons as guardian. A person named as a guardian in the will who was a minor when the will was probated may, on becoming an adult, qualify and receive letters of guardianship if:

(1) letters have been issued to the named guardians in the will who are adults; and

(2) the person is not otherwise disqualified from receiving letters.

Added by Acts 2011, 82nd Leg., ch. 823 (H.B. 2759), § 1.02, eff. Jan. 1, 2014.

## § 1203.105. Appointment of Formerly Ill or Absent Guardian Named in Will

(a) This section applies only to a person named as guardian in a will who was ill or absent from the state when the testator died or the will was proved and, as a result, could not:

(1) present the will for probate not later than the 30th day after the testator's death; or

(2) accept and qualify as guardian not later than the 20th day after the date the will was probated.

(b) A person to whom this section applies may accept and qualify as guardian not later than the 60th day after the date the person recovers from illness or returns to the state if proof is presented to the court that the person was ill or absent.

(c) If a person accepts and qualifies as guardian under Subsection (b) and letters of guardianship have been issued to another person, the other person's letters shall be revoked.

Added by Acts 2011, 82nd Leg., ch. 823 (H.B. 2759), § 1.02, eff. Jan. 1, 2014.

## § 1203.106. Appointment When Will Discovered After Grant of Letters

If, after letters of guardianship have been issued, it is discovered that the decedent left a lawful will, the letters shall be revoked and proper letters shall be issued to a person entitled to the letters.

Added by Acts 2011, 82nd Leg., ch. 823 (H.B. 2759), § 1.02, eff. Jan. 1, 2014.

## § 1203.107. Appointment on Removal of Litigation Conflict

The court may appoint as successor guardian a spouse, parent, or child of a proposed ward who was disqualified from serving as guardian because of a litigation conflict under Section 1104.354(1) on the removal of the conflict that caused the disqualification if the spouse, parent, or child is otherwise qualified to serve as a guardian.

Added by Acts 2011, 82nd Leg., ch. 823 (H.B. 2759), § 1.02, eff. Jan. 1, 2014.

## § 1203.108. Appointment of Department of Aging and Disability Services as Successor Guardian

(a) In this section, "department" means the Department of Aging and Disability Services.

(b) The court may appoint the department as a successor guardian of the person or estate, or both, of a ward who has been adjudicated as totally incapacitated if:

(1) there is no less-restrictive alternative to continuation of the guardianship;

(2) there is no family member or other suitable person, including a guardianship program, willing and able to serve as the ward's successor guardian;

(3) the ward is located more than 100 miles from the court that created the guardianship;

(4) the ward has private assets or access to government benefits to pay for the ward's needs;

(5) the department is served with citation and a hearing is held regarding the department's appointment as proposed successor guardian; and

(6) the appointment of the department does not violate a limitation imposed by Subsection (c).

(c) The number of appointments under Subsection (b) is subject to an annual limit of 55. The appointments must be distributed equally or as equally as possible among the health and human services regions of this state. The department, at the department's discretion, may establish a different distribution scheme to promote the efficient use and administration of resources.

(d) If the department is named as a proposed successor guardian in an application in which the department is not the applicant, citation must be issued and served on the department as provided by Section 1051.103(5).

Added by Acts 2011, 82nd Leg., ch. 823 (H.B. 2759), § 1.02, eff. Jan. 1, 2014.

## SUBCHAPTER D. SUCCESSOR GUARDIANS FOR WARDS OF GUARDIANSHIP PROGRAMS OR GOVERNMENTAL ENTITIES

### § 1203.151. Notice of Availability of Successor Guardian

(a) If a guardianship program or governmental entity serving as a guardian for a ward under this title becomes aware of a family member or friend of the ward, or any other interested person, who is willing and able to serve as the ward's successor guardian, the program or entity shall notify the court in which the guardianship is pending of the individual's willingness and ability to serve.

(b) If, while serving as a guardian for a ward under this title, the Department of Aging and Disability Services becomes aware of a guardianship program or private professional guardian willing and able to serve as the ward's successor guardian, and the department is not aware of a family member or friend of the ward, or any other interested person, who is willing and able to serve in that capacity, the department shall notify the court in which the guardianship is pending of the guardianship program's or private professional guardian's willingness and ability to serve.

Added by Acts 2011, 82nd Leg., ch. 823 (H.B. 2759), § 1.02, eff. Jan. 1, 2014.

### § 1203.152. Determination of Proposed Successor Guardian's Qualification to Serve

When the court is notified of the existence of a proposed successor guardian under Section 1203.151(a), or the court otherwise becomes aware of a family member, a friend, or any other interested person who is willing and able to serve as a successor guardian for a ward of a guardianship program or governmental entity, the court shall determine whether the proposed successor guardian is qualified to serve under this title as the ward's successor guardian.

Added by Acts 2011, 82nd Leg., ch. 823 (H.B. 2759), § 1.02, eff. Jan. 1, 2014.

### § 1203.153. Application to Appoint Successor Guardian

(a) If the court finds under Section 1203.152 that the proposed successor guardian for a ward is not disqualified from being appointed as the ward's successor guardian under Subchapter H, Chapter 1104, and that the appointment is in the ward's best interests, the guardianship program or governmental entity serving as the ward's guardian or the court, on the court's own motion, may file an application to appoint the individual as the ward's successor guardian.

(b) Service of notice on an application filed under this section shall be made as directed by the court.

Added by Acts 2011, 82nd Leg., ch. 823 (H.B. 2759), § 1.02, eff. Jan. 1, 2014.

## SUBCHAPTER E. PROCEDURES AFTER RESIGNATION, REMOVAL, OR DEATH OF GUARDIAN

### § 1203.201. Payment to Ward While Office of Guardian is Vacant

(a) A debtor, obligor, or payor may pay or tender money or another thing of value falling due to a ward while the office of guardian is vacant to the court clerk for the credit of the ward.

(b) Payment or tender under Subsection (a) discharges the debtor, obligor, or payor of the obligation for all purposes to the extent and purpose of the payment or tender.

(c) The court clerk shall issue a receipt for any payment or tender accepted under this section.

Added by Acts 2011, 82nd Leg., ch. 823 (H.B. 2759), § 1.02, eff. Jan. 1, 2014.

## § 1203.202. Rights, Powers, and Duties of Successor Guardian

(a) A successor guardian has the rights and powers and is subject to all the duties of the predecessor.

(b) A guardian who accepts appointment and qualifies after letters of guardianship have been granted on the estate shall:

(1) succeed in like manner to the predecessor; and

(2) administer the estate in like manner as if the guardian's administration were a continuation of the former administration.

(c) A successor guardian may:

(1) make himself or herself, and be made, a party to a suit prosecuted by or against the successor's predecessor;

(2) settle with the predecessor and receive and give a receipt for any portion of the estate property that remains in the successor's possession; or

(3) commence a suit on the bond or bonds of the predecessor, in the successor's own name and capacity, for all the estate property that:

(A) came into the predecessor's possession; and

(B) has not been accounted for by the predecessor.

Added by Acts 2011, 82nd Leg., ch. 823 (H.B. 2759), § 1.02, eff. Jan. 1, 2014.

## § 1203.203. Successor Guardian to Return Inventory, Appraisement, and List of Claims

(a) A successor guardian who has qualified to succeed a former guardian shall, in the manner required of an original appointee:

(1) make and return to the court an inventory, appraisement, and list of claims of the estate not later than the 30th day after the date the successor qualifies; and

(2) return additional inventories, appraisements, and lists of claims.

(b) On the application of any person interested in the estate, the court shall, in an order appointing a successor guardian, appoint an appraiser as in an original appointment of a guardian.

Added by Acts 2011, 82nd Leg., ch. 823 (H.B. 2759), § 1.02, eff. Jan. 1, 2014.

## CHAPTER 1204. FINAL SETTLEMENT, ACCOUNTING, AND DISCHARGE

### SUBCHAPTER A. TIME FOR SETTLEMENT OF GUARDIANSHIP

### SUBCHAPTER B. PAYMENT OF CERTAIN EXPENSES AND DEBTS

### SUBCHAPTER C. ACCOUNT FOR FINAL SETTLEMENT

### SUBCHAPTER D. CLOSING OF GUARDIANSHIP AND DISCHARGE OF GUARDIAN

### SUBCHAPTER E. FAILURE OF GUARDIAN TO ACT

## SUBCHAPTER A. TIME FOR SETTLEMENT OF GUARDIANSHIP

### § 1204.001. Settlement of Guardianship

(a) A guardianship shall be settled and closed as provided by this section and Section 1202.001.

(b) A guardianship of the estate of a ward shall be settled when:

(1) the ward dies;

(2) a minor ward becomes an adult by:

(A) becoming 18 years of age;

(B) removal of disabilities of minority according to the law of this state; or

(C) marriage;

(3) an incapacitated ward is decreed as provided by law to have been restored to full legal capacity;

(4) the spouse of a married ward has qualified as survivor in community and the ward does not own separate property;

(5) the ward's estate is exhausted;

(6) the foreseeable income accruing to the ward or to the ward's estate is so negligible that maintaining the guardianship in force would be burdensome;

(7) all of the assets of the estate have been placed in a management trust under Chapter 1301 or have been transferred to a pooled trust subaccount in accordance with a court order issued as provided by Chapter 1302, and the court determines that a guardianship of the ward's estate is no longer necessary; or

(8) the court determines for any other reason that a guardianship for the ward is no longer necessary.

(c) In a case arising under Subsection (b)(6), the court may authorize the income to be paid to a parent, or other person who has acted as guardian of the ward, to assist in the maintenance of the ward and without liability to account to the court for the income.

(d) If the estate of a minor ward consists only of cash or cash equivalents in an amount of $100,000 or less, the guardianship of the estate may be terminated and the assets paid to the county clerk of the county in which the guardianship proceeding is pending, and the clerk shall manage the funds as provided by Chapter 1355.

(e) In the settlement of a guardianship of the estate, the court may appoint an attorney ad litem to represent the ward's interests and may allow the attorney ad litem reasonable compensation to be taxed as costs.

Added by Acts 2011, 82nd Leg., ch. 823 (H.B. 2759), § 1.02, eff. Jan. 1, 2014. Amended by Acts 2013, 83rd Leg., ch. 161 (S.B. 1093), § 6.059, eff. Jan. 1, 2014.

### § 1204.002. Appointment of Attorney ad Litem to Represent Ward in Final Settlement Under Certain Circumstances

(a) The court may appoint an attorney ad litem to represent the ward's interest in the final settlement with the guardian if:

(1) the ward is deceased and there is no executor or administrator of the ward's estate;

(2) the ward is a nonresident; or

(3) the ward's residence is unknown.

(b) The court shall allow the attorney ad litem appointed under this section reasonable compensation out of the ward's estate for any services provided by the attorney.

Added by Acts 2011, 82nd Leg., ch. 823 (H.B. 2759), § 1.02, eff. Jan. 1, 2014.

## SUBCHAPTER B. PAYMENT OF CERTAIN EXPENSES AND DEBTS

### § 1204.051. Funeral Arrangements and Other Debts; Account for Final Settlement on Complaint of Personal Representative

Before a guardianship of the person or estate of a ward is closed on the ward's death, the guardian may, subject to the court's approval, make all funeral arrangements and pay the funeral expenses and all other debts out of the deceased ward's estate. If a personal representative of the estate of a deceased ward is appointed, the court shall on the written complaint of the personal representative have the guardian of the deceased ward cited to appear and present an account for final settlement as provided by Section 1204.101.

Added by Acts 2011, 82nd Leg., ch. 823 (H.B. 2759), § 1.02, eff. Jan. 1, 2014.

### § 1204.052. Taxes and Expenses of Administration; Sale of Estate Property

Notwithstanding any other provision of this title, a probate court in which proceedings to declare heirship are maintained may order:

(1) the guardian to pay any taxes or expenses of administering the estate; and

(2) the sale of property in the ward's estate, when necessary, to:

(A) pay the taxes or expenses of administering the estate; or

(B) distribute the estate among the heirs.

Added by Acts 2011, 82nd Leg., ch. 823 (H.B. 2759), § 1.02, eff. Jan. 1, 2014.

### § 1204.053. Inheritance Taxes; Limitation on Closing Estate

If the guardian has been ordered to pay inheritance taxes under this code, a deceased ward's estate may not be closed unless the account for final settlement shows and the court finds that all inheritance taxes due and owing to this state with respect to all interests and property passing through the guardian's possession have been paid.

Added by Acts 2011, 82nd Leg., ch. 823 (H.B. 2759), § 1.02, eff. Jan. 1, 2014.

### SUBCHAPTER C.  ACCOUNT FOR FINAL SETTLEMENT

### § 1204.101.  Verified Account Required

A guardian of the estate shall present to the court the guardian's verified account for final settlement when the guardianship of the estate is required to be settled.

Added by Acts 2011, 82nd Leg., ch. 823 (H.B. 2759), § 1.02, eff. Jan. 1, 2014.

### § 1204.102.  Contents of Account

(a) Except as provided by Subsection (b), it is sufficient for an account for final settlement to:

(1) refer to the inventory without describing each item of property in detail; and

(2) refer to and adopt any guardianship proceeding concerning sales, renting, leasing for mineral development, or any other transaction on behalf of the guardianship estate, including an exhibit, account, or voucher previously filed and approved, without restating the particular items.

(b) An account for final settlement shall be accompanied by proper vouchers supporting each item included in the account for which the guardian has not already accounted and, either by reference to any proceeding described by Subsection (a) or by a statement of the facts, must show:

(1) the property, rents, revenues, and profits received by the guardian, and belonging to the ward, during the term of the guardianship;

(2) the disposition made of the property, rents, revenues, and profits;

(3) any expenses and debts against the estate that remain unpaid;

(4) any estate property that remains in the guardian's possession;

(5) that the guardian has paid all required bond premiums;

(6) the tax returns the guardian has filed during the guardianship;

(7) the amount of taxes the ward owed during the guardianship that the guardian has paid;

(8) a complete account of the taxes the guardian has paid during the guardianship, including:

(A) the amount of the taxes;

(B) the date the guardian paid the taxes; and

(C) the name of the governmental entity to which the guardian paid the taxes;

(9) a description of all current delinquencies in the filing of tax returns and the payment of taxes, including a reason for each delinquency; and

(10) other facts as appear necessary to a full and definite understanding of the exact condition of the guardianship.

Added by Acts 2011, 82nd Leg., ch. 823 (H.B. 2759), § 1.02, eff. Jan. 1, 2014.

### § 1204.103.  Certain Debts Excluded From Settlement Computation

In the settlement of any of the accounts of the guardian of the estate, all debts due the estate that the court is satisfied could not have been collected by due diligence and that have not been collected shall be excluded from the computation.

Added by Acts 2011, 82nd Leg., ch. 823 (H.B. 2759), § 1.02, eff. Jan. 1, 2014.

### § 1204.104.  Guardian to Account for Ward's Labor or Services

(a) Subject to Subsection (b), the guardian of a ward shall account for:

(1) the reasonable value of labor or services provided by the ward; or

(2) the proceeds of labor or services provided by the ward.

(b) The guardian is entitled to reasonable credits for the board, clothing, and maintenance of the ward.

Added by Acts 2011, 82nd Leg., ch. 823 (H.B. 2759), § 1.02, eff. Jan. 1, 2014.

### § 1204.105. Citation and Notice on Presentation of Account

(a) On presentation of an account for final settlement by a guardian of the estate of a ward, the county clerk shall issue citation to the persons and in the manner provided by this section.

(b) Citation issued under Subsection (a) must contain:

(1) a statement that an account for final settlement has been presented;

(2) the time and place the court will consider the account; and

(3) a statement requiring the person cited to appear and contest the account, if the person determines contesting the account is proper.

(c) Except as provided by Subsection (d) or (e), the county clerk shall:

(1) issue a citation to be personally served on a ward if:

(A) the ward is 14 years of age or older;

(B) the ward is a living resident of this state; and

(C) the ward's residence is known;

(2) issue a citation to be personally served on the executor or administrator of a deceased ward's estate, if one has been appointed; and

(3) issue a citation to a ward or the ward's estate by publication, or by posting if directed by written court order, if:

(A) the ward's residence is unknown;

(B) the ward is not a resident of this state; or

(C) the ward is deceased and no representative of the ward's estate has been appointed and has qualified in this state.

(d) The ward, in person or by attorney, may waive by writing filed with the county clerk the issuance and personal service of citation required by Subsection (c)(1).

(e) Service of citation is not required under Subsection (c)(2) if the executor or administrator is the same person as the guardian.

(f) The court may allow the waiver of notice of an account for final settlement in a guardianship proceeding.

(g) The court by written order shall require additional notice if the court considers the additional notice necessary.

Added by Acts 2011, 82nd Leg., ch. 823 (H.B. 2759), § 1.02, eff. Jan. 1, 2014.

### § 1204.106. Examination of and Hearing on Account

(a) On the court's satisfaction that citation has been properly served on all persons interested in the guardianship estate, the court shall examine the account for final settlement and the accompanying vouchers.

(b) After hearing all exceptions or objections to the account and evidence in support of or against the account, the court shall audit and settle the account and, if necessary, restate the account.

Added by Acts 2011, 82nd Leg., ch. 823 (H.B. 2759), § 1.02, eff. Jan. 1, 2014.

### § 1204.107. Assets Becoming Due Pending Final Settlement; Receipt and Discharge

(a) This section does not apply to money or another thing of value held under Section 1105.153.

(b) Until the order of final discharge of the guardian is entered in the judge's guardianship docket, money or another thing of value falling due to the ward or the ward's estate while the account for final settlement is pending may be paid or tendered to the emancipated ward, the guardian, or the personal representative of the deceased ward's estate. The ward, guardian, or personal representative to whom the money or other thing of value is paid or tendered shall issue a receipt for the money or other thing of value, and the obligor or payor is discharged of the obligation for all purposes.

Added by Acts 2011, 82nd Leg., ch. 823 (H.B. 2759), § 1.02, eff. Jan. 1, 2014.

### § 1204.108. Delivery of Ward's Property in Possession of Guardian of the Person on Settlement of Guardianship of the Estate

(a) If the guardianship of a ward is required to be settled as provided by Section 1204. 001, the guardian of the person shall deliver all of the ward's property in the guardian's possession or control to the emancipated ward or other person entitled to the property. If the ward is deceased, the guardian shall deliver the property to the personal representative of the deceased ward's estate or other person entitled to the property.

(b) If none of the ward's property is in the guardian of the person's possession or control, the guardian shall, not later than the 60th day after the date the guardianship is required to be settled, file with the court a sworn affidavit that states:

(1) the reason the guardianship was terminated; and

(2) to whom the ward's property in the guardian's possession was delivered.

(c) The judge may issue orders as necessary for the best interests of the ward or the deceased ward's estate.

(d) This section does not discharge a guardian of the person from liability for breach of the guardian's fiduciary duties.

Added by Acts 2011, 82nd Leg., ch. 823 (H.B. 2759), § 1.02, eff. Jan. 1, 2014.

### § 1204.109.  Delivery of Remaining Estate Property

On final settlement of a guardianship estate, the court shall order that any part of the estate that remains in the guardian's possession be delivered to:

(1) the ward;

(2) the personal representative of the ward's estate, if the ward is deceased and a personal representative has been appointed;  or

(3) any other person legally entitled to the estate.

Added by Acts 2011, 82nd Leg., ch. 823 (H.B. 2759), § 1.02, eff. Jan. 1, 2014.

## SUBCHAPTER D.  CLOSING OF GUARDIANSHIP AND DISCHARGE OF GUARDIAN

### § 1204.151.  Discharge of Guardian When no Estate Property Remains

The court shall enter an order discharging a guardian from the guardian's trust and closing the guardianship estate if, on final settlement of the estate, none of the estate remains in the guardian's possession.

Added by Acts 2011, 82nd Leg., ch. 823 (H.B. 2759), § 1.02, eff. Jan. 1, 2014.

### § 1204.152.  Discharge of Guardian When Estate Fully Administered

The court shall enter an order discharging a guardian of the estate from the guardian's trust and declaring the estate closed when:

(1) the guardian has fully administered the estate in accordance with this title and the court's orders;

(2) the guardian's account for final settlement has been approved;  and

(3) the guardian has delivered all of the estate remaining in the guardian's possession to any person entitled to receive the estate.

Added by Acts 2011, 82nd Leg., ch. 823 (H.B. 2759), § 1.02, eff. Jan. 1, 2014.

## SUBCHAPTER E.  FAILURE OF GUARDIAN TO ACT

### § 1204.201.  Failure to Present Final Account or Report

(a) The court may, on the court's own motion, and shall, on the written complaint of the emancipated ward or anyone interested in the ward or the ward's estate, have the guardian who is charged with the duty of presenting a final account or report cited to appear and present the account or report within the time specified in the citation if the guardian failed or neglected to present the account or report at the proper time.

(b) If a written complaint has not been filed by anyone interested in the guardianship of the person or estate of a minor or deceased ward, on or after the third anniversary of the date the minor ward reaches the age of majority or the date the ward dies, as applicable, the court may remove the estate from the court's active docket without a final accounting and without appointing a successor personal representative.

(c) If a complaint has not been filed by anyone interested in the estate of a ward whose whereabouts are unknown to the court, on or after the fourth anniversary of the date the ward's whereabouts became unknown to the court, the court may remove the estate from the court's active docket without a final accounting and without appointing a successor personal representative.

Added by Acts 2011, 82nd Leg., ch. 823 (H.B. 2759), § 1.02, eff. Jan. 1, 2014.

## § 1204.202. Liability for Failure to Deliver Estate Property

(a) On final settlement or termination of the guardianship of the estate, if the guardian neglects when legally demanded to deliver a portion of the estate or any funds or money in the guardian's possession ordered to be delivered to a person entitled to that property, the person may file with the court clerk a written complaint alleging:

(1) the fact of the neglect;

(2) the date of the person's demand; and

(3) other relevant facts.

(b) After the filing of a complaint under Subsection (a), the court clerk shall issue a citation to be served personally on the guardian. The citation must:

(1) apprise the guardian of the complaint; and

(2) cite the guardian to appear before the court and answer, if the guardian desires, at a time designated in the citation.

(c) If at the hearing the court finds that the citation was properly served and returned, and that the guardian is guilty of the neglect charged, the court shall enter an order to that effect.

(d) If the court enters an order under Subsection (c), the guardian is liable to the person who filed the complaint under Subsection (a) for damages at the rate of 10 percent of the amount or appraised value of the money or estate withheld, per month, for each month or fraction of a month that the estate or money of a guardianship of the estate, or on termination of guardianship of the person, or funds is or has been withheld by the guardian after the date of demand. Damages under this subsection may be recovered in any court of competent jurisdiction.

Added by Acts 2011, 82nd Leg., ch. 823 (H.B. 2759), § 1.02, eff. Jan. 1, 2014.

# SUBTITLE G. SPECIAL TYPES OF GUARDIANSHIPS

## CHAPTER 1251. TEMPORARY GUARDIANSHIPS

### SUBCHAPTER A. APPOINTMENT OF TEMPORARY GUARDIAN GENERALLY

### SUBCHAPTER B. TEMPORARY GUARDIANSHIP PENDING CHALLENGE OR CONTEST OF CERTAIN GUARDIANSHIP APPLICATIONS

### SUBCHAPTER C. POWERS AND DUTIES OF TEMPORARY GUARDIANS

### SUBCHAPTER D. EXPIRATION AND CLOSING OF TEMPORARY GUARDIANSHIP

## SUBCHAPTER A. APPOINTMENT OF TEMPORARY GUARDIAN GENERALLY

### § 1251.001. Appointment of Temporary Guardian

(a) A court shall appoint a temporary guardian, with limited powers as the circumstances of the case require, if the court:

(1) is presented with substantial evidence that a person may be an incapacitated person; and

(2) has probable cause to believe that the person, the person's estate, or both require the immediate appointment of a guardian.

(b) The person for whom a temporary guardian is appointed under this chapter retains all rights and powers that are not specifically granted to the person's temporary guardian by court order.

Added by Acts 2011, 82nd Leg., ch. 823 (H.B. 2759), § 1.02, eff. Jan. 1, 2014.

### § 1251.002. No Presumption of Incapacity

A person for whom a temporary guardian is appointed under this chapter may not be presumed to be incapacitated.

Added by Acts 2011, 82nd Leg., ch. 823 (H.B. 2759), § 1.02, eff. Jan. 1, 2014.

## § 1251.003. Application

(a) A sworn, written application for the appointment of a temporary guardian shall be filed before the court appoints a temporary guardian.

(b) The application must state:

(1) the name and address of the person who is the subject of the guardianship proceeding;

(2) the danger to the person or property alleged to be imminent;

(3) the type of appointment and the particular protection and assistance being requested;

(4) the facts and reasons supporting the allegations and requests;

(5) the proposed temporary guardian's name, address, and qualification;

(6) the applicant's name, address, and interest; and

*Text of subsec. (b)(7) effective until Sept. 1, 2014*

(7) if applicable, that the proposed temporary guardian is a private professional guardian who is certified under Subchapter C, Chapter 111, Government Code, and has complied with the requirements of Subchapter G, Chapter 1104.

*Text of subsec. (b)(7) effective Sept. 1, 2014*

(7) if applicable, that the proposed temporary guardian is a private professional guardian who is certified under Subchapter C, Chapter 155, Government Code, and has complied with the requirements of Subchapter G, Chapter 1104.

Added by Acts 2011, 82nd Leg., ch. 823 (H.B. 2759), § 1.02, eff. Jan. 1, 2014. Amended by Acts 2013, 83rd Leg., ch. 42 (S.B. 966), § 2.22, eff. Sept. 1, 2014.

## § 1251.004. Appointment of Attorney

On the filing of an application for temporary guardianship, the court shall appoint an attorney to represent the proposed ward in all guardianship proceedings in which independent counsel has not been retained by or on behalf of the proposed ward.

Added by Acts 2011, 82nd Leg., ch. 823 (H.B. 2759), § 1.02, eff. Jan. 1, 2014.

## § 1251.005. Notice of Application

(a) On the filing of an application for temporary guardianship, the clerk shall issue notice to be served on:

(1) the proposed ward;

(2) the proposed ward's appointed attorney; and

(3) the proposed temporary guardian named in the application, if that person is not the applicant.

(b) The notice must describe:

(1) the rights of the parties; and

(2) the date, time, place, purpose, and possible consequences of a hearing on the application.

(c) A copy of the application must be attached to the notice.

Added by Acts 2011, 82nd Leg., ch. 823 (H.B. 2759), § 1.02, eff. Jan. 1, 2014.

## § 1251.006. Scheduling of Hearing

(a) Immediately after an application for a temporary guardianship is filed, the court shall issue an order setting a certain date for the hearing on the application.

(b) Unless postponed as provided by Subsection (c), a hearing shall be held not later than the 10th day after the date the application for temporary guardianship is filed.

(c) The proposed ward or the proposed ward's attorney may consent to postpone the hearing on the application for temporary guardianship for a period not to exceed 30 days after the date the application is filed.

(d) An application for temporary guardianship takes precedence over all matters except older matters of the same character.

Added by Acts 2011, 82nd Leg., ch. 823 (H.B. 2759), § 1.02, eff. Jan. 1, 2014.

## § 1251.007. Motion for Dismissal of Application

(a) Subject to Subsection (b), the proposed ward or the proposed ward's attorney may appear and move for the dismissal of the application for temporary guardianship.

(b) At least one day before making a motion under Subsection (a), the proposed ward or the proposed ward's attorney shall provide notice to the party who filed the application for temporary guardianship.

(c) If a motion is made for dismissal of the application for temporary guardianship, the court shall hear and determine the motion as expeditiously as justice requires.

Added by Acts 2011, 82nd Leg., ch. 823 (H.B. 2759), § 1.02, eff. Jan. 1, 2014.

## § 1251.008. Rights of Proposed Ward at Hearing

At a hearing under this subchapter, the proposed ward has the right to:

(1) receive prior notice;

(2) be represented by counsel;

(3) be present;

(4) present evidence;

(5) confront and cross-examine witnesses; and

(6) a closed hearing if requested by the proposed ward or the proposed ward's attorney.

Added by Acts 2011, 82nd Leg., ch. 823 (H.B. 2759), § 1.02, eff. Jan. 1, 2014.

## § 1251.009. Appearance by Proposed Temporary Guardian in Certain Circumstances

If the applicant for a temporary guardianship is not the proposed temporary guardian, a temporary guardianship may not be granted before a hearing on the application required by Section 1251.006(b) unless the proposed temporary guardian appears in court.

Added by Acts 2011, 82nd Leg., ch. 823 (H.B. 2759), § 1.02, eff. Jan. 1, 2014.

## § 1251.010. Order Appointing Temporary Guardian

(a) The court shall appoint a temporary guardian by written order if, at the conclusion of the hearing required by Section 1251.006(b), the court determines that the applicant has established that there is substantial evidence that the proposed ward is an incapacitated person, that there is imminent danger that the proposed ward's physical health or safety will be seriously impaired, or that the proposed ward's estate will be seriously damaged or dissipated unless immediate action is taken.

(b) The court shall assign to the temporary guardian only those powers and duties that are necessary to protect the proposed ward against the imminent danger shown.

(c) The order appointing the temporary guardian must describe:

(1) the reasons for the temporary guardianship; and

(2) the powers and duties of the temporary guardian.

Added by Acts 2011, 82nd Leg., ch. 823 (H.B. 2759), § 1.02, eff. Jan. 1, 2014.

## § 1251.011. Certain Agency as Temporary Guardian

A court may not ordinarily appoint the Department of Aging and Disability Services as a temporary guardian under this chapter. The appointment of the department as a temporary guardian under this chapter should be made only as a last resort.

Added by Acts 2011, 82nd Leg., ch. 823 (H.B. 2759), § 1.02, eff. Jan. 1, 2014.

## § 1251.012. Temporary Guardian's Bond

The court shall set bond for a temporary guardian according to Chapter 1105.

Added by Acts 2011, 82nd Leg., ch. 823 (H.B. 2759), § 1.02, eff. Jan. 1, 2014.

## § 1251.013. Court Costs

If the court appoints a temporary guardian after the hearing required by Section 1251.006(b), all court costs, including attorney's fees, may be assessed as provided by Sections 1155.054 and 1155.151.

Added by Acts 2011, 82nd Leg., ch. 823 (H.B. 2759), § 1.02, eff. Jan. 1, 2014. Amended by Acts 2013, 83rd Leg., ch. 982 (H.B. 2080), § 24, eff. Jan. 1, 2014.

Section 36 of Acts 2013, 83rd Leg., ch. 982 (H.B. 2080) provides:

"(a) Except as otherwise provided by this section, the changes in law made by this Act apply to:

"(1) a guardianship created before, on, or after the effective date [Jan. 1, 2014] of this Act; and

"(2) an application for a guardianship pending on, or filed on or after, the effective date of this Act.

"(b) The changes in law made by this Act to Sections 1301.054, 1301.055, 1301.057(b), (c), and (d), 1301.058, 1301.101, and 1301.102(a), Estates Code, apply only to an application for the creation, modification, or termination of a management trust that is filed on or after the effective date of this Act. An application described by this subsection that is filed before the effective date of this Act is governed by the law in effect on the date the application was filed, and the former law is continued in effect for that purpose.

"(c) The changes in law made by this Act to Sections 1301.103 and 1301.154(a), Estates Code, and by Section 1301.202(a–1), Estates Code, as added by this Act, apply to a management trust created before, on, or after the effective date of this Act.

"(d) The changes in law made by this Act to Section 1102.003, Estates Code, apply to a guardianship proceeding that is commenced on or after the effective date of this Act. A guardianship proceeding commenced before that date is governed by the law in effect on the date the proceeding was commenced, and the former law is continued in effect for that purpose."

## SUBCHAPTER B. TEMPORARY GUARDIANSHIP PENDING CHALLENGE OR CONTEST OF CERTAIN GUARDIANSHIP APPLICATIONS

## § 1251.051. Authority to Appoint Temporary Guardian or Grant Restraining Order

The court, on the court's own motion or on the motion of any interested party, may appoint a temporary guardian or grant a temporary restraining order under Rule 680, Texas Rules of Civil Procedure, or both, without issuing additional citation if:

(1) an application for a temporary guardianship, for the conversion of a temporary guardianship to a permanent guardianship, or for a permanent guardianship is challenged or contested; and

(2) the court finds that the appointment or the issuance of the order is necessary to protect the proposed ward or the proposed ward's estate.

Added by Acts 2011, 82nd Leg., ch. 823 (H.B. 2759), § 1.02, eff. Jan. 1, 2014.

### § 1251.052. Qualification and Duration of Certain Temporary Guardianships

(a) A temporary guardian appointed under Section 1251.051 must qualify in the same form and manner required of a guardian under this title.

(b) The term of a temporary guardian appointed under Section 1251.051 expires:

(1) at the conclusion of the hearing challenging or contesting the application; or

(2) on the date a permanent guardian appointed by the court for the proposed ward qualifies to serve as the ward's guardian.

Added by Acts 2011, 82nd Leg., ch. 823 (H.B. 2759), § 1.02, eff. Jan. 1, 2014.

## SUBCHAPTER C. POWERS AND DUTIES OF TEMPORARY GUARDIANS

### § 1251.101. Authority of Temporary Guardian

(a) When the temporary guardian files the oath and bond required under this title, the court order appointing the temporary guardian takes effect without the necessity for issuance of letters of guardianship.

(b) The clerk shall note compliance with the oath and bond requirements by the appointed temporary guardian on a certificate attached to the order.

(c) The order appointing the temporary guardian is evidence of the temporary guardian's authority to act within the scope of the powers and duties stated in the order.

(d) The clerk may not issue certified copies of the order until the oath and bond requirements are satisfied.

Added by Acts 2011, 82nd Leg., ch. 823 (H.B. 2759), § 1.02, eff. Jan. 1, 2014.

### § 1251.102. Applicability of Guardianship Provisions

The provisions of this title relating to the guardianship of the persons and estates of incapacitated persons apply to the temporary guardianship of the persons and estates of incapacitated persons, to the extent the provisions may be made applicable.

Added by Acts 2011, 82nd Leg., ch. 823 (H.B. 2759), § 1.02, eff. Jan. 1, 2014.

## SUBCHAPTER D. EXPIRATION AND CLOSING OF TEMPORARY GUARDIANSHIP

### § 1251.151. Duration of Temporary Guardianship

Except as provided by Section 1251.052, a temporary guardianship may not remain in effect for more than 60 days.

Added by Acts 2011, 82nd Leg., ch. 823 (H.B. 2759), § 1.02, eff. Jan. 1, 2014.

### § 1251.152. Accounting

(a) At the expiration of a temporary guardianship, the temporary guardian shall file with the court clerk:

(1) a sworn list of all estate property that has come into the temporary guardian's possession;

(2) a return of all sales made by the temporary guardian; and

(3) a full exhibit and account of all the temporary guardian's acts as temporary guardian.

(b) The court shall act on the list, return, exhibit, and account filed under Subsection (a).

Added by Acts 2011, 82nd Leg., ch. 823 (H.B. 2759), § 1.02, eff. Jan. 1, 2014.

### § 1251.153. Delivery of Estate; Discharge of Temporary Guardian

(a) When temporary letters expire or cease to be effective for any reason, the court immediately shall enter an order requiring the temporary guardian to deliver the estate remaining in the temporary guardian's possession to the person legally entitled to possession of the estate.

(b) On proof of delivery under Subsection (a):

(1) the temporary guardian shall be discharged; and

(2) the sureties on the temporary guardian's bond shall be released as to future liability.

Added by Acts 2011, 82nd Leg., ch. 823 (H.B. 2759), § 1.02, eff. Jan. 1, 2014.

## CHAPTER 1252. GUARDIANSHIPS FOR NONRESIDENT WARDS

### SUBCHAPTER A. RESIDENT GUARDIAN OF NONRESIDENT WARD'S ESTATE

### SUBCHAPTER A. RESIDENT GUARDIAN OF NONRESIDENT WARD'S ESTATE

### § 1252.001. Granting of Guardianship of Estate for Nonresident

(a) A guardianship of the estate of a nonresident incapacitated person who owns property in this state may be granted, if necessary, in the same manner as for the property of a resident of this state.

(b) A court in the county in which the principal estate of the nonresident incapacitated person is located has jurisdiction to appoint the guardian.

Added by Acts 2011, 82nd Leg., ch. 823 (H.B. 2759), § 1.02, eff. Jan. 1, 2014.

### § 1252.002. Court Actions and Orders Concerning Estate

The court shall take all actions and make all necessary orders with respect to the estate described by Section 1252.001 of a nonresident ward for the maintenance, support, care, or education of the ward out of the proceeds of the estate, in the same manner as if the ward were a resident of this state sent abroad by the court for education or treatment.

Added by Acts 2011, 82nd Leg., ch. 823 (H.B. 2759), § 1.02, eff. Jan. 1, 2014.

### § 1252.003. Closing Resident Guardianship

The court shall close a resident guardianship of an estate granted under this subchapter if a qualified nonresident guardian of the estate later qualifies in this state under Section 1252.051 as a nonresident guardian.

Added by Acts 2011, 82nd Leg., ch. 823 (H.B. 2759), § 1.02, eff. Jan. 1, 2014.

### SUBCHAPTER B. NONRESIDENT GUARDIAN OF NONRESIDENT WARD'S ESTATE

### § 1252.051. Appointment and Qualification of Nonresident Guardian

(a) A nonresident of this state may be appointed and qualified as guardian or coguardian of a nonresident ward's estate located in this state in the same manner provided by this title for the appointment and qualification of a resident guardian of the estate of an incapacitated person if:

(1) a court of competent jurisdiction in the geographical jurisdiction in which the nonresident resides appointed the nonresident guardian;

(2) the nonresident is qualified as guardian or as a fiduciary legal representative by any name known in the foreign jurisdiction of the property or estate of the ward located in the jurisdiction of the foreign court; and

(3) the nonresident, with the written application for appointment, files in the county court of a county of this state in which all or part of the nonresident ward's estate is located a complete transcript of the proceedings from the records of the court in which the nonresident applicant was appointed.

(b) The transcript required by Subsection (a)(3) must:

(1) show the applicant's appointment and qualification as guardian or other fiduciary legal representative of the ward's property or estate;

(2) be certified to and attested by the clerk of the foreign court or the court officer charged by law with custody of the court records, under the court seal, if any; and

(3) have attached a certificate of the judge, chief justice, or presiding magistrate of the foreign court certifying that the attestation of the clerk or legal custodian of the court records is in correct form.

Added by Acts 2011, 82nd Leg., ch. 823 (H.B. 2759), § 1.02, eff. Jan. 1, 2014.

## § 1252.052. Appointment; Issuance of Letters of Guardianship

(a) If a nonresident applicant meets the requirements of Section 1252.051, without the necessity of notice or citation, the court shall enter an order appointing the nonresident as guardian or coguardian of a nonresident ward's estate located in this state.

(b) After the nonresident applicant qualifies in the manner required of resident guardians and files with the court a power of attorney appointing a resident agent to accept service of process in all actions or proceedings with respect to the estate, the clerk shall issue the letters of guardianship to the nonresident guardian.

Added by Acts 2011, 82nd Leg., ch. 823 (H.B. 2759), § 1.02, eff. Jan. 1, 2014.

## § 1252.053. Inventory and Appraisement; Administration of Estate

After qualification, a nonresident guardian:

(1) shall file an inventory and appraisement of the ward's estate in this state subject to the court's jurisdiction, as in ordinary cases; and

(2) is subject to the applicable provisions of this code governing the handling and settlement of an estate by a resident guardian.

Added by Acts 2011, 82nd Leg., ch. 823 (H.B. 2759), § 1.02, eff. Jan. 1, 2014.

## § 1252.054. Delivery of Estate to Certain Guardians

The court may order a resident guardian who has any of the ward's estate to deliver the estate to a qualified and acting guardian of the ward.

Added by Acts 2011, 82nd Leg., ch. 823 (H.B. 2759), § 1.02, eff. Jan. 1, 2014.

## § 1252.055. Removal of Ward's Property From State by Nonresident Guardian

Regardless of whether qualified under this title, a nonresident guardian may remove personal property of the ward from this state if:

(1) the removal does not conflict with the tenure of the property or the terms of the guardianship under which the property is held; and

(2) all known debts against the estate in this state are paid or secured by a bond payable to and approved by the judge of the court in which guardianship proceedings are pending in this state.

Added by Acts 2011, 82nd Leg., ch. 823 (H.B. 2759), § 1.02, eff. Jan. 1, 2014.

## CHAPTER 1253. INTERSTATE GUARDIANSHIPS

## SUBCHAPTER A.  TRANSFER OF GUARDIANSHIP TO FOREIGN JURISDICTION

## § 1253.001. Application to Transfer Guardianship to Foreign Jurisdiction

A guardian of the person or estate may apply to the court that has jurisdiction over the guardianship to transfer the guardianship to a court in a foreign jurisdiction to which the ward has permanently moved.

Added by Acts 2011, 82nd Leg., ch. 823 (H.B. 2759), § 1.02, eff. Jan. 1, 2014.

## § 1253.002.  Notice of Application

Notice of an application to transfer a guardianship under this subchapter shall be:

(1)  served personally on the ward;  and

(2)  given to the foreign court to which the guardianship is to be transferred.

Added by Acts 2011, 82nd Leg., ch. 823 (H.B. 2759), § 1.02, eff. Jan. 1, 2014.

## § 1253.003.  Determination Regarding Transfer of Guardianship

(a)  On the court's own motion or on the motion of the ward or any interested person, the court shall hold a hearing to consider an application to transfer a guardianship under this subchapter.

(b)  The court shall transfer a guardianship to a foreign court if the court determines the transfer is in the best interests of the ward.  The transfer of the guardianship must be made contingent on the acceptance of the guardianship in the foreign jurisdiction.

(c)  The court shall coordinate efforts with the appropriate foreign court to facilitate the orderly transfer of the guardianship.

Added by Acts 2011, 82nd Leg., ch. 823 (H.B. 2759), § 1.02, eff. Jan. 1, 2014.

## SUBCHAPTER B.  RECEIPT AND ACCEPTANCE OF FOREIGN GUARDIANSHIP

## § 1253.051.  Application for Receipt and Acceptance of Foreign Guardianship

A guardian appointed by a foreign court to represent an incapacitated person who is residing in this state or intends to move to this state may file an application with a court in which the ward resides or intends to reside to have the guardianship transferred to the court.  The application must have attached a certified copy of all papers of the guardianship filed and recorded in the foreign court.

Added by Acts 2011, 82nd Leg., ch. 823 (H.B. 2759), § 1.02, eff. Jan. 1, 2014.  Amended by Acts 2011, 82nd Leg., 1st C.S., ch. 4 (S.B. 1), § 66A.02, eff. Jan. 1, 2014.

## § 1253.052.  Notice of Application

Notice of an application for receipt and acceptance of a foreign guardianship under this subchapter shall be:

(1)  served personally on the ward;  and

(2)  given to the foreign court from which the guardianship is to be transferred.

Added by Acts 2011, 82nd Leg., ch. 823 (H.B. 2759), § 1.02, eff. Jan. 1, 2014.

## § 1253.053.  Determination Regarding Receipt and Acceptance of Foreign Guardianship

(a)  The court shall hold a hearing to:

(1)  consider an application for receipt and acceptance of a foreign guardianship under this subchapter;  and

(2)  consider modifying the administrative procedures or requirements of the proposed transferred guardianship in accordance with local and state law.

(b)  In reviewing the application, the court should determine:

(1)  that the proposed guardianship is not a collateral attack on an existing or proposed guardianship in another jurisdiction in this or another state;  and

(2)  for a guardianship in which a court in one or more states may have jurisdiction, that the application has been filed in the court that is best suited to consider the matter.

(c)  The court shall grant the application if the transfer of the guardianship from the foreign jurisdiction is in the best interests of the ward.

(d)  In granting the application, the court shall give full faith and credit to the provisions of the foreign guardianship order concerning the determination of the ward's incapacity and the rights, powers, and duties of the guardian.

(e)  The court shall coordinate efforts with the appropriate foreign court to facilitate the orderly transfer of the guardianship.

(f)  At the time of granting an application for receipt and acceptance of a foreign guardianship, the court may also modify the administrative procedures or requirements of the transferred guardianship in accordance with local and state law.

Added by Acts 2011, 82nd Leg., ch. 823 (H.B. 2759), § 1.02, eff. Jan. 1, 2014.  Amended by Acts 2011, 82nd Leg., 1st C.S., ch. 4 (S.B. 1), § 66A.03, eff. Jan. 1, 2014.

## § 1253.054.  [Blank]

## § 1253.055.  Guardianship Transfer Proceedings Filed in Two or More Courts

If an application for receipt and acceptance of a foreign guardianship under this subchapter is filed in two or more courts with jurisdiction, the proceeding shall be heard in the court with jurisdiction over the application filed on the earliest date, if venue is otherwise proper in that court. A court that does not have venue to hear the application shall transfer the proceeding to the proper court.

Added by Acts 2011, 82nd Leg., ch. 823 (H.B. 2759), § 1.02, eff. Jan. 1, 2014.

### § 1253.056.  Construction With Other Law

The denial of an application for receipt and acceptance of a guardianship under this subchapter does not affect the right of a guardian appointed by a foreign court to file an application to be appointed guardian of the incapacitated person under Section 1101.001.

Added by Acts 2011, 82nd Leg., ch. 823 (H.B. 2759), § 1.02, eff. Jan. 1, 2014.

## SUBCHAPTER C.  GUARDIANSHIP PROCEEDINGS FILED IN THIS STATE AND IN FOREIGN JURISDICTION

### § 1253.101.  Delay of Certain Guardianship Proceedings

A court in which a guardianship proceeding is filed and in which venue of the proceeding is proper may delay further action in the proceeding in that court if:

(1) another guardianship proceeding involving a matter at issue in the proceeding filed in the court is subsequently filed in a court in a foreign jurisdiction; and

(2) venue of the proceeding in the foreign court is proper.

Added by Acts 2011, 82nd Leg., ch. 823 (H.B. 2759), § 1.02, eff. Jan. 1, 2014.

### § 1253.102.  Determination of Venue; Action Following Determination

(a) A court that delays further action in a guardianship proceeding under Section 1253.101 shall determine whether venue of the proceeding is more suitable in that court or in the foreign court.

(b) In making a determination under Subsection (a), the court may consider:

(1) the interests of justice;

(2) the best interests of the ward or proposed ward;

(3) the convenience of the parties;  and

(4) the preference of the ward or proposed ward, if the ward or proposed ward is 12 years of age or older.

(c) The court shall resume the guardianship proceeding delayed under Section 1253.101 if the court determines under this section that venue is more suitable in that court. If the court determines that venue is more suitable in the foreign court, the court shall, with the consent of the foreign court, transfer the proceeding to that foreign court.

Added by Acts 2011, 82nd Leg., ch. 823 (H.B. 2759), § 1.02, eff. Jan. 1, 2014. Amended by Acts 2011, 82nd Leg., 1st C.S., ch. 4 (S.B. 1), § 66A.04, eff. Jan. 1, 2014.

### § 1253.103.  Necessary Orders

A court that delays further action in a guardianship proceeding under Section 1253.101 may issue any order the court considers necessary to protect the proposed ward or the proposed ward's estate.

Added by Acts 2011, 82nd Leg., ch. 823 (H.B. 2759), § 1.02, eff. Jan. 1, 2014.

## SUBCHAPTER D.  DETERMINATION OF MOST APPROPRIATE FORUM FOR CERTAIN GUARDIANSHIP PROCEEDINGS

### § 1253.151.  Determination of Acquisition of Jurisdiction in This State Due to Unjustifiable Conduct

If at any time a court of this state determines that it acquired jurisdiction of a proceeding for the appointment of a guardian of the person or estate, or both, of a ward or proposed ward because of unjustifiable conduct, the court may:

(1) decline to exercise jurisdiction;

(2) exercise jurisdiction for the limited purpose of fashioning an appropriate remedy to ensure the health, safety, and welfare of the ward or proposed ward or the protection of the ward's or proposed ward's property or prevent a repetition of the unjustifiable conduct, including staying the proceeding until a petition for the appointment of a guardian or issuance of a protective order is filed in a court of another state having jurisdiction; or

(3) continue to exercise jurisdiction after considering:

(A) the extent to which the ward or proposed ward and all persons required to be notified of the proceedings have acquiesced in the exercise of the court's jurisdiction;

(B) whether the court of this state is a more appropriate forum than the court of any other state after considering the factors described by Section 1253.102(b); and

(C) whether the court of any other state would have jurisdiction under the factual circumstances of the matter.

Added by Acts 2011, 82nd Leg., 1st C.S., ch. 4 (S.B. 1), § 66A.05, eff. Jan. 1, 2014.

### § 1253.152.  Assessment of Expenses Against Party

(a) If a court of this state determines that it acquired jurisdiction of a proceeding for the appointment of a guardian of the person or estate, or both, of a ward or proposed ward because a party seeking to invoke the court's jurisdiction engaged in unjustifiable conduct, the court may assess against that party necessary and reasonable expenses, including attorney's fees, investigative fees, court costs, communication expenses, witness fees and expenses, and travel expenses.

(b) The court may not assess fees, costs, or expenses of any kind against this state or a governmental subdivision, agency, or instrumentality of this state unless authorized by other law.

Added by Acts 2011, 82nd Leg., 1st C.S., ch. 4 (S.B. 1), § 66A.05, eff. Jan. 1, 2014.

## SUBTITLE H.  COURT–AUTHORIZED TRUSTS AND ACCOUNTS

### CHAPTER 1301.  MANAGEMENT TRUSTS

#### SUBCHAPTER A.  GENERAL PROVISIONS

#### SUBCHAPTER A.  GENERAL PROVISIONS

### § 1301.001.  Definition

In this chapter, "management trust" means a trust created under Section 1301.053 or 1301.054.

Added by Acts 2011, 82nd Leg., ch. 823 (H.B. 2759), § 1.02, eff. Jan. 1, 2014.

### § 1301.002.  Applicability of Texas Trust Code

(a) A management trust is subject to Subtitle B, Title 9, Property Code.

(b) To the extent of a conflict between Subtitle B, Title 9, Property Code, and a provision of this chapter or of a management trust, the provision of this chapter or of the trust controls.

Added by Acts 2011, 82nd Leg., ch. 823 (H.B. 2759), § 1.02, eff. Jan. 1, 2014.

#### SUBCHAPTER B.  CREATION OF MANAGEMENT TRUSTS

### § 1301.051.  Eligibility to Apply for Creation of Trust

The following persons may apply for the creation of a trust under this subchapter:

(1) the guardian of a ward;

(2) an attorney ad litem or guardian ad litem appointed to represent a ward or the ward's interests;

(3) a person interested in the welfare of an alleged incapacitated person who does not have a guardian;

(4) an attorney ad litem or guardian ad litem appointed to represent an alleged incapacitated person who does not have a guardian; or

(5) a person who has only a physical disability.

Added by Acts 2011, 82nd Leg., ch. 823 (H.B. 2759), § 1.02, eff. Jan. 1, 2014. Amended by Acts 2013, 83rd Leg., ch. 161 (S.B. 1093), § 6.060, eff. Jan. 1, 2014.

## § 1301.052. Venue for Proceeding Involving Trust for an Alleged Incapacitated Person

(a) An application for the creation of a trust under Section 1301.054 for an alleged incapacitated person must be filed in the same court in which a proceeding for the appointment of a guardian for the person is pending, if any.

(b) If a proceeding for the appointment of a guardian for an alleged incapacitated person is not pending on the date an application is filed for the creation of a trust under Section 1301.054 for the person, venue for a proceeding to create a trust must be determined in the same manner as venue for a proceeding for the appointment of a guardian is determined under Section 1023.001.

Added by Acts 2011, 82nd Leg., ch. 823 (H.B. 2759), § 1.02, eff. Jan. 1, 2014. Amended by Acts 2013, 83rd Leg., ch. 161 (S.B. 1093), § 6.061, eff. Jan. 1, 2014; Acts 2013, 83rd Leg., ch. 982 (H.B. 2080), § 25, eff. Jan. 1, 2014.

Section 36 of Acts 2013, 83rd Leg., ch. 982 (H.B. 2080) provides:

"(a) Except as otherwise provided by this section, the changes in law made by this Act apply to:

"(1) a guardianship created before, on, or after the effective date [Jan. 1, 2014] of this Act; and

"(2) an application for a guardianship pending on, or filed on or after, the effective date of this Act.

"(b) The changes in law made by this Act to Sections 1301.054, 1301.055, 1301.057(b), (c), and (d), 1301.058, 1301.101, and 1301.102(a), Estates Code, apply only to an application for the creation, modification, or termination of a management trust that is filed on or after the effective date of this Act. An application described by this subsection that is filed before the effective date of this Act is governed by the law in effect on the date the application was filed, and the former law is continued in effect for that purpose.

"(c) The changes in law made by this Act to Sections 1301.103 and 1301.154(a), Estates Code, and by Section 1301.202(a–1), Estates Code, as added by this Act, apply to a management trust created before, on, or after the effective date of this Act.

"(d) The changes in law made by this Act to Section 1102.003, Estates Code, apply to a guardianship proceeding that is commenced on or after the effective date of this Act. A guardianship proceeding commenced before that date is governed by the law in effect on the date the proceeding was commenced, and the former law is continued in effect for that purpose."

## § 1301.053. Creation of Trust

(a) On application by an appropriate person as provided by Section 1301.051 and subject to Section 1301.054(a), if applicable, the court with jurisdiction over the proceedings may enter an order that creates a trust for the management of the funds of the person with respect to whom the application is filed if the court finds that the creation of the trust is in the person's best interests.

(b) The court may maintain a trust created under this section under the same cause number as the guardianship proceeding, if the person for whom the trust is created is a ward or proposed ward.

Added by Acts 2011, 82nd Leg., ch. 823 (H.B. 2759), § 1.02, eff. Jan. 1, 2014. Amended by Acts 2013, 83rd Leg., ch. 161 (S.B. 1093), § 6.062, eff. Jan. 1, 2014.

## § 1301.054. Creation of Trust for Incapacitated Person Without Guardian

(a) On application by an appropriate person as provided by Section 1301.051 and regardless of whether an application for guardianship has been filed on the alleged incapacitated person's behalf, a proper court exercising probate jurisdiction may enter an order that creates a trust for the management of the estate of an alleged incapacitated person who does not have a guardian if the court, after a hearing, finds that:

(1) the person is an incapacitated person; and

(2) the creation of the trust is in the incapacitated person's best interests.

(b) The court shall conduct the hearing to determine incapacity under Subsection (a) using the same procedures and evidentiary standards as are required in a hearing for the appointment of a guardian for a proposed ward.

(c) Except as provided by Subsection (c–1), the court shall appoint an attorney ad litem and, if necessary, may appoint a guardian ad litem, to represent the interests of the alleged incapacitated person in the hearing to determine incapacity under Subsection (a).

(c–1) If the application for the creation of the trust is filed by a person who has only a physical disability, the court may, but is not required to, appoint an attorney ad litem or guardian ad litem to represent the interests of the person in the hearing to determine incapacity under Subsection (a).

(d) The court may maintain a trust created under this section under the same cause number as the guardianship proceeding, if the person for whom the trust is created is a ward or proposed ward.

Added by Acts 2011, 82nd Leg., ch. 823 (H.B. 2759), § 1.02, eff. Jan. 1, 2014. Amended by Acts 2013, 83rd Leg., ch. 161 (S.B. 1093), § 6.063, eff. Jan. 1, 2014; Acts 2013, 83rd Leg., ch. 982 (H.B. 2080), § 26, eff. Jan. 1, 2014.

Section 36 of Acts 2013, 83rd Leg., ch. 982 (H.B. 2080) provides:

"(a) Except as otherwise provided by this section, the changes in law made by this Act apply to:

"(1) a guardianship created before, on, or after the effective date [Jan. 1, 2014] of this Act; and

"(2) an application for a guardianship pending on, or filed on or after, the effective date of this Act.

"(b) The changes in law made by this Act to Sections 1301.054, 1301.055, 1301.057(b), (c), and (d), 1301.058, 1301.101, and 1301.102(a), Estates Code, apply only to an application for the creation, modification, or termination of a management trust that is filed on or after the effective date of this Act. An application described by this subsection that is filed before the effective date of this Act is governed by the law in effect on the date the application was filed, and the former law is continued in effect for that purpose.

"(c) The changes in law made by this Act to Sections 1301.103 and 1301.154(a), Estates Code, and by Section 1301.202(a–1), Estates Code, as added by this Act, apply to a management trust created before, on, or after the effective date of this Act.

"(d) The changes in law made by this Act to Section 1102.003, Estates Code, apply to a guardianship proceeding that is commenced on or after the effective date of this Act. A guardianship proceeding commenced before that date is governed by the law in effect on the date the proceeding was commenced, and the former law is continued in effect for that purpose."

### § 1301.055. Authority of Court to Appoint Guardian Instead of Creating Trust

If, after a hearing under Section 1301.054, the court finds that the person for whom the application was filed is an incapacitated person but that it is not in the incapacitated person's best interests for the court to create a trust under this subchapter for the incapacitated person's estate, the court may appoint a guardian of the person or estate, or both, for the incapacitated person without commencing a separate proceeding for that purpose.

Added by Acts 2011, 82nd Leg., ch. 823 (H.B. 2759), § 1.02, eff. Jan. 1, 2014. Amended by Acts 2013, 83rd Leg., ch. 982 (H.B. 2080), § 27, eff. Jan. 1, 2014.

Section 36 of Acts 2013, 83rd Leg., ch. 982 (H.B. 2080) provides:

"(a) Except as otherwise provided by this section, the changes in law made by this Act apply to:

"(1) a guardianship created before, on, or after the effective date [Jan. 1, 2014] of this Act; and

"(2) an application for a guardianship pending on, or filed on or after, the effective date of this Act.

"(b) The changes in law made by this Act to Sections 1301.054, 1301.055, 1301.057(b), (c), and (d), 1301.058, 1301.101, and 1301.102(a), Estates Code, apply only to an application for the creation, modification, or termination of a management trust that is filed on or after the effective date of this Act. An application described by this subsection that is filed before the effective date of this Act is governed by the law in effect on the date the application was filed, and the former law is continued in effect for that purpose.

"(c) The changes in law made by this Act to Sections 1301.103 and 1301.154(a), Estates Code, and by Section 1301.202(a–1), Estates Code, as added by this Act, apply to a management trust created before, on, or after the effective date of this Act.

"(d) The changes in law made by this Act to Section 1102.003, Estates Code, apply to a guardianship proceeding that is commenced on or after the effective date of this Act. A guardianship proceeding commenced before that date is governed by the law in effect on the date the proceeding was commenced, and the former law is continued in effect for that purpose."

### § 1301.056. Contents of Order Creating Trust

An order creating a management trust must:

(1) direct any person or entity holding property that belongs to the person for whom the trust is created or to which that person is entitled to deliver all or part of that property to a person or corporate fiduciary appointed as trustee of the trust; and

(2) include terms and limitations placed on the trust.

Added by Acts 2011, 82nd Leg., ch. 823 (H.B. 2759), § 1.02, eff. Jan. 1, 2014. Amended by Acts 2013, 83rd Leg., ch. 161 (S.B. 1093), § 6.064, eff. Jan. 1, 2014.

### § 1301.057. Appointment of Trustee

(a) In this section, "financial institution" means a financial institution, as defined by Section 201.101, Finance Code, that has trust powers and exists and does business under the laws of this state, another state, or the United States.

(b) Except as provided by Subsection (c), the court shall appoint a financial institution to serve as trustee of a management trust, other than a management trust created for a person who has only a physical disability.

(c) The court may appoint a person or entity described by Subsection (d) to serve as trustee of a management trust created for a ward or incapacitated person instead of appointing a financial institution to serve in that capacity if the court finds:

(1) that the appointment is in the best interests of the person for whom the trust is created; and

(2) if the value of the trust's principal is more than $150,000, that the applicant for the creation of the trust, after the exercise of due diligence, has been unable to find a financial institution in the geographic area willing to serve as trustee.

(d) The following are eligible for appointment as trustee of a management trust created for a ward or incapacitated person under Subsection (c):

(1) an individual, including an individual who is certified as a private professional guardian;

(2) a nonprofit corporation qualified to serve as a guardian; and

(3) a guardianship program.

Added by Acts 2011, 82nd Leg., ch. 823 (H.B. 2759), § 1.02, eff. Jan. 1, 2014. Amended by Acts 2013, 83rd Leg., ch. 161 (S.B. 1093), § 6.065, eff. Jan. 1, 2014; Acts 2013, 83rd Leg., ch. 982 (H.B. 2080), § 28, eff. Jan. 1, 2014.

Section 36 of Acts 2013, 83rd Leg., ch. 982 (H.B. 2080) provides:

"(a) Except as otherwise provided by this section, the changes in law made by this Act apply to:

"(1) a guardianship created before, on, or after the effective date [Jan. 1, 2014] of this Act; and

"(2) an application for a guardianship pending on, or filed on or after, the effective date of this Act.

"(b) The changes in law made by this Act to Sections 1301.054, 1301.055, 1301.057(b), (c), and (d), 1301.058, 1301.101, and 1301.102(a), Estates Code, apply only to an application for the creation, modification, or termination of a management trust that is filed on or after the effective date of this Act. An application described by this subsection that is filed before the effective date of this Act is governed by the law in effect on the date the application was filed, and the former law is continued in effect for that purpose.

"(c) The changes in law made by this Act to Sections 1301.103 and 1301.154(a), Estates Code, and by Section 1301.202(a–1), Estates Code, as added by this Act, apply to a management trust created before, on, or after the effective date of this Act.

"(d) The changes in law made by this Act to Section 1102.003, Estates Code, apply to a guardianship proceeding that is commenced on or after the effective date of this Act. A guardianship proceeding commenced before that date is governed by the law in effect on the date the proceeding was commenced, and the former law is continued in effect for that purpose."

## § 1301.058. Bond Requirements for Trustees

(a) The following serve without giving a bond in accordance with the trust terms required by Sections 1301.101(a)(4) and (a–1):

(1) a trustee of a management trust that is a corporate fiduciary; and

(2) any other trustee of a management trust created for a person who has only a physical disability.

(b) Except as provided by Subsection (a), the court shall require a person serving as trustee of a management trust to file with the county clerk a bond that:

(1) is in an amount equal to the value of the trust's principal and projected annual income; and

(2) meets the conditions the court determines are necessary.

Added by Acts 2011, 82nd Leg., ch. 823 (H.B. 2759), § 1.02, eff. Jan. 1, 2014. Amended by Acts 2013, 83rd Leg., ch. 982 (H.B. 2080), § 29, eff. Jan. 1, 2014.

Section 36 of Acts 2013, 83rd Leg., ch. 982 (H.B. 2080) provides:

"(a) Except as otherwise provided by this section, the changes in law made by this Act apply to:

"(1) a guardianship created before, on, or after the effective date [Jan. 1, 2014] of this Act; and

"(2) an application for a guardianship pending on, or filed on or after, the effective date of this Act.

"(b) The changes in law made by this Act to Sections 1301.054, 1301.055, 1301.057(b), (c), and (d), 1301.058, 1301.101, and 1301.102(a), Estates Code, apply only to an application for the creation, modification, or termination of a management trust that is filed on or after the effective date of this Act. An application described by this subsection that is filed before the effective date of this Act is governed by the law in effect on the date the application was filed, and the former law is continued in effect for that purpose.

"(c) The changes in law made by this Act to Sections 1301.103 and 1301.154(a), Estates Code, and by Section 1301.202(a–1), Estates Code, as added by this Act, apply to a management trust created before, on, or after the effective date of this Act.

"(d) The changes in law made by this Act to Section 1102.003, Estates Code, apply to a guardianship proceeding that is commenced on or after the effective date of this Act. A guardianship proceeding commenced before that date is governed by the law in effect on the date the proceeding was commenced, and the former law is continued in effect for that purpose."

## SUBCHAPTER C. TERMS OF MANAGEMENT TRUST

## § 1301.101. Required Terms

(a) Except as provided by Subsection (c), a management trust created for a ward or incapacitated person must provide that:

(1) the ward, incapacitated person, or person who has only a physical disability is the sole beneficiary of the trust;

(2) the trustee may disburse an amount of the trust's principal or income as the trustee determines is necessary to spend for the health, education, maintenance, or support of the person for whom the trust is created;

(3) the trust income that the trustee does not disburse under Subdivision (2) must be added to the trust principal;

(4) a trustee that is a corporate fiduciary serves without giving a bond; and

(5) subject to the court's approval and Subsection (b), a trustee is entitled to receive reasonable compensation for services the trustee provides to the person for whom the trust is created as the person's trustee.

(a–1) A management trust created for a person who has only a physical disability must provide that the trustee of the trust:

(1) serves without giving a bond; and

(2) is entitled to receive, without the court's approval, reasonable compensation for services the trustee provides to the person as the person's trustee.

(b) A trustee's compensation under Subsection (a)(5) must be:

(1) paid from the management trust's income, principal, or both; and

(2) determined, paid, reduced, and eliminated in the same manner as compensation of a guardian under Subchapter A, Chapter 1155.

(c) The court creating or modifying a management trust may omit or modify otherwise applicable terms required by Subsection (a), (a–1), or (b) if the court is creating the trust for a person who has only a physical disability, or if the court determines that the omission or modification:

(1) is necessary and appropriate for the person for whom the trust is created to be eligible to receive public benefits or assistance under a state or federal program that is not otherwise available to the person; or

(2) is in the best interests of the person for whom the trust is created.

Added by Acts 2011, 82nd Leg., ch. 823 (H.B. 2759), § 1.02, eff. Jan. 1, 2014. Amended by Acts 2013, 83rd Leg., ch. 161 (S.B. 1093), § 6.066, eff. Jan. 1, 2014; Acts 2013, 83rd Leg., ch. 982 (H.B. 2080), § 30, eff. Jan. 1, 2014.

Section 36 of Acts 2013, 83rd Leg., ch. 982 (H.B. 2080) provides:

"(a) Except as otherwise provided by this section, the changes in law made by this Act apply to:

"(1) a guardianship created before, on, or after the effective date [Jan. 1, 2014] of this Act; and

"(2) an application for a guardianship pending on, or filed on or after, the effective date of this Act.

"(b) The changes in law made by this Act to Sections 1301.054, 1301.055, 1301.057(b), (c), and (d), 1301.058, 1301.101, and 1301.102(a), Estates Code, apply only to an application for the creation, modification, or termination of a management trust that is filed on or after the effective date of this Act. An application described by this subsection that is filed before the effective date of this Act is governed by the law in effect on the date the application was filed, and the former law is continued in effect for that purpose.

"(c) The changes in law made by this Act to Sections 1301.103 and 1301.154(a), Estates Code, and by Section 1301.202(a–1), Estates Code, as added by this Act, apply to a management trust created before, on, or after the effective date of this Act.

"(d) The changes in law made by this Act to Section 1102.003, Estates Code, apply to a guardianship proceeding that is commenced on or after the effective date of this Act. A guardianship proceeding commenced before that date is governed by the law in effect on the date the proceeding was commenced, and the former law is continued in effect for that purpose."

## § 1301.102.  Optional Terms

(a) A management trust created for a ward or incapacitated person may provide that the trustee make a distribution, payment, use, or application of trust funds for the health, education, maintenance, or support of the person for whom the trust is created or of another person whom the person for whom the trust is created is legally obligated to support:

(1) as necessary and without the intervention of:

(A) a guardian or other representative of the ward; or

(B) a representative of the incapacitated person or person who has only a physical disability; and

(2) to:

(A) the ward's guardian;

(B) a person who has physical custody of the person for whom the trust is created or of another person whom the person for whom the trust is created is legally obligated to support; or

(C) a person providing a good or service to the person for whom the trust is created or to another person whom the person for whom the trust is created is legally obligated to support.

(b) The court may include additional provisions in a management trust on the trust's creation or modification under this chapter if the court determines the addition does not conflict with Section 1301.101.

Added by Acts 2011, 82nd Leg., ch. 823 (H.B. 2759), § 1.02, eff. Jan. 1, 2014. Amended by Acts 2013, 83rd Leg., ch. 161 (S.B. 1093), § 6.067, eff. Jan. 1, 2014; Acts 2013, 83rd Leg., ch. 982 (H.B. 2080), § 31, eff. Jan. 1, 2014.

Section 36 of Acts 2013, 83rd Leg., ch. 982 (H.B. 2080) provides:

"(a) Except as otherwise provided by this section, the changes in law made by this Act apply to:

"(1) a guardianship created before, on, or after the effective date [Jan. 1, 2014] of this Act; and

"(2) an application for a guardianship pending on, or filed on or after, the effective date of this Act.

"(b) The changes in law made by this Act to Sections 1301.054, 1301.055, 1301.057(b), (c), and (d), 1301.058, 1301.101, and 1301.102(a), Estates Code, apply only to an application for the creation, modification, or termination of a management trust that is filed on or after the effective date of this Act. An application described by this subsection that is filed before the effective date of this Act is governed by the law in effect on the date the application was filed, and the former law is continued in effect for that purpose.

"(c) The changes in law made by this Act to Sections 1301.103 and 1301.154(a), Estates Code, and by Section 1301.202(a–1), Estates Code, as added by this Act, apply to a management trust created before, on, or after the effective date of this Act.

"(d) The changes in law made by this Act to Section 1102.003, Estates Code, apply to a guardianship proceeding that is commenced on or after the effective date of this Act. A guardianship proceeding commenced before that date is governed by the law in effect on the date the proceeding was commenced, and the former law is continued in effect for that purpose."

## § 1301.103.  Enforceability of Certain Terms

A provision in a management trust created for a ward or incapacitated person that relieves a trustee from a duty or liability imposed by this chapter or Subtitle B, Title 9, Property Code, is enforceable only if:

(1) the provision is limited to specific facts and circumstances unique to the property of that trust and is not applicable generally to the trust; and

(2) the court creating or modifying the trust makes a specific finding that there is clear and convincing evidence that the inclusion of the provision is in the best interests of the trust beneficiary.

Added by Acts 2011, 82nd Leg., ch. 823 (H.B. 2759), § 1.02, eff. Jan. 1, 2014. Amended by Acts 2013, 83rd Leg., ch. 982 (H.B. 2080), § 32, eff. Jan. 1, 2014.

Section 36 of Acts 2013, 83rd Leg., ch. 982 (H.B. 2080) provides:

"(a) Except as otherwise provided by this section, the changes in law made by this Act apply to:

"(1) a guardianship created before, on, or after the effective date [Jan. 1, 2014] of this Act; and

"(2) an application for a guardianship pending on, or filed on or after, the effective date of this Act.

"(b) The changes in law made by this Act to Sections 1301.054, 1301.055, 1301.057(b), (c), and (d), 1301.058, 1301.101, and 1301.102(a), Estates Code, apply only to an application for the creation, modification, or termination of a management trust that is filed on or after the effective date of this Act. An application described by this subsection that is filed before the effective date of this Act is governed by the law in effect on the date the application was filed, and the former law is continued in effect for that purpose.

"(c) The changes in law made by this Act to Sections 1301.103 and 1301.154(a), Estates Code, and by Section 1301.202(a–1), Estates Code, as added by this Act, apply to a management trust created before, on, or after the effective date of this Act.

"(d) The changes in law made by this Act to Section 1102.003, Estates Code, apply to a guardianship proceeding that is commenced on or after the effective date of this Act. A guardianship proceeding commenced before that date is governed by the law in effect on the date the proceeding was commenced, and the former law is continued in effect for that purpose."

## SUBCHAPTER D. ADMINISTRATION OF MANAGEMENT TRUSTS

### § 1301.151. Jurisdiction Over Trust Matters

A court that creates a management trust has the same jurisdiction to hear matters relating to the trust as the court has with respect to guardianship and other matters covered by this title.

Added by Acts 2011, 82nd Leg., ch. 823 (H.B. 2759), § 1.02, eff. Jan. 1, 2014.

### § 1301.152. Court's Authority to Discharge Guardian of Estate

On or at any time after the creation of a management trust, the court may discharge the guardian of the ward's estate if the court determines that the discharge is in the ward's best interests.

Added by Acts 2011, 82nd Leg., ch. 823 (H.B. 2759), § 1.02, eff. Jan. 1, 2014.

### § 1301.153. Investment in Texas Tomorrow Fund

The trustee of a management trust may invest trust funds in the Texas tomorrow fund established by Subchapter F, Chapter 54, Education Code, if the trustee determines that investment is in the best interest of the ward or incapacitated person for whom the trust is created.

Added by Acts 2011, 82nd Leg., ch. 823 (H.B. 2759), § 1.02, eff. Jan. 1, 2014.

### § 1301.1535. Initial Accounting by Certain Trustees Required

(a) This section applies only to a trustee of a management trust created for a person for whom a guardianship proceeding is pending on the date the trust is created.

(b) Not later than the 30th day after the date a trustee to which this section applies receives property into the trust, the trustee shall file with the court in which the guardianship proceeding is pending a report describing all property held in the trust on the date of the report and specifying the value of the property on that date.

Added by Acts 2013, 83rd Leg., ch. 161 (S.B. 1093), § 6.068, eff. Jan. 1, 2014.

### § 1301.154. Annual Accounting

(a) Except as provided by Subsection (d), the trustee of a management trust created for a ward shall prepare and file with the court an annual accounting of transactions in the trust in the same manner and form that is required of a guardian of the estate under this title.

(b) The trustee of a management trust created for a ward shall provide a copy of the annual account to the guardian of the ward's estate or person.

(c) The annual account is subject to court review and approval in the same manner that is required of an annual account prepared by a guardian under this title.

(d) The court may not require a trustee of a trust created for a person who has only a physical disability to prepare and file with the court the annual accounting as described by Subsection (a).

Added by Acts 2011, 82nd Leg., ch. 823 (H.B. 2759), § 1.02, eff. Jan. 1, 2014. Amended by Acts 2013, 83rd Leg., ch. 161 (S.B. 1093), § 6.069, eff. Jan. 1, 2014; Acts 2013, 83rd Leg., ch. 982 (H.B. 2080), § 33, eff. Jan. 1, 2014.

Section 36 of Acts 2013, 83rd Leg., ch. 982 (H.B. 2080) provides:

"(a) Except as otherwise provided by this section, the changes in law made by this Act apply to:

"(1) a guardianship created before, on, or after the effective date [Jan. 1, 2014] of this Act; and

"(2) an application for a guardianship pending on, or filed on or after, the effective date of this Act.

"(b) The changes in law made by this Act to Sections 1301.054, 1301.055, 1301.057(b), (c), and (d), 1301.058, 1301.101, and 1301.102(a), Estates Code, apply only to an application for the creation, modification, or termination of a management trust that is filed on or after the effective date of this Act. An application described by this subsection that is filed before the effective date of this Act is governed by the law in effect on the date the application was filed, and the former law is continued in effect for that purpose.

"(c) The changes in law made by this Act to Sections 1301.103 and 1301.154(a), Estates Code, and by Section 1301.202(a–1), Estates Code, as added by this Act, apply to a management trust created before, on, or after the effective date of this Act.

"(d) The changes in law made by this Act to Section 1102.003, Estates Code, apply to a guardianship proceeding that is commenced on or after the effective date of this Act. A guardianship proceeding commenced before that date is governed by the law in effect on the date the proceeding was commenced, and the former law is continued in effect for that purpose."

### § 1301.155. Appointment of Successor Trustee

The court may appoint a successor trustee if the trustee of a management trust resigns, becomes ineligible, or is removed.

Added by Acts 2011, 82nd Leg., ch. 823 (H.B. 2759), § 1.02, eff. Jan. 1, 2014.

### § 1301.156. Liability of Certain Persons for Conduct of Trustee

The guardian of the person or of the estate of a ward for whom a management trust is created or the surety on the guardian's bond is not liable for an act or omission of the trustee of the trust.

Added by Acts 2011, 82nd Leg., ch. 823 (H.B. 2759), § 1.02, eff. Jan. 1, 2014.

### SUBCHAPTER E. MODIFICATION, REVOCATION, OR TERMINATION OF MANAGEMENT TRUSTS

### § 1301.201. Modification or Revocation of Trust

(a) The court may modify or revoke a management trust at any time before the date of the trust's termination.

(b) The following may not revoke a management trust:

(1) the ward for whom the trust is created or the guardian of the ward's estate;

(2) the incapacitated person for whom the trust is created; or

(3) the person who has only a physical disability for whom the trust is created.

Added by Acts 2011, 82nd Leg., ch. 823 (H.B. 2759), § 1.02, eff. Jan. 1, 2014. Amended by Acts 2013, 83rd Leg., ch. 161 (S.B. 1093), § 6.070, eff. Jan. 1, 2014.

### § 1301.202. Transfer to Pooled Trust Subaccount

(a) If the court determines that it is in the best interests of the person for whom a management trust is created, the court may order the transfer of all property in the management trust to a pooled trust subaccount established in accordance with Chapter 1302.

(a–1) For purposes of a proceeding to determine whether to transfer property from a management trust to a pooled trust subaccount, the court may, but is not required to, appoint an attorney ad litem or guardian ad litem to represent the interests of a person who has only a physical disability for whom the management trust was created.

(b) The transfer of property from the management trust to the pooled trust subaccount shall be treated as a continuation of the management trust and may not be treated as the establishment of a new trust for purposes of 42 U.S.C. Section 1396p(d)(4)(A) or (C) or otherwise for purposes of the management trust beneficiary's eligibility for medical assistance under Chapter 32, Human Resources Code.

(c) The court may not allow termination of the management trust from which property is transferred under this section until all of the property in the management trust has been transferred to the pooled trust subaccount.

Added by Acts 2011, 82nd Leg., ch. 823 (H.B. 2759), § 1.02, eff. Jan. 1, 2014. Amended by Acts 2013, 83rd Leg., ch. 161 (S.B. 1093), § 6.071, eff. Jan. 1, 2014; Acts 2013, 83rd Leg., ch. 982 (H.B. 2080), § 34, eff. Jan. 1, 2014.

Section 36 of Acts 2013, 83rd Leg., ch. 982 (H.B. 2080) provides:

"(a) Except as otherwise provided by this section, the changes in law made by this Act apply to:

"(1) a guardianship created before, on, or after the effective date [Jan. 1, 2014] of this Act; and

"(2) an application for a guardianship pending on, or filed on or after, the effective date of this Act.

"(b) The changes in law made by this Act to Sections 1301.054, 1301.055, 1301.057(b), (c), and (d), 1301.058, 1301.101, and 1301.102(a), Estates Code, apply only to an application for the creation, modification, or termination of a management trust that is filed on or after the effective date of this Act. An application described by this subsection that is filed before the effective date of this Act is governed by the law in effect on the date the application was filed, and the former law is continued in effect for that purpose.

"(c) The changes in law made by this Act to Sections 1301.103 and 1301.154(a), Estates Code, and by Section 1301.202(a–1), Estates Code, as added by this Act, apply to a management trust created before, on, or after the effective date of this Act.

"(d) The changes in law made by this Act to Section 1102.003, Estates Code, apply to a guardianship proceeding that is commenced on or after the effective date of this Act. A guardianship proceeding commenced before that date is governed by the law in effect on the date the proceeding was commenced, and the former law is continued in effect for that purpose."

### § 1301.203. Termination of Trust

(a) If the person for whom a management trust is created is a minor, the trust terminates on:

(1) the earlier of:

(A) the person's death; or

(B) the person's 18th birthday; or

(2) the date provided by court order, which may not be later than the person's 25th birthday.

(b) If the person for whom a management trust is created is not a minor, the trust terminates:

(1) according to the terms of the trust;

(2) on the date the court determines that continuing the trust is no longer in the person's best interests, subject to Section 1301.202(c); or

(3) on the person's death.

Added by Acts 2011, 82nd Leg., ch. 823 (H.B. 2759), § 1.02, eff. Jan. 1, 2014. Amended by Acts 2013, 83rd Leg., ch. 161 (S.B. 1093), § 6.072, eff. Jan. 1, 2014.

## § 1301.204. Distribution of Trust Property

(a) Unless otherwise provided by the court and except as provided by Subsection (b), the trustee of a management trust shall:

(1) prepare a final account in the same form and manner that is required of a guardian under Sections 1204.101 and 1204.102; and

(2) on court approval, distribute the principal or any undistributed income of the trust to:

(A) the ward or incapacitated person when the trust terminates on the trust's own terms;

(B) the successor trustee on appointment of a successor trustee; or

(C) the representative of the deceased ward's or incapacitated person's estate on the ward's or incapacitated person's death.

(b) The court may not require a trustee of a trust created for a person who has only a physical disability to prepare and file with the court a final account as described by Subsection (a)(1). The trustee shall distribute the principal and any undistributed income of the trust in the manner provided by Subsection (a)(2) for a trust the beneficiary of which is a ward or incapacitated person.

Added by Acts 2011, 82nd Leg., ch. 823 (H.B. 2759), § 1.02, eff. Jan. 1, 2014. Amended by Acts 2013, 83rd Leg., ch. 161 (S.B. 1093), § 6.073, eff. Jan. 1, 2014.

## CHAPTER 1302. POOLED TRUST SUBACCOUNTS

## § 1302.001. Definitions

In this chapter:

(1) "Beneficiary" means a person for whom a subaccount is established.

(2) "Medical assistance" means benefits and services under the medical assistance program administered under Chapter 32, Human Resources Code.

(3) "Pooled trust" means a trust that meets the requirements of 42 U.S.C. Section 1396p(d)(4)(C) for purposes of exempting the trust from the applicability of 42 U.S.C. Section 1396p(d) in determining the eligibility of a person who is disabled for medical assistance.

(4) "Subaccount" means an account in a pooled trust established solely for the benefit of a beneficiary.

Added by Acts 2011, 82nd Leg., ch. 823 (H.B. 2759), § 1.02, eff. Jan. 1, 2014.

## § 1302.002. Application to Establish Subaccount

The following persons may apply to the court for the establishment of a subaccount for the benefit of a minor or other incapacitated person, an alleged incapacitated person, or a disabled person who is not an incapacitated person:

(1) the guardian of the incapacitated person;

(2) a person who has filed an application for the appointment of a guardian for the alleged incapacitated person;

(3) an attorney ad litem or guardian ad litem appointed to represent:

(A) the incapacitated person who is a ward or that person's interests; or

(B) the alleged incapacitated person who does not have a guardian; or

(4) the disabled person.

Added by Acts 2011, 82nd Leg., ch. 823 (H.B. 2759), § 1.02, eff. Jan. 1, 2014. Amended by Acts 2013, 83rd Leg., ch. 161 (S.B. 1093), § 6.074, eff. Jan. 1, 2014.

## § 1302.003. Appointment of Attorney ad Litem

(a) The court shall appoint an attorney ad litem for a person who is a minor or has a mental disability and who is the subject of an application under Section 1302.002.

(b) The attorney ad litem is entitled to a reasonable fee and reimbursement of expenses to be paid from the person's property.

Added by Acts 2011, 82nd Leg., ch. 823 (H.B. 2759), § 1.02, eff. Jan. 1, 2014.

### § 1302.004. Establishment of Subaccount

If the court finds that it is in the best interests of a person who is the subject of an application under Section 1302.002, the court may order:

(1) the establishment of a subaccount of which the person is the beneficiary; and

(2) the transfer to the subaccount of any of the person's property on hand or accruing to the person.

Added by Acts 2011, 82nd Leg., ch. 823 (H.B. 2759), § 1.02, eff. Jan. 1, 2014.

### § 1302.005. Terms of Subaccount

Unless the court orders otherwise, the terms governing the subaccount must provide that:

(1) the subaccount terminates on the earliest of the date of:

(A) the beneficiary's 18th birthday, if the beneficiary is not disabled on that date and was a minor at the time the subaccount was established;

(B) the beneficiary's death; or

(C) a court order terminating the subaccount; and

(2) on termination, any property remaining in the beneficiary's subaccount after making any required payments to satisfy the amounts of medical assistance reimbursement claims for medical assistance provided to the beneficiary under this state's medical assistance program and other states' medical assistance programs shall be distributed to:

(A) the beneficiary, if on the date of termination the beneficiary is living and is not incapacitated;

(B) the beneficiary's guardian, if on the date of termination the beneficiary is living and is incapacitated; or

(C) the personal representative of the beneficiary's estate, if on the date of termination the beneficiary is deceased.

Added by Acts 2011, 82nd Leg., ch. 823 (H.B. 2759), § 1.02, eff. Jan. 1, 2014.

### § 1302.006. Fees and Reporting

(a) The manager or trustee of a pooled trust may:

(1) assess fees against a subaccount of that pooled trust that is established under this chapter, in accordance with the manager's or trustee's standard fee structure; and

(2) pay fees assessed under Subdivision (1) from the subaccount.

(b) If required by the court, the manager or trustee of the pooled trust shall file a copy of the annual report of account with the court clerk.

Added by Acts 2011, 82nd Leg., ch. 823 (H.B. 2759), § 1.02, eff. Jan. 1, 2014.

### § 1302.007. Jurisdiction Exclusive

Notwithstanding any other law, the court that orders the establishment of a subaccount for a beneficiary has exclusive jurisdiction of a subsequent proceeding or action that relates to both the beneficiary and the subaccount, and the proceeding or action may be brought only in that court.

Added by Acts 2011, 82nd Leg., ch. 823 (H.B. 2759), § 1.02, eff. Jan. 1, 2014.

## SUBTITLE I. OTHER SPECIAL PROCEEDINGS AND ALTERNATIVES TO GUARDIANSHIP

### CHAPTER 1351. SALE OF PROPERTY OF CERTAIN INCAPACITATED PERSONS

SUBCHAPTER A. SALE OF MINOR'S INTEREST IN PROPERTY WITHOUT GUARDIANSHIP

## SUBCHAPTER A. SALE OF MINOR'S INTEREST IN PROPERTY WITHOUT GUARDIANSHIP

### § 1351.001. Authority to Sell Minor's Interest in Property Without Guardianship

A parent or managing conservator of a minor who is not a ward may apply to the court under this subchapter for an order to sell an interest of the minor in property without being appointed guardian if the net value of the interest does not exceed $100,000.

Added by Acts 2011, 82nd Leg., ch. 823 (H.B. 2759), § 1.02, eff. Jan. 1, 2014.

### § 1351.002. Application; Venue

(a) A parent or managing conservator shall apply to the court under oath for the sale of property under this subchapter.

(b) An application must contain:

(1) the minor's name;

(2) a legal description of the real property or a description that identifies the personal property, as applicable;

(3) the minor's interest in the property;

(4) the purchaser's name;

(5) a statement that the sale of the minor's interest in the property is for cash; and

(6) a statement that all money received by the parent or managing conservator shall be used for the minor's use and benefit.

(c) Venue for the application is the same as venue for an application for the appointment of a guardian for a minor.

Added by Acts 2011, 82nd Leg., ch. 823 (H.B. 2759), § 1.02, eff. Jan. 1, 2014.

### § 1351.003. Hearing; Requirements for Sale

(a) On receipt of an application under this subchapter, the court shall set the application for hearing on a date not earlier than five days from the date the application was filed.

(b) The court may cause citation to be issued if the court considers citation necessary.

(c) At the time of the hearing, the court shall order the sale of the property if the court is satisfied from the evidence that the sale is in the minor's best interests. The court may require an independent appraisal of the property to be sold to establish the minimum sale price.

Added by Acts 2011, 82nd Leg., ch. 823 (H.B. 2759), § 1.02, eff. Jan. 1, 2014.

### § 1351.004. Payment of Sale Proceeds Into Court Registry

If the court enters an order of sale of property as provided by this subchapter, the purchaser of the property shall pay the proceeds of the sale belonging to the minor into the court registry.

Added by Acts 2011, 82nd Leg., ch. 823 (H.B. 2759), § 1.02, eff. Jan. 1, 2014.

### § 1351.005. Withdrawal of Sale Proceeds From Registry Not Prohibited

This subchapter does not prevent the sale proceeds deposited into the court registry under Section 1351.004 from being withdrawn from the court registry under Chapter 1355.

Added by Acts 2011, 82nd Leg., ch. 823 (H.B. 2759), § 1.02, eff. Jan. 1, 2014.

### § 1351.006. Disaffirmation of Sale Prohibited

A minor may not disaffirm a sale of property made in accordance with a court order under this subchapter.

Added by Acts 2011, 82nd Leg., ch. 823 (H.B. 2759), § 1.02, eff. Jan. 1, 2014.

## SUBCHAPTER B. SALE OF WARD'S PROPERTY WITHOUT GUARDIANSHIP OF THE ESTATE

### § 1351.051. Applicability of Subchapter

This subchapter applies only to a ward who has a guardian of the person but does not have a guardian of the estate.

Added by Acts 2011, 82nd Leg., ch. 823 (H.B. 2759), § 1.02, eff. Jan. 1, 2014.

### § 1351.052. Authority to Sell Ward's Interest in Property Without Appointment as Guardian of the Estate

A guardian of the person of a ward may apply to the court under this subchapter for an order to sell an interest in property in the ward's estate without being appointed guardian of the ward's estate if the net value of the interest does not exceed $100,000.

Added by Acts 2011, 82nd Leg., ch. 823 (H.B. 2759), § 1.02, eff. Jan. 1, 2014.

## § 1351.053. Application; Venue

(a) An application under this subchapter must:

(1) be under oath; and

(2) contain the information required by Section 1351.002(b).

(b) For purposes of Subsection (a)(2), references in Section 1351.002(b) to:

(1) "minor" are replaced with references to "ward"; and

(2) "parent or managing conservator" are replaced with references to "guardian of the person."

(c) Venue for the application is the same as venue for an application for the appointment of a guardian for the ward.

Added by Acts 2011, 82nd Leg., ch. 823 (H.B. 2759), § 1.02, eff. Jan. 1, 2014.

## § 1351.054. Hearing

(a) On receipt of an application under this subchapter, the court shall set the application for hearing on a date not earlier than five days from the date the application was filed.

(b) The court may cause citation to be issued if the court considers citation necessary.

(c) The procedures and evidentiary requirements for the hearing are the same as the procedures and evidentiary requirements for a hearing of an application filed under Subchapter A.

Added by Acts 2011, 82nd Leg., ch. 823 (H.B. 2759), § 1.02, eff. Jan. 1, 2014.

## § 1351.055. Payment of Sale Proceeds Into Court Registry

If the court enters an order of sale of property as provided by this subchapter, the purchaser of the property shall pay the proceeds of the sale belonging to the ward into the court registry.

Added by Acts 2011, 82nd Leg., ch. 823 (H.B. 2759), § 1.02, eff. Jan. 1, 2014.

## § 1351.056. Withdrawal of Sale Proceeds From Registry Not Prohibited

This subchapter does not prevent the sale proceeds deposited into the court registry under Section 1351.055 from being withdrawn from the court registry under Chapter 1355.

Added by Acts 2011, 82nd Leg., ch. 823 (H.B. 2759), § 1.02, eff. Jan. 1, 2014.

## § 1351.057. Disaffirmation of Sale Prohibited

A ward may not disaffirm a sale of property made in accordance with a court order under this subchapter.

Added by Acts 2011, 82nd Leg., ch. 823 (H.B. 2759), § 1.02, eff. Jan. 1, 2014.

## CHAPTER 1352. MORTGAGE OF MINOR'S INTEREST IN RESIDENCE HOMESTEAD

### SUBCHAPTER A. GENERAL PROVISIONS

### SUBCHAPTER A. GENERAL PROVISIONS

## § 1352.001. Definitions

In this chapter:

(1) "Home equity loan" means a loan made under Section 50(a)(6), Article XVI, Texas Constitution.

(2) "Residence homestead" has the meaning assigned by Section 11.13, Tax Code.

Added by Acts 2011, 82nd Leg., ch. 823 (H.B. 2759), § 1.02, eff. Jan. 1, 2014.

## SUBCHAPTER B.  MORTGAGE OF MINOR'S INTEREST WITHOUT GUARDIANSHIP

### § 1352.051.  Applicability of Subchapter

This subchapter applies only to a minor who:

(1) is not a ward; and

(2) has an interest in a residence homestead.

Added by Acts 2011, 82nd Leg., ch. 823 (H.B. 2759), § 1.02, eff. Jan. 1, 2014.

### § 1352.052.  Authority to Mortgage Minor's Interest Without Guardianship

(a) If the net value of a minor's interest in a residence homestead does not exceed $100,000, a parent, subject to Subsection (b), or managing conservator of the minor may apply to the court under this subchapter for an order authorizing the parent or managing conservator to receive on the minor's behalf, without being appointed guardian, an extension of credit that is secured wholly or partly by a lien on the homestead.

(b) A parent of a minor may file an application under this subchapter only if the parent has a homestead interest in the property that is the subject of the application.

Added by Acts 2011, 82nd Leg., ch. 823 (H.B. 2759), § 1.02, eff. Jan. 1, 2014.

### § 1352.053.  Application; Venue

(a) A parent or managing conservator shall apply to the court under oath for the authority to encumber the residence homestead as provided by this subchapter.

(b) The application must contain:

(1) the minor's name and address;

(2) a legal description of the property constituting the homestead;

(3) a description of the minor's ownership interest in the property constituting the homestead;

(4) the fair market value of the property constituting the homestead;

(5) the amount of the home equity loan;

(6) the purpose or purposes for which the home equity loan is being sought;

(7) a detailed description of the proposed expenditure of the loan proceeds to be received by the parent or managing conservator on the minor's behalf; and

(8) a statement that all loan proceeds received by the parent or managing conservator on the minor's behalf through a home equity loan authorized under this subchapter shall be used in a manner that is for the minor's benefit.

(c) Venue for the application is the same as venue for an application for the appointment of a guardian for a minor.

Added by Acts 2011, 82nd Leg., ch. 823 (H.B. 2759), § 1.02, eff. Jan. 1, 2014.

### § 1352.054.  Hearing; Requirements to Mortgage Minor's Interest

(a) On receipt of an application under this subchapter, the court shall set the application for hearing on a date not earlier than the fifth day after the date the application is filed.

(b) The court may cause citation to be issued if the court considers citation necessary.

(c) At the time of the hearing, the court, on approval of the surety bond required by Section 1352.055, shall authorize the parent or managing conservator to receive the extension of credit sought in the application if the court is satisfied from a preponderance of the evidence that the encumbrance is:

(1) for a purpose described by Section 1352.056(1) or (2); and

(2) in the minor's best interests.

Added by Acts 2011, 82nd Leg., ch. 823 (H.B. 2759), § 1.02, eff. Jan. 1, 2014.

### § 1352.055.  Surety Bond; Discharge of Sureties

(a) Before a hearing under Section 1352.054 is held, the parent or managing conservator shall file with the county clerk a surety bond.  The bond must be:

(1) in an amount at least equal to two times the amount of the proposed home equity loan;

(2) payable to and approved by the court; and

(3) conditioned on the parent or managing conservator:

(A) using the proceeds of the home equity loan attributable to the minor's interest solely for the purposes authorized by Section 1352.056; and

(B) making payments on the minor's behalf toward the outstanding balance of the home equity loan.

(b) After the first anniversary of the date a parent or managing conservator executes a home equity loan authorized under this subchapter, the court may, on motion of the borrower, reduce the amount of the surety bond required under this section to an amount that is not less than the loan's outstanding balance.

(c) The court may not discharge the person's sureties from all further liability under a surety bond until the court:

(1) approves the filing of the parent's or managing conservator's reports required under Sections 1352.057 and 1352.058;

(2) finds that the parent or managing conservator used loan proceeds resulting from the minor's interest solely for the purposes authorized by Section 1352.056; and

(3) is presented with satisfactory evidence that the home equity loan has been repaid and is no longer considered an outstanding obligation.

Added by Acts 2011, 82nd Leg., ch. 823 (H.B. 2759), § 1.02, eff. Jan. 1, 2014.

### § 1352.056.  Use of Proceeds

Proceeds of a home equity loan that is the subject of an application under Section 1352.053 that are attributable to the minor's interest may be spent only to:

(1) make improvements to the homestead;

(2) pay for the minor's education or medical expenses; or

(3) pay the loan's outstanding balance.

Added by Acts 2011, 82nd Leg., ch. 823 (H.B. 2759), § 1.02, eff. Jan. 1, 2014.

### § 1352.057.  Annual Report

A parent or managing conservator executing a home equity loan on a minor's behalf under this subchapter shall file an annual report with the court regarding the transaction.

Added by Acts 2011, 82nd Leg., ch. 823 (H.B. 2759), § 1.02, eff. Jan. 1, 2014.

### § 1352.058.  Sworn Report of Expenditures

When the parent or managing conservator has spent the proceeds of a home equity loan authorized under this subchapter, the parent or managing conservator shall file with the county clerk a sworn report accounting for the proceeds.

Added by Acts 2011, 82nd Leg., ch. 823 (H.B. 2759), § 1.02, eff. Jan. 1, 2014.

### § 1352.059.  Disaffirmation of Home Equity Loan Prohibited

A minor may not disaffirm a home equity loan authorized by the court under this subchapter.

Added by Acts 2011, 82nd Leg., ch. 823 (H.B. 2759), § 1.02, eff. Jan. 1, 2014.

## SUBCHAPTER C.  MORTGAGE OF MINOR WARD'S INTEREST WITHOUT GUARDIANSHIP OF THE ESTATE

### § 1352.101.  Applicability of Subchapter

This subchapter applies only to a minor ward who:

(1) has a guardian of the person but does not have a guardian of the estate; and

(2) has an interest in a residence homestead.

Added by Acts 2011, 82nd Leg., ch. 823 (H.B. 2759), § 1.02, eff. Jan. 1, 2014.

### § 1352.102.  Authority to Mortgage Minor Ward's Interest Without Guardianship of the Estate

If the net value of a minor ward's interest in a residence homestead does not exceed $100,000, the guardian of the person of the ward may apply to the court under this subchapter for an order authorizing the guardian to receive on the ward's behalf an extension of credit that is secured wholly or partly by a lien on the homestead.

Added by Acts 2011, 82nd Leg., ch. 823 (H.B. 2759), § 1.02, eff. Jan. 1, 2014.

### § 1352.103.  Application; Venue

(a) An application under this subchapter must contain the information required by Section 1352.053(b).

(b) For purposes of Subsection (a), references in Section 1352.053(b) to "parent or managing conservator" are replaced with references to "guardian of the person."

(c) Venue for the application is the same as venue for an application for the appointment of a guardian for a ward.

Added by Acts 2011, 82nd Leg., ch. 823 (H.B. 2759), § 1.02, eff. Jan. 1, 2014.

### § 1352.104.  Hearing; Requirements to Mortgage Minor Ward's Interest

(a) On receipt of an application under this subchapter, the court shall set the application for hearing on a date not earlier than the fifth day after the date the application is filed.

(b) The court may cause citation to be issued if the court considers citation necessary.

(c) The procedures and evidentiary requirements for a hearing of an application filed under this subchapter are the same as the procedures and evidentiary requirements for a hearing of an application filed under Subchapter B.

(d) At the time of the hearing, the court, on approval of the surety bond required by Section 1352.105, shall authorize the guardian to receive the extension of credit sought in the application if the court is satisfied from a preponderance of the evidence that the encumbrance is:

(1) for a purpose described by Section 1352.106(1) or (2); and

(2) in the minor ward's best interests.

Added by Acts 2011, 82nd Leg., ch. 823 (H.B. 2759), § 1.02, eff. Jan. 1, 2014.

### § 1352.105. Surety Bond; Discharge of Sureties

(a) Before a hearing under Section 1352.104 is held, the guardian of the person shall file a surety bond with the county clerk to the same extent and in the same manner as a parent or managing conservator of a minor is required to file a surety bond under Section 1352.055.

(b) The court may not discharge the guardian's sureties from all further liability under a bond required by this section or another provision of this title until the court:

(1) finds that the guardian used loan proceeds resulting from the minor ward's interest solely for the purposes authorized by Section 1352.106; and

(2) is presented with satisfactory evidence that the home equity loan has been repaid and is no longer considered an outstanding obligation.

Added by Acts 2011, 82nd Leg., ch. 823 (H.B. 2759), § 1.02, eff. Jan. 1, 2014.

### § 1352.106. Use of Proceeds

Proceeds of a home equity loan that is the subject of an application under Section 1352.102 that are attributable to the minor ward's interest may be spent only to:

(1) make improvements to the homestead;

(2) pay for the ward's education or maintenance expenses; or

(3) pay the loan's outstanding balance.

Added by Acts 2011, 82nd Leg., ch. 823 (H.B. 2759), § 1.02, eff. Jan. 1, 2014.

### § 1352.107. Annual Accounting

A guardian of the person executing a home equity loan on a minor ward's behalf must account for the transaction, including the expenditure of the loan proceeds, in the annual account required by Subchapter A, Chapter 1163.

Added by Acts 2011, 82nd Leg., ch. 823 (H.B. 2759), § 1.02, eff. Jan. 1, 2014.

### § 1352.108. Disaffirmation of Home Equity Loan Prohibited

A minor ward may not disaffirm a home equity loan authorized by the court under this subchapter.

Added by Acts 2011, 82nd Leg., ch. 823 (H.B. 2759), § 1.02, eff. Jan. 1, 2014.

## CHAPTER 1353. MANAGEMENT AND CONTROL OF INCAPACITATED SPOUSE'S PROPERTY

## SUBCHAPTER A.  APPOINTMENT OF COMMUNITY ADMINISTRATOR OR GUARDIAN OF THE ESTATE

### § 1353.001.  Effect of Subchapter

(a) The manner in which community property is administered under this subchapter does not affect:

(1) the duties and obligations between spouses, including the duty to support the other spouse; and

(2) the rights of any creditor of either spouse.

(b) This subchapter does not partition community property between an incapacitated spouse and a spouse who is not incapacitated.

Added by Acts 2011, 82nd Leg., ch. 823 (H.B. 2759), § 1.02, eff. Jan. 1, 2014.

### § 1353.002.  Spouse as Community Administrator

(a) Except as provided by Section 1353.004, when a spouse is judicially declared to be incapacitated, the other spouse, in the capacity of surviving partner of the marital partnership, acquires full power to manage, control, and dispose of the entire community estate, including the part of the community estate that the incapacitated spouse legally has the power to manage in the absence of the incapacity, as community administrator without an administration.

(b) The spouse who is not incapacitated is presumed to be suitable and qualified to serve as community administrator.

Added by Acts 2011, 82nd Leg., ch. 823 (H.B. 2759), § 1.02, eff. Jan. 1, 2014.

### § 1353.003.  Appointment of Guardian of the Estate to Administer Separate Property

(a) Except as provided by Section 1353.004, when a spouse who owns separate property is judicially declared to be incapacitated, the court shall appoint the other spouse or another person or entity, in the order of precedence established under Subchapter C, Chapter 1104, as guardian of the estate to administer only the separate property of the incapacitated spouse.

(b) The qualification of a guardian of the estate of the separate property of an incapacitated spouse under Subsection (a) does not deprive the spouse who is not incapacitated of the right to manage, control, and dispose of the entire community estate as provided by this title.

Added by Acts 2011, 82nd Leg., ch. 823 (H.B. 2759), § 1.02, eff. Jan. 1, 2014.

### § 1353.004.  Appointment of Guardian of the Estate Under Certain Circumstances

(a) This section applies only if:

(1) a spouse who is not incapacitated is removed as community administrator; or

(2) the court finds that the spouse who is not incapacitated:

(A) would be disqualified to serve as guardian under Subchapter H, Chapter 1104; or

(B) is not suitable to serve as the community administrator for any other reason.

(b) The court shall appoint a guardian of the estate for the incapacitated spouse if the court:

(1) has not appointed a guardian of the estate under Section 1353.003(a); or

(2) has appointed the spouse who is not incapacitated as the guardian of the estate under Section 1353.003(a).

(c) After considering the financial circumstances of the spouses and any other relevant factors, the court may order the spouse who is not incapacitated to deliver to the guardian of the estate of the incapacitated spouse not more than one-half of the community property that is subject to the spouses' joint management, control, and disposition under Section 3.102, Family Code.

(d) The court shall authorize the guardian of the estate of the incapacitated spouse to administer:

(1) any separate property of the incapacitated spouse;

(2) any community property that is subject to the incapacitated spouse's sole management, control, and disposition under Section 3.102, Family Code;

(3) any community property delivered to the guardian of the estate under Subsection (c); and

(4) any income earned on property described by this section.

(e) Community property administered by a guardian of the estate under Subsection (d) is considered the incapacitated spouse's community property, subject to the incapacitated spouse's sole management, control, and disposition under Section 3.102, Family Code.

Added by Acts 2011, 82nd Leg., ch. 823 (H.B. 2759), § 1.02, eff. Jan. 1, 2014.

### § 1353.005. Administration of Certain Property by Non–incapacitated Spouse

(a) On a person's removal as community administrator or on qualification of a guardian of the estate of the person's incapacitated spouse under Section 1353.004, as appropriate, a spouse who is not incapacitated shall continue to administer:

(1) the person's own separate property;

(2) any community property that is subject to the person's sole management, control, and disposition under Section 3.102, Family Code;

(3) either:

(A) any community property subject to the spouses' joint management, control, and disposition under Section 3.102, Family Code; or

(B) if the person is required to deliver a portion of that community property described by Paragraph (A) to the guardian of the estate of the person's incapacitated spouse under Section 1353.004(c), only the portion of the community property remaining after delivery; and

(4) any income earned on property described by this section the person is authorized to administer.

(b) Community property administered under this section by a spouse who is not incapacitated is considered that spouse's community property, subject to that spouse's sole management, control, and disposition under Section 3.102, Family Code.

Added by Acts 2011, 82nd Leg., ch. 823 (H.B. 2759), § 1.02, eff. Jan. 1, 2014.

### § 1353.006. Effect of Court Order on Creditors' Claims

A court order that directs the administration of community property under Section 1353.004 or 1353.005 does not affect the enforceability of a creditor's claim existing on the date the court renders the order.

Added by Acts 2011, 82nd Leg., ch. 823 (H.B. 2759), § 1.02, eff. Jan. 1, 2014.

### SUBCHAPTER B. DUTIES OF COMMUNITY ADMINISTRATORS AND GUARDIANS OF THE ESTATE

### § 1353.051. Inventory and Appraisement by Community Administrator

(a) On its own motion or on the motion of an interested person for good cause shown, the court may order a community administrator to file a verified, full, and detailed inventory and appraisement of:

(1) any community property that is subject to the incapacitated spouse's sole management, control, and disposition under Section 3.102, Family Code;

(2) any community property subject to the spouses' joint management, control, and disposition under Section 3.102, Family Code; and

(3) any income earned on property described by this subsection.

(b) An inventory and appraisement ordered under this section must be:

(1) prepared in the same form and manner that is required of a guardian under Section 1154.051; and

(2) filed not later than the 90th day after the date the order is issued.

Added by Acts 2011, 82nd Leg., ch. 823 (H.B. 2759), § 1.02, eff. Jan. 1, 2014.

### § 1353.052. Account by Community Administrator

(a) At any time after the expiration of 15 months after the date a community administrator's spouse is judicially declared to be incapacitated, the court, on its own motion or on the motion of an interested person for good cause shown, may order the community administrator to prepare and file an account of:

(1) any community property that is subject to the incapacitated spouse's sole management, control, and disposition under Section 3.102, Family Code;

(2) any community property subject to the spouses' joint management, control, and disposition under Section 3.102, Family Code; and

(3) any income earned on property described by this subsection.

(b) An account ordered under Subsection (a) must be:

(1) prepared in the same form and manner that is required of a guardian under Subchapter A, Chapter 1163, except that the community administrator is not required to file the account annually with the county clerk; and

(2) filed not later than the 60th day after the date the order is issued.

(c) After an initial account has been filed by a community administrator under this section, the court, on the motion of an interested person for good cause shown, may order the community administrator to file subsequent periodic accounts at intervals of not less than 12 months.

Added by Acts 2011, 82nd Leg., ch. 823 (H.B. 2759), § 1.02, eff. Jan. 1, 2014.

### § 1353.053. Disclosure of Certain Lawsuits to the Court by Community Administrator

A person whose spouse is judicially declared to be incapacitated and who acquires the power to manage, control, and dispose of the entire community estate under Section 1353.002(a) shall inform the court in writing of any suit filed by or on behalf of the person that:

(1) is a suit for dissolution of the marriage of the person and the person's incapacitated spouse; or

(2) names the incapacitated spouse as a defendant.

Added by Acts 2011, 82nd Leg., ch. 823 (H.B. 2759), § 1.02, eff. Jan. 1, 2014.

### § 1353.054. Delivery of Community Property by Guardian of the Estate to Community Administrator

A guardian of the estate of an incapacitated married person who, as guardian, is administering community property as part of the ward's estate, shall deliver on demand the community property to the spouse who is not incapacitated if the spouse becomes community administrator under Section 1353.002(a).

Added by Acts 2011, 82nd Leg., ch. 823 (H.B. 2759), § 1.02, eff. Jan. 1, 2014.

### SUBCHAPTER C. REMOVAL OR TERMINATION OF POWERS OF COMMUNITY ADMINISTRATOR

### § 1353.101. Grounds for Removal of Community Administrator

A court may remove a community administrator if:

(1) the community administrator fails to comply with a court order for:

(A) an inventory and appraisement under Section 1353.051; or

(B) an account or subsequent account under Section 1353.052;

(2) sufficient grounds appear to support belief that the community administrator has misapplied or embezzled, or is about to misapply or embezzle, all or part of the property committed to the community administrator's care;

(3) the community administrator is proved to have been guilty of gross misconduct or gross mismanagement in the performance of duties as community administrator; or

(4) the community administrator:

(A) becomes an incapacitated person;

(B) is sentenced to the penitentiary; or

(C) for any other reason becomes legally incapacitated from properly performing the community administrator's fiduciary duties.

Added by Acts 2011, 82nd Leg., ch. 823 (H.B. 2759), § 1.02, eff. Jan. 1, 2014.

### § 1353.102. Procedure for Removal of Community Administrator

(a) A court may remove a community administrator on the court's own motion or on the motion of an interested person, after the community administrator has been cited by personal service to answer at a time and place specified in the notice.

(b) The removal order must:

(1) state the cause of removal; and

(2) direct the disposition of the assets remaining in the name or under the control of the removed community administrator.

(c) A community administrator who defends an action for the removal of the community administrator in good faith, regardless of whether successful, is entitled to recover from the incapacitated spouse's part of the community estate the community administrator's necessary expenses and disbursements in the removal proceedings, including reasonable attorney's fees.

Added by Acts 2011, 82nd Leg., ch. 823 (H.B. 2759), § 1.02, eff. Jan. 1, 2014.

### § 1353.103. Termination of Community Administrator's Powers on Recovery of Capacity

The special powers of management, control, and disposition vested in the community administrator by this title terminate when a court of competent jurisdiction by decree finds that the mental capacity of the incapacitated spouse has been recovered.

Added by Acts 2011, 82nd Leg., ch. 823 (H.B. 2759), § 1.02, eff. Jan. 1, 2014.

## SUBCHAPTER D.   APPOINTMENT OF ATTORNEY AD LITEM

### § 1353.151.   Appointment of Attorney ad Litem for Incapacitated Spouse

(a) The court shall appoint an attorney ad litem to represent the interests of an incapacitated spouse in a proceeding to remove a community administrator or other proceeding brought under this chapter.

(b) The attorney ad litem may demand from the community administrator an account or inventory and appraisement of the incapacitated spouse's part of the community estate being managed by the community administrator.

(c) A community administrator shall comply with a demand made under this section not later than the 60th day after the date the community administrator receives the demand.

(d) An account or inventory and appraisement returned under this section must be prepared in the form and manner required by the attorney ad litem. The attorney ad litem may require the community administrator to file the account or inventory and appraisement with the court.

Added by Acts 2011, 82nd Leg., ch. 823 (H.B. 2759), § 1.02, eff. Jan. 1, 2014.

## CHAPTER 1354.   RECEIVERSHIP FOR ESTATES OF CERTAIN INCAPAC- ITATED PERSONS

### § 1354.001.   Appointment of Receiver

(a) A judge of a probate court in the county in which an incapacitated person resides or in which the incapacitated person's endangered estate is located shall, with or without application, enter an order appointing a suitable person as receiver to take charge of the estate if:

(1) it appears that all or part of the estate of the incapacitated person is in danger of injury, loss, or waste and in need of a guardianship or other representative;

(2) there is no guardian of the estate who is qualified in this state; and

(3) a guardian is not needed.

(b) The court order must specify the duties and powers of the receiver the judge considers necessary for the protection, conservation, and preservation of the estate.

(c) The clerk shall enter an order issued under this section in the judge's guardianship docket.

Added by Acts 2011, 82nd Leg., ch. 823 (H.B. 2759), § 1.02, eff. Jan. 1, 2014.

### § 1354.002.   Bond

(a) A court order issued under Section 1354.001 shall require a receiver appointed under that section to give a bond, as in ordinary receiverships, in an amount the judge considers necessary to protect the estate.

(b) The person appointed as receiver shall:

(1) make and submit a bond for the judge's approval; and

(2) file the bond, when approved, with the clerk.

Added by Acts 2011, 82nd Leg., ch. 823 (H.B. 2759), § 1.02, eff. Jan. 1, 2014.

### § 1354.003.   Powers and Duties of Receiver

The person appointed as receiver shall take charge of the endangered estate as provided by the powers and duties vested in the person by the order of appointment and subsequent orders of the judge.

Added by Acts 2011, 82nd Leg., ch. 823 (H.B. 2759), § 1.02, eff. Jan. 1, 2014.

### § 1354.004.   Expenditures by Receiver

(a) If, while the receivership is pending, the needs of the incapacitated person require the use of the income or corpus of the estate for the education, clothing, or subsistence of the person, the judge shall, with or without application, enter an order in the judge's guardianship docket that appropriates an amount of income or corpus sufficient for that purpose.

(b) The receiver shall use the amount appropriated by the court to pay a claim for the education, clothing, or subsistence of the incapacitated person that is presented to the judge for approval and ordered by the judge to be paid.

Added by Acts 2011, 82nd Leg., ch. 823 (H.B. 2759), § 1.02, eff. Jan. 1, 2014.

## § 1354.005. Use of Excess Estate Assets

(a) A receiver who, while the receivership is pending, has possession of an amount of money belonging to the incapacitated person in excess of the amount needed for current necessities and expenses may, under direction of the judge, invest, lend, or contribute all or part of the excess money in the manner, for the security, and on the terms provided by this title for investments, loans, or contributions by guardians.

(b) The receiver shall report to the judge all transactions made under this section in the same manner that a report is required of a guardian under this title.

Added by Acts 2011, 82nd Leg., ch. 823 (H.B. 2759), § 1.02, eff. Jan. 1, 2014.

## § 1354.006. Receiver's Expenses, Account, and Compensation

(a) All necessary expenses incurred by a receiver in administering the estate may be reported monthly to the judge in the form of a sworn statement of account that includes a report of:

(1) the receiver's acts;

(2) the condition of the estate;

(3) the status of the threatened danger to the estate; and

(4) the progress made toward abatement of the danger.

(b) If the judge is satisfied that the statement is correct and reasonable in all respects, the judge shall promptly enter an order approving the expenses and authorizing reimbursement of the receiver from the estate funds in the receiver's possession.

(c) A receiver shall be compensated for services provided in the receiver's official capacity in the same manner and amount provided by this title for similar services provided by a guardian of an estate.

Added by Acts 2011, 82nd Leg., ch. 823 (H.B. 2759), § 1.02, eff. Jan. 1, 2014.

## § 1354.007. Closing Receivership; Notice

(a) When the threatened danger has abated and the estate is no longer liable to injury, loss, or waste because there is no guardian or other representative of the estate, the receiver shall:

(1) report to the judge; and

(2) file with the clerk a full and final sworn account of:

(A) all property of the estate received by the receiver;

(B) all property of the estate in the receiver's possession while the receivership was pending;

(C) all sums paid out;

(D) all acts performed by the receiver with respect to the estate; and

(E) all property of the estate remaining in the receiver's possession on the date of the report.

(b) On the filing of the report, the clerk shall:

(1) issue and cause to be posted a notice to all persons interested in the welfare of the incapacitated person; and

(2) give personal notice to the person who has custody of the incapacitated person to appear before the judge at a time and place specified in the notice and contest the report and account if the person desires.

Added by Acts 2011, 82nd Leg., ch. 823 (H.B. 2759), § 1.02, eff. Jan. 1, 2014.

## § 1354.008. Discharge of Receiver

(a) If, on hearing the receiver's report and account, the judge is satisfied that the danger of injury, loss, or waste to the estate has abated and that the report and account are correct, the judge shall:

(1) enter an order finding that the danger of injury, loss, or waste to the estate has abated; and

(2) direct the receiver to deliver the estate to:

(A) the person from whom the receiver took possession as receiver;

(B) the person who has custody of the incapacitated person; or

(C) another person the judge finds is entitled to possession of the estate.

(b) A person who receives the estate under Subsection (a) shall execute and file with the clerk an appropriate receipt for the estate that is delivered to the person.

(c) The judge's order shall discharge the receivership and the sureties on the receiver's bond.

(d) If the judge is not satisfied that the danger has abated, or is not satisfied with the receiver's report and account, the judge shall enter an order continuing the receivership in effect until the judge is satisfied that the danger has abated or is satisfied with the report and account.

Added by Acts 2011, 82nd Leg., ch. 823 (H.B. 2759), § 1.02, eff. Jan. 1, 2014.

## § 1354.009.  Record

An order, bond, report, account, or notice in a receivership proceeding must be recorded in the judge's guardianship docket.

Added by Acts 2011, 82nd Leg., ch. 823 (H.B. 2759), § 1.02, eff. Jan. 1, 2014.

## CHAPTER 1355.  PAYMENT OF CERTAIN CLAIMS WITHOUT GUARDIANSHIP

### SUBCHAPTER A.  PAYMENT OF CLAIMS TO CERTAIN INCAPACITATED PERSONS AND FORMER WARDS

**Section**
1355.001.  Payment of Claims to Resident Creditor.
1355.002.  Payment of Claims to Nonresident Creditor.

### SUBCHAPTER B.  ADMINISTRATION OF MONEY

1355.051.  Investment of Money by Clerk.
1355.052.  Annual Report.

### SUBCHAPTER C.  WITHDRAWAL OF MONEY

1355.101.  Applicability of Subchapter.
1355.102.  Custodian of Resident Creditor.
1355.103.  Withdrawal of Money by Custodian;  Bond.
1355.104.  Custodian's Report.
1355.105.  Withdrawal of Money by Creditor or Creditor's Heir or Representative.

### SUBCHAPTER D.  USE OF MONEY BY ELEEMOSYNARY INSTITUTION FOR BENEFIT OF RESIDENT

1355.151.  Applicability of Subchapter.
1355.152.  Payment of Money to Institution.
1355.153.  Deposit of Money in Trust.
1355.154.  Death of Resident or Depletion of Money.

## SUBCHAPTER A.  PAYMENT OF CLAIMS TO CERTAIN INCAPACITATED PERSONS AND FORMER WARDS

### § 1355.001.  Payment of Claims to Resident Creditor

(a) In this section, "resident creditor" means a person who:

(1) is a resident of this state;  and

(2) is entitled to money in an amount that is $100,000 or less, the right to which is liquidated and is uncontested in any pending lawsuit.

(b) This section applies only to a resident creditor who:

(1) is an incapacitated person or the former ward of a guardianship terminated under Chapter 1204;  and

(2) does not have a legal guardian of the creditor's estate.

(c) A debtor who owes money to a resident creditor to whom this section applies may pay the money to the county clerk of the county in which the creditor resides to the account of the creditor.  When making a payment under this subsection, a debtor shall give to the clerk:

(1) the creditor's name;

(2) the creditor's social security identification number;

(3) the nature of the creditor's disability;

(4) the creditor's post office address;  and

(5) if the creditor is a minor, the creditor's age.

(d) The receipt for the money signed by the county clerk is binding on the resident creditor as of the date of receipt and to the extent of the payment.

(e) The county clerk shall:

(1) by letter mailed to the address given under Subsection (c)(4), apprise the resident creditor that the deposit was made;  and

(2) on receipt of the payment, bring the payment to the court's attention.

Added by Acts 2011, 82nd Leg., ch. 823 (H.B. 2759), § 1.02, eff. Jan. 1, 2014.

### § 1355.002.  Payment of Claims to Nonresident Creditor

(a) In this section, "creditor" means a person who is entitled to money in an amount that is not more than $100,000 owing as a result of transactions in this state, the right to which is liquidated and is uncontested in any pending lawsuit in this state.

(b) This section applies only to a creditor who is a nonresident minor, a nonresident person who is adjudged by a court of competent jurisdiction to be incapacitated, or the former ward of a guardianship terminated under Chapter 1204 who has no legal guardian qualified in this state.

(c) A debtor in this state who owes money to a creditor to whom this section applies may pay the money:

(1) to the creditor's guardian qualified in the domiciliary jurisdiction; or

(2) to the county clerk of:

(A) any county in this state in which real property owned by the creditor is located; or

(B) if the creditor is not known to own real property in this state, the county in which the debtor resides.

(d) A payment made under this section is for the creditor's account and for the creditor's use and benefit.

(e) A receipt for payment signed by the county clerk is binding on the creditor as of the date and to the extent of payment if the receipt states:

(1) the creditor's name; and

(2) the creditor's post office address, if the address is known.

(f) A county clerk who receives a payment under Subsection (c) shall handle the money in the same manner as provided for a payment to the account of a resident creditor under Sections 1355.001, 1355.051, 1355.052, 1355.102, 1355.103, and 1355.104. Those sections apply to the handling and disposition of money or any increase, dividend, or income paid to the clerk for the use, benefit, and account of the creditor to whom this section applies.

Added by Acts 2011, 82nd Leg., ch. 823 (H.B. 2759), § 1.02, eff. Jan. 1, 2014.

## SUBCHAPTER B. ADMINISTRATION OF MONEY

### § 1355.051. Investment of Money by Clerk

(a) On receipt of a payment under Section 1355.001, the county clerk shall invest the money as authorized under this title under court order in the name and for the account of the minor or other person entitled to the money.

(b) The county clerk shall credit any increase, dividend, or income from an investment made under this chapter to the account of the minor or other person entitled to the investment.

Added by Acts 2011, 82nd Leg., ch. 823 (H.B. 2759), § 1.02, eff. Jan. 1, 2014.

### § 1355.052. Annual Report

Not later than March 1 of each year, the court clerk shall make a written report to the court of the status of an investment made by the county clerk under Section 1355.051. The report must contain:

(1) the amount of the original investment or the value of the investment at the last annual report, whichever is later;

(2) any increase, dividend, or income from the investment since the last annual report;

(3) the total amount of the investment and all increases, dividends, or income at the date of the report; and

(4) the name of the depository or the type of investment.

Added by Acts 2011, 82nd Leg., ch. 823 (H.B. 2759), § 1.02, eff. Jan. 1, 2014.

## SUBCHAPTER C. WITHDRAWAL OF MONEY

### § 1355.101. Applicability of Subchapter

Except as provided by Section 1355.105, this subchapter applies only to a resident creditor to whom Section 1355.001 applies.

Added by Acts 2011, 82nd Leg., ch. 823 (H.B. 2759), § 1.02, eff. Jan. 1, 2014.

### § 1355.102. Custodian of Resident Creditor

(a) The following may serve as custodian of a resident creditor under this section:

(1) a parent of the creditor;

(2) the unestranged spouse of the creditor; or

(3) if there is no spouse and both of the creditor's parents are dead or nonresidents of this state, the person who:

(A) resides in this state; and

(B) has actual custody of the creditor.

(b) An unestranged spouse residing in this state shall be given priority over a creditor's parent to serve as custodian under this subchapter.

Added by Acts 2011, 82nd Leg., ch. 823 (H.B. 2759), § 1.02, eff. Jan. 1, 2014.

### § 1355.103. Withdrawal of Money by Custodian; Bond

(a) A resident creditor's custodian may withdraw the money from the court clerk for the creditor's use and benefit if the custodian files with the clerk:

(1) a written application; and

(2) a bond approved by the county judge.

(b) A custodian's bond must be:

(1) twice the amount of the money to be withdrawn by the custodian;

(2) payable to the judge or the judge's successors in office; and

(3) conditioned that the custodian will:

(A) use the money for the resident creditor's benefit under the court's direction; and

(B) when legally required, faithfully account to the resident creditor and the creditor's heirs or legal representatives for the money and any increase to the money on:

(i) the removal of the creditor's disability;

(ii) the creditor's death; or

(iii) the appointment of a guardian for the creditor.

(c) A custodian may not receive a fee or commission for taking care of, handling, or spending money withdrawn by the custodian.

Added by Acts 2011, 82nd Leg., ch. 823 (H.B. 2759), § 1.02, eff. Jan. 1, 2014.

### § 1355.104. Custodian's Report

(a) The custodian shall file with the county clerk a sworn report of the custodian's accounting when the custodian has:

(1) spent the money in accordance with the court's directions; or

(2) otherwise complied with the terms of the custodian's bond by accounting for the money and any increase in the money.

(b) The filing of a custodian's report, when approved by the court, operates as a discharge of the person as custodian and of the person's sureties from all further liability under the bond.

(c) The court shall satisfy itself that the custodian's report is true and correct and may require proof as in other cases.

Added by Acts 2011, 82nd Leg., ch. 823 (H.B. 2759), § 1.02, eff. Jan. 1, 2014.

### § 1355.105. Withdrawal of Money by Creditor or Creditor's Heir or Representative

(a) On presentation to the court clerk of an order of a county or probate court of the county in which the money is held, money that is not withdrawn by an authorized person as provided by this chapter may be withdrawn by:

(1) the creditor, after termination of the creditor's disability;

(2) a subsequent personal representative of the creditor; or

(3) the creditor's heirs.

(b) A withdrawal under Subsection (a) may be made at any time and without a special bond for that purpose.

(c) The order presented under Subsection (a) must direct the court clerk to deliver the money to the creditor, the creditor's personal representative, or the creditor's heirs named in the order.

(d) Before the court may issue an order under this section, the person's identity and credentials must be proved to the court's satisfaction.

Added by Acts 2011, 82nd Leg., ch. 823 (H.B. 2759), § 1.02, eff. Jan. 1, 2014.

## SUBCHAPTER D. USE OF MONEY BY ELEEMOSYNARY INSTITUTION FOR BENEFIT OF RESIDENT

### § 1355.151. Applicability of Subchapter

This subchapter applies only to money of a resident of an eleemosynary institution of this state that is on deposit in a court registry and does not exceed $10,000.

Added by Acts 2011, 82nd Leg., ch. 823 (H.B. 2759), § 1.02, eff. Jan. 1, 2014.

### § 1355.152. Payment of Money to Institution

(a) The judge of a county court, district court, or other court of this state may by order direct the court clerk to pay money to an eleemosynary institution of this state for the use and benefit of a resident of the institution if the court receives satisfactory proof by affidavit or otherwise that the resident:

(1) is a person who has a mental disability, an incapacitated person, or a person whose mental illness or mental incapacity renders the person incapable of caring for himself or herself and of managing the person's property and financial affairs; and

(2) has no known legal guardian appointed for the resident's estate.

(b) The affidavit under Subsection (a) may be executed by the superintendent, business manager, or field representative of the institution of which the person is a resident.

(c) The institution to which the payment is made under Subsection (a) may not be required to give bond or security for receiving the money from the court registry.

(d) The receipt from the institution for a payment, or the canceled check or warrant by which the payment was made:

(1) is sufficient evidence of the disposition of the payment; and

(2) relieves the court clerk from further responsibility for the disposition.

Added by Acts 2011, 82nd Leg., ch. 823 (H.B. 2759), § 1.02, eff. Jan. 1, 2014.

### § 1355.153. Deposit of Money in Trust

(a) On receipt of money under this subchapter, an eleemosynary institution shall deposit all of the money received to the resident's trust account.

(b) Money deposited in a trust account may be used only:

(1) by or for the personal use of the owner of the trust account, under the rules or custom of the institution in the expenditure of money by a resident; or

(2) by the responsible officer of the institution, for the resident's use and benefit.

Added by Acts 2011, 82nd Leg., ch. 823 (H.B. 2759), § 1.02, eff. Jan. 1, 2014.

### § 1355.154. Death of Resident or Depletion of Money

(a) After the expenditure of all money in a resident's trust account, or after the resident's death, the responsible officer of the eleemosynary institution shall furnish a statement of expenditures of the money to the resident's nearest relative who is entitled to receive the statement.

(b) A copy of the statement described by Subsection (a) shall be filed with the court that first granted the order to dispose of the money in accordance with this title.

(c) The balance of a trust account of a resident of an eleemosynary institution who dies may be applied to:

(1) the resident's burial expenses; or

(2) the care, support, and treatment account of the resident at the institution.

Added by Acts 2011, 82nd Leg., ch. 823 (H.B. 2759), § 1.02, eff. Jan. 1, 2014.

## CHAPTER 1356. COURT APPROVAL OF CERTAIN ARTS AND ENTERTAINMENT, ADVERTISEMENT, AND SPORTS CONTRACTS

### SUBCHAPTER A. GENERAL PROVISIONS

### SUBCHAPTER A. GENERAL PROVISIONS

### § 1356.001. Definitions

In this chapter:

(1) "Advertise" means to solicit or induce the purchase of consumer goods or services through electronic or print media, including:

(A) radio;

(B) television;

(C) computer; or

(D) direct mail.

(2) "Advertisement contract" means a contract under which a person is employed or agrees to advertise consumer goods or services.

(3) "Artist" means:

(A) an actor who performs in a motion picture, theatrical, radio, television, or other entertainment production;

(B) a musician or musical director;

(C) a director or producer of a motion picture, theatrical, radio, television, or other entertainment production;

(D) a writer;

(E) a cinematographer;

(F) a composer, lyricist, or arranger of musical compositions;

(G) a dancer or choreographer of musical productions;

(H) a model; or

(I) any other individual who provides similar professional services in a motion picture, theatrical, radio, television, or other entertainment production.

(4) "Arts and entertainment contract" means a contract under which:

(A) an artist is employed or agrees to provide services in a motion picture, theatrical, radio, television, or other entertainment production; or

(B) a person agrees to purchase, secure, sell, lease, license, or otherwise dispose of literary, musical, or dramatic tangible or intangible property or any rights in that property for use in the field of entertainment, including:

(i) a motion picture;

(ii) television;

(iii) the production of phonograph records; or

(iv) theater.

(5) "Consumer goods" means goods used or bought for use primarily for personal, family, or household purposes.

(6) "Net earnings," with respect to a minor, means the total amount to be received for the services of the minor under a contract less:

(A) the amount required by law to be paid as taxes to any government or governmental agency;

(B) a reasonable amount to be spent for the support, care, maintenance, education, and training of the minor;

(C) fees and expenses paid in connection with procuring the contract or maintaining employment of the minor; and

(D) attorney's fees for services provided in connection with the contract or any other business of the minor.

(7) "Sports contract" means a contract under which an athlete is employed or agrees to participate, compete, or engage in a sports or athletic activity at a professional or amateur sports event or athletic event.

Added by Acts 2011, 82nd Leg., ch. 823 (H.B. 2759), § 1.02, eff. Jan. 1, 2014.

## § 1356.002.  Duration of Contract of a Minor

This chapter may not be construed to authorize a contract that binds a minor after the seventh anniversary of the date of the contract.

Added by Acts 2011, 82nd Leg., ch. 823 (H.B. 2759), § 1.02, eff. Jan. 1, 2014.

## SUBCHAPTER B.  COURT ACTION REGARDING CERTAIN CONTRACTS

### § 1356.051.  Approval of Certain Contracts of a Minor

(a) On the petition of the guardian of the estate of a minor, a court may issue an order approving for purposes of this chapter an arts and entertainment contract, advertisement contract, or sports contract that is entered into by the minor.

(b) Approval of a contract under this section extends to the contract as a whole and each term and provision of the contract, including any optional or conditional contract provision relating to the extension or termination of the contract's term.

(c) A court may withhold approval of a contract in which part of the minor's net earnings will be set aside as provided by Section 1356.054 until the guardian of the minor's estate executes and files with the court written consent to the issuance of the order.

Added by Acts 2011, 82nd Leg., ch. 823 (H.B. 2759), § 1.02, eff. Jan. 1, 2014.

### § 1356.052.  Notice Required

Before the court may approve a contract under Section 1356.051, the guardian of the minor's estate must provide the other party to the contract notice of the petition and an opportunity to request a hearing in the manner provided by the court.

Added by Acts 2011, 82nd Leg., ch. 823 (H.B. 2759), § 1.02, eff. Jan. 1, 2014.

### § 1356.053.  Necessary Parties to Proceeding

Each parent of a minor for whom a proceeding is brought under Section 1356.051 is a necessary party to the proceeding.

Added by Acts 2011, 82nd Leg., ch. 823 (H.B. 2759), § 1.02, eff. Jan. 1, 2014.

### § 1356.054.  Set–aside and Preservation of Portion of Net Earnings

(a) Notwithstanding any other law, in an order issued under Section 1356.051, the court may require that a portion of the net earnings of the minor under the contract be set aside and preserved for the benefit of the minor in a trust created under Section 1301.053

or 1301.054 or a similar trust created under the laws of another state.

(b) The amount to be set aside under this section must be reasonable as determined by the court.

Added by Acts 2011, 82nd Leg., ch. 823 (H.B. 2759), § 1.02, eff. Jan. 1, 2014.

### § 1356.055. Valid Contract Not Voidable

A contract approved under Section 1356.051 that is otherwise valid is not voidable solely on the ground that it was entered into by a person during the age of minority.

Added by Acts 2011, 82nd Leg., ch. 823 (H.B. 2759), § 1.02, eff. Jan. 1, 2014.

### § 1356.056. Guardian ad Litem

The court may appoint a guardian ad litem for a minor who has entered into an arts and entertainment contract, advertisement contract, or sports contract if the court finds that the appointment would be in the best interest of the minor.

Added by Acts 2011, 82nd Leg., ch. 823 (H.B. 2759), § 1.02, eff. Jan. 1, 2014.

# HEALTH AND SAFETY CODE

## TITLE 2. HEALTH

## SUBTITLE H. PUBLIC HEALTH PROVISIONS

### CHAPTER 166. ADVANCE DIRECTIVES

## SUBCHAPTER A.  GENERAL PROVISIONS

### § 166.001.  Short Title

This chapter may be cited as the Advance Directives Act.

Added by Acts 1999, 76th Leg., ch. 450, § 1.02, eff. Sept. 1, 1999.

### § 166.002.  Definitions

In this chapter:

(1) "Advance directive" means:

(A) a directive, as that term is defined by Section 166.031;

(B) an out-of-hospital DNR order, as that term is defined by Section 166.081; or

(C) a medical power of attorney under Subchapter D.¹

(2) "Artificial nutrition and hydration" means the provision of nutrients or fluids by a tube inserted in a vein, under the skin in the subcutaneous tissues, or in the stomach (gastrointestinal tract).

(3) "Attending physician" means a physician selected by or assigned to a patient who has primary responsibility for a patient's treatment and care.

(4) "Competent" means possessing the ability, based on reasonable medical judgment, to understand and appreciate the nature and consequences of a treatment decision, including the significant benefits and harms of and reasonable alternatives to a proposed treatment decision.

(5) "Declarant" means a person who has executed or issued a directive under this chapter.

(5–a) "Digital signature" means an electronic identifier intended by the person using it to have the same force and effect as the use of a manual signature.

(5–b) "Electronic signature" means a facsimile, scan, uploaded image, computer-generated image, or other electronic representation of a manual signature that is intended by the person using it to have the same force and effect of law as a manual signature.

(6) "Ethics or medical committee" means a committee established under Sections 161.031–161.033.

(7) "Health care or treatment decision" means consent, refusal to consent, or withdrawal of consent to health care, treatment, service, or a procedure to maintain, diagnose, or treat an individual's physical or mental condition, including such a decision on behalf of a minor.

(8) "Incompetent" means lacking the ability, based on reasonable medical judgment, to understand and appreciate the nature and consequences of a treatment decision, including the significant benefits and harms of and reasonable alternatives to a proposed treatment decision.

(9) "Irreversible condition" means a condition, injury, or illness:

(A) that may be treated but is never cured or eliminated;

(B) that leaves a person unable to care for or make decisions for the person's own self; and

(C) that, without life-sustaining treatment provided in accordance with the prevailing standard of medical care, is fatal.

(10) "Life-sustaining treatment" means treatment that, based on reasonable medical judgment, sustains the life of a patient and without which the patient will die. The term includes both life-sustaining medications and artificial life support, such as mechanical breathing machines, kidney dialysis treatment, and artificial nutrition and hydration. The term does not include the administration of pain management medication or the performance of a medical procedure considered to be necessary to provide comfort care, or any other medical care provided to alleviate a patient's pain.

(11) "Medical power of attorney" means a document delegating to an agent authority to make health care decisions executed or issued under Subchapter D.

(12) "Physician" means:

(A) a physician licensed by the Texas State Board of Medical Examiners; or

(B) a properly credentialed physician who holds a commission in the uniformed services of the United States and who is serving on active duty in this state.

(13) "Terminal condition" means an incurable condition caused by injury, disease, or illness that according to reasonable medical judgment will produce death within six months, even with available life-sustaining treatment provided in accordance with the prevailing standard of medical care. A patient who has been admitted to a program under which the person receives hospice services provided by a home and community support services agency licensed under Chapter 142 is presumed to have a terminal condition for purposes of this chapter.

(14) "Witness" means a person who may serve as a witness under Section 166.003.

(15) "Cardiopulmonary resuscitation" means any medical intervention used to restore circulatory or respiratory function that has ceased.

Added by Acts 1999, 76th Leg., ch. 450, § 1.02, eff. Sept. 1, 1999. Amended by Acts 2003, 78th Leg., ch. 1228, § 1, eff. June 20, 2003; Acts 2009, 81st Leg., ch. 461, § 1, eff. Sept. 1, 2009.

¹ V.T.C.A., Health & Safety Code § 166.151 et seq.

## § 166.003. Witnesses

In any circumstance in which this chapter requires the execution of an advance directive or the issuance of a nonwritten advance directive to be witnessed:

(1) each witness must be a competent adult; and

(2) at least one of the witnesses must be a person who is not:

(A) a person designated by the declarant to make a treatment decision;

(B) a person related to the declarant by blood or marriage;

(C) a person entitled to any part of the declarant's estate after the declarant's death under a will or codicil executed by the declarant or by operation of law;

(D) the attending physician;

(E) an employee of the attending physician;

(F) an employee of a health care facility in which the declarant is a patient if the employee is providing direct patient care to the declarant or is an officer, director, partner, or business office employee of the health care facility or of any parent organization of the health care facility; or

(G) a person who, at the time the written advance directive is executed or, if the directive is a nonwritten directive issued under this chapter, at the time the nonwritten directive is issued, has a claim against any part of the declarant's estate after the declarant's death.

Added by Acts 1999, 76th Leg., ch. 450, § 1.02, eff. Sept. 1, 1999.

## § 166.004. Statement Relating to Advance Directive

(a) In this section, "health care provider" means:

(1) a hospital;

(2) an institution licensed under Chapter 242, including a skilled nursing facility;

(3) a home and community support services agency;

(4) a personal care facility; and

(5) a special care facility.

(b) A health care provider shall maintain written policies regarding the implementation of advance directives. The policies must include a clear and precise statement of any procedure the health care provider is unwilling or unable to provide or withhold in accordance with an advance directive.

(c) Except as provided by Subsection (g), the health care provider shall provide written notice to an individual of the written policies described by Subsection (b). The notice must be provided at the earlier of:

(1) the time the individual is admitted to receive services from the health care provider; or

(2) the time the health care provider begins providing care to the individual.

(d) If, at the time notice is to be provided under Subsection (c), the individual is incompetent or otherwise incapacitated and unable to receive the notice required by this section, the provider shall provide the required written notice, in the following order of preference, to:

(1) the individual's legal guardian;

(2) a person responsible for the health care decisions of the individual;

(3) the individual's spouse;

(4) the individual's adult child;

(5) the individual's parent; or

(6) the person admitting the individual.

(e) If Subsection (d) applies and except as provided by Subsection (f), if a health care provider is unable, after diligent search, to locate an individual listed by Subsection (d), the health care provider is not required to provide the notice.

(f) If an individual who was incompetent or otherwise incapacitated and unable to receive the notice required by this section at the time notice was to be provided under Subsection (c) later becomes able to receive the notice, the health care provider shall provide the written notice at the time the individual becomes able to receive the notice.

(g) This section does not apply to outpatient hospital services, including emergency services.

Added by Acts 1999, 76th Leg., ch. 450, § 1.02, eff. Sept. 1, 1999.

## § 166.005. Enforceability of Advance Directives Executed in Another Jurisdiction

An advance directive or similar instrument validly executed in another state or jurisdiction shall be given the same effect as an advance directive validly executed under the law of this state. This section does not authorize the administration, withholding, or withdrawal of health care otherwise prohibited by the laws of this state.

Added by Acts 1999, 76th Leg., ch. 450, § 1.02, eff. Sept. 1, 1999.

## § 166.006. Effect of Advance Directive on Insurance Policy and Premiums

(a) The fact that a person has executed or issued an advance directive does not:

(1) restrict, inhibit, or impair in any manner the sale, procurement, or issuance of a life insurance policy to that person; or

(2) modify the terms of an existing life insurance policy.

(b) Notwithstanding the terms of any life insurance policy, the fact that life-sustaining treatment is withheld or withdrawn from an insured qualified patient under this chapter does not legally impair or invalidate that person's life insurance policy and may not be a factor for the purpose of determining, under the life insurance policy, whether benefits are payable or the cause of death.

(c) The fact that a person has executed or issued or failed to execute or issue an advance directive may not be considered in any way in establishing insurance premiums.

Added by Acts 1999, 76th Leg., ch. 450, § 1.02, eff. Sept. 1, 1999.

## § 166.007. Execution of Advance Directive May Not be Required

A physician, health facility, health care provider, insurer, or health care service plan may not require a person to execute or issue an advance directive as a condition for obtaining insurance for health care services or receiving health care services.

Added by Acts 1999, 76th Leg., ch. 450, § 1.02, eff. Sept. 1, 1999.

## § 166.008. Conflict Between Advance Directives

To the extent that a treatment decision or an advance directive validly executed or issued under this chapter conflicts with another treatment decision or an advance directive executed or issued under this chapter, the treatment decision made or instrument executed later in time controls.

Added by Acts 1999, 76th Leg., ch. 450, § 1.02, eff. Sept. 1, 1999.

## § 166.009. Certain Life-Sustaining Treatment Not Required

This chapter may not be construed to require the provision of life-sustaining treatment that cannot be provided to a patient without denying the same treatment to another patient.

Added by Acts 1999, 76th Leg., ch. 450, § 1.02, eff. Sept. 1, 1999.

## § 166.010. Applicability of Federal Law Relating to Child Abuse and Neglect

This chapter is subject to applicable federal law and regulations relating to child abuse and neglect to the extent applicable to the state based on its receipt of federal funds.

Added by Acts 2003, 78th Leg., ch. 1228, § 2, eff. June 20, 2003.

## § 166.011. Digital or Electronic Signature

(a) For an advance directive in which a signature by a declarant, witness, or notary public is required or used, the declarant, witness, or notary public may sign the directive or a written revocation of the directive using:

(1) a digital signature that:

(A) uses an algorithm approved by the department;

(B) is unique to the person using it;

(C) is capable of verification;

(D) is under the sole control of the person using it;

(E) is linked to data in a manner that invalidates the digital signature if the data is changed;

(F) persists with the document and not by association in separate files; and

(G) is bound to a digital certificate; or

(2) an electronic signature that:

(A) is capable of verification;

(B) is under the sole control of the person using it;

(C) is linked to data in a manner that invalidates the electronic signature if the data is changed; and

(D) persists with the document and not by association in separate files.

(b) In approving an algorithm for purposes of Subsection (a)(1)(A), the department may consider an algorithm approved by the National Institute of Standards and Technology.

(c) The executive commissioner of the Health and Human Services Commission by rule shall modify the advance directive forms required under this chapter as necessary to provide for the use of a digital or electronic signature that complies with the requirements of this section.

Added by Acts 2009, 81st Leg., ch. 461, § 2, eff. Sept. 1, 2009.

## SUBCHAPTER B. DIRECTIVE TO PHYSICIANS

*Acts 1999, 76th Leg., ch. 450, § 1.03 redesignated Chapter 672, Health & Safety Code as this Subchapter B.*

### § 166.031. Definitions

In this subchapter:

(1) "Directive" means an instruction made under Section 166.032, 166.034, or 166.035 to administer, withhold, or withdraw life-sustaining treatment in the event of a terminal or irreversible condition.

(2) "Qualified patient" means a patient with a terminal or irreversible condition that has been diagnosed and certified in writing by the attending physician.

Acts 1989, 71st Leg., ch. 678, § 1, eff. Sept. 1, 1989. Amended by Acts 1991, 72nd Leg., ch. 14, § 208, eff. Sept. 1, 1991; Acts 1993, 73rd Leg., ch. 107, § 5.04, eff. Aug. 30, 1993. Renumbered from V.T.C.A., Heath & Safety Code § 672.002 and amended by Acts 1999, 76th Leg., ch. 450, § 1.03, eff. Sept. 1, 1999.

### § 166.032. Written Directive by Competent Adult; Notice to Physician

(a) A competent adult may at any time execute a written directive.

(b) Except as provided by Subsection (b–1), the declarant must sign the directive in the presence of two witnesses who qualify under Section 166.003, at least one of whom must be a witness who qualifies under Section 166.003(2). The witnesses must sign the directive.

(b–1) The declarant, in lieu of signing in the presence of witnesses, may sign the directive and have the signature acknowledged before a notary public.

(c) A declarant may include in a directive directions other than those provided by Section 166.033 and may

designate in a directive a person to make a treatment decision for the declarant in the event the declarant becomes incompetent or otherwise mentally or physically incapable of communication.

(d) A declarant shall notify the attending physician of the existence of a written directive. If the declarant is incompetent or otherwise mentally or physically incapable of communication, another person may notify the attending physician of the existence of the written directive. The attending physician shall make the directive a part of the declarant's medical record.

Acts 1989, 71st Leg., ch. 678, § 1, eff. Sept. 1, 1989. Amended by Acts 1991, 72nd Leg., ch. 14, § 209, eff. Sept. 1, 1991; Acts 1997, 75th Leg., ch. 291, § 1, eff. Jan. 1, 1998. Renumbered from V.T.C.A., Health & Safety Code § 672.003 and amended by Acts 1999, 76th Leg., ch. 450, § 1.03, eff. Sept. 1, 1999. Amended by Acts 2009, 81st Leg., ch. 461, § 3, eff. Sept. 1, 2009.

### § 166.033. Form of Written Directive

A written directive may be in the following form:

#### DIRECTIVE TO PHYSICIANS AND FAMILY OR SURROGATES

Instructions for completing this document:

This is an important legal document known as an Advance Directive. It is designed to help you communicate your wishes about medical treatment at some time in the future when you are unable to make your wishes known because of illness or injury. These wishes are usually based on personal values. In particular, you may want to consider what burdens or hardships of treatment you would be willing to accept for a particular amount of benefit obtained if you were seriously ill.

You are encouraged to discuss your values and wishes with your family or chosen spokesperson, as well as your physician. Your physician, other health care provider, or medical institution may provide you with various resources to assist you in completing your advance directive. Brief definitions are listed below and may aid you in your discussions and advance planning. Initial the treatment choices that best reflect your personal preferences. Provide a copy of your directive to your physician, usual hospital, and family or spokesperson. Consider a periodic review of this document. By periodic review, you can best assure that the directive reflects your preferences.

In addition to this advance directive, Texas law provides for two other types of directives that can be important during a serious illness. These are the

Medical Power of Attorney and the Out-of-Hospital Do-Not-Resuscitate Order. You may wish to discuss these with your physician, family, hospital representative, or other advisers. You may also wish to complete a directive related to the donation of organs and tissues.

## DIRECTIVE

I, _____, recognize that the best health care is based upon a partnership of trust and communication with my physician. My physician and I will make health care decisions together as long as I am of sound mind and able to make my wishes known. If there comes a time that I am unable to make medical decisions about myself because of illness or injury, I direct that the following treatment preferences be honored:

If, in the judgment of my physician, I am suffering with a terminal condition from which I am expected to die within six months, even with available life-sustaining treatment provided in accordance with prevailing standards of medical care:

_____ I request that all treatments other than those needed to keep me comfortable be discontinued or withheld and my physician allow me to die as gently as possible; OR

_____ I request that I be kept alive in this terminal condition using available life-sustaining treatment. (THIS SELECTION DOES NOT APPLY TO HOSPICE CARE.)

If, in the judgment of my physician, I am suffering with an irreversible condition so that I cannot care for myself or make decisions for myself and am expected to die without life-sustaining treatment provided in accordance with prevailing standards of care:

_____ I request that all treatments other than those needed to keep me comfortable be discontinued or withheld and my physician allow me to die as gently as possible; OR

_____ I request that I be kept alive in this irreversible condition using available life-sustaining treatment. (THIS SELECTION DOES NOT APPLY TO HOSPICE CARE.)

Additional requests: (After discussion with your physician, you may wish to consider listing particular treatments in this space that you do or do not want in specific circumstances, such as artificial nutrition and fluids, intravenous antibiotics, etc. Be sure to state whether you do or do not want the particular treatment.)

_____

_____

_____

After signing this directive, if my representative or I elect hospice care, I understand and agree that only those treatments needed to keep me comfortable would be provided and I would not be given available life-sustaining treatments.

If I do not have a Medical Power of Attorney, and I am unable to make my wishes known, I designate the following person(s) to make treatment decisions with my physician compatible with my personal values:

1._____
2._____

(If a Medical Power of Attorney has been executed, then an agent already has been named and you should not list additional names in this document.)

If the above persons are not available, or if I have not designated a spokesperson, I understand that a spokesperson will be chosen for me following standards specified in the laws of Texas. If, in the judgment of my physician, my death is imminent within minutes to hours, even with the use of all available medical treatment provided within the prevailing standard of care, I acknowledge that all treatments may be withheld or removed except those needed to maintain my comfort. I understand that under Texas law this directive has no effect if I have been diagnosed as pregnant. This directive will remain in effect until I revoke it. No other person may do so.

Signed _____ Date _____ City, County, State of Residence _____

Two competent adult witnesses must sign below, acknowledging the signature of the declarant. The witness designated as Witness 1 may not be a person designated to make a treatment decision for the patient and may not be related to the patient by blood or marriage. This witness may not be entitled to any part of the estate and may not have a claim against the estate of the patient. This witness may not be the attending physician or an employee of the attending physician. If this witness is an employee of a health care facility in which the patient is being cared for, this witness may not be involved in providing direct patient care to the patient. This witness may not be an officer, director, partner, or business office employee of a health care facility in which the patient is being cared for or of any parent organization of the health care facility.

Witness 1 _____ Witness 2 _____

Definitions:

"Artificial nutrition and hydration" means the provision of nutrients or fluids by a tube inserted in a vein, under the skin in the subcutaneous tissues, or in the stomach (gastrointestinal tract).

"Irreversible condition" means a condition, injury, or illness:

(1) that may be treated, but is never cured or eliminated;

(2) that leaves a person unable to care for or make decisions for the person's own self; and

(3) that, without life-sustaining treatment provided in accordance with the prevailing standard of medical care, is fatal.

Explanation: Many serious illnesses such as cancer, failure of major organs (kidney, heart, liver, or lung), and serious brain disease such as Alzheimer's dementia may be considered irreversible early on. There is no cure, but the patient may be kept alive for prolonged periods of time if the patient receives life-sustaining treatments. Late in the course of the same illness, the disease may be considered terminal when, even with treatment, the patient is expected to die. You may wish to consider which burdens of treatment you would be willing to accept in an effort to achieve a particular outcome. This is a very personal decision that you may wish to discuss with your physician, family, or other important persons in your life.

"Life-sustaining treatment" means treatment that, based on reasonable medical judgment, sustains the life of a patient and without which the patient will die. The term includes both life-sustaining medications and artificial life support such as mechanical breathing machines, kidney dialysis treatment, and artificial hydration and nutrition. The term does not include the administration of pain management medication, the performance of a medical procedure necessary to provide comfort care, or any other medical care provided to alleviate a patient's pain.

"Terminal condition" means an incurable condition caused by injury, disease, or illness that according to reasonable medical judgment will produce death within six months, even with available life-sustaining treatment provided in accordance with the prevailing standard of medical care.

Explanation: Many serious illnesses may be considered irreversible early in the course of the illness, but they may not be considered terminal until the disease is fairly advanced. In thinking about terminal illness and its treatment, you again may wish to consider the relative benefits and burdens of treatment and discuss your wishes with your physician, family, or other important persons in your life.

Acts 1989, 71st Leg., ch. 678, § 1, eff. Sept. 1, 1989. Amended by Acts 1991, 72nd Leg., ch. 14, § 209, eff. Sept. 1, 1991; Acts 1997, 75th Leg., ch. 291, § 2, eff. Jan. 1, 1998. Renumbered from V.T.C.A., Health & Safety Code § 672.004 and amended by Acts 1999, 76th Leg., ch. 450, § 1.03, eff. Sept. 1, 1999.

### § 166.034. Issuance of Nonwritten Directive by Competent Adult Qualified Patient

(a) A competent qualified patient who is an adult may issue a directive by a nonwritten means of communication.

(b) A declarant must issue the nonwritten directive in the presence of the attending physician and two witnesses who qualify under Section 166.003, at least one of whom must be a witness who qualifies under Section 166.003(2).

(c) The physician shall make the fact of the existence of the directive a part of the declarant's medical record, and the names of the witnesses shall be entered in the medical record.

Acts 1989, 71st Leg., ch. 678, § 1, eff. Sept. 1, 1989. Renumbered from V.T.C.A., Health & Safety Code § 672.005 and amended by Acts 1999, 76th Leg., ch. 450, § 1.03, eff. Sept. 1, 1999.

### § 166.035. Execution of Directive on Behalf of Patient Younger Than 18 Years of Age

The following persons may execute a directive on behalf of a qualified patient who is younger than 18 years of age:

(1) the patient's spouse, if the spouse is an adult;

(2) the patient's parents; or

(3) the patient's legal guardian.

Acts 1989, 71st Leg., ch. 678, § 1, eff. Sept. 1, 1989. Renumbered from V.T.C.A., Health & Safety Code § 672.006 by Acts 1999, 76th Leg., ch. 450, § 1.03, eff. Sept. 1, 1999.

### § 166.036. Notarized Document Not Required; Requirement of Specific Form Prohibited

(a) Except as provided by Section 166.032(b–1), a written directive executed under Section 166.033 or

166.035 is effective without regard to whether the document has been notarized.

(b) A physician, health care facility, or health care professional may not require that:

(1) a directive be notarized; or

(2) a person use a form provided by the physician, health care facility, or health care professional.

Added by Acts 1999, 76th Leg., ch. 450, § 1.03, eff. Sept. 1, 1999. Amended by Acts 2009, 81st Leg., ch. 461, § 4, eff. Sept. 1, 2009.

### § 166.037. Patient Desire Supersedes Directive

The desire of a qualified patient, including a qualified patient younger than 18 years of age, supersedes the effect of a directive.

Acts 1989, 71st Leg., ch. 678, § 1, eff. Sept. 1, 1989. Renumbered from V.T.C.A., Health & Safety Code § 672.007 and amended by Acts 1999, 76th Leg., ch. 450, § 1.03, eff. Sept. 1, 1999.

### § 166.038. Procedure When Declarant is Incompetent or Incapable of Communication

(a) This section applies when an adult qualified patient has executed or issued a directive and is incompetent or otherwise mentally or physically incapable of communication.

(b) If the adult qualified patient has designated a person to make a treatment decision as authorized by Section 166.032(c), the attending physician and the designated person may make a treatment decision in accordance with the declarant's directions.

(c) If the adult qualified patient has not designated a person to make a treatment decision, the attending physician shall comply with the directive unless the physician believes that the directive does not reflect the patient's present desire.

Acts 1989, 71st Leg., ch. 678, § 1, eff. Sept. 1, 1989. Renumbered from V.T.C.A., Health & Safety Code § 672.008 and amended by Acts 1999, 76th Leg., ch. 450, § 1.03, eff. Sept. 1, 1999.

### § 166.039. Procedure When Person Has Not Executed or Issued a Directive and is Incompetent or Incapable of Communication

(a) If an adult qualified patient has not executed or issued a directive and is incompetent or otherwise mentally or physically incapable of communication, the attending physician and the patient's legal guardian or an agent under a medical power of attorney may make a treatment decision that may include a decision to withhold or withdraw life-sustaining treatment from the patient.

(b) If the patient does not have a legal guardian or an agent under a medical power of attorney, the attending physician and one person, if available, from one of the following categories, in the following priority, may make a treatment decision that may include a decision to withhold or withdraw life-sustaining treatment:

(1) the patient's spouse;

(2) the patient's reasonably available adult children;

(3) the patient's parents; or

(4) the patient's nearest living relative.

(c) A treatment decision made under Subsection (a) or (b) must be based on knowledge of what the patient would desire, if known.

(d) A treatment decision made under Subsection (b) must be documented in the patient's medical record and signed by the attending physician.

(e) If the patient does not have a legal guardian and a person listed in Subsection (b) is not available, a treatment decision made under Subsection (b) must be concurred in by another physician who is not involved in the treatment of the patient or who is a representative of an ethics or medical committee of the health care facility in which the person is a patient.

(f) The fact that an adult qualified patient has not executed or issued a directive does not create a presumption that the patient does not want a treatment decision to be made to withhold or withdraw life-sustaining treatment.

(g) A person listed in Subsection (b) who wishes to challenge a treatment decision made under this section must apply for temporary guardianship under Section 875, Texas Probate Code. The court may waive applicable fees in that proceeding.

Acts 1989, 71st Leg., ch. 678, § 1, eff. Sept. 1, 1989. Amended by Acts 1997, 75th Leg., ch. 291, § 3, eff. Jan. 1, 1998. Renumbered from V.T.C.A., Health & Safety Code § 672.009 and amended by Acts 1999, 76th Leg., ch. 450, § 1.03, eff. Sept. 1, 1999.

### § 166.040. Patient Certification and Prerequisites for Complying with Directive

(a) An attending physician who has been notified of the existence of a directive shall provide for the declarant's certification as a qualified patient on diagnosis of a terminal or irreversible condition.

(b) Before withholding or withdrawing life-sustaining treatment from a qualified patient under this subchapter, the attending physician must determine that the steps proposed to be taken are in accord with this subchapter and the patient's existing desires.

Acts 1989, 71st Leg., ch. 678, § 1, eff. Sept. 1, 1989. Amended by Acts 1991, 72nd Leg., 1st C.S., ch. 14, § 6.01, eff. Nov. 12, 1991. Renumbered from V.T.C.A., Health & Safety Code § 672.010 and amended by Acts 1999, 76th Leg., ch. 450, § 1.03, eff. Sept. 1, 1999.

### § 166.041. Duration of Directive

A directive is effective until it is revoked as prescribed by Section 166.042.

Acts 1989, 71st Leg., ch. 678, § 1, eff. Sept. 1, 1989. Renumbered from V.T.C.A., Health & Safety Code § 672.011 and amended by Acts 1999, 76th Leg., ch. 450, § 1.03, eff. Sept. 1, 1999.

### § 166.042. Revocation of Directive

(a) A declarant may revoke a directive at any time without regard to the declarant's mental state or competency. A directive may be revoked by:

(1) the declarant or someone in the declarant's presence and at the declarant's direction canceling, defacing, obliterating, burning, tearing, or otherwise destroying the directive;

(2) the declarant signing and dating a written revocation that expresses the declarant's intent to revoke the directive; or

(3) the declarant orally stating the declarant's intent to revoke the directive.

(b) A written revocation executed as prescribed by Subsection (a)(2) takes effect only when the declarant or a person acting on behalf of the declarant notifies the attending physician of its existence or mails the revocation to the attending physician. The attending physician or the physician's designee shall record in the patient's medical record the time and date when the physician received notice of the written revocation and shall enter the word "VOID" on each page of the copy of the directive in the patient's medical record.

(c) An oral revocation issued as prescribed by Subsection (a)(3) takes effect only when the declarant or a person acting on behalf of the declarant notifies the attending physician of the revocation. The attending physician or the physician's designee shall record in the patient's medical record the time, date, and place of the revocation, and, if different, the time, date, and place that the physician received notice of the revocation. The attending physician or the physician's designees shall also enter the word "VOID" on each page

of the copy of the directive in the patient's medical record.

(d) Except as otherwise provided by this subchapter, a person is not civilly or criminally liable for failure to act on a revocation made under this section unless the person has actual knowledge of the revocation.

Acts 1989, 71st Leg., ch. 678, § 1, eff. Sept. 1, 1989. Renumbered from V.T.C.A., Health & Safety Code § 672.012 and amended by Acts 1999, 76th Leg., ch. 450, § 1.03, eff. Sept. 1, 1999.

### § 166.043. Reexecution of Directive

A declarant may at any time reexecute a directive in accordance with the procedures prescribed by Section 166.032, including reexecution after the declarant is diagnosed as having a terminal or irreversible condition.

Acts 1989, 71st Leg., ch. 678, § 1, eff. Sept. 1, 1989. Renumbered from V.T.C.A., Health & Safety Code § 672.013 and amended by Acts 1999, 76th Leg., ch. 450, § 1.03, eff. Sept. 1, 1999.

### § 166.044. Limitation of Liability for Withholding or Withdrawing Life-Sustaining Procedures

(a) A physician or health care facility that causes life-sustaining treatment to be withheld or withdrawn from a qualified patient in accordance with this subchapter is not civilly liable for that action unless the physician or health care facility fails to exercise reasonable care when applying the patient's advance directive.

(b) A health professional, acting under the direction of a physician, who participates in withholding or withdrawing life-sustaining treatment from a qualified patient in accordance with this subchapter is not civilly liable for that action unless the health professional fails to exercise reasonable care when applying the patient's advance directive.

(c) A physician, or a health professional acting under the direction of a physician, who participates in withholding or withdrawing life-sustaining treatment from a qualified patient in accordance with this subchapter is not criminally liable or guilty of unprofessional conduct as a result of that action unless the physician or health professional fails to exercise reasonable care when applying the patient's advance directive.

(d) The standard of care that a physician, health care facility, or health care professional shall exercise under this section is that degree of care that a physician, health care facility, or health care professional, as applicable, of ordinary prudence and skill would have exercised under the same or similar circumstances in the same or a similar community.

Acts 1989, 71st Leg., ch. 678, § 1, eff. Sept. 1, 1989. Renumbered from V.T.C.A., Health & Safety Code § 672.015 and amended by Acts 1999, 76th Leg., ch. 450, § 1.03, eff. Sept. 1, 1999.

### § 166.045.  Liability for Failure to Effectuate Directive

(a) A physician, health care facility, or health care professional who has no knowledge of a directive is not civilly or criminally liable for failing to act in accordance with the directive.

(b) A physician, or a health professional acting under the direction of a physician, is subject to review and disciplinary action by the appropriate licensing board for failing to effectuate a qualified patient's directive in violation of this subchapter or other laws of this state.  This subsection does not limit remedies available under other laws of this state.

(c) If an attending physician refuses to comply with a directive or treatment decision and does not wish to follow the procedure established under Section 166.046, life-sustaining treatment shall be provided to the patient, but only until a reasonable opportunity has been afforded for the transfer of the patient to another physician or health care facility willing to comply with the directive or treatment decision.

(d) A physician, health professional acting under the direction of a physician, or health care facility is not civilly or criminally liable or subject to review or disciplinary action by the person's appropriate licensing board if the person has complied with the procedures outlined in Section 166.046.

Acts 1989, 71st Leg., ch. 678, § 1, eff. Sept. 1, 1989. Renumbered from V.T.C.A., Health & Safety Code § 672.016 and amended by Acts 1999, 76th Leg., ch. 450, § 1.03, eff. Sept. 1, 1999.

### § 166.046.  Procedure if Not Effectuating a Directive or Treatment Decision

(a) If an attending physician refuses to honor a patient's advance directive or a health care or treatment decision made by or on behalf of a patient, the physician's refusal shall be reviewed by an ethics or medical committee.  The attending physician may not be a member of that committee.  The patient shall be given life-sustaining treatment during the review.

(b) The patient or the person responsible for the health care decisions of the individual who has made the decision regarding the directive or treatment decision:

(1) may be given a written description of the ethics or medical committee review process and any other policies and procedures related to this section adopted by the health care facility;

(2) shall be informed of the committee review process not less than 48 hours before the meeting called to discuss the patient's directive, unless the time period is waived by mutual agreement;

(3) at the time of being so informed, shall be provided:

(A) a copy of the appropriate statement set forth in Section 166.052; and

(B) a copy of the registry list of health care providers and referral groups that have volunteered their readiness to consider accepting transfer or to assist in locating a provider willing to accept transfer that is posted on the website maintained by the Texas Health Care Information Council under Section 166.053; and

(4) is entitled to:

(A) attend the meeting; and

(B) receive a written explanation of the decision reached during the review process.

(c) The written explanation required by Subsection (b)(2)(B) must be included in the patient's medical record.

(d) If the attending physician, the patient, or the person responsible for the health care decisions of the individual does not agree with the decision reached during the review process under Subsection (b), the physician shall make a reasonable effort to transfer the patient to a physician who is willing to comply with the directive.  If the patient is a patient in a health care facility, the facility's personnel shall assist the physician in arranging the patient's transfer to:

(1) another physician;

(2) an alternative care setting within that facility; or

(3) another facility.

(e) If the patient or the person responsible for the health care decisions of the patient is requesting life-sustaining treatment that the attending physician has decided and the review process has affirmed is inappropriate treatment, the patient shall be given available life-sustaining treatment pending transfer under

Subsection (d). The patient is responsible for any costs incurred in transferring the patient to another facility. The physician and the health care facility are not obligated to provide life-sustaining treatment after the 10th day after the written decision required under Subsection (b) is provided to the patient or the person responsible for the health care decisions of the patient unless ordered to do so under Subsection (g).

(e-1) If during a previous admission to a facility a patient's attending physician and the review process under Subsection (b) have determined that life-sustaining treatment is inappropriate, and the patient is readmitted to the same facility within six months from the date of the decision reached during the review process conducted upon the previous admission, Subsections (b) through (e) need not be followed if the patient's attending physician and a consulting physician who is a member of the ethics or medical committee of the facility document on the patient's re-admission that the patient's condition either has not improved or has deteriorated since the review process was conducted.

(f) Life-sustaining treatment under this section may not be entered in the patient's medical record as medically unnecessary treatment until the time period provided under Subsection (e) has expired.

(g) At the request of the patient or the person responsible for the health care decisions of the patient, the appropriate district or county court shall extend the time period provided under Subsection (e) only if the court finds, by a preponderance of the evidence, that there is a reasonable expectation that a physician or health care facility that will honor the patient's directive will be found if the time extension is granted.

(h) This section may not be construed to impose an obligation on a facility or a home and community support services agency licensed under Chapter 142 or similar organization that is beyond the scope of the services or resources of the facility or agency. This section does not apply to hospice services provided by a home and community support services agency licensed under Chapter 142.

Added by Acts 1999, 76th Leg., ch. 450, § 1.03, eff. Sept. 1, 1999. Amended by Acts 2003, 78th Leg., ch. 1228, §§ 3, 4, eff. June 20, 2003.

### § 166.047. Honoring Directive Does Not Constitute Offense of Aiding Suicide

A person does not commit an offense under Section 22.08, Penal Code, by withholding or withdrawing life-sustaining treatment from a qualified patient in accordance with this subchapter.

Acts 1989, 71st Leg., ch. 678, § 1, eff. Sept. 1, 1989. Renumbered from V.T.C.A., Health & Safety Code § 672.017 and amended by Acts 1999, 76th Leg., ch. 450, § 1.03, eff. Sept. 1, 1999.

### § 166.048. Criminal Penalty; Prosecution

(a) A person commits an offense if the person intentionally conceals, cancels, defaces, obliterates, or damages another person's directive without that person's consent. An offense under this subsection is a Class A misdemeanor.

(b) A person is subject to prosecution for criminal homicide under Chapter 19, Penal Code, if the person, with the intent to cause life-sustaining treatment to be withheld or withdrawn from another person contrary to the other person's desires, falsifies or forges a directive or intentionally conceals or withholds personal knowledge of a revocation and thereby directly causes life-sustaining treatment to be withheld or withdrawn from the other person with the result that the other person's death is hastened.

Acts 1989, 71st Leg., ch. 678, § 1, eff. Sept. 1, 1989. Renumbered from V.T.C.A., Health & Safety Code § 672.018 and amended by Acts 1999, 76th Leg., ch. 450, § 1.03, eff. Sept. 1, 1999.

### § 166.049. Pregnant Patients

A person may not withdraw or withhold life-sustaining treatment under this subchapter from a pregnant patient.

Acts 1989, 71st Leg., ch. 678, § 1, eff. Sept. 1, 1989. Renumbered from V.T.C.A., Health & Safety Code § 672.019 and amended by Acts 1999, 76th Leg., ch. 450, § 1.03, eff. Sept. 1, 1999.

### § 166.050. Mercy Killing Not Condoned

This subchapter does not condone, authorize, or approve mercy killing or permit an affirmative or deliberate act or omission to end life except to permit the natural process of dying as provided by this subchapter.

Acts 1989, 71st Leg., ch. 678, § 1, eff. Sept. 1, 1989. Renumbered from V.T.C.A., Health & Safety Code § 672.020 and amended by Acts 1999, 76th Leg., ch. 450, § 1.03, eff. Sept. 1, 1999.

### § 166.051. Legal Right or Responsibility Not Affected

This subchapter does not impair or supersede any legal right or responsibility a person may have to effect the withholding or withdrawal of life-sustaining treatment in a lawful manner, provided that if an attending physician or health care facility is unwilling to honor a patient's advance directive or a treatment decision to provide life-sustaining treatment, life-sustaining treatment is required to be provided the patient, but only until a reasonable opportunity has been afforded for transfer of the patient to another physician or health care facility willing to comply with the advance directive or treatment decision.

Acts 1989, 71st Leg., ch. 678, § 1, eff. Sept. 1, 1989. Renumbered from V.T.C.A., Health & Safety Code § 672.021 and amended by Acts 1999, 76th Leg., ch. 450, § 1.03, eff. Sept. 1, 1999.

### § 166.052. Statements Explaining Patient's Right to Transfer

(a) In cases in which the attending physician refuses to honor an advance directive or treatment decision requesting the provision of life-sustaining treatment, the statement required by Section 166.046(b)(2)(A) shall be in substantially the following form:

When There Is A Disagreement About Medical Treatment: The Physician Recommends Against Life–Sustaining Treatment That You Wish To Continue

You have been given this information because you have requested life-sustaining treatment,* which the attending physician believes is not appropriate. This information is being provided to help you understand state law, your rights, and the resources available to you in such circumstances. It outlines the process for resolving disagreements about treatment among patients, families, and physicians. It is based upon Section 166.046 of the Texas Advance Directives Act, codified in Chapter 166 of the Texas Health and Safety Code.

When an attending physician refuses to comply with an advance directive or other request for life-sustaining treatment because of the physician's judgment that the treatment would be inappropriate, the case will be reviewed by an ethics or medical committee. Life–sustaining treatment will be provided through the review.

You will receive notification of this review at least 48 hours before a meeting of the committee related to your case. You are entitled to attend the meeting. With your agreement, the meeting may be held sooner than 48 hours, if possible.

You are entitled to receive a written explanation of the decision reached during the review process.

If after this review process both the attending physician and the ethics or medical committee conclude that life-sustaining treatment is inappropriate and yet you continue to request such treatment, then the following procedure will occur:

1. The physician, with the help of the health care facility, will assist you in trying to find a physician and facility willing to provide the requested treatment.

2. You are being given a list of health care providers and referral groups that have volunteered their readiness to consider accepting transfer, or to assist in locating a provider willing to accept transfer, maintained by the Texas Health Care Information Council. You may wish to contact providers or referral groups on the list or others of your choice to get help in arranging a transfer.

3. The patient will continue to be given life-sustaining treatment until he or she can be transferred to a willing provider for up to 10 days from the time you were given the committee's written decision that life-sustaining treatment is not appropriate.

4. If a transfer can be arranged, the patient will be responsible for the costs of the transfer.

5. If a provider cannot be found willing to give the requested treatment within 10 days, life-sustaining treatment may be withdrawn unless a court of law has granted an extension.

6. You may ask the appropriate district or county court to extend the 10–day period if the court finds that there is a reasonable expectation that a physician or health care facility willing to provide life-sustaining treatment will be found if the extension is granted.

* "Life-sustaining treatment" means treatment that, based on reasonable medical judgment, sustains the life of a patient and without which the patient will die. The term includes both life-sustaining medications and artificial life support, such as mechanical breathing machines, kidney dialysis treatment, and artificial nutrition and hydration. The term does not include the administration of pain management medication or the performance of a medical procedure considered to be necessary to provide comfort care, or any other medical care provided to alleviate a patient's pain.

(b) In cases in which the attending physician refuses to comply with an advance directive or treatment decision requesting the withholding or withdrawal of life-sustaining treatment, the statement required by Section 166.046(b)(3)(A) shall be in substantially the following form:

When There Is A Disagreement About Medical Treatment: The Physician Recommends Life–Sustaining Treatment That You Wish To Stop

You have been given this information because you have requested the withdrawal or withholding of life-sustaining treatment* and the attending physician refuses to comply with that request. The information is being provided to help you understand state law, your rights, and the resources available to you in such circumstances. It outlines the process for resolving disagreements about treatment among patients, families, and physicians. It is based upon Section 166.046 of the Texas Advance Directives Act, codified in Chapter 166 of the Texas Health and Safety Code.

When an attending physician refuses to comply with an advance directive or other request for withdrawal or withholding of life-sustaining treatment for any reason, the case will be reviewed by an ethics or medical committee. Life–sustaining treatment will be provided through the review.

You will receive notification of this review at least 48 hours before a meeting of the committee related to your case. You are entitled to attend the meeting. With your agreement, the meeting may be held sooner than 48 hours, if possible.

You are entitled to receive a written explanation of the decision reached during the review process.

If you or the attending physician do not agree with the decision reached during the review process, and the attending physician still refuses to comply with your request to withhold or withdraw life-sustaining treatment, then the following procedure will occur:

1. The physician, with the help of the health care facility, will assist you in trying to find a physician and facility willing to withdraw or withhold the life-sustaining treatment.

2. You are being given a list of health care providers and referral groups that have volunteered their readiness to consider accepting transfer, or to assist in locating a provider willing to accept transfer, maintained by the Texas Health Care Information Council. You may wish to contact providers or referral groups on the list or others of your choice to get help in arranging a transfer.

* "Life-sustaining treatment" means treatment that, based on reasonable medical judgment, sustains the life of a patient and without which the patient will die.

The term includes both life-sustaining medications and artificial life support, such as mechanical breathing machines, kidney dialysis treatment, and artificial nutrition and hydration. The term does not include the administration of pain management medication or the performance of a medical procedure considered to be necessary to provide comfort care, or any other medical care provided to alleviate a patient's pain.

(c) An attending physician or health care facility may, if it chooses, include any additional information concerning the physician's or facility's policy, perspective, experience, or review procedure.

Added by Acts 2003, 78th Leg., ch. 1228, § 5, eff. June 20, 2003.

### § 166.053. Registry to Assist Transfers

(a) The Texas Health Care Information Council shall maintain a registry listing the identity of and contact information for health care providers and referral groups, situated inside and outside this state, that have voluntarily notified the council they may consider accepting or may assist in locating a provider willing to accept transfer of a patient under Section 166.045 or 166.046.

(b) The listing of a provider or referral group in the registry described in this section does not obligate the provider or group to accept transfer of or provide services to any particular patient.

(c) The Texas Health Care Information Council shall post the current registry list on its website in a form appropriate for easy comprehension by patients and persons responsible for the health care decisions of patients and shall provide a clearly identifiable link from its home page to the registry page. The list shall separately indicate those providers and groups that have indicated their interest in assisting the transfer of:

(1) those patients on whose behalf life-sustaining treatment is being sought;

(2) those patients on whose behalf the withholding or withdrawal of life-sustaining treatment is being sought; and

(3) patients described in both Subdivisions (1) and (2).

(d) The registry list described in this section shall include the following disclaimer:

"This registry lists providers and groups that have indicated to the Texas Health Care Information Council their interest in assisting the transfer of patients in the circumstances described, and is provided for information purposes only. Neither the Texas Health Care Information Council nor the State of Texas endorses or assumes any responsibility for any representation, claim, or act of the listed providers or groups."

Added by Acts 2003, 78th Leg., ch. 1228, § 5, eff. June 20, 2003.

## SUBCHAPTER C.   OUT-OF-HOSPITAL DO-NOT-RESUSCITATE ORDERS

*Acts 1999, 76th Leg., ch. 450, § 1.04 redesignated Chapter 674, Health & Safety Code as this Subchapter C.*

### § 166.081.   Definitions

In this subchapter:

(1) Repealed by Acts 2003, 78th Leg., ch. 1228, § 8.

(2) "DNR identification device" means an identification device specified by the board under Section 166.101 that is worn for the purpose of identifying a person who has executed or issued an out-of-hospital DNR order or on whose behalf an out-of-hospital DNR order has been executed or issued under this subchapter.

(3) "Emergency medical services" has the meaning assigned by Section 773.003.

(4) "Emergency medical services personnel" has the meaning assigned by Section 773.003.

(5) "Health care professionals" means physicians, physician assistants, nurses, and emergency medical services personnel and, unless the context requires otherwise, includes hospital emergency personnel.

(6) "Out-of-hospital DNR order":

(A) means a legally binding out-of-hospital do-not-resuscitate order, in the form specified by the board under Section 166.083, prepared and signed by the attending physician of a person, that documents the instructions of a person or the person's legally authorized representative and directs health care professionals acting in an out-of-hospital setting not to initiate or continue the following life-sustaining treatment:

(i) cardiopulmonary resuscitation;

(ii) advanced airway management;

(iii) artificial ventilation;

(iv) defibrillation;

(v) transcutaneous cardiac pacing; and

(vi) other life-sustaining treatment specified by the board under Section 166.101(a); and

(B) does not include authorization to withhold medical interventions or therapies considered necessary to provide comfort care or to alleviate pain or to provide water or nutrition.

(7) "Out-of-hospital setting" means a location in which health care professionals are called for assistance, including long-term care facilities, in-patient hospice facilities, private homes, hospital outpatient or emergency departments, physician's offices, and vehicles during transport.

(8) "Proxy" means a person designated and authorized by a directive executed or issued in accordance with Subchapter B to make a treatment decision for another person in the event the other person becomes incompetent or otherwise mentally or physically incapable of communication.

(9) "Qualified relatives" means those persons authorized to execute or issue an out-of-hospital DNR order on behalf of a person who is incompetent or otherwise mentally or physically incapable of communication under Section 166.088.

(10) "Statewide out-of-hospital DNR protocol" means a set of statewide standardized procedures adopted by the board under Section 166.101(a) for withholding cardiopulmonary resuscitation and certain other life-sustaining treatment by health care professionals acting in out-of-hospital settings.

Added by Acts 1995, 74th Leg., ch. 965, § 10, eff. June 16, 1995.   Renumbered from V.T.C.A., Health & Safety Code § 674.001 and amended by Acts 1999, 76th Leg., ch. 450, § 1.04, eff. Sept. 1, 1999; Acts 2003, 78th Leg., ch. 1228, § 8, eff. June 20, 2003.

### § 166.082.   Out-of-Hospital DNR Order;   Directive to Physicians

(a) A competent person may at any time execute a written out-of-hospital DNR order directing health care professionals acting in an out-of-hospital setting to withhold cardiopulmonary resuscitation and certain other life-sustaining treatment designated by the board.

(b) Except as provided by this subsection, the declarant must sign the out-of-hospital DNR order in the presence of two witnesses who qualify under Section 166.003, at least one of whom must be a witness who qualifies under Section 166.003(2). The witnesses must sign the order. The attending physician of the declarant must sign the order and shall make the fact of the existence of the order and the reasons for execution of the order a part of the declarant's medical record. The declarant, in lieu of signing in the presence of witnesses, may sign the out-of-hospital DNR order and have the signature acknowledged before a notary public.

(c) If the person is incompetent but previously executed or issued a directive to physicians in accordance with Subchapter B,[1] the physician may rely on the directive as the person's instructions to issue an out-of-hospital DNR order and shall place a copy of the directive in the person's medical record. The physician shall sign the order in lieu of the person signing under Subsection (b) and may use a digital or electronic signature authorized under Section 166.011.

(d) If the person is incompetent but previously executed or issued a directive to physicians in accordance with Subchapter B designating a proxy, the proxy may make any decisions required of the designating person as to an out-of-hospital DNR order and shall sign the order in lieu of the person signing under Subsection (b).

(e) If the person is now incompetent but previously executed or issued a medical power of attorney designating an agent, the agent may make any decisions required of the designating person as to an out-of-hospital DNR order and shall sign the order in lieu of the person signing under Subsection (b).

(f) The board, on the recommendation of the department, shall by rule adopt procedures for the disposition and maintenance of records of an original out-of-hospital DNR order and any copies of the order.

(g) An out-of-hospital DNR order is effective on its execution.

Added by Acts 1995, 74th Leg., ch. 965, § 10, eff. June 16, 1995. Renumbered from V.T.C.A., Health & Safety Code § 674.002 and amended by Acts 1999, 76th Leg., ch. 450, § 1.04, eff. Sept. 1, 1999. Amended by Acts 2009, 81st Leg., ch. 461, § 5, eff. Sept. 1, 2009.

[1] V.T.C.A., Health & Safety Code § 166.031 et seq.

## § 166.083. Form of Out-of-Hospital DNR Order

(a) A written out-of-hospital DNR order shall be in the standard form specified by board rule as recommended by the department.

(b) The standard form of an out-of-hospital DNR order specified by the board must, at a minimum, contain the following:

(1) a distinctive single-page format that readily identifies the document as an out-of-hospital DNR order;

(2) a title that readily identifies the document as an out-of-hospital DNR order;

(3) the printed or typed name of the person;

(4) a statement that the physician signing the document is the attending physician of the person and that the physician is directing health care professionals acting in out-of-hospital settings, including a hospital emergency department, not to initiate or continue certain life-sustaining treatment on behalf of the person, and a listing of those procedures not to be initiated or continued;

(5) a statement that the person understands that the person may revoke the out-of-hospital DNR order at any time by destroying the order and removing the DNR identification device, if any, or by communicating to health care professionals at the scene the person's desire to revoke the out-of-hospital DNR order;

(6) places for the printed names and signatures of the witnesses or the notary public's acknowledgment and for the printed name and signature of the attending physician of the person and the medical license number of the attending physician;

(7) a separate section for execution of the document by the legal guardian of the person, the person's proxy, an agent of the person having a medical power of attorney, or the attending physician attesting to the issuance of an out-of-hospital DNR order by nonwritten means of communication or acting in accordance with a previously executed or previously issued directive to physicians under Section 166.082(c) that includes the following:

(A) a statement that the legal guardian, the proxy, the agent, the person by nonwritten means of communication, or the physician directs that each listed life-sustaining treatment should not be initiated or continued in behalf of the person; and

(B) places for the printed names and signatures of the witnesses and, as applicable, the legal guardian, proxy, agent, or physician;

(8) a separate section for execution of the document by at least one qualified relative of the person when the person does not have a legal guardian, proxy, or agent having a medical power of attorney and is incompetent or otherwise mentally or physically incapable of communication, including:

(A) a statement that the relative of the person is qualified to make a treatment decision to withhold cardiopulmonary resuscitation and certain other designated life-sustaining treatment under Section 166.088 and, based on the known desires of the person or a determination of the best interest of the person, directs that each listed life-sustaining treatment should not be initiated or continued in behalf of the person; and

(B) places for the printed names and signatures of the witnesses and qualified relative of the person;

(9) a place for entry of the date of execution of the document;

(10) a statement that the document is in effect on the date of its execution and remains in effect until the death of the person or until the document is revoked;

(11) a statement that the document must accompany the person during transport;

(12) a statement regarding the proper disposition of the document or copies of the document, as the board determines appropriate; and

(13) a statement at the bottom of the document, with places for the signature of each person executing the document, that the document has been properly completed.

(c) The board may, by rule and as recommended by the department, modify the standard form of the out-of-hospital DNR order described by Subsection (b) in order to accomplish the purposes of this subchapter.

(d) A photocopy or other complete facsimile of the original written out-of-hospital DNR order executed under this subchapter may be used for any purpose for which the original written order may be used under this subchapter.

Added by Acts 1995, 74th Leg., ch. 965, § 10, eff. June 16, 1995. Renumbered from V.T.C.A., Health & Safety Code § 674.003 and amended by Acts 1999, 76th Leg., ch. 450, § 1.04, eff. Sept. 1, 1999. Amended by Acts 2009, 81st Leg., ch. 461, § 6, eff. Sept. 1, 2009.

### § 166.084. Issuance of Out-of-Hospital DNR Order by Nonwritten Communication

(a) A competent person who is an adult may issue an out-of-hospital DNR order by nonwritten communication.

(b) A declarant must issue the nonwritten out-of-hospital DNR order in the presence of the attending physician and two witnesses who qualify under Section 166.003, at least one of whom must be a witness who qualifies under Section 166.003(2).

(c) The attending physician and witnesses shall sign the out-of-hospital DNR order in the place of the document provided by Section 166.083(b)(7) and the attending physician shall sign the document in the place required by Section 166.083(b)(13). The physi-

cian shall make the fact of the existence of the out-of-hospital DNR order a part of the declarant's medical record and the names of the witnesses shall be entered in the medical record.

(d) An out-of-hospital DNR order issued in the manner provided by this section is valid and shall be honored by responding health care professionals as if executed in the manner provided by Section 166.082.

Added by Acts 1995, 74th Leg., ch. 965, § 10, eff. June 16, 1995. Renumbered from V.T.C.A., Health & Safety Code § 674.004 and amended by Acts 1999, 76th Leg., ch. 450, § 1.04, eff. Sept. 1, 1999.

### § 166.085. Execution of Out–of–Hospital DNR Order on Behalf of a Minor

(a) The following persons may execute an out-of-hospital DNR order on behalf of a minor:

(1) the minor's parents;

(2) the minor's legal guardian; or

(3) the minor's managing conservator.

(b) A person listed under Subsection (a) may not execute an out-of-hospital DNR order unless the minor has been diagnosed by a physician as suffering from a terminal or irreversible condition.

Added by Acts 1995, 74th Leg., ch. 965, § 10, eff. June 16, 1995. Renumbered from V.T.C.A., Health & Safety Code § 674.005 by Acts 1999, 76th Leg., ch. 450, § 1.04, eff. Sept. 1, 1999. Amended by Acts 2003, 78th Leg., ch. 1228, § 6, eff. June 20, 2003.

### § 166.086. Desire of Person Supersedes Out-of-Hospital DNR Order

The desire of a competent person, including a competent minor, supersedes the effect of an out-of-hospital DNR order executed or issued by or on behalf of the person when the desire is communicated to responding health care professionals as provided by this subchapter.

Added by Acts 1995, 74th Leg., ch. 965, § 10, eff. June 16, 1995. Renumbered from V.T.C.A., Health & Safety Code § 674.006 and amended by Acts 1999, 76th Leg., ch. 450, § 1.04, eff. Sept. 1, 1999.

### § 166.087. Procedure When Declarant is Incompetent or Incapable of Communication

(a) This section applies when a person 18 years of age or older has executed or issued an out-of-hospital DNR order and subsequently becomes incompetent or otherwise mentally or physically incapable of communication.

(b) If the adult person has designated a person to make a treatment decision as authorized by Section

166.032(c), the attending physician and the designated person shall comply with the out-of-hospital DNR order.

(c) If the adult person has not designated a person to make a treatment decision as authorized by Section 166.032(c), the attending physician shall comply with the out-of-hospital DNR order unless the physician believes that the order does not reflect the person's present desire.

Added by Acts 1995, 74th Leg., ch. 965, § 10, eff. June 16, 1995. Renumbered from V.T.C.A., Health & Safety Code § 674.007 and amended by Acts 1999, 76th Leg., ch. 450, § 1.04, eff. Sept. 1, 1999.

### § 166.088. Procedure When Person Has Not Executed or Issued Out-of-Hospital DNR Order and is Incompetent or Incapable of Communication

(a) If an adult person has not executed or issued an out-of-hospital DNR order and is incompetent or otherwise mentally or physically incapable of communication, the attending physician and the person's legal guardian, proxy, or agent having a medical power of attorney may execute an out-of-hospital DNR order on behalf of the person.

(b) If the person does not have a legal guardian, proxy, or agent under a medical power of attorney, the attending physician and at least one qualified relative from a category listed by Section 166.039(b), subject to the priority established under that subsection, may execute an out-of-hospital DNR order in the same manner as a treatment decision made under Section 166.039(b).

(c) A decision to execute an out-of-hospital DNR order made under Subsection (a) or (b) must be based on knowledge of what the person would desire, if known.

(d) An out-of-hospital DNR order executed under Subsection (b) must be made in the presence of at least two witnesses who qualify under Section 166.003, at least one of whom must be a witness who qualifies under Section 166.003(2).

(e) The fact that an adult person has not executed or issued an out-of-hospital DNR order does not create a presumption that the person does not want a treatment decision made to withhold cardiopulmonary resuscitation and certain other designated life-sustaining treatment designated by the board.

(f) If there is not a qualified relative available to act for the person under Subsection (b), an out-of-hospital DNR order must be concurred in by another physi-cian who is not involved in the treatment of the patient or who is a representative of the ethics or medical committee of the health care facility in which the person is a patient.

(g) A person listed in Section 166.039(b) who wishes to challenge a decision made under this section must apply for temporary guardianship under Section 875, Texas Probate Code. The court may waive applicable fees in that proceeding.

Added by Acts 1995, 74th Leg., ch. 965, § 10, eff. June 16, 1995. Renumbered from V.T.C.A., Health & Safety Code § 674.008 and amended by Acts 1999, 76th Leg., ch. 450, § 1.04, eff. Sept. 1, 1999.

### § 166.089. Compliance With Out-of-Hospital DNR Order

(a) When responding to a call for assistance, health care professionals shall honor an out-of-hospital DNR order in accordance with the statewide out-of-hospital DNR protocol and, where applicable, locally adopted out-of-hospital DNR protocols not in conflict with the statewide protocol if:

(1) the responding health care professionals discover an executed or issued out-of-hospital DNR order form on their arrival at the scene; and

(2) the responding health care professionals comply with this section.

(b) If the person is wearing a DNR identification device, the responding health care professionals must comply with Section 166.090.

(c) The responding health care professionals must establish the identity of the person as the person who executed or issued the out-of-hospital DNR order or for whom the out-of-hospital DNR order was executed or issued.

(d) The responding health care professionals must determine that the out-of-hospital DNR order form appears to be valid in that it includes:

(1) written responses in the places designated on the form for the names, signatures, and other information required of persons executing or issuing, or witnessing or acknowledging as applicable, the execution or issuance of, the order;

(2) a date in the place designated on the form for the date the order was executed or issued; and

(3) the signature or digital or electronic signature of the declarant or persons executing or issuing the order and the attending physician in the appropriate places designated on the form for indicating that the order form has been properly completed.

(e) If the conditions prescribed by Subsections (a) through (d) are not determined to apply by the responding health care professionals at the scene, the out-of-hospital DNR order may not be honored and life-sustaining procedures otherwise required by law or local emergency medical services protocols shall be initiated or continued. Health care professionals acting in out-of-hospital settings are not required to accept or interpret an out-of-hospital DNR order that does not meet the requirements of this subchapter.

(f) The out-of-hospital DNR order form or a copy of the form, when available, must accompany the person during transport.

(g) A record shall be made and maintained of the circumstances of each emergency medical services response in which an out-of-hospital DNR order or DNR identification device is encountered, in accordance with the statewide out-of-hospital DNR protocol and any applicable local out-of-hospital DNR protocol not in conflict with the statewide protocol.

(h) An out-of-hospital DNR order executed or issued and documented or evidenced in the manner prescribed by this subchapter is valid and shall be honored by responding health care professionals unless the person or persons found at the scene:

(1) identify themselves as the declarant or as the attending physician, legal guardian, qualified relative, or agent of the person having a medical power of attorney who executed or issued the out-of-hospital DNR order on behalf of the person; and

(2) request that cardiopulmonary resuscitation or certain other life-sustaining treatment designated by the board be initiated or continued.

(i) If the policies of a health care facility preclude compliance with the out-of-hospital DNR order of a person or an out-of-hospital DNR order issued by an attending physician on behalf of a person who is admitted to or a resident of the facility, or if the facility is unwilling to accept DNR identification devices as evidence of the existence of an out-of-hospital DNR order, that facility shall take all reasonable steps to notify the person or, if the person is incompetent, the person's guardian or the person or persons having authority to make health care treatment decisions on behalf of the person, of the facility's policy and shall take all reasonable steps to effect the transfer of the person to the person's home or to a facility where the provisions of this subchapter can be carried out.

Added by Acts 1995, 74th Leg., ch. 965, § 10, eff. June 16, 1995. Renumbered from V.T.C.A., Health & Safety Code § 674.009 and amended by Acts 1999, 76th Leg., ch. 450, § 1.04, eff. Sept. 1, 1999. Amended by Acts 2009, 81st Leg., ch. 461, § 7, eff. Sept. 1, 2009.

## § 166.090.  DNR Identification Device

(a) A person who has a valid out-of-hospital DNR order under this subchapter may wear a DNR identification device around the neck or on the wrist as prescribed by board rule adopted under Section 166.101.

(b) The presence of a DNR identification device on the body of a person is conclusive evidence that the person has executed or issued a valid out-of-hospital DNR order or has a valid out-of-hospital DNR order executed or issued on the person's behalf. Responding health care professionals shall honor the DNR identification device as if a valid out-of-hospital DNR order form executed or issued by the person were found in the possession of the person.

Added by Acts 1995, 74th Leg., ch. 965, § 10, eff. June 16, 1995. Renumbered from V.T.C.A., Health & Safety Code § 674.010 and amended by Acts 1999, 76th Leg., ch. 450, § 1.04, eff. Sept. 1, 1999.

## § 166.091.  Duration of Out-of-Hospital DNR Order

An out-of-hospital DNR order is effective until it is revoked as prescribed by Section 166.092.

Added by Acts 1995, 74th Leg., ch. 965, § 10, eff. June 16, 1995. Renumbered from V.T.C.A., Health & Safety Code § 674.011 and amended by Acts 1999, 76th Leg., ch. 450, § 1.04, eff. Sept. 1, 1999.

## § 166.092.  Revocation of Out-of-Hospital DNR Order

(a) A declarant may revoke an out-of-hospital DNR order at any time without regard to the declarant's mental state or competency. An order may be revoked by:

(1) the declarant or someone in the declarant's presence and at the declarant's direction destroying the order form and removing the DNR identification device, if any;

(2) a person who identifies himself or herself as the legal guardian, as a qualified relative, or as the agent of the declarant having a medical power of attorney who executed the out-of-hospital DNR order or another person in the person's presence and at the person's direction destroying the order form and removing the DNR identification device, if any;

(3) the declarant communicating the declarant's intent to revoke the order; or

(4) a person who identifies himself or herself as the legal guardian, a qualified relative, or the agent of the declarant having a medical power of attorney

who executed the out-of-hospital DNR order orally stating the person's intent to revoke the order.

(b) An oral revocation under Subsection (a)(3) or (a)(4) takes effect only when the declarant or a person who identifies himself or herself as the legal guardian, a qualified relative, or the agent of the declarant having a medical power of attorney who executed the out-of-hospital DNR order communicates the intent to revoke the order to the responding health care professionals or the attending physician at the scene. The responding health care professionals shall record the time, date, and place of the revocation in accordance with the statewide out-of-hospital DNR protocol and rules adopted by the board and any applicable local out-of-hospital DNR protocol. The attending physician or the physician's designee shall record in the person's medical record the time, date, and place of the revocation and, if different, the time, date, and place that the physician received notice of the revocation. The attending physician or the physician's designee shall also enter the word "VOID" on each page of the copy of the order in the person's medical record.

(c) Except as otherwise provided by this subchapter, a person is not civilly or criminally liable for failure to act on a revocation made under this section unless the person has actual knowledge of the revocation.

Added by Acts 1995, 74th Leg., ch. 965, § 10, eff. June 16 1995. Renumbered from V.T.C.A., Health & Safety Code § 674.012 and amended by Acts 1999, 76th Leg., ch. 450, § 1.04, eff. Sept. 1, 1999.

### § 166.093. Reexecution of Out-of-Hospital DNR Order

A declarant may at any time reexecute or reissue an out-of-hospital DNR order in accordance with the procedures prescribed by Section 166.082, including reexecution or reissuance after the declarant is diagnosed as having a terminal or irreversible condition.

Added by Acts 1995, 74th Leg., ch. 965, § 10, eff. June 16, 1995. Renumbered from V.T.C.A., Health & Safety Code § 674.013 and amended by Acts 1999, 76th Leg., ch. 450, § 1.04, eff. Sept. 1, 1999.

### § 166.094. Limitation on Liability for Withholding Cardiopulmonary Resuscitation and Certain Other Life-Sustaining Procedures

(a) A health care professional or health care facility or entity that in good faith causes cardiopulmonary resuscitation or certain other life-sustaining treatment designated by the board to be withheld from a person in accordance with this subchapter is not civilly liable for that action.

(b) A health care professional or health care facility or entity that in good faith participates in withholding cardiopulmonary resuscitation or certain other life-sustaining treatment designated by the board from a person in accordance with this subchapter is not civilly liable for that action.

(c) A health care professional or health care facility or entity that in good faith participates in withholding cardiopulmonary resuscitation or certain other life-sustaining treatment designated by the board from a person in accordance with this subchapter is not criminally liable or guilty of unprofessional conduct as a result of that action.

(d) A health care professional or health care facility or entity that in good faith causes or participates in withholding cardiopulmonary resuscitation or certain other life-sustaining treatment designated by the board from a person in accordance with this subchapter and rules adopted under this subchapter is not in violation of any other licensing or regulatory laws or rules of this state and is not subject to any disciplinary action or sanction by any licensing or regulatory agency of this state as a result of that action.

Added by Acts 1995, 74th Leg., ch. 965, § 10, eff. June 16, 1995. Renumbered from V.T.C.A., Health & Safety Code § 674.016 and amended by Acts 1999, 76th Leg., ch. 450, § 1.04, eff. Sept. 1, 1999.

### § 166.095. Limitation on Liability for Failure to Effectuate Out-of-Hospital DNR Order

(a) A health care professional or health care facility or entity that has no actual knowledge of an out-of-hospital DNR order is not civilly or criminally liable for failing to act in accordance with the order.

(b) A health care professional or health care facility or entity is subject to review and disciplinary action by the appropriate licensing board for failing to effectuate an out-of-hospital DNR order. This subsection does not limit remedies available under other laws of this state.

(c) If an attending physician refuses to execute or comply with an out-of-hospital DNR order, the physician shall inform the person, the legal guardian or qualified relatives of the person, or the agent of the person having a medical power of attorney and, if the person or another authorized to act on behalf of the person so directs, shall make a reasonable effort to transfer the person to another physician who is willing to execute or comply with an out-of-hospital DNR order.

Added by Acts 1995, 74th Leg., ch. 965, § 10, eff. June 16, 1995. Renumbered from V.T.C.A., Health & Safety Code § 674.017 and amended by Acts 1999, 76th Leg., ch. 450, § 1.04, eff. Sept. 1, 1999.

### § 166.096. Honoring Out-of-Hospital DNR Order Does Not Constitute Offense of Aiding Suicide

A person does not commit an offense under Section 22.08, Penal Code, by withholding cardiopulmonary resuscitation or certain other life-sustaining treatment designated by the board from a person in accordance with this subchapter.

Added by Acts 1995, 74th Leg., ch. 965, § 10, eff. June 16, 1995. Renumbered from V.T.C.A., Health & Safety Code § 674.018 and amended by Acts 1999, 76th Leg., ch. 450, § 1.04, eff. Sept. 1, 1999.

### § 166.097. Criminal Penalty; Prosecution

(a) A person commits an offense if the person intentionally conceals, cancels, defaces, obliterates, or damages another person's out-of-hospital DNR order or DNR identification device without that person's consent or the consent of the person or persons authorized to execute or issue an out-of-hospital DNR order on behalf of the person under this subchapter. An offense under this subsection is a Class A misdemeanor.

(b) A person is subject to prosecution for criminal homicide under Chapter 19, Penal Code, if the person, with the intent to cause cardiopulmonary resuscitation or certain other life-sustaining treatment designated by the board to be withheld from another person contrary to the other person's desires, falsifies or forges an out-of-hospital DNR order or intentionally conceals or withholds personal knowledge of a revocation and thereby directly causes cardiopulmonary resuscitation and certain other life-sustaining treatment designated by the board to be withheld from the other person with the result that the other person's death is hastened.

Added by Acts 1995, 74th Leg., ch. 965, § 10, eff. June 16, 1995. Renumbered from V.T.C.A., Health & Safety Code § 674.019 and amended by Acts 1999, 76th Leg., ch. 450, § 1.04, eff. Sept. 1, 1999.

### § 166.098. Pregnant Persons

A person may not withhold cardiopulmonary resuscitation or certain other life-sustaining treatment designated by the board under this subchapter from a

person known by the responding health care professionals to be pregnant.

Added by Acts 1995, 74th Leg., ch. 965, § 10, eff. June 16, 1995. Renumbered from V.T.C.A., Health & Safety Code § 674.020 and amended by Acts 1999, 76th Leg., ch. 450, § 1.04, eff. Sept. 1, 1999.

### § 166.099. Mercy Killing Not Condoned

This subchapter does not condone, authorize, or approve mercy killing or permit an affirmative or deliberate act or omission to end life except to permit the natural process of dying as provided by this subchapter.

Added by Acts 1995, 74th Leg., ch. 965, § 10, eff. June 16, 1995. Renumbered from V.T.C.A., Health & Safety Code § 674.021 and amended by Acts 1999, 76th Leg., ch. 450, § 1.04, eff. Sept. 1, 1999.

### § 166.100. Legal Right or Responsibility Not Affected

This subchapter does not impair or supersede any legal right or responsibility a person may have under a constitution, other statute, regulation, or court decision to effect the withholding of cardiopulmonary resuscitation or certain other life-sustaining treatment designated by the board.

Added by Acts 1995, 74th Leg., ch. 965, § 10, eff. June 16, 1995. Renumbered from V.T.C.A., Health & Safety Code § 674.022 and amended by Acts 1999, 76th Leg., ch. 450, § 1.04, eff. Sept. 1, 1999.

### § 166.101. Duties of Department and Board

(a) The board shall, on the recommendation of the department, adopt all reasonable and necessary rules to carry out the purposes of this subchapter, including rules:

(1) adopting a statewide out-of-hospital DNR order protocol that sets out standard procedures for the withholding of cardiopulmonary resuscitation and certain other life-sustaining treatment by health care professionals acting in out-of-hospital settings;

(2) designating life-sustaining treatment that may be included in an out-of-hospital DNR order, including all procedures listed in Sections 166.081(6)(A)(i) through (v); and

(3) governing recordkeeping in circumstances in which an out-of-hospital DNR order or DNR identification device is encountered by responding health care professionals.

(b) The rules adopted by the board under Subsection (a) are not effective until approved by the Texas State Board of Medical Examiners.

(c) Local emergency medical services authorities may adopt local out-of-hospital DNR order protocols if the local protocols do not conflict with the statewide out-of-hospital DNR order protocol adopted by the board.

(d) The board by rule shall specify a distinctive standard design for a necklace and a bracelet DNR identification device that signifies, when worn by a person, that the possessor has executed or issued a valid out-of-hospital DNR order under this subchapter or is a person for whom a valid out-of-hospital DNR order has been executed or issued.

(e) The department shall report to the board from time to time regarding issues identified in emergency medical services responses in which an out-of-hospital DNR order or DNR identification device is encountered. The report may contain recommendations to the board for necessary modifications to the form of the standard out-of-hospital DNR order or the designated life-sustaining procedures listed in the standard out-of-hospital DNR order, the statewide out-of-hospital DNR order protocol, or the DNR identification devices.

Added by Acts 1995, 74th Leg., ch. 965, § 10, eff. June 16, 1995. Renumbered from V.T.C.A., Health & Safety Code § 674.023 and amended by Acts 1999, 76th Leg., ch. 450, § 1.04, eff. Sept. 1, 1999.

### § 166.102. Physician's DNR Order May be Honored by Health Care Personnel Other Than Emergency Medical Services Personnel

(a) Except as provided by Subsection (b), a licensed nurse or person providing health care services in an out-of-hospital setting may honor a physician's do-not-resuscitate order.

(b) When responding to a call for assistance, emergency medical services personnel:

(1) shall honor only a properly executed or issued out-of-hospital DNR order or prescribed DNR identification device in accordance with this subchapter; and

(2) have no duty to review, examine, interpret, or honor a person's other written directive, including a written directive in the form prescribed by Section 166.033.

Added by Acts 2003, 78th Leg., ch. 1228, § 7, eff. June 20, 2003. Amended by Acts 2011, 82nd Leg., ch. 710 (H.B. 577), § 1, eff. June 17, 2011.

## SUBCHAPTER D. MEDICAL POWER OF ATTORNEY

### § 166.151. Definitions

In this subchapter:

(1) "Adult" means a person 18 years of age or older or a person under 18 years of age who has had the disabilities of minority removed.

(2) "Agent" means an adult to whom authority to make health care decisions is delegated under a medical power of attorney.

(3) "Health care provider" means an individual or facility licensed, certified, or otherwise authorized to administer health care, for profit or otherwise, in the ordinary course of business or professional practice and includes a physician.

(4) "Principal" means an adult who has executed a medical power of attorney.

(5) "Residential care provider" means an individual or facility licensed, certified, or otherwise authorized to operate, for profit or otherwise, a residential care home.

Added by Acts 1991, 72nd Leg., ch. 16, § 3.02(a), eff. Aug. 26, 1991. Renumbered from V.T.C.A., Civil Practice & Remedies Code § 135.001 and amended by Acts 1999, 76th Leg., ch. 450, § 1.05, eff. Sept. 1, 1999.

### § 166.152. Scope and Duration of Authority

(a) Subject to this subchapter or any express limitation on the authority of the agent contained in the medical power of attorney, the agent may make any health care decision on the principal's behalf that the principal could make if the principal were competent.

(b) An agent may exercise authority only if the principal's attending physician certifies in writing and files the certification in the principal's medical record that, based on the attending physician's reasonable medical judgment, the principal is incompetent.

(c) Notwithstanding any other provisions of this subchapter, treatment may not be given to or withheld from the principal if the principal objects regardless of whether, at the time of the objection:

(1) a medical power of attorney is in effect; or

(2) the principal is competent.

(d) The principal's attending physician shall make reasonable efforts to inform the principal of any proposed treatment or of any proposal to withdraw or withhold treatment before implementing an agent's advance directive.

(e) After consultation with the attending physician and other health care providers, the agent shall make a health care decision:

(1) according to the agent's knowledge of the principal's wishes, including the principal's religious and moral beliefs; or

(2) if the agent does not know the principal's wishes, according to the agent's assessment of the principal's best interests.

(f) Notwithstanding any other provision of this subchapter, an agent may not consent to:

(1) voluntary inpatient mental health services;

(2) convulsive treatment;

(3) psychosurgery;

(4) abortion; or

(5) neglect of the principal through the omission of care primarily intended to provide for the comfort of the principal.

(g) The power of attorney is effective indefinitely on execution as provided by this subchapter and delivery of the document to the agent, unless it is revoked as provided by this subchapter or the principal becomes competent. If the medical power of attorney includes an expiration date and on that date the principal is incompetent, the power of attorney continues to be effective until the principal becomes competent unless it is revoked as provided by this subchapter.

Added by Acts 1991, 72nd Leg., ch. 16, § 3.02(a), eff. Aug. 26, 1991. Renumbered from V.T.C.A., Civil Practice & Remedies Code § 135.002 and amended by Acts 1999, 76th Leg., ch. 450, § 1.05, eff. Sept. 1, 1999.

### § 166.153. Persons Who May Not Exercise Authority of Agent

A person may not exercise the authority of an agent while the person serves as:

(1) the principal's health care provider;

(2) an employee of the principal's health care provider unless the person is a relative of the principal;

(3) the principal's residential care provider; or

(4) an employee of the principal's residential care provider unless the person is a relative of the principal.

Added by Acts 1991, 72nd Leg., ch. 16, § 3.02(a), eff. Aug. 26, 1991. Renumbered from V.T.C.A., Civil Practice & Remedies Code § 135.003 by Acts 1999, 76th Leg., ch. 450, § 1.05, eff. Sept. 1, 1999.

### § 166.154. Execution

(a) Except as provided by Subsection (b), the medical power of attorney must be signed by the principal in the presence of two witnesses who qualify under Section 166. 003, at least one of whom must be a witness who qualifies under Section 166.003(2). The witnesses must sign the document.

(b) The principal, in lieu of signing in the presence of the witnesses, may sign the medical power of attorney and have the signature acknowledged before a notary public.

(c) If the principal is physically unable to sign, another person may sign the medical power of attorney with the principal's name in the principal's presence and at the principal's express direction. The person may use a digital or electronic signature authorized under Section 166.011.

Added by Acts 1991, 72nd Leg., ch. 16, § 3.02(a), eff. Aug. 26, 1991. Renumbered from V.T.C.A., Civil Practice & Remedies Code § 135.004 and amended by Acts 1999, 76th Leg., ch. 450, § 1.05, eff. Sept. 1, 1999. Amended by Acts 2009, 81st Leg., ch. 461, § 8, eff. Sept. 1, 2009.

### § 166.155. Revocation

(a) A medical power of attorney is revoked by:

(1) oral or written notification at any time by the principal to the agent or a licensed or certified health or residential care provider or by any other act evidencing a specific intent to revoke the power, without regard to whether the principal is competent or the principal's mental state;

(2) execution by the principal of a subsequent medical power of attorney; or

(3) the divorce of the principal and spouse, if the spouse is the principal's agent, unless the medical power of attorney provides otherwise.

(b) A principal's licensed or certified health or residential care provider who is informed of or provided with a revocation of a medical power of attorney shall immediately record the revocation in the principal's medical record and give notice of the revocation to the agent and any known health and residential care providers currently responsible for the principal's care.

Added by Acts 1991, 72nd Leg., ch. 16, § 3.02(a), eff. Aug. 26, 1991. Renumbered from V.T.C.A., Civil Practice & Remedies Code § 135.005 and amended by Acts 1999, 76th Leg., ch. 450, § 1.05, eff. Sept. 1, 1999.

## § 166.156. Appointment of Guardian

(a) On motion filed in connection with a petition for appointment of a guardian or, if a guardian has been appointed, on petition of the guardian, a probate court shall determine whether to suspend or revoke the authority of the agent.

(b) The court shall consider the preferences of the principal as expressed in the medical power of attorney.

(c) During the pendency of the court's determination under Subsection (a), the guardian has the sole authority to make any health care decisions unless the court orders otherwise. If a guardian has not been appointed, the agent has the authority to make any health care decisions unless the court orders otherwise.

(d) A person, including any attending physician or health or residential care provider, who does not have actual knowledge of the appointment of a guardian or an order of the court granting authority to someone other than the agent to make health care decisions is not subject to criminal or civil liability and has not engaged in unprofessional conduct for implementing an agent's health care decision.

Added by Acts 1991, 72nd Leg., ch. 16, § 3.02(a), eff. Aug. 26, 1991. Renumbered from V.T.C.A., Civil Practice & Remedies Code § 135.006 and amended by Acts 1999, 76th Leg., ch. 450, § 1.05, eff. Sept. 1, 1999.

## § 166.157. Disclosure of Medical Information

Subject to any limitations in the medical power of attorney, an agent may, for the purpose of making a health care decision:

(1) request, review, and receive any information, oral or written, regarding the principal's physical or mental health, including medical and hospital records;

(2) execute a release or other document required to obtain the information; and

(3) consent to the disclosure of the information.

Added by Acts 1991, 72nd Leg., ch. 16, § 3.02(a), eff. Aug. 26, 1991. Renumbered from V.T.C.A., Civil Practice & Remedies Code § 135.007 and amended by Acts 1999, 76th Leg., ch. 450, § 1.05, eff. Sept. 1, 1999.

## § 166.158. Duty of Health or Residential Care Provider

(a) A principal's health or residential care provider and an employee of the provider who knows of the existence of the principal's medical power of attorney shall follow a directive of the principal's agent to the extent it is consistent with the desires of the principal, this subchapter, and the medical power of attorney.

(b) The attending physician does not have a duty to verify that the agent's directive is consistent with the principal's wishes or religious or moral beliefs.

(c) A principal's health or residential care provider who finds it impossible to follow a directive by the agent because of a conflict with this subchapter or the medical power of attorney shall inform the agent as soon as is reasonably possible. The agent may select another attending physician. The procedures established under Sections 166.045 and 166.046 apply if the agent's directive concerns providing, withholding, or withdrawing life-sustaining treatment.

(d) This subchapter may not be construed to require a health or residential care provider who is not a physician to act in a manner contrary to a physician's order.

Added by Acts 1991, 72nd Leg., ch. 16, § 3.02(a), eff. Aug. 26, 1991. Renumbered from V.T.C.A., Civil Practice & Remedies Code § 135.008 and amended by Acts 1999, 76th Leg., ch. 450, § 1.05, eff. Sept. 1, 1999.

## § 166.159. Discrimination Relating to Execution of Medical Power of Attorney

A health or residential care provider, health care service plan, insurer issuing disability insurance, self-insured employee benefit plan, or nonprofit hospital service plan may not:

(1) charge a person a different rate solely because the person has executed a medical power of attorney;

(2) require a person to execute a medical power of attorney before:

(A) admitting the person to a hospital, nursing home, or residential care home;

(B) insuring the person; or

(C) allowing the person to receive health or residential care; or

(3) refuse health or residential care to a person solely because the person has executed a medical power of attorney.

Added by Acts 1991, 72nd Leg., ch. 16, § 3.02(a), eff. Aug. 26, 1991. Renumbered from V.T.C.A., Civil Practice & Remedies Code § 135.009 and amended by Acts 1999, 76th Leg., ch. 450, § 1.05, eff. Sept. 1, 1999.

## § 166.160.   Limitation on Liability

(a) An agent is not subject to criminal or civil liability for a health care decision if the decision is made in good faith under the terms of the medical power of attorney and the provisions of this subchapter.

(b) An attending physician, health or residential care provider, or a person acting as an agent for or under the physician's or provider's control is not subject to criminal or civil liability and has not engaged in unprofessional conduct for an act or omission if the act or omission:

(1) is done in good faith under the terms of the medical power of attorney, the directives of the agent, and the provisions of this subchapter; and

(2) does not constitute a failure to exercise reasonable care in the provision of health care services.

(c) The standard of care that the attending physician, health or residential care provider, or person acting as an agent for or under the physician's or provider's control shall exercise under Subsection (b) is that degree of care that an attending physician, health or residential care provider, or person acting as an agent for or under the physician's or provider's control, as applicable, of ordinary prudence and skill would have exercised under the same or similar circumstances in the same or similar community.

(d) An attending physician, health or residential care provider, or person acting as an agent for or under the physician's or provider's control has not engaged in unprofessional conduct for:

(1) failure to act as required by the directive of an agent or a medical power of attorney if the physician, provider, or person was not provided with a copy of the medical power of attorney or had no knowledge of a directive; or

(2) acting as required by an agent's directive if the medical power of attorney has expired or been revoked but the physician, provider, or person does not have knowledge of the expiration or revocation.

Added by Acts 1991, 72nd Leg., ch. 16, § 3.02(a), eff. Aug. 26, 1991.   Renumbered from V.T.C.A., Civil Practice & Remedies Code § 135.010 and amended by Acts 1999, 76th Leg., ch. 450, § 1.05, eff. Sept. 1, 1999.

## § 166.161.   Liability for Health Care Costs

Liability for the cost of health care provided as a result of the agent's decision is the same as if the health care were provided as a result of the principal's decision.

Added by Acts 1991, 72nd Leg., ch. 16, § 3.02(a), eff. Aug. 26, 1991.   Renumbered from V.T.C.A., Civil Practice & Remedies Code § 135.011 by Acts 1999, 76th Leg., ch. 450, § 1.05, eff. Sept. 1, 1999.

## § 166.162.   Disclosure Statement

A medical power of attorney is not effective unless the principal, before executing the medical power of attorney, signs a statement that the principal has received a disclosure statement and has read and understood its contents.

Added by Acts 1991, 72nd Leg., ch. 16, § 3.02(a), eff. Aug. 26, 1991.   Renumbered from V.T.C.A., Civil Practice & Remedies Code § 135.014 and amended by Acts 1999, 76th Leg., ch. 450, § 1.05, eff. Sept. 1, 1999.

## § 166.163.   Form of Disclosure Statement

The disclosure statement must be in substantially the following form:

### INFORMATION CONCERNING THE MEDICAL POWER OF ATTORNEY

THIS IS AN IMPORTANT LEGAL DOCUMENT. BEFORE SIGNING THIS DOCUMENT, YOU SHOULD KNOW THESE IMPORTANT FACTS:

Except to the extent you state otherwise, this document gives the person you name as your agent the authority to make any and all health care decisions for you in accordance with your wishes, including your religious and moral beliefs, when you are no longer capable of making them yourself. Because "health care" means any treatment, service, or procedure to maintain, diagnose, or treat your physical or mental condition, your agent has the power to make a broad range of health care decisions for you. Your agent may consent, refuse to consent, or withdraw consent to medical treatment and may make decisions about withdrawing or withholding life-sustaining treatment. Your agent may not consent to voluntary inpatient mental health services, convulsive treatment, psychosurgery, or abortion. A physician must comply with your agent's instructions or allow you to be transferred to another physician.

Your agent's authority begins when your doctor certifies that you lack the competence to make health care decisions.

Your agent is obligated to follow your instructions when making decisions on your behalf. Unless you state otherwise, your agent has the same authority to make decisions about your health care as you would have had.

It is important that you discuss this document with your physician or other health care provider before you sign it to make sure that you understand the nature and range of decisions that may be made on your behalf. If you do not have a physician, you should talk with someone else who is knowledgeable about these issues and can answer your questions. You do not need a lawyer's assistance to complete this document, but if there is anything in this document that you do not understand, you should ask a lawyer to explain it to you.

The person you appoint as agent should be someone you know and trust. The person must be 18 years of age or older or a person under 18 years of age who has had the disabilities of minority removed. If you appoint your health or residential care provider (e.g., your physician or an employee of a home health agency, hospital, nursing home, or residential care home, other than a relative), that person has to choose between acting as your agent or as your health or residential care provider; the law does not permit a person to do both at the same time.

You should inform the person you appoint that you want the person to be your health care agent. You should discuss this document with your agent and your physician and give each a signed copy. You should indicate on the document itself the people and institutions who have signed copies. Your agent is not liable for health care decisions made in good faith on your behalf.

Even after you have signed this document, you have the right to make health care decisions for yourself as long as you are able to do so and treatment cannot be given to you or stopped over your objection. You have the right to revoke the authority granted to your agent by informing your agent or your health or residential care provider orally or in writing or by your execution of a subsequent medical power of attorney. Unless you state otherwise, your appointment of a spouse dissolves on divorce.

This document may not be changed or modified. If you want to make changes in the document, you must make an entirely new one.

You may wish to designate an alternate agent in the event that your agent is unwilling, unable, or ineligible to act as your agent. Any alternate agent you designate has the same authority to make health care decisions for you.

THIS POWER OF ATTORNEY IS NOT VALID UNLESS:

(1) YOU SIGN IT AND HAVE YOUR SIGNATURE ACKNOWLEDGED BEFORE A NOTARY PUBLIC; OR

(2) YOU SIGN IT IN THE PRESENCE OF TWO COMPETENT ADULT WITNESSES.

THE FOLLOWING PERSONS MAY NOT ACT AS ONE OF THE WITNESSES:

(1) the person you have designated as your agent;

(2) a person related to you by blood or marriage;

(3) a person entitled to any part of your estate after your death under a will or codicil executed by you or by operation of law;

(4) your attending physician;

(5) an employee of your attending physician;

(6) an employee of a health care facility in which you are a patient if the employee is providing direct patient care to you or is an officer, director, partner, or business office employee of the health care facility or of any parent organization of the health care facility; or

(7) a person who, at the time this power of attorney is executed, has a claim against any part of your estate after your death.

Added by Acts 1991, 72nd Leg., ch. 16, § 3.02(a), eff. Aug. 26, 1991. Renumbered from V.T.C.A., Civil Practice & Remedies Code § 135.015 and amended by Acts 1999, 76th Leg., ch. 450, § 1.05, eff. Sept. 1, 1999. Amended by Acts 2013, 83rd Leg., ch. 134 (S.B. 651), § 1, eff. Jan. 1, 2014.

### § 166.164. Form of Medical Power of Attorney

The medical power of attorney must be in substantially the following form:

MEDICAL POWER OF ATTORNEY
DESIGNATION OF HEALTH
CARE AGENT.

I, _____ (insert your name) appoint:

Name:_____

Address:_____

Phone_____

as my agent to make any and all health care decisions for me, except to the extent I state otherwise in this document. This medical power of attorney takes effect if I become unable to make my own health care decisions and this fact is certified in writing by my physician.

LIMITATIONS ON THE DECISION–MAKING AUTHORITY OF MY AGENT ARE AS FOLLOWS:

_____

### DESIGNATION OF ALTERNATE AGENT.

(You are not required to designate an alternate agent but you may do so. An alternate agent may make the same health care decisions as the designated agent if the designated agent is unable or unwilling to act as your agent. If the agent designated is your spouse, the designation is automatically revoked by law if your marriage is dissolved.)

If the person designated as my agent is unable or unwilling to make health care decisions for me, I designate the following persons to serve as my agent to make health care decisions for me as authorized by this document, who serve in the following order:

A. First Alternate Agent
   Name:_____
   Address:_____
      Phone _____
B. Second Alternate Agent
   Name:_____
   Address:_____
      Phone _____
   The original of this document is kept at:
   _____
   _____
   _____

The following individuals or institutions have signed copies:

   Name:_____
   Address:_____
   _____
   Name:_____
   Address:_____
   _____

### DURATION.

I understand that this power of attorney exists indefinitely from the date I execute this document unless I establish a shorter time or revoke the power of attorney. If I am unable to make health care decisions for myself when this power of attorney expires, the authority I have granted my agent continues to exist until the time I become able to make health care decisions for myself.

(IF APPLICABLE) This power of attorney ends on the following date: _____

### PRIOR DESIGNATIONS REVOKED.

I revoke any prior medical power of attorney.

### ACKNOWLEDGMENT OF DISCLOSURE STATEMENT.

I have been provided with a disclosure statement explaining the effect of this document. I have read and understand that information contained in the disclosure statement.

(YOU MUST DATE AND SIGN THIS POWER OF ATTORNEY. YOU MAY SIGN IT AND HAVE YOUR SIGNATURE ACKNOWLEDGED BEFORE A NOTARY PUBLIC OR YOU MAY SIGN IT IN THE PRESENCE OF TWO COMPETENT ADULT WITNESSES.)

SIGNATURE ACKNOWLEDGED BEFORE NOTARY

I sign my name to this medical power of attorney on _____ day of _____ (month, year) at

_____
(City and State)

_____
(Signature)

_____
(Print Name)

State of Texas
County of _____
This instrument was acknowledged before me on _____
(date) by _____ (name of person acknowledging).

_____
NOTARY PUBLIC, State of Texas
Notary's printed name:

_____
My commission expires:

_____

. OR

SIGNATURE IN PRESENCE OF TWO COMPETENT ADULT WITNESSES

I sign my name to this medical power of attorney on _____ day of _____ (month, year) at

_____
(City and State)

_____
(Signature)

_____
(Print Name)

STATEMENT OF FIRST WITNESS.

I am not the person appointed as agent by this document. I am not related to the principal by blood or marriage. I would not be entitled to any portion of the principal's estate on the principal's death. I am not the attending physician of the principal or an employee of the attending physician. I have no claim against any portion of the principal's estate on the principal's death. Furthermore, if I am an employee of a health care facility in which the principal is a patient, I am not involved in providing direct patient care to the principal and am not an officer, director, partner, or business office employee of the health care facility or of any parent organization of the health care facility.

Signature:_____
Print
Name:_____
Date:_____
Address:_____

SIGNATURE OF SECOND WITNESS.
Signature:_____
Print
Name:_____
Date:_____
Address:_____

Added by Acts 1991, 72nd Leg., ch. 16, § 3.02(a), eff. Aug. 26, 1991. Renumbered from V.T.C.A., Civil Practice & Remedies Code § 135.016 and amended by Acts 1999, 76th Leg., ch. 450, § 1.05, eff. Sept. 1, 1999. Amended by Acts 2013, 83rd Leg., ch. 134 (S.B. 651), § 1, eff. Jan. 1, 2014.

Section 4 of Acts 2013, 83rd Leg., ch. 134 (S.B. 651) provides:

"The change in law made by this Act to Section 166.164, Health and Safety Code, does not affect the validity of a document executed under that section before the effective date [Jan. 1, 2014] of this section. A document executed before the effective date of this section is governed by the law in effect on the date the document was executed, and that law continues in effect for that purpose."

### § 166.165. Civil Action

(a) A person who is a near relative of the principal or a responsible adult who is directly interested in the principal, including a guardian, social worker, physician, or clergyman, may bring an action to request that the medical power of attorney be revoked because the principal, at the time the medical power of attorney was signed:

(1) was not competent; or

(2) was under duress, fraud, or undue influence.

(a–1) In a county in which there is no statutory probate court, an action under this section shall be brought in the district court. In a county in which there is a statutory probate court, the statutory probate court and the district court have concurrent jurisdiction over an action brought under this section.

(b) The action may be brought in the county of the principal's residence or the residence of the person bringing the action.

(c) During the pendency of the action, the authority of the agent to make health care decisions continues in effect unless the court orders otherwise.

Added by Acts 1991, 72nd Leg., ch. 16, § 3.02(a), eff. Aug. 26, 1991. Renumbered from V.T.C.A., Civil Practice & Remedies Code § 135.017 and amended by Acts 1999, 76th Leg., ch. 450, § 1.05, eff. Sept. 1, 1999. Amended by Acts 2013, 83rd Leg., ch. 134 (S.B. 651), § 2, eff. Sept. 1, 2013.

Section 5 of Acts 2013, 83rd Leg., ch. 134 (S.B. 651) provides:

"The change in law made by this Act to Section 166.165, Health and Safety Code, applies to an action brought under that section on or after the effective date [Sept. 1, 2013] of this Act, regardless of whether the power of attorney was executed before, on, or after the effective date of this Act."

### § 166.166. Other Rights or Responsibilities Not Affected

This subchapter does not limit or impair any legal right or responsibility that any person, including a physician or health or residential care provider, may have to make or implement health care decisions on behalf of a person, provided that if an attending physician or health care facility is unwilling to honor a patient's advance directive or a treatment decision to provide life-sustaining treatment, life-sustaining treatment is required to be provided the patient, but only until a reasonable opportunity has been afforded for transfer of the patient to another physician or health care facility willing to comply with the advance directive or treatment decision.

Added by Acts 1991, 72nd Leg., ch. 16, § 3.02(a), eff. Aug. 26, 1991. Renumbered from V.T.C.A., Civil Practice & Remedies Code § 135.018 and amended by Acts 1999, 76th Leg., ch. 450, § 1.05, eff. Sept. 1, 1999.

*

# APPENDIX: TEXAS PROBATE CODE

*The Texas Probate Code was repealed and the Estates Code enacted effective January 1, 2014, by Acts 2009, 81st Leg., ch. 680, § 1 et seq.; Acts 2011, 82nd Leg., ch. 823 (H.B. 2759), § 1 et seq.; Acts 2011, 82nd Leg., ch. 1338 (S.B. 1198), § 1 et seq.*

*This appendix contains the text of the Probate Code as the Code existed prior to January 1, 2014.*

## CHAPTER I

## GENERAL PROVISIONS

**Section**

**Section**

## § 1. Short Title

This Act shall be known, and may be cited, as the "Texas Probate Code."

Acts 1955, 54th Leg., p. 88, ch. 55, eff. Jan. 1, 1956.

## § 2. Effective Date and Application

**(a) Effective Date.** This Code shall take effect and be in force on and after January 1, 1956. The procedure herein prescribed shall govern all probate proceedings in county and probate courts brought after the effective date of this Act, and also all further procedure in proceedings in probate then pending, except to the extent that in the opinion of the court, with respect to proceedings in probate then pending, its application in particular proceedings or parts thereof would not be feasible or would work injustice, in which event the former procedure shall apply.

**(b) Rights Not Affected.** No act done in any proceeding commenced before this Code takes effect, and no accrued right, shall be impaired by the provisions of this Code. When a right is acquired, extinguished, or barred upon the expiration of a prescribed period of time which has commenced to run by the provision of any statute in force before this Code takes effect, such provision shall remain in force and be deemed a part of this Code with respect to such right. All things properly done under any previously existing statute prior to the taking effect of this Code shall be treated as valid. Where citation or other process or notice is issued and served in compliance with existing statutes prior to the taking effect of this Code, the party upon whom such citation or other process has been served shall have the time provided for under such previously existing statutes in which to comply therewith.

**(c) Subdivisions Have No Legal Effect.** The division of this Code into Chapters, Parts, Sections, Subsections, and Paragraphs is solely for convenience and shall have no legal effect.

**(d) Severability.** If any provision of this Code, or the application thereof to any person or circumstance, is held invalid, such invalidity shall not affect other provisions or applications of the Code which can be given effect without the invalid provision or application, and to this end the provisions of this Code are declared to be severable, and the Legislature hereby states that it would have enacted such portions of the Code which can lawfully be given effect regardless of the possible invalidity of other provisions of the Code.

**(e) Nature of Proceeding.** The administration of the estate of a decedent, from the filing of the application for probate and administration, or for administration, until the decree of final distribution and the discharge of the last personal representative, shall be considered as one proceeding for purposes of jurisdiction. The entire proceeding is a proceeding in rem.

Acts 1955, 54th Leg., p. 88, ch. 55, eff. Jan. 1, 1956. Amended by Acts 1993, 73rd Leg., ch. 957, § 2, eff. Sept. 1, 1993.

## § 3. Definitions and Use of Terms

Except as otherwise provided by Chapter XIII of this Code, when used in this Code, unless otherwise apparent from the context:

(a) "Authorized corporate surety" means a domestic or foreign corporation authorized to do business in the State of Texas for the purpose of issuing surety, guaranty or indemnity bonds guaranteeing the fidelity of executors and administrators.

(b) "Child" includes an adopted child, whether adopted by any existing or former statutory procedure or by acts of estoppel, but, unless expressly so stated herein, does not include a child who has no presumed father.

(c) "Claims" include liabilities of a decedent which survive, including taxes, whether arising in contract or in tort or otherwise, funeral expenses, the expense of a tombstone, expenses of administration, estate and inheritance taxes, and debts due such estates.

(d) "Corporate fiduciary" means a financial institution as defined by Section 201.101, Finance Code, having trust powers, existing or doing business under the laws of this state, another state, or the United States, which is authorized by law to act under the order or appointment of any court of record, without giving bond, as receiver, trustee, executor, administrator, or, although without general depository powers, depository for any moneys paid into court, or to become sole guarantor or surety in or upon any bond required to be given under the laws of this state.

(e) "County Court" and "Probate Court" are synonymous terms and denote county courts in the exercise of their probate jurisdiction, courts created by statute and authorized to exercise original probate jurisdiction, and district courts exercising probate jurisdiction in contested matters.

(f) "County Judge," "Probate Judge," and "Judge" denote the presiding judge of any court having original jurisdiction over probate proceedings, whether it be a county court in the exercise of its probate jurisdiction, a court created by statute and authorized to exercise probate jurisdiction, or a district court exercising probate jurisdiction in contested matters.

(g) "Court" denotes and includes both a county court in the exercise of its probate jurisdiction, a court created by statute and authorized to exercise original probate jurisdiction, or a district court exercising original probate jurisdiction in contested matters.

(h) "Devise," when used as a noun, includes a testamentary disposition of real or personal property, or of both. When used as a verb, "devise" means to dispose of real or personal property, or of both, by will.

(i) "Devisee" includes legatee.

(j) "Distributee" denotes a person entitled to the estate of a decedent under a lawful will, or under the statutes of descent and distribution.

(k) "Docket" means the probate docket.

(*l*) "Estate" denotes the real and personal property of a decedent, both as such property originally existed and as from time to time changed in form by sale, reinvestment, or otherwise, and as augmented by any accretions and additions thereto (including any property to be distributed to the representative of the decedent by the trustee of a trust which terminates upon the decedent's death) and substitutions therefor, and as diminished by any decreases therein and distributions therefrom.

(m) "Exempt property" refers to that property of a decedent's estate which is exempt from execution or forced sale by the Constitution or laws of this State, and to the allowance in lieu thereof.

(n) Repealed by Acts 1995, 74th Leg., ch. 1039, § 73(1), eff. Sept. 1, 1995.

(o) "Heirs" denote those persons, including the surviving spouse, who are entitled under the statutes of descent and distribution to the estate of a decedent who dies intestate.

(p) "Incapacitated" or "Incapacitated person" means:

(1) a minor;

(2) an adult individual who, because of a physical or mental condition, is substantially unable to provide food, clothing, or shelter for himself or herself, to care for the individual's own physical health, or to manage the individual's own financial affairs; or

(3) a person who must have a guardian appointed to receive funds due the person from any governmental source.

(q) "Independent executor" means the personal representative of an estate under independent administration as provided in Section 145 of this Code. The term "independent executor" includes the term "independent administrator."

(r) "Interested persons" or "persons interested" means heirs, devisees, spouses, creditors, or any others having a property right in, or claim against, the estate being administered; and anyone interested in the welfare of an incapacitated person, including a minor.

(s) "Legacy" includes any gift or devise by will, whether of personalty or realty. "Legatee" includes any person entitled to a legacy under a will.

(t) "Minors" are all persons under eighteen years of age who have never been married or who have not had disabilities of minority removed for general purposes.

(u) Repealed by Acts 2009, 81st Leg., ch. 602, § 19(2).

(v) "Mortgage" or "Lien" includes deed of trust, vendor's lien, chattel mortgage, mechanic's, materialman's or laborer's lien, judgment, attachment or garnishment lien, pledge by hypothecation, and Federal or State tax liens.

(w) "Net estate" means the real and personal property of a decedent, exclusive of homestead rights, exempt property, the family allowance and enforceable claims against the estate.

(x) "Person" includes natural persons and corporations.

(y) Repealed by Acts 1995, 74th Leg., ch. 1039, § 73(1), eff. Sept. 1, 1995.

(z) "Personal property" includes interests in goods, money, choses in action, evidence of debts, and chattels real.

(aa) "Personal representative" or "Representative" includes executor, independent executor, administrator, independent administrator, temporary administrator, together with their successors. The inclusion of independent executors herein shall not be held to subject such representatives to control of the courts in probate matters with respect to settlement of estates except as expressly provided by law.

(bb) "Probate proceeding" is synonymous with the terms "Probate matter," "Proceeding in probate," and "Proceedings for probate." The term means a matter or proceeding related to the estate of a decedent and includes:

(1) the probate of a will, with or without administration of the estate;

(2) the issuance of letters testamentary and of administration;

(3) an heirship determination or small estate affidavit, community property administration, and homestead and family allowances;

(4) an application, petition, motion, or action regarding the probate of a will or an estate administration, including a claim for money owed by the decedent;

(5) a claim arising from an estate administration and any action brought on the claim;

(6) the settling of a personal representative's account of an estate and any other matter related to the settlement, partition, or distribution of an estate; and

(7) a will construction suit.

(cc) "Property" includes both real and personal property.

(dd) "Real property" includes estates and interests in lands, corporeal or incorporeal, legal or equitable, other than chattels real.

(ee) "Surety" includes both personal and corporate sureties.

(ff) "Will" includes codicil; it also includes a testamentary instrument which merely:

(1) appoints an executor or guardian;

(2) directs how property may not be disposed of; or

(3) revokes another will.

(gg) The singular number includes the plural; the plural number includes the singular.

(hh) The masculine gender includes the feminine and neuter.

(ii) "Statutory probate court" means a statutory court designated as a statutory probate court under Chapter 25,

**Text of Texas Probate Code effective until January 1, 2014**

Government Code. A county court at law exercising probate jurisdiction is not a statutory probate court under this Code unless the court is designated a statutory probate court under Chapter 25, Government Code.

(jj) "Next of kin" includes an adopted child or his or her descendents and the adoptive parent of the adopted child.

(kk) "Charitable organization" means:

(1) a nonprofit corporation, trust, community chest, fund, foundation, or other entity that is exempt from federal income tax under Section 501(c)(3) of the Internal Revenue Code of 1986 [1] because the entity is organized and operated exclusively for religious, charitable, scientific, educational, or literary purposes, testing for public safety, prevention of cruelty to children or animals, or promotion of amateur sports competition; or

(2) any other entity or organization that is organized and operated exclusively for the purposes listed in Section 501(c)(3) of the Internal Revenue Code of 1986.

(*ll*) "Governmental agency of the state" means:

(1) an incorporated city or town, a county, a public school district, a special-purpose district or authority, or a district, county, or justice of the peace court;

(2) a board, commission, department, office, or other agency in the executive branch of state government, including an institution of higher education as defined by Section 61.003, Education Code;

(3) the legislature or a legislative agency; and

(4) the supreme court, the court of criminal appeals, a court of appeals, or the State Bar of Texas or another judicial agency having statewide jurisdiction.

(mm) "Ward" is a person for whom a guardian has been appointed.

Acts 1955, 54th Leg., p. 88, ch. 55, eff. Jan. 1, 1956. Amended by Acts 1957, 55th Leg., p. 53, ch. 31, § 2(a), eff. Aug. 22, 1957; Acts 1961, 57th Leg., p. 44, ch. 30, § 2, eff. Aug. 28, 1961; Acts 1969, 61st Leg., p. 1703, ch. 556, § 1, eff. June 10, 1969; Acts 1969, 61st Leg., p. 1922, ch. 641, § 1, eff. June 12, 1969; Acts 1975, 64th Leg., p. 104, ch. 45, § 1, eff. Sept. 1, 1975; Acts 1975, 64th Leg., p. 2195, ch. 701, § 1, eff. June 21, 1975; Acts 1977, 65th Leg., p. 1061, ch. 390, §§ 1, 2, eff. Sept. 1, 1977; Acts 1979, 66th Leg., p. 1740, ch. 713, § 1, eff. Aug. 27, 1979; Acts 1985, 69th Leg., ch. 159, §§ 1, 2, eff. Sept. 1, 1985; Acts 1985, 69th Leg., ch. 591, § 1, eff. Sept. 1, 1985; Acts 1989, 71st Leg., ch. 375, § 33, eff. Sept. 1, 1989; Acts 1989, 71st Leg., ch. 1035, § 1, eff. Sept. 1, 1989; Acts 1991, 72nd Leg., ch. 14, § 284(96), eff. Sept. 1, 1991; Acts 1991, 72nd Leg., ch. 895, § 1, eff. Sept. 1, 1991; Acts 1993, 73rd Leg., ch. 957, § 3, eff. Sept. 1, 1993; Acts 1995, 74th Leg., ch. 1039, §§ 4, 73(1), eff. Sept. 1, 1995; Acts 1997, 75th Leg., ch. 52, § 1, eff. Sept. 1, 1997; Acts 1999, 76th Leg., ch. 344, § 6.001, eff. Sept. 1, 1999; Acts 1999, 76th Leg., ch. 379, § 1, eff. Sept. 1, 1999.

Subsec. (r) amended by Acts 2007, 80th Leg., ch. 1170, § 1.01, eff. Sept. 1, 2007; Subsec. (u) repealed by Acts 2009, 81st Leg., ch. 602, § 19(2), eff. June 19, 2009; Subsec. (bb) amended by Acts 2009, 81st Leg., ch. 1351, § 12(a), eff. Sept. 1, 2009.

[1] 26 U.S.C.A. § 501(c)(3).

## § 4. Repealed by Acts 2009, 81st Leg., ch. 1351, § 12(h), eff. Sept. 1, 2009

## § 4A. General Probate Court Jurisdiction; Appeals

(a) All probate proceedings must be filed and heard in a court exercising original probate jurisdiction. The court exercising original probate jurisdiction also has jurisdiction of all matters related to the probate proceeding as specified in Section 4B of this code for that type of court.

(b) A probate court may exercise pendent and ancillary jurisdiction as necessary to promote judicial efficiency and economy.

(c) A final order issued by a probate court is appealable to the court of appeals.

Added by Acts 2009, 81st Leg., ch. 1351, § 12(b), eff. Sept. 1, 2009.

## § 4B. Matters Related to Probate Proceeding

(a) For purposes of this code, in a county in which there is no statutory probate court or county court at law exercising original probate jurisdiction, a matter related to a probate proceeding includes:

(1) an action against a personal representative or former personal representative arising out of the representative's performance of the duties of a personal representative;

(2) an action against a surety of a personal representative or former personal representative;

(3) a claim brought by a personal representative on behalf of an estate;

(4) an action brought against a personal representative in the representative's capacity as personal representative;

(5) an action for trial of title to real property that is estate property, including the enforcement of a lien against the property; and

(6) an action for trial of the right of property that is estate property.

(b) For purposes of this code, in a county in which there is no statutory probate court, but in which there is a county court at law exercising original probate jurisdiction, a matter related to a probate proceeding includes:

(1) all matters and actions described in Subsection (a) of this section;

(2) the interpretation and administration of a testamentary trust if the will creating the trust has been admitted to probate in the court; and

(3) the interpretation and administration of an inter vivos trust created by a decedent whose will has been admitted to probate in the court.

(c) For purposes of this code, in a county in which there is a statutory probate court, a matter related to a probate proceeding includes:

(1) all matters and actions described in Subsections (a) and (b) of this section; and

(2) any cause of action in which a personal representative of an estate pending in the statutory probate court is a party in the representative's capacity as personal representative.

Added by Acts 2009, 81st Leg., ch. 1351, § 12(b), eff. Sept. 1, 2009.

### § 4C. Original Jurisdiction for Probate Proceedings

(a) In a county in which there is no statutory probate court or county court at law exercising original probate jurisdiction, the county court has original jurisdiction of probate proceedings.

(b) In a county in which there is no statutory probate court, but in which there is a county court at law exercising original probate jurisdiction, the county court at law exercising original probate jurisdiction and the county court have concurrent original jurisdiction of probate proceedings, unless otherwise provided by law. The judge of a county court may hear probate proceedings while sitting for the judge of any other county court.

(c) In a county in which there is a statutory probate court, the statutory probate court has original jurisdiction of probate proceedings.

Added by Acts 2009, 81st Leg., ch. 1351, § 12(b), eff. Sept. 1, 2009.

### § 4D. Jurisdiction of Contested Probate Proceeding in County with No Statutory Probate Court or Statutory County Court

(a) In a county in which there is no statutory probate court or county court at law exercising original probate jurisdiction, when a matter in a probate proceeding is contested, the judge of the county court may, on the judge's own motion, or shall, on the motion of any party to the proceeding, according to the motion:

(1) request the assignment of a statutory probate court judge to hear the contested matter, as provided by Section 25.0022, Government Code; or

(2) transfer the contested matter to the district court, which may then hear the contested matter as if originally filed in the district court.

(b) If a party to a probate proceeding files a motion for the assignment of a statutory probate court judge to hear a contested matter in the proceeding before the judge of the county court transfers the contested matter to a district court under this section, the county judge shall grant the motion for the assignment of a statutory probate court judge and may not transfer the matter to the district court unless the party withdraws the motion.

(b–1) If a judge of a county court requests the assignment of a statutory probate court judge to hear a contested matter in a probate proceeding on the judge's own motion or on the motion of a party to the proceeding as provided by this section, the judge may request that the statutory probate court judge be assigned to the entire proceeding on the judge's own motion or on the motion of a party.

(c) A party to a probate proceeding may file a motion for the assignment of a statutory probate court judge under this section before a matter in the proceeding becomes contested, and the motion is given effect as a motion for assignment of a statutory probate court judge under Subsection (a) of this section if the matter later becomes contested.

(d) Notwithstanding any other law, a transfer of a contested matter in a probate proceeding to a district court under any authority other than the authority provided by this section:

(1) is disregarded for purposes of this section; and

(2) does not defeat the right of a party to the proceeding to have the matter assigned to a statutory probate court judge in accordance with this section.

(e) A statutory probate court judge assigned to a contested matter in a probate proceeding or to the entire proceeding under this section has the jurisdiction and authority granted to a statutory probate court by this code. A statutory probate court judge assigned to hear only the contested matter in a probate proceeding shall, on resolution of the matter, including any appeal of the matter, return the matter to the county court for further proceedings not inconsistent with the orders of the statutory probate court or court of appeals, as applicable. A statutory probate court judge assigned to the entire probate proceeding as provided by Subsection (b–1) of this section shall, on resolution of the contested matter in the proceeding, including any appeal of the matter, return the entire proceeding to the county court for further proceedings not inconsistent with the orders of the statutory probate court or court of appeals, as applicable.

(f) A district court to which a contested matter is transferred under this section has the jurisdiction and authority granted to a statutory probate court by this code. On resolution of a contested matter transferred to the district court under this section, including any appeal of the matter, the district court shall return the matter to the county court for further proceedings not inconsistent with the orders of the district court or court of appeals, as applicable.

(g) If only the contested matter in a probate proceeding is assigned to a statutory probate court judge under this section, or if the contested matter in a probate proceeding is transferred to a district court under this section, the county court shall continue to exercise jurisdiction over the management of the estate, other than a contested matter, until final disposition of the contested matter is made in accordance with this section. Any matter related to a probate proceeding in which a contested matter is transferred to a district court may be brought in the district court. The district court in which a matter related to the proceeding is filed may, on its own motion or on the motion of any party, find that the matter is not a contested matter and transfer the matter to the county court with jurisdiction of the management of the estate.

(h) If a contested matter in a probate proceeding is transferred to a district court under this section, the district court has jurisdiction of any contested matter in the proceeding that is subsequently filed, and the county court shall transfer those contested matters to the district court. If a statutory probate court judge is assigned under this section to hear a contested matter in a probate proceeding, the statutory probate court judge shall be assigned to hear any contested matter in the proceeding that is subsequently filed.

(i) The clerk of a district court to which a contested matter in a probate proceeding is transferred under this section may perform in relation to the contested matter any function a county clerk may perform with respect to that type of matter.

Added by Acts 2009, 81st Leg., ch. 1351, § 12(b), eff. Sept. 1, 2009. Subsec. (b–1) added and subsecs. (e) and (g) amended by Acts 2011, 82nd Leg., ch. 1338 (S.B. 1198), § 1.01, eff. Sept. 1, 2011.

### § 4E. Jurisdiction of Contested Probate Proceeding in County with No Statutory Probate Court

(a) In a county in which there is no statutory probate court, but in which there is a county court at law exercising original probate jurisdiction, when a matter in a probate proceeding is contested, the judge of the county court may, on the judge's own motion, or shall, on the motion of any party to the proceeding, transfer the contested matter to the county court at law. In addition, the judge of the county court, on the judge's own motion or on the motion of a party to the proceeding, may transfer the entire proceeding to the county court at law.

(b) A county court at law to which a proceeding is transferred under this section may hear the proceeding as if originally filed in that court. If only a contested matter in the proceeding is transferred, on the resolution of the matter, the matter shall be returned to the county court for further proceedings not inconsistent with the orders of the county court at law.

Added by Acts 2009, 81st Leg., ch. 1351, § 12(b), eff. Sept. 1, 2009.

### § 4F. Exclusive Jurisdiction of Probate Proceeding in County with Statutory Probate Court

(a) In a county in which there is a statutory probate court, the statutory probate court has exclusive jurisdiction of all probate proceedings, regardless of whether contested or uncontested. A cause of action related to the probate proceeding must be brought in a statutory probate court unless the jurisdiction of the statutory probate court is concurrent with the jurisdiction of a district court as provided by Section 4H of this code or with the jurisdiction of any other court.

(b) This section shall be construed in conjunction and in harmony with Section 145 of this code and all other sections of this code relating to independent executors, but may not be construed to expand the court's control over an independent executor.

Added by Acts 2009, 81st Leg., ch. 1351, § 12(b), eff. Sept. 1, 2009.

### § 4G. Jurisdiction of Statutory Probate Court with Respect to Trusts and Powers of Attorney

In a county in which there is a statutory probate court, the statutory probate court has jurisdiction of:

(1) an action by or against a trustee;

(2) an action involving an inter vivos trust, testamentary trust, or charitable trust;

(3) an action against an agent or former agent under a power of attorney arising out of the agent's performance of the duties of an agent; and

(4) an action to determine the validity of a power of attorney or to determine an agent's rights, powers, or duties under a power of attorney.

Added by Acts 2009, 81st Leg., ch. 1351, § 12(b), eff. Sept. 1, 2009.

### § 4H. Concurrent Jurisdiction With District Court

A statutory probate court has concurrent jurisdiction with the district court in:

(1) a personal injury, survival, or wrongful death action by or against a person in the person's capacity as a personal representative;

(2) an action by or against a trustee;

(3) an action involving an inter vivos trust, testamentary trust, or charitable trust, including a charitable trust as defined by Section 123.001, Property Code;

(4) an action involving a personal representative of an estate in which each other party aligned with the personal representative is not an interested person in that estate;

(5) an action against an agent or former agent under a power of attorney arising out of the agent's performance of the duties of an agent; and

(6) an action to determine the validity of a power of attorney or to determine an agent's rights, powers, or duties under a power of attorney.

Added by Acts 2009, 81st Leg., ch. 1351, § 12(b), eff. Sept. 1, 2009. Subd. (3) amended by Acts 2011, 82nd Leg., ch. 1338 (S.B. 1198), § 1.02, eff. Sept. 1, 2011.

### § 5. Repealed by Acts 2011, 82nd Leg., ch. 1338 (S.B. 1198), § 1.42(b), eff. Sept. 1, 2011

### § 5A. Repealed by Acts 2009, 81st Leg., ch. 1351, § 12(h), eff. Sept. 1, 2009

### § 5B. Transfer to Statutory Probate Court of Proceeding Related to Probate Proceeding

(a) A judge of a statutory probate court, on the motion of a party to the action or on the motion of a person interested in an estate, may transfer to the judge's court from a district, county, or statutory court a cause of action related to a probate proceeding pending in the statutory probate court or a cause of action in which a personal representative of an estate pending in the statutory probate court is a party and may consolidate the transferred cause of action with the other proceedings in the statutory probate court relating to that estate.

(b) Notwithstanding any other provision of this chapter, the proper venue for an action by or against a personal representative for personal injury, death, or property damages is determined under Section 15.007, Civil Practice and Remedies Code.

Added by Acts 1983, 68th Leg., p. 5228, ch. 958, § 1, eff. Sept. 1, 1983. Amended by Acts 1999, 76th Leg., ch. 1431, § 1, eff. Sept. 1, 1999; Acts 2003, 78th Leg., ch. 204, § 3.06, eff. Sept. 1, 2003; Subsec. (a) amended by Acts 2009, 81st Leg., ch. 1351, § 12(c), eff. Sept. 1, 2009; Sec. head amended by Acts 2011, 82nd Leg., ch. 1338 (S.B. 1198), § 1.03, eff. Sept. 1, 2011.

### § 5C. Actions to Collect Delinquent Property Taxes

(a) This section applies only to a decedent's estate that:

(1) is being administered in a pending probate proceeding;

(2) owns or claims an interest in property against which a taxing unit has imposed ad valorem taxes that are delinquent; and

(3) is not being administered as an independent administration under Section 145 of this code.

(b) Notwithstanding any provision of this code to the contrary, if the probate proceedings are pending in a foreign jurisdiction or in a county other than the county in which the taxes were imposed, a suit to foreclose the lien securing payment of the taxes or to enforce personal liability for the taxes must be brought under Section 33.41, Tax Code, in a court of competent jurisdiction in the county in which the taxes were imposed.

(c) If the probate proceedings have been pending for four years or less in the county in which the taxes were imposed, the taxing unit may present a claim for the delinquent taxes against the estate to the personal representative of the estate in the probate proceedings.

(d) If the taxing unit presents a claim against the estate under Subsection (c) of this section:

(1) the claim of the taxing unit is subject to each applicable provision in Parts 4 and 5, Chapter VIII, of this code [1] that relates to a claim or the enforcement of a claim in a probate proceeding; and

(2) the taxing unit may not bring a suit in any other court to foreclose the lien securing payment of the taxes or to enforce personal liability for the delinquent taxes before the first day after the fourth anniversary of the date the application for the probate proceeding was filed.

(e) To foreclose the lien securing payment of the delinquent taxes, the taxing unit must bring a suit under Section 33.41, Tax Code, in a court of competent jurisdiction for the county in which the taxes were imposed if:

(1) the probate proceedings have been pending in that county for more than four years; and

(2) the taxing unit did not present a delinquent tax claim under Subsection (c) of this section against the estate in the probate proceeding.

(f) In a suit brought under Subsection (e) of this section, the taxing unit:

(1) shall make the personal representative of the decedent's estate a party to the suit; and

(2) may not seek to enforce personal liability for the taxes against the estate of the decedent.

Added by Acts 1999, 76th Leg., ch. 1481, § 36, eff. Sept. 1, 1999.

[1] V.A.T.S. Probate Code, § 294 et seq. and V.A.T.S. Probate Code, § 331 et seq.

### § 6. Venue: Probate of Wills and Granting of Letters Testamentary and of Administration

Wills shall be admitted to probate, and letters testamentary or of administration shall be granted:

(1) in the county where the decedent resided, if the decedent had a domicile or fixed place of residence in this State;

(2) if the decedent had no domicile or fixed place of residence in this State but died in this State, then either in the county where the decedent's principal estate was at the time of the decedent's death, or in the county where decedent died; or

(3) if the decedent had no domicile or fixed place of residence in this State, and died outside the limits of this State:

(A) in any county in this State where the decedent's nearest of kin reside; or

(B) if there are no kindred of the decedent in this State, then in the county where the decedent's principal estate was situated at the time of the decedent's death.

Acts 1955, 54th Leg., p. 88, ch. 55, eff. Jan. 1, 1956. Amended by Acts 2011, 82nd Leg., ch. 1338 (S.B. 1198), § 1.04, eff. Sept. 1, 2011.

### § 6A. Venue: Action Related to Probate Proceeding in Statutory Probate Court

Except as provided by Section 6B of this code, venue for any cause of action related to a probate proceeding pending in a statutory probate court is proper in the statutory probate court in which the decedent's estate is pending.

Added by Acts 2011, 82nd Leg., ch. 1338 (S.B. 1198), § 1.05, eff. Sept. 1, 2011.

### § 6B. Venue: Certain Actions Involving Personal Representative

Notwithstanding any other provision of this chapter, the proper venue for an action by or against a personal representative for personal injury, death, or property damages is determined under Section 15.007, Civil Practice and Remedies Code.

Added by Acts 2011, 82nd Leg., ch. 1338 (S.B. 1198), § 1.05, eff. Sept. 1, 2011.

## § 6C. Venue: Heirship Proceedings

(a) Venue for a proceeding to determine a decedent's heirs is in:

(1) the court of the county in which a proceeding admitting the decedent's will to probate or administering the decedent's estate was most recently pending; or

(2) the court of the county in which venue would be proper for commencement of an administration of the decedent's estate under Section 6 of this code if:

(A) no will of the decedent has been admitted to probate in this state and no administration of the decedent's estate has been granted in this state; or

(B) the proceeding is commenced by the trustee of a trust holding assets for the benefit of the decedent.

(b) Notwithstanding Subsection (a) of this section and Section 6 of this code, if there is no administration pending of the estate of a deceased ward who died intestate, venue for a proceeding to determine the deceased ward's heirs is in the probate court in which the guardianship proceedings with respect to the ward's estate were pending on the date of the ward's death. A proceeding described by this subsection may not be brought as part of the guardianship proceedings with respect to the ward's estate, but rather must be filed as a separate cause in which the court may determine the heirs' respective shares and interests in the estate as provided by the laws of this state.

Added by Acts 2011, 82nd Leg., ch. 1338 (S.B. 1198), § 1.05, eff. Sept. 1, 2011.

## § 6D. Venue: Certain Actions Involving Breach of Fiduciary Duty

Notwithstanding any other provision of this chapter, venue for a proceeding brought by the attorney general alleging breach of a fiduciary duty by a charitable entity or a fiduciary or managerial agent of a charitable trust is determined under Section 123.005, Property Code.

Added by Acts 2011, 82nd Leg., ch. 1338 (S.B. 1198), § 1.05, eff. Sept. 1, 2011.

## § 7. Repealed by Acts 1993, 73rd Leg., ch. 905, § 15, eff. Sept. 1, 1993; Acts 1993, 73rd Leg., ch. 957, § 75(1), eff. Sept. 1, 1993

## § 8. Concurrent Venue in Probate Proceeding

(a) Concurrent Venue. When two or more courts have concurrent venue of a probate proceeding, the court in which the application for the proceeding is first filed shall have and retain jurisdiction of the proceeding to the exclusion of the other court or courts. The proceeding shall be deemed commenced by the filing of an application averring facts sufficient to confer venue; and the proceeding first legally commenced shall extend to all of the property of the decedent or the decedent's estate. Provided, however, that a bona fide purchaser of real property in reliance on any such subsequent proceeding, without knowledge of its invalidity, shall be protected in such purchase unless before the purchase the decree admitting the will to probate, determining heirship, or granting administration in the prior proceeding is recorded in the office of the county clerk of the county in which such property is located.

(b) Probate Proceedings in More Than One County. If probate proceedings involving the same estate are commenced in more than one county, each proceeding commenced in a county other than the county in which a proceeding was first commenced is stayed until final determination of venue by the court in the county where first commenced. If the proper venue is finally determined to be in another county, the clerk, after making and retaining a true copy of the entire file in the case, shall transmit the original file to the proper county, and the proceeding shall thereupon be had in the proper county in the same manner as if the proceeding had originally been instituted therein.

(c) Jurisdiction to Determine Venue. Subject to Subsections (a) and (b) of this section, a court in which an application for a probate proceeding is filed has jurisdiction to determine venue for the proceeding and for any matter related to the proceeding. A court's determination under this subsection is not subject to collateral attack.

Acts 1955, 54th Leg., p. 88, ch. 55, eff. Jan. 1, 1956. Amended by Acts 1983, 68th Leg., p. 4754, ch. 833, § 1, eff. Sept. 1, 1983; Acts 1987, 70th Leg., ch. 786, § 1, eff. Aug. 31, 1987. Subsec. (c)(2) amended by Acts 2003, 78th Leg., ch. 1060, § 5, eff. Sept. 1, 2003; Subsecs. (a), (b), (c), and (e) amended by Acts 2007, 80th Leg., ch. 1170, § 2.01, eff. Sept. 1, 2007. Amended by Acts 2009, 81st Leg., ch. 602, § 1, eff. June 19, 2009; Acts 2011, 82nd Leg., ch. 1338 (S.B. 1198), § 1.06, eff. Sept. 1, 2011.

## § 8A. Transfer of Venue in Probate Proceeding

(a) Transfer for Want of Venue. If it appears to the court at any time before the final decree in a probate proceeding that the proceeding was commenced in a court which did not have priority of venue over such proceeding, the court shall, on the application of any interested person, transfer the proceeding to the proper county by transmitting to the proper court in such county the original file in such case, together with certified copies of all entries in the judge's probate docket theretofore made, and the proceeding in such county shall be completed in the same manner as if the proceeding had originally been instituted therein; but, if the question as to priority of venue is not raised before final decree in the proceedings is announced, the finality of such decree shall not be affected by any error in venue.

(b) Transfer for Convenience. If it appears to the court at any time before a probate proceeding is concluded that it would be in the best interest of the estate or, if there is no administration of the estate, that it would be in the best interest of the heirs or beneficiaries of the decedent's will, the court, in its discretion, may order the proceeding transferred to the proper court in any other county in this State. The clerk of the court from which the proceeding is transferred shall transmit to the court to which the proceeding is transferred the original file in the proceeding and a certified copy of the index.

Acts 1955, 54th Leg., p. 88, ch. 55, eff. Jan. 1, 1956. Amended by Acts 1983, 68th Leg., p. 4754, ch. 833, § 1, eff. Sept. 1, 1983; Acts 1987, 70th Leg., ch. 786, § 1, eff. Aug. 31, 1987. Subsec. (c)(2) amended by Acts 2003, 78th Leg., ch. 1060, § 5, eff. Sept. 1, 2003; Subsecs. (a), (b), (c), and (e) amended by Acts 2007, 80th Leg., ch. 1170, § 2.01, eff. Sept. 1, 2007. Amended by Acts 2009, 81st Leg., ch. 602, § 1, eff. June 19, 2009. Redesignated from V.A.T.S. Probate Code, § 8(c)(1), (2) and amended by Acts 2011, 82nd Leg., ch. 1338 (S.B. 1198), § 1.06, eff. Sept. 1, 2011.

## § 8B. Validation of Prior Proceedings

When a probate proceeding is transferred to another county under any provision of Section 8 or 8A of this Code, all orders entered in connection with the proceeding shall be valid and shall be recognized in the second court, provided such orders were made and entered in conformance with the procedure prescribed by this Code.

Acts 1955, 54th Leg., p. 88, ch. 55, eff. Jan. 1, 1956. Amended by Acts 1983, 68th Leg., p. 4754, ch. 833, § 1, eff. Sept. 1, 1983. Redesignated from V.A.T.S. Probate Code, § 8(d) and amended by Acts 2011, 82nd Leg., ch. 1338 (S.B. 1198), § 1.06, eff. Sept. 1, 2011.

## § 9. Defects in Pleading

No defect of form or substance in any pleading in probate shall be held by any court to invalidate such pleading, or any order based upon such pleading, unless the defect has been timely objected to and called to the attention of the court in which such proceedings were or are pending.

Acts 1955, 54th Leg., p. 88, ch. 55, eff. Jan. 1, 1956.

## § 10. Persons Entitled to Contest Proceedings

Any person interested in an estate may, at any time before any issue in any proceeding is decided upon by the court, file opposition thereto in writing and shall be entitled to process for witnesses and evidence, and to be heard upon such opposition, as in other suits.

Acts 1955, 54th Leg., p. 88, ch. 55, eff. Jan. 1, 1956.

## § 10A. Necessary Party

(a) An institution of higher education as defined by Section 61.003, Education Code, a private institution of higher education, or a charitable organization is a necessary party to a will contest or will construction suit involving a will in which the institution or organization is a distributee.

(b) If an institution or organization is a necessary party under Subsection (a) of this section, the court shall serve the institution or organization in the manner provided for service on other parties by this code.

Added by Acts 1989, 71st Leg., ch. 1035, § 4, eff. Sept. 1, 1989. Amended by Acts 1991, 72nd Leg., ch. 675, § 1, eff. Sept. 1, 1991.

## § 10B. Communications or Records Relating to Decedent's Condition Before Death

Notwithstanding the Medical Practice Act (Article 4495b, Vernon's Texas Civil Statutes), a person who is a party to a will contest or a proceeding in which a party relies on the mental or testamentary capacity of a decedent before the decedent's death as part of the party's claim or defense is entitled to production of all communications or records relevant to the decedent's condition before the decedent's death. On receipt of a subpoena of communications or records under this section and proof of filing of the will contest or proceeding, by file-stamped copy, the appropriate physician, hospital, medical facility, custodian of records, or other person in possession of the communications or records shall release the communications or records to the party requesting the records without further authorization.

Added by Acts 1997, 75th Leg., ch. 1302, § 2, eff. Sept. 1, 1997. Amended by Acts 1999, 76th Leg., ch. 855, § 1, eff. Sept. 1, 1999.

## § 10C. Effect of Filing or Contesting Pleading

(a) The filing or contesting in probate court of any pleading relating to a decedent's estate does not constitute tortious interference with inheritance of the estate.

(b) This section does not abrogate any rights of a person under Rule 13, Texas Rules of Civil Procedure, or Chapter 10, Civil Practice and Remedies Code.

Added by Acts 2003, 78th Leg., ch. 1060, § 6, eff. Sept. 1, 2003.

## § 11. Applications and Other Papers to be Filed With Clerk

All applications for probate proceedings, complaints, petitions and all other papers permitted or required by law to be filed in the court in probate matters, shall be filed with the county clerk of the proper county who shall file the same and endorse on each paper the date filed and the docket number, and his official signature.

Acts 1955, 54th Leg., p. 88, ch. 55, eff. Jan. 1, 1956.

## § 11A. Exemption from Probate Fees for Estates of Certain Military Servicemembers

(a) In this section, "combat zone" means an area that the president of the United States by executive order designates for purposes of 26 U.S.C. Section 112 as an area in which armed forces of the United States are or have engaged in combat.

(b) Notwithstanding any other law, the clerk of a county court may not charge, or collect from, the estate of a decedent any of the following fees if the decedent died while in active service as a member of the armed forces of the United States in a combat zone:

(1) a fee for or associated with the filing of the decedent's will for probate; and

(2) a fee for any service rendered by the probate court regarding the administration of the decedent's estate.

Added by Acts 2007, 80th Leg., ch. 940, § 1, eff. June 15, 2007.

**Text of Texas Probate Code effective until January 1, 2014**

## § 11B. Exemption from Probate Fees for Estates of Certain Law Enforcement Officers, Firefighters, and Others

(a) In this section:

(1) "Eligible decedent" means an individual listed in Section 615.003, Government Code.

(2) "Line of duty" and "personal injury" have the meanings assigned by Section 615.021(e), Government Code.

(b) Notwithstanding any other law, the clerk of a court may not charge, or collect from, the estate of an eligible decedent any of the following fees if the decedent died as a result of a personal injury sustained in the line of duty in the individual's position as described by Section 615.003, Government Code:

(1) a fee for or associated with the filing of the decedent's will for probate; and

(2) a fee for any service rendered by the court regarding the administration of the decedent's estate.

Added by Acts 2011, 82nd Leg., ch. 614 (S.B. 543), § 1.01, eff. Sept. 1, 2011.

## § 12. Costs and Security Therefor

**(a) Applicability of Laws Regulating Costs.** The provisions of law regulating costs in ordinary civil cases shall apply to all matters in probate when not expressly provided for in this Code.

**(b) Security for Costs Required, When.** When any person other than the personal representative of an estate files an application, complaint, or opposition in relation to the estate, he may be required by the clerk to give security for the probable cost of such proceeding before filing the same; or any one interested in the estate, or any officer of the court, may, at any time before the trial of such application, complaint, or opposition, obtain from the court, upon written motion, an order requiring such party to give security for the probable costs of such proceeding. The rules governing civil suits in the county court respecting this subject shall control in such cases.

**(c) Suit for Fiduciary.** No security for costs shall be required of an executor or administrator appointed by a court of this state in any suit brought by him in his fiduciary character.

Acts 1955, 54th Leg., p. 88, ch. 55, eff. Jan. 1, 1956. Amended by Acts 1985, 69th Leg., ch. 959, § 4, eff. Sept. 1, 1985; Acts 1993, 73rd Leg., ch. 957, § 7, eff. Sept. 1, 1993.

## § 13. Judge's Probate Docket

The county clerk shall keep a record book to be styled "Judge's Probate Docket," and shall enter therein:

(a) The name of each person upon whose person or estate proceedings are had or sought to be had.

(b) The name of the executor or administrator or of the applicant for letters.

(c) The date of the filing of the original application for probate proceedings.

(d) A notation of each order, judgment, decree, and proceeding had in each estate, with the date thereof.

(e) A number for each estate upon the docket in the order in which proceedings are commenced, and each paper filed in an estate shall be given the corresponding docket number of the estate.

Acts 1955, 54th Leg., p. 88, ch. 55, eff. Jan. 1, 1956. Amended by Acts 1993, 73rd Leg., ch. 957, § 8, eff. Sept. 1, 1993; Acts 2009, 81st Leg., ch. 602, § 2, eff. June 19, 2009.

## § 14. Claim Docket

The county clerk shall also keep a record book to be styled "Claim Docket," and shall enter therein all claims presented against an estate for approval by the court. This docket shall be ruled in sixteen columns at proper intervals from top to bottom, with a short note of the contents at the top of each column. One or more pages shall be assigned to each estate. The following information shall be entered in the respective columns beginning with the first or marginal column: The names of claimants in the order in which their claims are filed; the amount of the claim; its date; the date of filing; when due; the date from which it bears interest; the rate of interest; when allowed by the executor or administrator; the amount allowed; the date of rejection; when approved; the amount approved; when disapproved; the class to which the claim belongs; when established by judgment of a court; the amount of such judgment.

Acts 1955, 54th Leg., p. 88, ch. 55, eff. Jan. 1, 1956. Amended by Acts 1993, 73rd Leg., ch. 957, § 9, eff. Sept. 1, 1993.

## § 15. Case Files

The county clerk shall maintain a case file for each decedent's estate in which a probate proceeding has been filed. The case file must contain all orders, judgments, and proceedings of the court and any other probate filing with the court, including all:

(1) applications for the probate of wills and for the granting of administration;

(2) citations and notices, whether published or posted, with the returns thereon;

(3) wills and the testimony upon which the same are admitted to probate, provided that the substance only of depositions shall be recorded;

(4) bonds and official oaths;

(5) inventories, appraisements, and lists of claims;

(5–a) affidavits in lieu of inventories, appraisements, and lists of claims;

(6) exhibits and accounts;

(7) reports of hiring, renting, or sale;

(8) applications for sale or partition of real estate and reports of sale and of commissioners of partition;

(9) applications for authority to execute leases for mineral development, or for pooling or unitization of lands, royalty, or other interest in minerals, or to lend or invest money; and

(10) reports of lending or investing money.

Acts 1955, 54th Leg., p. 88, ch. 55, eff. Jan. 1, 1956. Amended by Acts 1993, 73rd Leg., ch. 957, § 10, eff. Sept. 1, 1993; Acts 1999, 76th Leg., ch. 67, § 1, eff. Sept. 1, 1999; Subd. (5-a) added by Acts 2011, 82nd Leg., ch. 1338 (S.B. 1198), § 1.07, eff. Sept. 1, 2011.

### § 16.  Probate Fee Book

The county clerk shall keep a record book styled "Probate Fee Book," and shall enter therein each item of costs which accrues to the officers of the court, together with witness fees, if any, showing the party to whom the costs or fees are due, the date of the accrual of the same, the estate or party liable therefor, and the date on which any such costs or fees are paid.

Acts 1955, 54th Leg., p. 88, ch. 55, eff. Jan. 1, 1956.

### § 17.  Maintaining Records in Lieu of Record Books

In lieu of keeping the record books described by Sections 13, 14, and 16 of this code, the county clerk may maintain the information relating to a person's or estate's probate proceedings maintained in those record books on a computer file, on microfilm, in the form of a digitized optical image, or in another similar form of data compilation.

Added by Acts 1999, 76th Leg., ch. 67, § 1, eff. Sept. 1, 1999.

### § 17A.  Index

The county clerk shall properly index the records and keep the index open for public inspection, but may not release the index from the clerk's custody.

Acts 1955, 54th Leg., p. 88, ch. 55, eff. Jan. 1, 1956. Renumbered from V.A.T.S. Probate Code, § 17 and amended by Acts 1999, 76th Leg., ch. 67, § 1, eff. Sept. 1, 1999.

### § 18.  Use of Records as Evidence

The record books or individual case files, including records on a computer file, on microfilm, in the form of a digitized optical image, or in another similar form of data compilation described in preceding sections of this code, or certified copies or reproductions of the records, shall be evidence in any court of this state.

Acts 1955, 54th Leg., p. 88, ch. 55, eff. Jan. 1, 1956. Amended by Acts 1999, 76th Leg., ch. 67, § 1, eff. Sept. 1, 1999.

### § 19.  Call of the Dockets

The judge of the court in which probate proceedings are pending, at such times as he shall determine, shall call the estates of decedents in their regular order upon both the probate and claim dockets and make such orders as shall be necessary.

Acts 1955, 54th Leg., p. 88, ch. 55, eff. Jan. 1, 1956. Amended by Acts 1993, 73rd Leg., ch. 957, § 11, eff. Sept. 1, 1993.

### § 20.  Clerk May Set Hearings

Whenever, on account of the county judge's absence from the county seat, or his being on vacation, disqualified, ill, or deceased, such judge is unable to designate the time and place for hearing a probate matter pending in his court, authority is hereby vested in the county clerk of the county in which such matter is pending to designate such time and place, entering such setting on the judge's docket and certifying thereupon why such judge is not acting by himself. If, after service of such notices and citations as required by law with reference to such time and place of hearing has been perfected, no qualified judge is present for the hearing, the same shall automatically be continued from day to day until a qualified judge is present to hear and determine the matter.

Acts 1955, 54th Leg., p. 88, ch. 55, eff. Jan. 1, 1956.

### § 21.  Trial by Jury

In all contested probate and mental illness proceedings in the district court or in the county court or statutory probate court, county court at law or other statutory court exercising probate jurisdiction, the parties shall be entitled to trial by jury as in other civil actions.

Acts 1955, 54th Leg., p. 88, ch. 55, eff. Jan. 1, 1956. Amended by Acts 1973, 63rd Leg., p. 1685, ch. 610, § 2.

### § 22.  Evidence

In proceedings arising under the provisions of this Code, the rules relating to witnesses and evidence that govern in the District Court shall apply so far as practicable except that where a will is to be probated, and in other probate matters where there is no opposing party or attorney of record upon whom notice and copies of interrogatories may be served, service may be had by posting notice of intention to take depositions for a period of ten days as provided in this Code governing posting of notices. When such notice is filed with the clerk, a copy of the interrogatories shall also be filed, and at the expiration of ten days, commission may issue for taking the depositions, and the judge may file cross-interrogatories where no one appears, if he so desires.

Acts 1955, 54th Leg., p. 88, ch. 55, eff. Jan. 1, 1956.

### § 23.  Decrees

All decisions, orders, decrees, and judgments of the county court in probate matters shall be rendered in open court except in cases where it is otherwise specially provided.

Acts 1955, 54th Leg., p. 88, ch. 55, eff. Jan. 1, 1956. Amended by Acts 2009, 81st Leg., ch. 602, § 3, eff. June 19, 2009.

### § 24.  Enforcement of Orders

The county or probate judge may enforce obedience to all his lawful orders against executors and administrators by attachment and imprisonment, but no such imprisonment shall exceed three days for any one offense, unless otherwise expressly so provided in this Code.

Acts 1955, 54th Leg., p. 88, ch. 55, eff. Jan. 1, 1956. Amended by Acts 1993, 73rd Leg., ch. 957, § 12, eff. Sept. 1, 1993.

### § 25. Executions

Executions in probate matters shall be directed "to any sheriff or any constable within the State of Texas," made returnable in sixty days, and shall be attested and signed by the clerk officially under the seal of the court. All proceedings under such executions shall be governed by the laws regulating proceedings under executions issued from the District Court so far as applicable. Provided, however, that no execution directed to the sheriff or any constable of a specific county within this State shall be held defective if such execution was properly executed within such county by such officer.

Acts 1955, 54th Leg., p. 88, ch. 55, eff. Jan. 1, 1956.

### § 26. Attachments for Property

Whenever complaint in writing, under oath, shall be made to the county or probate judge by any person interested in the estate of a decedent that the executor or administrator is about to remove said estate, or any part thereof, beyond the limits of the State, such judge may order a writ to issue, directed "to any sheriff or any constable within the State of Texas," commanding him to seize such estate, or any part thereof, and hold the same subject to such further orders as such judge shall make on such complaint. No such writ shall issue unless the complainant shall give bond, in such sum as the judge shall require, payable to the executor or administrator of such estate, conditioned for the payment of all damages and costs that shall be recovered for the wrongful suing out of such writ. Provided, however, that no writ of attachment directed to the sheriff or any constable of a specific county within this State shall be held defective if such writ was properly executed within such county by such officer.

Acts 1955, 54th Leg., p. 88, ch. 55, eff. Jan. 1, 1956. Amended by Acts 1993, 73rd Leg., ch. 957, § 13, eff. Sept. 1, 1993.

### § 27. Enforcement of Specific Performance

When any person shall sell property and enter into bond or other written agreement to make title thereto, and shall depart this life without having made such title, the owner of such bond or written agreement or his legal representatives, may file a complaint in writing in the court of the county where the letters testamentary or of administration on the estate of the deceased obligor were granted, and cause the personal representative of such estate to be cited to appear at a date stated in the citation and show cause why specific performance of such bond or written agreement should not be decreed. Such bond or other written agreement shall be filed with such complaint, or good cause shown under oath why the same cannot be filed; and if it cannot be so filed, the same or the substance thereof shall be set forth in the complaint. After the service of the citation, the court shall hear such complaint and the evidence thereon, and, if satisfied from the proof that such bond or written agreement was legally executed by the testator or intestate, and that the complainant has a right to demand specific performance thereof, a decree shall be made ordering the personal representative to make title to the property, according to the tenor of the obligation, fully describing the property in such decree. When a conveyance is made under the provisions of this Section, it shall refer to and identify the decree of the court authorizing it, and, when delivered, shall vest in the person to whom made all the right and title which the testator or intestate had to the property conveyed; and such conveyance shall be prima facie evidence that all requirements of the law have been complied with in obtaining the same.

Acts 1955, 54th Leg., p. 88, ch. 55, eff. Jan. 1, 1956.

### § 28. Personal Representative to Serve Pending Appeal of Appointment

Pending appeals from orders or judgments appointing administrators or temporary administrators, the appointees shall continue to act as such and shall continue the prosecution of any suits then pending in favor of the estate.

Acts 1955, 54th Leg., p. 88, ch. 55, eff. Jan. 1, 1956. Amended by Acts 1975, 64th Leg., p. 2196, ch. 701, § 3, eff. June 21, 1975; Acts 1993, 73rd Leg., ch. 957, § 14, eff. Sept. 1, 1993.

### § 29. Appeal Bonds of Personal Representatives

When an appeal is taken by an executor or administrator, no bond shall be required, unless such appeal personally concerns him, in which case he must give the bond.

Acts 1955, 54th Leg., p. 88, ch. 55, eff. Jan. 1, 1956. Amended by Acts 1993, 73rd Leg., ch. 957, § 15, eff. Sept. 1, 1993.

### § 30. Repealed by Acts 1975, 64th Leg., p. 2197, ch. 701, § 7, eff. June 21, 1975

### § 31. Bill of Review

Any person interested may, by a bill of review filed in the court in which the probate proceedings were had, have any decision, order, or judgment rendered by the court, or by the judge thereof, revised and corrected on showing error therein; but no process or action under such decision, order or judgment shall be stayed except by writ of injunction, and no bill of review shall be filed after two years have elapsed from the date of such decision, order, or judgment.

Acts 1955, 54th Leg., p. 88, ch. 55, eff. Jan. 1, 1956. Amended by Acts 1993, 73rd Leg., ch. 957, § 16, eff. Sept. 1, 1993.

### § 32. Common Law Applicable

The rights, powers and duties of executors and administrators shall be governed by the principles of the common law, when the same do not conflict with the provisions of the statutes of this State.

Acts 1955, 54th Leg., p. 88, ch. 55, eff. Jan. 1, 1956. Amended by Acts 1993, 73rd Leg., ch. 957, § 17, eff. Sept. 1, 1993.

§ 33. **Issuance, Contents, Service, and Return of Citation, Notices, and Writs in Probate Matters**

(a) **When Citation or Notice Necessary.** No person need be cited or otherwise given notice except in situations in which this Code expressly provides for citation or the giving of notice; provided, however, that even though this Code does not expressly provide for citation, or the issuance or return of notice in any probate matter, the court may, in its discretion, require that notice be given, and prescribe the form and manner of service and return thereof.

(b) **Issuance by the Clerk or by Personal Representative.** The county clerk shall issue necessary citations, writs, and process in probate matters, and all notices not required to be issued by personal representatives, without any order from the court, unless such order is required by a provision of this Code.

(c) **Contents of Citation, Writ, and Notice.** Citation and notices issued by the clerk shall be signed and sealed by him, and shall be styled "The State of Texas." Notices required to be given by a personal representative shall be in writing and shall be signed by the representative in his official capacity. All citations and notices shall be directed to the person or persons to be cited or notified, shall be dated, and shall state the style and number of the proceeding, the court in which it is pending, and shall describe generally the nature of the proceeding or matter to which the citation or notice relates. No precept directed to an officer is necessary. A citation or notice shall direct the person or persons cited or notified to appear by filing a written contest or answer, or to perform other acts required of him or them and shall state when and where such appearance or performance is required. No citation or notice shall be held to be defective because it contains a precept directed to an officer authorized to serve it. All writs and other process except citations and notices shall be directed "To any sheriff or constable within the State of Texas," but shall not be held defective because directed to the sheriff or any constable of a specific county if properly served within the named county by such officer.

(d) **Where No Specific Form of Notice, Service, or Return is Prescribed, or When Provisions Are Insufficient or Inadequate.** In all situations in which this Code requires that notice be given, or that a person be cited, and in which a specific method of giving such notice or of citing such person, or a specific method of service and return of such citation or notice is not given, or an insufficient or inadequate provision appears with respect to any of such matters, or when any interested person so requests, such notice or citation shall be issued, served, and returned in such manner as the court, by written order, shall direct in accordance with this Code and the Texas Rules of Civil Procedure, and shall have the same force and effect as if the manner of service and return had been specified in this Code.

(e) **Service of Citation or Notice Upon Personal Representatives.** Except in instances in which this Code expressly provides another method of service, any notice or citation required to be served upon any personal representative or receiver shall be served by the clerk issuing such citation or notice. The clerk shall serve the same by sending the original thereof by registered or certified mail to the attorney of record for the personal representative or receiver, but if there is no attorney of record, to the personal representative or receiver.

(f) **Methods of Serving Citations and Notices.**

(1) **Personal Service.** Where it is provided that personal service shall be had with respect to a citation or notice, any such citation or notice must be served upon the attorney of record for the person to be cited. Notwithstanding the requirement of personal service, service may be made upon such attorney by any of the methods hereinafter specified for service upon an attorney. If there is no attorney of record in the proceeding for such person, or if an attempt to make service upon the attorney was unsuccessful, a citation or notice directed to a person within this State must be served by the sheriff or constable upon the person to be cited or notified, in person, by delivering to him a true copy of such citation or notice at least ten (10) days before the return day thereof, exclusive of the date of service. Where the person to be cited or notified is absent from the State, or is a nonresident, such citation or notice may be served by any disinterested person competent to make oath of the fact. Said citation or notice shall be returnable at least ten (10) days after the date of service, exclusive of the date of service. The return of the person serving the citation or notice shall be endorsed on or attached to same; it shall show the time and place of service, certify that a true copy of the citation or notice was delivered to the person directed to be served, be subscribed and sworn to before some officer authorized by the laws of this State to take affidavits, under the hand and official seal of such officer, and returned to the county clerk who issued same. If in either case such citation or notice is returned with the notation that the person sought to be served, whether within or without this State, cannot be found, the clerk shall issue a new citation or notice directed to the person or persons sought to be served and service shall be by publication.

(2) **Posting.** When citation or notice is required to be posted, it shall be posted by the sheriff or constable at the courthouse door of the county in which the proceedings are pending, or at the place in or near the courthouse where public notices customarily are posted, for not less than ten (10) days before the return day thereof, exclusive of the date of posting. The clerk shall deliver the original and a copy of such citation or notice to the sheriff or any constable of the proper county, who shall post said copy as herein prescribed and return the original to the clerk, stating in a written return thereon the time when and the place where he posted such copy. The date of posting shall be the date of service. When posting of notice by a personal representative is authorized or required, the method herein prescribed shall be followed, such notices to be issued in the name of the representative, addressed and delivered to, posted and returned by, the proper officer, and filed with the clerk.

(3) **Publication.** When a person is to be cited or notified by publication, the citation or notice shall be published once in a newspaper of general circulation in the county in which the proceedings are pending, and said publication shall be not less than ten (10) days before the return day thereof, exclusive of the date of publication. The date of publication which said newspaper bears shall be the date of service. If no newspaper is published, printed, or of general circulation, in the county where citation or notice is to be had, service of such citation or notice shall be by posting.

(4) **Mailing.**

(A) When any citation or notice is required or permitted to be served by registered or certified mail, other than notices required to be given by personal representatives, the clerk shall issue such citation or notice and shall serve the same by sending the original thereof by registered or certified mail. Any notice required to be given by a personal representative by registered or certified mail shall be issued by him, and he shall serve the same by sending the original thereof by registered or certified mail. In either case the citation or notice shall be mailed with instructions to deliver to the addressee only, and with return receipt requested. The envelope containing such citation or notice shall be addressed to the attorney of record in the proceeding for the person to be cited or notified, but if there is none, or if returned undelivered, then to the person to be cited or notified. A copy of such citation or notice, together with the certificate of the clerk, or of the personal representative, as the case may be, showing the fact and date of mailing, shall be filed and recorded. If a receipt is returned, it shall be attached to the certificate.

(B) When any citation or notice is required or permitted to be served by ordinary mail, the clerk, or the personal representative when required by statute or by order of the court, shall serve the same by mailing the original to the person to be cited or notified. A copy of such citation or notice, together with a certificate of the person serving the same showing the fact and time of mailing, shall be filed and recorded.

(C) When service is made by mail, the date of mailing shall be the date of service. Service by mail shall be made not less than twenty (20) days before the return day thereof, exclusive of the date of service.

(D) If a citation or notice served by mailing is returned undelivered, a new citation or notice shall be issued, and such citation or notice shall be served by posting.

(g) **Return of Citation or Notice.** All citations and notices issued by the clerk and served by personal service, by mail, by posting, or by publication, shall be returnable to the court from which issued on the first Monday after the service is perfected.

(h) **Sufficiency of Return in Cases of Posting.** In any probate matter where citation or notice is required to be served by posting, and such citation or notice is issued in conformity with the applicable provision of this Code, the

citation or notice and the service and return thereof shall be sufficient and valid if any sheriff or constable posts a copy or copies of such citation or notice at the place or places prescribed by this Code on a day which is sufficiently prior to the return day named in such citation or notice for the period of time for which such citation or notice is required to be posted to elapse before the return day of such citation or notice, and the fact that such sheriff or constable makes his return on such citation or notice and returns same into court before the period of time elapses for which such citation or notice is required to be posted, shall not affect the sufficiency or validity of such citation or notice or the service or return thereof, even though such return is made, and such citation or notice is returned into court, on the same day it is issued.

(i) **Proof of Service.** Proof of service in all cases requiring notice or citation, whether by publication, posting, mailing, or otherwise, shall be filed before the hearing. Proof of service made by a sheriff or constable shall be made by the return of service. Service made by a private person shall be proved by the affidavit of the person. Proof of service by publication shall be made by the affidavit of the publisher or that of an employee of the publisher, which affidavit shall show the date the issue of the newspaper bore, and have attached to or embodied in it a copy of the published notice or citation. In the case of service by mail, proof shall be made by the certificate of the clerk, or the affidavit of the personal representative or other person making such service, stating the fact and time of mailing. In the case of service by registered or certified mail, the return receipt shall be attached to the certificate, if a receipt has been returned.

(j) **Request for Notice.** At any time after an application is filed for the purpose of commencing any proceeding in probate, including, but not limited to, a proceeding for the probate of a will, grant of letters testamentary or of administration and determination of heirship, any person interested in the estate may file with the clerk a request in writing that he be notified of any and all, or of any specifically designated, motions, applications, or pleadings filed by any person, or by any particular persons specifically designated in the request. The fees and costs for such notices shall be borne by the person requesting them, and the clerk may require a deposit to cover the estimated costs of furnishing such person with the notice or notices requested. The clerk shall thereafter send to such person by ordinary mail copies of any of the documents specified in the request. Failure of the clerk to comply with the request shall not invalidate any proceeding.

Acts 1955, 54th Leg., p. 88, ch. 55, eff. Jan. 1, 1956. Amended by Acts 1957, 55th Leg., p. 53, ch. 31, § 1, eff. Aug. 22, 1957; Acts 1971, 62nd Leg., p. 967, ch. 173, § 1, eff. Jan. 1, 1972; Acts 1993, 73rd Leg., ch. 957, § 18, eff. Sept. 1, 1993.

### § 34. Service on Attorney

If any attorney shall have entered his appearance of record for any party in any proceeding in probate, all citations and notices required to be served on the party in such proceeding shall be served on the attorney, and such service shall be in lieu of service upon the party for whom the attorney appears. All notices served on attorneys in accordance with this section may be served by registered or certified mail or by delivery to the attorney in person. They may be served by a party to the proceeding or his attorney of record, or by the proper sheriff or constable, or by any other person competent to testify. A written statement by an attorney of record, or the return of the officer, or the affidavit of any other person showing service shall be prima facie evidence of the fact of service.

Acts 1955, 54th Leg., p. 88, ch. 55, eff. Jan. 1, 1956. Amended by Acts 1971, 62nd Leg., p. 970, ch. 173, § 2, eff. Jan. 1, 1972.

### § 34A. Attorneys Ad Litem

Except as provided by Section 53(c) of this code, the judge of a probate court may appoint an attorney ad litem to represent the interests of a person having a legal disability, a nonresident, an unborn or unascertained person, or an unknown heir in any probate proceeding. Each attorney ad litem appointed under this section is entitled to reasonable compensation for services in the amount set by the court and to be taxed as costs in the proceeding.

Added by Acts 1983, 68th Leg., p. 747, ch. 178, § 1, eff. Aug. 29, 1983. Amended by Acts 1987, 70th Leg., ch. 467, § 1, eff. Sept. 1, 1987; Acts 1993, 73rd Leg., ch. 957, § 19, eff. Sept. 1, 1993; Acts 2001, 77th Leg., ch. 664, § 1, eff. Sept. 1, 2001.

### § 35. Waiver of Notice

Any person legally competent who is interested in any hearing in a proceeding in probate may, in person or by attorney, waive in writing notice of such hearing. A trustee may make such a waiver on behalf of the beneficiary of his trust. A consul or other representative of a foreign government, whose appearance has been entered as provided by law on behalf of any person residing in a foreign country, may make such waiver of notice on behalf of such person. Any person who submits to the jurisdiction of the court in any hearing shall be deemed to have waived notice thereof.

Acts 1955, 54th Leg., p. 88, ch. 55, eff. Jan. 1, 1956. Amended by Acts 1993, 73rd Leg., ch. 957, § 20, eff. Sept. 1, 1993.

### § 36. Duty and Responsibility of Judge

(a) It shall be the duty of each county and probate court to use reasonable diligence to see that personal representatives of estates being administered under orders of the court and other officers of the court perform the duty enjoined upon them by law pertaining to such estates. The judge shall annually, if in his opinion the same be necessary, examine the condition of each of said estates and the solvency of the bonds of personal representatives of estates. He shall, at any time he finds that the personal representative's bond is not sufficient to protect such estate, require such personal representatives to execute a new bond in accordance with law. In each case, he shall notify the personal representative, and the sureties on the bond, as provided by law; and should damage or loss result to estates through the gross neglect of the judge to use reasonable diligence in the

performance of his duty, he shall be liable on his bond to those damaged by such neglect.

(b) The court may request an applicant or court-appointed fiduciary to produce other information identifying an applicant, decedent, or personal representative, including social security numbers, in addition to identifying information the applicant or fiduciary is required to produce under this code. The court shall maintain the information required under this subsection, and the information may not be filed with the clerk.

Acts 1955, 54th Leg., p. 88, ch. 55, eff. Jan. 1, 1956. Amended by Acts 1975, 64th Leg., p. 979, ch. 375, § 1, eff. June 19, 1975; Acts 1993, 73rd Leg., ch. 957, § 21, eff. Sept. 1, 1993; Acts 1997, 75th Leg., ch. 1302, § 3, eff. Sept. 1, 1997.

### § 36A. Repealed by Acts 1993, 73rd Leg., ch. 49, § 2, eff. Sept. 1, 1993

### § 36B. Examination of Documents or Safe Deposit Box With Court Order

(a) A judge of a court having probate jurisdiction of a decedent's estate may order a person to permit a court representative named in the order to examine a decedent's documents or safe deposit box if it is shown to the judge that:

(1) the person may possess or control the documents or that the person leased the safe deposit box to the decedent; and

(2) the documents or safe deposit box may contain a will of the decedent, a deed to a burial plot in which the decedent is to be buried, or an insurance policy issued in the decedent's name and payable to a beneficiary named in the policy.

(b) The court representative shall examine the decedent's documents or safe deposit box in the presence of:

(1) the judge ordering the examination or an agent of the judge; and

(2) the person who has possession or control of the documents or who leased the safe deposit box or, if the person is a corporation, an officer of the corporation or an agent of an officer.

Added by Acts 1981, 67th Leg., 1st C.S., p. 193, ch. 17, art. 3, § 1, eff. Sept. 1, 1981.

### § 36C. Delivery of Document With Court Order

(a) A judge who orders an examination by a court representative of a decedent's documents or safe deposit box under Section 36B of this code may order the person who possesses or controls the documents or who leases the safe deposit box to permit the court representative to take possession of the following documents:

(1) a will of the decedent;

(2) a deed to a burial plot in which the decedent is to be buried; or

(3) an insurance policy issued in the decedent's name and payable to a beneficiary named in the policy.

(b) The court representative shall deliver:

(1) the will to the clerk of a court that has probate jurisdiction and that is located in the same county as the court of the judge who ordered the examination;

(2) the burial plot deed to the person designated by the judge in the order for the examination; or

(3) the insurance policy to a beneficiary named in the policy.

(c) A court clerk to whom a will is delivered under Subsection (b) of this section shall issue a receipt for the will to the court representative who delivers it.

Added by Acts 1981, 67th Leg., 1st C.S., p. 193, ch. 17, art. 3, § 1, eff. Sept. 1, 1981.

### § 36D. Examination of Document or Safe Deposit Box Without Court Order

(a) A person who possesses or controls a document delivered by a decedent for safekeeping or who leases a safe deposit box to a decedent may permit any of the following persons to examine the document or the contents of the safe deposit box:

(1) the spouse of the decedent;

(2) a parent of the decedent;

(3) a descendant of the decedent who is at least 18 years old; or

(4) a person named as executor of the decedent's estate in a copy of a document that the person has and that appears to be a will of the decedent.

(b) The examination shall be conducted in the presence of the person who possesses or controls the document or who leases the safe deposit box or, if the person is a corporation, an officer of the corporation.

Added by Acts 1981, 67th Leg., 1st C.S., p. 193, ch. 17, art. 3, § 1, eff. Sept. 1, 1981.

### § 36E. Delivery of Document Without Court Order

(a) A person who permits an examination of a decedent's document or safe deposit box under Section 36D of this code may deliver:

(1) a document appearing to be the decedent's will to the clerk of a court that has probate jurisdiction and that is located in the county in which the decedent resided or to the person named in the document as an executor of the decedent's estate;

(2) a document appearing to be a deed to a burial plot in which the decedent is to be buried or appearing to give burial instructions to the person making the examination; or

(3) a document appearing to be an insurance policy on the decedent's life to a beneficiary named in the policy.

(b) A person who has leased a safe deposit box to the decedent shall keep a copy of a document appearing to be a will that the person delivers under Subsection (a) of this section. The person shall keep the copy for four years after the day of delivery.

(c) A person may not deliver a document under Subsection (a) of this section unless requested to do so by the person examining the document and unless the person examining the document issues a receipt for the document to the person who is to deliver it.

Added by Acts 1981, 67th Leg., 1st C.S., p. 193, ch. 17, art. 3, § 1, eff. Sept. 1, 1981.

### § 36F. Restriction on Removal of Contents of Safe Deposit Box

A person may not remove the contents of a decedent's safe deposit box except as provided by Section 36C or 36E of this code or except as provided by another law.

Added by Acts 1981, 67th Leg., 1st C.S., p. 193, ch. 17, art. 3, § 1, eff. Sept. 1, 1981.

## CHAPTER II

## DESCENT AND DISTRIBUTION

### § 37. Passage of Title Upon Intestacy and Under a Will

When a person dies, leaving a lawful will, all of his estate devised or bequeathed by such will, and all powers of appointment granted in such will, shall vest immediately in the devisees or legatees of such estate and the donees of such powers; and all the estate of such person, not devised or bequeathed, shall vest immediately in his heirs at law; subject, however, to the payment of the debts of the testator or intestate, except such as is exempted by law, and subject to the payment of court-ordered child support payments that are delinquent on the date of the person's death; and whenever a person dies intestate, all of his estate shall vest immediately in his heirs at law, but with the exception aforesaid shall still be liable and subject in their hands to the payment of the debts of the intestate and the delinquent child support payments; but upon the issuance of letters testamentary or of administration upon any such estate, the executor or administrator shall have the right to possession of the estate as it existed at the death of the testator or intestate, with the exception aforesaid; and he shall recover possession of and hold such estate in trust to be disposed of in accordance with the law.

Acts 1955, 54th Leg., p. 88, ch. 55, eff. Jan. 1, 1956. Amended by Acts 1969, 61st Leg., p. 1703, ch. 556, § 2, eff. June 10, 1969; Acts 1981, 67th Leg., p. 2537, ch. 674, § 3, eff. Sept. 1, 1981.

### § 37A. Means of Evidencing Disclaimer or Renunciation of Property or Interest Receivable From a Decedent

**(a) Persons Who May Disclaim.** Any person, or the guardian of an incapacitated person, the personal representative of a deceased person, or the guardian ad litem of an unborn or unascertained person, with prior court approval of the court having, or which would have, jurisdiction over such guardian, personal representative, or guardian ad litem, or any independent executor of a deceased person, without prior court approval, or an attorney in fact or agent appointed under a durable power of attorney authorizing disclaimers that is executed by a principal, who may be entitled to receive any property as a beneficiary and who intends to effect disclaimer irrevocably on or after September 1, 1977, of the whole or any part of such property shall evidence same as herein provided.

**(b) Effective Date of Disclaimer.** A disclaimer evidenced as provided by this section shall be effective as of the death of decedent and shall relate back for all purposes to the death of the decedent and is not subject to the claims of any creditor of the disclaimant.

**(c) Effect of Disclaimer.** Unless the decedent's will provides otherwise, the property subject to the disclaimer shall pass as if the person disclaiming or on whose behalf a disclaimer is made had predeceased the decedent and a future interest that would otherwise take effect in possession or enjoyment after the termination of the estate or interest that is disclaimed takes effect as if the disclaiming beneficiary had predeceased the decedent.

**(d) Ineffective Disclaimer.** Failure to comply with the provisions of this section shall render such disclaimer ineffective except as an assignment of such property to those who would have received same had the person attempting the disclaimer died prior to the decedent.

**(e) Definitions.** The term "property" as used in this section shall include all legal and equitable interests, powers, and property, whether present or future, whether vested or contingent, and whether beneficial or burdensome, in whole or in part. The term "disclaimer" as used in this section shall include "renunciation." In this section "beneficiary" includes a person who would have been entitled, if the person had not made a disclaimer, to receive property as a result of the death of another person by inheritance, under a will, by

an agreement between spouses for community property with a right of survivorship, by a joint tenancy with a right of survivorship, or by any other survivorship agreement, account, or interest in which the interest of the decedent passes to a surviving beneficiary, by an insurance, annuity, endowment, employment, deferred compensation, or other contract or arrangement, or under a pension, profit sharing, thrift, stock bonus, life insurance, survivor income, incentive, or other plan or program providing retirement, welfare, or fringe benefits with respect to an employee or a self-employed individual.

**(f) Subsequent Disclaimers.** Nothing in this section shall be construed to preclude a subsequent disclaimer by any person who shall be entitled to property as a result of a disclaimer.

**(g) Form of Disclaimer.** In the case of property receivable by a beneficiary, the disclaimer shall be evidenced by a written memorandum, acknowledged before a notary public or other person authorized to take acknowledgements of conveyances of real estate.

**(h) Time for Filing of Disclaimer.** Unless the beneficiary is a charitable organization or governmental agency of the state, a written memorandum of disclaimer disclaiming a present interest shall be filed not later than nine months after the death of the decedent and a written memorandum of disclaimer disclaiming a future interest may be filed not later than nine months after the event determining that the taker of the property or interest is finally ascertained and his interest is indefeasibly vested. If the beneficiary is a charitable organization or a governmental agency of the state, a written memorandum of disclaimer disclaiming a present or future interest shall be filed not later than the later of:

(1) the first anniversary of the date the beneficiary receives the notice required by Section 128A of this code; or

(2) the expiration of the six-month period following the date the personal representative files:

(A) the inventory, appraisement, and list of claims due or owing to the estate; or

(B) the affidavit in lieu of the inventory, appraisement, and list of claims.

**(h–1) Filing of Disclaimer.** The written memorandum of disclaimer shall be filed in the probate court in which the decedent's will has been probated or in which proceedings have been commenced for the administration of the decedent's estate or which has before it an application for either of the same; provided, however, if the administration of the decedent's estate is closed, or after the expiration of one year following the date of the issuance of letters testamentary in an independent administration, or if there has been no will of the decedent probated or filed for probate, or if no administration of the decedent's estate has been commenced, or if no application for administration of the decedent's estate has been filed, the written memorandum of disclaimer shall be filed with the county clerk of the county of the decedent's residence, or, if the decedent is not a resident of this state but real property or an interest therein located in this state is disclaimed, a written memorandum of disclaimer shall be filed with the county clerk of the county in which such real property or interest therein is located, and recorded by such county clerk in the deed records of that county.

**(i) Notice of Disclaimer.** Unless the beneficiary is a charitable organization or governmental agency of the state, copies of any written memorandum of disclaimer shall be delivered in person to, or shall be mailed by registered or certified mail to and received by, the legal representative of the transferor of the interest or the holder of legal title to the property to which the disclaimer relates not later than nine months after the death of the decedent or, if the interest is a future interest, not later than nine months after the date the person who will receive the property or interest is finally ascertained and the person's interest is indefeasibly vested. If the beneficiary is a charitable organization or government agency of the state, the notices required by this section shall be filed not later than the later of:

(1) the first anniversary of the date the beneficiary receives the notice required by Section 128A of this code; or

(2) the expiration of the six-month period following the date the personal representative files:

(A) the inventory, appraisement, and list of claims due or owing to the estate; or

(B) the affidavit in lieu of the inventory, appraisement, and list of claims.

**(j) Power to Provide for Disclaimer.** Nothing herein shall prevent a person from providing in a will, insurance policy, employee benefit agreement, or other instrument for the making of disclaimers by a beneficiary of an interest receivable under that instrument and for the disposition of disclaimed property in a manner different from the provisions hereof.

**(k) Irrevocability of Disclaimer.** Any disclaimer filed and served under this section shall be irrevocable.

**(l) Partial Disclaimer.** Any person who may be entitled to receive any property as a beneficiary may disclaim such property in whole or in part, including but not limited to specific powers of invasion, powers of appointment, and fee estate in favor of life estates; and a partial disclaimer or renunciation, in accordance with the provisions of this section, shall be effective whether the property so renounced or disclaimed constitutes a portion of a single, aggregate gift or constitutes part or all of a separate, independent gift; provided, however, that a partial disclaimer shall be effective only with respect to property expressly described or referred to by category in such disclaimer; and provided further, that a partial disclaimer of property which is subject to a burdensome interest created by the decedent's will shall not be effective unless such property constitutes a gift which is separate and distinct from undisclaimed gifts.

**(m) Partial Disclaimer by Spouse.** Without limiting Subsection (l) of this section, a disclaimer by the decedent's surviving spouse of a transfer by the decedent is not a disclaimer by the surviving spouse of all or any part of any other transfer from the decedent to or for the benefit of the surviving spouse, regardless of whether the property or interest that would have passed under the disclaimed transfer passes because of the disclaimer to or for the benefit of the surviving spouse by the other transfer.

**(n) Disclaimer After Acceptance.** No disclaimer shall be effective after the acceptance of the property by the beneficiary. For the purpose of this subsection, acceptance shall occur only if the person making such disclaimer has previously taken possession or exercised dominion and control of such property in the capacity of beneficiary.

**(o) Interest in Trust Property.** A beneficiary who accepts an interest in a trust is not considered to have a direct or indirect interest in trust property that relates to a licensed or permitted business and over which the beneficiary exercises no control. Direct or indirect beneficial ownership of not more than five percent of any class of equity securities that is registered under the Securities Exchange Act of 1934 shall not be deemed to be an ownership interest in the business of the issuer of such securities within the meaning of any statute, pursuant thereto.

**(p) Extension of Time for Certain Disclaimers.** Notwithstanding the periods prescribed by Subsections (h) and (i) of this section, a disclaimer with respect to an interest in property passing by reason of the death of a decedent dying after December 31, 2009, but before December 17, 2010, may be executed and filed, and notice of the disclaimer may be given, not later than nine months after December 17, 2010. A disclaimer filed and for which notice is given during this extended period is valid and shall be treated as if the disclaimer had been filed and notice had been given within the periods prescribed by Subsections (h) and (i) of this section. This subsection does not apply to a disclaimer made by a beneficiary that is a charitable organization or governmental agency of the state.

Added by Acts 1971, 62nd Leg., p. 2954, ch. 979, § 1, eff. Aug. 30, 1971. Amended by Acts 1977, 65th Leg., p. 1918, ch. 769, § 1, eff. Aug. 29, 1977; Acts 1979, 66th Leg., p. 1741, ch. 713, § 4, eff. Aug. 27, 1979; Acts 1987, 70th Leg., ch. 467, § 2, eff. Sept. 1, 1987; Acts 1991, 72nd Leg., ch. 895, § 2, eff. Sept. 1, 1991; Acts 1993, 73rd Leg., ch. 846, § 1, eff. Sept. 1, 1993; Acts 1995, 74th Leg., ch. 1039, § 5, eff. Sept. 1, 1995; Acts 2007, 80th Leg., ch. 1170, § 3.01, eff. Sept. 1, 2007; Subsec. (h) amended and divided as subsecs. (h) and (h–1) by Acts 2011, 82nd Leg., ch. 1338 (S.B. 1198), § 1.08, eff. June 17, 2011; Subsec. (i) amended by Acts 2011, 82nd Leg., ch. 1338 (S.B. 1198), § 1.08, eff. Sept. 1, 2011; Subsec. (p) added by Acts 2011, 82nd Leg., ch. 1338 (S.B. 1198), § 1.08, eff. Sept. 1, 2011.

### Leading CLE/Law Review Publications

Akers, Estate Administration—A Summary of Practical Tax–Planning Ideas, 1998 Adv. Est. Plan & Probate, Tab D.

Bailey, Release of the Heir's Expectancy, 33 Tex. L. Rev. 423 (1955).

Cenatiempo, Disclaimers in Light of 2001 Tax Act, 2002 Adv. Est. Plan. & Probate, ch. 24.

Donoghue, Disclaimers in Estate and Post–Mortem Planning, 1995 Adv. Est. Plan. & Probate.

Henkel, Drafting for Disclaimers, 1994 Adv. Est. Plan. & Probate.

Schwartzel, Qualified Disclaimers Under the New Regulations, 1988 Adv. Est. Plan. & Probate.

## § 37B. Assignment of Property Received from a Decedent

(a) A person entitled to receive property or an interest in property from a decedent under a will, by inheritance, or as a beneficiary under a life insurance contract, and who does not disclaim the property under Section 37A of this code, may assign the property or interest in property to any person.

(b) The assignment may, at the request of the assignor, be filed as provided for the filing of a disclaimer under Section 37A(h) of this code. The filing requires the service of notice under Section 37A(i) of this code.

(c) Failure to comply with the provisions of Section 37A of this code does not affect an assignment under this section.

(d) An assignment under this section is a gift to the assignee and is not a disclaimer or renunciation under Section 37A of this code.

(e) An assignment that would defeat a spendthrift provision imposed in a trust may not be made under this section.

Added by Acts 1985, 69th Leg., ch. 880, § 1, eff. Sept. 1, 1985. Amended by Acts 2007, 80th Leg., ch. 1170, § 3.02, eff. Sept. 1, 2007.

## § 37C. Satisfaction of Devise

(a) Property given to a person by a testator during the testator's lifetime is considered a satisfaction, either wholly or partly, of a devise to the person if:

(1) the testator's will provides for deduction of the lifetime gift;

(2) the testator declares in a contemporaneous writing that the lifetime gift is to be deducted from or is in satisfaction of the devise; or

(3) the devisee acknowledges in writing that the lifetime gift is in satisfaction of the devise.

(b) Property given in partial satisfaction of a devise shall be valued as of the earlier of the date on which the devisee acquires possession of or enjoys the property or the date on which the testator dies.

Added by Acts 2003, 78th Leg., ch. 1060, § 7, eff. Sept. 1, 2003.

## § 38. Persons Who Take Upon Intestacy

(a) **Intestate Leaving No Husband or Wife.** Where any person, having title to any estate, real, personal or mixed, shall die intestate, leaving no husband or wife, it shall descend and pass in parcenary to his kindred, male and female, in the following course:

1. To his children and their descendants.

2. If there be no children nor their descendants, then to his father and mother, in equal portions. But if only the father or mother survive the intestate, then his estate shall be divided into two equal portions, one of which shall pass to

such survivor, and the other half shall pass to the brothers and sisters of the deceased, and to their descendants; but if there be none such, then the whole estate shall be inherited by the surviving father or mother.

3. If there be neither father nor mother, then the whole of such estate shall pass to the brothers and sisters of the intestate, and to their descendants.

4. If there be none of the kindred aforesaid, then the inheritance shall be divided into two moieties, one of which shall go to the paternal and the other to the maternal kindred, in the following course: To the grandfather and grandmother in equal portions, but if only one of these be living, then the estate shall be divided into two equal parts, one of which shall go to such survivor, and the other shall go to the descendant or descendants of such deceased grandfather or grandmother. If there be no such descendants, then the whole estate shall be inherited by the surviving grandfather or grandmother. If there be no surviving grandfather or grandmother, then the whole of such estate shall go to their descendants, and so on without end, passing in like manner to the nearest lineal ancestors and their descendants.

(b) **Intestate Leaving Husband or Wife.** Where any person having title to any estate, real, personal or mixed, other than a community estate, shall die intestate as to such estate, and shall leave a surviving husband or wife, such estate of such intestate shall descend and pass as follows:

1. If the deceased have a child or children, or their descendants, the surviving husband or wife shall take one-third of the personal estate, and the balance of such personal estate shall go to the child or children of the deceased and their descendants. The surviving husband or wife shall also be entitled to an estate for life, in one-third of the land of the intestate, with remainder to the child or children of the intestate and their descendants.

2. If the deceased have no child or children, or their descendants, then the surviving husband or wife shall be entitled to all the personal estate, and to one-half of the lands of the intestate, without remainder to any person, and the other half shall pass and be inherited according to the rules of descent and distribution; provided, however, that if the deceased has neither surviving father nor mother nor surviving brothers or sisters, or their descendants, then the surviving husband or wife shall be entitled to the whole of the estate of such intestate.

Acts 1955, 54th Leg., p. 88, ch. 55, eff. Jan. 1, 1956.

## § 39. No Distinction Because of Property's Source

There shall be no distinction in regulating the descent and distribution of the estate of a person dying intestate between property which may have been derived by gift, devise or descent from the father, and that which may have been derived by gift, devise or descent from the mother; and all the estate to which such intestate may have had title at the time of death shall descend and vest in the heirs of such person in the same manner as if he had been the original purchaser thereof.

Acts 1955, 54th Leg., p. 88, ch. 55, eff. Jan. 1, 1956.

### § 40.  Inheritance by and From an Adopted Child

For purposes of inheritance under the laws of descent and distribution, an adopted child shall be regarded as the child of the parent or parents by adoption, such adopted child and its descendants inheriting from and through the parent or parents by adoption and their kin the same as if such child were the natural child of such parent or parents by adoption, and such parent or parents by adoption and their kin inheriting from and through such adopted child the same as if such child were the natural child of such parent or parents by adoption.  The natural parent or parents of such child and their kin shall not inherit from or through said child, but, except as provided by Section 162.507(c), Family Code, the child shall inherit from and through its natural parent or parents.  Nothing herein shall prevent any parent by adoption from disposing of his property by will according to law.  The presence of this Section specifically relating to the rights of adopted children shall in no way diminish the rights of such children, under the laws of descent and distribution or otherwise, which they acquire by virtue of their inclusion in the definition of "child" which is contained in this Code.

Acts 1955, 54th Leg., p. 88, ch. 55, eff. Jan. 1, 1956.  Amended by Acts 1989, 71st Leg., ch. 375, § 34, eff. Sept. 1, 1989.
Amended by Acts 2005, 79th Leg., ch. 169, § 2, eff. Sept. 1, 2005.

### § 41.  Matters Affecting and Not Affecting the Right to Inherit

(a) **Persons Not in Being.**  No right of inheritance shall accrue to any persons other than to children or lineal descendants of the intestate, unless they are in being and capable in law to take as heirs at the time of the death of the intestate.

(b) **Heirs of Whole and Half Blood.**  In situations where the inheritance passes to the collateral kindred of the intestate, if part of such collateral be of the whole blood, and the other part be of the half blood only, of the intestate, each of those of half blood shall inherit only half so much as each of those of the whole blood; but if all be of the half blood, they shall have whole portions.

(c) **Alienage.**  No person is disqualified to take as an heir because he or a person through whom he claims is or has been an alien.

(d) **Convicted Persons and Suicides.**  No conviction shall work corruption of blood or forfeiture of estate, except in the case of a beneficiary in a life insurance policy or contract who is convicted and sentenced as a principal or accomplice in wilfully bringing about the death of the insured, in which case the proceeds of such insurance policy or contract shall be paid as provided in the Insurance Code of this State, as same now exists or is hereafter amended;  nor shall there be any forfeiture by reason of death by casualty; and the estates of those who destroy their own lives shall descend or vest as in the case of natural death.

(e) **Parent–Child Relationship.**  A probate court may declare that the parent of a child under 18 years of age may not inherit from or through the child under the laws of descent and distribution if the court finds by clear and convincing evidence that the parent has:

(1) voluntarily abandoned and failed to support the child in accordance with the parent's obligation or ability for at least three years before the date of the child's death, and did not resume support for the child before that date;

(2) voluntarily and with knowledge of the pregnancy, abandoned the mother of the child beginning at a time during her pregnancy with the child and continuing through the birth, failed to provide adequate support or medical care for the mother during the period of abandonment before the birth of the child, and remained apart from and failed to support the child since birth; or

(3) been convicted or has been placed on community supervision, including deferred adjudication community supervision, for being criminally responsible for the death or serious injury of a child under the following sections of the Penal Code or adjudicated under Title 3, Family Code, for conduct that caused the death or serious injury of a child and that would constitute a violation of one of the following sections of the Penal Code:

(A) Section 19.02 (murder);

(B) Section 19.03 (capital murder);

(C) Section 19.04 (manslaughter);

(D) Section 21.11 (indecency with a child);

(E) Section 22.01 (assault);

(F) Section 22.011 (sexual assault);

(G) Section 22.02 (aggravated assault);

(H) Section 22.021 (aggravated sexual assault);

(I) Section 22.04 (injury to a child, elderly individual, or disabled individual);

(J) Section 22.041 (abandoning or endangering child);

(K) Section 25.02 (prohibited sexual conduct);

(L) Section 43.25 (sexual performance by a child); or

(M) Section 43.26 (possession or promotion of child pornography).

(f) **Treatment of Certain Relationships.**  On a determination that the parent of a child may not inherit from or through the child under Subsection (e) of this section, the parent shall be treated as if the parent predeceased the child for purposes of:

(1) inheritance under the laws of descent and distribution; and

**Text of Texas Probate Code effective until January 1, 2014**

(2) any other cause of action based on parentage.

Acts 1955, 54th Leg., p. 88, ch. 55, eff. Jan. 1, 1956. Amended by Acts 1969, 61st Leg., p. 1922, ch. 641, § 2, eff. June 12, 1969.

Subsecs. (e), (f) amended by Acts 2007, 80th Leg., ch. 1412, § 2, eff. Sept. 1, 2007.

## § 42. Inheritance Rights of Children

(a) **Maternal Inheritance.** For the purpose of inheritance, a child is the child of his biological or adopted mother, so that he and his issue shall inherit from his mother and from his maternal kindred, both descendants, ascendants, and collaterals in all degrees, and they may inherit from him and his issue.

(b) **Paternal Inheritance.** (1) For the purpose of inheritance, a child is the child of his biological father if the child is born under circumstances described by Section 160.201, Family Code, is adjudicated to be the child of the father by court decree as provided by Chapter 160, Family Code,[1] was adopted by his father, or if the father executed an acknowledgment of paternity as provided by Subchapter D, Chapter 160, Family Code, or a like statement properly executed in another jurisdiction, so that he and his issue shall inherit from his father and from his paternal kindred, both descendants, ascendants, and collaterals in all degrees, and they may inherit from him and his issue. A person claiming to be a biological child of the decedent, who is not otherwise presumed to be a child of the decedent, or claiming inheritance through a biological child of the decedent, who is not otherwise presumed to be a child of the decedent, may petition the probate court for a determination of right of inheritance. If the court finds by clear and convincing evidence that the purported father was the biological father of the child, the child is treated as any other child of the decedent for the purpose of inheritance and he and his issue may inherit from his paternal kindred, both descendants, ascendants, and collaterals in all degrees, and they may inherit from him and his issue. This section does not permit inheritance by a purported father of a child, whether recognized or not, if the purported father's parental rights have been terminated.

(2) A person who purchases for valuable consideration any interest in real or personal property of the heirs of a decedent, who in good faith relies on the declarations in an affidavit of heirship that does not include a child who at the time of the sale or contract of sale of the property is not a presumed child of the decedent and has not under a final court decree or judgment been found to be entitled to treatment under this subsection as a child of the decedent, and who is without knowledge of the claim of that child, acquires good title to the interest that the person would have received, as purchaser, in the absence of any claim of the child not included in the affidavit. This subdivision does not affect the liability, if any, of the heirs for the proceeds of any sale described by this subdivision to the child who was not included in the affidavit of heirship.

(c) **Homestead Rights, Exempt Property, and Family Allowances.** A child as provided by Subsections (a) and (b) of this section is a child of his mother, and a child of his father, for the purpose of determining homestead rights, distribution of exempt property, and the making of family allowances.

(d) **Marriages Void and Voidable.** The issue of marriages declared void or voided by annulment shall be treated in the same manner as issue of a valid marriage.

Acts 1955, 54th Leg., p. 88, ch. 55, eff. Jan. 1, 1956. Amended by Acts 1977, 65th Leg., p. 762, ch. 290, § 1, eff. May 28, 1977; Acts 1979, 66th Leg., p. 40, ch. 24, § 25, eff. Aug. 27, 1979; Acts 1979, 66th Leg., p. 1743, ch. 713, § 5, eff. Aug. 27, 1979; Acts 1987, 70th Leg., ch. 464, § 1, eff. Sept. 1, 1987; Acts 1989, 71st Leg., ch. 375, § 35, eff. Sept. 1, 1989; Acts 1997, 75th Leg., ch. 165, § 7.54, eff. Sept. 1, 1997; Acts 1997, 75th Leg., ch. 1302, § 4, eff. Sept. 1, 1997; Acts 2001, 77th Leg., ch. 821, § 2.18, eff. June 14, 2001.

[1] V.T.C.A., Family Code § 160.301 et seq.

## § 43. Determination of Per Capita and Per Stirpes Distribution

When the intestate's children, descendants, brothers, sisters, uncles, aunts, or any other relatives of the deceased standing in the first or same degree alone come into the distribution upon intestacy, they shall take per capita, namely: by persons; and, when a part of them being dead and a part living, the descendants of those dead shall have right to distribution upon intestacy, such descendants shall inherit only such portion of said property as the parent through whom they inherit would be entitled to if alive.

Acts 1955, 54th Leg., p. 88, ch. 55, eff. Jan. 1, 1956. Amended by Acts 1991, 72nd Leg., ch. 895, § 3, eff. Sept. 1, 1991.

## § 44. Advancements

(a) If a decedent dies intestate as to all or a portion of the decedent's estate, property the decedent gave during the decedent's lifetime to a person who, on the date of the decedent's death, is the decedent's heir, or property received by a decedent's heir under a nontestamentary transfer under Chapter XI of this code[1] is an advancement against the heir's intestate share only if:

(1) the decedent declared in a contemporaneous writing or the heir acknowledged in writing that the gift or nontestamentary transfer is an advancement; or

(2) the decedent's contemporaneous writing or the heir's written acknowledgment otherwise indicates that the gift or nontestamentary transfer is to be taken into account in computing the division and distribution of the decedent's intestate estate.

(b) For purposes of Subsection (a) of this section, property that is advanced is valued at the time the heir came into possession or enjoyment of the property or at the time of the decedent's death, whichever occurs first.

(c) If the recipient of the property fails to survive the decedent, the property is not taken into account in computing the division and distribution of the decedent's intestate estate, unless the decedent's contemporaneous writing provides otherwise.

Acts 1955, 54th Leg., p. 88, ch. 55, eff. Jan. 1, 1956. Amended by Acts 1993, 73rd Leg., ch. 846, § 4, eff. Sept. 1, 1993.

¹ V.A.T.S. Probate Code, § 436 et seq.

## § 45.  Community Estate

(a) On the intestate death of one of the spouses to a marriage, the community property estate of the deceased spouse passes to the surviving spouse if:

(1) no child or other descendant of the deceased spouse survives the deceased spouse; or

(2) all surviving children and descendants of the deceased spouse are also children or descendants of the surviving spouse.

(b) On the intestate death of one of the spouses to a marriage, if a child or other descendant of the deceased spouse survives the deceased spouse and the child or descendant is not a child or descendant of the surviving spouse, one-half of the community estate is retained by the surviving spouse and the other one-half passes to the children or descendants of the deceased spouse. The descendants shall inherit only such portion of said property to which they would be entitled under Section 43 of this code. In every case, the community estate passes charged with the debts against it.

Acts 1955, 54th Leg., p. 88, ch. 55, eff. Jan. 1, 1956. Amended by Acts 1991, 72nd Leg., ch. 895, § 4, eff. Sept. 1, 1991; Acts 1993, 73rd Leg., ch. 846, § 33, eff. Sept. 1, 1993.

## § 46.  Joint Tenancies

(a) If two or more persons hold an interest in property jointly, and one joint owner dies before severance, the interest of the decedent in the joint estate shall not survive to the remaining joint owner or owners but shall pass by will or intestacy from the decedent as if the decedent's interest had been severed. The joint owners may agree in writing, however, that the interest of any joint owner who dies shall survive to the surviving joint owner or owners, but no such agreement shall be inferred from the mere fact that the property is held in joint ownership.

(b) Subsection (a) does not apply to agreements between spouses regarding their community property. Agreements between spouses regarding rights of survivorship in community property are governed by Part 3 of Chapter XI of this code.¹

Acts 1955, 54th Leg., p. 88, ch. 55, eff. Jan. 1, 1956. Amended by Acts 1961, 57th Leg., p. 233, ch. 120, § 1, eff. May 15, 1961; Acts 1969, 61st Leg., p. 1922, ch. 641, § 3, eff. June 12, 1969; Acts 1981, 67th Leg., p. 895, ch. 319, § 1, eff. Sept. 1, 1981; Acts 1987, 70th Leg., ch. 678, § 2; Acts 1989, 71st Leg., ch. 655, § 1, eff. Aug. 28, 1989.

¹ V.A.T.S. Probate Code, § 451 et seq.

## § 47.  Requirement of Survival by 120 Hours

(a) **Survival of Heirs.** A person who fails to survive the decedent by 120 hours is deemed to have predeceased the decedent for purposes of homestead allowance, exempt property, and intestate succession, and the decedent's heirs are determined accordingly, except as otherwise provided in this section. If the time of death of the decedent or of the person who would otherwise be an heir, or the times of death of both, cannot be determined, and it cannot be established that the person who would otherwise be an heir has survived the decedent by 120 hours, it is deemed that the person failed to survive for the required period. This subsection does not apply where its application would result in the escheat of an intestate estate.

(b) **Disposal of Community Property.** When a husband and wife have died, leaving community property, and neither the husband nor wife survived the other by 120 hours, one-half of all community property shall be distributed as if the husband had survived, and the other one-half thereof shall be distributed as if the wife had survived. The provisions of this subsection apply to proceeds of life or accident insurance which are community property and become payable to the estate of either the husband or the wife, as well as to other kinds of community property.

(c) **Survival of Devisees or Beneficiaries.** A devisee who does not survive the testator by 120 hours is treated as if he predeceased the testator, unless the will of the decedent contains some language dealing explicitly with simultaneous death or deaths in a common disaster, or requiring that the devisee survive the testator or survive the testator for a stated period in order to take under the will. If property is so disposed of that the right of a beneficiary to succeed to any interest therein is conditional upon his surviving another person, the beneficiary shall be deemed not to have survived unless he or she survives the person by 120 hours. However, if any interest in property is given alternatively to one of two or more beneficiaries, with the right of each to take being dependent upon his surviving the other or others, and all shall die within a period of less than 120 hours, the property shall be divided into as many equal portions as there are beneficiaries, and those portions shall be distributed respectively to those who would have taken in the event that each beneficiary had survived.

(d) **Joint Owners.** If any real or personal property, including community property with a right of survivorship, shall be so owned that one of two joint owners is entitled to the whole on the death of the other, and neither survives the other by 120 hours, these assets shall be distributed one-half as if one joint owner had survived and the other one-half as if the other joint owner had survived. If there are more than two joint owners and all have died within a period of less than 120 hours, these assets shall be divided into as many equal portions as there are joint owners and these portions shall be distributed respectively to those who would have taken in the event that each joint owner survived.

(e) **Insured and Beneficiary.** When the insured and a beneficiary in a policy of life or accident insurance have died within a period of less than 120 hours, the insured shall be deemed to have survived the beneficiary for the purpose of determining the rights under the policy of the beneficiary or beneficiaries as such. The provisions of this subsection shall not prevent the application of subsection (b) above to the proceeds of life or accident insurance which are community property.

**(f) Instruments Providing Different Disposition.** When provision has been made in the case of wills, living trusts, deeds, or contracts of insurance, or any other situation, for disposition of property different from the provisions of this Section, this Section shall not apply.

Acts 1955, 54th Leg., p. 88, ch. 55, eff. Jan. 1, 1956. Amended by Acts 1965, 59th Leg., p. 279, ch. 119, § 1, eff. Aug. 30, 1965; Acts 1979, 66th Leg., p. 1743, ch. 713, § 6, eff. Aug. 27, 1979; Acts 1993, 73rd Leg., ch. 846, § 5, eff. Sept. 1, 1993.

### Cross References

Prior Death of Legatee, V.T.C.A., Estates Code § 255.152.

## § 47A. Marriage Voidable Based on Mental Incapacity

(a) If a proceeding under Chapter 6, Family Code, to declare a marriage void based on the lack of mental capacity of one of the parties to the marriage is pending on the date of death of one of those parties, or if a guardianship proceeding in which a court is requested under Chapter 6, Family Code, to declare a ward's or proposed ward's marriage void based on the lack of mental capacity of the ward or proposed ward is pending on the date of death of the ward or proposed ward, the court may make the determination and declare the marriage void after the decedent's death. In making that determination after the decedent's death, the court shall apply the standards for an annulment prescribed by Section 6.108(a), Family Code.

(b) Subject to Subsection (c) of this section, if a proceeding described by Subsection (a) of this section is not pending on the date of a decedent's death, an interested person may file an application with the court requesting that the court void the marriage of the decedent if, on the date of the decedent's death, the decedent was married, and that marriage commenced not earlier than three years before the decedent's date of death. The notice applicable to a proceeding for a declaratory judgment under Chapter 37, Civil Practice and Remedies Code, applies to a proceeding under this subsection.

(c) An application requesting that the court void a decedent's marriage authorized by Subsection (b) of this section may not be filed after the first anniversary of the date of the decedent's death.

(d) Except as provided by Subsection (e) of this section, in a proceeding brought under Subsection (b) of this section, the court shall declare the decedent's marriage void if the court finds that, on the date the marriage occurred, the decedent did not have the mental capacity to:

(1) consent to the marriage; and

(2) understand the nature of the marriage ceremony, if a ceremony occurred.

(e) In a proceeding brought under Subsection (b) of this section, a court that makes a finding described by Subsection (d) of this section may not declare the decedent's marriage void if the court finds that, after the date the marriage occurred, the decedent:

(1) gained the mental capacity to recognize the marriage relationship; and

(2) did recognize the marriage relationship.

(f) If the court declares a decedent's marriage void in a proceeding described by Subsection (a) of this section or brought under Subsection (b) of this section, the other party to the marriage is not considered the decedent's surviving spouse for purposes of any law of this state.

Added by Acts 2007, 80th Leg., ch. 1170, § 4.01, eff. Sept. 1, 2007.

## CHAPTER III

## DETERMINATION OF HEIRSHIP

## § 48. Proceedings to Declare Heirship

(a) When a person dies intestate owning or entitled to real or personal property in Texas, and there shall have been no administration in this State upon the person's estate; or when it is necessary for the trustee of a trust holding assets for the benefit of a decedent to determine the heirs of the decedent; or when there has been a will probated in this State or elsewhere, or an administration in this State upon the estate of such decedent, and any real or personal property in this State has been omitted from such will or from such administration, or no final disposition thereof has been made in such administration, the court of the county in which venue would be proper under Section 6C of this code may determine and declare in the manner hereinafter provided who are the heirs and only heirs of such decedent, and their respective shares and interests, under the laws of this State, in the estate of such decedent or, if applicable, in the trust, and proceedings therefor shall be known as proceedings to declare heirship.

(b) If an application for determination of heirship is filed within four (4) years from the date of the death of the decedent, the applicant may request that the court determine whether a necessity for administration exists. The court shall hear evidence upon the issue and make a determination thereof in its judgment.

(c) Repealed by Acts 2011, 82nd Leg., ch. 1338 (S.B. 1198), § 1.42(a).

Acts 1955, 54th Leg., p. 88, ch. 55, eff. Jan. 1, 1956. Amended by Acts 1971, 62nd Leg., p. 971, ch. 173, § 4, eff. Jan. 1, 1972; Acts 1977, 65th Leg., p. 1521, ch. 616, § 1, eff. Aug. 29, 1977. Subsec. (a) amended by Acts 2007, 80th Leg., ch. 1170, § 2.02, eff. Sept. 1, 2007; Sec. heading and Subsec. (a) amended by Acts 2011, 82nd Leg., ch. 1338 (S.B. 1198), §§ 1.09, 1.10, eff. Sept. 1, 2011; Subsec. (c) repealed by Acts 2011, 82nd Leg., ch. 1338 (S.B. 1198), § 1.42(a), eff. Sept. 1, 2011.

## § 49. Who May Institute Proceedings to Declare Heirship

(a) Such proceedings may be instituted and maintained under a circumstance specified in Section 48(a) of this code by the qualified personal representative of the estate of such decedent, by a party seeking the appointment of an independent administrator under Section 145 of this code, by the trustee of a trust holding assets for the benefit of the decedent, by any person or persons claiming to be a secured creditor or the owner of the whole or a part of the estate of such decedent, or by the guardian of the estate of a ward, if the proceedings are instituted and maintained in the probate court in which the proceedings for the guardianship of the estate were pending at the time of the death of the ward. In such a case an application shall be filed in a proper court stating the following information:

(1) the name of the decedent and the time and place of death;

(2) the names and residences of the decedent's heirs, the relationship of each heir to the decedent, and the true interest of the applicant and each of the heirs in the estate of the decedent or in the trust, as applicable;

(3) all the material facts and circumstances within the knowledge and information of the applicant that might reasonably tend to show the time or place of death or the names or residences of all heirs, if the time or place of death or the names or residences of all the heirs are not definitely known to the applicant;

(4) a statement that all children born to or adopted by the decedent have been listed;

(5) a statement that each marriage of the decedent has been listed with the date of the marriage, the name of the spouse, and if the marriage was terminated, the date and place of termination, and other facts to show whether a spouse has had an interest in the property of the decedent;

(6) whether the decedent died testate and if so, what disposition has been made of the will;

(7) a general description of all the real and personal property belonging to the estate of the decedent or held in trust for the benefit of the decedent, as applicable; and

(8) an explanation for the omission of any of the foregoing information that is omitted from the application.

(b) Such application shall be supported by the affidavit of each applicant to the effect that, insofar as is known to such applicant, all the allegations of such application are true in substance and in fact and that no such material fact or circumstance has, within the affiant's knowledge, been omitted from such application. The unknown heirs of such decedent, all persons who are named in the application as heirs of such decedent, and all persons who are, at the date of the filing of the application, shown by the deed records of the county in which any of the real property described in such application is situated to own any share or interest in any such real property, shall be made parties in such proceeding.

Acts 1955, 54th Leg., p. 88, ch. 55, eff. Jan. 1, 1956. Amended by Acts 1971, 62nd Leg., p. 971, ch. 173, § 4, eff. Jan. 1, 1972; Acts 1977, 65th Leg., p. 1522, ch. 616, § 2, eff. Aug. 29, 1977; Acts 1979, 66th Leg., p. 1744, ch. 713, § 7, eff. Aug. 27, 1979; Acts 1983, 68th Leg., p. 629, ch. 139, § 1, eff. Sept. 1, 1983; Acts 1985, 69th Leg., ch. 693, § 1, eff. Sept. 1, 1985; Subsec. (a) amended by Acts 2011, 82nd Leg., ch. 1338 (S.B. 1198), § 1.11, eff. Sept. 1, 2011.

## § 50. Notice

(a) Citation shall be served by registered or certified mail upon all distributees 12 years of age or older whose names and addresses are known, or whose names and addresses can be learned through the exercise of reasonable diligence, provided that the court may in its discretion require that service of citation shall be made by personal service upon some or all of those named as distributees in the application. Citation shall be served as provided by this subsection on the parent, managing conservator, or guardian of a distributee who is younger than 12 years of age, if the name and address of the parent, managing conservator, or guardian is known or can be reasonably ascertained.

(b) If the address of a person or entity on whom citation is required to be served cannot be ascertained, citation shall be served on the person or entity by publication in the county in which the proceedings are commenced, and if the decedent resided in another county, then a citation shall also be published in the county of the decedent's last residence. To determine whether there are any other heirs, citation shall also be served on unknown heirs by publication in the manner provided by this subsection.

(c) Except in proceedings in which there is service of citation by publication as provided by Subsection (b) of this section, citation shall also be posted in the county in which the proceedings are commenced and in the county of the decedent's last residence.

(d) A party to the proceedings who has executed the application need not be served by any method.

(e) A parent, managing conservator, guardian, attorney ad litem, or guardian ad litem of a distributee who is at least 12 years of age but younger than 19 years of age may not waive citation required to be served on the distributee under this section.

Acts 1955, 54th Leg., p. 88, ch. 55, eff. Jan. 1, 1956. Amended by Acts 1971, 62nd Leg., p. 971, ch. 173, § 4, eff. Jan. 1, 1972; Acts 1979, 66th Leg., p. 1745, ch. 713, § 8, eff. Aug. 29, 1979; Acts 1997, 75th Leg., ch. 1130, § 1, eff. Sept. 1, 1997; Acts 2001, 77th Leg., ch. 664, § 2, eff. Sept. 1, 2001.

## § 51. Transfer of Proceeding When Will Probated or Administration Granted

If an administration upon the estate of any such decedent shall be granted in the State, or if the will of such decedent shall be admitted to probate in this State, after the institution of a proceeding to declare heirship, the court in which such proceeding is pending shall, by an order entered of record therein, transfer the cause to the court of the county in which such administration shall have been granted, or such will shall have been probated, and thereupon the clerk of the court in which such proceeding was originally filed shall send to the clerk of the court named in such order, a certified transcript of all pleadings, entries in the judge's probate docket, and orders of the court in such cause. The clerk of the court to which such cause shall be transferred shall file the transcript and record the same in the judge's probate docket of that court and shall docket such cause, and the same shall thereafter proceed as though originally filed in that court. The court, in its discretion, may consolidate the cause so transferred with the pending proceeding.

Acts 1955, 54th Leg., p. 88, ch. 55, eff. Jan. 1, 1956. Amended by Acts 1971, 62nd Leg., p. 971, ch. 173, § 4, eff. Jan. 1, 1972; Acts 2009, 81st Leg., ch. 602, § 4, eff. June 19, 2009.

## § 52. Recorded Instruments as Prima Facie Evidence

(a) A statement of facts concerning the family history, genealogy, marital status, or the identity of the heirs of a decedent shall be received in a proceeding to declare heirship, or in a suit involving title to real or personal property, as prima facie evidence of the facts therein stated, if the statement is contained in either an affidavit or any other instrument legally executed and acknowledged or sworn to before, and certified by, an officer authorized to take acknowledgments or oaths as applicable, or any judgment of a court of record, and if the affidavit or instrument has been of record for five years or more in the deed records of any county in this state in which such real or personal property is located at the time the suit is instituted, or in the deed records of any county of this state in which the decedent had his domicile or fixed place of residence at the time of his death. If there is any error in the statement of facts in such recorded affidavit or instrument, the true facts may be proved by anyone interested in the proceeding in which said affidavit or instrument is offered in evidence.

(b) An affidavit of facts concerning the identity of heirs of a decedent as to an interest in real property that is filed in a proceeding or suit described by Subsection (a) of this section may be in the form described by Section 52A of this code.

(c) An affidavit of facts concerning the identity of heirs of a decedent does not affect the rights of an omitted heir or a creditor of the decedent as otherwise provided by law. This statute shall be cumulative of all other statutes on the same subject, and shall not be construed as abrogating any right to present evidence or to rely on an affidavit of facts conferred by any other statute or rule of law.

Acts 1955, 54th Leg., p. 88, ch. 55, eff. Jan. 1, 1956. Amended by Acts 1969, 61st Leg., p. 1922, ch. 641, § 4, eff. June 12, 1969; Acts 1991, 72nd Leg., ch. 895, § 5, eff. Sept. 1, 1991; Acts 1999, 76th Leg., ch. 1538, § 1, eff. Sept. 1, 1999.

## § 52A. Form of Affidavit of Facts Concerning Identity of Heirs

An affidavit of facts concerning the identity of heirs of a decedent may be in substantially the following form:

### AFFIDAVIT OF FACTS CONCERNING THE IDENTITY OF HEIRS

Before me, the undersigned authority, on this day personally appeared _____ ("Affiant") (insert name of affiant) who, being first duly sworn, upon his/her oath states:

1. My name is _____ (insert name of affiant), and I live at _____ (insert address of affiant's residence). I am personally familiar with the family and marital history of _____ ("Decedent") (insert name of decedent), and I have personal knowledge of the facts stated in this affidavit.

2. I knew decedent from _____ (insert date) until _____ (insert date). Decedent died on _____ (insert date of death). Decedent's place of death was _____ (insert place of death). At the time of decedent's death, decedent's residence was _____ (insert address of decedent's residence).

3. Decedent's marital history was as follows: _____ (insert marital history and, if decedent's spouse is deceased, insert date and place of spouse's death).

4. Decedent had the following children: _____ (insert name, birth date, name of other parent, and current address of child or date of death of child and descendants of deceased child, as applicable, for each child).

5. Decedent did not have or adopt any other children and did not take any other children into decedent's home or raise any other children, except: _____ (insert name of child or names of children, or state "none").

6. (Include if decedent was not survived by descendants.) Decedent's mother was: _____ (insert name, birth date, and current address or date of death of mother, as applicable).

7. (Include if decedent was not survived by descendants.) Decedent's father was: _____ (insert name, birth date, and current address or date of death of father, as applicable).

8. (Include if decedent was not survived by descendants or by both mother and father.) Decedent had the following siblings: _____ (insert name, birth date, and current address or date of death of each sibling and parents of each sibling and descendants of each deceased sibling, as applicable, or state "none").

9. (Optional.) The following persons have knowledge regarding the decedent, the identity of decedent's children, if any, parents, or siblings, if any: _____ (insert names of persons with knowledge, or state "none").

10. Decedent died without leaving a written will. (Modify statement if decedent left a written will.)

11. There has been no administration of decedent's estate. (Modify statement if there has been administration of decedent's estate.)

12. Decedent left no debts that are unpaid, except: _____ (insert list of debts, or state "none").

13. There are no unpaid estate or inheritance taxes, except: _____ (insert list of unpaid taxes, or state "none").

14. To the best of my knowledge, decedent owned an interest in the following real property: _____ (insert list of real property in which decedent owned an interest, or state "none").

15. (Optional.) The following were the heirs of decedent: _____ (insert names of heirs).

16. (Insert additional information as appropriate, such as size of the decedent's estate.)

Signed this ___ day of _____, ___.

_____
(signature of affiant)

State of _____
County of _____

Sworn to and subscribed to before me on _____ (date) by _____ (insert name of affiant).

_____
(signature of notarial officer)

(Seal, if any, of notary) _____

_____
(printed name)

My commission expires: _____

Added by Acts 1999, 76th Leg., ch. 1538, § 2, eff. Sept. 1, 1999.

### § 53. Evidence; Unknown Parties and Incapacitated Persons

(a) The court in its discretion may require all or any part of the evidence admitted in a proceeding to declare heirship to be reduced to writing, and subscribed and sworn to by the witnesses, respectively, and filed in the cause, and recorded in the judge's probate docket.

(b) If it appears to the court that there are or may be living heirs whose names or whereabouts are unknown, or that any defendant is an incapacitated person, the court may, in its discretion, appoint an attorney ad litem or guardian ad litem to represent the interests of any such persons. The court may not appoint an attorney ad litem or guardian ad litem unless the court finds that the appointment is necessary to protect the interests of the living heir or incapacitated person.

(c) The court shall appoint an attorney ad litem to represent the interests of unknown heirs.

Acts 1955, 54th Leg., p. 88, ch. 55, eff. Jan. 1, 1956. Amended by Acts 1971, 62nd Leg., p. 971, ch. 173, § 4, eff. Jan. 1, 1972; Acts 1995, 74th Leg., ch. 1039, § 6, eff. Sept. 1, 1995; Acts 2001, 77th Leg., ch. 664, §§ 3, 4, eff. Sept. 1, 2001; Acts 2009, 81st Leg., ch. 602, § 5, eff. June 19, 2009.

### § 53A. Order for Genetic Testing Authorized

(a) In a proceeding to declare heirship under this chapter, the court may, on the court's own motion, and shall, on the request of a party to the proceeding, order one or more specified individuals to submit to genetic testing as provided for in Subchapter F, Chapter 160, Family Code. If two or more individuals are ordered to be tested, the court may order that the testing of those individuals be done concurrently or sequentially. The court may enforce an order under this subsection by contempt.

(b) Subject to any assessment of costs following the proceeding in accordance with Rule 131, Texas Rules of Civil Procedure, the cost of genetic testing ordered under Subsection (a) of this section must be advanced:

(1) by a party to the proceeding who requests the testing;

(2) as agreed by the parties and approved by the court; or

(3) as ordered by the court.

(c) Subject to Subsection (d) of this section, the court shall order genetic testing subsequent to the testing conducted under Subsection (a) of this section if:

(1) a party to the proceeding contests the results of the genetic testing ordered under Subsection (a) of this section; and

(2) the party contesting the results requests that additional testing be conducted.

(d) If the results of the genetic testing ordered under Subsection (a) of this section identify a tested individual as an heir of the decedent, the court may order additional genetic testing in accordance with Subsection (c) of this section only if the party contesting those results pays for the additional testing in advance.

(e) If a sample of an individual's genetic material that could identify another individual as the decedent's heir is not available for purposes of conducting genetic testing under this section, the court, on a finding of good cause and that the need for genetic testing outweighs the legitimate interests of the individual to be tested, may order any of the following other individuals to submit a sample of genetic material for the testing under circumstances the court considers just:

(1) a parent, sibling, or child of the individual whose genetic material is not available; or

(2) any other relative of that individual, as necessary to conduct the testing.

(f) On good cause shown, the court may order:

(1) genetic testing of a deceased individual under this section; and

(2) if necessary, removal of the remains of the deceased individual as provided by Section 711.004, Health and Safety Code, for that testing.

(g) An individual commits an offense if the individual intentionally releases an identifiable sample of the genetic material of another individual that was provided for purposes of genetic testing ordered under this section, the release is for a purpose not related to the proceeding to declare heirship, and the release was not ordered by the court or done in accordance with written permission obtained from the individual who provided the sample. An offense under this subsection is a Class A misdemeanor.

Added by Acts 2007, 80th Leg., ch. 566, § 1, eff. Sept. 1, 2007.

## § 53B. Results of Genetic Testing; Admissibility

(a) A report of the results of genetic testing ordered under Section 53A of this chapter:

(1) must comply with the requirements for a report prescribed by Section 160.504, Family Code; and

(2) is admissible in a proceeding to declare heirship under this chapter as evidence of the truth of the facts asserted in the report.

(b) The presumption under Section 160.505, Family Code, applies to the results of genetic testing ordered under this section, and the presumption may be rebutted as provided by that section.

(c) A party to the proceeding who contests the results of genetic testing may call one or more genetic testing experts to testify in person or by telephone, videoconference, deposition, or another method approved by the court. Unless otherwise ordered by the court, the party offering the testimony bears the expense for the expert testifying.

Added by Acts 2007, 80th Leg., ch. 566, § 1, eff. Sept. 1, 2007.

## § 53C. Use of Genetic Testing Results in Certain Proceedings to Declare Heirship

(a) This section applies in a proceeding to declare heirship of a decedent only with respect to an individual who:

(1) petitions the court for a determination of right of inheritance as authorized by Section 42(b) of this code; and

(2) claims to be a biological child of the decedent, but with respect to whom a parent-child relationship with the dece-

dent was not established as provided by Section 160.201, Family Code, or who claims inheritance through a biological child of the decedent, if a parent-child relationship between the individual through whom the inheritance is claimed and the decedent was not established as provided by Section 160.201, Family Code.

(b) Unless the results of genetic testing of another individual who is an heir of the decedent are admitted as rebuttal evidence, the court shall find that the individual described by Subsection (a) of this section is an heir of the decedent if the results of genetic testing ordered under Section 53A of this chapter identify a tested individual who is an heir of the decedent as the ancestor of the individual described by Subsection (a) of this section.

(c) Unless the results of genetic testing of another individual who is an heir of the decedent are admitted as rebuttal evidence, the court shall find that the individual described by Subsection (a) of this section is not an heir of the decedent if the results of genetic testing ordered under Section 53A of this chapter exclude a tested individual who is an heir of the decedent as the ancestor of the individual described by Subsection (a) of this section.

(d) If the results of genetic testing ordered under Section 53A of this chapter do not identify or exclude a tested individual as the ancestor of the individual described by Subsection (a) of this section:

(1) the court may not dismiss the proceeding to declare heirship; and

(2) the results of the genetic testing and other relevant evidence are admissible in the proceeding.

Added by Acts 2007, 80th Leg., ch. 566, § 1, eff. Sept. 1, 2007.

## § 53D. Additional Orders Authorized

On the request of an individual determined by the results of genetic testing to be the heir of a decedent and for good cause shown, the court may:

(1) order the name of the individual to be changed; and

(2) if the court orders a name change under Subdivision (1) of this section, order the bureau of vital statistics to issue an amended birth record for the individual.

Added by Acts 2007, 80th Leg., ch. 566, § 1, eff. Sept. 1, 2007.

## § 53E. Proceedings and Records Public

A proceeding under this chapter involving genetic testing is open to the public as in other civil cases, and papers and records in the proceeding are available for public inspection.

Added by Acts 2007, 80th Leg., ch. 566, § 1, eff. Sept. 1, 2007.

## § 54. Judgment

The judgment of the court in a proceeding to declare heirship shall declare the names and places of residence of the heirs of the decedent, and their respective shares and interests in the real and personal property of such decedent.

If the proof is in any respect deficient, the judgment shall so state.

Acts 1955, 54th Leg., p. 88, ch. 55, eff. Jan. 1, 1956. Amended by Acts 1971, 62nd Leg., p. 971, ch. 173, § 4, eff. Jan. 1, 1972.

## § 55. Effect of Judgment

(a) Such judgment shall be a final judgment, and may be appealed or reviewed within the same time limits and in the same manner as may other judgments in probate matters at the instance of any interested person. If any person who is an heir of the decedent is not served with citation by registered or certified mail, or by personal service, he may at any time within four years from the date of such judgment have the same corrected by bill of review, or upon proof of actual fraud, after the passage of any length of time, and may recover from the heirs named in the judgment, and those claiming under them who are not bona fide purchasers for value, his just share of the property or its value.

(b) Although such judgment may later be modified, set aside, or nullified, it shall nevertheless be conclusive in any suit between any heir omitted from the judgment and a bona fide purchaser for value who has purchased real or personal property after entry of the judgment without actual notice of the claim of the omitted heir. Similarly, any person who has delivered funds or property of the decedent to the persons declared to be heirs in the judgment, or has engaged in any other transaction with them, in good faith, after entry of such judgment, shall not be liable therefor to any person.

(c) If the court states in its judgment that there is no necessity for administration on the estate, such recital shall constitute authorization to all persons owing any money to the estate of the decedent, or having custody of any property of such estate, or acting as registrar or transfer agent of any evidence of interest, indebtedness, property, or right belonging to the estate, and to persons purchasing from or otherwise dealing with the heirs as determined in the judgment, to pay, deliver, or transfer such property or evidence of property rights to such heirs, or to purchase property from such heirs, without liability to any creditor of the estate or other person. Such heirs shall be entitled to enforce their right to payment, delivery, or transfer by suit. Nothing in this chapter shall affect the rights or remedies of the creditors of the decedent except as provided in this subsection.

Acts 1955, 54th Leg., p. 88, ch. 55, eff. Jan. 1, 1956. Amended by Acts 1971, 62nd Leg., p. 971, ch. 173, § 4, eff. Jan. 1, 1972; Acts 1979, 66th Leg., p. 1746, ch. 713, § 9, eff. Aug. 29, 1979.

## § 56. Filing of Certified Copy of Judgment

A certified copy of such judgment may be filed for record in the office of the county clerk of the county in which any of the real property described in such judgment is situated, and recorded in the deed records of such county, and indexed in the name of such decedent as grantor and of the heirs named in such judgment as grantees; and, from and after such filing, such judgment shall constitute constructive notice of the facts set forth therein.

Acts 1955, 54th Leg., p. 88, ch. 55, eff. Jan. 1, 1956.

# CHAPTER IV

## EXECUTION AND REVOCATION OF WILLS

## § 57. Who May Execute a Will

Every person who has attained the age of eighteen years, or who is or has been lawfully married, or who is a member of the armed forces of the United States or of the auxiliaries thereof or of the maritime service at the time the will is made, being of sound mind, shall have the right and power to make a last will and testament, under the rules and limitations prescribed by law.

Acts 1955, 54th Leg., p. 88, ch. 55, eff. Jan. 1, 1956. Amended by Acts 1967, 60th Leg., p. 801, ch. 334, § 1, eff. Aug. 28, 1967.

## § 58. Interests Which May Pass Under a Will

(a) Every person competent to make a last will and testament may thereby devise and bequeath all the estate, right, title, and interest in property the person has at the time of the person's death, subject to the limitations prescribed by law.

(b) A person who makes a last will and testament may:

(1) disinherit an heir; and

(2) direct the disposition of property or an interest passing under the will or by intestacy.

(c) A legacy of personal property does not include any contents of the property unless the will directs that the contents are included in the legacy. A devise of real property does not include any personal property located on or associated with the real property or any contents of personal property located on the real property unless the will directs that the personal property or contents are included in the devise.

(d) In this section:

(1) "Contents" means tangible personal property, other than titled personal property, found inside of or on a specifically bequeathed or devised item. The term includes clothing, pictures, furniture, coin collections, and other items of tangible personal property that do not require a formal transfer of title and that are located in another item of tangible personal property such as a cedar chest or other furniture.

(2) "Titled personal property" includes all tangible personal property represented by a certificate of title, certificate of ownership, written label, marking, or designation that signifies ownership by a person. The term includes a motor vehicle, motor home, motorboat, or other similar property that requires a formal transfer of title.

Acts 1955, 54th Leg., p. 88, ch. 55, eff. Jan. 1, 1956. Amended by Acts 1991, 72nd Leg., ch. 895, § 6, eff. Sept. 1, 1991; Acts 1993, 73rd Leg., ch. 846, § 6, eff. Sept. 1, 1993; Acts 1995, 74th Leg., ch. 642, § 1, eff. Sept. 1, 1995.

## § 58a. Devises or Bequests to Trustees

(a) A testator may validly devise or bequeath property in a will to the trustee of a trust established or to be established:

(1) during the testator's lifetime by the testator, by the testator and another person, or by another person, including a funded or unfunded life insurance trust, in which the settlor has reserved any or all rights of ownership of the insurance contracts; or

(2) at the testator's death by the testator's devise or bequest to the trustee, if the trust is identified in the testator's will and its terms are in a written instrument, other than a will, that is executed before, with, or after the execution of the testator's will or in another person's will if that other person has predeceased the testator, regardless of the existence, size, or character of the corpus of the trust.

(b) A devise or bequest is not invalid because the trust is amendable or revocable or because the trust was amended after the execution of the will or the testator's death.

(c) Unless the testator's will provides otherwise, property devised or bequeathed to a trust described by Subsection (a) of this section is not held under a testamentary trust of the testator. The property becomes a part of the trust to which it is devised or bequeathed and must be administered and disposed of in accordance with the provisions of the instrument establishing the trust, including any amendments to the instrument made before or after the testator's death.

(d) Unless the testator's will provides otherwise, a revocation or termination of the trust before the testator's death causes the devise or bequest to lapse.

Added by Acts 1961, 57th Leg., p. 43, ch. 29, § 1. Amended by Acts 1993, 73rd Leg., ch. 846, § 7, eff. Sept. 1, 1993.

## § 58b. Devises and Bequests That Are Void

(a) A devise or bequest of property in a will is void if the devise or bequest is made to:

(1) an attorney who prepares or supervises the preparation of the will;

(2) a parent, descendant of a parent, or employee of the attorney described by Subdivision (1) of this subsection; or

(3) a spouse of an individual described by Subdivision (1) or (2) of this subsection.

(b) This section does not apply to:

(1) a devise or bequest made to a person who:

(A) is the testator's spouse;

(B) is an ascendant or descendant of the testator; or

(C) is related within the third degree by consanguinity or affinity to the testator; or

(2) a bona fide purchaser for value from a devisee in a will.

Added by Acts 1997, 75th Leg., ch. 1054, § 1, eff. Sept. 1, 1997. Amended by Acts 2001, 77th Leg., ch. 527, § 1, eff. June 11, 2001. Subsec. (a) amended by Acts 2005, 79th Leg., ch. 551, § 2, eff. Sept. 1, 2005.

## § 58c. Exercise of Power of Appointment

A testator may not exercise a power of appointment through a residuary clause in the testator's will or through a will providing for general disposition of all the testator's property unless:

(1) the testator makes a specific reference to the power in the will; or

(2) there is some other indication in writing that the testator intended to include the property subject to the power in the will.

Added by Acts 2003, 78th Leg., ch. 1060, § 8, eff. Sept. 1, 2003.

## § 59. Requisites of a Will

(a) Every last will and testament, except where otherwise provided by law, shall be in writing and signed by the testator in person or by another person for him by his direction and in his presence, and shall, if not wholly in the handwriting of the testator, be attested by two or more credible witnesses above the age of fourteen years who shall subscribe their names thereto in their own handwriting in the presence of the testator. Such a will or testament may, at the time of its execution or at any subsequent date during the lifetime of the testator and the witnesses, be made self-proved, and the testimony of the witnesses in the probate thereof may be made unnecessary, by the affidavits of the testator and the attesting witnesses, made before an officer authorized to administer oaths. Provided that nothing shall require an affidavit or certificate of any testator or testatrix as a prerequisite to self-proof of a will or testament other than the certificate set out below. The affidavits shall be evidenced by a certificate, with official seal affixed, of such officer attached or annexed to such will or testament in form and contents substantially as follows:

THE STATE OF TEXAS

COUNTY OF _____

Before me, the undersigned authority, on this day personally appeared _____, _____, and _____, known to me to be the testator and the witnesses, respectively, whose names are subscribed to the annexed or foregoing instrument in their respective capacities, and, all of said persons being by me duly sworn, the said _____, testator, declared to me and to the said witnesses in my presence that said instrument is his last will and testament, and that he had willingly made and executed it as his free act and deed; and the said witnesses, each on his oath stated to me, in the presence and hearing of the said testator, that the said testator had declared to them that said instrument is his last will and testament, and that he executed same as such and wanted each of them to sign it as a witness; and upon their oaths each witness stated further that they did sign the same as witnesses in the presence of the said testator and at his request; that he was at that time eighteen years of age or over (or being under such age, was or had been lawfully married, or was then a member of the armed forces of the United States or of an auxiliary thereof or of the Maritime Service) and was of sound mind; and that each of said witnesses was then at least fourteen years of age.

_____
Testator
_____
Witness
_____
Witness

Subscribed and sworn to before me by the said _____, testator, and by the said _____ and _____, witnesses, this _____ day of _____ A.D. _____
(SEAL)

(Signed) _____
(Official Capacity of Officer)

(a–1) As an alternative to the self-proving of a will by the affidavits of the testator and the attesting witnesses under Subsection (a) of this section, a will may be simultaneously executed, attested, and made self-proved before an officer authorized to administer oaths, and the testimony of the witnesses in the probate of the will may be made unnecessary, with the inclusion in the will of the following in form and contents substantially as follows:

I, _____, as testator, after being duly sworn, declare to the undersigned witnesses and to the undersigned authority that this instrument is my will, that I have willingly made and executed it in the presence of the undersigned witnesses, all of whom were present at the same time, as my free act and deed, and that I have requested each of the undersigned witnesses to sign this will in my presence and in the presence of each other. I now sign this will in the presence of the attesting witnesses and the undersigned authority on this _____ day of _____, 20_____.

_____
Testator

The undersigned, _____ and _____, each being above fourteen years of age, after being duly sworn, declare to the testator and to the undersigned authority that the testator declared to us that this instrument is the testator's will and that the testator requested us to act as witnesses to the testator's will and signature. The testator then signed this will in our presence, all of us being present at the same time. The testator is eighteen years of age or over (or being under such age, is or has been lawfully married, or is a member of the armed forces of the United States or of an auxiliary thereof or of the Maritime Service), and we believe the testator to be of sound mind. We now sign our names as attesting witnesses in the presence of the testator, each other, and the undersigned authority on this _____ day of _____, 20_____.

_____
Witness
_____
Witness

Subscribed and sworn to before me by the said _____, testator, and by the said _____ and _____, witnesses, this _____ day of _____, 20_____.
(SEAL)

(Signed) _____
(Official Capacity of Officer)

(b) An affidavit in form and content substantially as provided by Subsection (a) of this section is a "self-proving affidavit." A will with a self-proving affidavit subscribed and sworn to by the testator and witnesses attached or annexed to the will, or a will simultaneously executed, attested, and made self-proved as provided by Subsection (a–1) of this section, is a "self-proved will." Substantial compliance with the form provided by Subsection (a) or (a–1) of this section shall suffice to cause the will to be self-proved. For this purpose, an affidavit that is subscribed and acknowledged by the testator and subscribed and sworn to by the witnesses would suffice as being in substantial compliance. A signature on a self-proving affidavit as provided by Subsection (a) of this section is considered a signature to the will if necessary to prove that the will was signed by the testator or witnesses, or both, but in that case, the will may not be considered a self-proved will.

(c) A self-proved will may be admitted to probate without the testimony of any subscribing witness, but otherwise it shall be treated no differently than a will not self-proved. In particular and without limiting the generality of the foregoing, a self-proved will may be contested, or revoked or amended by a codicil in exactly the same fashion as a will not self-proved.

Acts 1955, 54th Leg., p. 88, ch. 55, eff. Jan. 1, 1956. Amended by Acts 1961, 57th Leg., p. 936, ch. 412, § 1, eff. June 17, 1961; Acts 1969, 61st Leg., p. 1922, ch. 641, § 5, eff. June 12, 1969; Acts 1971, 62nd Leg., p. 974, ch. 173, § 5, eff. Jan. 1, 1972; Acts 1991, 72nd Leg., ch. 895, § 7, eff. Sept. 1, 1991; Subsecs. (a), (b) amended by and Subsec. (a–1) added by Acts 2011, 82nd Leg., ch. 1338 (S.B. 1198), § 1.12, eff. Sept. 1, 2011.

## § 59A. Contracts Concerning Succession

(a) A contract to make a will or devise, or not to revoke a will or devise, if executed or entered into on or after September 1, 1979, can be established only by:

(1) provisions of a written agreement that is binding and enforceable; or

(2) provisions of a will stating that a contract does exist and stating the material provisions of the contract.

(b) The execution of a joint will or reciprocal wills does not by itself suffice as evidence of the existence of a contract.

Added by Acts 1979, 66th Leg., p. 1746, ch. 713, § 10, eff. Aug. 27, 1979.

Subsec. (a) amended by Acts 2003, 78th Leg., ch. 1060, § 9, eff. Sept. 1, 2003.

## § 60. Exception Pertaining to Holographic Wills

Where the will is written wholly in the handwriting of the testator, the attestation of the subscribing witnesses may be dispensed with. Such a will may be made self-proved at any time during the testator's lifetime by the attachment or annexation thereto of an affidavit by the testator to the effect that the instrument is his last will; that he was at least eighteen years of age when he executed it (or, if under such age, was or had been lawfully married, or was then a member of the armed forces of the United States or of an auxiliary thereof or of the Maritime Service); that he was of sound mind; and that he has not revoked such instrument.

Acts 1955, 54th Leg., p. 88, ch. 55, eff. Jan. 1, 1956. Amended by Acts 1969, 61st Leg., p. 1922, ch. 641, § 6, eff. June 12, 1969.

## § 61. Bequest to Witness

Should any person be a subscribing witness to a will, and also be a legatee or devisee therein, if the will cannot be otherwise established, such bequest shall be void, and such witness shall be allowed and compelled to appear and give his testimony in like manner as if no such bequest had been made. But, if in such case the witness would have been entitled to a share of the estate of the testator had there been no will, he shall be entitled to as much of such share as shall not exceed the value of the bequest to him in the will.

Acts 1955, 54th Leg., p. 88, ch. 55, eff. Jan. 1, 1956.

## § 62. Corroboration of Testimony of Interested Witness

In the situation covered by the preceding Section, the bequest to the subscribing witness shall not be void if his testimony proving the will is corroborated by one or more disinterested and credible persons who testify that the testimony of the subscribing witness is true and correct, and such subscribing witness shall not be regarded as an incompetent or non-credible witness under Section 59 of this Code.

Acts 1955, 54th Leg., p. 88, ch. 55, eff. Jan. 1, 1956.

## § 63. Revocation of Wills

No will in writing, and no clause thereof or devise therein, shall be revoked, except by a subsequent will, codicil, or declaration in writing, executed with like formalities, or by the testator destroying or canceling the same, or causing it to be done in his presence.

Acts 1955, 54th Leg., p. 88, ch. 55, eff. Jan. 1, 1956.

## § 64. Forfeiture Clause

A provision in a will that would cause a forfeiture of or void a devise or provision in favor of a person for bringing any court action, including contesting a will, is enforceable unless in a court action determining whether the forfeiture clause should be enforced, the person who brought the action contrary to the forfeiture clause establishes by a preponderance of the evidence that:

(1) just cause existed for bringing the action; and

(2) the action was brought and maintained in good faith.

Added by Acts 2009, 81st Leg., ch. 414, § 1, eff. June 19, 2009. Amended by Acts 2011, 82nd Leg., ch. 1338 (S.B. 1198), § 1.13, eff. Sept. 1, 2011; Acts 2013, 83rd Leg., ch. 351 (H.B. 2380), § 1.01, eff. Sept. 1, 2013.

## § 65. Repealed by Acts 2007, 80th Leg., ch. 1170, § 5.05, eff. September 1, 2007

## § 66. Repealed by Acts 1979, 66th Leg., p. 1746, ch. 713, § 11, eff. Aug. 27, 1979

## § 67. Pretermitted Child

(a) Whenever a pretermitted child is not mentioned in the testator's will, provided for in the testator's will, or otherwise provided for by the testator, the pretermitted child shall succeed to a portion of the testator's estate as provided by Subsection (a)(1) or (a)(2) of this section, except as limited by Subsection (e) of this section.

(1) If the testator has one or more children living when he executes his last will, and:

(A) No provision is made therein for any such child, a pretermitted child succeeds to the portion of the testator's separate and community estate to which the pretermitted child would have been entitled pursuant to Section 38(a) of this code had the testator died intestate without a surviving spouse owning only that portion of his estate not devised or bequeathed to the other parent of the pretermitted child.

(B) Provision, whether vested or contingent, is made therein for one or more of such children, a pretermitted child is entitled to share in the testator's estate as follows:

(i) The portion of the testator's estate to which the pretermitted child is entitled is limited to the disposition made to children under the will.

(ii) The pretermitted child shall receive such share of the testator's estate, as limited in Subparagraph (i), as he would have received had the testator included all pretermitted children with the children upon whom benefits were conferred under the will, and given an equal share of such benefits to each such child.

(iii) To the extent that it is feasible, the interest of the pretermitted child in the testator's estate shall be of the same character, whether an equitable or legal life estate or in fee, as the interest that the testator conferred upon his children under the will.

(2) If the testator has no child living when he executes his last will, the pretermitted child succeeds to the portion of the testator's separate and community estate to which the pretermitted child would have been entitled pursuant to Section 38(a) of this code had the testator died intestate without a surviving spouse owning only that portion of his estate not devised or bequeathed to the other parent of the pretermitted child.

(b) The pretermitted child may recover the share of the testator's estate to which he is entitled either from the other children under Subsection (a)(1)(B) or the testamentary beneficiaries under Subsections (a)(1)(A) and (a)(2) other than the other parent of the pretermitted child, ratably, out of the portions of such estate passing to such persons under the will. In abating the interests of such beneficiaries, the character of the testamentary plan adopted by the testator shall be preserved to the maximum extent possible.

(c) A "pretermitted child," as used in this section, means a child of a testator who, during the lifetime of the testator, or after his death, is born or adopted after the execution of the will of the testator.

(d) For the purposes of this section, a child is provided for or a provision is made for a child if a disposition of property to or for the benefit of the pretermitted child, whether vested or contingent, is made:

(1) in the testator's will, including a devise or bequest to a trustee as authorized by Section 58(a) of this code; or

(2) outside the testator's will and is intended to take effect at the testator's death.

(e) If a pretermitted child's other parent is not the surviving spouse of the testator, the portion of the testator's estate to which the pretermitted child is entitled under Subsection (a)(1)(A) or (a)(2) of this section may not reduce the portion of the testator's estate passing to the testator's surviving spouse by more than one-half.

Acts 1955, 54th Leg., p. 88, ch. 55, eff. Jan. 1, 1956. Amended by Acts 1989, 71st Leg., ch. 1035, § 5, eff. Sept. 1, 1989; Acts 1991, 72nd Leg., ch. 895, § 8, eff. Sept. 1, 1993; Acts 1993, 73rd Leg., ch. 846, § 8, eff. Sept. 1, 1993. Subsec. (a) amended by Acts 2003, 78th Leg., ch. 1060, § 10, eff. Sept. 1, 2003; Subsecs. (a) and (b) amended and subsec. (e) added by Acts 2011, 82nd Leg., ch. 1338 (S.B. 1198), § 1.14, eff. Sept. 1, 2011.

## § 68. Prior Death of Legatee

(a) If a devisee who is a descendant of the testator or a descendant of a testator's parent is deceased at the time of the execution of the will, fails to survive the testator, or is treated as if the devisee predeceased the testator by Section 47 of this code or otherwise, the descendants of the devisee who survived the testator by 120 hours take the devised property in place of the devisee. The property shall be divided into as many shares as there are surviving descendants in the nearest degree of kinship to the devisee and deceased persons in the same degree whose descendants survived the testator. Each surviving descendant in the nearest degree receives one share, and the share of each deceased person in the same degree is divided among his descendants by representation. For purposes of this section, a person who would have been a devisee under a class gift if the person had survived the testator is treated as a devisee unless the person died before the date the will was executed.

(b) Except as provided by Subsection (a) of this section, if a devise or bequest, other than a residuary devise or bequest, fails for any reason, the devise or bequest becomes a part of the residuary estate.

(c) Except as provided by Subsection (a) of this section, if the residuary estate is devised to two or more persons and the share of one of the residuary devisees fails for any reason, the residuary devisee's share passes to the other residuary devisees, in proportion to the residuary devisee's interest in the residuary estate.

(d) Except as provided by Subsection (a) of this section, if all residuary devisees are dead at the time of the execution of the will, fail to survive the testator, or are treated as if they predeceased the testator, the residuary estate passes as if the testator had died intestate.

(e) This section applies unless the testator's last will and testament provides otherwise. For example, a devise or bequest in the testator's will such as "to my surviving children" or "to such of my children as shall survive me" prevents the application of Subsection (a) of this section.

Acts 1955, 54th Leg., p. 88, ch. 55, eff. Jan. 1, 1956. Amended by Acts 1991, 72nd Leg., ch. 895, § 9, eff. Sept. 1, 1991; Acts 1993, 73rd Leg., ch. 846, § 9, eff. Sept. 1, 1993.

## § 69. Will Provisions Made Before Dissolution of Marriage

(a) In this section, "relative" means an individual who is related to another individual by consanguinity or affinity, as determined under Sections 573.022 and 573.024, Government Code, respectively.

(b) If, after making a will, the testator's marriage is dissolved, whether by divorce, annulment, or a declaration that the marriage is void, all provisions in the will, including all fiduciary appointments, shall be read as if the former spouse and each relative of the former spouse who is not a relative of the testator failed to survive the testator, unless the will expressly provides otherwise.

(c) A person whose marriage to the decedent has been dissolved, whether by divorce, annulment, or a declaration that the marriage is void, is not a surviving spouse unless, by virtue of a subsequent marriage, the person is married to the decedent at the time of death and the subsequent marriage is not declared void under Section 47A of this code.

Acts 1955, 54th Leg., p. 88, ch. 55, eff. Jan. 1, 1956. Amended by Acts 1979, 66th Leg., p. 1746, ch. 713, § 12, eff. Aug. 27, 1979; Acts 1995, 74th Leg., ch. 642, § 2, eff. Sept. 1, 1995; Acts 1997, 75th Leg., ch. 1302, § 5, eff. Sept. 1, 1997.

Amended by Acts 2007, 80th Leg., ch. 1170, § 4.02, eff. Sept. 1, 2007.

## § 69A. Changing Wills

(a) A court may not prohibit a person from executing a new will or a codicil to an existing will.

(b) Notwithstanding Section 3(g) of this code, in this section, "court" means a constitutional county court, district court, or statutory county court, including a statutory probate court.

Added by Acts 1993, 73rd Leg., ch. 120, § 1, eff. Sept. 1, 1993.

## § 70. Repealed by Acts 2011, 82nd Leg., ch. 1338 (S.B. 1198), § 1.42(a), eff. Sept. 1, 2011

## § 70A. Increase in Securities; Accessions

(a) Unless the will clearly provides otherwise, a devise of securities that are owned by the testator on the date of execution of the will includes the following additional securities subsequently acquired by the testator as a result of the testator's ownership of the devised securities:

(1) securities of the same organization acquired because of action initiated by the organization or any successor, related, or acquiring organization, including stock splits, stock dividends, and new issues of stock acquired in a reorganization, redemption, or exchange, other than securities acquired through the exercise of purchase options or through a plan of reinvestment; and

(2) securities of another organization acquired as a result of a merger, consolidation, reorganization, or other distribution by the organization or any successor, related, or acquiring organization, including stock splits, stock dividends, and new issues of stock acquired in a reorganization, redemption, or exchange, other than securities acquired through the exercise of purchase options or through a plan of reinvestment.

(b) Unless the will clearly provides otherwise, a devise of securities does not include a cash distribution relating to the securities and accruing before death, whether or not the distribution is paid before death.

(c) In this section:

(1) "Securities" has the meaning assigned by Section 4, The Securities Act (Article 581–4, Vernon's Texas Civil Statutes), and its subsequent amendments.

(2) "Stock" means securities.

Added by Acts 1993, 73rd Leg., ch. 846, § 10, eff. Sept. 1, 1993.

## § 71. Deposit of Will With Court During Testator's Lifetime

(a) **Deposit of Will.** A will may be deposited by the person making it, or by another person for him, with the county clerk of the county of the testator's residence. Before accepting any will for deposit, the clerk may require such proof as shall be satisfactory to him concerning the testator's identity and residence. The clerk, on being paid a fee of Five Dollars therefor, shall receive and keep the will, and shall give a certificate of deposit for it. All wills so filed shall be numbered by the clerk in consecutive order, and all certificates of deposit shall bear like numbers respectively.

(b) **How Will Shall Be Enclosed.** Every will intended to be deposited with a county clerk shall be enclosed in a sealed wrapper, which shall have indorsed thereon "Will of," followed by the name, address and signature of the testator. The wrapper must also be indorsed with the name and current address of each person who shall be notified of the deposit of the will after the death of the testator.

(c) **Index To Be Kept of All Wills Deposited.** Each county clerk shall keep an index of all wills so deposited with him.

(d) **To Whom Will Shall Be Delivered.** During the lifetime of the testator, a will so deposited shall be delivered only to the testator, or to another person authorized by him by a sworn written order. Upon delivery of the will to the testator or to a person so authorized by him, the certificate of deposit issued for the will shall be surrendered by the person to whom delivery of the will is made; provided, however, that in lieu of the surrender of such certificate, the clerk may, in his discretion, accept and file an affidavit by the testator to the effect that the certificate of deposit has been lost, stolen, or destroyed.

(e) **Proceedings Upon Death of Testator.** If there shall be submitted to the clerk an affidavit to the effect that the testator of any will deposited with the clerk has died, or if the clerk shall receive any other notice or proof of the death of such testator which shall suffice to convince him that the testator is deceased, the clerk shall notify by registered mail with return receipt requested the person or persons named on the indorsement of the wrapper of the will that the will is on deposit in his office, and, upon request, he shall deliver the will to such person or persons, taking a receipt therefor. If the notice by registered mail is returned undelivered, or if a clerk has accepted a will which does not specify on the wrapper the person or persons to whom it shall be delivered, the clerk shall open the wrapper and inspect the will. If an executor is named in the will, he shall be notified by registered mail, with return receipt requested, that the will is on deposit, and, upon request, the clerk shall deliver the will to the person so named as executor. If no executor is named in the will, or if the person so named is deceased, or fails to take the will within thirty days after the clerk's notice to him is mailed, or if notice to the person so named is returned undelivered, the clerk shall give notice by registered mail, with return receipt requested, to the devisees and legatees named in the will that the will is on deposit, and, upon request, the clerk shall deliver the will to any or all of such devisees and legatees.

**(f) Depositing Has No Legal Significance.** These provisions for the depositing of a will during the lifetime of a testator are solely for the purpose of providing a safe and convenient repository for such a will, and no will which has been so deposited shall be treated for purposes of probate any differently than any will which has not been so deposited. In particular, and without limiting the generality of the foregoing, a will which is not deposited shall be admitted to probate upon proof that it is the last will and testament of the testator, notwithstanding the fact that the same testator has on deposit with the court a prior will which has been deposited in accordance with the provisions of this Code.

**(g) Depositing Does Not Constitute Notice.** The fact that a will has been deposited as provided herein shall not constitute notice of any character, constructive or otherwise, to any person as to the existence of such will or as to the contents thereof.

Acts 1955, 54th Leg., p. 88, ch. 55, eff. Jan. 1, 1956.
Amended by Acts 2007, 80th Leg., ch. 275, § 1, eff. June 15, 2007.

### § 71A. No Right to Exoneration of Debts; Exception

(a) Except as provided by Subsection (b) of this section, a specific devise passes to the devisee subject to each debt secured by the property that exists on the date of the testator's death, and the devisee has no right to exoneration from the testator's estate for payment of the debt.

(b) A specific devise does not pass to the devisee subject to a debt described by Subsection (a) of this section if the will in which the devise is made specifically states that the devise passes without being subject to the debt. A general provision in the will stating that debts are to be paid is not a specific statement for purposes of this subsection.

(c) Subsection (a) of this section does not affect the rights of creditors provided under this code or the rights of other persons or entities provided under Part 3, Chapter VIII, of this code. If a creditor elects to have a debt described by Subsection (a) of this section allowed and approved as a matured secured claim, the claim shall be paid in accordance with Section 306(c–1) of this code.

Added by Acts 2005, 79th Leg., ch. 551, § 3, eff. Sept. 1, 2005.

### CHAPTER V

### PROBATE AND GRANT OF ADMINISTRATION

PART 1. ESTATES OF DECEDENTS

**Text of Texas Probate Code effective until January 1, 2014**

## PART 1.   ESTATES OF DECEDENTS

### § 72.   Proceedings Before Death; Administration in Absence of Direct Evidence of Death; Distribution; Limitation of Liability; Restoration of Estate; Validation of Proceedings

(a) The probate of a will or administration of an estate of a living person shall be void; provided, however, that the court shall have jurisdiction to determine the fact, time and place of death, and where application is made for the grant of letters testamentary or of administration upon the estate of a person believed to be dead and there is no direct evidence that such person is dead but the death of such person shall be proved by circumstantial evidence to the satisfaction of the court, such letters shall be granted. Distribution of the estate to the persons entitled thereto shall not be made by the personal representative until after the expiration of three (3) years from the date such letters are granted. If in a subsequent action such person shall be proved by direct evidence to have been living at any time subsequent to the date of grant of such letters, neither the personal representative nor anyone who shall deliver said estate or any part thereof to another under orders of the court shall be liable therefor; and provided further, that such person shall be entitled to restoration of said estate or the residue thereof with the rents and profits therefrom, except real or personal property sold by the personal representative or any distributee, his successors or assigns, to bona fide purchasers for value, in which case the right of such person to the restoration shall be limited to the proceeds of such sale or the residue thereof with the increase thereof. In no event shall the bonds of such personal representative be void provided, however, that the surety shall have no liability for any acts of the personal representative which were done in compliance with or approved by an order of the court. Probate proceedings upon estates of persons believed to be dead brought prior to the effective date of this Act and all such probate proceedings then pending, except such probate proceedings contested in any litigation pending on the effective date of this Act, are hereby validated insofar as the court's finding of death of such person is concerned.

(b) In any case in which the fact of death must be proved by circumstantial evidence, the court, at the request of any interested person, may direct that citation be issued to the person supposed to be dead, and served upon him by publication and by posting, and by such additional means as the court may by its order direct. After letters testamentary or of administration have been issued, the court may also direct the personal representative to make a search for the person supposed to be dead by notifying law enforcement agencies and public welfare agencies in appropriate locations that such person has disappeared, and may further direct that the applicant engage the services of an investigative agency to make a search for such person. The expenses of search and notices shall be taxed as costs and shall be paid out of the property of the estate.

Acts 1955, 54th Leg., p. 88, ch. 55, eff. Jan. 1, 1956.  Amended by Acts 1959, 56th Leg., p. 950, ch. 442, § 1, eff. May 30, 1959; Acts 1971, 62nd Leg., p. 975, ch. 173, § 7, eff. Jan. 1, 1972.

### § 73.   Period for Probate

(a) No will shall be admitted to probate after the lapse of four years from the death of the testator unless it be shown by proof that the party applying for such probate was not in default in failing to present the same for probate within the four years aforesaid; and in no case shall letters testamentary be issued where a will is admitted to probate after the lapse of four years from the death of the testator.

(b) If any person shall purchase real or personal property from the heirs of a decedent more than four years from the date of the death of the decedent, for value, in good faith, and without knowledge of the existence of a will, such purchaser shall be held to have good title to the interest which such heir or heirs would have had in the absence of a will, as against the claims of any devisees or legatees under any will which may thereafter be offered for probate.

Acts 1955, 54th Leg., p. 88, ch. 55, eff. Jan. 1, 1956.  Amended by Acts 1971, 62nd Leg., p. 976, ch. 173, § 8, eff. Jan. 1, 1972.

### § 74.   Time to File Application for Letters Testamentary or Administration

All applications for the grant of letters testamentary or of administration upon an estate must be filed within four years after the death of the testator or intestate; provided, that this section shall not apply in any case where administration is necessary in order to receive or recover funds or other property due to the estate of the decedent.

Acts 1955, 54th Leg., p. 88, ch. 55, eff. Jan. 1, 1956.  Amended by Acts 1971, 62nd Leg., p. 976, ch. 173, § 8, eff. Jan. 1, 1972.

## § 75. Duty and Liability of Custodian of Will

Upon receiving notice of the death of a testator, the person having custody of the testator's will shall deliver it to the clerk of the court which has jurisdiction of the estate. On sworn written complaint that any person has the last will of any testator, or any papers belonging to the estate of a testator or intestate, the county judge shall cause said person to be cited by personal service to appear before him and show cause why he should not deliver such will to the court for probate, or why he should not deliver such papers to the executor or administrator. Upon the return of such citation served, unless delivery is made or good cause shown, if satisfied that such person had such will or papers at the time of filing the complaint, such judge may cause him to be arrested and imprisoned until he shall so deliver them. Any person refusing to deliver such will or papers shall also be liable to any person aggrieved for all damages sustained as a result of such refusal, which damages may be recovered in any court of competent jurisdiction.

Acts 1955, 54th Leg., p. 88, ch. 55, eff. Jan. 1, 1956.

## § 76. Persons Who May Make Application

An executor named in a will or any interested person may make application to the court of a proper county:

(a) For an order admitting a will to probate, whether the same is written or unwritten, in his possession or not, is lost, is destroyed, or is out of the State.

(b) For the appointment of the executor named in the will.

(c) For the appointment of an administrator, if no executor is designated in the will, or if the person so named is disqualified, or refuses to serve, or is dead, or resigns, or if there is no will. An application for probate may be combined with an application for the appointment of an executor or administrator; and a person interested in either the probate of the will or the appointment of a personal representative may apply for both.

Acts 1955, 54th Leg., p. 88, ch. 55, eff. Jan. 1, 1956.

## § 77. Order of Persons Qualified to Serve

Letters testamentary or of administration shall be granted to persons who are qualified to act, in the following order:

(a) To the person named as executor in the will of the deceased.

(b) To the surviving husband or wife.

(c) To the principal devisee or legatee of the testator.

(d) To any devisee or legatee of the testator.

(e) To the next of kin of the deceased, the nearest in order of descent first, and so on, and next of kin includes a person and his descendants who legally adopted the deceased or who have been legally adopted by the deceased.

(f) To a creditor of the deceased.

(g) To any person of good character residing in the county who applies therefor.

(h) To any other person not disqualified under the following Section. When applicants are equally entitled, letters shall be granted to the applicant who, in the judgment of the court, is most likely to administer the estate advantageously, or they may be granted to any two or more of such applicants.

Acts 1955, 54th Leg., p. 88, ch. 55, eff. Jan. 1, 1956. Amended by Acts 1979, 66th Leg., p. 1763, ch. 713, § 34, eff. Aug. 27, 1979.

## § 78. Persons Disqualified to Serve as Executor or Administrator

No person is qualified to serve as an executor or administrator who is:

(a) An incapacitated person;

(b) A convicted felon, under the laws either of the United States or of any state or territory of the United States, or of the District of Columbia, unless such person has been duly pardoned, or his civil rights restored, in accordance with law;

(c) A non-resident (natural person or corporation) of this State who has not appointed a resident agent to accept service of process in all actions or proceedings with respect to the estate, and caused such appointment to be filed with the court;

(d) A corporation not authorized to act as a fiduciary in this State; or

(e) A person whom the court finds unsuitable.

Acts 1955, 54th Leg., p. 88, ch. 55, eff. Jan. 1, 1956. Amended by Acts 1957, 55th Leg., p. 53, ch. 31, § 2a, eff. Aug. 22, 1957; Acts 1969, 61st Leg., p. 1922, ch. 641, § 7, eff. June 12, 1969; Acts 1995, 74th Leg., ch. 1039, § 7, eff. Sept. 1, 1995.

## § 79. Waiver of Right to Serve

The surviving husband or wife, or, if there be none, the heirs or any one of the heirs of the deceased to the exclusion of any person not equally entitled, may, in open court, or by power of attorney duly authenticated and filed with the county clerk of the county where the application is filed, renounce his right to letters testamentary or of administration in favor of another qualified person, and thereupon the court may grant letters to such person.

Acts 1955, 54th Leg., p. 88, ch. 55, eff. Jan. 1, 1956.

## § 80. Prevention of Administration

(a) Method of Prevention. When application is made for letters of administration upon an estate by a creditor, and other interested persons do not desire an administration thereupon, they can defeat such application:

(1) By the payment of the claim of such creditor; or

(2) By proof to the satisfaction of the court that such claim is fictitious, fraudulent, illegal, or barred by limitation; or

(3) By executing a bond payable to, and to be approved by, the judge in double the amount of such creditor's debt, conditioned that the obligors will pay the debt of such applicant upon the establishment thereof by suit in any court in the county having jurisdiction of the amount.

**(b) Filing of Bond.** The bond provided for, when given and approved, shall be filed with the county clerk, and any creditor for whose protection it was executed may sue thereon in his own name for the recovery of his debt.

**(c) Bond Secured by Lien.** A lien shall exist on all of the estate in the hands of the distributees of such estate, and those claiming under them with notice of such lien, to secure the ultimate payment of the bond provided for herein.

Acts 1955, 54th Leg., p. 88, ch. 55, eff. Jan. 1, 1956.

### § 81.  Contents of Application for Letters Testamentary

(a) For Probate of a Written Will. A written will shall, if within the control of the applicant, be filed with the application for its probate, and shall remain in the custody of the county clerk unless removed therefrom by order of a proper court. An application for probate of a written will shall state:

(1) The name and domicile of each applicant.

(2) The name, age if known, and domicile of the decedent, and the fact, time, and place of death.

(3) Facts showing that the court has venue.

(4) That the decedent owned real or personal property, or both, describing the same generally, and stating its probable value.

(5) The date of the will, the name and residence of the executor named therein, if any, and if none be named, then the name and residence of the person to whom it is desired that letters be issued, and also the names and residences of the subscribing witnesses, if any.

(6) Whether a child or children born or adopted after the making of such will survived the decedent, and the name of each such survivor, if any.

(7) That such executor or applicant, or other person to whom it is desired that letters be issued, is not disqualified by law from accepting letters.

(8) Whether a marriage of the decedent was ever dissolved after the will was made and if so, when and from whom.

(9) Whether the state, a governmental agency of the state, or a charitable organization is named by the will as a devisee.

The foregoing matters shall be stated and averred in the application to the extent that they are known to the applicant, or can with reasonable diligence be ascertained by him, and if any of such matters is not stated or averred in the application, the application shall set forth the reason why such matter is not so stated and averred.

**(b) For Probate of Written Will Not Produced.** When a written will cannot be produced in court, in addition to the requirements of Subsection (a) hereof, the application shall state:

(1) The reason why such will cannot be produced.

(2) The contents of such will, as far as known.

(3) The date of such will and the executor appointed therein, if any, as far as known.

(4) The name, age, marital status, and address, if known, and the relationship to the decedent, if any, of each devisee, and of each person who would inherit as an heir in the absence of a valid will, and, in cases of partial intestacy, of each heir.

(c)  Repealed by Acts 2007, 80th leg., ch. 1170, § 5.05.

Acts 1955, 54th Leg., p. 88, ch. 55, eff. Jan. 1, 1956.  Amended by Acts 1971, 62nd Leg., p. 976, ch. 173, § 9, eff. Jan. 1, 1972; Acts 1987, 70th Leg., ch. 463, § 1, eff. Sept. 1, 1987; Acts 1989, 71st Leg., ch. 1035, § 6, eff. Sept. 1, 1989; Acts 1997, 75th Leg., ch. 1302, § 6, eff. Sept. 1, 1997; subsec. (c) repealed by Acts 2007, 80th Leg., ch. 1170, § 5.05, eff. Sept. 1, 2007; subsec. (a)(8) amended by Acts 2009, 81st Leg., ch. 633, § 1, eff. Sept. 1, 2009; subsec. (a)(8) amended by Acts 2011, 82nd Leg., ch. 1338 (S.B. 1198), § 1.15, eff. Sept. 1, 2011.

### § 82.  Contents of Application for Letters of Administration

An application for letters of administration when no will is alleged to exist shall state:

(a) The name and domicile of the applicant, relationship to the decedent, if any, and that the applicant is not disqualified by law to act as administrator;

(b) The name and intestacy of the decedent, and the fact, time and place of death;

(c) Facts necessary to show venue in the court to which the application is made;

(d) Whether the decedent owned real or personal property, with a statement of its probable value;

(e) The name, age, marital status and address, if known, and the relationship, if any, of each heir to the decedent;

(f) If known by the applicant at the time of the filing of the application, whether children were born to or adopted by the decedent, with the name and the date and place of birth of each;

(g) If known by the applicant at the time of the filing of the application, whether the decedent was ever divorced, and if so, when and from whom; and

(h) That a necessity exists for administration of the estate, alleging the facts which show such necessity.

Acts 1955, 54th Leg., p. 88, ch. 55, eff. Jan. 1, 1956.  Amended by Acts 1979, 66th Leg., p. 1746, ch. 713, § 13, eff. Aug. 27, 1979; Acts 1987, 70th Leg., ch. 463, § 2, eff. Sept. 1, 1987; Acts 1997, 75th Leg., ch. 1302, § 7, eff. Sept. 1, 1997.

Amended by Acts 2007, 80th Leg., ch. 1170, § 5.01, eff. Sept. 1, 2007.

### § 83.  Procedure Pertaining to a Second Application

(a) Where Original Application Has Not Been Heard. If, after an application for the probate of a will or for the appointment of a general personal representative has been filed, and before such application has been heard, an application for the probate of a will of the decedent, not theretofore presented for probate, is filed, the court shall hear both applications together and determine what instrument, if any, should be admitted to probate, or whether the decedent died intestate. The court may not sever or bifurcate the proceeding on the applications.

**(b) Where First Will Has Been Admitted to Probate.** If, after a will has been admitted to probate, an application for the probate of a will of the decedent, not theretofore presented for probate, is filed, the court shall determine whether the former probate should be set aside, and whether such other will should be admitted to probate, or whether the decedent died intestate.

**(c) Where Letters of Administration Have Been Granted.** Whenever letters of administration shall have been granted upon an estate, and it shall afterwards be discovered that the deceased left a lawful will, such will may be proved in the manner provided for the proof of wills; and, if an executor is named in such will, and he is not disqualified, he shall be allowed to qualify and accept as such executor, and the letters previously granted shall be revoked; but, if no such executor be named in the will, or if the executor named be disqualified, be dead, or shall renounce the executorship, or shall fail or be unable to accept and qualify within twenty days after the date of the probate of the will, or shall fail for a period of thirty days after the discovery of such will to present it for probate, then administration with the will annexed of the estate of such testator shall be granted as in other cases. All acts done by the first administrator, prior to the qualification of the executor or of the administrator with the will annexed, shall be as valid as if no such will had been discovered.

Acts 1955, 54th Leg., p. 88, ch. 55, eff. Jan. 1, 1956.

Subsec. (c) amended by Acts 2007, 80th Leg., ch. 1170, § 7.01, eff. Sept. 1, 2007; subsec. (a) amended by Acts 2011, 82nd Leg., ch. 1338 (S.B. 1198), § 1.16, eff. Sept. 1, 2011.

### § 84.  Proof of Written Will Produced in Court

**(a) Self–Proved Will.** (1) If a will is self-proved as provided in Section 59 of this Code or, if executed in another state or a foreign country, is self-proved in accordance with the laws of the state or foreign country of the testator's domicile at the time of the execution, no further proof of its execution with the formalities and solemnities and under the circumstances required to make it a valid will shall be necessary.

(2) For purposes of Subdivision (1) of this subsection, a will is considered self-proved if the will, or an affidavit of the testator and attesting witnesses attached or annexed to the will, provides that:

(A) the testator declared that the testator signed the instrument as the testator's will, the testator signed it willingly or willingly directed another to sign for the testator, the testator executed the will as the testator's free and voluntary act for the purposes expressed in the instrument, the testator is of sound mind and under no constraint or undue influence, and the testator is eighteen years of age or over or, if under that age, was or had been lawfully married, or was then a member of the armed forces of the United States, an auxiliary of the armed forces of the United States, or the United States Maritime Service; and

(B) the witnesses declared that the testator signed the instrument as the testator's will, the testator signed it willingly or willingly directed another to sign for the testator, each of the witnesses, in the presence and hearing of the testator, signed the will as witness to the testator's signing, and to the best of their knowledge the testator was of sound mind and under no constraint or undue influence, and the testator was eighteen years of age or over or, if under that age, was or had been lawfully married, or was then a member of the armed forces of the United States, an auxiliary of the armed forces of the United States, or the United States Maritime Service.

**(b) Attested Written Will.** If not self-proved as provided in this Code, an attested written will produced in court may be proved:

(1) By the sworn testimony or affidavit of one or more of the subscribing witnesses thereto, taken in open court.

(2) If all the witnesses are non-residents of the county, or those who are residents are unable to attend court, by the sworn testimony of any one or more of them by deposition, either written or oral, taken in the same manner and under the same rules as depositions taken in other civil actions; or, if no opposition in writing to such will is filed on or before the date set for hearing thereon, then by the sworn testimony or affidavit of two witnesses taken in open court, or by deposition in the manner provided herein, to the signature or the handwriting evidenced thereby of one or more of the attesting witnesses, or of the testator, if he signed the will; or, if it be shown under oath to the satisfaction of the court that, diligent search having been made, only one witness can be found who can make the required proof, then by the sworn testimony or affidavit of such one taken in open court, or by deposition in the manner provided herein, to such signatures or handwriting.

(3) If none of the witnesses is living, or if all of such witnesses are members of the armed forces of the United States of America or of any auxiliary thereof, or of the armed forces reserve of the United States of America or of any auxiliary thereof, or of the Maritime Service, and are beyond the jurisdiction of the court, by two witnesses to the handwriting of one or both of the subscribing witnesses thereto, or of the testator, if signed by him, and such proof may be either by sworn testimony or affidavit taken in open court, or by deposition, either written or oral, taken in the same manner and under the same rules as depositions taken in other civil actions; or, if it be shown under oath to the satisfaction of the court that, diligent search having been made, only one witness can be found who can make the required proof, then by the sworn testimony or

affidavit of such one taken in open court, or by deposition in the manner provided herein, to such signatures or handwriting.

**(c) Holographic Will.** If not self-proved as provided in this Code, a will wholly in the handwriting of the testator may be proved by two witnesses to his handwriting, which evidence may be by sworn testimony or affidavit taken in open court, or, if such witnesses are non-residents of the county or are residents who are unable to attend court, by deposition, either written or oral, taken in the same manner and under the same rules as depositions taken in other civil actions.

**(d) Depositions if No Contest Filed.** If no contest has been filed, depositions for the purpose of establishing a will may be taken in the same manner as provided in this Code for the taking of depositions where there is no opposing party or attorney of record upon whom notice and copies of interrogatories may be served; and, in such event, this Subsection, rather than the preceding portions of this Section which provide for the taking of depositions under the same rules as depositions in other civil actions, shall be applicable.

Subsec. (a) amended by Acts 2011, 82nd Leg., ch. 1338 (S.B. 1198), § 1.17, eff. Sept. 1, 2011.

Acts 1955, 54th Leg., p. 88, ch. 55, eff. Jan. 1, 1956.

Amended by Acts 2003, 78th Leg., ch. 1060, § 11, eff. Sept. 1, 2003; Subsec. (a) amended by Acts 2011, 82nd Leg., ch. 1338 (S.B. 1198), § 1.17, eff. Sept. 1, 2011.

### § 85.  Proof of Written Will Not Produced in Court

A written will which cannot be produced in court shall be proved in the same manner as provided in the preceding Section for an attested written will or an holographic will, as the case may be, and the same amount and character of testimony shall be required to prove such will as is required to prove a written will produced in court; but, in addition thereto, the cause of its non-production must be proved, and such cause must be sufficient to satisfy the court that it cannot by any reasonable diligence be produced, and the contents of such will must be substantially proved by the testimony of a credible witness who has read the will, has heard the will read, or can identify a copy of the will.

Acts 1955, 54th Leg., p. 88, ch. 55, eff. Jan. 1, 1956.

Amended by Acts 2007, 80th Leg., ch. 1170, § 6.01, eff. Sept. 1, 2007.

### § 86.  Repealed by Acts 2007, 80th Leg., ch. 1170, § 5.05, eff. Sept. 1, 2007

### § 87.  Testimony to Be Committed to Writing

All testimony taken in open court upon the hearing of an application to probate a will shall be committed to writing at the time it is taken, and subscribed, and sworn to in open court by the witness or witnesses, and filed by the clerk; provided, however, that in any contested case, the court may, upon agreement of the parties, and in the event of no agreement on its own motion, dismiss this requirement.

Acts 1955, 54th Leg., p. 88, ch. 55, eff. Jan. 1, 1956.  Amended by Acts 1971, 62nd Leg., p. 976, ch. 173, § 9, eff. Jan. 1, 1972.

### § 88.  Proof Required for Probate and Issuance of Letters Testamentary or of Administration

**(a) General Proof.** Whenever an applicant seeks to probate a will or to obtain issuance of letters testamentary or of administration, he must first prove to the satisfaction of the court:

(1) That the person is dead, and that four years have not elapsed since his decease and prior to the application; and

(2) That the court has jurisdiction and venue over the estate; and

(3) That citation has been served and returned in the manner and for the length of time required by this Code; and

(4) That the person for whom letters testamentary or of administration are sought is entitled thereto by law and is not disqualified.

**(b) Additional Proof for Probate of Will.** To obtain probate of a will, the applicant must also prove to the satisfaction of the court:

(1) If the will is not self-proved as provided by this Code, that the testator, at the time of executing the will, was at least eighteen years of age, or was or had been lawfully married, or was a member of the armed forces of the United States or of the auxiliaries thereof, or of the Maritime Service of the United States, and was of sound mind; and

(2) If the will is not self-proved as provided by this Code, that the testator executed the will with the formalities and solemnities and under the circumstances required by law to make it a valid will; and

(3) That such will was not revoked by the testator.

**(c) Additional Proof for Issuance of Letters Testamentary.** If letters testamentary are to be granted, it must appear to the court that proof required for the probate of the will has been made, and, in addition, that the person to whom the letters are to be granted is named as executor in the will.

**(d) Additional Proof for Issuance of Letters of Administration.** If letters of administration are to be granted, the applicant must also prove to the satisfaction of the court that there exists a necessity for an administration upon such estate.

**(e) Proof Required Where Prior Letters Have Been Granted.** If letters testamentary or of administration have previously been granted upon the estate, the applicant need show only that the person for whom letters are sought is entitled thereto by law and is not disqualified.

Acts 1955, 54th Leg., p. 88, ch. 55, eff. Jan. 1, 1956.  Amended by Acts 1969, 61st Leg., p. 1922, ch. 641, § 8, eff. June 12, 1969.

### § 89.  Action of Court on Probated Will

Upon the completion of hearing of an application for the probate of a will, if the Court be satisfied that such will should be admitted to probate, an order to that effect shall be entered.  Certified copies of such will and the order, or of

**Text of Texas Probate Code effective until January 1, 2014**

the record thereof, and the record of testimony, may be recorded in other counties, and may be used in evidence, as the original might be, on the trial of the same matter in any other court, when taken there by appeal or otherwise.

Acts 1955, 54th Leg., p. 88, ch. 55, eff. Jan. 1, 1956.  Amended by Acts 1961, 57th Leg., p. 1072, ch. 480, § 1, eff. Aug. 28, 1961;  Acts 1983, 68th Leg., p. 1155, ch. 260, § 1, eff. Sept. 1, 1983;  Acts 1993, 73rd Leg., ch. 846, § 11, eff. Sept. 1, 1993.

### § 89A.  Contents of Application for Probate of Will as Muniment of Title

(a) A written will shall, if within the control of the applicant, be filed with the application for probate as a muniment of title, and shall remain in the custody of the county clerk unless removed from the custody of the clerk by order of a proper court.  An application for probate of a will as a muniment of title shall state:

(1) The name and domicile of each applicant.

(2) The name, age if known, and domicile of the decedent, and the fact, time, and place of death.

(3) Facts showing that the court has venue.

(4) That the decedent owned real or personal property, or both, describing the property generally, and stating its probable value.

(5) The date of the will, the name and residence of the executor named in the will, if any, and the names and residences of the subscribing witnesses, if any.

(6) Whether a child or children born or adopted after the making of such will survived the decedent, and the name of each such survivor, if any.

(7) That there are no unpaid debts owing by the estate of the testator, excluding debts secured by liens on real estate.

(8) Whether a marriage of the decedent was ever dissolved after the will was made and if so, when and from whom.

(9) Whether the state, a governmental agency of the state, or a charitable organization is named by the will as a devisee.

The foregoing matters shall be stated and averred in the application to the extent that they are known to the applicant, or can with reasonable diligence be ascertained by the applicant, and if any of such matters is not stated or averred in the application, the application shall set forth the reason why such matter is not so stated and averred.

(b) When a written will cannot be produced in court, in addition to the requirements of Subsection (a) of this section, the application shall state:

(1) The reason why such will cannot be produced.

(2) The contents of such will, to the extent known.

(3) The date of such will and the executor appointed in the will, if any, to the extent known.

(4) The name, age, marital status, and address, if known, and the relationship to the decedent, if any, of each devisee, and of each person who would inherit as an heir in the

absence of a valid will, and, in cases of partial intestacy, of each heir.

(c) Repealed by Acts 2007, 80th leg., ch. 1170, § 5.05.

Added by Acts 1997, 75th Leg., ch. 540, § 1, eff. Sept. 1, 1997. Amended by Acts 2001, 77th Leg., ch. 10, § 1, eff. Sept. 1, 2001. Subsec. (c) repealed by Acts 2007, 80th Leg., ch. 1170, § 5.05, eff. Sept. 1, 2007; subsec. (a)(8) amended by Acts 2009, 81st Leg., ch. 634, § 1, eff. Sept. 1, 2009.  Subsec. (a)(8) amended by Acts 2011, 82nd Leg., ch. 1338 (S.B. 1198), § 1.18, eff. Sept. 1, 2011.

### § 89B.  Proof Required for Probate of a Will as a Muniment of Title

(a) General Proof.  Whenever an applicant seeks to probate a will as a muniment of title, the applicant must first prove to the satisfaction of the court:

(1) That the person is dead, and that four years have not elapsed since the person's death and prior to the application; and

(2) That the court has jurisdiction and venue over the estate; and

(3) That citation has been served and returned in the manner and for the length of time required by this Code; and

(4) That there are no unpaid debts owing by the estate of the testator, excluding debts secured by liens on real estate.

(b) To obtain probate of a will as a muniment of title, the applicant must also prove to the satisfaction of the court:

(1) If the will is not self-proved as provided by this Code, that the testator, at the time of executing the will, was at least 18 years of age, or was or had been lawfully married, or was a member of the armed forces of the United States or of the auxiliaries of the armed forces of the United States, or of the Maritime Service of the United States, and was of sound mind; and

(2) If the will is not self-proved as provided by this Code, that the testator executed the will with the formalities and solemnities and under the circumstances required by law to make it a valid will; and

(3) That such will was not revoked by the testator.

Added by Acts 1997, 75th Leg., ch. 540, § 1 eff. Sept. 1, 1997.

### § 89C.  Probate of Wills as Muniments of Title

(a) In each instance where the court is satisfied that a will should be admitted to probate, and where the court is further satisfied that there are no unpaid debts owing by the estate of the testator, excluding debts secured by liens on real estate, or for other reason finds that there is no necessity for administration upon such estate, the court may admit such will to probate as a muniment of title.

(b) If a person who is entitled to property under the provisions of the will cannot be ascertained solely by reference to the will or if a question of construction of the will exists, on proper application and notice as provided by Chapter 37, Civil Practice and Remedies Code, the court may hear evidence and include in the order probating the will as a muniment of title a declaratory judgment construing the will or determining those persons who are entitled to receive property under the will and the persons' shares or interests in the estate. The judgment is conclusive in any suit between any person omitted from the judgment and a bona fide purchaser for value who has purchased real or personal property after entry of the judgment without actual notice of the claim of the omitted person to an interest in the estate. Any person who has delivered property of the decedent to a person declared to be entitled to the property under the judgment or has engaged in any other transaction with the person in good faith after entry of the judgment is not liable to any person for actions taken in reliance on the judgment.

(c) The order admitting a will to probate as a muniment of title shall constitute sufficient legal authority to all persons owing any money to the estate of the decedent, having custody of any property, or acting as registrar or transfer agent of any evidence of interest, indebtedness, property, or right belonging to the estate, and to persons purchasing from or otherwise dealing with the estate, for payment or transfer, without liability, to the persons described in such will as entitled to receive the particular asset without administration. The person or persons entitled to property under the provisions of such wills shall be entitled to deal with and treat the properties to which they are so entitled in the same manner as if the record of title thereof were vested in their names.

(d) Unless waived by the court, before the 181st day, or such later day as may be extended by the court, after the date a will is admitted to probate as a muniment of title, the applicant for probate of the will shall file with the clerk of the court a sworn affidavit stating specifically the terms of the will that have been fulfilled and the terms of the will that have been unfulfilled. Failure of the applicant for probate of the will to file such affidavit shall not otherwise affect title to property passing under the terms of the will.

Added by Acts 1993, 73rd Leg., ch. 846, § 12, eff. Sept. 1, 1993. Renumbered from V.A.T.S. Probate Code, § 89A by Acts 1997, 75th Leg., ch. 540, § 1, eff. Sept. 1, 1997.

## § 90. Custody of Probated Wills

All original wills, together with the probate thereof, shall be deposited in the office of the county clerk of the county wherein the same shall have been probated, and shall there remain, except during such time as they may be removed for inspection to another place upon order by the court where probated. If the court shall order an original will to be removed to another place for inspection, the person removing such original will shall give a receipt therefor, and the clerk of the court shall make and retain a copy of such original will.

Acts 1955, 54th Leg., p. 88, ch. 55, eff. Jan. 1, 1956.

## § 91. When Will Not in Custody of Court

If for any reason a written will is not in the custody of the court, the court shall find the contents thereof by written order, and certified copies of same as so established by the court may be recorded in other counties, and may be used in evidence, as in the case of certified copies of written wills in the custody of the court.

Acts 1955, 54th Leg., p. 88, ch. 55, eff. Jan. 1, 1956.
Amended by Acts 2007, 80th Leg., ch. 1170, § 5.02, eff. Sept. 1, 2007.

## § 92. Period for Probate Does Not Affect Settlement

Where letters testamentary or of administration shall have once been granted, any person interested in the administration of the estate may proceed, after any lapse of time, to compel settlement of the estate when it does not appear from the record that the administration thereof has been closed.

Acts 1955, 54th Leg., p. 88, ch. 55, eff. Jan. 1, 1956.

## § 93. Period for Contesting Probate

After a will has been admitted to probate, any interested person may institute suit in the proper court to contest the validity thereof, within two years after such will shall have been admitted to probate, and not afterward, except that any interested person may institute suit in the proper court to cancel a will for forgery or other fraud within two years after the discovery of such forgery or fraud, and not afterward. Provided, however, that incapacitated persons shall have two years after the removal of their disabilities within which to institute such contest.

Acts 1955, 54th Leg., p. 88, ch. 55, eff. Jan. 1, 1956. Amended by Acts 2001, 77th Leg., ch. 292, § 3, eff. May 23, 2001.

## § 94. No Will Effectual Until Probated

Except as hereinafter provided with respect to foreign wills, no will shall be effectual for the purpose of proving title to, or the right to the possession of, any real or personal property disposed of by the will, until such will has been admitted to probate.

Acts 1955, 54th Leg., p. 88, ch. 55, eff. Jan. 1, 1956.

## PART 2. PROCEDURE PERTAINING TO FOREIGN WILLS

## § 95. Probate of Foreign Will Accomplished by Filing and Recording

(a) Foreign Will May Be Probated. The written will of a testator who was not domiciled in Texas at the time of his death which would affect any real or personal property in this State, may be admitted to probate upon proof that it stands probated or established in any of the United States, its territories, the District of Columbia, or any foreign nation.

(b) Application and Citation.

(1) Will probated in domiciliary jurisdiction. If a foreign will has been admitted to probate or established in the jurisdiction in which the testator was domiciled at the time of

his death, the application need state only that probate is requested on the basis of the authenticated copy of the foreign proceedings in which the will was probated or established. No citation or notice is required.

**(2) Will probated in non-domiciliary jurisdiction.** If a foreign will has been admitted to probate or established in any jurisdiction other than the domicile of the testator at the time of his death, the application for its probate shall contain all of the information required in an application for the probate of a domestic will, and shall also set out the name and address of each devisee and each person who will be entitled to a portion of the estate as an heir in the absence of a will. Citations shall be issued and served on each such devisee and heir by registered or certified mail.

**(c) Copy of Will and Proceedings To Be Filed.** A copy of the will and of the judgment, order, or decree by which it was admitted to probate or otherwise established, attested by and with the original signature of the clerk of the court or of such other official as has custody of such will or is in charge of probate records, with the seal of the court affixed, if there is a seal, together with a certificate containing the original signature of the judge or presiding magistrate of such court that the said attestation is in due form, shall be filed with the application. Original signatures shall not be required for recordation in the deed records pursuant to Sections 96 through 99 or Section 107 of this code.

**(d) Probate Accomplished by Recording.**

**(1) Will admitted in domiciliary jurisdiction.** If the will has been probated or established in the jurisdiction in which the testator was domiciled at the time of his death, it shall be the ministerial duty of the clerk to record such will and the evidence of its probate or establishment in the judge's probate docket. No order of the court is necessary. When so filed and recorded, the will shall be deemed to be admitted to probate, and shall have the same force and effect for all purposes as if the original will had been probated by order of the court, subject to contest in the manner and to the extent hereinafter provided.

**(2) Will admitted in non-domiciliary jurisdiction.** If the will has been probated or established in another jurisdiction not the domicile of the testator, its probate in this State may be contested in the same manner as if the testator had been domiciled in this State at the time of his death. If no contest is filed, the clerk shall record such will and the evidence of its probate or establishment in the judge's probate docket, and no order of the court shall be necessary. When so filed and recorded, it shall be deemed to be admitted to probate, and shall have the same force and effect for all purposes as if the original will had been probated by order of the court, subject to contest in the manner and to the extent hereafter provided.

**(e) Effect of Foreign Will on Local Property.** If a foreign will has been admitted to probate or established in the jurisdiction in which the testator was domiciled at the time of his death, such will, when probated as herein provid-

ed, shall be effectual to dispose of both real and personal property in this State irrespective of whether such will was executed with the formalities required by this Code.

**(f) Protection of Purchasers.** When a foreign will has been probated in this State in accordance with the procedure prescribed in this section for a will that has been admitted to probate in the domicile of the testator, and it is later proved in a proceeding brought for that purpose that the foreign jurisdiction in which the will was admitted to probate was not in fact the domicile of the testator, the probate in this State shall be set aside. If any person has purchased property from the personal representative or any legatee or devisee, in good faith and for value, or otherwise dealt with any of them in good faith, prior to the commencement of the proceeding, his title or rights shall not be affected by the fact that the probate in this State is subsequently set aside.

Acts 1955, 54th Leg., p. 88, ch. 55, eff. Jan. 1, 1956. Amended by Acts 1971, 62nd Leg., p. 976, ch. 173, § 9, eff. Jan. 1, 1972; Acts 1999, 76th Leg., ch. 755, § 1, eff. Sept. 1, 1999; Acts 2009, 81st Leg., ch. 602, § 6, eff. June 19, 2009.

### § 96. Filing and Recording Foreign Will in Deed Records

When any will or testamentary instrument conveying or in any manner disposing of land in this State has been duly probated according to the laws of any of the United States, or territories thereof, or the District of Columbia, or of any country out of the limits of the United States, a copy thereof and of its probate which bears the attestation, seal and certificate required by the preceding Section, may be filed and recorded in the deed records in any county of this State in which said real estate is situated, in the same manner as deeds and conveyances are required to be recorded under the laws of this State, and without further proof or authentication; provided that the validity of such a will or testamentary instrument filed under this Section may be contested in the manner and to the extent hereinafter provided.

Acts 1955, 54th Leg., p. 88, ch. 55, eff. Jan. 1, 1956.

### § 97. Proof Required for Recording in Deed Records

A copy of such foreign will or testamentary instrument, and of its probate attested as provided above, together with the certificate that said attestation is in due form, shall be prima facie evidence that said will or testamentary instrument has been duly admitted to probate, according to the laws of the state, territory, district, or country wherein it has allegedly been admitted to probate, and shall be sufficient to authorize the same to be recorded in the deed records in the proper county or counties in this State.

Acts 1955, 54th Leg., p. 88, ch. 55, eff. Jan. 1, 1956. Amended by Acts 1969, 61st Leg., p. 1925, ch. 641, § 9, eff. June 12, 1969.

### § 98. Effect of Recording Copy of Will in Deed Records

Every such foreign will, or testamentary instrument, and the record of its probate, which shall be attested and proved, as hereinabove provided, and delivered to the county clerk of the proper county in this State to be recorded in the deed records, shall take effect and be valid and effectual as a deed of conveyance of all property in this State covered by said foreign will or testamentary instrument; and the record thereof shall have the same force and effect as the record of deeds or other conveyances of land from the time when such instrument is delivered to the clerk to be recorded, and from that time only.

Acts 1955, 54th Leg., p. 88, ch. 55, eff. Jan. 1, 1956. Amended by Acts 1969, 61st Leg., p. 1925, ch. 641, § 9, eff. June 12, 1969.

## § 99. Recording in Deed Records Serves as Notice of Title

The record of any such foreign will, or testamentary instrument, and of its probate, duly attested and proved and filed for recording in the deed records of the proper county, shall be notice to all persons of the existence of such will or testamentary instrument, and of the title or titles conferred thereby.

Acts 1955, 54th Leg., p. 88, ch. 55, eff. Jan. 1, 1956. Amended by Acts 1969, 61st Leg., p. 1925, ch. 641, § 9, eff. June 12, 1969.

## § 100. Contest of Foreign Wills

**(a) Will Admitted in Domiciliary Jurisdiction.** A foreign will that has been admitted to probate or established in the jurisdiction in which the testator was domiciled at the time of his death, and either admitted to probate in this State or filed in the deed records of any county of this State, may be contested by any interested person but only upon the following grounds:

(1) That the foreign proceedings were not authenticated in the manner required for ancillary probate or recording in the deed records.

(2) That the will has been finally rejected for probate in this State in another proceeding.

(3) That the probate of the will has been set aside in the jurisdiction in which the testator died domiciled.

**(b) Will Probated in Non-Domiciliary Jurisdiction.** A foreign will that has been admitted to probate or established in any jurisdiction other than that of the testator's domicile at the time of his death may be contested on any grounds that are the basis for the contest of a domestic will. If a will has been probated in this State in accordance with the procedure applicable for the probate of a will that has been admitted in the state of domicile, without the service of citation required for a will admitted in another jurisdiction that is not the domicile of the testator, and it is proved that the foreign jurisdiction in which the will was probated was not in fact the domicile of the testator, the probate in this State shall be set aside. If otherwise entitled, the will may be reprobated in accordance with the procedure prescribed for the probate of a will admitted in a non-domiciliary jurisdiction, or it may be admitted to original probate in this State in the same or a subsequent proceeding.

**(c) Time and Method.** A foreign will that has been admitted to ancillary probate in this State or filed in the deed records in this State may be contested by the same procedures, and within the same time limits, as wills admitted to probate in this State in original proceedings.

Acts 1955, 54th Leg., p. 88, ch. 55, eff. Jan. 1, 1956. Amended by Acts 1971, 62nd Leg., p. 976, ch. 173, § 9, eff. Jan. 1, 1972.

## § 101. Notice of Contest of Foreign Will

Within the time permitted for the contest of a foreign will in this State, verified notice may be filed and recorded in the judge's probate docket of the court in this State in which the will was probated, or the deed records of any county in this State in which such will was recorded, that proceedings have been instituted to contest the will in the foreign jurisdiction where it was probated or established. Upon such filing and recording, the force and effect of the probate or recording of the will shall cease until verified proof is filed and recorded that the foreign proceedings have been terminated in favor of the will, or that such proceedings were never actually instituted.

Acts 1955, 54th Leg., p. 88, ch. 55, eff. Jan. 1, 1956. Amended by Acts 1969, 61st Leg., p. 1925, ch. 641, § 9, eff. June 12, 1969; Acts 2009, 81st Leg., ch. 602, § 7, eff. June 19, 2009.

## § 102. Effect of Rejection of Will in Domiciliary Proceedings

Final rejection of a will or other testamentary instrument from probate or establishment in the jurisdiction in which the testator was domiciled shall be conclusive in this State, except where the will or other testamentary instrument has been rejected solely for a cause which is not ground for rejection of a will of a testator who died domiciled in this State, in which case the will or testamentary instrument may nevertheless be admitted to probate or continue to be effective in this State.

Acts 1955, 54th Leg., p. 88, ch. 55, eff. Jan. 1, 1956. Amended by Acts 1971, 62nd Leg., p. 976, ch. 173, § 9, eff. Jan. 1, 1972.

## § 103. Original Probate of Foreign Will in This State

Original probate of the will of a testator who died domiciled outside this State which, upon probate, may operate upon any property in this State, and which is valid under the laws of this State, may be granted in the same manner as the probate of other wills is granted under this Code, if the will does not stand rejected from probate or establishment in the jurisdiction where the testator died domiciled, or if it stands rejected from probate or establishment in the jurisdiction where the testator died domiciled solely for a cause which is not ground for rejection of a will of a testator who died domiciled in this State. The court may delay passing on the application for probate of a foreign will pending the result of probate or establishment, or of a contest thereof, at the domicile of the testator.

Acts 1955, 54th Leg., p. 88, ch. 55, eff. Jan. 1, 1956.

## § 104. Proof of Foreign Will in Original Probate Proceeding

If a testator dies domiciled outside this State, a copy of his will, authenticated in the manner required by this Code, shall be sufficient proof of the contents of the will to admit it to probate in an original proceeding in this State if no objection is made thereto. This Section does not authorize the probate of any will which would not otherwise be admissible to probate, or, in case objection is made to the will, relieve the proponent from offering proof of the contents and legal sufficiency of the will as otherwise required, except that the original will need not be produced unless the court so orders.

Acts 1955, 54th Leg., p. 88, ch. 55, eff. Jan. 1, 1956. Amended by Acts 1969, 61st Leg., p. 1925, ch. 641, § 9, eff. June 12, 1969.

## § 105. Executor of Will Probated in Another Jurisdiction

When a foreign will is admitted to ancillary probate in accordance with Section 95 of this Code, the executor named in such will shall be entitled to receive, upon application, letters testamentary upon proof that he has qualified as such in the jurisdiction in which the will was admitted to probate, and that he is not disqualified to serve as executor in this State. After such proof is made, the court shall enter an order directing that ancillary letters testamentary be issued to him. If letters of administration have previously been granted by such court in this State to any other person, such letters shall be revoked upon the application of the executor after personal service of citation upon the person to whom such letters were granted.

Acts 1955, 54th Leg., p. 88, ch. 55, eff. Jan. 1, 1956. Amended by Acts 1969, 61st Leg., p. 1925, ch. 641, § 9, eff. June 12, 1969.

## § 105A. Appointment and Service of Foreign Banks and Trust Companies in Fiduciary Capacity

(a) A corporate fiduciary that does not have its main office or a branch office in this state, hereinafter called "foreign corporate fiduciaries", having the corporate power to so act, may be appointed and may serve in the State of Texas as trustee (whether of a personal or corporate trust), executor, administrator, guardian of the estate, or in any other fiduciary capacity, whether the appointment be by will, deed, agreement, declaration, indenture, court order or decree, or otherwise, when and to the extent that the home state of the corporate fiduciary grants authority to serve in like fiduciary capacity to a corporate fiduciary whose home state is this state.

(b) Before qualifying or serving in the State of Texas in any fiduciary capacity, as aforesaid, such a foreign corporate fiduciary shall file in the office of the Secretary of the State of the State of Texas (1) a copy of its charter, articles of incorporation or of association, and all amendments thereto, certified by its secretary under its corporate seal; (2) a duly executed instrument in writing, by its terms of indefinite duration and irrevocable, appointing the Secretary of State and his successors its agent for service of process upon whom all notices and processes issued by any court of this state may be served in any action or proceeding relating to any trust, estate, fund or other matter within this state with respect to which such foreign corporate fiduciary is acting in any fiduciary capacity, including the acts or defaults of such foreign corporate fiduciary with respect to any such trust, estate or fund; and (3) a written certificate of designation, which may be changed from time to time thereafter by the filing of a new certificate of designation, specifying the name and address of the officer, agent or other person to whom such notice or process shall be forwarded by the Secretary of State. Upon receipt of such notice or process, it shall be the duty of the Secretary of State forthwith to forward same by registered or certified mail to the officer, agent or other person so designated. Service of notice or process upon the Secretary of State as agent for such a foreign corporate fiduciary shall in all ways and for all purposes have the same effect as if personal service had been had within this state upon such foreign corporate fiduciary.

(c) Any foreign corporate fiduciary acting in a fiduciary capacity in this state in strict accordance with the provisions of this Section shall not be deemed to be doing business in the State of Texas within the meaning of Article 8.01 of the Texas Business Corporation Act; and shall be deemed qualified to serve in such capacity under the provisions of Section 105 of this Code.

(d) The provisions hereof are in addition to, and not a limitation on, the provisions of Subtitle F or G, Title 3, Finance Code.[1]

(e) Any foreign corporate fiduciary which shall violate any provision of this Section 105a shall be guilty of a misdemeanor and, upon conviction thereof, shall be subject to a fine of not exceeding Five Thousand Dollars ($5,000.00), and may, in the discretion of the court, be prohibited from thereafter serving in this state in any fiduciary capacity.

Added by Acts 1961, 57th Leg., p. 46, ch. 31, § 1, eff. Aug. 28, 1961. Amended by Acts 1995, 74th Leg., ch. 914, § 10, eff. Sept. 1, 1995; Acts 1997, 75th Leg., ch. 769, § 5, eff. Sept. 1, 1997; Acts 1999, 76th Leg., ch. 344, § 6.002, eff. Sept. 1, 1999; Acts 2001, 77th Leg., ch. 1420, § 6.029, eff. Sept. 1, 2001.

[1] V.T.C.A., Finance Code §§ 181.001 or 201.001 et seq.

## § 106. When Foreign Executor to Give Bond

A foreign executor shall not be required to give bond if the will appointing him so provides. If the will does not exempt him from giving bond, the provisions of this Code with respect to the bonds of domestic representatives shall be applicable.

Acts 1955, 54th Leg., p. 88, ch. 55, eff. Jan. 1, 1956. Amended by Acts 1971, 62nd Leg., p. 976, ch. 173, § 9, eff. Jan. 1, 1972.

## § 107. Power of Sale of Foreign Executor or Trustee

When by any foreign will recorded in the deed records of any county in this state in the manner provided herein, power is given an executor or trustee to sell any real or personal property situated in this state, no order of a court of this state shall be necessary to authorize such executor or trustee to make such sale and execute proper conveyance, and whenever any particular directions are given by a testator in any such will respecting the sale of any such property situated in this state, belonging to his estate, the same shall be followed unless such directions have been annulled or suspended by order of a court of competent jurisdiction.

Acts 1955, 54th Leg., p. 88, ch. 55, eff. Jan. 1, 1956. Amended by Acts 1969, 61st Leg., p. 1925, ch. 641, § 9, eff. June 12, 1969.

### § 107A. Suit for the Recovery of Debts by a Foreign Executor or Administrator

(a) On giving notice by registered or certified mail to all creditors of the decedent in this state who have filed a claim against the estate of the decedent for a debt due to the creditor, a foreign executor or administrator of a person who was a nonresident at the time of death may prosecute a suit in this state for the recovery of debts due to the decedent.

(b) The plaintiff's letters testamentary or letters of administration granted by a competent tribunal, properly authenticated, shall be filed with the suit.

(c) By filing suit in this state for the recovery of a debt due to the decedent, a foreign executor or administrator submits personally to the jurisdiction of the courts of this state in a proceeding relating to the recovery of a debt due by his decedent to a resident of this state. Jurisdiction under this subsection is limited to the money or value of personal property recovered in this state by the foreign executor or administrator.

(d) Suit may not be maintained in this state by a foreign executor or administrator if there is an executor or administrator of the decedent qualified by a court of this state or if there is pending in this state an application for appointment as an executor or administrator.

Added by Acts 1977, 65th Leg., p. 1190, ch. 457, § 1, eff. Aug. 29, 1977.

### PART 3. EMERGENCY INTERVENTION PROCEEDINGS; FUNERAL AND BURIAL EXPENSES

### § 108. Time to File Emergency Application

An applicant may file an application requesting emergency intervention by a court exercising probate jurisdiction to provide for the payment of funeral and burial expenses or the protection and storage of personal property owned by the decedent that was located in rented accommodations on the date of the decedent's death with the clerk of the court in the county of domicile of the decedent or the county in which the rental accommodations that contain the decedent's personal property are located. The application must be filed not earlier than the third day after the date of the decedent's death and not later than the 90th day after the date of the decedent's death.

Added by Acts 1993, 73rd Leg., ch. 712, § 7, eff. Sept. 1, 1993. Amended by Acts 1995, 74th Leg., ch. 642, § 6, eff. Sept. 1, 1995. Renumbered from V.A.T.S. Probate Code, § 520 and amended by Acts 1997, 75th Leg., ch. 199, § 1, eff. Sept. 1, 1997.

### § 109. Eligible Applicants for Emergency Intervention

A person qualified to serve as an administrator under Section 77 of this code may file an emergency intervention application.

Added by Acts 1993, 73rd Leg., ch. 712, § 7, eff. Sept. 1, 1993. Renumbered from V.A.T.S., Probate Code § 521 and amended by Acts 1997, 75th Leg., ch. 199, § 1, eff. Sept. 1, 1997.

### § 110. Requirements for Emergency Intervention

An applicant may file an emergency application with the court under Section 108 of this code only if an application has not been filed and is not pending under Section 81, 82, 137, or 145 of this code and the applicant:

(1) needs to obtain funds for the funeral and burial of the decedent; or

(2) needs to gain access to rental accommodations in which the decedent's personal property is located and the applicant has been denied access to those accommodations.

Added by Acts 1995, 74th Leg., ch. 642, § 7, eff. Sept. 1, 1995. Renumbered from V.A.T.S., Probate Code § 521A and amended by Acts 1997, 75th Leg., ch. 199, § 1, eff. Sept. 1, 1997.

### § 111. Contents of Emergency Intervention Application for Funeral and Burial Expenses

(a) An application for emergency intervention to obtain funds needed for a decedent's funeral and burial expenses must be sworn and must contain:

(1) the name, address, and interest of the applicant;

(2) the facts showing an immediate necessity for the issuance of an emergency intervention order under this section by the court;

(3) the date of the decedent's death, place of death, decedent's residential address, and the name and address of the funeral home holding the decedent's remains;

(4) any known or ascertainable heirs and devisees of the decedent and the reason:

(A) the heirs and devisees cannot be contacted; or

(B) the heirs and devisees have refused to assist in the decedent's burial;

(5) a description of funeral and burial procedures necessary and a statement from the funeral home that contains a detailed and itemized description of the cost of the funeral and burial procedures; and

(6) the name and address of an individual, entity, or financial institution, including an employer, that is in possession of any funds of or due to the decedent, and related account numbers and balances, if known by the applicant.

(b) The application shall also state whether there are any written instructions from the decedent relating to the type and manner of funeral or burial the decedent would like to have. The applicant shall attach the instructions, if available, to the application and shall fully comply with the instructions. If written instructions do not exist, the applicant may not permit the decedent's remains to be cremated unless the applicant obtains the court's permission to cremate the decedent's remains.

Added by Acts 1993, 73rd Leg., ch. 712, § 7, eff. Sept. 1, 1993. Amended by Acts 1995, 74th Leg., ch. 642, § 8, eff. Sept. 1, 1995. Renumbered from V.A.T.S., Probate Code § 522 and amended by Acts 1997, 75th Leg., ch. 199, § 1, eff. Sept. 1, 1997.
Subsec. (a) amended by Acts 2007, 80th Leg., ch. 1170, § 8.01, eff. June 15, 2007.

### § 112. Contents for Emergency Intervention Application for Access to Personal Property

An application for emergency intervention to gain access to rental accommodations of a decedent at the time of the decedent's death that contain the decedent's personal property must be sworn and must contain:

(1) the name, address, and interest of the applicant;

(2) the facts showing an immediate necessity for the issuance of an emergency intervention order by the court;

(3) the date and place of the decedent's death, the decedent's residential address, and the name and address of the funeral home holding the decedent's remains;

(4) any known or ascertainable heirs and devisees of the decedent and the reason:

(A) the heirs and devisees cannot be contacted; or

(B) the heirs and devisees have refused to assist in the protection of the decedent's personal property;

(5) the type and location of the decedent's personal property and the name of the person in possession of the property; and

(6) the name and address of the owner or manager of the decedent's rental accommodations and whether access to the accommodations is necessary.

Added by Acts 1995, 74th Leg., ch. 642, § 9, eff. Sept. 1, 1995. Renumbered from V.A.T.S., Probate Code § 522A and amended by Acts 1997, 75th Leg., ch. 199, § 1, eff. Sept. 1, 1997.
Amended by Acts 2007, 80th Leg., ch. 1170, § 8.02, eff. June 15, 2007.

### § 112A. Repealed by Acts 1995, 74th Leg., ch. 1039, § 73(1), eff. Sept. 1, 1995

### § 113. Orders of Emergency Intervention

(a) If the court determines on review of an application filed under Section 108 of this code that emergency intervention is necessary to obtain funds needed for a decedent's funeral and burial expenses, the court may order funds of the decedent held by an employer, individual, or financial institution to be paid directly to a funeral home only for reasonable and necessary attorney's fees for the attorney who obtained the order granted under this section, for court costs for obtaining the order, and for funeral and burial expenses not to exceed $5,000 as ordered by the court to provide the decedent with a reasonable, dignified, and appropriate funeral and burial.

(b) If the court determines on review of an application filed under Section 108 of this code that emergency intervention is necessary to gain access to accommodations rented by the decedent at the time of the decedent's death that contain the decedent's personal property, the court may order one or more of the following:

(1) the owner or agent of the rental accommodations shall grant the applicant access to the accommodations at a reasonable time and in the presence of the owner or agent;

(2) the applicant and owner or agent of the rental accommodations shall jointly prepare and file with the court a list that generally describes the decedent's property found at the premises;

(3) the applicant or the owner or agent of the rental accommodations may remove and store the decedent's property at another location until claimed by the decedent's heirs;

(4) the applicant has only the powers that are specifically stated in the order and that are necessary to protect the decedent's property that is the subject of the application; or

(5) funds of the decedent held by an employer, individual, or financial institution to be paid to the applicant for reasonable and necessary attorney's fees and court costs for obtaining the order.

(c) The court clerk may issue certified copies of an emergency intervention order on request of the applicant only until the 90th day after the date the order was signed or the date a personal representative is qualified, whichever occurs first.

(d) A person who is furnished with a certified copy of an emergency intervention order within the period described by Subsection (c) of this section is not personally liable for the person's actions that are taken in accordance with and in reliance on the order.

Added by Acts 1993, 73rd Leg., ch. 712, § 7, eff. Sept. 1, 1993. Amended by Acts 1995, 74th Leg., ch. 642, § 10, eff. Sept. 1, 1995. Renumbered from V.A.T.S., Probate Code § 523 and amended by Acts 1997, 75th Leg., ch. 199, § 1, eff. Sept. 1, 1997.

### § 113A. Repealed by Acts 1993, 73rd Leg., ch. 957, § 75(2), eff. Sept. 1, 1993

### § 114. Termination

(a) All power and authority of an applicant under an emergency intervention order cease to be effective or enforceable on the 90th day after the date the order was issued or on the date a personal representative is qualified, whichever occurs first.

(b) If a personal representative has not been appointed when an emergency intervention order issued under Section

113(b) of this code ceases to be effective, a person who is in possession of the decedent's personal property that is the subject of the order, without incurring civil liability, may:

(1) release the property to the decedent's heirs; or

(2) dispose of the property under Subchapter C, Chapter 54, Property Code,[1] or Section 7.209 or 7.210, Business & Commerce Code.

Added by Acts 1993, 73rd Leg., ch. 712, § 7, eff. Sept. 1, 1993. Amended by Acts 1995, 74th Leg., ch. 642, § 11, eff. Sept. 1, 1995. Renumbered from V.A.T.S. Probate Code, § 524 and amended by Acts 1997, 75th Leg., ch. 199, § 1, eff. Sept. 1, 1997.

[1] V.T.C.A., Property Code § 54.041 et seq.

### § 115. Limitation on Right of Surviving Spouse to Control Deceased's Burial or Cremation

(a) An application under this section may be filed by:

(1) the executor of the deceased's will; or

(2) the next of kin of the deceased, the nearest in order of descent first, and so on, and next of kin includes the deceased's descendants who legally adopted the deceased or who have been legally adopted by the deceased.

(b) An application under this section must be under oath and must establish:

(1) whether the deceased died intestate or testate;

(2) the surviving spouse is alleged to be a principal or accomplice in a wilful act which resulted in the death of the deceased; and

(3) good cause exists to limit the right of the surviving spouse to control the burial and interment or cremation of the deceased spouse.

(c) After notice and hearing, without regard to whether the deceased died intestate or testate, and subject to the prohibition described by Section 711.002(*l*), Health and Safety Code, a court may limit the right of a surviving spouse, whether or not the spouse has been designated by the deceased's will as the executor of a deceased spouse's estate, to control the burial and interment or cremation of the deceased spouse if the court finds that there is good cause to believe that the surviving spouse is the principal or an accomplice in a wilful act which resulted in the death of the deceased spouse.

(d) If the court limits the surviving spouse's right of control, as provided by Subsection (c), the court shall designate and authorize a person to make burial or cremation arrangements.

Added by Acts 1995, 74th Leg., ch. 642, § 12, eff. Sept. 1, 1995. Renumbered from V.A.T.S. Probate Code, § 525 and amended by Acts 1997, 75th Leg., ch. 199, § 1, eff. Sept. 1, 1997. Amended by Acts 2011, 82nd Leg., ch. 707 (H.B. 549), § 2, eff. June 12, 2011.

### §§ 116, 117. Repealed by Acts 1993, 73rd Leg., ch. 957, § 75(2), eff. Sept. 1, 1993

### § 118. Repealed by Acts 1993, 73rd Leg., ch. 957, § 75(2), eff. Sept. 1, 1993; Acts 1995, 74th Leg., ch. 1039, § 73(1), eff. Sept. 1, 1995

### §§ 118A to 123. Repealed by Acts 1993, 73rd Leg., ch. 957, § 75(2), eff. Sept. 1, 1993

### § 123A. Repealed by Acts 1995, 74th Leg., ch. 1039, § 73(1), eff. Sept. 1, 1995

### §§ 124 to 127. Repealed by Acts 1993, 73rd Leg., ch. 957, § 75(2), eff. Sept. 1, 1993

### § 127A. Repealed by Acts 1993, 73rd Leg., ch. 957, § 75(2), eff. Sept. 1, 1993; Acts 1995, 74th Leg., ch. 1039, § 73(1), eff. Sept. 1, 1995

## PART 4. CITATIONS AND NOTICES

### § 128. Citations With Respect to Applications for Probate or for Issuance of Letters

**(a) Where Application Is for Probate of a Written Will Produced in Court or for Letters of Administration.** When an application for the probate of a written will produced in court, or for letters of administration, is filed with the clerk, he shall issue a citation to all parties interested in such estate, which citation shall be served by posting and shall state:

(1) That such application has been filed, and the nature of it.

(2) The name of the deceased and of the applicant.

(3) The time when such application will be acted upon.

(4) That all persons interested in the estate should appear at the time named therein and contest said application, should they desire to do so.

**(b) Where Application Is for Probate of a Written Will Not Produced.** When the application is for the probate of a written will which cannot be produced in court, the clerk shall issue a citation to all parties interested in such estate, which citation shall contain substantially the statements made in the application for probate, and the time when, place where, and the court before which such application will be acted upon. If the heirs of the testator be residents of this state, and their residence be known, the citation shall be served upon them by personal service. Service of such citation may be made by publication in the following cases:

(1) When the heirs are non-residents of this state; or

(2) When their names or their residences are unknown; or

(3) When they are transient persons.

**(c) No Action Until Service Is Had.** No application for the probate of a will or for the issuance of letters shall be acted upon until service of citation has been made in the manner provided herein.

Acts 1955, 54th Leg., p. 88, ch. 55, eff. Jan. 1, 1956.

Subsec. (b) amended by Acts 2007, 80th Leg., ch. 1170, § 5.03, eff. Sept. 1, 2007.

### § 128A.   Notice to Certain Beneficiaries After Probate of Will

(a) In this section, "beneficiary" means a person, entity, state, governmental agency of the state, charitable organization, or trustee of a trust entitled to receive property under the terms of a decedent's will, to be determined for purposes of this section with the assumption that each person who is alive on the date of the decedent's death survives any period required to receive the bequest as specified by the terms of the will. The term does not include a person, entity, state, governmental agency of the state, charitable organization, or trustee of a trust that would be entitled to receive property under the terms of a decedent's will on the occurrence of a contingency that has not occurred as of the date of the decedent's death.

(a–1) This section does not apply to the probate of a will as a muniment of title.

(b) Except as provided by Subsection (d) of this section, not later than the 60th day after the date of an order admitting a decedent's will to probate, the personal representative of the decedent's estate, including an independent executor or independent administrator, shall give notice that complies with Subsection (e) of this section to each beneficiary named in the will whose identity and address are known to the personal representative or, through reasonable diligence, can be ascertained. If, after the 60th day after the date of the order, the personal representative becomes aware of the identity and address of a beneficiary who was not given notice on or before the 60th day, the personal representative shall give the notice as soon as possible after becoming aware of that information.

(c) Notwithstanding the requirement under Subsection (b) of this section that the personal representative give the notice to the beneficiary, the personal representative shall give the notice with respect to a beneficiary described by this subsection as follows:

(1) if the beneficiary is a trustee of a trust, to the trustee, unless the personal representative is the trustee, in which case the personal representative shall, except as provided by Subsection (c–1) of this section, give the notice to the person or class of persons first eligible to receive the trust income, to be determined for purposes of this subdivision as if the trust were in existence on the date of the decedent's death;

(2) if the beneficiary has a court-appointed guardian or conservator, to that guardian or conservator;

(3) if the beneficiary is a minor for whom no guardian or conservator has been appointed, to a parent of the minor; and

(4) if the beneficiary is a charity that for any reason cannot be notified, to the attorney general.

(c–1) The personal representative is not required to give the notice otherwise required by Subsection (c)(1) of this section to a person eligible to receive trust income at the sole discretion of the trustee of a trust if:

(1) the personal representative has given the notice to an ancestor of the person who has a similar interest in the trust; and

(2) no apparent conflict exists between the ancestor and the person eligible to receive trust income.

(d) A personal representative is not required to give the notice otherwise required by this section to a beneficiary who:

(1) has made an appearance in the proceeding with respect to the decedent's estate before the will was admitted to probate;

(2) is entitled to receive aggregate gifts under the will with an estimated value of $2,000 or less;

(3) has received all gifts to which the beneficiary is entitled under the will not later than the 60th day after the date of the order admitting the decedent's will to probate; or

(4) has received a copy of the will that was admitted to probate or a written summary of the gifts to the beneficiary under the will and has waived the right to receive the notice in an instrument that:

(A) either acknowledges the receipt of the copy of the will or includes the written summary of the gifts to the beneficiary under the will;

(B) is signed by the beneficiary; and

(C) is filed with the court.

(e) The notice required by this section must include:

(1) the name and address of the beneficiary to whom the notice is given or, for a beneficiary described by Subsection (c) of this section, the name and address of the beneficiary for whom the notice is given and of the person to whom the notice is given;

(2) the decedent's name;

(3) a statement that the decedent's will has been admitted to probate;

(4) a statement that the beneficiary to whom or for whom the notice is given is named as a beneficiary in the will;

(5) the personal representative's name and contact information; and

(6) either:

(A) a copy of the will that was admitted to probate and the order admitting the will to probate; or

(B) a summary of the gifts to the beneficiary under the will, the court in which the will was admitted to probate, the docket number assigned to the estate, the date the will was admitted to probate, and, if different, the date the court appointed the personal representative.

(f) The notice required by this section must be sent by registered or certified mail, return receipt requested.

(g) Not later than the 90th day after the date of an order admitting a will to probate, the personal representative shall file with the clerk of the court in which the decedent's estate is pending a sworn affidavit of the personal representative, or a certificate signed by the personal representative's attorney, stating:

(1) for each beneficiary to whom notice was required to be given under this section, the name and address of the beneficiary to whom the personal representative gave the notice or, for a beneficiary described by Subsection (c) of this section, the name and address of the beneficiary and of the person to whom the notice was given;

(2) the name and address of each beneficiary to whom notice was not required to be given under Subsection (d)(2), (3), or (4) of this section;

(3) the name of each beneficiary whose identity or address could not be ascertained despite the personal representative's exercise of reasonable diligence; and

(4) any other information necessary to explain the personal representative's inability to give the notice to or for any beneficiary as required by this section.

(h) The affidavit or certificate required by Subsection (g) of this section may be included with any pleading or other document filed with the clerk of the court, including the inventory, appraisement, and list of claims, an affidavit in lieu of the inventory, appraisement, and list of claims, or an application for an extension of the deadline to file the inventory, appraisement, and list of claims or an affidavit in lieu of the inventory, appraisement, and list of claims, provided that the pleading or other document with which the affidavit or certificate is included is filed not later than the date the affidavit or certificate is required to be filed as provided by Subsection (g) of this section.

Added by Acts 1989, 71st Leg., ch. 1035, § 7, eff. Sept. 1, 1989.
Amended by Acts 2007, 80th Leg., ch. 801, § 1, eff. Sept. 1, 2007; Subsec. (a) amended by Acts 2007, 80th Leg., ch. 1170, § 5.04, eff. Sept. 1, 2007; Acts 2011, 82nd Leg., ch. 1338 (S.B. 1198), § 1.18, eff. Sept. 1, 2011.

### § 128B. Notice to Heirs on Application to Probate Will After Four Years

(a) Except as provided by Subsection (b) of this section, an applicant for the probate of a will under Section 73(a) of this code must give notice by service of process to each of the testator's heirs whose address can be ascertained by the applicant with reasonable diligence. The notice must be given before the probate of the testator's will.

(b) Notice under Subsection (a) of this section is not required to be provided to an heir who has delivered to the court an affidavit signed by the heir stating that the heir does not object to the offer of the testator's will for probate.

(c) The notice required by this section and an affidavit described by Subsection (b) of this section must also contain a statement that:

(1) the testator's property will pass to the testator's heirs if the will is not admitted to probate; and

(2) the person offering the testator's will for probate may not be in default for failing to present the will for probate during the four-year period immediately following the testator's death.

(d) If the address of any of the testator's heirs cannot be ascertained by the applicant with reasonable diligence, the court shall appoint an attorney ad litem to protect the interests of the unknown heirs after an application for the probate of a will is made under Section 73(a) of this code.

(e) In the case of an application for the probate of a will of a testator who has had another will admitted to probate, this section applies to a beneficiary of the testator's probated will instead of the testator's heirs.

Added by Acts 1999, 76th Leg., ch. 855, § 2, eff. Sept. 1, 1999.
Section heading amended by Acts 2007, 80th Leg., ch. 801, § 2, eff. Sept. 1, 2007.

### § 129. Validation of Prior Modes of Service of Citation

(a) In all cases where written wills produced in court have been probated prior to June 14, 1927, after publication of citation as provided by the then Article 28 of the Revised Civil Statutes of Texas (1925), without service of citation, the action of the courts in admitting said wills to probate is hereby validated in so far as service of citation is concerned.

(b) In all cases where written wills produced in court have been probated or letters of administration have been granted prior to May 18, 1939, after citation, as provided by the then Article 3334, Title 54, of the Revised Civil Statutes of Texas (1925), without service of citation as provided for in the then Article 3336, Title 54, of the Revised Civil Statutes of Texas (1925) as amended by Acts 1935, 44th Legislature, page 659, Chapter 273, Section 1, such service of citation and the action of the court in admitting said wills to probate and granting administration upon estates, are hereby validated in so far as service of citation is concerned.

(c) In all cases where written wills have been probated or letters of administration granted, prior to June 12, 1941, upon citation or notice duly issued by the clerk in conformance with the requirements of the then Article 3333 of Title 54 of the Revised Civil Statutes of Texas (1925), as amended, but not directed to the sheriff or any constable of the county wherein the proceeding was pending, and such citation or notice having been duly posted by the sheriff or any constable of said county and returned for or in the time, manner, and form required by law, such citation or notice and return thereof and the action of the court in admitting said wills to probate or granting letters of administration upon estates, are hereby validated in so far as said citation or notice, and the issuance, service and return thereof are concerned.

Acts 1955, 54th Leg., p. 88, ch. 55, eff. Jan. 1, 1956.

§ 129A.  Service by Publication or Other Substituted Service

Notwithstanding any other provisions of this part of this chapter, if an attempt to make service under this part of this chapter is unsuccessful, service may be made in the manner provided by Rule 109 or 109a, Texas Rules of Civil Procedure, for the service of a citation on a party by publication or other substituted service.

Added by Acts 1993, 73rd Leg., ch. 712, § 2, eff. Sept. 1, 1993.

§ 130.  Repealed by Acts 1993, 73rd Leg., ch. 905, § 15, eff. Sept. 1, 1993; Acts 1993, 73rd Leg., ch. 957, § 75(1), eff. Sept. 1, 1993

PART 5.  LIMITED GUARDIANSHIP PROCEEDINGS [REPEALED]

§§ 130A to 130O.  Repealed by Acts 1993, 73rd Leg., ch. 905, § 15, eff. Sept. 1, 1993; Acts 1993, 73rd Leg., ch. 957, § 75(2), eff. Sept. 1, 1993

CHAPTER VI

SPECIAL TYPES OF ADMINISTRATION

PART 1.  TEMPORARY ADMINISTRATION IN THE INTEREST OF ESTATES OF DEPENDENTS

§ 131.  Repealed by Acts 1993, 73rd Leg., ch. 957, § 75(1), eff. Sept. 1, 1993

§ 131A.  Appointment of Temporary Administrators

(a) If a county judge determines that the interest of a decedent's estate requires the immediate appointment of a personal representative, he shall, by written order, appoint a temporary administrator with limited powers as the circumstances of the case require.  The duration of the appointment must be specified in the court's order and may not exceed 180 days unless the appointment is made permanent as provided by Subsection (j) of this section.

(b) Any person may file with the clerk of the court a written application for the appointment of a temporary administrator of a decedent's estate under this section.  The application must be verified and must include the information required by Section 81 of this code if the decedent died testate or Section 82 of this code if the decedent died intestate and an affidavit that sets out:

(1) the name, address, and interest of the applicant;

(2) the facts showing an immediate necessity for the appointment of a temporary administrator;

(3) the requested powers and duties of the temporary administrator;

(4) a statement that the applicant is entitled to letters of temporary administration and is not disqualified by law from serving as a temporary administrator; and

(5) a description of the real and personal property that the applicant believes to be in the decedent's estate.

(c) An order of appointment must:

(1) designate the appointee as "temporary administrator" of the decedent's estate for the specified period;

(2) define the powers conferred on the appointee; and

(3) set the amount of bond to be given by the appointee.

(d) Not later than the third business day after the date of the order, the appointee shall file with the county clerk a bond in the amount ordered by the court. In this subsection, "business day" means a day other than a Saturday, Sunday, or holiday recognized by this state.

(e) Not later than the third day after the date on which an appointee qualifies, the county clerk shall issue to the appointee letters of appointment that set forth the powers to be exercised by the appointee as ordered by the court.

(f) On the date that the county clerk issues letters of appointment, the county clerk shall post a notice of the appointment to all interested persons on the courthouse door.

(g) On the date the county clerk issues letters of appointment, the appointee shall notify the known heirs of the decedent of his appointment by certified mail, return receipt requested.

(h) A notice required by Subsection (f) or (g) of this section must state that:

(1) an interested person or an heir may request a hearing to contest the appointment not later than the 15th day after the date that the letters of appointment are issued;

(2) if no contest is made within the period specified by the notice, the appointment will continue for the time specified in the order of appointment; and

(3) the court may make the appointment permanent.

(i) If an interested person or an heir requests a hearing to contest the appointment of a temporary administrator, a hearing shall be held and a determination made not later than the 10th day after the date the request was made. If a request is not made on or before the 15th day after the date that the letters of appointment are issued, the appointment of a temporary administrator continues for the period specified in the order, unless made permanent under Subsection (j) of this section. During the pendency of a contest of the appointment of a temporary administrator, the temporary appointee shall continue to act as administrator of the estate to the extent of the powers conferred by his appointment. If the court sets aside the appointment, the court may require the temporary administrator to prepare and file, under oath, a complete exhibit of the condition of the estate and detail the disposition the temporary administrator has made of the property of the estate.

(j) At the conclusion of the term of appointment of a temporary administrator, the court may, by written order, make the appointment permanent if the permanent appointment is in the interest of the estate.

Added by Acts 1987, 70th Leg., ch. 460, § 2, eff. Sept. 1, 1987. Amended by Acts 1989, 71st Leg., ch. 1035, § 8, eff. Sept. 1, 1989; Acts 1997, 75th Leg., ch. 540, § 2, eff. Sept. 1, 1997; Acts 2005, 79th Leg., ch. 765, § 1, eff. June 17, 2005.

## § 132. Temporary Administration Pending Contest of a Will or Administration

(a) **Appointment of Temporary Administrator.** Pending a contest relative to the probate of a will or the granting of letters of administration, the court may appoint a temporary administrator, with such limited powers as the circumstances of the case require; and such appointment may continue in force until the termination of the contest and the appointment of an executor or administrator with full powers. The power of appointment in this Subsection is in addition to the court's power of appointment under Section 131A of this Code.

(b) **Additional Powers Relative to Claims.** When temporary administration has been granted pending a will contest, or pending a contest on an application for letters of administration, the court may, at any time during the pendency of the contest, confer upon the temporary administrator all the power and authority of a permanent administrator with respect to claims against the estate, and in such case the court and the temporary administrator shall act in the same manner as in permanent administration in connection with such matters as the approval or disapproval of claims, the payment of claims, and the making of sales of real or personal property for the payment of claims; provided, however, that in the event such power and authority is conferred upon a temporary administrator, he shall be required to give bond in the full amount required of a permanent administrator. The provisions of this Subsection are cumulative and shall not be construed to exclude the right of the court to order a temporary administrator to do any and all of the things covered by this Subsection in other cases where the doing of such things shall be necessary or expedient to preserve the estate pending final determination of the contest.

Acts 1955, 54th Leg., p. 88, ch. 55, eff. Jan. 1, 1956. Amended by Acts 1987, 70th Leg., ch. 460, § 3, eff. Sept. 1, 1987.

## § 133. Powers of Temporary Administrators

Temporary administrators shall have and exercise only such rights and powers as are specifically expressed in the order of the court appointing them, and as may be expressed in subsequent orders of the court. Where a court, by a subsequent order, extends the rights and powers of a temporary administrator, it may require additional bond commensurate with such extension. Any acts performed by temporary administrators that are not so expressly authorized shall be void.

Acts 1955, 54th Leg., p. 88, ch. 55, eff. Jan. 1, 1956. Amended by Acts 1993, 73rd Leg., ch. 957, § 25, eff. Sept. 1, 1993.

### § 134. Accounting

At the expiration of a temporary appointment, the appointee shall file with the clerk of the court a sworn list of all property of the estate which has come into his hands, a return of all sales made by him, and a full exhibit and account of all his acts as such appointee.

Acts 1955, 54th Leg., p. 88, ch. 55, eff. Jan. 1, 1956.

### § 135. Closing Temporary Administration

The list, return, exhibit, and account so filed shall be acted upon by the court and, whenever temporary letters shall expire or cease to be of effect for any cause, the court shall immediately enter an order requiring such temporary appointee forthwith to deliver the estate remaining in his possession to the person or persons legally entitled to its possession. Upon proof of such delivery, the appointee shall be discharged and the sureties on his bond released as to any future liability.

Acts 1955, 54th Leg., p. 88, ch. 55, eff. Jan. 1, 1956. Amended by Acts 1993, 73rd Leg., ch. 957, § 26, eff. Sept. 1, 1993.

### PART 2. RECEIVERSHIP FOR MINORS AND INCOMPETENTS [REPEALED]

### § 136. Repealed by Acts 1993, 73rd Leg., ch. 957, § 75(3), eff. Sept. 1, 1993

### PART 3. SMALL ESTATES

### § 137. Collection of Small Estates Upon Affidavit

(a) The distributees of the estate of a decedent who dies intestate shall be entitled thereto, to the extent that the assets, exclusive of homestead and exempt property, exceed the known liabilities of said estate, exclusive of liabilities secured by homestead and exempt property, without awaiting the appointment of a personal representative when:

(1) No petition for the appointment of a personal representative is pending or has been granted; and

(2) Thirty days have elapsed since the death of the decedent; and

(3) The value of the entire assets of the estate, not including homestead and exempt property, does not exceed $50,000; and

(4) There is filed with the clerk of the court having jurisdiction and venue an affidavit sworn to by two disinterested witnesses, by all such distributees that have legal capacity, and, if the facts warrant, by the natural guardian or next of kin of any minor or the guardian of any other

incapacitated person who is also a distributee, which affidavit shall be examined by the judge of the court having jurisdiction and venue; and

(5) The affidavit shows the existence of the foregoing conditions and includes a list of all of the known assets and liabilities of the estate, the names and addresses of the distributees, and the relevant family history facts concerning heirship that show the distributees' rights to receive the money or property of the estate or to have such evidences of money, property, or other rights of the estate as are found to exist transferred to them as heirs or assignees; and

(6) The judge, in the judge's discretion, finds that the affidavit conforms to the terms of this section and approves the affidavit; and

(7) A copy of the affidavit, certified to by said clerk, is furnished by the distributees of the estate to the person or persons owing money to the estate, having custody or possession of property of the estate, or acting as registrar, fiduciary or transfer agent of or for evidences of interest, indebtedness, property, or other right belonging to the estate.

(b) This section does not affect the disposition of property under the terms of a will or other testamentary document nor, except as provided by Subsection (c) of this section, does it transfer title to real property.

(c) Title to a decedent's homestead that is the only real property in a decedent's estate may be transferred on an affidavit that meets the requirements of this section. An affidavit that is used to transfer title to a homestead under this section must be recorded in the deed records of a county in which the homestead is located. A bona fide purchaser for value may rely on a recorded affidavit under this section. A bona fide purchaser for value without actual or constructive notice of an heir who is not disclosed in a recorded affidavit under this section acquires title to a homestead free of the interests of the undisclosed heir, but the bona fide purchaser remains subject to any claim a creditor of the decedent has by law. A purchaser has constructive notice of an heir who is not disclosed in a recorded affidavit under this section if an affidavit, judgment of heirship, or title transaction in the chain of title in the deed records identifies the heir of the decedent who is not disclosed in the affidavit as an heir of the decedent. An heir who is not disclosed in a recorded affidavit under this section may recover from an heir who receives consideration from a purchaser in a transfer for value of title to a homestead passing under the affidavit.

(d) If the judge approves the affidavit under this section, the affidavit is to be recorded as an official public record under Chapter 194,[1] Local Government Code. If the county has not adopted a microfilm or microphotographic process under Chapter 194, Local Government Code, the county clerk shall provide and keep in his office an appropriate book labeled "Small Estates," with an accurate index showing the name of the decedent and reference to land, if any, involved, in which he shall record every such affidavit so filed, upon being paid his legal recording fee.

Acts 1955, 54th Leg., p. 88, ch. 55, eff. Jan. 1, 1956. Amended by Acts 1957, 55th Leg., p. 53, ch. 31, § 4, eff. Aug. 22, 1957; Acts 1969, 61st Leg., p. 1978, ch. 670, § 1, eff. Sept. 1, 1969; Acts 1975, 64th Leg., p. 1402, ch. 543, § 1, eff. Sept. 1, 1975; Acts 1977, 65th Leg., p. 361, ch. 177, § 1, eff. May 20, 1977; Acts 1979, 66th Leg., p. 1747, ch. 713, § 14, eff. Aug. 27, 1979; Acts 1983, 68th Leg., p. 4560, ch. 757, § 1, eff. Sept. 1, 1983; Acts 1993, 73rd Leg., ch. 594, § 1, eff. Sept. 1, 1993; Acts 1995, 74th Leg., ch. 642, § 3, eff. Sept. 1, 1995; Acts 1995, 74th Leg., ch. 1039, § 8, eff. Sept. 1, 1995; Acts 1997, 75th Leg., ch. 540, § 3, eff. Sept. 1, 1997.

[1] Repealed, see, now, V.T.C.A., Local Government Code § 204.001 et seq.

## § 138. Effect of Affidavit

The person making payment, delivery, transfer or issuance pursuant to the affidavit described in the preceding Section shall be released to the same extent as if made to a personal representative of the decedent, and shall not be required to see to the application thereof or to inquire into the truth of any statement in the affidavit, but the distributees to whom payment, delivery, transfer, or issuance is made shall be answerable therefor to any person having a prior right and be accountable to any personal representative thereafter appointed. In addition, the person or persons who execute the affidavit shall be liable for any damage or loss to any person which arises from any payment, delivery, transfer, or issuance made in reliance on such affidavit. If the person to whom such affidavit is delivered refuses to pay, deliver, transfer, or issue the property as above provided, such property may be recovered in an action brought for such purpose by or on behalf of the distributees entitled thereto, upon proof of the facts required to be stated in the affidavit.

Acts 1955, 54th Leg., p. 88, ch. 55, eff. Jan. 1, 1956. Amended by Acts 1995, 74th Leg., ch. 642, § 4, eff. Sept. 1, 1995.

## § 139. Application for Order of No Administration

If the value of the entire assets of an estate, not including homestead and exempt property, does not exceed the amount to which the surviving spouse, minor children, and adult incapacitated children of the decedent are entitled as a family allowance, there may be filed by or on behalf of the surviving spouse, minor children, or adult incapacitated children an application in any court of proper venue for administration, or, if an application for the appointment of a personal representative has been filed but not yet granted, then in the court where such application has been filed, requesting the court to make a family allowance and to enter an order that no administration shall be necessary. The application shall state the names of the heirs or devisees, a list of creditors of the estate together with the amounts of the claims so far as the same are known, and a description of all real and personal property belonging to the estate, together with the estimated value thereof according to the best knowledge and information of the applicant, and the liens and encumbrances thereon, with a prayer that the court make a family allowance and that, if the entire assets of the estate, not including homestead and exempt property, are thereby exhausted, the

same be set aside to the surviving spouse, minor children, and adult incapacitated children, as in the case of other family allowances provided for by this Code.

Acts 1955, 54th Leg., p. 88, ch. 55, eff. Jan. 1, 1956. Amended by Acts 2011, 82nd Leg., ch. 810 (H.B. 2492), § 1.01, eff. Sept. 1, 2011.

## § 140. Hearing and Order Upon the Application

Upon the filing of an application for no administration such as that provided for in the preceding Section, the court may hear the same forthwith without notice, or at such time and upon such notice as the court requires. Upon the hearing of the application, if the court finds that the facts contained therein are true and that the expenses of last illness, funeral charges, and expenses of the proceeding have been paid or secured, the court shall make a family allowance and, if the entire assets of the estate, not including homestead and exempt property, are thereby exhausted, shall order that no administration be had of the estate and shall assign to the surviving spouse, minor children, and adult incapacitated children the whole of the estate, in the same manner and with the same effect as provided in this Code for the making of family allowances to the surviving spouse, minor children, and adult incapacitated children.

Acts 1955, 54th Leg., p. 88, ch. 55, eff. Jan. 1, 1956. Amended by Acts 2011, 82nd Leg., ch. 810 (H.B. 2492), § 1.01, eff. Sept. 1, 2011.

## § 141. Effect of Order

The order that no administration be had on the estate shall constitute sufficient legal authority to all persons owing any money, having custody of any property, or acting as registrar or transfer agent of any evidence of interest, indebtedness, property, or right, belonging to the estate, and to persons purchasing from or otherwise dealing with the estate, for payment or transfer to the persons described in the order as entitled to receive the estate without administration, and the persons so described in the order shall be entitled to enforce their right to such payment or transfer by suit.

Acts 1955, 54th Leg., p. 88, ch. 55, eff. Jan. 1, 1956.

## § 142. Proceeding to Revoke Order

At any time within one year after the entry of an order of no administration, and not thereafter, any interested person may file an application to revoke the same, alleging that other property has been discovered, or that property belonging to the estate was not included in the application for no administration, or that the property described in the application was incorrectly valued, and that if said property were added, included, or correctly valued, as the case may be, the total value of the property would exceed that necessary to justify the court in ordering no administration. Upon proof of any of such grounds, the court shall revoke the order of no administration. In case of any contest as to the value of any property, the court may appoint two appraisers to appraise the same in accordance with the procedure hereinafter provided for inventories and appraisements, and the appraisement of such appraisers shall be received in evidence but shall not be conclusive.

Acts 1955, 54th Leg., p. 88, ch. 55, eff. Jan. 1, 1956.

### § 143. Summary Proceedings for Small Estates After Personal Representative Appointed

Whenever, after the inventory, appraisement, and list of claims or the affidavit in lieu of the inventory, appraisement, and list of claims has been filed by a personal representative, it is established that the estate of a decedent, exclusive of the homestead and exempt property and family allowance to the surviving spouse, minor children, and adult incapacitated children, does not exceed the amount sufficient to pay the claims of Classes One to Four, inclusive, as claims are hereinafter classified, the personal representative shall, upon order of the court, pay the claims in the order provided and to the extent permitted by the assets of the estate subject to the payment of such claims, and thereafter present the personal representative's account with an application for the settlement and allowance thereof. Thereupon the court, with or without notice, may adjust, correct, settle, allow or disallow such account, and, if the account is settled and allowed, may decree final distribution, discharge the personal representative, and close the administration.

Acts 1955, 54th Leg., p. 88, ch. 55, eff. Jan. 1, 1956. Amended by Acts 2011, 82nd Leg., ch. 810 (H.B. 2492), § 1.01, eff. Sept. 1, 2011; Acts 2011, 82nd Leg., ch. 1338 (S.B. 1198), § 1.20, eff. Sept. 1, 2011.

### § 144. Repealed by Acts 1993, 73rd Leg., ch. 957, § 75(1), eff. Sept. 1, 1993

## PART 4.  INDEPENDENT ADMINISTRATION

### § 145.  Independent Administration

(a) Independent administration of an estate may be created as provided in Subsections (b) through (e) of this section.

(b) Any person capable of making a will may provide in his will that no other action shall be had in the county court in relation to the settlement of his estate than the probating and recording of his will, and the return of an inventory, appraisement, and list of claims of his estate.

(c) In situations where an executor is named in a decedent's will, but the will does not provide for independent administration of the decedent's estate as provided in Subsection (b) of this section, all of the distributees of the decedent may agree on the advisability of having an independent administration and collectively designate in the application for probate of the decedent's will the executor named in the will to serve as independent executor and request in the application that no other action shall be had in the county court in relation to the settlement of the decedent's estate other than the probating and recording of the decedent's will, and the return of an inventory, appraisement, and list of claims of the decedent's estate. In such case the county court shall enter an order granting independent administration and appointing the person, firm, or corporation designated in the application as independent executor, unless the

county court finds that it would not be in the best interest of the estate to do so.

(d) In situations where no executor is named in the decedent's will, or in situations where each executor named in the will is deceased or is disqualified to serve as executor or indicates by affidavit filed with the application for administration of the decedent's estate his inability or unwillingness to serve as executor, all of the distributees of the decedent may agree on the advisability of having an independent administration and collectively designate in the application for probate of the decedent's will a qualified person, firm, or corporation to serve as independent administrator and request in the application that no other action shall be had in the county court in relation to the settlement of the decedent's estate other than the probating and recording of the decedent's will, and the return of an inventory, appraisement, and list of claims of the decedent's estate. In such case the county court shall enter an order granting independent administration and appointing the person, firm, or corporation designated in the application as independent administrator, unless the county court finds that it would not be in the best interest of the estate to do so.

(e) All of the distributees of a decedent dying intestate may agree on the advisability of having an independent administration and collectively designate in the application for administration of the decedent's estate a qualified person, firm, or corporation to serve as independent administrator and request in the application that no other action shall be had in the county court in relation to the settlement of the decedent's estate other than the return of an inventory, appraisement, and list of claims of the decedent's estate. In such case the county court shall enter an order granting independent administration and appointing the person, firm, or corporation designated in the application as independent administrator, unless the county court finds that it would not be in the best interest of the estate to do so.

(f) In those cases where an independent administration is sought under the provisions of Subsections (c) through (e) above, all distributees shall be served with citation and notice of the application for independent administration unless the distributee waives the issuance or service of citation or enters an appearance in court.

(g) The court may not appoint an independent administrator to serve in an intestate administration unless and until the parties seeking appointment of the independent administrator have been determined, through a proceeding to declare heirship under Chapter III of this code, to constitute all of the decedent's heirs.

(h) When an independent administration has been created, and the order appointing an independent executor has been entered by the county court, and the inventory, appraisement, and list aforesaid has been filed by the executor and approved by the county court or an affidavit in lieu of the inventory, appraisement, and list of claims has been filed by the executor, as long as the estate is represented by an independent executor, further action of any nature shall not be had in the county court except where this Code specifically and explicitly provides for some action in the county court.

(i) If a distributee described in Subsections (c) through (e) of this section is an incapacitated person, the guardian of the person of the distributee may sign the application on behalf of the distributee. If the county court finds that either the granting of independent administration or the appointment of the person, firm, or corporation designated in the application as independent executor would not be in the best interests of the incapacitated person, then, notwithstanding anything to the contrary in Subsections (c) through (e) of this section, the county court shall not enter an order granting independent administration of the estate. If such distributee who is an incapacitated person has no guardian of the person, the county court may appoint a guardian ad litem to make application on behalf of the incapacitated person if the county court considers such an appointment necessary to protect the interest of the distributees. Alternatively, if the distributee who is an incapacitated person is a minor and has no guardian of the person, the natural guardian or guardians of the minor may consent on the minor's behalf if there is no conflict of interest between the minor and the natural guardian or guardians.

(j) If a trust is created in the decedent's will, the person or class of persons first eligible to receive the income from the trust, when determined as if the trust were to be in existence on the date of the decedent's death, shall, for the purposes of Subsections (c) and (d) of this section, be deemed to be the distributee or distributees on behalf of such trust, and any other trust or trusts coming into existence upon the termination of such trust, and are authorized to apply for independent administration on behalf of the trusts without the consent or agreement of the trustee or any other beneficiary of the trust, or the trustee or any beneficiary of any other trust which may come into existence upon the termination of such trust. If a trust beneficiary who is considered to be a distributee under this subsection is an incapacitated person, the trustee or cotrustee may file the application or give the consent, provided that the trustee or cotrustee is not the person proposed to serve as the independent executor.

(k) If a life estate is created either in the decedent's will or by law, the life tenant or life tenants, when determined as if the life estate were to commence on the date of the decedent's death, shall, for the purposes of Subsections (c) through (e) of this section, be deemed to be the distributee or distributees on behalf of the entire estate created, and are authorized to apply for independent administration on behalf of the estate without the consent or approval of any remainderman.

(l) If a decedent's will contains a provision that a distributee must survive the decedent by a prescribed period of time in order to take under the decedent's will, then, for the purposes of determining who shall be the distributee under Subsections (c), (d), (h), and (i) of this section, it shall be presumed that the distributees living at the time of the filing

of the application for probate of the decedent's will survived the decedent by the prescribed period.

(m) In the case of all decedents, whether dying testate or intestate, for the purposes of determining who shall be the distributees under Subsections (c), (d), (e), (h), and (i) of this section, it shall be presumed that no distributee living at the time the application for independent administration is filed shall subsequently disclaim any portion of such distributee's interest in the decedent's estate.

(n) If a distributee of a decedent's estate should die and if by virtue of such distributee's death such distributee's share of the decedent's estate shall become payable to such distributee's estate, then the deceased distributee's personal representative may sign the application for independent administration of the decedent's estate under Subsections (c), (d), (e), (h), and (i) of this section.

(o) Notwithstanding anything to the contrary in this section, a person capable of making a will may provide in his will that no independent administration of his estate may be allowed. In such case, his estate, if administered, shall be administered and settled under the direction of the county court as other estates are required to be settled.

(p) If an independent administration of a decedent's estate is created pursuant to Subsections (c), (d), or (e) of this section, then, unless the county court shall waive bond on application for waiver, the independent executor shall be required to enter into bond payable to and to be approved by the judge and his or her successors in a sum that is found by the judge to be adequate under all circumstances, or a bond with one surety in a sum that is found by the judge to be adequate under all circumstances, if the surety is an authorized corporate surety. This subsection does not repeal any other section of this Code.

(q) Absent proof of fraud or collusion on the part of a judge, no judge may be held civilly liable for the commission of misdeeds or the omission of any required act of any person, firm, or corporation designated as an independent executor or independent administrator under Subsections (c), (d), and (e) of the section. Section 36 of this code does not apply to the appointment of an independent executor or administrator under Subsection (c), (d), or (e) of this section.

(r) A person who declines to serve or resigns as independent executor or administrator of a decedent's estate may be appointed an executor or administrator of the estate if the estate will be administered and settled under the direction of the court.

Acts 1955, 54th Leg., p. 88, ch. 55, eff. Jan. 1, 1956. Amended by Acts 1957, 55th Leg., p. 53, ch. 31, § 2(b); Acts 1977, 65th Leg., p. 1061, ch. 390, § 3, eff. Sept. 1, 1977; Acts 1979, 66th Leg., p. 1750, ch. 713, § 16, eff. Aug. 27, 1979; Acts 1991, 72nd Leg., ch. 895, § 10, eff. Sept. 1, 1991; Acts 1993, 73rd Leg., ch. 846, § 15, eff. Sept. 1, 1993; Acts 1995, 74th Leg., ch. 1039, § 9, eff. Sept. 1, 1995; Subsecs. (g) to (j) amended by Acts 2011, 82nd Leg., ch. 1338 (S.B. 1198), § 1.21, eff. Sept. 1, 2011.

**Text of Texas Probate Code effective until January 1, 2014**

## § 145A. Granting Power of Sale by Agreement

In a situation in which a decedent does not have a will or a decedent's will does not contain language authorizing the personal representative to sell real property or contains language that is not sufficient to grant the representative that authority, the court may include in an order appointing an independent executor under Section 145 of this code any general or specific authority regarding the power of the independent executor to sell real property that may be consented to by the beneficiaries who are to receive any interest in the real property in the application for independent administration or in their consents to the independent administration. The independent executor, in such event, may sell the real property under the authority granted in the court order without the further consent of those beneficiaries.

Added by Acts 2011, 82nd Leg., ch. 1338 (S.B. 1198), § 1.22, eff. Sept. 1, 2011.

## § 145B. Independent Executors May Act Without Court Approval

Unless this code specifically provides otherwise, any action that a personal representative subject to court supervision may take with or without a court order may be taken by an independent executor without a court order. The other provisions of this part are designed to provide additional guidance regarding independent administrations in specified situations, and are not designed to limit by omission or otherwise the application of the general principles set forth in this part.

Added by Acts 2011, 82nd Leg., ch. 1338 (S.B. 1198), § 1.22, eff. Sept. 1, 2011.

## § 145C. Power of Sale of Estate Property

(a) Definition. In this section, "independent executor" does not include an independent administrator.

(b) General. Unless limited by the terms of a will, an independent executor, in addition to any power of sale of estate property given in the will, and an independent administrator have the same power of sale for the same purposes as a personal representative has in a supervised administration, but without the requirement of court approval. The procedural requirements applicable to a supervised administration do not apply.

(c) Protection of Person Purchasing Estate Property. (1) A person who is not a devisee or heir is not required to inquire into the power of sale of estate property of the independent executor or independent administrator or the propriety of the exercise of the power of sale if the person deals with the independent executor or independent administrator in good faith and:

(A) a power of sale is granted to the independent executor in the will;

(B) a power of sale is granted under Section 145A of this code in the court order appointing the independent executor or independent administrator; or

(C) the independent executor or independent administrator provides an affidavit, executed and sworn to under oath and recorded in the deed records of the county where the property is located, that the sale is necessary or advisable for any of the purposes described in Section 341(1) of this code.

(2) As to acts undertaken in good faith reliance, the affidavit described by Subsection (c)(1)(C) of this section is conclusive proof, as between a purchaser of property from an estate, and the personal representative of the estate or the heirs and distributees of the estate, with respect to the authority of the independent executor or independent administrator to sell the property. The signature or joinder of a devisee or heir who has an interest in the property being sold as described in this section is not necessary for the purchaser to obtain all right, title, and interest of the estate in the property being sold.

(3) This section does not relieve the independent executor or independent administrator from any duty owed to a devisee or heir in relation, directly or indirectly, to the sale.

(d) No Limitations. This section does not limit the authority of an independent executor or independent administrator to take any other action without court supervision or approval with respect to estate assets that may take place in a supervised administration, for purposes and within the scope otherwise authorized by this code, including the authority to enter into a lease and to borrow money.

Added by Acts 2011, 82nd Leg., ch. 1338 (S.B. 1198), § 1.22, eff. Sept. 1, 2011.

## § 146. Payment of Claims and Delivery of Exemptions and Allowances

(a) Duty of the Independent Executor. An independent executor, in the administration of an estate, independently of and without application to, or any action in or by the court:

(1) shall give the notices required under Sections 294 and 295;

(2) may give the notice permitted under Section 294(d) and bar a claim under that subsection;

(3) shall approve, classify, and pay, or reject, claims against the estate in the same order of priority, classification, and proration prescribed in this Code; and

(4) shall set aside and deliver to those entitled thereto exempt property and allowances for support, and allowances in lieu of exempt property, as prescribed in this Code, to the same extent and result as if the independent executor's actions had been accomplished in, and under orders of, the court.

(a-1) Statement in Notice of Claim. To be effective, the notice provided under Subsection (a)(2) of this section must include, in addition to the other information required by Section 294(d) of this code, a statement that a claim may be effectively presented by only one of the methods prescribed by this section.

(b) Secured Claims for Money. Within six months after the date letters are granted or within four months after the date notice is received under Section 295 of this code, whichever is later, a creditor with a claim for money secured by real or personal property of the estate must give notice to the independent executor of the creditor's election to have the creditor's claim approved as a matured secured claim to be paid in due course of administration. In addition to giving the notice within this period, a creditor whose claim is secured by real property shall record a notice of the creditor's election under this subsection in the deed records of the county in which the real property is located. If no election to be a matured secured creditor is made, or the election is made, but not within the prescribed period, or is made within the prescribed period but the creditor has a lien against real property and fails to record notice of the claim in the deed records as required within the prescribed period, the claim shall be a preferred debt and lien against the specific property securing the indebtedness and shall be paid according to the terms of the contract that secured the lien, and the claim may not be asserted against other assets of the estate. The independent executor may pay the claim before the claim matures if paying the claim before maturity is in the best interest of the estate.

(b–1) Matured Secured Claims. (1) A claim approved as a matured secured claim under Subsection (b) of this section remains secured by any lien or security interest against the specific property securing payment of the claim but subordinated to the payment from the property of claims having a higher classification under Section 322 of this code. However, the secured creditor:

(A) is not entitled to exercise any remedies in a manner that prevents the payment of the higher priority claims and allowances; and

(B) during the administration of the estate, is not entitled to exercise any contractual collection rights, including the power to foreclose, without either the prior written approval of the independent executor or court approval.

(2) Subdivision (1) of this subsection may not be construed to suspend or otherwise prevent a creditor with a matured secured claim from seeking judicial relief of any kind or from executing any judgment against an independent executor. Except with respect to real property, any third party acting in good faith may obtain good title with respect to an estate asset acquired through a secured creditor's extrajudicial collection rights, without regard to whether the creditor had the right to collect the asset or whether the creditor acted improperly in exercising those rights during an estate administration due to having elected matured secured status.

(3) If a claim approved or established by suit as a matured secured claim is secured by property passing to one or more devisees in accordance with Section 71A of this code, the independent executor shall collect from the devisees the amount of the debt and pay that amount to the claimant or shall sell the property and pay out of the sale proceeds the claim and associated expenses of sale consistent with the provisions of Section 306(c–1) of this code applicable to court supervised administrations.

(b–2) Preferred Debt and Lien Claims. During an independent administration, a secured creditor whose claim is a preferred debt and lien against property securing the indebtedness under Subsection (b) of this section is free to exercise any judicial or extrajudicial collection rights, including the right to foreclosure and execution; provided, however, that the creditor does not have the right to conduct a nonjudicial foreclosure sale within six months after letters are granted.

(b–3) Certain Unsecured Claims; Barring of Claims. An unsecured creditor who has a claim for money against an estate and who receives a notice under Section 294(d) of this code shall give to the independent executor notice of the nature and amount of the claim not later than the 120th day after the date the notice is received or the claim is barred.

(b–4) Notices Required by Creditors. Notice to the independent executor required by Subsections (b) and (b–3) of this section must be contained in:

(1) a written instrument that is hand-delivered with proof of receipt, or mailed by certified mail, return receipt requested with proof of receipt, to the independent executor or the executor's attorney;

(2) a pleading filed in a lawsuit with respect to the claim; or

(3) a written instrument or pleading filed in the court in which the administration of the estate is pending.

(b–5) Filing Requirements Applicable. Subsection (b–4) of this section does not exempt a creditor who elects matured secured status from the filing requirements of Subsection (b) of this section, to the extent those requirements are applicable.

(b–6) Statute of Limitations. Except as otherwise provided by Section 16.062, Civil Practice and Remedies Code, the running of the statute of limitations shall be tolled only by a written approval of a claim signed by an independent executor, a pleading filed in a suit pending at the time of the decedent's death, or a suit brought by the creditor against the independent executor. In particular, the presentation of a statement or claim, or a notice with respect to a claim, to an independent executor does not toll the running of the statute of limitations with respect to that claim.

(b–7) Other Claim Procedures of Code Generally Do Not Apply. Except as otherwise provided by this section, the procedural provisions of this code governing creditor claims in supervised administrations do not apply to independent administrations. By way of example, but not as a limitation:

(1) Section 313 of this code does not apply to independent administrations, and consequently a creditor's claim may not be barred solely because the creditor failed to file a suit not later than the 90th day after the date an independent execu-

tor rejected the claim or with respect to a claim for which the independent executor takes no action; and

(2) Sections 306(f)–(k) of this code do not apply to independent administrations.

(c) Liability of Independent Executor.  An independent executor, in the administration of an estate, may pay at any time and without personal liability a claim for money against the estate to the extent approved and classified by the personal representative if:

(1) the claim is not barred by limitations;  and

(2) at the time of payment, the independent executor reasonably believes the estate will have sufficient assets to pay all claims against the estate.

(d) Notice Required of Unsecured Creditor.  An unsecured creditor who has a claim for money against an estate and receives a notice under Section 294(d) shall give notice to the independent executor of the nature and amount of the claim not later than the 120th day after the date on which the notice is received or the claim is barred.

(e) Placement of Notice.  Notice required by Subsections (b) and (d) must be contained in:

(1) a written instrument that is hand-delivered with proof of receipt or mailed by certified mail, return receipt requested, to the independent executor or the executor's attorney;

(2) a pleading filed in a lawsuit with respect to the claim; or

(3) a written instrument or pleading filed in the court in which the administration of the estate is pending.

Acts 1955, 54th Leg., p. 88, ch. 55, eff. Jan. 1, 1956.  Amended by Acts 1957, 55th Leg., p. 53, ch. 31, § 2(c), eff. Aug. 21, 1957; Acts 1995, 74th Leg., ch. 1054, § 1, eff. Jan. 1, 1996; Acts 1997, 75th Leg., ch. 1302, § 8, eff. Sept. 1, 1997; Subsec. (b) amended and Subsecs. (a–1) and (b–1) to (b–7) added by Acts 2011, 82nd Leg., ch. 1338 (S.B. 1198), § 1.23, eff. Sept. 1, 2011.

## § 147.  Enforcement of Claims by Suit

Any person having a debt or claim against the estate may enforce the payment of the same by suit against the independent executor;  and, when judgment is recovered against the independent executor, the execution shall run against the estate of the decedent in the hands of the independent executor which is subject to such debt.  The independent executor shall not be required to plead to any suit brought against him for money until after six months from the date that an independent administration was created and the order appointing an independent executor was entered by the county court.

Acts 1955, 54th Leg., p. 88, ch. 55, eff. Jan. 1, 1956.  Amended by Acts 1975, 64th Leg., p. 980, ch. 376, § 1, eff. June 19, 1975; Acts 1977, 65th Leg., p. 1064, ch. 390, § 4, eff. Sept. 1, 1977.

## § 148.  Requiring Heirs to Give Bond

When an independent administration is created and the order appointing an independent executor is entered by the county court, any person having a debt against such estate may, by written complaint filed in the county court where such order was entered, cause all distributees of the estate, heirs at law, and other persons entitled to any portion of such estate under the will, if any, to be cited by personal service to appear before such county court and execute a bond for an amount equal to the amount of the creditor's claim or the full value of such estate, as shown by the inventory and list of claims, whichever is the smaller, such bond to be payable to the judge, and his successors, and to be approved by said judge, and conditioned that all obligors shall pay all debts that shall be established against such estate in the manner provided by law.  Upon the return of the citation served, unless such person so entitled to any portion of the estate, or some of them, or some other person for them, shall execute such bond to the satisfaction of the county court, such estate shall thereafter be administered and settled under the direction of the county court as other estates are required to be settled.  If the bond is executed and approved, the independent administration shall proceed.  Creditors of the estate may sue on such bond, and shall be entitled to judgment thereon for the amount of their debt, or they may have their action against those in possession of the estate.

Acts 1955, 54th Leg., p. 88, ch. 55, eff. Jan. 1, 1956.  Amended by Acts 1977, 65th Leg., p. 1064, ch. 390, § 5, eff. Sept. 1, 1977; Acts 1979, 66th Leg., p. 1750, ch. 713, § 17, eff. Aug. 27, 1979.

## § 149.  Requiring Independent Executor to Give Bond

When it has been provided by will, regularly probated, that an independent executor appointed by such will shall not be required to give bond for the management of the estate devised by such will, the direction shall be observed, unless it be made to appear at any time that such independent executor is mismanaging the property, or has betrayed or is about to betray his trust, or has in some other way become disqualified, in which case, upon proper proceedings had for that purpose, as in the case of executors or administrators acting under orders of the court, such executor may be required to give bond.

Acts 1955, 54th Leg., p. 88, ch. 55, eff. Jan. 1, 1956.

## § 149A.  Accounting

(a) Interested Person May Demand Accounting.  At any time after the expiration of fifteen months from the date that an independent administration was created and the order appointing an independent executor was entered by the county court, any person interested in the estate may demand an accounting from the independent executor.  The independent executor shall thereupon furnish to the person or persons making the demand an exhibit in writing, sworn and subscribed by the independent executor, setting forth in detail:

1.  The property belonging to the estate which has come into his hands as executor.

2.  The disposition that has been made of such property.

3.  The debts that have been paid.

**Text of Texas Probate Code effective until January 1, 2014**

4. The debts and expenses, if any, still owing by the estate.

5. The property of the estate, if any, still remaining in his hands.

6. Such other facts as may be necessary to a full and definite understanding of the exact condition of the estate.

7. Such facts, if any, that show why the administration should not be closed and the estate distributed.

Any other interested person shall, upon demand, be entitled to a copy of any exhibit or accounting that has been made by an independent executor in compliance with this section.

(b) **Enforcement of Demand.** Should the independent executor not comply with a demand for an accounting authorized by this section within sixty days after receipt of the demand, the person making the demand may compel compliance by an action in the county court, as that term is defined by Section 3 of this code. After a hearing, the court shall enter an order requiring the accounting to be made at such time as it deems proper under the circumstances.

(c) **Subsequent Demands.** After an initial accounting has been given by an independent executor, any person interested in an estate may demand subsequent periodic accountings at intervals of not less than twelve months, and such subsequent demands may be enforced in the same manner as an initial demand.

(d) **Remedies Cumulative.** The right to an accounting accorded by this section is cumulative of any other remedies which persons interested in an estate may have against the independent executor thereof.

Added by Acts 1971, 62nd Leg., p. 980, ch. 173, § 10, eff. Jan. 1, 1972. Amended by Acts 1973, 63rd Leg., p. 412, ch. 184, § 1, eff. May 25, 1973; Acts 1977, 65th Leg., p. 1065, ch. 390, § 6, eff. Sept. 1, 1977; Acts 1999, 76th Leg., ch. 855, § 3, eff. Sept. 1, 1999.

### § 149B. Accounting and Distribution

(a) In addition to or in lieu of the right to an accounting provided by Section 149A of this code, at any time after the expiration of two years from the date the court clerk first issues letters testamentary or of administration to any personal representative of an estate, a person interested in the estate then subject to independent administration may petition the county court, as that term is defined by Section 3 of this code, for an accounting and distribution. The court may order an accounting to be made with the court by the independent executor at such time as the court deems proper. The accounting shall include the information that the court deems necessary to determine whether any part of the estate should be distributed.

(b) On receipt of the accounting and, after notice to the independent executor and a hearing, unless the court finds a continued necessity for administration of the estate, the court shall order its distribution by the independent executor to the persons entitled to the property. If the court finds there is a continued necessity for administration of the estate, the court shall order the distribution of any portion of the estate that the court finds should not be subject to further administration by the independent executor. If any portion of the estate that is ordered to be distributed is incapable of distribution without prior partition or sale, the court shall order partition and distribution, or sale, in the manner provided for the partition and distribution of property incapable of division in estates administered under the direction of the county court.

(c) If all the property in the estate is ordered distributed by the executor and the estate is fully administered, the court also may order the independent executor to file a final account with the court and may enter an order closing the administration and terminating the power of the independent executor to act as executor.

Added by Acts 1979, 66th Leg., p. 1751, ch. 713, § 18, eff. Aug. 27, 1979. Amended by Acts 1985, 69th Leg., ch. 882, § 1, eff. Aug. 26, 1985; Acts 1987, 70th Leg., ch. 760, § 1, eff. Aug. 31, 1987; Acts 1987, 70th Leg., ch. 565, § 1, eff. June 18, 1987; Acts 1999, 76th Leg., ch. 855, § 4, eff. Sept. 1, 1999; Subsec. (a) amended by Acts 2011, 82nd Leg., ch. 1338 (S.B. 1198), § 1.24, eff. Sept. 1, 2011.

### § 149C. Removal of Independent Executor

(a) The county court, as that term is defined by Section 3 of this code, on its own motion or on motion of any interested person, after the independent executor has been cited by personal service to answer at a time and place fixed in the notice, may remove an independent executor when:

(1) the independent executor fails to return within ninety days after qualification, unless such time is extended by order of the court, either an inventory of the property of the estate and list of claims that have come to the independent executor's knowledge or an affidavit in lieu of the inventory, appraisement, and list of claims;

(2) sufficient grounds appear to support belief that the independent executor has misapplied or embezzled, or that the independent executor is about to misapply or embezzle, all or any part of the property committed to the independent executor's care;

(3) the independent executor fails to make an accounting which is required by law to be made;

(4) the independent executor fails to timely file the affidavit or certificate required by Section 128A of this code;

(5) the independent executor is proved to have been guilty of gross misconduct or gross mismanagement in the performance of the independent executor's duties;

(6) the independent executor becomes an incapacitated person, or is sentenced to the penitentiary, or from any other cause becomes legally incapacitated from properly performing the independent executor's fiduciary duties; or

(7) the independent executor becomes incapable of properly performing the independent executor's fiduciary duties due to a material conflict of interest.

(b) The order of removal shall state the cause of removal and shall direct by order the disposition of the assets remaining in the name or under the control of the removed executor. The order of removal shall require that letters issued to the removed executor shall be surrendered and that all letters shall be canceled of record. If an independent executor is removed by the court under this section, the court may, on application, appoint a successor independent executor as provided by Section 154A of this code.

(c) An independent executor who defends an action for his removal in good faith, whether successful or not, shall be allowed out of the estate his necessary expenses and disbursements, including reasonable attorney's fees, in the removal proceedings.

(d) Costs and expenses incurred by the party seeking removal incident to removal of an independent executor appointed without bond, including reasonable attorney's fees and expenses, may be paid out of the estate.

Added by Acts 1979, 66th Leg., p. 1751, ch. 713, § 19, eff. Aug. 27, 1979. Amended by Acts 1987, 70th Leg., ch. 719, § 1, eff. Aug. 31, 1987; Acts 1989, 71st Leg., ch. 1035, § 10, eff. Sept. 1, 1989; Acts 1995, 74th Leg., ch. 1039, § 10, eff. Sept. 1, 1995; Acts 1999, 76th Leg., ch. 855, § 5, eff. Sept. 1, 1999.
Subsec. (a) amended by Acts 2007, 80th Leg., ch. 801, § 3, eff. Sept. 1, 2007; Subsec. (a)(1) and (7) amended by Acts 2011, 82nd Leg., ch. 1338 (S.B. 1198), § 1.25, eff. Sept. 1, 2011.

### § 149D. Distribution of Remaining Estate Pending Judicial Discharge

(a) On or before filing an action under Section 149E of this code, the independent executor must distribute to the beneficiaries of the estate any of the remaining assets or property of the estate that remains in the hands of the independent executor after all of the estate's debts have been paid, except for a reasonable reserve of assets that the independent executor may retain in a fiduciary capacity pending court approval of the final account.

(b) The court may review the amount of assets on reserve and may order the independent executor to make further distributions under this section.

Added by Acts 1999, 76th Leg., ch. 855, § 6, eff. Sept. 1, 1999.

### § 149E. Judicial Discharge of Independent Executor

(a) After an estate has been administered and if there is no further need for an independent administration of the estate, the independent executor of the estate may file an action for declaratory judgment under Chapter 37, Civil Practice and Remedies Code, seeking to discharge the independent executor from any liability involving matters relating to the past administration of the estate that have been fully and fairly disclosed.

(b) On the filing of an action under this section, each beneficiary of the estate shall be personally served with citation, except for a beneficiary who has waived the issuance and service of citation.

(c) In a proceeding under this section, the court may require the independent executor to file a final account that includes any information the court considers necessary to

adjudicate the independent executor's request for a discharge of liability. The court may audit, settle, or approve a final account filed under this subsection.

Added by Acts 1999, 76th Leg., ch. 855, § 6, eff. Sept. 1, 1999.

### § 149F. Court Costs and Other Charges Related to Final Account in Judicial Discharge

(a) Except as ordered by the court, the independent executor is entitled to pay from the estate legal fees, expenses, or other costs of a proceeding incurred in relation to a final account required under Section 149E of this code.

(b) The independent executor shall be personally liable to refund any amount not approved by the court as a proper charge against the estate.

Added by Acts 1999, 76th Leg., ch. 855, § 6, eff. Sept. 1, 1999.

### § 149G. Rights and Remedies Cumulative

The rights and remedies conferred by Sections 149D, 149E, and 149F of this code are cumulative of other rights and remedies to which a person interested in the estate may be entitled under law.

Added by Acts 1999, 76th Leg., ch. 855, § 6, eff. Sept. 1, 1999.

### § 150. Partition and Distribution or Sale of Property Incapable of Division

If the will does not distribute the entire estate of the testator, or provide a means for partition of said estate, or if no will was probated, the independent executor may file his final account in the county court in which the will was probated, or if no will was probated, in the county court in which the order appointing the independent executor was entered, and ask for either partition and distribution of the estate or an order of sale of any portion of the estate alleged by the independent executor and found by the court to be incapable of a fair and equal partition and distribution, or both; and the same either shall be partitioned and distributed or shall be sold, or both, in the manner provided for the partition and distribution of property and the sale of property incapable of division in estates administered under the direction of the county court.

Acts 1955, 54th Leg., p. 88, ch. 55, eff. Jan. 1, 1956. Amended by Acts 1977, 65th Leg., p. 1065, ch. 390, § 7, eff. Sept. 1, 1977; Acts 1979, 66th Leg., p. 1752, ch. 713, § 20, eff. Aug. 27, 1979.

### § 151. Closing Independent Administration by Closing Report or Notice of Closing Estate

(a) Filing of Closing Report or Notice of Closing Estate. When all of the debts known to exist against the estate have been paid, or when they have been paid so far as the assets in the hands of the independent executor will permit, when there is no pending litigation, and when the independent executor has distributed to the persons entitled thereto all assets of the estate, if any, remaining after payment of debts, the independent executor may file with the court a closing report or a notice of closing of the estate.

(a–1) Closing Report. An independent executor may file a closing report verified by affidavit that:

(1) shows:

(A) the property of the estate which came into the possession of the independent executor;

(B) the debts that have been paid;

(C) the debts, if any, still owing by the estate;

(D) the property of the estate, if any, remaining on hand after payment of debts; and

(E) the names and residences of the persons to whom the property of the estate, if any, remaining on hand after payment of debts has been distributed; and

(2) includes signed receipts or other proof of delivery of property to the distributees named in the closing report if the closing report reflects that there was property remaining on hand after payment of debts.

(b) Notice of Closing Estate. (1) Instead of filing a closing report under Subsection (a–1) of this section, an independent executor may file a notice of closing estate verified by affidavit that states:

(A) that all debts known to exist against the estate have been paid or have been paid to the extent permitted by the assets in the independent executor's possession;

(B) that all remaining assets of the estate, if any, have been distributed; and

(C) the names and addresses of the distributees to whom the property of the estate, if any, remaining on hand after payment of debts has been distributed.

(2) Before filing the notice, the independent executor shall provide to each distributee of the estate a copy of the notice of closing estate. The notice of closing estate filed by the independent executor must include signed receipts or other proof that all distributees have received a copy of the notice of closing estate.

(c) Effect of Filing Closing Report or Notice of Closing Estate. (1) The independent administration of an estate is considered closed 30 days after the date of the filing of a closing report or notice of closing estate unless an interested person files an objection with the court within that time. If an interested person files an objection within the 30–day period, the independent administration of the estate is closed when the objection has been disposed of or the court signs an order closing the estate.

(2) The closing of an independent administration by filing of a closing report or notice of closing estate terminates the power and authority of the independent executor, but shall not relieve the independent executor from liability for any mismanagement of the estate or from liability for any false statements contained in the report or notice.

(3) When a closing report or notice of closing estate has been filed, persons dealing with properties of the estate, or with claims against the estate, shall deal directly with the distributees of the estate; and the acts of the distributees with respect to the properties or claims shall in all ways be valid and binding as regards the persons with whom they deal, notwithstanding any false statements made by the independent executor in the report or notice.

(4) If the independent executor is required to give bond, the independent executor's filing of the closing report and proof of delivery, if required, automatically releases the sureties on the bond from all liability for the future acts of the principal. The filing of a notice of closing estate does not release the sureties on the bond of an independent executor.

(d) Authority to Transfer Property of a Decedent After Filing the Closing Report or Notice of Closing Estate. An independent executor's closing report or notice of closing estate shall constitute sufficient legal authority to all persons owing any money, having custody of any property, or acting as registrar or transfer agent or trustee of any evidence of interest, indebtedness, property, or right that belongs to the estate, for payment or transfer without additional administration to the distributees described in the will as entitled to receive the particular asset or who as heirs at law are entitled to receive the asset. The distributees described in the will as entitled to receive the particular asset or the heirs at law entitled to receive the asset may enforce their right to the payment or transfer by suit.

(e) Delivery Subject to Receipt or Proof of Delivery. An independent executor may not be required to deliver tangible or intangible personal property to a distributee unless the independent executor receives, at or before the time of delivery of the property, a signed receipt or other proof of delivery of the property to the distributee. An independent executor may not require a waiver or release from the distributee as a condition of delivery of property to a distributee.

Acts 1955, 54th Leg., p. 88, ch. 55, eff. Jan. 1, 1956. Amended by Acts 1979, 66th Leg., p. 1752, ch. 713, § 21, eff. Aug. 27, 1979; Acts 1991, 72nd Leg., ch. 895, § 11, eff. Sept. 1, 1991; Acts 1995, 74th Leg., ch. 642, § 5, eff. Sept. 1, 1995. Subsec. (e) repealed by Acts 2007, 80th Leg., ch. 301, § 7, eff. Sept. 1, 2007. Amended by Acts 2011, 82nd Leg., ch. 1338 (S.B. 1198), § 1.26, eff. Sept. 1, 2011.

## § 152. Closing Independent Administration Upon Application by Distributee

(a) At any time after an estate has been fully administered and there is no further need for an independent administration of such estate, any distributee may file an application to close the administration; and, after citation upon the independent executor, and upon hearing, the court may enter an order:

(1) requiring the independent executor to file a verified report meeting the requirements of Section 151(a) of this code;

(2) closing the administration;

(3) terminating the power of the independent executor to act as such; and

(4) releasing the sureties on any bond the independent executor was required to give from all liability for the future acts of the principal.

(b) The order of the court closing the independent administration shall constitute sufficient legal authority to all persons owing any money, having custody of any property, or acting as registrar or transfer agent or trustee of any evidence of interest, indebtedness, property, or right that belongs to the estate, for payment or transfer without additional administration to the persons described in the will as entitled to receive the particular asset or who as heirs at law are entitled to receive the asset. The persons described in the will as entitled to receive the particular asset or the heirs at law entitled to receive the asset may enforce their right to the payment or transfer by suit.

Acts 1955, 54th Leg., p. 88, ch. 55, eff. Jan. 1, 1956. Amended by Acts 1979, 66th Leg., p. 1752, ch. 713, § 22, eff. Aug. 27, 1979; Acts 1991, 72nd Leg., ch. 895, § 12, eff. Sept. 1, 1991.

### § 153. Issuance of Letters

At any time before the authority of an independent executor has been terminated in the manner set forth in the preceding Sections, the clerk shall issue such number of letters testamentary as the independent executor shall request.

Acts 1955, 54th Leg., p. 88, ch. 55, eff. Jan. 1, 1956.

### § 154. Powers of an Administrator Who Succeeds an Independent Executor

**(a) Grant of Powers by Court.** Whenever a person has died, or shall die, testate, owning property in Texas, and such person's will has been or shall be admitted to probate by the proper court, and such probated will names an independent executor or executors, or trustees acting in the capacity of independent executors, to execute the terms and provisions of said will, and such will grants to such independent executor, or executors, or trustees acting in the capacity of independent executors, the power to raise or borrow money and to mortgage, and such independent executor, or executors, or trustees, have died or shall die, resign, fail to qualify, or be removed from office, leaving unexecuted parts or portions of the will of the testator, and an administrator with the will annexed is appointed by the court having jurisdiction of the estate, and an administrator's bond is filed and approved by the court, then in all such cases, the court may, in addition to the powers conferred upon such administrator under other provisions of the laws of Texas, authorize, direct, and empower such administrator to do and perform the acts and deeds, clothed with the rights, powers, authorities, and privileges, and subject to the limitations, set forth in the subsequent portions of this Section.

**(b) Power to Borrow Money and Mortgage or Pledge Property.** The court, upon application, citation, and hearing, may, by its order, authorize, direct, and empower such administrator to raise or borrow such sums of money and incur such obligations and debts as the court shall, in its said order, direct, and to renew and extend same from time to time, as the court, upon application and order, shall provide; and, if authorized by the court's order, to secure such loans, obligations, and debts, by pledge or mortgage upon property or assets of the estate, real, personal, or mixed, upon such terms and conditions, and for such duration of time, as the court shall deem to be to the best interest of the estate, and by its order shall prescribe; and all such loans, obligations, debts, pledges, and mortgages shall be valid and enforceable against the estate and against such administrator in his official capacity.

**(c) Powers Limited to Those Granted by the Will.** The court may order and authorize such administrator to have and exercise the powers and privileges set forth in the preceding Subsections hereof only to the extent that same are granted to or possessed by the independent executor, or executors, or trustees acting in the capacity of independent executors, under the terms of the probated will of such deceased person, and then only in such cases as it appears, at the hearing of the application, that at the time of the appointment of such administrator, there are outstanding and unpaid obligations and debts of the estate, or of the independent executor, or executors, or trustees, chargeable against the estate, or unpaid expenses of administration, or when the court appointing such administrator orders the business of such estate to be carried on and it becomes necessary, from time to time, under orders of the court, for such administrator to borrow money and incur obligations and indebtedness in order to protect and preserve the estate.

**(d) Powers Other Than Those Relating to Borrowing Money and Mortgaging or Pledging Property.** The court, in addition, may, upon application, citation, and hearing, order, authorize and empower such administrator to assume, exercise, and discharge, under the orders and directions of said court, made from time to time, all or such part of the rights, powers, and authorities vested in and delegated to, or possessed by, the independent executor, or executors, or trustees acting in the capacity of independent executors, under the terms of the will of such deceased person, as the court finds to be to the best interest of the estate and shall, from time to time, order and direct.

**(e) Application for Grant of Powers.** The granting to such administrator by the court of some, or all, of the powers and authorities set forth in this Section shall be upon application filed by such administrator with the county clerk, setting forth such facts as, in the judgment of the administrator, require the granting of the power or authority requested.

**(f) Citation.** Upon the filing of such application, the clerk shall issue citation to all persons interested in the estate, stating the nature of the application, and requiring such persons to appear on the return day named in such citation and show cause why such application should not be granted, should they choose to do so. Such citation shall be served by posting.

**(g) Hearing and Order.** The court shall hear such application and evidence thereon, upon the return day named in the citation, or thereafter, and, if satisfied a necessity exists and that it would be to the best interest of the estate to grant said application in whole or in part, the court shall so order; otherwise, the court shall refuse said application.

Acts 1955, 54th Leg., p. 88, ch. 55, eff. Jan. 1, 1956.

### § 154A. Court-Appointed Successor Independent Executor

(a) If the will of a person who dies testate names an independent executor who, having qualified, fails for any reason to continue to serve, or is removed for cause by the court, and the will does not name a successor independent executor or if each successor executor named in the will fails for any reason to qualify as executor or indicates by affidavit filed with the application for an order continuing independent administration his inability or unwillingness to serve as successor independent executor, all of the distributees of the decedent as of the filing of the application for an order continuing independent administration may apply to the county court for the appointment of a qualified person, firm, or corporation to serve as successor independent executor. If the county court finds that continued administration of the estate is necessary, the county court shall enter an order continuing independent administration and appointing the person, firm, or corporation designated in the application as successor independent executor, unless the county court finds that it would not be in the best interest of the estate to do so. Such successor shall serve with all of the powers and privileges granted to his predecessor independent executor.

(b) If a distributee described in this section is an incapacitated person, the guardian of the person of the distributee may sign the application on behalf of the distributee. If the county court finds that either the continuing of independent administration or the appointment of the person, firm, or corporation designated in the application as successor independent executor would not be in the best interest of the incapacitated person, then, notwithstanding anything to the contrary in Subsection (a) of this section, the county court shall not enter an order continuing independent administration of the estate. If the distributee is an incapacitated person and has no guardian of the person, the court may appoint a guardian ad litem to make application on behalf of the incapacitated person if the county court considers such an appointment necessary to protect the interest of such distributee.

(c) If a trust is created in the decedent's will, the person or class of persons first eligible to receive the income from the trust, determined as if the trust were to be in existence on the date of the filing of the application for an order continuing independent administration, shall, for the purposes of this section, be deemed to be the distributee or distributees on behalf of such trust, and any other trust or trusts coming into existence upon the termination of such trust, and are authorized to apply for an order continuing independent administration on behalf of the trust without the consent or agreement of the trustee or any other beneficiary of the trust, or the trustee or any beneficiary of any other trust which may come into existence upon the termination of such trust.

(d) If a life estate is created either in the decedent's will or by law, and if a life tenant is living at the time of the filing of the application for an order continuing independent administration, then the life tenant or life tenants, determined as if the life estate were to commence on the date of the filing of the application for an order continuing independent administration, shall, for the purposes of this section, be deemed to the distributee or distributees on behalf of the entire estate created, and are authorized to apply for an order continuing independent administration on behalf of the estate without the consent or approval of any remainderman.

(e) If a decedent's will contains a provision that a distributee must survive the decedent by a prescribed period of time in order to take under the decedent's will, for the purposes of determining who shall be the distributee under this section, it shall be presumed that the distributees living at the time of the filing of the application for an order continuing independent administration of the decedent's estate survived the decedent for the prescribed period.

(f) In the case of all decedents, whether dying testate or intestate, for the purposes of determining who shall be the distributees under this section, it shall be presumed that no distributee living at the time the application for an order continuing independent administration of the decedent's estate is filed shall subsequently disclaim any portion of such distributee's interest in the decedent's estate.

(g) If a distributee of a decedent's estate should die, and if by virtue of such distributee's death such distributee's share of the decedent's estate shall become payable to such distributee's estate, then the deceased distributee's personal representative may sign the application for an order continuing independent administration of the decedent's estate under this section.

(h) If a successor independent executor is appointed pursuant to this section, then, unless the county court shall waive bond on application for waiver, the successor independent executor shall be required to enter into bond payable to and to be approved by the judge and his or her successors in a sum that is found by the judge to be adequate under all circumstances, or a bond with one surety in a sum that is found by the judge to be adequate under all circumstances, if the surety is an authorized corporate surety.

(i) Absent proof of fraud or collusion on the part of a judge, the judge may not be held civilly liable for the commission of misdeeds or the omission of any required act of any person, firm, or corporation designated as a successor independent executor under this section. Section 36 of this code does not apply to an appointment of a successor independent executor under this section.

Added by Acts 1977, 65th Leg., p. 1066, ch. 390, § 8, eff. Sept. 1, 1977. Amended by Acts 1979, 66th Leg., p. 1753, ch. 713, § 23, eff. Aug. 27, 1979; Acts 1993, 73rd Leg., ch. 846, § 16, eff. Sept. 1, 1993; Acts 1995, 74th Leg., ch. 1039, § 11, eff. Sept. 1, 1995.

## PART 5. ADMINISTRATION OF COMMUNITY PROPERTY

### § 155. No Necessity For Administration of Community Property

When a husband or wife dies intestate and the community property passes to the survivor, no administration thereon shall be necessary. Nothing in this part of this chapter prohibits the administration of community property under other provisions of this code relating to the administration of an estate.

Acts 1955, 54th Leg., p. 88, ch. 55, eff. Jan. 1, 1956. Amended by Acts 1971, 62nd Leg., p. 980, ch. 173, § 11, eff. Jan. 1, 1972.

Amended by Acts 2007, 80th Leg., ch. 301, § 1, eff. Sept. 1, 2007.

### § 156. Liability of Community Property for Debts

The community property subject to the sole or joint management, control, and disposition of a spouse during marriage continues to be subject to the liabilities of that spouse upon death. In addition, the interest that the deceased spouse owned in any other nonexempt community property passes to his or her heirs or devisees charged with the debts which were enforceable against such deceased spouse prior to his or her death. The surviving spouse or personal representative shall keep a separate, distinct account of all community debts allowed or paid in the administration and settlement of such estate.

Acts 1955, 54th Leg., p. 88, ch. 55, eff. Jan. 1, 1956. Amended by Acts 1971, 62nd Leg., p. 980, ch. 173, § 11, eff. Jan. 1, 1972.

Amended by Acts 2007, 80th Leg., ch. 301, § 2, eff. Sept. 1, 2007.

### § 157. Repealed by Acts 1993, 73rd Leg., ch. 957, § 75(1), eff. Sept. 1, 1993; Acts 1995, 74th Leg., ch. 1039, § 73(1), eff. Sept. 1, 1995

### § 158. Repealed by Acts 1993, 73rd Leg., ch. 957, § 75(1), eff. Sept. 1, 1993

### § 159. Repealed by Acts 1995, 74th Leg., ch. 1039, § 73(1), eff. Sept. 1, 1995

### § 160. Powers of Surviving Spouse When No Administration is Pending

(a) When no one has qualified as executor or administrator of the estate of a deceased spouse, the surviving spouse, whether the husband or wife, as the surviving partner of the marital partnership has power to sue and be sued for the recovery of community property; to sell, mortgage, lease, and otherwise dispose of community property for the purpose of paying community debts; to collect claims due to the community estate; and has such other powers as shall be necessary to preserve the community property, discharge community obligations, and wind up community affairs.

(b) If an affidavit stating that the affiant is the surviving spouse and that no one has qualified as executor or administrator of the estate of the deceased spouse is furnished to a person owing money to the community estate for current wages at the time of the death of the deceased spouse, the person making payment or delivering to the affiant the deceased spouse's final paycheck for wages, including unpaid sick pay or vacation pay, if any, is released from liability to the same extent as if the payment or delivery was made to a personal representative of the deceased spouse. The person is not required to inquire into the truth of the affidavit. The affiant to whom the payment or delivery is made is answerable to any person having a prior right and is accountable to any personal representative who is appointed. The affiant is liable for any damage or loss to any person that arises from a payment or delivery made in reliance on the affidavit.

(c) This section does not affect the disposition of the property of the deceased spouse.

Acts 1955, 54th Leg., p. 88, ch. 55, eff. Jan. 1, 1956. Amended by Acts 1993, 73rd Leg., ch. 846, § 17, eff. Sept. 1, 1993.

Subsec. (a) amended by Acts 2007, 80th Leg., ch. 301, § 3, eff. Sept. 1, 2007.

### §§ 161 to 167. Repealed by Acts 2007, 80th Leg., ch. 301, § 7, eff. Sept. 1, 2007

### § 168. Accounting by Survivor

The survivor shall keep a fair and full account and statement of all community debts and expenses paid by him, and of the disposition made of the community property; and, upon final partition of such estate, shall deliver to the heirs, devisees or legatees of the deceased spouse their interest in such estate, and the increase and profits of the same, after deducting therefrom the proportion of the community debts chargeable thereto, unavoidable losses, necessary and reasonable expenses, and a reasonable commission for the management of the same. The survivor may not be liable for losses sustained by the estate, except when the survivor has been guilty of gross negligence or bad faith.

Acts 1955, 54th Leg., p. 88, ch. 55, eff. Jan. 1, 1956. Amended by Acts 1971, 62nd Leg., p. 982, ch. 173, § 13, eff. Jan. 1, 1972.

Amended by Acts 2007, 80th Leg., ch. 301, § 4, eff. Sept. 1, 2007.

### §§ 169 to 175. Repealed by Acts 2007, 80th Leg., ch. 301, § 7, eff. Sept. 1, 2007

### § 176. Remarriage of Surviving Spouse

The remarriage of a surviving spouse shall not terminate the surviving spouse's powers as a surviving partner.

Acts 1955, 54th Leg., p. 88, ch. 55, eff. Jan. 1, 1956. Amended by Acts 1979, 66th Leg., p. 39, ch. 24, § 23, eff. Aug. 27, 1979.

Amended by Acts 2007, 80th Leg., ch. 301, § 5, eff. Sept. 1, 2007.

### § 177. Distribution of Powers Among Personal Representatives and Surviving Spouse

When a personal representative of the estate of a deceased spouse has duly qualified, the personal representative is authorized to administer, not only the separate property of the deceased spouse, but also the community property which was by law under the management of the deceased spouse during the continuance of the marriage and all of the community property that was by law under the joint control of the

**Text of Texas Probate Code effective until January 1, 2014**

spouses during the continuance of the marriage. The surviving spouse, as surviving partner of the marital partnership, is entitled to retain possession and control of all community property which was legally under the sole management of the surviving spouse during the continuance of the marriage and to exercise over that property all the powers elsewhere in this part of this code authorized to be exercised by the surviving spouse when there is no administration pending on the estate of the deceased spouse. The surviving spouse may by written instrument filed with the clerk waive any right to exercise powers as community survivor, and in such event the personal representative of the deceased spouse shall be authorized to administer upon the entire community estate.

Acts 1955, 54th Leg., p. 88, ch. 55, eff. Jan. 1, 1956. Amended by Acts 1971, 62nd Leg., p. 982, ch. 173, § 13, eff. Jan. 1, 1972; Acts 2001, 77th Leg., ch. 10, § 2, eff. Sept. 1, 2001.
Amended by Acts 2007, 80th Leg., ch. 301, § 6, eff. Sept. 1, 2007.

# CHAPTER VII

## EXECUTORS AND ADMINISTRATORS

**Section**
246, 247. Repealed.

## PART 1.  APPOINTMENT AND ISSUANCE OF LETTERS

### § 178.  When Letters Testamentary or of Administration Shall Be Granted

**(a) Letters Testamentary.**  When a will has been probated, the court shall, within twenty days thereafter, grant letters testamentary, if permitted by law, to the executor or executors appointed by such will, if any there be, or to such of them as are not disqualified, and are willing to accept the trust and qualify according to law.

**(b) Letters of Administration.**  When a person shall die intestate, or where no executor is named in a will, or where the executor is dead or shall fail to accept and qualify within twenty days after the probate of the will, or shall fail for a period of thirty days after the death of the testator to present the will for probate and the court finds there was no good cause for not presenting the will for probate during that period, then administration of the estate of such intestate, or administration with the will annexed of the estate of such testator, shall be granted, should administration appear to be necessary.  No administration of any estate shall be granted unless there exists a necessity therefor, such necessity to be determined by the court hearing the application.  Such necessity shall be deemed to exist if two or more debts exist against the estate, or if or when it is desired to have the county court partition the estate among the distributees, or if the administration is necessary to receive or recover funds or other property due the estate, but mention of these three instances of necessity for administration shall not prevent the court from finding other instances of necessity upon proof before it.

**(c) Failure to Issue Letters Within Prescribed Time.**  Failure of a court to issue letters testamentary within the twenty day period prescribed by this Section shall not affect the validity of any letters testamentary which are issued subsequent to such period, in accordance with law.

Acts 1955, 54th Leg., p. 88, ch. 55, eff. Jan. 1, 1956.

Subsec. (b) amended by Acts 2007, 80th Leg., ch. 1170, § 7.02, eff. Sept. 1, 2007.

### § 179.  Opposition to Grant of Letters of Administration

When application is made for letters of administration, any interested person may at any time before the application is granted, file the person's opposition thereto in writing, and may apply for the grant of letters to the person or to any other person; and, upon the trial, the court shall grant letters to the person that may seem best entitled to them, having regard to applicable provisions of this Code, without further notice than that of the original application.

Acts 1955, 54th Leg., p. 88, ch. 55, eff. Jan. 1, 1956.

Amended by Acts 2007, 80th Leg., ch. 1170, § 7.03, eff. Sept. 1, 2007.

### § 180.  Effect of Finding That No Necessity for Administration Exists

When application is filed for letters of administration and the court finds that there exists no necessity for administration of the estate, the court shall recite in its order refusing the application that no necessity for administration exists.  An order of the court containing such recital shall constitute sufficient legal authority to all persons owing any money, having custody of any property, or acting as registrar or transfer agent of any evidence of interest, indebtedness, property, or right belonging to the estate, and to persons purchasing or otherwise dealing with the estate, for payment or transfer to the distributees of the decedent, and such distributees shall be entitled to enforce their right to such payment or transfer by suit.

Acts 1955, 54th Leg., p. 88, ch. 55, eff. Jan. 1, 1956.

### § 181.  Orders Granting Letters Testamentary or of Administration

When letters testamentary or of administration are granted, the court shall make an order to that effect, which shall specify:

(a) The name of the testator or intestate;  and

(b) The name of the person to whom the grant of letters is made;  and

(c) If bond is required, the amount thereof;  and

(d) If any interested person shall apply to the court for the appointment of an appraiser or appraisers, or if the court deems an appraisal necessary, the name of not less than one nor more than three disinterested persons appointed to appraise the estate and return such appraisement to the court;  and

(e) That the clerk shall issue letters in accordance with said order when the person to whom said letters are granted shall have qualified according to law.

Acts 1955, 54th Leg., p. 88, ch. 55, eff. Jan. 1, 1956.  Amended by Acts 1967, 60th Leg., p. 1815, ch. 697, § 1, eff. Aug. 28, 1967;  Acts 1969, 61st Leg., p. 1922, ch. 641, § 10, eff. June 12, 1969.

### § 182.  When Clerk Shall Issue Letters

Whenever an executor or administrator has been qualified in the manner required by law, the clerk of the court granting the letters testamentary or of administration shall forthwith issue and deliver the letters to such executor or administrator.  When two or more persons qualify as executors or administrators, letters shall be issued to each of them so qualifying.

Acts 1955, 54th Leg., p. 88, ch. 55, eff. Jan. 1, 1956.

### § 183.  What Constitutes Letters

Letters testamentary or of administration shall be a certificate of the clerk of the court granting the same, attested by the seal of such court, and stating that the executor or administrator, as the case may be, has duly qualified as such as the law requires, the date of such qualification, and the name of the deceased.

Acts 1955, 54th Leg., p. 88, ch. 55, eff. Jan. 1, 1956.

## §§ 184, 185. Repealed by Acts 1993, 73rd Leg., ch. 957, § 75(1), eff. Sept. 1, 1993

## § 186. Letters or Certificate Made Evidence

Letters testamentary or of administration or a certificate of the clerk of the court which granted the same, under the seal of such court, that said letters have been issued, shall be sufficient evidence of the appointment and qualification of the personal representative of an estate and of the date of qualification.

Acts 1955, 54th Leg., p. 88, ch. 55, eff. Jan. 1, 1956. Amended by Acts 1993, 73rd Leg., ch. 957, § 28, eff. Sept. 1, 1993.

## § 187. Issuance of Other Letters

When letters have been destroyed or lost, the clerk shall issue other letters in their stead, which shall have the same force and effect as the original letters. The clerk shall also issue any number of letters as and when requested by the person or persons who hold such letters.

Acts 1955, 54th Leg., p. 88, ch. 55, eff. Jan. 1, 1956.

## § 188. Rights of Third Persons Dealing With Executors or Administrators

When an executor or administrator, legally qualified as such, has performed any acts as such executor or administrator in conformity with his authority and the law, such acts shall continue to be valid to all intents and purposes, so far as regards the rights of innocent purchasers of any of the property of the estate from such executor or administrator, for a valuable consideration, in good faith, and without notice of any illegality in the title to the same, notwithstanding such acts or the authority under which they were performed may afterward be set aside, annulled, and declared invalid.

Acts 1955, 54th Leg., p. 88, ch. 55, eff. Jan. 1, 1956.

## PART 2. OATHS AND BONDS OF PERSONAL REPRESENTATIVES

## § 189. How Executors and Administrators Shall Qualify

A personal representative shall be deemed to have duly qualified when he shall have taken and filed his oath and made the required bond, had the same approved by the judge, and filed it with the clerk. In case of an executor who is not required to make bond, he shall be deemed to have duly qualified when he shall have taken and filed his oath required by law.

Acts 1955, 54th Leg., p. 88, ch. 55, eff. Jan. 1, 1956. Amended by Acts 1993, 73rd Leg., ch. 957, § 29, eff. Sept. 1, 1993.

## § 190. Oaths of Executors and Administrators

**(a) Executor, or Administrator With Will Annexed.** Before the issuance of letters testamentary or of administra-

tion with the will annexed, the person named as executor, or appointed administrator with the will annexed, shall take and subscribe an oath in form substantially as follows: "I do solemnly swear that the writing which has been offered for probate is the last will of _____, so far as I know or believe, and that I will well and truly perform all the duties of executor of said will (or of administrator with the will annexed, as the case may be) of the estate of said _____."

**(b) Administrator.** Before the issuance of letters of administration, the person appointed administrator shall take and subscribe an oath in form substantially as follows: "I do solemnly swear that _____, deceased, died without leaving any lawful will (or that the named executor in any such will is dead or has failed to offer the same for probate, or to accept and qualify as executor, within the time required, as the case may be), so far as I know or believe, and that I will well and truly perform all the duties of administrator of the estate of said deceased."

**(c) Temporary Administrator.** Before the issuance of temporary letters of administration, the person appointed temporary administrator shall take and subscribe an oath in form substantially as follows: "I do solemnly swear that I will well and truly perform the duties of temporary administrator of the estate of _____, deceased, in accordance with the law, and with the order of the court appointing me such administrator."

**(d) Filing and Recording of Oaths.** All such oaths may be taken before any officer authorized to administer oaths, and shall be filed with the clerk of the court granting the letters, and shall be recorded in the judge's probate docket.

Acts 1955, 54th Leg., p. 88, ch. 55, eff. Jan. 1, 1956. Subsec. (b) amended by Acts 2007, 80th Leg., ch. 1170, § 7.04, eff. Sept. 1, 2007; Subsec. (d) amended by Acts 2009, 81st Leg., ch. 602, § 8, eff. June 19, 2009.

## § 191. Repealed by Acts 1993, 73rd Leg., ch. 957, § 75(1), eff. Sept. 1, 1993

## § 192. Time for Taking Oath and Giving Bond

The oath of a personal representative may be taken and subscribed, or his bond may be given and approved, at any time before the expiration of twenty days after the date of the order granting letters testamentary or of administration, as the case may be, or before such letters shall have been revoked for a failure to qualify within the time allowed. All such oaths may be taken before any person authorized to administer oaths under the laws of this State.

Acts 1955, 54th Leg., p. 88, ch. 55, eff. Jan. 1, 1956. Amended by Acts 1993, 73rd Leg., ch. 957, § 30, eff. Sept. 1, 1993.

## § 193. Repealed by Acts 1993, 73rd Leg., ch. 957, § 75(1), eff. Sept. 1, 1993

## § 194. Bonds of Personal Representatives of Estates

Except when bond is not required under the provisions of this Code, before the issuance of letters testamentary or of administration, the recipient of letters shall enter into bond conditioned as required by law, payable to the county judge or probate judge of the county in which the probate proceedings are pending and to his successors in office. Such bonds shall bear the written approval of either of such judges in his official capacity, and shall be executed and approved in accordance with the following rules:

**1. Court to Fix Penalty.** The penalty of the bond shall be fixed by the judge, in an amount deemed sufficient to protect the estate and its creditors, as hereinafter provided.

**2. Bond to Protect Creditors Only, When.** If the person to whom letters testamentary or of administration is granted is also entitled to all of the decedent's estate, after payment of debts, the bond shall be in an amount sufficient to protect creditors only, notwithstanding the rules applicable generally to bonds of personal representatives of estates.

**3. Before Fixing Penalty, Court to Hear Evidence.** In any case where a bond is, or shall be, required of a personal representative of an estate, the court shall, before fixing the penalty of the bond, hear evidence and determine:

(a) The amount of cash on hand and where deposited, and the amount of cash estimated to be needed for administrative purposes, including operation of a business, factory, farm or ranch owned by the estate, and expenses of administration for one (1) year; and

(b) The revenue anticipated to be received in the succeeding twelve (12) months from dividends, interest, rentals, or use of real or personal property belonging to the estate and the aggregate amount of any installments or periodical payments to be collected; and

(c) The estimated value of certificates of stock, bonds, notes, or securities of the estate or ward, the name of the depository, if any, in which said assets are held for safekeeping, the face value of life insurance or other policies payable to the person on whose estate administration is sought, or to such estate, and such other personal property as is owned by the estate, or by one under disability; and

(d) The estimated amount of debts due and owing by the estate or ward.

**4. Penalty of Bond.** The penalty of the bond shall be fixed by the judge in an amount equal to the estimated value of all personal property belonging to the estate, or to the person under disability, together with an additional amount to cover revenue anticipated to be derived during the succeeding twelve (12) months from interest, dividends, collectible claims, the aggregate amount of any installments or periodical payments exclusive of income derived or to be derived from federal social security payments, and rentals for use of real and personal property; provided, that the penalty of the original bond shall be reduced in proportion to the amount of cash or value of securities or other assets authorized or required to be deposited or placed in safekeeping by order of court, or voluntarily made by the representative or by his sureties as hereinafter provided in Subdivisions 6 and 7 hereof.

**5. Agreement as to Deposit of Assets.** It shall be lawful, and the court may require such action when deemed in the best interest of an estate, for a personal representative to agree with the surety or sureties, either corporate or personal, for the deposit of any or all cash, and safekeeping of other assets of the estate in a financial institution as defined by Section 201.101, Finance Code, with its main office or a branch office in this state and qualified to act as a depository in this State under the laws of this State or of the United States, if such deposit is otherwise proper, in such manner as to prevent the withdrawal of such moneys or other assets without the written consent of the surety, or an order of the court made on such notice to the surety as the court shall direct. No such agreement shall in any manner release from or change the liability of the principal or sureties as established by the terms of the bond.

**6. Deposits Authorized or Required, When.** Cash or securities or other personal assets of an estate or which an estate is entitled to receive may, and if deemed by the court in the best interest of such estate shall, be deposited or placed in safekeeping as the case may be, in one or more of the depositories hereinabove described upon such terms as shall be prescribed by the court. The court in which the proceedings are pending, upon its own motion, or upon written application of the representative or of any other person interested in the estate may authorize or require additional assets of the estate then on hand or as they accrue during the pendency of the probate proceedings to be deposited or held in safekeeping as provided above. The amount of the bond of the personal representative shall be reduced in proportion to the cash so deposited, or the value of the securities or other assets placed in safekeeping. Such cash so deposited, or securities or other assets held in safekeeping, or portions thereof, may be withdrawn from a depository only upon order of the court, and the bond of the personal representative shall be increased in proportion to the amount of cash or the value of securities or other assets so authorized to be withdrawn.

**7. Representative May Deposit Cash or Securities of His Own in Lieu of Bond.** It shall be lawful for the personal representative of an estate, in lieu of giving surety or sureties on any bond which shall be required of him, or for the purpose of reducing the amount of such bond, to deposit out of his own assets cash or securities acceptable to the court, with a depository such as named above or with any other corporate depository approved by the court, if such deposit is otherwise proper, said deposit to be equal in amount or value to the amount of the bond required, or the bond reduced by the value of assets so deposited.

**8. Rules Applicable to Making and Handling Deposits in Lieu of Bond or to Reduce Penal Sum of Bond.** (a) A receipt for a deposit in lieu of surety or sureties shall be issued by the depository, showing the amount of cash or, if securities, the amount and description thereof, and agreeing not to disburse or deliver the same except upon receipt of a certified copy of an order of the court in which the proceedings are pending, and such receipt shall be attached to the representative's bond and be delivered to and filed by the county clerk after approval by the judge.

(b) The amount of cash or securities on deposit may be increased or decreased, by order of the court from time to time, as the interest of the estate shall require.

(c) Deposits in lieu of sureties on bonds, whether of cash or securities, may be withdrawn or released only on order of a court having jurisdiction.

(d) Creditors shall have the same rights against the representative and such deposits as are provided for recovery against sureties on a bond.

(e) The court may on its own motion, or upon written application by the representative or by any other person interested in the estate, require that adequate bond be given by the representative in lieu of such deposit, or authorize withdrawal of the deposit and substitution of a bond with sureties therefor. In either case, the representative shall file a sworn statement showing the condition of the estate, and unless the same be filed within twenty (20) days after being personally served with notice of the filing of an application by another, or entry of the court's motion, he shall be subject to removal as in other cases. The deposit may not be released or withdrawn until the court has been satisfied as to the condition of the estate, has determined the amount of bond, and has received and approved the bond.

**9. Withdrawal of Deposits When Estate Closed.** Upon the closing of an estate, any such deposit or portion thereof remaining on hand, whether of the assets of the representative, or of the assets of the estate, or of the surety, shall be released by order of court and paid over to the person or persons entitled thereto. No writ of attachment or garnishment shall lie against the deposit, except as to claims of creditors of the estate being administered, or persons interested therein, including distributees and wards, and then only in the event distribution has been ordered by the court, and to the extent only of such distribution as shall have been ordered.

**10. Who May Act as Sureties.** The surety or sureties on said bonds may be authorized corporate sureties, or personal sureties.

**11. Procedure When Bond Exceeds Fifty Thousand Dollars ($50,000).** When any such bond shall exceed Fifty Thousand Dollars ($50,000) in penal sum, the court may require that such bond be signed by two (2) or more authorized corporate sureties, or by one such surety and two (2) or more good and sufficient personal sureties. The estate shall pay the cost of a bond with corporate sureties.

**12. Qualifications of Personal Sureties.** If the sureties be natural persons, there shall not be less than two (2), each of whom shall make affidavit in the manner prescribed in this Code, and the judge shall be satisfied that he owns property within this State, over and above that exempt by law, sufficient to qualify as a surety as required by law. Except as provided by law, only one surety is required if the surety is an authorized corporate surety; provided, a personal surety,

instead of making affidavit, or creating a lien on specific real estate when such is required, may, in the same manner as a personal representative, deposit his own cash or securities, in lieu of pledging real property as security, subject, so far as applicable, to the provisions covering such deposits when made by personal representatives.

**13. Bonds of Temporary Appointees.** In case of a temporary administrator, the bond shall be in such sum as the judge shall direct.

**14. Increased or Additional Bonds When Property Sold, Rented, Leased for Mineral Development, or Money Borrowed or Invested.** The provisions in this Section with respect to deposit of cash and safekeeping of securities shall cover, so far as they may be applicable, the orders to be entered by the court when real or personal property of an estate has been authorized to be sold or rented, or money borrowed thereon, or when real property, or an interest therein, has been authorized to be leased for mineral development or subjected to unitization, the general bond having been found insufficient.

Acts 1955, 54th Leg., p. 88, ch. 55, eff. Jan. 1, 1956. Amended by Acts 1957, 55th Leg., p. 53, ch. 31, § 6(b), eff. Aug. 22, 1957; Acts 1971, 62nd Leg., p. 983, ch. 173, § 14, eff. Jan. 1, 1972; Acts 1979, 66th Leg., p. 1754, ch. 713, § 25, eff. Aug. 27, 1979; Acts 1993, 73rd Leg., ch. 957, § 31, eff. Sept. 1, 1993; Acts 1999, 76th Leg., ch. 344, § 6.003, eff. Sept. 1, 1999.

**§ 195. When No Bond Required**

**(a) By Will.** Whenever any will probated in a Texas court directs that no bond or security be required of the person or persons named as executors, the court finding that such person or persons are qualified, letters testamentary shall be issued to the persons so named, without requirement of bond.

**(b) Corporate Fiduciary Exempted From Bond.** If a personal representative is a corporate fiduciary, as said term is defined in this Code, no bond shall be required.

Acts 1955, 54th Leg., p. 88, ch. 55, eff. Jan. 1, 1956. Amended by Acts 1995, 74th Leg., ch. 1039, § 12, eff. Sept. 1, 1995.

**§ 196. Form of Bond**

The following form, or the same in substance, may be used for the bonds of personal representatives:

"The State of Texas

"County of _____

"Know all men by these presents that we, A. B., as principal, and E. F., as sureties, are held and firmly bound unto the county (or probate) judge of the County of _____, and his successors in office, in the sum of _____ Dollars; conditioned that the above bound A. B., who has been appointed executor of the last will and testament of J. C., deceased (or has been appointed by the said judge of _____ County, administrator with the will annexed of the estate of J. C., deceased, or has been appointed by the said judge of _____ County, administrator of the estate of J. C., deceased, or has been appointed by the said judge of _____ County, temporary administrator of the estate of J. C., deceased, as the case may be), shall well and truly perform all of the duties required of him by law under said appointment."

Acts 1955, 54th Leg., p. 88, ch. 55, eff. Jan. 1, 1956. Amended by Acts 1993, 73rd Leg., ch. 957, § 32, eff. Sept. 1, 1993.

### § 197. Bonds to Be Filed

All bonds required by preceding provisions of this Code shall be subscribed by both principals and sureties, and, when approved by the court, be filed with the clerk.

Acts 1955, 54th Leg., p. 88, ch. 55, eff. Jan. 1, 1956.

### § 198. Bonds of Joint Representatives

When two or more persons are appointed representatives of the same estate or person and are required by the provisions of this Code or by the court to give a bond, the court may require either a separate bond from each or one joint bond from all of them.

Acts 1955, 54th Leg., p. 88, ch. 55, eff. Jan. 1, 1956.

### § 199. Bonds of Married Persons

When a married person is appointed personal representative, the person may, jointly with, or without, his or her spouse, execute such bond as the law requires; and such bond shall bind the person's separate estate, but shall bind his or her spouse only if signed by the spouse.

Acts 1955, 54th Leg., p. 88, ch. 55, eff. Jan. 1, 1956. Amended by Acts 1979, 66th Leg., p. 39, ch. 24, § 24, eff. Aug. 27, 1979.

### § 200. Bond of Married Person Under Eighteen Years of Age

When a person under eighteen years of age who is or has been married shall accept and qualify as executor or administrator, any bond required to be executed by him shall be as valid and binding for all purposes as if he were of lawful age.

Acts 1955, 54th Leg., p. 88, ch. 55, eff. Jan. 1, 1956. Amended by Acts 1975, 64th Leg., p. 105, ch. 45, § 3, eff. Sept. 1, 1975; Acts 1993, 73rd Leg., ch. 957, § 33, eff. Sept. 1, 1993.

### § 201. (a) Affidavit of Personal Surety; (b) Lien on Specific Property, When Required; (c) Subordination of Lien Authorized

**(a) Affidavit of Personal Surety.** Before the judge may consider a bond with personal sureties, each person offered as surety shall execute an affidavit stating the amount of his assets, reachable by creditors, of a value over and above his liabilities, the total of the worth of such sureties to be equal to at least double the amount of the bond, and such affidavit shall be presented to the judge for his consideration and, if approved, shall be attached to and form part of the bond.

**(b) Lien on Specific Property, When Required.** If the judge finds that the estimated value of personal property of the estate which cannot be deposited or held in safekeeping as hereinabove provided is such that personal sureties cannot be accepted without the creation of a specific lien on real property of such sureties, he shall enter an order requiring

that each surety designate real property owned by him within this State subject to execution, of a value over and above all liens and unpaid taxes, equal at least to the amount of the bond, giving an adequate legal description of such property, all of which shall be incorporated in an affidavit by the surety, approved by the judge, and be attached to and form part of the bond. If compliance with such order is not had, the judge may in his discretion require that the bond be signed by an authorized corporate surety, or by such corporate surety and two (2) or more personal sureties.

**(c) Subordination of Lien Authorized.** If a personal surety who has been required to create a lien on specific real estate desires to lease such property for mineral development, he may file his written application in the court in which the proceedings are pending, requesting subordination of such lien to the proposed lease, and the judge of such court may, in his discretion, enter an order granting such application. A certified copy of such order, filed and recorded in the deed records of the proper county, shall be sufficient to subordinate such lien to the rights of a lessee, in the proposed lease.

Acts 1955, 54th Leg., p. 88, ch. 55, eff. Jan. 1, 1956. Amended by Acts 1957, 55th Leg., p. 53, ch. 31, § 6(c).

### § 202. Bond as Lien on Real Property of Surety

When a personal surety has been required by the court to create a lien on specific real property as a condition of his acceptance as surety on a bond, a lien on the real property of the surety in this State which is described in the affidavit of the surety, and only upon such property, shall arise as security for the performance of the obligation of the bond. The clerk of the court shall, before letters are issued to the representative, cause to be mailed to the office of the county clerk of each county in which is located any real property as set forth in the affidavit of the surety, a statement signed by the clerk, giving a sufficient description of such real property, the name of the principal and sureties, the amount of the bond, and the name of the estate and the court in which the bond is given. The county clerk to whom such statement is sent shall record the same in the deed records of the county. All such recorded statements shall be duly indexed in such manner that the existence and character of the liens may conveniently be determined, and such recording and indexing of such statement shall constitute and be constructive notice to all persons of the existence of such lien on such real property situated in such county, effective as of date of such indexing.

Acts 1955, 54th Leg., p. 88, ch. 55, eff. Jan. 1, 1956. Amended by Acts 1957, 55th Leg., p. 53, ch. 31, § 6(d).

### § 203. When New Bond May Be Required

A personal representative may be required to give a new bond in the following cases:

(a) When the sureties upon the bond, or any one of them, shall die, remove beyond the limits of the state, or become insolvent; or

(b) When, in the opinion of the court, the sureties upon any such bond are insufficient; or

(c) When, in the opinion of the court, any such bond is defective; or

(d) When the amount of any such bond is insufficient; or

(e) When the sureties, or any one of them, petitions the court to be discharged from future liability upon such bond; or

(f) When the bond and the record thereof have been lost or destroyed.

Acts 1955, 54th Leg., p. 88, ch. 55, eff. Jan. 1, 1956.

### § 204. Demand for New Bond by Interested Person

Any person interested in an estate may, upon application in writing filed with the county clerk of the county where the probate proceedings are pending, alleging that the bond of the personal representative is insufficient or defective, or has been, together with the record thereof, lost or destroyed, cause such representative to be cited to appear and show cause why he should not give a new bond.

Acts 1955, 54th Leg., p. 88, ch. 55, eff. Jan. 1, 1956.

### § 205. Judge to Require New Bond

When it shall be known to him that any such bond is in any respect insufficient or that it has, together with the record thereof, been lost or destroyed, the judge shall:

(1) without delay and without notice enter an order requiring the representative to give a new bond; or

(2) without delay cause the representative to be cited to show cause why he should not give a new bond.

Acts 1955, 54th Leg., p. 88, ch. 55, eff. Jan. 1, 1956. Amended by Acts 2007, 80th Leg., ch. 683, § 1, eff. Sept. 1, 2007.

### § 206. Order Requiring New Bond

(a) The order entered under Section 205(1) of this code must state the reasons for requiring a new bond, the amount of the new bond, and the time within which the new bond must be given, which may not be earlier than the 10th day after the date of the order. If the personal representative opposes the order, the personal representative may demand a hearing on the order. The hearing must be held before the expiration of the time within which the new bond must be given.

(b) Upon the return of a citation ordering a personal representative to show cause why he should not give a new bond, the judge shall, on the day named therein for the hearing of the matter, proceed to inquire into the sufficiency of the reasons for requiring a new bond; and, if satisfied that a new bond should be required, he shall enter an order to that effect, stating in such order the amount of such new

bond, and the time within which it shall be given, which shall not be later than twenty days from the date of such order.

Acts 1955, 54th Leg., p. 88, ch. 55, eff. Jan. 1, 1956. Amended by Acts 2007, 80th Leg., ch. 683, § 1, eff. Sept. 1, 2007.

### § 207. Order Suspends Powers of Personal Representative

When a personal representative is required to give a new bond, the order requiring such bond shall have the effect to suspend his powers, and he shall not thereafter pay out any money of said estate or do any other official act, except to preserve the property of the estate, until such new bond has been given and approved.

Acts 1955, 54th Leg., p. 88, ch. 55, eff. Jan. 1, 1956.

### § 208. Decrease in Amount of Bond

A personal representative required to give bond may at any time file with the clerk a written application to the court to have his bond reduced. Forthwith the clerk shall issue and cause to be posted notice to all persons interested and to the surety or sureties on the bond, apprising them of the fact and nature of the application and of the time when the judge will hear the application. The judge, in his discretion, upon the submission of proof that a smaller bond than the one in effect will be adequate to meet the requirements of the law and protect the estate, and upon the approval of an accounting filed at the time of the application, may permit the filing of a new bond in a reduced amount.

Acts 1955, 54th Leg., p. 88, ch. 55, eff. Jan. 1, 1956.

### § 209. Discharge of Sureties Upon Execution of New Bond

When a new bond has been given and approved, an order shall be entered discharging the sureties upon the former bond from all liability for the future acts of the principal.

Acts 1955, 54th Leg., p. 88, ch. 55, eff. Jan. 1, 1956.

### § 210. Release of Sureties Before Estate Fully Administered

The sureties upon the bond of a personal representative, or any one of them, may at any time file with the clerk a petition to the court in which the proceedings are pending, praying that such representative be required to give a new bond and that petitioners be discharged from all liability for the future acts of such representative; whereupon, such representative shall be cited to appear and give a new bond.

Acts 1955, 54th Leg., p. 88, ch. 55, eff. Jan. 1, 1956.

### § 211. Release of Lien Before Estate Fully Administered

If a personal surety who has given a lien on specific real property as security applies to the court to have the lien released, the court shall order the release requested, if the court is satisfied that the bond is sufficient without the lien on such property, or if sufficient other real or personal property of the surety is substituted on the same terms and conditions required for the lien which is to be released. If such personal surety who requests the release of the lien does not offer a lien on other real or personal property, and if the court is not satisfied of the sufficiency of the bond without the substitution of other property, the court shall order the personal representative to appear and give a new bond.

Acts 1955, 54th Leg., p. 88, ch. 55, eff. Jan. 1, 1956.

### § 212. Release of Recorded Lien on Surety's Property

A certified copy of the court's order describing the property, and releasing the lien, filed with the county clerk of the county where the property is located, and recorded in the deed records, shall have the effect of cancelling the lien on such property.

Acts 1955, 54th Leg., p. 88, ch. 55, eff. Jan. 1, 1956.

### § 213. Revocation of Letters for Failure to Give Bond

If at any time a personal representative fails to give bond as required by the court, within the time fixed by this Code, another person may be appointed in his stead.

Acts 1955, 54th Leg., p. 88, ch. 55, eff. Jan. 1, 1956.

### § 214. Executor Without Bond Required to Give Bond

Where no bond is required of an executor appointed by will, any person having a debt, claim, or demand against the estate, to the justice of which oath has been made by himself, his agent, or attorney, or any other person interested in such estate, whether in person or as the representative of another, may file a complaint in writing in the court where such will is probated, and the court shall thereupon cite such executor to appear and show cause why he should not be required to give bond.

Acts 1955, 54th Leg., p. 88, ch. 55, eff. Jan. 1, 1956. Amended by Acts 1993, 73rd Leg., ch. 957, § 34, eff. Sept. 1, 1993.

### § 215. Order Requiring Bond

Upon hearing such complaint, if it appears to the court that such executor is wasting, mismanaging, or misapplying such estate, and that thereby a creditor may probably lose his debt, or that thereby some person's interest in the estate may be diminished or lost, the court shall enter an order requiring such executor to give bond within ten days from the date of such order.

Acts 1955, 54th Leg., p. 88, ch. 55, eff. Jan. 1, 1956. Amended by Acts 1993, 73rd Leg., ch. 957, § 34, eff. Sept. 1, 1993.

### § 216. Bond in Such Case

Such bond shall be for an amount sufficient to protect the estate and its creditors, to be approved by, and payable to, the judge, conditioned that said executor will well and truly administer such estate, and that he will not waste, mismanage, or misapply the same.

Acts 1955, 54th Leg., p. 88, ch. 55, eff. Jan. 1, 1956. Amended by Acts 1993, 73rd Leg., ch. 957, § 34, eff. Sept. 1, 1993.

### § 217. Failure to Give Bond

Should the executor fail to give such bond within ten days after the order requiring him to do so, then if the judge does not extend the time, he shall, without citation, remove such executor and appoint some competent person in his stead who shall administer the estate according to the provisions of such will or the law, and who, before he enters upon the administration of said estate, shall take the oath required of an administrator with the will annexed, and shall give bond in the same manner and in the same amount provided in this Code for the issuance of original letters of administration.

Acts 1955, 54th Leg., p. 88, ch. 55, eff. Jan. 1, 1956. Amended by Acts 1993, 73rd Leg., ch. 957, § 34, eff. Sept. 1, 1993.

### § 218. Bonds Not Void Upon First Recovery

The bonds of personal representative shall not become void upon the first recovery, but may be put in suit and prosecuted from time to time until the whole amount thereof shall have been recovered.

Acts 1955, 54th Leg., p. 88, ch. 55, eff. Jan. 1, 1956.

### § 219. Repealed by Acts 1957, 55th Leg., p. 53, ch. 31, § 13, eff. Aug. 22, 1957

## PART 3. REVOCATION OF LETTERS, DEATH, RESIGNATION, AND REMOVAL

### § 220. Appointment of Successor Representative

**(a) Because of Death, Resignation or Removal.** When a person duly appointed a personal representative fails to qualify, or, after qualifying, dies, resigns, or is removed, the court may, upon application appoint a successor if there be necessity therefor, and such appointment may be made prior to the filing of, or action upon, a final accounting. In case of death, the legal representatives of the deceased person shall account for, pay, and deliver to the person or persons legally entitled to receive the same, all the property of every kind belonging to the estate entrusted to his care, at such time and in such manner as the court shall order. Upon the finding that a necessity for the immediate appointment of a successor representative exists, the court may appoint such successor without citation or notice.

**(b) Because of Existence of Prior Right.** Where letters have been granted to one, and another whose right thereto is prior and who has not waived such right and is qualified, applies for letters, the letters previously granted shall be revoked and other letters shall be granted to the applicant.

**(c) When Named Executor Becomes an Adult.** If one named in a will as executor is not an adult when the will is probated and letters in any capacity have been granted to another, such nominated executor, upon proof that he has become an adult and is not otherwise disqualified, shall be entitled to have such former letters revoked and appropriate letters granted to him. And if the will names two or more persons as executor, any one or more of whom are minors when such will is probated, and letters have been issued to such only as are adults, said minor or minors, upon becoming adults, if not otherwise disqualified, shall be permitted to qualify and receive letters.

**(d) Upon Return of Sick or Absent Executor.** If one named in a will as executor was sick or absent from the State when the testator died, or when the will was proved, and therefore could not present the will for probate within thirty days after the testator's death, or accept and qualify as executor within twenty days after the probate of the will, he may accept and qualify as executor within sixty days after his return or recovery from sickness, upon proof to the court that he was absent or ill; and, if the letters have been issued to others, they shall be revoked.

**(e) When Will Is Discovered After Administration Granted.** If it is discovered after letters of administration have been issued that the deceased left a lawful will, the letters shall be revoked and proper letters issued to the person or persons entitled thereto.

**(f) When Application and Service Necessary.** Except when otherwise expressly provided in this Code, letters shall not be revoked and other letters granted except upon application, and after personal service of citation on the person, if living, whose letters are sought to be revoked, that he appear and show cause why such application should not be granted.

**(g) Payment or Tender of Money Due During Vacancy.** Money or other thing of value falling due to an estate while the office of the personal representative is vacant may be paid, delivered, or tendered to the clerk of the court for credit of the estate, and the debtor, obligor, or payor shall thereby be discharged of the obligation for all purposes to the extent and purpose of such payment or tender. If the clerk accepts such payment or tender, he shall issue a proper receipt therefor.

Acts 1955, 54th Leg., p. 88, ch. 55, eff. Jan. 1, 1956. Amended by Acts 1969, 61st Leg., p. 1922, ch. 641, § 11, eff. June 12, 1969; Acts 1993, 73rd Leg., ch. 957, § 35, eff. Sept. 1, 1993.

## § 221. Resignation

**(a) Application to Resign.** A personal representative who wishes to resign his trust shall file with the clerk his written application to the court to that effect, accompanied by a full and complete exhibit and final account, duly verified, showing the true condition of the estate entrusted to his care.

**(b) Successor Representatives.** If the necessity exists, the court may immediately accept a resignation and appoint a successor, but shall not discharge the person resigning, or release him or the sureties on his bond until final order or judgment shall have been rendered on his final account.

**(c) Citation.** Upon the filing of an application to resign, supported by exhibit and final account, the clerk shall call the

application to the attention of the judge, who shall set a date for a hearing upon the matter. The clerk shall then issue a citation to all interested persons, showing that proper application has been filed, and the time and place set for hearing, at which time said persons may appear and contest the exhibit and account. The citation shall be posted, unless the court directs that it be published.

**(d) Hearing.** At the time set for hearing, unless it has been continued by the court, if the court finds that citation has been duly issued and served, he shall proceed to examine such exhibit and account, and hear all evidence for and against the same, and shall, if necessary, restate, and audit and settle the same. If the court is satisfied that the matters entrusted to the applicant have been handled and accounted for in accordance with law, he shall enter an order of approval, and require that the estate remaining in the possession of the applicant, if any, be delivered to the person or persons entitled by law to receive it.

**(e) Requisites of Discharge.** No resigning personal representative shall be discharged until the application has been heard, the exhibit and account examined, settled, and approved, and until he has satisfied the court that he has delivered the estate, if there be any remaining in his possession, or has complied with all lawful orders of the court with relation to his trust.

**(f) Final Discharge.** When the resigning applicant has complied in all respects with the orders of the court, an order shall be made accepting the resignation, discharging the applicant, and, if he is under bond, his sureties.

Acts 1955, 54th Leg., p. 88, ch. 55, eff. Jan. 1, 1956. Amended by Acts 1993, 73rd Leg., ch. 957, § 36, eff. Sept. 1, 1993.

## § 221A. Change of Resident Agent

(a) A personal representative may change its resident agent to accept service of process in a probate proceeding or other action relating to the estate by filing a statement of the change titled "Designation of Successor Resident Agent" with the court in which the probate proceeding is pending. The statement must contain the names and addresses of the:

(1) personal representative;

(2) resident agent; and

(3) successor resident agent.

(b) The designation of a successor resident agent made in a statement filed under this section takes effect on the date on which the statement is filed with the court.

Added by Acts 1999, 76th Leg., ch. 855, § 7, eff. Sept. 1, 1999.

## § 221B. Resignation of Resident Agent

(a) A resident agent of a personal representative may resign as the resident agent by giving notice to the personal representative and filing with the court in which the probate proceeding is pending a statement titled "Resignation of Resident Agent" that:

(1) contains the name of the personal representative;

(2) contains the address of the personal representative most recently known by the resident agent;

(3) states that notice of the resignation has been given to the personal representative and that the personal representative has not designated a successor resident agent; and

(4) contains the date on which the notice of the resignation was given to the personal representative.

(b) The resident agent shall send, by certified mail, return receipt requested, a copy of a resignation statement filed under Subsection (a) of this section to:

(1) the personal representative at the address most recently known by the agent; and

(2) each party in the case or the party's attorney or other designated representative of record.

(c) The resignation of a resident agent takes effect on the date on which the court enters an order accepting the agent's resignation. A court may not enter an order accepting the agent's resignation unless the agent complies with the requirements of this section.

Added by Acts 1999, 76th Leg., ch. 855, § 7, eff. Sept. 1, 1999.

## § 222. Removal

**(a) Without Notice.** (1) The court, on its own motion or on motion of any interested person, and without notice, may remove any personal representative, appointed under provisions of this Code, who:

(A) Neglects to qualify in the manner and time required by law;

(B) Fails to return within ninety days after qualification, unless such time is extended by order of the court, an inventory of the property of the estate and list of claims that have come to his knowledge;

(C) Having been required to give a new bond, fails to do so within the time prescribed;

(D) Absents himself from the State for a period of three months at one time without permission of the court, or removes from the State;

(E) Cannot be served with notices or other processes because of the fact that the:

(i) personal representative's whereabouts are unknown;

(ii) personal representative is eluding service; or

(iii) personal representative is a nonresident of this state who does not have a resident agent to accept service of process in any probate proceeding or other action relating to the estate; or

(F) Has misapplied, embezzled, or removed from the State, or is about to misapply, embezzle, or remove from the State, all or any part of the property committed to the personal representative's care.

(2) The court may remove a personal representative under Paragraph (F), Subdivision (1), of this subsection only on the presentation of clear and convincing evidence given under oath.

**(b) With Notice.** The court may remove a personal representative on its own motion or on the complaint of any interested person, after the personal representative has been cited by personal service to answer at a time and place fixed in the notice, when:

(1) Sufficient grounds appear to support belief that the personal representative has misapplied, embezzled, or removed from the state, or that the personal representative is about to misapply, embezzle, or remove from the state, all or any part of the property committed to the personal representative's care;

(2) The personal representative fails to return any account which is required by law to be made;

(3) The personal representative fails to obey any proper order of the court having jurisdiction with respect to the performance of the personal representative's duties;

(4) The personal representative is proved to have been guilty of gross misconduct, or mismanagement in the performance of the personal representative's duties;

(5) The personal representative becomes an incapacitated person, or is sentenced to the penitentiary, or from any other cause becomes incapable of properly performing the duties of the personal representative's trust;

(6) As executor or administrator, the personal representative fails to make a final settlement within three years after the grant of letters, unless the time be extended by the court upon a showing of sufficient cause supported by oath; or

(7) As executor or administrator, the personal representative fails to timely file the affidavit or certificate required by Section 128A of this code.

**(c) Order of Removal.** The order of removal shall state the cause thereof. It shall require that any letters issued to the one removed shall, if he has been personally served with citation, be surrendered, and that all such letters be cancelled of record, whether delivered or not. It shall further require, as to all the estate remaining in the hands of a removed person, delivery thereof to the person or persons entitled thereto, or to one who has been appointed and has qualified as successor representative.

Acts 1955, 54th Leg., p. 88, ch. 55, eff. Jan. 1, 1956. Amended by Acts 1969, 61st Leg., p. 1922, ch. 641, § 11, eff. June 12, 1969; Acts 1989, 71st Leg., ch. 1035, § 11, eff. Sept. 1, 1989; Acts 1993, 73rd Leg., ch. 905, § 11, eff. Sept. 1, 1993; Acts 1993, 73rd Leg., ch. 957, § 37, eff. Sept. 1, 1993; Acts 1995, 74th Leg., ch. 1039, § 13, eff. Sept. 1, 1995; Acts 1999, 76th Leg., ch. 855, § 8, eff. Sept. 1, 1999. Subsec. (b) amended by Acts 2007, 80th Leg., ch. 801, § 4, eff. Sept. 1, 2007.

## § 222A. Reinstatement After Removal

(a) Not later than the 10th day after the date the court signs the order of removal, a personal representative who is removed under Subsection (a)(1)(F) or (G), Section 222, of this code may file an application with the court for a hearing to determine whether the personal representative should be reinstated.

(b) On the filing of an application for a hearing under this section, the court clerk shall issue a notice stating that the application for reinstatement was filed, the name of the decedent, and the name of the applicant. The clerk shall issue the notice to the applicant and to the successor representative of the decedent's estate. The notice must cite all persons interested in the estate to appear at the time and place stated in the notice if they wish to contest the application.

(c) If, at the conclusion of a hearing under this section, the court is satisfied by a preponderance of the evidence that the applicant did not engage in the conduct that directly led to the applicant's removal, the court shall set aside an order appointing a successor representative, if any, and shall enter an order reinstating the applicant as personal representative of the ward or estate.

(d) If the court sets aside the appointment of a successor representative under this section, the court may require the successor representative to prepare and file, under oath, an accounting of the estate and to detail the disposition the successor has made of the property of the estate.

Added by Acts 1993, 73rd Leg., ch. 905, § 12, eff. Sept. 1, 1993. Subsec. (b) amended by Acts 2003, 78th Leg., ch. 1060, § 12, eff. Sept. 1, 2003.

## PART 4. SUBSEQUENT PERSONAL REPRESENTATIVES

### § 223. Further Administration With or Without Will Annexed

Whenever any estate is unrepresented by reason of the death, removal, or resignation of the personal representative of such estate, the court shall grant further administration of the estate when necessary, and with the will annexed where there is a will, upon application therefor by a qualified person interested in the estate. Such appointments shall be made on notice and after hearing, as in case of original appointments, except that when the court finds that there is a necessity for the immediate appointment of a successor representative, such successor may be appointed upon application but without citation or notice.

Acts 1955, 54th Leg., p. 88, ch. 55, eff. Jan. 1, 1956. Amended by Acts 1969, 61st Leg., p. 1922, ch. 641, § 11, eff. June 12, 1969.

### § 224. Successors Succeed to Prior Rights, Powers, and Duties

When a representative of the estate not administered succeeds another, he shall be clothed with all rights, powers, and duties of his predecessor, except such rights and powers conferred on the predecessor by will which are different from those conferred by this Code on personal representatives generally. Subject to this exception, the successor shall proceed to administer such estate in like manner as if his administration were a continuation of the former one. He

shall be required to account for all the estate which came into the hands of his predecessor and shall be entitled to any order or remedy which the court has power to give in order to enforce the delivery of the estate and the liability of the sureties of his predecessor for so much as is not delivered. He shall be excused from accounting for such of the estate as he has failed to recover after due diligence.

Acts 1955, 54th Leg., p. 88, ch. 55, eff. Jan. 1, 1956.

### § 225. Additional Powers of Successor Appointee

In addition, such appointee may make himself, and may be made, a party to suits prosecuted by or against his predecessors. He may settle with the predecessor, and receive and receipt for all such portion of the estate as remains in his hands. He may bring suit on the bond or bonds of the predecessor in his own name and capacity, for all the estate that came into the hands of the predecessor and has not been accounted for by him.

Acts 1955, 54th Leg., p. 88, ch. 55, eff. Jan. 1, 1956.

### § 226. Subsequent Executors Also Succeed to Prior Rights and Duties

Whenever an executor shall accept and qualify after letters of administration shall have been granted upon the estate, such executor shall, in like manner, succeed to the previous administrator, and he shall administer the estate in like manner as if his administration were a continuation of the former one, subject, however, to any legal directions of the testator contained in the will in relation to the estate.

Acts 1955, 54th Leg., p. 88, ch. 55, eff. Jan. 1, 1956. Amended by Acts 1993, 73rd Leg., ch. 957, § 38, eff. Sept. 1, 1993.

### § 227. Successors Return of Inventory, Appraisement, and List of Claims or Affidavit in Lieu of Inventory, Appraisement, and List of Claims

An appointee who has been qualified to succeed to a prior personal representative shall make and return to the court an inventory, appraisement, and list of claims of the estate or, if the appointee is an independent executor, shall make and return to the court that document or file an affidavit in lieu of the inventory, appraisement, and list of claims, within ninety days after being qualified, in like manner as is provided for original appointees; and he shall also in like manner return additional inventories, appraisements, and lists of claims or file additional affidavits. In all orders appointing successor representatives of estates, the court shall appoint appraisers as in original appointments upon the application of any person interested in the estate.

Acts 1955, 54th Leg., p. 88, ch. 55, eff. Jan. 1, 1956. Amended by Acts 1969, 61st Leg., p. 1922, ch. 641, § 11, eff. June 12, 1969; Acts 2011, 82nd Leg., ch. 1338 (S.B. 1198), § 1.27, eff. Sept. 1, 2011.

## PART 5. GENERAL POWERS OF PERSONAL REPRESENTATIVES

### §§ 228, 229. Repealed by Acts 1993, 73rd Leg., ch. 957, § 75(1), eff. Sept. 1, 1993

## § 230. Care of Property of Estates

The executor or administrator shall take care of the property of the estate of his testator or intestate as a prudent man would take of his own property, and if there be any buildings belonging to the estate, he shall keep the same in good repair, extraordinary casualties excepted, unless directed not to do so by an order of the court.

Acts 1955, 54th Leg., p. 88, ch. 55, eff. Jan. 1, 1956.  Amended by Acts 1975, 64th Leg., p. 268, ch. 114, § 1, eff. April 30, 1975; Acts 1993, 73rd Leg., ch. 957, § 39, eff. Sept. 1, 1993.

## § 231. Repealed by Acts 1993, 73rd Leg., ch. 957, § 75(1), eff. Sept. 1, 1993

## § 232. Representative of Estate Shall Take Possession of Personal Property and Records

The personal representative of an estate, immediately after receiving letters, shall collect and take into possession the personal property, record books, title papers, and other business papers of the estate, and all such in his possession shall be delivered to the person or persons legally entitled thereto when the administration has been closed or a successor has received letters.

Acts 1955, 54th Leg., p. 88, ch. 55, eff. Jan. 1, 1956.

## § 233. Collection of Claims and Recovery of Property

(a) Every personal representative of an estate shall use ordinary diligence to collect all claims and debts due the estate and to recover possession of all property of the estate to which its owners have claim or title, provided there is a reasonable prospect of collecting such claims or of recovering such property.  If he wilfully neglects to use such diligence, he and the sureties on his bond shall be liable, at the suit of any person interested in the estate, for the use of the estate, for the amount of such claims or the value of such property as has been lost by such neglect.

(b) Except as provided by Subsection (c) of this section, a personal representative may enter into a contract to convey, or may convey, a contingent interest in any property sought to be recovered, not exceeding one-third thereof, for services of attorneys, subject only to approval of the court in which the estate is being administered.

(c) A personal representative, including an independent executor or independent administrator, may convey or contract to convey for services of an attorney a contingent interest that exceeds one-third of the property sought to be recovered under this section only on the approval of the court in which the estate is being administered.  The court must approve a contract entered into or conveyance made under this section before an attorney performs any legal services.  A contract entered into or conveyance made in violation of this section is void, unless the court ratifies or reforms the contract or documents relating to the conveyance to the extent necessary to cause the contract or conveyance to meet the requirements of this section.

(d) In approving a contract or conveyance under Subsection (b) or (c) of this section for services of an attorney, the court shall consider:

(1) the time and labor that will be required, the novelty and difficulty of the questions to be involved, and the skill that will be required to perform the legal services properly;

(2) the fee customarily charged in the locality for similar legal services;

(3) the value of property recovered or sought to be recovered by the personal representative under this section;

(4) the benefits to the estate that the attorney will be responsible for securing;  and

(5) the experience and ability of the attorney who will be performing the services.

(e) On satisfactory proof to the court, a personal representative of an estate is entitled to all necessary and reasonable expenses incurred by the personal representative in collecting or attempting to collect a claim or debt owed to the estate or in recovering or attempting to recover property to which the estate has a title or claim.

Acts 1955, 54th Leg., p. 88, ch. 55, eff. Jan. 1, 1956.  Amended by Acts 1993, 73rd Leg., ch. 848, § 1, eff. Sept. 1, 1993.

## § 233A. Suits by Executors or Administrators

Suits for the recovery of personal property, debts, or damages and suits for title or possession of lands or for any right attached to or growing out of the same or for injury or damage done thereto may be instituted by executors or administrators appointed in this state; and judgment in such cases shall be conclusive, but may be set aside by any person interested for fraud or collusion on the part of such executor or administrator.

Added by Acts 1985, 69th Leg., ch. 959, § 3, eff. Sept. 1, 1985.  Amended by Acts 1993, 73rd Leg., ch. 957, § 40, eff. Sept. 1, 1993.

## § 234. Exercise of Powers With and Without Court Order

(a) Powers To Be Exercised Under Order of the Court. The personal representative of the estate of any person may, upon application and order authorizing same, renew or extend any obligation owing by or to such estate.  When a personal representative deems it for the interest of the estate, he may, upon written application to the court, and by order granting authority:

(1) Purchase or exchange property;

(2) Take claims or property for the use and benefit of the estate in payment of any debt due or owing to the estate;

(3) Compound bad or doubtful debts due or owing to the estate;

(4) Make compromises or settlements in relation to property or claims in dispute or litigation;

(5) Compromise or pay in full any secured claim which has been allowed and approved as required by law against the

estate by conveying to the holder of such claim the real estate or personalty securing the same, in full payment, liquidation, and satisfaction thereof, and in consideration of cancellation of notes, deeds of trust, mortgages, chattel mortgages, or other evidences of liens securing the payment of such claim;

(6) Abandon the administration of property of the estate that is burdensome or worthless. Abandoned real or personal property may be foreclosed by a secured party, trustee, or mortgagee without further order of the court.

**(b) Powers To Be Exercised Without Court Order.** The personal representative of the estate of any person may, without application to or order of the court, exercise the powers listed below, provided, however, that a personal representative under court control may apply and obtain an order if doubtful of the propriety of the exercise of any such powers:

(1) Release liens upon payment at maturity of the debt secured thereby;

(2) Vote stocks by limited or general proxy;

(3) Pay calls and assessments;

(4) Insure the estate against liability in appropriate cases;

(5) Insure property of the estate against fire, theft, and other hazards;

(6) Pay taxes, court costs, bond premiums.

Acts 1955, 54th Leg., p. 88, ch. 55, eff. Jan. 1, 1956. Amended by Acts 1971, 62nd Leg., p. 984, ch. 173, § 15, eff. Jan. 1, 1972; Acts 1997, 75th Leg., ch. 1302, § 9, eff. Sept. 1, 1997.

### § 235. Possession of Property Held in Common Ownership

If the estate holds or owns any property in common, or as part owner with another, the representative of the estate shall be entitled to possession thereof in common with the other part owner or owners in the same manner as other owners in common or joint owners would be entitled.

Acts 1955, 54th Leg., p. 88, ch. 55, eff. Jan. 1, 1956.

### § 236. Repealed by Acts 1993, 73rd Leg., ch. 957, § 75(1), eff. Sept. 1, 1993; Acts 1995, 74th Leg., ch. 1039, § 73(1), eff. Sept. 1, 1995

### § 236A. Repealed by Acts 1995, 74th Leg., ch. 1039, § 73(1), eff. Sept. 1, 1995

### § 237. Repealed by Acts 1993, 73rd Leg., ch. 957, § 75(1), eff. Sept. 1, 1993

### § 238. Operation of Farm, Ranch, Factory, or Other Business

(a) In this section, "business" includes a farm, ranch, or factory.

(b) A court, after notice to all interested persons and a hearing, may order the personal representative of an estate to operate a business that is part of the estate and may grant the personal representative the powers to operate the business that the court determines are appropriate, after considering the factors listed in Subsection (f) of this section, if:

(1) the disposition of the business has not been specifically directed by the decedent's will;

(2) it is not necessary to sell the business at once for the payment of debts or other lawful purposes; and

(3) the court determines that the operation of the business by the personal representative is in the best interest of the estate.

(c) A personal representative who is granted the power to operate a business in an order entered under this section has the powers granted under Section 234(b) of this code, regardless of whether the order specifies that the personal representative has those powers, unless the order specifically provides that the personal representative does not have one or more of the powers listed in that section.

(d) In addition to the powers granted to the personal representative under Section 234(b) of this code, subject to any specific limitation on those powers in accordance with Subsection (c) of this section, an order entered under this section may grant the personal representative one or more of the following powers:

(1) the power to hire, pay, and terminate the employment of employees of the business;

(2) the power to incur debt on behalf of the business, including debt secured by liens against assets of the business or estate, if permitted or directed in the order;

(3) the power to purchase and sell property in the ordinary course of the operation of the business, including the power to purchase and sell real property if the court finds that the principal purpose of the business is the purchasing and selling of real property and the order states that finding;

(4) the power to enter into a lease or contract, the term of which may extend beyond the settlement of the estate, but only to the extent granting that power appears to be consistent with the speedy settlement of the estate; and

(5) any other power the court finds is necessary with respect to the operation of the business.

(e) If the order entered under this section gives the personal representative the power to purchase, sell, lease, or otherwise encumber real or personal property:

(1) the purchase, sale, lease, or encumbrance is governed by the terms of the order; and

(2) the personal representative is not required to comply with any other provision of this code regarding the purchase, sale, lease, or encumbrance, including provisions requiring citation or notice.

(f) In determining which powers to grant a personal representative in an order entered under this section, the court shall consider the following factors:

(1) the condition of the estate and the business;

(2) the necessity that may exist for the future sale of the business or of business property to provide for payment of debts or claims against the estate or other lawful expenditures with respect to the estate;

(3) the effect of the order on the speedy settlement of the estate; and

(4) the best interests of the estate.

(g) A personal representative who operates a business under an order entered under this section has the same fiduciary duties as a personal representative who does not operate a business that is part of an estate. The personal representative shall:

(1) in operating the business, consider:

(A) the condition of the estate and the business;

(B) the necessity that may exist for the future sale of the business or of business property to provide for payment of debts or claims against the estate or other lawful expenditures with respect to the estate;

(C) the effect of the order on the speedy settlement of the estate; and

(D) the best interests of the estate; and

(2) report to the court with respect to the operation and condition of the business as part of the accounts required by Parts 11 and 12, Chapter VIII, of this code, unless the court orders the reports regarding the business to be made more frequently or in a different manner or form.

(h) Before purchasing, selling, leasing, or otherwise encumbering any real property of the business in accordance with an order entered under this section, the personal representative shall file a notice in the real property records of the county in which the real property is located. The notice must state:

(1) the name of the decedent;

(2) the county of the court in which the decedent's estate is pending;

(3) the cause number assigned to the pending estate;

(4) that one or more orders have been entered under this section; and

(5) a description of the property that is the subject of the purchase, sale, lease, or other encumbrance.

(i) For purposes of determining a personal representative's powers with respect to a purchase, sale, lease, or other encumbrance of real property of a business that is part of an estate, a third party who deals in good faith with a personal representative with respect to the transaction may rely on the notice under Subsection (h) of this section and an order that is entered under this section and filed as part of the estate records maintained by the clerk of the court in which the estate is pending.

Acts 1955, 54th Leg., p. 88, ch. 55, eff. Jan. 1, 1956. Amended by Acts 1993, 73rd Leg., ch. 957, § 41, eff. Sept. 1, 1993; Acts 2007, 80th Leg., ch. 668, § 1, eff. Sept. 1, 2007.

### § 238A.  Administration of Partnership Interest by Personal Representative

If the decedent was a partner in a general partnership and the articles of partnership provide that, on the death of a partner, his or her executor or other personal representative shall be entitled to the place of the deceased partner in the firm, the executor or other personal representative so contracting to come into the partnership shall, to the extent allowed by law, be liable to third persons only to the extent of the deceased partner's capital in the partnership and the estate's assets held by the executor or other personal representative. This section does not exonerate an executor or other personal representative from liability for his or her negligence.

Added by Acts 1979, 66th Leg., p. 71, ch. 46, § 1, eff. April 11, 1979.

### § 239.  Payment or Credit of Income

In all cases where the estate of a deceased person is being administered under the direction, control, and orders of a court in the exercise of its probate jurisdiction, upon the application of the executor or administrator of said estate, or of any interested party, after notice thereof has been given by posting, if it appears from evidence introduced at the hearing upon said application, and the court finds, that the reasonable market value of the assets of the estate then on hand, exclusive of the annual income therefrom, is at least twice the aggregate amount of all unpaid debts, administration expenses, and legacies, and that no creditor or legatee of the estate has then appeared and objected, the court may order and direct the executor or administrator to pay to, or credit to the account of, those persons who the court finds will own the assets of the estate when the administration thereon is completed, and in the same proportions, such part of the annual net income received by or accruing to said estate, as the court believes and finds can conveniently be paid to such owners without prejudice to the rights of creditors, legatees, or other interested parties. Nothing herein contained shall authorize the court to order paid over to such owners of the estate any part of the corpus or principal of the estate, except as otherwise provided by sections of this Code; provided, however, in this connection, bonuses, rentals, and royalties received for, or from, an oil, gas, or other mineral lease shall be treated and regarded as income, and not as corpus or principal.

Acts 1955, 54th Leg., p. 88, ch. 55, eff. Jan. 1, 1956. Amended by Acts 1973, 63rd Leg., p. 407, ch. 182, § 1, eff. May 25, 1973.

### § 240.  Joint Executors or Administrators

Should there be more than one executor or administrator of the same estate at the same time, the acts of one of them as such executor or administrator shall be as valid as if all had acted jointly; and, in case of the death, resignation or removal of an executor or administrator, if there be a co-executor or co-administrator of such estate, he shall proceed with the administration as if no such death, resignation or removal had occurred. Provided, however, that this Section shall not be construed to authorize one of several executors or administrators to convey real estate, but in such case all the executors or administrators who have qualified as such and are acting as such shall join in the conveyance, unless the court, after due hearing, authorizes less than all to act.

Acts 1955, 54th Leg., p. 88, ch. 55, eff. Jan. 1, 1956.

## PART 6. COMPENSATION, EXPENSES, AND COURT COSTS

### § 241. Compensation of Personal Representatives

(a) Executors, administrators, and temporary administrators shall be entitled to receive a commission of five per cent (5%) on all sums they may actually receive in cash, and the same per cent on all sums they may actually pay out in cash, in the administration of the estate on a finding by the court that the executor or administrator has taken care of and managed the estate in compliance with the standards of this code; provided, no commission shall be allowed for receiving funds belonging to the testator or intestate which were on hand or were held for the testator or intestate at the time of his death in a financial institution or a brokerage firm, including cash or a cash equivalent held in a checking account, savings account, certificate of deposit, or money market account; nor for collecting the proceeds of any life insurance policy; nor for paying out cash to the heirs or legatees as such; provided, further, however, that in no event shall the executor or administrator be entitled in the aggregate to more than five per cent (5%) of the gross fair market value of the estate subject to administration. If the executor or administrator manages a farm, ranch, factory, or other business of the estate, or if the compensation as calculated above is unreasonably low, the court may allow him reasonable compensation for his services, including unusual effort to collect funds or life insurance. For this purpose, the county court shall have jurisdiction to receive, consider, and act on applications from independent executors. The court may, on application of an interested person or on its own motion, deny a commission allowed by this subsection in whole or in part if:

(1) the court finds that the executor or administrator has not taken care of and managed estate property prudently; or

(2) the executor or administrator has been removed under Section 149C or 222 of this code.

(b) **Definition.** In this section, "financial institution" means an organization authorized to do business under state or federal laws relating to financial institutions, including banks and trust companies, savings banks, building and loan associations, savings and loan companies or associations, and credit unions.

Acts 1955, 54th Leg., p. 88, ch. 55, eff. Jan. 1, 1956. Amended by Acts 1957, 55th Leg., p. 53, ch. 31, § 8; Acts 1987, 70th Leg., ch. 919, § 1, eff. Sept. 1, 1987; Acts 1991, 72nd Leg., ch. 468, §§ 1, 2, eff. Sept. 1, 1991; Acts 1993, 73rd Leg., ch. 957, § 42, eff. Sept. 1, 1993.

### § 242. Expenses Allowed

Personal representatives of estates shall also be entitled to all necessary and reasonable expenses incurred by them in the preservation, safekeeping, and management of the estate, and in collecting or attempting to collect claims or debts, and in recovering or attempting to recover property to which the estate has a title or claim, and all reasonable attorney's fees, necessarily incurred in connection with the proceedings and management of such estate, on satisfactory proof to the court.

Acts 1955, 54th Leg., p. 88, ch. 55, eff. Jan. 1, 1956.

### § 243. Allowance for Defending Will

When any person designated as executor in a will or an alleged will, or as administrator with the will or alleged will annexed, defends it or prosecutes any proceeding in good faith, and with just cause, for the purpose of having the will or alleged will admitted to probate, whether successful or not, he shall be allowed out of the estate his necessary expenses and disbursements, including reasonable attorney's fees, in such proceedings. When any person designated as a devisee, legatee, or beneficiary in a will or an alleged will, or as administrator with the will or alleged will annexed, defends it or prosecutes any proceeding in good faith, and with just cause, for the purpose of having the will or alleged will admitted to probate, whether successful or not, he may be allowed out of the estate his necessary expenses and disbursements, including reasonable attorney's fees, in such proceedings.

Acts 1955, 54th Leg., p. 88, ch. 55, eff. Jan. 1, 1956. Amended by Acts 1983, 68th Leg., p. 5227, ch. 957, § 1, eff. Sept. 1, 1983; Acts 1987, 70th Leg., ch. 462, § 1, eff. Sept. 1, 1987.

### § 244. Expense Accounts

All expense charges shall be made in writing, showing specifically each item of expense and the date thereof, and shall be verified by affidavit of the representative, filed with the clerk and entered on the claim docket, and shall be acted on by the court in like manner as other claims against the estate.

Acts 1955, 54th Leg., p. 88, ch. 55, eff. Jan. 1, 1956.

### § 245. When Costs Are Adjudged Against Representative

When a personal representative neglects to perform a required duty or if a personal representative is removed for cause, the personal representative and the sureties on the personal representative's bond are liable for:

(1) costs of removal and other additional costs incurred that are not authorized expenditures, as defined by this code; and

(2) reasonable attorney's fees incurred in removing the personal representative or in obtaining compliance regarding any statutory duty the personal representative has neglected.

Acts 1955, 54th Leg., p. 88, ch. 55, eff. Jan. 1, 1956. Amended by Acts 1977, 65th Leg., p. 1171, ch. 448, § 3, eff. Aug. 29, 1977; Acts 1983, 68th Leg., p. 631, ch. 140, § 1, eff. Aug. 29, 1983.

Amended by Acts 2003, 78th Leg., ch. 1060, § 13, eff. Sept. 1, 2003.

§§ 246, 247.  Repealed by Acts 1993, 73rd Leg., ch. 957, § 75(1), eff. Sept. 1, 1993

## CHAPTER VIII

## PROCEEDINGS DURING ADMINISTRATION

**Text of Texas Probate Code effective until January 1, 2014**

# PROCEEDINGS DURING ADMINISTRATION

**Text of Texas Probate Code effective until January 1, 2014**

## PART 1. INVENTORY, APPRAISEMENT, AND LIST OF CLAIMS

### § 248. Appointment of Appraisers

At any time after the grant of letters testamentary or of administration, the court for good cause on its own motion or on the motion of an interested party shall appoint not less than one nor more than three disinterested persons, citizens of the county in which letters were granted, to appraise the property of the estate. In such event and when part of the estate is situated in a county other than the county in which letters were granted, if the court shall deem necessary it may appoint not less than one nor more than three disinterested persons, citizens of the county where such part of the estate is situated, to appraise the property of the estate situated therein.

Acts 1955, 54th Leg., p. 88, ch. 55, eff. Jan. 1, 1956. Amended by Acts 1967, 60th Leg., p. 1815, ch. 697, § 2, eff. Aug. 28, 1967; Acts 1993, 73rd Leg., ch. 957, § 44, eff. Sept. 1, 1993; Acts 2005, 79th Leg., ch. 765, § 2, eff. June 17, 2005; Acts 2005, 79th Leg. ch. 701, § 1, eff. Sept. 1, 2005.

### § 249. Failure of Appraisers to Serve

If any appraiser so appointed shall fail or refuse to act, the court shall by a like order or orders remove such appraiser and appoint another appraiser or appraisers, as the case shall require.

Acts 1955, 54th Leg., p. 88, ch. 55, eff. Jan. 1, 1956. Amended by Acts 1967, 60th Leg., p. 1816, ch. 697, § 3, eff. Aug. 28, 1967.

### § 250. Inventory and Appraisement; Affidavit in Lieu of Inventory, Appraisement, and List of Claims

(a) Within ninety days after the representative's qualification, unless a longer time shall be granted by the court, the representative shall prepare and file with the clerk of court a verified, full, and detailed inventory, in one written instrument, of all the property of such estate which has come to the representative's possession or knowledge, which inventory shall include:

(1) all real property of the estate situated in the State of Texas; and

(2) all personal property of the estate wherever situated.

(b) The representative shall set out in the inventory the representative's appraisement of the fair market value of each item thereof as of the date of death in the case of grant of letters testamentary or of administration, as the case may be; provided that if the court shall appoint an appraiser or appraisers of the estate, the representative shall determine the fair market value of each item of the inventory with the assistance of such appraiser or appraisers and shall set out in the inventory such appraisement. The inventory shall specify what portion of the property, if any, is separate property and what portion, if any, is community property. Such inventory, when approved by the court and duly filed with the clerk of court, shall constitute for all purposes the inventory and appraisement of the estate referred to in this Code. The court for good cause shown may require the filing of the inventory and appraisement at a time prior to ninety days after the qualification of the representative.

(c) Notwithstanding Subsection (a) of this section, if there are no unpaid debts, except for secured debts, taxes, and administration expenses, at the time the inventory is due, including any extensions, an independent executor may file with the court clerk, in lieu of the inventory, appraisement, and list of claims, an affidavit stating that all debts, except for secured debts, taxes, and administration expenses, are paid and that all beneficiaries have received a verified, full, and detailed inventory. The affidavit in lieu of the inventory, appraisement, and list of claims must be filed within the 90–day period prescribed by Subsection (a) of this section, unless the court grants an extension.

(d) In this section, "beneficiary" means a person, entity, state, governmental agency of the state, charitable organization, or trust entitled to receive real or personal property:

(1) under the terms of a decedent's will, to be determined for purposes of this subsection with the assumption that each person who is alive on the date of the decedent's death survives any period required to receive the bequest as specified by the terms of the will; or

(2) as an heir of the decedent.

(e) If the independent executor files an affidavit in lieu of filing an inventory, appraisement, and list of claims as authorized under Subsection (c) of this section:

(1) any person interested in the estate, including a possible heir of the decedent or a beneficiary under a prior will of the decedent, is entitled to receive a copy of the inventory, appraisement, and list of claims from the independent executor on written request;

(2) the independent executor may provide a copy of the inventory, appraisement, and list of claims to any person the independent executor believes in good faith may be a person interested in the estate without liability to the estate or its beneficiaries; and

(3) a person interested in the estate may apply to the court for an order compelling compliance with Subdivision (1) of this subsection and the court, in its discretion, may compel the independent executor to provide a copy of the inventory, appraisement, and list of claims to the interested person or may deny the application.

Acts 1955, 54th Leg., p. 88, ch. 55, eff. Jan. 1, 1956. Amended by Acts 1967, 60th Leg., p. 1816, ch. 697, § 4, eff. Aug. 28, 1967; Acts 1993, 73rd Leg., ch. 957, § 45, eff. Sept. 1, 1993; Acts 2011, 82nd Leg., ch. 1338 (S.B. 1198), § 1.28, eff. Sept. 1, 2011.

### § 251. List of Claims

There shall also be made out and attached to said inventory a full and complete list of all claims due or owing to the estate, which shall state:

(a) The name of each person indebted to the estate and his address when known.

(b) The nature of such debt, whether by note, bill, bond, or other written obligation, or by account or verbal contract.

(c) The date of such indebtedness, and the date when the same was or will be due.

(d) The amount of each claim, the rate of interest thereon, and time for which the same bears interest.

(e) In the case of decedent's estate, which of such claims are separate property and which are of the community.

(f) Repealed by Acts 2011, 82nd Leg., ch. 1338 (S.B. 1198), § 1.42(a).

Acts 1955, 54th Leg., p. 88, ch. 55, eff. Jan. 1, 1956. Subsec. (f) repealed by Acts 2011, 82nd Leg., ch. 1338 (S.B. 1198), § 1.42(a), eff. Sept. 1, 2011.

## § 252. Affidavit to be Attached

The representative of the estate shall also attach to such inventory and list of claims his affidavit subscribed and sworn to before an officer in the county authorized by law to administer oaths, that the said inventory and list of claims are a true and complete statement of the property and claims of the estate that have come to his knowledge.

Acts 1955, 54th Leg., p. 88, ch. 55, eff. Jan. 1, 1956.

## § 253. Fees of Appraisers

Each appraiser appointed by the court, as herein authorized, shall be entitled to receive a minimum compensation of Five Dollars ($5) per day, payable out of the estate, for each day that he actually serves in performance of his duties as such.

Acts 1955, 54th Leg., p. 88, ch. 55, eff. Jan. 1, 1956. Amended by Acts 1957, 55th Leg., p. 53, ch. 31, § 9.

## § 254. Repealed by Acts 1967, 60th Leg., p. 1816, ch. 697, § 6, eff. Aug. 28, 1967

## § 255. Action by the Court

Upon return of the inventory, appraisement, and list of claims, the judge shall examine and approve, or disapprove, them, as follows:

(a) **Order of Approval.** Should the judge approve the inventory, appraisement, and list of claims, he shall issue an order to that effect.

(b) **Order of Disapproval.** Should the judge not approve the inventory, appraisement, or list of claims, or any of them, an order to that effect shall be entered, and it shall further require the return of another inventory, appraisement, and list of claims, or whichever of them is disapproved, within a time specified in such order, not to exceed twenty days from the date of the order; and the judge may also, if deemed necessary, appoint new appraisers.

Acts 1955, 54th Leg., p. 88, ch. 55, eff. Jan. 1, 1956.

## § 256. Discovery of Additional Property

(a) If, after the filing of the inventory and appraisement, property or claims not included in the inventory shall come to the possession or knowledge of the representative, the representative shall forthwith file with the clerk of court a verified, full, and detailed supplemental inventory and appraisement.

(b) If, after the filing of an affidavit in lieu of the inventory and appraisement, property or claims not included in the inventory given to the beneficiaries shall come to the possession or knowledge of the representative, the representative shall forthwith file with the clerk of court a supplemental affidavit in lieu of the inventory and appraisement stating that all beneficiaries have received a verified, full, and detailed supplemental inventory and appraisement.

Acts 1955, 54th Leg., p. 88, ch. 55, eff. Jan. 1, 1956. Amended by Acts 1967, 60th Leg., p. 1816, ch. 697, § 5, eff. Aug. 28, 1967; Acts 2011, 82nd Leg., ch. 1338 (S.B. 1198), § 1.29, eff. Sept. 1, 2011.

## § 257. Additional Inventory or List of Claims Required by Court

Any representative of an estate, on the written complaint of any interested person that property or claims of the estate have not been included in the inventory and list of claims filed, shall be cited to appear before the court in which the cause is pending and show cause why he should not be required to make and return an additional inventory or list of claims, or both. After hearing such complaint, and being satisfied of the truth thereof, the court shall enter its order requiring such additional inventory or list of claims, or both, to be made and returned in like manner as original inventories, and within such time, not to exceed twenty days, from the date of said order, as may be fixed by the court, but to include only property or claims theretofore not inventoried or listed.

Acts 1955, 54th Leg., p. 88, ch. 55, eff. Jan. 1, 1956.

## § 258. Correction Required When Inventory, Appraisement, or List of Claims Erroneous or Unjust

Any person interested in an estate who deems an inventory, appraisement, or list of claims returned therein erroneous or unjust in any particular may file a complaint in writing setting forth and pointing out the alleged erroneous or unjust items, and cause the representative to be cited to appear before the court and show cause why such errors should not be corrected. If, upon the hearing of such complaint, the court be satisfied from the evidence that the inventory, appraisement, or list of claims is erroneous or unjust in any particular as alleged in the complaint, an order shall be entered specifying the erroneous or unjust items and the corrections to be made, and appointing appraisers to make a new appraisement correcting such erroneous or unjust items and requiring the return of said new appraisement within twenty days from the date of the order. The court may also, on its own motion or that of the personal representative of the estate, have a new appraisal made for the purposes above set out.

Acts 1955, 54th Leg., p. 88, ch. 55, eff. Jan. 1, 1956.

### § 259. Effect of Reappraisement

When any reappraisement is made, returned, and approved by the court, it shall stand in place of the original appraisement. Not more than one reappraisement shall be made, but any person interested in the estate may object to the reappraisement either before or after it is approved, and if the court finds that the reappraisement is erroneous or unjust, the court shall appraise the property upon the basis of the evidence before it.

Acts 1955, 54th Leg., p. 88, ch. 55, eff. Jan. 1, 1956.

### § 260. Failure of Joint Personal Representatives to Return an Inventory, Appraisement, and List of Claims or Affidavit in Lieu of Inventory, Appraisement, and List of Claims

If there be more than one representative qualified as such, any one or more of them, on the neglect of the others, may make and return an inventory and appraisement and list of claims or file an affidavit in lieu of an inventory, appraisement, and list of claims; and the representative so neglecting shall not thereafter interfere with the estate or have any power over same; but the representative so returning the inventory, appraisement, and list of claims or filing the affidavit in lieu of an inventory, appraisement, and list of claims shall have the whole administration, unless, within sixty days after the return or the filing, the delinquent or delinquents shall assign to the court in writing and under oath a reasonable excuse which the court may deem satisfactory; and if no excuse is filed or if the excuse filed is not deemed sufficient, the court shall enter an order removing any and all such delinquents and revoking their letters.

Acts 1955, 54th Leg., p. 88, ch. 55, eff. Jan. 1, 1956. Amended by Acts 2011, 82nd Leg., ch. 1338 (S.B. 1198), § 1.30, eff. Sept. 1, 2011.

### § 261. Use of Inventories, Appraisements, and Lists of Claims as Evidence

All inventories, appraisements, and lists of claims which have been taken, returned, and approved in accordance with law, or the record thereof, or copies of either the originals or the record thereof, duly certified under the seal of the county court affixed by the clerk, may be given in evidence in any of the courts of this State in any suit by or against the representative of the estate, but shall not be conclusive for or against him, if it be shown that any property or claims of the estate are not shown therein, or that the value of the property or claims of the estate actually was in excess of that shown in the appraisement and list of claims.

Acts 1955, 54th Leg., p. 88, ch. 55, eff. Jan. 1, 1956.

## PART 2. WITHDRAWING ESTATES OF DECEASED PERSONS FROM ADMINISTRATION

### § 262. Executor or Administrator Required to Report on Condition of Estate

At any time after the return of inventory, appraisement, and list of claims of a deceased person, any one entitled to a portion of the estate may, by a written complaint filed in the court in which such case is pending, cause the executor or administrator of the estate to be cited to appear and render under oath an exhibit of the condition of the estate.

Acts 1955, 54th Leg., p. 88, ch. 55, eff. Jan. 1, 1956.

### § 263. Bond Required to Withdraw Estate From Administration

When the executor or administrator has rendered the required exhibit, the persons entitled to such estate, or any of them, or any persons for them, may execute and deliver to the court a bond payable to the judge, and his successors in office, to be approved by the court, for an amount equal to at least double the gross appraised value of the estate as shown by the appraisement and list of claims returned, conditioned that the persons who execute such bond shall pay all the debts against the estate not paid that have been or shall be allowed by the executor or administrator and approved by the court, or that have been or shall be established by suit against said estate, and will pay to the executor or administrator any balance that shall be found to be due him by the judgment of the court on his exhibit.

Acts 1955, 54th Leg., p. 88, ch. 55, eff. Jan. 1, 1956.

### § 264. Court's Order

When such bond has been given and approved, the court shall thereupon enter an order directing and requiring the executor or administrator to deliver forthwith to all persons entitled to any portion of the estate the portion or portions of such estate to which they are entitled.

Acts 1955, 54th Leg., p. 88, ch. 55, eff. Jan. 1, 1956.

### § 265. Order of Discharge

When an estate has been so withdrawn from further administration, an order shall be entered discharging the executor or administrator and declaring the administration closed.

Acts 1955, 54th Leg., p. 88, ch. 55, eff. Jan. 1, 1956.

### § 266. Lien on Property of Estate Withdrawn From Administration

A lien shall exist on all of the estate withdrawn from administration in the hands of the distributees, and those claiming under them with notice of such lien, to secure the ultimate payment of the aforesaid bond and of the debts and claims secured thereby.

Acts 1955, 54th Leg., p. 88, ch. 55, eff. Jan. 1, 1956.

### § 267. Partition of Estate Withdrawn From Administration

Any person entitled to any portion of the estate withdrawn from further administration may, on written application to the court, cause a partition and distribution to be made among the persons entitled thereto, in accordance with the provisions of this Code pertaining to the partition and distribution of estates.

Acts 1955, 54th Leg., p. 88, ch. 55, eff. Jan. 1, 1956.

### § 268. Creditors May Sue on Bond

Any creditor of an estate withdrawn from administration whose debt or claim is unpaid and is not barred by limitation shall have the right to sue on the bond in his own name, and shall be entitled to judgment thereon for such debt or claim as he shall establish against the estate.

Acts 1955, 54th Leg., p. 88, ch. 55, eff. Jan. 1, 1956.

### § 269. Creditors May Sue Distributees

Any creditor of an estate withdrawn from administration whose debt or claim is unpaid and is not barred by limitation may sue any distributee who has received any of the estate, or he may sue all the distributees together, but no one of such distributees shall be liable beyond his just proportion according to the amount of the estate he shall have received in the distribution.

Acts 1955, 54th Leg., p. 88, ch. 55, eff. Jan. 1, 1956.

### PART 3. SETTING APART HOMESTEAD AND OTHER EXEMPT PROPERTY, AND FIXING THE FAMILY ALLOWANCE

### § 270. Liability of Homestead for Debts

The homestead shall not be liable for the payment of any of the debts of the estate, except for:

(1) the purchase money thereof;

(2) the taxes due thereon;

(3) work and material used in constructing improvements thereon if the requirements of Section 50(a)(5), Article XVI, Texas Constitution, are met;

(4) an owelty of partition imposed against the entirety of the property by court order or by a written agreement of the parties to the partition, including a debt of one spouse in favor of the other spouse resulting from a division or an award of a family homestead in a divorce proceeding;

(5) the refinance of a lien against a homestead, including a federal tax lien resulting from the tax debt of both spouses, if the homestead is a family homestead, or from the tax debt of the decedent;

(6) an extension of credit on the homestead if the requirements of Section 50(a)(6), Article XVI, Texas Constitution, are met; or

(7) a reverse mortgage.

Acts 1955, 54th Leg., p. 88, ch. 55, eff. Jan. 1, 1956. Amended by Acts 1979, 66th Leg., p. 35, ch. 24, § 1, eff. Aug. 27, 1979; Acts 1999, 76th Leg., ch. 487, § 1, eff. Sept. 1, 1999; Acts 1999, 76th Leg., ch. 855, § 9, eff. Sept. 1, 1999.

### § 271. Exempt Property to Be Set Apart

(a) Unless an affidavit is filed under Subsection (b) of this section, immediately after the inventory, appraisement, and list of claims have been approved or after the affidavit in lieu of the inventory, appraisement, and list of claims has been filed, the court shall, by order, set apart:

(1) the homestead for the use and benefit of the surviving spouse and minor children; and

(2) all other property of the estate that is exempt from execution or forced sale by the constitution and laws of this state for the use and benefit of the surviving spouse, minor children, unmarried adult children remaining with the family of the deceased, and each other adult child who is incapacitated.

(b) Before the approval of the inventory, appraisement, and list of claims or, if applicable, before the filing of the affidavit in lieu of the inventory, appraisement, and list of claims:

(1) a surviving spouse or any person who is authorized to act on behalf of minor children of the deceased may apply to the court to have exempt property, including the homestead, set aside by filing an application and a verified affidavit listing all of the property that the applicant claims is exempt; and

(2) any unmarried adult child remaining with the family of the deceased, any other adult child who is incapacitated, or a person who is authorized to act on behalf of the adult incapacitated child may apply to the court to have all exempt property other than the homestead set aside by filing an application and a verified affidavit listing all of the other property that the applicant claims is exempt.

(c) An applicant under Subsection (b) of this section bears the burden of proof by a preponderance of the evidence at any hearing on the application. The court shall set aside property of the decedent's estate that the court finds is exempt.

Acts 1955, 54th Leg., p. 88, ch. 55, eff. Jan. 1, 1956. Amended by Acts 1979, 66th Leg., p. 35, ch. 24, § 2, eff. Aug. 27, 1979; Acts 1993, 73rd Leg., ch. 846, § 18, eff. Sept. 1, 1993; Acts 2005, 79th Leg., ch. 551, § 4, eff. Sept. 1, 2005. Subsecs. (a) and (b) amended by Acts 2011, 82nd Leg., ch. 810 (H.B. 2492), § 1.02, eff. Sept. 1, 2011; Subsecs. (a) and (b) amended by Acts 2011, 82nd Leg., ch. 1338 (S.B. 1198), § 1.31, eff. Sept. 1, 2011.

### § 272. To Whom Delivered

The exempt property set apart to the surviving spouse and children shall be delivered by the executor or administrator without delay as follows: (a) If there be a surviving spouse and no children, or if the children, including any adult incapacitated children, be the children of the surviving spouse, the whole of such property shall be delivered to the surviving spouse. (b) If there be children and no surviving spouse, such property, except the homestead, shall be delivered to the guardian of each of those children who is a minor, to each of those children who is of lawful age and not incapacitated, and to the guardian of each of those children who is an incapacitated adult or to another appropriate person, as determined by the court, on behalf of the adult incapacitated child if there is no guardian. (c) If there be children of the deceased of whom the surviving spouse is not the parent, the share of such children in such exempted property, except the homestead, shall be delivered to the guardian of each of those children who is a minor, to each of those children who is of lawful age and not incapacitated, and to the guardian of each of those children who is an incapacitated adult or to another appropriate person, as determined by the court, on behalf of the adult incapacitated child if there is no guardian. (d) In all cases, the homestead shall be delivered to the surviving spouse, if there be one, and if there be no surviving spouse, to the guardian of the minor children.

Acts 1955, 54th Leg., p. 88, ch. 55, eff. Jan. 1, 1956. Amended by Acts 1979, 66th Leg., p. 35, ch. 24, § 3, eff. Aug. 27, 1979; Acts 2005, 79th Leg., ch. 551, § 5, eff. Sept. 1, 2005; Acts 2011, 82nd Leg., ch. 810 (H.B. 2492), § 1.03, eff. Sept. 1, 2011.

### § 273. Allowance in Lieu of Exempt Property

In case there should not be among the effects of the deceased all or any of the specific articles exempted from execution or forced sale by the Constitution and laws of this state, the court shall make a reasonable allowance in lieu thereof, to be paid to such surviving spouse and children, or such of them as there are, as hereinafter provided. The allowance in lieu of a homestead shall in no case exceed $45,000 and the allowance for other exempted property shall in no case exceed $30,000, exclusive of the allowance for the support of the surviving spouse, minor children, and adult incapacitated children which is hereinafter provided for.

Acts 1955, 54th Leg., p. 88, ch. 55, eff. Jan. 1, 1956. Amended by Acts 1977, 65th Leg., p. 351, ch. 172, § 1, eff. Aug. 29, 1977; Acts 1979, 66th Leg., p. 35, ch. 24, § 4, eff. Aug. 27, 1979; Acts 1993, 73rd Leg., ch. 846, § 19, eff. Sept. 1, 1993; Acts 2011, 82nd Leg., ch. 810 (H.B. 2492), § 1.03, eff. Sept. 1, 2011; Acts 2013, 83rd Leg., ch. 647 (H.B. 789), § 1.01, eff. Sept. 1, 2013.

### § 274. How Allowance Paid

The allowance made in lieu of any of the exempted property shall be paid either in money out of the funds of the estate that come to the hands of the executor or administrator, or in any property of the deceased that such surviving spouse, children who are of lawful age, guardian of children who are minors, or guardian of each adult incapacitated child or other appropriate person, as determined by the court, on behalf of the adult incapacitated child if there is no guardian, shall choose to take at the appraisement, or a part thereof, or both, as they shall select; provided, however, that property specifically bequeathed or devised to another may be so taken, or may be sold to raise funds for the allowance as

hereinafter provided, only if the other available property shall be insufficient to provide the allowance.

Acts 1955, 54th Leg., p. 88, ch. 55, eff. Jan. 1, 1956. Amended by Acts 1979, 66th Leg., p. 36, ch. 24, § 5, eff. Aug. 27, 1979; Acts 2011, 82nd Leg., ch. 810 (H.B. 2492), § 1.03, eff. Sept. 1, 2011.

### § 275. To Whom Allowance Paid

The allowance in lieu of exempt property shall be paid by the executor or administrator, as follows:

(a) If there be a surviving spouse and no children, or if all the children, including any adult incapacitated children, be the children of the surviving spouse, the whole shall be paid to such surviving spouse.

(b) If there be children and no surviving spouse, the whole shall be equally divided among them and each of their shares shall be paid as follows:

(1) if the child is of lawful age and not incapacitated, to the child;

(2) if the child is a minor, to the child's guardian; or

(3) if the child is an incapacitated adult, to the adult incapacitated child's guardian or another appropriate person, as determined by the court, on behalf of the adult incapacitated child if there is no guardian.

(c) If there be a surviving spouse, and children of the deceased, some of whom are not children of the surviving spouse, the surviving spouse shall receive one-half of the whole, plus the shares of the children of whom the survivor is the parent, and the remaining shares shall be paid with respect to each of the children of whom the survivor is not the parent as follows:

(1) if the child is an adult who is not incapacitated, to the child;

(2) if the child is a minor, to the child's guardian; or

(3) if the child is an incapacitated adult, to the adult incapacitated child's guardian or another appropriate person, as determined by the court, on behalf of the adult incapacitated child if there is no guardian.

Acts 1955, 54th Leg., p. 88, ch. 55, eff. Jan. 1, 1956. Amended by Acts 1979, 66th Leg., p. 36, ch. 24, § 6, eff. Aug. 27, 1979; Acts 2011, 82nd Leg., ch. 810 (H.B. 2492), § 1.03, eff. Sept. 1, 2011.

### § 276. Sale to Raise Allowance

If there be no property of the deceased that such surviving spouse or children are willing to take for such allowance, or not a sufficiency, and there be no funds, or not sufficient funds, of the estate in the hands of such executor or administrator to pay such allowance, or any part thereof, the court, on the application in writing of such surviving spouse and children, or of a person authorized to represent any of those children, shall order a sale of so much of the estate for cash as will be sufficient to raise the amount of such allowance, or a part thereof, as the case requires.

Acts 1955, 54th Leg., p. 88, ch. 55, eff. Jan. 1, 1956. Amended by Acts 1979, 66th Leg., p. 36, ch. 24, § 7, eff. Aug. 27, 1979; Acts 2011, 82nd Leg., ch. 810 (H.B. 2492), § 1.03, eff. Sept. 1, 2011.

## § 277. Preference of Liens

If property upon which there is a valid subsisting lien or encumbrance shall be set apart to the surviving spouse or children as exempt property, or appropriated to make up allowances made in lieu of exempt property or for the support of the surviving spouse or children, the debts secured by such lien shall, if necessity requires, be either paid or continued as against such property. This provision applies to all estates, whether solvent or insolvent.

Acts 1955, 54th Leg., p. 88, ch. 55, eff. Jan. 1, 1956. Amended by Acts 1979, 66th Leg., p. 36, ch. 24, § 8, eff. Aug. 27, 1979.

## § 278. When Estate Is Solvent

If, upon a final settlement of the estate, it shall appear that the same is solvent, the exempted property, except the homestead or any allowance in lieu thereof, shall be subject to partition and distribution among the heirs and distributees of such estate in like manner as the other property of the estate.

Acts 1955, 54th Leg., p. 88, ch. 55, eff. Jan. 1, 1956.

## § 279. When Estate is Insolvent

Should the estate, upon final settlement, prove to be insolvent, the title of the surviving spouse and children to all the property and allowances set apart or paid to them under the provisions of this Code shall be absolute, and shall not be taken for any of the debts of the estate except as hereinafter provided.

Acts 1955, 54th Leg., p. 88, ch. 55, eff. Jan. 1, 1956. Amended by Acts 1979, 66th Leg., p. 37, ch. 24, § 9, eff. Aug. 27, 1979.

## § 280. Exempt Property Not Considered in Determining Solvency

In ascertaining whether an estate is solvent or insolvent, the exempt property set apart to the surviving spouse or children, or the allowance in lieu thereof, and the family allowance hereinafter provided for, shall not be estimated or considered as assets of the estate.

Acts 1955, 54th Leg., p. 88, ch. 55, eff. Jan. 1, 1956. Amended by Acts 1979, 66th Leg., p. 37, ch. 24, § 10, eff. Aug. 27, 1979.

## § 281. Exempt Property Liable for Certain Debts

The exempt property, other than the homestead or any allowance made in lieu thereof, shall be liable for the payment of Class 1 claims, but such property shall not be liable for any other debts of the estate.

Acts 1955, 54th Leg., p. 88, ch. 55, eff. Jan. 1, 1956. Amended by Acts 1997, 75th Leg., ch. 1302, § 10, eff. Sept. 1, 1997.

## § 282. Nature of Homestead Property Immaterial

The homestead rights of the surviving spouse and children of the deceased are the same whether the homestead be the separate property of the deceased or community property between the surviving spouse and the deceased, and the respective interests of such surviving spouse and children shall be the same in one case as in the other.

Acts 1955, 54th Leg., p. 88, ch. 55, eff. Jan. 1, 1956. Amended by Acts 1979, 66th Leg., p. 37, ch. 24, § 11, eff. Aug. 27, 1979.

## § 283. Homestead Rights of Surviving Spouse

On the death of the husband or wife, leaving a spouse surviving, the homestead shall descend and vest in like manner as other real property of the deceased and shall be governed by the same laws of descent and distribution.

Acts 1955, 54th Leg., p. 88, ch. 55, eff. Jan. 1, 1956. Amended by Acts 1979, 66th Leg., p. 37, ch. 24, § 12, eff. Aug. 27, 1979.

## § 284. When Homestead Not Partitioned

The homestead shall not be partitioned among the heirs of the deceased during the lifetime of the surviving spouse, or so long as the survivor elects to use or occupy the same as a homestead, or so long as the guardian of the minor children of the deceased is permitted, under the order of the proper court having jurisdiction, to use and occupy the same.

Acts 1955, 54th Leg., p. 88, ch. 55, eff. Jan. 1, 1956. Amended by Acts 1979, 66th Leg., p. 37, ch. 24, § 13, eff. Aug. 27, 1979.

## § 285. When Homestead Can Be Partitioned

When the surviving spouse dies or sells his or her interest in the homestead, or elects no longer to use or occupy the same as a homestead, or when the proper court no longer permits the guardian of the minor children to use and occupy the same as a homestead, it may be partitioned among the respective owners thereof in like manner as other property held in common.

Acts 1955, 54th Leg., p. 88, ch. 55, eff. Jan. 1, 1956. Amended by Acts 1979, 66th Leg., p. 37, ch. 24, § 14, eff. Aug. 27, 1979.

## § 286. Family Allowance to Surviving Spouses, Minors, and Adult Incapacitated Children

(a) Unless an affidavit is filed under Subsection (b) of this section, immediately after the inventory, appraisement, and list of claims have been approved or the affidavit in lieu of the inventory, appraisement, and list of claims has been filed, the court shall fix a family allowance for the support of the surviving spouse, minor children, and adult incapacitated children of the deceased.

(b) Before the approval of the inventory, appraisement, and list of claims or, if applicable, before the filing of the affidavit in lieu of the inventory, appraisement, and list of claims, a surviving spouse or any person who is authorized to act on behalf of minor children or adult incapacitated children of the deceased may apply to the court to have the court fix the family allowance by filing an application and a verified affidavit describing the amount necessary for the maintenance of the surviving spouse, minor children, and adult incapacitated children for one year after the date of the death of the decedent and describing the spouse's separate property and any property that minor children or adult incapacitated children have in their own right. The applicant bears the burden of proof by a preponderance of the evidence at any hearing on the application. The court shall fix a family allowance for the support of the surviving spouse, minor children, and adult incapacitated children of the deceased.

Acts 1955, 54th Leg., p. 88, ch. 55, eff. Jan. 1, 1956. Amended by Acts 1979, 66th Leg., p. 38, ch. 24, § 15, eff. Aug. 27, 1979; Acts 1993, 73rd Leg., ch. 846, § 20, eff. Sept. 1, 1993; Acts 2011, 82nd Leg., ch. 810 (H.B. 2492), § 1.03, eff. Sept. 1, 2011; Acts 2011, 82nd Leg., ch. 1338 (S.B. 1198), § 1.32, eff. Sept. 1, 2011.

### § 287. Amount of Family Allowance

Such allowance shall be of an amount sufficient for the maintenance of such surviving spouse, minor children, and adult incapacitated children for one year from the time of the death of the testator or intestate. The allowance shall be fixed with regard to the facts or circumstances then existing and those anticipated to exist during the first year after such death. The allowance may be paid either in a lump sum or in installments, as the court shall order.

Acts 1955, 54th Leg., p. 88, ch. 55, eff. Jan. 1, 1956. Amended by Acts 1979, 66th Leg., p. 38, ch. 24, § 16, eff. Aug. 27, 1979; Acts 2011, 82nd Leg., ch. 810 (H.B. 2492), § 1.03, eff. Sept. 1, 2011.

### § 288. When Family Allowance Not Made

No such allowance shall be made for the surviving spouse when the survivor has separate property adequate to the survivor's maintenance; nor shall such allowance be made for the minor children or adult incapacitated children when they have property in their own right adequate to their maintenance.

Acts 1955, 54th Leg., p. 88, ch. 55, eff. Jan. 1, 1956. Amended by Acts 1979, 66th Leg., p. 38, ch. 24, § 17, eff. Aug. 27, 1979; Acts 2011, 82nd Leg., ch. 810 (H.B. 2492), § 1.03, eff. Sept. 1, 2011.

### § 289. Order Fixing Family Allowance

When an allowance has been fixed, an order shall be entered stating the amount thereof, providing how the same shall be payable, and directing the executor or administrator to pay the same in accordance with law.

Acts 1955, 54th Leg., p. 88, ch. 55, eff. Jan. 1, 1956.

### § 290. Family Allowance Preferred

The family allowance made for the support of the surviving spouse, minor children, and adult incapacitated children of the deceased shall be paid in preference to all other debts or charges against the estate, except Class 1 claims.

Acts 1955, 54th Leg., p. 88, ch. 55, eff. Jan. 1, 1956. Amended by Acts 1979, 66th Leg., p. 38, ch. 24, § 18, eff. Aug. 27, 1979; Acts 1997, 75th Leg., ch. 1302, § 11, eff. Sept. 1, 1997; Acts 2011, 82nd Leg., ch. 810 (H.B. 2492), § 1.03, eff. Sept. 1, 2011.

### § 291. To Whom Family Allowance Paid

The executor or administrator shall apportion and pay the family allowance:

(a) To the surviving spouse, if there be one, for the use of the survivor and the minor children and adult incapacitated children, if such children be the survivor's.

(b) If the surviving spouse is not the parent of such minor children and adult incapacitated children, or of some of them, the portion of such allowance necessary for the support of such minor child or children of which the survivor is not the parent shall be paid to the guardian or guardians of such child or children who are minors, and to the guardian of each adult incapacitated child or another appropriate person, as determined by the court, on behalf of the adult incapacitated child if there is no guardian.

(c) If there be no surviving spouse, the allowance to the minor child or children shall be paid to the guardian or guardians of such minor child or children, and the allowance to each adult incapacitated child shall be paid to the guardian of the adult incapacitated child or another appropriate person, as determined by the court, on behalf of the adult incapacitated child if there is no guardian.

(d) If there be a surviving spouse and no minor child or adult incapacitated child, the entire allowance shall be paid to the surviving spouse.

Acts 1955, 54th Leg., p. 88, ch. 55, eff. Jan. 1, 1956. Amended by Acts 1979, 66th Leg., p. 38, ch. 24, § 19, eff. Aug. 27, 1979; Acts 2011, 82nd Leg., ch. 810 (H.B. 2492), § 1.03, eff. Sept. 1, 2011.

### § 292. May Take Property for Family Allowance

The surviving spouse, the guardian of the minor children, or the guardian of an adult incapacitated child or another appropriate person, as determined by the court, on behalf of the adult incapacitated child if there is no guardian, as the case may be, shall have the right to take in payment of such allowance, or any part thereof, any of the personal property of the estate at its appraised value as shown by the appraisement; provided, however, that property specifically devised or bequeathed to another may be so taken, or may be sold to raise funds for the allowance as hereinafter provided, only if the other available property shall be insufficient to provide the allowance.

Acts 1955, 54th Leg., p. 88, ch. 55, eff. Jan. 1, 1956. Amended by Acts 1979, 66th Leg., p. 39, ch. 24, § 20, eff. Aug. 27, 1979; Acts 2011, 82nd Leg., ch. 810 (H.B. 2492), § 1.03, eff. Sept. 1, 2011.

### § 293. Sale to Raise Funds for Family Allowance

If there be no personal property of the deceased that the surviving spouse or guardian is willing to take for such allowance, or not a sufficiency of them, and if there be no funds or not sufficient funds in the hands of such executor or administrator to pay such allowance, or any part thereof, then the court, as soon as the inventory, appraisement, and list of claims are returned and approved or, if applicable, the affidavit in lieu of the inventory, appraisement, and list of claims is filed, shall order a sale of so much of the estate for cash as will be sufficient to raise the amount of such allowance, or a part thereof, as the case requires.

Acts 1955, 54th Leg., p. 88, ch. 55, eff. Jan. 1, 1956. Amended by Acts 1979, 66th Leg., p. 39, ch. 24, § 21, eff. Aug. 27, 1979; Acts 2011, 82nd Leg., ch. 1338 (S.B. 1198), § 1.33, eff. Sept. 1, 2011.

## PART 4.  PRESENTMENT AND PAYMENT OF CLAIMS

### § 294.  Notice by Representative of Appointment

**(a) Giving of Notice Required.** Within one month after receiving letters, personal representatives of estates shall send to the comptroller of public accounts by certified or registered mail if the decedent remitted or should have remitted taxes administered by the comptroller of public accounts and publish in some newspaper, printed in the county where the letters were issued, if there be one, a notice requiring all persons having claims against the estate being administered to present the same within the time prescribed by law. The notice shall include the date of issuance of letters held by the representative, the address to which claims may be presented, and an instruction of the representative's choice that claims be addressed in care of the representative, in care of the representative's attorney, or in care of "Representative, Estate of _____" (naming the estate).

**(b) Proof of Publication.** A copy of such printed notice, together with the affidavit of the publisher, duly sworn to and subscribed before a proper officer, to the effect that the notice was published as provided in this Code for the service of citation or notice by publication, shall be filed in the court where the cause is pending.

**(c) When No Newspaper Printed in the County.** When no newspaper is printed in the county, the notice shall be posted and the return made and filed as required by this Code.

**(d) Permissive Notice to Unsecured Creditors.** At any time before an estate administration is closed, the personal representative may give notice by certified or registered mail, with return receipt requested, to an unsecured creditor having a claim for money against the estate expressly stating that the creditor must present a claim within four months after the date of the receipt of the notice or the claim is barred, if the claim is not barred by the general statutes of limitation. The notice must include:

(1) the dates of issuance of letters held by the representative;

(2) the address to which claims may be presented; and

(3) an instruction of the representative's choice that the claim be addressed in care of:

(A) the representative;

(B) the representative's attorney; or

(C) "Representative, Estate of " (naming the estate).

Acts 1955, 54th Leg., p. 88, ch. 55, eff. Jan. 1, 1956. Amended by Acts 1981, 67th Leg., p. 243, ch. 102, § 9, eff. Aug. 31, 1981; Acts 1991, 72nd Leg., ch. 464, § 1, eff. Aug. 26, 1991; Acts 1995, 74th Leg., ch. 1054, § 2, eff. Jan. 1, 1996.

### § 295.  Notice to Holders of Secured Claims

**(a) When notice required for secured claimants.** Within two months after receiving letters, the personal representative of an estate shall give notice of the issuance of such letters to each and every person known to the personal representative to have a claim for money against the estate of a decedent that is secured by real or personal property of the estate. Within a reasonable time after the personal representative obtains actual knowledge of the existence of a person having a secured claim for money and to whom notice was not previously given, the personal representative shall give notice to the person of the issuance of letters.

**(b) How notice shall be given.** The notice stating the original grant of letters shall be given by mailing same by certified or registered mail, with return receipt requested, addressed to the record holder of such indebtedness or claim at the record holder's last known post office address.

**(c) Proof of service of notice.** A copy of each notice required by Subsection (a) of this section and a copy of the return receipt and an affidavit of the representative, stating that said notice was mailed as required by law, giving the name of the person to whom the notice was mailed, if not shown on the notice or receipt, shall be filed with the clerk of the court from which letters were issued.

Acts 1955, 54th Leg., p. 88, ch. 55, eff. Jan. 1, 1956. Amended by Acts 1987, 70th Leg., ch. 461, § 1, eff. Sept. 1, 1987; Acts 1991, 72nd Leg., ch. 895, § 13, eff. Sept. 1, 1991; Acts 1993, 73rd Leg., ch. 957, § 46, eff. Sept. 1, 1993; Acts 1995, 74th Leg., ch. 1054, § 3, eff. Jan. 1, 1996.

### § 296.  One Notice Sufficient

If the notices required by the two preceding Sections have been given by a former representative, or by one where several are acting, that shall be sufficient, and need not be repeated by any successor or co-representative.

Acts 1955, 54th Leg., p. 88, ch. 55, eff. Jan. 1, 1956.

### § 297.  Penalty for Failure to Give Notice

If the representative fails to give the notices required in preceding Sections, or to cause such notices to be given, the representative and the sureties on the representative's bond shall be liable for any damage which any person suffers by reason of such neglect, unless it appears that such person had notice otherwise.

Acts 1955, 54th Leg., p. 88, ch. 55, eff. Jan. 1, 1956. Amended by Acts 1995, 74th Leg., ch. 1054, § 4, eff. Jan. 1, 1996.

### § 298.  Claims Against Estates of Decedents

**(a) Time for Presentation of Claims.** A claim may be presented to the personal representative at any time before the estate is closed if suit on the claim has not been barred by the general statutes of limitation. If a claim of an unsecured creditor for money is not presented within four months after the date of receipt of the notice permitted by Section 294(d), the claim is barred.

**(b) Claims Barred by Limitation Not to Be Allowed or Approved.** No claims for money against a decedent, or against the estate of the decedent, on which a suit is barred under Subsection (a) of this section, Section 313, or Section 317(a) or by a general statute of limitation applicable thereto shall be allowed by a personal representative. If allowed by the representative and the court is satisfied that the claim is barred or that limitation has run, the claim shall be disapproved.

Acts 1955, 54th Leg., p. 88, ch. 55, eff. Jan. 1, 1956. Amended by Acts 1971, 62nd Leg., p. 2992, ch. 988, § 1, eff. June 15, 1971; Acts 1993, 73rd Leg., ch. 957, § 47, eff. Sept. 1, 1993; Acts 1995, 74th Leg., ch. 1054, § 5, eff. Jan. 1, 1996.

### § 299. Tolling of General Statutes of Limitation

The general statutes of limitation are tolled on the date:

(1) a claim for money is filed or deposited with the clerk; or

(2) suit is brought against the personal representative of an estate with respect to a claim of the estate that is not required to be presented to the personal representative.

Acts 1955, 54th Leg., p. 88, ch. 55, eff. Jan. 1, 1956. Amended by Acts 1997, 75th Leg., ch. 1302, § 12, eff. Sept. 1, 1997.

### § 300. Repealed by Acts 1995, 74th Leg., ch. 1054, § 29, eff. Jan. 1, 1996

### § 301. Claims for Money Must be Authenticated

No personal representative of a decedent's estate shall allow, and the court shall not approve, a claim for money against such estate, unless such claim be supported by an affidavit that the claim is just and that all legal offsets, payments, and credits known to the affiant have been allowed. If the claim is not founded on a written instrument or account, the affidavit shall also state the facts upon which the claim is founded. A photostatic copy of any exhibit or voucher necessary to prove a claim may be offered with and attached to the claim in lieu of the original.

Acts 1955, 54th Leg., p. 88, ch. 55, eff. Jan. 1, 1956. Amended by Acts 1993, 73rd Leg., ch. 957, § 48, eff. Sept. 1, 1993; Acts 1995, 74th Leg., ch. 1054, § 6, eff. Jan. 1, 1996.

### § 302. When Defects of Form Are Waived

Any defect of form, or claim of insufficiency of exhibits or vouchers presented, shall be deemed waived by the personal representative unless written objection thereto has been made within thirty days after presentment of the claim, and filed with the county clerk.

Acts 1955, 54th Leg., p. 88, ch. 55, eff. Jan. 1, 1956.

### § 303. Evidence Concerning Lost or Destroyed Claims

If evidence of a claim is lost or destroyed, the claimant or an authorized representative or agent of the claimant, may make affidavit to the fact of such loss or destruction, stating the amount, date, and nature of the claim and when due, and that the same is just, and that all legal offsets, payments and credits known to the affiant have been allowed, and that the claimant is still the owner of the claim; and the claim must be proved by disinterested testimony taken in open court, or by oral or written deposition, before the claim is approved. If such claim is allowed or approved without such affidavit, or if it is approved without satisfactory proof, such allowance or approval shall be void.

Acts 1955, 54th Leg., p. 88, ch. 55, eff. Jan. 1, 1956. Amended by Acts 1995, 74th Leg., ch. 1054, § 7, eff. Jan. 1, 1996.

### § 304. Authentication of Claim by Others Than Individual Owners

An authorized officer or representative of a corporation or other entity shall make the affidavit required to authenticate a claim of such corporation or entity. When an affidavit is made by an officer of a corporation, or by an executor, administrator, trustee, assignee, agent, representative, or attorney, it shall be sufficient to state in such affidavit that the person making it has made diligent inquiry and examination, and that he believes that the claim is just and that all legal offsets, payments, and credits made known to the affiant have been allowed.

Acts 1955, 54th Leg., p. 88, ch. 55, eff. Jan. 1, 1956. Amended by Acts 1993, 73rd Leg., ch. 957, § 49, eff. Sept. 1, 1993; Acts 1995, 74th Leg., ch. 1054, § 8, eff. Jan. 1, 1996.

### § 305. Repealed by Acts 1993, 73rd Leg., ch. 957, § 75(1), eff. Sept. 1, 1993

### § 306. Method of Handling Secured Claims for Money

**(a) Specifications of Claim.** When a secured claim for money against an estate is presented, the claimant shall specify therein, in addition to all other matters required to be specified in claims:

(1) Whether it is desired to have the claim allowed and approved as a matured secured claim to be paid in due course of administration, in which event it shall be so paid if allowed and approved; or

(2) Whether it is desired to have the claim allowed, approved, and fixed as a preferred debt and lien against the specific property securing the indebtedness and paid according to the terms of the contract which secured the lien, in which event it shall be so allowed and approved if it is a valid lien; provided, however, that the personal representative may pay said claim prior to maturity if it is for the best interest of the estate to do so.

**(b) Time for Specification of Secured Claim.** Within six months after the date letters are granted, or within four months after the date notice is received under Section 295 of this code, whichever is later, the secured creditor may present the creditor's claim and shall specify whether the claim is to be allowed and approved under Paragraph (1) or (2) of Subsection (a) of this section. If a secured claim is not presented within the time prescribed by this subsection or if the claim is presented without specifying how the claim is to be paid, it shall be treated as a claim to be paid in accordance with Paragraph (2) of Subsection (a) hereof.

**(c) Matured Secured Claims.** If a claim has been allowed and approved as a matured secured claim under Paragraph (1) of Subsection (a) of this section, the claim shall be paid in due course of administration and the secured creditor is not entitled to exercise any other remedies in a manner that prevents the preferential payment of claims and allowances described by Paragraphs (1) through (3) of Section 320(a) of this code.

**(c–1)** If a claimant presents a secured claim against an estate for a debt that would otherwise pass with the property securing the debt to one or more devisees in accordance with Section 71A(a) of this code and the claim is allowed and approved as a matured secured claim under Subsection (a)(1) of this section, the personal representative shall collect from the devisees the amount of the debt and pay that amount to the claimant in satisfaction of the claim. Each devisee's share of the debt is an amount equal to a fraction representing the devisee's ownership interest in the property, multiplied by the amount of the debt. If the personal representative is unable to collect from the devisees an amount sufficient to pay the debt, the personal representative shall sell the property securing the debt, subject to Part 5 of this chapter. The personal representative shall use the sale proceeds to pay the debt and any expenses associated with the sale and shall distribute the remaining sale proceeds to each devisee in an amount equal to a fraction representing the devisee's ownership interest in the property, multiplied by the amount of the remaining sale proceeds. If the sale proceeds are insufficient to pay the debt and any expenses associated with the sale, the difference between the sum of the amount of the debt and the expenses associated with the sale and the sale proceeds shall be paid under Subsection (c) of this section.

**(d) Approved Claim as Preferred Lien Against Property.** When an indebtedness has been allowed and approved under Paragraph (2) of Subsection (a) hereof, no further claim shall be made against other assets of the estate by reason thereof, but the same thereafter shall remain a preferred lien against the property securing same, and the property shall remain security for the debt in any distribution or sale thereof prior to final maturity and payment of the debt.

**(e) Payment of Maturities on Preferred Debt and Lien Claims.** If property securing a claim allowed, approved, and fixed under Paragraph (2) of Subsection (a) hereof is not sold or distributed within six months from the date letters are granted, the representative of the estate shall promptly pay all maturities which have accrued on the debt according to the terms thereof, and shall perform all the terms of any contract securing same. If the representative defaults in such payment or performance, on application of the claimholder, the court shall:

(1) require the sale of said property subject to the unmatured part of such debt and apply the proceeds of the sale to the liquidation of the maturities;

(2) require the sale of the property free of the lien and apply the proceeds to the payment of the whole debt; or

(3) authorize foreclosure by the claimholder as provided by Subsections (f) through (k) of this section.

**(f) Foreclosure of Preferred Liens.** An application by a claimholder under Subsection (e) of this section to foreclose the claimholder's lien or security interest on property securing a claim that has been allowed, approved, and fixed under Paragraph (2) of Subsection (a) of this section shall be supported by affidavit of the claimholder that:

(1) describes the property or part of the property to be sold by foreclosure;

(2) describes the amounts of the claimholder's outstanding debt;

(3) describes the maturities that have accrued on the debt according to the terms of the debt;

(4) describes any other debts secured by a mortgage, lien, or security interest against the property that are known by the claimholder;

(5) contains a statement that the claimholder has no knowledge of the existence of any debts secured by the property other than those described by the application; and

(6) requests permission for the claimholder to foreclose the claimholder's mortgage, lien, or security interest.

**(g) Citation.** On the filing of an application, the clerk shall issue citation by personal service to the personal representative and to any person described by the application as having other debts secured by a mortgage, lien, or security interest against the property and by posting to any other person interested in the estate. The citation must require the person to appear and show cause why foreclosure should or should not be permitted.

**(h) Setting of Hearing on Application.** When an application is filed, the clerk shall immediately notify the judge. The judge shall schedule in writing a date for a hearing on the application. The judge may, by entry on the docket or otherwise, continue the hearing for a reasonable time to allow an interested person to obtain an appraisal or other evidence concerning the fair market value of the property that is the subject of the application. If the interested person requests an unreasonable time for a continuance, the person must show good cause for the continuance.

**(i) Hearing.** (1) At the hearing, if the court finds that there is a default in payment or performance under the contract that secures the payment of the claim, the court shall:

(A) require the sale of the property subject to the unmatured part of the debt and apply the proceeds of the sale to the liquidation of the maturities;

(B) require the sale of the property free of the lien and apply the proceeds to the payment of the whole debt; or

(C) authorize foreclosure by the claimholder as provided by Subsection (f) of this section.

(2) When the court grants a claimholder the right of foreclosure, the court shall authorize the claimholder to foreclose the claimholder's mortgage, lien, or security interest in accordance with the provisions of the document creating the mortgage, lien, or security interest or in any other manner allowed by law. In the discretion of the court and based on the evidence presented at the hearing, the court may fix a minimum price for the property to be sold by foreclosure that does not exceed the fair market value of the property. If the court fixes a minimum price, the property may not be sold at the foreclosure sale for a lower price.

**(j) Appeal.** Any person interested in the estate may appeal an order issued under Subsection (i)(1)(C) of this section.

**(k) Unsuccessful Foreclosure.** If a foreclosure sale authorized under this section is conducted and the property is not sold because no bid at the sale met the minimum price set by the court, the claimholder may file another application under Subsection (f) of this section. The court may, in the court's discretion, eliminate or modify the minimum price requirement and grant permission for another foreclosure sale.

Acts 1955, 54th Leg., p. 88, ch. 55, eff. Jan. 1, 1956. Amended by Acts 1993, 73rd Leg., ch. 957, § 50, eff. Sept. 1, 1993; Acts 1995, 74th Leg., ch. 1054, § 9, eff. Jan. 1, 1996; Acts 1997, 75th Leg., ch. 1302, § 13, eff. Sept. 1, 1997. Subsec. (c-1) added by Acts 2005, 79th Leg., ch. 551, § 6, eff. Sept. 1, 2005.

### § 307. Claims Providing for Attorney's Fees

If the instrument evidencing or supporting a claim provides for attorney's fees, then the claimant may include as a part of the claim the portion of such fee that he has paid or contracted to pay to an attorney to prepare, present, and collect such claim.

Acts 1955, 54th Leg., p. 88, ch. 55, eff. Jan. 1, 1956.

### § 308. Depositing Claims With Clerk

Claims may also be presented by depositing same, with vouchers and necessary exhibits and affidavit attached, with the clerk, who, upon receiving same, shall advise the representative of the estate, or the representative's attorney, by letter mailed to the representative's last known address, of the deposit of same. Should the representative fail to act on said claim within thirty days after it is deposited, then it shall be presumed to be rejected. Failure of the clerk to give notice as required herein shall not affect the validity of the presentment or the presumption of rejection because not

acted upon within said thirty day period. The clerk shall enter a deposited claim on the claim docket.

Acts 1955, 54th Leg., p. 88, ch. 55, eff. Jan. 1, 1956. Amended by Acts 1995, 74th Leg., ch. 1054, § 10, eff. Jan. 1, 1996.

### § 309. Memorandum of Allowance or Rejection of Claim

When a duly authenticated claim against an estate is presented to the representative, or deposited with the clerk as heretofore provided, the representative shall, within thirty days after the claim is presented or deposited, endorse thereon, annex thereto, or file with the clerk a memorandum signed by the representative, stating the date of presentation or depositing of the claim, and that the representative allows or rejects it, or what portion thereof the representative allows or rejects.

Acts 1955, 54th Leg., p. 88, ch. 55, eff. Jan. 1, 1956. Amended by Acts 1995, 74th Leg., ch. 1054, § 11, eff. Jan. 1, 1996.

### § 310. Failure to Endorse or Annex Memorandum

The failure of a representative of an estate to timely allow or reject a claim under Section 309 of this code shall constitute a rejection of the claim. If the claim is thereafter established by suit, the costs shall be taxed against the representative, individually, or the representative may be removed on the written complaint of any person interested in the claim, after personal service of citation, hearing, and proof, as in other cases of removal.

Acts 1955, 54th Leg., p. 88, ch. 55, eff. Jan. 1, 1956. Amended by Acts 1995, 74th Leg., ch. 1054, § 12, eff. Jan. 1, 1996.

### § 311. When Claims Entered in Docket

After a claim against an estate has been presented to and allowed or rejected by the personal representative, in whole or in part, the claim must be filed with the county clerk of the proper county. The clerk shall enter the claim on the claim docket.

Acts 1955, 54th Leg., p. 88, ch. 55, eff. Jan. 1, 1956. Amended by Acts 1971, 62nd Leg., p. 2992, ch. 988, § 2, eff. June 15, 1971; Acts 1993, 73rd Leg., ch. 957, § 51, eff. Sept. 1, 1993; Acts 1995, 74th Leg., ch. 1054, § 13, eff. Jan. 1, 1996.

### § 312. Contest of Claims, Action by Court, and Appeals

**(a) Contest of Claims.** Any person interested in an estate may, at any time before the court has acted upon a claim, appear and object in writing to the approval of the same, or any part thereof, and in such case the parties shall be entitled to process for witnesses, and the court shall hear proof and render judgment as in ordinary suits.

**(b) Court's Action Upon Claims.** All claims which have been allowed and entered upon the claim docket for a period of ten days shall be acted upon by the court and be either approved in whole or in part or rejected, and they shall also at the same time be classified by the court.

**(c) Hearing on Claims.** Although a claim may be properly authenticated and allowed, if the court is not satisfied that it is just, the court shall examine the claimant and the personal representative under oath, and hear other evidence necessary to determine the issue. If not then convinced that the claim is just, the court shall disapprove it.

**(d) Order of the Court.** When the court has acted upon a claim, the court shall also endorse thereon, or annex thereto, a written memorandum dated and signed officially, stating the exact action taken upon such claim, whether approved or disapproved, or approved in part or rejected in part, and stating the classification of the claim. Such orders shall have the force and effect of final judgments.

**(e) Appeal.** When a claimant or any person interested in an estate shall be dissatisfied with the action of the court upon a claim, the claimant or person may appeal therefrom to the courts of appeals, as from other judgments of the county court in probate matters.

Acts 1955, 54th Leg., p. 88, ch. 55, eff. Jan. 1, 1956. Amended by Acts 1975, 64th Leg., p. 2196, ch. 701, § 4, eff. June 21, 1975; Acts 1993, 73rd Leg., ch. 957, § 52, eff. Sept. 1, 1993; Acts 1995, 74th Leg., ch. 1054, § 14, eff. Jan. 1, 1996.

### § 313. Suit on Rejected Claim

When a claim or a part thereof has been rejected by the representative, the claimant shall institute suit thereon in the court of original probate jurisdiction in which the estate is pending within ninety days after such rejection, or the claim shall be barred. When a rejected claim is sued on, the endorsement made on or annexed thereto, or any memorandum of rejection filed with respect to the claim, shall be taken to be true without further proof, unless denied under oath. When a rejected claim or part thereof has been established by suit, no execution shall issue, but the judgment shall be filed in the court in which the cause is pending, entered upon the claim docket, classified by the court, and handled as if originally allowed and approved in due course of administration.

Acts 1955, 54th Leg., p. 88, ch. 55, eff. Jan. 1, 1956. Amended by Acts 1975, 64th Leg., p. 2196, ch. 701, § 5, eff. June 21, 1975; Acts 1995, 74th Leg., ch. 1054, § 15, eff. Jan. 1, 1996; Acts 2001, 77th Leg., ch. 10, § 3, eff. Sept. 1, 2001.

### § 314. Presentment of Claims a Prerequisite for Judgment

No judgment shall be rendered in favor of a claimant upon any claim for money which has not been legally presented to the representative of an estate, and rejected by the representative or by the court, in whole or in part.

Acts 1955, 54th Leg., p. 88, ch. 55, eff. Jan. 1, 1956. Amended by Acts 1993, 73rd Leg., ch. 957, § 53, eff. Sept. 1, 1993; Acts 1995, 74th Leg., ch. 1054, § 16, eff. Jan. 1, 1996.

### § 315. Costs of Suit With Respect to Claims

All costs incurred in the probate court with respect to claims shall be taxed as follows:

(a) If allowed and approved, the estate shall pay the costs.

(b) If allowed, but disapproved, the claimant shall pay the costs.

(c) If rejected, but established by suit, the estate shall pay the costs.

(d) If rejected, but not established by suit, the claimant shall pay the costs, except as provided by Section 310 of this code.

(e) In suits to establish a claim after rejection in part, if the claimant fails to recover judgment for a greater amount than was allowed or approved, the claimant shall pay all costs.

Acts 1955, 54th Leg., p. 88, ch. 55, eff. Jan. 1, 1956. Amended by Acts 1995, 74th Leg., ch. 1054, § 17, eff. Jan. 1, 1996.

### § 316. Claims Against Personal Representatives

The naming of an executor in a will shall not operate to extinguish any just claim which the deceased had against the person named as executor; and, in all cases where a personal representative is indebted to the testator or intestate, the representative shall account for the debt in the same manner as if it were cash in the representative's hands; provided, however, that if said debt was not due at the time of receiving letters, the representative shall be required to account for it only from the date when it becomes due.

Acts 1955, 54th Leg., p. 88, ch. 55, eff. Jan. 1, 1956. Amended by Acts 1995, 74th Leg., ch. 1054, § 18, eff. Jan. 1, 1996.

### § 317. Claims by Personal Representatives

**(a) By Executors or Administrators.** The foregoing provisions of this Code relative to the presentation of claims against an estate shall not be construed to apply to any claim of a personal representative against the testator or intestate; but a personal representative holding such claim shall file the same in the court granting the letters, verified by affidavit as required in other cases, within six months after the representative has qualified, or such claim shall be barred.

**(b) Action on Such Claims.** When a claim by a personal representative has been filed with the court within the required time, such claim shall be entered upon the claim docket and acted upon by the court in the same manner as in other cases, and, when the claim has been acted upon by the court, an appeal from the judgment of the court may be taken as in other cases.

**(c) Provisions Not Applicable to Certain Claims.** The foregoing provisions relative to the presentment of claims shall not be so construed as to apply to a claim:

(1) of any heir, devisee, or legatee who claims in such capacity;

(2) that accrues against the estate after the granting of letters for which the representative of the estate has contracted; or

(3) for delinquent ad valorem taxes against a decedent's estate that is being administered in probate in:

(A) a county other than the county in which the taxes were imposed; or

(B) the same county in which the taxes were imposed, if the probate proceedings have been pending for more than four years.

Acts 1955, 54th Leg., p. 88, ch. 55, eff. Jan. 1, 1956. Amended by Acts 1993, 73rd Leg., ch. 957, § 54, eff. Sept. 1, 1993; Acts 1995, 74th Leg., ch. 1054, § 19, eff. Jan. 1, 1996; Acts 1999, 76th Leg., ch. 1481, § 37, eff. Sept. 1, 1999.

### § 318. Claims Not Allowed After Order for Partition and Distribution

No claim for money against the estate of a decedent shall be allowed by a personal representative and no suit shall be instituted against the representative on any such claim, after an order for final partition and distribution has been made; but, after such an order has been made, the owner of any claim not barred by the laws of limitation shall have an action thereon against the heirs, devisees, legatees, or creditors of the estate, limited to the value of the property received by them in distributions from the estate.

Acts 1955, 54th Leg., p. 88, ch. 55, eff. Jan. 1, 1956. Amended by Acts 1995, 74th Leg., ch. 1054, § 20, eff. Jan. 1, 1996.

### § 319. Claims Not to Be Paid Unless Approved

No claim for money against the estate of a decedent, or any part thereof, shall be paid until it has been approved by the court or established by the judgment of a court of competent jurisdiction.

Acts 1955, 54th Leg., p. 88, ch. 55, eff. Jan. 1, 1956. Amended by Acts 1993, 73rd Leg., ch. 957, § 55, eff. Sept. 1, 1993.

### § 320. Order of Payment of Claims and Allowances

(a) **Priority of Payments.** Personal representatives, when they have funds in their hands belonging to the estate, shall pay in the following order:

(1) Funeral expenses and expenses of last sickness, in an amount not to exceed Fifteen Thousand Dollars.

(2) Allowances made to the surviving spouse and children, or to either.

(3) Expenses of administration and the expenses incurred in the preservation, safekeeping, and management of the estate.

(4) Other claims against the estate in the order of their classification.

(b) **Sale of Mortgaged Property.** If a personal representative has the proceeds of a sale that has been made for the satisfaction of a mortgage, lien, or security interest, and the proceeds, or any part of the proceeds, are not required for the payment of any debts against the estate that have a preference over the mortgage, lien, or security interest, the personal representative shall pay the proceeds to any holder of a mortgage, lien, or security interest. If there is more than one mortgage, lien, or security interest against the property, the personal representative shall pay the holders in the order of the holders' priority. If the personal representative fails to pay proceeds under this subsection, a holder,

on proof of the failure to pay, may obtain an order from the court directing the payment to be made.

(c) **Claimant's Petition.** A claimant whose claim has not been paid may petition the court for determination of his claim at any time before it is barred by the applicable statute of limitations and upon due proof procure an order for its allowance and payment from the estate.

(d) **Permissive Order of Payment.** After the sixth month after the date letters are granted and on application by the personal representative stating that the personal representative has no actual knowledge of any outstanding enforceable claims against the estate other than the claims already approved and classified by the court, the court may order the personal representative to pay any claim that is allowed and approved.

Acts 1955, 54th Leg., p. 88, ch. 55, eff. Jan. 1, 1956. Amended by Acts 1975, 64th Leg., p. 1818, ch. 554, § 1, eff. Sept. 1, 1975; Acts 1977, 65th Leg., p. 352, ch. 173, § 1, eff. Aug. 29, 1977; Acts 1979, 66th Leg., p. 1876, ch. 758, § 1, eff. Aug. 27, 1979. Amended by Acts 1987, 70th Leg., ch. 461, § 2, eff. Sept. 1, 1987; Acts 1993, 73rd Leg., ch. 957, § 56, eff. Sept. 1, 1993; Acts 1995, 74th Leg., ch. 1054, § 21, eff. Jan. 1, 1996; Acts 1997, 75th Leg., ch. 540, § 4, eff. Sept. 1, 1997; Acts 1997, 75th Leg., ch. 1361, § 1, eff. Sept. 1, 1997.

### § 320A. Funeral Expenses

When personal representatives pay claims for funeral expenses and for items incident thereto, such as tombstones, grave markers, crypts or burial plots, they shall charge the whole of such claims to the decedent's estate and shall charge no part thereof to the community share of a surviving spouse.

Added by Acts 1967, 60th Leg., p. 768, ch. 321, § 1, eff. May 27, 1967. Amended by Acts 1995, 74th Leg., ch. 1054, § 22, eff. Jan. 1, 1996.

### § 321. Deficiency of Assets

When there is a deficiency of assets to pay all claims of the same class, other than secured claims for money, the claims in such class shall be paid pro rata, as directed by the court, and in the order directed. No personal representative shall be allowed to pay the claims, whether the estate is solvent or insolvent, except with the pro rata amount of the funds of the estate that have come to hand.

Acts 1955, 54th Leg., p. 88, ch. 55, eff. Jan. 1, 1956. Amended by Acts 1993, 73rd Leg., ch. 957, § 57, eff. Sept. 1, 1993; Acts 1995, 74th Leg., ch. 1054, § 23, eff. Jan. 1, 1996.

### § 322. Classification of Claims Against Estate of Decedent

Claims against an estate of a decedent shall be classified and have priority of payment, as follows:

Class 1. Funeral expenses and expenses of last sickness for a reasonable amount to be approved by the court, not to exceed a total of Fifteen Thousand Dollars, with any excess to be classified and paid as other unsecured claims.

Class 2. Expenses of administration and expenses incurred in the preservation, safekeeping, and management of the estate, including fees and expenses awarded under Section 243 of this code, and unpaid expenses of administration awarded in a guardianship of the decedent.

Class 3. Secured claims for money under Section 306(a)(1), including tax liens, so far as the same can be paid out of the proceeds of the property subject to such mortgage or other lien, and when more than one mortgage, lien, or security interest shall exist upon the same property, they shall be paid in order of their priority.

Class 4. Claims for the principal amount of and accrued interest on delinquent child support and child support arrearages that have been confirmed and reduced to money judgment, as determined under Subchapter F, Chapter 157, Family Code,[1] and claims for unpaid child support obligations under Section 154.015, Family Code.

Class 5. Claims for taxes, penalties, and interest due under Title 2, Tax Code;[2] Chapter 8, Title 132, Revised Statutes;[3] Section 81.111, Natural Resources Code; the Municipal Sales and Use Tax Act (Chapter 321, Tax Code); Section 451.404, Transportation Code; or Subchapter I, Chapter 452, Transportation Code.[4]

Class 6. Claims for the cost of confinement established by the Texas Department of Criminal Justice under Section 501.017, Government Code.

Class 7. Claims for repayment of medical assistance payments made by the state under Chapter 32, Human Resources Code, to or for the benefit of the decedent.

Class 8. All other claims.

Acts 1955, 54th Leg., p. 88, ch. 55, eff. Jan. 1, 1956. Amended by Acts 1971, 62nd Leg., p. 2992, ch. 988, § 3, eff. June 15, 1971; Acts 1979, 66th Leg., p. 869, ch. 394, § 1, eff. Aug. 27, 1979; Acts 1981, 67th Leg., p. 242, ch. 102, § 8, eff. Aug. 31, 1981; Acts 1981, 67th Leg., p. 1785, ch. 389, §§ 38A, 39(*l* ), eff. Jan. 1, 1982; Acts 1987, 70th Leg., ch. 1049, § 51, eff. Sept. 1, 1987; Acts 1987, 70th Leg., ch. 1052, § 2.07, eff. Sept. 1, 1987; Acts 1989, 71st Leg., ch. 2, § 14.27(a)(6), eff. Aug. 28, 1989; Acts 1989, 71st Leg., ch. 1035, § 13, eff. Sept. 1, 1989; Acts 1995, 74th Leg., ch. 1054, § 24, eff. Jan. 1, 1996; Acts 1997, 75th Leg., ch. 165, § 30.243, eff. Sept. 1, 1997; Acts 1997, 75th Leg., ch. 1361, § 2, eff. Sept. 1, 1997; Acts 1999, 76th Leg., ch. 69, § 1, eff. Sept. 1, 1999. Amended by Acts 2003, 78th Leg., ch. 1060, § 14, eff. Sept. 1, 2003; Acts 2005, 79th Leg., ch. 551, § 7, eff. Sept. 1, 2005; Acts 2007, 80th Leg., ch. 1404, § 3, eff. Sept. 1, 2007; Acts 2009, 81st Leg., ch. 87, § 25.151, eff. Sept. 1, 2009; Sec. head amended by Acts 2011, 82nd Leg., ch. 1338 (S.B. 1198), § 1.34, eff. Sept. 1, 2011.

[1] V.T.C.A., Family Code § 157.261 et seq.

[2] V.T.C.A., Tax Code § 101.001 et seq.

[3] Vernon's Ann.Civ.St. art. 8801 et seq.

[4] V.T.C.A., Transportation Code § 452.401 et seq.

### § 322A. Apportionment of Taxes

(a) In this section:

(1) "Estate" means the gross estate of a decedent as determined for the purpose of estate taxes.

(2) "Estate tax" means any estate, inheritance, or death tax levied or assessed on the property of a decedent's estate, because of the death of a person, imposed by federal, state, local, or foreign law, including the federal estate tax and the additional inheritance tax imposed by Chapter 211, Tax Code, and including interest and penalties imposed in addition to those taxes. Estate tax does not include a tax imposed under Section 2701(d)(1)(A), Internal Revenue Code of 1986 (26 U.S.C. Section 2701(d)).

(3) "Person" includes a trust, natural person, partnership, association, joint stock company, corporation, government, political subdivision, or governmental agency.

(4) "Person interested in the estate" means a person, or a fiduciary on behalf of that person, who is entitled to receive, or who has received, from a decedent or because of the death of the decedent, property included in the decedent's estate for purposes of the estate tax, but does not include a creditor of the decedent or of the decedent's estate.

(5) "Representative" means the representative, executor, or administrator of an estate, or any other person who is required to pay estate taxes assessed against the estate.

(b)(1) The representative shall charge each person interested in the estate a portion of the total estate tax assessed against the estate. The portion of each estate tax that is charged to each person interested in the estate must represent the same ratio as the taxable value of that person's interest in the estate included in determining the amount of the tax bears to the total taxable value of all the interests of all persons interested in the estate included in determining the amount of the tax. In apportioning an estate tax under this subdivision, the representative shall disregard a portion of the tax that is apportioned under the law imposing the tax, otherwise apportioned by federal law, or apportioned as otherwise provided by this section.

(2) Subdivision (1) of this subsection does not apply to the extent the decedent in a written inter vivos or testamentary instrument disposing of or creating an interest in property specifically directs the manner of apportionment of estate tax or grants a discretionary power of apportionment to another person. A direction for the apportionment or nonapportionment of estate tax is limited to the estate tax on the property passing under the instrument unless the instrument is a will that provides otherwise.

(3) If under Subdivision (2) of this subsection directions for the apportionment of an estate tax in two or more instruments executed by the same person conflict, the instrument disposing of or creating an interest in the property to be taxed controls. If directions for the apportionment of estate tax in two or more instruments executed by different persons conflict, the direction of the person in whose estate the property is included controls.

(4) Subdivisions (2) and (3) of this subsection do not grant or enlarge the power of a person to apportion estate tax to property passing under an instrument created by another person in excess of the estate tax attributable to the property. Subdivisions (2) and (3) of this subsection do not apply to the extent federal law directs a different manner of apportionment.

(c) Any deduction, exemption, or credit allowed by law in connection with the estate tax inures to a person interested in the estate as provided by Subsections (d)–(f) of this section.

(d) If the deduction, exemption, or credit is allowed because of the relationship of the person interested in the estate to the decedent, or because of the purpose of the gift, the deduction, exemption, or credit inures to the person having the relationship or receiving the gift, unless that person's interest in the estate is subject to a prior present interest that is not allowable as a deduction. The estate tax apportionable to the person having the present interest shall be paid from the corpus of the gift or the interest of the person having the relationship.

(e) A deduction for property of the estate that was previously taxed and a credit for gift taxes or death taxes of a foreign country that were paid by the decedent or his estate inures proportionally to all persons interested in the estate who are liable for a share of the estate tax.

(f) A credit for inheritance, succession, or estate taxes, or taxes of a similar nature applicable to property or interests includable in the estate, inures to the persons interested in the estate who are chargeable with payment of a portion of those taxes to the extent that the credit reduces proportionately those taxes.

(g) To the extent that property passing to or in trust for a surviving spouse or a charitable, public, or similar gift or devise is not an allowable deduction for purposes of the estate tax solely because of an inheritance tax or other death tax imposed on and deductible from the property, the property is not included in the computation provided for by Subsection (b) of this section, and to that extent no apportionment is made against the property. The exclusion provided by this subsection does not apply if the result would be to deprive the estate of a deduction otherwise allowable under Section 2053(d), Internal Revenue Code of 1986,[1] relating to deductions for state death taxes on transfers for public, charitable, or religious uses.

(h) Except as provided by Subsection (i)(3) of this section, an interest in income, an estate for years or for life, or another temporary interest in any property or fund is not subject to apportionment. The estate tax apportionable to the temporary interest and the remainder, if any, is chargeable against the corpus of the property or the funds that are subject to the temporary interest and remainder.

(i)(1) In this subsection, "qualified real property" has the meaning assigned by Section 2032A, Internal Revenue Code of 1986 (26 U.S.C. Section 2032A).

(2) If an election is made under Section 2032A, Internal Revenue Code of 1986 (26 U.S.C. Section 2032A), the representative shall apportion estate taxes according to the amount of federal estate tax that would be payable if the election were not made. The amount of the reduction of the estate tax resulting from the election shall be applied to reduce the amount of the estate tax allocated based on the value of the qualified real property that is the subject of the election. If the amount applied to reduce the taxes allocated based on the value of the qualified real property is greater than the amount of those taxes, the excess shall be applied to the portion of the taxes allocated for all other property. This amount is to be apportioned under Subsection (b)(1) of this section.

(3) If additional federal estate tax is imposed under Section 2032A(c), Internal Revenue Code of 1986 (26 U.S.C. Section 2032A) because of an early disposition or cessation of a qualified use, the additional tax shall be equitably apportioned among the persons who have an interest in the portion of the qualified real property to which the additional tax is attributable in proportion to their interests. The additional tax is a charge against such qualified real property. If the qualified real property is split between one or more life or term interests and remainder interests, the additional tax shall be apportioned to each person whose action or cessation of use caused the imposition of additional tax, unless all persons with an interest in the qualified real property agree in writing to dispose of the property, in which case the additional tax shall be apportioned among the remainder interests.

(j) Repealed by Acts 2003, 78th Leg., ch. 1060, § 16.

(k) If the date for the payment of any portion of an estate tax is extended, the amount of the extended tax shall be apportioned to the persons who receive the specific property that gives rise to the extension. Those persons are entitled to the benefits and shall bear the burdens of the extension.

(l) If federal law directs the apportionment of the federal estate tax, a similar state tax shall be apportioned in the same manner.

(m) Interest on an extension of estate tax and interest and penalties on a deficiency shall be apportioned equitably to reflect the benefits and burdens of the extension or deficiency and of any tax deduction associated with the interest and penalties, but if the assessment or penalty and interest is due to delay caused by the negligence of the representative, the representative shall be charged with the amount of assessed penalty and interest.

(n) If property includable in an estate does not come into possession of the representative obligated to pay the estate tax, the representative shall recover from each person interested in the estate the amount of the estate tax apportioned to the person under this section or assign to persons affected by the tax obligation the representative's right of recovery. The obligation to recover a tax under this subsection does not apply if:

(1) the duty is waived by the parties affected by the tax obligation or by the instrument under which the representative derives powers; or

(2) in the reasonable judgment of the representative, proceeding to recover the tax is not cost-effective.

(o) If a representative cannot collect from a person interested in the estate an unpaid amount of estate tax apportioned to the person, the amount not collected shall be apportioned among the other persons interested in the estate who are subject to apportionment in the same manner as provided by Subsection (b)(1) of this section. A person who is charged with or who pays an apportioned amount under this subsection because another person failed to pay an amount of estate tax apportioned to the person has a right of reimbursement for that amount from the person who failed to pay the tax. The representative may enforce the right of reimbursement, or the person who is charged with or who pays an apportioned amount under this subsection may enforce the right of reimbursement directly by an assignment from the representative. A person assigned the right under this subsection is subrogated to the rights of the representative. A representative who has a right of reimbursement may petition a court to determine the right of reimbursement.

(p) This section shall be applied after giving effect to any disclaimers made in accordance with Section 37A of this code.

(q) Interest and penalties assessed against the estate by a taxing authority shall be apportioned among and charged to the persons interested in the estate in the manner provided by Subsection (b) of this section, unless, on application by any person interested in the estate, the court determines that the proposed apportionment is not equitable or that the assessment of interest or penalties was caused by a breach of fiduciary duty of a representative. If the apportionment is not equitable, the court may apportion interest and penalties in an equitable manner. If the assessment of interest or penalties was caused by a breach of fiduciary duty of a representative, the court may charge the representative with the amount of the interest and penalties assessed attributable to his conduct.

(r) Expenses reasonably incurred by a representative in determination of the amount, apportionment, or collection of the estate tax shall be apportioned among and charged to persons interested in the estate in the manner provided by Subsection (b) of this section unless, on application by any person interested in the estate, the court determines that the proposed apportionment is not equitable. If the court determines that the assessment is not equitable, the court may apportion the expenses in an equitable manner.

(s) For the purposes of this section, "court" means a court in which proceedings for administration of the estate are pending or have been completed or, if no proceedings are pending or have been completed, a court in which venue lies for the administration of the estate of the decedent.

(t) A representative who has possession of any property of an estate that is distributable to a person interested in the estate may withhold from that property an amount equal to the person's apportioned share of the estate tax.

(u) A representative shall recover from any person interested in the estate the unpaid amount of the estate tax apportioned and charged to the person under this section, unless the representative determines in good faith that an attempt to recover this amount would be economically impractical.

(v) A representative required to recover unpaid amounts of estate tax apportioned to persons interested in the estate under this section may not be required to initiate the necessary actions until the expiration of 90 days after the date of the final determination of the amount of the estate tax by the Internal Revenue Service. A representative who initiates an action under this section within a reasonable time after the 90-day period is not subject to any liability or surcharge because any portion of the estate tax apportioned to any person interested in the estate was collectible at a time following the death of the decedent but thereafter became uncollectible.

(w) A representative acting in another state may initiate an action in a court of this state to recover a proportionate amount of the federal estate tax, of an estate tax payable to another state, or of a death duty due by a decedent's estate to another state, from a person interested in the estate who is domiciled in this state or owns property in this state subject to attachment or execution. In the action, a determination of apportionment by the court having jurisdiction of the administration of the decedent's estate in the other state is prima facie correct. This section applies only if the state in which the determination of apportionment was made affords a substantially similar remedy.

(x) A reference in this section to a section of the Internal Revenue Code of 1986 refers to the section as it exists at the time in question. The reference also includes a corresponding section of a subsequent Internal Revenue Code and the referenced section as renumbered if it is renumbered.

(y) The prevailing party in an action initiated by a person for the collection of estate taxes from a person interested in the estate to whom estate taxes were apportioned and charged under Subsection (b) of this section shall be awarded necessary expenses, including reasonable attorney's fees.

Added by Acts 1987, 70th Leg., ch. 742, § 1, eff. Sept. 1, 1987. Amended by Acts 1991, 72nd Leg., ch. 410, § 1, eff. Sept. 1, 1991; Subsec. (j) repealed by Acts 2003, 78th Leg., ch. 1060, § 16, eff. Sept. 1, 2003.

[1] 26 U.S.C.A. § 2053(d).

## § 322B.  Abatement of Bequests

(a) Except as provided by Subsections (b)–(d) of this section, a decedent's property is liable for debts and expenses of administration other than estate taxes, and bequests abate in the following order:

(1) property not disposed of by will, but passing by intestacy;

(2) personal property of the residuary estate;

(3) real property of the residuary estate;

(4) general bequests of personal property;

(5) general devises of real property;

(6) specific bequests of personal property; and

(7) specific devises of real property.

(b) This section does not affect the requirements for payment of a claim of a secured creditor who elects to have the claim continued as a preferred debt and lien against specific property under Section 306 of this code.

(c) This section does not apply to the payment of estate taxes under Section 322A of this code.

(d) A decedent's intent, as expressed in a will, controls over the abatement of bequests provided by this section.

Added by Acts 1987, 70th Leg., ch. 742, § 2, eff. Sept. 1, 1987.

## § 323.  Joint Obligation

When two or more persons are jointly bound for the payment of a debt, or for any other purpose, upon the death of any of the persons so bound, the decedent's estate shall be charged by virtue of such obligation in the same manner as if the obligors had been bound severally as well as jointly.

Acts 1955, 54th Leg., p. 88, ch. 55, eff. Jan. 1, 1956.  Amended by Acts 1995, 74th Leg., ch. 1054, § 25, eff. Jan. 1, 1996.

## § 324.  Representatives Not to Purchase Claims

It shall be unlawful, and cause for removal, for a personal representative whether acting under appointment by will or under orders of the court, to purchase for the personal representative's own use or for any purposes whatsoever, any claim against the estate the personal representative represents.  Upon written complaint by any person interested in the estate, and satisfactory proof of violation of this provision, after citation and hearing, the court shall enter its order cancelling the claim, and no part thereof shall be paid out of the estate; and the court may, in the court's discretion, remove such representative.

Acts 1955, 54th Leg., p. 88, ch. 55, eff. Jan. 1, 1956.  Amended by Acts 1993, 73rd Leg., ch. 957, § 58, eff. Sept. 1, 1993; Acts 1995, 74th Leg., ch. 1054, § 26, eff. Jan. 1, 1996.

## § 325.  Repealed by Acts 1995, 74th Leg., ch. 1054, § 29, eff. Jan. 1, 1996

## § 326.  Owner May Obtain Order for Payment

Any creditor of an estate of a decedent whose claim, or part thereof, has been approved by the court or established by suit, may, at any time after twelve months from the granting of letters testamentary, upon written application and proof showing that the estate has on hand sufficient available funds, obtain an order directing that payment be made; or, if there are no available funds, and if to await the receipt of funds from other sources would unreasonably delay payment, the court shall then order sale of property of the estate sufficient to pay the claim; provided, the representative of the estate shall have first been cited on such written complaint to appear and show cause why such order should not be made.

Acts 1955, 54th Leg., p. 88, ch. 55, eff. Jan. 1, 1956.

## § 327.  Repealed by Acts 1995, 74th Leg., ch. 1054, § 29, eff. Jan. 1, 1996

## § 328.  Liability for Nonpayment of Claims

(a) Procedure to Force Payment.  If any representative of an estate shall fail to pay on demand any money ordered by the court to be paid to any person, except to the State Treasury, when there are funds of the estate available, the person or claimant entitled to such payment, upon affidavit of the demand and failure to pay, shall be authorized to have execution issued against the property of the estate for the amount due, with interest and costs; or

(b) Penalty Against Representative.  Upon return of the execution not satisfied, or merely upon the affidavit of demand and failure to pay, the court may cite the representative and the sureties on the representative's bond to show cause why they should not be held liable for such debt, interest, costs, and damages.  Upon return of citation duly served, if good cause to the contrary be not shown, the court shall render judgment against the representative and sureties so cited, in favor of the holder of such claim, for the amount theretofore ordered to be paid or established by suit, and remaining unpaid, together with interest and costs, and also for damages upon the amount neglected to be paid, at the rate of five per cent per month for each month, or fraction thereof, that the payment was neglected to be paid after demand made therefor, which damages may be collected in any court of competent jurisdiction.

Acts 1955, 54th Leg., p. 88, ch. 55, eff. Jan. 1, 1956.  Amended by Acts 1995, 74th Leg., ch. 1054, § 27, eff. Jan. 1, 1996.

## § 329.  Borrowing Money

(a) Circumstances Under Which Money May Be Borrowed.  Any real or personal property of an estate may be mortgaged or pledged by deed of trust or otherwise as security for an indebtedness, under order of the court, when necessary for any of the following purposes:

(1) For the payment of any ad valorem, income, gift, estate, inheritance, or transfer taxes upon the transfer of an estate or due from a decedent or the estate, regardless of whether such taxes are assessed by a state, or any of its political subdivisions, or by the federal government or by a foreign country; or

(2) For payment of expenses of administration, including sums necessary for operation of a business, farm, or ranch owned by the estate; or

(3) For payment of claims allowed and approved, or established by suit, against the estate; or

(4) To renew and extend a valid, existing lien.

(b) Procedure for Borrowing Money.  When it is necessary to borrow money for any of the aforementioned purposes, or to create or extend a lien upon property of the estate as security, a sworn application for such authority shall be filed with the court, stating fully and in detail the circumstances which the representative of the estate believes make necessary the granting of such authority. Thereupon, the clerk shall issue and cause to be posted a citation to all interested persons, stating the nature of the application and requiring such persons, if they choose so to do, to appear and show cause, if any, why such application should not be granted.

**(c) Order Authorizing Such Borrowing, or Extension of Lien.** The court, if satisfied by the evidence adduced at the hearing upon said application that it is to the interest of the estate to borrow money, or to extend and renew an existing lien, shall issue its order to that effect, setting out the terms and conditions of the authority granted; provided, however, the loan or renewal shall not be for a term longer than three years from the granting of original letters to the representative of such estate, but the court may authorize an extension of such lien for not more than one additional year without further citation or notice. If a new lien is created on property of an estate, the court may require that the representative's general bond be increased, or an additional bond given, for the protection of the estate and the creditors, as for the sale of real property belonging to the estate.

Acts 1955, 54th Leg., p. 88, ch. 55, eff. Jan. 1, 1956. Amended by Acts 1973, 63rd Leg., p. 408, ch. 182, § 3, eff. May 25, 1973; Acts 1987, 70th Leg., ch. 766, § 1, eff. Aug. 31, 1987; Acts 1993, 73rd Leg., ch. 957, § 59, eff. Sept. 1, 1993; Acts 1995, 74th Leg., ch. 1054, § 28, eff. Jan. 1, 1996.

**§ 330. Repealed by Acts 1993, 73rd Leg., ch. 957, § 75(1), eff. Sept. 1, 1993**

### PART 5. SALES

### § 331. Court Must Order Sales

Except as hereinafter provided, no sale of any property of an estate shall be made without an order of court authorizing the same. The court may order property sold for cash or on credit, at public auction or privately, as it may consider most to the advantage of the estate, except when otherwise specially provided herein.

Acts 1955, 54th Leg., p. 88, ch. 55, eff. Jan. 1, 1956.

### § 332. Sales Authorized by Will

Whenever by the terms of a will an executor is authorized to sell any property of the testator, no order of court shall be necessary to authorize the executor to make such sale, and the sale may be made at public auction or privately as the executor deems to be in the best interest of the estate and may be made for cash or upon such credit terms as the executor shall determine; provided, that when particular directions are given by a testator in his will respecting the sale of any property belonging to his estate, the same shall be followed, unless such directions have been annulled or suspended by order of the court.

Acts 1955, 54th Leg., p. 88, ch. 55, eff. Jan. 1, 1956.

### § 333. Certain Personal Property to Be Sold

(a) The representative of an estate, after approval of inventory and appraisement, shall promptly apply for an order of the court to sell at public auction or privately, for cash or on credit not exceeding six months, all of the estate that is liable to perish, waste, or deteriorate in value, or that will be an expense or disadvantage to the estate if kept. Property exempt from forced sale, specific legacies, and personal property necessary to carry on a farm, ranch, factory, or any other business which it is thought best to operate, shall not be included in such sales.

(b) In determining whether to order the sale of an asset under Subsection (a) of this section, the court shall consider:

(1) the representative's duty to take care of and manage the estate as a person of ordinary prudence, discretion, and intelligence would exercise in the management of the person's own affairs; and

(2) whether the asset constitutes an asset that a trustee is authorized to invest under Chapter 117 or Subchapter F, Chapter 113, Property Code.[1]

Added by Acts 1955, 54th Leg., p. 88, ch. 55, eff. Jan. 1, 1956. Amended by Acts 1993, 73rd Leg., ch. 846, § 21, eff. Sept. 1, 1993. Subsec. (b)(2) amended by Acts 2003, 78th Leg., ch. 1103, § 14, eff. Jan. 1, 2004.

[1] V.T.C.A., Property Code § 113.171 et seq.

### § 334. Sales of Other Personal Property

Upon application by the personal representative of the estate or by any interested person, the court may order the sale of any personal property of the estate not required to be sold by the preceding Section, including growing or harvested crops or livestock, but not including exempt property or specific legacies, if the court finds that so to do would be in the best interest of the estate in order to pay expenses of administration, funeral expenses, expenses of last illness, allowances, or claims against the estate, from the proceeds of the sale of such property. In so far as possible, applications and orders for the sale of personal property shall conform to the requirements hereinafter set forth for applications and orders for the sale of real estate.

Acts 1955, 54th Leg., p. 88, ch. 55, eff. Jan. 1, 1956.

### § 335. Special Provisions Pertaining to Livestock

When the personal representative of an estate has in his possession any livestock which he deems necessary or to the advantage of the estate to sell, he may, in addition to any other method provided by law for the sale of personal property, obtain authority from the court in which the estate is pending to sell such livestock through a bonded livestock commission merchant, or a bonded livestock auction commission merchant. Such authority may be granted by the court upon written and sworn application by the personal representative, or by any person interested in the estate, describing the livestock sought to be sold, and setting out the reasons why it is deemed necessary or to the advantage of the estate that the application be granted. The court shall forthwith consider any such application, and may, in its discretion, hear evidence for or against the same, with or without notice, as the facts warrant. If the application be granted, the court shall enter its order to that effect, and shall authorize delivery of the livestock to any bonded livestock commission merchant or bonded livestock auction commission merchant for sale in the regular course of business. The commission merchant shall be paid his usual and customary charges, not to exceed five per cent of the sale price, for the sale of such livestock. A report of such sale, supported by a verified copy of the merchant's account of sale, shall be made promptly by the personal representative to the court, but no order of confirmation by the court is required to pass title to the purchaser of such livestock.

Acts 1955, 54th Leg., p. 88, ch. 55, eff. Jan. 1, 1956. Amended by Acts 2001, 77th Leg., ch. 443, § 1, eff. Sept. 1, 2001.

### § 336. Sales of Personal Property at Public Auction

All sales of personal property at public auction shall be made after notice has been issued by the representative of the estate and posted as in case of posting for original proceedings in probate, unless the court shall otherwise direct.

Acts 1955, 54th Leg., p. 88, ch. 55, eff. Jan. 1, 1956.

### § 337. Sales of Personal Property on Credit

No more than six months credit may be allowed when personal property is sold at public auction, based upon the date of such sale. The purchaser shall be required to give his note for the amount due, with good and solvent personal security, before delivery of such property can be made to him, but security may be waived if delivery is not to be made until the note, with interest, has been paid.

Acts 1955, 54th Leg., p. 88, ch. 55, eff. Jan. 1, 1956.

### § 338. Sale of Mortgaged Property

Any creditor holding a claim secured by a valid mortgage or other lien, which has been allowed and approved or established by suit, may obtain from the court in which the estate is pending an order that said property, or so much thereof as necessary to satisfy his claim, shall be sold, by filing his written application therefor. Upon the filing of such application, the clerk shall issue citation requiring the representative of the estate to appear and show cause why such application should not be granted. If it appears to the court that it would be advisable to discharge the lien out of the general assets of the estate or that it be refinanced, he may so order; otherwise, he shall grant the application and order that the property be sold at public or private sale, as deemed best, as in ordinary cases of sales of real estate.

Acts 1955, 54th Leg., p. 88, ch. 55, eff. Jan. 1, 1956.

### § 339. Sales of Personal Property to be Reported; Decree Vests Title

All sales of personal property shall be reported to the court, and the laws regulating sales of real estate as to confirmation or disapproval of sales shall apply, but no conveyance shall be necessary. The decree confirming the sale of personal property shall vest the right and title of the estate of the intestate in the purchaser who has complied with the terms of the sale, and shall be prima facie evidence that all requirements of the law in making the sale have been met. The representative of an estate may, upon request, issue a bill of sale without warranty to the purchaser as evidence of title, the expense thereof to be borne by the purchaser.

Acts 1955, 54th Leg., p. 88, ch. 55, eff. Jan. 1, 1956. Amended by Acts 1993, 73rd Leg., ch. 957, § 60, eff. Sept. 1, 1993.

### § 339A. Repealed by Acts 1993, 73rd Leg., ch. 957, § 75(1), eff. Sept. 1, 1993

### § 340. Selection of Real Property to Be Sold for Payment of Debts

Real property of the estate which is selected to be sold for the payment of expenses or claims shall be that which the court deems most advantageous to the estate to be sold.

Acts 1955, 54th Leg., p. 88, ch. 55, eff. Jan. 1, 1956.

### § 341. Application for Sale of Real Estate

Application may be made to the court for an order to sell property of the estate when it appears necessary or advisable in order to:

(1) Pay expenses of administration, funeral expenses and expenses of last sickness of decedents, and allowances and claims against the estates of decedents.

(2) Dispose of any interest in real property of the estate of a decedent, when it is deemed to the best interest of the estate to sell such interest.

Acts 1955, 54th Leg., p. 88, ch. 55, eff. Jan. 1, 1956. Amended by Acts 1969, 61st Leg., p. 2030, ch. 695, § 1, eff. June 12, 1969; Acts 1973, 63rd Leg., p. 408, ch. 182, § 4, eff. May 25, 1973; Acts 1975, 64th Leg., p. 975, ch. 372, § 1, eff. June 19, 1975; Acts 1975, 64th Leg., p. 976, ch. 373, § 1, eff. June 19, 1975; Acts 1979, 66th Leg., p. 1755, ch. 713, § 27, eff. Aug. 27, 1979; Acts 1993, 73rd Leg., ch. 957, § 61, eff. Sept. 1, 1993.

### § 342. Contents of Application for Sale of Real Estate

An application for the sale of real estate shall be in writing, shall describe the real estate or interest in or part thereof sought to be sold, and shall be accompanied by an exhibit, verified by affidavit, showing fully and in detail the condition of the estate, the charges and claims that have been approved or established by suit, or that have been rejected and may yet be established, the amount of each such claim, the property of the estate remaining on hand liable for the payment of such claims, and any other facts tending to show the necessity or advisability of such sale.

Acts 1955, 54th Leg., p. 88, ch. 55, eff. Jan. 1, 1956.

## § 343. Repealed by Acts 2007, 80th Leg., ch. 1170, § 9.05, eff. Sept. 1, 2007

## § 344. Citation on Application

Upon the filing of such application and exhibit, the clerk shall issue a citation to all persons interested in the estate, describing the land or interest or part thereof sought to be sold, and informing them of the right under Section 345 of this code to file an opposition to the sale during the period prescribed by the court as shown in the citation, if they so elect. Service of such citation shall be by posting.

Acts 1955, 54th Leg., p. 88, ch. 55, eff. Jan. 1, 1956.

Amended by Acts 2007, 80th Leg., ch. 1170, § 9.01, eff. Sept. 1, 2007.

## § 345. Opposition to Application

When an application for an order of sale is made, any person interested in the estate may, during the period provided in the citation issued under Section 344 of this code, file his opposition to the sale, in writing, or may make application for the sale of other property of the estate.

Acts 1955, 54th Leg., p. 88, ch. 55, eff. Jan. 1, 1956. Amended by Acts 2007, 80th Leg., ch. 1170, § 9.02, eff. Sept. 1, 2007.

## § 345A. Hearing on Application and Any Opposition

(a) The clerk of a court in which an application for an order of sale is filed shall immediately call to the attention of the judge any opposition to the sale that is filed during the period provided in the citation issued under Section 344 of this code. The court shall hold a hearing on an application if an opposition to the sale is filed during the period provided in the citation.

(b) A hearing on an application for an order of sale is not required under this section if no opposition to the application is filed during the period provided in the citation. The court, in its discretion, may determine that a hearing is necessary on the application even if no opposition was filed during that period.

(c) If the court orders a hearing under Subsection (a) or (b) of this section, the court shall designate in writing a date and time for hearing the application and any opposition, together with the evidence pertaining to the application and opposition. The clerk shall issue a notice to the applicant and to each person who files an opposition to the sale, if applicable, of the date and time of the hearing.

(d) The judge may, by entries on the docket, continue a hearing held under this section from time to time until the judge is satisfied concerning the application.

Added by Acts 2007, 80th Leg., ch. 1170, § 9.03, eff. Sept. 1, 2007.

## § 346. Order of Sale

If satisfied that the sale of the property of the estate described in the application is necessary or advisable, the court shall order the sale to be made; otherwise, the court may deny the application and may, if it deems best, order the sale of other property the sale of which would be more advantageous to the estate. An order for the sale of real estate shall specify:

(a) The property to be sold, giving such description as will identify it; and

(b) Whether the property is to be sold at public auction or at private sale, and, if at public auction, the time and place of such sale; and

(c) The necessity or advisability of the sale and its purpose; and

(d) Except in cases in which no general bond is required, that, having examined the general bond of the representative of the estate, the court finds it to be sufficient as required by law, or finds the same to be insufficient and specifies the necessary or increased bond, as the case may be; and

(e) That the sale shall be made and the report returned in accordance with law; and

(f) The terms of the sale.

Acts 1955, 54th Leg., p. 88, ch. 55, eff. Jan. 1, 1956.

Introductory paragraph amended by Acts 2007, 80th Leg., ch. 1170, § 9.04, eff. Sept. 1, 2007.

## § 347. Procedure When Representative Neglects to Apply for Sale

When the representative of an estate neglects to apply for an order to sell sufficient property to pay the charges and claims against the estate that have been allowed and approved, or established by suit, any interested person may, upon written application, cause such representative to be cited to appear and make a full exhibit of the condition of such estate, and show cause why a sale of the property should not be ordered. Upon hearing such application, if the court is satisfied that a sale of the property is necessary or advisable in order to satisfy such claims, it shall enter an order of sale as provided in the preceding Section.

Acts 1955, 54th Leg., p. 88, ch. 55, eff. Jan. 1, 1956.

## § 348. Permissible Terms of Sale of Real Estate

(a) For Cash or Credit. The real estate may be sold for cash, or for part cash and part credit, or the equity in land securing an indebtedness may be sold subject to such indebtedness, or with an assumption of such indebtedness, at public or private sale, as appears to the court to be for the best interest of the estate. When real estate is sold partly on credit, the cash payment shall not be less than one-fifth of the purchase price, and the purchaser shall execute a note for the deferred payments payable in monthly, quarterly, semi-annual or annual installments, of such amounts as appears to the court to be for the best interest of the estate, to bear interest from date at a rate of not less than four percent (4%) per annum, payable as provided in such note. Default in the payment of principal or interest, or any part thereof when due, shall, at the election of the holder of such note, mature the whole debt. Such note shall be secured by vendor's lien retained in the deed and in the note upon the property sold, and be further secured by deed of trust upon the property sold, with the usual provisions for foreclosure and sale upon failure to make the payments provided in the deed and notes.

**(b) Reconveyance Upon Redemption.** When an estate owning real estate by virtue of foreclosure of vendor's lien or mortgage belonging to the estate, either by judicial sale or by a foreclosure suit or through sale under deed of trust or by acceptance of a deed in cancellation of a lien or mortgage owned by the estate, and it appears to the court that an application to redeem the property foreclosed upon has been made by the former owner of the real estate to any corporation or agency now created or hereafter to be created by any Act or Acts of the Congress of the United States or of the State of Texas in connection with legislation for the relief of owners of mortgaged or encumbered homes, farms, ranches, or other real estate, and it further appears to the court that it would be to the best interest of the estate to own bonds of one of the above named federal or state corporations or agencies instead of the real estate, then upon proper application and proof, the court may dispense with the provisions of credit sales as provided above, and may order reconveyance of the property to the former mortgage debtor, or former owner, reserving vendor's lien notes for the total amount of the indebtedness due or for the total amount of bonds which the corporation or agency above named is under its rules and regulations allowed to advance, and, upon obtaining such an order, it shall be proper for the representative to indorse and assign the notes so obtained over to any one of the corporations or agencies above named in exchange for bonds of that corporation or agency.

Acts 1955, 54th Leg., p. 88, ch. 55, eff. Jan. 1, 1956. Amended by Acts 1959, 56th Leg., p. 636, ch. 290, § 1, eff. May 30, 1959.

### § 349. Public Sales of Real Estate

**(a) Notice of Sale.** Except as hereinafter provided, all public sales of real estate shall be advertised by the representative of the estate by a notice published in the county in which the estate is pending, as provided in this Code for publication of notices or citations. Reference shall be made to the order of sale, the time, place, and the required terms of sale, and a brief description of the property to be sold shall be given. It need not contain field notes, but if rural property, the name of the original survey, the number of acres, its locality in the county, and the name by which the land is generally known, if any, shall be given.

**(b) Method of Sale.** All public sales of real estate shall be made at public auction to the highest bidder.

**(c) Time and Place of Sale.** All such sales shall be made in the county in which the proceedings are pending, at the courthouse door of said county, or other place in such county where sales of real estate are specifically authorized to be made, on the first Tuesday of the month after publication of notice shall have been completed, between the hours of ten o'clock A.M. and four o'clock P.M., provided, that if deemed advisable by the court, he may order such sale to be made in the county in which the land is situated, in which event notice shall be published both in such county and in the county where the proceedings are pending.

**(d) Continuance of Sales.** If sales are not completed on the day advertised, they may be continued from day to day by making public announcement verbally of such continuance at the conclusion of the sale each day, such continued sales to be within the same hours as hereinbefore prescribed. If sales are so continued, the fact shall be shown in the report of sale made to the court.

**(e) Failure of Bidder to Comply.** When any person shall bid off property of an estate offered for sale at public auction, and shall fail to comply with the terms of sale, such property shall be readvertised and sold without any further order; and the person so defaulting shall be liable to pay to the representative of the estate, for its benefit, ten per cent of the amount of his bid, and also any deficiency in price on the second sale, such amounts to be recovered by such representative by suit in any court having jurisdiction of the amount claimed, in the county in which the sale was made.

Acts 1955, 54th Leg., p. 88, ch. 55, eff. Jan. 1, 1956.

### § 350. Private Sales of Real Estate

All private sales of real estate shall be made in such manner as the court directs in its order of sale, and no further advertising, notice, or citation concerning such sale shall be required, unless the court shall direct otherwise.

Acts 1955, 54th Leg., p. 88, ch. 55, eff. Jan. 1, 1956. Amended by Acts 1979, 66th Leg., p. 1755, ch. 713, § 29, eff. Aug. 27, 1979.

### § 351. Sales of Easements and Right of Ways

It shall be lawful to sell and convey easements and rights of ways on, under, and over the lands of an estate being administered under orders of a court, regardless of whether the proceeds of such a sale are required for payment of charges or claims against the estate, or for other lawful purposes. The procedure for such sales shall be the same as now or hereafter provided by law for sales of real property of estates of decedents at private sale.

Acts 1955, 54th Leg., p. 88, ch. 55, eff. Jan. 1, 1956. Amended by Acts 1993, 73rd Leg., ch. 957, § 62, eff. Sept. 1, 1993.

### § 352. Representative Purchasing Property of the Estate

(a) Except as provided by Subsection (b), (c), or (d) of this section, the personal representative of an estate shall not become the purchaser, directly or indirectly, of any property of the estate sold by him, or by any co-representative if one be acting.

(b) A personal representative of an estate may purchase property from the estate if the will, duly admitted to probate, appointing the personal representative expressly authorizes the sale.

(c) A personal representative of a decedent may purchase property from the estate of the decedent in compliance with the terms of a written executory contract signed by the decedent, including a contract for deed, earnest money contract, buy/sell agreement, or stock purchase or redemption agreement.

(d) After issuing the notice required by this subsection, a personal representative of an estate, including an independent administrator, may purchase property from the estate on the court's determination that the sale is in the best interest of the estate. The personal representative shall give notice by certified mail, return receipt requested, unless the court requires another form of notice, to each distributee of a deceased person's estate and to each creditor whose claim remains unsettled after presenting a claim within six months of the original grant of letters. The court may require additional notice or it may allow for the waiver of the notice required for a sale made under this subsection.

(e) If a purchase is made in violation of this section, any person interested in the estate may file a written complaint with the court in which the proceedings are pending, and upon service of citation upon the representative, after hearing and proof, such sale shall be by the court declared void, and shall be set aside by the court and the property ordered to be reconveyed to the estate. All costs of the sale, protest, and suit, if found necessary, shall be adjudged against the representative.

Acts 1955, 54th Leg., p. 88, ch. 55, eff. Jan. 1, 1956. Amended by Acts 1985, 69th Leg., ch. 709, § 1, eff. Aug. 26, 1985; Acts 1989, 71st Leg., ch. 651, § 1, eff. June 14, 1989; Acts 1991, 72nd Leg., ch. 895, § 14, eff. Sept. 1, 1991; Acts 1993, 73rd Leg., ch. 957, § 63, eff. Sept. 1, 1993.

## § 353.  Reports of Sale

All sales of real property of an estate shall be reported to the court ordering the same within thirty days after the sales are made. Reports shall be in writing, sworn to, and filed with the clerk, and noted on the probate docket. They shall show:

(a) The date of the order of sale.

(b) The property sold, describing it.

(c) The time and place of sale.

(d) The name of the purchaser.

(e) The amount for which each parcel of property or interest therein was sold.

(f) The terms of the sale, and whether made at public auction or privately.

(g) Whether the purchaser is ready to comply with the order of sale.

Acts 1955, 54th Leg., p. 88, ch. 55, eff. Jan. 1, 1956.

## § 354.  Bond on Sale of Real Estate

If the personal representative of the estate is not required by this Code to furnish a general bond, the sale may be confirmed by the court if found to be satisfactory and in accordance with law. Otherwise, before any sale of real estate is confirmed, the court shall determine whether the general bond of said representative is sufficient to protect the estate after the proceeds of the sale are received. If the court so finds, the sale may be confirmed. If the general bond be found insufficient, the sale shall not be confirmed until and unless the general bond be increased to the amount required by the court, or an additional bond given, and approved by the court. The increase, or the additional bond, shall be equal to the amount for which such real estate is sold, plus, in either instance, such additional sum as the court shall find necessary and fix for the protection of the estate; provided, that where the real estate sold is encumbered by a lien to secure a claim against the estate and is sold to the owner or holder of such secured claim and is in full payment, liquidation, and satisfaction thereof, no increased general bond or additional bond shall be required except for the amount of cash, if any, actually paid to the representative of the estate in excess of the amount necessary to pay, liquidate, and satisfy such claim in full.

Acts 1955, 54th Leg., p. 88, ch. 55, eff. Jan. 1, 1956.

## § 355.  Action of Court on Report of Sale

After the expiration of five days from the filing of a report of sale, the court shall inquire into the manner in which the sale was made, hear evidence in support of or against such report, and determine the sufficiency or insufficiency of the representative's general bond, if any has been required and given; and, if he is satisfied that the sale was for a fair price, was properly made and in conformity with law, and has approved any increased or additional bond which may have been found necessary to protect the estate, the court shall enter a decree confirming such sale, showing conformity with the foregoing provisions of the Code, and authorizing the conveyance of the property to be made by the representative of the estate upon compliance by the purchaser with the terms of the sale, detailing such terms. If the court is not satisfied that the sale was for a fair price, was properly made, and in conformity with law, an order shall be made setting the same aside and ordering a new sale to be made, if necessary. The action of the court in confirming or disapproving a report of sale shall have the force and effect of a final judgment; and any person interested in the estate or in the sale shall have the right to have such decrees reviewed as in other final judgments in probate proceedings.

Acts 1955, 54th Leg., p. 88, ch. 55, eff. Jan. 1, 1956. Amended by Acts 1975, 64th Leg., p. 2197, ch. 701, § 6, eff. June 21, 1975.

## § 356.  Deed Conveys Title to Real Estate

When real estate is sold, the conveyance shall be by proper deed which shall refer to and identify the decree of the court confirming the sale. Such deed shall vest in the purchaser all right, title, and interest of the estate to such property, and shall be prima facie evidence that said sale has met all applicable requirements of the law.

Acts 1955, 54th Leg., p. 88, ch. 55, eff. Jan. 1, 1956.

### § 357. Delivery of Deed, Vendor's and Deed of Trust Lien

After a sale is confirmed by the court and the terms of sale have been complied with by the purchaser, the representative of the estate shall forthwith execute and deliver to the purchaser a proper deed conveying the property. If the sale is made partly on credit, the vendor's lien securing the purchase money note or notes shall be expressly retained in said deed, and in no event waived, and before actual delivery of said deed to purchaser, he shall execute and deliver to the representative of the estate a vendor's lien note or notes, with or without personal sureties as the court shall have ordered, and also a deed of trust or mortgage on the property as further security for the payment of said note or notes. Upon completion of the transaction, the personal representative shall promptly file or cause to be filed and recorded in the appropriate records in the county where the land is situated said deed of trust or mortgage.

Acts 1955, 54th Leg., p. 88, ch. 55, eff. Jan. 1, 1956.

### § 358. Penalty for Neglect

Should the representative of an estate neglect to comply with the preceding Section, or to file the deed of trust securing such lien in the proper county, he and the sureties on his bond shall, after complaint and citation, be held liable for the use of the estate, for all damages resulting from such neglect, which damages may be recovered in any court of competent jurisdiction, and he may be removed by the court.

Acts 1955, 54th Leg., p. 88, ch. 55, eff. Jan. 1, 1956.

### PART 6. HIRING AND RENTING

### § 359. Hiring or Renting Without Order of Court

The personal representative of an estate may, without order of court, rent any of its real property or hire out any of its personal property, either at public auction or privately, as may be deemed in the best interest of the estate, for a period not to exceed one year.

Acts 1955, 54th Leg., p. 88, ch. 55, eff. Jan. 1, 1956.

### § 360. Liability of Personal Representative

If property of the estate is hired or rented without an order of court, the personal representative shall be required to account to the estate for the reasonable value of the hire or rent of such property, to be ascertained by the court upon satisfactory evidence, upon sworn complaint of any person interested in the estate.

Acts 1955, 54th Leg., p. 88, ch. 55, eff. Jan. 1, 1956.

### § 361. Order to Hire or Rent

Representatives of estates, if they prefer, may, and, if the proposed rental period exceeds one year, shall, file a written application with the court setting forth the property sought to be hired or rented. If the court finds that it would be to the interest of the estate, he shall grant the application and issue an order which shall describe the property to be hired or rented, state whether such hiring or renting shall be at public auction or privately, whether for cash or on credit, and, if on credit, the extent of same and the period for which the property may be rented. If to be hired or rented at public auction, the court shall also prescribe whether notice thereof shall be published or posted.

Acts 1955, 54th Leg., p. 88, ch. 55, eff. Jan. 1, 1956.

### § 362. Procedure in Case of Neglect to Rent Property

Any person interested in an estate may file his written and sworn complaint in a court where such estate is pending, and cause the personal representative of such estate to be cited to appear and show cause why he did not hire or rent any property of the estate, and the court, upon hearing such complaint, shall make such order as seems for the best interest of the estate.

Acts 1955, 54th Leg., p. 88, ch. 55, eff. Jan. 1, 1956.

### § 363. When Property is Hired or Rented on Credit

When property is hired or rented on credit, possession thereof shall not be delivered until the hirer or renter has executed and delivered to the representative of the estate a note with good personal security for the amount of such hire or rent; and, if any such property so hired or rented is delivered without receiving such security, the representative and the sureties on his bond shall be liable for the full amount of such hire or rent; provided, that when the hire or rental is payable in installments, in advance of the period of time to which they relate, this Section shall not apply.

Acts 1955, 54th Leg., p. 88, ch. 55, eff. Jan. 1, 1956.

### § 364. Property Hired or Rented to Be Returned in Good Condition

All property hired or rented, with or without an order of court, shall be returned to the possession of the estate in as good condition, reasonable wear and tear excepted, as when hired or rented, and it shall be the duty and responsibility of the representative of the estate to see that this is done, to report to the court any loss, damage or destruction of property hired or rented, and to ask for authority to take such action as is necessary; failing so to do, he and the sureties on his bond shall be liable to the estate for any loss or damage suffered through such fault.

Acts 1955, 54th Leg., p. 88, ch. 55, eff. Jan. 1, 1956.

### § 365. Report of Hiring or Renting

(a) When any property of the estate with an appraised value of Three Thousand Dollars or more has been hired or rented, the representative shall, within thirty days thereafter, file with the court a sworn and written report, stating:

(1) The property involved and its appraised value.

(2) The date of hiring or renting, and whether at public auction or privately.

(3) The name of the person or persons hiring or renting such property.

(4) The amount of such hiring or rental.

(5) Whether the hiring or rental was for cash or on credit, and, if on credit, the length of time, the terms, and the security taken therefor.

(b) When the value of the property involved is less than Three Thousand Dollars, the hiring or renting thereof may be reported upon in the next annual or final account which shall be filed as required by law.

Acts 1955, 54th Leg., p. 88, ch. 55, eff. Jan. 1, 1956.

### § 366. Action of Court on Report

At any time after five days from the time such report of hiring or renting is filed, it shall be examined by the court and approved and confirmed by order of the court if found just and reasonable; but, if disapproved, the estate shall not be bound and the court may order another offering of the property for hire or rent, in the same manner and subject to the same rules heretofore provided. If the report has been approved and it later appears that, by reason of any fault of the representative of the estate, the property has not been hired or rented for its reasonable value, the court shall cause the representative of the estate and his sureties to appear and show cause why the reasonable value of hire or rent of such property shall not be adjudged against him.

Acts 1955, 54th Leg., p. 88, ch. 55, eff. Jan. 1, 1956.

### PART 7. MINERAL LEASES, POOLING OR UNITIZATION AGREEMENTS, AND OTHER MATTERS RELATING TO MINERAL PROPERTIES

### § 367. Mineral Leases After Public Notice

(a) **Certain Words and Terms Defined.** As used throughout in this Part of this Chapter, the words "land" or "interest in land" include minerals or any interest in any of such minerals in place. The word "property" includes land, minerals in place, whether solid, liquid or gaseous, as well as an interest of any kind in such property, including royalty, owned by the estate. "Mineral development" includes exploration, by geophysical or by any other means, drilling, mining, developing, and operating, and producing and saving oil, other liquid hydrocarbons, gas (including all liquid hydrocarbons in the gaseous phase in the reservoir), gaseous elements, sulphur, metals, and all other minerals, solid or otherwise.

(b) **Mineral Leases, With or Without Pooling or Unitization.** Personal representatives of the estates of decedents, appointed and qualified under the laws of this State,

and acting solely under orders of court, may be authorized by the court in which the probate proceedings on such estates are pending to make, execute, and deliver leases, with or without unitization clauses or pooling provisions, providing for the exploration for, and development and production of, oil, other liquid hydrocarbons, gas (including all liquid hydrocarbons in the gaseous phase), metals, and other solid minerals, and other minerals, or any of such minerals in place, belonging to such estates.

(c) **Rules Concerning Applications, Orders, Notices, and Other Essential Matters.** All such leases, with or without pooling provisions or unitization clauses, shall be made and entered into pursuant to and in conformity with the following rules:

**1. Contents of Application.** The representative of the estate shall file with the county clerk of the county where the probate proceeding is pending his written application, addressed to the court or the judge of such court, asking for authority to lease property of the estate for mineral exploration and development, with or without pooling provisions or unitization clauses. The application shall (a) describe the property fully enough by reference to the amount of acreage, the survey name or number, or abstract number, or other description adequately identifying the property and its location in the county in which situated; (b) specify the interest thought to be owned by the estate, if less than the whole, but asking for authority to include all interest owned by the estate, if that be the intention; and (c) set out the reasons why such particular property of the estate should be leased. Neither the name of any proposed lessee, nor the terms, provisions, or form of any desired lease, need be set out or suggested in any such application for authority to lease for mineral development.

**2. Order Designating Time and Place for Hearing Application.**

(a) **Duties of Clerk and Judge.** When an application to lease, as above prescribed, is filed, the county clerk shall immediately call the filing of such application to the attention of the court, and the judge shall promptly make and enter a brief order designating the time and place for the hearing of such application.

(b) **Continuance of Hearing.** If the hearing is not had at the time originally designated by the court or by timely order or orders of continuance duly entered, then, in such event, the hearing shall be automatically continued, without further notice, to the same hour or time the following day (except Sundays and holidays on which the county courthouse is officially closed to business) and from day to day until the application is finally acted upon and disposed of by order of the court. No notice of such automatic continuance shall be required.

**3. Notice of Application to Lease, Service of Notice, and Proof of Service.**

(a) **Notice and Its Contents.** The personal representative, and not the county clerk, shall give notice in writing of the time designated by the judge for the hearing on the application to lease. The notice shall be directed to all persons interested in the estate. It shall state the date on which the application was filed, describe briefly the property sought to be leased, specifying the fractional interest sought to be leased if less than the entire interest in the tract or tracts identified, state the time and place designated by the judge for the hearing, and be dated.

**(b) Service of Notice.** The personal representative shall give at least ten days notice, exclusive of the date of notice and of the date set for hearing, by publication in one issue of a newspaper of general circulation in the county in which the proceeding is pending, or, if there be no such newspaper, then by posting by the personal representative or at his instance. The date of notice when published shall be the date the newspaper bears.

**4. Preceding Requirements Mandatory.** In the absence of: (a) a written order originally designating a time and place for hearing; (b) a notice issued by the personal representative of the estate in compliance with such order; and (c) proof of publication or posting of such notice as required, any order of the judge or court authorizing any acts to be performed pursuant to said application shall be null and void.

**5. Hearing on Application to Lease and Order Thereon.** At the time and place designated for the hearing, or at any time to which it shall have been continued as hereinabove provided, the judge shall hear such application, requiring proof as to the necessity or advisability of leasing for mineral development the property described in the application and in the notice; and, if he is satisfied that the application is in due form, that notice has been duly given in the manner and for the time required by law, that the proof of necessity or advisability of leasing is sufficient, and that the application should be granted, then an order shall be entered so finding, and authorizing the making of one or more leases, with or without pooling provisions or unitization clauses (with or without cash consideration if deemed by the court to be in the best interest of the estate) affecting and covering the property, or portions thereof, described in the application. Said order authorizing leasing shall also set out the following mandatory contents:

(a) The name of the lessee.

(b) The actual cash consideration, if any, to be paid by the lessee.

(c) Finding that the personal representative is exempted by law from giving bond, if that be a fact and if not a fact, then a finding as to whether or not the representative's general bond on file is sufficient to protect the personal property on hand, inclusive of any cash bonus to be paid, if any. If the court finds the general bond insufficient to meet these requirements, the order shall show the amount of increased or additional bond required to cover the deficiency.

(d) A complete exhibit copy, either written or printed, of each lease thus authorized to be made, shall either be set out

in the order or attached thereto and incorporated by reference in said order and made a part thereof. It shall show the name of the lessee, the date of the lease, an adequate description of the property being leased, the delay rental, if any, to be paid to defer commencement of operations, and all other terms and provisions authorized; provided, that if no date of the lease appears in such exhibit copy, or in the court's order, then the date of the court's order shall be considered for all purposes as the date of the authorized lease, and if the name and address of the depository bank, or either of them, for receiving rental is not shown in said exhibit copy, the same may be inserted or caused to be inserted in the lease by the estate's personal representative at the time of its execution, or at any other time agreeable to the lessee, his successors, or assigns.

**6. Conditional Validity of Lease; Bond; Time of Execution; Confirmation Not Needed.** If, upon the hearing of an application for authority to lease, the court shall grant the same as above provided, the personal representative of the estate shall then be fully authorized to make, within thirty days after date of the judge's order, but not afterwards unless an extension be granted by the court upon sworn application showing good cause, the lease or leases as evidenced by the aforesaid true exhibit copies, in accordance with said order; but, unless the personal representative is not required to give a general bond, no such lease, for which a cash consideration is required, though ordered, executed, and delivered, shall be valid unless the order authorizing same actually makes findings with respect to the general bond, and, in case such bond has been found insufficient, then unless and until the bond has been increased, or an additional bond given, as required by the court's order, with the sureties required by law, has been approved by the judge and filed with the clerk of the court in which the proceedings are pending. In the event two or more leases on different lands are authorized by the same order, the general bond shall be increased, or additional bonds given, to cover all. It shall not be necessary for the judge to make any order confirming such leases.

**7. Term of Lease Binding.** Every such lease, when executed and delivered in compliance with the rules hereinabove set out, shall be valid and binding upon the property or interest therein owned by the estate and covered by the lease for the full duration of the term as provided therein, subject only to its terms and conditions, even though the primary term shall extend beyond the date when the estate shall have been closed in accordance with law; provided the authorized primary term shall not exceed five (5) years, subject to terms and provisions of the lease extending it beyond the primary term by paying production, by bona fide drilling or reworking operations, whether in or on the same or additional well or wells, with no cessation of operations of more than sixty (60) consecutive days before production has been restored or obtained, or by the provisions of the lease relating to a shut-in gas well.

**7(a). Validation of Certain Provisions of Leases Heretofore Executed by Personal Representatives.** As to any valid mineral lease heretofore executed and delivered in compliance with the provisions of the Texas Probate Code and which lease is still in force, any provisions of any such lease continuing such lease in force after its five (5) year primary term by a shut-in gas well are hereby validated; provided, however, that this provision shall not be applicable to any such provision of any such lease which is involved in any lawsuit pending in this state on the effective date of this Act wherein the validity of such provision is an issue.

**8. Amendment of Leases.** Any oil, gas, and mineral lease heretofore or hereafter executed by a personal representative pursuant to the Texas Probate Code may be amended by an instrument which provides that a shut-in gas well on the land covered by the lease or on land pooled with all or some part thereof shall continue such lease in force after its five (5) year primary term. Such instrument shall be executed by the personal representative, with the approval of the court, and on such terms and conditions as may be prescribed therein.

Acts 1955, 54th Leg., p. 88, ch. 55, eff. Jan. 1, 1956. Amended by Acts 1957, 55th Leg., p. 53, ch. 31, § 10(a), eff. Aug. 22, 1957; Acts 1961, 57th Leg., p. 441, ch. 215, §§ 1 to 3, eff. May 25, 1961; Acts 1993, 73rd Leg., ch. 957, § 64, eff. Sept. 1, 1993.

## § 368. Mineral Leases at Private Sale

**(a) Authorization Allowed.** Notwithstanding the preceding mandatory requirements for setting a time and place for hearing of an application to lease and the issuance, service, and return of notice, the court may authorize the making of oil, gas, and mineral leases at private sale (without public notice or advertising) if, in the opinion of the court, sufficient facts are set out in the application required above to show that it would be more advantageous to the estate that a lease be made privately and without compliance with said mandatory requirements mentioned above. Leases so authorized may include pooling provisions or unitization clauses as in other cases.

**(b) Action of the Court When Public Advertising Not Required.** At any time after the expiration of five (5) days and prior to the expiration of ten (10) days from the date of filing and without an order setting time and place of hearing, the court shall hear the application to lease at private sale and shall inquire into the manner in which the proposed lease has been or will be made, and shall hear evidence for or against the same; and, if satisfied that the lease has been or will be made for a fair and sufficient consideration and on fair terms, and has been or will be properly made in conformity with law, the court shall enter an order authorizing the execution of such lease without the necessity of advertising, notice, or citation, said order complying in all other respects with the requirements essential to the validity of mineral leases as hereinabove set out, as if advertising or notice were required. No order confirming a lease or leases made at private sale need be issued, but no such lease shall be valid until the increased or additional bond required by the court, if any, has been approved by the court and filed with the clerk of the court.

Acts 1955, 54th Leg., p. 88, ch. 55, eff. Jan. 1, 1956. Amended by Acts 1957, 55th Leg., p. 53, ch. 31, § 10(b).

## § 369. Pooling or Unitization of Royalty or Minerals

**(a) Authorization for Pooling or Unitization.** When an existing lease or leases on property owned by the estate does not adequately provide for pooling or unitization, the court may authorize the commitment of royalty or mineral interests in oil, liquid hydrocarbons, gas (including all liquid hydrocarbons in the gaseous phase in the reservoir), gaseous elements, and other minerals, or any one or more of them, owned by the estate being administered, to agreements that provide for the operation of areas as a pool or unit for the exploration, development, and production of all such minerals, where the court finds that the pool or unit to which the agreement relates will be operated in such a manner as to protect correlative rights, or to prevent the physical or economic waste of oil, liquid hydrocarbons, gas (including all liquid hydrocarbons in the gaseous phase in the reservoir), gaseous elements, or other mineral subject thereto, and that it is to the best interest of the estate to execute the agreement. Any agreement so authorized to be executed may, among other things, provide:

(1) That operations incident to the drilling of or production from a well upon any portion of a pool or unit shall be deemed for all purposes to be the conduct of operations upon or production from each separately owned tract in the pool or unit.

(2) That any lease covering any part of the area committed to a pool or unit shall continue in force in its entirety as long as oil, gas, or other mineral subject to the agreement is produced in paying quantities from any part of the pooled or unitized area, or as long as operations are conducted as provided in the lease on any part of the pooled or unitized area, or as long as there is a shut-in gas well on any part of the pooled or unitized area, if the presence of such shut-in gas well is a ground for continuation of the lease by the terms of said lease.

(3) That the production allocated by the agreement to each tract included in a pool or unit shall, when produced, be deemed for all purposes to have been produced from such tract by a well drilled thereon.

(4) That the royalties provided for on production from any tract or portion thereof within the pool or unit shall be paid only on that portion of the production allocated to the tract in accordance with the agreement.

(5) That the dry gas, before or after extraction of hydrocarbons, may be returned to a formation underlying any lands or leases committed to the agreement, and that no royalties are required to be paid on the gas so returned.

(6) That gas obtained from other sources or other lands may be injected into a formation underlying any lands or leases committed to the agreement, and that no royalties are

required to be paid on the gas so injected when same is produced from the unit.

(b) Procedure for Authorizing Pooling or Unitization. Pooling or unitization, when not adequately provided for by an existing lease or leases on property owned by the estate, may be authorized by the court in which the proceedings are pending pursuant to and in conformity with the following rules:

(1) Contents of Application. The personal representative of the estate shall file with the county clerk of the county where the probate proceeding is pending his written application for authority (a) to enter into pooling or unitization agreements supplementing, amending, or otherwise relating to, any existing lease or leases covering property owned by the estate, or (b) to commit royalties or other interest in minerals, whether subject to lease or not, to a pooling or unitization agreement. The application shall also (c) describe the property sufficiently, as required in original application to lease, (d) describe briefly the lease or leases, if any, to which the interest of the estate is subject, and (e) set out the reasons why the proposed agreement concerning such property should be made. A true copy of the proposed agreement shall be attached to the application and by reference made a part thereof, but the agreement shall not be recorded in the judge's probate docket. The clerk shall immediately, after such application is filed, call it to the attention of the judge.

(2) Notice Not Necessary. No notice of the filing of such application by advertising, citation, or otherwise, is required.

(3) Hearing of Application. A hearing on such application may be held by the judge at any time agreeable to the parties to the proposed agreement, and the judge shall hear proof and satisfy himself as to whether or not it is to the best interest of the estate that the proposed agreement be authorized. The hearing may be continued from day to day and from time to time as the court finds to be necessary.

(4) Action of Court and Contents of Order. If the court finds that the pool or unit to which the agreement relates will be operated in such a manner as to protect correlative rights or to prevent the physical or economic waste of oil, liquid hydrocarbons, gas (including all liquid hydrocarbons in the gaseous phase in the reservoir), gaseous elements, or other mineral subject thereto; that it is to the best interest of the estate that the agreement be executed; and that the agreement conforms substantially with the permissible provisions of Subsection (a) hereof, he shall enter an order setting out the findings made by him, authorizing execution of the agreement (with or without payment of cash consideration according to the agreement). If cash consideration is to be paid for the agreement, findings as to the necessity of increased or additional bond, as in making of leases upon payment of the cash bonus therefor, shall also be made, and no such agreement shall be valid until the increased or additional bond required by the court, if any, has been approved by the judge and filed with the clerk. The date of

the court's order shall be the effective date of the agreement, if not stipulated in such agreement.

Acts 1955, 54th Leg., p. 88, ch. 55, eff. Jan. 1, 1956. Amended by Acts 1961, 57th Leg., p. 441, ch. 215, § 4, eff. May 25, 1961; Acts 2009, 81st Leg., ch. 602, § 9, eff. June 19, 2009.

### § 370. Special Ancillary Instruments Which May Be Executed Without Court Order

As to any valid mineral lease or pooling or unitization agreement, executed on behalf of the estate prior to the effective date of this Code, or pursuant to its provisions, or by a former owner of land, minerals, or royalty affected thereby, the personal representative of the estate which is being administered may, without further order of the court, and without consideration, execute division orders, transfer orders, instruments of correction, instruments designating depository banks for the reception of delay rentals or shut-in gas well royalty to accrue or become payable under the terms of any such lease or leases, and similar instruments pertaining to any such lease or agreement and the property covered thereby.

Acts 1955, 54th Leg., p. 88, ch. 55, eff. Jan. 1, 1956. Amended by Acts 1957, 55th Leg., p. 53, ch. 31, § 10(c).

### § 371. Procedure When Representative of Estate Neglects to Apply for Authority

When the personal representative of an estate shall neglect to apply for authority to subject property of the estate to a lease for mineral development, pooling or unitization, or to commit royalty or other interest in minerals to pooling or unitization, any person interested in the estate may, upon written application filed with the county clerk, cause such representative to be cited to show cause why it is not for the best interest of the estate for such a lease to be made, or such an agreement entered into. The clerk shall immediately call the filing of such application to the attention of the judge of the court in which the probate proceedings are pending, and the judge shall set a time and place for a hearing on the application, and the representative of the estate shall be cited to appear and show cause why the execution of such lease or agreement should not be ordered. Upon hearing, if satisfied from the proof that it would be in the best interest of the estate, the court shall enter an order requiring the personal representative forthwith to file his application to subject such property of the estate to a lease for mineral development, with or without pooling or unitization provisions, or to commit royalty or other minerals to unitization, as the case may be. The procedure prescribed with respect to original application to lease, or with respect to original application for authority to commit royalty or minerals to pooling or unitization, whichever is appropriate, shall then be followed.

Acts 1955, 54th Leg., p. 88, ch. 55, eff. Jan. 1, 1956.

## § 372. Validation of Certain Leases and Pooling or Unitization Agreements Based on Previous Statutes

All presently existing leases on the oil, gas, or other minerals, or one or more of them, belonging to the estates of decedents, and all agreements with respect to pooling, or unitization thereof, or one or more of them, or any interest therein, with like properties of others having been authorized by the court having venue, and executed and delivered by the executors, administrators, or other fiduciaries of their estates in substantial conformity to the rules set forth in statutes heretofore existing, providing for only seven days notice in some instances, and also for a brief order designating a time and place for hearing, are hereby validated in so far as said period of notice is concerned, and in so far as the absence of any order setting a time and place for hearing is concerned; provided, this shall not apply to any lease or pooling or unitization agreement involved in any suit pending on the effective date of this Code wherein either the length of time of said notice or the absence of such order is in issue.

Acts 1955, 54th Leg., p. 88, ch. 55, eff. Jan. 1, 1956. Amended by Acts 1993, 73rd Leg., ch. 957, § 65, eff. Sept. 1, 1993.

## PART 8. PARTITION AND DISTRIBUTION OF ESTATES OF DECEDENTS

### § 373. Application for Partition and Distribution of Estates of Decedents

(a) **Who May Apply.** At any time after the expiration of twelve months after the original grant of letters testamentary or of administration, the executor or administrator, or the heirs, devisees, or legatees of the estate, or any of them, may, by written application filed in the court in which the estate is pending, request the partition and distribution of the estate.

(b) **Contents of Application.** The application shall state:

(1) The name of the person whose estate is sought to be partitioned and distributed; and

(2) The names and residences of all persons entitled to shares of such estate, and whether adults or minors; and, if these facts be unknown to the applicant, it shall be so stated in the application; and

(3) The reasons why partition and distribution should be had.

(c) **Partial Distribution.** At any time after the original grant of letters testamentary or of administration, and the filing and approval of the inventory, the executor or administrator, or the heirs, devisees, or legatees of the estate, or any of them, may, by written application filed in the court in which the estate is pending, request a distribution of any portion of the estate. All interested parties shall be personally cited, as in other distributions, including known creditors. The court may upon proper citation and hearing distribute any portion of the estate it deems advisable. In the event a distribution is to be made to one or more heirs or

devisees, and not to all the heirs or devisees, the court shall require a refunding bond in an amount to be determined by the court to be filed with the court and, upon its approval, the court shall order the distribution of that portion of the estate, unless such requirement is waived in writing and the waiver is filed with the court by all interested parties. This section shall apply to corpus as well as income, notwithstanding any other provisions of this Code.

Acts 1955, 54th Leg., p. 88, ch. 55, eff. Jan. 1, 1956. Amended by Acts 1973, 63rd Leg., p. 408, ch. 182, § 2, eff. May 25, 1973.

### § 374. Citation of Interested Persons

Upon the filing of such application, the clerk shall issue a citation which shall state the name of the person whose estate is sought to be partitioned and distributed, and the date upon which the court will hear the application, and the citation shall require all persons interested in the estate to appear and show cause why such partition and distribution should not be made. Such citation shall be personally served upon each person residing in the state entitled to a share of the estate whose address is known; and, if there be any such persons whose identities or addresses are not known, or who are not residents of this state, or are residents of but absent from this state, such citation shall be served by publication.

Acts 1955, 54th Leg., p. 88, ch. 55, eff. Jan. 1, 1956.

### § 375. Citation of Executor or Administrator

When application for partition and distribution is made by any person other than the executor or administrator, such representative shall also be cited to appear and answer the application and to file in court a verified exhibit and account of the condition of the estate, as in the case of final settlements.

Acts 1955, 54th Leg., p. 88, ch. 55, eff. Jan. 1, 1956.

### § 376. Repealed by Acts 1993, 73rd Leg., ch. 957, § 75(1), eff. Sept. 1, 1993

### § 377. Facts to Be Ascertained Upon Hearing

At the hearing upon the application for partition and distribution, the court shall ascertain:

(a) The residue of the estate subject to partition and distribution, which shall be ascertained by deducting from the entire assets of such estate remaining on hand the amount of all debts and expenses of every kind which have been approved or established by judgment, but not paid, or which may yet be established by judgment, and also the probable future expenses of administration.

(b) The persons who are by law entitled to partition and distribution, and their respective shares.

(c) Whether advancements have been made to any of the persons so entitled and their nature and value. If advancements have been made, the court shall require the same to be placed in hotchpotch as required by the law governing intestate succession.

Acts 1955, 54th Leg., p. 88, ch. 55, eff. Jan. 1, 1956.

### § 378. Decree of the Court

If the court is of the opinion that the estate should be partitioned and distributed, it shall enter a decree which shall state:

(a) The name and address, if known, of each person entitled to a share of the estate, specifying those who are known to be minors, and the names of their guardians, or the guardians ad litem, and the name of the attorney appointed to represent those who are unknown or who are not residents of the state.

(b) The proportional part of the estate to which each is entitled.

(c) A full description of all the estate to be distributed.

(d) That the executor or administrator retain in his hands for the payment of all debts, taxes, and expenses of administration a sufficient amount of money or property for that purpose, specifying the amount of money or the property to be so retained.

Acts 1955, 54th Leg., p. 88, ch. 55, eff. Jan. 1, 1956.

### § 378A. Satisfaction of Pecuniary Bequests

(a) Unless the governing instrument provides otherwise, if an executor, administrator, or trustee is authorized under the will or trust of a decedent to satisfy a pecuniary bequest, devise, or transfer in trust with assets at their value for federal estate tax purposes, in satisfaction of a gift intended to qualify, or that otherwise would qualify, for a United States estate tax marital deduction, the executor, administrator, or trustee, in order to implement the bequest, devise, or transfer, shall distribute assets, including cash, fairly representative of appreciation or depreciation in the value of all property available for distribution in satisfaction of the pecuniary bequest, devise, or transfer.

(b) Unless the governing instrument provides otherwise, if a will or trust contains a pecuniary bequest, devise, or transfer that may be satisfied by distributing assets in kind and if the executor, administrator, or trustee determines to fund the bequest, devise, or transfer by distributing assets in kind, the property shall, for the purpose of funding the bequest, devise, or transfer, be valued at its value on the date or dates of distribution.

Added by Acts 1987, 70th Leg., ch. 1110, § 1, eff. Sept. 1, 1987. Amended by Acts 1991, 72nd Leg., ch. 895, § 15, eff. Sept. 1, 1991.

### § 378B. Allocation of Income and Expenses During Administration of Decedent's Estate

(a) Except as provided by Subsection (b) of this section and unless the will provides otherwise, all expenses incurred in connection with the settlement of a decedent's estate, including debts, funeral expenses, estate taxes, penalties relating to estate taxes, and family allowances, shall be charged against the principal of the estate. Fees and expenses of an attorney, accountant, or other professional advisor, commissions and expenses of a personal representative, court costs, and all other similar fees or expenses relating to the administration of the estate and interest relating to estate taxes shall be allocated between the income and principal of the estate as the executor determines in its discretion to be just and equitable.

(b) Unless the will provides otherwise, income from the assets of a decedent's estate that accrues after the death of the testator and before distribution, including income from property used to discharge liabilities, shall be determined according to the rules applicable to a trustee under the Texas Trust Code (Subtitle B, Title 9, Property Code)[1] and distributed as provided by Chapter 116, Property Code, and Subsections (c) and (d) of this section.

(c) The income from the property bequeathed or devised to a specific devisee shall be distributed to the devisee after reduction for property taxes, ordinary repairs, insurance premiums, interest accrued after the death of the testator, other expenses of management and operation of the property, and other taxes, including the taxes imposed on the income that accrues during the period of administration and that is payable to the devisee.

(d) The balance of the net income shall be distributed to all other devisees after reduction for the balance of property taxes, ordinary repairs, insurance premiums, interest accrued, other expenses of management and operation of all property from which the estate is entitled to income, and taxes imposed on income that accrues during the period of administration and that is payable or allocable to the devisees, in proportion to the devisees' respective interests in the undistributed assets of the estate.

(e), (f) Repealed by Acts 2003, 78th Leg., ch. 659, § 4, eff. Jan. 1, 2004.

(g) Income received by a trustee under this section shall be treated as income of the trust as provided by Section 116.101, Property Code.

(h) In this section, "undistributed assets" includes funds used to pay debts, administration expenses, and federal and state estate, inheritance, succession, and generation-skipping transfer taxes until the date of payment of the debts, expenses, and taxes. Except as required by Sections 2055 and 2056 of the Internal Revenue Code of 1986 (26 U.S.C. Secs. 2055 and 2056), and its subsequent amendments, the frequency and method of determining the beneficiaries' respective interests in the undistributed assets of the estate shall be in the executor's sole and absolute discretion. The executor may consider all relevant factors, including administrative convenience and expense and the interests of the various beneficiaries of the estate in order to reach a fair and equitable result among beneficiaries.

(i) Chapter 116, Property Code, prevails to the extent of any conflict between this section and Chapter 116, Property Code.

Added by Acts 1993, 73rd Leg., ch. 846, § 24, eff. Sept. 1, 1993.
Subsecs. (a), (b), (d) and (g) amended by Acts 2003, 78th Leg., ch. 659, § 3, eff. Jan. 1, 2004; Subsecs. (e), (f) amended by Acts 2003, ch. 659, § 4, eff. Jan. 1, 2004; Subsec. (f) amended by Acts 2003, 78th Leg., ch. 1060, § 15, eff. Sept. 1, 2003; Subsec. (i) added by Acts 2003, 78th Leg., ch. 659, § 3, eff. Jan. 1, 2004.

[1] V.T.C.A., Property Code § 111.001 et seq.

## § 379. Partition When Estate Consists of Money or Debts Only

If the estate to be distributed shall consist only of money or debts due the estate, or both, the court shall fix the amount to which each distributee is entitled, and shall order the payment and delivery thereof by the executor or administrator.

Acts 1955, 54th Leg., p. 88, ch. 55, eff. Jan. 1, 1956.

## § 380. Partition and Distribution When Property Is Capable of Division

(a) **Appointment of Commissioners.** If the estate does not consist entirely of money or debts due the estate, or both, the court shall appoint three or more discreet and disinterested persons as commissioners, to make a partition and distribution of the estate, unless the court has already determined that the estate is incapable of partition.

(b) **Writ of Partition and Service Thereof.** When commissioners are appointed, the clerk shall issue a writ of partition directed to the commissioners appointed, commanding them to proceed forthwith to make partition and distribution in accordance with the decree of the court, a copy of which decree shall accompany the writ, and also command them to make due return of said writ, with their proceedings under it, on a date named in the writ. Such writ shall be served by delivering the same and the accompanying copy of the decree of partition to any one of the commissioners appointed, and by notifying the other commissioners, verbally or otherwise, of their appointment, and such service may be made by any person.

(c) **Partition by Commissioners.** The commissioners shall make a fair, just, and impartial partition and distribution of the estate in the following order:

(1) Of the land or other property, by allotting to each distributee a share in each parcel or shares in one or more parcels, or one or more parcels separately, either with or without the addition of a share or shares of other parcels, as shall be most for the interest of the distributees; provided, the real estate is capable of being divided without manifest injury to all or any of the distributees.

(2) If the real estate is not capable of a fair, just and equal division in kind, but may be made so by allotting to one or more of the distributees a proportion of the money or other personal property to supply the deficiency or deficiencies, the commissioners shall have power to make, as nearly as may be, an equal division of the real estate and supply the deficiency of any share or shares from the money or other property.

(3) The commissioners shall proceed to make a like division in kind, as nearly as may be, of the money and other personal property, and shall determine by lot, among equal shares, to whom each particular share shall belong.

(d) **Report of Commissioners.** The commissioners, having divided the whole or any part of the estate, shall make to the court a written sworn report containing a statement of the property divided by them, and also a particular description of the property allotted to each distributee, and its value. If it be real estate that has been divided, the report shall contain a general plat of said land with the division lines plainly set down and with the number of acres in each share. The report of a majority of the commissioners shall be sufficient.

(e) **Action of the Court.** Upon the return of such report, the court shall examine the same carefully and hear all exceptions and objections thereto, and evidence in favor of or against the same, and if it be informal, it shall cause said informality to be corrected. If such division shall appear to have been fairly made according to law, and no valid exceptions are taken to it, the court shall approve it, and shall enter a decree vesting title in the distributees of their respective shares or portions of the property as set apart to them by the commissioners; otherwise, the court may set aside said report and division and order a new partition to be made.

(f) **Delivery of Property.** When the report of commissioners to make partition has been approved and ordered to be recorded, the court shall order the executor or administrator to deliver to the distributees their respective shares of the estate on demand, including all the title deeds and papers belonging to the same.

(g) **Fees of Commissioners.** Commissioners thus appointed who actually serve in partitioning and distributing an estate shall be entitled to receive Five Dollars each for every day that they are necessarily engaged in the performance of their duties as such commissioners, to be taxed and paid as other costs in cases of partition.

Acts 1955, 54th Leg., p. 88, ch. 55, eff. Jan. 1, 1956.

## § 381. Partition and Distribution When Property of an Estate Is Incapable of Division

(a) **Finding by the Court.** When, in the opinion of the court, the whole or any portion of an estate is not capable of a fair and equal partition and distribution, the court shall make a special finding in writing, specifying therein the property incapable of division.

(b) **Order of Sale.** When the court has found that the whole or any portion of the estate is not capable of fair and equal division, it shall order a sale of all property which it has found not to be capable of such division. Such sale shall be made by the executor or administrator in the same manner as when sales of real estate are made for the purpose of satisfying debts of the estate, and the proceeds of such sale, when collected, shall be distributed by the court among those entitled thereto.

**(c) Purchase by Distributee.** At such sale, if any distributee shall buy any of the property, he shall be required to pay or secure only such amount of his bid as exceeds the amount of his share of such property.

**(d) Applicability of Provisions Relating to Sales of Real Estate.** The provisions of this Code relative to reports of sales of real estate, the giving of an increased general or additional bond upon sales of real estate, and to the vesting of title to the property sold by decree or by deed, shall also apply to sales made under this Section.

Acts 1955, 54th Leg., p. 88, ch. 55, eff. Jan. 1, 1956.

### § 382. Property Located in Another County

**(a) Court May Order Sale.** When any portion of the estate to be partitioned lies in another county and cannot be fairly partitioned without prejudice to the interests of the distributees, the commissioners may report such facts to the court in writing; whereupon, if satisfied that the said property cannot be fairly divided, or that its sale would be more advantageous to the distributees, the court may order a sale thereof, which sale shall be conducted in the same manner as is provided in this Code for the sale of property which is not capable of fair and equal division.

**(b) Court May Appoint Additional Commissioners.** If the court is not satisfied that such property cannot be fairly and advantageously divided, or that its sale would be more advantageous to the distributees, three or more commissioners may be appointed in each county where any portion of the estate so reported is situated, and the same proceedings shall be had thereon as are provided in this Code for commissioners to make partition.

Acts 1955, 54th Leg., p. 88, ch. 55, eff. Jan. 1, 1956.

### § 383. Repealed by Acts 1993, 73rd Leg., ch. 957, § 75(1), eff. Sept. 1, 1993

### § 384. Damages for Neglect to Deliver Property

If any executor or administrator shall neglect to deliver to the person entitled thereto, when demanded, any portion of an estate ordered to be delivered, such person may file with the clerk of the court his written complaint alleging the fact of such neglect, the date of his demand, and other relevant facts, whereupon the clerk shall issue a citation to be served personally on such representative, apprising him of the complaint and citing him to appear before the court and answer, if he so desires, at the time designated in the citation. If at the hearing the court finds that the citation was duly served and returned and that the representative is guilty of such neglect, the court shall enter an order to that effect, and the representative shall be liable to such complainant in damages at the rate of ten per cent of the amount or appraised value of the share so withheld, per month, for each and every

month or fraction thereof that the share is and/or has been so withheld after date of demand, which damages may be recovered in any court of competent jurisdiction.

Acts 1955, 54th Leg., p. 88, ch. 55, eff. Jan. 1, 1956.

### § 385. Partition of Community Property

**(a) Application for Partition.** When a husband or wife shall die leaving any community property, the survivor may, at any time after letters testamentary or of administration have been granted, and an inventory, appraisement, and list of the claims of the estate have been returned or an affidavit in lieu of the inventory, appraisement, and list of claims has been filed, make application in writing to the court which granted such letters for a partition of such community property.

**(b) Bond and Action of the Court.** The survivor shall execute and deliver to the judge of said court a bond with a corporate surety or two or more good and sufficient personal sureties, payable to and approved by said judge, for an amount equal to the value of the survivor's interest in such community property, conditioned for the payment of one-half of all debts existing against such community property, and the court shall proceed to make a partition of said community property into two equal moieties, one to be delivered to the survivor and the other to the executor or administrator of the deceased. The provisions of this Code respecting the partition and distribution of estates shall apply to such partition so far as the same are applicable.

**(c) Lien Upon Property Delivered.** Whenever such partition is made, a lien shall exist upon the property delivered to the survivor to secure the payment of the aforementioned bond; and any creditor of said community estate may sue in his own name on such bond, and shall have judgment thereon for one-half of such debt as he shall establish, and for the other one-half he shall be entitled to be paid by the executor or administrator of the deceased.

Acts 1955, 54th Leg., p. 88, ch. 55, eff. Jan. 1, 1956. Subsec. (a) amended by Acts 2011, 82nd Leg., ch. 1338 (S.B. 1198), § 1.35, eff. Sept. 1, 2011.

### § 386. Partition of Property Jointly Owned

Any person having a joint interest with the estate of a decedent in any property, real or personal, may make application to the court from which letters testamentary or of administration have been granted thereon to have a partition thereof, whereupon the court shall make a partition of said property between the applicant and the estate of the deceased; and all the provisions of this Code in relation to the partition and distribution of estates shall govern partition hereunder, so far as the same are applicable.

Acts 1955, 54th Leg., p. 88, ch. 55, eff. Jan. 1, 1956.

### § 387. Expense of Partition

Expense of partition of the estate of a decedent shall be paid by the distributees pro rata. The portion of the estate allotted each distributee shall be liable for his portion of such expense, and, if not paid, the court may order execution therefor in the names of the persons entitled thereto.

Acts 1955, 54th Leg., p. 88, ch. 55, eff. Jan. 1, 1956.

## PART 9.  PARTITION OF WARD'S ESTATE IN REALTY [REPEALED]

§ 388.  **Repealed by Acts 1993, 73rd Leg., ch. 957, § 75(4), eff. Sept. 1, 1993**

## PART 10.  INVESTMENTS, LOANS, AND CONTRIBUTIONS OF ESTATES OF WARDS

§ 389.  **Repealed by Acts 2003, 78th Leg., ch. 549, § 35, eff. Sept. 1, 2003**

§§ 389A to 398.  **Repealed by Acts 1993, 73rd Leg., ch. 957, § 75(4), eff. Sept. 1, 1993**

## PART 10A.  STOCKS, BONDS AND OTHER PERSONAL PROPERTY

§ 398A.  **Holding of Stocks, Bonds and Other Personal Property by Personal Representatives in Name of Nominee**

Unless otherwise provided by will, a personal representative may cause stocks, bonds, and other personal property of an estate to be registered and held in the name of a nominee without mention of the fiduciary relationship in any instrument or record constituting or evidencing title thereto. The personal representative is liable for the acts of the nominee with respect to any property so registered. The records of the personal representative shall at all times show the ownership of the property. Any property so registered shall be in the possession and control of the personal representative at all times and be kept separate from his individual property.

Added by Acts 1969, 61st Leg., p. 2106, ch. 719, § 1, eff. Sept. 1, 1969.

## PART 11.  ANNUAL ACCOUNTS AND OTHER EXHIBITS

§ 399.  **Annual Accounts Required**

**(a) Estates of Decedents Being Administered Under Order of Court.** The personal representative of the estate of a decedent being administered under order of court shall, upon the expiration of twelve (12) months from the date of qualification and receipt of letters, return to the court an exhibit in writing under oath setting forth a list of all claims against the estate that were presented to him within the period covered by the account, specifying which have been allowed by him, which have been paid, which have been rejected and the date when rejected, which have been sued upon, and the condition of the suit, and show:

(1) All property that has come to his knowledge or into his possession not previously listed or inventoried as property of the estate.

(2) Any changes in the property of the estate which have not been previously reported.

(3) A complete account of receipts and disbursements for the period covered by the account, and the source and nature thereof, with receipts of principal and income to be shown separately.

(4) A complete, accurate and detailed description of the property being administered, the condition of the property and the use being made thereof, and, if rented, the terms upon and the price for which rented.

(5) The cash balance on hand and the name and location of the depository wherein such balance is kept; also, any other sums of cash in savings accounts or other form, deposited subject to court order, and the name and location of the depository thereof.

(6) A detailed description of personal property of the estate, which shall, with respect to bonds, notes, and other securities, include the names of obligor and obligee, or if payable to bearer, so state; the date of issue and maturity; the rate of interest; serial or other identifying numbers; in what manner the property is secured; and other data necessary to identify the same fully, and how and where held for safekeeping.

(7) A statement that, during the period covered by the account, all tax returns due have been filed and that all taxes due and owing have been paid and a complete account of the amount of the taxes, the date the taxes were paid, and the governmental entity to which the taxes were paid.

(8) If any tax return due to be filed or any taxes due to be paid are delinquent on the filing of the account, a description of the delinquency and the reasons for the delinquency.

(9) A statement that the personal representative has paid all the required bond premiums for the accounting period.

**(b) Annual Reports Continue Until Estate Closed.** Each personal representative of the estate of a decedent shall continue to file annual accounts conforming to the essential requirements of those in Subsection (a) hereof as to changes in the assets of the estate after rendition of the former account so that the true condition of the estate, with respect to money, securities, and other property, can be ascertained by the court or by any interested person, by adding to the balances forward the receipts, and then subtracting the disbursements. The description of property sufficiently described in an inventory or previous account may be by reference thereto.

**(c) Supporting Vouchers, etc., Attached to Accounts.** Annexed to all annual accounts of representatives of estates shall be:

(1) Proper vouchers for each item of credit claimed in the account, or, in the absence of such voucher, the item must be supported by evidence satisfactory to the court. Original vouchers may, upon application, be returned to the representative after approval of his account.

(2) An official letter from the bank or other depository in which the money on hand of the estate is deposited, showing the amounts in general or special deposits.

(3) Proof of the existence and possession of securities owned by the estate, or shown by the accounting, as well as other assets held by a depository subject to orders of the court, the proof to be by one of the following means:

a. By an official letter from the bank or other depository wherein said securities or other assets are held for safekeeping; provided, that if such depository is the representative, the official letter shall be signed by a representative of such depository other than the one verifying the account; or

b. By a certificate of an authorized representative of the corporation which is surety on the representative's bonds; or

c. By a certificate of the clerk or a deputy clerk of a court of record in this State; or

d. By an affidavit of any other reputable person designated by the court upon request of the representative or other interested party.

Such certificate or affidavit shall be to the effect that the affiant has examined the assets exhibited to him by the representative as assets of the estate in which the accounting is made, and shall describe the assets by reference to the account or otherwise sufficiently to identify those so exhibited, and shall state the time when and the place where exhibited. In lieu of using a certificate or an affidavit, the representative may exhibit the securities to the judge of the court who shall endorse on the account, or include in his order with respect thereto, a statement that the securities shown therein as on hand were in fact exhibited to him, and that those so exhibited were the same as those shown in the account, or note any variance. If the securities are exhibited at any place other than where deposited for safekeeping, it shall be at the expense and risk of the representative. The court may require additional evidence as to the existence and custody of such securities and other personal property as in his discretion he shall deem proper; and may require the representative to exhibit them to the court, or any person designated by him, at any time at the place where held for safekeeping.

**(d) Verification of Account.** The representative filing the account shall attach thereto his affidavit that it contains a correct and complete statement of the matters to which it relates.

Acts 1955, 54th Leg., p. 88, ch. 55, eff. Jan. 1, 1956. Amended by Acts 1957, 55th Leg., p. 53, ch. 31, § 11(a); Acts 1993, 73rd Leg., ch. 712, § 4, eff. Sept. 1, 1993; Acts 1993, 73rd Leg., ch. 957, § 66, eff. Sept. 1, 1993; Acts 1997, 75th Leg., ch. 1403, § 1, eff. Sept. 1, 1997.

### § 400. Penalty for Failure to File Annual Account

Should any personal representative of an estate fail to return any annual account required by preceding sections of this Code, any person interested in said estate may, upon written complaint, or the court upon its own motion may, cause the personal representative to be cited to return such account, and show cause for such failure. If he fails to return said account after being so cited, or fails to show good cause for his failure so to do, the court, upon hearing, may revoke the letters of such representative, and may fine him in a sum not to exceed Five Hundred Dollars ($500). He and his sureties shall be liable for any fine imposed, and for all damages and costs sustained by reason of such failure, which may be recovered in any court of competent jurisdiction.

Acts 1955, 54th Leg., p. 88, ch. 55, eff. Jan. 1, 1956. Amended by Acts 1957, 55th Leg., p. 53, ch. 31, § 11(b); Acts 1993, 73rd Leg., ch. 957, § 67, eff. Sept. 1, 1993.

### § 401. Action Upon Annual Accounts

These rules shall govern the handling of annual accounts:

(a) They shall be filed with the county clerk, and the filing thereof shall be noted forthwith upon the judge's docket.

(b) Before being considered by the judge, the account shall remain on file ten (10) days.

(c) At any time after the expiration of ten (10) days after the filing of an annual account, the judge shall consider same, and may continue the hearing thereon until fully advised as to all items of said account.

(d) No accounting shall be approved unless possession of cash, listed securities, or other assets held in safekeeping or on deposit under order of court has been proved as required by law.

(e) If the account be found incorrect, it shall be corrected. When corrected to the satisfaction of the court, it shall be approved by an order of court, and the court shall then act with respect to unpaid claims, as follows:

(1) Order for Payment of Claims in Full. If it shall appear from the exhibit, or from other evidence, that the estate is wholly solvent, and that the representative has in his hands sufficient funds for the payment of every character of claims against the estate, the court shall order immediate payment to be made of all claims allowed and approved or established by judgment.

(2) Order for Pro Rata Payment of Claims. If it shall appear from the account, or from other evidence, that the funds on hand are not sufficient for the payment of all the said claims, or if the estate is insolvent and the personal representative has any funds on hand, the court shall order such funds to be applied to the payment of all claims having a preference in the order of their priority if they, or any of them, be still unpaid, and then to the payment pro rata of the other claims allowed and approved or established by final judgment, taking into consideration also the claims that were presented within twelve (12) months after the granting of administration, and those which are in suit or on which suit may yet be instituted.

Acts 1955, 54th Leg., p. 88, ch. 55, eff. Jan. 1, 1956. Amended by Acts 1957, 55th Leg., p. 53, ch. 31, § 11(c).

**Text of Texas Probate Code effective until January 1, 2014**

## § 402.  Additional Exhibits of Estates of Decedents

At any time after the expiration of fifteen months from the original grant of letters to an executor or administrator, any interested person may, by a complaint in writing filed in the court in which the estate is pending, cause the representative to be cited to appear and make an exhibit in writing under oath, setting forth fully, in connection with previous exhibits, the condition of the estate he represents; and, if it shall appear to the court by said exhibit, or by other evidence, that said representative has any funds of the estate in his hands subject to distribution among the creditors of the estate, the court shall order the same to be paid out to them according to the provisions of this Code; or any representative may voluntarily present such exhibit to the court; and, if he has any of the funds of the estate in his hands subject to distribution among the creditors of the estate, a like order shall be made.

Acts 1955, 54th Leg., p. 88, ch. 55, eff. Jan. 1, 1956.

## § 403.  Penalty for Failure to File Exhibits or Reports

Should any personal representative fail to file any exhibit or report required by this Code, any person interested in the estate may, upon written complaint filed with the clerk of the court, cause him to be cited to appear and show cause why he should not file such exhibit or report; and, upon hearing, the court may order him to file such exhibit or report, and, unless good cause be shown for such failure, the court may revoke the letters of such personal representative and may fine him in an amount not to exceed One Thousand Dollars.

Acts 1955, 54th Leg., p. 88, ch. 55, eff. Jan. 1, 1956.

### PART 12.  FINAL SETTLEMENT, ACCOUNTING, AND DISCHARGE

## § 404.  Closing Administration of Estates of Decedents

Administration of the estates of decedents shall be settled and closed when all the debts known to exist against the estate of a deceased person have been paid, or when they have been paid so far as the assets in the hands of an administrator or executor of such estate will permit, and when there is no further need for administration.

Acts 1955, 54th Leg., p. 88, ch. 55, eff. Jan. 1, 1956.  Amended by Acts 1975, 64th Leg., p. 104, ch. 45, § 2, eff. Sept. 1, 1975; Acts 1985, 69th Leg., ch. 881, § 2, eff. Aug. 26, 1985; Acts 1989, 71st Leg., ch. 1035, § 15, eff. Sept. 1, 1989; Acts 1993, 73rd Leg., ch. 712, § 5, eff. Sept. 1, 1993; Acts 1993, 73rd Leg., ch. 957, § 68, eff. Sept. 1, 1993; Acts 1999, 76th Leg., ch. 826, § 1, eff. June 18, 1999.

## §§ 404A, 404B.  Repealed by Acts 1993, 73rd Leg., ch. 957, § 75(1), eff. Sept. 1, 1993

## § 405.  Account for Final Settlement of Estates of Decedents

When administration of the estate of a decedent is to be settled and closed, the personal representative of such estate shall present to the court his verified account for final settlement.  In such account it shall be sufficient to refer to the inventory without describing each item of property in detail, and to refer to and adopt any and all proceedings had in the administration concerning sales, renting or hiring, leasing for mineral development, or any other transactions on behalf of the estate including exhibits, accounts, and vouchers previously filed and approved, without restating the particular items thereof.  Each final account, however, shall be accompanied by proper vouchers in support of each item thereof not already accounted for and shall show, either by reference to any proceedings authorized above or by statement of the facts:

1.   The property belonging to the estate which has come into the hands of the executor or administrator.

2.   The disposition that has been made of such property.

3.   The debts that have been paid.

4.   The debts and expenses, if any, still owing by the estate.

5.   The property of the estate, if any, still remaining on hand.

6.   The persons entitled to receive such estate, their relationship to the decedent, and their residence, if known, and whether adults or minors, and, if minors, the names of their guardians, if any.

7.   All advancements or payments that have been made, if any, by the executor or administrator from such estate to any such person.

8.   The tax returns due that have been filed and the taxes due and owing that have been paid and a complete account of the amount of taxes, the date the taxes were paid, and the governmental entity to which the taxes were paid.

9.   If any tax return due to be filed or any taxes due to be paid are delinquent on the filing of the account, a description of the delinquency and the reasons for the delinquency.

10.   The personal representative has paid all required bond premiums.

Acts 1955, 54th Leg., p. 88, ch. 55, eff. Jan. 1, 1956.  Amended by Acts 1993, 73rd Leg., ch. 712, § 6, eff. Sept. 1, 1993; Acts 1993, 73rd Leg., ch. 957, § 69, eff. Sept. 1, 1993; Acts 1997, 75th Leg., ch. 1403, § 2, eff. Sept. 1, 1997.

## § 405A.  Delivery of Property

The court may permit a resident executor or administrator who has any of the estate of a ward to deliver the estate to a duly qualified and acting guardian of the ward.

Added by Acts 1995, 74th Leg., ch. 1039, § 14, eff. Sept. 1, 1995.

## § 406.  Procedure in Case of Neglect or Failure to File Final Account; Payments Due Meantime

(a) If a personal representative charged with the duty of filing a final account fails or neglects so to do at the proper time, the court shall, upon its own motion, or upon the written complaint of any one interested in the decedent's estate which has been administered, cause such representative to be cited to appear and present such account within the time specified in the citation.

(b) If the whereabouts of the personal representative and heirs of a decedent are unknown and a complaint has not been filed by anyone interested in the decedent's estate, the court may, on or after the fourth anniversary after the last date on which letters testamentary or of administration are issued by the court clerk, close the estate without a final accounting and without appointing a successor personal representative.

Acts 1955, 54th Leg., p. 88, ch. 55, eff. Jan. 1, 1956. Amended by Acts 1979, 66th Leg., p. 1876, ch. 758, § 3, eff. Aug. 27, 1979; Acts 1993, 73rd Leg., ch. 898, § 1, eff. June 19, 1993; Acts 1993, 73rd Leg., ch. 957, § 70, eff. Sept. 1, 1993; Acts 1999, 76th Leg., ch. 827, § 1, eff. Sept. 1, 1999.

### § 407. Citation Upon Presentation of Account for Final Settlement

Upon the filing of an account for final settlement by temporary or permanent personal representatives of the estates of decedents, citation shall contain a statement that such final account has been filed, the time and place when it will be considered by the court, and a statement requiring the person or persons cited to appear and contest the same if they see proper. Such citation shall be issued by the county clerk to the persons and in the manner set out below.

1. In case of the estates of deceased persons, notice shall be given by the personal representative to each heir or beneficiary of the decedent by certified mail, return receipt requested, unless another type of notice is directed by the court by written order. The notice must include a copy of the account for final settlement.

2. If the court deems further additional notice necessary, it shall require the same by written order. In its discretion, the court may allow the waiver of notice of an account for final settlement in a proceeding concerning a decedent's estate.

Acts 1955, 54th Leg., p. 88, ch. 55, eff. Jan. 1, 1956. Amended by Acts 1959, 56th Leg., p. 641, ch. 294, § 1, eff. May 30, 1959; Acts 1979, 66th Leg., p. 1755, ch. 713, § 30, eff. Aug. 27, 1979; Acts 1983, 68th Leg., p. 4558, ch. 756, § 1, eff. Sept. 1, 1983; Acts 1993, 73rd Leg., ch. 957, § 71, eff. Sept. 1, 1993.

### § 408. Action of the Court

(a) **Action Upon Account.** Upon being satisfied that citation has been duly served upon all persons interested in the estate, the court shall examine the account for final settlement and the vouchers accompanying the same, and, after hearing all exceptions or objections thereto, and evidence in support of or against such account, shall audit and settle the same, and restate it if that be necessary.

(b) **Distribution of Remaining Property.** Upon final settlement of an estate, if there be any of such estate remaining in the hands of the personal representative, the court shall order that a partition and distribution be made among the persons entitled to receive such estate.

(c) **Discharge of Representative When No Property Remains.** If, upon such settlement, there be none of the estate remaining in the hands of the representative, he shall be discharged from his trust and the estate ordered closed.

(d) **Discharge When Estate Fully Administered.** Whenever the representative of an estate has fully administered the same in accordance with this Code and the orders of the court, and his final account has been approved, and he has delivered all of said estate remaining in his hands to the person or persons entitled to receive the same, it shall be the duty of the court to enter an order discharging such representative from his trust, and declaring the estate closed.

Acts 1955, 54th Leg., p. 88, ch. 55, eff. Jan. 1, 1956. Amended by Acts 1979, 66th Leg., p. 1877, ch. 758, § 4, eff. Aug. 27, 1979; Acts 1993, 73rd Leg., ch. 957, § 72, eff. Sept. 1, 1993.

### § 409. Money Becoming Due Pending Final Discharge

Until the order of final discharge of the personal representative is entered in the judge's probate docket, money or other thing of value falling due to the estate while the account for final settlement is pending may be paid, delivered, or tendered to the personal representative, who shall issue receipt therefor, and the obligor and/or payor shall be thereby discharged of the obligation for all purposes.

Acts 1955, 54th Leg., p. 88, ch. 55, eff. Jan. 1, 1956. Amended by Acts 1993, 73rd Leg., ch. 957, § 73, eff. Sept. 1, 1993; Acts 2009, 81st Leg., ch. 602, § 10, eff. June 19, 2009.

### § 410. Inheritance Taxes Must be Paid

No final account of an executor or administrator shall be approved, and no estate of a decedent shall be closed, unless the final account shows, and the court finds, that all inheritance taxes due and owing to the State of Texas with respect to all interests and properties passing through the hands of the representative have been paid.

Acts 1955, 54th Leg., p. 88, ch. 55, eff. Jan. 1, 1956. Amended by Acts 1989, 71st Leg., ch. 1035, § 16, eff. Sept. 1, 1989.

### § 411. Repealed by Acts 1993, 73rd Leg., ch. 957, § 75(1), eff. Sept. 1, 1993

### § 412. Offsets, Credits, and Bad Debts

In the settlement of any of the accounts of the personal representative of an estate, all debts due the estate which the court is satisfied could not have been collected by due diligence, and which have not been collected, shall be excluded from the computation.

Acts 1955, 54th Leg., p. 88, ch. 55, eff. Jan. 1, 1956.

### § 413. Repealed by Acts 1993, 73rd Leg., ch. 957, § 75(1), eff. Sept. 1, 1993

### § 414. Procedure if Representative Fails to Deliver Estate

If any personal representative of an estate, upon final settlement, shall neglect to deliver to the person entitled thereto when demanded any portion of an estate or any funds or money in his hands ordered to be delivered, such person may file with the clerk of the court his written complaint alleging the fact of such neglect, the date of his demand, and other relevant facts, whereupon the clerk shall issue a citation to be served personally upon such representative, apprising him of the complaint and citing him to appear before the court and answer, if he so desires, at the time designated in the citation. If at the hearing the court finds that the citation was duly served and returned and that the representative is guilty of the neglect charged, the court shall enter an order to that effect, and the representative shall be liable to such person in damages at the rate of ten per cent of the amount or appraised value of the money or estate so withheld, per month, for each and every month or fraction thereof that said estate or money or funds is and/or has been so withheld after date of demand, which damages may be recovered in any court of competent jurisdiction.

Acts 1955, 54th Leg., p. 88, ch. 55, eff. Jan. 1, 1956. Amended by Acts 1993, 73rd Leg., ch. 957, § 74, eff. Sept. 1, 1993.

## CHAPTER IX

## SPECIFIC PROVISIONS RELATING TO PERSONS OF UNSOUND MIND AND HABITUAL DRUNKARDS [REPEALED]

**§§ 415 to 426.   Repealed by Acts 1993, 73rd Leg., ch. 905, § 17, eff. Sept. 1, 1993; Acts 1993, 73rd Leg., ch. 957, § 75(5), eff. Sept. 1, 1993**

## CHAPTER X

## PAYMENT OF ESTATES INTO STATE TREASURY

## § 427.   When Estates to Be Paid Into State Treasury

If any person entitled to a portion of an estate, except a resident minor without a guardian, shall not demand his portion from the executor or administrator within six months after an order of court approving the report of commissioners of partition, or within six months after the settlement of the final account of an executor or administrator, as the case may be, the court by written order shall require the executor or administrator to pay so much of said portion as is in money to the comptroller; and such portion as is in other property he shall order the executor or administrator to sell on such terms as the court thinks best, and, when the proceeds of such sale are collected, the court shall order the same to be paid to the comptroller, in all such cases allowing

the executor or administrator reasonable compensation for his services.   A suit to recover proceeds of the sale is governed by Section 433 of this Code.

Acts 1955, 54th Leg., p. 88, ch. 55, eff. Jan. 1, 1956. Amended by Acts 1991, 72nd Leg., ch. 153, § 27, eff. Sept. 1, 1991; Acts 1997, 75th Leg., ch. 1423, § 15.01, eff. Sept. 1, 1997.

## § 428.   Indispensability of Comptroller as Party

The comptroller is an indispensable party to any judicial or administrative proceeding concerning the disposition and handling of any portion of an estate that is or may be payable to the comptroller under Section 427 of this Code. Whenever an order shall be made by the court for an executor or administrator to pay any funds to the comptroller under Section 427 of this Code, the clerk of the court in which such order is made shall serve on the comptroller by personal service of citation a certified copy of such order within five days after the same has been made.

Acts 1955, 54th Leg., p. 88, ch. 55, eff. Jan. 1, 1956. Amended by Acts 1991, 72nd Leg., ch. 153, § 27, eff. Sept. 1, 1991; Acts 1997, 75th Leg., ch. 1423, § 15.02, eff. Sept. 1, 1997.

## § 429.   Penalty for Neglect to Notify Comptroller

Any clerk who shall neglect to have served on the comptroller by personal citation a certified copy of any such order within the time prescribed by Section 428 of this Code shall be liable in a penalty of One Hundred Dollars, to be recovered in an action in the name of the state, after personal service of citation, on the information of any citizen, one-half of which penalty shall be paid to the informer and the other one-half to the state.

Acts 1955, 54th Leg., p. 88, ch. 55, eff. Jan. 1, 1956. Amended by Acts 1991, 72nd Leg., ch. 153, § 27, eff. Sept. 1, 1991; Acts 1997, 75th Leg., ch. 1423, § 15.03, eff. Sept. 1, 1997.

## § 430.   Receipt of Comptroller

Whenever an executor or administrator pays the comptroller any funds of the estate he represents, under the preceding provisions of this Code, he shall take from the comptroller a receipt for such payment, with official seal attached, and shall file the same with the clerk of the court ordering such payment; and such receipt shall be recorded in the judge's probate docket.

Acts 1955, 54th Leg., p. 88, ch. 55, eff. Jan. 1, 1956. Amended by Acts 1997, 75th Leg., ch. 1423, § 15.04, eff. Sept. 1, 1997; Acts 2009, 81st Leg., ch. 602, § 11, eff. June 19, 2009.

## § 431.   Penalty for Failure to Make Payments to Comptroller

When an executor or administrator fails to pay to the comptroller any funds of an estate which he has been ordered by the court so to pay, within 30 days after such order has been made, such executor or administrator shall, after personal service of citation charging such failure and after proof thereof, be liable to pay out of his own estate to the comptroller damages thereon at the rate of five per cent per month for each month, or fraction thereof, that he fails to make such payment after 30 days from such order, which damages may be recovered in any court of competent jurisdiction.

Acts 1955, 54th Leg., p. 88, ch. 55, eff. Jan. 1, 1956. Amended by Acts 1991, 72nd Leg., ch. 153, § 28, eff. Sept. 1, 1991; Acts 1997, 75th Leg., ch. 1423, § 15.05, eff. Sept. 1, 1997.

### § 432. Comptroller May Enforce Payment and Collect Damages.

The Comptroller shall have the right in the name of the state to apply to the court in which the order for payment was made to enforce the payment of funds which the executor or administrator has failed to pay to him pursuant to order of court, together with the payment of any damages that shall have accrued under the provisions of the preceding section of this code, and the court shall enforce such payment in like manner as other orders of payment are required to be enforced. The comptroller shall also have the right to institute suit in the name of the state against such executor or administrator, and the sureties on his bond, for the recovery of the funds so ordered to be paid and such damages as have accrued. The county attorney or criminal district attorney of the county, the district attorney of the district, or the attorney general, at the election of the comptroller and with the approval of the attorney general, shall represent the comptroller in all such proceedings, and shall also represent the interests of the state in all other matters arising under any provisions of this Code.

Acts 1955, 54th Leg., p. 88, ch. 55, eff. Jan. 1, 1956. Amended by Acts 1991, 72nd Leg., ch. 153, § 28, eff. Sept. 1, 1991; Acts 1997, 75th Leg., ch. 1423, § 15.06, eff. Sept. 1, 1997.

### § 433. Suit for the Recovery of Funds Paid to the Comptroller

(a) Mode of Recovery. When funds of an estate have been paid to the comptroller, any heir, devisee, or legatee of the estate, or their assigns, or any of them, may recover the portion of such funds to which he, she, or they are entitled. The person claiming such funds shall institute suit on or before the fourth anniversary of the date of the order requiring payment to the comptroller, by petition filed in the district court of Travis County, against the comptroller, setting forth the plaintiff's right to such funds, and the amount claimed by him.

(b) Citation. Upon the filing of such petition, the clerk shall issue a citation for the comptroller, to be served by personal service, to appear and represent the interest of the state in such suit. As the comptroller elects and with the approval of the attorney general, the attorney general, the county attorney or criminal district attorney for the county, or the district attorney for the district shall represent the comptroller.

(c) Procedure. The proceedings in such suit shall be governed by the rules for other civil suits; and, should the plaintiff establish his right to the funds claimed, he shall have a judgment therefor, which shall specify the amount to which

he is entitled; and a certified copy of such judgment shall be sufficient authority for the comptroller to pay the same.

(d) Costs. The costs of any such suit shall in all cases be adjudged against the plaintiff, and he may be required to secure the costs.

Acts 1955, 54th Leg., p. 88, ch. 55, eff. Jan. 1, 1956. Amended by Acts 1991, 72nd Leg., ch. 153, § 29, eff. Sept. 1, 1991; Acts 1997, 75th Leg., ch. 1423, § 15.07, eff. Sept. 1, 1997.

### REPEAL OF LAWS—EMERGENCY CLAUSE

### § 434. Repeal of Laws Supplanted by This Code

The following statutes and laws of this State are supplanted by the provisions of this Code and are hereby repealed:

(a) Title 48 of the Revised Civil Statutes of Texas of 1925, as amended, and all Articles contained in said Title, as said Articles are amended; [1] Article 932 of the Revised Civil Statutes of Texas of 1925; [2] and Chapter 196, Acts of the 52nd Legislature (1951), page 322; [3] and

(b) Title 129 of the Revised Civil Statutes of Texas of 1925, as amended, and all Articles contained in said Title, as said Articles are amended; [4] and

(1) Sections 1 and 2 of Chapter 196, Acts of the 42nd Legislature (1931), page 329; [5] and

(2) Section 1 of Chapter 297, Acts of the 49th Legislature (1945), page 469; [6] and

(3) Sections 1 and 2 of Chapter 170, Acts of the 50th Legislature (1947), page 275; [7] and

(4) Section 1 of Chapter 120, Acts of the 51st Legislature (1949), page 218; [8] and

(c) Title 54 of the Revised Civil Statutes of Texas of 1925, as amended, and all Articles contained in said Title, as said Articles are amended; [9] and

(1) Acts of the 39th Legislature (1925), Section 1 of Chapter 82, page 253; [10] and

(2) Acts of the 40th Legislature (1927): Section 1 of Chapter 50, page 74; [11] Sections 1, 2 and 3 of Chapter 81, page 123; [12] Section 1 of Chapter 92, page 142; [13] Section 1 of Chapter 152, page 223; [14] and Section 1 of Chapter 244, page 362; [15] and

(3) Acts of the 41st Legislature (1929): Sections 1 and 2 of Chapter 29, page 63; [16] Section 1 of Chapter 63, page 130; [17] Section 2 of Chapter 100, page 235; [18] Section 1 of Chapter 132; page 288; [19] and Section 1 of Chapter 48, First Called Session, page 107; [20] and

(4) Acts of the 42nd Legislature (1931): Chapter 52, page 79; [21] Section 1 of Chapter 59, page 93; [22] Chapter 123, page 210; [20] Section 1 of Chapter 234, page 389; [23] Section 1 of

Chapter 235, page 390; [24] Section 1 of Chapter 236, page 391; [25] and Section 1 of Chapter 35a, page 842; [26] and

(5) Acts of the 43rd Legislature, Third Called Session (1934): Section 1 of Chapter 25, page 48; [27] and

(6) Acts of the 44th Legislature (1935): Section 1 of Chapter 247, page 634; [28] Section 1 of Chapter 248, page 635; [18] Section 1 of Chapter 250, page 637; [29] Section 1 of Chapter 251, page 638; [30] Section 1 of Chapter 252, page 638; [31] Section 1 of Chapter 253, page 639; [32] Section 1 of Chapter 266, page 654; [33] Section 1 of Chapter 272, page 658; [34] Section 1 of Chapter 273, page 659; [35] Sections 1 and 2 of Chapter 277, page 662; [36] Section 1 of Chapter 278, page 664; [37] Section 1 of Chapter 280, page 665; [38] and Chapter 446, Second Called Session, page 1729; [39] and

(7) Acts of the 45th Legislature (1937): Section 1 of Chapter 193, page 391; [40] and Section 1 of Chapter 250, page 499; [41] and

(8) Acts of the 46th Legislature (1939): H.B.No.656, page 318; [42] H.B.No.158, page 319; [35] H.B.No.31, page 320; [43] and S.B.No.141, page 321; [44] and

(9) Acts of the 47th Legislature (1941): Section 1 of Chapter 382, page 633; [45] and Chapter 521, page 845; [46] and

(10) Acts of the 48th Legislature (1943): Section 1 of Chapter 234, page 356; [47] and

(11) Acts of the 49th Legislature (1945): Section 1 of Chapter 214, page 296; [48] Section 1 of Chapter 296, page 468; [49] Section 2 of Chapter 297, page 469; [50] and Sections 1 and 2 of Chapter 316, page 525; [16] and

(12) Acts of the 50th Legislature (1947): Section 1 of Chapter 401, page 942; [51] and

(13) Acts of the 52nd Legislature (1951): Chapter 37, page 62; [52] and

(d) Title 69 of the Revised Civil Statutes of Texas of 1925, as amended, and all Articles contained in said Title, as said Articles are amended; [53] and

(1) Acts of the 39th Legislature (1925): Section 1 of Chapter 156, page 367; [54] and Section 1 of Chapter 134, page 338; [55] and

(2) Acts of the 40th Legislature (1927): Section 1 of Chapter 16, page 22; [56] Section 2 of Chapter 31, page 43; [57] Section 1 of Chapter 164, page 237; [58] and Sections 1, 2 and 3 of Chapter 179, page 257; [59] and

(3) Acts of the 41st Legislature (1929): Section 1 of Chapter 31, page 65; [60] Chapter 126, page 281; [61] Sections 1 and 2 of Chapter 127, page 282; [62] Sections 1 and 2 of Chapter 128, page 283; [63] Sections 1 and 2 of Chapter 129, page 284; [64] Sections 1 and 2 of Chapter 130, page 285; [65] Sections 1, 2, 3, 4, 5 and 6 of Chapter 131, page 286; [66] Section 1 of Chapter 133, page 289; [67] and Chapter 305, page 684; [68] and

(4) Acts of the 42nd Legislature (1931): Section 1 of Chapter 237, page 392; [69] and

(5) Acts of the 43rd Legislature (1933): Chapter 47, page 93; [70] Chapter 239, page 838; [71] and Section 1 of Chapter 26, Third Called Session (1934), page 49; [57] and

(6) Acts of the 44th Legislature (1935): Section 1 of Chapter 13, page 5; [72] Section 1 of Chapter 79, page 196; [73] Section 1 of Chapter 84, page 206; [74] Section 1 of Chapter 254, page 640; [75] Section 1 of Chapter 279, page 664; [76] and

(7) Acts of the 45th Legislature (1937): Chapter 289, page 579; [77] Chapter 336, page 673; [68] Sections 1 and 2 of Chapter 27, First Called Session, page 1803; [78] and Section 1 of Chapter 54, Second Called Session, page 1964; [68] and

(8) Acts of the 46th Legislature (1939): S.B.No.189, page 340; [54] and

(9) Acts of the 47th Legislature (1941): Section 3 of Chapter 303, page 480; [79] and Sections 1, 2, 3, 4, 5, 6 and 7 of Chapter 541, page 867; [80] and

(10) Acts of the 48th Legislature (1943): Section 1 of Chapter 56, page 65; [68] Chapter 281, page 414; [81] and Section 1 of Chapter 378, page 684; [82] and

(11) Acts of the 49th Legislature (1945): Sections 3, 4 and 5 of Chapter 316, page 525; [83] and

(12) Acts of the 50th Legislature (1947): Section 1 of Chapter 39, page 51; [81] and Section 1 of Chapter 256, page 453; [84] and

(13) Acts of the 51st Legislature (1949): Section 1 of Chapter 499, page 923; [85] Section 1 of Chapter 556, page 1093; [86] Chapter 456, page 842; [87] and Section 3 of Chapter 259, page 447; [88] and

(14) Acts of the 52nd Legislature (1951): Section 1 of Chapter 34, page 56.[58]

(15) Acts of the 53rd Legislature (1953): Section 1 of Chapter 70, page 104.[89]

Acts 1955, 54th Leg., p. 88, ch. 55, eff. Jan. 1, 1956.

[1] Vernon's Ann.Civ.St. arts. 2570 to 2583.
[2] Vernon's Ann.Civ.St. art. 932.
[3] Vernon's Ann.Civ.St. art. 2583a.
[4] Vernon's Ann.Civ.St. arts. 8281 to 8305.
[5] Vernon's Ann.Civ.St. arts. 8291, 8292.
[6] Vernon's Ann.Civ.St. art. 8281.
[7] Vernon's Ann.Civ.St. arts. 8283, 8284.
[8] Vernon's Ann.Civ.St. art. 8293.
[9] Vernon's Ann.Civ.St. arts. 3290 to 3703.
[10] Vernon's Ann.Civ.St. art. 3678.
[11] Vernon's Ann.Civ.St. art. 3654.
[12] Vernon's Ann.Civ.St. arts. 3334, 3334a, 3336.
[13] Vernon's Ann.Civ.St. art. 3351.
[14] Vernon's Ann.Civ.St. art. 3386.
[15] Vernon's Ann.Civ.St. art. 3597a.
[16] Vernon's Ann.Civ.St. arts. 3386, 3576.
[17] Vernon's Ann.Civ.St. art. 3393a.
[18] Vernon's Ann.Civ.St. art. 3334.
[19] Vernon's Ann.Civ.St. art. 3325.
[20] Vernon's Ann.Civ.St. art. 3310a.
[21] Vernon's Ann.Civ.St. art. 3515a.
[22] Vernon's Ann.Civ.St. art. 3293–A.

[23] Vernon's Ann.Civ.St. art. 3531.

[24] Vernon's Ann.Civ.St. art. 3690.

[25] Vernon's Ann.Civ.St. art. 3492.

[26] Probably should read: "and Section 1 of Chapter 352, page 842". Vernon's Ann.Civ.St. art. 3432a.

[27] Vernon's Ann.Civ.St. art. 3369.

[28] Vernon's Ann.Civ.St. art. 3311.

[29] Vernon's Ann.Civ.St. art. 3576.

[30] Vernon's Ann.Civ.St. art. 3321.

[31] Vernon's Ann.Civ.St. art. 3420.

[32] Vernon's Ann.Civ.St. art. 3476.

[33] Vernon's Ann.Civ.St. art. 3396.

[34] Vernon's Ann.Civ.St. art. 3337.

[35] Vernon's Ann.Civ.St. art. 3336.

[36] Vernon's Ann.Civ.St. arts. 3430, 3576 note.

[37] Vernon's Ann.Civ.St. art. 3417.

[38] Vernon's Ann.Civ.St. art. 3317.

[39] Vernon's Ann.Civ.St. arts. 3456A to 3456I.

[40] Vernon's Ann.Civ.St. arts. 3410–a, 3410–b.

[41] Vernon's Ann.Civ.St. art. 3605.

[42] Vernon's Ann.Civ.St. art. 3334b.

[43] Vernon's Ann.Civ.St. art. 3370.

[44] Vernon's Ann.Civ.St. arts. 3393a, 3396.

[45] Vernon's Ann.Civ.St. art. 3432b.

[46] Vernon's Ann.Civ.St. arts. 3333a, 3333a note.

[47] Vernon's Ann.Civ.St. art. 3554a.

[48] Vernon's Ann.Civ.St. art. 3310b.

[49] Vernon's Ann.Civ.St. art. 3344.

[50] Vernon's Ann.Civ.St. art. 3348.

[51] Vernon's Ann.Civ.St. art. 3683a.

[52] Vernon's Ann.Civ.St. art. 3582a.

[53] Vernon's Ann.Civ.St. arts. 4102 to 4329.

[54] Vernon's Ann.Civ.St. art. 4225.

[55] Vernon's Ann.Civ.St. arts. 4195, 4196.

[56] Vernon's Ann.Civ.St. art. 4231.

[57] Vernon's Ann.Civ.St. art. 4195a.

[58] Vernon's Ann.Civ.St. art. 4192.

[59] Vernon's Ann.Civ.St. arts. 4102, 4111, 4123.

[60] Vernon's Ann.Civ.St. art. 4111.

[61] Vernon's Ann.Civ.St. art. 4227a.

[62] Vernon's Ann.Civ.St. art. 4233.

[63] Vernon's Ann.Civ.St. art. 4143.

[64] Vernon's Ann.Civ.St. art. 4234.

[65] Vernon's Ann.Civ.St. art. 4148.

[66] Vernon's Ann.Civ.St. arts. 4282 to 4284.

[67] Vernon's Ann.Civ.St. art. 4142.

[68] Vernon's Ann.Civ.St. art. 4180.

[69] Vernon's Ann.Civ.St. art. 4200.

[70] Probably should read: "Chapter 47, page 96". Vernon's Ann.Civ.St. art. 4295a.

[71] Vernon's Ann.Civ.St. art. 4223a.

[72] Probably should read: "Section 1 of Chapter 13, page 35". Vernon's Ann.Civ.St. art. 4204.

[73] Vernon's Ann.Civ.St. art. 4216.

[74] Vernon's Ann.Civ.St. art. 4201.

[75] Vernon's Ann.Civ.St. art. 4115.

[76] Vernon's Ann.Civ.St. art. 4291.

[77] Vernon's Ann.Civ.St. art. 4112a.

[78] Vernon's Ann.Civ.St. arts. 4285, 4286.

[79] Vernon's Ann.Civ.St. art. 4203.

[80] Vernon's Ann.Civ.St. arts. 4113, 4114, 4116, 4117, 4121 to 4123, 4128, 4228, 4229, 4272, 4123a, 4123a–1.

[81] Vernon's Ann.Civ.St. art. 4296.

[82] Vernon's Ann.Civ.St. arts. 4201, 4216.

[83] Vernon's Ann.Civ.St. arts. 4141, 4201, 4216.

[84] Vernon's Ann.Civ.St. art. 4141.

[85] Vernon's Ann.Civ.St. art. 4123a–1.

[86] Vernon's Ann.Civ.St. art. 4168.

[87] Probably should read "Chapter 458, page 842". Vernon's Ann.Civ.St. art. 4192b.

[88] Probably should read "Section 3 of Chapter 259, page 477". Vernon's Ann.Civ.St. art. 6008b, § 3.

[89] Vernon's Ann.Civ.St. art. 4285.

## § 435.  Emergency Clause

The need for revision of the probate statutes of this state creates an emergency and an imperative public necessity that the Constitutional Rule requiring bills to be read on three several days in each House be suspended, and said Rule is hereby suspended, and this Act shall take effect and be in force from and after its passage, and it is so enacted.

Acts 1955, 54th Leg., p. 88, ch. 55, eff. Jan. 1, 1956.

## CHAPTER XI

## NONTESTAMENTARY TRANSFERS

PART 1.  MULTIPLE–PARTY ACCOUNTS

**Text of Texas Probate Code effective until January 1, 2014**

## PART 1. MULTIPLE–PARTY ACCOUNTS

### § 436. Definitions

In this part:

(1) "Account" means a contract of deposit of funds between a depositor and a financial institution, and includes a checking account, savings account, certificate of deposit, share account, and other like arrangement.

(2) "Beneficiary" means a person named in a trust account as one for whom a party to the account is named as trustee.

(2–a) "Charitable organization" means any corporation, community chest, fund, or foundation that is exempt from federal income tax under Section 501(a) of the Internal Revenue Code of 1986 by being listed as an exempt organization in Section 501(c)(3) of that code.

(3) "Financial institution" means an organization authorized to do business under state or federal laws relating to financial institutions, including, without limitation, banks and trust companies, savings banks, building and loan associations, savings and loan companies or associations, credit unions, and brokerage firms that deal in the sales and purchases of stocks, bonds, and other types of securities.

(4) "Joint account" means an account payable on request to one or more of two or more parties whether or not there is a right of survivorship.

(5) "Multiple-party account" means a joint account, a convenience account, a P.O.D. account, or a trust account. It does not include accounts established for deposit of funds of a partnership, joint venture, or other association for business purposes, or accounts controlled by one or more persons as the duly authorized agent or trustee for a corporation, unincorporated association, charitable or civic organization, or a regular fiduciary or trust account where the relationship is established other than by deposit agreement.

(6) "Net contribution" of a party to a joint account as of any given time is the sum of all deposits made to that account by or for him, less all withdrawals made by or for him which have not been paid to or applied to the use of any other party, plus a pro rata share of any interest or dividends included in the current balance. The term includes, in addition, any proceeds of deposit life insurance added to the account by reason of the death of the party whose net contribution is in question.

(7) "Party" means a person who, by the terms of the account, has a present right, subject to request, to payment from a multiple-party account. A P.O.D. payee, including a charitable organization, or beneficiary of a trust account is a party only after the account becomes payable to the P.O.D payee or beneficiary by reason of the P.O.D payee or beneficiary surviving the original payee or trustee. Unless the context otherwise requires, it includes a guardian, personal representative, or assignee, including an attaching creditor, of a party. It also includes a person identified as a trustee of an account for another whether or not a beneficiary is named, but it does not include a named beneficiary unless the beneficiary has a present right of withdrawal.

(8) "Payment" of sums on deposit includes withdrawal, payment on check or other directive of a party, and any pledge of sums on deposit by a party and any set-off, or reduction or other disposition of all or part of an account pursuant to a pledge.

(9) "Proof of death" includes a certified copy of a death certificate or the judgment or order of a court in a proceeding where the death of a person is proved by circumstantial evidence to the satisfaction of the court as provided by Section 72 of this code.

(10) "P.O.D. account" means an account payable on request to one person during lifetime and on his death to one or more P.O.D. payees, or to one or more persons during their lifetimes and on the death of all of them to one or more P.O.D. payees.

(11) "P.O.D. payee" means a person or charitable organization designated on a P.O.D. account as one to whom the account is payable on request after the death of one or more persons.

(12) "Request" means a proper request for withdrawal, or a check or order for payment, which complies with all conditions of the account, including special requirements concerning necessary signatures and regulations of the financial institution, but if the financial institution conditions withdrawal or payment on advance notice, for purposes of this part the request for withdrawal or payment is treated as immediately effective and a notice of intent to withdraw is treated as a request for withdrawal.

(13) "Sums on deposit" means the balance payable on a multiple-party account including interest, dividends, and in addition any deposit life insurance proceeds added to the account by reason of the death of a party.

(14) "Trust account" means an account in the name of one or more parties as trustee for one or more beneficiaries where the relationship is established by the form of the account and the deposit agreement with the financial institution and there is no subject of the trust other than the sums on deposit in the account. It is not essential that payment to the beneficiary be mentioned in the deposit agreement. A trust account does not include a regular trust account under a testamentary trust or a trust agreement which has significance apart from the account, or a fiduciary account arising from a fiduciary relation such as attorney-client.

(15) "Withdrawal" includes payment to a third person pursuant to check or other directive of a party.

Added by Acts 1979, 66th Leg., p. 1756, ch. 713, § 31, eff. Aug. 27, 1979. Amended by Acts 1993, 73rd Leg., ch. 846, § 25, eff. Sept. 1, 1993; Subds. (7) and (11) amended by and subd. (2–a) added by Acts 2011, 82nd Leg., ch. 1338 (S.B. 1198), § 1.36, eff. Sept. 1, 2011.

### § 437. Ownership as Between Parties and Others

The provisions of Sections 438 through 440 of this code that concern beneficial ownership as between parties, or as between parties and P.O.D. payees or beneficiaries of multiple-party accounts, are relevant only to controversies between these persons and their creditors and other successors, and have no bearing on the power of withdrawal of these persons as determined by the terms of account contracts.

Added by Acts 1979, 66th Leg., p. 1756, ch. 713, § 31, eff. Aug. 27, 1979. Amended by Acts 1981, 67th Leg., p. 895, ch. 319, § 2, eff. Sept. 1, 1981.

## § 438. Ownership During Lifetime

(a) A joint account belongs, during the lifetime of all parties, to the parties in proportion to the net contributions by each to the sums on deposit, unless there is clear and convincing evidence of a different intent.

(b) A P.O.D. account belongs to the original payee during his lifetime and not to the P.O.D. payee or payees. If two or more parties are named as original payees, during their lifetimes rights as between them are governed by Subsection (a) of this section.

(c) Unless a contrary intent is manifested by the terms of the account or the deposit agreement or there is other clear and convincing evidence of an irrevocable trust, a trust account belongs beneficially to the trustee during his lifetime, and if two or more parties are named as trustee on the account, during their lifetimes beneficial rights as between them are governed by Subsection (a) of this section. If there is an irrevocable trust, the account belongs beneficially to the beneficiary.

Added by Acts 1979, 66th Leg., p. 1756, ch. 713, § 31, eff. Aug. 27, 1979.

## § 438A. Convenience Account

(a) If an account is established at a financial institution by one or more parties in the names of the parties and one or more convenience signers and the terms of the account provide that the sums on deposit are paid or delivered to the parties or to the convenience signers "for the convenience" of the parties, the account is a convenience account.

(b) The making of a deposit in a convenience account does not affect the title to the deposit.

(c) A party to a convenience account is not considered to have made a gift of the deposit or of any additions or accruals to the deposit to a convenience signer.

(d) On the death of the last surviving party, a convenience signer shall have no right of survivorship in the account and ownership of the account remains in the estate of the last surviving party.

(e) If an addition is made to the account by anyone other than a party, the addition and accruals to the addition are considered to have been made by a party.

(f) All deposits to a convenience account and additions and accruals to the deposits may be paid to a party or to a convenience signer. The financial institution is completely released from liability for a payment made from the account before the financial institution receives notice in writing signed by a party not to make the payment in accordance with the terms of the account. After receipt of the notice from a party, the financial institution may require a party to approve any further payments from the account.

(g) If the financial institution makes a payment of the sums on deposit in a convenience account to a convenience signer after the death of the last surviving party and before the financial institution has received written notice of the last surviving party's death, the financial institution is completely released from liability for the payment. If a financial institution makes payment to the personal representative of the deceased last surviving party's estate after the death of the last surviving party and before service on the financial institution of a court order prohibiting payment, the financial institution is released to the extent of the payment from liability to any person claiming a right to the funds. The receipt by the representative to whom payment is made is a complete release and discharge of the financial institution.

Added by Acts 1993, 73rd Leg., ch. 795, § 1, eff. Aug. 30, 1993; Acts 1993, 73rd Leg., ch. 846, § 27, eff. Sept. 1, 1993.
Subsecs. (a) and (c) to (g) amended by Acts 2003, 78th Leg., ch. 658, § 1, eff. Sept. 1, 2003.

## § 438B. Convenience Signer on Other Accounts

(a) An account established by one or more parties at a financial institution that is not designated as a convenience account, but is instead designated as a single-party account or another type of multiple-party account, may provide that the sums on deposit may be paid or delivered to the parties or to one or more convenience signers "for the convenience of the parties."

(b) Except as provided by Subsection (c) of this section:

(1) the provisions of Section 438A of this chapter apply to an account described by Subsection (a) of this section, including provisions relating to the ownership of the account during the lifetimes and on the deaths of the parties and provisions relating to the powers and duties of the financial institution at which the account is established; and

(2) any other law relating to a convenience signer applies to a convenience signer designated as provided by this section to the extent the law applies to a convenience signer on a convenience account.

(c) On the death of the last surviving party to an account that has a convenience signer designated as provided by this section, the convenience signer does not have a right of survivorship in the account and the estate of the last surviving party owns the account unless the convenience signer is also designated as a P.O.D. payee or as a beneficiary.

Added by Acts 2009, 81st Leg., ch. 929, § 1, eff. June 19, 2009.

## § 439. Right of Survivorship

(a) Sums remaining on deposit at the death of a party to a joint account belong to the surviving party or parties against the estate of the decedent if, by a written agreement signed by the party who dies, the interest of such deceased party is made to survive to the surviving party or parties. Notwithstanding any other law, an agreement is sufficient to confer an absolute right of survivorship on parties to a joint account under this subsection if the agreement states in substantially the following form: "On the death of one party to a joint account, all sums in the account on the date of the death vest in and belong to the surviving party as his or her separate property and estate." A survivorship agreement will not be inferred from the mere fact that the account is a joint account or that the account is designated as JT TEN, Joint Tenancy, or joint, or with other similar language. If there are two or more surviving parties, their respective ownerships during lifetime shall be in proportion to their previous ownership interests under Section 438 of this code augmented by an equal share for each survivor of any interest the decedent may have owned in the account immediately before his death, and the right of survivorship continues between the surviving parties if a written agreement signed by a party who dies so provides.

(b) If the account is a P.O.D. account and there is a written agreement signed by the original payee or payees, on the death of the original payee or on the death of the survivor of two or more original payees, any sums remaining on deposit belong to the P.O.D. payee or payees if surviving, or to the survivor of them if one or more P.O.D. payees die before the original payee. If two or more P.O.D. payees survive, there is no right of survivorship in event of death of a P.O.D. payee thereafter unless the terms of the account or deposit agreement expressly provide for survivorship between them.

(c) If the account is a trust account and there is a written agreement signed by the trustee or trustees, on death of the trustee or the survivor of two or more trustees, any sums remaining on deposit belong to the person or persons named as beneficiaries, if surviving, or to the survivor of them if one or more beneficiaries die before the trustee dies. If two or more beneficiaries survive, there is no right of survivorship in event of death of any beneficiary thereafter unless the terms of the account or deposit agreement expressly provide for survivorship between them.

(d) In other cases, the death of any party to a multiple-party account has no effect on beneficial ownership of the account other than to transfer the rights of the decedent as part of his estate.

Added by Acts 1979, 66th Leg., p. 1756, ch. 713, § 31, eff. Aug. 27, 1979. Amended by Acts 1987, 70th Leg., ch. 297, § 1, eff. Aug. 31, 1987; Acts 1993, 73rd Leg., ch. 846, § 26, eff. Sept. 1, 1993; Subsec. (a) amended by Acts 2011, 82nd Leg., ch. 1338 (S.B. 1198), § 1.37, eff. Sept. 1, 2011.

## § 439A. Uniform Single-Party or Multiple-Party Account Form

(a) A contract of deposit that contains provisions substantially the same as in the form provided by Subsection (b) of this section establishes the type of account selected by a party. The provisions of this part of Chapter XI of this code govern an account selected under the form. A contract of deposit that does not contain provisions substantially the same as in the form provided by Subsection (b) of this section is governed by the provisions of this chapter applicable to the account that most nearly conforms to the depositor's intent.

(b) A financial institution may use the following form to establish the type of account selected by a party:

UNIFORM SINGLE–PARTY OR MULTIPLE–PARTY ACCOUNT SELECTION FORM NOTICE: The type of account you select may determine how property passes on your death. Your will may not control the disposition of funds held in some of the following accounts. You may choose to designate one or more convenience signers on an account, even if the account is not a convenience account. A designated convenience signer may make transactions on your behalf during your lifetime, but does not own the account during your lifetime. The designated convenience signer owns the account on your death only if the convenience signer is also designated as a P.O.D. payee or trust account beneficiary.

Select one of the following accounts by placing your initials next to the account selected:

____ (1) SINGLE–PARTY ACCOUNT WITHOUT "P.O.D." (PAYABLE ON DEATH) DESIGNATION. The party to the account owns the account. On the death of the party, ownership of the account passes as a part of the party's estate under the party's will or by intestacy.

Enter the name of the party:

_____

Enter the name(s) of the convenience signer(s), if you want one or more convenience signers on this account:

_____

_____

____ (2) SINGLE–PARTY ACCOUNT WITH "P.O.D." (PAYABLE ON DEATH) DESIGNATION. The party to the account owns the account. On the death of the party, ownership of the account passes to the P.O.D. beneficiaries of the account. The account is not a part of the party's estate.

Enter the name of the party:

_____

Enter the name or names of the P.O.D. beneficiaries:

_____

_____

Enter the name(s) of the convenience signer(s), if you want one or more convenience signers on this account:

_____

_____

____ (3) MULTIPLE–PARTY ACCOUNT WITHOUT RIGHT OF SURVIVORSHIP. The parties to the account own the account in proportion to the parties' net contributions to the account. The financial institution may pay any sum in the account to a party at any time. On the death of a party, the party's ownership of the account passes as a part of the party's estate under the party's will or by intestacy.

Enter the names of the parties:

_____

_____

_____

Enter the name(s) of the convenience signer(s), if you want one or more convenience signers on this account:

_____

_____

\_\_\_ (4) MULTIPLE–PARTY ACCOUNT WITH RIGHT OF SURVIVORSHIP. The parties to the account own the account in proportion to the parties' net contributions to the account. The financial institution may pay any sum in the account to a party at any time. On the death of a party, the party's ownership of the account passes to the surviving parties.

Enter the names of the parties:

_____

_____

Enter the name(s) of the convenience signer(s), if you want one or more convenience signers on this account:

_____

_____

\_\_\_ (5) MULTIPLE–PARTY ACCOUNT WITH RIGHT OF SURVIVORSHIP AND P.O.D. (PAYABLE ON DEATH) DESIGNATION. The parties to the account own the account in proportion to the parties' net contributions to the account. The financial institution may pay any sum in the account to a party at any time. On the death of the last surviving party, the ownership of the account passes to the P.O.D. beneficiaries.

Enter the names of the parties:

_____

_____

Enter the name or names of the P.O.D. beneficiaries:

_____

_____

Enter the name(s) of the convenience signer(s), if you want one or more convenience signers on this account:

_____

_____

\_\_\_ (6) CONVENIENCE ACCOUNT. The parties to the account own the account. One or more convenience signers to the account may make account transactions for a party. A convenience signer does not own the account. On the death of the last surviving party, ownership of the account passes as a part of the last surviving party's estate under the last surviving party's will or by intestacy. The financial institution may pay funds in the account to a convenience signer before the financial institution receives notice of the death of the last surviving party. The payment to a convenience signer does not affect the parties' ownership of the account.

Enter the names of the parties:

_____

_____

Enter the name(s) of the convenience signer(s):

_____

_____

\_\_\_ (7) TRUST ACCOUNT. The parties named as trustees to the account own the account in proportion to the parties' net contributions to the account. A trustee may withdraw funds from the account. A beneficiary may not withdraw funds from the account before all trustees are deceased. On the death of the last surviving trustee, the ownership of the account passes to the beneficiary. The trust account is not a part of a trustee's estate and does not pass under the trustee's will or by intestacy, unless the trustee survives all of the beneficiaries and all other trustees.

Enter the name or names of the trustees:

_____

_____

Enter the name or names of the beneficiaries:

_____

_____

Enter the name(s) of the convenience signer(s), if you want one or more convenience signers on this account:

_____

_____

(c) A financial institution shall be deemed to have adequately disclosed the information provided in this section if the financial institution uses the form set forth in Subsection (b) of this section. If a financial institution varies the format of the form set forth in Subsection (b) of this section, then such financial institution may make disclosures in the account agreement or in any other form which adequately discloses the information provided in this section.

(d) A financial institution may combine any of the provisions and vary the format of the selections form and notices described in Subsection (b) of this section provided that the customer receives adequate disclosure of the ownership rights and there is appropriate indication of the names of the parties. This may be accomplished in a universal account form with options listed for selection and additional disclosures provided in the account agreement, or in any other manner which adequately discloses the information provided in this section.

Added by Acts 1993, 73rd Leg., ch. 795, § 2, eff. Aug. 30, 1993. Subsec. (b) amended by Acts 2003, 78th Leg., ch. 658, § 2, eff. Sept. 1, 2003. Subsecs. (a) and (b) amended by Acts 2009, 81st Leg., ch. 929, § 2, eff. June 19, 2009.

## § 440. Effect of Written Notice to Financial Institution

The provisions of Section 439 of this code as to rights of survivorship are determined by the form of the account at the death of a party. Notwithstanding any other provision of the law, this form may be altered by written order given by a party to the financial institution to change the form of the account or to stop or vary payment under the terms of the account. The order or request must be signed by a party, received by the financial institution during the party's lifetime, and not countermanded by other written order of the same party during his lifetime.

Added by Acts 1979, 66th Leg., p. 1756, ch. 713, § 31, eff. Aug. 27, 1979.

## § 441. Accounts and Transfers Nontestamentary

Transfers resulting from the application of Section 439 of this code are effective by reason of the account contracts involved and this statute and are not to be considered as testamentary or subject to the testamentary provisions of this code.

Added by Acts 1979, 66th Leg., p. 1756, ch. 713, § 31, eff. Aug. 27, 1979.

## § 442. Rights of Creditors; Pledge of Account

No multiple-party account will be effective against an estate of a deceased party to transfer to a survivor sums needed to pay debts, taxes, and expenses of administration, including statutory allowances to the surviving spouse and minor children, if other assets of the estate are insufficient. No multiple-party account will be effective against the claim of a secured creditor who has a lien on the account. A party to a multiple-party account may pledge the account or otherwise create a security interest in the account without the joinder of, as appropriate, a P.O.D. payee, a beneficiary, a convenience signer, or any other party to a joint account, regardless of whether there is a right of survivorship. A convenience signer may not pledge or otherwise create a security interest in an account. Not later than the 30th day after the date on which a security interest on a multiple-party account is perfected, a secured creditor that is a financial institution the accounts of which are insured by the Federal Deposit Insurance Corporation shall provide written notice of the pledge of the account to any other party to the account who did not create the security interest. The notice must be sent by certified mail to any other party at the last address the party provided to the depository bank and is not required to be provided to a P.O.D. payee, a beneficiary, or a convenience signer. A party, P.O.D. payee, or beneficiary who receives payment from a multiple-party account after the death of a deceased party shall be liable to account to the deceased party's personal representative for amounts the decedent owned beneficially immediately before his death to the extent necessary to discharge the claims and charges mentioned above remaining unpaid after application of the decedent's estate, but is not liable in an amount greater than the amount that the party, P.O.D. payee, or beneficiary received from the multiple-party account. No proceeding to assert this liability shall be commenced unless the personal representative has received a written demand by a surviving spouse, a creditor, or one acting for a minor child of the decedent, and no proceeding shall be commenced later than two years following the death of the decedent. Sums recovered by the personal representative shall be administered as part of the decedent's estate. This section shall not affect the right of a financial institution to make payment on multiple-party accounts according to the terms thereof, or make it liable to the estate of a deceased party unless before payment the institution received written notice from the personal representative stating the sums needed to pay debts, taxes, claims, and expenses of administration.

Added by Acts 1979, 66th Leg., p. 1756, ch. 713, § 31, eff. Aug. 27, 1979. Amended by Acts 2003, 78th Leg., ch. 564, § 1, eff. Sept. 1, 2003.

## § 443. Protection of Financial Institutions

Sections 444 through 449 of this code govern the liability of financial institutions that make payments as provided in this chapter and the set-off rights of the institutions.

Added by Acts 1979, 66th Leg., p. 1756, ch. 713, § 31, eff. Aug. 27, 1979.

## § 444. Payment on Signature of One Party

Financial institutions may enter into multiple-party accounts to the same extent that they may enter into single-party accounts. A multiple-party account may be paid, on request, to any one or more of the parties. A financial institution shall not be required to inquire as to the source of funds received for deposit to a multiple-party account, or to inquire as to the proposed application of any sum withdrawn from an account, for purposes of establishing net contributions.

Added by Acts 1979, 66th Leg., p. 1756, ch. 713, § 31, eff. Aug. 27, 1979.

## § 445. Payment of Joint Account After Death or Disability

Any sums in a joint account may be paid, on request, to any party without regard to whether any other party is incapacitated or deceased at the time the payment is demanded, but payment may not be made to the personal representative or heirs of a deceased party unless proofs of death are presented to the financial institution showing that the decedent was the last surviving party or unless there is no right of survivorship under Section 439 of this code. A financial institution that pays a sum from a joint account to a surviving party to that account pursuant to a written agreement under Section 439(a) of this code is not liable to an heir, devisee, or beneficiary of the decedent's estate.

Added by Acts 1979, 66th Leg., p. 1756, ch. 713, § 31, eff. Aug. 27, 1979. Amended by Acts 1987, 70th Leg., ch. 297, § 2, eff. Aug. 31, 1987.

## § 446. Payment of P.O.D. Account

A P.O.D. account may be paid, on request, to any original party to the account. Payment may be made, on request, to the P.O.D. payee or to the personal representative or heirs of a deceased P.O.D. payee upon presentation to the financial institution of proof of death showing that the P.O.D. payee survived all persons named as original payees. Payment may be made to the personal representative or heirs of a deceased original payee if proof of death is presented to the financial institution showing that his decedent was the survivor of all other persons named on the account either as an original payee or as P.O.D. payee.

Added by Acts 1979, 66th Leg., p. 1756, ch. 713, § 31, eff. Aug. 27, 1979.

## § 447. Payment of Trust Account

A trust account may be paid, on request, to any trustee. Unless the financial institution has received written notice that the beneficiary has a vested interest not dependent upon his surviving the trustee, payment may be made to the personal representative or heirs of a deceased trustee if proof of death is presented to the financial institution showing that his decedent was the survivor of all other persons named on the account either as trustee or beneficiary. Payment may be made, on request, to the beneficiary upon presentation to the financial institution of proof of death showing that the beneficiary or beneficiaries survived all persons named as trustees.

Added by Acts 1979, 66th Leg., p. 1756, ch. 713, § 31, eff. Aug. 27, 1979.

## § 448. Discharge from Claims

Payment made as provided by Section 444, 445, 446, or 447 of this code discharges the financial institution from all claims for amounts so paid whether or not the payment is consistent with the beneficial ownership of the account as between parties, P.O.D. payees, or beneficiaries, or their successors. The protection here given does not extend to payments made after a financial institution has received written notice from any party able to request present payment to the effect that withdrawals in accordance with the terms of the account should not be permitted. Unless the notice is withdrawn by the person giving it, the successor of any deceased party must concur in any demand for withdrawal if the financial institution is to be protected under this section. No other notice or any other information shown to have been available to a financial institution shall affect its right to the protection provided here. The protection here provided shall have no bearing on the rights of parties in disputes between themselves or their successors concerning

the beneficial ownership of funds in, or withdrawn from, multiple-party accounts.

Added by Acts 1979, 66th Leg., p. 1756, ch. 713, § 31, eff. Aug. 27, 1979.

## § 449. Set-Off to Financial Institution

Without qualifying any other statutory right to set-off or lien and subject to any contractual provision, if a party to a multiple-party account is indebted to a financial institution, the financial institution has a right to set-off against the account in which the party has or had immediately before his death a present right of withdrawal. The amount of the account subject to set-off is that proportion to which the debtor is, or was immediately before his death, beneficially entitled, and in the absence of proof of net contributions, to an equal share with all parties having present rights of withdrawal.

Added by Acts 1979, 66th Leg., p. 1756, ch. 713, § 31, eff. Aug. 27, 1979.

## PART 2. PROVISIONS RELATING TO EFFECT OF DEATH

## § 450. Provisions for Payment or Transfer at Death

(a) Any of the following provisions in an insurance policy, contract of employment, bond, mortgage, promissory note, deposit agreement, employees' trust, retirement account, deferred compensation arrangement, custodial agreement, pension plan, trust agreement, conveyance of real or personal property, securities, accounts with financial institutions as defined in Part 1 of this chapter, mutual fund account, or any other written instrument effective as a contract, gift, conveyance, or trust is deemed to be nontestamentary, and this code does not invalidate the instrument or any provision:

(1) that money or other benefits theretofore due to, controlled, or owned by a decedent shall be paid after his death to a person designated by the decedent in either the instrument or a separate writing, including a will, executed at the same time as the instrument or subsequently;

(2) that any money due or to become due under the instrument shall cease to be payable in event of the death of the promisee or the promissor before payment or demand; or

(3) that any property which is the subject of the instrument shall pass to a person designated by the decedent in either the instrument or a separate writing, including a will, executed at the same time as the instrument or subsequently.

(b) Nothing in this section limits the rights of creditors under other laws of this state.

(c) In this section:

(1) "Employees' trust" means:

(A) a trust that forms a part of a stock-bonus, pension, or profit-sharing plan under Section 401, Internal Revenue Code of 1954 (26 U.S.C.A. Sec. 401 (1986));

(B) a pension trust under Chapter 111, Property Code; and

(C) an employer-sponsored benefit plan or program, or any other retirement savings arrangement, including a pension plan created under Section 3, Employee Retirement Income Security Act of 1974 (29 U.S.C.A. Sec. 1002 (1986)), regardless of whether the plan, program, or arrangement is funded through a trust.

(2) "Individual retirement account" means a trust, custodial arrangement, or annuity under Section 408(a) or (b), Internal Revenue Code of 1954 (26 U.S.C.A. Sec. 408 (1986)).

(3) "Retirement account" means a retirement-annuity contract, an individual retirement account, a simplified employee pension, or any other retirement savings arrangement.

(4) "Retirement-annuity contract" means an annuity contract under Section 403, Internal Revenue Code of 1954 (26 U.S.C.A. Sec. 403 (1986)).

(5) "Simplified employee pension" means a trust, custodial arrangement, or annuity under Section 408, Internal Revenue Code of 1954 (26 U.S.C.A. Sec. 408 (1986)).

Added by Acts 1979, 66th Leg., p. 1756, ch. 713, § 31, eff. Aug. 27, 1979. Amended by Acts 1987, 70th Leg., ch. 94, §§ 1, 2, eff. Aug. 31, 1987; Acts 1997, 75th Leg., ch. 1302, § 14, eff. Sept. 1, 1997; Acts 2001, 77th Leg., ch. 284, § 1, eff. May 22, 2001.

## PART 3.  COMMUNITY PROPERTY WITH RIGHT OF SURVIVORSHIP

### § 451.  Right of Survivorship

At any time, spouses may agree between themselves that all or part of their community property, then existing or to be acquired, becomes the property of the surviving spouse on the death of a spouse.

Added by Acts 1989, 71st Leg., ch. 655, § 2, eff. Aug. 28, 1989.

### § 452.  Formalities

(a) An agreement between spouses creating a right of survivorship in community property must be in writing and signed by both spouses. If an agreement in writing is signed by both spouses, the agreement shall be sufficient to create a right of survivorship in the community property described in the agreement if it includes any of the following phrases:

(1) "with right of survivorship";

(2) "will become the property of the survivor";

(3) "will vest in and belong to the surviving spouse"; or

(4) "shall pass to the surviving spouse."

(b) An agreement that otherwise meets the requirements of this part, however, shall be effective without including any of those phrases.

(c) A survivorship agreement will not be inferred from the mere fact that the account is a joint account or that the account is designated as JT TEN, Joint Tenancy, or joint, or with other similar language.

Added by Acts 1989, 71st Leg., ch. 655, § 2, eff. Aug. 28, 1989. Amended by Acts 2011, 82nd Leg., ch. 1338 (S.B. 1198), § 1.38, eff. Sept. 1, 2011.

### § 453.  Ownership and Management During Marriage

Property subject to an agreement between spouses creating a right of survivorship in community property remains community property during the marriage of the spouses. Such an agreement does not affect the rights of the spouses concerning management, control, and disposition of the property subject to the agreement unless the agreement provides otherwise.

Added by Acts 1989, 71st Leg., ch. 655, § 2, eff. Aug. 28, 1989.

### § 454.  Transfers Nontestamentary

Transfers at death resulting from agreements made in accordance with this part of this code are effective by reason of the agreement involved and are not testamentary transfers. Such transfers are not subject to the provisions of this code applicable to testamentary transfers except as expressly provided otherwise in this code.

Added by Acts 1989, 71st Leg., ch. 655, § 2, eff. Aug. 28, 1989.

### § 455.  Revocation

An agreement between spouses made in accordance with this part of this code may be revoked in accordance with the terms of the agreement. If the agreement does not provide a method for revocation, the agreement may be revoked by a written instrument signed by both spouses or by a written instrument signed by one spouse and delivered to the other spouse. The agreement may be revoked with respect to specific property subject to the agreement by the disposition of such property by one or both of the spouses if such disposition is not inconsistent with specific terms of the agreement and applicable law.

Added by Acts 1989, 71st Leg., ch. 655, § 2, eff. Aug. 28, 1989.

### § 456.  Proof of Agreement

(a) **Application for Adjudication.** An agreement between spouses creating a right of survivorship in community property that satisfies the requirements of this part is effective without an adjudication. After the death of a spouse, however, the surviving spouse or the personal representative of the surviving spouse may apply to the court for an order stating that the agreement satisfies the requirements of this code and is effective to create a right of survivorship in community property. The original agreement shall be filed with the application for an adjudication. An application for an adjudication under this section must include:

(1) the name and domicile of the surviving spouse;

(2) the name and former domicile of the decedent and the fact, time, and place of death;

(3) facts establishing venue in the court; and

(4) the social security number of the decedent, if known.

**(b) Proof Required.** An applicant for an adjudication under this section must prove to the satisfaction of the court:

(1) that the spouse whose community property interest is at issue is dead;

(2) that the court has jurisdiction and venue;

(3) that the agreement was executed with the formalities required by law;

(4) that the agreement was not revoked; and

(5) that citation has been served and returned in the manner and for the length of time required by this code.

**(c) Method of Proof.** The deceased spouse's signature to the agreement may be proved by the sworn testimony of one witness taken in open court, by the affidavit of one witness, or by the deposition of one witness, either written or oral, taken in the same manner and under the same rules as depositions in other civil actions. If the surviving spouse is competent to make an oath, the surviving spouse's signature to the agreement may be proved by the sworn testimony of the surviving spouse taken in open court, by the affidavit of the surviving spouse, or by the deposition of the surviving spouse either written or oral, taken in the same manner and under the same rules as depositions in other civil actions. If the surviving spouse is not competent to make an oath, the surviving spouse's signature to the agreement may be proved in the manner provided above for the proof of the deceased spouse's signature.

**(d) Venue.** An application for an adjudication under this section must be filed in the county of proper venue for administration of the deceased spouse's estate.

Added by Acts 1989, 71st Leg., ch. 655, § 2, eff. Aug. 28, 1989.

### § 457. Action of Court on Agreement

On completion of a hearing on an application under Section 456 of this code, if the court is satisfied that the requisite proof has been made, an order adjudging the agreement valid shall be entered. Certified copies of the agreement and order may be recorded in other counties and may be used in evidence, as the original might be, on the trial of the same matter in any other court, on appeal or otherwise.

Added by Acts 1989, 71st Leg., ch. 655, § 2, eff. Aug. 28, 1989.

### § 458. Effect of Order

An agreement between spouses creating a right of survivorship in community property that satisfies the requirements of this code is effective and enforceable without an adjudication. If an order adjudging such an agreement valid is obtained, however, the order shall constitute sufficient authority to all persons owing money, having custody of any property, or acting as registrar or transfer agent of any

evidence of interest, indebtedness, property, or right, that is subject to the provisions of the agreement, and to persons purchasing from or otherwise dealing with the surviving spouse for payment or transfer to the surviving spouse, and the surviving spouse may enforce his or her right to such payment or transfer.

Added by Acts 1989, 71st Leg., ch. 655, § 2, eff. Aug. 28, 1989.

### § 459. Custody of Adjudicated Agreements

An original agreement creating a right of survivorship in community property that has been adjudicated together with the order adjudging it valid shall be deposited in the office of the county clerk of the county in which it was adjudicated and shall remain there, except during such time when it may be removed for inspection to another place on order of the court where adjudicated. If the court orders an original agreement to be removed to another place for inspection, the person removing the original agreement shall give a receipt therefor, and the clerk of the court shall make and retain a copy of the original agreement.

Added by Acts 1989, 71st Leg., ch. 655, § 2, eff. Aug. 28, 1989.

### § 460. Protection of Persons or Entities Acting Without Knowledge or Notice

**(a) Personal Representatives.** If the personal representative of a decedent's estate has no actual knowledge of the existence of an agreement creating a right of survivorship in community property in the decedent's surviving spouse, the personal representative shall not be liable to the surviving spouse or to any person claiming from the surviving spouse for selling, exchanging, distributing, or otherwise disposing of the property or an interest therein.

**(b) Purchaser without Notice of Survivorship Agreement.**

(1) If any person or entity purchases real or personal property from a person claiming from a decedent more than six months after the date of the decedent's death, for value, and without notice of the existence of an agreement creating a right of survivorship in the property in the decedent's surviving spouse, the purchaser shall have good title to the interest which the person claiming from the decedent would have had in the absence of the agreement, as against the claims of the surviving spouse or any person claiming from the surviving spouse.

(2) If any person or entity purchases real or personal property from the personal representative of a decedent's estate, for value, and without notice of the existence of an agreement creating a right of survivorship in the property in the decedent's surviving spouse, the purchaser shall have good title to the interest which the personal representative would have had the power to convey in the absence of the agreement, as against the claims of the surviving spouse or any person claiming from the surviving spouse.

**(c) Purchaser without Notice of Revocation of Survivorship Agreement.** If any person or entity purchases real or personal property from a decedent's surviving spouse more than six months after the date of the decedent's death, for value, and:

(1) with respect to real or personal property, the purchaser has received an original or certified copy of an agreement purporting to create a right of survivorship in such property in the decedent's surviving spouse, purportedly signed by the decedent and the surviving spouse; or

(2) with respect to real property, an agreement purporting to create a right of survivorship in such property in the decedent's surviving spouse, purportedly signed by the decedent and the surviving spouse, is properly recorded in a county in which a part of the property is located; and the purchaser has no notice that the agreement was revoked, the purchaser shall have good title to the interest which the surviving spouse would have had in the absence of a revocation of the agreement, as against the claims of the personal representative of the decedent's estate and all persons claiming from the decedent or the personal representative of the decedent's estate.

**(d) Debtors, Transfer Agents, and Other Persons Acting without Notice of Survivorship Agreement.** If any person or entity owing money to a decedent or having custody of any property or acting as registrar or transfer agent of any evidence of interest, indebtedness, property, or right which was owned by a decedent prior to death has no actual knowledge of an agreement creating a right of survivorship in such property in the decedent's surviving spouse, that person or entity may pay or transfer such property to the personal representative of the decedent's estate or to the heirs, legatees, or devisees of the decedent's estate if no administration is pending on the estate, and the person or entity shall be discharged from all claims for amounts or property so paid or transferred.

**(e) Debtors, Transfer Agents, and Persons Acting without Notice of Revocation of Survivorship Agreement.** If any person or entity owing money to a decedent or having custody of any property or acting as registrar or transfer agent of any evidence of interest, indebtedness, property, or right which was owned by a decedent prior to death is presented with the original or a certified copy of an agreement creating a right of survivorship in such property in the decedent's surviving spouse, purportedly signed by the decedent and the decedent's surviving spouse and if such person or entity has no actual knowledge that the agreement was revoked, that person or entity may pay or transfer such property to the decedent's surviving spouse and shall be discharged from all claims for amounts or property so paid or transferred.

**(f) Definitions.** Under this section:

(1) a person or entity has "actual knowledge" of an agreement creating a right of survivorship in community property or of the revocation of such an agreement only if the person or entity has received written notice or has received the original or a certified copy of the agreement or revoking instrument;

(2) a person or entity has "notice" of an agreement creating a right of survivorship in community property or the revocation of such an agreement if the person or entity has actual knowledge of the agreement or revocation or, with respect to real property, if the agreement or revoking instrument is properly recorded in the county in which the real property is located; and

(3) a "certified copy" is a copy of an official record or of a document authorized by law to be recorded or filed and actually recorded or filed in a public office, certified as correct in accordance with the provisions of Rule 902 of the Texas Rules of Civil Evidence.

**(g) Other Cases.** Except as expressly provided in this section, the provisions of this section do not affect the rights of a surviving spouse or person claiming from the surviving spouse in disputes with persons claiming from a decedent or the successors of any of them concerning a beneficial interest in property or the proceeds therefrom, subject to a right of survivorship pursuant to an agreement that satisfies the requirements of this code.

Added by Acts 1989, 71st Leg., ch. 655, § 2, eff. Aug. 28, 1989.

## § 461. Rights of Creditors

The provisions of Part 1 of this chapter govern the rights of creditors in multiple-party accounts, as defined by Section 436 of Part 1. Except as expressly provided above in this section, the community property subject to the sole or joint management, control, and disposition of a spouse during marriage continues to be subject to the liabilities of that spouse upon death without regard to a right of survivorship in the decedent's surviving spouse under an agreement made in accordance with the provisions of this part. The surviving spouse shall be liable to account to the deceased spouse's personal representative for the property received by the surviving spouse pursuant to a right of survivorship to the extent necessary to discharge such liabilities. No proceeding to assert such a liability shall be commenced unless the personal representative has received a written demand by a creditor, and no proceeding shall be commenced later than two years following the death of the decedent. Property recovered by the personal representative shall be administered as part of the decedent's estate. This section does not affect the protection given to persons and entities under Section 460 of this code unless, before payment or transfer to the surviving spouse, the person or entity received a written notice from the decedent's personal representative stating the amount needed to satisfy the decedent's liabilities.

Added by Acts 1989, 71st Leg., ch. 655, § 2, eff. Aug. 28, 1989.

## § 462. Coordination With Part 1 of Chapter XI

The provisions of Part 1 of this chapter apply to multiple-party accounts held by spouses with a right of survivorship to the extent that such provisions are not inconsistent with the provisions of this part.

Added by Acts 1989, 71st Leg., ch. 655, § 2, eff. Aug. 28, 1989.

## CHAPTER XI–A

### PROVISIONS APPLICABLE TO CERTAIN NONTESTAMENTARY TRANSFERS

### § 471. Definitions

In this chapter:

(1) "Disposition or appointment of property" includes a transfer of property or provision of any other benefit to a beneficiary under a trust instrument.

(2) "Divorced individual" means an individual whose marriage has been dissolved, whether by divorce, annulment, or a declaration that the marriage is void.

(2–a) "Relative" means an individual who is related to another individual by consanguinity or affinity, as determined under Sections 573.022 and 573.024, Government Code, respectively.

(3) "Revocable," with respect to a disposition, appointment, provision, or nomination, means a disposition to, appointment of, provision in favor of, or nomination of an individual's spouse in a trust instrument executed by the individual before the dissolution of the individual's marriage to the spouse that the individual was solely empowered by law or by the trust instrument to revoke, regardless of whether the individual had the capacity to exercise the power at that time.

Added by Acts 2005, 79th Leg., ch. 551, § 8, eff. Sept. 1, 2005. Subd. (2) amended and subd. (2–a) added by Acts 2011, 82nd Leg., ch. 1338 (S.B. 1198), § 1.39, eff. Sept. 1, 2011.

### § 472. Revocation of Certain Nontestamentary Transfers on Dissolution of Marriage

(a) Except as otherwise provided by a court order, the express terms of a trust instrument executed by a divorced individual before the individual's marriage was dissolved, or an express provision of a contract relating to the division of the marital estate entered into between a divorced individual and the individual's former spouse before, during, or after the marriage, the dissolution of the marriage revokes the following:

(1) a revocable disposition or appointment of property made by a divorced individual to the individual's former spouse or any relative of the former spouse who is not a relative of the divorced individual in a trust instrument executed before the dissolution of the marriage;

(2) a provision in a trust instrument executed by a divorced individual before the dissolution of the marriage that confers a general or special power of appointment on the individual's former spouse or any relative of the former spouse who is not a relative of the divorced individual; and

(3) a nomination in a trust instrument executed by a divorced individual before the dissolution of the marriage that nominates the individual's former spouse or any relative of the former spouse who is not a relative of the divorced individual to serve in a fiduciary or representative capacity, including as a personal representative, executor, trustee, conservator, agent, or guardian.

(b) After the dissolution of a marriage, an interest granted in a provision of a trust instrument that is revoked under Subsection (a)(1) or (2) of this section passes as if the former spouse of the divorced individual who executed the trust instrument and each relative of the former spouse who is not a relative of the divorced individual disclaimed the interest granted in the provision, and an interest granted in a provision of a trust instrument that is revoked under Subsection (a)(3) of this section passes as if the former spouse and each relative of the former spouse who is not a relative of the divorced individual died immediately before the dissolution of the marriage.

Added by Acts 2005, 79th Leg., ch. 551, § 8, eff. Sept. 1, 2005. Amended by Acts 2011, 82nd Leg., ch. 1338 (S.B. 1198), § 1.40, eff. Sept. 1, 2011.

### § 473. Liability for Certain Payments, Benefits, and Property

(a) A bona fide purchaser of property from a divorced individual's former spouse or any relative of the former spouse who is not a relative of the divorced individual or a person who receives from a divorced individual's former spouse or any relative of the former spouse who is not a relative of the divorced individual a payment, benefit, or property in partial or full satisfaction of an enforceable obligation:

(1) is not required by this chapter to return the payment, benefit, or property; and

(2) is not liable under this chapter for the amount of the payment or the value of the property or benefit.

(b) A divorced individual's former spouse or any relative of the former spouse who is not a relative of the divorced individual who, not for value, receives a payment, benefit, or property to which the former spouse or the relative of the former spouse who is not a relative of the divorced individual is not entitled as a result of Section 472(a) of this code:

(1) shall return the payment, benefit, or property to the person who is otherwise entitled to the payment, benefit, or property as provided by this chapter; or

(2) is personally liable to the person described by Subdivision (1) of this subsection for the amount of the payment or the value of the benefit or property received.

Added by Acts 2005, 79th Leg., ch. 551, § 8, eff. Sept. 1, 2005. Amended by Acts 2011, 82nd Leg., ch. 1338 (S.B. 1198), § 1.40, eff. Sept. 1, 2011.

## CHAPTER XII

## DURABLE POWER OF ATTORNEY ACT

## § 481. Short Title

This chapter may be cited as the Durable Power of Attorney Act.

Added by Acts 1993, 73rd Leg., ch. 49, § 1, eff. Sept. 1, 1993.

## § 482. Definition

A "durable power of attorney" means a written instrument that:

(1) designates another person as attorney in fact or agent;

(2) is signed by an adult principal;

(3) contains the words "This power of attorney is not affected by subsequent disability or incapacity of the principal," or "This power of attorney becomes effective on the disability or incapacity of the principal," or similar words showing the principal's intent that the authority conferred on the attorney in fact or agent shall be exercised notwithstanding the principal's subsequent disability or incapacity; and

(4) is acknowledged by the principal before an officer authorized to take acknowledgments to deeds of conveyance and to administer oaths under the laws of this state or any other state.

Added by Acts 1993, 73rd Leg., ch. 49, § 1, eff. Sept. 1, 1993.

## § 483. Duration

A durable power of attorney does not lapse because of the passage of time unless the instrument creating the power of attorney specifically states a time limitation.

Added by Acts 1993, 73rd Leg., ch. 49, § 1, eff. Sept. 1, 1993.

## § 484. Effect of Acts by Attorney in Fact or Agent During Incapacity of Principal

All acts done by an attorney in fact or agent pursuant to a durable power of attorney during any period of disability or incapacity of the principal have the same effect and inure to the benefit of and bind the principal and the principal's successors in interest as if the principal were not disabled or incapacitated.

Added by Acts 1993, 73rd Leg., ch. 49, § 1, eff. Sept. 1, 1993.

## § 485. Relation of Attorney in Fact or Agent to Court-Appointed Guardian of Estate

(a) If, after execution of a durable power of attorney, a court of the principal's domicile appoints a permanent guardian of the estate of the principal, the powers of the attorney in fact or agent terminate on the qualification of the guardian of the estate, and the attorney in fact or agent shall deliver to the guardian of the estate all assets of the estate of the ward in the attorney's or agent's possession and shall account to the guardian of the estate as the attorney or agent would to the principal had the principal terminated his powers.

(b) If, after execution of a durable power of attorney, a court of the principal's domicile appoints a temporary guardian of the estate of the principal, the court may suspend the powers of the attorney in fact or agent on the qualification of the temporary guardian of the estate until the date on which the term of the temporary guardian expires.

(c) Subsection (b) of this section may not be construed to prohibit the application for or issuance of a temporary restraining order under applicable law.

Added by Acts 1993, 73rd Leg., ch. 49, § 1, eff. Sept. 1, 1993. Amended by Acts 2001, 77th Leg., ch. 217, § 1, eff. Sept. 1, 2001.

## § 485A. Effect of Principal's Divorce or Marriage Annulment if Former Spouse is Attorney in Fact or Agent

If, after execution of a durable power of attorney, the principal is divorced from a person who has been appointed the principal's attorney in fact or agent or the principal's marriage to a person who has been appointed the principal's attorney in fact or agent is annulled, the powers of the attorney in fact or agent granted to the principal's former spouse shall terminate on the date on which the divorce or annulment of marriage is granted by a court, unless otherwise expressly provided by the durable power of attorney.

Added by Acts 1997, 75th Leg., ch. 455, § 1, eff. Sept. 1, 1997.

## § 486. Knowledge of Death, Guardian of Estate, Revocation, Divorce, or Marriage Annulment; Good-Faith Acts

(a) The revocation by, the death of, or the qualification of a guardian of the estate of a principal who has executed a durable power of attorney does not revoke or terminate the agency as to the attorney in fact, agent, or other person who, without actual knowledge of the termination of the power by revocation, by the principal's death, or by the qualification of a guardian of the estate of the principal, acts in good faith under or in reliance on the power.

(b) The divorce of a principal from a person who has been appointed the principal's attorney in fact or agent before the date on which the divorce is granted or the annulment of the marriage of a principal and a person who has been appointed the principal's attorney in fact or agent before the date the annulment is granted does not revoke or terminate the agency as to a person other than the principal's former spouse if the person acts in good faith under or in reliance on the power.

(c) Any action taken under this section, unless otherwise invalid or unenforceable, binds successors in interest of the principal.

Added by Acts 1993, 73rd Leg., ch. 49, § 1, eff. Sept. 1, 1993. Amended by Acts 1997, 75th Leg., ch. 455, § 2, eff. Sept. 1, 1997.

## § 487. Affidavit of Lack of Knowledge or Termination of Power; Recording; Good-Faith Reliance

(a) As to acts undertaken in good-faith reliance on the durable power of attorney, an affidavit executed by the attorney in fact or agent under a durable power of attorney stating that the attorney in fact or agent did not have at the time of exercise of the power actual knowledge of the termination of the power by revocation, by the principal's death, by the principal's divorce or the annulment of the marriage of the principal if the attorney in fact or agent was the principal's spouse, or by the qualification of a guardian of the estate of the principal is conclusive proof as between the attorney in fact or agent and a person other than the principal or the principal's personal representative dealing with the attorney in fact or agent of the nonrevocation or nontermination of the power at that time.

(b) As to acts undertaken in good-faith reliance on the durable power of attorney, an affidavit executed by the attorney in fact or agent under a durable power of attorney stating that the principal is disabled or incapacitated, as defined by the power, is conclusive proof as between the attorney in fact or agent and a person other than the principal or the principal's personal representative dealing with the attorney in fact or agent of the disability or incapacity of the principal at that time.

(c) If the exercise of the power of attorney requires execution and delivery of any instrument that is to be recorded, an affidavit executed under Subsection (a) or (b) of this section, when authenticated for record, may also be recorded.

(d) This section does not affect any provision in a durable power of attorney for its termination by expiration of time or occurrence of an event other than express revocation.

(e) When a durable power of attorney is used, a third party who relies in good faith on the acts of an attorney in fact or agent within the scope of the power of attorney is not liable to the principal.

Added by Acts 1993, 73rd Leg., ch. 49, § 1, eff. Sept. 1, 1993. Amended by Acts 1997, 75th Leg., ch. 455, § 3, eff. Sept. 1, 1997.

## § 487A. Effect of Bankruptcy Proceeding

After execution of a durable power of attorney, the filing of a voluntary or involuntary petition in bankruptcy in connection with the principal's debts does not revoke or terminate the agency as to the principal's attorney in fact or agent. Any act the attorney in fact or agent may undertake with respect to the principal's property is subject to the limitations and requirements of the United States Bankruptcy Code until a final determination is made in the bankruptcy proceeding.

Added by Acts 2001, 77th Leg., ch. 73, § 1, eff. Sept. 1, 2001.

## § 488. Revocation of Durable Power of Attorney

Unless otherwise provided by the durable power of attorney, a revocation of a durable power of attorney is not effective as to a third party relying on the power of attorney until the third party receives actual notice of the revocation.

Added by Acts 1993, 73rd Leg., ch. 49, § 1, eff. Sept. 1, 1993.

**Text of Texas Probate Code effective until January 1, 2014**

## § 489. Recording Durable Power of Attorney for Real Property Transactions

A durable power of attorney for a real property transaction requiring the execution and delivery of an instrument that is to be recorded, including a release, assignment, satisfaction, mortgage, security agreement, deed of trust, encumbrance, deed of conveyance, oil, gas, or other mineral lease, memorandum of a lease, lien, or other claim or right to real property, shall be recorded in the office of the county clerk of the county in which the property is located.

Added by Acts 1993, 73rd Leg., ch. 49, § 1, eff. Sept. 1, 1993.

## § 489B. Duty to Inform and Account

(a) The attorney in fact or agent is a fiduciary and has a duty to inform and to account for actions taken pursuant to the power of attorney.

(b) The attorney in fact or agent shall timely inform the principal of all actions taken pursuant to the power of attorney. Failure of the attorney in fact or agent to inform timely, as to third parties, shall not invalidate any action of the attorney in fact or agent.

(c) The attorney in fact or agent shall maintain records of each action taken or decision made by the attorney in fact or agent.

(d) The principal may demand an accounting by the attorney in fact or agent. Unless otherwise directed by the principal, the accounting shall include:

(1) the property belonging to the principal that has come to the attorney in fact's or agent's knowledge or into the attorney in fact's or agent's possession;

(2) all actions taken or decisions made by the attorney in fact or agent;

(3) a complete account of receipts, disbursements, and other actions of the attorney in fact or agent, including their source and nature, with receipts of principal and income shown separately;

(4) a listing of all property over which the attorney in fact or agent has exercised control, with an adequate description of each asset and its current value if known to the attorney in fact or agent;

(5) the cash balance on hand and the name and location of the depository where the balance is kept;

(6) all known liabilities; and

(7) such other information and facts known to the attorney in fact or agent as may be necessary to a full and definite understanding of the exact condition of the property belonging to the principal.

(e) Unless directed otherwise by the principal, the attorney in fact or agent shall also provide to the principal all documentation regarding the principal's property.

(f) The attorney in fact or agent shall maintain all records until delivered to the principal, released by the principal, or discharged by a court.

(g) If the attorney in fact or agent fails or refuses to inform the principal, provide documentation, or deliver the accounting within 60 days (or such longer or shorter time that the principal demands or a court may order), the principal may file suit to compel the attorney in fact or agent to deliver the accounting, to deliver the assets, or to terminate the power of attorney.

(h) This section shall not limit the right of the principal to terminate the power of attorney or to make additional requirements of or to give additional instructions to the attorney in fact or agent.

(i) Wherever in this chapter a principal is given an authority to act, that shall include not only the principal but also any person designated by the principal, a guardian of the estate of the principal, or other personal representative of the principal.

(j) The rights set out in this section and chapter are cumulative of any other rights or remedies the principal may have at common law or other applicable statutes and not in derogation of those rights.

Added by Acts 2001, 77th Leg., ch. 1056, § 1, eff. Sept. 1, 2001.

## § 490. Statutory Durable Power of Attorney

(a) The following form is known as a "statutory durable power of attorney." A person may use a statutory durable power of attorney to grant an attorney in fact or agent powers with respect to a person's property and financial matters. A power of attorney in substantially the following form has the meaning and effect prescribed by this chapter. The validity of a power of attorney as meeting the requirements of a statutory durable power of attorney is not affected by the fact that one or more of the categories of optional powers listed in the form are struck or the form includes specific limitations on or additions to the attorney in fact's or agent's powers.

The following form is not exclusive, and other forms of power of attorney may be used.

### STATUTORY DURABLE POWER OF ATTORNEY

NOTICE: THE POWERS GRANTED BY THIS DOCUMENT ARE BROAD AND SWEEPING. THEY ARE EXPLAINED IN THE DURABLE POWER OF ATTORNEY ACT, CHAPTER XII, TEXAS PROBATE CODE. IF YOU HAVE ANY QUESTIONS ABOUT THESE POWERS, OBTAIN COMPETENT LEGAL ADVICE. THIS DOCUMENT DOES NOT AUTHORIZE ANYONE TO MAKE MEDICAL AND OTHER HEALTH-CARE DECISIONS FOR YOU. YOU MAY REVOKE THIS POWER OF ATTORNEY IF YOU LATER WISH TO DO SO.

I, _____ (insert your name and address), appoint _____ (insert the name and address of the person appointed) as my agent (attorney-in-fact) to act for me in any lawful way with respect to all of the following powers except for a power that I have crossed out below.

TO WITHHOLD A POWER, YOU MUST CROSS OUT EACH POWER WITHHELD.

Real property transactions;

Tangible personal property transactions;

Stock and bond transactions;

Commodity and option transactions;

Banking and other financial institution transactions;

Business operating transactions;

Insurance and annuity transactions;

Estate, trust, and other beneficiary transactions;

Claims and litigation;

Personal and family maintenance;

Benefits from social security, Medicare, Medicaid, or other governmental programs or civil or military service;

Retirement plan transactions;

Tax matters.

IF NO POWER LISTED ABOVE IS CROSSED OUT, THIS DOCUMENT SHALL BE CONSTRUED AND INTERPRETED AS A GENERAL POWER OF ATTORNEY AND MY AGENT (ATTORNEY IN FACT) SHALL HAVE THE POWER AND AUTHORITY TO PERFORM OR UNDERTAKE ANY ACTION I COULD PERFORM OR UNDERTAKE IF I WERE PERSONALLY PRESENT.

SPECIAL INSTRUCTIONS:

Special instructions applicable to gifts (initial in front of the following sentence to have it apply):

I grant my agent (attorney in fact) the power to apply my property to make gifts, except that the amount of a gift to an individual may not exceed the amount of annual exclusions allowed from the federal gift tax for the calendar year of the gift.

ON THE FOLLOWING LINES YOU MAY GIVE SPECIAL INSTRUCTIONS LIMITING OR EXTENDING THE POWERS GRANTED TO YOUR AGENT.

_____
_____
_____
_____
_____
_____
_____
_____
_____

UNLESS YOU DIRECT OTHERWISE ABOVE, THIS POWER OF ATTORNEY IS EFFECTIVE IMMEDIATELY AND WILL CONTINUE UNTIL IT IS REVOKED.

CHOOSE ONE OF THE FOLLOWING ALTERNATIVES BY CROSSING OUT THE ALTERNATIVE NOT CHOSEN:

(A) This power of attorney is not affected by my subsequent disability or incapacity.

(B) This power of attorney becomes effective upon my disability or incapacity.

YOU SHOULD CHOOSE ALTERNATIVE (A) IF THIS POWER OF ATTORNEY IS TO BECOME EFFECTIVE ON THE DATE IT IS EXECUTED.

IF NEITHER (A) NOR (B) IS CROSSED OUT, IT WILL BE ASSUMED THAT YOU CHOSE ALTERNATIVE (A).

If Alternative (B) is chosen and a definition of my disability or incapacity is not contained in this power of attorney, I shall be considered disabled or incapacitated for purposes of this power of attorney if a physician certifies in writing at a date later than the date this power of attorney is executed that, based on the physician's medical examination of me, I am mentally incapable of managing my financial affairs. I authorize the physician who examines me for this purpose to disclose my physical or mental condition to another person for purposes of this power of attorney. A third party who accepts this power of attorney is fully protected from any action taken under this power of attorney that is based on the determination made by a physician of my disability or incapacity.

I agree that any third party who receives a copy of this document may act under it. Revocation of the durable power of attorney is not effective as to a third party until the third party receives actual notice of the revocation. I agree to indemnify the third party for any claims that arise against the third party because of reliance on this power of attorney.

If any agent named by me dies, becomes legally disabled, resigns, or refuses to act, I name the following (each to act alone and successively, in the order named) as successor(s) to that agent: _____

Signed this _____ day of _____, 19___

_____
(your signature)

State of _____

County of _____

This document was acknowledged before me on
_____(date) by _____

(name of principal)

_____

(signature of notarial officer)

(Seal, if any, of notary)

_____

(printed name)

My commission expires: _____

THE ATTORNEY IN FACT OR AGENT, BY ACCEPTING OR ACTING UNDER THE APPOINTMENT, ASSUMES THE FIDUCIARY AND OTHER LEGAL RESPONSIBILITIES OF AN AGENT.

(b) A statutory durable power of attorney is legally sufficient under this chapter if the wording of the form complies substantially with Subsection (a) of this section, the form is properly completed, and the signature of the principal is acknowledged.

(c) Repealed by Acts 1997, 75th Leg., ch. 455, § 7, eff. Sept. 1, 1997.

Added by Acts 1993, 73rd Leg., ch. 49, § 1, eff. Sept. 1, 1993. Amended by Acts 1997, 75th Leg., ch. 455, § 4, eff. Sept. 1, 1997; Acts 1997, 75th Leg., ch. 455, § 7, eff. Sept. 1, 1997.

## § 491.  Construction of Powers Generally

The principal, by executing a statutory durable power of attorney that confers authority with respect to any class of transactions, empowers the attorney in fact or agent for that class of transactions to:

(1) demand, receive, and obtain by litigation, action, or otherwise any money or other thing of value to which the principal is, may become, or may claim to be entitled;

(2) conserve, invest, disburse, or use any money or other thing of value received on behalf of the principal for the purposes intended;

(3) contract in any manner with any person, on terms agreeable to the attorney in fact or agent, to accomplish a purpose of a transaction and perform, rescind, reform, release, or modify the contract or another contract made by or on behalf of the principal;

(4) execute, acknowledge, seal, and deliver a deed, revocation, mortgage, lease, notice, check, release, or other instrument the agent considers desirable to accomplish a purpose of a transaction;

(5) prosecute, defend, submit to arbitration, settle, and propose or accept a compromise with respect to a claim existing in favor of or against the principal or intervene in an action or litigation relating to the claim;

(6) seek on the principal's behalf the assistance of a court to carry out an act authorized by the power of attorney;

(7) engage, compensate, and discharge an attorney, accountant, expert witness, or other assistant;

(8) keep appropriate records of each transaction, including an accounting of receipts and disbursements;

(9) prepare, execute, and file a record, report, or other document the attorney in fact or agent considers necessary or desirable to safeguard or promote the principal's interest under a statute or governmental regulation;

(10) reimburse the attorney in fact or agent for expenditures made in exercising the powers granted by the durable power of attorney;  and

(11) in general, do any other lawful act that the principal may do with respect to a transaction.

Added by Acts 1993, 73rd Leg., ch. 49, § 1, eff. Sept. 1, 1993.

## § 492.  Construction of Power Relating to Real Property Transactions

In a statutory durable power of attorney, the language conferring authority with respect to real property transactions empowers the attorney in fact or agent without further reference to a specific description of the real property to:

(1) accept as a gift or as security for a loan or reject, demand, buy, lease, receive, or otherwise acquire an interest in real property or a right incident to real property;

(2) sell, exchange, convey with or without covenants, quitclaim, release, surrender, mortgage, encumber, partition, consent to partitioning, subdivide, apply for zoning, rezoning, or other governmental permits, plat or consent to platting, develop, grant options concerning, lease or sublet, or otherwise dispose of an estate or interest in real property or a right incident to real property;

(3) release, assign, satisfy, and enforce by litigation, action, or otherwise a mortgage, deed of trust, encumbrance, lien, or other claim to real property that exists or is claimed to exist;

(4) do any act of management or of conservation with respect to an interest in real property, or a right incident to real property, owned or claimed to be owned by the principal, including power to:

(A) insure against a casualty, liability, or loss;

(B) obtain or regain possession or protect the interest or right by litigation, action, or otherwise;

(C) pay, compromise, or contest taxes or assessments or apply for and receive refunds in connection with them;

(D) purchase supplies, hire assistance or labor, or make repairs or alterations in the real property;  and

(E) manage and supervise an interest in real property, including the mineral estate, by, for example, entering into a lease for oil, gas, and mineral purposes, making contracts for development of the mineral estate, or making pooling and unitization agreements;

(5) use, develop, alter, replace, remove, erect, or install structures or other improvements on real property in which the principal has or claims to have an estate, interest, or right;

(6) participate in a reorganization with respect to real property or a legal entity that owns an interest in or right incident to real property, receive and hold shares of stock or obligations received in a plan or reorganization, and act with respect to the shares or obligations, including:

(A) selling or otherwise disposing of the shares or obligations;

(B) exercising or selling an option, conversion, or similar right with respect to the shares or obligations; and

(C) voting the shares or obligations in person or by proxy;

(7) change the form of title of an interest in or right incident to real property; and

(8) dedicate easements or other real property in which the principal has or claims to have an interest to public use, with or without consideration.

Added by Acts 1993, 73rd Leg., ch. 49, § 1, eff. Sept. 1, 1993. Amended by Acts 1997, 75th Leg., ch. 455, § 5, eff. Sept. 1, 1997.

### § 493. Construction of Power Relating to Tangible Personal Property Transactions

In a statutory durable power of attorney, the language conferring general authority with respect to tangible personal property transactions empowers the attorney in fact or agent to:

(1) accept as a gift or as security for a loan, reject, demand, buy, receive, or otherwise acquire ownership or possession of tangible personal property or an interest in tangible personal property;

(2) sell, exchange, convey with or without covenants, release, surrender, mortgage, encumber, pledge, hypothecate, create a security interest in, pawn, grant options concerning, lease or sublet to others, or otherwise dispose of tangible personal property or an interest in tangible personal property;

(3) release, assign, satisfy, or enforce by litigation, action, or otherwise a mortgage, security interest, encumbrance, lien, or other claim on behalf of the principal, with respect to tangible personal property or an interest in tangible personal property; and

(4) do an act of management or conservation with respect to tangible personal property or an interest in tangible personal property on behalf of the principal, including:

(A) insuring against casualty, liability, or loss;

(B) obtaining or regaining possession or protecting the property or interest by litigation, action, or otherwise;

(C) paying, compromising, or contesting taxes or assessments or applying for and receiving refunds in connection with taxes or assessments;

(D) moving from place to place;

(E) storing for hire or on a gratuitous bailment; and

(F) using, altering, and making repairs or alterations.

Added by Acts 1993, 73rd Leg., ch. 49, § 1, eff. Sept. 1, 1993.

### § 494. Construction of Power Relating to Stock and Bond Transactions

In a statutory durable power of attorney, the language conferring authority with respect to stock and bond transactions empowers the attorney in fact or agent to buy, sell, and exchange stocks, bonds, mutual funds, and all other types of securities and financial instruments other than commodity futures contracts and call and put options on stocks and stock indexes, receive certificates and other evidences of ownership with respect to securities, exercise voting rights with respect to securities in person or by proxy, enter into voting trusts, and consent to limitations on the right to vote.

Added by Acts 1993, 73rd Leg., ch. 49, § 1, eff. Sept. 1, 1993.

### § 495. Construction of Power Relating to Commodity and Option Transactions

In a statutory durable power of attorney, the language conferring authority with respect to commodity and option transactions empowers the attorney in fact or agent to buy, sell, exchange, assign, settle, and exercise commodity futures contracts and call and put options on stocks and stock indexes traded on a regulated options exchange and establish, continue, modify, or terminate option accounts with a broker.

Added by Acts 1993, 73rd Leg., ch. 49, § 1, eff. Sept. 1, 1993.

### § 496. Construction of Power Relating to Banking and Other Financial Institution Transactions

In a statutory durable power of attorney, the language conferring authority with respect to banking and other financial institution transactions empowers the attorney in fact or agent to:

(1) continue, modify, or terminate an account or other banking arrangement made by or on behalf of the principal;

(2) establish, modify, or terminate an account or other banking arrangement with a bank, trust company, savings and loan association, credit union, thrift company, brokerage firm, or other financial institution selected by the attorney in fact or agent;

(3) hire a safe deposit box or space in a vault;

(4) contract to procure other services available from a financial institution as the attorney in fact or agent considers desirable;

(5) withdraw by check, order, or otherwise money or property of the principal deposited with or left in the custody of a financial institution;

(6) receive bank statements, vouchers, notices, or similar documents from a financial institution and act with respect to them;

(7) enter a safe deposit box or vault and withdraw or add to the contents;

(8) borrow money at an interest rate agreeable to the attorney in fact or agent and pledge as security real or personal property of the principal necessary to borrow, pay, renew, or extend the time of payment of a debt of the principal;

(9) make, assign, draw, endorse, discount, guarantee, and negotiate promissory notes, bills of exchange, checks, drafts, or other negotiable or nonnegotiable paper of the principal, or payable to the principal or the principal's order, to receive the cash or other proceeds of those transactions, to accept a draft drawn by a person on the principal, and to pay the principal when due;

(10) receive for the principal and act on a sight draft, warehouse receipt, or other negotiable or nonnegotiable instrument;

(11) apply for and receive letters of credit, credit cards, and traveler's checks from a financial institution and give an indemnity or other agreement in connection with letters of credit; and

(12) consent to an extension of the time of payment with respect to commercial paper or a financial transaction with a financial institution.

Added by Acts 1993, 73rd Leg., ch. 49, § 1, eff. Sept. 1, 1993.

### § 497. Construction of Power Relating to Business Operation Transactions

In a statutory durable power of attorney, the language conferring authority with respect to business operating transactions empowers the attorney in fact or agent to:

(1) operate, buy, sell, enlarge, reduce, or terminate a business interest;

(2) to the extent that an agent is permitted by law to act for a principal and subject to the terms of the partnership agreement:

(A) perform a duty or discharge a liability or exercise a right, power, privilege, or option that the principal has, may have, or claims to have under a partnership agreement, whether or not the principal is a general or limited partner;

(B) enforce the terms of a partnership agreement by litigation, action, or otherwise; and

(C) defend, submit to arbitration, settle, or compromise litigation or an action to which the principal is a party because of membership in the partnership;

(3) exercise in person or by proxy or enforce by litigation, action, or otherwise a right, power, privilege, or option the principal has or claims to have as the holder of a bond, share, or other instrument of similar character and defend, submit to arbitration, settle, or compromise a legal proceeding to which the principal is a party because of a bond, share, or similar instrument;

(4) with respect to a business owned solely by the principal:

(A) continue, modify, renegotiate, extend, and terminate a contract made with an individual or a legal entity, firm, association, or corporation by or on behalf of the principal with respect to the business before execution of the power of attorney;

(B) determine:

(i) the location of its operation;

(ii) the nature and extent of its business;

(iii) the methods of manufacturing, selling, merchandising, financing, accounting, and advertising employed in its operation;

(iv) the amount and types of insurance carried; and

(v) the mode of engaging, compensating, and dealing with its accountants, attorneys, and other agents and employees;

(C) change the name or form of organization under which the business is operated and enter into a partnership agreement with other persons or organize a corporation to take over all or part of the operation of the business; and

(D) demand and receive money due or claimed by the principal or on the principal's behalf in the operation of the business and control and disburse the money in the operation of the business;

(5) put additional capital into a business in which the principal has an interest;

(6) join in a plan of reorganization, consolidation, or merger of the business;

(7) sell or liquidate a business or part of it at the time and on the terms that the attorney in fact or agent considers desirable;

(8) establish the value of a business under a buy-out agreement to which the principal is a party;

(9) prepare, sign, file, and deliver reports, compilations of information, returns, or other papers with respect to a business that are required by a governmental agency, department, or instrumentality or that the attorney in fact or agent considers desirable and make related payments; and

(10) pay, compromise, or contest taxes or assessments and do any other act that the attorney in fact or agent considers desirable to protect the principal from illegal or unnecessary taxation, fines, penalties, or assessments with respect to a business, including attempts to recover, in any manner permitted by law, money paid before or after the execution of the power of attorney.

Added by Acts 1993, 73rd Leg., ch. 49, § 1, eff. Sept. 1, 1993.

## § 498. Construction of Power Relating to Insurance Transactions

In a statutory durable power of attorney, the language conferring authority with respect to insurance and annuity transactions empowers the attorney in fact or agent to:

(1) continue, pay the premium or assessment on, modify, rescind, release, or terminate a contract procured by or on behalf of the principal that insures or provides an annuity to either the principal or another person, whether or not the principal is a beneficiary under the contract;

(2) procure new, different, or additional contracts of insurance and annuities for the principal or the principal's spouse, children, and other dependents and select the amount, type of insurance or annuity, and mode of payment;

(3) pay the premium or assessment on or modify, rescind, release, or terminate a contract of insurance or annuity procured by the attorney in fact or agent;

(4) designate the beneficiary of the contract, except that an attorney in fact or agent may be named a beneficiary of the contract or an extension, renewal, or substitute for the contract only to the extent the attorney in fact or agent was named as a beneficiary under a contract procured by the principal before executing the power of attorney;

(5) apply for and receive a loan on the security of the contract of insurance or annuity;

(6) surrender and receive the cash surrender value;

(7) exercise an election;

(8) change the manner of paying premiums;

(9) change or convert the type of insurance contract or annuity with respect to which the principal has or claims to have a power described in this section;

(10) change the beneficiary of a contract of insurance or annuity, except that the attorney in fact or agent may be designated a beneficiary only to the extent authorized by Subdivision (4) of this section;

(11) apply for and procure government aid to guarantee or pay premiums of a contract of insurance on the life of the principal;

(12) collect, sell, assign, hypothecate, borrow on, or pledge the interest of the principal in a contract of insurance or annuity; and

(13) pay from proceeds or otherwise, compromise or contest, or apply for refunds in connection with a tax or assessment levied by a taxing authority with respect to a contract of insurance or annuity or its proceeds or liability accruing because of the tax or assessment.

Added by Acts 1993, 73rd Leg., ch. 49, § 1, eff. Sept. 1, 1993.

## § 499. Construction of Power Relating to Estate, Trust, and Other Beneficiary Transactions

In a statutory durable power of attorney, the language conferring authority with respect to estate, trust, and other beneficiary transactions empowers the attorney in fact or agent to act for the principal in all matters that affect a trust, probate estate, guardianship, conservatorship, escrow, custodianship, or other fund from which the principal is, may become, or claims to be entitled, as a beneficiary, to a share or payment, including to:

(1) accept, reject, disclaim, receive, receipt for, sell, assign, release, pledge, exchange, or consent to a reduction in or modification of a share in or payment from the fund;

(2) demand or obtain by litigation, action, or otherwise money or any other thing of value to which the principal is, may become, or claims to be entitled because of the fund;

(3) initiate, participate in, or oppose a legal or judicial proceeding to ascertain the meaning, validity, or effect of a deed, will, declaration of trust, or other instrument or transaction affecting the interest of the principal;

(4) initiate, participate in, or oppose a legal or judicial proceeding to remove, substitute, or surcharge a fiduciary;

(5) conserve, invest, disburse, or use anything received for an authorized purpose; and

(6) transfer all or part of an interest of the principal in real property, stocks, bonds, accounts with financial institutions, insurance, and other property to the trustee of a revocable trust created by the principal as settlor.

Added by Acts 1993, 73rd Leg., ch. 49, § 1, eff. Sept. 1, 1993.

## § 500. Construction of Power Relating to Claims and Litigation

In a statutory durable power of attorney, the language conferring general authority with respect to claims and litigation empowers the attorney in fact or agent to:

(1) assert and prosecute before a court or administrative agency a claim, a claim for relief, a counterclaim, or an offset or defend against an individual, a legal entity, or a government, including suits to recover property or other thing of value, to recover damages sustained by the principal, to eliminate or modify tax liability, or to seek an injunction, specific performance, or other relief;

(2) bring an action to determine adverse claims, intervene in an action or litigation, and act as amicus curiae;

(3) in connection with an action or litigation, procure an attachment, garnishment, libel, order of arrest, or other preliminary, provisional, or intermediate relief and use an available procedure to effect or satisfy a judgment, order, or decree;

(4) in connection with an action or litigation, perform any lawful act the principal could perform, including acceptance of tender, offer of judgment, admission of facts, submission of a controversy on an agreed statement of facts, consent to examination before trial, and binding of the principal in litigation;

(5) submit to arbitration, settle, and propose or accept a compromise with respect to a claim or litigation;

(6) waive the issuance and service of process on the principal, accept service of process, appear for the principal, designate persons on whom process directed to the principal may be served, execute and file or deliver stipulations on the principal's behalf, verify pleadings, seek appellate review, procure and give surety and indemnity bonds, contract and pay for the preparation and printing of records and briefs, or receive and execute and file or deliver a consent, waiver, release, confession of judgment, satisfaction of judgment, notice, agreement, or other instrument in connection with the prosecution, settlement, or defense of a claim or litigation;

(7) act for the principal with respect to bankruptcy or insolvency proceedings, whether voluntary or involuntary, concerning the principal or some other person, with respect to a reorganization proceeding or a receivership or application for the appointment of a receiver or trustee that affects an interest of the principal in real or personal property or other thing of value; and

(8) pay a judgment against the principal or a settlement made in connection with a claim or litigation and receive and conserve money or other thing of value paid in settlement of or as proceeds of a claim or litigation.

Added by Acts 1993, 73rd Leg., ch. 49, § 1, eff. Sept. 1, 1993.

### § 501. Construction of Power Relating to Personal and Family Maintenance

In a statutory durable power of attorney, the language conferring authority with respect to personal and family maintenance empowers the attorney in fact or agent to:

(1) perform the acts necessary to maintain the customary standard of living of the principal, the principal's spouse and children, and other individuals customarily or legally entitled to be supported by the principal, including providing living quarters by purchase, lease, or other contract, or paying the operating costs, including interest, amortization payments, repairs, and taxes on premises owned by the principal and occupied by those individuals;

(2) provide for the individuals described by Subdivision (1) of this section normal domestic help, usual vacations and travel expenses, and funds for shelter, clothing, food, appropriate education, and other current living costs;

(3) pay necessary medical, dental, and surgical care, hospitalization, and custodial care for the individuals described by Subdivision (1) of this section;

(4) continue any provision made by the principal, for the individuals described by Subdivision (1) of this section, for automobiles or other means of transportation, including registering, licensing, insuring, and replacing the automobiles or other means of transportation;

(5) maintain or open charge accounts for the convenience of the individuals described by Subdivision (1) of this section and open new accounts the attorney in fact or agent considers desirable to accomplish a lawful purpose; and

(6) continue payments incidental to the membership or affiliation of the principal in a church, club, society, order, or other organization or to continue contributions to those organizations.

Added by Acts 1993, 73rd Leg., ch. 49, § 1, eff. Sept. 1, 1993.

### § 502. Construction of Power Relating to Benefits From Certain Governmental Programs or Civil or Military Service

In a statutory durable power of attorney, the language conferring authority with respect to benefits from social security, Medicare, Medicaid, or other governmental programs or civil or military service empowers the attorney in fact or agent to:

(1) execute vouchers in the name of the principal for allowances and reimbursements payable by the United States, a foreign government, or a state or subdivision of a state to the principal, including allowances and reimbursements for transportation of the individuals described by Section 501(1) of this code, and for shipment of their household effects;

(2) take possession and order the removal and shipment of property of the principal from a post, warehouse, depot, dock, or other place of storage or safekeeping, either governmental or private, and execute and deliver a release, voucher, receipt, bill of lading, shipping ticket, certificate, or other instrument for that purpose;

(3) prepare, file, and prosecute a claim of the principal to a benefit or assistance, financial or otherwise, to which the principal claims to be entitled under a statute or governmental regulation;

(4) prosecute, defend, submit to arbitration, settle, and propose or accept a compromise with respect to any benefits the principal may be entitled to receive; and

(5) receive the financial proceeds of a claim of the type described in this section and conserve, invest, disburse, or use anything received for a lawful purpose.

Added by Acts 1993, 73rd Leg., ch. 49, § 1, eff. Sept. 1, 1993.

### § 503. Construction of Power Relating to Retirement Plan Transactions

(a) In a statutory durable power of attorney, the language conferring authority with respect to retirement plan transactions empowers the attorney in fact or agent to do any lawful act the principal may do with respect to a transaction relating to a retirement plan, including to:

(1) apply for service or disability retirement benefits;

(2) select payment options under any retirement plan in which the principal participates, including plans for self-employed individuals;

(3) designate or change the designation of a beneficiary or benefits payable by a retirement plan, except that an attorney in fact or agent may be named a beneficiary only to the extent the attorney in fact or agent was a named beneficiary

under the retirement plan before the durable power of attorney was executed;

(4) make voluntary contributions to retirement plans if authorized by the plan;

(5) exercise the investment powers available under any self-directed retirement plan;

(6) make "rollovers" of plan benefits into other retirement plans;

(7) borrow from, sell assets to, and purchase assets from retirement plans if authorized by the plan;

(8) waive the right of the principal to be a beneficiary of a joint or survivor annuity if the principal is a spouse who is not employed;

(9) receive, endorse, and cash payments from a retirement plan;

(10) waive the right of the principal to receive all or a portion of benefits payable by a retirement plan; and

(11) request and receive information relating to the principal from retirement plan records.

(b) In this section, "retirement plan" means:

(1) an employee pension benefit plan as defined by Section 1002, Employee Retirement Income Security Act of 1974 (ERISA) (29 U.S.C. Section 1002), without regard to the provisions of Section (2)(B) of that section;

(2) a plan that does not meet the definition of an employee benefit plan under ERISA because the plan does not cover common law employees;

(3) a plan that is similar to an employee benefit plan under ERISA, regardless of whether it is covered by Title I of ERISA, including a plan that provides death benefits to the beneficiary of employees; and

(4) an individual retirement account or annuity or a self-employed pension plan or similar plan or account.

Added by Acts 1993, 73rd Leg., ch. 49, § 1, eff. Sept. 1, 1993. Amended by Acts 1997, 75th Leg., ch. 455, § 6, eff. Sept. 1, 1997.

## § 504.  Construction of Power Relating to Tax Matters

In a statutory durable power of attorney, the language conferring authority with respect to tax matters empowers the attorney in fact or agent to:

(1) prepare, sign, and file federal, state, local, and foreign income, gift, payroll, Federal Insurance Contributions Act, and other tax returns, claims for refunds, requests for extension of time, petitions regarding tax matters, and any other tax-related documents, including receipts, offers, waivers, consents, including consents and agreements under Section 2032A, Internal Revenue Code of 1986 (26 U.S.C. Section 2032A), closing agreements, and any power of attorney form required by the Internal Revenue Service or other taxing authority with respect to a tax year on which the statute of limitations has not run and 25 tax years following that tax year;

(2) pay taxes due, collect refunds, post bonds, receive confidential information, and contest deficiencies determined by the Internal Revenue Service or other taxing authority;

(3) exercise any election available to the principal under federal, state, local, or foreign tax law;  and

(4) act for the principal in all tax matters for all periods before the Internal Revenue Service and any other taxing authority.

Added by Acts 1993, 73rd Leg., ch. 49, § 1, eff. Sept. 1, 1993.

## § 505.  Existing Interest; Foreign Interests

The powers described in Sections 492 through 504 of this code may be exercised equally with respect to an interest the principal has at the time the durable power of attorney is executed or acquires later, whether or not the property is located in this state and whether or not the powers are exercised or the durable power of attorney is executed in this state.

Added by Acts 1993, 73rd Leg., ch. 49, § 1, eff. Sept. 1, 1993.

## § 506.  Uniformity of Application and Construction

This chapter shall be applied and construed to effect its general purpose to make uniform the law with respect to the subject of this chapter among states enacting it.

Added by Acts 1993, 73rd Leg., ch. 49, § 1, eff. Sept. 1, 1993.

## §§ 507 to 510.  Repealed by Acts 1997, 75th Leg., ch. 540, § 5, eff. Sept. 1, 1997

## §§ 520 to 525.  Renumbered as V.A.T.S. Probate Code, §§ 108 to 115 by Acts 1997, 75th Leg., ch. 199, § 1, eff. Sept. 1, 1997

# CHAPTER XIII

# GUARDIANSHIP

PART 1.  GENERAL PROVISIONS
SUBPART A.  DEFINITIONS; PURPOSE; APPLICABILITY;
PROCEEDINGS IN REM

# GUARDIANSHIP

**Text of Texas Probate Code effective until January 1, 2014**

**Text of Texas Probate Code effective until January 1, 2014**

# GUARDIANSHIP

**Text of Texas Probate Code effective until January 1, 2014**

# APPENDIX: PROBATE CODE

**Text of Texas Probate Code effective until January 1, 2014**

## PART 1.  GENERAL PROVISIONS

### SUBPART A.  DEFINITIONS; PURPOSE; APPLICABILITY; PROCEEDINGS IN REM

### § 601.  Definitions

In this chapter:

(1) "Attorney ad litem" means an attorney who is appointed by a court to represent and advocate on behalf of a proposed ward, an incapacitated person, or an unborn person in a guardianship proceeding.

(2) "Authorized corporate surety" means a domestic or foreign corporation authorized to do business in this state to issue surety, guaranty, or indemnity bonds guaranteeing the fidelity of guardians.

(3) "Child" includes a biological or adopted child, whether adopted by a parent under a statutory procedure or by acts of estoppel.

(4) "Claims" includes a liability against the estate of a minor or an incapacitated person and debts due to the estate of a minor or an incapacitated person.

(5) "Community administrator" means a spouse who is authorized to manage, control, and dispose of the entire community estate on the judicial declaration of incapacity of the other spouse, including the part of the community estate that the other spouse legally has the power to manage in the absence of the incapacity.

(6) "Corporate fiduciary" means a financial institution as defined by Section 201.101, Finance Code, having trust powers, existing or doing business under the laws of this state, another state, or the United States, that is authorized by law to act under the order or appointment of any court of record, without giving bond, as a guardian, receiver, trustee, executor, or administrator, or, although without general depository powers, as a depository for any money paid into court, or to become sole guarantor or surety in or on any bond required to be given under the laws of this state.

(7) "Court investigator" means a person appointed by a statutory probate court under Section 25.0025, Government Code.

(8) "Court" or "probate court" means a county court in the exercise of its probate jurisdiction, a court created by statute and authorized to exercise original probate jurisdiction, or a district court exercising original probate jurisdiction in contested matters.

(9) "Estate" or "guardianship estate" means the real and personal property of a ward or deceased ward, both as the property originally existed and as has from time to time changed in form by sale, reinvestment, or otherwise, and as augmented by any accretions and additions to (including any property to be distributed to the representative of the deceased ward by the trustee of a trust that terminates on the ward's death) or substitutions for the property, and as diminished by any decreases to or distributions from the property.

(10) "Exempt property" refers to that property of a deceased ward's estate that is exempt from execution or forced sale by the constitution or laws of this state, and to the allowance in lieu of the property.

(11) "Guardian" means a person who is appointed guardian under Section 693 of this code, or a temporary or successor guardian. Except as expressly provided otherwise, "guardian" includes the guardian of the estate and the guardian of the person of an incapacitated person.

(12) "Guardian ad litem" means a person who is appointed by a court to represent the best interests of an incapacitated person in a guardianship proceeding.

(12–a) "Guardianship Certification Board" means the Guardianship Certification Board established under Chapter 111, Government Code.

(13) "Guardianship program" has the meaning assigned by Section 111.001, Government Code.

(14) "Incapacitated person" means:

(A) a minor;

(B) an adult individual who, because of a physical or mental condition, is substantially unable to provide food, clothing, or shelter for himself or herself, to care for the individual's own physical health, or to manage the individual's own financial affairs; or

(C) a person who must have a guardian appointed to receive funds due the person from any governmental source.

(15) "Interested persons" or "persons interested" means an heir, devisee, spouse, creditor, or any other person having a property right in, or claim against, the estate being administered or a person interested in the welfare of an incapacitated person, including a minor.

(16) "Minor" means a person who is younger than 18 years of age and who has never been married or who has not had the person's disabilities of minority removed for general purposes.

(17) Repealed by Acts 2009, 81st Leg., ch. 602, § 19(2).

(18) "Mortgage" or "lien" includes a deed of trust; vendor's lien; chattel mortgage; mechanic's, materialman's, or laborer's lien; judgment, attachment, or garnishment lien; pledge by hypothecation; and a federal or state tax lien.

(19) "Next of kin" includes an adopted child, the descendants of an adopted child, and the adoptive parent of an adopted child.

(20) "Parent" means the mother of a child, a man presumed to be the biological father of a child, a man who has been adjudicated to be the biological father of a child by a court of competent jurisdiction, or an adoptive mother or father of a child, but does not include a parent as to whom the parent-child relationship has been terminated.

(21) "Person" includes natural persons, corporations, and guardianship programs.

(22) "Personal property" includes an interest in goods, money, choses in action, evidence of debts, and chattels real.

(23) "Personal representative" or "representative" includes a guardian, and a successor guardian.

(24) "Private professional guardian" has the meaning assigned by Section 111.001, Government Code.

(25) The term "guardianship proceeding" means a matter or proceeding related to a guardianship or any other matter covered by this chapter, including:

(A) the appointment of a guardian of a minor or other incapacitated person, including an incapacitated adult for whom another court obtained continuing, exclusive jurisdiction in a suit affecting the parent-child relationship when the person was a child;

(B) an application, petition, or motion regarding guardianship or an alternative to guardianship under this chapter;

(C) a mental health action; and

(D) an application, petition, or motion regarding a trust created under Section 867 of this code.

(26) "Property" includes both real and personal property.

(27) "Proposed ward" means a person alleged to be incapacitated in a guardianship proceeding.

(28) "Real property" includes estates and interests in lands, corporeal or incorporeal, legal or equitable, other than chattels real.

(29) "Statutory probate court" means a statutory court designated as a statutory probate court under Chapter 25, Government Code. A county court at law exercising probate jurisdiction is not a statutory probate court under this chapter unless the court is designated a statutory probate court under Chapter 25, Government Code.

(30) "Surety" includes a personal and a corporate surety.

(31) "Ward" is a person for whom a guardian has been appointed.

(32) The singular number includes the plural; the plural number includes the singular.

(33) The masculine gender includes the feminine and neuter.

Added by Acts 1993, 73rd Leg., ch. 957, § 1, eff. Sept. 1, 1993. Amended by Acts 1995, 74th Leg., ch. 1039, § 15, eff. Sept. 1, 1995; Acts 1997, 75th Leg., ch. 1376, § 1, eff. Sept. 1, 1997; Acts 1997, 75th Leg., ch. 52, § 2, eff. Sept. 1, 1997; Acts 1999, 76th Leg., ch. 344, § 6.005, eff. Sept. 1, 1999; Acts 1999, 76th Leg., ch. 379, § 2, eff. Sept. 1, 1999; Acts 2001, 77th Leg., ch. 217, § 2, eff. Sept. 1, 2001. Subd. (12-a) added by Acts 2005, 79th Leg., ch. 268, § 3.05, eff. Sept. 1, 2005; Subd. (13) amended by Acts 2005, 79th Leg., ch. 268, § 3.05, eff. Sept. 1, 2005; Subd. (24) amended by Acts 2005, 79th Leg., ch. 268, § 3.05, eff. Sept. 1, 2005. Amended by by Acts 2009, 81st Leg., ch. 602, § 19(2), eff. June 19, 2009. Subd. (25) amended by Acts 2011, 82nd Leg., ch. 1085 (S.B. 1196), § 1, eff. Sept. 1, 2011.

## § 602. Policy; Purpose of Guardianship

A court may appoint a guardian with full authority over an incapacitated person or may grant a guardian limited authority over an incapacitated person as indicated by the incapacitated person's actual mental or physical limitations and only as necessary to promote and protect the well-being of the person. If the person is not a minor, the court may not use age as the sole factor in determining whether to appoint a guardian for the person. In creating a guardianship that gives a guardian limited power or authority over an incapacitated person, the court shall design the guardianship to encourage the development or maintenance of maximum self-reliance and independence in the incapacitated person.

Added by Acts 1993, 73rd Leg., ch. 957, § 1, eff. Sept. 1, 1993.

## § 603. Laws Applicable to Guardianships

(a) To the extent applicable and not inconsistent with other provisions of this code, the laws and rules governing estates of decedents apply to and govern guardianships.

(b) A reference in other sections of this code or in other law to a person who is mentally, physically, or legally incompetent, a person who is judicially declared incompetent, an incompetent or an incompetent person, a person of unsound mind, or a habitual drunkard means an incapacitated person.

Added by Acts 1993, 73rd Leg., ch. 957, § 1, eff. Sept. 1, 1993.

## § 604. Proceeding In Rem

From the filing of the application for the appointment of a guardian of the estate or person, or both, until the guardianship is settled and closed under this chapter, the administration of the estate of a minor or other incapacitated person is one proceeding for purposes of jurisdiction and is a proceeding in rem.

Added by Acts 1993, 73rd Leg., ch. 957, § 1, eff. Sept. 1, 1993.

PART 2. GUARDIANSHIP PROCEEDINGS
AND MATTERS

SUBPART A. JURISDICTION

## § 605. General Probate Court Jurisdiction in Guardianship Proceedings; Appeals

(a) All guardianship proceedings must be filed and heard in a court exercising original probate jurisdiction. The court exercising original probate jurisdiction also has jurisdiction of all matters related to the guardianship proceeding as specified in Section 606A of this code for that type of court.

(b) A probate court may exercise pendent and ancillary jurisdiction as necessary to promote judicial efficiency and economy.

(c) A final order issued by a probate court is appealable to the court of appeals.

Added by Acts 1993, 73rd Leg., ch. 957, § 1, eff. Sept. 1, 1993. Amended by Acts 2011, 82nd Leg., ch. 1085 (S.B. 1196), § 2, eff. Sept. 1, 2011.

## § 606. Repealed by Acts 2011, 82nd Leg., ch. 1085 (S.B. 1196), § 42, eff. Sept. 1, 2011

## § 606A. Matters Related to Guardianship Proceeding

(a) For purposes of this code, in a county in which there is no statutory probate court, a matter related to a guardianship proceeding includes:

(1) the granting of letters of guardianship;

(2) the settling of an account of a guardian and all other matters relating to the settlement, partition, or distribution of a ward's estate;

(3) a claim brought by or against a guardianship estate;

(4) an action for trial of title to real property that is guardianship estate property, including the enforcement of a lien against the property;

(5) an action for trial of the right of property that is guardianship estate property;

(6) after a guardianship of the estate of a ward is required to be settled as provided by Section 745 of this code:

(A) an action brought by or on behalf of the former ward against a former guardian of the ward for alleged misconduct arising from the performance of the person's duties as guardian;

(B) an action calling on the surety of a guardian or former guardian to perform in place of the guardian or former guardian, which may include the award of a judgment against the guardian or former guardian in favor of the surety;

(C) an action against a former guardian of the former ward that is brought by a surety that is called on to perform in place of the former guardian;

(D) a claim for the payment of compensation, expenses, and court costs, and any other matter authorized under Subpart H, Part 2, of this chapter; and

(E) a matter related to an authorization made or duty performed by a guardian under Subpart C, Part 4, of this chapter; and

(7) the appointment of a trustee for a trust created under Section 867 of this code, the settling of an account of the trustee, and all other matters relating to the trust.

(b) For purposes of this code, in a county in which there is a statutory probate court, a matter related to a guardianship proceeding includes:

(1) all matters and actions described in Subsection (a) of this section;

(2) a suit, action, or application filed against or on behalf of a guardianship or a trustee of a trust created under Section 867 of this code; and

(3) a cause of action in which a guardian in a guardianship pending in the statutory probate court is a party.

Added by Acts 2011, 82nd Leg., ch. 1085 (S.B. 1196), § 3, eff. Sept. 1, 2011.

§ 607. Repealed by Acts 2011, 82nd Leg., ch. 1085 (S.B. 1196), § 42, eff. Sept. 1, 2011

### § 607A. Original Jurisdiction for Guardianship Proceedings

(a) In a county in which there is no statutory probate court or county court at law exercising original probate jurisdiction, the county court has original jurisdiction of guardianship proceedings.

(b) In a county in which there is no statutory probate court, but in which there is a county court at law exercising original probate jurisdiction, the county court at law exercising original probate jurisdiction and the county court have concurrent original jurisdiction of guardianship proceedings, unless otherwise provided by law. The judge of a county court may hear guardianship proceedings while sitting for the judge of any other county court.

(c) In a county in which there is a statutory probate court, the statutory probate court has original jurisdiction of guardianship proceedings.

Added by Acts 2011, 82nd Leg., ch. 1085 (S.B. 1196), § 3, eff. Sept. 1, 2011.

### § 607B. Jurisdiction of Contested Guardianship Proceeding in County With no Statutory Probate Court or County Court at Law

(a) In a county in which there is no statutory probate court or county court at law exercising original probate jurisdiction, when a matter in a guardianship proceeding is contested, the judge of the county court may, on the judge's own motion, or shall, on the motion of any party to the proceeding, according to the motion:

(1) request the assignment of a statutory probate court judge to hear the contested matter, as provided by Section 25.0022, Government Code; or

(2) transfer the contested matter to the district court, which may then hear the contested matter as if originally filed in the district court.

(b) If a party to a guardianship proceeding files a motion for the assignment of a statutory probate court judge to hear a contested matter in the proceeding before the judge of the county court transfers the contested matter to a district court under this section, the county judge shall grant the motion for the assignment of a statutory probate court judge and may not transfer the matter to the district court unless the party withdraws the motion.

(c) If a judge of a county court requests the assignment of a statutory probate court judge to hear a contested matter in a guardianship proceeding on the judge's own motion or on the motion of a party to the proceeding as provided by this section, the judge may request that the statutory probate court judge be assigned to the entire proceeding on the judge's own motion or on the motion of a party.

(d) A party to a guardianship proceeding may file a motion for the assignment of a statutory probate court judge under this section before a matter in the proceeding becomes contested, and the motion is given effect as a motion for assignment of a statutory probate court judge under Subsection (a) of this section if the matter later becomes contested.

(e) Notwithstanding any other law, a transfer of a contested matter in a guardianship proceeding to a district court under any authority other than the authority provided by this section:

(1) is disregarded for purposes of this section; and

(2) does not defeat the right of a party to the proceeding to have the matter assigned to a statutory probate court judge in accordance with this section.

(f) A statutory probate court judge assigned to a contested matter in a guardianship proceeding or to the entire proceeding under this section has the jurisdiction and authority granted to a statutory probate court by this code. A statutory probate court judge assigned to hear only the contested matter in a guardianship proceeding shall, on resolution of the matter, including any appeal of the matter, return the matter to the county court for further proceedings not inconsistent with the orders of the statutory probate court or court of appeals, as applicable. A statutory probate court judge assigned to the entire guardianship proceeding as provided by Subsection (c) of this section shall, on resolution of the contested matter in the proceeding, including any appeal of the matter, return the entire proceeding to the county court for further proceedings not inconsistent with the orders of the statutory probate court or court of appeals, as applicable.

(g) A district court to which a contested matter in a guardianship proceeding is transferred under this section has the jurisdiction and authority granted to a statutory probate court by this code. On resolution of a contested matter transferred to the district court under this section, including any appeal of the matter, the district court shall return the matter to the county court for further proceedings not inconsistent with the orders of the district court or court of appeals, as applicable.

(h) If only the contested matter in a guardianship proceeding is assigned to a statutory probate court judge under this section, or if the contested matter in a guardianship proceeding is transferred to a district court under this section, the county court shall continue to exercise jurisdiction over the management of the guardianship, other than a contested matter, until final disposition of the contested matter is made in accordance with this section. Any matter related to a guardianship proceeding in which a contested matter is transferred to a district court may be brought in the district court. The district court in which a matter related to the proceeding is filed may, on the court's own motion or on the motion of any party, find that the matter is not a contested matter and transfer the matter to the county court with jurisdiction of the management of the guardianship.

(i) If a contested matter in a guardianship proceeding is transferred to a district court under this section, the district court has jurisdiction of any contested matter in the proceeding that is subsequently filed, and the county court shall transfer those contested matters to the district court. If a statutory probate court judge is assigned under this section to hear a contested matter in a guardianship proceeding, the statutory probate court judge shall be assigned to hear any contested matter in the proceeding that is subsequently filed.

(j) The clerk of a district court to which a contested matter in a guardianship proceeding is transferred under this section may perform in relation to the transferred matter any function a county clerk may perform with respect to that type of matter.

Added by Acts 2011, 82nd Leg., ch. 1085 (S.B. 1196), § 3, eff. Sept. 1, 2011.

### § 607C. Jurisdiction of Contested Guardianship Proceeding in County With no Statutory Probate Court

(a) In a county in which there is no statutory probate court, but in which there is a county court at law exercising original probate jurisdiction, when a matter in a guardianship proceeding is contested, the judge of the county court may, on the judge's own motion, or shall, on the motion of any party to the proceeding, transfer the contested matter to the county court at law. In addition, the judge of the county court, on the judge's own motion or on the motion of a party to the proceeding, may transfer the entire proceeding to the county court at law.

(b) A county court at law to which a proceeding is transferred under this section may hear the proceeding as if originally filed in that court. If only a contested matter in the proceeding is transferred, on the resolution of the matter, the matter shall be returned to the county court for further proceedings not inconsistent with the orders of the county court at law.

Added by Acts 2011, 82nd Leg., ch. 1085 (S.B. 1196), § 3, eff. Sept. 1, 2011.

### § 607D. Exclusive Jurisdiction of Guardianship Proceeding in County with Statutory Probate Court

(a) In a county in which there is a statutory probate court, the statutory probate court has exclusive jurisdiction of all guardianship proceedings, regardless of whether contested or uncontested.

(b) A cause of action related to a guardianship proceeding of which the statutory probate court has exclusive jurisdiction as provided by Subsection (a) of this section must be brought in the statutory probate court unless the jurisdiction of the statutory probate court is concurrent with the jurisdiction of a district court as provided by Section 607E of this code or with the jurisdiction of any other court.

Added by Acts 2011, 82nd Leg., ch. 1085 (S.B. 1196), § 3, eff. Sept. 1, 2011.

### § 607E. Concurrent Jurisdiction with District Court

A statutory probate court has concurrent jurisdiction with the district court in:

(1) a personal injury, survival, or wrongful death action by or against a person in the person's capacity as a guardian; and

(2) an action involving a guardian in which each other party aligned with the guardian is not an interested person in the guardianship.

Added by Acts 2011, 82nd Leg., ch. 1085 (S.B. 1196), § 3, eff. Sept. 1, 2011.

### § 608. Transfer of Proceeding by Statutory Probate Court

(a) A judge of a statutory probate court, on the motion of a party to the action or of a person interested in the guardianship, may:

(1) transfer to the judge's court from a district, county, or statutory court a cause of action that is a matter related to a guardianship proceeding pending in the statutory probate court, including a cause of action that is a matter related to a guardianship proceeding pending in the statutory probate court and in which the guardian, ward, or proposed ward in the pending guardianship proceeding is a party; and

(2) consolidate the transferred cause of action with the guardianship proceeding to which it relates and any other proceedings in the statutory probate court that are related to the guardianship proceeding.

(b) Notwithstanding any other provision of this chapter, the proper venue for an action by or against a guardian, ward, or proposed ward for personal injury, death, or property damages is determined under Section 15.007, Civil Practice and Remedies Code.

Added by Acts 1993, 73rd Leg., ch. 957, § 1, eff. Sept. 1, 1993. Amended by Acts 1999, 76th Leg., ch. 1431, § 2, eff. Sept. 1, 1999; Acts 2003, 78th Leg., ch. 549, § 7, eff. Sept. 1, 2003; Acts 2011, 82nd Leg., ch. 1085 (S.B. 1196), § 4, eff. Sept. 1, 2011.

### § 609. Transfer of Contested Guardianship of the Person of a Minor

(a) If an interested person contests an application for the appointment of a guardian of the person of a minor or an interested person seeks the removal of a guardian of the person of a minor, the judge, on the judge's own motion, may transfer all matters related to the guardianship proceeding to a court of competent jurisdiction in which a suit affecting the parent-child relationship under the Family Code is pending.

(b) The probate court that transfers a proceeding under this section to a court with proper jurisdiction over suits affecting the parent-child relationship shall send to the court to which the transfer is made the complete files in all matters affecting the guardianship of the person of the minor and certified copies of all entries in the judge's guardianship docket. The transferring court shall keep a copy of the transferred files. If the transferring court retains jurisdiction of the guardianship of the estate of the minor or of another minor who was the subject of the suit, the court shall send a copy of the complete files to the court to which the transfer is made and shall keep the original files.

(c) The court to which a transfer is made under this section shall apply the procedural and substantive provisions of the Family Code, including Sections 155.005 and 155.205, in regard to enforcing an order rendered by the court from which the proceeding was transferred.

Added by Acts 1993, 73rd Leg., ch. 957, § 1, eff. Sept. 1, 1993. Amended by Acts 1997, 75th Leg., ch. 77, § 1, eff. Sept. 1, 1997; Acts 1997, 75th Leg., ch. 165, § 7.55, eff. Sept. 1, 1997; Acts 2009, 81st Leg., ch. 602, § 12, eff. June 19, 2009. Subsec. (a) amended by Acts 2011, 82nd Leg., ch. 1085 (S.B. 1196), § 5, 6, eff. Sept. 1, 2011.

## SUBPART B. VENUE

### § 610. Venue for Appointment of Guardian

(a) Except as otherwise authorized by this section, a proceeding for the appointment of a guardian for the person or estate, or both, of an incapacitated person shall be brought in the county in which the proposed ward resides or is located on the date the application is filed or in the county in which the principal estate of the proposed ward is located.

(b) A proceeding for the appointment of a guardian for the person or estate, or both, of a minor may be brought:

(1) in the county in which both the minor's parents reside;

(2) if the parents do not reside in the same county, in the county in which the parent who is the sole managing conservator of the minor resides, or in the county in which the parent who is the joint managing conservator with the greater period of physical possession of and access to the minor resides;

(3) if only one parent is living and the parent has custody of the minor, in the county in which that parent resides;

(4) if both parents are dead but the minor was in the custody of a deceased parent, in the county in which the last surviving parent having custody resided; or

(5) if both parents of a minor child have died in a common disaster and there is no evidence that the parents died other than simultaneously, in the county in which both deceased parents resided at the time of their simultaneous deaths if they resided in the same county.

(c) A proceeding for the appointment of a guardian who was appointed by will may be brought in the county in which the will was admitted to probate or in the county of the appointee's residence if the appointee resides in this state.

(d) Repealed by Acts 1999, 76th Leg., ch. 379, § 10, eff. Sept. 1, 1999.

Added by Acts 1993, 73rd Leg., ch. 957, § 1, eff. Sept. 1, 1993. Amended by Acts 1999, 76th Leg., ch. 379, § 10, eff. Sept. 1, 1999.

### § 611. Concurrent Venue and Transfer for Want of Venue

(a) If two or more courts have concurrent venue of a guardianship proceeding, the court in which an application for a guardianship proceeding is initially filed has and retains jurisdiction of the proceeding. A proceeding is considered commenced by the filing of an application alleging facts sufficient to confer venue, and the proceeding initially legally commenced extends to all of the property of the guardianship estate.

(b) If a guardianship proceeding is commenced in more than one county, it shall be stayed except in the county in which it was initially commenced until final determination of proper venue is made by the court in the county in which it was initially commenced.

(c) If it appears to the court at any time before the guardianship is closed that the proceeding was commenced in a court that did not have venue over the proceeding, the court shall, on the application of any interested person, transfer the proceeding to the proper county.

(d) When a proceeding is transferred to another county under a provision of this chapter, all orders entered in connection with the proceeding shall be valid and shall be recognized in the court to which the guardianship was ordered transferred, if the orders were made and entered in conformance with the procedures prescribed by this code.

Added by Acts 1993, 73rd Leg., ch. 957, § 1, eff. Sept. 1, 1993. Subsec. (a) amended by Acts 2011, 82nd Leg., ch. 1085 (S.B. 1196), § 7, eff. Sept. 1, 2011.

### § 612. Application for Transfer of Guardianship to Another County

When a guardian or any other person desires to transfer the transaction of the business of the guardianship from one county to another, the person shall file a written application in the court in which the guardianship is pending stating the reason for the transfer.

Added by Acts 1993, 73rd Leg., ch. 957, § 1, eff. Sept. 1, 1993. Amended by Acts 2011, 82nd Leg., 1st C.S., ch. 4 (S.B. 1), § 66.01, eff. Sept. 28, 2011.

### § 613. Notice

(a) On filing an application to transfer a guardianship to another county, the sureties on the bond of the guardian shall be cited by personal service to appear and show cause why the application should not be granted.

(b) If an application is filed by a person other than the guardian, the guardian shall be cited by personal service to appear and show cause why the application should not be granted.

Added by Acts 1993, 73rd Leg., ch. 957, § 1, eff. Sept. 1, 1993. Amended by Acts 2011, 82nd Leg., 1st C.S., ch. 4 (S.B. 1), § 66.02, eff. Sept. 28, 2011.

### § 614.  Court Action

(a) On hearing an application under Section 612 of this code, if good cause is not shown to deny the application and it appears that transfer of the guardianship is in the best interests of the ward, the court shall enter an order authorizing the transfer on payment on behalf of the estate of all accrued costs.

(b) In an order entered under Subsection (a) of this section, the court shall require the guardian, not later than the 20th day after the date the order is entered, to:

(1) give a new bond payable to the judge of the court to which the guardianship is transferred; or

(2) file a rider to an existing bond noting the court to which the guardianship is transferred.

Added by Acts 1993, 73rd Leg., ch. 957, § 1, eff. Sept. 1, 1993. Amended by Acts 2011, 82nd Leg., 1st C.S., ch. 4 (S.B. 1), § 66.03, eff. Sept. 28, 2011.

### § 615.  Transfer of Record

When an order of transfer is made under Section 614 of this code, the clerk shall record any unrecorded papers of the guardianship required to be recorded.  On payment of the clerk's fee, the clerk shall transmit to the county clerk of the county to which the guardianship was ordered transferred:

(1) the case file of the guardianship proceedings; and

(2) a certified copy of the index of the guardianship records.

Added by Acts 1993, 73rd Leg., ch. 957, § 1, eff. Sept. 1, 1993. Amended by Acts 2005, 79th Leg., ch. 200, § 1, eff. Sept. 1, 2005; Acts 2011, 82nd Leg., 1st C.S., ch. 4 (S.B. 1), § 66.03, eff. Sept. 28, 2011.

### § 616.  Transfer Effective

The order transferring a guardianship does not take effect until:

(1) the case file and a certified copy of the index required by Section 615 of this code are filed in the office of the county clerk of the county to which the guardianship was ordered transferred; and

(2) a certificate under the clerk's official seal and reporting the filing of the case file and a certified copy of the index is filed in the court ordering the transfer by the county clerk of the county to which the guardianship was ordered transferred.

Added by Acts 1993, 73rd Leg., ch. 957, § 1, eff. Sept. 1, 1993. Amended by Acts 2005, 79th Leg., ch. 200, § 2, eff. Sept. 1, 2005; Acts 2011, 82nd Leg., 1st C.S., ch. 4 (S.B. 1), § 66.03, eff. Sept. 28, 2011.

### § 617.  Continuation of Guardianship

When a guardianship is transferred from one county to another in accordance with this subpart, the guardianship proceeds in the court to which it was transferred as if it had been originally commenced in that court.  It is not necessary to record in the receiving court any of the papers in the case that were recorded in the court from which the case was transferred.

Added by Acts 1993, 73rd Leg., ch. 957, § 1, eff. Sept. 1, 1993. Amended by Acts 2011, 82nd Leg., 1st C.S., ch. 4 (S.B. 1), § 66.03, eff. Sept. 28, 2011.

### § 618.  New Guardian Appointed on Transfer

If it appears to the court that transfer of the guardianship is in the best interests of the ward, but that because of the transfer it is not in the best interests of the ward for the guardian of the estate to continue to serve in that capacity, the court may in its order of transfer revoke the letters of guardianship and appoint a new guardian, and the former guardian shall account for and deliver the estate as provided by this chapter in a case in which a guardian resigns.

Added by Acts 1993, 73rd Leg., ch. 957, § 1, eff. Sept. 1, 1993. Amended by Acts 2011, 82nd Leg., 1st C.S., ch. 4 (S.B. 1), § 66.03, eff. Sept. 28, 2011.

### § 619.  Review of Transferred Guardianship

Not later than the 90th day after the date the transfer of the guardianship takes effect under Section 616 of this code, the court to which the guardianship was transferred shall hold a hearing to consider modifying the rights, duties, and powers of the guardian or any other provisions of the transferred guardianship.

Added by Acts 2011, 82nd Leg., 1st C.S., ch. 4 (S.B. 1), § 66.04, eff. Sept. 28, 2011.

### SUBPART C.  DUTIES AND RECORDS OF CLERK

### § 621.  Application and Other Papers to be Filed With Clerk

(a) An application for a guardianship proceeding or a complaint, petition, or other paper permitted or required by law to be filed in the court in a guardianship proceeding shall be filed with the county clerk of the proper county.

(b) The county clerk shall file the paper received under this section and endorse on each paper the date filed, the docket number, and the clerk's official signature.

Added by Acts 1993, 73rd Leg., ch. 957, § 1, eff. Sept. 1, 1993. Subsec. (a) amended by Acts 2011, 82nd Leg., ch. 1085 (S.B. 1196), § 8, eff. Sept. 1, 2011.

## § 622.   Costs and Security

(a) The laws regulating costs in ordinary civil cases apply to a guardianship proceeding unless otherwise expressly provided by this chapter.

(b) When a person other than the guardian, attorney ad litem, or guardian ad litem files an application, complaint, or opposition in relation to a guardianship proceeding, the clerk may require the person to give security for the probable costs of the proceeding before filing. A person interested in the guardianship or in the welfare of the ward, or an officer of the court, at any time before the trial of an application, complaint, or opposition in relation to a guardianship proceeding, may obtain from the court, on written motion, an order requiring the person who filed the application, complaint, or opposition to give security for the probable costs of the proceeding. The rules governing civil suits in the county court relating to this subject control in these cases.

(c) No security for costs shall be required of a guardian, attorney ad litem, or guardian ad litem appointed under this chapter by a court of this state in any suit brought by the guardian, attorney ad litem, or guardian ad litem in their respective fiduciary capacities.

Added by Acts 1993, 73rd Leg., ch. 957, § 1, eff. Sept. 1, 1993. Subsecs. (a) and (b) amended by Acts 2011, 82nd Leg., ch. 1085 (S.B. 1196), § 9, eff. Sept. 1, 2011.

## § 623.   Judge's Guardianship Docket

(a) The county clerk shall keep a record book to be styled "Judge's Guardianship Docket" and shall enter in the record book:

(1) the name of each person on whose person or estate a proceeding is had or is sought to be had;

(2) the name of the guardian of the estate or person or of the applicant for letters;

(3) the date the original application for a guardianship proceeding was filed;

(4) a notation, including the date, of each order, judgment, decree, and proceeding in each estate; and

(5) a number of each guardianship on the docket in the order in which a proceeding is commenced.

(b) Each paper filed in a guardianship proceeding shall be given the corresponding docket number of the estate.

Added by Acts 1993, 73rd Leg., ch. 957, § 1, eff. Sept. 1, 1993. Amended by Acts 2009, 81st Leg., ch. 602, § 13, eff. June 19, 2009.

## § 624.   Claim Docket

The county clerk shall keep a record book to be styled "Claim Docket" and shall enter in the claim docket all claims presented against a guardianship for court approval. The claim docket shall be ruled in 16 columns at proper intervals from top to bottom, with a short note of the contents at the top of each column. One or more pages shall be assigned to each guardianship. The following information shall be entered in the respective columns beginning with the first or marginal column: The names of claimants in the order in which their claims are filed; the amount of the claim; its date; the date of filing; when due; the date from which it bears interest; the rate of interest; when allowed by the guardian; the amount allowed; the date of rejection; when approved; the amount approved; when disapproved; the class to which the claim belongs; when established by judgment of a court; the amount of the judgment.

Added by Acts 1993, 73rd Leg., ch. 957, § 1, eff. Sept. 1, 1993.

## § 625.   Case Files

The county clerk shall maintain a case file for each person's filed guardianship proceedings. The case file must contain all orders, judgments, and proceedings of the court and any other guardianship filing with the court, including all:

(1) applications for the granting of guardianship;

(2) citations and notices, whether published or posted, with the returns on the citations and notices;

(3) bonds and official oaths;

(4) inventories, appraisements, and lists of claims;

(5) exhibits and accounts;

(6) reports of hiring, renting, or sale;

(7) applications for sale or partition of real estate and reports of sale and of commissioners of partition;

(8) applications for authority to execute leases for mineral development, or for pooling or unitization of lands, royalty, or other interest in minerals, or to lend or invest money;

(9) reports of lending or investing money; and

(10) reports of guardians of the persons.

Added by Acts 1993, 73rd Leg., ch. 957, § 1, eff. Sept. 1, 1993. Amended by Acts 1999, 76th Leg., ch. 67, § 2, eff. Sept. 1, 1999.

## § 626.   Guardianship Fee Book

The county clerk shall keep a record book styled "Guardianship Fee Book" and shall enter in the guardianship fee book each item of costs that accrue to the officers of the court, with witness fees, if any, showing the:

(1) party to whom the costs or fees are due;

(2) date of the accrual of the costs or fees;

(3) guardianship or party liable for the costs or fees; and

(4) date on which the costs or fees are paid.

Added by Acts 1993, 73rd Leg., ch. 957, § 1, eff. Sept. 1, 1993.

## § 627.   Maintaining Records in Lieu of Record Books

In lieu of keeping the record books described by Sections 623, 624, and 626 of this code, the county clerk may maintain the information relating to a person's guardianship proceeding maintained in those record books on a computer file, on microfilm, in the form of a digitized optical image, or in another similar form of data compilation.

Added by Acts 1999, 76th Leg., ch. 67, § 2, eff. Sept. 1, 1999.

### § 627A. Index

The county clerk shall properly index the records and keep the index open for public inspection but may not release the index from the clerk's custody.

Added by Acts 1993, 73rd Leg., ch. 957, § 1, eff. Sept. 1, 1993. Renumbered from V.A.T.S. Probate Code, § 627 and amended by Acts 1999, 76th Leg., ch. 67, § 2, eff. Sept. 1, 1999.

### § 628. Use of Records as Evidence

The record books or individual case files, including records on a computer file, on microfilm, in the form of a digitized optical image, or in another similar form of data compilation described in other sections of this chapter, or certified copies or reproductions of the records, shall be evidence in any court of this state.

Added by Acts 1993, 73rd Leg., ch. 957, § 1, eff. Sept. 1, 1993. Amended by Acts 1999, 76th Leg., ch. 67, § 2, eff. Sept. 1, 1999.

### § 629. Call of the Dockets

The judge of the court in which a guardianship proceeding is pending, as the judge determines, shall call guardianship proceedings in their regular order on both the guardianship and claim dockets and shall make necessary orders.

Added by Acts 1993, 73rd Leg., ch. 957, § 1, eff. Sept. 1, 1993. Amended by Acts 2011, 82nd Leg., ch. 1085 (S.B. 1196), § 10, eff. Sept. 1, 2011.

### § 630. Clerk May Set Hearings

If the judge is absent from the county seat or is on vacation, disqualified, ill, or deceased and is unable to designate the time and place for hearing a guardianship proceeding pending in the judge's court, the county clerk of the county in which the proceeding is pending may designate the time and place for hearing, entering the setting on the judge's docket and certifying on the docket the reason that the judge is not acting to set the hearing. If a qualified judge is not present for the hearing, after service of the notices and citations required by law with reference to the time and place of hearing has been perfected, the hearing is automatically continued from day to day until a qualified judge is present to hear and make a determination in the proceeding.

Added by Acts 1993, 73rd Leg., ch. 957, § 1, eff. Sept. 1, 1993. Amended by Acts 2011, 82nd Leg., ch. 1085 (S.B. 1196), § 11, eff. Sept. 1, 2011.

### § 631. Clerk's Duties

(a) If the proper venue is finally determined to be in another county, the clerk, after making and retaining a true copy of the entire file in the case, shall transmit the original file to the proper county, and a proceeding shall be held in the proper county in the same manner as if the proceeding had originally been instituted in the proper county.

(b) By transmitting to the proper court in the proper county for venue purposes the original file in the case, with certified copies of all entries in the judge's guardianship docket made in the file, an administration of the guardianship in the proper county for venue purposes shall be completed in the same manner as if the proceeding had originally been instituted in that county.

(c) The clerk of the court from which the proceeding is transferred shall transmit to the court to which the proceeding is transferred the original file in the proceeding and a certified copy of the entries in the judge's guardianship docket that relate to the proceeding.

Added by Acts 1993, 73rd Leg., ch. 957, § 1, eff. Sept. 1, 1993. Amended by Acts 2009, 81st Leg., ch. 602, § 14, eff. June 19, 2009.

## SUBPART D. SERVICE AND NOTICE

### § 632. Issuance, Contents, Service, and Return of Citation, Notices, and Writs in Guardianship Proceedings

(a) A person does not need to be cited or otherwise given notice in a guardianship proceeding except in situations in which this chapter expressly provides for citation or the giving of notice. If this chapter does not expressly provide for citation or the issuance or return of notice in a guardianship proceeding, the court may require that notice be given. If the court requires that notice be given, the court shall prescribe the form and manner of service and return of service.

(b) Unless a court order is required by a provision of this chapter, the county clerk shall issue without a court order necessary citations, writs, and process in guardianship proceedings and all notices not required to be issued by guardians.

(c) A citation and notice issued by the clerk shall be signed and sealed by the clerk and shall be styled "The State of Texas." A notice required to be given by a guardian shall be in writing and signed by the guardian in the guardian's official capacity. A citation or notice shall be dated and directed to the person that is being cited or notified and must state the style and number of the proceeding and the court in which the proceeding is pending and must describe generally the nature of the proceeding or matter to which the citation or notice relates. A precept directed to an officer is not necessary. A citation or notice must direct the person cited or notified to appear by filing a written contest or answer or perform other required acts. A citation or notice must state when and where an appearance or performance by a person cited or notified is required. A citation or notice is not defective because it contains a precept directed to an officer authorized to serve it. A writ or other process other than a citation or notice shall be directed "To any sheriff or constable within the State of Texas" and may not be held defective because it is directed to the sheriff or any constable of a specific county if the writ or other process is properly served within the named county by an officer authorized to serve it.

(d) In all situations in which this chapter requires that notice be given or that a person be cited, and in which a specific method of giving the notice or citing the person, or a specific method of service and return of the citation or notice is not given, or an insufficient or inadequate provision appears with respect to any matter relating to citation or notice, or on request of an interested person, notice or citation shall be issued, served, and returned in the manner the court, by written order, directs in accordance with this chapter and the Texas Rules of Civil Procedure and has the same force and effect as if the manner of service and return had been specified in this chapter.

(e) Except in instances in which this chapter expressly provides for another method of service, a notice or citation required to be served on a guardian or receiver shall be served by the clerk that issues the citation or notice. The clerk shall serve the citation or notice by sending the original citation or notice by registered or certified mail to the attorney of record for the guardian or receiver or to the guardian or receiver, if the guardian or receiver does not have an attorney of record.

(f)(1) In cases in which it is provided that personal service shall be had with respect to a citation or notice, the citation or notice must be served on the attorney of record for the person who is being cited or notified. Notwithstanding the requirement of personal service, service may be made on the attorney by any method specified under this chapter for service on an attorney. If there is no attorney of record in the proceeding for the person who is being cited or notified, or if an attempt to make service on the attorney was unsuccessful, a citation or notice directed to a person within this state must be served in person by the sheriff or constable on the person who is being cited or notified by delivering to the person a true copy of the citation or notice at least 10 days before the return day on the citation or notice, exclusive of the date of service. If the person who is being cited or notified is absent from the state or is a nonresident, the citation or notice may be served by a disinterested person competent to make oath of the fact. The citation or notice served by a disinterested person shall be returnable at least 10 days after the date of service, exclusive of the date of service. The return of the person serving the citation or notice shall be endorsed on or attached to the citation or notice. The return must show the time and place of service, certify that a true copy of the citation or notice was delivered to the person directed to be served, be subscribed and sworn to before an officer authorized by the laws of this state to take affidavits, under the hand and official seal of the officer, and returned to the county clerk who issued the citation or notice. If the citation or notice is returned with the notation that the person sought to be served, whether or not within this state, cannot be found, the clerk shall issue a new citation or notice directed to the person sought to be served and service shall be by publication.

(2) When citation or notice is required to be posted, the sheriff or constable shall post the citation or notice at the courthouse door of the county in which the proceeding is pending, or at the place in or near the courthouse where public notices customarily are posted, for at least 10 days before the return day of the citation or notice, exclusive of the date of posting. The clerk shall deliver the original and a copy of the citation or notice to the sheriff or a constable of the proper county, who shall post the copy as prescribed by this section and return the original to the clerk, stating in a written return of the copy the time when and the place where the sheriff or constable posted the copy. The date of posting is the date of service. When posting of notice by a guardian is authorized or required, the method prescribed by this section shall be followed. The notice is to be issued in the name of the guardian, addressed and delivered to, posted and returned by, the proper officer, and filed with the clerk.

(3) When a person is to be cited or notified by publication, the citation or notice shall be published once in a newspaper of general circulation in the county in which the proceeding is pending, and the publication shall be not less than 10 days before the return date of the citation or notice, exclusive of the date of publication. The date of publication of the newspaper in which the citation or notice is published appears is the date of service. If there is no newspaper of general circulation published or printed in the county in which citation or notice is to be had, service of the citation or notice shall be by posting.

(4)(A) When a citation or notice is required or permitted to be served by registered or certified mail, other than a notice required to be given by a guardian, the clerk shall issue the citation or notice and shall serve the citation or notice by sending the original citation or notice by registered or certified mail. A guardian shall issue notice required to be given by the guardian by registered or certified mail, and the guardian shall serve the notice by sending the original notice by registered or certified mail. The citation or notice shall be mailed return receipt requested with instructions to deliver to the addressee only. The envelope containing the citation or notice shall be addressed to the attorney of record in the proceeding for the person who is being cited or notified, but if there is no attorney of record, or if the citation or notice is returned undelivered, the envelope containing the citation or notice shall be addressed to the person who is being cited or notified. A copy of the citation or notice and the certificate of the clerk or guardian showing the fact and date of mailing shall be filed and recorded. If a receipt is returned, it shall be attached to the certificate.

(B) When a citation or notice is required or permitted to be served by ordinary mail, the clerk or the guardian when required by statute or court order, shall serve the citation or notice by mailing the original to the person being cited or notified. A copy of the citation or notice and a certificate of the person serving the citation or notice that shows the fact and time of mailing shall be filed and recorded.

(C) When service is made by mail, the date of mailing is the date of service. Service by mail must be made not less than 20 days before the return day of the citation or notice, exclusive of the date of service.

Text of Texas Probate Code effective until January 1, 2014

(D) If a citation or notice served by mail is returned undelivered, a new citation or notice shall be issued, and the new citation or notice shall be served by posting.

(g) A citation or notice issued by the clerk and served by personal service, by mail, by posting, or by publication shall be returned to the court from which the citation or notice was issued on the first Monday after the service is perfected.

(h) In a guardianship proceeding in which citation or notice is required to be served by posting and issued in conformity with the applicable provision of this code, the citation or notice and the service of and return of the citation or notice is sufficient and valid if a sheriff or constable posts a copy of the citation or notice at the place or places prescribed by this chapter on a day that is sufficiently before the return day contained in the citation or notice for the period of time for which the citation or notice is required to be posted to elapse before the return day of the citation or notice. The sufficiency or validity of the citation or notice or the service of or return of the service of the citation or notice is not affected by the fact that the sheriff or constable makes the return on the citation or notice and returns the citation or notice to the court before the period elapses for which the citation or notice is required to be posted, even though the return is made, and the citation or notice is returned to the court, on the same day it is issued.

(i) Proof of service by publication, posting, mailing, or otherwise in all cases requiring notice or citation shall be filed before a hearing. Proof of service made by a sheriff or constable shall be made by the return of service. Service made by a private person shall be proved by the person's affidavit. Proof of service by publication shall be made by an affidavit of the publisher or of an employee of the publisher that shows the issue date of the newspaper that carried the notice or citation and that has attached to or embodied in the affidavit a copy of the notice or citation. Proof of service by mail shall be made by the certificate of the clerk, or the affidavit of the guardian or other person that makes the service that states the fact and time of mailing. The return receipt must be attached to the certificate, if a receipt has been returned if service is made by registered or certified mail.

(j) At any time after an application is filed for the purpose of commencing a guardianship proceeding, a person interested in the estate or welfare of a ward or an incapacitated person may file with the clerk a written request that the person be notified of any or all specifically designated motions, applications, or pleadings filed by any person, or by a person specifically designated in the request. The person who makes the request is responsible for the fees and costs associated with the documents specified in the request. The clerk may require a deposit to cover the estimated costs of furnishing the person with the requested notice. The clerk by ordinary mail shall send to the requesting person a copy of any document specified in the request. A proceeding is not invalid if the clerk fails to comply with the request under this subsection.

Added by Acts 1993, 73rd Leg., ch. 957, § 1, eff. Sept. 1, 1993. Sec. heading, subsecs. (a), (b) and (h) amended by Acts 2011, 82nd Leg., ch. 1085 (S.B. 1196), §§ 12, 13, eff. Sept. 1, 2011.

## § 633. Notice and Citation

(a) On the filing of an application for guardianship, notice shall be issued and served as provided by this section.

(b) The court clerk shall issue a citation stating that the application for guardianship was filed, the name of the proposed ward, the name of the applicant, and the name of the person to be appointed guardian as provided in the application, if that person is not the applicant. The citation must cite all persons interested in the welfare of the proposed ward to appear at the time and place stated in the notice if they wish to contest the application and must contain a clear and conspicuous statement informing those interested persons of the right provided under Section 632(j) of this code to be notified of any or all motions, applications, or pleadings relating to the application for the guardianship or any subsequent guardianship proceeding involving the ward after the guardianship is created, if any. The citation shall be posted.

(c) The sheriff or other officer shall personally serve citation to appear and answer the application for guardianship on:

(1) a proposed ward who is 12 years of age or older;

(2) the parents of a proposed ward if the whereabouts of the parents are known or can be reasonably ascertained;

(3) any court-appointed conservator or person having control of the care and welfare of the proposed ward;

(4) a proposed ward's spouse if the whereabouts of the spouse are known or can be reasonably ascertained; and

(5) the person named in the application to be appointed guardian, if that person is not the applicant.

(c–1) The citation served as provided by Subsection (c) of this section must contain the statement regarding the right provided under Section 632(j) of this code that is required in the citation issued under Subsection (b) of this section.

(d) The applicant shall mail a copy of the application for guardianship and a notice containing the information required in the citation issued under Subsection (b) of this section by registered or certified mail, return receipt requested, or by any other form of mail that provides proof of delivery, to the following persons, if their whereabouts are known or can be reasonably ascertained:

(1) all adult children of a proposed ward;

(2) all adult siblings of a proposed ward;

(3) the administrator of a nursing home facility or similar facility in which the proposed ward resides;

(4) the operator of a residential facility in which the proposed ward resides;

(5) a person whom the applicant knows to hold a power of attorney signed by the proposed ward;

(6) a person designated to serve as guardian of the proposed ward by a written declaration under Section 679 of this code, if the applicant knows of the existence of the declaration;

(7) a person designated to serve as guardian of the proposed ward in the probated will of the last surviving parent of the ward;

(8) a person designated to serve as guardian of the proposed ward by a written declaration of the proposed ward's last surviving parent, if the declarant is deceased and the applicant knows of the existence of the declaration; and

(9) each person named as another relative within the third degree by consanguinity in the application for guardianship as required by Section 682(10) or (12) of this code if the proposed ward's spouse and each of the proposed ward's parents, adult siblings, and adult children are deceased or there is no spouse, parent, adult sibling, or adult child.

(d–1) The applicant shall file with the court:

(1) a copy of any notice required by Subsection (d) of this section and the proofs of delivery of the notice; and

(2) an affidavit sworn to by the applicant or the applicant's attorney stating:

(A) that the notice was mailed as required by Subsection (d) of this section; and

(B) the name of each person to whom the notice was mailed, if the person's name is not shown on the proof of delivery.

(e) A person other than the proposed ward who is entitled to receive notice or personal service of citation under Subsections (c) and (d) of this section may choose, in person or by attorney ad litem, by writing filed with the clerk, to waive the receipt of notice or the issuance and personal service of citation.

(f) The court may not act on an application for the creation of a guardianship until the Monday following the expiration of the 10–day period beginning the date service of notice and citation has been made as provided by Subsections (b), (c), and (d)(1) of this section and the applicant has complied with Subsection (d–1) of this section. The validity of a guardianship created under this chapter is not affected by the failure of the applicant to comply with the requirements of Subsections (d)(2)–(9) of this section.

(g) It is not necessary for a person who files an application for the creation of a guardianship under this chapter to be served with citation or waive the issuance and personal service of citation under this section.

Added by Acts 1995, 74th Leg., ch. 1039, § 18, eff. Sept. 1, 1995. Amended by Acts 1997, 75th Leg., ch. 77, § 2, eff. Sept. 1, 1997; Acts 1999, 76th Leg., ch. 379, § 3, eff. Sept. 1, 1999; Acts 1999, 76th Leg., ch. 997, § 1, eff. Sept. 1, 1999; Acts 2001, 77th Leg., ch. 940, § 1, eff. Sept. 1, 2001; Acts 2001, 77th Leg., ch. 1174, § 2, eff. Sept. 1, 2001. Subsecs. (d), (f) amended by Acts 2003, 78th Leg., ch. 549, § 8, eff. Sept. 1, 2003; Subsec. (d–1) added by Acts 2003, 78th Leg., ch. 549, § 8; Subsecs. (b) and (d) amended by Acts 2011, 82nd Leg., ch. 599 (S.B. 220), § 6, eff. Sept. 1, 2011; Subsec. (c–1) added by Acts 2011, 82nd Leg., ch. 599 (S.B. 220), § 6, eff. Sept. 1, 2011.

### § 634. Service on Attorney

(a) If an attorney has entered an appearance on record for a party in a guardianship proceeding, a citation or notice required to be served on the party shall be served on the attorney. Service on the attorney of record is in lieu of service on the party for whom the attorney appears. Except as provided by Section 633(e) of this code, an attorney ad litem may not waive personal service of citation.

(b) A notice served on an attorney under this section may be served by registered or certified mail, return receipt requested, by any other form of mail requiring proof of delivery, or by delivery to the attorney in person. A party to the proceeding or the party's attorney of record, an appropriate sheriff or constable, or another person who is competent to testify may serve notice or citation to an attorney under this section.

(c) A written statement by an attorney of record, the return of the officer, or the affidavit of a person that shows service is prima facie evidence of the fact of service.

Added by Acts 1993, 73rd Leg., ch. 957, § 1, eff. Sept. 1, 1993. Amended by Acts 2003, 78th Leg., ch. 549, § 9, eff. Sept. 1, 2003.

### § 635. Waiver of Notice

A competent person who is interested in a hearing in a guardianship proceeding, in person or by attorney, may waive in writing notice of the hearing. A consul or other representative of a foreign government, whose appearance has been entered as provided by law on behalf of a person residing in a foreign country, may waive notice on behalf of the person. A person who submits to the jurisdiction of the court in a hearing is deemed to have waived notice of the hearing.

Added by Acts 1993, 73rd Leg., ch. 957, § 1, eff. Sept. 1, 1993.

### § 636. Notices to Department of Veterans Affairs by Guardians

When an annual or other account of funds, or an application for the expenditure of or investment of funds is filed by a guardian whose ward is a beneficiary of the Department of Veterans Affairs, or when a claim against the estate of a ward who is a beneficiary of the Department of Veterans Affairs is filed, the court shall set a date for the hearing of the account, application, petition, or claim to be held not less than 20 days from the date of the filing of the account, application, petition, or claim. The person who files the account, application, petition, or claim shall give notice of the date of the filing to the office of the Department of Veterans Affairs in whose territory the court is located by mailing to the office a certified copy of the account, application, petition, or claim not later than five days after the date of the filing. An office of the Department of Veterans Affairs, through its attorney, may waive the service of notice and the time within which a hearing may be had in those cases.

Added by Acts 1993, 73rd Leg., ch. 957, § 1, eff. Sept. 1, 1993. Amended by Acts 1995, 74th Leg., ch. 1039, § 19, eff. Sept. 1, 1995.

## SUBPART E. TRIAL AND HEARING MATTERS

### § 641. Defects in Pleading

A court may not invalidate a pleading in a guardianship proceeding or an order based on the pleading based on a defect of form or substance in the pleading, unless the defect has been timely objected to and called to the attention of the court in which the proceeding was or is pending.

Added by Acts 1993, 73rd Leg., ch. 957, § 1, eff. Sept. 1, 1993. Amended by Acts 2011, 82nd Leg., ch. 1085 (S.B. 1196), § 14, eff. Sept. 1, 2011.

### § 642. Standing to Commence or Contest Proceeding

(a) Except as provided by Subsection (b) of this section, any person has the right to commence any guardianship proceeding, including a proceeding for complete restoration of a ward's capacity or modification of a ward's guardianship, or to appear and contest any guardianship proceeding or the appointment of a particular person as guardian.

(b) A person who has an interest that is adverse to a proposed ward or incapacitated person may not:

(1) file an application to create a guardianship for the proposed ward or incapacitated person;

(2) contest the creation of a guardianship for the proposed ward or incapacitated person;

(3) contest the appointment of a person as a guardian of the person or estate, or both, of the proposed ward or incapacitated person; or

(4) contest an application for complete restoration of a ward's capacity or modification of a ward's guardianship.

(c) The court shall determine by motion in limine the standing of a person who has an interest that is adverse to a proposed ward or incapacitated person.

Added by Acts 1993, 73rd Leg., ch. 957, § 1, eff. Sept. 1, 1993. Amended by Acts 1995, 74th Leg., ch. 1039, § 20, eff. Sept. 1, 1995; Acts 1999, 76th Leg., ch. 829, § 2, eff. Sept. 1, 1999.

### § 643. Trial by Jury

A party in a contested guardianship proceeding is entitled, on request, to a jury trial.

Added by Acts 1993, 73rd Leg., ch. 957, § 1, eff. Sept. 1, 1993.

### § 644. Hearing by Submission

(a) A court may consider by submission a motion or application filed under this chapter unless the proceeding is:

(1) contested; or

(2) an application for the appointment of a guardian.

(b) The burden of proof at a hearing on a motion or application that is being considered by the court on submission is on the party who is seeking relief under the motion or application.

(c) The court may consider a person's failure to file a response to a motion or application that may be considered on submission as a representation that the person does not oppose the motion or application.

(d) A person's request for oral argument is not a response to a motion or application under this section.

(e) The court, on its own motion, may order oral argument on a motion or application that may be considered by submission.

Added by Acts 1993, 73rd Leg., ch. 957, § 1, eff. Sept. 1, 1993. Amended by Acts 1995, 74th Leg., ch. 1039, § 21, eff. Sept. 1, 1995.

### § 645. Guardians Ad Litem

(a) The judge may appoint a guardian ad litem to represent the interests of an incapacitated person in a guardianship proceeding.

(b) A guardian ad litem is entitled to reasonable compensation for services in the amount set by the court to be taxed as costs in the proceeding.

(c) A guardian ad litem is an officer of the court. The guardian ad litem shall protect the incapacitated person in a manner that will enable the court to determine what action will be in the best interests of the incapacitated person.

(d) If a guardian ad litem is appointed under Section 681(4) of this code, the fees and expenses of the guardian ad litem are costs of the litigation proceeding that made the appointment necessary.

(e) In the interest of judicial economy, the court may appoint as guardian ad litem under Section 681(4) of this code the person who has been appointed attorney ad litem under Section 646 of this code or the person who is serving as an ad litem for the benefit of the ward in any other proceeding.

(f) The term of appointment of a guardian ad litem made in a proceeding for the appointment of a guardian expires, without a court order, on the date the court either appoints a guardian or denies the application for appointment of a guardian, unless the court determines that the continued appointment of the guardian ad litem is in the ward's best interest.

Added by Acts 1993, 73rd Leg., ch. 957, § 1, eff. Sept. 1, 1993. Subsec. (f) added by Acts 2007, 80th Leg., ch. 614, § 1, eff. Sept. 1, 2007.

## § 645A. Immunity

(a) A guardian ad litem appointed under Section 645, 683, or 694A of this code to represent the interests of an incapacitated person in a guardianship proceeding involving the creation, modification, or termination of a guardianship is not liable for civil damages arising from a recommendation made or an opinion given in the capacity of guardian ad litem.

(b) Subsection (a) of this section does not apply to a recommendation or opinion that is:

(1) wilfully wrongful;

(2) given with conscious indifference or reckless disregard to the safety of another;

(3) given in bad faith or with malice; or

(4) grossly negligent.

Added by Acts 2003, 78th Leg., ch. 622, § 1, eff. Sept. 1, 2003.

## § 646. Appointment of Attorney ad Litem and Interpreter

(a) In a proceeding under this chapter for the appointment of a guardian, the court shall appoint an attorney ad litem to represent the interests of the proposed ward. The attorney shall be supplied with copies of all of the current records in the case and may have access to all of the proposed ward's relevant medical, psychological, and intellectual testing records.

(b) To be eligible for appointment as an attorney ad litem, a person must have the certification required by Section 647A of this code.

(c) A person whose certificate has expired must obtain a new certificate to be eligible for appointment as an attorney ad litem.

(d) At the time of the appointment of the attorney ad litem, the court shall also appoint a language interpreter or a sign interpreter if necessary to ensure effective communication between the proposed ward and the attorney.

(e) The term of appointment of an attorney ad litem appointed under this section expires, without a court order, on the date the court appoints a guardian in accordance with Section 693 of this code, appoints a successor guardian, or denies the application for appointment of a guardian, unless the court determines that the continued appointment of the attorney ad litem is in the ward's best interest.

(f) The term of appointment of an attorney ad litem appointed under this section continues after the court appoints a temporary guardian under Section 875 of this code unless a court order provides for the termination or expiration of the attorney ad litem's appointment.

Added by Acts 1993, 73rd Leg., ch. 957, § 1, eff. Sept. 1, 1993. Amended by Acts 1995, 74th Leg., ch. 1039, §§ 22, 74, eff. Sept. 1, 1995; Acts 1999, 76th Leg., ch. 379, § 4, eff. Sept. 1, 1999; Acts 1999, 76th Leg., ch. 716, § 1, eff. Sept. 1, 1999.
Subsec. (e) added by Acts 2007, 80th Leg., ch. 614, § 2, eff. Sept. 1, 2007; Subsec. (e) amended and subsec. (f) added by Acts 2011, 82nd Leg., ch. 1085 (S.B. 1196), § 15, eff. Sept. 1, 2011.

## § 646A. Representation of Ward or Proposed Ward by Attorney

(a) The following persons may at any time retain an attorney who holds a certificate required by Section 647A of this code to represent the person's interests in a guardianship matter instead of having those interests represented by an attorney ad litem appointed under Section 646 of this code or another provision of this chapter:

(1) a ward who retains the power to enter into a contract under the terms of the guardianship, subject to Section 694K of this code; and

(2) a proposed ward for purposes of a proceeding for the appointment of a guardian as long as the proposed ward has capacity to contract.

(b) If the court finds that the ward or the proposed ward has capacity to contract, the court may remove an attorney ad litem appointed under Section 646 of this code or any other provision of this chapter that requires the court to appoint an attorney ad litem to represent the interests of a ward or proposed ward and appoint a ward or a proposed ward's retained counsel.

Added by Acts 2011, 82nd Leg., ch. 599 (S.B. 220), § 7, eff. Sept. 1, 2011.

## § 647. Duties of Attorney Ad Litem

(a) An attorney ad litem appointed under Section 646 of this code to represent a proposed ward shall, within a reasonable time before the hearing, interview the proposed ward. To the greatest extent possible, the attorney shall discuss with the proposed ward the law and facts of the case, the proposed ward's legal options regarding disposition of the case, and the grounds on which guardianship is sought.

(b) Before the hearing, the attorney shall review the application for guardianship, certificates of current physical, medical, and intellectual examinations, and all of the proposed ward's relevant medical, psychological, and intellectual testing records.

Added by Acts 1993, 73rd Leg., ch. 957, § 1, eff. Sept. 1, 1993.

## § 647A. Certification Requirement for Certain Court-Appointed Attorneys

(a) A court-appointed attorney in any guardianship proceeding must be certified by the State Bar of Texas or a person or other entity designated by the state bar as having successfully completed a course of study in guardianship law and procedure sponsored by the state bar or its designee.

(b) For certification under this section, the state bar shall require three hours of credit.

(c) Except as provided by Subsection (e) of this section, a certificate issued under this section expires on the second anniversary of the date the certificate is issued.

(d) To be eligible to be appointed by a court to represent a person at a guardianship proceeding, an attorney whose certificate has expired must obtain a new certificate.

(e) A new certificate obtained by a person who previously has been issued a certificate under this section expires on the fourth anniversary of the date the new certificate is issued if the person has been certified each of the four years immediately preceding the date the new certificate is issued.

Added by Acts 1999, 76th Leg., ch. 716, § 2, eff. Sept. 1, 1999.

## § 648. Court Visitor Program

(a) Each statutory probate court shall operate a court visitor program to assess the conditions of wards and proposed wards. Another court that has jurisdiction over a guardianship proceeding may operate a court visitor program in accordance with the population needs and financial abilities of the jurisdiction. A court that operates a court visitor program shall use persons willing to serve without compensation to the greatest extent possible.

(b) On request by any interested person, including a ward or proposed ward, or on its own motion, and at any time before the appointment of a guardian or during the pendency of a guardianship of the person or estate, a court may appoint a court visitor to evaluate the ward or proposed ward and provide a written report that substantially complies with Subsection (c) of this section.

(c) A court visitor's report must include:

(1) a description of the nature and degree of capacity and incapacity of the ward or proposed ward, including the medical history of the ward or proposed ward, if reasonably available and not waived by the court;

(2) a medical prognosis and a list of the treating physicians of the ward or proposed ward, when appropriate;

(3) a description of the living conditions and circumstances of the ward or proposed ward;

(4) a description of the social, intellectual, physical, and educational condition of the ward or proposed ward;

(5) a statement that the court visitor has personally visited or observed the ward or proposed ward;

(6) a statement of the date of the most recent visit by the guardian, if one has been appointed;

(7) a recommendation as to any modifications needed in the guardianship or proposed guardianship, including removal or denial of the guardianship; and

(8) any other information required by the court.

(d) The court visitor shall file the report not later than the 14th day after the date of the evaluation conducted by the court visitor, and the court visitor making the report must swear, under penalty of perjury, to its accuracy to the best of the court visitor's knowledge and belief.

(e) A court visitor who has not expressed a willingness to serve without compensation is entitled to reasonable compensation for services in an amount set by the court and to be taxed as costs in the proceeding.

(f) This section does not apply to a guardianship that is created only because it is necessary for a person to have a guardian appointed to receive funds from a governmental source.

Added by Acts 1993, 73rd Leg., ch. 957, § 1, eff. Sept. 1, 1993. Amended by Acts 1995, 74th Leg., ch. 1039, § 23, eff. Sept. 1, 1995.

## § 648A. Duties of Court Investigator

(a) On the filing of an application for guardianship under Section 682 of this code, a court investigator shall investigate the circumstances alleged in the application to determine whether a less restrictive alternative than guardianship is appropriate.

(b) A court investigator shall:

(1) supervise the court visitor program established under Section 648 of this code and in that capacity serve as the chief court visitor;

(2) investigate a complaint received from any person about a guardianship and report to the judge, if necessary; and

(3) perform other duties as assigned by the judge or required by this code.

(c) After making an investigation under Subsection (a) or (b) of this section, a court investigator shall file with the court a report of the court investigator's findings and conclusions. Disclosure to a jury of the contents of a court investigator's report is subject to the Texas Rules of Civil Evidence. In a contested case, the court investigator shall provide copies of the report to the attorneys for the parties before the earlier of:

(1) the seventh day after the day the report is completed; or

(2) the 10th day before the day the trial is scheduled to begin.

(d) Nothing in this section supersedes any duty or obligation of another to report or investigate abuse or neglect under any statute of this state.

Added by Acts 1995, 74th Leg., ch. 1039, § 24, eff. Sept. 1, 1995. Amended by Acts 1999, 76th Leg., ch. 829, § 3, eff. Sept. 1, 1999.

## § 649. Evidence

In a guardianship proceeding, the rules relating to witnesses and evidence that govern in the district court apply as far as practicable. If there is no opposing party or attorney of record on whom to serve notice and copies of interrogatories, service may be had by posting notice of the intention to take depositions for a period of 10 days as provided by this chapter in the provisions governing a posting of notice. When notice by posting under this section is filed with the clerk, a copy of the interrogatories shall also be filed. At the expiration of the 10-day period, commission may issue for taking the depositions and the judge may file cross-interrogatories if no person appears.

Added by Acts 1993, 73rd Leg., ch. 957, § 1, eff. Sept. 1, 1993.

## § 650. Decrees

A decision, order, decree, or judgment of the court in a guardianship proceeding must be rendered in open court, except in a case in which it is otherwise expressly provided.

Added by Acts 1993, 73rd Leg., ch. 957, § 1, eff. Sept. 1, 1993. Amended by Acts 2009, 81st Leg., ch. 602, § 15, eff. June 19, 2009; Acts 2011, 82nd Leg., ch. 1085 (S.B. 1196), § 16, eff. Sept. 1, 2011.

## § 651. Enforcement of Orders

The judge may enforce obedience to an order entered against a guardian by attachment and imprisonment. An imprisonment of a guardian may not exceed three days for any one offense, unless expressly provided otherwise in this chapter.

Added by Acts 1993, 73rd Leg., ch. 957, § 1, eff. Sept. 1, 1993.

## § 652. Location of Hearing

(a) Except as provided by Subsection (b) of this section, the judge may hold a hearing on a guardianship matter involving an adult ward or adult proposed ward at any suitable location in the county in which the guardianship matter is pending. The hearing should be held in a physical setting that is not likely to have a harmful effect on the ward or proposed ward.

(b) On the request of the adult proposed ward, the adult ward, or the attorney of the proposed ward or ward, the hearing may not be held under the authority of this section at a place other than the courthouse.

Added by Acts 2011, 82nd Leg., ch. 1085 (S.B. 1196), § 17, eff. Sept. 1, 2011.

## SUBPART F. POST–TRIAL MATTERS

## § 653. Execution

An execution in a guardianship proceeding shall be directed "To any sheriff or any constable within the State of Texas," made returnable in 60 days, and attested and signed by the clerk officially under the seal of the court. A proceeding under an execution in a guardianship proceeding is governed so far as applicable by the laws regulating a proceeding under an execution issued from the district court. An execution directed to the sheriff or a constable of a specific county in this state may not be held defective if the execution was properly executed within the county by the officer to whom the direction for execution was given.

Added by Acts 1993, 73rd Leg., ch. 957, § 1, eff. Sept. 1, 1993. Amended by Acts 2011, 82nd Leg., ch. 1085 (S.B. 1196), § 18, eff. Sept. 1, 2011.

## § 654. Attachment for Property

When a complaint in writing and under oath that the guardian is about to remove the estate or any part of the estate beyond the limits of the state is made to the judge by a person interested in the estate of a minor or other incapacitated person, the judge may order a writ to issue, directed "To any sheriff or any constable within the State of Texas," commanding the sheriff or constable to seize the estate or any part of the estate and to hold the estate subject to further court order. The judge may not issue a writ unless the complainant gives a bond, in the sum the judge requires, payable to the guardian of the estate and conditioned on payment of all damages and costs that shall be recovered for a wrongful suit out of the writ. A writ of attachment directed to the sheriff or a constable of a specific county in this state is not defective if the writ was properly executed within the county by the officer to whom the direction to seize the estate was given.

Added by Acts 1993, 73rd Leg., ch. 957, § 1, eff. Sept. 1, 1993.

## § 655. Guardian to Serve Pending Appeal of Appointment

Pending an appeal from an order or judgment appointing a guardian, an appointee shall continue to act as guardian and shall continue the prosecution of a pending suit in favor of the guardianship.

Added by Acts 1993, 73rd Leg., ch. 957, § 1, eff. Sept. 1, 1993.

## § 656. Appeal Bond of Guardian

When a guardian appeals, a bond is not required, unless the appeal personally concerns the guardian, in which case the guardian must give the bond.

Added by Acts 1993, 73rd Leg., ch. 957, § 1, eff. Sept. 1, 1993.

## § 657. Bill of Review

A person interested, including a ward, by bill of review filed in the court in which a guardianship proceeding took place, may have a decision, order, or judgment rendered by the court, revised and corrected if an error is shown on the decision, order, or judgment. A process or action under the decision, order, or judgment is not stayed except by writ of injunction. A bill of review may not be filed after two years have elapsed from the date of the decision, order, or judgment. A person with a disability has two years after the removal of the person's respective disability to apply for a bill of review.

Added by Acts 1993, 73rd Leg., ch. 957, § 1, eff. Sept. 1, 1993.

## SUBPART G. LETTERS OF GUARDIANSHIP

## § 659. Issuance of Letters of Guardianship

(a) When a person who is appointed guardian has qualified under Section 699 of this code, the clerk shall issue to the guardian a certificate under seal, stating the fact of the appointment, of the qualification, the date of the appointment and qualification, and the date the letters of guardianship expire. The certificate issued by the clerk constitutes letters of guardianship.

(b) All letters of guardianship expire one year and four months after the date of issuance unless renewed.

(c) The clerk may not renew letters of guardianship relating to the appointment of a guardian of the estate until the court receives and approves the guardian's annual accounting. The clerk may not renew letters of guardianship relating to the appointment of a guardian of the person until the court receives and approves the annual report. If the guardian's annual accounting or annual report is disapproved or not timely filed, the clerk may not issue further letters of guardianship to the delinquent guardian unless ordered by the court.

(d) Regardless of the date the court approves an annual accounting or annual report for purposes of this section, a renewal relates back to the date the original letters of guardianship are issued, unless the accounting period has been changed as provided by this chapter, in which case a renewal relates back to the first day of the accounting period.

Added by Acts 1993, 73rd Leg., ch. 957, § 1, eff. Sept. 1, 1993.
Amended by Acts 1995, 74th Leg., ch. 1039, § 25, eff. Sept. 1, 1995.

### § 660. Letters or Order Made Evidence

(a) Letters of guardianship or a certificate under seal of the clerk of the court that granted the letters issued under Section 659 of this code is sufficient evidence of the appointment and qualification of the guardian and of the date of qualification.

(b) The court order that appoints the guardian is evidence of the authority granted to the guardian and of the scope of the powers and duties that the guardian may exercise only after the date letters of guardianship or a certificate has been issued under Section 659 of this code.

Added by Acts 1993, 73rd Leg., ch. 957, § 1, eff. Sept. 1, 1993.
Amended by Acts 1995, 74th Leg., ch. 1039, § 26, eff. Sept. 1, 1995.

### § 661. Issuance of New Letters

When letters of guardianship have been destroyed or lost, the clerk shall issue new letters that have the same force and effect as the original letters. The clerk shall also issue any number of letters on request of the person who holds the letters.

Added by Acts 1993, 73rd Leg., ch. 957, § 1, eff. Sept. 1, 1993.

### § 662. Rights of Third Persons Dealing With Guardian

When a guardian who has qualified performs any act as guardian that is in conformity with the guardian's authority and the law, the guardian's act continues to be valid for all intents and purposes in regard to the rights of an innocent purchaser of the property of the guardianship estate who purchased the property from the guardian for a valuable consideration, in good faith, and without notice of any illegality in the title to the property, even if the guardian's act or the authority under which the act was performed may later be set aside, annulled, or declared invalid.

Added by Acts 1993, 73rd Leg., ch. 957, § 1, eff. Sept. 1, 1993.

### § 663. Validation of Certain Letters of Guardianship

All presently existing letters of guardianship issued to a nonresident guardian, with or without the procedure provided in this subpart, in whole or in part, and with or without a notice or citation required of resident guardians, are validated as of each letter's date, insofar as the absence of the procedure, notice, or citations is concerned. An otherwise valid conveyance, mineral lease, or other act of a nonresident guardian qualified and acting in connection with the letters of guardianship under supporting orders of a county or probate court of this state are validated. This section does not apply to any letters, conveyance, lease, or other act of a nonresident guardian under this section if the absence of the procedure, notice, or citation involving the letters, conveyance, lease, or other act of the nonresident guardian is an issue in a lawsuit pending in this state on September 1, 1993.

Added by Acts 1993, 73rd Leg., ch. 957, § 1, eff. Sept. 1, 1993.

### SUBPART H. COMPENSATION, EXPENSES, AND COURT COSTS

### § 665. Compensation of Guardians and Temporary Guardians

(a) The court may authorize compensation for a guardian or a temporary guardian serving as a guardian of the person alone from available funds of the ward's estate or other funds available for that purpose. The court may set the compensation in an amount not exceeding five percent of the ward's gross income.

(a–1) In determining whether to authorize compensation for a guardian under this section, the court shall consider the ward's monthly income from all sources and whether the ward receives medical assistance under the state Medicaid program.

(b) The guardian or temporary guardian of an estate is entitled to reasonable compensation on application to the court at the time the court approves any annual accounting or final accounting filed by the guardian or temporary guardian under this chapter. A fee of five percent of the gross income of the ward's estate and five percent of all money paid out of the estate, subject to the award of an additional amount under Subsection (c) of this section following a review under Subsection (c)(1) of this section, is considered reasonable under this subsection if the court finds that the guardian or temporary guardian has taken care of and managed the estate in compliance with the standards of this chapter.

(c) On application of an interested person or on its own motion, the court may:

(1) review and modify the amount of compensation authorized under Subsection (a) or (b) of this section if the court finds that the amount is unreasonably low when considering the services rendered as guardian or temporary guardian; and

(2) authorize compensation for the guardian or temporary guardian in an estimated amount the court finds reasonable that is to be paid on a quarterly basis before the guardian or temporary guardian files an annual or final accounting if the

court finds that delaying the payment of compensation until the guardian or temporary guardian files an accounting would create a hardship for the guardian or temporary guardian.

(d) A finding of unreasonably low compensation may not be established under Subsection (c) of this section solely because the amount of compensation is less than the usual and customary charges of the person or entity serving as guardian or temporary guardian. A court that authorizes payment of estimated quarterly compensation under Subsection (c) of this section may later reduce or eliminate the guardian's or temporary guardian's compensation if, on review of an annual or final accounting or otherwise, the court finds that the guardian or temporary guardian:

(1) received compensation in excess of the amount permitted under this section;

(2) has not adequately performed the duties required of a guardian or temporary guardian under this chapter;  or

(3) has been removed for cause.

(d–1) If a court reduces or eliminates a guardian's or temporary guardian's compensation as provided by Subsection (d) of this section, the guardian or temporary guardian and the surety on the guardian's or temporary guardian's bond are liable to the guardianship estate for any excess compensation received.

(e) The court, on application of an interested person or on its own motion, may deny a fee authorized under this section in whole, or in part, if:

(1) the court finds that the guardian or temporary guardian has not adequately performed the duties required of a guardian or temporary guardian under this chapter;  or

(2) the guardian or temporary guardian has been removed for cause.

(f) Except as provided by Subsection (c) of this section for a fee that is determined by the court to be unreasonably low, the aggregate fee of the guardian of the person and guardian of the estate may not exceed an amount equal to five percent of the gross income of the ward's estate plus five percent of all money paid out of the estate.

(g) If the estate of a ward is insufficient to pay for the services of a private professional guardian or a licensed attorney serving as guardian of the ward's person, the court may authorize compensation for that guardian if funds in the county treasury are budgeted for that purpose.

(h) In this section:

(1) "Gross income" does not include Department of Veterans Affairs or Social Security benefits received by a ward.

(2) "Money paid out" does not include any money loaned, invested, or paid over on the settlement of the guardianship or a tax-motivated gift made by the ward.

Added by Acts 1993, 73rd Leg., ch. 957, § 1, eff. Sept. 1, 1993. Amended by Acts 1995, 74th Leg., ch. 1039, § 27, eff. Sept. 1, 1995; Acts 1999, 76th Leg., ch. 905, § 1, eff. Sept. 1, 1999; Acts 2001, 77th Leg., ch. 217, § 3, eff. Sept. 1, 2001; Acts 2001, 77th Leg., ch. 953, § 1, eff. Sept. 1, 2001; Acts 2009, 81st Leg., ch. 930, § 1, eff. Sept. 1, 2009.

### § 665A.   Payment for Professional Services

The court shall order the payment of a fee set by the court as compensation to the attorneys, mental health professionals, and interpreters appointed under this chapter, as applicable, to be taxed as costs in the case. If after examining the proposed ward's assets the court determines the proposed ward is unable to pay for services provided by an attorney, a mental health professional, or an interpreter appointed under this chapter, as applicable, the county is responsible for the cost of those services.

Added by Acts 1995, 74th Leg., ch. 1039, § 28, eff. Sept. 1, 1995. Amended by Acts 2007, 80th Leg., ch. 614, § 3, eff. Sept. 1, 2007.

### § 665B.   Payment of Attorney's Fees to Attorney Representing Applicant

(a) A court that creates a guardianship or creates a management trust under Section 867 of this code for a ward under this chapter, on request of a person who filed an application to be appointed guardian of the proposed ward, an application for the appointment of another suitable person as guardian of the proposed ward, or an application for the creation of the management trust, may authorize the payment of reasonable and necessary attorney's fees, as determined by the court, to an attorney who represents the person who filed the application at the application hearing, regardless of whether the person is appointed the ward's guardian or whether a management trust is created, from:

(1) available funds of the ward's estate or management trust, if created; or

(2) subject to Subsection (c) of this section, the county treasury if:

(A) the ward's estate or, if created, management trust, is insufficient to pay for the services provided by the attorney; and

(B) funds in the county treasury are budgeted for that purpose.

(b) The court may not authorize attorney's fees under this section unless the court finds that the applicant acted in good faith and for just cause in the filing and prosecution of the application.

(c) The court may authorize the payment of attorney's fees from the county treasury under Subsection (a) of this section only if the court is satisfied that the attorney to whom the fees will be paid has not received, and is not seeking, payment for the services described by that subsection from any other source.

Added by Acts 1995, 74th Leg., ch. 1039, § 28, eff. Sept. 1, 1995. Amended by Acts 1999, 76th Leg., ch. 905, § 2, eff. Sept. 1, 1999; Acts 2003, 78th Leg., ch. 549, § 10, eff. Sept. 1, 2003; Acts 2009, 81st Leg., ch. 314, § 1, eff. Sept. 1, 2009; Acts 2009, 81st Leg., ch. 930, §§ 2, 3, eff. Sept. 1, 2009.

## § 665C. Compensation for Collection of Claims and Recovery of Property

(a) Except as provided by Subsection (b) of this section, a guardian of an estate may enter into a contract to convey, or may convey, a contingent interest in any property sought to be recovered, not exceeding one-third thereof for services of attorneys, subject only to the approval of the court in which the estate is being administered.

(b) A guardian of an estate may convey or contract to convey for services of attorneys a contingent interest that exceeds one-third of the property sought to be recovered under this section only on the approval of the court in which the estate is being administered. The court must approve a contract entered into or conveyance made under this section before an attorney performs any legal services. A contract entered into or conveyance made in violation of this section is void, unless the court ratifies or reforms the contract or documents relating to the conveyance to the extent necessary to cause the contract or conveyance to meet the requirements of this section.

(c) In approving a contract or conveyance under Subsection (a) or (b) of this section for services of an attorney, the court shall consider:

(1) the time and labor that will be required, the novelty and difficulty of the questions to be involved, and the skill that will be required to perform the legal services properly;

(2) the fee customarily charged in the locality for similar legal services;

(3) the value of property recovered or sought to be recovered by the personal representative under this section;

(4) the benefits to the estate that the attorney will be responsible for securing; and

(5) the experience and ability of the attorney who will be performing the services.

(d) On satisfactory proof to the court, a guardian of an estate is entitled to all necessary and reasonable expenses incurred by the guardian in collecting or attempting to collect a claim or debt owed to the estate or in recovering or attempting to recover property to which the estate has a title or claim.

Added by Acts 1995, 74th Leg., ch. 1039, § 28, eff. Sept. 1, 1995.

## § 665D. Compensation and Payment of Attorney's Fees of Attorney Serving as Guardian

(a) Notwithstanding any other provision of this subpart, an attorney who serves as guardian and who also provides legal services in connection with the guardianship is not entitled to compensation for the guardianship services or payment of attorney's fees for the legal services from the ward's estate or other funds available for that purpose unless the attorney files with the court a detailed description of the services performed that identifies which of the services provided were guardianship services and which were legal services.

(b) An attorney described by Subsection (a) of this section is not entitled to payment of attorney's fees for guardianship services that are not legal services.

(c) The court shall set the compensation of an attorney described by Subsection (a) of this section for the performance of guardianship services in accordance with Section 665 of this code. The court shall set attorney's fees for an attorney described by Subsection (a) of this section for legal services provided in accordance with Sections 665A, 665B, and 666 of this code.

Added by Acts 2009, 81st Leg., ch. 930, § 4, eff. Sept. 1, 2009.

## § 666. Expenses Allowed

A guardian is entitled to be reimbursed from the guardianship estate for all necessary and reasonable expenses incurred in performing any duty as a guardian, including reimbursement for the payment of reasonable attorney's fees necessarily incurred by the guardian in connection with the management of the estate or any other matter in the guardianship.

Added by Acts 1993, 73rd Leg., ch. 957, § 1, eff. Sept. 1, 1993. Amended by Acts 2001, 77th Leg., ch. 953, § 2, eff. Sept. 1, 2001; Acts 2011, 82nd Leg., ch. 1085 (S.B. 1196), § 19, eff. Sept. 1, 2011.

## § 667. Expense Account

All expense charges shall be:

(1) in writing, showing specifically each item of expense and the date of the expense;

(2) verified by affidavit of the guardian;

(3) filed with the clerk; and

(4) paid only if the payment is authorized by court order.

Added by Acts 1993, 73rd Leg., ch. 957, § 1, eff. Sept. 1, 1993. Amended by Acts 2001, 77th Leg., ch. 953, § 3, eff. Sept. 1, 2001.

## § 668. Costs Adjudged Against Guardian

When costs are incurred because a guardian neglects to perform a required duty or if a guardian is removed for cause, the guardian and the sureties on the guardian's bond are liable for:

(1) costs of removal and other additional costs incurred that are not authorized expenditures under this chapter; and

(2) reasonable attorney's fees incurred in removing the guardian or in obtaining compliance regarding any statutory duty the guardian has neglected.

Added by Acts 1993, 73rd Leg., ch. 957, § 1, eff. Sept. 1, 1993.

## § 669. Costs Against Guardianship

(a) Except as provided by Subsection (b) of this section, in a guardianship proceeding, the cost of the proceeding, including the cost of the guardian ad litem or court visitor, shall be paid out of the guardianship estate, or, if the estate is insufficient to pay for the cost of the proceeding, the cost of the proceeding shall be paid out of the county treasury, and the judgment of the court shall be issued accordingly.

(b) If a court denies an application for the appointment of a guardian under this chapter based on the recommendation of a court investigator, the applicant shall pay the cost of the proceeding.

Added by Acts 1993, 73rd Leg., ch. 957, § 1, eff. Sept. 1, 1993. Amended by Acts 1995, 74th Leg., ch. 1039, § 29, eff. Sept. 1, 1995; Subsec. (a) amended by Acts 2011, 82nd Leg., ch. 1085 (S.B. 1196), § 20, eff. Sept. 1, 2011.

## § 670. Compensation of Certain Guardians; Certain Other Guardianship Costs

(a) In this section:

(1) "Applied income" means the portion of the earned and unearned income of a recipient of medical assistance or, if applicable, the recipient and the recipient's spouse, that is paid under the medical assistance program to an institution or long-term care facility in which the recipient resides.

(2) "Medical assistance" has the meaning assigned by Section 32.003, Human Resources Code.

(b) Notwithstanding any other provision of this chapter and to the extent permitted by federal law, a court that appoints a guardian for a recipient of medical assistance who has applied income may order the following to be deducted as an additional personal needs allowance in the computation of the recipient's applied income in accordance with Section 32.02451, Human Resources Code:

(1) compensation to the guardian in an amount not to exceed $175 per month;

(2) costs directly related to establishing or terminating the guardianship, not to exceed $1,000 except as provided by Subsection (c) of this section; and

(3) other administrative costs related to the guardianship, not to exceed $1,000 during any three-year period.

(c) Costs ordered to be deducted under Subsection (b)(2) of this section may include compensation and expenses for an attorney ad litem or guardian ad litem and reasonable attorney's fees for an attorney representing the guardian. The costs ordered to be paid may exceed $1,000 if the costs in excess of that amount are supported by documentation acceptable to the court and the costs are approved by the court.

(d) A court may not order:

(1) that the deduction for compensation and costs under Subsection (b) of this section take effect before the later of:

(A) the month in which the court order issued under that subsection is signed; or

(B) the first month of medical assistance eligibility for which the recipient is subject to a copayment; or

(2) a deduction for services provided before the effective date of the deduction as provided by Subdivision (1) of this subsection.

Added by Acts 2009, 81st Leg., ch. 859, § 2, eff. Sept. 1, 2009. Amended by Acts 2011, 82nd Leg., ch. 599 (S.B. 220), § 8, eff. Sept. 1, 2011.

## SUBPART I. DUTY AND RESPONSIBILITY OF COURT

## § 671. Judge's Duty

(a) The court shall use reasonable diligence to determine whether a guardian is performing all of the duties required of the guardian that pertain to the guardian's ward.

(b) The judge, at least annually, shall examine the well-being of each ward of the court and the solvency of the bonds of the guardians of the estates.

(c) If after examining the solvency of a guardian's bond under this section a judge determines that the guardian's bond is not sufficient to protect the ward or the ward's estate, the judge shall require the guardian to execute a new bond.

(d) The judge shall notify the guardian and the sureties on the bond as provided by law. If damage or loss results to a guardianship or ward because of gross neglect of the judge to use reasonable diligence in the performance of the judge's duty under this section, the judge shall be liable on the judge's bond to those damaged by the judge's neglect.

(e) The court may request an applicant or court-appointed fiduciary to produce other information identifying an applicant, ward, or guardian, including social security numbers, in addition to identifying information the applicant or fiduciary is required to produce under this code. The court shall maintain the information required under this subsection, and the information may not be filed with the clerk.

Added by Acts 1993, 73rd Leg., ch. 957, § 1, eff. Sept. 1, 1993. Amended by Acts 1997, 75th Leg., ch. 77, § 3, eff. Sept. 1, 1997.

## § 672. Annual Determination Whether Guardianship Should be Continued, Modified, or Terminated

(a) A court in which a guardianship proceeding is pending shall review annually each guardianship in which the application to create the guardianship was filed after September 1, 1993, and may review annually any other guardianship to determine whether the guardianship should be continued, modified, or terminated.

(b) In reviewing a guardianship as provided by Subsection (a) of this section, a statutory probate court may:

(1) review any report prepared by a court investigator under Section 648A or 694A(c) of this code;

(2) review any report prepared by a guardian ad litem under Section 694A(c) of this code;

(3) review any report prepared by a court visitor under Section 648 of this code;

(4) conduct a hearing; or

(5) review an annual account prepared under Section 741 of this code or a report prepared under Section 743 of this code.

(c) In reviewing a guardianship as provided by Subsection (a) of this section, a court that is not a statutory probate court may use any appropriate method determined by the court according to the court's caseload and the resources available to the court.

(d) A determination under this section must be in writing and filed with the clerk.

(e) This section does not apply to a guardianship that is created only because it is necessary for a person to have a guardian appointed to receive funds from a governmental source.

Added by Acts 1995, 74th Leg., ch. 1039, § 30, eff. Sept. 1, 1995.
Subsec. (b) amended by Acts 2005, 79th Leg., ch. 200, § 3, eff. Sept. 1, 2005.

## SUBPART J. LIABILITY OF GUARDIAN

### § 673. Liability of Guardian for Conduct of Ward

A person is not liable to a third person solely because the person has been appointed guardian of a ward under this chapter.

Added by Acts 1993, 73rd Leg., ch. 957, § 1, eff. Sept. 1, 1993.
Section heading amended by Acts 2005, 79th Leg., ch. 268, § 3.07, eff. Sept. 1, 2005.

### § 674. Immunity of Guardianship Program

A guardianship program is not liable for civil damages arising from an action taken or omission made by a person while providing guardianship services to a ward on behalf of the guardianship program, unless the action or omission:

(1) was wilfully wrongful;

(2) was taken or made with conscious indifference or reckless disregard to the safety of the incapacitated person or another;

(3) was taken or made in bad faith or with malice; or

(4) was grossly negligent.

Added by Acts 2005, 79th Leg., ch. 268, § 3.08, eff. Sept. 1, 2005.

## PART 3. APPOINTMENT AND QUALIFICATION OF GUARDIANS

## SUBPART A. APPOINTMENT

### § 675. Rights and Powers Retained by Ward

An incapacitated person for whom a guardian is appointed retains all legal and civil rights and powers except those designated by court order as legal disabilities by virtue of having been specifically granted to the guardian.

Added by Acts 1993, 73rd Leg., ch. 957, § 1, eff. Sept. 1, 1993.

### § 676. Guardians of Minors

(a) Except as provided by Section 680 of this code, the selection of a guardian for a minor is governed by this section.

(b) If the parents live together, both parents are the natural guardians of the person of the minor children by the marriage, and one of the parents is entitled to be appointed guardian of the children's estates. If the parents disagree as to which parent should be appointed, the court shall make the appointment on the basis of which parent is better qualified to serve in that capacity. If one parent is dead, the survivor is the natural guardian of the person of the minor children and is entitled to be appointed guardian of their estates. The rights of parents who do not live together are equal, and the guardianship of their minor children shall be assigned to one or the other, considering only the best interests of the children.

(c) In appointing a guardian for a minor orphan:

(1) if the last surviving parent did not appoint a guardian, the nearest ascendant in the direct line of the minor is entitled to guardianship of both the person and the estate of the minor;

(2) if more than one ascendant exists in the same degree in the direct line, one ascendant shall be appointed, according to circumstances and considering the best interests of the minor;

(3) if the minor has no ascendant in the direct line, the nearest of kin shall be appointed, and if there are two or more persons in the same degree of kinship, one shall be appointed, according to circumstances and considering the best interests of the minor; and

(4) if no relative of the minor is eligible to be guardian, or if no eligible person applies to be guardian, the court shall appoint a qualified person as guardian.

(d) Notwithstanding Subsection (b) of this section and Section 690 of this code, the surviving parent of a minor may by will or written declaration appoint any eligible person to be guardian of the person of the parent's minor children after the death of the parent or in the event of the parent's incapacity.

(e) After the death of the surviving parent of a minor or if the court finds the surviving parent is an incapacitated person, as appropriate, the court shall appoint the person designated in the will or declaration to serve as guardian of the person of the parent's minor children in preference to those otherwise entitled to serve as guardian under this chapter unless the court finds that the designated guardian is disqualified, is dead, refuses to serve, or would not serve the best interests of the minor children.

(f) On compliance with this chapter, an eligible person is also entitled to be appointed guardian of the children's estates after the death of the parent or in the event of the parent's incapacity.

(g) The powers of a person appointed to serve as the designated guardian of the person or estate, or both, of a minor child solely because of the incapacity of the minor's surviving parent and in accordance with this section and Section 677A of this code terminate when a probate court enters an order finding that the surviving parent is no longer an incapacitated person.

Added by Acts 1993, 73rd Leg., ch. 957, § 1, eff. Sept. 1, 1993. Amended by Acts 1995, 74th Leg., ch. 304, § 1, eff. Sept. 1, 1995; Acts 2001, 77th Leg., ch. 217, § 4, eff. Sept. 1, 2001.

### § 677. Guardians of Persons Other Than Minors

(a) The court shall appoint a guardian for a person other than a minor according to the circumstances and considering the best interests of the ward. If the court finds that two or more eligible persons are equally entitled to be appointed guardian:

(1) the ward's spouse is entitled to the guardianship in preference to any other person if the spouse is one of the eligible persons;

(2) the eligible person nearest of kin to the ward is entitled to the guardianship if the ward's spouse is not one of the eligible persons; or

(3) the court shall appoint the eligible person who is best qualified to serve as guardian if:

(A) the persons entitled to serve under Subdivisions (1) and (2) of this section refuse to serve;

(B) two or more persons entitled to serve under Subdivision (2) of this section are related in the same degree of kinship to the ward; or

(C) neither the ward's spouse or any person related to the ward is an eligible person.

(b) The surviving parent of an adult individual who is an incapacitated person may by will or written declaration appoint an eligible person to be guardian of the person of the adult individual after the parent's death or in the event of the parent's incapacity if the parent is the guardian of the person of the adult individual.

(c) After the death of the surviving parent of an adult individual who is an incapacitated person or if the court finds the surviving parent becomes an incapacitated person after being appointed the individual's guardian, as appropriate, the court shall appoint the person designated in the will or declaration to serve as guardian in preference to those otherwise entitled to serve as guardian under this chapter unless the court finds that the designated guardian is disqualified, is dead, refuses to serve, or would not serve the best interests of the adult individual.

(d) On compliance with this chapter, the eligible person appointed under Subsection (c) of this section is also entitled to be appointed guardian of the adult individual's estate after the death of the individual's parent or in the event of the parent's incapacity if the individual's parent is the guardian of the individual's estate.

(e) The powers of a person appointed to serve as the designated guardian of the person or estate, or both, of an adult individual solely because of the incapacity of the individual's surviving parent and in accordance with this section and Section 677A of this code terminate when a probate court enters an order finding that the surviving parent is no longer an incapacitated person and reappointing the surviving parent as the individual's guardian.

Added by Acts 1993, 73rd Leg., ch. 957, § 1, eff. Sept. 1, 1993. Amended by Acts 1995, 74th Leg., ch. 304, § 2, eff. Sept. 1, 1995; Acts 2001, 77th Leg., ch. 217, § 5, eff. Sept. 1, 2001.

### § 677A. Written Declarations by Certain Parents to Appoint Guardians for Their Children

(a) A written declaration appointing an eligible person to be guardian of the person of the parent's child under Section 676(d) or 677(b) of this code must be signed by the declarant and be:

(1) written wholly in the handwriting of the declarant; or

(2) attested to in the presence of the declarant by at least two credible witnesses 14 years of age or older who are not named as guardian or alternate guardian in the declaration.

(b) A declaration that is not written wholly in the handwriting of the declarant may be signed by another person for the declarant under the direction of and in the presence of the declarant.

(c) A declaration described by Subsection (a)(2) of this section may have attached a self-proving affidavit signed by the declarant and the witnesses attesting to the competence of the declarant and the execution of the declaration.

(d) The declaration and any self-proving affidavit may be filed with the court at any time after the application for appointment of a guardian is filed and before a guardian is appointed.

(e) If the designated guardian does not qualify, is dead, refuses to serve, resigns, or dies after being appointed guardian, or is otherwise unavailable to serve as guardian, the court shall appoint the next eligible designated alternate guardian named in the declaration. If the guardian and all alternate guardians do not qualify, are dead, refuse to serve, or later die or resign, the court shall appoint another person to serve as otherwise provided by this code.

(f) The declarant may revoke a declaration in any manner provided for the revocation of a will under Section 63 of this code, including the subsequent reexecution of the declaration in the manner required for the original declaration.

(g) A declaration and affidavit may be in any form adequate to clearly indicate the declarant's intention to designate a guardian for the declarant's child. The following form may, but need not, be used:

## DECLARATION OF APPOINTMENT OF GUARDIAN FOR MY CHILDREN IN THE EVENT OF MY DEATH OR INCAPACITY

I, _____, make this Declaration to appoint as guardian for my child or children, listed as follows, in the event of my death or incapacity:

_____    _____

_____    _____

_____    _____

(add blanks as appropriate)

I designate _____ to serve as guardian of the person of my (child or children), _____ as first alternate guardian of the person of my (child or children), _____ as second alternate guardian of the person of my (child or children), and _____ as third alternate guardian of the person of my (child or children).

I direct that the guardian of the person of my (child or children) serve (with or without) bond.

(If applicable) I designate _____ to serve as guardian of the estate of my (child or children), _____ as first alternate guardian of the estate of my (child or children), _____ as second alternate guardian of the estate of my (child or children), and _____ as third alternate guardian of the estate of my (child or children).

If any guardian or alternate guardian dies, does not qualify, or resigns, the next named alternate guardian becomes guardian of my (child or children).

Signed this _____ day of _____, 20__.

_____
Declarant

_____    _____
Witness                 Witness

### SELF–PROVING AFFIDAVIT

Before me, the undersigned authority, on this date personally appeared _____, the declarant, and _____ and _____ as witnesses, and all being duly sworn, the declarant said that the above instrument was his or her Declaration of Appointment of Guardian for the Declarant's Children in the Event of Declarant's Death or Incapacity and that the declarant had made and executed it for the purposes expressed in the declaration. The witnesses declared to me that they are each 14 years of age or older, that they saw the declarant sign the declaration, that they signed the declaration as witnesses, and that the declarant appeared to them to be of sound mind.

_____
Declarant

_____    _____
Affiant                 Affiant

Subscribed and sworn to before me by _____, the above named declarant, and _____ (names of affiants) affiants, on this ___ day of _____, 20__.

_____
Notary Public in and for the State of Texas
My Commission expires:

_____

(h) In this section, "self-proving affidavit" means an affidavit the form and content of which substantially complies with the requirements of Subsection (g) of this section.

(i) As an alternative to the self-proving affidavit authorized by Subsection (g) of this section, a declaration of appointment of a guardian for the declarant's children in the event of the declarant's death or incapacity may be simultaneously executed, attested, and made self-proved by including the following in substantially the same form and with substantially the same contents:

I, _____, as declarant, after being duly sworn, declare to the undersigned witnesses and to the undersigned authority that this instrument is my Declaration of Appointment of Guardian for My Children in the Event of My Death or Incapacity, and that I have made and executed it for the purposes expressed in the declaration. I now sign this declaration in the presence of the attesting witnesses and the undersigned authority on this ___ day of _____, 20__.

_____
Declarant

The undersigned, _____ and _____, each being 14 years of age or older, after being duly sworn, declare to the declarant and to the undersigned authority that the declarant declared to us that this instrument is the declarant's Declaration of Appointment of Guardian for the Declarant's Children in the Event of Declarant's Death or Incapacity and that the declarant executed it for the purposes expressed in the declaration. The declarant then signed this declaration and we believe the declarant to be of sound mind. We now sign our names as attesting witnesses on this ___ day of _____, 20__.

_____
Witness

_____
Witness

Subscribed and sworn to before me by the above named declarant, and affiants, this ___ day of _____, 20__.

_____
Notary Public in and for the State of Texas
My Commission Expires:_____

**Text of Texas Probate Code effective until January 1, 2014**

(j) A declaration that is executed as provided by Subsection (i) of this section is considered self-proved to the same extent a declaration executed with a self-proving affidavit under Subsection (g) of this section is considered self-proved.

Added by Acts 1995, 74th Leg., ch. 304, § 3, eff. Sept. 1, 1995. Amended by Acts 1997, 75th Leg., ch. 77, § 4, eff. Sept. 1, 1997; Acts 1999, 76th Leg., ch. 1078, § 2, eff. Sept. 1, 1999; Acts 2001, 77th Leg., ch. 217, § 6, eff. Sept. 1, 2001; Acts 2009, 81st Leg., ch. 930, § 5, eff. Sept. 1, 2009.

### § 677B. Proof of Written Declaration of Certain Parents to Designate Childrens' Guardian

(a) In this section:

(1) "Declaration" means a written declaration of a person that:

(A) appoints a guardian for the person's child under Section 676(d) or 677(b) of this code; and

(B) satisfies the requirements of Section 677A of this code.

(2) "Self-proving affidavit" means an affidavit the form and content of which substantially complies with the requirements of Section 677A(g) of this code.

(3) "Self-proving declaration" includes a self-proving affidavit that is attached or annexed to a declaration.

(b) If a declaration is self-proved, the court may admit the declaration into evidence without the testimony of witnesses attesting to the competency of the declarant and the execution of the declaration. Additional proof of the execution of the declaration with the formalities and solemnities and under the circumstances required to make it a valid declaration is not necessary.

(c) At any time during the declarant's lifetime, a written declaration described by Section 677A(a)(1) of this code may be made self-proved in the same form and manner a will written wholly in the handwriting of a testator is made self-proved under Section 60 of this code.

(d) A properly executed and witnessed self-proving declaration and affidavit, including a declaration and affidavit described by Section 677A(c) of this code, are prima facie evidence that the declarant was competent at the time the declarant executed the declaration and that the guardian named in the declaration would serve the best interests of the ward.

(e) A written declaration described by Section 677A(a)(1) of this code that is not self-proved may be proved in the same manner a will written wholly in the handwriting of the testator is proved under Section 84 of this code.

(f) A written declaration described by Section 677A(a)(2) of this code that is not self-proved may be proved in the same manner an attested written will produced in court is proved under Section 84 of this code.

Added by Acts 2001, 77th Leg., ch. 217, § 7, eff. Sept. 1, 2001.

### § 678. Presumption Concerning Best Interest

It is presumed not to be in the best interests of a ward to appoint a person as guardian of the ward if the person has been finally convicted of any sexual offense, sexual assault, aggravated assault, aggravated sexual assault, injury to a child, to an elderly individual, or to a disabled individual, abandoning or endangering a child, or incest.

Added by Acts 1993, 73rd Leg., ch. 957, § 1, eff. Sept. 1, 1993. Amended by Acts 1995, 74th Leg., ch. 612, § 1, eff. Aug. 28, 1995.

### § 679. Designation of Guardian Before Need Arises

(a) A person other than an incapacitated person may designate by a written declaration persons to serve as guardian of the person of the declarant or the estate of the declarant if the declarant becomes incapacitated. The declaration must be signed by the declarant and be:

(1) written wholly in the handwriting of the declarant; or

(2) attested to in the presence of the declarant by at least two credible witnesses 14 years of age or older who are not named as guardian or alternate guardian in the declaration.

(b) A declarant may, in the declaration, disqualify named persons from serving as guardian of the declarant's person or estate, and the persons named may not be appointed guardian under any circumstances.

(c) A declaration that is not written wholly in the handwriting of a declarant may be signed by another person for the declarant under the direction of and in the presence of the declarant.

(d) A declaration described by Subsection (a)(2) of this section may have attached a self-proving affidavit signed by the declarant and the witnesses attesting to the competence of the declarant and the execution of the declaration.

(e) The declaration and any self-proving affidavit may be filed with the court at any time after the application for appointment of a guardian is filed and before a guardian is appointed.

(f) Unless the court finds that the person designated in the declaration to serve as guardian is disqualified or would not serve the best interests of the ward, the court shall appoint the person as guardian in preference to those otherwise entitled to serve as guardian under this code. If the designated guardian does not qualify, is dead, refuses to serve, resigns, or dies after being appointed guardian, or is otherwise unavailable to serve as guardian, the court shall appoint the next eligible designated alternate guardian named in the declaration. If the guardian and all alternate guardians do not qualify, are dead, refuse to serve, or later die or resign, the court shall appoint another person to serve as otherwise provided by this code.

(g) The declarant may revoke a declaration in any manner provided for the revocation of a will under Section 63 of this code, including the subsequent reexecution of the declaration in the manner required for the original declaration.

**Text of Texas Probate Code effective until January 1, 2014**

(h) If a declarant designates the declarant's spouse to serve as guardian under this section, and the declarant is subsequently divorced from that spouse before a guardian is appointed, the provision of the declaration designating the spouse has no effect.

(i) A declaration and affidavit may be in any form adequate to clearly indicate the declarant's intention to designate a guardian. The following form may, but need not, be used:

### DECLARATION OF GUARDIAN IN THE EVENT OF LATER INCAPACITY OR NEED OF GUARDIAN

I, _____, make this Declaration of Guardian, to operate if the need for a guardian for me later arises.

1. I designate _____ to serve as guardian of my person, _____ as first alternate guardian of my person, _____ as second alternate guardian of my person, and _____ as third alternate guardian of my person.

2. I designate _____ to serve as guardian of my estate, _____ as first alternate guardian of my estate, _____ as second alternate guardian of my estate, and _____ as third alternate guardian of my estate.

3. If any guardian or alternate guardian dies, does not qualify, or resigns, the next named alternate guardian becomes my guardian.

4. I expressly disqualify the following persons from serving as guardian of my person: _____, _____, and _____.

5. I expressly disqualify the following persons from serving as guardian of my estate: _____, _____, and _____.

Signed this ___ day of _____, 20___.

_____
Declarant

_____    _____
Witness                       Witness

### SELF–PROVING AFFIDAVIT

Before me, the undersigned authority, on this date personally appeared _____, the declarant, and _____ and _____ as witnesses, and all being duly sworn, the declarant said that the above instrument was his or her Declaration of Guardian and that the declarant had made and executed it for the purposes expressed in the declaration. The witnesses declared to me that they are each 14 years of age or older, that they saw the declarant sign the declaration, that they signed the declaration as witnesses, and that the declarant appeared to them to be of sound mind.

_____
Declarant

_____    _____
Affiant                        Affiant

Subscribed and sworn to before me by the above named declarant and affiants on this ___ day of _____, 20___.

_____
Notary Public in and for the State of Texas
My Commission expires:

_____

(j) In this section, "self-proving affidavit" means an affidavit the form and content of which substantially complies with the requirements of Subsection (i) of this section.

(k) As an alternative to the self-proving affidavit authorized by Subsection (i) of this section, a Declaration of Guardian in the Event of Later Incapacity or Need of Guardian may be simultaneously executed, attested, and made self-proved by including the following in substantially the same form and with substantially the same contents:

I, _____, as declarant, after being duly sworn, declare to the undersigned witnesses and to the undersigned authority that this instrument is my Declaration of Guardian in the Event of Later Incapacity or Need of Guardian, and that I have made and executed it for the purposes expressed in the declaration. I now sign this declaration in the presence of the attesting witnesses and the undersigned authority on this ___ day of _____, 20___.

_____
Declarant

The undersigned, _____ and _____, each being 14 years of age or older, after being duly sworn, declare to the declarant and to the undersigned authority that the declarant declared to us that this instrument is the declarant's Declaration of Guardian in the Event of Later Incapacity or Need of Guardian and that the declarant executed it for the purposes expressed in the declaration. The declarant then signed this declaration and we believe the declarant to be of sound mind. We now sign our names as attesting witnesses on this ___ day of _____, 20___.

_____
Witness

_____
Witness

Subscribed and sworn to before me by the above named declarant, and affiants, this ___ day of _____, 20___.

_____
Notary Public in and for the State of Texas
My Commission Expires:_____

(l) A declaration that is executed as provided by Subsection (k) of this section is considered self-proved to the same extent a declaration executed with a self-proving affidavit under Subsection (i) of this section is considered self-proved.

Added by Acts 1993, 73rd Leg., ch. 957, § 1, eff. Sept. 1, 1993. Amended by Acts 2001, 77th Leg., ch. 217, § 8, eff. Sept. 1, 2001; Acts 2009, 81st Leg., ch. 930, § 6, eff. Sept. 1, 2009.

## § 679A. Proof of Written Declaration to Designate Guardian Before Need Arises

(a) In this section:

(1) "Declaration" means a written declaration of a person that:

(A) designates another person to serve as a guardian of the person or estate of the declarant; and

(B) satisfies the requirements of Section 679 of this code.

(2) "Self-proving affidavit" means an affidavit the form and content of which substantially complies with the requirements of Section 679(i) of this code.

(3) "Self-proving declaration" includes a self-proving affidavit that is attached or annexed to a declaration.

(b) If a declaration is self-proved, the court may admit the declaration into evidence without the testimony of witnesses attesting to the competency of the declarant and the execution of the declaration. Additional proof of the execution of the declaration with the formalities and solemnities and under the circumstances required to make it a valid declaration is not necessary.

(c) At any time during the declarant's lifetime, a written declaration described by Section 679(a)(1) of this code may be made self-proved in the same form and manner a will written wholly in the handwriting of a testator is made self-proved under Section 60 of this code.

(d) A properly executed and witnessed self-proving declaration and affidavit, including a declaration and affidavit described by Section 679(d) of this code, are prima facie evidence that the declarant was competent at the time the declarant executed the declaration and that the guardian named in the declaration would serve the best interests of the ward.

(e) A written declaration described by Section 679(a)(1) of this code that is not self-proved may be proved in the same manner a will written wholly in the handwriting of the testator is proved under Section 84 of this code.

(f) A written declaration described by Section 679(a)(2) of this code that is not self-proved may be proved in the same manner an attested written will produced in court is proved under Section 84 of this code.

Added by Acts 2001, 77th Leg., ch. 217, § 9, eff. Sept. 1, 2001.

## § 680. Selection of Guardian by Minor

(a) When an application is filed for the guardianship of the person or estate, or both, of a minor at least 12 years of age, the minor, by writing filed with the clerk, may choose the guardian if the court approves the choice and finds that the choice is in the best interest of the minor.

(b) A minor at least 12 years of age may select another guardian of either the minor's person or estate, or both, if the minor has a guardian appointed by the court or the minor has a guardian appointed by will or written declaration of the parent of the minor and that guardian dies, resigns, or is removed from guardianship. If the court is satisfied that the person selected is suitable and competent and that the appointment of the person is in the best interest of the minor, it shall make the appointment and revoke the letters of guardianship of the former guardian. The minor shall make the selection by filing an application in open court in person or by attorney.

Added by Acts 1993, 73rd Leg., ch. 957, § 1, eff. Sept. 1, 1993. Amended by Acts 1995, 74th Leg., ch. 1039, § 31, eff. Sept. 1, 1995.

## § 681. Persons Disqualified to Serve as Guardians

A person may not be appointed guardian if the person is:

(1) a minor;

(2) a person whose conduct is notoriously bad;

(3) an incapacitated person;

(4) a person who is a party or whose parent is a party to a lawsuit concerning or affecting the welfare of the proposed ward, unless the court:

(A) determines that the lawsuit claim of the person who has applied to be appointed guardian is not in conflict with the lawsuit claim of the proposed ward; or

(B) appoints a guardian ad litem to represent the interests of the proposed ward throughout the litigation of the ward's lawsuit claim;

(5) a person indebted to the proposed ward unless the person pays the debt before appointment;

(6) a person asserting a claim adverse to the proposed ward or the proposed ward's property, real or personal;

(7) a person who, because of inexperience, lack of education, or other good reason, is incapable of properly and prudently managing and controlling the ward or the ward's estate;

(8) a person, institution, or corporation found unsuitable by the court;

(9) a person disqualified in a declaration made under Section 679 of this code;

(10) a nonresident person who has not filed with the court the name of a resident agent to accept service of process in all actions or proceedings relating to the guardianship; or

(11) a person who does not have the certification to serve as guardian that is required by Section 697B of this code.

Added by Acts 1993, 73rd Leg., ch. 957, § 1, eff. Sept. 1, 1993. Amended by Acts 1995, 74th Leg., ch. 1039, § 32, eff. Sept. 1, 1995; Acts 2009, 81st Leg., ch. 509, § 1, eff. Sept. 1, 2009.

## § 682. Application; Contents

Any person may commence a proceeding for the appointment of a guardian by filing a written application in a court having jurisdiction and venue. The application must be sworn to by the applicant and state:

(1) the name, sex, date of birth, and address of the proposed ward;

(2) the name, relationship, and address of the person the applicant desires to have appointed as guardian;

(3) whether guardianship of the person or estate, or both, is sought;

(4) the nature and degree of the alleged incapacity, the specific areas of protection and assistance requested, and the limitation or termination of rights requested to be included in the court's order of appointment, including a termination of:

(A) the right of a proposed ward who is 18 years of age or older to vote in a public election; and

(B) the proposed ward's eligibility to hold or obtain a license to operate a motor vehicle under Chapter 521, Transportation Code;

(5) the facts requiring that a guardian be appointed and the interest of the applicant in the appointment;

(6) the nature and description of any guardianship of any kind existing for the proposed ward in any other state;

(7) the name and address of any person or institution having the care and custody of the proposed ward;

(8) the approximate value and description of the proposed ward's property, including any compensation, pension, insurance, or allowance to which the proposed ward may be entitled;

(9) the name and address of any person whom the applicant knows to hold a power of attorney signed by the proposed ward and a description of the type of power of attorney;

(10) if the proposed ward is a minor and if known by the applicant:

(A) the name of each parent of the proposed ward and state the parent's address or that the parent is deceased;

(B) the name and age of each sibling, if any, of the proposed ward and state the sibling's address or that the sibling is deceased; and

(C) if each of the proposed ward's parents and adult siblings are deceased, the names and addresses of the proposed ward's other living relatives who are related to the proposed ward within the third degree by consanguinity and who are adults;

(11) if the proposed ward is a minor, whether the minor was the subject of a legal or conservatorship proceeding within the preceding two-year period and, if so, the court involved, the nature of the proceeding, and the final disposition, if any, of the proceeding;

(12) if the proposed ward is an adult and if known by the applicant:

(A) the name of the proposed ward's spouse, if any, and state the spouse's address or that the spouse is deceased;

(B) the name of each of the proposed ward's parents and state the parent's address or that the parent is deceased;

(C) the name and age of each of the proposed ward's siblings, if any, and state the sibling's address or that the sibling is deceased;

(D) the name and age of each of the proposed ward's children, if any, and state the child's address or that the child is deceased; and

(E) if the proposed ward's spouse and each of the proposed ward's parents, adult siblings, and adult children are deceased, or, if there is no spouse, parent, adult sibling, or adult child, the names and addresses of the proposed ward's other living relatives who are related to the proposed ward within the third degree by consanguinity and who are adults;

(13) facts showing that the court has venue over the proceeding; and

(14) if applicable, that the person whom the applicant desires to have appointed as a guardian is a private professional guardian who is certified under Subchapter C, Chapter 111, Government Code, and has complied with the requirements of Section 697 of this code.

Added by Acts 1993, 73rd Leg., ch. 957, § 1, eff. Sept. 1, 1993. Amended by Acts 1997, 75th Leg., ch. 77, § 5, eff. Sept. 1, 1997; Acts 1997, 75th Leg., ch. 1376, § 2, eff. Sept. 1, 1997; Acts 1999, 76th Leg., ch. 829, § 4, eff. Sept. 1, 1999; Acts 2003, 78th Leg., ch. 549, § 11, eff. Sept. 1, 2003; Subd. (14) amended by Acts 2005, 79th Leg., ch. 268, § 3.09, eff. Sept. 1, 2005; Subd. (4) amended by Acts 2007, 80th Leg., ch. 614, § 4, eff. Sept. 1, 2007; Subds. (10)(C) and (12)(E) amended by Acts 2011, 82nd Leg., ch. 599 (S.B. 220), § 9, eff. Sept. 1, 2011.

## § 682A. Application for Appointment of Guardian for Certain Persons

(a) If a minor is a person who, because of incapacity, will require a guardianship after the ward is no longer a minor, a person may file an application under Section 682 of this code for the appointment of a guardian of the person or the estate, or both, of the proposed ward not earlier than the 180th day before the proposed ward's 18th birthday. If the application is heard before the proposed ward's 18th birthday, a guardianship created under this section may not take effect and the person appointed guardian may not give a bond or take the oath as required under Section 700 or 702 of this code until the proposed ward's 18th birthday.

(a–1) Notwithstanding any other law, if the applicant who files an application under Subsection (a) of this section or Section 682 of this code is a person who was appointed conservator of a disabled child and the proceeding is a guardianship proceeding described by Section 601(25)(A) of this code in which the proposed ward is the incapacitated adult with respect to whom another court obtained continuing, exclusive jurisdiction in a suit affecting the parent-child relationship when the person was a child, the applicant may present to the court a written letter or certificate that meets the requirements of Section 687(a) of this code.

(a–2) If, on receipt of the letter or certificate described by Subsection (a–1) of this section, the court is able to make the findings required by Section 684 of this code, the court, notwithstanding Section 677 of this code, shall appoint the conservator as guardian without conducting a hearing and shall, to the extent possible, preserve the terms of possession and access to the ward that applied before the court obtained jurisdiction of the guardianship proceeding.

(b) Notwithstanding Section 694(b) of this code, the guardianship of the person of a minor who is the subject of an application for the appointment of a guardian of the person filed under Subsection (a) of this section is settled and closed when:

(1) the court, after a hearing on the application, determines that the appointment of a guardian of the person for the proposed ward is not necessary; or

(2) the guardian appointed by the court after a hearing on the application has qualified under Section 699 of this code.

Added by Acts 1999, 76th Leg., ch. 904, § 1, eff. Sept. 1, 1999. Amended by Acts 2001, 77th Leg., ch. 217, § 10, eff. Sept. 1, 2001. Subsecs. (a–1) and (a–2) added by Acts 2007, 80th Leg., ch. 453, § 3, eff. June 16, 2007; Subsecs. (a–1) and (a–2) amended by Acts 2011, 82nd Leg., ch. 1085 (S.B. 1196), § 21, eff. Sept. 1, 2011.

## § 683. Court's Initiation of Guardianship Proceedings

(a) If a court has probable cause to believe that a person domiciled or found in the county in which the court is located is an incapacitated person, and the person does not have a guardian in this state, the court shall appoint a guardian ad litem or court investigator to investigate the person's conditions and circumstances to determine whether the person is an incapacitated person and whether a guardianship is necessary. If after the investigation the guardian ad litem or court investigator believes that the person is an incapacitated person and that a guardianship is necessary, the guardian ad litem or court investigator shall file an application for the appointment of a guardian of the person or estate, or both, for the person.

(b) To establish probable cause under this section, the court may require:

(1) an information letter about the person believed to be incapacitated that is submitted by an interested person and satisfies the requirements of Section 683A of this code; or

(2) a written letter or certificate from a physician who has examined the person believed to be incapacitated that satisfies the requirements of Section 687(a) of this code, except that the letter must be dated not earlier than the 120th day before the date of the appointment of a guardian ad litem or court investigator under Subsection (a) of this section and be based on an examination the physician performed not earlier than the 120th day before that date.

(c) A court that appoints a guardian ad litem under Subsection (a) of this section may authorize compensation of the guardian ad litem from available funds of the proposed ward's estate, regardless of whether a guardianship is created for the proposed ward. If after examining the ward's or proposed ward's assets the court determines the ward or proposed ward is unable to pay for services provided by the guardian ad litem, the court may authorize compensation from the county treasury.

Added by Acts 1993, 73rd Leg., ch. 957, § 1, eff. Sept. 1, 1993. Amended by Acts 1999, 76th Leg., ch. 905, § 3, eff. Sept. 1, 1999. Amended by Acts 2007, 80th Leg., ch. 614, § 5, eff. Sept. 1, 2007.

## § 683A. Information Letter

An information letter under Section 683(b)(1) of this code about a person believed to be incapacitated may:

(1) include the name, address, telephone number, county of residence, and date of birth of the person;

(2) state whether the residence of the person is a private residence, health care facility, or other type of residence;

(3) describe the relationship between the interested person and the person;

(4) contain the names and telephone numbers of any known friends and relatives of the person;

(5) state whether a guardian of the person or estate of the person has been appointed in this state;

(6) state whether the person has executed a power of attorney and, if so, the designee's name, address, and telephone number;

(7) describe any property of the person, including the estimated value of that property;

(8) list any amount and source of monthly income of the person; and

(9) describe the nature and degree of the person's alleged incapacity and include a statement of whether the person is in imminent danger of serious impairment to the person's physical health, safety, or estate.

Added by Acts 1999, 76th Leg., ch. 905, § 4, eff. Sept. 1, 1999.

## § 684. Findings Required

(a) Before appointing a guardian, the court must find by clear and convincing evidence that:

(1) the proposed ward is an incapacitated person;

(2) it is in the best interest of the proposed ward to have the court appoint a person as guardian of the proposed ward; and

(3) the rights of the proposed ward or the proposed ward's property will be protected by the appointment of a guardian.

(b) Before appointing a guardian, the court must find by a preponderance of the evidence that:

(1) the court has venue of the case;

(2) the person to be appointed guardian is eligible to act as guardian and is entitled to appointment, or, if no eligible person entitled to appointment applies, the person appointed is a proper person to act as guardian;

(3) if a guardian is appointed for a minor, the guardianship is not created for the primary purpose of enabling the minor to establish residency for enrollment in a school or school district for which the minor is not otherwise eligible for enrollment; and

(4) the proposed ward is totally without capacity as provided by this code to care for himself or herself and to manage the individual's property, or the proposed ward lacks the capacity to do some, but not all, of the tasks necessary to care for himself or herself or to manage the individual's property.

(c) The court may not grant an application to create a guardianship unless the applicant proves each element required by this code. A determination of incapacity of an adult proposed ward, other than a person who must have a guardian appointed to receive funds due the person from any governmental source, must be evidenced by recurring acts or occurrences within the preceding six-month period and not by isolated instances of negligence or bad judgment.

(d) A court may not appoint a guardian of the estate of a minor when a payment of claims is made under Section 887 of this code.

(e) A certificate of the executive head or a representative of the bureau, department, or agency of the government, to the effect that the appointment of a guardian is a condition precedent to the payment of any funds due the proposed ward from that governmental entity, is prima facie evidence of the necessity for the appointment of a guardian.

Added by Acts 1993, 73rd Leg., ch. 957, § 1, eff. Sept. 1, 1993. Amended by Acts 1995, 74th Leg., ch. 1039, § 33, eff. Sept. 1, 1995; Acts 1997, 75th Leg., ch. 1376, § 3, eff. Sept. 1, 1997; Acts 1999, 76th Leg., ch. 379, § 5, eff. Sept. 1, 1999.

## § 685. Hearing for Appointment of Guardian; Right to Jury Trial

(a) A proposed ward must be present at a hearing to appoint a guardian unless the court, on the record or in the order, determines that a personal appearance is not necessary. The court may close the hearing if the proposed ward or the proposed ward's counsel requests a closed hearing.

(b) The proposed ward is entitled, on request, to a jury trial.

(c) At the hearing, the court shall:

(1) inquire into the ability of any allegedly incapacitated adult person to feed, clothe, and shelter himself or herself, to care for the individual's own physical health, and to manage the individual's property or financial affairs;

(2) ascertain the age of any proposed ward who is a minor;

(3) inquire into the governmental reports for any person who must have a guardian appointed to receive funds due the person from any governmental source; and

(4) inquire into the qualifications, abilities, and capabilities of the person seeking to be appointed guardian.

Added by Acts 1993, 73rd Leg., ch. 957, § 1, eff. Sept. 1, 1993. Amended by Acts 1995, 74th Leg., ch. 1039, § 34, eff. Sept. 1, 1995; Acts 1999, 76th Leg., ch. 379, § 6, eff. Sept. 1, 1999.

## § 686. Use of Records in Hearing to Appoint Guardian

(a) Before a hearing may be held for the appointment of a guardian, current and relevant medical, psychological, and intellectual testing records of the proposed ward must be provided to the attorney ad litem appointed to represent the proposed ward unless:

(1) the proposed ward is a minor or a person who must have a guardian appointed to receive funds due the person from any governmental source; or

(2) the court makes a finding on the record that no current or relevant records exist and examining the proposed ward for the purpose of creating the records is impractical.

(b) Current medical, psychological, and intellectual testing records are a sufficient basis for a determination of guardianship.

(c) The findings and recommendations contained in the medical, psychological, and intellectual testing records are not binding on the court.

Added by Acts 1993, 73rd Leg., ch. 957, § 1, eff. Sept. 1, 1993. Amended by Acts 1999, 76th Leg., ch. 379, § 7, eff. Sept. 1, 1999.

## § 687. Examinations and Reports

(a) Except as provided by Subsection (c) of this section, the court may not grant an application to create a guardianship for an incapacitated person, other than a minor or person for whom it is necessary to have a guardian appointed only to receive funds from a governmental source, unless the applicant presents to the court a written letter or certificate from a physician licensed in this state that is dated not earlier than the 120th day before the date of the filing of the application and based on an examination the physician performed not earlier than the 120th day before the date of the filing of the application. The letter or certificate must:

(1) describe the nature, degree, and severity of incapacity, including functional deficits, if any, regarding the proposed ward's ability to:

(A) handle business and managerial matters;

(B) manage financial matters;

(C) operate a motor vehicle;

(D) make personal decisions regarding residence, voting, and marriage; and

(E) consent to medical, dental, psychological, or psychiatric treatment;

(2) provide an evaluation of the proposed ward's physical condition and mental function and summarize the proposed ward's medical history if reasonably available;

(3) state how or in what manner the proposed ward's ability to make or communicate responsible decisions concerning himself or herself is affected by the person's physical or mental health, including the proposed ward's ability to:

(A) understand or communicate;

(B) recognize familiar objects and individuals;

(C) perform simple calculations;

(D) reason logically; and

(E) administer to daily life activities;

(4) state whether any current medication affects the demeanor of the proposed ward or the proposed ward's ability to participate fully in a court proceeding;

(5) describe the precise physical and mental conditions underlying a diagnosis of a mental disability, and state whether the proposed ward would benefit from supports and services that would allow the individual to live in the least restrictive setting;

(6) in providing a description under Subdivision (1) of this subsection regarding the proposed ward's ability to operate a motor vehicle and make personal decisions regarding voting, state whether in the physician's opinion the proposed ward:

(A) has the mental capacity to vote in a public election; and

(B) has the ability to safely operate a motor vehicle; and

(7) include any other information required by the court.

(b) If the court determines it is necessary, the court may appoint the necessary physicians to examine the proposed ward. The court must make its determination with respect to the necessity for a physician's examination of the proposed ward at a hearing held for that purpose. Not later than the fourth day before the date of the hearing, the applicant shall give to the proposed ward and the proposed ward's attorney ad litem written notice specifying the purpose and the date and time of the hearing. A physician who examines the proposed ward, other than a physician or psychologist who examines the proposed ward under Subsection (c)(2) of this section, shall make available to an attorney ad litem appointed to represent the proposed ward, for inspection, a written letter or certificate from the physician that complies with the requirements of Subsection (a) of this section.

(c) If the basis of the proposed ward's alleged incapacity is mental retardation, the court may not grant an application to create a guardianship for the proposed ward unless the applicant presents to the court a written letter or certificate that:

(1) complies with Subsection (a) of this section; or

(2) shows that:

(A) not earlier than 24 months before the date of the hearing, the proposed ward has been examined by a physician or psychologist licensed in this state or certified by the Department of Aging and Disability Services to perform the examination, in accordance with rules of the executive commissioner of the Health and Human Services Commission governing examinations of that kind; and

(B) the physician's or psychologist's written findings and recommendations to the court include a statement as to whether the physician or psychologist has made a determination of mental retardation in accordance with Section 593.005, Health and Safety Code.

Added by Acts 1995, 74th Leg., ch. 1039, § 35, eff. Sept. 1, 1995. Amended by Acts 1999, 76th Leg., ch. 379, § 8, eff. Sept. 1, 1999; Acts 2001, 77th Leg., ch. 1174, § 3, eff. Sept. 1, 2001. Subsec. (c) amended by Acts 2003, 78th Leg., ch. 549, § 12, eff. Sept. 1, 2003; Subsec. (a) amended by Acts 2007, 80th Leg., ch. 614, § 6, eff. Sept. 1, 2007. Amended by Acts 2009, 81st Leg., ch. 575, § 1, eff. Sept. 1, 2009; Subsec. (c) amended by Acts 2011, 82nd Leg., ch. 1085 (S.B. 1196), § 22, eff. Sept. 1, 2011.

### §§ 688, 688A. Repealed by Acts 1995, 74th Leg., ch. 1039, § 73(1), eff. Sept. 1, 1995

### § 689. Preference of Ward

Before appointing a guardian, the court shall make a reasonable effort to consider the incapacitated person's preference of the person to be appointed guardian and, to the extent not inconsistent with other provisions of this chapter, shall give due consideration to the preference indicated by the incapacitated person.

Added by Acts 1993, 73rd Leg., ch. 957, § 1, eff. Sept. 1, 1993.

### § 690. Persons Appointed Guardian

Only one person may be appointed as guardian of the person or estate, but one person may be appointed guardian of the person and another of the estate, if it is in the best interest of the ward. Nothing in this section prohibits the joint appointment, if the court finds it to be in the best interest of the ward, of:

(1) a husband and wife;

(2) joint managing conservators;

(3) coguardians appointed under the laws of a jurisdiction other than this state; or

(4) both parents of an adult who is incapacitated if the incapacitated person:

(A) has not been the subject of a suit affecting the parent-child relationship; or

(B) has been the subject of a suit affecting the parent-child relationship and both of the incapacitated person's parents were named as joint managing conservators in the suit but are no longer serving in that capacity.

Added by Acts 1993, 73rd Leg., ch. 957, § 1, eff. Sept. 1, 1993. Amended by Acts 1995, 74th Leg., ch. 1039, § 36, eff. Sept. 1, 1995. Amended by Acts 2007, 80th Leg., ch. 614, § 7, eff. Sept. 1, 2007.

**§ 691. Repealed by Acts 1997, 75th Leg., ch. 809, § 2, eff. Sept. 1, 1997**

**§ 692. Dismissal of Application**

If it is found that an adult person possesses the capacity to care for himself or herself and to manage the individual's property as would a reasonably prudent person, the court shall dismiss the application for guardianship.

Added by Acts 1993, 73rd Leg., ch. 957, § 1, eff. Sept. 1, 1993. Amended by Acts 1995, 74th Leg., ch. 1039, § 38, eff. Sept. 1, 1995.

**§ 693. Order of Court**

(a) If it is found that the proposed ward is totally without capacity to care for himself or herself, to manage the individual's property, to operate a motor vehicle, and to vote in a public election, the court may appoint a guardian of the individual's person or estate, or both, with full authority over the incapacitated person except as provided by law. An order appointing a guardian under this subsection must contain findings of fact and specify:

(1) the information required by Subsection (c) of this section;

(2) that the guardian has full authority over the incapacitated person;

(3) if necessary, the amount of funds from the corpus of the person's estate the court will allow the guardian to expend for the education and maintenance of the person under Section 776 of this code;

(4) whether the person is totally incapacitated because of a mental condition; and

(5) that the person does not have the capacity to operate a motor vehicle and to vote in a public election.

(b) If it is found that the person lacks the capacity to do some, but not all, of the tasks necessary to care for himself or herself or to manage the individual's property, the court may appoint a guardian with limited powers and permit the individual to care for himself or herself or to manage the individual's property commensurate with the individual's ability. An order appointing a guardian under this subsection must contain findings of fact and specify:

(1) the information required by Subsection (c) of this section;

(2) the specific powers, limitations, or duties of the guardian with respect to the care of the person or the management of the person's property by the guardian;

(3) if necessary, the amount of funds from the corpus of the person's estate the court will allow the guardian to expend for the education and maintenance of the person under Section 776 of this code; and

(4) whether the person is incapacitated because of a mental condition and, if so, whether the person retains the right to vote in a public election or maintains eligibility to hold or obtain a license to operate a motor vehicle under Chapter 521, Transportation Code.

(c) The order of the court appointing a guardian must specify:

(1) the name of the person appointed;

(2) the name of the ward;

(3) whether the guardian is of the person or the estate, or of both, of the ward;

(4) the amount of any bond required;

(5) if it is a guardianship of the estate and the court deems an appraisal is necessary, one or more but not more than three disinterested persons to appraise the estate and to return the appraisement to the court; and

(6) that the clerk will issue letters of guardianship to the person appointed when the person has qualified according to law.

(d) An order appointing a guardian may not duplicate or conflict with the powers and duties of any other guardian.

(e) An order appointing a guardian or a successor guardian may specify a period of not more than one year during which a petition for adjudication that the incapacitated person no longer requires the guardianship may not be filed without special leave.

Added by Acts 1993, 73rd Leg., ch. 957, § 1, eff. Sept. 1, 1993. Amended by Acts 1995, 74th Leg., ch. 1039, § 39, eff. Sept. 1, 1995.

Subsecs. (a) and (b) amended by Acts 2007, 80th Leg., ch. 614, § 8, eff. Sept. 1, 2007.

**§ 694. Term of Appointment of Guardian**

(a) Unless otherwise discharged as provided by law, a guardian remains in office until the estate is closed.

(b) The guardianship shall be settled and closed when the incapacitated person:

(1) dies and, if the person was married, the person's spouse qualifies as survivor in community;

(2) is found by the court to have full capacity to care for himself or herself and to manage the person's property;

(3) is no longer a minor; or

(4) no longer must have a guardian appointed to receive funds due the person from any governmental source.

(c) An order appointing a guardian or a successor guardian may specify a period of not more than one year during which a petition for adjudication that the incapacitated person no longer requires the guardianship may not be filed without special leave.

(d) A request for an order under this section may be made by informal letter to the court. A person who knowingly interferes with the transmission of the request to the court may be adjudged guilty of contempt of court.

(e) If a nonresident guardian of a nonresident ward qualifies as guardian under this chapter, the guardianship of any resident guardian may be terminated.

(f) Repealed by Acts 1999, 76th Leg., ch. 379, § 10, eff. Sept. 1, 1999.

Added by Acts 1993, 73rd Leg., ch. 957, § 1, eff. Sept. 1, 1993. Amended by Acts 1995, 74th Leg., ch. 1039, § 40, eff. Sept. 1, 1995; Acts 1999, 76th Leg., ch. 379, §§ 9, 10, eff. Sept. 1, 1999.

### § 694A.  Complete Restoration of Ward's Capacity or Modification of Guardianship

(a) A ward or any person interested in the ward's welfare may file a written application with the court for an order:

(1) finding that the ward is no longer an incapacitated person and ordering the settlement and closing of the guardianship;

(2) finding that the ward lacks the capacity to do some or all of the tasks necessary to provide food, clothing, or shelter for himself or herself, to care for the ward's own physical health, or to manage the ward's own financial affairs and granting additional powers or duties to the guardian;  or

(3) finding that the ward has the capacity to do some, but not all, of the tasks necessary to provide food, clothing, or shelter for himself or herself, to care for the ward's own physical health, or to manage the ward's own financial affairs and:

(A) limiting the powers or duties of the guardian;  and

(B) permitting the ward to care for himself or herself or to manage the ward's own financial affairs commensurate with the ward's ability.

(b) A ward may make a request for an order under this section by informal letter to the court.  A person who knowingly interferes with the transmission of the request to the court may be adjudged guilty of contempt of court.

(c) On receipt of an informal letter under Subsection (b) of this section, the court shall appoint the court investigator or a guardian ad litem to investigate the circumstances of the ward, including any circumstances alleged in the informal letter, to determine whether the ward is no longer an incapacitated person or whether a modification of the guardianship is necessary.  The court investigator or guardian ad litem shall file with the court a report of the investigation's findings and conclusions and, if the court investigator or the guardian ad litem determines that it is in the best interest of the ward to terminate or modify the guardianship, the court investigator or guardian ad litem, as appropriate, shall file an application under Subsection (a) of this section on the ward's behalf.  A guardian ad litem appointed under this subsection may also be appointed by the court to serve as attorney ad litem under Section 694C of this code.

(d) When an application is filed under this section, citation shall be served on the ward's guardian and on the ward if the ward is not the applicant.

(e) Except as otherwise provided by the court, on good cause shown by the applicant, a person may not reapply for complete restoration of a ward's capacity or modification of a ward's guardianship before the first anniversary of the date of the hearing on the last preceding application.

Added by Acts 1995, 74th Leg., ch. 1039, § 41, eff. Sept. 1, 1995. Amended by Acts 1999, 76th Leg., ch. 829, § 5, eff. Sept. 1, 1999. Subsec. (c) amended by Acts 2005, 79th Leg., ch. 200, § 4, eff. Sept. 1, 2005.

### § 694B.  Contents of Application

An application filed under Section 694A of this code must be sworn to by the applicant and must:

(1) contain the name, sex, date of birth, and address of the ward;

(2) contain the name and address of any person serving as guardian of the person of the ward on the date the application is filed;

(3) contain the name and address of any person serving as guardian of the estate of the ward on the date the application is filed;

(4) state the nature and description of the ward's guardianship;

(5) state the specific areas of protection and assistance and any limitation of rights that exist;

(6) state whether the relief being sought is:

(A) a restoration of the ward's capacity because the ward is no longer an incapacitated person;

(B) the granting of additional powers or duties to the guardian;  or

(C) the limitation of powers granted to or duties performed by the guardian;

(7) if the relief being sought under the application is described by Subdivision (6)(B) or (C) of this section, state:

(A) the nature and degree of the ward's incapacity;

(B) the specific areas of protection and assistance to be provided to the ward and requested to be included in the court's order;  and

(C) any limitation of the ward's rights requested to be included in the court's order;

(8) state the approximate value and description of the ward's property, including any compensation, pension, insurance, or allowance to which the ward is or may be entitled; and

(9) if the ward is 60 years of age or older, contain the names and addresses, to the best of the applicant's knowledge, of the ward's spouse, siblings, and children or, if there is no known spouse, sibling, or child, the names and addresses of the ward's next of kin.

Added by Acts 1999, 76th Leg., ch. 829, § 6, eff. Sept. 1, 1999.

### § 694C.  Appointment of Attorney Ad Litem

(a) The court shall appoint an attorney ad litem to represent a ward in a proceeding for the complete restoration of the ward's capacity or for the modification of the ward's guardianship.

(b) Unless otherwise provided by the court, an attorney ad litem appointed under this section shall represent the ward only for purposes of the restoration or modification proceeding.

(c) An attorney ad litem appointed under this section is entitled to reasonable compensation for services in the amount set by the court to be taxed as costs in the proceeding, regardless of whether the proceeding results in the restoration of the ward's capacity or a modification of the ward's guardianship.

Added by Acts 1999, 76th Leg., ch. 829, § 6, eff. Sept. 1, 1999.

Subsec. (c) added by Acts 2007, 80th Leg., ch. 614, § 9, eff. Sept. 1, 2007.

### § 694D.  Hearing

(a) At a hearing on an application for complete restoration of a ward's capacity or modification of a ward's guardianship, the court shall consider only evidence regarding the ward's mental or physical capacity at the time of the hearing that is relevant to the restoration of capacity or modification of the guardianship, as appropriate.

(b) The party who filed the application has the burden of proof at the hearing.

Added by Acts 1999, 76th Leg., ch. 829, § 6, eff. Sept. 1, 1999.

### § 694E.  Findings Required

(a) Before ordering the settlement and closing of the guardianship under an application filed under Section 694A of this code, the court must find by a preponderance of the evidence that the ward is no longer partially or fully incapacitated.

(b) Before granting additional powers to the guardian or requiring the guardian to perform additional duties under an application filed under Section 694A of this code, the court must find by a preponderance of the evidence that the current nature and degree of the ward's incapacity warrants a modification of the guardianship and that some or all of the ward's rights need to be further restricted.

(c) Before limiting the powers granted to or duties required to be performed by the guardian under an application filed under Section 694A of this code, the court must find by a preponderance of the evidence that the current nature and degree of the ward's incapacity warrants a modification of the guardianship and that some of the ward's rights need to be restored.

Added by Acts 1999, 76th Leg., ch. 829, § 6, eff. Sept. 1, 1999.

### § 694F.  Examinations and Reports Relating to Complete Restoration of Ward's Capacity or Modification of Guardianship

(a) The court may not grant an order completely restoring a ward's capacity or modifying a ward's guardianship under an application filed under Section 694A of this code unless, in addition to other requirements prescribed by this code, the applicant presents to the court a written letter or certificate from a physician licensed in this state that is dated not earlier than the 120th day before the date of the filing of the application or dated after the date on which the application was filed but before the date of the hearing.  The letter or certificate must:

(1) describe the nature and degree of incapacity, including the medical history if reasonably available, or state that, in the physician's opinion, the ward has the capacity to provide food, clothing, and shelter for himself or herself, to care for the ward's own physical health, and to manage the financial affairs of the ward;

(2) provide a medical prognosis specifying the estimated severity of any incapacity;

(3) state how or in what manner the ward's ability to make or communicate responsible decisions concerning himself or herself is affected by the person's physical or mental health;

(4) state whether any current medication affects the demeanor of the ward or the ward's ability to participate fully in a court proceeding;

(5) describe the precise physical and mental conditions underlying a diagnosis of senility, if applicable; and

(6) include any other information required by the court.

(b) If the court determines it is necessary, the court may appoint the necessary physicians to examine the ward in the same manner and to the same extent as a ward is examined by a physician under Section 687 of this code.

Added by Acts 1999, 76th Leg., ch. 829, § 6, eff. Sept. 1, 1999.

### § 694G.  Order of Complete Restoration of Ward's Capacity

If the court finds that a ward is no longer an incapacitated person, the order completely restoring the ward's capacity must contain findings of fact and specify:

(1) the information required by Section 694J of this code;

(2) that the ward is no longer an incapacitated person;

(3) that there is no further need for a guardianship of the person or estate of the ward;

(3–a) if the ward's incapacity resulted from a mental condition, that the ward's mental capacity is completely restored;

(4) that the guardian is required to:

(A) immediately settle the guardianship in accordance with this chapter; and

(B) deliver all of the remaining guardianship estate to the ward; and

(5) that the clerk shall revoke letters of guardianship when the guardianship is finally settled and closed.

Added by Acts 1999, 76th Leg., ch. 829, § 6, eff. Sept. 1, 1999. Amended by Acts 2001, 77th Leg., ch. 484, § 2, eff. Sept. 1, 2001; Acts 2001, 77th Leg., ch. 1174, § 4, eff. Sept. 1, 2001. Amended by Acts 2007, 80th Leg., ch. 614, § 10, eff. Sept. 1, 2007.

### § 694H. Modification of Guardianship

If the court finds that a guardian's powers or duties should be expanded or limited, the order modifying the guardianship must contain findings of fact and specify:

(1) the information required by Section 694J of this code;

(2) the specific powers, limitations, or duties of the guardian with respect to the care of the ward or the management of the property of the ward, as appropriate;

(3) the specific areas of protection and assistance to be provided to the ward;

(4) any limitation of the ward's rights;

(5) if the ward's incapacity resulted from a mental condition, whether the ward retains the right to vote; and

(6) that the clerk shall modify the letters of guardianship to the extent applicable to conform to the order.

Added by Acts 1999, 76th Leg., ch. 829, § 6, eff. Sept. 1, 1999. Amended by Acts 2007, 80th Leg., ch. 614, § 10, eff. Sept. 1, 2007.

### § 694I. Dismissal of Application

If the court finds that a modification of the ward's guardianship is not necessary, including that the ward's capacity has not been restored, the court shall dismiss the application and enter an order that contains findings of fact and specifies:

(1) the information required by Section 694J of this code; and

(2) that the powers, limitations, or duties of the guardian with respect to the care of the ward or the management of the ward's property will remain unchanged.

Added by Acts 1999, 76th Leg., ch. 829, § 6, eff. Sept. 1, 1999.

### § 694J. Contents of Order

(a) A court order entered with respect to a request made under Section 694A of this code to completely restore a ward's capacity or modify a ward's guardianship must:

(1) contain the name of the guardian;

(2) contain the name of the ward; and

(3) state whether the type of guardianship being addressed at the proceeding is a:

(A) guardianship of the person;

(B) guardianship of the estate; or

(C) guardianship of both the person and the estate.

(b) In an order described by this section, the court may not grant a power to a guardian or require the guardian to perform a duty that is a power granted to or a duty required to be performed by another guardian.

Added by Acts 1999, 76th Leg., ch. 829, § 6, eff. Sept. 1, 1999.

### § 694K. Attorney Retained on Ward's Behalf

(a) A ward may retain an attorney for a proceeding involving the complete restoration of the ward's capacity or modification of the ward's guardianship.

(b) The court may order that compensation for services provided by an attorney retained under this section be paid from funds in the ward's estate only if the court finds that the attorney had a good-faith belief that the ward had the capacity necessary to retain the attorney's services.

Added by Acts 1999, 76th Leg., ch. 829, § 6, eff. Sept. 1, 1999.

### § 694L. Payment for Guardians Ad Litem

As provided by Section 645(b) of this code, a guardian ad litem appointed in a proceeding involving the complete restoration of a ward's capacity or modification of a ward's guardianship is entitled to reasonable compensation for services in the amount set by the court to be taxed as costs in the proceeding, regardless of whether the proceeding results in the restoration of the ward's capacity or modification of the ward's guardianship.

Added by Acts 2007, 80th Leg., ch. 614, § 11, eff. Sept. 1, 2007.

### § 695. Appointment of Successor Guardian

(a) If a guardian dies, resigns, or is removed, the court may, on application and on service of notice as directed by the court, appoint a successor guardian. On a finding that a necessity for the immediate appointment of a successor guardian exists, the court may appoint a successor guardian without citation or notice.

(b) A successor guardian has the powers and rights and is subject to all of the duties of the preceding guardian.

(c) The court may appoint the Department of Aging and Disability Services as a successor guardian of the person or estate, or both, of a ward who has been adjudicated as totally incapacitated if:

(1) there is no less restrictive alternative to continuation of the guardianship;

(2) there is no family member or other suitable person, including a guardianship program, willing and able to serve as the ward's successor guardian;

(3) the ward is located more than 100 miles from the court that created the guardianship;

(4) the ward has private assets or access to government benefits to pay for the needs of the ward;

(5) the department is served with citation and a hearing is held regarding the department's appointment as proposed successor guardian; and

(6) the appointment of the department does not violate a limitation imposed by Subsection (d) of this section.

(d) The number of appointments under Subsection (c) of this section is subject to an annual limit of 55. The appointments must be distributed equally or as near as equally as possible among the health and human services regions of this state. The Department of Aging and Disability Services at its discretion may establish a different distribution scheme to promote the efficient use and administration of resources.

(e) If the Department of Aging and Disability Services is named as a proposed successor guardian in an application in which the department is not the applicant, citation must be issued and served on the department as provided by Section 633(c)(5) of this code.

Added by Acts 1993, 73rd Leg., ch. 957, § 1, eff. Sept. 1, 1993. Amended by Acts 2007, 80th Leg., ch. 614, § 12, eff. Sept. 1, 2007; Subsecs. (c), (d), and (e) added by Acts 2009, 81st Leg., ch. 726, § 3, eff. June 19, 2009.

## § 695A. Successor Guardians for Wards of Guardianship Programs or Governmental Entities

(a) If a guardianship program or governmental entity serving as a guardian for a ward under this chapter becomes aware of a family member or friend of the ward or any other interested person who is willing and able to serve as the ward's successor guardian, the program or entity shall notify the court in which the guardianship is pending of the individual's willingness and ability.

(a–1) If, while serving as a guardian for a ward under this chapter, the Department of Aging and Disability Services becomes aware of a guardianship program or private professional guardian willing and able to serve as the ward's successor guardian and the department is not aware of a family member or friend of the ward or any other interested person who is willing and able to serve as the ward's successor guardian, the department shall notify the court in which the guardianship is pending of the guardianship program's or private professional guardian's willingness and ability to serve.

(b) When the court is notified of the existence of a proposed successor guardian under Subsection (a) of this section or the court otherwise becomes aware of a family member, friend, or any other interested person who is willing and able to serve as a successor guardian for a ward of a guardianship program or governmental entity, the court shall determine whether the proposed successor guardian is qualified to serve under this chapter as the ward's successor guardian.

(c) If the court finds under Subsection (b) of this section that the proposed successor guardian for a ward is not disqualified from being appointed as the ward's successor guardian under Section 681 of this code and that the appointment is in the ward's best interests, the guardianship program or governmental entity serving as the ward's guardian or the court, on the court's own motion, may file an application to appoint the individual as the ward's successor guard-

ian. Service of notice on an application filed under this subsection shall be made as directed by the court.

Added by Acts 1999, 76th Leg., ch. 906, § 1, eff. Sept. 1, 1999.
Subsec. (a-1) added by Acts 2005, 79th Leg., ch. 268, § 3.10, eff. Sept. 1, 2005.

## § 696. Appointment of Private Professional Guardians

A court may not appoint a private professional guardian to serve as a guardian or permit a private professional guardian to continue to serve as a guardian under this code if the private professional guardian:

(1) has not complied with the requirements of Section 697 of this code; or

(2) is not certified as provided by Section 697B of this code.

Added by Acts 1993, 73rd Leg., ch. 957, § 1, eff. Sept. 1, 1993.
Amended by Acts 2005, 79th Leg., ch. 268, § 3.11, eff. Sept. 1, 2005.

## § 696A. Appointment of Public Guardians

(a) An individual employed by or contracting with a guardianship program must be certified as provided by Section 697B of this code to provide guardianship services to a ward of the guardianship program.

(b) An employee of the Department of Aging and Disability Services must be certified as provided by Section 697B of this code to provide guardianship services to a ward of the department.

Added by Acts 2005, 79th Leg., ch. 268, § 3.12, eff. Sept. 1, 2005.

## § 696B. Appointment of Family Members or Friends

A family member or friend of an incapacitated person is not required to be certified under Subchapter C, Chapter 111, Government Code, or any other law to serve as the person's guardian.

Added by Acts 2005, 79th Leg., ch. 268, § 3.12, eff. Sept. 1, 2005.

## § 697. Registration of Private Professional Guardians

(a) A private professional guardian must apply annually to the clerk of the county having venue over the proceeding for the appointment of a guardian for a certificate of registration. The application must include a sworn statement containing the following information concerning a private professional guardian or each person who represents or plans to represent the interests of a ward as a guardian on behalf of the private professional guardian:

(1) educational background and professional experience;

(2) three or more professional references;

(3) the names of all of the wards the private professional guardian or person is or will be serving as a guardian;

(4) the aggregate fair market value of the property of all wards that is being or will be managed by the private professional guardian or person;

(5) place of residence, business address, and business telephone number;

(6) whether the private professional guardian or person has ever been removed as a guardian by the court or resigned as a guardian in a particular case, and, if so, a description of the circumstances causing the removal or resignation, and the style of the suit, the docket number, and the court having jurisdiction over the proceeding; and

(7) the certification number or provisional certification number issued by the Guardianship Certification Board to the private professional guardian or person.

(b) The application must be accompanied by a nonrefundable fee set by the clerk in an amount necessary to cover the cost of administering this section.

(c) The term of the registration begins on the date that the requirements are met and extends through December 31 of the initial year. After the initial year of registration, the term of the registration begins on January 1 and ends on December 31 of each year. A renewal application must be completed during December of the year preceding the year for which the renewal is requested.

(d) The clerk shall bring the information received under this section to the judge's attention for review. The judge shall use the information only in determining whether to appoint, remove, or continue the appointment of a private professional guardian.

(e) Not later than January 31 of each year, the clerk shall submit to the Guardianship Certification Board the names and business addresses of private professional guardians who have satisfied the registration requirements under this section during the preceding year.

Added by Acts 1993, 73rd Leg., ch. 957, § 1, eff. Sept. 1, 1993. Amended by Acts 1999, 76th Leg., ch. 1116, § 2, eff. Sept. 1, 1999; Subsecs. (a), (c), (e) amended by Acts 2005, 79th Leg., ch. 268, § 3.13, eff. Sept. 1, 2005; subsecs. (a) and (e) amended by Acts 2009, 81st Leg., ch. 510, § 2, eff. Sept. 1, 2009.

### § 697A. List of Certain Public Guardians Maintained by County Clerks or Guardianship Certification Board

(a) Not later than January 31 of each year, each guardianship program operating in a county shall submit to the county clerk a copy of the report submitted to the Guardianship Certification Board under Section 111.044, Government Code.

(b) Not later than January 31 of each year, the Department of Aging and Disability Services shall submit to the Guardianship Certification Board a statement containing:

(1) the name, address, and telephone number of each department employee who is or will be providing guardianship services to a ward or proposed ward on behalf of the department; and

(2) the name of each county in which each employee named in Subdivision (1) of this subsection is providing or is authorized to provide those services.

Added by Acts 2005, 79th Leg., ch. 268, § 3.14, eff. Sept. 1, 2005. Amended by Acts 2007, 80th Leg., ch. 361, §§ 1 and 2, eff. Sept. 1, 2007; Acts 2009, 81st Leg., ch. 510, § 3, eff. Sept. 1, 2009.

### § 697B. Certification Requirement for Private Professional Guardians and Public Guardians

(a) The following persons must be certified under Subchapter C, Chapter 111, Government Code:

(1) an individual who is a private professional guardian;

(2) an individual who will represent the interests of a ward as a guardian on behalf of a private professional guardian;

(3) an individual providing guardianship services to a ward of a guardianship program on the program's behalf, except as provided by Subsection (d) of this section; and

(4) an employee of the Department of Aging and Disability Services providing guardianship services to a ward of the department.

(b) A person whose certification has expired must obtain a new certification under Subchapter C, Chapter 111, Government Code, to be allowed to provide or continue to provide guardianship services to a ward under this code.

(c) The court shall notify the Guardianship Certification Board if the court becomes aware of a person who is not complying with the terms of a certification issued under Subchapter C, Chapter 111, Government Code, or with the standards and rules adopted under that subchapter.

(d) An individual volunteering with a guardianship program or with the Department of Aging and Disability Services is not required to be certified as provided by this section to provide guardianship services or other services under Section 161.114, Human Resources Code, on the program's or the department's behalf.

(e) In this section, "certified" includes holding a provisional certificate under Section 111.0421, Government Code.

Added by Acts 2005, 79th Leg., ch. 268, § 3.14, eff. Sept. 1, 2005. Subsec. (e) added by Acts 2007, 80th Leg., ch. 16, § 3, eff. April 25, 2007; Subsec. (d) amended by Acts 2011, 82nd Leg., ch. 599 (S.B. 220), § 10, eff. Sept. 1, 2011.

### § 698. Access to Criminal History Records

(a) Except as provided by Subsections (a–1), (a–5), and (a–6) of this section, the clerk of the county having venue over the proceeding for the appointment of a guardian shall obtain criminal history record information that is maintained by the Department of Public Safety or the Federal Bureau of Investigation identification division relating to:

(1) a private professional guardian;

(2) each person who represents or plans to represent the interests of a ward as a guardian on behalf of the private professional guardian;

(3) each person employed by a private professional guardian who will:

(A) have personal contact with a ward or proposed ward;

(B) exercise control over and manage a ward's estate; or

(C) perform any duties with respect to the management of a ward's estate;

(4) each person employed by or volunteering or contracting with a guardianship program to provide guardianship services to a ward of the program on the program's behalf; or

(5) any other person proposed to serve as a guardian under this chapter, including a proposed temporary guardian and a proposed successor guardian, other than the ward's or proposed ward's family member or an attorney.

(a–1) The Department of Aging and Disability Services shall obtain criminal history record information that is maintained by the Department of Public Safety or the Federal Bureau of Investigation identification division relating to each individual who is or will be providing guardianship services to a ward of or referred by the department, including:

(1) an employee of or an applicant selected for an employment position with the Department of Aging and Disability Services;

(2) a volunteer or an applicant selected to volunteer with the Department of Aging and Disability Services;

(3) an employee of or an applicant selected for an employment position with a business entity or other person that contracts with the Department of Aging and Disability Services to provide guardianship services to a ward referred by the department; and

(4) a volunteer or an applicant selected to volunteer with a business entity or other person described by Subdivision (3) of this subsection.

(a–2) The information in Subsection (a–1) of this section regarding applicants for employment positions must be obtained before an offer of employment, and the information regarding applicant volunteers must be obtained before the person's contact with a ward of or referred by the Department of Aging and Disability Services.

(a–3) The information in Subsection (a–1) of this section regarding employees or volunteers providing guardianship services must be obtained annually.

(a–4) The Department of Aging and Disability Services shall provide the information obtained under Subsection (a–1) of this section to:

(1) the clerk of the county having venue over the guardianship proceeding at the request of the court; and

(2) the Guardianship Certification Board at the request of the board.

(a–5) Not later than the 10th day before the date of the hearing to appoint a guardian, a person may submit to the clerk a copy of the person's criminal history record information required under Subsection (a)(5) of this section that the person obtains from the Department of Public Safety or the Federal Bureau of Investigation not earlier than the 30th day before the date of the hearing.

(a–6) The clerk described by Subsection (a) of this section is not required to obtain criminal history record information for a person who holds a certificate issued under Section 111.042, Government Code, or a provisional certificate issued under Section 111.0421, Government Code, if the Guardianship Certification Board conducted a criminal history check on the person before issuing or renewing the certificate. The board shall provide to the clerk at the court's request the criminal history record information that was obtained from the Department of Public Safety or the Federal Bureau of Investigation.

(b) The criminal history record information obtained or provided under Subsection (a), (a–5), or (a–6) of this section is for the exclusive use of the court and is privileged and confidential. The criminal history record information may not be released or otherwise disclosed to any person or agency except on court order or consent of the person being investigated. The county clerk may destroy the criminal history information records after the records are used for the purposes authorized by this section.

(b–1) The criminal history record information obtained under Subsection (a–4) of this section is for the exclusive use of the court or Guardianship Certification Board, as appropriate, and is privileged and confidential. The information may not be released or otherwise disclosed to any person or agency except on court order, with the consent of the person being investigated, or as authorized by Subsection (a–6) of this section or Section 411.1386(a–6), Government Code. The county clerk or Guardianship Certification Board may destroy the criminal history record information after the information is used for the purposes authorized by this section.

(c) The court shall use the information obtained under this section only in determining whether to:

(1) appoint, remove, or continue the appointment of a private professional guardian, a guardianship program, or the Department of Aging and Disability Services; or

(2) appoint any other person proposed to serve as a guardian under this chapter, including a proposed temporary guardian and a proposed successor guardian, other than the ward's or proposed ward's family member or an attorney.

(c–1) Criminal history record information obtained by the Guardianship Certification Board under Subsection (a–4)(2) of this section may be used for any purpose related to the issuance, denial, renewal, suspension, or revocation of a certificate issued by the board.

(d) A person commits an offense if the person releases or discloses any information received under this section without the authorization prescribed by Subsection (b) or (b–1) of this section. An offense under this subsection is a Class A misdemeanor.

(e) The clerk may charge a $10 fee to recover the costs of obtaining criminal history information records authorized by Subsection (a) of this section.

(f) This section does not prohibit the Department of Aging and Disability Services from obtaining and using criminal history record information as provided by other law.

Added by Acts 1993, 73rd Leg., ch. 957, § 1, eff. Sept. 1, 1993. Amended by Acts 1999, 76th Leg., ch. 1116, § 3, eff. Sept. 1, 1999. Subsecs. (a), (c) amended by Acts 2005, 79th Leg., ch. 268, § 3.15, eff. Sept. 1, 2005; Acts 2007, 80th Leg., ch. 361, § 3, eff. Sept. 1, 2007; Subsecs. (a), (b), and (b–1) amended by and subsec. (a–1) added by Acts 2009, 81st Leg., ch. 511, § 3, eff. June 19, 2009.

## SUBPART B.　QUALIFICATION

### § 699.　How Guardians Qualify

A guardian is deemed to have duly qualified when the guardian has taken and filed the oath required under Section 700 of this code, has made the required bond, and has filed it with the clerk, and has the bond approved by the judge. A guardian who is not required to make bond, is deemed to have duly qualified when the guardian has taken and filed the required oath.

Added by Acts 1993, 73rd Leg., ch. 957, § 1, eff. Sept. 1, 1993.

### § 700.　Oath of Guardian

(a) The guardian shall take an oath to discharge faithfully the duties of guardian for the person or estate, or both, of a ward.

(b) A representative of the Department of Aging and Disability Services shall take the oath required by Subsection (a) of this section if the department is appointed guardian.

Added by Acts 1993, 73rd Leg., ch. 957, § 1, eff. Sept. 1, 1993. Amended by Acts 1997, 75th Leg., ch. 1022, § 101, eff. Sept. 1, 1997. Subsec. (b) amended by Acts 2005, 79th Leg., ch. 268, § 3.16, eff. Sept. 1, 2005.

### § 701.　Time for Taking Oath and Giving Bond

Except as provided by Section 682A(a) of this code, the oath of a guardian may be taken and subscribed, or the bond of a guardian may be given and approved, at any time before the expiration of the 20th day after the date of the order granting letters of guardianship, or before the letters have been revoked for a failure to qualify within the time allowed. An oath may be taken before any person authorized to administer oaths under the laws of this state.

Added by Acts 1993, 73rd Leg., ch. 957, § 1, eff. Sept. 1, 1993. Amended by Acts 2001, 77th Leg., ch. 217, '§ 11, eff. Sept. 1, 2001.

### § 702.　Bond Required of Guardian of the Person or Estate

(a) Except as provided by Subsections (b) and (c) of this section, a guardian of the person or of the estate of a ward is required to give bond.

(b) A bond is not required to be given by a guardian that is:

(1) a corporate fiduciary, as defined by Section 601 of this code; or

(2) a guardianship program operated by a county.

(c) When a will that is made by a surviving parent and is probated in a court in this state or a written declaration that is made by a surviving parent directs that the guardian appointed in the will or declaration serve without bond, the court finding that the person is qualified shall issue letters of guardianship of the person to the person named to be appointed guardian in the will or declaration without requirement of bond. The court may not waive the requirement of a bond for the guardian of the estate of a ward, regardless of whether a surviving parent's will or declaration directs the court to waive the bond.

Added by Acts 1993, 73rd Leg., ch. 957, § 1, eff. Sept. 1, 1993. Amended by Acts 1995, 74th Leg., ch. 642, § 13, eff. Sept. 1, 1995; Acts 1995, 74th Leg., ch. 1039, § 42, eff. Sept. 1, 1995; Acts 1997, 75th Leg., ch. 924, § 1, eff. Sept. 1, 1997; Acts 1999, 76th Leg., ch. 1078, § 1, eff. Sept. 1, 1999; Acts 2001, 77th Leg., ch. 217, § 12, eff. Sept. 1, 2001.

### § 702A.　Types of Bonds Acceptable for Guardian of the Person

(a) This section applies only to a bond required to be posted by a guardian of the person of a ward when there is no guardian of the ward's estate.

(b) To ensure the performance of the guardian's duties, the court may accept only:

(1) a corporate surety bond;

(2) a personal surety bond;

(3) a deposit of money instead of a surety bond; or

(4) a personal bond.

(c) In determining the appropriate type and amount of bond to set for the guardian, the court shall consider:

(1) the familial relationship of the guardian to the ward;

(2) the guardian's ties to the community;

(3) the guardian's financial condition;

(4) the guardian's past history of compliance with the court; and

(5) the reason the guardian may have previously been denied a corporate surety bond.

Added by Acts 1997, 75th Leg., ch. 924, § 2, eff. Sept. 1, 1997.

### § 703.　Bond of Guardian of the Estate

(a) Except when bond is not required under this chapter, before being issued letters of guardianship of estates, the recipient of letters shall give a bond that is conditioned as required by law and that is payable to the judge of the county in which the guardianship proceedings are pending or to the judge's successors in office. A bond of the guardian of the estate must have the written approval of either of the judges in the judge's official capacity and shall be executed and approved in accordance with Subsections (b)–(q) of this section.

(b) The judge shall set the penalty of the bond in an amount that is sufficient to protect the guardianship and its creditors, as provided by this chapter.

(c) If a bond is or will be required of a guardian of an estate, the court, before setting the penalty of the bond, shall hear evidence and determine:

(1) the amount of cash on hand and where deposited, and the amount of cash estimated to be needed for administrative purposes, including the operation of a business, factory, farm, or ranch owned by the guardianship estate, and administrative expenses for one year;

(2) the revenue anticipated to be received in the succeeding 12 months from dividends, interest, rentals, or use of real or personal property belonging to the guardianship estate and the aggregate amount of any installments or periodic payments to be collected;

(3) the estimated value of certificates of stock, bonds, notes, or securities of the ward, the name of the depository in which the stocks, bonds, notes, or securities of the ward are held for safekeeping, the face value of life insurance or other policies payable to the person on whose guardianship administration is sought or to the person's estate, and other personal property that is owned by the guardianship, or by a person with a disability; and

(4) the estimated amount of debts due and owing by the ward.

(d) The judge shall set the penalty of the bond in an amount equal to the estimated value of all personal property belonging to the ward, with an additional amount to cover revenue anticipated to be derived during the succeeding 12 months from interest, dividends, collectible claims, the aggregate amount of any installments or periodic payments exclusive of income derived or to be derived from federal social security payments, and rentals for use of real and personal property, provided that the penalty of the original bond shall be reduced in proportion to the amount of cash or value of securities or other assets authorized or required to be deposited or placed in safekeeping by court order, or voluntarily made by the guardian or by the sureties on the bond of the guardian as provided in Subsections (f) and (g) of this section.

(e) If the court considers it to be in the best interests of the ward, the court may require that the guardian and the corporate or personal sureties on the bond of the guardian of the ward agree to deposit any or all cash and safekeeping of other assets of the guardianship estate in a financial institution as defined by Section 201.101, Finance Code, with its main office or a branch office in this state and qualified to act as a depository in this state under the laws of this state or of the United States, and, if the depository is otherwise proper, the court may require the deposit to be made in a manner so

as to prevent the withdrawal of the money or other assets in the guardianship estate without the written consent of the surety or on court order made on the notice to the surety. An agreement made by a guardian and the sureties on the bond of the guardian under this section does not release from liability or change the liability of the principal or sureties as established by the terms of the bond.

(f) Cash, securities, or other personal assets of a ward that a ward is entitled to receive may, and if it is deemed by the court in the best interests of the ward shall, be deposited or placed in safekeeping in one or more of the depositories described in this section on the terms prescribed by the court. The court in which the guardianship proceeding is pending, on its own motion or on written application of the guardian or of any other person interested in the ward, may authorize or require additional assets of the guardianship estate then on hand or as they accrue during the pendency of the guardianship proceeding to be deposited or held in safekeeping as provided by this section. The amount of the guardian's bond shall be reduced in proportion to the cash deposited or the value of the securities or other assets placed in safekeeping. Cash that is deposited, securities or other assets held in safekeeping, or portions of the cash, securities, or other assets held in safekeeping may be withdrawn from a depository only on court order. The bond of the guardian shall be increased in proportion to the amount of cash or the value of securities or other assets that are authorized to be withdrawn.

(g) In lieu of giving a surety or sureties on a bond that is required of the guardian, or for purposes of reducing the amount of the bond, the guardian of an estate may deposit out of the guardian's own assets cash or securities that are acceptable to the court with a financial institution as defined by Section 201.101, Finance Code, with its main office or a branch office in this state. If the deposit is otherwise proper, the deposit must be equal in amount or value to the amount of the bond required or the bond shall be reduced by the value of assets that are deposited.

(h) The depository shall issue a receipt for a deposit in lieu of a surety showing the amount of cash or, if securities, the amount and description of the securities and agreeing not to disburse or deliver the cash or securities except on receipt of a certified copy of an order of the court in which the proceeding is pending. The receipt must be attached to the guardian's bond and be delivered to and filed by the county clerk after the receipt is approved by the judge.

(i) The amount of cash or securities on deposit may be increased or decreased by court order from time to time as the interests of the guardianship shall require.

(j) A cash or security deposit in lieu of a surety on the bond may be withdrawn or released only on order of a court that has jurisdiction.

(k) A creditor has the same rights against the guardian and the deposits as are provided for recovery against sureties on a bond.

(*l*) The court on its own motion or on written application by the guardian or any other person interested in the guardianship may require that the guardian give adequate bond in lieu of the deposit or may authorize withdrawal of the deposit and substitution of a bond with sureties on the bond. In either case, the guardian shall file a sworn statement showing the condition of the guardianship. The guardian is subject to removal as in other cases if the guardian does not file the sworn statement before the 21st day after the guardian is personally served with notice of the filing of the application or before the 21st day after the date the court enters its motion. The deposit may not be released or withdrawn until the court is satisfied as to the condition of the guardianship estate, determines the amount of bond, and receives and approves the bond.

(m) On the closing of a guardianship, a deposit or a portion of a deposit that remains on hand, whether of the assets of the guardian, the guardianship, or surety, shall be released by court order and paid to the person entitled to the assets. A writ of attachment or garnishment does not lie against the deposit except as to claims of creditors of the guardianship being administered or of persons interested in the guardianship, including distributees and wards, and only if the court has ordered distribution, and only to the extent of the ordered distribution.

(n) The surety on the bond may be an authorized corporate or personal surety.

(o) When the bond is more than $50,000, the court may require that the bond be signed by two or more authorized corporate sureties or by one corporate surety and two or more good and sufficient personal sureties. The guardianship shall pay the cost of a bond with corporate sureties.

(p) If the sureties are natural persons, there may not be less than two sureties, each of whom shall make affidavit in the manner prescribed by this chapter. The judge must be satisfied that each surety owns property in this state, over and above that exempt by law, sufficient to qualify as a surety as required by law. Except as otherwise provided by law, only one surety is required if the surety is an authorized corporate surety. A personal surety, instead of making an affidavit or creating a lien on specific real estate when an affidavit or lien is required, may deposit the personal surety's own cash or securities in the same manner as a guardian in lieu of pledging real property as security, subject to the provisions covering the deposits when made by guardians.

(q) If the guardian is a temporary guardian, the judge shall set the amount of the bond.

(r) The provisions of this section relating to the deposit of cash and safekeeping of securities cover, as far as they may apply, the orders entered by the court when:

(1) real or personal property of a guardianship has been authorized to be sold or rented;

(2) money is borrowed from the guardianship;

(3) real property, or an interest in real property, has been authorized to be leased for mineral development or made subject to unitization;

(4) the general bond has been found insufficient; or

(5) money is borrowed or invested on behalf of a ward.

(s) In determining the amount of the bond, the court may not take into account the assets of the estate that are placed in a management trust under Subpart N, Part 4,[1] of this code.

Added by Acts 1993, 73rd Leg., ch. 957, § 1, eff. Sept. 1, 1993. Amended by Acts 1999, 76th Leg., ch. 344, § 6.006, eff. Sept. 1, 1999.

[1] V.A.T.S. Probate Code, § 867 et seq.

### § 704. Form of Bond

The following form, or the same in substance, may be used for the bonds of guardians:

"The State of Texas

"County of _____

"Know all men by these presents that we, A. B., as principal, and E. F., as sureties, are held and firmly bound to the county judge of the County of ____ and his successors in office, in the sum of $_____; conditioned that the above bound A. B., who has been appointed by the judge of the county as guardian or temporary guardian of the person or of the estate, or both, _____, stating in each case whether or not the person is a minor or an incapacitated person other than a minor, shall well and truly perform all of the duties required of the guardian or temporary guardian of the estate by law under appointment."

Added by Acts 1993, 73rd Leg., ch. 957, § 1, eff. Sept. 1, 1993.

### § 705. Bond to be Filed

A bond required under this chapter shall be subscribed by the principals and sureties, and shall be filed with the clerk when approved by the court.

Added by Acts 1993, 73rd Leg., ch. 957, § 1, eff. Sept. 1, 1993.

### § 706. Bond of Joint Guardians

When two or more persons are appointed guardians and are required to give a bond by the court or under this chapter, the court may require either a separate bond from each person or one joint bond from all of the persons.

Added by Acts 1993, 73rd Leg., ch. 957, § 1, eff. Sept. 1, 1993.

### § 707. Bond of Married Persons

When a married person is appointed guardian, the person may jointly execute, with or without, the person's spouse, the bond required by law. The bond shall bind the person's separate estate and may bind the person's spouse only if the bond is signed by the spouse.

Added by Acts 1993, 73rd Leg., ch. 957, § 1, eff. Sept. 1, 1993.

## § 708. Bond of Married Person Younger Than 18 Years of Age

When a person who is younger than 18 years of age and is or has been married accepts and qualifies as guardian, a bond required to be executed by the person shall be as valid and binding for all purposes as if the person were of lawful age.

Added by Acts 1993, 73rd Leg., ch. 957, § 1, eff. Sept. 1, 1993.

## § 708A. Bond of Guardianship Program

The judge may require a guardianship program that is appointed guardian under this chapter to file one bond that:

(1) meets all the conditions required under this chapter; and

(2) is in an amount that is sufficient to protect the guardianship and the creditors of the guardianship of all of the wards of the guardianship program.

Added by Acts 1993, 73rd Leg., ch. 957, § 1, eff. Sept. 1, 1993.

## § 709. Affidavit of Personal Surety; Lien on Specific Property When Required; Subordination of Lien Authorized

(a) Before a judge considers a bond with a personal surety, each personal surety shall execute an affidavit stating the amount of the surety's assets, reachable by creditors, of a value over and above the surety's liabilities. The total of the surety's worth must be equal to at least double the amount of the bond. The affidavit shall be presented to the judge for the judge's consideration and, if approved, shall be attached to and form part of the bond.

(b) If the judge finds that the estimated value of personal property of the guardianship that cannot be deposited or held in safekeeping as provided by this section is such that personal sureties cannot be accepted without the creation of a specific lien on the real property of the sureties, the judge shall enter an order requiring that each surety designate real property owned by the surety in this state subject to execution. The designated property must be of a value over and above all liens and unpaid taxes, equal at least to the amount of the bond, giving an adequate legal description of the property, all of which shall be incorporated in an affidavit by the surety, approved by the judge, and attached to and form part of the bond. If the surety does not comply with the order, the judge may require that the bond be signed by an authorized corporate surety or by an authorized corporate surety and two or more personal sureties.

(c) If a personal surety who has been required to create a lien on specific real estate desires to lease the real property for mineral development, the personal surety may file the surety's written application in the court in which the proceeding is pending to request subordination of the lien to the proposed lease. The judge of the court in which the proceeding is pending may enter an order granting the application. A certified copy of an order entered under this subsection that is filed and recorded in the deed records of the proper county is sufficient to subordinate the lien to the rights of a lessee in the proposed lease.

Added by Acts 1993, 73rd Leg., ch. 957, § 1, eff. Sept. 1, 1993.

## § 710. Bond as Lien on Real Property of Surety

When a personal surety is required by the court to create a lien on specific real property as a condition of the personal surety's acceptance as surety on a bond, a lien on the surety's real property in this state that is described in the affidavit of the surety, and only on the property, shall arise as security for the performance of the obligation of the bond. Before letters are issued to the guardian, the clerk of the court shall mail to the office of the county clerk of each county in which any real property set forth in the surety's affidavit is located a statement signed by the clerk that gives a sufficient description of the real property, the name of the principal and sureties, the amount of the bond, the name of the guardianship, and the court in which the bond is given. The county clerk to whom such statement is sent shall record the statement in the deed records of the county. The recorded statement shall be duly indexed in such a manner that the existence and character of a lien may conveniently be determined, and the recording and indexing of the statement is constructive notice to a person of the existence of the lien on the real property located in the county, effective as of the date of the indexing.

Added by Acts 1993, 73rd Leg., ch. 957, § 1, eff. Sept. 1, 1993.

## § 711. When New Bond May be Required

A guardian may be required to give a new bond when:

(1) one of the sureties on the bond dies, removes beyond the limits of the state, or becomes insolvent;

(2) in the opinion of the court, the sureties on the bond are insufficient;

(3) in the opinion of the court, the bond is defective;

(4) the amount of the bond is insufficient;

(5) one of the sureties petitions the court to be discharged from future liability on the bond; or

(6) the bond and the record of the bond has been lost or destroyed.

Added by Acts 1993, 73rd Leg., ch. 957, § 1, eff. Sept. 1, 1993.

## § 712. Demand for New Bond by Interested Person

A person interested in a guardianship may allege, on application in writing that is filed with the county clerk of the county in which the guardianship proceeding is pending, that the guardian's bond is insufficient or defective or has been, with the record of the bond, lost or destroyed, and may cause the guardian to be cited to appear and show cause why the guardian should not give a new bond.

Added by Acts 1993, 73rd Leg., ch. 957, § 1, eff. Sept. 1, 1993.

## § 713. Judge to Require New Bond

When it is made known to a judge that a bond is insufficient or that the bond has, with the record of the bond, been lost or destroyed, the judge shall:

(1) without delay and without notice enter an order requiring the guardian to give a new bond; or

(2) without delay cause the guardian to be cited to show cause why the guardian should not give a new bond.

Added by Acts 1993, 73rd Leg., ch. 957, § 1, eff. Sept. 1, 1993.
Amended by Acts 2007, 80th Leg., ch. 683, § 2, eff. Sept. 1, 2007.

## § 714. Order Requiring New Bond

(a) The order entered under Section 713(1) of this code must state the reasons for requiring a new bond, the amount of the new bond, and the time within which the new bond must be given, which may not be earlier than the 10th day after the date of the order. If the guardian opposes the order, the guardian may demand a hearing on the order. The hearing must be held before the expiration of the time within which the new bond must be given.

(b) On the return of a citation ordering a guardian to show cause why the guardian should not give a new bond, the judge on the day contained in the return of citation as the day for the hearing of the matter, shall proceed to inquire into the sufficiency of the reasons for requiring a new bond. If the judge is satisfied that a new bond should be required, the judge shall enter an order to that effect that states the amount of the new bond and the time within which the new bond shall be given, which may not be later than 20 days from the date of the order issued by the judge under this subsection.

Added by Acts 1993, 73rd Leg., ch. 957, § 1, eff. Sept. 1, 1993.
Amended by Acts 2007, 80th Leg., ch. 683, § 2, eff. Sept. 1, 2007.

## § 715. Order Suspends Powers of Guardians

When a guardian is required to give a new bond, the order requiring the bond has the effect of suspending the guardian's powers, and the guardian may not pay out any money of the guardianship or do any other official act, except to preserve the property of the guardianship, until a new bond has been given and approved.

Added by Acts 1993, 73rd Leg., ch. 957, § 1, eff. Sept. 1, 1993.

## § 716. Decrease in Amount of Bond

A guardian required to give bond at any time may file with the clerk a written application to the court to have the bond reduced. After an application has been filed by the guardian under this section, the clerk shall issue and cause to be posted notice to all persons interested in the estate and to a surety on the bond, apprising the persons and surety of the fact and nature of the application and of the time at which the judge will hear the application. The judge may permit the filing of a new bond in a reduced amount on the submission of proof that a smaller bond than the one in effect will be adequate to meet the requirements of the law and protect the guardianship and on the approval of an accounting filed at the time of the application.

Added by Acts 1993, 73rd Leg., ch. 957, § 1, eff. Sept. 1, 1993.

## § 717. Discharge of Sureties on Execution of New Bond

When a new bond has been given and approved, the judge shall enter an order discharging the sureties on the former bond from all liability for the future acts of the principal.

Added by Acts 1993, 73rd Leg., ch. 957, § 1, eff. Sept. 1, 1993.

## § 718. Release of Sureties Before Guardianship Fully Administered

A surety on the guardian's bond at any time may file with the clerk a petition with the court in which the proceeding is pending, praying that the guardian be required to give a new bond and that the petitioner be discharged from all liability for the future acts of the guardian. If a petition is filed, the guardian shall be cited to appear and give a new bond.

Added by Acts 1993, 73rd Leg., ch. 957, § 1, eff. Sept. 1, 1993.

## § 719. Release of Lien Before Guardianship Fully Administered

If a personal surety who has given a lien on specific real property as security applies to the court to have the lien released, the court shall order the release requested if the court is satisfied that the bond is sufficient without the lien on the property or if sufficient other real or personal property of the surety is substituted on the same terms and conditions required for the lien that is to be released. If the personal surety who requests the release of the lien does not offer a lien on other real or personal property and if the court is not satisfied that the bond is sufficient without the substitution of other property, the court shall order the guardian to appear and give a new bond.

Added by Acts 1993, 73rd Leg., ch. 957, § 1, eff. Sept. 1, 1993.

## § 720. Release of Recorded Lien on Surety's Property

A certified copy of the court order that describes the property, releases the lien, and is filed with the county clerk and recorded in the deed records of the county in which the property is located has the effect of cancelling the lien on the property.

Added by Acts 1993, 73rd Leg., ch. 957, § 1, eff. Sept. 1, 1993.

## § 721. Revocation of Letters for Failure to Give Bond

If a guardian of a ward fails to give the bond required by the court within the time required under this chapter, another person may be appointed guardian of the ward.

Added by Acts 1993, 73rd Leg., ch. 957, § 1, eff. Sept. 1, 1993.

## § 722. Guardian Without Bond Required to Give Bond

If a bond is not required of an individual guardian of the estate, a person who has a debt, claim, or demand against the guardianship, to the justice of which oath has been made by the person, the person's agent or attorney, or any other person interested in the guardianship, in person or as the representative of another person, may file a complaint under oath in writing in the court in which the guardian was appointed, and the court, after a complaint is filed under this section, shall cite the guardian to appear and show cause why the guardian should not be required to give bond.

Added by Acts 1993, 73rd Leg., ch. 957, § 1, eff. Sept. 1, 1993.

### § 723. Order Requiring Bond

On hearing a complaint under Section 722 of this code, if it appears to the court that a guardian is wasting, mismanaging, or misapplying the guardianship estate and that a creditor may probably lose his debt, or that a person's interest in the guardianship may be diminished or lost, the court shall enter an order requiring the guardian to give a bond not later than the 10th day after the date of the order.

Added by Acts 1993, 73rd Leg., ch. 957, § 1, eff. Sept. 1, 1993.

### § 724. Amount of Bond

A bond that is required under Section 723 of this code shall be in an amount that is sufficient to protect the guardianship and its creditors. The bond shall be approved by and payable to the judge and shall be conditioned that the guardian will well and truly administer the guardianship and that the guardian will not waste, mismanage, or misapply the guardianship estate.

Added by Acts 1993, 73rd Leg., ch. 957, § 1, eff. Sept. 1, 1993.

### § 725. Failure to Give Bond

If the guardian fails to give the bond required under Section 723 of this code, and the judge does not extend the time, the judge, without citation, shall remove the guardian and appoint a competent person as guardian of the ward who:

(1) shall administer the guardianship according to the provisions of a will or law;

(2) shall take the oath required of a guardian as the case may be before the person enters on the administration of the guardianship; and

(3) shall give bond in the same manner and in the same amount provided in this chapter for the issuance of original letters of guardianship.

Added by Acts 1993, 73rd Leg., ch. 957, § 1, eff. Sept. 1, 1993.

### § 726. Bonds Not Void on First Recovery

The bond of a guardian is not void on the first recovery, but the bond may be sued on and prosecuted from time to time until the whole amount of the bond is recovered.

Added by Acts 1993, 73rd Leg., ch. 957, § 1, eff. Sept. 1, 1993.

PART 4. ADMINISTRATION OF GUARDIANSHIP

SUBPART A. INVENTORY, APPRAISEMENT, AND LIST OF CLAIMS

### § 727. Appointment of Appraisers

After letters of guardianship of the estate have been granted and on its own motion or on the motion of any interested person, the court for good cause shown shall appoint at least one but not more than three disinterested persons who are citizens of the county in which letters were granted to appraise the property of the ward. If the court appoints an appraiser under this section and part of the estate is located in a county other than the county in which letters were granted, the court may appoint at least one but not more than three disinterested persons who are citizens of the county in which the part of the estate is located to appraise the property of the estate located in the county if the court considers it necessary to appoint an appraiser.

Added by Acts 1993, 73rd Leg., ch. 957, § 1, eff. Sept. 1, 1993.
Amended by Acts 2005, 79th Leg., ch. 701, § 2, eff. Sept. 1, 2005.

### § 728. Failure of Appraiser to Serve

If an appraiser appointed under Section 727 of this code fails or refuses to act, the court shall remove the appraiser and appoint one or more appraisers.

Added by Acts 1993, 73rd Leg., ch. 957, § 1, eff. Sept. 1, 1993.

### § 729. Inventory and Appraisement

(a) Not later than the 30th day after the date the guardian of the estate qualifies as guardian, unless a longer time is granted by the court, the guardian of the estate shall file with the clerk of the court a verified, full, and detailed inventory, in one written instrument, of all the property of the ward that has come into the guardian's possession or knowledge. The inventory filed by the guardian under this section must include:

(1) all real property of the ward that is located in this state; and

(2) all personal property of the ward wherever located.

(b) The guardian shall set out in the inventory the guardian's appraisement of the fair market value of each item of the property on the date of the grant of letters of guardianship. If the court appoints an appraiser of the estate, the guardian shall determine the fair market value of each item of the inventory with the assistance of the appraiser and shall set out in the inventory the appraisement made by the appraiser.

(c) An inventory made under this section must specify:

(1) what portion of the property is separate property and what portion is community property; and

(2) if any of the property is owned in common with other persons, the interest owned by the ward.

(d) The inventory, when approved by the court and duly filed with the clerk of court, is for purposes of this chapter the inventory and appraisement of the estate referred to in this chapter.

(e) The court for good cause shown may require the filing of the inventory and appraisement at a time not later than the 30th day after the date of qualification of the guardian.

Added by Acts 1993, 73rd Leg., ch. 957, § 1, eff. Sept. 1, 1993. Subsecs. (a), (e) amended by Acts 2003, 78th Leg., ch. 549, § 13, eff. Sept. 1, 2003; Subsec. (c) amended by Acts 2011, 82nd Leg., ch. 1085 (S.B. 1196), § 23, eff. Sept. 1, 2011.

## § 730. List of Claims

The guardian shall make and attach to an inventory under Section 729 of this code a full and complete list of all claims due or owing to the ward that must state:

(1) the name of each person indebted to the ward and the address of the person if known;

(2) the nature of the debt, whether it is a note, bill, bond, or other written obligation or whether it is an account or verbal contract;

(3) the date of the indebtedness and the date when the debt is or was due;

(4) the amount of each claim, the rate of interest on each claim, and time for which the claim bears interest; and

(5) what portion of the claim is held in common with others and the interest of the estate in the claim.

Added by Acts 1993, 73rd Leg., ch. 957, § 1, eff. Sept. 1, 1993. Amended by Acts 2011, 82nd Leg., ch. 1085 (S.B. 1196), § 24, eff. Sept. 1, 2011.

## § 731. Affidavit Attached

The guardian of the estate shall attach to the inventory and list of claims the guardian's affidavit subscribed and sworn to before an officer in the county authorized by law to administer oaths that the inventory and list of claims are a true and complete statement of the property and claims of the estate that have come to the guardian's knowledge.

Added by Acts 1993, 73rd Leg., ch. 957, § 1, eff. Sept. 1, 1993.

## § 732. Appraiser Fees

An appraiser appointed by the court is entitled to receive a reasonable fee for the performance of the appraiser's duties as an appraiser that are to be paid out of the estate.

Added by Acts 1993, 73rd Leg., ch. 957, § 1, eff. Sept. 1, 1993.

## § 733. Court Action

(a) On return of the inventory, appraisement, and list of claims, the judge shall examine and approve or disapprove the inventory, appraisement, or list of claims as follows:

(1) if the judge approves the inventory, appraisement, and list of claims, the judge shall issue an order to that effect; and

(2) if the judge does not approve the inventory, appraisement, or list of claims, the judge shall enter an order to that effect.

(b) The court order shall require the return of another inventory, appraisement, and list of claims, or whichever of them is disapproved, within a time specified in the order but not later than 20 days after the date of the order. The judge may appoint new appraisers if the judge deems it necessary.

Added by Acts 1993, 73rd Leg., ch. 957, § 1, eff. Sept. 1, 1993.

## § 734. Discovery of Additional Property

The guardian of the estate shall promptly file with the clerk of court a verified, full, and detailed supplemental inventory and appraisement if property or claims that are not included in the inventory come to the guardian's possession or knowledge after the guardian files the inventory and appraisement required under Section 729 of this code.

Added by Acts 1993, 73rd Leg., ch. 957, § 1, eff. Sept. 1, 1993.

## § 735. Additional Inventory or List of Claims

(a) On the written complaint of an interested person that property or claims of the estate have not been included in the inventory and list of claims filed by the guardian, the guardian of an estate shall be cited to appear before the court in which the cause is pending and show cause why the guardian should not be required to make and return an additional inventory or list of claims, or both.

(b) After hearing a complaint filed under this section and being satisfied of the truth of the complaint, the court shall enter an order requiring the additional inventory or list of claims, or both, to be made and returned in like manner as the original inventory, not later than 20 days after the date of the order, as may be set by the court. The additional inventory or list of claims must include only property or claims that were not inventoried or listed by the guardian.

Added by Acts 1993, 73rd Leg., ch. 957, § 1, eff. Sept. 1, 1993.

## § 736. Correction When Inventory, Appraisement, or List of Claims Erroneous or Unjust

A person interested in an estate who deems an inventory, appraisement, or list of claims returned by the guardian erroneous or unjust in any particular form may file a written complaint that sets forth and points out the alleged erroneous or unjust items and cause the guardian to be cited to appear before the court and show cause why the errors should not be corrected. On the hearing of a complaint filed under this section, if the court is satisfied from the evidence that the inventory, appraisement, or list of claims is erroneous or unjust in any particular form as alleged in the complaint, the court shall enter an order that specifies the erroneous or unjust items and the corrections to be made and that appoints an appraiser to make a new appraisement correcting the erroneous or unjust items and requires the return of the new appraisement not later than the 20th day after the date of the order. The court may also, on its own motion or on motion of the guardian of the estate, have a new appraisal made for the purposes described by this section.

Added by Acts 1993, 73rd Leg., ch. 957, § 1, eff. Sept. 1, 1993.

### § 737. Effect of Reappraisement

When a reappraisement is made, returned, and approved by the court, the reappraisement stands in place of the original appraisement. Not more than one reappraisement shall be made, but any person interested in the estate may object to the reappraisement before or after the reappraisement is approved. If the court finds that the reappraisement is erroneous or unjust, the court shall appraise the property on the basis of the evidence before the court.

Added by Acts 1993, 73rd Leg., ch. 957, § 1, eff. Sept. 1, 1993.

### § 738. Failure of Joint Guardians to Return an Inventory, Appraisement, and List of Claims

If there is more than one qualified guardian of the estate, one or more of the guardians, on the neglect of the other guardians, may make and return an inventory and appraisement and list of claims. The guardian so neglecting may not thereafter interfere with the estate or have any power over the estate. The guardian that returns an inventory, appraisement, and list of claims has the whole administration, unless, not later than the 60th day after the date of return, each of the delinquent guardians assigns to the court in writing and under oath a reasonable excuse that the court may deem satisfactory. If no excuse is filed or if the excuse filed by a delinquent guardian is insufficient, the court shall enter an order removing the delinquent guardian and revoking the guardian's letters.

Added by Acts 1993, 73rd Leg., ch. 957, § 1, eff. Sept. 1, 1993.

### § 739. Use of Inventories, Appraisements, and Lists of Claims as Evidence

All inventories, appraisements, and lists of claims that have been taken, returned, and approved in accordance with the law, or the record of an inventory, appraisement, or list of claims, or copies of either the originals or the record, duly certified under the seal of the county court affixed by the clerk, may be given in evidence in any of the courts of this state in any suit by or against the guardian of the estate, but may not be conclusive for or against the guardian of the estate if it is shown that any property or claims of the estate are not shown in the inventory, appraisement, or list of claims or that the value of the property or claims of the estate actually was in excess of the value shown in the appraisement and list of claims.

Added by Acts 1993, 73rd Leg., ch. 957, § 1, eff. Sept. 1, 1993.

## SUBPART B. ANNUAL ACCOUNTS, REPORTS, AND OTHER EXHIBITS

### § 741. Annual Accounts Required

(a) Not later than the 60th day after the expiration of 12 months from the date of qualification, unless the court extends that time period, the guardian of the estate of a ward shall return to the court an exhibit in writing under oath setting forth a list of all claims against the estate that were presented to the guardian within the period covered by the account and specifying which claims have been allowed, paid, or rejected by the guardian and the date when any claim was rejected and which claims have been the subject of a lawsuit and the status of the lawsuit, and showing:

(1) all property that has come to the guardian's knowledge or into the guardian's possession that has not been previously listed or inventoried as property of the ward;

(2) any changes in the property of the ward that have not been previously reported;

(3) a complete account of receipts and disbursements for the period covered by the account, and the source and nature of the receipts and disbursements, with receipts of principal and income shown separately;

(4) a complete, accurate, and detailed description of the property being administered, the condition of the property, and the use being made of the property and, if rented, the terms of the rental and the price for which the property is being rented;

(5) the cash balance on hand and the name and location of the depository where the cash balance is kept and any other sums of cash in savings accounts or other form, deposited subject to court order, and the name and location of the depository of the cash; and

(6) a detailed description of personal property of the estate, that, with respect to bonds, notes, and other securities, includes the names of obligor and obligee, or if payable to bearer, so state; the date of issue and maturity; the rate of interest; serial or other identifying numbers; in what manner the property is secured; and other data necessary to identify the same fully, and how and where held for safekeeping.

(b) A guardian of the estate shall file annual accounts conforming to the essential requirements of those in Subsection (a) of this section as to changes in the assets of the estate after rendition of the former account so that the true condition of the estate, with respect to money or securities or other property, can be ascertained by the court or by any interested person, by adding to the balances forward the receipts, and then subtracting the disbursements. The description of property sufficiently described in an inventory or previous account may be by reference to the property.

(c) The following shall be annexed to all annual accounts of guardians of estates:

(1) proper vouchers for each item of credit claimed in the account, or, in the absence of a voucher, the item must be supported by evidence satisfactory to the court, and original vouchers may, on application, be returned to the guardian after approval of the guardian's account;

(2) an official letter from the bank or other depository in which the money on hand of the estate or ward is deposited that shows the amounts in general or special deposits; and

(3) proof of the existence and possession of securities owned by the estate, or shown by the accounting, and other assets held by a depository subject to court order, the proof by one of the following means:

(A) an official letter from the bank or other depository that holds the securities or other assets for safekeeping; provided, that if the depository is the representative, the official letter shall be signed by a representative of the depository other than the depository that verifies the account;

(B) a certificate of an authorized representative of the corporation that is the surety on the representative's bonds;

(C) a certificate of the clerk or a deputy clerk of a court of record in this state; or

(D) an affidavit of any other reputable person designated by the court on request of the guardian or other interested party.

(d) A certificate or affidavit under this section shall be to the effect that the affiant has examined the assets exhibited to the affiant by the guardian as assets of the estate in which the accounting is made, shall describe the assets by reference to the account or otherwise sufficiently to identify those assets exhibited, and shall state the time when and the place where the assets were exhibited. Instead of using a certificate or an affidavit, the representative may exhibit the securities to the judge of the court who shall endorse on the account, or include in the judge's order with respect to the account, a statement that the securities shown to the judge as on hand were in fact exhibited to the judge and that those securities exhibited to the judge were the same as those shown in the account, or note any variance. If the securities are exhibited at any place other than where deposited for safekeeping, it shall be at the expense and risk of the representative. The judge may require additional evidence as to the existence and custody of the securities and other personal property as in the judge's discretion the judge considers proper, and the judge may require the representative to exhibit the securities to the judge, or any person designated by the judge, at any time at the place where the securities are held for safekeeping.

(e) The guardian of the estate filing the account shall attach to the account the guardian's affidavit that:

(1) the account contains a correct and complete statement of the matters to which the account relates;

(2) the guardian has paid the bond premium for the next accounting period;

(3) the guardian has filed all tax returns of the ward due during the accounting period; and

(4) the guardian has paid all taxes the ward owed during the accounting period, showing:

(A) the amount of the taxes;

(B) the date the guardian paid the taxes; and

(C) the name of the governmental entity to which the guardian paid the taxes.

(f) If the guardian, on the ward's behalf, has not filed a tax return or paid taxes that are due on the filing of the account under this section, the guardian of the estate filing the account shall attach to the account a description of the taxes and the reasons for the guardian's failure to file the return or pay the taxes.

(g) If the estate produces negligible or fixed income, the court has the power to waive the filing of annual accounts, and the court may permit the guardian to receive all income and apply it to the support, maintenance, and education of the ward and account to the court for income and corpus of the estate when the estate must be closed.

Added by Acts 1993, 73rd Leg., ch. 957, § 1, eff. Sept. 1, 1993.

## § 742.　Action on Annual Accounts

(a) The rules in this section govern the handling of annual accounts.

(b) Annual accounts shall be filed with the county clerk, and the filing of the accounts shall be noted on the judge's docket.

(c) Before being considered by the judge, the account must remain on file for 10 days.

(d) After the expiration of 10 days after the filing of an annual account, the judge shall consider the annual account, and may continue the hearing on the account until the judge is fully advised as to all items of the account.

(e) An accounting may not be approved unless possession of cash, listed securities, or other assets held in safekeeping or on deposit under court order has been proved as required by law.

(f) If an account is found to be incorrect, it shall be corrected. When corrected to the satisfaction of the court, the account shall be approved by a court order, and the court shall act with respect to unpaid claims, as follows:

(1) if it appears from the exhibit, or from other evidence, that the estate is wholly solvent, and that the guardian has sufficient funds for the payment of every claim against the estate, the court shall order immediate payment made of all claims allowed and approved or established by judgment; and

(2) if it appears from the account, or from other evidence, that the funds on hand are not sufficient for the payment of all the claims, or if the estate is insolvent and the guardian has any funds on hand, the court shall order the funds to be applied to the payment of all claims having a preference in the order of their priority if any claim is still unpaid, and then to the payment pro rata of the other claims allowed and approved or established by final judgment, taking into consideration also the claims that were presented not later than

12 months after the date of the granting of letters of guardianship and those claims that are in suit or on which suit may yet be instituted.

Added by Acts 1993, 73rd Leg., ch. 957, § 1, eff. Sept. 1, 1993. Amended by Acts 1995, 74th Leg., ch. 1039, § 43, eff. Sept. 1, 1995.

### § 743. Reports of Guardians of the Person

(a) The guardian of the person of a ward shall return to the court a sworn, written report showing each item of receipts and disbursements for the support and maintenance of the ward, the education of the ward when necessary, and support and maintenance of the ward's dependents, when authorized by order of court.

(b) The guardian of the person, whether or not there is a separate guardian of the estate, shall submit to the court an annual report by sworn affidavit that contains the following information:

(1) the guardian's current name, address, and phone number;

(2) the ward's current:

(A) name, address, and phone number; and

(B) age and date of birth;

(3) the type of home in which the ward resides, described as the ward's own; a nursing, guardian's, foster, or boarding home; a relative's home, and the ward's relationship to the relative; a hospital or medical facility; or other type of residence;

(4) the length of time the ward has resided in the present home and, if there has been a change in the ward's residence in the past year, the reason for the change;

(5) the date the guardian most recently saw the ward, and how frequently the guardian has seen the ward in the past year;

(6) a statement indicating whether or not the guardian has possession or control of the ward's estate;

(7) the following statements concerning the ward's health during the past year:

(A) whether the ward's mental health has improved, deteriorated, or remained unchanged, and a description if there has been a change; and

(B) whether the ward's physical health has improved, deteriorated, or remained unchanged, and a description if there has been a change;

(8) a statement concerning whether or not the ward has regular medical care, and the ward's treatment or evaluation by any of the following persons during the last year, including the name of that person, and the treatment involved:

(A) a physician;

(B) a psychiatrist, psychologist, or other mental health care provider;

(C) a dentist;

(D) a social or other caseworker; or

(E) another individual who provided treatment;

(9) a description of the ward's activities during the past year, including recreational, educational, social, and occupational activities, or if no activities are available or if the ward is unable or has refused to participate in them, a statement to that effect;

(10) the guardian's evaluation of the ward's living arrangements as excellent, average, or below average, including an explanation if the conditions are below average;

(11) the guardian's evaluation of whether the ward is content or unhappy with the ward's living arrangements;

(12) the guardian's evaluation of unmet needs of the ward;

(13) a statement of whether or not the guardian's power should be increased, decreased, or unaltered, including an explanation if a change is recommended;

(14) a statement that the guardian has paid the bond premium for the next reporting period; and

(15) any additional information the guardian desires to share with the court regarding the ward, including whether the guardian has filed for emergency detention of the ward under Subchapter A, Chapter 573, Health and Safety Code, and if applicable, the number of times the guardian has filed and the dates of the applications.

(c) If the ward is deceased, the guardian shall provide the court with the date and place of death, if known, in lieu of the information about the ward otherwise required to be provided in the annual report.

(d) Unless the judge is satisfied that the facts stated are true, he shall issue orders as are necessary for the best interests of the ward.

(e) If the judge is satisfied that the facts stated in the report are true, the court shall approve the report.

(f) The court on the court's own motion may waive the costs and fees related to the filing of a report approved under Subsection (e) of this section.

(g) Once each year for the duration of the guardianship, a guardian of the person shall file the report that contains the information required by Subsections (a) and (b) of this section. Except as provided by Subsection (h) of this section, the report must cover a 12-month reporting period that begins on the date the guardian qualifies to serve.

(h) The court may change a reporting period for purposes of this section but may not extend a reporting period so that it covers more than 12 months.

(i) Each report is due not later than the 60th day after the date on which the reporting period ends.

**Text of Texas Probate Code effective until January 1, 2014**

(j) A guardian of the person may complete and file the report required under this section without the assistance of an attorney.

Added by Acts 1993, 73rd Leg., ch. 957, § 1, eff. Sept. 1, 1993. Amended by Acts 1995, 74th Leg., ch. 1039, §§ 44, 45, eff. Sept. 1, 1995; Acts 1997, 75th Leg., ch. 1403, § 3, eff. Sept. 1, 1997; Acts 1999, 76th Leg., ch. 905, § 5, eff. Sept. 1, 1999.

Subsec. (b) amended by Acts 2003, 78th Leg., ch. 692, § 1, eff. Sept. 1, 2003.

### § 744. Penalty for Failure to File Accountings, Exhibits, or Reports

If a guardian fails to file any accounting, exhibit, report of the guardian of the person, or other report required by this chapter, any person interested in the estate may, on written complaint filed with the clerk of the court, or the court on its own motion, may cause the guardian to be cited to appear and show cause why the guardian should not file the account, exhibit, or report; and, on hearing, the court may order the guardian to file the account, exhibit, or report, and, unless good cause is shown for the failure to file the account, exhibit, or report, the court may fine the guardian an amount not to exceed $1,000, revoke the letters of the guardian, or fine the guardian an amount not to exceed $1,000 and revoke the letters of the guardian.

Added by Acts 1993, 73rd Leg., ch. 957, § 1, eff. Sept. 1, 1993. Amended by Acts 1995, 74th Leg., ch. 1039, § 46, eff. Sept. 1, 1995.

### SUBPART C.   FINAL SETTLEMENT, ACCOUNTING, AND DISCHARGE

### § 745. Settling Guardianships of the Estate

(a) A guardianship of the estate of a ward shall be settled when:

(1) a minor ward dies or becomes an adult by becoming 18 years of age, or by removal of disabilities of minority according to the law of this state, or by marriage;

(2) an incapacitated ward dies, or is decreed as provided by law to have been restored to full legal capacity;

(3) the spouse of a married ward has qualified as survivor in community and the ward owns no separate property;

(4) the estate of a ward becomes exhausted;

(5) the foreseeable income accruing to a ward or to the ward's estate is so negligible that maintaining the guardianship in force would be burdensome;

(6) all of the assets of the estate have been placed in a management trust under Subpart N of this part, or have been transferred to a pooled trust subaccount in accordance with a court order issued as provided by Subpart I, Part 5, of this chapter, and the court determines that a guardianship of the ward's estate is no longer necessary; or

(7) the court determines for any other reason that a guardianship for the ward is no longer necessary.

(b) In a case arising under Subsection (a)(5) of this section, the court may authorize the income to be paid to a parent, or other person who has acted as guardian of the ward, to assist in the maintenance of the ward and without liability to account to the court for the income.

(c) When the estate of a minor ward consists only of cash or cash equivalents in an amount of $100,000 or less, the guardianship of the estate may be terminated and the assets paid to the county clerk of the county in which the guardianship proceeding is pending, and the clerk shall manage the funds as provided by Section 887 of this code.

(d) In the settlement of a guardianship, the court may appoint an attorney ad litem to represent the interests of the ward, and may allow the attorney ad litem reasonable compensation to be taxed as costs.

Added by Acts 1993, 73rd Leg., ch. 957, § 1, eff. Sept. 1, 1993. Amended by Acts 1995, 74th Leg., ch. 1039, § 47, eff. Sept. 1, 1995; Acts 2001, 77th Leg., ch. 127, § 1, eff. Sept. 1, 2001; Acts 2001, 77th Leg., ch. 217, § 13, eff. Sept. 1, 2001; Acts 2001, 77th Leg., ch. 484, §§ 3, 4, eff. Sept. 1, 2001; Acts 2001, 77th Leg., ch. 1174, § 5, eff. Sept. 1, 2001.

Subsec. (c) amended by Acts 2003, 78th Leg., ch. 549, § 14, eff. Sept. 1, 2003; Subsecs. (a) and (d) amended by Acts 2011, 82nd Leg., ch. 1085 (S.B. 1196), § 25, eff. Sept. 1, 2011.

### § 746. Payment of Funeral Expenses and Other Debts on Death of Ward

Before the guardianship of a person or estate of a ward is closed on the death of a ward, the guardian, subject to the approval of the court, may make all funeral arrangements, pay for the funeral expenses out of the estate of the deceased ward, and pay all other debts out of the estate. If a personal representative of the estate of a deceased ward is appointed, the court shall on the written complaint of the personal representative cause the guardian to be cited to appear and present a final account as provided in Section 749 of this code.

Added by Acts 1993, 73rd Leg., ch. 957, § 1, eff. Sept. 1, 1993. Amended by Acts 2001, 77th Leg., ch. 484, § 5, eff. Sept. 1, 2001.

### § 747. Termination of Guardianship of the Person

(a) When the guardianship of an incapacitated person is required to be settled as provided by Section 745 of this code, the guardian of the person shall deliver all property of the ward in the possession or control of the guardian to the emancipated ward or other person entitled to the property. If the ward is deceased, the guardian shall deliver the property to the personal representative of the deceased ward's estate or other person entitled to the property.

(b) If there is no property of the ward in the possession or control of the guardian of the person, the guardian shall, not later than the 60th day after the date on which the guardianship is required to be settled, file with the court a sworn affidavit that states the reason the guardianship was terminated and to whom the property of the ward in the guardian's possession was delivered. The judge may issue orders as necessary for the best interests of the ward or of the estate of a deceased ward. This section does not discharge a guardian of the person from liability for breach of the guardian's fiduciary duties.

Added by Acts 1993, 73rd Leg., ch. 957, § 1, eff. Sept. 1, 1993. Amended by Acts 2001, 77th Leg., ch. 484, § 6, eff. Sept. 1, 2001.

Subsec. (b) amended by Acts 2003, 78th Leg., ch. 586, § 1, eff. Sept. 1, 2003.

### § 748. Payment by Guardian of Taxes or Expenses

Notwithstanding any other provision of this chapter, a probate court in which proceedings to declare heirship are maintained may order the payment by the guardian of any and all taxes or expenses of administering the estate and may order the sale of properties in the ward's estate, when necessary, for the purpose of paying the taxes or expenses of administering the estate or for the purpose of distributing the estate among the heirs.

Added by Acts 1993, 73rd Leg., ch. 957, § 1, eff. Sept. 1, 1993.

### § 749. Account for Final Settlement of Estates of Wards

When a guardianship of the estate is required to be settled, the guardian shall present to the court the guardian's verified account for final settlement. In the account it shall be sufficient to refer to the inventory without describing each item of property in detail and to refer to and adopt any and all guardianship proceedings that concern sales, renting or hiring, leasing for mineral development, or any other transaction on behalf of the guardianship estate, including an exhibit, account, or voucher previously filed and approved, without restating the particular items. Each final account shall be accompanied by proper vouchers in support of each item not already accounted for and shall show, either by reference to any proceedings authorized above or by statement of the facts:

(1) the property, rents, revenues, and profits received by the guardian, and belonging to the ward, during the term of the guardianship;

(2) the disposition made of the property, rents, revenues, and profits;

(3) the expenses and debts against the estate that remain unpaid, if any;

(4) the property of the estate that remains in the hands of the guardian, if any;

(5) that the guardian has paid all required bond premiums;

(6) the tax returns the guardian has filed during the guardianship;

(7) the amount of taxes the ward owed during the guardianship that the guardian has paid;

(8) a complete account of the taxes the guardian has paid during the guardianship, including the amount of the taxes, the date the guardian paid the taxes, and the name of the governmental entity to which the guardian paid the taxes;

(9) a description of all current delinquencies in the filing of tax returns and the payment of taxes and a reason for each delinquency; and

(10) other facts as appear necessary to a full and definite understanding of the exact condition of the guardianship.

Added by Acts 1993, 73rd Leg., ch. 957, § 1, eff. Sept. 1, 1993. Amended by Acts 1997, 75th Leg., ch. 1403, § 4, eff. Sept. 1, 1997; Acts 2001, 77th Leg., ch. 484, § 7, eff. Sept. 1, 2001.

### § 750. Procedure in Case of Neglect or Failure to File Final Account or Report

(a) If a guardian charged with the duty of filing a final account or report fails or neglects so to do at the proper time, the court may, on the court's own motion, or on the written complaint of the emancipated ward or anyone interested in the ward or the ward's estate, shall cause the guardian to be cited to appear and present the account or report within the time specified in the citation.

(b) If a written complaint has not been filed by anyone interested in the guardianship of a person or estate of a minor or deceased ward, the court may, on or after the third anniversary after the date of the death of the ward or after the date the minor reaches the age of majority, remove the estate from the court's active docket without a final accounting and without appointing a successor personal representative.

(c) If a complaint has not been filed by anyone interested in the estate of a ward whose whereabouts are unknown to the court, the court may, on or after the fourth anniversary after the ward's whereabouts became unknown to the court, remove the estate from the court's active docket without a final accounting and without appointing a successor personal representative.

Added by Acts 1993, 73rd Leg., ch. 957, § 1, eff. Sept. 1, 1993.

### § 751. Citation on Presentation of Account for Final Settlement

(a) On the filing of an account for final settlement by a guardian of the estate of a ward, citation must contain a statement that the final account has been filed, the time and place when it will be considered by the court, and a statement requiring the person cited to appear and contest the final account if the person determines it is proper. The county clerk shall issue the citation to the following persons and in the manner provided by this section.

(b) If a ward is a living resident of this state who is 14 years of age or older, and the ward's residence is known, the ward shall be cited by personal service, unless the ward, in person or by attorney, by writing filed with the clerk, waives the issuance and personal service of citation.

(c) If one who has been a ward is deceased, the ward's executor or administrator, if one has been appointed, shall be personally served, but no service is required if the executor or administrator is the same person as the guardian.

(d) If a ward's residence is unknown, or if the ward is a nonresident of this state, or if the ward is deceased and no representative of the ward's estate has been appointed and qualified in this state, the citation to the ward or to the ward's estate shall be by publication, unless the court by written order directs citation by posting.

(e) If the court deems further additional notice necessary, it shall require the additional notice by written order. In its discretion, the court may allow the waiver of notice of an account for final settlement in a guardianship proceeding.

Added by Acts 1993, 73rd Leg., ch. 957, § 1, eff. Sept. 1, 1993.

### § 752. Court Action; Closing of Guardianship of Ward's Estate

(a) On being satisfied that citation has been duly served on all persons interested in the estate, the court shall examine the account for final settlement and the vouchers accompanying the account. After hearing all exceptions or objections to the account and evidence in support of or against the account, the court shall audit and settle the same, and restate it if that is necessary.

(b) On final settlement of an estate, if there is any part of the estate remaining in the hands of the guardian, the court shall order that it be delivered, in case of a ward, to the ward, or in the case of a deceased ward, to the personal representative of the deceased ward's estate if one has been appointed, or to any other person legally entitled to the estate.

(c) If on final settlement of an estate there is no part of the estate remaining in the hands of the guardian, the court shall discharge the guardian from the guardian's trust and order the estate closed.

(d) When the guardian of an estate has fully administered the estate in accordance with this chapter and the orders of the court and the guardian's final account has been approved, and the guardian has delivered all of the estate remaining in the guardian's hands to any person entitled to receive the estate, the court shall enter an order discharging the guardian from the guardian's trust, and declaring the estate closed.

Added by Acts 1993, 73rd Leg., ch. 957, § 1, eff. Sept. 1, 1993. Amended by Acts 2001, 77th Leg., ch. 484, § 8, eff. Sept. 1, 2001.

### § 753. Money Becoming Due Pending Final Discharge

Money or any other thing of value falling due to the estate or ward while the account for final settlement is pending, other than money or any other thing of value held under Section 703(c) of this code, until the order of final discharge of the guardian is entered in the judge's guardianship docket, may be paid, delivered, or tendered to the emancipated ward, the guardian, or the personal representative of the deceased ward's estate, who shall issue a receipt for the money or other thing of value, and the obligor or payor shall be discharged of the obligation for all purposes.

Added by Acts 1993, 73rd Leg., ch. 957, § 1, eff. Sept. 1, 1993. Amended by Acts 2009, 81st Leg., ch. 602, § 16, eff. June 19, 2009.

### § 754. Inheritance Taxes Must be Paid

If the guardian has been ordered to make payment of inheritance taxes under this code, an estate of a deceased ward may not be closed unless the final account shows and the court finds that all inheritance taxes due and owing to this state with respect to all interests and properties passing through the hands of the guardian have been paid.

Added by Acts 1993, 73rd Leg., ch. 957, § 1, eff. Sept. 1, 1993.

### § 755. Appointment of Attorney to Represent Ward

When the ward is dead and there is no executor or administrator of the ward's estate, or when the ward is a nonresident, or the ward's residence is unknown, the court may appoint an attorney ad litem to represent the interest of the ward in the final settlement with the guardian, and shall allow the attorney reasonable compensation out of the ward's estate for any services provided by the attorney.

Added by Acts 1993, 73rd Leg., ch. 957, § 1, eff. Sept. 1, 1993.

### § 756. Offsets, Credits, and Bad Debts

In the settlement of any of the accounts of the guardian of an estate, all debts due the estate that the court is satisfied could not have been collected by due diligence, and that have not been collected, shall be excluded from the computation.

Added by Acts 1993, 73rd Leg., ch. 957, § 1, eff. Sept. 1, 1993.

### § 757. Accounting for Labor or Services of a Ward

The guardian of a ward shall account for the reasonable value of the labor or services of the ward of the guardian, or the proceeds of the labor or services, if the labor or services have been rendered by the ward, but the guardian is entitled to reasonable credits for the board, clothing, and maintenance of the ward.

Added by Acts 1993, 73rd Leg., ch. 957, § 1, eff. Sept. 1, 1993.

### § 758. Procedure if Representative Fails to Deliver Estate

If a guardian, on final settlement or termination of the guardianship of the estate, neglects to deliver to the person entitled when legally demanded any portion of the estate or any funds or money in the hands of the guardian ordered to be delivered, a person entitled to the estate, funds, or money may file with the clerk of the court a written complaint alleging the fact of the guardian's neglect, the date of the person's demand, and other relevant facts. After the person files a complaint under this section, the clerk shall issue a citation to be served personally on the guardian, appraising the guardian of the complaint and citing the guardian to appear before the court and answer, if the guardian desires, at the time designated in the citation. If at the hearing the court finds that the citation was duly served and returned and that the guardian is guilty of the neglect charged, the court shall enter an order to that effect, and the guardian shall be liable to the person who filed the complaint in damages at the rate of 10 percent of the amount or appraised value of the money or estate withheld, per month, for each month or fraction of a month that the estate or money of a guardianship of the estate, or on termination of guardianship of the person, or funds is or has been withheld by the guardian after the date of demand, which damages may be recovered in any court of competent jurisdiction.

Added by Acts 1993, 73rd Leg., ch. 957, § 1, eff. Sept. 1, 1993.

## SUBPART D. REVOCATION OF LETTERS, DEATH, RESIGNATION, AND REMOVAL

### § 759. Appointment of Successor Guardian

(a) In case of the death of the guardian of the person or of the estate of a ward, a personal representative of the deceased guardian shall account for, pay, and deliver to a person legally entitled to receive the property, all the property belonging to the guardianship that is entrusted to the care of the representative, at the time and in the manner as the court orders.

(b) If letters have been granted to a person, and another person whose right to be appointed successor guardian is prior and who has not waived the right and is qualified, applies for letters, the letters previously granted shall be revoked and other letters shall be granted to the applicant.

(c) If a person named in a will as guardian is not an adult when the will is probated and letters in any capacity have been granted to another person, the nominated guardian, on proof that the nominated guardian has become an adult and is not otherwise disqualified from serving as a guardian, is entitled to have the former letters revoked and appropriate letters granted to the nominated guardian. If the will names two or more persons as guardian, any one or more of whom are minors when the will is probated and letters have been issued to the persons who are adults, a minor, on becoming an adult, if not otherwise disqualified, is permitted to qualify and receive letters.

(d) If a person named in a will as guardian was ill or absent from the state when the testator died, or when the will was proved, and for that reason could not present the will for probate not later than the 30th day after the testator's death, or accept and qualify as guardian not later than the 20th day after the date the will was probated, the person may accept and qualify as guardian not later than the 60th day after the person's return or recovery from illness, on proof to the court that the person was absent or ill. If the letters have been issued to another person, the letters shall be revoked.

(e) If it is discovered after letters of guardianship have been issued that the deceased person left a lawful will, the letters shall be revoked and proper letters of guardianship issued to a person entitled to receive the letters.

(f) Except when otherwise expressly provided in this chapter, letters may not be revoked except on application, and after personal service of citation on the person whose letters are sought to be revoked, that the person appear and show cause why the application should not be granted.

(g) Money or any other thing of value falling due to a ward while the office of the guardian is vacant may be paid, delivered, or tendered to the clerk of the court for credit of the ward, and the debtor, obligor, or payor shall be discharged of the obligation for all purposes to the extent and purpose of the payment or tender. If the clerk accepts the payment or tender, the clerk shall issue a proper receipt for the payment or tender.

(h) The court may appoint as successor guardian a spouse, parent, or child of a proposed ward who has been disqualified from serving as guardian because of a litigation conflict under Section 681(4) of this code on removal of the conflict that caused the initial disqualification if the spouse, parent, or child is otherwise qualified to serve as a guardian.

Added by Acts 1993, 73rd Leg., ch. 957, § 1, eff. Sept. 1, 1993. Amended by Acts 1995, 74th Leg., ch. 1039, § 48, eff. Sept. 1, 1995. Subsecs. (a) and (f) amended by Acts 2007, 80th Leg., ch. 614, § 13, eff. Sept. 1, 2007.

### § 760. Resignation

(a) A guardian of the estate who wishes to resign the guardian's trust shall file with the clerk a written application to the court to that effect, accompanied by a full and complete exhibit and final account, duly verified, showing the true condition of the guardianship estate entrusted to the guardian's care. A guardian of the person who wishes to resign the guardian's trust shall file with the clerk a written application to the court to that effect, accompanied by a report setting forth the information required in the annual report required under this chapter, duly verified, showing the condition of the ward entrusted to the guardian's care.

(b) If the necessity exists, the court may immediately accept a resignation and appoint a successor without citation or notice but may not discharge the person resigning as guardian of the estate or release the person or the sureties on the person's bond until final order or judgment is rendered on the final account of the guardian.

(c) On the filing of an application to resign, supported by an exhibit and final account, the clerk shall call the application to the attention of the judge, who shall set a date for a hearing on the matter. The clerk shall then issue a citation to all interested persons, showing that proper application has been filed and the time and place set for hearing, at which time the interested persons may appear and contest the exhibit and account or report. The citation shall be posted, unless the court directs that it be published.

(d) At the time set for hearing, unless it has been continued by the court, if the court finds that citation has been duly issued and served, the court shall proceed to examine the exhibit and account or report and hear all evidence for and against the exhibit, account, or report and shall, if necessary, restate, and audit and settle the exhibit, account, or report. If the court is satisfied that the matters entrusted to the applicant have been handled and accounted for in accordance with the law, the court shall enter an order of approval and require that the estate remaining in the possession of the applicant, if any, be delivered to the person entitled by law to receive it. A guardian of the person is required to comply with all orders of the court concerning the ward of the guardian.

(e) A resigning guardian may not be discharged until the application has been heard, the exhibit and account or report examined, settled, and approved, and the guardian has satisfied the court that the guardian has delivered the estate, if there is any part of the estate remaining in the possession of the guardian, or has complied with all orders of the court with relation to the guardian's trust.

(f) When the resigning guardian has complied in all respects with the orders of the court, an order shall be made accepting the resignation, discharging the applicant, and, if the applicant is under bond, the sureties of the guardian.

(g) The court at any time may order a resigning guardian who has all or part of the estate of a ward to deliver all or part of the ward's estate to a person who has been appointed and has qualified as successor guardian.

Added by Acts 1993, 73rd Leg., ch. 957, § 1, eff. Sept. 1, 1993. Amended by Acts 1995, 74th Leg., ch. 1039, § 49, eff. Sept. 1, 1995.

Subsec. (b) amended by Acts 2007, 80th Leg., ch. 614, § 14, eff. Sept. 1, 2007.

### § 760A.  Change of Resident Agent

(a) A guardian may change its resident agent to accept service of process in a guardianship proceeding or other matter relating to the guardianship by filing a statement of the change entitled "Designation of Successor Resident Agent" with the court in which the guardianship proceeding is pending. The statement must contain the names and addresses of the:

(1) guardian;

(2) resident agent; and

(3) successor resident agent.

(b) The designation of a successor resident agent made in a statement filed under this section takes effect on the date on which the statement is filed with the court.

Added by Acts 2001, 77th Leg., ch. 217, § 14, eff. Sept. 1, 2001.

### § 760B.  Resignation of Resident Agent

(a) A resident agent of a guardian may resign as the resident agent by giving notice to the guardian and filing with the court in which the guardianship proceeding is pending a statement entitled "Resignation of Resident Agent" that:

(1) contains the name of the guardian;

(2) contains the address of the guardian most recently known by the resident agent;

(3) states that notice of the resignation has been given to the guardian and that the guardian does not have a resident agent; and

(4) contains the date on which the notice of the resignation was given to the guardian.

(b) The resident agent shall send, by certified mail, return receipt requested, a copy of a resignation statement filed under Subsection (a) of this section to:

(1) the guardian at the address most recently known by the agent; and

(2) each party in the case or the party's attorney or other designated representative of record.

(c) The resignation of a resident agent takes effect on the date on which the court enters an order accepting the agent's resignation. A court may not enter an order accepting the agent's resignation unless the agent complies with the requirements of this section.

Added by Acts 2001, 77th Leg., ch. 217, § 14, eff. Sept. 1, 2001.

### § 761.  Removal

(a) The court, on its own motion or on motion of any interested person, including the ward, and without notice, may remove any guardian appointed under this chapter who:

(1) neglects to qualify in the manner and time required by law;

(2) fails to return within 30 days after qualification, unless the time is extended by order of the court, an inventory of the property of the guardianship estate and list of claims that have come to the guardian's knowledge;

(3) having been required to give a new bond, fails to do so within the time prescribed;

(4) absents himself or herself from the state for a period of three months at one time without permission of the court, or removes from the state;

(5) cannot be served with notices or other processes because of the fact that:

(A) the guardian's whereabouts are unknown;

(B) the guardian is eluding service; or

(C) the guardian is a nonresident of this state who does not have a resident agent to accept service of process in any guardianship proceeding or other matter relating to the guardianship;

(6) has misapplied, embezzled, or removed from the state, or is about to misapply, embezzle, or remove from the state, all or any part of the property committed to the guardian's care;

(7) has engaged in conduct with respect to the ward that would be considered to be abuse, neglect, or exploitation, as those terms are defined by Section 48.002, Human Resources Code, if engaged in with respect to an elderly or disabled person, as defined by that section; or

(8) has neglected to educate or maintain the ward as liberally as the means of the ward and the condition of the ward's estate permit.

*Text of subsec. (a–1) as added by Acts 2011,*
*82nd Leg., ch. 599 (S.B. 220), § 11*

(a–1) In a proceeding to remove a guardian under Subsection (a)(6), (7), or (8) of this section, the court shall appoint a guardian ad litem as provided by Section 645 of this code and an attorney ad litem. The attorney ad litem has the duties prescribed by Section 647 of this code. In the interest of judicial economy, the court may appoint the same person as guardian ad litem and attorney ad litem unless a conflict exists between the interests to be represented by the guardian ad litem and attorney ad litem.

*Text of subsec. (a–1), as added by Acts 2011,*
*82nd Leg., ch. 1218 (S.B. 481), § 1*

(a–1) The court clerk shall issue notice of an order rendered by the court removing a guardian under Subsection (a)(1), (2), (3), (4), (6), (7), or (8) of this section. The notice must:

(1) state the names of the ward and the removed guardian;

(2) state the date the court signed the order of removal;

(3) contain the following statement printed in 12–point bold font:

"If you have been removed from serving as guardian under Section 761(a)(6) or (7), Texas Probate Code, you have the right to contest the order of removal by filing an application with the court for a hearing under Section 762, Texas Probate Code, to determine whether you should be reinstated as guardian. The application must be filed not later than the 30th day after the date the court signed the order of removal.";

(4) contain as an attachment a copy of the order of removal; and

(5) be personally served on the removed guardian not later than the seventh day after the date the court signed the order of removal.

(b) The court may remove a personal representative under Subsection (a)(6) or (7) of this section only on the presentation of clear and convincing evidence given under oath.

(c) The court may remove a guardian on its own motion, or on the complaint of an interested person, after the guardian has been cited by personal service to answer at a time and place set in the notice, when:

(1) sufficient grounds appear to support belief that the guardian has misapplied, embezzled, or removed from the state, or that the guardian is about to misapply, embezzle, or remove from the state, all or any part of the property committed to the care of the guardian;

(2) the guardian fails to return any account or report that is required by law to be made;

(3) the guardian fails to obey any proper order of the court having jurisdiction with respect to the performance of the guardian's duties;

(4) the guardian is proved to have been guilty of gross misconduct or mismanagement in the performance of the duties of the guardian;

(5) the guardian becomes incapacitated, or is sentenced to the penitentiary, or from any other cause becomes incapable of properly performing the duties of the guardian's trust;

(6) the guardian has engaged in conduct with respect to the ward that would be considered to be abuse, neglect, or exploitation, as those terms are defined by Section 48.002, Human Resources Code, if engaged in with respect to an elderly or disabled person, as defined by that section;

(6–a) the guardian neglects to educate or maintain the ward as liberally as the means of the ward's estate and the ward's ability or condition permit;

(7) the guardian interferes with the ward's progress or participation in programs in the community;

(8) the guardian fails to comply with the requirements of Section 697 of this code;

(9) the court determines that, because of the dissolution of the joint guardians' marriage, the termination of the guardians' joint appointment and the continuation of only one of the joint guardians as the sole guardian is in the best interest of the ward; or

(10) the guardian would be ineligible for appointment as a guardian under Section 681 of this code.

(c–1) In addition to the authority granted to the court under Subsection (c) of this section, the court may, on the complaint of the Guardianship Certification Board, remove a guardian who would be ineligible for appointment under Section 681 of this code because of the guardian's failure to maintain the certification required under Section 697B of this code. The guardian shall be cited to appear and contest the request for removal under this subsection in the manner provided by Subsection (c) of this section.

(d) The order of removal shall state the cause of the removal. It must require that any letters issued to the person who is removed shall, if the removed person has been personally served with citation, be surrendered and that all those letters be cancelled of record, whether or not delivered. It must further require, as to all the estate remaining in the hands of a removed person, delivery of the estate to the person or persons entitled to the estate, or to one who has been appointed and has qualified as successor guardian, and as to the person of a ward, that control be relinquished as required in the order.

(e) If a joint guardian is removed under Subsection (c)(9) of this section, the other joint guardian is entitled to continue to serve as the sole guardian unless removed for a reason other than the dissolution of the joint guardians' marriage.

(f) If the necessity exists, the court may immediately appoint a successor guardian without citation or notice but may not discharge the person removed as guardian of the estate or release the person or the sureties on the person's bond until final order or judgment is rendered on the final account of the guardian. Subject to an order of the court, a successor guardian has the rights and powers of the removed guardian.

(g) The court at any time may order a person removed as guardian under this section who has all or part of the estate of a ward to deliver all or part of the ward's estate to a person who has been appointed and has qualified as successor guardian.

(h) The appointment of a successor guardian under Subsection (f) of this section does not preclude an interested person from filing an application to be appointed guardian of the ward for whom the successor guardian was appointed. The court shall hold a hearing on an application filed under the circumstances described by this subsection. At the conclusion of the hearing, the court may set aside the appointment of the successor guardian and appoint the applicant as the ward's guardian if the applicant is not disqualified and after considering the requirements of Section 676 or 677 of this code, as applicable.

(i) If the court sets aside the appointment of the successor guardian under this section, the court may require the successor guardian to prepare and file, under oath, an accounting of the estate and to detail the disposition the successor has made of the estate property.

Added by Acts 1993, 73rd Leg., ch. 957, § 1, eff. Sept. 1, 1993. Amended by Acts 1995, 74th Leg., ch. 1039, § 50, eff. Sept. 1, 1995; Acts 2001, 77th Leg., ch. 217, § 15, eff. Sept. 1, 2001. Subsec. (a) amended by Acts 2005, 79th Leg., ch. 5, § 1, eff. April 27, 2005; Subsecs. (a) and (c) amended by Acts 2005, 79th Leg., ch. 127, § 1, eff. Sept. 1, 2005; Subsec. (a) amended by Acts 2005, 79th Leg., ch. 200, § 5, eff. Sept. 1, 2005; Subsecs. (c) and (f) amended by Acts 2007, 80th Leg., ch. 614, § 15, eff. Sept. 1, 2007; Subsec. (c–1) added by Acts 2009, 81st Leg., ch. 509, § 2, eff. Sept. 1, 2009; Subsecs. (a), (c) and (f) amended by Acts 2011, 82nd Leg., ch. 599 (S.B. 220), § 11, eff. Sept. 1, 2011; Subsecs. (a–1), (h) and (i) added by Acts 2011, 82nd Leg., ch. 599 (S.B. 220), § 11, eff. Sept. 1, 2011; Subsec. (a–1) added by Acts 2011, 82nd Leg., ch. 1218 (S.B. 481), § 1, eff. Sept. 1, 2011.

### § 762. Reinstatement After Removal

(a) Not later than the 30th day after the date the court signs the order of removal, a guardian who is removed under Section 761(a)(6) or (7) of this code may file an application with the court for a hearing to determine whether the guardian should be reinstated.

(b) On the filing of an application for a hearing under this section, the court clerk shall issue a notice stating that the application for reinstatement was filed, the name of the ward, and the name of the applicant. The clerk shall issue the notice to the applicant, the ward, a person interested in the welfare of the ward or the ward's estate, and, if applicable, a person who has control of the care and custody of the ward. The notice must cite all persons interested in the estate or welfare of the ward to appear at the time and place stated in the notice if they wish to contest the application.

(c) The court shall hold a hearing on an application for reinstatement under this section as soon as practicable after the application is filed, but not later than the 60th day after the date the court signed the order of removal. If, at the conclusion of the hearing, the court is satisfied by a preponderance of the evidence that the applicant did not engage in the conduct that directly led to the applicant's removal, the court shall set aside an order appointing a successor guardian, if any, and shall enter an order reinstating the applicant as guardian of the ward or estate.

(d) If the court sets aside the appointment of a successor guardian under this section, the court may require the successor guardian to prepare and file, under oath, an accounting of the estate and to detail the disposition the successor has made of the property of the estate.

Added by Acts 1993, 73rd Leg., ch. 957, § 1, eff. Sept. 1, 1993. Subsec. (b) amended by Acts 2003, 78th Leg., ch. 549, § 15, eff. Sept. 1, 2003. Amended by Acts 2011, 82nd Leg., ch. 1218 (S.B. 481), § 2, eff. Sept. 1, 2011.

### § 763. Additional Powers of Successor Guardian

In addition, a successor guardian may make himself, and may be made, a party to a suit prosecuted by or against the predecessor of the successor guardian. The successor guardian may settle with the predecessor and receive and receipt for all the portion of the estate as remains in the hands of the successor guardian. The successor guardian may bring suit on the bond or bonds of the predecessor in the guardian's own name and capacity for all the estate that came into the hands of the predecessor and has not been accounted for by the predecessor.

Added by Acts 1993, 73rd Leg., ch. 957, § 1, eff. Sept. 1, 1993.

### § 764. Subsequent Guardians Succeed to Prior Rights and Duties

Whenever a guardian shall accept and qualify after letters of guardianship are granted on the estate, the guardian shall, in like manner, succeed to the previous guardian, and the guardian shall administer the estate in like manner as if the administration by the guardian were a continuation of the former one.

Added by Acts 1993, 73rd Leg., ch. 957, § 1, eff. Sept. 1, 1993.

### § 765. Successors' Return of Inventory, Appraisement, and List of Claims

A successor guardian who has qualified to succeed a prior guardian shall make and return to the court an inventory, appraisement, and list of claims of the estate, not later than the 30th day after the date the successor guardian qualifies as guardian, in the same manner as is required of an original appointee. The successor guardian shall in like manner as is required of an original appointee return additional inventories, appraisements, and lists of claims. In all orders appointing a successor guardian, the court shall appoint an appraiser as in original appointments on the application of any person interested in the estate.

Added by Acts 1993, 73rd Leg., ch. 957, § 1, eff. Sept. 1, 1993.
Amended by Acts 2003, 78th Leg., ch. 549, § 16, eff. Sept. 1, 2003.

## SUBPART E.  GENERAL DUTIES AND POWERS OF GUARDIANS

### § 767.  Powers and Duties of Guardians of the Person

(a) The guardian of the person is entitled to take charge of the person of the ward, and the duties of the guardian correspond with the rights of the guardian.  A guardian of the person has:

(1) the right to have physical possession of the ward and to establish the ward's legal domicile;

(2) the duty to provide care, supervision, and protection for the ward;

(3) the duty to provide the ward with clothing, food, medical care, and shelter;

(4) the power to consent to medical, psychiatric, and surgical treatment other than the in-patient psychiatric commitment of the ward;  and

(5) on application to and order of the court, the power to establish a trust in accordance with 42 U.S.C. Section 1396p(d)(4)(B), as amended, and direct that the income of the ward as defined by that section be paid directly to the trust, solely for the purpose of the ward's eligibility for medical assistance under Chapter 32, Human Resources Code.

(b) Notwithstanding Subsection (a)(4) of this section, a guardian of the person of a ward has the power to personally transport the ward or to direct the ward's transport by emergency medical services or other means to an inpatient mental health facility for a preliminary examination in accordance with Subchapters A and C, Chapter 573, Health and Safety Code.

Added by Acts 1993, 73rd Leg., ch. 957, § 1, eff. Sept. 1, 1993; Amended by Acts 2003, 78th Leg., ch. 549, § 17, eff. Sept. 1, 2003; Acts 2003, 78th Leg., ch. 692, § 2, eff. Sept. 1, 2003; Subsec. (a) amended by Acts 2005, 79th Leg., ch. 268, § 3.17, eff. Sept. 1, 2005; Acts 2009, 81st Leg., ch. 930, § 7, eff. Sept. 1, 2009.

### § 768.  General Powers and Duties of Guardian of the Estate

The guardian of the estate of a ward is entitled to the possession and management of all property belonging to the ward, to collect all debts, rentals, or claims that are due to the ward, to enforce all obligations in favor of the ward, and to bring and defend suits by or against the ward;  but, in the management of the estate, the guardian is governed by the provisions of this chapter.  It is the duty of the guardian of the estate to take care of and manage the estate as a prudent person would manage the person's own property, except as otherwise provided by this chapter.  The guardian of the estate shall account for all rents, profits, and revenues that

the estate would have produced by such prudent management.

Added by Acts 1993, 73rd Leg., ch. 957, § 1, eff. Sept. 1, 1993.
Amended by Acts 2003, 78th Leg., ch. 549, § 18, eff. Sept. 1, 2003.

### § 769.  Summary of Powers of Guardian of Person and Estate

The guardian of both the person of and estate of a ward has all the rights and powers and shall perform all the duties of the guardian of the person and of the guardian of the estate.

Added by Acts 1993, 73rd Leg., ch. 957, § 1, eff. Sept. 1, 1993.

### § 770.  Care of Ward;  Commitment

(a) The guardian of an adult may expend funds of the guardianship as provided by court order to care for and maintain the incapacitated person.  The guardian may apply for residential care and services provided by a public or private facility on behalf of an incapacitated person who has decision-making ability if the person agrees to be placed in the facility.  The guardian shall report the condition of the person to the court at regular intervals at least annually, unless the court orders more frequent reports.  If the person is receiving residential care in a public or private residential care facility, the guardian shall include in any report to the court a statement as to the necessity for continued care in the facility.

(b) Except as provided by Subsection (c) or (d) of this section, a guardian may not voluntarily admit an incapacitated person to a public or private in-patient psychiatric facility or to a residential facility operated by the Texas Department of Mental Health and Mental Retardation for care and treatment.  If care and treatment in a psychiatric or a residential facility are necessary, the person or the person's guardian may:

(1) apply for services under Section 593.027 or 593.028, Health and Safety Code;

(2) apply to a court to commit the person under Subtitle D, Title 7, Health and Safety Code (Persons with Mental Retardation Act),[1] Subtitle C, Title 7, Health and Safety Code (Texas Mental Health Code),[2] or Chapter 462, Health and Safety Code;  or

(3) transport the ward to an inpatient mental health facility for a preliminary examination in accordance with Subchapters A and C, Chapter 573, Health and Safety Code.

(c) A guardian of a person younger than 18 years of age may voluntarily admit the ward to a public or private inpatient psychiatric facility for care and treatment.

(d) A guardian of a person may voluntarily admit an incapacitated person to a residential care facility for emergency care or respite care under Section 593.027 or 593.028, Health and Safety Code.

Added by Acts 1993, 73rd Leg., ch. 957, § 1, eff. Sept. 1, 1993. Subsec. (b) amended by Acts 2003, 78th Leg., ch. 692, § 3, eff. Sept. 1, 2003; Subsec. (c) amended by Acts 2011, 82nd Leg., ch. 1085 (S.B. 1196), § 26, eff. Sept. 1, 2011.

1 V.T.C.A., Health & Safety Code § 591.001 et seq.
2 V.T.C.A., Health & Safety Code § 571.001 et seq.

### § 770A. Administration of Medication

(a) In this section, "psychoactive medication" has the meaning assigned by Section 574.101, Health and Safety Code.

(b) If a person under a protective custody order as provided by Subchapter B, Chapter 574, Health and Safety Code, is a ward who is not a minor, the guardian of the person of the ward may consent to the administration of psychoactive medication as prescribed by the ward's treating physician regardless of the ward's expressed preferences regarding treatment with psychoactive medication.

Added by Acts 2003, 78th Leg., ch. 692, § 4, eff. Sept. 1, 2003.

### SUBPART F. SPECIFIC DUTIES AND POWERS OF GUARDIANS

### § 771. Guardian of Estate: Possession of Personal Property and Records

The guardian of an estate, immediately after receiving letters of guardianship, shall collect and take into possession the personal property, record books, title papers, and other business papers of the ward and shall deliver the personal property, books, or papers, of the ward to a person who is legally entitled to that property when the guardianship has been closed or a successor guardian has received letters.

Added by Acts 1993, 73rd Leg., ch. 957, § 1, eff. Sept. 1, 1993.

### § 772. Collection of Claims and Recovery of Property

Every guardian of an estate shall use ordinary diligence to collect all claims and debts due the ward and to recover possession of all property of the ward to which the ward has claim or title, if there is a reasonable prospect of collecting the claims or of recovering the property. If the guardian wilfully neglects to use ordinary diligence, the guardian and the sureties on the guardian's bond shall be liable, at the suit of any person interested in the estate, for the use of the estate, for the amount of the claims or for the value of the property that has been lost due to the guardian's neglect.

Added by Acts 1993, 73rd Leg., ch. 957, § 1, eff. Sept. 1, 1993. Amended by Acts 1995, 74th Leg., ch. 1039, § 51, eff. Sept. 1, 1995.

### § 773. Suit by Guardian of Estate

A guardian of a ward's estate appointed in this state may institute suits for the recovery of personal property, debts, or damages and suits for title to or possession of land or for any right attached to or growing out of the same or for injury or damage done. Judgment in those cases shall be conclusive

but may be set aside by any person interested for fraud or collusion on the part of the guardian.

Added by Acts 1993, 73rd Leg., ch. 957, § 1, eff. Sept. 1, 1993. Amended by Acts 1995, 74th Leg., ch. 1039, § 52, eff. Sept. 1, 1995.

### § 774. Exercise of Power With or Without Court Order

(a) On application, and if authorized by an order, the guardian of the estate may renew or extend any obligation owed by or to the ward. On written application to the court and when a guardian of the estate deems it is in the best interest of the estate, the guardian may, if authorized by an order of the court:

(1) purchase or exchange property;

(2) take a claim or property for the use and benefit of the estate in payment of a debt due or owing to the estate;

(3) compound a bad or doubtful debt due or owing to the estate;

(4) make a compromise or a settlement in relation to property or a claim in dispute or litigation;

(5) compromise or pay in full any secured claim that has been allowed and approved as required by law against the estate by conveying to the holder of the secured claim the real estate or personalty securing the claim, in full payment, liquidation, and satisfaction of the claim, and in consideration of cancellation of a note, deed of trust, mortgage, chattel mortgage, or other evidence of a lien that secures the payment of the claim;

(6) abandon worthless or burdensome property and the administration of that property. Abandoned real or personal property may be foreclosed on by a secured party, trustee, or mortgagee without further order of the court;

(7) purchase a prepaid funeral benefits contract; and

(8) establish a trust in accordance with 42 U.S.C. Section 1396p(d)(4)(B), as amended, and direct that the income of the ward as defined by that section be paid directly to the trust, solely for the purpose of the ward's eligibility for medical assistance under Chapter 32, Human Resources Code.

(b) The guardian of the estate of a person, without application to or order of the court, may exercise the following powers provided, however, that a guardian may apply and obtain an order if doubtful of the propriety of the exercise of any such power:

(1) release a lien on payment at maturity of the debt secured by the lien;

(2) vote stocks by limited or general proxy;

(3) pay calls and assessments;

(4) insure the estate against liability in appropriate cases;

(5) insure property of the estate against fire, theft, and other hazards; and

(6) pay taxes, court costs, and bond premiums.

Added by Acts 1993, 73rd Leg., ch. 957, § 1, eff. Sept. 1, 1993. Amended by Acts 1997, 75th Leg., ch. 77, § 6, eff. Sept. 1, 1997; Acts 2001, 77th Leg., ch. 305, § 1, eff. Sept. 1, 2001.

Subsec. (a) amended by Acts 2003, 78th Leg., ch. 549, § 19, eff. Sept. 1, 2003.

### § 775. Possession of Property Held in Common Ownership

If the ward holds or owns any property in common, or as part owner with another person, the guardian of the estate is entitled to possession of the property of the ward held or owned in common with a part owner in the same manner as another owner in common or joint owner would be entitled.

Added by Acts 1993, 73rd Leg., ch. 957, § 1, eff. Sept. 1, 1993.

### § 776. Amounts Allowable for Education and Maintenance of Ward

(a) Subject to Section 777 of this code, if a monthly allowance for the ward was not ordered in the court's order appointing a guardian, the guardian of the estate shall file an application with the court requesting a monthly allowance to be expended from the income and corpus of the ward's estate for the education and maintenance of the ward and the maintenance of the ward's property.

(a–1) The guardian must file the application requesting the monthly allowance not later than the 30th day after the date on which the guardian qualifies as guardian or the date specified by the court, whichever is later. The application must clearly separate amounts requested for education and maintenance of the ward from amounts requested for maintenance of the ward's property.

(a–2) In determining the amount of the monthly allowance for the ward and the ward's property, the court shall consider the condition of the estate and the income and corpus of the estate necessary to pay the reasonably anticipated regular education and maintenance expenses of the ward and maintenance expenses of the ward's property. The court's order setting a monthly allowance must specify the types of expenditures the guardian may make on a monthly basis for the ward or the ward's property. An order setting a monthly allowance does not affect the guardian's duty to account for expenditures of the allowance in the annual account required by Section 741 of this code.

(a–3) When different persons have the guardianship of the person and estate of a ward, the court's order setting a monthly allowance must specify the amount, if any, set by the court for the education and maintenance of the ward that the guardian of the estate shall pay and the amount, if any, the guardian of the estate shall pay to the guardian of the person, at a time specified by the court, for the education and maintenance of the ward. If the guardian of the estate fails to pay to the guardian of the person the monthly allowance set by the court, the guardian of the estate shall be compelled to make the payment by court order after the guardian is duly cited to appear.

(b) When a guardian has in good faith expended funds from the income and corpus of the estate of the ward for support and maintenance of the ward and the expenditures exceed the monthly allowance authorized by the court, the guardian shall file a motion with the court requesting approval of the expenditures. The court may approve the excess expenditures if:

(1) the expenditures were made when it was not convenient or possible for the guardian to first secure court approval;

(2) the proof is clear and convincing that the expenditures were reasonable and proper;

(3) the court would have granted authority in advance to make the expenditures; and

(4) the ward received the benefits of the expenditures.

Added by Acts 1993, 73rd Leg., ch. 957, § 1, eff. Sept. 1, 1993. Amended by Acts 1995, 74th Leg., ch. 1039, § 53, eff. Sept. 1, 1995. Amended by Acts 2003, 78th Leg., ch. 549, § 20, eff. Sept. 1, 2003; Subsec. (a-3) amended by Acts 2005, 79th Leg., ch. 200, § 6, eff. Sept. 1, 2005.

### § 776A. Sums Allowable for Education and Maintenance of Ward's Spouse or Dependent

(a) Subject to Section 777 of this code and on application to the court, the court may order the guardian of the estate of a ward to expend funds from the ward's estate for the education and maintenance of the ward's spouse or dependent.

(b) In determining whether to order the expenditure of funds from a ward's estate for the ward's spouse or dependent, as appropriate, in accordance with this section, the court shall consider:

(1) the circumstances of the ward, the ward's spouse, and the ward's dependents;

(2) the ability and duty of the ward's spouse to support himself or herself and the ward's dependent;

(3) the size of the ward's estate;

(4) a beneficial interest the ward or the ward's spouse or dependent has in a trust; and

(5) an existing estate plan, including a trust or will, that provides a benefit to the ward's spouse or dependent.

(c) A person who makes an application to the court under this section shall mail notice of the application by certified mail to all interested persons.

Added by Acts 1997, 75th Leg., ch. 77, § 7, eff. Sept. 1, 1997.

### § 777. Sums Allowed Parents for Education and Maintenance of Minor Ward

(a) Except as provided by Subsection (b) of this section, a parent who is the guardian of the person of a ward who is 17 years of age or younger may not use the income or the corpus from the ward's estate for the ward's support, education, or maintenance.

(b) A court with proper jurisdiction may authorize the guardian of the person to spend the income or the corpus from the ward's estate to support, educate, or maintain the ward if the guardian presents clear and convincing evidence to the court that the ward's parents are unable without unreasonable hardship to pay for all of the expenses related to the ward's support.

Added by Acts 1993, 73rd Leg., ch. 957, § 1, eff. Sept. 1, 1993.

### § 778. Title of Wards Not to be Disputed

A guardian or the heirs, executors, administrators, or assigns of a guardian may not dispute the right of the ward to any property that came into the possession of the guardian as guardian of the ward, except property that is recovered from the guardian or property on which there is a personal action pending.

Added by Acts 1993, 73rd Leg., ch. 957, § 1, eff. Sept. 1, 1993.

### § 779. Operation of Farm, Ranch, Factory, or Other Business

If the ward owns a farm, ranch, factory, or other business and if the farm, ranch, factory, or other business is not required to be sold at once for the payment of debts or other lawful purposes, the guardian of the estate on order of the court shall carry on the operation of the farm, ranch, factory, or other business, or cause the same to be done, or rent the same, as shall appear to be for the best interests of the estate. In deciding, the court shall consider the condition of the estate and the necessity that may exist for the future sale of the property or business for the payment of a debt, claim, or other lawful expenditure and may not extend the time of renting any of the property beyond what appears consistent with the maintenance and education of a ward or the settlement of the estate of the ward.

Added by Acts 1993, 73rd Leg., ch. 957, § 1, eff. Sept. 1, 1993.

### § 780. Administration of Partnership Interest by Guardian

If the ward was a partner in a general partnership and the articles of partnership provide that, on the incapacity of a partner, the guardian of the estate of the partner is entitled to the place of the incapacitated partner in the firm, the guardian who contracts to come into the partnership shall, to the extent allowed by law, be liable to a third person only to the extent of the incapacitated partner's capital in the partnership and the assets of the estate of the partner that are held by the guardian. This section does not exonerate a guardian from liability for the negligence of the guardian.

Added by Acts 1993, 73rd Leg., ch. 957, § 1, eff. Sept. 1, 1993.

### § 781. Borrowing Money

(a) The guardian may mortgage or pledge any real or personal property of a guardianship estate by deed of trust or otherwise as security for an indebtedness, under court order, when necessary for any of the following purposes:

(1) for the payment of any ad valorem, income, gift, or transfer taxes due from a ward, regardless of whether the taxes are assessed by a state, a political subdivision of the state, the federal government, or a foreign country;

(2) for the payment of any expenses of administration, including sums necessary for the operation of a business, farm, or ranch owned by the estate;

(3) for the payment of any claims allowed and approved, or established by suit, against the ward or the estate of the ward;

(4) to renew and extend a valid, existing lien;

(5) to make improvements or repairs to the real estate of the ward if:

(A) the real estate of the ward is not revenue producing but could be made revenue producing by certain improvements and repairs; or

(B) the revenue from the real estate could be increased by making improvements or repairs to the real estate;

(6) court-authorized borrowing of money that the court finds to be in the best interests of the ward for the purchase of a residence for the ward or a dependent of the ward; and

(7) if the guardianship is kept open after the death of the ward, funeral expenses of the ward and expenses of the ward's last illness.

(a-1) The guardian of the estate may also receive an extension of credit on the ward's behalf that is secured, wholly or partly, by a lien on real property that is the homestead of the ward, under court order, when necessary to:

(1) make improvements or repairs to the homestead; or

(2) pay for education or medical expenses of the ward.

(a-2) Proceeds of a home equity loan described by Subsection (a-1) of this section may be used only for the purposes authorized under Subsection (a-1) of this section and to pay the outstanding balance of the loan.

(b) When it is necessary to borrow money for any of the purposes authorized under Subsection (a) or (a-1) of this section, or to create or extend a lien on property of the estate as security, a sworn application for the authority to borrow money shall be filed with the court, stating fully and in detail the circumstances that the guardian of the estate believes make necessary the granting of the authority. On the filing of an application under this subsection, the clerk shall issue and cause to be posted a citation to all interested persons, stating the nature of the application and requiring the interested persons to appear and show cause why the application should not be granted.

(c) If the court is satisfied by the evidence adduced at the hearing on the application that it is in the interest of the ward or the ward's estate to borrow money under Subsection (b) of this section, or to extend and renew an existing lien, the court shall issue an order to that effect, setting out the terms and conditions of the authority granted. The term of the loan or renewal shall be for the length of time that the court determines to be for the best interests of the ward or the ward's estate. If a new lien is created on the property of a guardianship estate, the court may require that the guardian's general bond be increased, or that an additional bond be given, for the protection of the guardianship estate and its creditors, as for the sale of real property belonging to the estate.

Added by Acts 1993, 73rd Leg., ch. 957, § 1, eff. Sept. 1, 1993. Subsec. (a-1) added by Acts 2005, 79th Leg., ch. 1204, § 1, eff. Sept. 1, 2005; Subsec. (a-2) added by Acts 2005, 79th Leg., ch. 1204, § 1, eff. Sept. 1, 2005; Subsec. (b) amended by Acts 2005, 79th Leg., ch. 1204, § 1, eff. Sept. 1, 2005.

### § 782. Powers, Duties, and Obligations of Guardian of Person Entitled to Government Funds

(a) A guardian of the person for whom it is necessary to have a guardian appointed to receive funds from a governmental source has the power to administer only the funds received from the governmental source, all earnings, interest, or profits derived from the funds, and all property acquired with the funds. The guardian has the power to receive the funds and pay out the expenses of administering the guardianship and the expenses for the support, maintenance, or education of the ward or the ward's dependents. Expenditures for the support, maintenance, or education of the ward or the ward's dependents may not exceed $12,000 during any 12-month period without the court's approval.

(b) All acts performed before September 1, 1993, by guardians of the estate of a person for whom it is necessary to have a guardian appointed to receive and disburse funds that are due the person from a governmental source are validated if the acts are performed in conformance with orders of a court that has venue with respect to the support, maintenance, and education of the ward or the ward's dependents and the investment of surplus funds of the ward under this chapter and if the validity of the act is not an issue in a probate proceeding or civil lawsuit that is pending on September 1, 1993.

Added by Acts 1993, 73rd Leg., ch. 957, § 1, eff. Sept. 1, 1993. Amended by Acts 1995, 74th Leg., ch. 1039, § 54, eff. Sept. 1, 1995.

### SUBPART G. CLAIMS PROCEDURES

### § 783. Notice by Guardian of Appointment

(a) Within one month after receiving letters, personal representatives of estates shall send to the comptroller of public accounts by certified or registered mail if the ward remitted or should have remitted taxes administered by the comptroller of public accounts and publish in some newspaper, printed in the county where the letters were issued, if there be one, a notice requiring all persons having a claim against the estate being administered to present the claim within the time prescribed by law. The notice must include the time of issuance of letters held by the representative, the address to which a claim may be presented, and an instruction of the

representative's choice that a claim be addressed in care of the representative, in care of the representative's attorney, or in care of "Representative, Estate of _____" (naming the estate).

(b) A copy of the printed notice, with the affidavit of the publisher, duly sworn to and subscribed before a proper officer, to the effect that the notice was published as provided in this chapter for the service of citation or notice by publication, shall be filed in the court in which the cause is pending.

(c) When no newspaper is printed in the county, the notice shall be posted and the return made and filed as required by this chapter.

Added by Acts 1993, 73rd Leg., ch. 957, § 1, eff. Sept. 1, 1993. Amended by Acts 1997, 75th Leg., ch. 77, § 8, eff. Sept. 1, 1997.

### § 784. Notice to Holders of Recorded Claims

(a) Within four months after receiving letters, the guardian of an estate shall give notice of the issuance of the letters to each and every person having a claim for money against the estate of a ward if the claim is secured by a deed of trust, mortgage, or vendor's, mechanic's or other contractor's lien on real estate belonging to the estate.

(b) Within four months after receiving letters, the guardian of an estate shall give notice of the issuance of the letters to each person having an outstanding claim for money against the estate of a ward if the guardian has actual knowledge of the claim.

(c) The notice stating the original grant of letter shall be given by mailing the notice by certified mail or registered letter, with return receipt requested, addressed to the record holder of the indebtedness or claim at the last known post office address of the record holder.

(d) A copy of each notice required by Subsection (a) of this section, with the return receipt and an affidavit of the representative, stating that the notice was mailed as required by law, giving the name of the person to whom the notice was mailed, if not shown on the notice or receipt, shall be filed in the court from which letters were issued.

(e) In the notice required by Subsection (b) of this section, the guardian of the estate may expressly state in the notice that the unsecured creditor must present a claim not later than the 120th day after the date on which the unsecured creditor receives the notice or the claim is barred, if the claim is not barred by the general statutes of limitation. The notice under this subsection must include:

(1) the address to which claims may be presented; and

(2) an instruction that the claim be filed with the clerk of the court issuing the letters of guardianship.

Added by Acts 1993, 73rd Leg., ch. 957, § 1, eff. Sept. 1, 1993. Amended by Acts 2001, 77th Leg., ch. 1174, § 6, eff. Sept. 1, 2001.

## § 785. One Notice Sufficient; Penalty for Failure to Give Notice

(a) If the notice required by Section 784 of this code has been given by a former representative, or by one when several representatives are acting, the notice given by the former representative or co-representative is sufficient and need not be repeated by any successor or co-representative.

(b) If the guardian fails to give the notice required in other sections of this chapter or to cause the notices to be given, the guardian and the sureties on the bond of the guardian shall be liable for any damage that any person suffers because of the neglect, unless it appears that the person had notice otherwise.

Added by Acts 1993, 73rd Leg., ch. 957, § 1, eff. Sept. 1, 1993.

## § 786. Claims Against Wards

(a) A claim may be presented to the guardian of the estate at any time when the estate is not closed and when suit on the claim has not been barred by the general statutes of limitation. A claim of an unsecured creditor for money that is not presented within the time prescribed by the notice of presentment permitted by Section 784(e) of this code is barred.

(b) A claim against a ward on which a suit is barred by a general statute of limitation applicable to the claim may not be allowed by a guardian. If allowed by the guardian and the court is satisfied that limitation has run, the claim shall be disapproved.

Added by Acts 1993, 73rd Leg., ch. 957, § 1, eff. Sept. 1, 1993.
Amended by Acts 2001, 77th Leg., ch. 1174, § 7, eff. Sept. 1, 2001.

## § 787. Tolling of General Statutes of Limitation

The general statutes of limitation are tolled:

(1) by filing a claim that is legally allowed and approved; or

(2) by bringing a suit on a rejected and disapproved claim not later than the 90th day after the date of rejection or disapproval.

Added by Acts 1993, 73rd Leg., ch. 957, § 1, eff. Sept. 1, 1993.

## § 788. Claims Must be Authenticated

Except as provided by Section 792 of this code, with respect to the payment of an unauthenticated claim by a guardian, a guardian of the estate may not allow and the court may not approve a claim for money against the estate, unless the claim is supported by an affidavit that the claim is just and that all legal offsets, payments, and credits known to the affiant have been allowed. If the claim is not founded on a written instrument or account, the affidavit must also state the facts on which the claim is founded. A photostatic copy of an exhibit or voucher necessary to prove a claim under

this section may be offered with and attached to the claim instead of the original.

Added by Acts 1993, 73rd Leg., ch. 957, § 1, eff. Sept. 1, 1993.
Amended by Acts 2005, 79th Leg., ch. 200, § 7, eff. Sept. 1, 2005.

## § 789. When Defects of Form are Waived

Any defect of form or claim of insufficiency of exhibits or vouchers presented is deemed waived by the guardian unless written objection to the form, exhibit, or voucher is made not later than the 30th day after the date of presentment of the claim and is filed with the county clerk.

Added by Acts 1993, 73rd Leg., ch. 957, § 1, eff. Sept. 1, 1993.

## § 790. Evidence Concerning Lost or Destroyed Claims

If evidence of a claim is lost or destroyed, the claimant or a representative of the claimant may make affidavit to the fact of the loss or destruction, stating the amount, date, and nature of the claim and when due, that the claim is just, that all legal offsets, payments, and credits known to the affiant have been allowed, and that the claimant is still the owner of the claim. The claim must be proved by disinterested testimony taken in open court, or by oral or written deposition, before the claim is approved. If the claim is allowed or approved without the affidavit or if the claim is approved without satisfactory proof, the allowance or approval is void.

Added by Acts 1993, 73rd Leg., ch. 957, § 1, eff. Sept. 1, 1993.

## § 791. Authentication of Claim by Others Than Individual Owners

The cashier, treasurer, or managing official of a corporation shall make the affidavit required to authenticate a claim of the corporation. When an affidavit is made by an officer of a corporation, or by an executor, administrator, guardian, trustee, assignee, agent, or attorney, it is sufficient to state in the affidavit that the person making the affidavit has made diligent inquiry and examination and that the person believes that the claim is just and that all legal offsets, payments, and credits made known to the person making the affidavit have been allowed.

Added by Acts 1993, 73rd Leg., ch. 957, § 1, eff. Sept. 1, 1993.

## § 792. Guardian's Payment of Unauthenticated Claims

A guardian may pay an unauthenticated claim against the estate of the guardian's ward that the guardian believes to be just, but the guardian and the sureties on the bond of the guardian shall be liable for the amount of any payment of the claim if the court finds that the claim is not just.

Added by Acts 1993, 73rd Leg., ch. 957, § 1, eff. Sept. 1, 1993.

## § 793. Method of Handling Secured Claims

(a) When a secured claim against a ward is presented, the claimant shall specify in the claim, in addition to all other matters required to be specified in claims:

(1) whether the claim shall be allowed and approved as a matured secured claim to be paid in due course of adminis-

tration, in which event it shall be so paid if allowed and approved; or

(2) whether the claim shall be allowed, approved, and fixed as a preferred debt and lien against the specific property securing the indebtedness and paid according to the terms of the contract that secured the lien, in which event it shall be so allowed and approved if it is a valid lien; provided, however, the guardian may pay the claim prior to maturity if it is in the best interests of the estate to do so.

(b) If a secured claim is not presented within the time provided by law, it shall be treated as a claim to be paid in accordance with Subsection (a)(2) of this section.

(c) When an indebtedness has been allowed and approved under Subsection (a)(2) of this section, no further claim shall be made against other assets of the estate because of the indebtedness, but the claim remains a preferred lien against the property securing the claim, and the property remains security for the debt in any distribution or sale of the property before final maturity and payment of the debt.

(d) If property that secures a claim allowed, approved, and fixed under Subsection (a)(2) of this section is not sold or distributed not later than the 12th month after the date letters of guardianship are granted, the guardian of the estate shall promptly pay all maturities that have accrued on the debt according to the terms of the maturities and shall perform all the terms of any contract securing the maturities. If the guardian defaults in the payment or performance, the court, on motion of the claim holder, shall require the sale of the property subject to the unmatured part of the debt and apply the proceeds of the sale to the liquidation of the maturities or, at the option of the claim holder, a motion may be made in a like manner to require the sale of the property free of the lien and to apply the proceeds to the payment of the whole debt.

Added by Acts 1993, 73rd Leg., ch. 957, § 1, eff. Sept. 1, 1993.

### § 794. Claims Providing for Attorney's Fees

If the instrument that evidences or supports a claim provides for attorney's fees, the claimant may include as a part of the claim the portion of the fee that the claimant has paid or contracted to pay to an attorney to prepare, present, and collect the claim.

Added by Acts 1993, 73rd Leg., ch. 957, § 1, eff. Sept. 1, 1993.

### § 795. Depositing Claims With Clerk

A claim may also be presented by depositing the claim, with vouchers and necessary exhibits and affidavit attached to the claim, with the clerk. The clerk, on receiving the claim, shall advise the guardian of the estate or the guardian's attorney by letter mailed to the last known address of the guardian of the deposit of the claim. If the guardian fails to act on the claim within 30 days after it is filed, the claim is presumed to be rejected. Failure of the clerk to give notice as required under this section does not affect the

validity of the presentment or the presumption of rejection of the claim because not acted on within the 30-day period.

Added by Acts 1993, 73rd Leg., ch. 957, § 1, eff. Sept. 1, 1993.

### § 796. Memorandum of Allowance or Rejection of Claim

When a duly authenticated claim against a guardianship estate is presented to the guardian or filed with the clerk as provided by this subpart, the guardian shall, not later than the 30th day after the date the claim is presented or filed, endorse or annex to the claim a memorandum signed by the guardian stating the time of presentation or filing of the claim and that the guardian allows or rejects the claim, or what portion of the claim the guardian allows or rejects.

Added by Acts 1993, 73rd Leg., ch. 957, § 1, eff. Sept. 1, 1993.

### § 797. Failure to Endorse or Annex Memorandum

The failure of a guardian of an estate to endorse on or annex to a claim presented to the guardian, or the failure of a guardian to allow or reject the claim or portion of the claim within 30 days after the claim was presented constitutes a rejection of the claim. If the claim is later established by suit, the costs shall be taxed against the guardian, individually, or the guardian may be removed as in other cases of removal on the written complaint of any person interested in the claim, after personal service of citation, hearing, and proof.

Added by Acts 1993, 73rd Leg., ch. 957, § 1, eff. Sept. 1, 1993.

### § 798. Claims Entered in Docket

After a claim against a ward's estate has been presented to and allowed by the guardian, either in whole or in part, the claim shall be filed with the county clerk of the proper county who shall enter it on the claim docket.

Added by Acts 1993, 73rd Leg., ch. 957, § 1, eff. Sept. 1, 1993.

### § 799. Contest of Claims, Action by Court, and Appeals

(a) Any person interested in a ward, at any time before the court has acted on a claim, may appear and object in writing to the approval of the claim, or any part of the claim. The parties are entitled to process for witnesses, and the court shall hear proof and render judgment as in ordinary suits.

(b) The court shall either approve in whole or in part or reject a claim that has been allowed and entered on the claim docket for a period of 10 days and shall at the same time classify the claim.

(c) Although a claim may be properly authenticated and allowed, if the court is not satisfied that it is just, the court shall examine the claimant and the guardian under oath and hear other evidence necessary to determine the issue. If after the examination and hearing the court is not convinced that the claim is just, the court shall disapprove the claim.

(d) When the court has acted on a claim, the court shall endorse on or annex to the claim a written memorandum dated and signed officially that states the exact action taken by the court on the claim, whether the court approved or disapproved the claim or approved in part or rejected in part the claim, and that states the classification of the claim. An order under this subsection has the force and effect of a final judgment.

(e) When a claimant or any person interested in a ward is dissatisfied with the action of the court on a claim, the claimant or person interested may appeal the action to the courts of appeals, as from other judgments of the county court in probate matters.

Added by Acts 1993, 73rd Leg., ch. 957, § 1, eff. Sept. 1, 1993.

### § 800. Suit on Rejected Claim

When a claim or a part of a claim has been rejected by the guardian, the claimant shall institute suit on the claim in the court of original probate jurisdiction in which the guardianship is pending or in any other court of proper jurisdiction not later than the 90th day after the date of the rejection of the claim or the claim is barred. When a rejected claim is sued on, the endorsement made on or annexed to the claim is taken to be true without further proof, unless denied under oath. When a rejected claim or part of a claim has been established by suit, no execution shall issue but the judgment shall be certified not later than the 30th day after the date of rendition if the judgment is from a court other than the court of original probate jurisdiction, filed in the court in which the cause is pending entered on the claim docket, classified by the court, and handled as if originally allowed and approved in due course of administration.

Added by Acts 1993, 73rd Leg., ch. 957, § 1, eff. Sept. 1, 1993.

### § 801. Presentment of Claims a Prerequisite for Judgment

(a) A judgment may not be rendered in favor of a claimant on any claim for money that has not been legally presented to the guardian of the estate of the ward and rejected by the guardian or by the court, in whole or in part.

(b) Subsection (a) does not apply to a claim for delinquent ad valorem taxes against the estate of a ward that is being administered in probate in a county other than the county in which the taxes were imposed.

Added by Acts 1993, 73rd Leg., ch. 957, § 1, eff. Sept. 1, 1993. Amended by Acts 1999, 76th Leg., ch. 1481, § 38, eff. Sept. 1, 1999.

### § 802. Costs of Suit With Respect to Claims

All costs incurred in the probate court with respect to claims are taxed as follows:

(1) if allowed and approved, the guardianship estate shall pay the costs;

(2) if allowed, but disapproved, the claimant shall pay the costs;

(3) if rejected, but established by suit, the guardianship estate shall pay the costs;

(4) if rejected, but not established by suit, the claimant shall pay the costs; or

(5) in suits to establish a claim after rejection in part, if the claimant fails to recover judgment for a greater amount than was allowed or approved, the claimant shall pay all costs.

Added by Acts 1993, 73rd Leg., ch. 957, § 1, eff. Sept. 1, 1993.

### § 803. Claims by Guardians

(a) A claim that a guardian of the person or estate held against the ward at the time of the appointment of the guardian, or that has since accrued, shall be verified by affidavit as required in other cases and presented to the clerk of the court in which the guardianship is pending. The clerk shall enter the claim on the claim docket, after which it shall take the same course as other claims.

(b) When a claim by a guardian has been filed with the court within the required time, the claim shall be entered on the claim docket and acted on by the court in the same manner as in other cases. When the claim has been acted on by the court, an appeal from the judgment of the court may be taken as in other cases.

Added by Acts 1993, 73rd Leg., ch. 957, § 1, eff. Sept. 1, 1993.

### § 804. Claims Not to be Paid Unless Approved

Except as provided for payment at the risk of a guardian of an unauthenticated claim, a claim for money against the estate of a ward or any part of a claim may not be paid until it has been approved by the court or established by the judgment of a court of competent jurisdiction.

Added by Acts 1993, 73rd Leg., ch. 957, § 1, eff. Sept. 1, 1993.

### § 805. Order of Payment of Claims

(a) The guardian shall pay a claim against the estate of the guardian's ward that has been allowed and approved or established by suit, as soon as practicable, in the following order, except as provided by Subsection (b) of this section:

(1) expenses for the care, maintenance, and education of the ward or the ward's dependents;

(2) funeral expenses of the ward and expenses of the ward's last illness, if the guardianship is kept open after the death of the ward as provided under this chapter, except that any claim against the estate of a ward that has been allowed and approved or established by suit before the death of the ward shall be paid before the funeral expenses and expenses of the last illness;

(3) expenses of administration; and

(4) other claims against the ward or the ward's estate.

(b) If the estate is insolvent, the guardian shall give first priority to the payment of a claim relating to the administration of the guardianship. The guardian shall pay other claims against the ward's estate in the order prescribed by Subsection (a) of this section.

(c) A claimant whose claim has not been paid may petition the court for determination of the claim at any time before it is barred by the applicable statute of limitations and on due proof procure an order for its allowance and payment from the estate.

Added by Acts 1993, 73rd Leg., ch. 957, § 1, eff. Sept. 1, 1993. Amended by Acts 1997, 75th Leg., ch. 1403, § 5, eff. Sept. 1, 1997.

### § 806. Deficiency of Assets

When there is a deficiency of assets to pay all claims of the same class, the claims in the same class shall be paid pro rata, as directed by the court, and in the order directed. A guardian may not be allowed to pay any claims, whether the estate is solvent or insolvent, except with the pro rata amount of the funds of the guardianship estate that have come to hand.

Added by Acts 1993, 73rd Leg., ch. 957, § 1, eff. Sept. 1, 1993.

### § 807. Guardian Not to Purchase Claims

A guardian may not purchase for the guardian's own use or for any purposes whatsoever a claim against the guardianship the guardian represents. On written complaint by a person interested in the guardianship estate and satisfactory proof of violation of this provision, the court after citation and hearing shall enter its order cancelling the claim and no part of the claim shall be paid out of the guardianship. The judge may remove the guardian for a violation of this section.

Added by Acts 1993, 73rd Leg., ch. 957, § 1, eff. Sept. 1, 1993.

### § 808. Proceeds of Sale of Mortgaged Property

When a guardian has on hand the proceeds of a sale that has been made for the satisfaction of a mortgage or other lien and the proceeds, or any part of the proceeds, are not required for the payment of any debts against the estate that have a preference over the mortgage or other lien, the guardian shall pay the proceeds to a holder of the mortgage or other lien. If the guardian fails to pay the proceeds as required by this section, the holder, on proof of the mortgage or other lien, may obtain an order from the court directing the payment to be made.

Added by Acts 1993, 73rd Leg., ch. 957, § 1, eff. Sept. 1, 1993.

### § 809. Liability for Nonpayment of Claims

(a) If a guardian of an estate fails to pay on demand any money ordered by the court to be paid to any person, except to the state treasury, when there are funds of the guardianship estate available, the person or claimant entitled to the payment, on affidavit of the demand and failure to pay, is authorized to have execution issued against the property of the guardianship for the amount due, with interest and costs.

(b) On return of the execution not satisfied, or merely on the affidavit of demand and failure to pay, the court may cite the guardian and the sureties on the bond of the guardian to show cause why the guardian or the sureties should not be held liable for the debt, interest, costs, or damages. On return of citation duly served, if good cause to the contrary is not shown, the court shall render judgment against the guardian and sureties that are cited under this subsection in favor of the holder of the claim for the unpaid amount ordered to be paid or established by suit, with interest and costs, and for damages on the amount neglected to be paid, at the rate of five percent per month for each month or fraction of a month that the payment was neglected to be paid after demand was made for payment. The damages may be collected in any court of competent jurisdiction.

Added by Acts 1993, 73rd Leg., ch. 957, § 1, eff. Sept. 1, 1993.

## SUBPART H. SALES

### § 811. Court Must Order Sales

Except as provided by this subpart, the sale of any property of the ward may not be made without an order of court authorizing the sale. The court may order property sold for cash or on credit, at public auction or privately, as it may consider most to the advantage of the estate, except when otherwise specifically provided in this chapter.

Added by Acts 1993, 73rd Leg., ch. 957, § 1, eff. Sept. 1, 1993.

### § 812. Certain Personal Property to be Sold

(a) The guardian of an estate, after approval of inventory and appraisement, shall promptly apply for an order of the court to sell at public auction or privately, for cash or on credit not exceeding six months, all of the estate that is liable to perish, waste, or deteriorate in value or that will be an expense or disadvantage to the estate if kept. Property exempt from forced sale, a specific legacy, or personal property necessary to carry on a farm, ranch, factory, or any other business that it is thought best to operate, may not be included in a sale under this section.

(b) In determining whether to order the sale of an asset under Subsection (a) of this section, the court shall consider:

(1) the guardian's duty to take care of and manage the estate as a person of ordinary prudence, discretion, and intelligence would exercise in the management of the person's own affairs; and

(2) whether the asset constitutes an asset that a trustee is authorized to invest under Chapter 117 or Subchapter F, Chapter 113, Property Code.[1]

Added by Acts 1993, 73rd Leg., ch. 957, § 1, eff. Sept. 1, 1993; Subsec. (b) amended by Acts 2003, 78th Leg., ch. 1103, § 15, eff. Jan. 1, 2004.

[1] V.T.C.A., Property Code § 113.171 et seq.

### § 813. Sales of Other Personal Property

On application by the guardian of the estate or by any interested person, the court may order the sale of any personal property of the estate not required to be sold by Section 812 of this code, including growing or harvested crops or livestock but not including exempt property, if the court finds that the sale of the property would be in the best interests of the ward or the ward's estate in order to pay expenses of the care, maintenance, and education of the ward or the ward's dependents, expenses of administration, allowances, or claims against the ward or the ward's estate, and funeral expenses of the ward and expenses of the ward's last illness, if the guardianship is kept open after the death of the ward, from the proceeds of the sale of the property. Insofar as possible, applications and orders for the sale of personal property must conform to the requirements set forth under this chapter for applications and orders for the sale of real estate.

Added by Acts 1993, 73rd Leg., ch. 957, § 1, eff. Sept. 1, 1993.

## § 814. Special Provisions Pertaining to Livestock

(a) When the guardian of an estate has in the guardian's possession any livestock that the guardian deems necessary or to the advantage of the estate to sell, the guardian may, in addition to any other method provided by law for the sale of personal property, obtain authority from the court in which the estate is pending to sell the livestock through a bonded livestock commission merchant or a bonded livestock auction commission merchant.

(b) On written and sworn application by the guardian or by any person interested in the estate that describes the livestock sought to be sold and that sets out the reasons why it is deemed necessary or to the advantage of the estate that the application be granted, the court may authorize the sale. The court shall consider the application and may hear evidence for or against the application, with or without notice, as the facts warrant.

(c) If the application is granted, the court shall enter its order to that effect and shall authorize delivery of the livestock to any bonded livestock commission merchant or bonded livestock auction commission merchant for sale in the regular course of business. The commission merchant shall be paid the merchant's usual and customary charges, not to exceed five percent of the sale price, for the sale of the livestock. A report of the sale, supported by a verified copy of the merchant's account of sale, shall be made promptly by the guardian to the court, but no order of confirmation by the court is required to pass title to the purchaser of the livestock.

Added by Acts 1993, 73rd Leg., ch. 957, § 1, eff. Sept. 1, 1993.
Amended by Acts 2003, 78th Leg., ch. 549, § 21, eff. Sept. 1, 2003.

## § 815. Sales of Personal Property at Public Auction

All sales of personal property at public auction shall be made after notice has been issued by the guardian of the estate and posted as in case of posting for original proceedings in probate, unless the court shall otherwise direct.

Added by Acts 1993, 73rd Leg., ch. 957, § 1, eff. Sept. 1, 1993.

## § 816. Sales of Personal Property on Credit

No more than six months' credit may be allowed when personal property is sold at public auction, based on the date of the sale. The purchaser shall be required to give his note for the amount due, with good and solvent personal security, before delivery of the property can be made to the purchaser, but security may be waived if delivery is not to be made until the note, with interest, has been paid.

Added by Acts 1993, 73rd Leg., ch. 957, § 1, eff. Sept. 1, 1993.

## § 817. Sale of Mortgaged Property

On the filing of a written application, a creditor who holds a claim that is secured by a valid mortgage or other lien and that has been allowed and approved or established by suit may obtain from the court in which the guardianship is pending an order that the property, or so much of the property as necessary to satisfy the creditor's claim, shall be sold. On the filing of the application, the clerk shall issue citation requiring the guardian of the estate to appear and show cause why an application filed under this section should not be granted. If it appears to the court that it would be advisable to discharge the lien out of the general assets of the estate or that it be refinanced, the court may so order. Otherwise, the court shall grant the application and order that the property be sold at public or private sale, as the court considers best, as in ordinary cases of sales of real estate.

Added by Acts 1993, 73rd Leg., ch. 957, § 1, eff. Sept. 1, 1993.

## § 818. Sales of Personal Property Reported; Decree Vests Title

All sales of personal property shall be reported to the court. The laws regulating the confirmation or disapproval of sales of real estate apply to sales of personal property, but no conveyance shall be necessary. The decree confirming the sale of personal property shall vest the right and title of the estate of the ward in the purchaser who has complied with the terms of the sale and shall be prima facie evidence that all requirements of the law in making the sale have been met. The guardian of an estate may, on request, issue a bill of sale without warranty to the purchaser as evidence of title. The expense of the bill of sale if requested is to be borne by the purchaser.

Added by Acts 1993, 73rd Leg., ch. 957, § 1, eff. Sept. 1, 1993.

## § 819. Selection of Real Property Sold for Payment of Debts

Real property of the ward that is selected to be sold for the payment of expenses or claims shall be that property that the court deems most advantageous to the guardianship to be sold.

Added by Acts 1993, 73rd Leg., ch. 957, § 1, eff. Sept. 1, 1993.

## § 820. Application For Sale of Real Estate

An application may be made to the court for an order to sell real property of the estate when it appears necessary or advisable in order to:

(1) pay expenses of administration, allowances, and claims against the ward or the ward's estate, and to pay funeral

expenses of the ward and expenses of the ward's last illness, if the guardianship is kept open after the death of the ward;

(2) make up the deficiency when the income of a ward's estate, the personal property of the ward's estate, and the proceeds of previous sales, are insufficient to pay for the education and maintenance of the ward or to pay debts against the estate;

(3) dispose of property of the ward's estate that consists in whole or in part of an undivided interest in real estate when it is deemed in the best interests of the estate to sell the interest;

(4) dispose of real estate of a ward, any part of which is nonproductive or does not produce sufficient revenue to make a fair return on the value of the real estate, when the improvement of the real estate with a view to making it productive is not deemed advantageous or advisable and it appears that the sale of the real estate and the investment of the money derived from the sale of the real estate would be in the best interests of the estate; or

(5) conserve the estate of a ward by selling mineral interest or royalties on minerals in place owned by a ward.

Added by Acts 1993, 73rd Leg., ch. 957, § 1, eff. Sept. 1, 1993.

## § 821. Contents of Application For Sale of Real Estate

An application for the sale of real estate shall be in writing, must describe the real estate or an interest in or part of the real estate sought to be sold, and shall be accompanied by an exhibit, verified by affidavit that shows fully and in detail:

(1) the condition of the estate;

(2) the charges and claims that have been approved or established by suit, or that have been rejected and may be established later;

(3) the amount of each claim that has been approved or established by suit, or that has been rejected but may be established later;

(4) the property of the estate remaining on hand liable for the payment of those claims; and

(5) any other facts that show the necessity or advisability of the sale.

Added by Acts 1993, 73rd Leg., ch. 957, § 1, eff. Sept. 1, 1993.

## § 822. Repealed by Acts 2007, 80th Leg., ch. 614, § 33, eff. Sept. 1, 2007

## § 823. Citation on Application

On the filing of an application for the sale of real estate under Section 820 of this code and exhibit, the clerk shall issue a citation to all persons interested in the guardianship that describes the land or interest or part of the land or interest sought to be sold and that informs the persons of the right under Section 824 of this code to file an opposition to the sale during the period prescribed by the court as shown in the citation, if they so elect. Service of citation shall be by posting.

Added by Acts 1993, 73rd Leg., ch. 957, § 1, eff. Sept. 1, 1993.
Amended by Acts 2007, 80th Leg., ch. 614, § 16, eff. Sept. 1, 2007.

## § 824. Opposition to Application

When an application for an order of sale is made, a person interested in the guardianship may, during the period provided in the citation issued under Section 823 of this code, file the person's opposition to the sale, in writing, or may make application for the sale of other property of the estate.

Added by Acts 1993, 73rd Leg., ch. 957, § 1, eff. Sept. 1, 1993.
Amended by Acts 2007, 80th Leg., ch. 614, § 17, eff. Sept. 1, 2007.

## § 824A. Hearing on Application and Any Opposition

(a) The clerk of a court in which an application for an order of sale is filed shall immediately call to the attention of the judge any opposition to the sale that is filed during the period provided in the citation issued under Section 823 of this code. The court shall hold a hearing on an application if an opposition to the sale is filed during the period provided in the citation.

(b) A hearing on an application for an order of sale is not required under this section if no opposition to the application is filed during the period provided in the citation. The court, in its discretion, may determine that a hearing is necessary on the application even if no opposition was filed during that period.

(c) If the court orders a hearing under Subsection (a) or (b) of this section, the court shall designate in writing a date and time for hearing the application and any opposition, together with the evidence pertaining to the application and opposition. The clerk shall issue a notice to the applicant and to each person who files an opposition to the sale, if applicable, of the date and time of the hearing.

(d) The judge may, by entries on the docket, continue a hearing held under this section from time to time until the judge is satisfied concerning the application.

Added by Acts 2007, 80th Leg., ch. 614, § 18, eff. Sept. 1, 2007.

## § 825. Order of Sale

If satisfied that the sale of the property of the guardianship described in the application made under Section 820 of this code is necessary or advisable, the court shall order the sale to be made. Otherwise, the court may deny the application and, if the court deems best, may order the sale of other property the sale of which would be more advantageous to the estate. An order for the sale of real estate must specify:

(1) the property to be sold, giving a description that will identify the property;

(2) whether the property is to be sold at public auction or at private sale, and, if at public auction, the time and place of the sale;

(3) the necessity or advisability of the sale and its purpose;

(4) except in cases in which no general bond is required, that, having examined the general bond of the representative of the estate, the court finds it to be sufficient as required by law, or finds the bond to be insufficient and specifies the necessary or increased bond;

(5) that the sale shall be made and the report returned in accordance with law; and

(6) the terms of the sale.

Added by Acts 1993, 73rd Leg., ch. 957, § 1, eff. Sept. 1, 1993. Amended by Acts 2007, 80th Leg., ch. 614, § 19, eff. Sept. 1, 2007.

### § 826. Procedure When Guardian Neglects to Apply For Sale

When the guardian of an estate neglects to apply for an order to sell sufficient property to pay the charges and claims against the estate that have been allowed and approved or established by suit, an interested person, on written application, may cause the guardian to be cited to appear and make a full exhibit of the condition of the estate, and show cause why a sale of the property should not be ordered. On hearing an application made under this section, if the court is satisfied that a sale of the property is necessary or advisable in order to satisfy the claims, it shall enter an order of sale as provided by Section 825 of this code.

Added by Acts 1993, 73rd Leg., ch. 957, § 1, eff. Sept. 1, 1993.

### § 827. Permissible Terms of Sale of Real Estate

(a) The real estate may be sold for cash, or for part cash and part credit, or the equity in land securing an indebtedness may be sold subject to the indebtedness, or with an assumption of the indebtedness, at public or private sale, as appears to the court to be in the best interests of the estate. When real estate is sold partly on credit, the cash payment may not be less than one-fifth of the purchase price, and the purchaser shall execute a note for the deferred payments payable in monthly, quarterly, semiannual or annual installments, of the amounts as appear to the court to be for the best interests of the guardianship, to bear interest from date at a rate of not less than four percent per annum, payable as provided in the note. Default in the payment of principal or interest, or any part of the payment when due, at the election of the holder of the note, matures the whole debt. The note shall be secured by vendor's lien retained in the deed and in the note on the property sold and shall be further secured by deed of trust on the property sold, with the usual provisions for foreclosure and sale on failure to make the payments provided in the deed and the note.

(b) When an estate owning real estate by virtue of foreclosure of a vendor's lien or mortgage belonging to the estate either by judicial sale or by a foreclosure suit, by sale under deed of trust, or by acceptance of a deed in cancellation of a lien or mortgage owned by the estate, and it appears to the court that an application to redeem the property foreclosed on has been made by the former owner of the real estate to any corporation or agency created by any act of the Congress of the United States or of this state in connection with

legislation for the relief of owners of mortgaged or encumbered homes, farms, ranches, or other real estate and that it would be in the best interests of the estate to own bonds of one of the above named federal or state corporations or agencies instead of the real estate, then on proper application and proof, the court may dispense with the provisions of credit sales as provided by Subsection (a) of this section, and may order reconveyance of the property to the former mortgage debtor, or former owner, reserving vendor's lien notes for the total amount of the indebtedness due or for the total amount of bonds that the corporation or agency above named is under its rules and regulations allowed to advance. On obtaining the order, it shall be proper for the guardian to endorse and assign the notes so obtained over to any one of the corporations or agencies above named in exchange for bonds of that corporation or agency.

Added by Acts 1993, 73rd Leg., ch. 957, § 1, eff. Sept. 1, 1993.

### § 828. Public Sale of Real Estate

(a) Except as otherwise provided by this chapter, all public sales of real estate shall be advertised by the guardian of the estate by a notice published in the county in which the estate is pending, as provided by this chapter for publication of notices or citations. A reference in the notice shall be made to the order of sale, the time, place, and the required terms of sale, and a brief description of the property to be sold. A reference made under this section does not have to contain field notes, but if the real estate consists of rural property, the name of the original survey, the number of acres, its locality in the county, and the name by which the land is generally known must be contained in the reference.

(b) All public sales of real estate shall be made at public auction to the highest bidder.

(c) All public sales of real estate shall be made in the county in which the guardianship proceedings are pending, at the courthouse door of the county, or at another place in the county where sales of real estate are specifically authorized to be made, on the first Tuesday of the month after publication of notice has been completed, between the hours of 10 a.m. and 4 p.m. If deemed advisable by the court, the court may order the sale to be made in the county in which the land is located, in which event notice shall be published both in that county and in the county in which the proceedings are pending.

(d) If a sale is not completed on the day advertised, the sale may be continued from day to day by making an oral public announcement of the continuance at the conclusion of the sale each day. The continued sale is to be made within the same hours as prescribed by Subsection (c) of this section. If sales are so continued, the fact shall be shown in the report of sale made to the court.

(e) When a person who bids on property of a guardianship estate offered for sale at public auction fails to comply with the terms of sale, the property shall be readvertised and sold without any further order. The person who defaults shall be liable to pay to the guardian of the estate, for the benefit of the estate, 10 percent of the amount of the person's bid and any deficiency in price on the second sale. The guardian shall recover the amounts by suit in any court in the county in which the sale was made that has jurisdiction over the amount claimed.

Added by Acts 1993, 73rd Leg., ch. 957, § 1, eff. Sept. 1, 1993.

### § 829. Private Sale of Real Estate

All private sales of real estate shall be made in the manner the court directs in its order of sale, and no further advertising, notice, or citation concerning the sale shall be required unless the court shall direct otherwise.

Added by Acts 1993, 73rd Leg., ch. 957, § 1, eff. Sept. 1, 1993.

### § 830. Sales of Easements and Rights of Way

The guardian may sell and convey easements and rights of way on, under, and over the land of a guardianship estate that is being administered under orders of a court, regardless of whether the proceeds of the sale are required for payment of charges or claims against the estate, or for other lawful purposes. The procedure for the sale is the same as provided by law for a sale of real property of wards at private sale.

Added by Acts 1993, 73rd Leg., ch. 957, § 1, eff. Sept. 1, 1993.

### § 831. Guardian Purchasing Property of the Estate

(a) Except as provided by Subsection (b) or (c) of this section, the guardian of an estate may not purchase, directly or indirectly, any property of the estate sold by the guardian, or by any co-representative of a guardian.

(b) A guardian may purchase property from the estate in compliance with the terms of a written executory contract signed by the ward before the ward became incapacitated, including a contract for deed, earnest money contract, buy/sell agreement, or stock purchase or redemption agreement.

(c) A guardian of an estate may purchase property from the estate on the court's determination that the sale is in the best interest of the estate. In the case of an application filed by the guardian of the estate of a ward, the court shall appoint an attorney ad litem to represent the ward with respect to the sale. The court may require notice for a sale made under this subsection.

(d) If a purchase is made in violation of this section, a person interested in the estate may file a written complaint with the court in which the guardianship proceedings are pending. On service of citation on the guardian and after hearing and proof, the court shall declare the sale void, set aside the sale, and order that the property be reconveyed to the estate. All costs of the sale, protest, and suit, if found necessary, shall be adjudged against the guardian.

Added by Acts 1993, 73rd Leg., ch. 957, § 1, eff. Sept. 1, 1993.
Subsec. (c) amended by Acts 2005, 79th Leg., ch. 200, § 8, eff. Sept. 1, 2005.

### § 832. Report of Sale

A sale of real property of an estate shall be reported to the court that orders the sale not later than the 30th day after the date the sale is made. A report must be in writing, sworn to, filed with the clerk, and noted on the probate docket. A report made under this section must contain:

(1) the date of the order of sale;

(2) a description of the property sold;

(3) the time and place of sale;

(4) the name of the purchaser;

(5) the amount for which each parcel of property or interest in the parcel of property was sold;

(6) the terms of the sale, and whether the sale was private or made at a public auction; and

(7) whether the purchaser is ready to comply with the order of sale.

Added by Acts 1993, 73rd Leg., ch. 957, § 1, eff. Sept. 1, 1993.

### § 833. Bond on Sale of Real Estate

If the guardian of the estate is not required by this chapter to furnish a general bond, the court may confirm the sale if the court finds the sale is satisfactory and in accordance with law. Otherwise, before a sale of real estate is confirmed, the court shall determine whether the general bond of the guardian is sufficient to protect the estate after the proceeds of the sale are received. If the court finds the bond is sufficient, the court may confirm the sale. If the general bond is found by the court to be insufficient, the court may not confirm the sale until the general bond is increased to the amount required by the court, or an additional bond is given and approved by the court. The increase in the amount of the bond, or the additional bond, shall be equal to the amount for which the real estate is sold in addition to any additional sum the court finds necessary and sets for the protection of the estate. If the real estate sold is encumbered by a lien to secure a claim against the estate, is sold to the owner or holder of the secured claim, and is in full payment, liquidation, and satisfaction of the claim, an increased general bond or additional bond may not be required except for the amount of cash actually paid to the guardian of the estate in excess of the amount necessary to pay, liquidate, and satisfy the claim in full.

Added by Acts 1993, 73rd Leg., ch. 957, § 1, eff. Sept. 1, 1993.

### § 834. Action of Court on Report of Sale

After the expiration of five days from the date a report of sale is filed under Section 832 of this code, the court shall inquire into the manner in which the sale was made, hear evidence in support of or against the report, and determine the sufficiency or insufficiency of the guardian's general bond, if any has been required and given. If the court is satisfied that the sale was for a fair price, was properly made, and conforms with the law and the court has approved any increased or additional bond that may have been found necessary to protect the estate, the court shall enter a decree confirming the sale showing conformity with other provisions of this chapter relating to the sale and authorizing the conveyance of the property to be made by the guardian of the estate on compliance by the purchaser with the terms of the sale, detailing those terms. If the court is not satisfied that the sale was for a fair price, was properly made, and conforms with the law, the court shall issue an order that sets the sale aside and order a new sale to be made, if necessary. The action of the court in confirming or disapproving a report of sale has the force and effect of a final judgment. Any person interested in the guardianship estate or in the sale has the right to have the decrees reviewed as in other final judgments in probate proceedings.

Added by Acts 1993, 73rd Leg., ch. 957, § 1, eff. Sept. 1, 1993.

## § 835.  Deed Conveys Title to Real Estate

When real estate is sold, the conveyance of real estate shall be by proper deed that refers to and identifies the decree of the court that confirmed the sale. The deed shall vest in the purchaser all right, title, and interest of the estate to the property and shall be prima facie evidence that the sale has met all applicable requirements of the law.

Added by Acts 1993, 73rd Leg., ch. 957, § 1, eff. Sept. 1, 1993.

## § 836.  Delivery of Deed, Vendor's Lien, and Deed of Trust Lien

After a sale is confirmed by the court and one purchaser has complied with the terms of sale, the guardian of the estate shall execute and deliver to the purchaser a proper deed conveying the property. If the sale is made partly on credit, the vendor's lien securing a purchase money note shall be expressly retained in the deed and may not be waived. Before actual delivery of the deed to the purchaser, the purchaser shall execute and deliver to the guardian of the estate a vendor's lien note, with or without personal sureties as the court has ordered and a deed of trust or mortgage on the property as further security for the payment of the note. On completion of the transaction, the guardian shall promptly file and record in the appropriate records in the county where the land is located the deed of trust or mortgage.

Added by Acts 1993, 73rd Leg., ch. 957, § 1, eff. Sept. 1, 1993.

## § 837.  Penalty for Neglect

If the guardian of an estate neglects to comply with Section 836 of this code or fails to file the deed of trust securing the lien in the proper county, the guardian, after complaint and citation, may be removed. The guardian and the sureties on the bond of the guardian shall be held liable for the use of the estate and for all damages resulting from the neglect of the guardian. Damages under this section may be recovered in a court of competent jurisdiction.

Added by Acts 1993, 73rd Leg., ch. 957, § 1, eff. Sept. 1, 1993.

## SUBPART I.  HIRING AND RENTING

## § 839.  Hiring or Renting Without Order of Court

The guardian of an estate, without court order, may rent any real property of the estate or hire out any personal property of the estate for one year or less, either at public auction or privately, as may be deemed in the best interests of the estate.

Added by Acts 1993, 73rd Leg., ch. 957, § 1, eff. Sept. 1, 1993.

## § 840.  Liability of Guardian

If property of the guardianship estate is hired or rented without court order, on the sworn complaint of any person interested in the estate, the guardian of the estate shall be required to account to the estate for the reasonable value of the hire or rent of the property to be ascertained by the court on satisfactory evidence.

Added by Acts 1993, 73rd Leg., ch. 957, § 1, eff. Sept. 1, 1993.

## § 841.  Order to Hire or Rent

A guardian of an estate may file a written application with the court setting forth the property sought to be hired or rented. If the proposed rental period is one year or more, the guardian of the estate shall file a written application with the court setting forth the property sought to be hired or rented. If the court finds that it would be in the interests of the estate, the court shall grant the application and issue an order that describes the property to be hired or rented and states whether the hiring or renting shall be at public auction or privately, whether for cash or on credit, and, if on credit, the extent of the credit and the period for which the property may be rented. If the property is to be hired or rented at public auction, the court shall prescribe whether notice shall be published or posted.

Added by Acts 1993, 73rd Leg., ch. 957, § 1, eff. Sept. 1, 1993.

## § 842.  Procedure in Case of Neglect to Rent Property

A person interested in a guardianship may file a written and sworn complaint in a court in which the estate is pending and cause the guardian of the estate to be cited to appear and show cause why the guardian did not hire or rent any property of the estate. The court, on hearing the complaint, shall make an order that is in the best interests of the estate.

Added by Acts 1993, 73rd Leg., ch. 957, § 1, eff. Sept. 1, 1993.

## § 843.  Property Hired or Rented on Credit

When property is hired or rented on credit, possession of the property may not be delivered until the hirer or renter has executed and delivered to the guardian of the estate a note with good personal security for the amount of the hire or rental. If the property that is hired or rented is delivered without the receipt of the security required under this section, the guardian and the sureties on the bond of the guardian shall be liable for the full amount of the hire or rental. This section does not apply to a hire or rental that is paid in installments in advance of the period of time to which they relate.

Added by Acts 1993, 73rd Leg., ch. 957, § 1, eff. Sept. 1, 1993.

### § 844. Property Hired or Rented Returned in Good Condition

All property that is hired or rented, with or without a court order, shall be returned to the possession of the guardianship in as good a condition, reasonable wear and tear excepted, as when the property was hired or rented. It shall be the duty and responsibility of the guardian of the estate to see that the property is returned as provided by this section, to report to the court any loss, damage, or destruction of property that is hired or rented under this chapter, and to ask for authority to take action as is necessary. If the guardian fails to act as required by this section, the guardian and the sureties on the bond of the guardian shall be liable to the guardianship for any loss or damage suffered through the fault of the guardian to act as required under this section.

Added by Acts 1993, 73rd Leg., ch. 957, § 1, eff. Sept. 1, 1993.

### § 845. Report of Hiring or Renting

(a) When any property of the guardianship estate with an appraised value of $3,000 or more has been hired or rented, the guardian of the estate, not later than the 30th day after the date of the hire or rental, shall file with the court a sworn and written report that states:

(1) the property involved and its appraised value;

(2) the date of hiring or renting, and whether at public auction or privately;

(3) the name of the person who hired or rented the property;

(4) the amount of the hiring or rental; and

(5) whether the hiring or rental was for cash or on credit, and, if on credit, the length of time, the terms, and the security taken for the hiring or rental.

(b) When the value of the property involved is less than $3,000, the hiring or renting of the property may be reported in the next annual or final account that is to be filed as required by law.

Added by Acts 1993, 73rd Leg., ch. 957, § 1, eff. Sept. 1, 1993.

### § 846. Court Action on Report

After five days from the time the report of the hiring or rental is filed, the court shall examine the report and shall approve and confirm the hiring or rental by court order if the court finds the hire or rental just and reasonable. If the court disapproves the hiring or rental, the guardianship may not be bound and the court may order another offering of the property for hire or rent in the same manner and subject to the same rules provided in this chapter for property for hire or rent. If the report has been approved by the court and it later appears that, due to the fault of the guardian of the estate, the property has not been hired or rented for its reasonable value, the court shall cause the guardian of the estate and the sureties on the bond of the guardian to appear and show cause why the reasonable value of the hire or rental of the property should not be adjudged against the guardian or sureties.

Added by Acts 1993, 73rd Leg., ch. 957, § 1, eff. Sept. 1, 1993.

## SUBPART J. MINERAL LEASES, POOLING OR UNITIZATION AGREEMENTS, AND OTHER MATTERS RELATING TO MINERAL PROPERTIES

### § 847. Mineral Leases After Public Notice

(a) In this subpart:

(1) "Land" or "interest in land" includes minerals or any interest in any of the minerals in place.

(2) "Mineral development" includes exploration, by geophysical or by any other means, drilling, mining, developing, and operating, and producing and saving oil, other liquid hydrocarbons, gas (including all liquid hydrocarbons in the gaseous phase in the reservoir), gaseous elements, sulphur, metals, and all other minerals, solid or otherwise.

(3) "Property" includes land, minerals in place, whether solid, liquid, or gaseous, as well as an interest of any kind in the property, including royalty, owned by the estate.

(b) A guardian acting solely under an order of a court, may be authorized by the court in which the guardianship proceeding is pending to make, execute, and deliver leases, with or without unitization clauses or pooling provisions, that provide for the exploration for, and development and production of, oil, other liquid hydrocarbons, gas (including all liquid hydrocarbons in the gaseous phase), metals, and other solid minerals, and other minerals, or any of those minerals in place, belonging to the estate.

(c) All leases authorized by Subsection (b) of this section, with or without pooling provisions or unitization clauses, shall be made and entered into pursuant to and in conformity with Subsections (d)–(m) of this section.

(d) The guardian of the estate shall file a written application with the court seeking authority to lease property of the estate for mineral exploration and development, with or without pooling provisions or unitization clauses. The name of any proposed lessee or the terms, provisions, or form of any desired lease do not need to be set out or suggested in the application. The application shall:

(1) describe the property fully enough by reference to the amount of acreage, the survey name or number, abstract number, or other description that adequately identifies the property and its location in the county in which the property is located;

(2) specify the interest thought to be owned by the estate if less than the whole, but asking for authority to include all interest owned by the estate if that is the intention; and

(3) set out the reasons why the particular property of the estate should be leased.

(e) When an application to lease is filed, under this section, the county clerk shall immediately call the filing of the application to the attention of the court. The judge shall promptly make and enter a brief order designating the time and place for the hearing of the application. If the hearing does not take place at the time originally designated by the court or by timely order of continuance duly entered, the hearing shall be automatically continued without further notice to the same hour or time the following day, except Sundays and holidays on which the county courthouse is officially closed to business, and from day to day until the application is finally acted on and disposed of by order of the court. No notice of the automatic continuance shall be required.

(f) The guardian shall give written notice directed to all persons interested in the estate of the time designated by the judge for the hearing on the application to lease. The notice must be dated, state the date on which the application was filed, describe briefly the property sought to be leased, specify the fractional interest sought to be leased if less than the entire interest in the tract identified, and state the time and place designated by the judge for the hearing. Exclusive of the date of notice and of the date set for hearing, the guardian shall give at least 10 days' notice by publishing in one issue of a newspaper of general circulation in the county in which the proceeding is pending or by posting if there is no newspaper in the county. Posting under this section may be done at the guardian's instance. The date of notice when published shall be the date the newspaper bears.

(g) A court order authorizing any acts to be performed pursuant to the application is null and void in the absence of:

(1) a written order originally designating a time and place for hearing;

(2) a notice issued by the guardian of the estate in compliance with the order; and

(3) proof of publication or posting of the notice as required.

(h) At the time and place designated for the hearing, or at any time to which the hearing has been continued as provided by this section, the judge shall hear the application and require proof as to the necessity or advisability of leasing for mineral development the property described in the application and in the notice. If the judge is satisfied that the application is in due form, that notice has been duly given in the manner and for the time required by law, that the proof of necessity or advisability of leasing is sufficient, and that the application should be granted, the judge shall enter an order so finding and authorizing the making of one or more leases, with or without pooling provisions or unitization clauses (with or without cash consideration if deemed by the court to be in the best interest of the estate) that affects and covers the property or portions of the property described in the application. The order that authorizes the leasing must also set out the following mandatory contents:

(1) the name of the lessee;

(2) the actual cash consideration, if any, to be paid by the lessee;

(3) a finding that the guardian is exempt by law from giving bond if that is a fact, and if the guardian is required to give a bond, then a finding as to whether or not the guardian's general bond on file is sufficient to protect the personal property on hand, inclusive of any cash bonus to be paid; but if the court finds the general bond is insufficient to meet these requirements, the order shall show the amount of increased or additional bond required to cover the deficiency;

(4) a complete exhibit copy, either written or printed, of each lease authorized to be made, either set out in, attached to, incorporated by reference in, or made a part of the order.

(i) An exhibit copy must show the name of the lessee, the date of the lease, an adequate description of the property being leased, the delay rental, if any, to be paid to defer commencement of operations, and all other terms and provisions authorized. If no date of the lease appears in the exhibit copy or in the court's order, then the date of the court's order is considered for all purposes as the date of the authorized lease. If the name and address of a depository bank for receiving rental is not shown in the exhibit copy, the name or address of the depository bank may be inserted or caused to be inserted in the lease by the estate's guardian at the time of its execution or at any other time agreeable to the lessee, his successors, or assigns.

(j) On the hearing of an application for authority to lease, if the court grants the authority to lease, the guardian of the estate is fully authorized to make, not later than the 30th day after the date of the judge's order, unless an extension is granted by the court on a sworn application showing good cause, the lease as evidenced by the true exhibit copies in accordance with the order. Unless the guardian is not required to give a general bond, a lease for which a cash consideration is required, though ordered, executed, and delivered, is not valid unless the order authorizing the lease actually makes a finding with respect to the general bond. If the general bond has been found insufficient, the lease is not valid until the bond has been increased or an additional bond given with the sureties required by law as required by the court order, has been approved by the judge, and has been filed with the clerk of the court in which the proceeding is pending. If two or more leases on different lands are authorized by the same order, the general bond shall be increased or additional bonds given to cover all. It is not necessary for the judge to make any order confirming the leases.

(k) Every lease when executed and delivered in compliance with the rules set out in this section shall be valid and binding on the property or interest owned by the estate and covered by the lease for the full duration of the term as provided in the lease and is subject only to its terms and conditions even though the primary term extends beyond the date when the estate is closed in accordance with law. In order for a lease to be valid and binding on the property or interest owned by the estate under this section, the authorized primary term in the lease may not exceed five years, subject to terms and provisions of the lease extending it beyond the primary term by paying production, by bona fide drilling or reworking operations, whether in or on the same or additional well or wells with no cessation of operations of more than 60 consecutive days before production has been restored or obtained, or by the provisions of the lease relating to a shut-in gas well.

(*l*) As to any existing valid mineral lease executed and delivered in compliance with this chapter before September 1, 1993, a provision of the lease continuing the lease in force after its five-year primary term by a shut-in gas well is validated, unless the validity of the provision is an issue in a lawsuit pending in this state on September 1, 1993.

(m) Any oil, gas, and mineral lease executed by a guardian under this chapter may be amended by an instrument that provides that a shut-in gas well on the land covered by the lease or on land pooled with all or some part of the land covered by the lease shall continue the lease in force after its five-year primary term. The instrument shall be executed by the guardian, with court approval, and on the terms and conditions as may be prescribed in the instrument.

Added by Acts 1993, 73rd Leg., ch. 957, § 1, eff. Sept. 1, 1993.

### § 848. Mineral Leases at Private Sale

(a) Notwithstanding the mandatory requirements for setting a time and place for hearing of an application to lease under Section 847 of this code and the issuance, service, and return of notice, the court may authorize the making of oil, gas, and mineral leases at private sale without public notice or advertising if, in the opinion of the court, sufficient facts are set out in the application to show that it would be more advantageous to the estate that a lease be made privately and without compliance with the mandatory requirements under Section 847 of this code. Leases authorized under this section may include pooling provisions or unitization clauses as in other cases.

(b) At any time after the expiration of five days and before the expiration of the 10th day after the date of filing and without an order setting the time and place of hearing, the court shall hear the application to lease at a private sale. The court shall inquire into the manner in which the proposed lease has been or will be made and shall hear evidence for or against the application. If the court is satisfied that the lease has been or will be made for a fair and sufficient consideration and on fair terms and has been or will be properly made in conformity with the law, the court shall enter an order authorizing the execution of the lease without the necessity of advertising, notice, or citation. An order entered under this subsection must comply in all other respects with the requirements essential to the validity of mineral leases set out in this chapter as if advertising or notice were required. An order that confirms a lease made at a private sale does not need to be issued. A lease made at a private sale is not valid until the increased or additional bond required by the court, if any, has been approved by the court and filed with the clerk of the court.

Added by Acts 1993, 73rd Leg., ch. 957, § 1, eff. Sept. 1, 1993.

### § 849. Pooling or Unitization of Royalty or Minerals

(a) When an existing lease on property owned by the estate does not adequately provide for pooling or unitization, the court may authorize the commitment of royalty or mineral interests in oil, liquid hydrocarbons, gas (including all liquid hydrocarbons in the gaseous phase in the reservoir), gaseous elements, and other minerals or any one or more of them owned by the estate being administered to agreements that provide for the operation of areas as a pool or unit for the exploration, development, and production of all those minerals, if the court finds that the pool or unit to which the agreement relates will be operated in such a manner as to protect correlative rights, or to prevent the physical or economic waste of oil, liquid hydrocarbons, gas (including all liquid hydrocarbons in the gaseous phase in the reservoir), gaseous elements, or other mineral subject thereto, and that it is in the best interests of the estate to execute the agreement. Any agreement so authorized to be executed may provide that:

(1) operations incident to the drilling of or production from a well on any portion of a pool or unit are deemed for all purposes to be the conduct of operations on or production from each separately owned tract in the pool or unit;

(2) any lease covering any part of the area committed to a pool or unit shall continue in force in its entirety as long as oil, gas, or other mineral subject to the agreement is produced in paying quantities from any part of the pooled or unitized area, as long as operations are conducted as provided in the lease on any part of the pooled or unitized area, or as long as there is a shut-in gas well on any part of the pooled or unitized area if the presence of the shut-in gas well is a ground for continuation of the lease on the terms of the lease;

(3) the production allocated by the agreement to each tract included in a pool or unit shall, when produced, be deemed for all purposes to have been produced from the tract by a well drilled on the tract;

(4) the royalties provided for on production from any tract or portion of a tract within the pool or unit shall be paid only on that portion of the production allocated to the tract in accordance with the agreement;

(5) the dry gas, before or after extraction of hydrocarbons, may be returned to a formation underlying any lands or leases committed to the agreement, and that no royalties are required to be paid on the gas so returned; and

(6) gas obtained from other sources or another tract of land may be injected into a formation underlying any land or lease committed to the agreement, and that no royalties are

required to be paid on the gas so injected when same is produced from the unit.

(b) Pooling or unitization, when not adequately provided for by an existing lease on property owned by the estate, may be authorized by the court in which the proceeding is pending pursuant to and in conformity with Subsections (c)–(g) of this section.

(c) The guardian of the estate shall file with the county clerk of the county in which the guardianship proceeding is pending the guardian's written application for authority to enter into a pooling or unitization agreement supplementing, amending, or otherwise relating to, any existing lease covering property owned by the estate, or to commit royalties or other interest in minerals, whether subject to lease or not, to a pooling or unitization agreement. The application must also describe the property sufficiently as required in the original application to lease, describe briefly the lease to which the interest of the estate is subject, and set out the reasons the proposed agreement concerning the property should be made. A true copy of the proposed agreement shall be attached to the application and by reference made a part of the application, but the agreement may not be recorded in the judge's guardianship docket. The clerk shall immediately, after the application is filed, call it to the attention of the judge.

(d) Notice of the filing of the application by advertising, citation, or otherwise is not required.

(e) The judge may hold a hearing on the application at a time that is agreeable to the parties to the proposed agreement. The judge shall hear proof and be satisfied as to whether it is in the best interests of the estate that the proposed agreement be authorized. The hearing may be continued from day to day and from time to time as the court finds to be necessary.

(f) If the court finds that the pool or unit to which the agreement relates will be operated in such a manner as to protect correlative rights or to prevent the physical or economic waste of oil, liquid hydrocarbons, gas (including all liquid hydrocarbons in the gaseous phase in the reservoir), gaseous elements, or other mineral subject to the pool or unit, that it is in the best interests of the estate that the agreement be executed, and that the agreement conforms substantially with the permissible provisions of Subsection (a) of this section, the court shall enter an order setting out the findings made by the court and authorizing execution of the agreement, with or without payment of cash consideration according to the agreement. If cash consideration is to be paid for the agreement, the court shall make a finding as to the necessity of increased or additional bond as a finding is made in the making of leases on payment of the cash bonus for the lease. The agreement is not valid until the increased or additional bond required by the court, if any, has been approved by the judge and filed with the clerk. If

the date is not stipulated in the agreement, the date of the court's order shall be the effective date of the agreement.

Added by Acts 1993, 73rd Leg., ch. 957, § 1, eff. Sept. 1, 1993. Amended by Acts 2009, 81st Leg., ch. 602, § 17, eff. June 19, 2009.

## § 850. Special Ancillary Instruments Executed Without Court Order

As to any valid mineral lease or pooling or unitization agreement, executed on behalf of the estate before September 1, 1993, pursuant to provisions, or by a former owner of land, minerals, or royalty affected by the lease, pooling, or unitization agreement, the guardian of the estate that is being administered, without further order of the court and without consideration, may execute division orders, transfer orders, instruments of correction, instruments designating depository banks for the reception of delay rentals or shut-in gas well royalty to accrue or become payable under the terms of the lease, or similar instruments pertaining to the lease or agreement and the property covered by the lease or agreement.

Added by Acts 1993, 73rd Leg., ch. 957, § 1, eff. Sept. 1, 1933.

## § 851. Procedure When Guardian of Estate Neglects to Apply for Authority

When the guardian of an estate neglects to apply for authority to subject property of the estate to a lease for mineral development, pooling, or unitization, or authority to commit royalty or other interest in minerals to pooling or unitization, any person interested in the estate, on written application filed with the county clerk, may cause the guardian to be cited to show cause why it is not in the best interests of the estate for the lease to be made or an agreement to be entered into. The clerk shall immediately call the filing of the application under this section to the attention of the judge of the court in which the guardianship proceeding is pending. The judge shall set a time and place for a hearing on the application. The guardian of the estate shall be cited to appear and show cause why the execution of the lease or agreement should not be ordered. On hearing and if satisfied from the proof that it would be in the best interests of the estate, the court shall enter an order requiring the guardian to file the guardian's application to subject the property of the estate to a lease for mineral development, with or without pooling or unitization provisions, or to commit royalty or other minerals to unitization, as the case may be. The procedures prescribed with respect to original application to lease or with respect to original application for authority to commit royalty or minerals to pooling or unitization shall be followed.

Added by Acts 1993, 73rd Leg., ch. 957, § 1, eff. Sept. 1, 1993.

## § 852. Validation of Certain Leases and Pooling or Unitization Agreements Based on Previous Statutes

All leases on the oil, gas, or other minerals existing on September 1, 1993, belonging to the estates of minors or other incapacitated persons and all agreements with respect to the pooling or unitization of oil, gas, or other minerals or any interest in oil, gas, or other minerals with like properties of others that have been authorized by the court having venue, executed, and delivered by a guardian or other fiduciary of the estate of a minor or incapacitated person in substantial conformity to the rules set forth in statutes on execution or delivery providing for only seven days' notice in some instances and for a brief order designating a time and place for hearing, are validated insofar as the period of notice or absence of an order setting a time and place for hearing is concerned, unless the length of time of the notice or the absence of the order is an issue in a lease or pooling or unitization agreement that is involved in a lawsuit pending on September 1, 1993.

Added by Acts 1993, 73rd Leg., ch. 957, § 1, eff. Sept. 1, 1993.

## SUBPART K. PARTITION OF WARD'S ESTATE IN REALTY

### § 853. Partition of Ward's Interest in Realty

(a) If a ward owns an interest in real estate in common with another part owner or one or more part owners, and if, in the opinion of the guardian of the estate, it is in the best interests of the ward's estate to partition the real estate, the guardian may agree on a partition with the other part owners subject to the approval of the court in which the guardianship proceeding is pending.

(b) When a guardian has reached an agreement with the other part owners on how to partition the real estate, the guardian shall file with the court an application to have the agreement approved. The application filed by the guardian under this subsection shall describe the land that is to be divided and shall state why it is in the best interests of the ward's estate to partition the real estate and shall show that the proposed partition agreement is fair and just to the ward's estate.

(c) When the application required by Subsection (b) of this section is filed, the county clerk shall immediately call the filing of the application to the attention of the judge of the court in which the guardianship proceeding is pending. The judge shall designate a day to hear the application. The application must remain on file at least 10 days before any orders are made, and the judge may continue the hearing from time to time until the judge is satisfied concerning the application.

(d) If the judge is satisfied that the proposed partition of the real estate is in the best interests of the ward's estate, the court shall enter an order approving the partition and directing the guardian to execute the necessary agreement for the purpose of carrying the order and partition into effect.

(e) When a guardian has executed an agreement or will execute an agreement to partition any land in which the ward has an interest without court approval as provided by this section, the guardian shall file with the court in which the guardianship proceedings are pending an application for the approval and ratification of the partition agreement. The application must refer to the agreement in such a manner that the court can fully understand the nature of the partition and the land being divided. The application must state that, in the opinion of the guardian, the agreement is fair and just to the ward's estate and is in the best interests of the estate. When the application is filed, a hearing shall be held on the application as provided by Subsection (c) of this section. If the court is of the opinion that the partition is fairly made and that the partition is in the best interests of the ward's estate, the court shall enter an order ratifying and approving the partition agreement. When the partition is ratified and approved, the partition shall be effective and binding as if originally executed after a court order.

(f) If the guardian of the estate of a ward is of the opinion that it is in the best interests of the ward's estate that any real estate that the ward owns in common with others should be partitioned, the guardian may bring a suit in the court in which the guardianship proceeding is pending against the other part owner or part owners for the partition of the real estate. The court, if after hearing the suit is satisfied that the necessity for the partition of the real estate exists, may enter an order partitioning the real estate to the owner of the real estate.

Added by Acts 1993, 73rd Leg., ch. 957, § 1, eff. Sept. 1, 1993.

## SUBPART L. INVESTMENTS AND LOANS OF ESTATES OF WARDS

### § 854. Guardian Required to Keep Estate Invested Under Certain Circumstances

(a) The guardian of the estate is not required to invest funds that are immediately necessary for the education, support, and maintenance of the ward or others the ward supports, if any, as provided by this chapter. The guardian of the estate shall invest any other funds and assets available for investment unless the court orders otherwise under this subpart.

(b) The court may, on its own motion or on written request of a person interested in the guardianship, cite the guardian to appear and show cause why the estate is not invested or not properly invested. At any time after giving notice to all parties, the court may conduct a hearing to protect the estate, except that the court may not hold a final hearing on whether the estate is properly invested until the 31st day after the date the guardian was originally cited to appear under this subsection. On the hearing of the court's motion or a request made under this section, the court shall render an order the court considers to be in the best interests of the ward.

(c) The court may appoint a guardian ad litem for the limited purpose of representing the ward's best interests with respect to the investment of the ward's property at a hearing under this section.

Added by Acts 2003, 78th Leg., ch. 549, § 22, eff. Sept. 1, 2003.

## § 855.  Standard for Management and Investments

(a) In acquiring, investing, reinvesting, exchanging, retaining, selling, supervising, and managing a ward's estate, a guardian of the estate shall exercise the judgment and care under the circumstances then prevailing that persons of ordinary prudence, discretion, and intelligence exercise in the management of their own affairs, considering the probable income from as well as the probable increase in value and the safety of their capital.  The guardian shall also consider all other relevant factors, including:

(1) the anticipated costs of supporting the ward;

(2) the ward's age, education, current income, ability to earn additional income, net worth, and liabilities;

(3) the nature of the ward's estate;  and

(4) any other resources reasonably available to the ward.

(a–1) In determining whether a guardian has exercised the standard of investment required by this section with respect to an investment decision, the court shall, absent fraud or gross negligence, take into consideration the investment of all the assets of the estate over which the guardian has management or control, rather than taking into consideration the prudence of only a single investment made by the guardian.

(b) A guardian of the estate is considered to have exercised the standard required by this section with respect to investing the ward's estate if the guardian invests in the following:

(1) bonds or other obligations of the United States;

(2) tax-supported bonds of this state;

(3) except as limited by Subsections (c) and (d) of this section, tax-supported bonds of a county, district, political subdivision, or incorporated city or town in this state;

(4) shares or share accounts of a state savings and loan association or savings bank with its main office or a branch office in this state if the payment of the shares or share accounts is insured by the Federal Deposit Insurance Corporation;

(5) the shares or share accounts of a federal savings and loan association or savings bank with its main office or a branch office in this state if the payment of the shares or share accounts is insured by the Federal Deposit Insurance Corporation;

(6) collateral bonds of companies incorporated under the laws of this state, having a paid-in capital of $1,000,000 or more, when the bonds are a direct obligation of the company that issues the bonds and are specifically secured by first mortgage real estate notes or other securities pledged with a trustee;  or

(7) interest-bearing time deposits that may be withdrawn on or before one year after demand in a bank that does business in this state where the payment of the time deposits is insured by the Federal Deposit Insurance Corporation.

(c) The bonds of a county, district, or subdivision may be purchased only if the net funded debt of the county, district, or subdivision that issues the bonds does not exceed 10 percent of the assessed value of taxable property in the county, district, or subdivision.

(d) The bonds of a city or town may be purchased only if the net funded debt of the city or town does not exceed 10 percent of the assessed value of taxable property in the city or town less that part of the debt incurred for acquisition or improvement of revenue-producing utilities, the revenues of which are not pledged to support other obligations of the city or town.

(e) The limitations in Subsections (c) and (d) of this section do not apply to bonds issued for road purposes in this state under Section 52, Article III, of the Texas Constitution that are supported by a tax unlimited as to rate or amount.

(f) In this section, "net funded debt" means the total funded debt less sinking funds on hand.

(g) The court may modify or eliminate the guardian's duty to keep the estate invested or the standard required by this section with regard to investments of estate assets on a showing by clear and convincing evidence that the modification or elimination is in the best interests of the ward and the ward's estate.

Added by Acts 1993, 73rd Leg., ch. 957, § 1, eff. Sept. 1, 1993. Amended by Acts 1999, 76th Leg., ch. 344, § 6.007, eff. Sept. 1, 1999.

Section heading amended by Acts 2003, 78th Leg., ch. 549, § 23, eff. Sept. 1, 2003;  Subsecs. (a), (b) amended by Acts 2003, 78th Leg., ch. 549, § 24, eff. Sept. 1, 2003;  Subsecs. (a-1), (g) added by Acts 2003, 78th Leg., ch. 549, § 24, eff. Sept. 1, 2003.

## § 855A.  Retention of Assets

(a) A guardian of the estate may retain without court approval until the first anniversary of the date of receipt any property received into the guardianship estate at its inception or added to the estate by gift, devise, inheritance, mutation, or increase, without regard to diversification of investments and without liability for any depreciation or loss resulting from the retention.  The guardian shall care for and manage the retained assets as a person of ordinary prudence, discretion, and intelligence would in caring for and managing the person's own affairs.

(b) On application and a hearing, the court may render an order authorizing the guardian to continue retaining the property after the period prescribed by Subsection (a) of this section if the retention is an element of the guardian's investment plan as provided by this subpart.

Added by Acts 2003, 78th Leg., ch. 549, § 25, eff. Sept. 1, 2003.

**Text of Texas Probate Code effective until January 1, 2014**

## § 855B. Procedure for Making Investments or Retaining Estate Assets

(a) Not later than the 180th day after the date on which the guardian of the estate qualified as guardian or another date specified by the court, the guardian shall:

(1) have estate assets invested according to Section 855(b) of this code; or

(2) file a written application with the court for an order:

(A) authorizing the guardian to:

(i) develop and implement an investment plan for estate assets;

(ii) invest in or sell securities under an investment plan developed under Subparagraph (i) of this paragraph;

(iii) declare that one or more estate assets must be retained, despite being underproductive with respect to income or overall return; or

(iv) loan estate funds, invest in real estate or make other investments, or purchase a life, term, or endowment insurance policy or an annuity contract; or

(B) modifying or eliminating the guardian's duty to invest the estate.

(a–1) The court may approve an investment plan under Subsection (a)(2) of this section without a hearing.

(b) If the court determines that the action requested in the application is in the best interests of the ward and the ward's estate, the court shall render an order granting the authority requested in the application or an order modifying or eliminating the guardian's duty to keep the estate invested. An order under this subsection must state in reasonably specific terms:

(1) the nature of the investment, investment plan, or other action requested in the application and authorized by the court, including, if applicable, the authority to invest in and sell securities in accordance with the objectives of the investment plan;

(2) when an investment must be reviewed and reconsidered by the guardian; and

(3) whether the guardian must report the guardian's review and recommendations to the court.

(c) The fact that an account or other asset is the subject of a specific or general gift under a ward's will, if any, or that a ward has funds, securities, or other property held with a right of survivorship does not prevent:

(1) a guardian of the estate from taking possession and control of the asset or closing the account; or

(2) the court from authorizing an action or modifying or eliminating a duty with respect to the possession, control, or investment of the account or other asset.

(d) The procedure prescribed by this section does not apply if a different procedure is prescribed for an investment or sale by a guardian. A guardian is not required to follow the procedure prescribed by this section with respect to an investment or sale that is specifically authorized by other law.

(e) A citation or notice is not necessary to invest in or sell securities under an investment plan authorized by the court under Subsection (b)(1) of this section.

Added by Acts 2003, 78th Leg., ch. 549, § 25, eff. Sept. 1, 2003. Subsecs. (a) and (b) amended and Subsec. (e) added by Acts 2005, 79th Leg., ch. 200, § 9, eff. Sept. 1, 2005; Subsecs. (a) and (b) amended and Subsec. (a–1) added by Acts 2007, 80th Leg., ch. 614, § 20, eff. Sept. 1, 2007.

## § 856. Repealed by Acts 2003, 78th Leg., ch. 549, § 35, eff. Sept. 1, 2003

## § 857. Investment in, or Continued Investment in, Life Insurance or Annuities.

(a) In this section, "life insurance company" means a stock or mutual legal reserve life insurance company that maintains the full legal reserves required under the laws of this state and that is licensed by the State Board of Insurance to transact the business of life insurance in this state.

(b) The guardian of the estate may invest in life, term, or endowment insurance policies, or in annuity contracts, or both, issued by a life insurance company or administered by the Veterans Administration, subject to conditions and limitations in this section.

(c) The guardian shall first apply to the court for an order that authorizes the guardian to make the investment. The application filed under this subsection must include a report that shows:

(1) in detail the financial condition of the estate at the time the application is made;

(2) the name and address of the life insurance company from which the policy or annuity contract is to be purchased and that the company is licensed by the State Board of Insurance to transact that business in this state on the date the application is filed, or that the policy or contract is administered by the Veterans Administration;

(3) a statement of the face amount and plan of the policy of insurance sought to be purchased and of the amount, frequency, and duration of the annuity payments to be provided by the annuity contract sought to be purchased;

(4) a statement of the amount, frequency, and duration of the premiums required by the policy or annuity contract; and

(5) a statement of the cash value of the policy or annuity contract at its anniversary nearest the 21st birthday of the ward, assuming that all premiums to the anniversary are paid and that there is no indebtedness against the policy or contract incurred in accordance with its terms.

(d) An insurance policy must be issued on the life of the ward, or the father, mother, spouse, child, brother, sister, grandfather, or grandmother of the ward or a person in whose life the ward may have an insurable interest.

(e) Only the ward, the ward's estate, or the father, mother, spouse, child, brother, sister, grandfather, or grandmother of the ward may be a beneficiary of the insurance policy and of the death benefit of the annuity contract, and the ward must be the annuitant in the annuity contract.

(f) The control of the policy or the annuity contract and of the incidents of ownership in the policy or annuity contract is vested in the guardian during the life and disability of the ward.

(g) The policy or annuity contract may not be amended or changed during the life and disability of the ward except on application to and order of the court.

(h) If a life, term, or endowment insurance policy or a contract of annuity is owned by the ward when a proceeding for the appointment of a guardian is begun, and it is made to appear that the company issuing the policy or contract of annuity is a life insurance company as defined by this section or the policy or contract is administered by the Veterans Administration, the policy or contract may be continued in full force and effect. All future premiums may be paid out of surplus funds of the ward's estate. The guardian shall apply to the court for an order to continue the policy or contract, or both, according to the existing terms of the policy or contract or to modify the policy or contract to fit any new developments affecting the welfare of the ward. Before any application filed under this subsection is granted, the guardian shall file a report in the court that shows in detail the financial condition of the ward's estate at the time the application is filed.

(i) The court, if satisfied by the application and the evidence adduced at the hearing that it is in the interests of the ward to grant the application, shall enter an order granting the application.

(j) A right, benefit, or interest that accrues under an insurance or annuity contract that comes under the provisions of this section shall become the exclusive property of the ward when the ward's disability is terminated.

Added by Acts 1993, 73rd Leg., ch. 957, § 1, eff. Sept. 1, 1993.
Amended by Acts 2003, 78th Leg., ch. 549, § 26, eff. Sept. 1, 2003.

### § 858. Loans and Security for Loans

(a) If, at any time, the guardian of the estate has on hand money belonging to the ward in an amount that provides a return that is more than is necessary for the education, support, and maintenance of the ward and others the ward supports, if applicable, the guardian may lend the money for a reasonable rate of interest. The guardian shall take the note of the borrower for the money that is loaned, secured by a mortgage with a power of sale on unencumbered real estate located in this state worth at least twice the amount of the note, or by collateral notes secured by vendor's lien notes, as collateral, or the guardian may purchase vendor's lien notes if at least one-half has been paid in cash or its equivalent on the land for which the notes were given.

(b) A guardian of the estate is considered to have obtained a reasonable rate of interest for a loan for purposes of Subsection (a) of this section if the rate of interest is at least equal to 120 percent of the applicable short-term, midterm, or long-term interest rate under Section 7520, Internal Revenue Code of 1986, as amended, for the month during which the loan was made.

(c) Except as provided by this subsection, a guardian of the estate who loans estate money with the court's approval on security approved by the court is not personally liable if the borrower is unable to repay the money and the security fails. If the guardian committed fraud or was negligent in making or managing the loan, including in collecting on the loan, the guardian and the guardian's surety are liable for the loss sustained by the guardianship estate as a result of the fraud or negligence.

(d) Except as provided by Subsection (e) of this section, a guardian of the estate who lends estate money may not pay or transfer any money to consummate the loan until the guardian:

(1) submits to an attorney for examination all bonds, notes, mortgages, abstracts, and other documents relating to the loan; and

(2) receives a written opinion from the attorney stating that the documents under Subdivision (1) of this subsection are regular and that the title to relevant bonds, notes, or real estate is clear.

(e) A guardian of the estate may obtain a mortgagee's title insurance policy on any real estate loan in lieu of an abstract and attorney's opinion under Subsection (d) of this section.

(f) The borrower shall pay attorney's fees for any legal services required by this section.

(g) Not later than the 30th day after the date the guardian of the estate loans money from the estate, the guardian shall file with the court a written report, accompanied by an affidavit, stating fully the facts related to the loan. This subsection does not apply to a loan made in accordance with a court order.

(h) This section does not apply to an investment in a debenture, bond, or other publicly traded debt security.

Added by Acts 1993, 73rd Leg., ch. 957, § 1, eff. Sept. 1, 1993.
Amended by Acts 2003, 78th Leg., ch. 549, § 27, eff. Sept. 1, 2003.

### § 859. Repealed by Acts 2003, 78th Leg., ch. 549, § 35, eff. Sept. 1, 2003

### § 860. Guardian's Investments in Real Estate

(a) The guardian of the estate may invest estate assets in real estate if:

(1) the guardian believes that the investment is in the best interests of the ward;

(2) there are on hand sufficient additional assets to provide a return sufficient to provide for:

(A) the education, support, and maintenance of the ward and others the ward supports, if applicable; and

(B) the maintenance, insurance, and taxes on the real estate in which the guardian wishes to invest;

(3) the guardian files a written application with the court requesting a court order authorizing the guardian to make the desired investment and stating the reasons why the guardian is of the opinion that the investment would be for the benefit of the ward; and

(4) the court renders an order authorizing the investment as provided by this section.

(b) When an application is filed by the guardian under this section, the judge's attention shall be called to the application, and the judge shall make investigation as necessary to obtain all the facts concerning the investment. The judge may not render an opinion or make an order on the application until 10 days from the date of the filing of the application have expired. On the hearing of the application, if the court is satisfied that the investment benefits the ward, the court shall issue an order that authorizes the guardian to make the investment. The order shall specify the investment to be made and contain other directions the court thinks are advisable.

(c) When a contract is made for the investment of money in real estate under court order, the guardian shall report the contract in writing to the courts. The court shall inquire fully into the contract. If satisfied that the investment will benefit the estate of the ward and that the title of the real estate is valid and unencumbered, the court may approve the contract and authorize the guardian to pay over the money in performance of the contract. The guardian may not pay any money on the contract until the contract is approved by court order to that effect.

(d) When the money of the ward has been invested in real estate, the title to the real estate shall be made to the ward. The guardian shall inventory, appraise, manage, and account for the real estate as other real estate of the ward.

Added by Acts 1993, 73rd Leg., ch. 957, § 1, eff. Sept. 1, 1993.
Subsec. (a) amended by Acts 2003, 78th Leg., ch. 549, § 28, eff. Sept. 1, 2003.

### § 861. Opinion of Attorney With Respect to Loans

When the guardian of the estate of a ward lends the money of the ward, the guardian may not pay over or transfer any money in consummation of the loan until the guardian has submitted to a reputable attorney for examination all bonds, notes, mortgages, documents, abstracts, and other papers pertaining to the loan and the guardian has received a written opinion from the attorney that all papers pertaining to the loan are regular and that the title to the bonds, notes, or real estate is good. The attorney's fee shall be paid by the borrower. The guardian may obtain a

mortgagee's title insurance policy on any real estate loan instead of an abstract and attorney's opinion.

Added by Acts 1993, 73rd Leg., ch. 957, § 1, eff. Sept. 1, 1993.
Amended by Acts 1995, 74th Leg., ch. 1039, § 55, eff. Sept. 1, 1995.

### § 862. Report of Loans

Not later than the 30th day after the date money belonging to a ward's estate is lent, the guardian of the ward's estate shall report to the court in writing, verified by affidavit, stating fully the facts of the loan, unless the loan was made pursuant to a court order.

Added by Acts 1993, 73rd Leg., ch. 957, § 1, eff. Sept. 1, 1993.
Amended by Acts 1995, 74th Leg., ch. 1039, § 56, eff. Sept. 1, 1995.

### § 863. Liability of Guardian and Guardian's Surety

(a) In addition to any other remedy authorized by law, if the guardian of the estate fails to invest or lend estate assets in the manner provided by this subpart, the guardian and the guardian's surety are liable for the principal and the greater of:

(1) the highest legal rate of interest on the principal during the period the guardian failed to invest or lend the assets; or

(2) the overall return that would have been made on the principal if the principal were invested in the manner provided by this subpart.

(b) In addition to the liability under Subsection (a) of this section, the guardian and the guardian's surety are liable for attorney's fees, litigation expenses, and costs related to a proceeding brought to enforce this section.

Added by Acts 1993, 73rd Leg., ch. 957, § 1, eff. Sept. 1, 1993.
Amended by Acts 2003, 78th Leg., ch. 549, § 29, eff. Sept. 1, 2003.

### § 864. Repealed by Acts 2003, 78th Leg., ch. 549, § 35, eff. Sept. 1, 2003

SUBPART M. TAX MOTIVATED, CHARITABLE, AND OTHER GIFTS

### § 865. Power to Make Certain Gifts and Transfers

(a) On application of the guardian of the estate or any interested person and after the posting of notice, the court, after hearing, may enter an order that authorizes the guardian to apply the principal or income of the ward's estate that is not required for the support of the ward or the ward's family during the ward's lifetime toward the establishment of an estate plan for the purpose of minimizing income, estate, inheritance, or other taxes payable out of the ward's estate, or to transfer a portion of the ward's estate as necessary to qualify the ward for government benefits and only to the extent allowed by applicable state or federal laws, including rules, regarding those benefits, on a showing that the ward will probably remain incapacitated during the ward's lifetime. On the ward's behalf, the court may authorize the guardian to make gifts or transfers described by this subsection, outright or in trust, of the ward's property to or for the benefit of:

(1) an organization to which charitable contributions may be made under the Internal Revenue Code and in which it is shown the ward would reasonably have an interest;

(2) the ward's spouse, descendant, or other person related to the ward by blood or marriage who are identifiable at the time of the order;

(3) a devisee under the ward's last validly executed will, trust, or other beneficial instrument if the instrument exists; and

(4) a person serving as guardian of the ward if the person is eligible under either Subdivision (2) or (3) of this subsection.

(b) The person making an application to the court under this section shall outline the proposed estate or other transfer plan and set forth all the benefits that are to be derived from the plan. The application must indicate that the planned disposition is consistent with the ward's intentions if the ward's intentions can be ascertained. If the ward's intentions cannot be ascertained, the ward will be presumed to favor reduction in the incidence of the various forms of taxation, the qualification for government benefits, and the partial distribution of the ward's estate as provided by this section.

(c) The court may appoint a guardian ad litem for the ward or any interested party at any stage of the proceedings if it is deemed advisable for the protection of the ward or the interested party.

(d) A subsequent modification of an approved plan may be made by similar application to the court.

(e) A person who makes an application to the court under this section shall mail notice of the application by certified mail to:

(1) all devisees under a will, trust, or other beneficial instrument relating to the ward's estate;

(2) the ward's spouse;

(3) the ward's dependents; and

(4) any other person as directed by the court.

(f) In an order entered under Subsection (a) of this section, the court may authorize the guardian to make gifts as provided by Subsection (a) of this section on an annual or other periodic basis without subsequent application to or order of the court if the court finds it to be in the best interest of the ward and the ward's estate. The court, on the court's own motion or on the motion of a person interested in the welfare of the ward, may modify or set aside an order entered under this subsection if the court finds that the ward's financial condition has changed in such a manner that authorizing the guardian to make gifts of the estate on a continuing basis is no longer in the best interest of the ward and the ward's estate.

Added by Acts 1993, 73rd Leg., ch. 957, § 1, eff. Sept. 1, 1993. Amended by Acts 1997, 75th Leg., ch. 77, § 9, eff. Sept. 1, 1997; Subsec. (f) added by Acts 2005, 79th Leg., ch. 256, § 1, eff. Sept. 1, 2005; Section heading and subsecs. (a) and (b) amended by Acts 2011, 82nd Leg., ch. 1085 (S.B. 1196), § 28, 29, eff. Sept. 1, 2011.

### § 865A. Inspection of Certain Instrument for Estate Planning Purposes

(a) On the filing of an application under Section 865 of this code, the guardian of the ward's estate may apply to the court for an order to seek an in camera inspection of a true copy of a will, codicil, trust, or other estate planning instrument of the ward as a means of obtaining access to the instrument for purposes of establishing an estate plan under Section 865 of this code.

(b) An application filed under this section must:

(1) be sworn to by the guardian;

(2) list all of the instruments requested for inspection; and

(3) state one or more reasons supporting the necessity to inspect each requested instrument for the purpose described by Subsection (a) of this section.

(c) A person who files an application under this section shall send a copy of the application to:

(1) each person who has custody of an instrument listed in the application;

(2) the ward's spouse;

(3) the ward's dependents;

(4) all devisees under a will, trust, or other beneficial instrument relating to the ward's estate; and

(5) any other person as directed by the court.

(d) Notice required by Subsection (c) of this section must be delivered by certified mail to a person described by Subsection (c)(2), (3), (4), or (5) of this section and by registered or certified mail to a person described by Subsection (c)(1) of this section. After the 10th day after the date on which the applicant complies with the notice requirement, the applicant may request that a hearing be held on the application. Notice of the date, time, and place of the hearing must be given by the applicant to each person described by Subsection (c)(1) of this section when the court sets a date for a hearing on the application.

(e) After the conclusion of a hearing on the application and on a finding that there is good cause for an in camera inspection of a requested instrument, the court shall direct the person that has custody of the requested will, codicil, trust, or other estate planning instrument to deliver a true copy of the instrument to the court for in camera inspection only. After conducting an in camera review of the instrument, the court, if good cause exists, shall release all or part of the instrument to the applicant only for the purpose described by Subsection (a) of this section.

(f) The court may appoint a guardian ad litem for the ward or an interested party at any stage of the proceedings if it is considered advisable for the protection of the ward or the interested party.

(g) An attorney does not violate the attorney-client privilege solely by complying with a court order to release an instrument subject to this section. Notwithstanding Section 22.004, Government Code, the supreme court may not amend or adopt rules in conflict with this subsection.

Added by Acts 2001, 77th Leg., ch. 217, § 16, eff. Sept. 1, 2001.

## § 866. Contributions

(a) The guardian of the estate may at any time file the guardian's sworn application in writing with the county clerk requesting an order from the court in which the guardianship is pending authorizing the guardian to contribute from the income of the ward's estate a specific amount of money as stated in the application, to one or more:

(1) designated corporations, trusts, or community chests, funds, or foundations, organized and operated exclusively for religious, charitable, scientific, literary, or educational purposes; or

(2) designated nonprofit federal, state, county, or municipal projects operated exclusively for public health or welfare.

(b) When an application is filed under this section, the county clerk shall immediately call the filing of the application to the attention of the judge of the court. The judge, by written order filed with the clerk, shall designate a day to hear the application. The application shall remain on file at least 10 days before the hearing is held. The judge may postpone or continue the hearing from time to time until the judge is satisfied concerning the application.

(c) On the conclusion of a hearing under this section, the court may enter an order authorizing the guardian to make a contribution from the income of the ward's estate to a particular donee designated in the application and order if the court is satisfied and finds from the evidence that:

(1) the amount of the proposed contribution stated in the application will probably not exceed 20 percent of the net income of the ward's estate for the current calendar year;

(2) the net income of the ward's estate for the current calendar year exceeds, or probably will exceed, $25,000;

(3) the full amount of the contribution, if made, will probably be deductible from the ward's gross income in determining the net income of the ward under applicable federal income tax laws and rules;

(4) the condition of the ward's estate justifies a contribution in the proposed amount; and

(5) the proposed contribution is reasonable in amount and is for a worthy cause.

Added by Acts 1993, 73rd Leg., ch. 957, § 1, eff. Sept. 1, 1993.

## SUBPART N. MANAGEMENT TRUSTS

## § 867. Creation of Management Trust

(a) In this section, "financial institution" means a financial institution, as defined by Section 201.101, Finance Code, that has trust powers and exists and does business under the laws of this or another state or the United States.

(a–1) The following persons may apply for the creation of a trust under this section:

(1) the guardian of the estate of a ward;

(2) the guardian of the person of a ward;

(3) the guardian of both the person of and estate of a ward;

(4) an attorney ad litem or guardian ad litem appointed to represent a ward or the ward's interests;

(5) a person interested in the welfare of an alleged incapacitated person who does not have a guardian;

(6) an attorney ad litem or guardian ad litem appointed to represent an alleged incapacitated person who does not have a guardian; or

(7) a person who has only a physical disability.

(b) On application by an appropriate person as provided by Subsection (a–1) of this section and subject to Subsection (b–1) of this section, if applicable, the court with jurisdiction over the proceedings may enter an order that creates a trust for the management of the funds of the person with respect to whom the application is filed if the court finds that the creation of the trust is in the person's best interests.

(b–1) On application by an appropriate person as provided by Subsection (a–1) of this section and regardless of whether an application for guardianship has been filed on the alleged incapacitated person's behalf, a proper court exercising probate jurisdiction may enter an order that creates a trust for the management of the estate of an alleged incapacitated person who does not have a guardian if the court, after a hearing, finds that:

(1) the person is an incapacitated person; and

(2) the creation of the trust is in the incapacitated person's best interests.

(b–2) If a proceeding for the appointment of a guardian for an alleged incapacitated person is pending, an application for the creation of a trust for the alleged incapacitated person under Subsection (b–1) of this section must be filed in the same court in which the guardianship proceeding is pending.

(b–3) The court shall conduct a hearing to determine incapacity under Subsection (b–1) of this section using the same procedures and evidentiary standards as required in a hearing for the appointment of a guardian for a proposed ward. The court shall appoint an attorney ad litem and, if necessary, may appoint a guardian ad litem, to represent the interests of the alleged incapacitated person in the proceeding.

(b–4) If, after a hearing, the court finds that a person for whom an application is filed under Subsection (b–1) of this section is an incapacitated person but that it is not in the incapacitated person's best interests to have the court create a management trust for the person's estate, the court may appoint a guardian of the person or estate, or both, for the incapacitated person without the necessity of instituting a separate proceeding for that purpose.

(b–5) Except as provided by Subsections (c) and (d) of this section, the court shall appoint a financial institution to serve as trustee of a trust created under this section.

(c) Subject to Subsection (d) of this section, if the court finds that it is in the best interests of the person for whom a trust is created under this section, the court may appoint a person or entity that meets the requirements of Subsection (e) of this section to serve as trustee of the trust instead of appointing a financial institution to serve in that capacity.

(d) If the value of the trust's principal is more than $150,000, the court may appoint a person or entity other than a financial institution in accordance with Subsection (c) of this section to serve as trustee of the trust only if the court, in addition to the finding required by that subsection, finds that the applicant for the creation of the trust, after the exercise of due diligence, has been unable to find a financial institution in the geographic area willing to serve as trustee.

(e) The following are eligible for appointment as trustee under Subsection (c) or (d) of this section:

(1) an individual, including an individual who is certified as a private professional guardian;

(2) a nonprofit corporation qualified to serve as a guardian; and

(3) a guardianship program.

(f) If a trust is created for a person, the order shall direct any person or entity holding property belonging to the person for whom the trust is created or to which that person is entitled to deliver all or part of the property to a person or corporate fiduciary appointed by the court as trustee of the trust. The order shall include terms, conditions, and limitations placed on the trust. The court may maintain the trust under the same cause number as the guardianship proceeding, if the person for whom the trust is created is a ward or proposed ward.

Added by Acts 1993, 73rd Leg., ch. 957, § 1, eff. Sept. 1, 1993. Amended by Acts 1995, 74th Leg., ch. 1039, § 57, eff. Sept. 1, 1995; Acts 1997, 75th Leg., ch. 1375, § 1, eff. Sept. 1, 1997; Acts 2001, 77th Leg., ch. 994, § 1, eff. Sept. 1, 2001; Subsecs. (a-1) and (b-1) to (b-5) added by Acts 2005, 79th Leg., ch. 1238, § 1, eff. Sept. 1, 2005; Subsecs. (b), (c), (d), and (f) amended by Acts 2005, 79th Leg., ch. 1238, § 1, eff. Sept. 1, 2005; Subsec. (b-1) amended by Acts 2007, 80th Leg., ch. 281, § 1, eff. Sept. 1, 2007; Acts 2009, 81st Leg., ch. 930, § 8, eff. Sept. 1, 2009; Subsecs. (a-1), (b), (c) and (f) amended by Acts 2011, 82nd Leg., ch. 1085 (S.B. 1196), § 30, eff. Sept. 1, 2011.

## § 867A.   Venue

If a proceeding for the appointment of a guardian for the alleged incapacitated person is not pending on the date the application is filed, venue for a proceeding to create a trust for an alleged incapacitated person under Section 867(b-1) of this code must be determined in the same manner as venue for a proceeding for the appointment of a guardian is determined under Section 610 of this code.

Added by Acts 2005, 79th Leg., ch. 1238, § 2, eff. Sept. 1, 2005.

## § 868.   Terms of Management Trust

(a) Except as provided by Subsection (d) of this section, a trust created under Section 867 of this code must provide that:

(1) the ward, incapacitated person, or person who has only a physical disability is the sole beneficiary of the trust;

(2) the trustee may disburse an amount of the trust's principal or income as the trustee determines is necessary to expend for the health, education, support, or maintenance of the person for whom the trust is created;

(3) the income of the trust that the trustee does not disburse under Subdivision (2) of this subsection must be added to the principal of the trust;

(4) if the trustee is a corporate fiduciary, the trustee serves without giving a bond; and

(5) the trustee, subject to the court's approval, is entitled to receive reasonable compensation for services that the trustee provided to the person for whom the trust is created as the person's trustee that is:

(A) to be paid from the trust's income, principal, or both; and

(B) determined, paid, reduced, and eliminated in the same manner as compensation of a guardian under Section 665 of this code.

(b) The trust may provide that a trustee make a distribution, payment, use, or application of trust funds for the health, education, support, or maintenance of the person for whom the trust is created or of another person whom the person for whom the trust is created is legally obligated to support, as necessary and without the intervention of a guardian or other representative of the ward or of a representative of the incapacitated person or person who has only a physical disability, to:

(1) the ward's guardian;

(2) a person who has physical custody of the person for whom the trust is created or another person whom the person for whom the trust is created is legally obligated to support; or

(3) a person providing a good or service to the person for whom the trust is created or another person whom the person for whom the trust is created is legally obligated to support.

(c) A provision in a trust created under Section 867 that relieves a trustee from a duty, responsibility, or liability imposed by this subpart or Subtitle B, Title 9, Property Code, is enforceable only if:

(1) the provision is limited to specific facts and circumstances unique to the property of that trust and is not applicable generally to the trust; and

(2) the court creating or modifying the trust makes a specific finding that there is clear and convincing evidence that the inclusion of the provision is in the best interests of the beneficiary of the trust.

(d) When creating or modifying a trust, the court may omit or modify terms required by Subsection (a)(1) or (2) of this section only if the court determines that the omission or modification:

(1) is necessary and appropriate for the person for whom the trust is created to be eligible to receive public benefits or assistance under a state or federal program that is not otherwise available to the person; and

(2) is in the best interests of the person for whom the trust is created.

(e) The court may include additional provisions in a trust created or modified under this section if the court determines an addition does not conflict with Subsection (a) and, if appropriate, Subsection (d) of this section.

(f) If the trustee determines that it is in the best interest of the ward or incapacitated person, the trustee may invest funds of the trust in the Texas tomorrow fund established by Subchapter F, Chapter 54, Education Code.[1]

Added by Acts 1993, 73rd Leg., ch. 957, § 1, eff. Sept. 1, 1993. Amended by Acts 1995, 74th Leg., ch. 1039, §§ 58, 59, eff. Sept. 1, 1995; Acts 1997, 75th Leg., ch. 1375, §§ 2, 6, eff. Sept. 1, 1997; Acts 1999, 76th Leg., ch. 94, § 2, eff. May 17, 1999; Acts 2001, 77th Leg., ch. 994, § 2, eff. Sept. 1, 2001; Subsec. (c) added by Acts 2003, 78th Leg., ch. 1154, § 4, eff. Sept. 1, 2003; Subsecs. (a), (b), (d), and (f) amended by Acts 2005, 79th Leg., ch. 1238, § 3, eff. Sept. 1, 2005; Acts 2009, 81st Leg., ch. 930, § 9, eff. Sept. 1, 2009; Subsecs. (a), (b) and (d) amended by Acts 2011, 82nd Leg., ch. 1085 (S.B. 1196), § 31, eff. Sept. 1, 2011.

[1] V.T.C.A., Education Code § 54.6001 et seq.

### § 868A. Discharge of Guardian of Estate and Continuation of Trust

On or at any time after the creation of a trust under this subpart, the court may discharge the guardian of the ward's estate if the court determines that the discharge is in the ward's best interests.

Added by Acts 1997, 75th Leg., ch. 1375, § 3, eff. Sept. 1, 1997. Amended by Acts 2003, 78th Leg., ch. 549, § 30, eff. Sept. 1, 2003.

### § 868B. Bond Requirement for Certain Trustees

The court shall require a person, other than a corporate fiduciary, serving as trustee to file with the county clerk a bond in an amount equal to the value of the trust's principal and projected annual income and with the conditions the court determines are necessary.

Added by Acts 2001, 77th Leg., ch. 994, § 3, eff. Sept. 1, 2001.

### § 868C. Transfer of Management Trust Property to Pooled Trust

(a) If the court determines that it is in the best interests of the person for whom a trust is created under Section 867 of this code, the court may order the transfer of all property in the trust to a subaccount of a pooled trust established in accordance with Subpart I, Part 5[1], of this chapter. The transfer of property from the management trust to the subaccount of the pooled trust shall be treated as a continuation of the management trust and may not be treated as the establishment of a new trust for purposes of 42 U.S.C. Section 1396p(d)(4)(A) or (C) or otherwise for purposes of the management trust beneficiary's eligibility for medical assistance under Chapter 32, Human Resources Code.

(b) The court may not allow termination of the management trust created under Section 867 of this code from which property is transferred under this section until all of the property in the management trust has been transferred to the subaccount of the pooled trust.

Added by Acts 2009, 81st Leg., ch. 930, § 10, eff. Sept. 1, 2009. Subsec. (a) amended by Acts 2011, 82nd Leg., ch. 1085 (S.B. 1196), § 32, eff. Sept. 1, 2011.

[1] V.A.T.S. Probate Code § 910 et seq.

### § 869. Trust Amendment, Modification, or Revocation

(a) The court may amend, modify, or revoke the trust at any time before the date of the trust's termination.

(b) The following may not revoke the trust:

(1) the ward for whom the trust is created or the guardian of the ward's estate;

(2) the incapacitated person for whom the trust is created; or

(3) the person who has only a physical disability for whom the trust is created.

Added by Acts 1993, 73rd Leg., ch. 957, § 1, eff. Sept. 1, 1993. Subsec. (b) amended by Acts 2005, 79th Leg., ch. 1238, § 4, eff. Sept. 1, 2005; Subsec. (b) amended by Acts 2011, 82nd Leg., ch. 1085 (S.B. 1196), § 33, eff. Sept. 1, 2011.

### § 869A. Successor Trustee

The court may appoint a successor trustee if the trustee resigns, becomes ineligible, or is removed.

Added by Acts 1995, 74th Leg., ch. 1039, § 60, eff. Sept. 1, 1995. Amended by Acts 2001, 77th Leg., ch. 994, § 4, eff. Sept. 1, 2001.

### § 869B. Applicability of Texas Trust Code

(a) A trust created under Section 867 of this code is subject to Subtitle B, Title 9, Property Code.[1]

(b) To the extent of a conflict between Subtitle B, Title 9, Property Code, and a provision of this subpart or of the trust, the provision of the subpart or trust controls.

Added by Acts 1997, 75th Leg., ch. 1375, § 3, eff. Sept. 1, 1997.

[1] V.T.C.A., Property Code § 111.001 et seq.

### § 869C. Jurisdiction Over Trust Matters

A court that creates a trust under Section 867 of this code has the same jurisdiction to hear matters relating to the trust as the court has with respect to guardianship and other matters covered by this chapter.

Added by Acts 1997, 75th Leg., ch. 1375, § 3, eff. Sept. 1, 1997. Amended by Acts 2005, 79th Leg., ch. 1238, § 5, eff. Sept. 1, 2005.

### § 870. Termination of Trust

(a) If the person for whom a trust is created under Section 867 of this code is a minor, the trust terminates:

(1) on the person's death or the person's 18th birthday, whichever is earlier; or

(2) on the date provided by court order, which may not be later than the person's 25th birthday.

(b) If the person for whom a trust is created under Section 867 of this code is not a minor, the trust terminates:

(1) according to the terms of the trust;

(2) on the date the court determines that continuing the trust is no longer in the person's best interests, subject to Section 868C(b) of this code; or

(3) on the person's death.

Added by Acts 1993, 73rd Leg., ch. 957, § 1, eff. Sept. 1, 1993. Amended by Acts 1995, 74th Leg., ch. 1039, § 61, eff. Sept. 1, 1995; Acts 1997, 75th Leg., ch. 1375, § 4, eff. Sept. 1, 1997; Acts 2005, 79th Leg., ch. 1238, § 6, eff. Sept. 1, 2005; Acts 2009, 81st Leg., ch. 930, § 11, eff. Sept. 1, 2009; Acts 2011, 82nd Leg., ch. 1085 (S.B. 1196), § 34, eff. Sept. 1, 2011.

### § 870A. Initial Accounting by Certain Trustees Required

(a) This section applies only to a trustee of a trust created under Section 867 of this code for a person for whom a guardianship proceeding is pending on the date the trust is created.

(b) Not later than the 30th day after the date a trustee to which this section applies receives property into the trust, the trustee shall file with the court in which the guardianship proceeding is pending a report describing all property held in the trust on the date of the report and specifying the value of the property on that date.

Added by Acts 2011, 82nd Leg., ch. 1085 (S.B. 1196), § 35, eff. Sept. 1, 2011.

### § 871. Annual Accounting

(a) Except as provided by Subsection (d) of this section, the trustee shall prepare and file with the court an annual accounting of transactions in the trust in the same manner and form that is required of a guardian under this chapter.

(b) If a trust has been created under this section for a ward, the trustee shall provide a copy of the annual account to the guardian of the ward's estate or person.

(c) The annual account is subject to court review and approval in the same manner that is required of an annual account prepared by a guardian under this chapter.

(d) The court may not require a trustee of a trust created for a person who has only a physical disability to prepare and file with the court the annual accounting as described by Subsection (a) of this section.

Added by Acts 1993, 73rd Leg., ch. 957, § 1, eff. Sept. 1, 1993. Subsec. (b) amended by Acts 2005, 79th Leg., ch. 1238, § 7, eff. Sept. 1, 2005; Subsec. (a) amended and subsec. (d) added by Acts 2011, 82nd Leg., ch. 1085 (S.B. 1196), § 36, eff. Sept. 1, 2011.

### § 872. Liability

The guardian of the person or of the estate of the ward or the surety on the bond of the guardian is not liable for an act or omission of the trustee.

Added by Acts 1993, 73rd Leg., ch. 957, § 1, eff. Sept. 1, 1993. Amended by Acts 1995, 74th Leg., ch. 1039, § 62, eff. Sept. 1, 1995.

### § 873. Distribution of Trust Property

(a) Unless otherwise provided by the court and except as provided by Subsection (b) of this section, the trustee shall:

(1) prepare a final account in the same form and manner that is required of a guardian under Section 749 of this code; and

(2) on court approval, distribute the principal or any undistributed income of the trust:

(A) to the ward or incapacitated person when the trust terminates on its own terms;

(B) to the successor trustee on appointment of a successor trustee; or

(C) to the representative of the deceased ward's or incapacitated person's estate on the ward's or incapacitated person's death.

(b) The court may not require a trustee of a trust created for a person who has only a physical disability to prepare and file with the court a final account as described by Subsection (a)(1) of this section. The trustee shall distribute the principal and any undistributed income of the trust in the manner provided by Subsection (a)(2) of this section for a trust the beneficiary of which is a ward or incapacitated person.

Added by Acts 1993, 73rd Leg., ch. 957, § 1, eff. Sept. 1, 1993. Amended by Acts 1995, 74th Leg., ch. 1039, § 63, eff. Sept. 1, 1995; Acts 2005, 79th Leg., ch. 1238, § 8, eff. Sept. 1, 2005; Acts 2011, 82nd Leg., ch. 1085 (S.B. 1196), § 37, eff. Sept. 1, 2011.

PART 5. SPECIAL PROCEEDINGS AND ORDERS

SUBPART A. TEMPORARY GUARDIANSHIPS

### § 874. Presumption of Incapacitation

The person for whom a temporary guardian is appointed under Section 875 of this code may not be presumed to be incapacitated.

Added by Acts 2005, 79th Leg., ch. 200, § 10, eff. Sept. 1, 2005.

### § 875. Temporary Guardian—Procedure

(a) If a court is presented with substantial evidence that a person may be a minor or other incapacitated person, and the court has probable cause to believe that the person or person's estate, or both, requires the immediate appointment of a guardian, the court shall appoint a temporary guardian with limited powers as the circumstances of the case require.

(b) The person retains all rights and powers that are not specifically granted to the person's temporary guardian by court order.

(c) A sworn, written application for the appointment of a temporary guardian shall be filed before the court appoints a temporary guardian. The application must state:

(1) the name and address of the person who is the subject of the guardianship proceeding;

(2) the danger to the person or property alleged to be imminent;

(3) the type of appointment and the particular protection and assistance being requested;

(4) the facts and reasons supporting the allegations and requests;

(5) the name, address, and qualification of the proposed temporary guardian;

(6) the name, address, and interest of the applicant; and

(7) if applicable, that the proposed temporary guardian is a private professional guardian who is certified under Subchapter C, Chapter 111, Government Code, and has complied with the requirements of Section 697 of this code.

(d) On the filing of an application for temporary guardianship, the court shall appoint an attorney to represent the proposed ward in all guardianship proceedings in which independent counsel has not been retained by or on behalf of the proposed ward.

(e) On the filing of an application for temporary guardianship, the clerk shall issue notice that shall be served on the respondent, the respondent's appointed attorney, and the proposed temporary guardian named in the application, if that person is not the applicant. The notice must describe the rights of the parties and the date, time, place, purpose, and possible consequences of a hearing on the application. A copy of the application must be attached to the notice.

(f)(1) A hearing shall be held not later than the 10th day after the date of the filing of the application for temporary guardianship unless the hearing date is postponed as provided by Subdivision (2) of this subsection. At a hearing under this section, the respondent has the right to:

(A) receive prior notice;

(B) have representation by counsel;

(C) be present;

(D) present evidence and confront and cross-examine witnesses; and

(E) a closed hearing if requested by the respondent or the respondent's attorney.

(2) The respondent or the respondent's attorney may consent to postpone the hearing on the application for temporary guardianship for a period not to exceed 30 days after the date of the filing of the application.

(3) Every application for temporary guardianship takes precedence over all matters except older matters of the same character.

(4) Immediately after an application for temporary guardianship is filed, the court shall issue an order that sets a certain date for hearing on the application for temporary guardianship.

(5) On one day's notice to the party who filed the application for temporary guardianship, the respondent or the respondent's attorney may appear and move for the dismissal of the application for temporary guardianship. If a motion is made for dismissal of the application for temporary guardianship, the court shall hear and determine the motion as expeditiously as the ends of justice require.

(6) If the applicant is not the proposed temporary guardian, a temporary guardianship may not be granted before a hearing on the application required by Subdivision (1) of this subsection unless the proposed temporary guardian appears in court.

(g) If at the conclusion of the hearing required by Subsection (f)(1) of this section the court determines that the applicant has established that there is substantial evidence that the person is a minor or other incapacitated person, that there is imminent danger that the physical health or safety of the respondent will be seriously impaired, or that the respondent's estate will be seriously damaged or dissipated unless immediate action is taken, the court shall appoint a temporary guardian by written order. The court shall assign to the temporary guardian only those powers and duties that are necessary to protect the respondent against the imminent danger shown. The court shall set bond according to Subpart B, Part 3, of this chapter. The reasons for the temporary guardianship and the powers and duties of the temporary guardian must be described in the order of appointment.

(h) Except as provided by Subsection (k) of this section, a temporary guardianship may not remain in effect for more than 60 days.

(i) If the court appoints a temporary guardian after the hearing required by Subsection (f)(1) of this section, all court costs, including attorney's fees, may be assessed as provided in Section 665A, 665B, or 669 of this code.

(j) The court may not customarily or ordinarily appoint the Department of Aging and Disability Services as a temporary guardian under this section. The appointment of the department as a temporary guardian under this section should be made only as a last resort.

(k) If an application for a temporary guardianship, for the conversion of a temporary guardianship to a permanent guardianship, or for a permanent guardianship is challenged or contested, the court, on the court's own motion or on the motion of any interested party, may appoint a temporary guardian or grant a temporary restraining order under Rule 680, Texas Rules of Civil Procedure, or both, without issuing additional citation if the court finds that the appointment or the issuance of the order is necessary to protect the proposed ward or the proposed ward's estate.

(*l*) A temporary guardian appointed under Subsection (k) of this section must qualify in the same form and manner required of a guardian under this code. The term of the temporary guardian expires at the conclusion of the hearing challenging or contesting the application or on the date a permanent guardian the court appoints for the proposed ward qualifies to serve as the ward's guardian.

Added by Acts 1993, 73rd Leg., ch. 957, § 1, eff. Sept. 1, 1993. Amended by Acts 1995, 74th Leg., ch. 76, § 8.074, eff. Sept. 1, 1995; Acts 1995, 74th Leg., ch. 1039, § 64, eff. Sept. 1, 1995; Acts 1999, 76th Leg., ch. 997, § 2, eff. Sept. 1, 1999; Acts 2001, 77th Leg., ch. 217, § 17, eff. Sept. 1, 2001; Subsecs. (b) to (g), (k) amended by Acts 2003, 78th Leg., ch. 277, § 1, eff. Sept. 1, 2003; Subsec. (*l*) added by Acts 2003, 78th Leg., ch. 277, § 1, eff. Sept. 1, 2003; Subsecs. (c), (j) amended by Acts 2005, 79th Leg., ch. 268, § 3.18, eff. Sept. 1, 2005; Acts 2009, 81st Leg., ch. 930, § 12, eff. Sept. 1, 2009.

### § 876. Authority of Temporary Guardian

When the temporary guardian files the oath and bond required under this chapter, the court order appointing the temporary guardian takes effect without the necessity for issuance of letters of guardianship. The clerk shall note compliance with oath and bond requirements by the appointed guardian on a certificate attached to the order. The order shall be evidence of the temporary guardian's authority to act within the scope of the powers and duties set forth in the order. The clerk may not issue certified copies of the order until the oath and bond requirements are satisfied.

Added by Acts 1993, 73rd Leg., ch. 957, § 1, eff. Sept. 1, 1993.

### § 877. Powers of Temporary Guardian

All the provisions of this chapter relating to the guardianship of persons and estates of incapacitated persons apply to a temporary guardianship of the persons and estates of incapacitated persons, insofar as the same may be made applicable.

Added by Acts 1993, 73rd Leg., ch. 957, § 1, eff. Sept. 1, 1993.

### § 878. Accounting

At the expiration of a temporary appointment, the appointee shall file with the clerk of the court a sworn list of all property of the estate that has come into the hands of the appointee, a return of all sales made by the appointee, and a full exhibit and account of all of the appointee's acts as temporary appointee.

Added by Acts 1993, 73rd Leg., ch. 957, § 1, eff. Sept. 1, 1993.

### § 879. Closing Temporary Guardianship

The court shall act on the list, return, exhibit, and account filed under Section 878 of this code. Whenever temporary letters expire or cease to be effective for any reason, the court shall immediately enter an order requiring the temporary appointee to deliver the estate remaining in the temporary appointee's possession to the person who is legally entitled to the possession of the estate. The temporary appointee shall be discharged and the sureties on the bond of the temporary appointee shall be released as to future liability on proof that the appointee delivered the property as required by this section.

Added by Acts 1993, 73rd Leg., ch. 957, § 1, eff. Sept. 1, 1993.

### SUBPART B. GUARDIANSHIPS FOR NONRESIDENTS

### § 881. Nonresident Guardian

(a) A nonresident of this state may be appointed and qualified as guardian or coguardian of a nonresident ward's estate located in this state in the same manner provided by this code for the appointment and qualification of a resident as guardian of the estate of an incapacitated person if:

(1) a court of competent jurisdiction in the geographical jurisdiction in which the nonresident resides appointed the nonresident guardian;

(2) the nonresident is qualified as guardian or as a fiduciary legal representative by whatever name known in the foreign jurisdiction of the property or estate of the ward located in the jurisdiction of the foreign court; and

(3) with the written application for appointment in the county court of any county in this state in which all or part of the ward's estate is located, the nonresident files a complete transcript of the proceedings from the records of the court in which the nonresident applicant was appointed, showing the applicant's appointment and qualification as the guardian or fiduciary legal representative of the ward's property or estate.

(b) The transcript required by Subsection (a) of this section must be certified to and attested by the clerk of the foreign court or the officer of the court charged by law with custody of the court records, under the court seal, if any. The certificate of the judge, chief justice, or presiding magistrate, as applicable, of the foreign court must be attached to the transcript, certifying that the attestation of the transcript by the clerk or legal custodian of the court records is in correct form.

(c) If the nonresident applicant meets the requirements of this section, without the necessity of any notice or citation, the court shall enter an order appointing the nonresident. After the nonresident applicant qualifies in the manner required of resident guardians and files with the court a power of attorney appointing a resident agent to accept service of process in all actions or proceedings with respect to the estate, the clerk shall issue the letters of guardianship to the nonresident guardian.

(d) After qualification, the nonresident guardian shall file an inventory and appraisement of the estate of the ward in this state subject to the jurisdiction of the court, as in ordinary cases, and is subject to all applicable provisions of this code with respect to the handling and settlement of estates by resident guardians.

(e) A resident guardian who has any of the estate of a ward may be ordered by the court to deliver the estate to a duly qualified and acting guardian of the ward.

Added by Acts 1993, 73rd Leg., ch. 957, § 1, eff. Sept. 1, 1993; Amended by Acts 1995, 74th Leg., ch. 1039, § 65, eff. Sept. 1, 1995.

### § 881A. Nonresident Guardian's Removal of Ward's Property From State

A nonresident guardian, regardless of whether the nonresident guardian is qualified under this code, may remove personal property of the ward out of the state if:

(1) the removal does not conflict with the tenure of the property or the terms and limitations of the guardianship under which the property is held; and

(2) all debts known to exist against the estate in this state are paid or secured by bond payable to and approved by the judge of the court in which guardianship proceedings are pending in this state.

Added by Acts 1995, 74th Leg., ch. 1039, § 66, eff. Sept. 1, 1995.

### § 882. Nonresident as Ward

Guardianship of the estate of a nonresident incapacitated person who owns property in this state may be granted, if necessary, in the same manner as for the property of a resident of this state. A court in the county in which the principal estate of the ward is located has jurisdiction to appoint a guardian. The court shall take all actions and make all necessary orders with respect to the estate of the ward for the maintenance, support, care, or education of the ward, out of the proceeds of the ward's estate, in the same manner as if the ward were a resident of this state and was sent abroad by the court for education or treatment. If a qualified nonresident guardian of the estate later qualifies in

this state under Section 881 of this code, the court shall close the resident guardianship.

Added by Acts 1993, 73rd Leg., ch. 957, § 1, eff. Sept. 1, 1993.

### SUBPART C.  INCAPACITATED SPOUSE AND COMMUNITY PROPERTY

### § 883.  Incapacitated Spouse

(a) Except as provided by Subsection (c) of this section, when a husband or wife is judicially declared to be incapacitated:

(1) the other spouse, in the capacity of surviving partner of the marital partnership, acquires full power to manage, control, and dispose of the entire community estate as community administrator, including the part of the community estate that the incapacitated spouse legally has the power to manage in the absence of the incapacity, without an administration; and

(2) if the incapacitated spouse owns separate property, the court shall appoint the other spouse or another person or entity, in the order of precedence established under Section 677 of this code, as guardian of the estate to administer only the separate property of the incapacitated spouse.

(b) The spouse who is not incapacitated is presumed to be suitable and qualified to serve as community administrator. The qualification of a guardian of the estate of the separate property of an incapacitated spouse as required under Subsection (a) of this section does not deprive the competent spouse of the right to manage, control, and dispose of the entire community estate as provided in this chapter.

(c) If a spouse who is not incapacitated is removed as community administrator or if the court finds that the spouse who is not incapacitated would be disqualified to serve as guardian under Section 681 of this code or is not suitable to serve as community administrator for any other reason, the court:

(1) shall appoint a guardian of the estate for the incapacitated spouse if the court:

(A) has not appointed a guardian of the estate under Subsection (a)(2) of this section; or

(B) has appointed the spouse who is not incapacitated as guardian of the estate under Subsection (a)(2) of this section;

(2) after taking into consideration the financial circumstances of the spouses and any other relevant factors, may order the spouse who is not incapacitated to deliver to the guardian of the estate of the incapacitated spouse a portion, not to exceed one-half, of the community property that is subject to the spouses' joint management, control, and disposition under Section 3.102, Family Code; and

(3) shall authorize the guardian of the estate of the incapacitated spouse to administer:

(A) any separate property of the incapacitated spouse;

**Text of Texas Probate Code effective until January 1, 2014**

(B) any community property that is subject to the incapacitated spouse's sole management, control, and disposition under Section 3.102, Family Code;

(C) any community property delivered to the guardian of the estate under Subdivision (2) of this subsection; and

(D) any income earned on property described in this subsection.

(d) On a person's removal as community administrator or on qualification of a guardian of the estate of the person's incapacitated spouse under Subsection (c) of this section, as appropriate, a spouse who is not incapacitated shall continue to administer:

(1) the person's own separate property;

(2) any community property that is subject to the person's sole management, control, and disposition under Section 3.102, Family Code;

(3) any community property subject to the spouses' joint management, control, and disposition under Section 3.102, Family Code, unless the person is required to deliver a portion of that community property to the guardian of the estate of the person's incapacitated spouse under Subsection (c)(2) of this section, in which event, the person shall continue to administer only the portion of the community property remaining after delivery; and

(4) any income earned on property described in this subsection the person is authorized to administer.

(e) The duties and obligations between spouses, including the duty to support the other spouse, and the rights of any creditor of either spouse are not affected by the manner in which community property is administered under this section.

(f) This section does not partition community property between an incapacitated spouse and a spouse who is not incapacitated.

(g) If the court renders an order directing the guardian of the estate of the incapacitated spouse to administer certain community property as provided by Subsection (c) of this section, the community property administered by the guardian is considered the incapacitated spouse's community property, subject to the incapacitated spouse's sole management, control, and disposition under Section 3.102, Family Code. If the court renders an order directing the spouse who is not incapacitated to administer certain community property as provided by Subsection (d) of this section, the community property administered by the spouse who is not incapacitated is considered that spouse's community property, subject to that spouse's sole management, control, and disposition under Section 3.102, Family Code.

(h) An order described by Subsection (g) of this section does not affect the enforceability of a creditor's claim existing on the date the court renders the order.

Added by Acts 1993, 73rd Leg., ch. 957, § 1, eff. Sept. 1, 1993. Amended by Acts 2001, 77th Leg., ch. 217, § 18, eff. Sept. 1, 2001. Subsecs. (f) to (h) added by Acts 2003, 78th Leg., ch. 549, § 31, eff. Sept. 1, 2003.

## § 883A.   Recovery of Capacity

The special powers of management, control, and disposition vested in the community administrator by this chapter shall terminate when the decree of a court of competent jurisdiction finds that the mental capacity of the incapacitated spouse has been recovered.

Added by Acts 1995, 74th Leg., ch. 1039, § 67, eff. Sept. 1, 1995. Amended by Acts 2001, 77th Leg., ch. 217, § 19, eff. Sept. 1, 2001.

## § 883B.   Accounting, Inventory, and Appraisement by Community Administrator

(a) On its own motion or on the motion of an interested person for good cause shown, the court may order a community administrator to file a verified, full, and detailed inventory and appraisement of:

(1) any community property that is subject to the incapacitated spouse's sole management, control, and disposition under Section 3.102, Family Code;

(2) any community property subject to the spouses' joint management, control, and disposition under Section 3.102, Family Code; and

(3) any income earned on property described in this subsection.

(b) At any time after the expiration of 15 months after the date that a community administrator's spouse is judicially declared to be incapacitated, the court, on its own motion or on the motion of an interested person for good cause shown, may order the community administrator to prepare and file an accounting of:

(1) any community property that is subject to the incapacitated spouse's sole management, control, and disposition under Section 3.102, Family Code;

(2) any community property subject to the spouses' joint management, control, and disposition under Section 3.102, Family Code; and

(3) any income earned on property described in this subsection.

(c) An inventory and appraisement ordered under Subsection (a) of this section must:

(1) be prepared in the same form and manner that is required of a guardian under Section 729 of this code; and

(2) be filed not later than the 90th day after the date on which the order is issued.

(d) An accounting ordered under Subsection (b) of this section must:

(1) be prepared in the same form and manner that is required of a guardian under Section 741 of this code, except that the requirement that an accounting be filed annually with the county clerk does not apply; and

(2) be filed not later than the 60th day after the date on which the order is issued.

(e) After an initial accounting has been filed by a community administrator under this section, the court, on the motion of an interested person for good cause shown, may order the community administrator to file subsequent periodic accountings at intervals of not less than 12 months.

Added by Acts 2001, 77th Leg., ch. 217, § 20, eff. Sept. 1, 2001.

### § 883C. Removal of Community Administrator

(a) A court, on its own motion or on the motion of an interested person and after the community administrator has been cited by personal service to answer at a time and place specified in the notice, may remove a community administrator if:

(1) the community administrator fails to comply with a court order for an inventory and appraisement, accounting, or subsequent accounting under Section 883B of this code;

(2) sufficient grounds appear to support belief that the community administrator has misapplied or embezzled, or that the community administrator is about to misapply or embezzle, all or any part of the property committed to the care of the community administrator;

(3) the community administrator is proved to have been guilty of gross misconduct or gross mismanagement in the performance of duties as community administrator; or

(4) the community administrator becomes an incapacitated person, is sentenced to the penitentiary, or for any other reason becomes legally incapacitated from properly performing the community administrator's fiduciary duties.

(b) The order of removal must state the cause of removal and shall direct by order the disposition of the assets remaining in the name or under the control of the removed community administrator.

(c) A community administrator who defends an action for the removal of the community administrator in good faith, regardless of whether successful, is entitled to recover from the incapacitated spouse's part of the community estate the community administrator's necessary expenses and disbursements in the removal proceedings, including reasonable attorney's fees.

Added by Acts 2001, 77th Leg., ch. 217, § 20, eff. Sept. 1, 2001.

### § 883D. Appointment of Attorney Ad Litem for Incapacitated Spouse

(a) The court shall appoint an attorney ad litem to represent the interests of an incapacitated spouse in a proceeding to remove a community administrator or other proceeding brought under this subpart.

(b) The attorney ad litem may demand from the community administrator an accounting or inventory and appraisement of the incapacitated spouse's part of the community estate being managed by the community administrator.

(c) A community administrator shall comply with a demand made under this section not later than the 60th day

after the date on which the community administrator receives the demand.

(d) An accounting or inventory and appraisement returned under this section must be prepared in the form and manner required by the attorney ad litem, and the attorney ad litem may require the community administrator to file the accounting and inventory and appraisement with the court.

Added by Acts 2001, 77th Leg., ch. 217, § 20, eff. Sept. 1, 2001.

### § 884. Delivery to Spouse

A guardian of the estate of an incapacitated married person who, as guardian, is administering community property as part of the estate of the ward, shall deliver on demand the community property to the spouse who is not incapacitated if the spouse becomes community administrator under Section 883 of this code.

Added by Acts 1993, 73rd Leg., ch. 957, § 1, eff. Sept. 1, 1993. Amended by Acts 2001, 77th Leg., ch. 217, § 21, eff. Sept. 1, 2001.

### § 884A. Lawsuit Information

A person whose spouse is judicially declared to be incapacitated and who acquires the power to manage, control, and dispose of the entire community estate under Section 883 of this code shall inform the court in writing of any suit filed by or on behalf of the person that:

(1) is a suit for dissolution of the marriage of the person and the person's incapacitated spouse; or

(2) names the incapacitated spouse as a defendant.

Added by Acts 2001, 77th Leg., ch. 217, § 22, eff. Sept. 1, 2001.

### SUBPART D. RECEIVERSHIP FOR MINORS AND OTHER INCAPACITATED PERSONS

### § 885. Receivership

(a) When the estate of a minor or other incapacitated person or any portion of the estate of the minor or other incapacitated person appears in danger of injury, loss, or waste and in need of a guardianship or other representative and there is no guardian of the estate who is qualified in this state and a guardian is not needed, the county judge of the county in which the minor or other incapacitated person resides or in which the endangered estate is located shall enter an order, with or without application, appointing a suitable person as receiver to take charge of the estate. The court order shall require a receiver appointed under this section to give bond as in ordinary receiverships in an amount the judge deems necessary to protect the estate. The court order shall specify the duties and powers of the receiver as the judge deems necessary for the protection, conservation, and preservation of the estate. The clerk shall enter an order made under this section in the judge's guardianship docket. The person who is appointed as receiver shall make and submit a bond for the judge's approval and shall file the bond, when approved, with the clerk. The person who is appointed receiver shall proceed to take charge of the endangered estate pursuant to the powers and duties vested in the person by the order of appointment and subsequent orders made by the judge.

(b) During the pendency of the receivership, when the needs of the minor or other incapacitated person require the use of the income or corpus of the estate for the education, clothing, or subsistence of the minor or other incapacitated person, the judge, with or without application, shall enter an order in the judge's guardianship docket that appropriates an amount of income or corpus that is sufficient for that purpose. The receiver shall use the amount appropriated by the court to pay a claim for the education, clothing, or subsistence of the minor or other incapacitated person that is presented to the judge for approval and ordered by the judge to be paid.

(c) During the pendency of the receivership, when the receiver has on hand an amount of money that belongs to the minor or other incapacitated person that is in excess of the amount needed for current necessities and expenses, the receiver, under direction of the judge, may invest, lend, or contribute the excess money or any portion of the money in the manner, for the security, and on the terms and conditions provided by this chapter for investments, loans, or contributions by guardians. The receiver shall report to the judge all transactions made under this subsection in the same manner that a report is required of a guardian under this chapter.

(d) All necessary expenses incurred by the receiver in administering the estate may be rendered monthly to the judge in the form of a sworn statement of account that includes a report of the receiver's acts, the condition of the estate, the status of the threatened danger to the estate, and the progress made toward abatement of the danger. If the judge is satisfied that the statement is correct and reasonable in all respects, the judge shall promptly enter an order approving the expenses and authorizing the receiver to be reimbursed from the funds of the estate in the receiver's hands. A receiver shall be compensated for services rendered in the receiver's official capacity in the same manner and amount as provided by this chapter for similar services rendered by guardians of estates.

(e) When the threatened danger has abated and the estate is no longer liable to injury, loss, or waste because there is no guardian or other representative of the estate, the receiver shall report to the judge, file with the clerk a full and final sworn account of all property of the estate the receiver received, had on hand when the receivership was pending, all sums paid out, all acts performed by the receiver with respect to the estate, and all property of the estate that remains in the receiver's hands on the date of the report. On the filing of the report, the clerk shall issue and cause to be posted a notice to all persons interested in the welfare of the minor or other incapacitated person and shall give personal notice to the person who has custody of the minor or other incapacitated person to appear before the judge at a time and place specified in the notice and contest the report and account if the person desires.

(f) If on hearing the receiver's report and account the judge is satisfied that the danger of injury, loss, or waste to the estate has abated and that the report and account are correct, the judge shall enter an order finding that the danger of injury, loss, or waste to the estate has abated and shall direct the receiver to deliver the estate to the person from whom the receiver took possession as receiver, to the person who has custody of the minor or other incapacitated person, or to another person as the judge may find is entitled to possession of the estate. A person who receives the estate under this subsection shall execute and file with the clerk an appropriate receipt for the estate that is delivered to the person. The judge's order shall discharge the receivership and the sureties on the bond of the receiver. If the judge is not satisfied that the danger has abated, or if the judge is not satisfied with the receiver's report and account, the judge shall enter an order that continues the receivership in effect until the judge is satisfied that the danger has abated or is satisfied with the report and account.

(g) An order or a bond, report, account, or notice in a receivership proceeding must be recorded in the judge's guardianship docket.

Added by Acts 1993, 73rd Leg., ch. 957, § 1, eff. Sept. 1, 1993. Amended by Acts 2009, 81st Leg., ch. 602, § 18, eff. June 19, 2009.

**§§ 886 to 886F. Repealed by Acts 1999, 76th Leg., ch. 1081, § 7, eff. Sept. 1, 1999**

### SUBPART E. PAYMENT OF CLAIMS WITHOUT GUARDIANSHIP

### § 887. Payment of Claims Without Guardianship and Administration of Terminated Guardianship Assets

(a) When a resident person who is a minor or other incapacitated person, or the former ward of a guardianship terminated under Subpart C, Part 4, of this code,[1] who are referred to in this section as "creditor," are without a legal guardian of the person's estate, and the person is entitled to money in an amount that is $100,000 or less, the right to which is liquidated and is uncontested in any pending lawsuit, the debtor may pay the money to the county clerk of the county in which the creditor resides to the account of the creditor, giving the creditor's name, the creditor's social security identification number, the nature of the creditor's disability, and, if the creditor is a minor, the minor's age, and the creditor's post-office address. The receipt for the money signed by the clerk is binding on the creditor as of the date of receipt and to the extent of the payment. The clerk, by letter mailed to the address given by the debtor, shall apprise the creditor of the fact that the deposit was made. On receipt of the payment by the clerk, the clerk shall call the receipt of the payment to the court's attention and shall invest the money as authorized under this chapter pursuant to court order in the name and for the account of the minor or other person entitled to the money. Any increase, dividend, or income from an investment made under this section shall be credited to the account of the minor or other person entitled to the investment. Any money that is deposited under the terms of this section that has not been paid out shall be subject to the provisions of this chapter not later than October 1, 1993.

(b) Not later than March 1 of each calendar year, the clerk of the court shall make a written report to the court of the status of an investment made by the clerk under this section. The report must contain:

(1) the amount of the original investment or the amount of the investment at the last annual report, whichever is later;

(2) any increase, dividend, or income from such investment since the last annual report;

(3) the total amount of the investment and all increases, dividends, or income at the date of the report; and

(4) the name of the depository or the type of investment.

(c) The father or mother, or unestranged spouse, of the creditor, with priority being given to the spouse who resides in this state or if there is no spouse and both father and mother are dead or are nonresidents of this state, then the person who resides in this state who has actual custody of the creditor, as custodian and on filing with the clerk written application and bond approved by the county judge of the county, may withdraw the money from the clerk for the use and benefit of the creditor, the bond to be in double the amount of the money and to be payable to the judge or the judge's successors in office and to be conditioned that the custodian will use the money for the creditor's benefit under directions of the court and that the custodian, when legally called on to do so, will faithfully account to the creditor and the creditor's heirs or legal representatives for the money and any increase to the money on the removal of the disability to which the creditor is subject, or on the creditor's death, or the appointment of a guardian for the creditor. A fee or commission may not be allowed to the custodian for taking care of, handling, or expending the money withdrawn by the custodian.

(d) When the custodian has expended the money in accordance with directions of the court or has otherwise complied with the terms of the custodian's bond by accounting for the money and any increase in the money, the custodian shall file with the county clerk of the county the custodian's sworn report of the custodian's accounting. The filing of the custodian's report, when approved by the court, operates as a discharge of the person as custodian and of the person's sureties from all further liability under the bond. The court shall satisfy itself that the report is true and correct and may require proof as in other cases.

(e) When a nonresident minor, a nonresident person who is adjudged by a court of competent jurisdiction to be incapacitated, or the former ward of a guardianship terminated under Subpart C, Part 4, of this code who has no legal guardian qualified in this state is entitled to money in an amount that is not more than $100,000 owing as a result of transactions within this state, the right to which is liquidated

and is uncontested in any pending lawsuit in this state, the debtor in this state may pay the money to the guardian of the creditor who is duly qualified in the domiciliary jurisdiction or to the county clerk of any county in this state in which real property owned by the nonresident person is located. If the person is not known to own any real property in any county in this state the debtor has the right to pay the money to the county clerk of the county of this state in which the debtor resides. In either case, the debtor's payment to the clerk is for the use and benefit and for the account of the nonresident creditor. The receipt for the payment signed by the clerk that recites the name of the creditor and the post office address of the creditor, if known, is binding on the creditor as of the date and to the extent of the payment. The clerk shall handle the money paid to the clerk by the debtor in the same manner as provided for cases of payments to the accounts of residents of this state under Subsections (a)–(d) of this section. All applicable provisions of Subsections (a)–(d) of this section apply to the handling and disposition of money or any increase, dividend, or income paid to the clerk for the use, benefit, and account of the nonresident creditor.

(f) If a person who is authorized to withdraw the money does not withdraw the money from the clerk as provided for in this section, the creditor, after termination of the creditor's disability, or the subsequent personal representative of the creditor or the creditor's heirs may withdraw, at any time and without special bond for the purpose, the money on simply exhibiting to the clerk an order of the county or probate court of the county where the money is held by the clerk that directs the clerk to deliver the money to the creditor, to the creditor's personal representative, or to the creditor's heirs named in the order. Before the court issues an order under this subsection, the person's identity and the person's credentials must be proved to the court's satisfaction.

(g) When it is made to appear to the judge of a county court, district court, or other court of this state, by an affidavit executed by the superintendent, business manager, or field representative of any eleemosynary institution of this state, that a certain inmate in the institution is a person who has a mental disability, an incapacitated person, or a person whose mental illness or mental incapacity, or both, renders the person incapable of caring for himself and of managing the person's own property and financial affairs, there is no known legal guardian appointed for the estate of the inmate, and there is on deposit in the court registry a certain sum of money that belongs to the inmate that does not exceed $10,000, the court may order the disposition of the funds as provided by this subsection. The court, on satisfactory proof by affidavit or otherwise that the inmate is a person who has a mental disability, an incapacitated person, or a person whose mental illness or mental incapacity, or both, renders the inmate incapable of caring for the inmate's self and of managing the inmate's own property and financial affairs and is without a legally appointed guardian of the inmate's estate, may by order direct the clerk of the court to pay the money to the institution for the use and benefit of the inmate. The state institution to which the payment is made may not be required to give bond or security for receiving the fund from the court registry, and the receipt from the state institution for the payment, or the canceled check or warrant by which the payment was made, shall be sufficient evidence of the disposition of the payment. The clerk of the court is relieved of further responsibility for the disposition. On receipt of the money, the institution shall deposit all of the amount of money received to the trust account of the inmate. The money deposited by the institution in the trust account is to be used by or for the personal use of the owner of the trust account under the rules or custom of the institution in the expenditure of the funds by the inmate or for the use and benefit of the inmate by the responsible officer of the institution. This subsection is cumulative of all other laws affecting the rights of a person who has a mental disability, an incapacitated person, or a person who has a mental illness and affecting money that belongs to the person as an inmate of a state eleemosynary institution. If the inmate dies leaving a balance in the inmate's trust account, the balance may be applied to the burial expenses of the inmate or applied to the care, support, and treatment account of the inmate at the eleemosynary institution. After the expenditure of all funds in the trust account or after the death of the inmate, the responsible officer shall furnish a statement of expenditures of the funds to the nearest relative who is entitled to receive the statement. A copy of the statement shall be filed with the court that first granted the order to dispose of the funds in accordance with the provisions of this chapter.

Added by Acts 1993, 73rd Leg., ch. 957, § 1, eff. Sept. 1, 1993. Amended by Acts 1997, 75th Leg., ch. 295, § 1, eff. Sept. 1, 1997; Acts 2001, 77th Leg., ch. 127, § 2, eff. Sept. 1, 2001; Acts 2001, 77th Leg., ch. 1174, § 8, eff. Sept. 1, 2001.

[1] V.A.T.S. Probate Code, § 745 et seq.

### SUBPART F. SALE OF PROPERTY OF MINORS AND CERTAIN WARDS

### § 889. Sale of Property of a Minor by a Parent Without Guardianship

(a) When a minor has an interest in real or personal property and the net value of the interest does not exceed $100,000, a natural or adoptive parent, or the managing conservator, of a minor who is not a ward may apply to the court for an order to sell the minor's interest in the property without being appointed guardian. A minor may not disaffirm a sale of property pursuant to a court order under this section.

(b) The parent shall apply to the court under oath for the sale of the property. Venue for the application under this section is the same as venue for an application for the appointment of a guardian for a minor. The application must contain:

(1) a legal description of the real property and a description that identifies the personal property;

(2) the name of the minor and the minor's interest in the property;

(3) the name of the purchaser;

(4) a statement that the sale of the minor's interest in the property is for cash; and

(5) a statement that all funds received by the parent shall be used for the use and benefit of the minor.

(c) On receipt of the application, the court shall set the application for hearing at a date not earlier than five days from the date of the filing of the application. If the court deems it necessary, the court may cause citation to be issued.

(d) At the time of the hearing of the application filed under this section, the court shall order the sale of the property if the court is satisfied from the evidence that the sale is in the best interests of the minor. The court may require an independent appraisal of the property to be sold to establish the minimum sale price.

(e) When the court enters the order of sale, the purchaser of the property shall pay the proceeds of the sale belonging to the minor into the court registry.

(f) Nothing in this section prevents the proceeds deposited in the registry from being withdrawn from the court registry under Section 887 of this code.

Added by Acts 1993, 73rd Leg., ch. 957, § 1, eff. Sept. 1, 1993. Amended by Acts 1995, 74th Leg., ch. 1039, §§ 68, 69, eff. Sept. 1, 1995; Acts 1997, 75th Leg., ch. 295, § 2, eff. Sept. 1, 1997; Acts 2001, 77th Leg., ch. 127, § 3, eff. Sept. 1, 2001; Acts 2001, 77th Leg., ch. 1174, § 9, eff. Sept. 1, 2001.

### § 889A. Mortgage of Residential Homestead Interest of a Minor Without Guardianship

(a) In this section:

(1) "Home equity loan" means a loan made under Section 50(a)(6), Article XVI, Texas Constitution.

(2) "Residence homestead" has the meaning assigned by Section 11.13, Tax Code.

(b) When a minor has an interest in a residence homestead and the net value of the interest does not exceed $100,000, a natural or adoptive parent, subject to Subsection (j) of this section, or the managing conservator, of a minor who is not a ward may apply to the court for an order authorizing the parent or managing conservator to receive, without being appointed guardian, an extension of credit on the minor's behalf that is secured, wholly or partly, by a lien on the homestead. Proceeds of the home equity loan attributable to the minor's interest may be used only to:

(1) make improvements to the homestead;

(2) pay for education or medical expenses of the minor; or

(3) pay the outstanding balance of the loan.

(c) The parent or managing conservator shall apply to the court under oath for the authority to encumber the residence homestead as provided by this section. Venue for the application is the same as venue for an application for the appointment of a guardian for a minor. The application must contain:

(1) the name and address of the minor;

(2) a legal description of the property constituting the homestead;

(3) a description of the minor's ownership interest in the property constituting the homestead;

(4) the name of the minor and the fair market value of the property constituting the homestead;

(5) the amount of the home equity loan;

(6) the purpose or purposes for which the home equity loan is being sought;

(7) a detailed description of the proposed expenditure of the loan proceeds to be received by the parent or managing conservator on the minor's behalf; and

(8) a statement that all loan proceeds received by the parent or managing conservator on the minor's behalf through a home equity loan authorized under this section shall be used in a manner that is for the minor's benefit.

(d) On receipt of the application, the court shall set the application for hearing at a date not earlier than the fifth day after the date the application is filed. If the court considers it necessary, the court may cause citation to be issued.

(e) Before the hearing, the parent or managing conservator shall file with the county clerk a surety bond in an amount at least equal to two times the amount of the proposed home equity loan. The bond must be:

(1) payable to and approved by the court; and

(2) conditioned on the parent or managing conservator:

(A) using the proceeds of the home equity loan attributable to the minor's interest solely for the purposes authorized by this section; and

(B) making payments on the minor's behalf toward the outstanding balance of the home equity loan.

(f) At the time of the hearing of the application filed under this section, the court, on approval of the bond required by Subsection (e) of this section, shall authorize the parent or managing conservator to receive the extension of credit sought in the application if the court is satisfied from a preponderance of the evidence that the encumbrance is for a purpose described by Subsection (b)(1) or (2) of this section and is in the minor's best interests.

(g) A parent or managing conservator executing a home equity loan on a minor's behalf under this section shall file an annual report with the court regarding the transaction. When the parent or managing conservator has expended the proceeds of a home equity loan authorized under this section, the parent or managing conservator, in addition, shall file with the county clerk a sworn report accounting for the proceeds.

(h) The court may not discharge the person's sureties from all further liability under the bond until the court:

(1) has approved the filing of the parent's or managing conservator's reports required under Subsection (g) of this section;

(2) finds that the parent or managing conservator used loan proceeds resulting from the minor's interest solely for the purposes authorized by this section; and

(3) has been presented with satisfactory evidence that the home equity loan has been repaid and is no longer considered an outstanding obligation.

(i) After the first anniversary of the date a parent or managing conservator executes a home equity loan authorized under this section, the court may, on motion of the borrower, reduce the amount of the surety bond required under this section to an amount that is not less than the outstanding balance of the loan.

(j) A parent of a minor may file an application under this section only if the parent has a homestead interest in the property that is the subject of the application.

(k) A minor may not disaffirm a home equity loan authorized by the court under this section.

Added by Acts 2005, 79th Leg., ch. 1204, § 2, eff. Sept. 1, 2005.

§ 890. Sale of Property of Ward Without Guardianship of the Estate

(a) This section applies only to a ward who has a guardian of the person but does not have a guardian of the estate.

(b) When a ward has an interest in real or personal property in an estate and the net value of the interest does not exceed $100,000, the guardian may apply under oath to the court for an order to sell the ward's interest in the property without being appointed guardian of the estate. A ward may not disaffirm a sale of property pursuant to a court order under this section.

(c) Venue for an application under this section is the same as venue for an application for the appointment of a guardian for the ward. The application must contain the same information required by Section 889(b) of this code.

(d) On receipt of the application, the court shall set the application for hearing at a date not earlier than five days from the date of the filing of the application. If the court considers it necessary, the court may cause citation to be issued.

(e) The procedures and evidentiary requirements for a hearing of an application filed under this section are the same as the procedures and evidentiary requirements for a hearing of an application filed under Section 889 of this code.

(f) When the court enters the order of sale, the purchaser of the property shall pay the proceeds of the sale belonging to the ward into the court registry.

(g) Nothing in this section prevents the proceeds deposited in the court registry from being withdrawn as prescribed by Section 887 of this code.

Added by Acts 1997, 75th Leg., ch. 295, § 4, eff. Sept. 1, 1997. Amended by Acts 2001, 77th Leg., ch. 127, § 4, eff. Sept. 1, 2001; Acts 2001, 77th Leg., ch. 1174, § 10, eff. Sept. 1, 2001.

### § 890A. Mortgage of Residential Homestead Interest of a Minor Ward

(a) In this section:

(1) "Home equity loan" means a loan made under Section 50(a)(6), Article XVI, Texas Constitution.

(2) "Residence homestead" has the meaning assigned by Section 11.13, Tax Code.

(b) This section applies only to a minor ward who has a guardian of the person but does not have a guardian of the estate.

(c) When a minor ward has an interest in a residence homestead and the net value of the interest does not exceed $100,000, the guardian of the person of the ward may apply to the court for an order authorizing the guardian to receive an extension of credit on the ward's behalf that is secured, wholly or partly, by a lien on the homestead. Proceeds of the home equity loan attributable to the minor's interest may be used only to:

(1) make improvements to the homestead;

(2) pay for the education or maintenance expenses of the ward; or

(3) pay the outstanding balance of the loan.

(d) Venue for the application is the same as venue for an application for the appointment of a guardian for a ward. The application must contain the same information required by Section 889A of this code.

(e) On receipt of the application, the court shall set the application for hearing at a date not earlier than the fifth day after the date the application is filed. If the court considers it necessary, the court may cause citation to be issued.

(f) The guardian of the person, before the hearing, shall file a surety bond with the county clerk to the same extent and in the same manner as a parent or managing conservator of a minor is required to provide a surety bond under Section 889A of this code.

(g) The procedures and evidentiary requirements for a hearing of an application filed under this section are the same as the procedures and evidentiary requirements for a hearing of an application filed under Section 889A of this code.

(h) At the time of the hearing of the application filed under this section, the court, on approval of a bond required by Subsection (f) of this section, shall authorize the guardian to receive the extension of credit sought in the application if the court is satisfied from a preponderance of the evidence that the encumbrance is for a purpose described by Subsec-

tion (c)(1) or (2) of this section and is in the ward's best interests.

(i) A guardian of the person executing a home equity loan on a ward's behalf must account for the transaction, including the expenditure of the loan proceeds, in the annual accounting required by Section 741 of this code.

(j) The court may not discharge a guardian's sureties from all further liability under a bond required by this section or another provision of this code until the court:

(1) finds that the guardian used loan proceeds resulting from the ward's interest solely for the purposes authorized by this section; and

(2) has been presented with satisfactory evidence that the home equity loan has been repaid and is no longer considered an outstanding obligation.

(k) A minor ward may not disaffirm a home equity loan authorized by the court under this section.

Added by Acts 2005, 79th Leg., ch. 1204, § 2, eff. Sept. 1, 2005.

## SUBPART G. INTERSTATE GUARDIANSHIPS

### § 891. Transfer of Guardianship to Foreign Jurisdiction

(a) A guardian of the person or estate of a ward may apply with the court that has jurisdiction over the guardianship to transfer the guardianship to a court in a foreign jurisdiction if the ward has moved permanently to the foreign jurisdiction.

(b) Notice of the application to transfer a guardianship under this section shall be served personally on the ward and shall be given to the foreign court to which the guardianship is to be transferred.

(c) On the court's own motion or on the motion of the ward or any interested person, the court shall hold a hearing to consider the application to transfer the guardianship.

(d) The court shall transfer a guardianship to a foreign court if the court determines the transfer is in the best interests of the ward. The transfer of the guardianship must be made contingent on the acceptance of the guardianship in the foreign jurisdiction. To facilitate the orderly transfer of the guardianship, the court shall coordinate efforts with the appropriate foreign court.

Added by Acts 2001, 77th Leg., ch. 479, § 1, eff. Sept. 1, 2001.

### § 892. Receipt and Acceptance of Foreign Guardianship

(a) A guardian appointed by a foreign court to represent an incapacitated person who is residing in this state or intends to move to this state may file an application with a court in which the ward resides or intends to reside to have the guardianship transferred to the court. The application must have attached a certified copy of all papers of the guardianship filed and recorded in the foreign court.

(b) Notice of the application for receipt and acceptance of a foreign guardianship under this section shall be served personally on the ward and shall be given to the foreign court from which the guardianship is to be transferred.

(c) If an application for receipt and acceptance of a foreign guardianship is filed in two or more courts with jurisdiction, the proceeding shall be heard in the court with jurisdiction over the application filed on the earliest date if venue is otherwise proper in that court. A court that does not have venue to hear the application shall transfer the proceeding to the proper court.

(d) In reviewing an application for receipt and acceptance of a foreign guardianship, the court should determine:

(1) that the proposed guardianship is not a collateral attack on an existing or proposed guardianship in another jurisdiction in this or another state; and

(2) for a guardianship in which a court in one or more states may have jurisdiction, that the application has been filed in the court that is best suited to consider the matter.

(e) The court shall hold a hearing to:

(1) consider the application for receipt and acceptance of a foreign guardianship; and

(2) consider modifying the administrative procedures or requirements of the proposed transferred guardianship in accordance with local and state law.

(f) The court shall grant an application for receipt and acceptance of a foreign guardianship if the transfer of the guardianship from the foreign jurisdiction is in the best interests of the ward. In granting an application under this subsection, the court shall give full faith and credit to the provisions of the foreign guardianship order concerning the determination of the ward's incapacity and the rights, powers, and duties of the guardian.

(f-1) At the time of granting an application for receipt and acceptance of a foreign guardianship, the court may also modify the administrative procedures or requirements of the transferred guardianship in accordance with local and state law.

(g) The court shall coordinate efforts with the appropriate foreign court to facilitate the orderly transfer of the guardianship.

(h) The denial of an application for receipt and acceptance of a guardianship under this section does not affect the right of a guardian appointed by a foreign court to file an application to be appointed guardian of the incapacitated person under Section 682 of this code.

Added by Acts 2001, 77th Leg., ch. 479, § 1, eff. Sept. 1, 2001. Amended by Acts 2011, 82nd Leg., 1st C.S., ch. 4 (S.B. 1), § 66.05, eff. Sept. 28, 2011.

**§ 893. Repealed by Acts 2011, 82nd Leg., 1st C.S., ch. 4 (S.B. 1), § 66.08, eff. Sept. 28, 2011**

**§ 894. Guardianship Proceedings Filed in This State and in Foreign Jurisdiction**

(a) A court in which a guardianship proceeding is filed and in which venue of the proceeding is proper may delay further action in the proceeding in that court if:

(1) another guardianship proceeding involving a matter at issue in the proceeding filed in the court is subsequently filed in a court in a foreign jurisdiction; and

(2) venue of the proceeding in the foreign court is proper.

(b) A court that delays further action in a guardianship proceeding under Subsection (a) of this section shall determine whether venue of the proceeding is more suitable in that court or in the foreign court. In making that determination, the court may consider:

(1) the interests of justice;

(2) the best interests of the ward or proposed ward;

(3) the convenience of the parties; and

(4) the preference of the ward or proposed ward, if the ward or proposed ward is 12 years of age or older.

(c) A court that delays further action under Subsection (a) of this section may issue any order it considers necessary to protect the proposed ward or the proposed ward's estate.

(d) The court shall resume the guardianship proceeding if the court determines that venue is more suitable in that court. If the court determines that venue is more suitable in the foreign court, the court shall, with the consent of the foreign court, transfer the proceeding to the foreign court.

Added by Acts 2007, 80th Leg., ch. 606, § 1, eff. June 15, 2007. Amended by Acts 2011, 82nd Leg., 1st C.S., ch. 4 (S.B. 1), § 66.06, eff. Sept. 28, 2011.

**§ 895. Determination of Most Appropriate Forum for Certain Guardianship Proceedings**

(a) If at any time a court of this state determines that it acquired jurisdiction of a proceeding for the appointment of a guardian of the person or estate, or both, of a ward or proposed ward because of unjustifiable conduct, the court may:

(1) decline to exercise jurisdiction;

(2) exercise jurisdiction for the limited purpose of fashioning an appropriate remedy to ensure the health, safety, and welfare of the ward or proposed ward or the protection of the ward's or proposed ward's property or prevent a repetition of the unjustifiable conduct, including staying the proceeding until a petition for the appointment of a guardian or issuance of a protective order is filed in a court of another state having jurisdiction; or

(3) continue to exercise jurisdiction after considering:

(A) the extent to which the ward or proposed ward and all persons required to be notified of the proceedings have acquiesced in the exercise of the court's jurisdiction;

(B) whether the court of this state is a more appropriate forum than the court of any other state after considering the factors described by Section 894(b) of this code; and

(C) whether the court of any other state would have jurisdiction under the factual circumstances of the matter.

(b) If a court of this state determines that it acquired jurisdiction of a proceeding for the appointment of a guardian of the person or estate, or both, of a ward or proposed ward because a party seeking to invoke the court's jurisdiction engaged in unjustifiable conduct, the court may assess against that party necessary and reasonable expenses, including attorney's fees, investigative fees, court costs, communication expenses, witness fees and expenses, and travel expenses. The court may not assess fees, costs, or expenses of any kind against this state or a governmental subdivision, agency, or instrumentality of this state unless authorized by other law.

Added by Acts 2011, 82nd Leg., 1st C.S., ch. 4 (S.B. 1), § 66.07, eff. Sept. 28, 2011.

## SUBPART H.　CONTRACTS IN ARTS, ENTERTAINMENT, ADVERTISEMENT, AND SPORTS

### § 901.　Definitions

In this subpart:

(1) "Advertise" means to solicit or induce, through print or electronic media, including radio, television, computer, or direct mail, to purchase consumer goods or services.

(2) "Advertisement contract" means a contract under which a person is employed or agrees to advertise consumer goods or services.

(3) "Artist" means:

(A) an actor who performs in a motion picture, theatrical, radio, television, or other entertainment production;

(B) a musician or musical director;

(C) a director or producer of a motion picture, theatrical, radio, television, or other entertainment production;

(D) a writer;

(E) a cinematographer;

(F) a composer, lyricist, or arranger of musical compositions;

(G) a dancer or choreographer of musical productions;

(H) a model; or

(I) any other individual who renders analogous professional services in a motion picture, theatrical, radio, television, or other entertainment production.

(4) "Arts and entertainment contract" means a contract under which:

(A) an artist is employed or agrees to render services in a motion picture, theatrical, radio, television, or other entertainment production; or

(B) a person agrees to purchase, secure, sell, lease, license, or otherwise dispose of literary, musical, or dramatic tangible or intangible property or any rights in that property for use in the field of entertainment, including a motion picture, television, the production of phonograph records, or theater.

(5) "Consumer goods" means goods that are used or bought for use primarily for personal, family, or household purposes.

(6) "Sports contract" means a contract under which an athlete is employed or agrees to participate, compete, or engage in a sports or athletic activity at a professional or amateur sports event or athletic event.

Added by Acts 2001, 77th Leg., ch. 799, § 1, eff. Sept. 1, 2001.

### § 902.　Construction

This subpart may not be construed to authorize the making of a contract that binds a minor beyond the seventh anniversary of the date of the contract.

Added by Acts 2001, 77th Leg., ch. 799, § 1, eff. Sept. 1, 2001.

### § 903.　Approval of Certain Contracts of Minors;　Not Voidable

(a) A court, on petition of the guardian of the estate of the minor, may enter an order approving for purposes of this subpart an arts and entertainment contract, advertisement contract, or sports contract that is entered into by a minor. The court may approve the contract only after the guardian of the minor's estate provides to the other party to the contract notice of the petition and an opportunity to request a hearing in the manner provided by the court.

(b) The approval of a contract under this section extends to the contract as a whole and any of the terms and provisions of the contract, including any optional or conditional provision in the contract relating to the extension or termination of its term.

(c) A court may withhold approval of a contract under which part of the minor's net earnings under the contract will be set aside as provided by Section 904 of this code until the guardian of the minor's estate executes and files with the court written consent to the making of the order.

(d) An otherwise valid contract approved under this section may not be voidable solely on the ground that it was entered into by a person during the age of minority.

(e) Each parent of the minor is a necessary party to a proceeding brought under this section.

Added by Acts 2001, 77th Leg., ch. 799, § 1, eff. Sept. 1, 2001.

### § 904.　Net Earnings of Minor;　Set Aside and Preservation

(a) In this section, "net earnings" means the total amount to be received for the services of the minor under the contract less:

(1) the sum required by law to be paid as taxes to any government or governmental agency;

(2) a reasonable sum to be expended for the support, care, maintenance, education, and training of the minor;

(3) fees and expenses paid in connection with procuring the contract or maintaining employment of the minor; and

(4) attorney's fees for services rendered in connection with the contract or any other business of the minor.

(b) Notwithstanding any other law, the court may require in an order approving a contract under Section 903 of this code that a portion of the net earnings of the minor under the contract be set aside and preserved for the benefit of the minor in a trust created under Section 867 of this code or a similar trust created under the laws of another state. The amount to be set aside under this subsection must be a reasonable amount as determined by the court.

Added by Acts 2001, 77th Leg., ch. 799, § 1, eff. Sept. 1, 2001.

### § 905. Guardian Ad Litem

The court may appoint a guardian ad litem for a minor who has entered into an arts and entertainment contract, advertisement contract, or sports contract if the court finds that appointment of the ad litem would be in the best interest of the minor.

Added by Acts 2001, 77th Leg., ch. 799, § 1, eff. Sept. 1, 2001.

### SUBPART I. ESTABLISHMENT OF POOLED TRUST SUBACCOUNTS; TRANSFERS

### § 910. Definitions

In this subpart:

(1) "Beneficiary" means a minor or other incapacitated person, an alleged incapacitated person, or a disabled person who is not an incapacitated person for whom a subaccount is established.

(2) "Medical assistance" means benefits and services under the medical assistance program administered under Chapter 32, Human Resources Code.

(3) "Pooled trust" means a trust that meets the requirements of 42 U.S.C. Section 1396p(d)(4)(C) for purposes of exempting the trust from the applicability of 42 U.S.C. Section 1396p(d) in determining the eligibility of a person who is disabled for medical assistance.

(4) "Subaccount" means an account in a pooled trust established solely for the benefit of a beneficiary.

Added by Acts 2009, 81st Leg., ch. 930, § 13, eff. Sept. 1, 2009. Subd. (a) amended by Acts 2011, 82nd Leg., ch. 1085 (S.B. 1196), § 38, eff. Sept. 1, 2011.

### § 911. Application

The following persons may apply to the court for the establishment of a subaccount for the benefit of a minor or other incapacitated person, an alleged incapacitated person, or a disabled person who is not an incapacitated person:

(1) the guardian of the incapacitated person;

(2) a person who has filed an application for the appointment of a guardian for the alleged incapacitated person;

(3) an attorney ad litem or guardian ad litem appointed to represent:

(A) the incapacitated person who is a ward or that person's interests; or

(B) the alleged incapacitated person who does not have a guardian; or

(4) the disabled person.

Added by Acts 2009, 81st Leg., ch. 930, § 13, eff. Sept. 1, 2009. Amended by Acts 2011, 82nd Leg., ch. 1085 (S.B. 1196), § 39, eff. Sept. 1, 2011.

### § 912. Appointment of Attorney Ad Litem

The court shall appoint an attorney ad litem for a person who is a minor or has a mental disability and who is the subject of an application under Section 911 of this code. The attorney ad litem is entitled to a reasonable fee and reimbursement of expenses to be paid from the person's property.

Added by Acts 2009, 81st Leg., ch. 930, § 13, eff. Sept. 1, 2009.

### § 913. Transfer

If the court finds that it is in the best interests of a person who is the subject of an application under Section 911 of this code, the court may order:

(1) the establishment of a subaccount of which the person is the beneficiary; and

(2) the transfer to the subaccount of any of the person's property on hand or accruing to the person.

Added by Acts 2009, 81st Leg., ch. 930, § 13, eff. Sept. 1, 2009.

### § 914. Terms of Subaccount

Unless the court orders otherwise, the terms governing the subaccount must provide that:

(1) the subaccount terminates on the earliest of the date of:

(A) the beneficiary's 18th birthday, if the beneficiary is not disabled on that date and was a minor at the time the subaccount was established;

(B) the beneficiary's death; or

(C) an order of the court terminating the subaccount; and

(2) on termination, any property remaining in the beneficiary's subaccount after making any required payments to satisfy the amounts of medical assistance reimbursement claims for medical assistance provided to the beneficiary under this state's medical assistance program and other states' medical assistance programs shall be distributed to:

(A) the beneficiary, if on the date of termination the beneficiary is living and is not incapacitated;

(B) the beneficiary's guardian, if on the date of termination the beneficiary is living and is incapacitated; or

(C) the personal representative of the beneficiary's estate, if the beneficiary is deceased on the date of termination.

Added by Acts 2009, 81st Leg., ch. 930, § 13, eff. Sept. 1, 2009.

### § 915.   Jurisdiction Exclusive

Notwithstanding any other law, the court that orders the establishment of a subaccount for a beneficiary has exclusive jurisdiction of a subsequent proceeding or action that relates to both the beneficiary and the subaccount, and the proceeding or action may only be brought in that court.

Added by Acts 2009, 81st Leg., ch. 930, § 13, eff. Sept. 1, 2009.

### § 916.   Fees and Accounting

(a) The manager or trustee of a pooled trust may:

(1) assess fees against a subaccount of that pooled trust established under this subpart in accordance with the manager's or trustee's standard fee structure; and

(2) pay those fees from the subaccount.

(b) If required by the court, the manager or trustee of the pooled trust shall file a copy of the annual report of account with the court clerk.

Added by Acts 2009, 81st Leg., ch. 930, § 13, eff. Sept. 1, 2009.

# INDEX

---

## Abbreviations

H & S . . . . . . . . . . . . . . . . . . . . . . Health and Safety Code
Est . . . . . . . . . . . . . . . . . . . . . . . . Estates Code

---

**ABANDONED OR UNCLAIMED PROP-
ERTY**
Escheat, generally, this index
Guardian and ward, powers and duties,
orders of court, **Est 1151.102**
Probate proceedings, personal representa-
tives, orders of court, **Est 351.051**

**ABANDONMENT**
Children and Minors, this index
Intestate succession, children and minors,
**Est 201.062**

**ABSENCE AND ABSENTEES**
Guardian and Ward, this index
Probate Proceedings, this index

**ABUSE**
Aged Persons, this index
Children and Minors, this index
Guardian and ward,
Presumptions, disqualification, **Est
1104.353**
Removal from office, **Est 1203.051,
1203.052**
Handicapped Persons, this index
Intestate succession, children and minors,
**Est 201.062**

**ABUSE OF CHILDREN**
Children and Minors, this index

**ACCIDENTS**
Casualty Insurance, generally, this index
Life, Health and Accident Insurance, gen-
erally, this index

**ACCOUNTANTS**
Power of Attorney, this index

**ACCOUNTS AND ACCOUNTING**
Community Property, this index
Custodians, indebtedness, incapacitated
persons, **Est 1355.104**
Definitions, multiple party accounts, pro-
bate proceedings, **Est 113.001**
Financial Institutions, this index
Guardian and Ward, this index
Intestate succession, multiple party ac-
counts, **Est 113.001 et seq.**
Power of Attorney, this index
Probate Proceedings, this index
Receivers and Receivership, this index
Trusts and Trustees, this index

**ACCOUNTS AND ACCOUNTING**
—Cont'd
Wills, multiple party accounts, **Est
113.001 et seq.**

**ACKNOWLEDGMENTS**
Probate proceedings, disclaimers, **Est
122.051**
Wills, lifetime gifts, satisfaction, **Est
255.101**

**ACTIONS AND PROCEEDINGS**
Community property,
Notice, incapacitated spouse, communi-
ty administrators, **Est 1353.053**
Surviving spouses, contracts, **Est
112.101 et seq.**
Costs, generally, this index
Escheat, this index
Evidence, generally, this index
Garnishment, generally, this index
Guardian Ad Litem, generally, this index
Guardian and Ward, this index
Injunctions, generally, this index
Jurisdiction, generally, this index
Parentage and Parentage Determination,
generally, this index
Paternity suits. Parentage and Parentage
Determination, generally, this index
Power of Attorney, this index
Privileges and Immunities, generally, this
index
Probate Proceedings, generally, this index
Process, generally, this index
Witnesses, generally, this index

**ACTIVE TRUSTS**
Trusts and Trustees, generally, this index

**ADDRESS**
Guardian and Ward, this index
Probate Proceedings, this index

**ADMINISTRATION OF SMALL ES-
TATES**
Probate Proceedings, this index

**ADMINISTRATIVE LAW AND PROCE-
DURE**
Power of attorney, **Est 752.110**

**ADMINISTRATOR DE BONIS NON**
Probate Proceedings, generally, this index

**ADMISSIBILITY OF EVIDENCE**
Evidence, generally, this index

**ADOPTION OF CHILDREN**
Intestate Succession, this index
Wills, pretermitted child, definitions, **Est
255.051**

**ADULTS**
Definitions, medical power of attorney, **H
& S 166.151**

**ADVANCE DIRECTIVE ACT**
Generally, **H & S 166.001 et seq.**

**ADVANCE DIRECTIVES**
Generally, **H & S 166.001 et seq.**
Abortion, medical power of attorney, **H &
S 166.152**
Abuse of children, federal law, applica-
tion of law, **H & S 166.010**
Accident, health or life insurance, **H & S
166.006**
Actions and proceedings, medical power
of attorney, revocation or suspension,
**H & S 166.165**
Age, **H & S 166.035**
Agents and agencies, out of hospital do
not resuscitate orders, **H & S 166.082**
Appeal and review, **H & S 166.046**
Beneficiaries, witnesses, **H & S 166.003**
Cancellation, revocation or suspension, **H
& S 166.042**
Certificates and certification, **H & S
166.040**
Medical power of attorney, **H & S
166.152**
Challenges, **H & S 166.039**
Out of hospital do not resuscitate or-
ders, **H & S 166.088**
Children and minors, **H & S 166.035**
Abuse of children, federal law, applica-
tion of law, **H & S 166.010**
Out of hospital do not resuscitate or-
ders, **H & S 166.085**
Claims against estate, witnesses, **H & S
166.003**
Communications, **H & S 166.034**
Competency, **H & S 166.038**
Competency, **H & S 166.038, 166.039**
Medical power of attorney, certificates
and certification, **H & S 166.152**

I–1

# INDEX

# INDEX

**CASUALTY INSURANCE**
Guardian and ward, powers and duties, **Est 1151.103**
Life, Health and Accident Insurance, generally, this index
Power of attorney, **Est 752.102**
Personal property, **Est 752.103**
Probate proceedings, personal representatives, powers and duties, **Est 351.052**

**CATASTROPHES**
Casualty Insurance, generally, this index

**CEMETERIES AND DEAD BODIES**
Cremations. Probate Proceedings, this index
Funerals, generally, this index
Probate proceedings, cremations, Emergencies, intervention, **Est 152.003**
Surviving spouses, rights, limitations, **Est 152.101, 152.102**

**CERTIFICATES AND CERTIFICATION**
Birth certificates. Vital Statistics, this index
Guardian and Ward, this index
Probate Proceedings, this index
Wills, this index

**CESTUI QUE TRUST**
Trusts and Trustees, generally, this index

**CHANGE OF NAME**
Names, this index

**CHARITABLE ORGANIZATIONS AND SOCIETIES**
Charities, generally, this index

**CHARITABLE TRUSTS**
Venue, breach of fiduciary duty, attorney general, **Est 33.005**

**CHARITIES**
Definitions, probate proceedings, **Est 22.003**
Multiple party accounts, **Est 113.001**
Guardian and ward,
Gifts, **Est 1162.051 et seq.**
Tax motivated gifts, **Est 1162.001 et seq.**
Inheritance taxes, apportionment, exemptions, **Est 124.007**
Probate Proceedings, this index
Wills, contests, necessary parties, **Est 55.052**

**CHATTELS**
Personal Property, generally, this index

**CHECKS**
Negotiable Instruments, this index

**CHILD ABUSE**
Abuse of children. Children and Minors, this index

**CHILD DAY CARE**
Power of attorney, **Est 752.111**

**CHILD SUPPORT**
Support, generally, this index

**CHILDREN AND MINORS**
Abandonment, guardian and ward, presumptions, disqualification, **Est 1104.353**
Abuse of children,
Advance directives, federal law, application of law, **H & S 166.010**
Guardian and ward, presumptions, disqualification, **Est 1104.353**
Intestate succession, **Est 201.062**
Actions affecting parent child relationship. Parentage and Parentage Determination, generally, this index
Actions and proceedings. Parentage and Parentage Determination, generally, this index
Advance directives, **H & S 166.035**
Out of hospital do not resuscitate orders, **H & S 166.085**
Advertisements, contracts, **Est 1356.001 et seq.**
Athletics, contracts, **Est 1356.001 et seq.**
Bonds (officers and fiduciaries), home equity loans, **Est 1352.055**
Children born out of wedlock. Parentage and Parentage Determination, generally, this index
Compensation and salaries, contracts, trusts and trustees, **Est 1356.054**
Conservators and conservatorship,
Deeds and conveyances, without guardianship, **Est 1351.001 et seq.**
Home equity loans, **Est 1352.001 et seq.**
Property, sales, without guardianship, **Est 1351.001 et seq.**
Revocation or suspension, **Est 123.052, 123.053**
Contracts, entertainment, advertisements, athletics, **Est 1356.001 et seq.**
Deeds and conveyances, without guardianship, **Est 1351.001 et seq.**
Definitions,
Contracts, **Est 1356.001**
Guardian and ward, **Est 1002.004, 1002.019, 1002.022**
Probate proceedings, **Est 22.004, 22.022**
Education, home equity loans, **Est 1352.056**
Employment. Labor and Employment, this index
Entertainment, contracts, **Est 1356.001 et seq.**
Guardian Ad Litem, generally, this index
Guardian and Ward, generally, this index
Hearings,
Home equity loans, **Est 1352.054**
Property, sales, without guardianship, **Est 1351.003**
Home equity loans. Venue, post
Illegitimate children. Parentage and Parentage Determination, generally, this index
Intestate Succession, this index
Labor and Employment, this index

**CHILDREN AND MINORS—Cont'd**
Legitimacy. Parentage and Parentage Determination, generally, this index
Medical care and treatment, home equity loans, **Est 1352.056**
Models, contracts, **Est 1356.001 et seq.**
Motion pictures, contracts, **Est 1356.001 et seq.**
Neglect. Abuse of children, generally, ante
Nonsupport. Support, generally, this index
Out of hospital do not resuscitate orders, **H & S 166.085**
Parentage and Parentage Determination, generally, this index
Probate Proceedings, this index
Property, sales, without guardianship, **Est 1351.001 et seq.**
Reports, home equity loans, **Est 1352.057, 1352.058**
Sales, property, without guardianship, **Est 1351.001 et seq.**
Support, generally, this index
Television and radio, contracts, **Est 1356.001 et seq.**
Termination of parent child relationship, intestate succession, paternal inheritance, **Est 201.052**
Trusts and Trustees, this index
Venue,
Home equity loans, **Est 1352.053**
Property, sales, without guardianship, **Est 1351.002**
Wills, this index
Work. Labor and Employment, this index

**CHILDREN BORN OUT OF WEDLOCK**
Parentage and Parentage Determination, generally, this index

**CITATION**
Escheat, this index
Guardian and Ward, this index
Probate Proceedings, this index
Wills, this index

**CIVIL PROCESS**
Process, generally, this index

**CIVIL RIGHTS**
Guardian and ward, ward, **Est 1151.001**

**CLAIM DOCKET**
Probate Proceedings, this index

**CLERKS**
County Clerks, generally, this index

**CODICILS**
Wills, this index

**COLLATERAL**
Guardian and ward, loans, investments, **Est 1161.203**

**COLLECTIONS**
Guardian and Ward, this index

I–5

# INDEX

**DECLARATIONS**—Cont'd
Living wills. Advance Directives, generally, this index

**DECLARATORY JUDGMENTS**
Probate Proceedings, this index
Wills, this index

**DEEDS AND CONVEYANCES**
Community property, surviving spouses, title to property, **Est 112.206**
Guardian and Ward, this index
Power of Attorney, this index
Records and Recordation, generally, this index
Wills, foreign wills, **Est 503.051**

**DEEDS OF TRUST**
Guardian and Ward, this index
Power of attorney, records and recordation, **Est 751.151**
Probate Proceedings, this index

**DEFERRED COMPENSATION**
Probate proceedings, exemptions, **Est 111.052**

**DEFINITIONS**
Words and Phrases, generally, this index

**DEPARTMENTS**
Definitions, guardian and ward,
Criminal history record information, **Est 1104.401**
Successor guardians, **Est 1203.108**

**DEPOSITIONS**
Guardian and Ward, this index
Probate Proceedings, this index
Wills, this index

**DEPOSITORIES**
Guardian and Ward, this index

**DEPOSITS**
Probate Proceedings, this index
Wills, this index

**DEPRECIATION**
Probate proceedings, sales, prevention, **Est 356.051**

**DEPRESSION**
Mental Health, generally, this index

**DESCENT AND DISTRIBUTION**
Intestate Succession, generally, this index

**DEVISES AND DEVISEES**
Gifts, generally, this index
Wills, generally, this index

**DIGITAL SIGNATURES**
Signatures, this index

**DIPLOMATIC AND CONSULAR OFFICERS**
Guardian and ward, notice, waiver, **Est 1051.251**

**DIRECTIVES**
Advance Directives, generally, this index

**DISABILITY**
Handicapped Persons, generally, this index

**DISABLED PERSONS**
Handicapped Persons, generally, this index

**DISCHARGE**
Probate Proceedings, this index

**DISCIPLINE**
Health Care Facilities and Services, this index
Health Care Professionals, this index
Physicians and Surgeons, this index

**DISCLAIMERS**
Annuities, **Est 122.001 et seq.**
Community property, **Est 122.001 et seq.**
Definitions, probate proceedings, **Est 122.001**
Financial institutions, accounts and accounting, joint tenants, survivors and survivorship, **Est 122.001 et seq.**
Guardian and ward, beneficiaries, **Est 122.001 et seq.**
Intestate Succession, this index
Joint Tenants, this index
Life, Health and Accident Insurance, this index
Probate Proceedings, this index
Retirement and pensions, **Est 122.001 et seq.**

**DISCLOSURE**
Financial Institutions, this index
Guardian and Ward, this index

**DISEASES**
Advance Directives, generally, this index
Medical power of attorney. Advance Directives, this index
Out of hospital do not resuscitate orders. Advance Directives, this index

**DISMISSAL AND NONSUIT**
Guardian and Ward, this index

**DISSOLUTION**
Receivers and Receivership, generally, this index

**DISSOLUTION OF MARRIAGE**
Marriage, this index

**DISTRICT CLERKS**
Records and recordation, open records. Records and Recordation, this index

**DISTRICT COURTS**
Concurrent jurisdiction, probate proceedings, **Est 32.007**
Costs, generally, this index
Guardian and Ward, this index

**DISTRICT COURTS**—Cont'd
Probate proceedings, jurisdiction, **Est 32.003**
Concurrent jurisdiction, **Est 32.007**

**DISTRICTS**
Open records. Records and Recordation, this index
Records and recordation, open records. Records and Recordation, this index

**DIVIDENDS**
Guardian and ward, bonds (officers and fiduciaries), amount, **Est 1105.154**

**DIVORCE**
Dissolution of marriage. Marriage, this index

**DNR ORDERS**
Advance Directives, generally, this index

**DO NOT RESUSCITATE ORDERS**
Advance Directives, generally, this index

**DOCKETS**
Definitions, probate proceedings, **Est 22.011**
Guardian and Ward, this index
Receivers and receivership, incapacitated persons, **Est 1354.009**

**DOCTORS**
Physicians and Surgeons, generally, this index

**DOMESTIC CORPORATIONS**
Corporations, generally, this index

**DOMESTIC VIOLENCE**
Guardian and ward,
Presumptions, disqualification, **Est 1104.353**
Protective orders, disqualification, **Est 1104.358**

**DOMICILE AND RESIDENCE**
Guardian and Ward, this index
Probate proceedings,
Foreign wills, vacating or setting aside, ancillary probate, **Est 501.008**
Nonprobate assets, application of law, **Est 111.054**

**DONATIONS**
Gifts, generally, this index

**DRUGS AND MEDICINE**
Guardian and ward, mental health, powers and duties, **Est 1151.054**
Mental Health, this index

**DUPLICATES AND COPIES**
Probate Proceedings, this index
Wills, this index

**DURABLE POWER OF ATTORNEY**
Generally, **Est 751.001 et seq.**
Power of Attorney, generally, this index

# INDEX

# INDEX

# INDEX

# INDEX

# INDEX

I–25

# INDEX

## HEALTH CARE PROFESSIONALS
Advance directives, out of hospital do not resuscitate orders, application of law, **H & S 166.102**

Definitions,
Advance directives, **H & S 166.004**
Medical power of attorney, **H & S 166.151**

Discipline,
Advance directives, **H & S 166.045**
Out of hospital do not resuscitate orders, **H & S 166.095**

Medical power of attorney. Advance Directives, this index

Notice, advance directives, **H & S 166.004**

Out of hospital do not resuscitate orders. Advance Directives, this index

Physicians and Surgeons, generally, this index

Policies, advance directives, **H & S 166.004**

Privileges and immunities,
Advance directives, **H & S 166.044, 166.045**
Out of hospital do not resuscitate orders, **H & S 166.094, 166.095**

Statements, advance directives, **H & S 166.004**

## HEALTH CARE PROVIDERS
Health Care Professionals, generally, this index

## HEALTH CARE SERVICES
Health Care Facilities and Services, generally, this index

## HEALTH FACILITIES
Health Care Facilities and Services, generally, this index

## HEALTH INSURANCE
Life, Health and Accident Insurance, generally, this index

## HEIRS
Action to determine. Probate Proceedings, this index

Descent and distribution. Intestate Succession, generally, this index

Indebtedness, withdrawals, incapacitated persons, county clerks, **Est 1355.105**

Intestate Succession, generally, this index

Probate Proceedings, generally, this index

Relatives, generally, this index

Wills, generally, this index

## HIGHER EDUCATION
Colleges and Universities, generally, this index

## HOLOGRAPHIC WILLS
Wills, this index

## HOME AND COMMUNITY SUPPORT SERVICES
Advance Directives, generally, this index
Medical power of attorney. Advance Directives, this index

## HOME AND COMMUNITY SUPPORT SERVICES—Cont'd
Notice, advance directives, **H & S 166.004**

Out of hospital do not resuscitate orders. Advance Directives, this index

Policies, advance directives, **H & S 166.004**

Statements, advance directives, **H & S 166.004**

## HOME CARE
Home and Community Support Services, generally, this index

## HOME EQUITY LOANS
Bonds (officers and fiduciaries), guardian and ward, guardian of person, **Est 1352.105**

Children and minors, **Est 1352.001 et seq.**

Definitions, children and minors, **Est 1352.001**

Evidence, guardian and ward, guardian of person, **Est 1352.104**

Guardian and Ward, this index

Hearings,
Children and minors, **Est 1352.054**
Guardian and ward, guardian of person, **Est 1352.104**

Venue,
Children and minors, **Est 1352.053**
Guardian and ward, **Est 1352.103**
Guardian of person, **Est 1352.103**

## HOME HEALTH AGENCIES
Home and Community Support Services, generally, this index

## HOME HEALTH SERVICES
Home and Community Support Services, generally, this index

## HOMESTEAD
Guardian and Ward, this index
Intestate succession, small estates, title to property, affidavits, **Est 205.006**
Probate Proceedings, this index

## HOMICIDE
Advance directives, **H & S 166.048**
Out of hospital do not resuscitate orders, **H & S 166.097**

Intestate succession, children and minors, **Est 201.062**

Out of hospital do not resuscitate orders, **H & S 166.097**

Probate proceedings, surviving spouses, funerals, rights, limitations, **Est 152.102**

## HOSPITALS
See, also, Health Care Facilities and Services, generally, this index

Advance Directives, generally, this index

Disagreements, life sustaining treatment, transfer of patients, **H & S 166.052**

Life sustaining treatment. Advance Directives, generally, this index

## HOSPITALS—Cont'd
Lists, life sustaining treatment, disagreements, transfer of patients, **H & S 166.053**

Medical power of attorney. Advance Directives, this index

Mental Health, generally, this index

Notice, advance directives, **H & S 166.004**

Out of hospital do not resuscitate orders. Advance Directives, this index

Policies, advance directives, **H & S 166.004**

Registry, life sustaining treatment, disagreements, transfer of patients, **H & S 166.053**

Statements, advance directives, **H & S 166.004**

Transfer of patients, life sustaining treatment, disagreements, **H & S 166.052**

## HOUSING
Equity. Home Equity Loans, generally, this index

Guardian and Ward, this index

Home Equity Loans, generally, this index

Loans,
Home Equity Loans, generally, this index

Mortgages, generally, this index

Power of attorney, **Est 752.111**

## HUMAN RESOURCES
Social Services, generally, this index

## HUMAN SERVICES
Social Services, generally, this index

## HUMAN SERVICES DEPARTMENT
Children and Minors, generally, this index

Handicapped Persons, generally, this index

Medical assistance. Social Services, this index

## HUSBAND AND WIFE
See, also, Marriage, generally, this index

Annulment of marriage. Marriage, this index

Community Property, generally, this index

Custodians, incapacitated persons, indebtedness, withdrawals, county clerks, **Est 1355.102**

Dissolution of marriage. Marriage, this index

Guardian and Ward, this index

Maintenance, power of attorney, **Est 752.111**

Probate Proceedings, this index

Property. Community Property, generally, this index

Support, generally, this index

Wills, this index

## HYPOMANIC DISORDERS
Mental Health, generally, this index

# INDEX

**IDENTITY AND IDENTIFICATION**
Guardian and Ward, this index
Out of hospital do not resuscitate orders, H & S 166.089, 166.090
Parentage and Parentage Determination, generally, this index
Probate proceedings, applicants, decedents, personal representatives, Est 351.355

**ILLEGITIMATE CHILDREN**
Parentage and Parentage Determination, generally, this index

**ILLNESS**
Guardian and Ward, this index
Probate proceedings, personal representatives, successors, Est 361.105

**IMMUNITIES**
Privileges and Immunities, generally, this index

**IMPRISONMENT**
Crimes and Offenses, generally, this index

**IMPROVEMENTS**
Probate proceedings, homestead, Est 102.004

**IN REM PROCEEDINGS**
Guardianship, Est 1022.002
Probate proceedings, Est 32.001

**INCAPACITATED PERSONS**
Guardian and Ward, generally, this index

**INCOME**
Guardian and Ward, this index
Inheritance taxes, apportionment, exemptions, Est 124.008
Probate Proceedings, this index
Trusts and trustees, Est 310.005

**INCOME TAX**
Power of attorney, Est 752.114

**INCOMPETENT PERSONS**
Mental Health, generally, this index

**INDEBTEDNESS**
Capacity, incapacitated persons, claims, Est 1355.001 et seq.
Claims, incapacitated persons, Est 1355.001 et seq.
Community Property, this index
County clerks, incapacitated persons, investments, payment, Est 1355.051
Custodians, incapacitated persons, withdrawals, county clerks, payment, Est 1355.101 et seq.
Garnishment, generally, this index
Guardian and Ward, this index
Handicapped persons, claims, incapacitated persons, Est 1355.001 et seq.
Heirs, withdrawals, incapacitated persons, county clerks, Est 1355.105
Incapacitated persons, claims, Est 1355.001 et seq.

**INDEBTEDNESS**—Cont'd
Mortgages, generally, this index
Nonresidents, incapacitated persons, claims, Est 1355.002
Payment, incapacitated persons, Est 1355.001 et seq.
Receivers and Receivership, generally, this index
Wills, this index
Withdrawals, incapacitated persons, county clerks, Est 1355.105

**INDEPENDENT ADMINISTRATION**
Probate Proceedings, this index

**INDEXES**
Guardian and ward, records and recordation, Est 1052.053
Wills, deposits, Est 252.004

**INDIVIDUAL RETIREMENT ACCOUNTS**
Definitions, nonprobate assets, Est 111.051

**INFANTS**
Children and Minors, generally, this index

**INHERITANCE**
Intestate Succession, generally, this index

**INHERITANCE TAXES**
Apportionment, Est 124.001 et seq.
Assignments, withholding, personal representatives, recovery, Est 124.014
Attorney fees, apportionment, Est 124.018
Charities, apportionment, exemptions, Est 124.007
Costs, apportionment, Est 124.018
Credit, apportionment, Est 124.006
Deductions, apportionment, Est 124.006
  Exclusions, Est 124.007
Deficiencies, apportionment, Est 124.010
Definitions, apportionment, Est 124.001
Estate for years, life estate, apportionment, exemptions, Est 124.008
Estates for years, estates for life, apportionment, exemptions, Est 124.008
Exemptions, apportionment, Est 124.006 et seq.
Fines and penalties, apportionment, Est 124.011
Foreign states, personal representatives, apportionment, withholding, Est 124.017
Guardian and Ward, this index
Income, apportionment, exemptions, Est 124.008
Interest, apportionment, Est 124.011
Internal Revenue Code, references, apportionment, Est 124.002
Personal representatives. Probate Proceedings, this index
Probate Proceedings, this index
Recovery, personal representatives, Est 124.014 et seq.

**INHERITANCE TAXES**—Cont'd
Time,
  Extensions, apportionment, Est 124.010
  Personal representatives, apportionment, withholding, Est 124.016
Withholding, personal representatives, Est 124.013

**INJUNCTIONS**
Guardian and Ward, this index
Power of attorney, Est 752.110
Probate proceedings, appeal and review, Est 55.252
Temporary restraining orders, guardian and ward, temporary guardians, Est 1251.051

**INJURIES**
Personal Injuries, generally, this index

**INSANE PERSONS**
Mental Health, generally, this index

**INSOLVENCY**
Guardian and ward,
  Bonds (officers and fiduciaries), new bonds, Est 1105.251
  Priorities and preferences, claims, Est 1157.103
Power of attorney, Est 752.110
Probate Proceedings, this index
Receivers and Receivership, generally, this index

**INSPECTION AND INSPECTORS**
Guardian and Ward, this index
Wills, this index

**INSTITUTIONS OF HIGHER EDUCATION**
Colleges and Universities, generally, this index

**INSURANCE**
Accidents. Casualty Insurance, generally, this index
Advance directives, H & S 166.006
  Medical power of attorney, H & S 166.159
Casualty Insurance, generally, this index
Catastrophes. Casualty Insurance, generally, this index
Guardian and Ward, this index
Health and accident insurance. Life, Health and Accident Insurance, generally, this index
Life, Health and Accident Insurance, generally, this index
Medical assistance. Social Services, this index
Medical insurance. Life, Health and Accident Insurance, generally, this index
Power of Attorney, this index
Prepaid funeral services. Funeral Directors and Embalmers, this index
Probate Proceedings, this index

# INDEX

## MEDICAL RECORDS
Guardian and Ward, this index
Probate proceedings, testamentary capacity, disclosure, **Est 55.101, 55.102**

## MEDICARE
Power of attorney, **Est 752.112**

## MENTAL EXAMINATIONS
Medical examinations. Mental Health, this index

## MENTAL HEALTH
Advance Directives, generally, this index
Commitments, guardian and ward, powers and duties, **Est 1151.053**
Drugs and medicine, guardian and ward, powers and duties, **Est 1151.054**
Guardian and ward,
  Annual reports, **Est 1163.101**
  Annulment of marriage, death, **Est 123.101 et seq.**
  Drugs and medicine, powers and duties, **Est 1151.054**
  Examinations and examiners, transportation, powers and duties, **Est 1151.051**
  Findings, **Est 1101.103**
  Full authority, findings, court orders, **Est 1101.151**
  Partial authority, findings, court orders, **Est 1101.152**
  Powers and duties,
    Commitment, **Est 1151.053**
    Drugs and medicine, **Est 1151.054**
    Transportation, examinations and examiners, **Est 1151.051**
  Retarded persons, post
Marriage, annulment of marriage, death, **Est 123.101 et seq.**
Medical examinations, guardian and ward, powers and duties, **Est 1151.053**
Medical power of attorney. Advance Directives, this index
Nursing and Convalescent Homes, this index
Out of hospital do not resuscitate orders. Advance Directives, this index
Personal Care Facilities, generally, this index
Probate Proceedings, this index
Retarded persons, guardian and ward, findings, **Est 1101.104**
Ward. Guardian and ward, generally, ante

## MENTAL HEALTH AND MENTAL RETARDATION DEPARTMENT
Mental Health, generally, this index
Retarded persons. Mental Health, this index
Texas State Hospitals and Special Schools. Mental Health, generally, this index

## MENTAL HEALTH CODE
Mental Health, generally, this index

## MENTAL ILLNESS
Mental Health, generally, this index

## MENTAL RETARDATION
Retarded persons. Mental Health, this index

## MENTALLY DEFICIENT AND MENTALLY ILL PERSONS
Mental Health, generally, this index

## MENTALLY ILL PERSONS
Mental Health, generally, this index

## MENTALLY RETARDED PERSONS
Retarded persons. Mental Health, this index

## MERGER AND CONSOLIDATION
Power of attorney, business and commerce, **Est 752.107**

## MICROFILM
Guardian and ward, records and recordation, **Est 1052.004**
Probate proceedings, records and recordation, **Est 52.004**

## MILITARY FORCES
Probate proceedings, fees, exemptions, **Est 53.053**
Wills, this index

## MINERAL LEASES
Leases. Mines and Minerals, this index

## MINERALS
Mines and Minerals, generally, this index

## MINES AND MINERALS
Definitions, probate proceedings, leases, **Est 358.001**
Guardian and Ward, this index
Leases,
  Definitions, probate proceedings, **Est 358.001**
  Power of attorney, **Est 752.102**
  Records and recordation, **Est 751.151**
  Probate Proceedings, this index
Pooling, probate proceedings, leases, **Est 358.151 et seq.**
Probate Proceedings, this index

## MINORS
Children and Minors, generally, this index

## MINUTES
Probate proceedings, signatures, judges, **Est 53.105**

## MISAPPROPRIATIONS OF MONEY
Embezzlement, generally, this index

## MISDEMEANORS
Crimes and Offenses, generally, this index

## MODELS
Children and minors, contracts, **Est 1356.001 et seq.**

## MODELS—Cont'd
Guardian and ward, contracts, **Est 1356.001 et seq.**

## MONEY
Escheat, **Est 551.002**
Nursing and Convalescent Homes, this index

## MONEY ORDERS
Power of attorney, **Est 752.106**

## MORTGAGES
Definitions,
  Guardian and ward, **Est 1002.020**
  Probate proceedings, **Est 22.024**
Equity. Home Equity Loans, generally, this index
Guardian and Ward, this index
Home Equity Loans, generally, this index
Power of Attorney, this index
Probate Proceedings, this index
Receivers and Receivership, generally, this index
Reverse mortgages, probate proceedings, homestead, **Est 102.004**
Second mortgages. Home Equity Loans, generally, this index

## MOTION PICTURES
Children and minors, contracts, **Est 1356.001 et seq.**
Guardian and ward, contracts, **Est 1356.001 et seq.**

## MOTIONS
Guardian and Ward, this index
Probate Proceedings, this index

## MOTOR VEHICLES
Guardian and Ward, this index
Power of attorney, **Est 752.111**

## MULTIPARTY ACCOUNT
Generally, **Est 113.001 et seq.**
Probate Proceedings, this index

## MUNICIPALITIES
Open records. Records and Recordation, this index
Records and recordation, open records. Records and Recordation, this index

## MUNIMENTS OF TITLE
Probate Proceedings, this index

## MURDER
Homicide, generally, this index

## MUTUAL FUNDS
Power of attorney, **Est 752.104**
Probate proceedings, exemptions, **Est 111.052**

## NAMES
Change of name, probate proceedings, genetics, tests, orders of court, **Est 204.201**
Guardian and Ward, this index

# INDEX

**NAMES**—Cont'd
Probate Proceedings, this index

**NATURAL DEATH**
Generally, H & S 166.001 et seq.
Advance Directives, generally, this index

**NEGLECT**
Guardian and ward, removal from office,
Est 1203.051, 1203.052

**NEGLIGENCE**
Guardian ad litem, Est 1054.056
Guardian and Ward, this index
Probate Proceedings, this index

**NEGOTIABLE INSTRUMENTS**
Checks, power of attorney, Est 752.106
Power of attorney, Est 752.106
Probate proceedings, exemptions, Est
111.052
Travelers checks, power of attorney, Est
752.106

**NEGOTIABLE PAPER**
Negotiable Instruments, generally, this index

**NEXT OF KIN**
Relatives, generally, this index

**NON COMPOS MENTIS**
Mental Health, generally, this index

**NONNEGOTIABLE INSTRUMENTS**
Negotiable Instruments, generally, this index

**NONPROFIT CORPORATIONS**
Guardian and ward, management trusts,
Est 1301.057

**NONPROFIT ORGANIZATIONS**
Guardian and ward, gifts, Est 1162.051 et
seq.

**NONRESIDENTS**
Foreign States, generally, this index
Guardian and Ward, this index
Handicapped persons, indebtedness, incapacitated persons, claims, Est
1355.002
Indebtedness, incapacitated persons,
claims, Est 1355.002
Probate Proceedings, this index

**NONSUPPORT**
Support, generally, this index

**NONTESTAMENTARY TRANSFERS**
Probate Proceedings, this index

**NOTARIES PUBLIC**
Advance Directives, this index
Guardian and ward, information letters,
Est 1102.003
Health care. Advance Directives, this index

**NOTICE**
Advance Directives, this index
Community Property, this index
Financial Institutions, this index
Guardian and Ward, this index
Health Care Professionals, this index
Home and Community Support Services,
this index
Hospitals, this index
Nursing and Convalescent Homes, this
index
Personal Care Facilities, this index
Probate Proceedings, this index
Receivers and Receivership, this index
Wills, this index

**NURSES AND NURSING**
Advance Directives, generally, this index
Home and Community Support Services,
generally, this index
Medical power of attorney. Advance Directives, this index
Out of hospital do not resuscitate orders.
Advance Directives, this index
Vocational nurses. Home and Community Support Services, generally, this
index

**NURSING AND CONVALESCENT
HOMES**
Advance Directives, generally, this index
Application of law, money, residents, payment, Est 1355.151
Death, money, residents, Est 1355.154
Funeral expenses, money, residents, Est
1355.154
Home and Community Support Services,
generally, this index
Medical power of attorney. Advance Directives, this index
Mental health, money, residents, payment, Est 1355.152
Money, residents, payment, Est 1355.151
et seq.
Notice, advance directives, H & S 166.004
Personal Care Facilities, generally, this
index
Policies, advance directives, H & S
166.004
Statements, advance directives, H & S
166.004
Trusts and trustees, money, residents,
payment, Est 1355.153

**NURSING HOMES**
Nursing and Convalescent Homes, generally, this index

**NUTRITION**
Home and Community Support Services,
generally, this index

**OATHS AND AFFIRMATIONS**
Definitions,
Guardian and ward, Est 1105.001
Personal representatives, Est 305.001
Guardian and Ward, this index
Probate Proceedings, this index

**OBSCENITY**
Intestate succession, children and minors,
Est 201.062

**OBSESSIVE COMPULSIVE DISORDERS**
Mental Health, generally, this index

**OCCUPATIONAL THERAPISTS**
Home and Community Support Services,
generally, this index

**OFFENSES**
Crimes and Offenses, generally, this index

**OFFICIAL BONDS**
Bonds (Officers and Fiduciaries), generally, this index

**OFFICIAL RECORDS**
Records and Recordation, generally, this
index

**OIL AND GAS**
Definitions,
Guardian and ward, Est 1160.001
Probate proceedings, mines and minerals, leases, Est 358.001
Guardian and Ward, this index
Probate Proceedings, this index

**OIL AND GAS LEASES**
Power of attorney, Est 752.102
Records and recordation, Est 751.151

**OLD AGE ASSISTANCE**
Social Services, generally, this index

**OPEN RECORDS**
Records and Recordation, this index

**OPINION AND EXPERT TESTIMONY**
Witnesses, this index

**ORAL ARGUMENT**
Guardian and ward, hearing by submission, Est 1055.051

**ORDERS OF COURT**
Community Property, this index
Guardian and Ward, this index
Probate Proceedings, this index
Receivers and Receivership, this index
Wills, this index

**ORPHANS**
Guardian and ward, Est 1104.052

**OTHER STATES**
Foreign States, generally, this index

**OUT OF HOSPITAL DO NOT RESUSCITATE ORDERS**
Advance Directives, this index

**OWNERS AND OWNERSHIP**
Title to Property, generally, this index

**P.O.D. ACCOUNTS**
Generally, Est 113.101 et seq.

# INDEX

**PALLIATIVE CARE**
Home and Community Support Services, generally, this index

**PARANOID DISORDERS**
Mental Health, generally, this index

**PARENT AND CHILD**
Children and Minors, generally, this index

**PARENTAGE AND PARENTAGE DE-TERMINATION**
Intestate succession,
Intended parents,
Maternal inheritance, **Est 201.051**
Paternal inheritance, **Est 201.052**
Paternal inheritance, **Est 201.052**
Probate proceedings, heirship, actions to determine, presumptions, tests, **Est 204.152**

**PARENTS**
Children and Minors, generally, this index

**PARTIES**
Definitions, multiple party accounts, probate proceedings, **Est 113.002**
Escheat, this index
Guardian and Ward, this index
Probate Proceedings, this index

**PARTITION**
Guardian and Ward, this index
Intestate Succession, this index
Power of attorney, **Est 752.102**
Probate Proceedings, this index

**PARTNERSHIPS**
Guardian and Ward, this index
Power of attorney, **Est 752.107**
Probate proceedings, personal representatives, powers and duties, **Est 351.104**

**PATERNITY**
Parentage and Parentage Determination, generally, this index

**PAYMENT**
Definitions, multiple party accounts, probate proceedings, **Est 113.001**
Financial institutions, accounts and accounting, **Est 113.201 et seq.**
Guardian and Ward, this index
Indebtedness, this index
Probate Proceedings, this index
Support, this index
Trusts and Trustees, this index

**PAYROLL TAXES**
Power of attorney, **Est 752.114**

**PEACE OFFICERS**
Exemptions, probate proceedings, fees, **Est 53.054**
Probate proceedings, exemptions, fees, **Est 53.054**

**PENDING ACTIONS**
Probate proceedings, personal representatives, powers and duties, **Est 351.053**

**PENSIONS AND RETIREMENT**
Retirement and Pensions, generally, this index

**PERFORMANCE BOND**
Bonds (Officers and Fiduciaries), generally, this index

**PERJURY**
Guardian and ward, annual reports, unsworn declarations, **Est 1163.1011**

**PERSONAL ASSISTANCE SERVICES**
Home and Community Support Services, generally, this index

**PERSONAL CARE FACILITIES**
Advance Directives, generally, this index
Notice, advance directives, **H & S 166.004**
Policies, advance directives, **H & S 166.004**
Statements, advance directives, **H & S 166.004**

**PERSONAL CARE FACILITY LICENSING ACT**
Personal Care Facilities, generally, this index

**PERSONAL INJURIES**
Advance Directives, generally, this index
Guardian and ward, concurrent jurisdiction, district courts, statutory probate courts, **Est 1022.006**
Jurisdiction, **Est 32.007**
Medical power of attorney. Advance Directives, this index
Out of hospital do not resuscitate orders. Advance Directives, this index
Probate proceedings, jurisdiction, **Est 32.007**

**PERSONAL PROPERTY**
Definitions,
Guardian and ward, **Est 1002.024**
Probate proceedings, **Est 22.028**
Escheat, generally, this index
Guardian and Ward, this index
Inheritance Taxes, generally, this index
Intestate Succession, this index
Power of attorney, **Est 752.103**
Probate Proceedings, this index
Receivers and Receivership, generally, this index
Wills, this index

**PERSONAL PROPERTY TAXATION**
Power of attorney, **Est 752.103**

**PERSONAL REPRESENTATIVES**
Guardian and Ward, this index
Probate Proceedings, this index

**PERSONAL SERVICE**
Process, generally, this index

**PERSONAL SURETIES**
Guardian and Ward, this index

**PERSONS**
Definitions,
Guardian and ward, **Est 1002.023**
Inheritance taxes, apportionment, **Est 124.001**
Probate proceedings, **Est 22.027**

**PERSONS WITH DISABILITIES**
Handicapped Persons, generally, this index

**PETITIONS**
Escheat, this index
Guardian and Ward, this index
Probate Proceedings, this index

**PHRASES**
Words and Phrases, generally, this index

**PHYSICAL EXAMINATIONS**
Guardian and ward,
Capacity, **Est 1101.103**
Investigations and investigators, probable cause, **Est 1102.002**

**PHYSICAL THERAPISTS**
Home and Community Support Services, generally, this index

**PHYSICALLY DISABLED PERSONS**
Handicapped Persons, generally, this index

**PHYSICIAN ASSISTANTS**
Advance Directives, generally, this index
Medical power of attorney. Advance Directives, this index
Out of hospital do not resuscitate orders. Advance Directives, this index

**PHYSICIANS AND SURGEONS**
Advance Directives, generally, this index
Definitions, advance directives, **H & S 166.002**
Discipline, advance directives, **H & S 166.045**
Guardian and Ward, this index
Living wills. Advance Directives, generally, this index
Medical power of attorney. Advance Directives, this index
Out of hospital do not resuscitate orders. Advance Directives, this index
Privileges and immunities,
Advance directives, **H & S 166.044, 166.045**
Medical power of attorney, **H & S 166.160**

**PLEADINGS**
Community property, surviving spouses, actions and proceedings, contracts, **Est 112.101**
Guardian and Ward, this index
Probate Proceedings, this index

# INDEX

# INDEX

# INDEX

# INDEX

# INDEX

# INDEX

# INDEX

# INDEX

# INDEX

# INDEX

## RECEIVERS AND RECEIVERSHIP
—Cont'd
Probate proceedings—Cont'd
Service of process, **Est 51.056**
Reports, incapacitated persons, discharge, **Est 1354.007**

## RECORDS AND RECORDATION
Advance Directives, this index
Community Property, this index
Guardian and Ward, this index
Intestate succession, small estates, affidavits, **Est 205.005**
Open records, probate proceedings, genetics, tests, heirship, actions to determine, **Est 204.001**
Out of hospital do not resuscitate orders, **H & S 166.082**
Power of Attorney, this index
Probate Proceedings, this index
Wills, this index

## REGISTERS AND REGISTRIES
Advance directives, life sustaining treatment, disagreements, transfers, **H & S 166.053**
Life sustaining treatment, hospitals, disagreements, transfer of patients, **H & S 166.053**

## REGISTRATION
Guardian and Ward, this index

## RELATIVES
Definitions,
    Guardian and ward, **Est 1002.021**
    Trusts and trustees, nontestamentary transfers, **Est 123.051**
    Wills, dissolution of marriage, **Est 123.001**
Guardian and Ward, this index
Probate proceedings,
    Heirship, actions to determine, genetics, tests, **Est 204.054**
    Personal representatives, priorities and preferences, **Est 304.001**

## RELEASE
Guardian and Ward, this index

## RELIGIOUS ORGANIZATIONS AND SOCIETIES
Guardian and ward, gifts, **Est 1162.051 et seq.**
Power of attorney, dues, **Est 752.111**

## REMARRIAGE
Marriage, this index

## REPORTS
Children and Minors, this index
County Clerks, this index
Custodians, indebtedness, incapacitated persons, **Est 1355.104**
Guardian and Ward, this index
Power of attorney, **Est 752.101**
Probate Proceedings, this index
Receivers and receivership, incapacitated persons, discharge, **Est 1354.007**

## RESIDENTIAL CARE FACILITIES
Advance Directives, generally, this index
Guardian and ward, powers and duties, **Est 1151.052, 1151.053**
Medical power of attorney.  Advance Directives, this index
Out of hospital do not resuscitate orders.  Advance Directives, this index

## RESPIRATORY CARE PRACTITIONERS
Home and Community Support Services, generally, this index

## RESPIRATORY FACILITIES
Home and Community Support Services, generally, this index

## RESPITE CARE
Home and Community Support Services, generally, this index

## REST HOMES
Nursing and Convalescent Homes, generally, this index

## RESTRAINING ORDERS
Injunctions, generally, this index

## RETARDED PERSONS
Mental Health, this index

## RETIREMENT AND PENSIONS
Definitions, power of attorney, **Est 752.113**
Disclaimers, **Est 122.001 et seq.**
Guardian and ward, applications, **Est 1101.001**
Power of attorney, **Est 752.113**
Probate proceedings, exemptions, **Est 111.052**

## REVERSE MORTGAGES
Mortgages, this index

## RIGHT OF WAY
Guardian and ward, sales, **Est 1158.501, 1158.502**
Probate proceedings, sales, **Est 356.501, 356.502**

## ROYALTIES
Probate Proceedings, this index

## RULES OF COURT
Probate proceedings, application,
    Rules of civil procedure, **Est 53.107**
    Rules of evidence, **Est 54.051**

## RUSK STATE HOSPITAL
Mental Health, generally, this index

## SAFE DEPOSIT BOXES
Power of attorney, **Est 752.106**
Probate proceedings, examinations and examiners, orders of court, **Est 151.001 et seq.**

## SALES
Bills of sale, probate proceedings, personal property, **Est 356.105**
Children and Minors, this index
Conservators and Conservatorship, this index
Escheat, this index
Guardian and Ward, this index
Power of Attorney, this index
Probate Proceedings, this index
Wills, this index

## SAN ANTONIO STATE HOSPITAL
Mental Health, generally, this index

## SAVINGS AND LOAN ASSOCIATIONS
Guardian and Ward, this index

## SCHOOLS AND SCHOOL DISTRICTS
Colleges and Universities, generally, this index
Guardian and ward, domicile and residence, findings, **Est 1101.101**
Open records.  Records and Recordation, this index
Records and recordation, open records.  Records and Recordation, this index
Trusts and trustees, open records.  Records and Recordation, this index

## SEALS
Probate proceedings, letters testamentary or of administration, **Est 306.005**

## SEARCHES AND SEIZURES
Probate proceedings, absence and absentees, presumptions, death, **Est 454.003**

## SECOND MORTGAGES
Home Equity Loans, generally, this index

## SECURED TRANSACTIONS
Guardian and ward, powers and duties, **Est 1151.201 et seq.**

## SECURITIES
Guardian and Ward, this index
Power of attorney, **Est 752.104**
Probate Proceedings, this index
Wills, **Est 255.251 et seq.**

## SECURITY
Bonds (Officers and Fiduciaries), generally, this index
Guardian and Ward, this index
Loans, this index

## SECURITY AGREEMENTS
Power of attorney, records and recordation, **Est 751.151**

## SECURITY BONDS
Bonds (Officers and Fiduciaries), generally, this index

## SECURITY INTEREST
Financial institutions, accounts and accounting, **Est 113.251**

# INDEX

# INDEX

# INDEX

# INDEX

†